Children Moving

TENTH EDITION

Children Moving

A REFLECTIVE APPROACH TO TEACHING PHYSICAL EDUCATION

George Graham
Pinehurst, North Carolina

Shirley Ann Holt/Hale (Ret.)
Linden Elementary School, Oak Ridge, Tennessee

Melissa Parker
University of Limerick, Limerick, Ireland

Tina Hall
Middle Tennessee State University, Murfreesboro, Tennessee

Kevin Patton
California State University, Chico, California

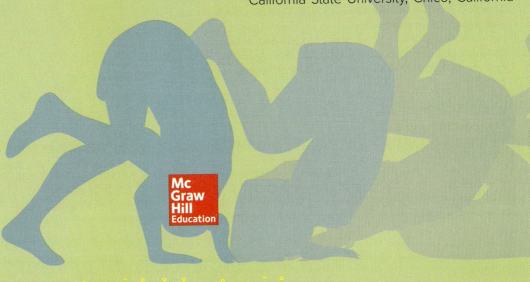

Mc
Graw
Hill
Education

CHILDREN MOVING: A REFLECTIVE APPROACH TO TEACHING PHYSICAL EDUCATION, TENTH EDITION

Published by McGraw-Hill Education, 2 Penn Plaza, New York, NY 10121. Copyright ©2020 by McGraw-Hill Education. All rights reserved. Printed in the United States of America. Previous editions ©2013, 2010, and 2008. No part of this publication may be reproduced or distributed in any form or by any means, or stored in a database or retrieval system, without the prior written consent of McGraw-Hill Education, including, but not limited to, in any network or other electronic storage or transmission, or broadcast for distance learning.

Some ancillaries, including electronic and print components, may not be available to customers outside the United States.

This book is printed on acid-free paper.

1 2 3 4 5 6 7 8 9 LWI 21 20 19

ISBN 978-0-07-802274-6 (bound edition)
MHID 0-07-802274-6 (bound edition)
ISBN 978-1-260-39217-3 (loose-leaf edition)
MHID 1-260-39217-1 (loose-leaf edition)

Product Developers: *Erika Lo*
Marketing Manager: *Meredith Leo*
Content Project Managers: *Lisa Bruflodt, Emily Windelborn*
Buyer: *Susan K. Culbertson*
Designer: *Beth Blech*
Content Licensing Specialist: *Beth Cray*
Cover Image: *boy running-©Shutterstock/Nowik Sylwia, girl jumping-©Shutterstock/Hibrida*
Compositor: *Cenveo® Publisher Services*

All credits appearing on page or at the end of the book are considered to be an extension of the copyright page.

Library of Congress Cataloging-in-Publication Data

Names: Graham, George, 1943- author.
Title: Children moving : a reflective approach to teaching physical education
  / George Graham, Pinehurst, NC, Shirley Ann Holt/Hale (Ret.), Linden
  Elementary School, Oak Ridge, Tennessee, Melissa Parker, University of
  Limerick, Tina Hall, Middle Tennessee State University, Kevin Patton,
  California State University, Chico.
Description: Tenth Edition. | New York : McGraw-Hill, an imprint of The
  McGraw-Hill Companies, Inc., [2019] | Audience: Ages: 18+ | Includes index.
Identifiers: LCCN 2018052785 | ISBN 9780078022746 (Hard Cover : acid-free
  paper)
Subjects: LCSH: Physical education for children–Study and teaching–United
  States. | Physical education for children–Curricula–United States. |
  Movement education–United States.
Classification: LCC GV443 .G73 2019 | DDC 372.86/044–dc23 LC record available at https://lccn.loc
  .gov/2018052785

The Internet addresses listed in the text were accurate at the time of publication. The inclusion of a website does not indicate an endorsement by the authors or McGraw-Hill Education, and McGraw-Hill Education does not guarantee the accuracy of the information presented at these sites.

mheducation.com/highered

To my wonderful family: Teresa, Nick, Tommy, Jackie, Verenda, Austin, Carter, Savanna, Lois and Natalie. I love you!
   GG

For the elementary physical education teachers of New York City, in their quest for quality programs for children
   SHH

For Tia Ziegler, Lizzy Ginger, Karla Drury, Nancy McNamee, and all the elementary physical education teachers in Weld County District 6 whose passion, courage, and tenacity remind me daily of what is possible!
   MP

For all future and current physical education specialists. Keep making a difference in the lives of children!
   TH

For Andrea, Nathan, Dillon, and Brian
   KP

CONTENTS

CHAPTER 22

Transferring Weight and Rolling   401

CHAPTER 25

Volleying and Dribbling   502

Volleying 503

PART SIX

Skill Theme Application   595

CHAPTER 28

Teaching Physical Fitness, Physical Activity, and Wellness   597

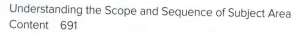

PART SEVEN

The Future   697

CHAPTER 33

Building Support for Your Program   699

CHAPTER 34

Physical Education for Tomorrow's Children   711

Children! Impressionable, innocent, enthusiastic, eager to learn, and all different. In fact, if you believe that all children are identical—same interests, same abilities, same size—then *Children Moving* is not the book for you. The authors of *Children Moving* recognize that each child is unique and different. One size does not fit all! The purpose of *Children Moving* is to guide you in the process of learning to teach a curriculum that is differentiated for a range of skill abilities and fitness levels. If all children were the same, we would be able to "package" a curriculum—the same games, gymnastic stunts, and dances you would do with all of the children as if they were identical. *Children Moving* will introduce you to a process of teaching—the reflective approach—that will provide the background for you to adapt, adjust, and modify lessons so they are interesting and worthwhile for all of the children you teach—from the lowest to the highest skill and fitness levels. The ultimate goal, of course, is to guide youngsters in the process of becoming physically active for a lifetime.

The importance of physical activity for one's health is recognized today as never before. As we write this 10th edition, virtually no one questions the value of participating in 60 minutes, or more, of physical activity each day. *Children Moving* focuses on building the competence and confidence in children that lead to a lifetime of physical activity. It's easy to recommend that children, and adults, become and remain physically active. As you may know, it's much harder to do it.

Children Moving is not simply a description of games and activities for kids. Instead it emphasizes the importance of children actually learning to move by focusing on skill themes that are used in virtually all sports and physical activities. This text contains rich progressions of field-tested learning experiences that have the potential to assist children in becoming good movers. Competent movers typically enjoy physical activity and are eager participants. In contrast, incompetent movers who are poorly skilled are far more likely to avoid physical activity. Each logical, developmentally appropriate skill theme progression is described with word-for-word examples of what teachers actually say to the children during the lessons. This is especially valuable for novice teachers and those with little experience teaching by skill themes.

In addition to providing detailed tasks that can be used to develop safe and child-centered lessons for the skill themes, *Children Moving* also devotes 10 chapters to the process of teaching (Parts 2 and 3). These pedagogical skills are based in the research literature and also years and years of teaching experience. If you want to become a good teacher, you understand effective teachers do a lot more than just keep kids "busy, happy, and good." They develop logical skill progressions that are the foundation of sports skills and physical activities and then they provide copious amounts of encouraging feedback that lets the children know how they are doing—and what they need to work on. They also create an environment that is safe and child-centered.

Children Moving is far more than a collection of fun, unrelated physical activities for children. If you wanted to be a popular parent, you might let your children eat nothing but desserts. Yet you know that doing so would be terrible for the health of your children. The authors of *Children Moving* feel the same about physical education. Simply playing a bunch of unrelated games with no progression or feedback is not in the children's best interest. For this reason, the authors of *Children Moving* have built on the literature about teaching and children to develop a solid, experience-tested, evidence-based approach to teaching children physical education. We hope you enjoy reading and implementing the skill theme approach. We also believe the children you teach will benefit enormously.

When the first edition of *Children Moving* was published in 1980, the skill theme approach was new to many in our profession. Today, an increasing number of teachers follow the developmentally appropriate guidelines and practices outlined in this book. We have blended the literature on effective teaching with research on physical activity and teacher preparation into a practical format designed to help you understand, and successfully implement, the skill theme approach with children—an approach that provides a program of physical education appropriate for all children, not just the athletically gifted or physically fit youngsters.

In 1980 the research documenting the benefits of physical activity and the importance of physical education in the school curricula was nonexistent, as was the universal lack of understanding about the importance of physical activity for children. Today, with the increasing epidemic of obesity and the associated health problems, there is little need to convince parents, administrators, and the medical community of the importance of regular physical activity for children.

It has now been more than two decades since the Surgeon General's report on physical activity and the first edition of the *National Standards for Physical Education* were published. Today they are landmark documents. It is common practice and in many states a requirement for programs of physical education to align their curricula with national or state standards with clear and obvious goals. In this era of increased accountability and testing, state legislatures and school districts are mandating that teachers document what students have and have not learned, often through high-stakes testing with highly publicized results. Physical education programs that do not have sound educational goals and practices guiding their instruction are more vulnerable than ever before.

Appropriate Instructional Practice Guidelines (2009), *Appropriate Instructional Practice Guidelines for Elementary School Physical Education* (third edition, 2009), and the *National Standards & Grade-Level Outcomes for K–12 Physical Education* (2014), all published by the Society of Health and Physical Educators (SHAPE America), offer counsel for the structure of quality physical education programs along with suggested content.

The authors of *Children Moving* have been involved with these and other national, regional, and state projects in various ways. Our involvement is one of the key reasons for the match between *Children Moving* and the recent national and state advances substantiating the importance of physical activity. This edition includes literally hundreds of practical learning experiences and assessments for reaching the goals and outcomes outlined in the combined editions of the *National Standards* and various state standards.

In this edition we have continued to expand, clarify, and update the content and teaching process. Our goal, however, is to keep the book both informal and practical. What we wrote in the preface to the first edition remains true today: "We are teachers of children first. And writers second. Individual insights gained during years of teaching experience and ideas to enhance teacher success are sprinkled throughout the text. We hope that by sharing these experiences with you we can help others to enrich the lives of children."

At the outset of the 10th edition, we want to thank those professors and instructors who have used *Children Moving* in the past. We think you will be pleased to see the major changes we have made to this edition. For students and teachers who are reading this text for the first time, you will be pleased to know that this edition is easier to understand, and use, than past editions. We have also continued to stay abreast of recent developments in our profession and, as you will see, these changes are reflected throughout this edition.

In this section of the Preface, we want to highlight some of the specific changes we have made to this edition of *Children Moving*. The introduction to the skill theme approach (Part 1) now contains revised chapters. Chapter 1 highlights the benefits of physical activity for children as well as the components of a quality physical education program for children. For the first time, Chapter 1 includes sample student learning indicators for movement concepts and skill themes. Chapter 2 identifies the characteristics of the skill theme approach, developmental appropriateness, and how fitness and the cognitive and affective learning domains are addressed. Chapter 3 has been updated with the 2014 *National Standards* and includes detailed discussion on the role of the grade-level outcomes in making teaching and planning decisions.

The three chapters in Part 2 of this edition focus specifically on the process of becoming a reflective teacher. Chapter 4 defines and gives examples of reflective teaching as well as new practical suggestions for addressing large class sizes and limited equipment. One of the tenets of reflective teaching is that we base our lessons on the skills, abilities, and interests of the children. Chapter 5 describes our system for determining the content the children are ready to learn based on their developmental needs and interests—an alternative to organizing the content by grade levels or age (generic levels of skill proficiency). Chapter 6 is an extremely important one as it conveys a four-part process describing how reflective teachers plan their lessons and programs to maximize the benefit for children. This chapter has been rewritten to align with requirements for designing standards-based lessons. As you will read in this chapter, planning in the skill theme approach involves a lot more than just finding games or activities that will keep the children active. The planning appendices that were formerly at the end of the text have been moved to the end of this chapter for ease of access.

Part 3 of *Children Moving* also focuses on the teaching skills (pedagogy) of effective teaching. The first two chapters describe the process of creating a positive learning environment with your classes (Chapter 7) and strategies for maintaining that environment after it has been created (Chapter 8). Chapter 7 describes the process of creating a child-centered atmosphere conducive to learning and includes sections on safety and legal liability. In this chapter we introduce the safety icon ⚠ as an alert for a strong emphasis on safety in a given situation. Chapter 8 introduces a multitude of strategies that can be used to help all students stay on task, take responsibility for their own learning, and ensure the environment that was created initially continues throughout the year. Chapter 9 describes a variety of instructional approaches teachers use to heighten children's ability to gradually become independent learners. An analysis is provided that allows teachers to determine how any given approach may be more or less appropriate than others based on the students' needs and the teacher's pedagogical skills. This chapter provides links of the various instructional approaches to specific learning experiences in the skill theme chapters. Chapter 10, "Adapting the Content for Diverse Learners," has been completely rewritten and has been moved from a later part in this book to Part 3. The authors support the philosophy of inclusion and provide teaching strategies for creating an inclusive environment as well as general implications for teaching the children who make up the diversity of our classrooms. The process of observing the children with understanding is a critical pedagogical skill in determining the lesson and program content that will be most beneficial to the children. Once again in the 10th edition, we have devoted an entire chapter to the observation process because we believe it is so important to becoming an effective reflective teacher (Chapter 11). Chapter 12 provides a plethora of practical ideas you can use to answer questions such as, Are the children I am teaching improving? Are they grasping the important concepts? Assessment icons 🅾 are used throughout the text to indicate performance assessments and to provide suggestions for checking for cognitive understanding. All assessment items are aligned with the *National Standards*. The final chapter in Part 3 (Chapter 13) is designed to assist you in analyzing your teaching to better understand your effectiveness and progress as a reflective teacher and lifelong learner.

The next two parts of the book provide detailed and practical examples of the movement concepts (Part 4) and skill themes (Part 5). Chapters 14-16 are the movement concept chapters ("Space Awareness," "Effort," and "Relationships") and include connections to the 2014 *National Standards & Grade-Level Outcomes for K–12 Physical Education* as well as new learning experiences. They are followed by the skill theme chapters (Chapters 17–27), which contain hundreds of learning experiences designed to help children develop the fundamental movement skills necessary for successful participation in and enjoyment of a variety of physical activities and sports. Changes in this edition include changes to Chapter 17, "Traveling," which has been reorganized and includes attention to detail on teaching locomotor skills in isolation and in combination. Also included are new learning experiences that apply locomotor skills in dance, gymnastics, and games.

The remaining skill themes chapters in this section (Chapters 18–27) all include connections to the 2014 *National Standards*, adaptations in the progression of tasks, as well as numerous new learning experiences.

Each skill theme chapter begins with an overview of the content followed by a description of a series of tasks, the critical elements necessary to succeed at these tasks, and challenges designed to maintain children's interest in learning the tasks. The tasks are organized according to the generic levels of skill proficiency in a spiral progression from beginning to advanced. Assessment options for the skill theme chapters are keyed to the assessment chapter (Chapter 12). Introduced in the ninth edition, many of the skill theme chapters make use of a photographic technique allowing us to provide movement sequences of many of the skill themes labeled with critical elements that are so important for children to learn the fundamental movement skills that are the building blocks for successful and enjoyable participation in sports and physical activities for a lifetime.

Part 6 includes the skill theme application chapters of: "Teaching Physical Fitness, Physical Activity, and Wellness" (Chapter 28), "Teaching Educational Dance and Rhythms" (Chapter 29), "Teaching Educational Gymnastics" (Chapter 30), and "Teaching Educational Games" (Chapter 31). Each of these chapters has been rewritten to be more user friendly to current teachers and teacher candidates.

These chapters describe predesigned and child-designed learning experiences, with a focus on teachers guiding children to develop their own games, gymnastic sequences, and dances. The last chapter in Part 6 (Chapter 32) provides examples of how classroom and physical education teachers can work together to reinforce literacy, mathematics, science, social studies, physical education, and other concepts that are taught in the classroom, in the gymnasium, and on the playground.

The final part of *Children Moving* (Part 7) contains two chapters. Chapter 33 describes some of the ways physical educators can garner support for their program for various constituents that are critical for the development of a thriving, contemporary program of physical education. Chapter 34 contains our dreams for the future. You may want to read this chapter any time. We think it says a great deal about the authors of *Children Moving* and our vision of the future.

New to This Edition

If you have read previous editions of *Children Moving*, you will see significant changes this time around. First, you have probably noticed we have added two new authors to the *Children Moving* team. We are delighted to welcome Tina Hall of Middle Tennessee State University and Kevin Patton from California State University, Chico. Tina and Kevin are long-time adopters of

Children Moving, and throughout the book, you will notice the new perspectives they bring to the writing team. Second, although no new chapters have been included, we have made major revisions in nearly every chapter. Additionally, we have reorganized the order of some of the chapters for better flow.

- A key feature of this new edition is updated content, which is reflected in the text discussions and in the references and readings.
- Sample student learning indicators for movement concepts and skill themes have been provided for the psychomotor domain (Chapter 1) and reinforced when addressing assessment (Chapter 12).
- The critical elements for each fundamental movement skill are listed within the skill theme chapters.
- Linkages of skill themes to the newly revised SHAPE America *National Standards & Grade-Level Outcomes for K–12 Physical Education* are provided for all skill themes and movement concepts.
- Included as an appendix to "Planning and Developing the Content" (Chapter 6), two sample school-year overviews based on the material in *Children Moving* have been added. This includes a two-day-a-week scope and sequence for an inexperienced class (grades K–2) and a two-day-a-week program (scope and sequence) for an experienced class (grades 3–6).
- Assessment information and examples have been enhanced in Chapter 12, including updated elementary report cards.
- New and revised learning tasks and assessment examples have been included throughout the movement concept chapters (14–16) as well as the skill theme chapters (17–27).
- "Adapting the Content for Diverse Learners" (Chapter 10) has been completely rewritten. The authors support the philosophy of inclusion and provide strategies for teaching all children who make up the diversity of our classrooms.
- "Teaching Educational Dance" (Chapter 29) has been rewritten to aid both the novice and the experienced teacher in developing the content of predesigned and child-designed dance. The chapter appendices include additional sample dance experiences.
- "Teaching Physical Fitness, Physical Activity, and Wellness" (Chapter 28) has been revised to include a detailed introduction to the Comprehensive School Physical Activity Plan (CSPAP).

Evidence-Based Support

This new edition highlights many examples of the latest research in the field, such as findings that suggest a connection between ongoing physical activity and obesity and between movement and learning.

Whenever possible, we have cited research evidence to support the skill theme approach. These citations are noted throughout the chapters, and complete references are included at the end of many chapters. In some instances you will see research cited that may be a number of years old. In these instances the research cited is relevant today, even though it was done some time ago. In other instances there are no recent relevant studies of which the authors are aware.

Successful Features

The Skill Theme Approach

The skill theme focus of this book guides teachers in helping children develop their fundamental movement skills with developmentally appropriate learning experiences that are directed toward their skill level rather than their grade level. Designed for both classroom teachers and physical education teachers, the skill theme approach highlights practical ways of teaching physical education to children.

Basic Teaching Skills

This book emphasizes the foundation for teaching skills with topics such as planning, organizing, assessing, and evaluating. It offers a strong background in educationally sound theory and explains how to apply that knowledge to become an effective teacher. The focus is on reflective teaching, which involves adjusting both the content and teaching process to match the needs of students.

Classroom Conversations

The scripted format of the skill theme chapters offers new teachers examples of real conversations that take place in the classroom or gymnasium. In this way teachers can learn how to participate in the different dialogues that are instrumental to child-centered education.

Advocacy of Physical Education

This text focuses on physical education and its relationship to physical fitness. Recognizing the value of physical education as a part of total fitness, this book incorporates the concepts of health-related fitness and wellness throughout all chapters. Virtually every movement concept and skill theme activity avoids asking the children to wait in lines or wait for turns.

Promotion of Inclusion

The idea of inclusion is central to *Children Moving*. Examples of how all individuals can be included in high-quality physical education are found throughout this text. In essence this is the foundation of the reflective teaching process described throughout the book.

Skill Theme Development

Our initial focus in the skill theme approach is on helping children develop and learn the fundamental movement skills. As children acquire these building blocks, they are placed into the contexts of educational dance, gymnastics, and games. Therefore, this text describes how skill themes develop from isolation to being combined with movement concepts and, finally, to being applied to dance, gymnastics, and small-sided games or sports.

Pedagogical Aids

Key Concepts   Each chapter begins with a list of Key Concepts to help students focus their attention on the main topics as they begin studying the chapter. This learning tool also offers an accessible and practical method of review.

Safety   Throughout the text discussions, the symbol ⚠ indicates a safety alert for a particular situation. This tool keeps the new teacher attuned to making safety a basic element in physical education activities and helps avoid accidents.

Critical Elements and Illustrations   Skill themes are presented with a listing of the critical elements of each. These critical elements are useful in observing the particular skill, in providing individual feedback for assistance, and in the selection of appropriate learning experiences for the children performing that skill. Many of these critical elements are illustrated in sequences of photos of children actually performing the skills.

Cues   Cues are brief phrases that can be used to help the children perform a skill more efficiently. A selection of cues—such as "Heads Up" or "Light on Your Feet"—is presented at the beginning of each series of tasks for skill themes and movement concepts. The teacher can select a cue that is appropriate to help children perform the skill correctly.

Tasks   The skill theme and movement concept chapters feature a suggested progression of tasks, or extensions, for children. Highlighted by the symbol 🅣, each task is worded in a conversational style that can be used to give instructions to the children about how to perform the task.

Challenges   Challenges are indicated by the symbol 🅒 in the skill theme and movement concept chapters. They are designed to maintain the children's interest in a particular task. Teachers can either use the challenges listed along with the tasks or create ones that seem appropriate for the children with whom they are working. Challenges allow the reflective teacher to avoid making tasks too difficult before the children are ready.

Assessment Ideas   Assessment tools are designed to see what students have learned in relation to the goals set by the teacher. The symbol ❓ identifies suggested assessments that can be used as part of a lesson (formative) rather than as a separate entity at the end of the unit (summative). These assessment ideas include an array of options, from checks for understanding to exit (or entrance) slips that can be used to quickly assess cognitive and affective learning, to teacher observation checklists and digital analysis to verify psychomotor skills.

Summaries   The chapter summaries highlight the major topics and concepts discussed in the chapter. They can be used for clarification or for review for examinations.

Reading Comprehension Questions   A set of questions appears at the end of each chapter that will allow you to test your understanding of the content. These questions also offer a means of reviewing and analyzing the material.

References/Suggested Readings   This list at the end of each chapter includes references that support the text discussion and additional sources for study and exploration.

Supplements

Test Bank

The test bank is designed for use with McGraw-Hill Connect or EZ Test computerized testing software. EZ Test is a flexible and easy-to-use electronic testing program that allows instructors to create tests from book-specific items. The test bank accommodates a wide range of question types, and instructors may add their own questions in either system. Multiple versions of the test can be created, and tests can be exported for use with course management systems. Additional help is available at www.mheducation.com/connect.

Lesson Planning for Elementary Physical Education: Meeting the National Standards & Grade-Level Outcomes (2016) by Shirley Ann Holt/Hale and Tina Hall.

These lesson plans are designed to offer learning experiences for children that assist them in developing a broad base of movement skills coupled with an enjoyment of physical activity that will translate into a physically active, healthy lifestyle for a lifetime. Some of the highlights are (1) instructional objectives attainable within a single lesson; (2) content development with a focus on a skill rather than on broad exploration; (3) maximum practice of the focus skill; (4) concentration on one cue at a time; (5) challenges throughout the lessons; and (6) both cognitive and performance assessments. Lesson plans are created for the movement concepts, the fundamental movement skills, and the components and concepts of health-related fitness.

McGraw Hill Education connect®

The 10th edition of *Children Moving* is now available online with Connect, McGraw-Hill Education's integrated assignment and assessment platform. Connect also offers SmartBook for the new edition, which is the first adaptive reading experience proven to improve grades and help students study more effectively. All of the title's ancillary content is available through Connect, including:

For the Instructor

- Instructor's manual
- Sample syllabi
- State curriculum guides
- Movement Framework Analysis eWheel
- Image bank
- Downloadable PowerPoint presentations
- Lesson plan Web sites
- Lecture outlines
- Links to professional resources

Assignable for Students

- State curriculum guides
- SHAPE America national standards & grade level outcomes
- Sample lesson plans

- National organizations and professional development resources
- Student success strategies
- Movement Framework Analysis eWheel
- Lesson plan template

McGraw-Hill Create™

Craft your teaching resources to match the way you teach! With McGraw-Hill Create™, you can easily rearrange chapters, combine material from other content sources, and quickly upload content you have written like your course syllabus or teaching notes. Find the content you need in Create by searching through thousands of leading McGraw-Hill textbooks. Arrange your book to fit your teaching style. Create even allows you to personalize your book's appearance by selecting the cover and adding your name, school, and course information. Order a Create book and you'll receive a complimentary print review copy in 3–5 business days or a complimentary electronic review copy (eComp) via email in minutes. Go to www.mcgrawhillcreate.com today and register to experience how McGraw-Hill Create empowers you to teach *your* students *your* way.

Acknowledgments

Children Moving continues to be a work in progress. Over the past 30 plus years, we have been fortunate to work with a number of dedicated professionals who have assisted and inspired us to continue to improve each edition. We would like to acknowledge many of the people who assisted us with this edition and previous ones. We are grateful for their efforts to work with us to continue to improve *Children Moving*.

- Eloise Elliott, West Virginia University, Morgantown, West Virginia, for writing Chapter 32, "Integrating the Skill Theme Approach Across the Curriculum," for the ninth and previous editions as well as for developing the instructor materials for the third through the sixth editions.
- Martin Block, University of Virginia, for his inspiration and shared philosophy concerning children with special needs.
- Rosa Edwards, Shawn Fortner, Liz Harkrader, Sharn Nicholson, John Pomeroy, Andy Lloyd, Larry Satchwell, Casey Jones, Lizzy Ginger, Karla Drury, Tia Ziegler, Nancy McNamee, and so many other children's physical education teachers—for your inspiration, dedication to children, and example in serving as role models for countless other teachers and thousands of children.

- The children at St. Mary's Elementary School, Grand Forks, North Dakota; Bluff Elementary School, Bluff, Utah; and The Accelerated School, Los Angeles, California, who continually added to our understanding of linking skill themes with the development of personal and social responsibility.
- The children at Linden Elementary School in Oak Ridge, Tennessee, who create as well as follow our dreams of physical education for children.
- Barbara Adamcik, for her ability to capture children's movement through photography.
- Derek Sine, Van Tucker, and the Visual Anthropology Department of California State University, Chico, for making the seemingly impossible possible with photography that brought to life the critical elements of skill. We dreamed it; you did it. The children of Beth Giese's fifth-/sixth-grade class at Hooker Oak Elementary School and youngsters from the greater Chico, California, area who selflessly endured our "do it one more time" photography sessions.
- Tia Ziegler and the children of Chappelow K–8 Magnet School, Evans, Colorado; Karla Drury, Lizzy Ginger, and the children of Shawsheen and Monfort Elementary Schools, Greeley, Colorado; and Nathan, Dillon, and Brian Patton for the children's drawings used throughout the book.
- Lans Hayes of Mayfield Publishing Company, who, in 1977, took a huge risk on four unknown authors with a radical idea.
- Danielle Chouhan, our developmental editor for her guidance, patience, gentle nagging, and support.
- The entire McGraw-Hill book team who worked on this edition: Erika Lo, Amy Oline, Danielle Ferrier, Maria McGreal, Lisa Bruflodt, Carrie Burger, and Beth Cray.
- We would like to offer special thanks to the countless teachers and students who have made so many positive and helpful comments since the first edition of *Children Moving* was published. Your support and encouragement continue to be much appreciated.
- Finally, we would like to thank the reviewers of this edition for their insights:

Jon Phillip Gray
University of Houston

Randy Votava
University of North Dakota

Nancy Magee Speed
The University of Southern Mississippi

Alysia Jenkins
Middle Tennessee State University

Jacqueline Williams
James Madison University

Jesse Rhoades
University of North Dakota

Roger S. Jackson
Wayne State University

Students—study more efficiently, retain more and achieve better outcomes. Instructors—focus on what you love—teaching.

SUCCESSFUL SEMESTERS INCLUDE CONNECT

FOR INSTRUCTORS

You're in the driver's seat.

Want to build your own course? No problem. Prefer to use our turnkey, prebuilt course? Easy. Want to make changes throughout the semester? Sure. And you'll save time with Connect's auto-grading too.

65%
Less Time Grading

They'll thank you for it.

Adaptive study resources like SmartBook® help your students be better prepared in less time. You can transform your class time from dull definitions to dynamic debates. Hear from your peers about the benefits of Connect at **www.mheducation.com/highered/connect**

Make it simple, make it affordable.

Connect makes it easy with seamless integration using any of the major Learning Management Systems—Blackboard®, Canvas, and D2L, among others—to let you organize your course in one convenient location. Give your students access to digital materials at a discount with our inclusive access program. Ask your McGraw-Hill representative for more information.

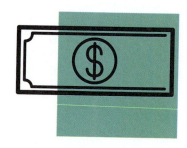

©Hill Street Studios/Tobin Rogers/Blend Images LLC

Solutions for your challenges.

A product isn't a solution. Real solutions are affordable, reliable, and come with training and ongoing support when you need it and how you want it. Our Customer Experience Group can also help you troubleshoot tech problems—although Connect's 99% uptime means you might not need to call them. See for yourself at **status.mheducation.com**

Effective, efficient studying.

Connect helps you be more productive with your study time and get better grades using tools like SmartBook, which highlights key concepts and creates a personalized study plan. Connect sets you up for success, so you walk into class with confidence and walk out with better grades.

©Shutterstock/wavebreakmedia

> " I really liked this app—it made it easy to study when you don't have your text-book in front of you. "

> - Jordan Cunningham,
> Eastern Washington University

Study anytime, anywhere.

Download the free ReadAnywhere app and access your online eBook when it's convenient, even if you're offline. And since the app automatically syncs with your eBook in Connect, all of your notes are available every time you open it. Find out more at **www.mheducation.com/readanywhere**

No surprises.

The Connect Calendar and Reports tools keep you on track with the work you need to get done and your assignment scores. Life gets busy; Connect tools help you keep learning through it all.

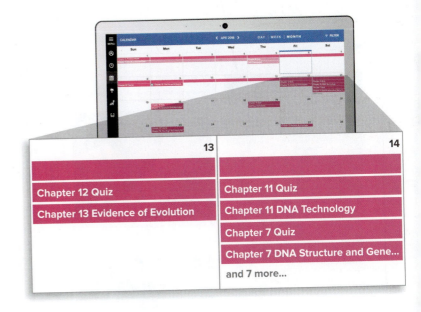

	13		14
	Chapter 12 Quiz		Chapter 11 Quiz
	Chapter 13 Evidence of Evolution		Chapter 11 DNA Technology
			Chapter 7 Quiz
			Chapter 7 DNA Structure and Gene...
			and 7 more...

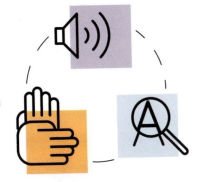

Learning for everyone.

McGraw-Hill works directly with Accessibility Services Departments and faculty to meet the learning needs of all students. Please contact your Accessibility Services office and ask them to email accessibility@mheducation.com, or visit **www.mheducation.com/accessibility** for more information.

Students, are you looking for practical teaching techniques? Working hard to develop the skill theme approach with children? Trying to improve your grade? The features in *Children Moving* will help you do this and more! Take a look.

Key Concepts

Each chapter, or each part in the skills theme chapters, begins with a list of key concepts to help you focus your attention on the main topics as you begin studying each chapter. This learning tool also offers an accessible and practical method of review.

24
CHAPTER

Throwing and Catching

Drawn by children at Monfort, Chappelow or Shawsheen Elementary Schools, Greeley, CO. Courtesy of Lizzy Ginger, Tia Ziegler.

---

68   PART 2 Becoming a Reflective Teacher

Key Concepts

- Reflective teachers constantly plan and revise their plans as they continue to strive to provide the most productive and meaningful learning experiences for children.
- Planning is divided into four steps in this chapter.
  - The first planning step is determining what you want students to learn over the entire program; this is the scope of the curriculum.
  - The second planning step is the development of learning indicators or benchmarks that allow reflective teachers to determine if the children are learning what is being taught.
  - The third planning step is to decide what you want students to learn each year of a program and the sequencing of the content of the program across and within each grade level.
  - The final planning step is the development of daily lesson plans that are interesting and beneficial to youngsters and achieve your objectives for the lesson.
- Ideally, lessons encourage students to be physically active during the majority of the lesson. Typically this occurs when children are able to be successful and consider the lesson fun.
- Just because a lesson is fun does not mean that it is a productive learning experience for children.

The second scenario involves children from another school with whom we work. In their photo diaries regarding physical education are two snippets about their experiences in physical education:

©Melissa Parker

"I learned that we have to shape our hands like a 'W' when catching a ball."

©Melissa Parker

"I learned that spread fingers help with dribbling."

We want to begin this important chapter with two scenarios. The first is a story one of our grandchildren told her father. Savanna, who was age eight, had just started playing organized after-school soccer. This is the conversation she had with her dad on the way to her first after-school soccer practice.

"Dad, I know how to play soccer."

Her dad responded, "That's great. Where did you learn to play soccer?"

Savanna answered, "In PE."

On the way home after her first 90-minute practice, Savanna had another conversation with her Dad who has played a lot of soccer.

"Dad, can you help me with my soccer?"

He replied, "That would be great. But I thought you already learned to play soccer in PE?"

She responded, "No, Dad, we don't learn anything in PE. We just play."

The authors of *Children Moving* sincerely hope you are a teacher that produces results like those illustrated in the second scenario—a teacher from whom children learn, not just one who "does activities" in their physical education classes.

One of the basic premises on which *Children Moving* is based is that youngsters are learning the fundamental movement skills that provide the foundation for success in sports and physical activity. This chapter provides a detailed explanation of how teachers plan their programs so that youngsters actually leave the program having learned some, ideally many, of the fundamental movement skills. While there is not

Box 22-2

Key Observation Points: Rolling Pattern

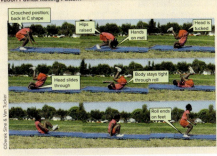

©Derek Sine & Van Tucker

Crouched position; back in C shape
Hips raised
Hands on mat
Head is tucked
Head slides through
Body stays tight through roll
Roll ends on feet

be round. This exploration includes rocking actions from the head to feet on the back and stomach. At this level, children are challenged when asked to perform actions such as rocking back and forth like a rocking chair or rolling in a stretched position like a log. Rocking in a ball-like position, in preparation for rolling, is also explored at this level. When a child first begins to roll, the arms and hands are of little use. The child may get over, but the whole body usually uncurls in the middle of the roll, and the child lands sitting down.

Making Curled Shapes

Setting: A mat, space on a mat, or a grassy area for each child; children positioned so they will not rock into each other (Figure 22.5)

Tasks/Challenges:
- On your mat, try to find as many ways as possible to curl your body so it is round. Three different ways would be good.

Rocking on Different Body Parts

Setting: A mat, space on a mat, or a a grassy area for each child; children positioned so they will not rock into each other

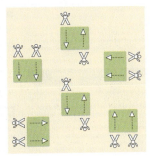

Figure 22.5 Mat positions that minimize the likelihood children will rock or roll into each other.

Illustration Program

Instructional full-color illustrations and photographs throughout the book enhance learning with an exciting visual appeal.

©Barbara Adamcik

Peer teaching provides the opportunity for children to analyze and teach a skill while learning to work with others.

the teacher can help them learn through her or his presentation of the task.

For peer teaching to be an effective instructional approach, follow several key points:

- The skill should be simple, the cues for observation clear, and the performance easily measured.
- Post the cues either on the wall or on individual cue cards so the peer teachers can remember them.
- Children need to have the skills of giving and receiving feedback from others. We have found it useful to demonstrate and role-play what this looks like and sounds like.
- Start small. You might consider including one peer-teaching task in a lesson and then expand.

> *Teaching was easy. All you did was tell them and they did it.*
>
> —Fourth grader after teaching a self-designed game to another group

Guided Discovery

The fourth instructional approach is guided discovery. Guided discovery is designed to facilitate children's critical thinking, as reflected in their movement responses, and to let them solve problems rather than copy the teacher's or another student's correct performance. Guided discovery also enhances student interest and motivation (Chen 2001). In this student-centered

approach, the teacher typically gives the task by asking questions. The teacher most often describes how the task will be practiced and some way to measure success, but exactly how to perform the task is left to the child to explore and interpret. For example, the teacher may say, "From your spot on the floor, try to kick the ball to the wall both in the air and on the ground." The child knows how to practice (from the spot on the floor, kick) and a little about success (to the wall, in the air, and on the ground), but the rest is left up to the child. Guided discovery really serves as an umbrella for two different types of discovery: convergent and divergent. One asks children to find a single answer to a task, whereas the other asks children to find multiple answers to a task.

Convergent Inquiry

Convergent inquiry encourages children to discover the same answer(s) to a series of questions the teacher asks. The teacher guides the children toward one or more correct answers. This approach has been successfully adapted to teaching game skills and strategies, and it is the fundamental principle underlying teaching games for understanding or the tactical approach to teaching games (Mitchell, Oslin, and Griffin 2013). Mosston and Ashworth (2008) suggested that children can discover ideas, similarities, dissimilarities, principles (governing rules), order or system, a particular physical activity or movement, how, why, limits (the dimensions of "how much," "how fast"), and other elements. When we want children to learn one of these elements, we often use the discovery approach to increase their involvement.

The following sequence illustrating Mosston and Ashworth's (2008, pp. 157–58) classic slanty rope technique is a very good example of convergent inquiry encouraging children to find ways to avoid eliminating others from activity.

Step 1: Ask two children to hold a rope for high jumping. Invariably they will hold the rope horizontally at a given height (for example, at hip level).

Step 2: Ask the group to jump over. Before they do so, you might want to ask the rope holders to decrease the height so that everybody can be successful.

Step 3: After everyone has cleared the height, you ask, "What shall we do now?" "Raise it!" "Raise it!" is the answer—always! (The success of the first jump motivates all to continue.)

Step 4: Ask the rope holders to raise the rope just a bit. The jumping is resumed.

Vignettes and Quotations

The authors and seasoned teachers provide real examples of experiences with students that relate to the topics discussed, for more insight into the dynamics of teaching.

Tasks/Challenges

The skill theme and movement concept chapters feature a suggested progression of tasks for children. Each task is worded in a conversational style that can be used to give instructions to the children about how to perform the task. Challenges are designed to maintain the children's interest in a particular task. Teachers can either use the challenges listed along with the tasks or create ones that seem appropriate for the children with whom they are working.

Transferring Weight to Hands Momentarily

Setting: Large gymnastics mats and/or small mats that will not slide as children transfer weight, scattered throughout general space

Tasks/Challenges:

- Transfer your weight from your feet to your hands to your feet, momentarily taking your weight on your hands only.

Wedge mats or folded or rolled mats may be easier for children just beginning to take weight on their hands and/or for those uncomfortable with transfer from standing position to mat on floor.

Transferring Weight onto and off Equipment

Setting: Low gymnastics equipment—benches, tables, balance beams, and so on—scattered throughout general space

⚠ Carefully examine all equipment to be used for gymnastics in elementary school physical education. Extended edges of gymnastics equipment and bases/supports of apparatus sometimes need extra padding to assure safety and prevention of injury for children.

Tasks/Challenges:

The focus for exploration of equipment at the precontrol level is safety—getting on and off equipment with personal safety and without creating an unsafe situation for others.

Control Level (GLSP): Learning Experiences Leading to Skill Development

Tasks at the control level are designed to help children transfer their weight to specific body parts—feet to back, to hands, to head and hands—as they travel, and in relation to gymnastics apparatus. Control of their bodies, i.e., safety throughout the weight transfer, is the goal at the control level.

A note about cues: *Although several cues are listed for many of the learning experiences, it's important to focus on only one cue at a time. This way, the children can really concentrate on that cue. Once you provide feedback to the children and observe that most have learned a cue, it's time to focus on another one.*

Transferring Weight from Feet to Hands to Feet

Setting: Lines marked or taped on the floor; children scattered throughout general space

Cues

| Strong Muscles | (Strong arms and shoulders—no collapse.) |
| Stretch Your Legs | (Extend your legs upward—stretch to the sky.) |

Tasks/Challenges:

- When we were exploring transferring weight, you practiced taking your weight on your hands and bringing your feet to the floor at the same place. Practice taking your weight on your hands and bringing your feet down safely (Figure 22.1) at a new place—to the right or the left of their original place.

- Now you are going to transfer your weight from your feet to your hands to travel across your line. Stand on one side of your line, transfer your weight to your hands, and bring your feet down on the other side. You will travel across the line by transferring your weight from feet to hands to feet.

   You may want to begin in a squat position with your feet on the floor and your hands on the other side of the line, or relatively close to your feet. Transfer your weight to your hands and bring your feet down a short distance away—just over the line.

- When you are comfortable taking your weight on your hands for a longer time and you are landing safely, kick your legs higher in the air to remain on your hands even longer.

- Stand at the side of your line, in a front-back stance. Extend your arms upward. Step forward with your lead foot, and transfer your weight to your hands. Bring your feet to the floor on the opposite side of your line. If you stretch your trunk and legs as you transfer your weight to one hand and then the other, you will begin to do a cartwheel (Figure 22.1).

Transferring Weight from Feet to Back with a Rocking Action

Setting: Large or small mats that will not slide, scattered throughout general space

Cues

| Rounded Back | (Curl your back and body for all rocking skills.) |

Tasks/Challenges:

- Transfer your weight from your feet to your back with a rocking action. Always return to your feet (Figure 22.1).

A young boy kicking a stone along the sidewalk as he walks home from school, a neighborhood game of kick the can, kickball on the school playground at recess, an aspiring athlete practicing the soccer (futbol) dribble, and the professional punter—all are executing a similar movement: the kick. This movement requires accuracy, body control, point of contact, force, and direction. Some children seem to perform the kick with intense concentration; others, effortlessly.

We try to give children a variety of opportunities to practice kicking so they'll develop a foundation of kicking skills they can use in different situations. For young children, the challenge is simply making contact with the ball; at the advanced level, the challenge is participation in dynamic group activities combining the skill of kicking with other skills and movement concepts. See Box 23-1 for linkages of the skill theme of kicking and punting to the *National Standards & Grade-Level Outcomes for K–12 Physical Education* (SHAPE America 2014).

Box 23-1

Kicking and Punting in the *National Standards & Grade-Level Outcomes for K–12 Physical Education*

Kicking and punting are referenced in the *National Standards & Grade-Level Outcomes for K–12 Physical Education* (SHAPE America 2014) under Standard 1: "Demonstrates competency in a variety of motor skills and movement patterns." The intent of the standard is developing the fundamental skills needed to enjoy participation in physical activities, with the mastery of movement fundamentals as the foundation for continued skill acquisition.

Sample grade-level outcomes from the *National Standards* include:

- Kicks a stationary ball from a stationary position, demonstrating two of the five critical elements of a mature pattern (K)
- Approaches a stationary ball and kicks it forward, demonstrating two of the five critical elements of a mature pattern (1)
- Uses a continuous running approach and kicks a moving ball, demonstrating three of the five critical elements of a mature pattern (2)
- Uses a continuous running approach and intentionally performs a kick along the ground and a kick in the air, demonstrating four of the five critical elements of a mature pattern for each (3)
- Uses a continuous running approach and kicks a stationary ball for accuracy (3)
- Kicks along the ground and in the air, and punts using mature patterns (4)
- Demonstrates mature patterns of kicking and punting in small-sided practice task environments (5)

* Suggested grade-level outcomes for student learning.

Skill Theme Development Progression

Kicking

Proficiency Level

Playing Cone Soccer
Playing Alley Soccer
Playing Soccer Keep-Away
Playing Mini Soccer
Kicking at a moving target
Kicking at small stationary targets

Utilization Level

Playing two-on-one soccer
Passing to a partner in general space
Kicking to a traveling partner
Kicking to a partner from various angles
Dribble and kick: playing soccer golf
Playing one-on-one soccer
Traveling and kicking for a goal
Performing a continuous dribble and change of direction
Changing directions: dribble

Control Level

Dribble: control of ball and body
Dribbling around stationary obstacles
Dribble: Traveling in pathways
Dribble: Starting and stopping
Dribbling the ball along the ground
Kicking/passing to a partner
Kicking to targets
Kicking at low targets
Kicking a rolling ball from a running approach
Kicking a rolling ball from a stationary position
Kicking to a distance zone
Kicking for distance along the ground and in the air
Kicking in the air
Kicking on the ground

Precontrol Level

Tap/dribble the ball
Approaching a stationary ball and kicking
Kicking a stationary ball from a stationary position

Skill Theme Development Sequences

The skill theme chapters contain hundreds of learning experiences designed to help children learn. Motor skills are organized according to the generic levels of skill proficiency in a spiral progression from beginning to advanced.

...vel but focus on the critical elements of the skill. ...arning experiences provide opportunities to learn to ...ibble in different places around the body and then ...ogress to dribbling and traveling while varying both ...rection and pathway. In all experiences, children are ...couraged to use both the preferred and nonpreferred ...ands.

A note about cues: *Although several cues are listed for ...any of the learning experiences, it's important to focus on ...ly one cue at a time. This way, the children can really ...ncentrate on that cue. Once you provide feedback to the ...ildren and observe that most have learned a cue, it's time ... focus on another one.*

...ribbling in Self-Space

...etting: Children scattered throughout general space, ...ch with a ball

Cues

Fingerpads	(Use the fingerpads, not finger-tips.)
Knees Bent	(Bend the knees slightly.)
Push, Push	(Push to the floor, snap the wrist at the end)
Opposite Foot	(Opposite foot slightly forward; see Figure 25.10.)

...asks/Challenges:

1. Dribble the ball with one hand.
2. Dribble the ball with the other hand.
3. Count the number of times you can dribble without losing control.
4. On the signal, begin dribbling with one hand. ...ntinue dribbling until the signal is given to stop.

Figure 25.10 Correct hand and body position for dribbling a ball.

Have children repeat each task with their nonpreferred hand throughout all levels of the skill. The proficient dribbler is equally skilled with each hand.

Continuous Dribbling

Setting: Children scattered in general space, each with a ball (either a smaller basketball or a playground ball)

Cues

Fingerpads	(Use the finger pads, not fingertips.)
Knees Bent	(Bend the knees slightly.)
Push, Push	(Push to the floor, snap the wrist at the end.)
Opposite Foot	(Opposite foot of the dribbling hand should be slightly forward.)

Tasks/Challenges:

1. Remember when you bounced a ball down so it came back up to you and then pushed it down again so the bounce continued? This continuous bounce is called a dribble. Practice dribbling now.
2. Practice until you can dribble the ball five times without losing control of it.
3. Say one letter of the alphabet for each time you dribble. Can you get to Z?

Tip: Children tend to dribble either with the whole palm or with the ends of the fingers. Besides using the term finger-pads, we have also found it useful to put chalk or tape on the fingerpads to help children learn the correct part of their fingers to use.

4. Point to which parts of your fingers are used for dribbling.
5. ***Student Drawing.*** Students are provided with a drawing of a handprint and are asked to color the portion of the hand used in mature dribbling. Students may also be asked to draw an entire person dribbling to show the overall critical elements of this movement task.

Criteria for Assessment

a. Correctly identifies position of hand used in mature dribbling.
b. Identifies the critical elements of dribbling.

NASPE (1995, pp. 20–21)

Dribbling at Different Levels

Setting: Children scattered throughout general space, each with a ball

Cues

Cues can be used to help children perform a skill more efficiently. A selection of cues is presented at the beginning of each series of tasks. The teacher can choose a cue that is appropriate for a particular child to make the task easier for that child to perform. Many of the cues are illustrated in color photographic sequences to allow the child to perform the skill correctly.

Assessment Ideas

Assessment tools are designed to see what students have learned in relation to the goals set by the teacher. These assessment ideas include an array of options from exit (or entrance) slips that can be used to quickly assess cognitive and affective learning to teacher observation checklists and digital analysis to verify psychomotor skills.

---

level of achievement. Reflective teachers are no different. As you know by now, becoming an excellent teacher takes many, many hours of hard work. Just because a teacher has 10 or 15 years of teaching experience and a master's degree does not mean he or she has become an excellent teacher. The process of reflective teaching is no different. *Children Moving* will guide you in the process of beginning to become a reflective teacher. We hope you find your journey both enjoyable and worthwhile.

Summary

Six major variables necessitate the need for reflective teaching, or differentiated instruction: the values of the teacher, class size, the number of class sessions per week, facilities and equipment, student behavior, and the context of the school. The reflective teacher considers the characteristics of each class and the abilities of the individual students. A reflective teacher doesn't expect all children to respond in the same way or to achieve the same level of skill. Reflective teachers continually observe and analyze, a process that enables them to revise their expectations and adapt all the components of the program, thereby constantly improving the program's effectiveness. The reflective approach requires that teachers constantly and accurately monitor their teaching as they attempt to design and implement a physical education program for a given school. Reflective teachers also have a wealth of content knowledge that allows them to adapt and modify tasks for individuals of varying abilities. The process of becoming a reflective teacher takes time, practice, and a commitment to lifelong learning. *Children Moving* is designed to guide you in this process.

Reading Comprehension Questions

1. What is reflective teaching? What are its basic characteristics?
2. What does a linear approach to teaching mean? What is a prepackaged curriculum? How is it different from the skill theme approach?
3. Provide three examples of how class size influences the way a teacher teaches a lesson.
4. Provide an example of a teacher who "rolls out the ball." Contrast that teacher with a reflective teacher. What do they do differently in their planning, teaching, and assessment of their teaching?
5. In the previous two chapters, you have learned about skill themes and movement concepts. Explain the difference(s) between skill themes and games like Duck, Duck, Goose or elimination dodgeball.
6. In your own words, explain the major implication of reflective teaching, or differentiated instruction.

References/Suggested Readings

Allen, D. 1975. The future of education: Where do we go from here? *Journal of Teacher Education* 26: 41–45.

Foster, H. L. 1974. *Ribbin', jivin' and playin' the dozens: The unrecognized dilemma of inner-city schools.* Cambridge, MA: Ballinger.

Good, T. L., B. J. Biddle, and J. E. Brophy. 1975. *Teachers make a difference.* New York: Holt, Rinehart & Winston.

Graham, G., E. Elliot, and S. Palmer. 2016. *Teaching children and adolescents physical education: Becoming a master teacher.* 4th ed. Champaign, IL: Human Kinetics.

Graham, G., M. Metzler, and G. Webster. 1991. Specialist and classroom teacher effectiveness in children's physical education: A 3-year study [monograph]. *Journal of Teaching in Physical Education* 4: 321–426.

Hall, T. J., and M. A. Smith. 2006. Teacher planning, instruction and reflection: What we know about teacher cognitive processes. *Quest* 58: 424–42.

Hastie, P. A., and Sanders, J. E. 1991. Effects of class size and equipment availability on student involvement in physical education. *The Journal of Experimental Education* 59: 212–24.

Locke, L. F. 1975, Spring. The ecology of the gymnasium: What the tourist never sees. *Southern Association for Physical Education of College Women Proceedings*, 38–50.

[NASPE] National Association for Sport and Physical Education. 2006. *Teaching large class sizes in physical education: guidelines and strategies* [Guidance document]. Reston, VA: NASPE.

Summaries

The chapter summaries highlight the major topics and concepts discussed in the chapter. They can be used for clarification or for review for examinations.

Reading Comprehension Questions

A set of questions appears at the end of each chapter to allow you to test your understanding of the content. This tool offers a means of reviewing and analyzing the material.

References/Suggested Readings

At the end of each chapter are references that support the text discussion and additional sources for study and exploration.

Appendix

The Appendix to chapter 6 offers two sample school-year overviews (scopes and sequences) based on the material in *Children Moving*. These overviews can be followed exactly as presented or used as a model for developing your own quality physical education program.

---

level of achievement. Reflective teachers are no different. As you know by now, becoming an excellent teacher takes many, many hours of hard work. Just because a teacher has 10 or 15 years of teaching experience and a master's degree does not mean he or she has become an excellent teacher. The process of reflective teaching is no different. *Children Moving* will guide you in the process of beginning to become a reflective teacher. We hope you find your journey both enjoyable and worthwhile.

Summary

Six major variables necessitate the need for reflective teaching, or differentiated instruction: the values of the teacher, class size, the number of class sessions per week, facilities and equipment, student behavior, and the context of the school. The reflective teacher considers the characteristics of each class and the abilities of the individual students. A reflective teacher doesn't expect all children to respond in the same way or to achieve the same level of skill. Reflective teachers continually observe and analyze, a process that enables them to revise their expectations and adapt all the components of the program, thereby constantly improving the program's effectiveness. The reflective approach requires that teachers constantly and accurately monitor their teaching as they attempt to design and implement a physical education program for a given school. Reflective teachers also have a wealth of content knowledge that allows them to adapt and modify tasks for individuals of varying abilities. The process of becoming a reflective teacher takes time, practice, and a commitment to lifelong learning. *Children Moving* is designed to guide you in this process.

Reading Comprehension Questions

1. What is reflective teaching? What are its basic characteristics?
2. What does a linear approach to teaching mean? What is a prepackaged curriculum? How is it different from the skill theme approach?
3. Provide three examples of how class size influences the way a teacher teaches a lesson.
4. Provide an example of a teacher who "rolls out the ball." Contrast that teacher with a reflective teacher. What do they do differently in their planning, teaching, and assessment of their teaching?
5. In the previous two chapters, you have learned about skill themes and movement concepts. Explain the difference(s) between skill themes and games like Duck, Duck, Goose or elimination dodgeball.
6. In your own words, explain the major implication of reflective teaching, or differentiated instruction.

References/Suggested Readings

Allen, D. 1975. The future of education: Where do we go from here? *Journal of Teacher Education* 26: 41–45.

Foster, H. L. 1974. *Ribbin', jivin' and playin' the dozens: The unrecognized dilemma of inner-city schools.* Cambridge, MA: Ballinger.

Good, T. L., B. J. Biddle, and J. E. Brophy. 1975. *Teachers make a difference.* New York: Holt, Rinehart & Winston.

Graham, G., E. Elliot, and S. Palmer. 2016. *Teaching children and adolescents physical education: Becoming a master teacher.* 4th ed. Champaign, IL: Human Kinetics.

Graham, G., M. Metzler, and G. Webster. 1991. Specialist and classroom teacher effectiveness in children's physical education: A 3-year study [monograph]. *Journal of Teaching in Physical Education* 4: 321–426.

Hall, T. J., and M. A. Smith. 2006. Teacher planning, instruction and reflection: What we know about teacher cognitive processes. *Quest* 58: 424–42.

Hastie, P. A., and Sanders, J. E. 1991. Effects of class size and equipment availability on student involvement in physical education. *The Journal of Experimental Education* 59: 212–24.

Locke, L. F. 1975, Spring. The ecology of the gymnasium: What the tourist never sees. *Southern Association for Physical Education of College Women Proceedings,* 38–50.

[NASPE] National Association for Sport and Physical Education. 2006. *Teaching large class sizes in physical education: guidelines and strategies* [Guidance document]. Reston, VA: NASPE.

Sample Two-Day-a-Week Lesson Topics for Lower Elementary Classes (72 Days a Year)

Week	Chapter	Day	
1	7	1	Establishing an Environment for Learning (pp. 95–119)
	7	2	Establishing an Environment for Learning (cont.) (pp. 99–119)
2	14	1	Exploring Self-Space (p. 245)
	14	2	Exploring General Space (p. 246)
3	14	1	Traveling in Different Directions (p. 249)
	14	2	Traveling and Freezing at Different Levels (p. 251)
4	28	1	Teaching Physical Fitness, Physical Activity, and Wellness (pp. 597–623)
	24	2	Throwing at a Large Target (p. 474)
5	24	1	Catching a Rolling Ball (p. 474); Catching from a Skilled Thrower (p. 474)
	17	2	Traveling with Different Locomotor Patterns (p. 305): Sliding; Galloping; Hopping; Skipping (p. 306)
6	17	1	Performing Locomotor Sequences (p. 308)
	18	2	Traveling to Flee (p. 327); Fleeing from a Partner (p. 328)
7	18	1	Traveling to Dodge (p. 327); Dodging the Obstacles (p. 329)
	23	2	Kicking a Stationary Ball from a Stationary Position (p. 441)
8	23	1	Approaching a Stationary Ball and Kicking (p. 441); Kicking in the Air (p. 478)
	23	2	Dropping, Bouncing, and Kicking Lightweight Balls (p. 458); Dropping and Punting (p. 458)
9	20	1	Jumping and Landing: Basic Patterns (p. 360)
	28	2	Teaching Physical Fitness, Physical Activity, and Wellness (pp. 597–623)
10	25	1	Volleying Balloons in the Air (p. 504)
	25	2	Volleying a Ball Upward (Underhand Pattern) (p. 506)
11	25	1	Bouncing a Ball Down (Dribbling) Continuously (p. 521)
	25	2	Dribbling and Walking (p. 521)
12	15	1	Exploring Time (p. 262)
	15	2	Exploring Force (p. 268)
13	15	1	Traveling and Changing Force Qualities (p. 268)
	7	2	Establishing an Environment for Learning (pp. 95–119)
14	14	1	Exploring Pathways (p. 252)
	14	2	Exploring Extensions (p. 256)
15	17	1	Moving to Rhythms (p. 309)
	28	2	Teaching Physical Fitness, Physical Activity, and Wellness (pp. 597–623)
16	26	1	Striking Down; Striking Up (pp. 542, 543)
	26	2	Striking Up and Down (p. 543)
17	20	1	Jumping over Low Obstacles: Hoops (p. 362); Jumping over Low Obstacles: Hurdles (p. 362)
	20	2	Jumping a Turned Rope (p. 363); Jumping a Self-Turned Rope (p. 364)
18	16	1	Identifying Body Parts (p. 277); Balancing on Matching and Nonmatching Parts (p. 278)
	16	2	Traveling and Freezing in Different Body Shapes (p. 280)
19	28	1	Teaching Physical Fitness, Physical Activity, and Wellness (pp. 597–623)
	17	2	Leaping (p. 309)
20	16	1	Over, Under, Around, In Front Of, and Behind Concepts (p. 285)
	17	2	Locomotors and Rhythm: The Follow-Me Dance (p. 311)
21	22	1	Rocking on Different Body Parts (p. 418); Rocking to Match a Partner (p. 419)
	22	2	Rolling Sideways (p. 419); Rolling Forward (p. 422)
22		1	Special Event
	16	2	Matching (p. 288); Mirroring (p. 289); Matching and Mirroring (p. 290)
23	21	1	Balancing on Different Bases of Support (pp. 377, 378)
	21	2	Balancing in Different Body Shapes (p. 378, 381)
24	22	1	Rolling in a Long, Narrow Position (Log Roll) (p. 419)
	22	2	Rocking Backward (p. 421)
25	22	1	Transferring Weight to Hands Momentarily (p. 404)
	22	2	Transferring Weight From Feet to Hands to Feet (p. 404)
26	24	1	Throwing Overhand (p. 476); Throwing Underhand (p. 476); Throwing Sidearm (p. 476)
	24	2	Throwing a Ball Against a Wall and Catching the Rebound (p. 484)

1
PART

Introduction and Content Overview

Trent

A quality program of physical education for children is much more than simply a bunch of activities that children enjoy for 30 minutes or so several times a week. A quality program of physical education has a definite purpose and long-term goals and is developmentally and instructionally appropriate; in short, it makes a difference for children that lasts well beyond elementary school. Part 1 of *Children Moving* contains the first three chapters and documents the importance of a quality program of physical education for children and also introduces you to the skill theme approach.

Chapter 1, "The Value and Purpose of Physical Education for Children," introduces three important themes as an introduction and overview to the book. The first two respond to the need for, and the importance of, physical activity and physical education for children. The last answer provides insights into the characteristics of a physical education program for children that is positive and guides them in the process of becoming physically active for a lifetime. As you will see, these themes are based on recent publications written by some of the leading experts in physical education and physical activity for children. Together they define a clear and unified direction providing outcomes for programs of physical education while also suggesting a process (developmentally appropriate) that is consistent with contemporary approaches for teaching children.

Chapter 2, "The Skill Theme Approach," answers many of the questions that teachers often ask when they are first exposed to the skill theme approach. Because the skill theme curriculum is organized by skills and concepts rather than by games, gymnastics, and dance, for example, some teachers initially find the approach confusing. In Chapter 2, we use a question-and-answer format to respond to these questions.

Then, Chapter 3, "Skill Themes, Movement Concepts, and the *National Standards*," defines the skill themes and movement concepts as the foundation of elementary physical education and *Children Moving*. The Movement Analysis Framework—The Wheel—shows the interaction of skill themes and movement concepts. Progression spirals are introduced to demonstrate the developmentally appropriate progression for each of the skill themes. Chapter 3 also shows the alignment of *Children Moving* with the National Standards & Grade-Level Outcomes (SHAPE America, 2014).

The Value and Purpose of Physical Education for Children

As the old man walked the beach at dawn, he noticed a young man ahead of him picking up starfish and flinging them into the sea. Finally catching up with the youth, he asked him why he was doing this. The answer was that the stranded starfish would die if left until the morning sun.

"But the beach goes on for miles and there are millions of starfish," countered the old man. "How can your effort make any difference?"

The young man looked at the starfish in his hand and then threw it to the safety of the waves. "It makes a difference to this one," he said.

—DONALD QUIMBY (1988)

If you don't take care of your body, where are you going to live?

—AUTHOR UNKNOWN

Drawn by children at Monfort, Chappelow or Shawsheen Elementary Schools, Greeley, CO. Courtesy of Lizzy Ginger; Tia Ziegler

Key Concepts

- The purpose of a quality program of physical education is to guide youngsters in the process of becoming physically active for a lifetime.

- Regular physical activity is important because it helps prevent obesity; promotes motor skill development and physical fitness; provides opportunities for setting goals, making new friends, and reducing stress; and may enhance academic performance.

- Physical activity and physical education are different: physical activity is a behavior; physical education is an educational program designed to help children learn to be physically active.

- Physical education is important because it can enhance movement skill development, self-efficacy, personal and social responsibility, cognitive development regarding skill and fitness, and leadership.

- Quality physical education is the foundation for a lifetime of physical activity and educates the whole child.

- Quality physical education programs have reasonable class sizes, a developmental and sequential curriculum, plenty of practice and movement opportunities, and adequate facilities and equipment; honor children's voices; and are clearly aligned with learning indicators.

What if you could give the children you teach a gift to help them live longer, happier, healthier lives? Of course you are thinking "Sure, I would like to do that." You also have numerous questions. What is involved? Would this program be for every child? Would it be expensive? How long would it take? Can I really do that?

As a teacher the gift you can give the children you teach is a love and enjoyment of physical activity that leads to fun, frequent participation in physical activity as children, adolescents, and adults. *Children Moving* describes, in detail, how to develop a quality program of elementary school physical education. Many experts believe programs like this provide a foundation to developing the competence that leads to confidence and the enjoyment of physical activity for a lifetime. This book provides a complete blueprint for teachers who are interested in starting children on the path to obtain the skills, knowledge, and dispositions that lead to a physically active lifestyle.

Children, especially young children, love to move. They enjoy squirming, wriggling, crawling, running, chasing, jumping, rolling, balancing, kicking, throwing, and many other activities. For parents and teachers

While it is true that physical activity participation for children is down, the opportunity to participate in activity is greater for elementary school children than at any other time in life. These opportunities to be physically active can be depicted as an hourglass. Although mediated by socioeconomic status, neighborhood, and gender, young children generally have a lot of opportunities to be physically active. Playgrounds, parks, and even a number of fast-food chains have equipment for children to climb on, over, around, and through. Young children also are encouraged to run and chase their friends and siblings. Many communities also have soccer, basketball, and softball or baseball leagues for young children. There are also opportunities to be on a swim team and take lessons in dance or martial arts. Unfortunately, once a youngster enters middle school, many of these opportunities are reduced, even if a child joins sport teams. Too often if a middle school sponsors sport teams, only a relatively few "make the team" and today's "traveling" teams limit participation to those who can afford it. The same is true at the high school level for sports and intramurals. If intramurals are offered, many are limited to team sports after school. In many schools it is not popular to play intramurals or have your parents drive you to a dance lesson. This reduction in opportunities to participate becomes clear when you look at the youth sport participation data. In 2016, 36,250,000 children aged 6 to 12 participated in youth sport; at the high school level, this participation dropped to 2,286,00 largely because of lack of opportunity (The Aspen Institute 2017). After high school, however, there are once again a plethora of physical activities for adults. They include weight and fitness clubs, recreation programs, and simply walking, jogging, or biking activities that were not in vogue in secondary school but are acceptable to adults.

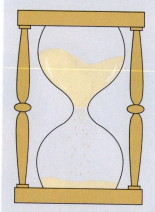

Physical Activity Hourglass

Preschool and elementary
Multitude of opportunities

Secondary school
Limited to school sports and intramurals

Adults
Multitude of opportunities

the challenge is getting the children to stop moving—for just a few minutes. And then, at about 10 or 12 years of age, this torrent of physical activity becomes a trickle for far too many children. Why? What can be done to encourage children, all children, to continue this enjoyment of movement into their teen and adult years? In short, what can teachers and schools do to encourage children to continue moving throughout their lifetime?

Children Moving attempts to provide answers to many of these questions. The goal of this book is to describe both a curriculum and the companion teaching skills designed to guide youngsters in the process of becoming physically active for a lifetime. There is general agreement that skillfulness, the ability to perform fundamental and sport-related movement skills, is an important prerequisite for adopting a physically active lifestyle (Clark 2007; Gallahue, Ozmun, and Goodway 2012). Our goal is also to teach children to value physical activity for all the benefits that are described later in this chapter—as well as the pure enjoyment and satisfaction that comes from successful and enjoyable participation.

Why are some adults physically active and others not? Although we do not have all the answers to this question, there is growing evidence that physically active children become physically active adolescents and adults (Barnett et al. 2008; Ennis 2011; Jaakkola and Washington 2013; Stodden, Langendorfer, and Roberton 2009). And we have a solid evidence base that physically active children, as well as adults, derive substantial benefits from being physically active (Reiner et al. 2013).

Children Moving is based on the premise that to truly enjoy many of the physical activities and sports in which adults participate, one needs a certain level of skillfulness or the development of fundamental motor/movement skills. Although the terms *fundamental motor skills* and *fundamental movement skills* can be used interchangeably, we have chosen to use *fundamental movement skills* throughout the remainder of this book. The ideal time to learn these fundamental movement skills is when children are young and they so enjoy moving in any form. One of the important characteristics of fundamental movement skills is that once they are learned, they are retained for a lifetime. Swimming and riding a bike are two good examples. While we may not be as adept at these skills if we have not done them for 20 years or so, our bodies (kinesthetic memory) don't forget. Thus the goal of *Children Moving* is to describe effective techniques and strategies to assist children in acquiring many of the fundamental movement skills that all children and adults use in sports and physical activities.

It is important to emphasize that quality programs do far more than simply provide opportunities for children to be physically active for the few minutes they are in physical education class (NASPE 2006). As will be explained throughout the book, in quality physical education programs, children are taught the fundamental movement skills used in all types of physical activities and sports—while also keeping the children physically active throughout the lesson (NASPE 2011).

It is analogous to teaching reading or mathematics; children learn the fundamental skills in elementary school and then apply them in middle school and high school—and throughout their lives. As you will learn in this book, physical education for children is far more than just playing a few games or learning a dance or two. Physical education provides learning experiences that lead to competence and confidence in physical activity and sports.

The Importance of Physical Activity

As stated earlier the goal of physical education is giving youngsters the psychomotor, cognitive, and affective skills for a lifetime of physical activity. Today, the benefits of being active and the health consequences of being physically inactive are well known. Since 1996, when the Surgeon General of the United States released his landmark report documenting the important contribution regular physical activity can make to good health (USDHHS 1996), the importance of physical activity has been recognized as never before (Box 1-1). In 2018, the U.S. Department of Health and Human Services (USDHHS) issued the newly revised *Physical Activity Guidelines for Americans*, which provide science-based recommendations to help persons age 6 or older improve their health through physical activity. The guidelines recommend that children and adolescents should have 60 minutes of moderate- or vigorous-intensity aerobic physical activity daily, muscle-strengthening activities at least three days a week, and bone strengthening activities at least three days a week (USDHHS 2018).

In 2017, the Centers for Disease Control and Prevention (CDC) outlined the following health benefits of regular physical activity:

- Controlling weight
- Reducing the risk of cardiovascular disease
- Reducing the risk for type 2 diabetes and metabolic syndrome
- Reducing the risk of some cancers
- Strengthening bones and muscles
- Improving mental health and mood
- Improving the ability to do daily activities and preventing falls for older adults
- Increasing the chances of living longer

In addition to the health benefits associated with regular physical activity listed above, there are also numerous social, psychological, and academic benefits (WHO 2018). They include:

Enhanced academic performance Movement can be used to reinforce the understanding of many subjects taught in the classroom. Kinesthetic learning

It is estimated that 70 percent of U.S. adults are overweight or obese.

©Noel Moore/Getty Images

Box 1-1

Significant Seminal Surgeon Report Linking Physical Activity and Health Benefits

Over 20 years ago, in 1996, the Surgeon General of the United States published a significant report that documented, for the first time, the relationship between regular physical activity and health. Here are some of the research-based observations in the report (USDHHS 1996). These findings have also been supported in the recently released document *Physical Activity Guidelines for Americans* (USDHHS 2018).

- Significant health benefits can be obtained by including a moderate amount of physical activity (e.g., 30 minutes of brisk walking or raking leaves, 15 minutes of running, or 45 minutes of volleyball) on most, if not all, days of the week. Through a modest increase in daily activity, most Americans can improve their health and quality of life (4).
- Additional health benefits can be gained through greater amounts of physical activity. People who can maintain a regular regimen of activity that is of longer duration or of more vigorous intensity are likely to derive greater benefit (4).
- Consistent influences on physical activity patterns among adults and young people include confidence in one's ability to engage in regular physical activity (e.g., self-efficacy), enjoyment of physical activity, support from others, positive beliefs concerning the benefits of physical activity, and lack of perceived barriers to physical activity (249).
- Physical activity appears to improve health-related quality of life by enhancing psychological well-being and by improving physical functioning in persons compromised by poor health (8).

of other subject content helps children grasp concepts in language arts, science, and math that they might struggle with in a more inactive classroom environment. In addition there is a growing body of evidence indicating that physical activity and fitness can benefit both health and academic performance for children (Pellicer-Chenoll et al. 2015). For example, physical activity can have both immediate and long-term benefits on academic performance. Almost immediately after engaging in physical activity, children are better able to concentrate on classroom tasks, which can enhance learning. Regular participation in physical activity and higher levels of physical fitness have been linked to improved academic performance and brain functions, such as attention and memory. These brain functions are the foundation for learning. Long-term studies have demonstrated that increases in physical activity,

resulting from greater time spent in physical education, were related to improved academic performance. Even single sessions of physical activity have been associated with better scores on academic tests, improved concentration, and more efficient transfers of information from short- to long-term memory (Castelli et al. 2015, p. 4).

> *Girls who do not participate in sports before the age of 10 have less than a 10 percent chance of doing so at age 25.*
>
> —**DONNA LOPIANO,** Women's Sports Foundation

Stress reduction Physical activity helps ease stress, tension, depression, and anxiety and may result in better attention in the classroom.

Social development Sports and physical activity are excellent ways to meet and make new friends. Confidence in one's physical abilities encourages youngsters, and later adults, to socialize more easily and fit into a variety of situations.

Adoption of other healthy behaviors Physical activity can increase the likelihood of other health-enhancing behaviors such as avoidance of tobacco, alcohol, and drug use.

The Importance of Physical Education

Clearly, the accumulated evidence suggests that youngsters who develop physically active lifestyles stand to gain enormous health, social, and emotional benefits, and yes, physical education does contribute to the recommended 60 minutes or more of daily physical education. So how does physical education relate to physical activity? Although some may incorrectly use the terms *physical activity* and *physical education* interchangeably, they are different in some very important ways. Physical activity is a behavior that involves bodily movement of any type and may include a variety of recreational, sport, and fitness activities. In contrast, physical education is an instructional program taught by teachers with professional credentials in physical education with the specific intent to develop physically literate individuals who have the knowledge, skills, and confidence to enjoy a lifetime of healthful physical activity (SHAPE America 2014). Put another way, physical education is a setting where students learn to be physically active, and physical activity programs provide opportunities for students to practice what they learn in physical education. Physical education is also guided by educational policy, has a structured and sequential curriculum, is developmentally and instructionally appropriate, and is driven by student assessment (Ballard et al. 2005). Physical activity participation provides an important component of physical education, as well as a means of achieving a healthy fitness

level (NASPE 2009). By thoughtfully examining the difference between the two, an understanding as to why both contribute to the development of healthy, active children can be achieved. In short, physical education programs are carefully planned with a focus on student learning and executed by teachers who hold themselves and students accountable for learning. Physical education programs provide for:

Skill development In physical education, children learn fundamental movement and sports skills that enable them to develop the competence that creates confidence and leads to safe and successful participation in a wide range of physical activities as adults.

Opportunities to develop health-related fitness In physical education, children are encouraged to improve their muscular and cardiovascular endurance, strength, and flexibility.

Personal and social responsibility Lessons provide students opportunities to develop and accept responsibility for their personal movement skill and health-related fitness development.

Appropriate Instructional Practice Guidelines for Elementary School Physical Education.

Over 25 years ago, the National Association for the Education of Young Children (NAEYC) published a series of articles and documents describing developmentally appropriate educational experiences for young children. The ideas in these documents were extremely popular with educators and parents and have now become common in all K–12 educational environments; physical education is no exception. *Appropriate Instructional Practice Guidelines for Elementary School Physical Education* describes developmentally and instructionally appropriate elementary school physical education experiences for children (NASPE 2009). This document, and the related middle and high school physical education guidelines (MASSPEC 2001, 2004), can be downloaded from the publications section of the SHAPE America Web site:

https://www.shapeamerica.org/upload/Appropriate-Instructional-Practice-Guidelines-K-12.pdf

Quality physical education is both developmentally and instructionally suitable for the specific children being served. Developmentally appropriate practices in physical education are those that recognize children's changing capacities to move and those that promote such change. A developmentally appropriate physical education program accommodates a variety of individual characteristics, such as developmental status, previous movement experiences, fitness and skill levels, body size, and age. Instructionally appropriate physical education incorporates the best-known practices, derived

from both research and experiences teaching children, into a program that maximizes opportunities for learning and success for all children (NASPE 2009, p. 3).

In addition to defining instructionally appropriate practices, these documents describe in easy-to-follow, straightforward terms the tenets of physical education that have evolved over the past three decades. They emphasize, for example, that:

- Children develop at different rates, and therefore educators should recognize these variances by designing experiences that allow for individual differences in abilities.
- For learning to occur, youngsters need lots of opportunities to practice a skill or movement at high rates of success.
- It is inappropriate to use exercise as punishment.
- The physical education curriculum should have a clear scope and sequence, with observable outcomes that can be assessed.
- Allowing captains to pick teams, overemphasizing competition, and giving fitness tests to one student at a time while the rest of the class watches are inappropriate educational practices.

These documents clearly make the point that physical education curricula that consist solely of large-group games, often played with one ball, are both developmentally and instructionally inappropriate.

The Physically Uneducated Adult

The physically uneducated adult may find themselves feeling uncomfortable and uncertain in physical activity settings. For example they may:

- Be overweight partly as a result of physical inactivity
- Have painful memories of being picked last when teams were chosen
- Remember being laughed at because they couldn't catch a softball or were afraid of a volleyball
- Recall being last whenever they ran laps
- Dread the memory of never being able to do even one pull-up on the physical fitness test
- Be uncomfortable starting and maintaining an exercise program
- Feel like a klutz and make excuses to avoid physical activity
- Believe that athletes were born that way
- Not understand there are virtually hundreds of ways to exercise and they would enjoy some of them

Goal setting School-based physical education provides a laboratory for helping youngsters understand the process of setting and achieving goals, especially health-related fitness goals.

Leadership and cooperation Physical education offers learning experiences that require students to work in groups or as a team to solve problems. These opportunities are an excellent laboratory for developing both leadership and cooperation skills.

Enhanced self-efficacy Physical education is a learning environment that leads to positive feelings of self-esteem.

Quality Physical Education and Children Moving

At this point in the chapter you may be asking how *Children Moving* relates to all that has been described? *Children Moving* introduces you to the skill theme approach designed for every child, from the least skilled child in a class to the highly skilled. The book explains the ways you can guide all children in positive directions, enabling them to develop the competence that leads to confidence in their physical abilities. This competence and confidence eventually culminate in a desire to regularly participate in physical activity because it has become an enjoyable and important part of their lives as children, as teens, and later as adults. *Children Moving* is about providing a blueprint, or road map, for developing a quality program of physical education. It is based on the literature, expert opinion, and more than 175 years of combined teaching experience by the authors. Quality programs of elementary physical education do not "just happen." So what is a quality physical education program?

Quality elementary physical education programs are designed to introduce youngsters to the fundamental movement skills that are the building blocks of enjoyable participation in physical activity and sport (Logan et al. 2017). In a quality physical education

Children enjoy seeing how they can take their weight on their hands on beautiful sunny day outside.

©Lars A. Niki

program, the teacher is actually *teaching*—providing learning tasks that are developmentally appropriate, assisting children to improve their skills by providing feedback and encouragement, and developing a sequential progression of learning experiences that results in progress and improvement. In short, a quality program teaches the skills, knowledge, and dispositions to be physically active for a lifetime.

In contrast, a substandard physical education program is one in which no actual teaching is occurring (i.e., there is no feedback, no demonstrations, and no episodes of instruction). Days and weeks are not connected in a second-rate program of physical education. Teachers focus on keeping children "busy, happy and good" (Placek 1983) and on students "doing" activities. Children in these programs see no connection between physical education in schools and physical activity outside of school (Parker et al. 2017). There is no intent for the students to learn! In a program like this, a teacher might tell you "the children love it." And some children do enjoy these programs, especially if they already possess the skills necessary to be successful in physical activity. However, children would also enjoy having pizza and ice cream for dinner every night; they might "love" the diet, but it certainly wouldn't be in their best interests.

Once again, we look to SHAPE America and Voices for Healthy Kids (2016) to expand on the brief definition of a quality physical education program and also guidelines developed by the USDHHS (2017) in its *School Health Index*. Some of the characteristics of a positive, or quality, program of physical education are straightforward and require little or no explanation. Others are lengthier because they are not as obvious or easily understood. The characteristics are bulleted, rather than numbered, because they are all important parts of a positive physical education program that leads to student learning of skills, knowledge, and dispositions to be physically active for a lifetime.

- *Time* Ideally children have physical education for at least 150 minutes each week (USDHHS 2017). This is especially important if they are to develop the fundamental movement skills that are so necessary for successful and enjoyable participation in sports and physical activities in later years (van der Mars 2006). SHAPE America recommends 150 minutes per week in elementary school and 225 minutes for middle and high school.
- *Class size* The number of children in a physical education class should be the same number as in the classroom.
- *Clear learning intentions* Teachers follow a carefully planned curriculum scope and sequence (pacing guide) based on standards or designed curricula

that progressively build on past experiences and incorporate new experiences when children are developmentally ready. See Box 1-3 for SHAPE America's standards for what students should know and be able to do as a result of a quality physical education program. (The Appendix included in Chapter 6 provides examples of curricular pacing guides based on the content in this book.)

- *Minimum of 50 percent MVPA* Physical education is a moving experience. In quality physical education programs, teachers find ways to actively engage all children in moderate to vigorous physical activity (MVPA) for the majority of every lesson while they are also learning movement and sports skills (USDHHS 2017).

Box 1-3

National Physical Education Standards

SHAPE America's *National Standards & Grade-Level Outcomes for K-12 Physical Education* define what a student should know and be able to do as a result of a highly effective physical education program. States and local school districts across the country use the *National Standards* to develop or revise existing standards, frameworks, and curricula.

Standard 1: The physically literate individual demonstrates competency in a variety of motor skills and movement patterns.

Standard 2: The physically literate individual applies knowledge of concepts, principles, strategies, and tactics related to movement and performance.

Standard 3: The physically literate individual demonstrates the knowledge and skills to achieve and maintain a health-enhancing level of physical activity and fitness.

Standard 4: The physically literate individual exhibits responsible personal and social behavior that respects self and others.

Standard 5: The physically literate individual recognizes the value of physical activity for health, enjoyment, challenge, self-expression, and/or social interaction.

Source: [SHAPE America] Society of Health and Physical Educators. 2014. *National standards & grade-level outcomes for K-12 physical education*. Champaign, IL: Human Kinetics, p. 12. With permission from the Society of Health and Physical Educators (SHAPE America), 1900 Association Drive, Reston, VA 20191.

The 60-Second One-Ball Test

Principals and parents typically do not have time to spend hours observing a physical education class to determine if it is a quality program. A rough estimate can be made in a short amount of time, however, by using the 60-second one-ball test. Here are the directions.

When you walk (or drive) by a physical education lesson, observe how many balls are in use (obviously this applies only to lessons in which balls are being used). If there is only one ball for an entire class of 20 youngsters or more, make a mental note. This typically takes less than 60 seconds, as the intent is not to observe an entire lesson. As you notice more lessons, keep track of the number of balls being used.

After observing five or more lessons, you will have an idea of the amount of practice opportunities children are getting in their physical education classes. If all the lessons use only one ball, then you know the amount of practice is severely limited, just as if a reading class was using only one book for an entire class. In contrast, if every child had a ball in the lessons you observed, then you know the teacher is attempting to maximize practice opportunities for children. Although this is hardly a scientific approach, it does provide one generalized indicator about the quality of a program.

©Stockbyte/Getty Images

Children derive lifetime benefits from becoming physically active.

- *Plenty of practice opportunities* In addition to being actively engaged, children also need plenty of opportunities to practice the skill or concept being taught that day (Rink 2003). Quality programs provide many practice opportunities (opportunities to learn) for children to develop their movement skills, sometimes alone, sometimes with a partner, and sometimes in small-sided games or with groups.
- *High rates of success* In addition to copious practice opportunities, teachers also design lessons so that youngsters of all abilities have high rates of success (Chapter 10) (Rink 2014). When youngsters, especially the unskilled, experience success, they are more likely to continue practicing and working to improve than when they fail continually. This is especially important in physical education because success and failure are so readily observable. For this reason, many programs have switched to the skill theme approach as described in *Children Moving*. Thus the highly skilled youngsters, all too often boys, are no longer allowed to dominate (Portman 1995), and physical education is for every youngster, especially the poorly coordinated, overweight, or awkward children who stand to benefit the most from a quality program of physical education.
- *Positive emotional environment* Quality physical education classes, in addition to promoting successful learning experiences, are also emotionally warm, nurturing environments in which children are encouraged to practice learning new fundamental movement skills and improve their physical fitness without feeling embarrassed or humiliated by the teacher or their peers.
- *Honors children's voices* Quality teachers listen to their students, recognizing the importance of honoring student voices when designing strategies to increase their participation and engagement (Cothran 2010; Graham 1995; Parker et al. 2017). This learner-centered approach does not mean that whatever students suggest is acceptable. Rather, teachers should focus on what students know, believe, can do, and bring to the learning situation and on how children understand, interpret, think, and feel about the content presented. Your choices as a teacher should be informed by students' perspectives because they are important for not only how curricula are managed and taught but also for understanding broader questions in relation to

Catching is a skill used in many sports and physical activities.

©Derek Sine & Van Tucker

movement choice and children's health (Macdonald et al. 2005).

- *Educates the whole child* While much of our emphasis to this point might have seemed to focus on learning physical skills, a quality physical education emphasizes learning with "the head, hands, and heart," or the cognitive, psychomotor, and affective domains. Physical education provides numerous opportunities for social and emotional learning experiences. A quality program equips children with the skills, knowledge, and dispositions to be physically active for a lifetime.
- *Teacher background.* The authors of *Children Moving* strongly support elementary physical education taught by specialist teachers who have an extensive background in the content and pedagogy of physical education for young children.
- *Realistic expectations* Teachers with an extensive background in children's physical education are able to develop realistic programs when their time is less than the recommended 150 minutes per week or if they have limited equipment. The emphasis is on "developing basic motor skills that allow participation in a variety of physical activities" (NCCD-PHP 1997, p. 209).

- *Adequate equipment and facilities* Ideally, every program has both an indoor and outdoor facility and a wide variety of equipment so children do not have to wait for turns to use equipment.
- *Meaningful* Quality physical education classes are also meaningful. Meaningful experiences are those that hold "personal significance" (Kretchmar 2007, p. 382). Children should see the relevance of physical education and enjoy and look forward to coming to class. In a recent review of literature examining meaningful experiences in physical education and youth sport, Beni, Fletcher, and Ní Chróinín (2016) identified five themes as central influences to young people's meaningful experiences in physical education and sport: social interaction, fun, challenge, motor competence, and personally relevant learning.
- *Focus on student learning* An important characteristic of quality physical education, and some would argue the most important characteristic, is that students are, in fact, learning (i.e., there are clear indicators that the students, parents, and teachers can observe). Just as reading and math teachers have clear, observable outcomes, so too do physical educators who are teaching for learning—as opposed to simply trying to keep children physically active.

Although there are a number of simple ways to assess student learning, one relatively straightforward way to judge what students have learned is through simple assessment tasks that ask children to do exactly what it is that you hope they have learned. We have chosen to call these student learning indicators. These student learning indicators can be used to determine if your students are actually learning a skill and can demonstrate their learning through quality movement. For example, if you were teaching a class to jump rope, you might say, "Let's see if you can jump your rope 10 times in a row without a miss. Ready, go." Quickly the teacher would know if most of the students were able to accomplish this challenge or if they needed to continue practicing the task because most of them could only jump two or three times in a row. Student learning indicators also let the teacher know which critical elements to focus on to guide students in becoming more skillful. In short, if children cannot accomplish the task, regardless of whether you taught it or not, go back and teach it again, with a clear focus on the cues designed to elicit the critical elements.

We have designed some sample student learning indicators unique to *Children Moving* and the skill theme approach (see Box 1-4). These would ideally be used at the end of the control level to determine if children were ready to progress to the use of a skill at the utilization level (see Chapter 5 for generic levels of skill

Box 1-4

Sample Student Learning Indicators for Movement Concept and Skill Themes: Psychomotor Domain Only

Chapter	Title	Indicators
13	Space Awareness	• Skip, hop, or gallop in a clockwise direction. Repeat in a counterclockwise direction. • Walk or run in a straight, curved, and zig-zag pathway. • Travel in general space while maintaining self-space (e.g., do not run into others).
14	Effort	• Walk or run contrasting fast and slow speeds. • Throw a ball to the wall two times using a light/soft force and then two times with a strong/hard force.
15	Relationships	• Demonstrate four different body shapes (wide, narrow, rounded, and twisted). • Make a nonsymmetrical shape matching the shape of a partner; make a nonsymmetrical shape mirroring the shape of a partner.
16	Traveling	• Run, hop, skip, gallop, and slide traveling in general space demonstrating correct technique. • Travel forward, backward, and sideways using a different locomotor pattern with each change of direction.
17	Chasing, Fleeing, and Dodging	• Demonstrate at least two strategies to avoiding being tagged (speed, fake, dart, vary pathways).
18	Bending, Stretching, Curling, and Twisting	• Demonstrate the four actions of bending, stretching, curling, and twisting. • Demonstrate at least one of the following actions: stretching to catch a ball, twisting to strike a ball with a bat, or a bending or curling action to transition between two balances.
19	Jumping and Landing	• Demonstrate the five different jump patterns. • Jump once for height and once for distance demonstrating three critical elements. • Jump a self-turned rope for at least 10 jumps without missing.
20	Balancing	• Demonstrate dynamic balance by traveling forward and backward on a low beam, bench, or 2-by-4-inch plank on the floor without stepping off. • Demonstrate at least five different balances (vary the base of support, level, or body shape) holding each balance still for 3 or more seconds. • Demonstrate at least one inverted balance holding the balance still for 3 or more seconds.
21	Transferring Weight and Rolling	• Demonstrate at least two different rolling actions (forward shoulder roll, forward roll, backward shoulder roll, egg roll, or log roll). • Transfer weight from feet to hands to feet in a cartwheel or round-off–like action.
22	Kicking and Punting	• Kick a stationary ball with a running approach so that the ball travels at least 20 feet in the air three out of five times. • Dribble a ball with feet in general space without losing control (avoids contact with other balls and students while continuing the dribble) for at least 1 minute. • Punt a ball with a step approach so that the ball travels at least 20 feet in the air three out of five times.
23	Throwing and Catching	• Throw a ball against a wall (from 15 feet away) with force and catch the rebound in the air or after one bounce three out of five times. • Overhand throw as far as you can demonstrating three critical elements.
24	Volleying and Dribbling	• Dribble a ball with preferred hand in general space without losing control (maintains dribble and avoids contact with others) for at least 1 minute. • Overhead or underhand volley a ball to a wall at least five times in a row.

Box 1-4 (continued)

Chapter	Title	Indicators
25	Striking with Rackets and Paddles	• Strike a ball with an underhand or forehand stroke against a wall for at least five consecutive hits.
26	Striking with Long Handled Implements	• Bat a ball from a tee so that the ball travels at least 20 feet in the air three out of five times.
		• Strike a ball (or puck) with a golf club, hockey stick, or pillow polo stick between two cones (positioned 6 feet apart) from 10 feet away, three out of five times.
		• Using a hockey stick, dribble a ball (or puck) in general space demonstrating control (avoids contact with other balls/pucks and students while continuing the dribble) for at least 1 minute.

proficiency). These indicators are not designed to replace the *National Standards* (SHAPE America 2014), but instead serve as progress markers (indicators) of student learning toward some of those identified outcomes. The indicators we designed only convey psychomotor learning; we are very conscious that cognitive and affective learning are equally important.

While we have provided a variety of sample indicators, student learning indicators are context specific. Some of these indicators will meet your needs as a teacher. Others will be too easy, too hard, or not a skill on which you have time to focus in your program. We would encourage you to create your own indicators of what you want your students to learn that are representative of the unique characteristics of your school and students; these may, and we would say should, also represent achievement in affective and cognitive domains (see Figure 12.1 for an example one school district developed). Additionally, the use of student learning indicators provides a convenient technique for informally and quickly assessing the progress children are making in your program (other, more detailed ideas for assessment are included in Chapter 12). These student learning indicators can also be shared with parents and administrators to document the progress your students are making.

We hope this chapter has helped you to understand why a quality physical education program can be so important in a youngster's life, especially for a child who is inclined not to be a physically active adolescent or adult. This chapter also provides an overview of the components of a quality, or positive, physical education.

The next two chapters describe in detail the components of the skill theme approach designed to maintain the love of movement that is so characteristic of young children into the middle and high school years.

Quality Physical Education Web Sites

Throughout the 10th edition of *Children Moving*, we will be referring to a variety of documents that can be accessed directly via the Internet. Three Internet sites that might be useful are PE Central, supportREALteachers, and SHAPE America. They are comprehensive Web sites for K–12 physical educators. Virtually all the documents referred to in this edition can be located through one of these sites. In addition there are links to the appropriate instructional practice documents, the Surgeon General's report, and the *National Standards & Grade-Level Outcomes for K-12 Physical Education* (SHAPE 2014). These sites also provide numerous developmentally appropriate lessons, assessment ideas, descriptions of best practices, conference and job announcements, kids' quotes, and links to many other Web sites. The Web address, or URL, for PE Central is www.pecentral.org; for supportREALteachers, it is www.support-realteachers.org; and for SHAPE America, it is www.shapeamerica.org. You will also find easy-to-use forms for sharing your lesson and assessment ideas with other physical educators. There are also multiple other sites. With any site, use due diligence to determine if the information is developmentally appropriate and aids in the development of skill themes.

Summary

Quality physical education programs for children have never been more important than they are today. The three overarching questions in this chapter provide an introduction to the program and teaching process described in the text. The responses to the questions taken from the recent literature (1) summarize the importance of physical activity, (2) establish the importance of physical education, and (3) define a quality physical education program for children as one that is developmentally and instructionally appropriate and results in learning the skills, knowledge, and dispositions that enable enjoyable participation in physical activity and sports.

Reading Comprehension Questions

1. Describe the difference between physical activity and physical education. Name at least three distinct differences.
2. The Physical Activity Hourglass suggests that opportunities for many youngsters are reduced once they enter secondary school. Analyze the opportunities for middle school and high school youth to be physically active in your community. Contrast the opportunities with those provided for young children. Describe what your community might do to create more environmental invitations to become physically active, especially for the youngsters who are not on athletic teams.
3. The purpose of a quality physical education program is described in this chapter. Explain your reasons for agreeing or disagreeing with the purpose.
4. A list of reasons children need quality physical education was provided. Which of those reasons do you think are most important? Least important? Explain your reasons.
5. Chapter 1 describes the characteristics of a quality physical education program. Make a three-column table listing these characteristics in the left-hand column. In the second column, grade your elementary school program on each of these characteristics from A to F. In the third column, explain your reason for each grade. If you did not have an elementary school physical education program, analyze your middle or high school physical education program.
6. Assume that someone asks you why youngsters need physical education. Prepare an argument using the information from this chapter to convince the person that physical education is as important as many other subjects in school.
7. It is recommended that children be physically active for 60 minutes or more most days of the week. Physical education classes are often 30 minutes in length. What would you recommend to a class of third graders about how they could acquire the recommended physical activity minutes on days they do not have physical education? Make five fun and interesting recommendations.

References/Suggested Readings

Ballard, K., D. Caldwell, C. Dunn, A. Hardison, J. Newkirk, M. Sanderson, S. Thaxton Vodicka, and C. Thomas. 2005. *Move more: North Carolina's recommended standards for physical activity in school.* Raleigh, NC: North Carolina Department of Health and Human Services, North Carolina Division of Public Health.

Barnett, L. M., P. J. Morgan, E. van Beurden, and J. R. Beard. 2008. Perceived sports competence mediates the relationship between childhood and adolescent motor skill proficiency and fitness. *International Journal of Behavioral Nutrition and Physical Activity* 10: 5–40.

Beni, S., T. Fletcher, and D. Ní Chróinín. 2017. Meaningful experiences in physical education and youth sport: A review of the literature. *Quest* 69(3): 291–312.

Castelli, D. M., E. M. Glowacki, J. M. Barcelona, H. G. Calvert, and J. Hwang. 2015. *Active education: Growing evidence on physical activity and academic performance.* Active Living Research [ALR], 1–5.

[CDC] Centers for Disease Control and Prevention. 2017. *Physical activity and health.* https://www.cdc.gov/physicalactivity/basics/pa-health/index.htm.

Clark, J. E. 2007. On the problems of motor skill development. *Journal of Physical Education, Recreation & Dance* 78(5): 39–44.

Cothran, D. 2010. Students' curricular values and experience. In *Young people's voices in physical education and youth sport*, ed. M. O'Sullivan and A. MacPhail, pp. 49–62. London: Routledge.

Ennis, C. E. 2011. Physical education curriculum priorities: Evidence for education and skillfulness. *Quest* 63: 5–18.

Gallahue, D., J. Ozmun, and J. Goodway. 2012. *Understanding motor development: Infants, children, adolescents, adults.* 7th ed. New York: McGraw-Hill Education.

Graham, G., ed. 1995. Physical education through students' eyes and in students' voices. *Journal of Teaching in Physical Education* 14(4): 363–485.

Jaakkola, T., and T. Washington. 2013. The relationship between fundamental movement skills and self-reported physical activity during Finnish junior high school. *Physical Education and Sport Pedagogy* 18(5): 492–505.

Kretchmar, R. S. 2007. What to do with meaning? A research conundrum for the 21st century. *Quest* 59: 373–83.

Logan, S. W., S. M. Ross, K. Chee, D. Stodden, and L. E. Robinson. 2017. Fundamental motor skills: A systematic review of terminology. *Journal of Sport Sciences* 36(7): 781–96.

Macdonald, D., S. A. Rodger, R. A. Abbott, J. M. Ziviana, and J. Jones. 2005. "I could do with a pair of wings": Perspectives on physical activity, bodies and health from young Australian children. *Sport, Education, and Society* 10: 195–209.

[MASSPEC] Middle and Secondary School Physical Education Council. 2001. *Appropriate practices for middle school physical education: A position statement of the National Association for Sport and Physical Education developed by the Middle and Secondary School Physical Education Council (MASSPEC).* Reston, VA: National Association for Sport and Physical Education. http://www.aahperd.org/naspe.

[MASSPEC] Middle and Secondary School Physical Education Council. 2004. *Appropriate practices for high school physical education: A position statement of the National Association for Sport and Physical Education Developed by the Middle and Secondary School Physical Education Council (MASSPEC).* Reston, VA: National Association for Sport and Physical Education. http://www.aahperd.org/naspe.

[NASPE] National Association for Sport and Physical Education. 2006. *Is it physical education or physical activity?* https://www.shapeamerica.org/publications/resources/teachingtools/qualtype/pa_vs_pe.aspx.

[NASPE] National Association for Sport and Physical Education. 2009. *Appropriate instructional practice guidelines for elementary school physical education.* 3rd ed. Reston, VA: National Association for Sport and Physical Education.

[NASPE] National Association for Sport and Physical Education. 2011. Key points of a quality physical education program. http://www.aahperd.org/naspe/publications/teachingTools/key-points-of-QPE.cfm.

[NCCDPHP] National Center for Chronic Disease Prevention and Health Promotion, Centers for Disease Control and Prevention. 1997. Guidelines for school and community programs to promote lifelong physical activity among your people. *Journal of School Health* 76(6): 202–19.

Parker, M., A. MacPhail, M. O'Sullivan, D. Ní Chróinín, and E. McEvoy. 2017. "Drawing" conclusions: Irish primary school children's understanding of physical education and physical activity opportunities outside of school. *European Physical Education Review* 1–18; DOI: 10.1177/1356336X16683898.

Pellicer-Chenoll, M., X. Garcia-Massó, J. Morales, P. Serra-Añó, M. Solana-Tramunt, L. González, and L. Toca-Herrera. 2015. Physical activity, physical fitness and academic achievement in adolescents: A self-organizing maps approach. *Health Education Research* 30(3): 436–48.

Placek, J. 1983. Conceptions of success in teaching: Busy, happy and good? In *Teaching in Physical Education,* ed. T. Templin and J. Olsen, pp. 46–56. Champaign, IL: Human Kinetics.

Portman, P. A. 1995. Who is having fun in physical education classes? Experiences of sixth grade students in elementary and middle schools. *Journal of Teaching in Physical Education* 14(4): 445–53.

Quimby, D. 1988. The starfish. *TEAM* 2(6).

Reiner, M., C. Niermann, D. Jekauc, and A. Woll. 2013. Long-term health benefits of physical activity: A systematic review of longitudinal studies. *BMC Public Health* 13: 1–9.

Rink, J. 2003. Effective instruction in physical education. In *Student learning in physical education,* 2nd ed., ed. S. Silverman and C. Ennis. Champaign, IL: Human Kinetics.

Rink, J. 2014. *Teaching Physical Education for Learning.* 7th ed. New York: McGraw-Hill.

[SHAPE America] Society of Health and Physical Educators. 2014. *National Standards & Grade-Level Outcomes for K-12 Physical Education.* Champaign, IL: Human Kinetics.

[SHAPE America and Voices for Healthy Kids] Society of Health and Physical Educators. 2016. *2016 Shape of the nation: Status of physical education in the USA.* Reston, VA: SHAPE America.

Stodden, D., S. Langendorfer, and M. A. Roberton. 2009. The association between skill competence and physical fitness in adults. *Research Quarterly for Exercise and Sports* 80: 229–33.

The Aspen Institute. 2017. Project Play 2020. https://www.aspenprojectplay.org/project-play-2020/.

[USDHHS] U.S. Department of Health and Human Services. 1996. *Physical activity and health: A report of the Surgeon General.* Atlanta: Centers for Disease Control and Prevention, National Center for Chronic Disease Prevention and Health Promotion.

[USDHHS] U.S. Department of Health and Human Services. 2018. *Physical activity guidelines for Americans.* 2nd ed. Washington, DC: U.S. Department of Health and Human Services. http://www.health.gov/paguidelines.

[USDHHS] U.S. Department of Health and Human Services. 2017. *School health index: A self-assessment and planning guide for elementary school.* Atlanta: Centers for Disease Control and Prevention. Available for free download from http://www.cdc.gov/HealthyYouth.

Van der Mars, H. 2006. Time and learning in physical education. In *The handbook of physical education*, ed. D. Kirk, D. Macdonald, and M. O'Sullivan, pp. 191–213. London: Sage.

[WHO] World Health Organization. 2018. *Global strategy on diet, physical activity and health: Physical activity and young people.* http://www.who.int/dietphysicalactivity/factsheet_young_people/en/.

The Skill Theme Approach

Motor skills do not develop miraculously from one day to the next or through maturation; they must be nurtured, promoted, and practiced. Physical education must promote both physical activity and motor skill development. If we want students to become physically active for life, we need to help them acquire the motor skills that will allow them to participate in a wide range of physical activities.

—JANE CLARK

Drawn by children at Monfort, Chappelow or Shawsheen Elementary Schools, Greeley, CO. Courtesy of Lizzy Ginger; Tia Ziegler

Key Concepts

- The skill theme approach describes both the content and pedagogy for physical education.

- The skill theme approach is based on developmentally appropriate principles that recognize children have different interests, abilities, and motor skills.

- The development of fundamental movement skills and their application to a variety of physical activities and sports create the basis for the skill theme approach.

- The Curriculum Diamond suggests the content to be taught in elementary school, middle school, and high school physical education programs.

- Children's abilities and interests as opposed to age or grade level are used to guide the selection of content in the skill theme approach.

- Skill themes are initially practiced in isolation; as children develop their movement skills, they practice them in games, gymnastics, dance, and sports contexts.

- Skill themes are revisited throughout the year rather than in units of several weeks.

- Cognitive, affective, and psychomotor concepts are interwoven throughout the skill theme approach rather than taught as isolated units.

Chapter 1 answered questions that provided important insights into why physical education is so important in children's lives today, followed by an overview of the characteristics of a quality, or positive, physical education program. This chapter also answers a question: What is the skill theme approach to children's physical education?

Over the years we have observed many elementary school teachers whose curriculum consists solely of games. Each day the children play a game or two. In these programs the teacher's role is to explain the game, provide the equipment, keep score, and referee. The teacher pays no attention to the development of movement skills. The highly skilled students in the classes are happy because they typically dominate the games. The poorly skilled children survive from day to day—devoid of both enjoyment and learning. The skill theme approach offers an alternative for teachers who want to make a difference in all children's lives by helping them become skillful movers who enjoy physical activities and sports.

The skill theme approach describes both the content (what to teach) of children's physical education (Parts 3 and 4 of *Children Moving* detail the curriculum) and the teaching process, or pedagogy (how to teach, which is described in Part 2). A question-and-answer format will help you understand the characteristics of the skill theme approach. You will discover how it differs from traditional games programs, and how dance, games, gymnastics, and physical fitness are incorporated in it.

What Are Skill Themes?

Skill themes are initially the fundamental movements that form the foundation for success in physical activities and sports in later years. Reflective teachers, as will be explained throughout the text, adapt the skill themes to match the ability level of the students in a class. Initially we focus on one skill at a time; in later grades as children become more skillful, skills are combined and used in more complex settings, such as those in dance, games, and gymnastics. The intent is to help children develop the building blocks for a variety of locomotor, nonmanipulative, and manipulative skills that provide the foundation to enjoyably and confidently play a sport, for example, or perform a dance consisting of an intricate set of movements. If you watch college or professional athletes practicing their sport, you will observe the skill themes in their most advanced stage, for example, throwing to a batter in baseball, striking a tennis ball, dancing with a partner, or diving and rolling in volleyball.

What Are the Characteristics of the Skill Theme Approach?

Four characteristics of the skill theme approach (content and pedagogy combined) clearly distinguish it from the games curriculum described earlier.

Characteristic 1

A major purpose of the skill theme approach is competence in performing a variety of locomotor, nonmanipulative, and manipulative movement skills. The skill theme approach links directly with National Standard 1 through the development of mature patterns/competency of fundamental movement skills. A skill theme curriculum is designed to develop skills competency and is not simply an introduction to a skill (Holt/Hale 2015).

Think of a sport or physical activity you know well. If you were asked to write a progression (a series of tasks) starting with novices (beginners) up to highly skilled athletes, you would be able to develop a series of tasks that would, over a period of years and with a lot of practice, lead to the students becoming highly skilled in that sport. This is the basic idea behind the skill theme approach. Each skill theme begins with the fundamental skills and concepts, is gradually combined with other skills (e.g., dribbling while running), and eventually leads to success and enjoyment in full-sided games (e.g., five-against-five basketball) during middle and high school years.

The skill theme approach reflects the growing concern that some, perhaps many, children who participate in programs that emphasize game playing rather than movement skill learning don't necessarily improve their motor ability (Graham 1987; Manross 2000). While studies documenting the impact of instruction provided in physical education classes on children's acquisition of fundamental movement skills is limited, the most promising results have come from programs

at the preschool level (e.g., Logan et al. 2012). A common theme of those programs is that they involved purposeful structuring of the learning environment to promote practice opportunities for fundamental movement skills (Hastie 2017). Just as we all benefited from being taught to read, spell, and write, children benefit from being instructed on how to reach advanced levels of fundamental movement skills (Barnett et al. 2016). The logical implication, of course, is that adults with inefficient movement skills tend to avoid physical activities that require them to use these poorly learned skills and as a consequence develop tendencies toward "couch potatoism." See Box 2-1 for one example of the difference in outcomes of the two approaches.

A basic assumption is that a curriculum that is "scoped and sequenced" by skill themes (see Appendix in Chapter 6) introduces students to the requisite skills for

Box 2-1

Critical Elements in the Skill Theme Approach

One of the sample grade-level outcomes in the *National Standards & Grade-Level Outcomes for K-12 Physical Education* suggests that a child "throws overhand using a mature pattern in nondynamic environments (closed skills) (S1.E14.4a)" (SHAPE America 2014, p. 6). In the skill theme approach, as you will see in later chapters, we focus on children learning the critical elements as they practice perfecting them. How would your students respond? Manross (2000) interviewed 25 children who had been taught using a skill theme approach (at Pendleton Elementary School) and 25 children whose curriculum consisted primarily of low-organized games (at Eckland). As part of his study he asked the children to identify the critical elements of the overhand throw. It was clear that the children being taught using the skill theme approach at Pendleton could describe many of the critical elements of a mature overhand throw, whereas the children at Eckland had not learned the critical elements. The table contains their responses.

Answer Stated	No. of Times
Pendleton (Skill Theme Approach)	
Turn your side to the target	17
Step with the opposite foot	15
Arm way back	10
Aim at target	9
Follow through	3
Step through with other foot	2
Let elbow lead	1
Twist body at waist	1
Bring arm straight over, not sidearm	1

Eckland (Low-Organized Games)	
Get straight in front of target	4
Hold ball with tight grip	3
Bring hand back behind shoulder	3
Follow through	2
Try your best	2
Don't know	2
Practice	2
Don't be scared of the ball	2
Take a forward step	2
Throw hard	2
Aim at target	2
Don't strain arm	2
Try to throw sidearm	1
Hold your hand straight	1
Work on stance	1
Don't throw hard	1
Pretend it is hot object	1
Don't get nervous	1
Keep mind on throwing	1
Make sure they see good	1
Have a strong arm	1
Keep eye on ball	1

enjoyably participating in adult versions of sports, dance, and the myriad other physical activities available today—and those that will be invented tomorrow. As physical educators we're able to help children learn these skills more quickly and with less frustration than they would if they attempted to learn the skills on their own.

The skill themes are generic in the sense that they are not tied to any single sport or activity. Rather, they transcend, or cut across, various forms of physical activity and structured sports. As shown in Figure 2.1, which illustrates a progression that might be used in introducing dribbling with hands, beginning tasks for each skill theme start at the most basic level. The children are asked to practice the movement skill—with no defenders, for example—and the fundamental critical elements are emphasized, such as throwing a ball hard against a wall while focusing on opposition (that is, stepping with the foot opposite the throwing hand). As children demonstrate the ability to perform the skill using the critical elements, the tasks require children to combine the skill with other skills and concepts,

such as throwing while running to a partner who is also running. When the children are ready, the skill theme tasks may involve developing dance and gymnastic routines with their classmates or playing small-sided games. Some skills (e.g., jumping and landing) are used in games, dance, gymnastics, and track and field, for example. Other skills such as dribbling are more specific to games or sports.

Although some skill themes are typically associated with a specific sport, most are used in a variety of sports or physical activities. This is illustrated by using the skill theme of dribbling with the hands (Chapter 25). Dribbling is typically associated with basketball. The initial dribbling tasks focus on children dribbling a ball in a self-space without traveling or moving. As they gain dribbling skill, children are challenged to dribble and travel in different pathways, at different speeds, and around stationary and eventually moving obstacles. If there is sufficient time for practice, eventually the children will be ready to dribble in complex situations that might be small-sided basketball games;

Figure 2.1 The skill theme of dribbling is initially studied as an isolated skill. As the children become more skillful, it is combined with other skills and concepts. Eventually, dribbling is used in teacher- or children-designed routines, games, or small-sided basketball games.

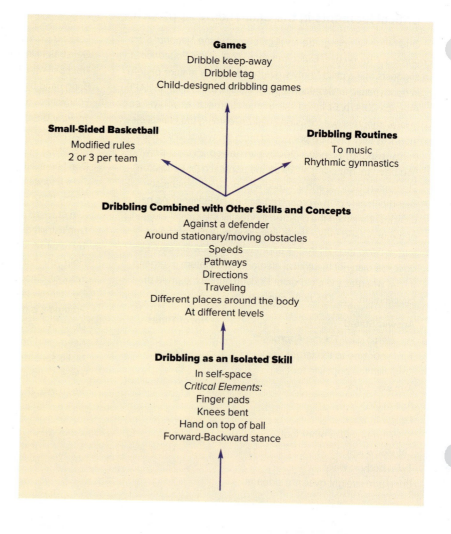

children may also be challenged to create dribbling routines to music or to dribble in keep-away or tag games. In some instances, the teacher designs the routine or game; in other instances, the children design their routine or invent their game. Figure 2.1 illustrates how the skill theme of dribbling is developed with youngsters based on the tasks described in Chapter 25.

Some skill theme chapters (e.g., Chapters 23, 24, and 25) include rules for games, but these rules are suggested as part of the skill theme progression for children at more advanced levels (e.g., utilization and proficiency levels, as described in Chapter 5). To reach the more advanced levels, the children will need to spend considerable time on tasks devoted to learning these skills—initially in rather static environments—before using them successfully within the dynamic setting of an organized game, for example. The sample student learning indicators discussed in Chapter 1 are examples of movement skills children should learn in your program that are prerequisites to success in the dynamic setting of an organized game. In this book, games are carefully selected (or designed) to enhance skill acquisition as part of a long-term progression rather than simply as a way to keep children busy, happy, and good for 30 minutes or so.

We also encourage teachers to explain to their classes that skillfulness typically involves practicing outside of school the skills taught in class. Unfortunately, in many physical education programs, there is just not enough time to devote to the skill themes and movement concepts to enable children to dramatically improve their skill levels. It is important that children understand this reality so they do not develop unrealistic expectations about how much practice it takes to become skillful.

In addition to including a progression (sequence) of tasks for developing each skill theme from the beginning through the advanced levels (Part 4), each chapter includes information (written descriptions, diagrams, and/or photos) to help the teacher observe children's use of the critical elements (this process is first described in Chapter 11) and to help the youngsters develop efficient and biomechanically correct movement patterns (see Chapter 12).

Characteristic 2

The skill theme approach is designed to provide experiences appropriate to a child's developmental level, as opposed to age or grade level.

One of the many challenges of effective teaching is matching the content of the lesson to students' abilities (Chapter 9). Both grade level and age are unreliable indices of ability. A second characteristic of the skill theme approach is that it uses the students' developmental level as a guide for selecting the content to be taught. It may be easier to use grade level or age as an indicator, but children develop at different rates (Gallahue, Ozmun, and Goodway 2012), and effective teachers attempt to take this into account.

The generic levels of skill proficiency (Chapter 5) serve as guides for assessing the children's abilities and then selecting tasks that are matched to their abilities. If the majority of children in a class, for example, were unable to hit a ball against a wall continually using a paddle so that it returned on a single bounce, we wouldn't require them to participate in a game requiring an even greater ability to strike the ball—for example, a game that required them to hit a ball to a partner (Chapter 26).

In the skill theme approach, the tasks are selected according to the children's abilities and not according to a predetermined calendar that implies all children of the same grade develop at the same rate. This is especially important, for example, when children's skill development may be limited because they have physical education classes only one or two days a week (SHAPE America and Voices for Healthy Kids 2016). In practice, this means that if an experienced teacher taught three consecutive fourth-grade classes using a skill theme approach, one class might be challenged with a more difficult series of tasks than another (Graham et al. 1993). And within each of the three fourth-grade classes, students might be challenged individually or in groups to undertake different tasks, as will be explained in Chapter 6.

We can use the skill of throwing (Chapter 24) to illustrate how a skill theme is developmentally sequenced. At the beginning levels (precontrol and control), children are encouraged to throw a ball hard or far. These tasks lead to the development of greater trunk rotation and foot–arm opposition, for example, which combine with other critical elements to form a mature (biomechanically efficient) throwing pattern. Throwing for distance, however, is only one type of throwing. As the children learn the components of an overhand throw for distance, they are challenged by tasks that involve throwing at targets, throwing to a partner, and throwing while moving. At more advanced levels (utilization and proficiency), they might be invited to participate in a game of Keep-Away involving throwing, such as two against two or three against one (three throwers, one defender). The effective teacher bases these decisions, however, on the children's readiness rather than on age or grade level. Throwing efficiently and effectively then becomes a focus that is interwoven and revisited as variations of throwing throughout the program.

Fitness is built into the skill theme approach as children hop in general space.

©Lars A. Niki

Characteristic 3

The scope and sequence of the skill themes are designed to reflect students' varying needs and interests over a period of years.

The third characteristic of the skill theme approach can be found within the scope and sequence recommendations (see Chapter 6 and the Appendix in Chapter 6). Rather than focusing on the same skill theme for

"Kick the ball back and forth with your partner; try to make it go through the arch" is a task skill theme teachers use to develop kicking skills.

©Lars A. Niki

several weeks (in a three- or six-week unit, for example), we focus on a skill theme for brief periods and then revisit it at various times during the year. In the motor learning literature, this is called distributed practice. At the beginning levels (precontrol and control), we might spend only two or three days in a row on a skill theme. In fact, we might not even spend an entire class period on a single skill theme. As children gain proficiency, expanding their movement repertoire, they become more interested in spending larger amounts of time (three or four days) on the same skill theme because the tasks are more complex and involved and their success rate is higher.

Revisiting the same skill theme several times during a year, as depicted in the progression spiral in Chapter 3, also allows the teacher to teach virtually the same lesson that was taught two or three months before. This is often necessary when the children's skill (use of critical elements) doesn't improve noticeably. A teacher who remains on the same skill theme for many days in a row, however, is tempted to make the tasks harder (in an effort to alleviate the children's and the teacher's boredom) than the children may be ready for. Revisitation is emphasized throughout *Children Moving*. The skill theme curriculum begins with the development of foundational skills and abilities and gradually, over the years, introduces more complex and difficult skills.

Characteristic 4

The skill theme approach emphasizes instructional alignment. The term *instructional alignment* refers to the alignment of what teachers intend for students to learn, how they determine student success, how they teach, and how students practice (Lund and Tannehill 2015). In this process, teachers first decide what students can learn in a lesson (objectives) and determine how student success will be determined (assessment). Next, they develop a series of tasks and challenges aligned with district, state, or national standards and designed to assist the children accomplish the lesson objective(s), and identify how content is to be delivered to students (instructional approach). According to Tannehill (2001, p. 19), a teacher "tells students what is important for them to know and be able to do, designs appropriate tasks that allow them to practice what you taught them, and assesses them on what they have been practicing." For example, if a teacher wants her class to learn the grapevine step, she would utilize an instructional approach to demonstrate and explain the step, devise tasks and challenges that allow them to practice it, and then assess their ability to do the grapevine to determine if they need more practice. This process, called instructional alignment, is emphasized throughout *Children Moving*.

What Is Developmentally Appropriate Physical Education?

Another characteristic of the skill theme approach is that it is developmentally appropriate (Appropriate Instructional Practice Guidelines, K-12, SHAPE America, 2009). Fundamental motor skills are the "building blocks" of more advanced, complex movements required to participate in sports, games, or other context-specific physical activity (Logan et al. 2017). The skill theme approach is developmentally appropriate because it reflects important motor development principles in curriculum design and in the teaching process. Some of the important motor development principles upon which *Children Moving* is based are briefly explained in the following sections.

Children Develop at Different Rates

One critical premise of motor skill development is that children develop at different rates. Some kindergarten children can skip; others are not ready to skip. Some are able to track a ball in motion; others are not visually ready yet. Developmentally appropriate physical education recognizes this premise and therefore does not expect all children to be able to perform the same task identically. As you will see in subsequent chapters detailing the skill theme approach, we recognize and value the developmental differences in children's abilities, although it's not easy with 25 or more children in a class.

Age Does Not Predict Motor Ability

If age was a predictor of motor ability, then all adults would be skillful athletes. Although there are certain advantages to aging (e.g., quicker reflexes, visual tracking ability), the only way individuals become skillful in fundamental movement skills is to use, or practice, them. Thus most adults are reasonably efficient at walking. Many, however, are inefficient at catching a ball or striking an object with a racket. They are inefficient because they have not used the skills regularly over a period of years and not because they do not have the potential to be skillful.

Children Develop Fundamental Movement Skills Naturally through Play

Children today have fewer and fewer opportunities to develop fundamental movement skills on their own. Television viewing, electronic games, the Internet, and fear of playing outside in many communities combine to mean fewer chances to be physically active. Although there is some evidence that fundamental movement skills may develop through informal play (hours and hours of basketball or soccer, for example), this possibility is becoming less and less probable in society today. The simple fact is that physical education is becoming increasingly important for children because their playtime is severely limited. This is especially true for overweight youngsters who have little or no physical activity built into their lives.

The Myth of the Natural Athlete

One sports myth is that there are natural athletes. Although some youngsters are physically (genetically) disposed to do better at some sports than others, the fact is that highly skilled children have participated in one or many sports from very early ages. Some children begin kindergarten with mature throwing and catching patterns, for example. They were not born this way. They played a lot of catch with parents, siblings, or friends from a young age and thus enter school more highly skilled than their peers. In time, however, their less-skilled peers can catch up if they, too, practice and use the motor skill thousands of times as they play with friends, on teams, or with a parent.

Differences in Physical Abilities between Boys and Girls

On average, boys are more physically active than girls (Cooper et al. 2015; USDHHS 1996). This may be one reason boys tend to be more highly skilled than girls in certain sports. Developmentally, however, girls have the potential to be equally as skillful as boys. As more and more girls play sports and become physically active, we can expect to see a decline in any gap that exists between physical abilities. As teachers we emphasize this continually in our programs so that the girls in our classes understand that skillfulness is a result of practice, not heredity or gender.

In summary, developmentally appropriate physical education (Appropriate Instructional Practice Guidelines, K–12, SHAPE America, 2009) recognizes that youngsters develop at different rates and have different abilities and that the environment plays a critical role in the development of fundamental movement skills. The chapter continues with a question-and-answer format that answers many questions typically asked when folks are initially introduced to the skill theme approach.

©Lars A. Niki

Games such as Duck, Duck, Goose are fun for a few, but most of the children are inactive.

Why Don't You Describe Such Activities as Duck, Duck, Goose, and Kickball?

We don't include many of the so-called traditional activities for three major reasons. First, activities such as these, in which children are singled out to perform solo with everyone watching them, can be both embarrassing and discouraging when the less-skilled children are "on center stage." Children (or adults, for that matter) who are embarrassed or made to feel inadequate are hardly motivated to participate. One of our primary goals is to encourage children to develop positive attitudes about themselves and about physical activity so they choose to be physically active throughout their lives. Games such as Duck, Duck, Goose, and kickball are developmentally inappropriate because they do not take into account the varying skill abilities of children within a class (SHAPE America 2009) and thereby force some children into situations that make them unhappy and may lead them to dislike physical activity.

Second, these games emphasize winning more than learning. Another of our primary goals is to help children develop the movement competence that enables them to enjoy and participate in physical activity successfully. While keeping score and attempting to win are enjoyable for some children, others prefer games and activities in which score is not kept. When children are encouraged to design their own games (Chapter 9), you will see that some keep score and others do not.

Finally, many of these traditional games encourage only a few youngsters to be physically active. The less-skilled, overweight, or less physically fit youngsters often find ways to avoid actively participating in games

with one ball or tag games with one person who is "it." The skill theme approach was designed with the underlying premise that children have different skill levels and abilities.

What Is the Curriculum Diamond?

The Curriculum Diamond (Figure 2.2) illustrates the concept of foundational movement skills leading to successful participation in sports and physical activities. It is intended to help physical educators think about and design curriculums that will guide youngsters in the process of becoming physically active for a lifetime. It is important to understand that it takes time and practice—a lot of practice—to successfully perform complex, sport-related skills in game, gymnastics, and dance contexts. In fact, it is virtually impossible to become proficient without the foundational movement skills described in the skill theme approach. Clearly, decisions about when to introduce different content will need to be based on the progress students make in a given program (e.g., number of days per week, length of the classes, equipment, and facilities).

The Curriculum Diamond suggests a curricular focus corresponding to the grade-level structure of most school districts across the United States—elementary, middle, and high school. (Grade levels are suggested in the model for illustration purposes only). It follows the recommendations of the Centers for Disease Control and Prevention (CDC 2011) and the *National Standards & Grade-Level Outcomes for K–12*

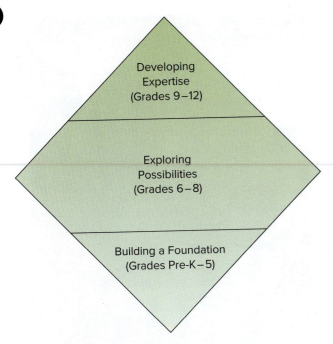

Figure 2.2 The Curriculum Diamond.

Physical Education (SHAPE America 2014) by developing a broad foundation of movement skills at the elementary and middle school levels and then focusing on proficiency in a few movement forms at the high school level. It provides a brief, albeit oversimplified, answer to the question: How can elementary, middle, and high school physical education programs work together to guide youngsters in the process of becoming physically active for a lifetime?

Building a Foundation (Preschool through Grade 5)

The bottom part of the diamond represents the earliest ages at which children are introduced to skill themes and movement concepts. The initial focus is on developing a functional (applied) understanding of the concepts of space awareness, effort, and relationships (Chapters 14–16). As children develop, they are introduced to skill themes designed to encourage and assist them in beginning to acquire the fundamental competencies that will become the foundation skills for many of the sports and physical activities they will pursue as adolescents and adults (Chapters 17–27). Notice that this section of the diamond widens as each layer is laid upon the foundational layer that precedes it. This is intended to represent how skill themes and concepts are combined in the upper elementary grades. (Some have suggested that a more appropriate geometric representation might be a trapezoid. This figure would

suggest that the skill themes and movement concepts would be wider at the base, representing a broader foundation, and gradually narrow toward the top. What do you think?

Exploring Possibilities (Grades 6–8)

In the middle school years, the focus shifts from building a foundation to using the skills and concepts in a variety of movement forms. Skills continue to be developed and learned, but the focus is on exposing students to a wide variety of sports and physical activities designed to stimulate interest in health-enhancing lifetime activities. Ideally this is the age when adolescents begin to discover the various sports and physical activities that are or are not personally appealing. Some youngsters, for example, like team sports; others may prefer individual sports. Others will enjoy yoga, dance, martial arts, or mountain biking. The goal is to introduce youngsters to many different movement forms and then assist them to discover the types of activities that are personally enjoyable and meaningful to them.

Developing Expertise (Grades 9–12)

Ideally the exposure to many movement options in middle school stimulates student interest in a handful of health-enhancing lifetime activities. When students enter high school, the diamond begins to narrow, suggesting that students will begin to make decisions about the activities they enjoy and desire to become proficient in. At this point students choose electives based on the possibilities they explored in middle school. As students approach the peak, the focus narrows. This is the time when students develop the expertise that enables them to participate in several activities enjoyably and confidently, thereby allowing them to accrue the benefits that come to those who remain physically active for a lifetime. This is the time when students refine the skill themes and movement concepts they learned in the early years for use in specific sports and physical activities.

Is It Difficult to Maintain Youngsters' Interest in a Program That Emphasizes the Fundamentals?

We hope by now you understand why skill themes are important as the building blocks for enjoyable participation in physical activities and sports. Some, who haven't been taught using a skill theme approach, wonder about maintaining children's interest in fundamentals. Ideally, children begin this program in preschool when this is really the only program they know, so their interest remains high. When we introduce skill themes to children in the fourth and fifth grades for the first time, some children initially have a difficult time adjusting, particularly the highly skilled who enjoy playing games they dominate. In time, however, children learn to enjoy this program because they're improving. Effective teachers also attempt to adjust the activities to the youngsters' skill level, and this makes the lessons more interesting. It is important to understand, however, that students do play games, albeit small sided, in the skills theme approach, but only when they have the necessary skills to do so. As you may have experienced, games, even small-sided ones, are no fun when you haven't learned the necessary skills to play them.

What Does "Adjusting the Activities" Mean?

"Adjusting the activities" is the concept of reflective teaching (Chapter 4). It means that the teacher adapts the lesson for the children rather than allowing them to fail. If a boy can't catch a ball, for example, he isn't going to enjoy playing a game of softball in which the score is kept and winning is important. Thus, we provide noncompetitive activities for this child in which he can succeed. In the same class, however, a girl may have played softball on a team for several years and be very good. We try to provide her with game-like activities related to softball in which she and a group of classmates may choose to keep score. For more effective learning in reading and math classes, children are grouped by ability (differentiated instruction). Although it's harder to do this in physical education, we do provide different tasks based on the youngsters' ability. This system for determining students' skill level is explained in Chapter 5 as are techniques like teaching by invitation and intratask variation (Chapter 7). In addition, the tasks in each skill theme chapter are organized into a logical sequence.

Where Is Fitness in the Skill Theme Approach?

Physical fitness is an important part of the skill theme approach. National Standard 3 (SHAPE America 2014) indicates that students should demonstrate both the knowledge and skills necessary to achieve and maintain a health-enhancing level of physical activity and fitness. As we explain in Chapter 28, fitness is interwoven throughout the program rather than confined to one

©Lars A. Niki

"Traveling under the shape made by your partner" is an example of developing the concept of the relationships with people in gymnastics.

separate unit. Our emphasis is not on training children so they score well on a physical fitness test battery. Our emphasis is three-fold: (1) We try to provide experiences that help children to understand and value the importance of health-related physical fitness and physical activity. (2) We design our lessons to help children enjoy physical activity so they choose to make it a part of their daily lives. (3) We provide children with the knowledge of the fitness components and the importance of each for good health. Thus, we provide children fitness within and beyond our physical education programs.

Where Does the Cognitive Domain Fit into the Skill Theme Approach?

The skill theme approach, as you will see, encourages children to think on their feet as they move. Thus, as with physical fitness, cognition is part of every lesson we teach. With this approach the focus is not only on children's physical movements but also on how and why they move certain ways as well as the most efficient and effective ways to do so. National Standard 2 indicates that students should have the ability to apply knowledge of concepts, principles, strategies, and tactics related to movement performance (SHAPE America 2014). An integral contribution of the skill theme approach is its focus on children developing a functional understanding of movement. This functional understanding, cognitive and performance, serves as the foundation for physical education experiences.

Where Does the Affective Domain Fit into the Skill Theme Approach?

In addition to providing high-quality learning experiences in the psychomotor and cognitive domains, the skill theme approach emphasizes the affective domain. As indicated in National Standard 4, exhibiting responsible personal and social behavior that respects self and others is an essential part of becoming physically literate (SHAPE America 2014). Because we believe children's feelings, emotions, and self-concept can never be ignored, we attempt to design our lessons so they are developmentally appropriate and recognize that children have different abilities, attitudes, and feelings about being in our classes. With respect to the affective domain, we carefully follow the appropriate practice guidelines (SHAPE America 2009) to ensure that children are treated fairly, compassionately, and equitably. It is important to note that responsible behavior is not an automatic by-product of the skill theme approach. Rather, it must be taught through thoughtfully designed lessons and promoted using a positive, emotionally safe learning environment for all children (Holt/Hale 2015).

From years of teaching and observing children's physical education classes, we are increasingly convinced that lifelong attitudes and feelings toward physical activity and exercise are developed during the elementary school years (Robinson et al. 2015; Stodden et al. 2008). We want children to enjoy and feel good about their participation in physical education. Thus, we focus on helping them develop competence, confidence, and a love of movement—resulting in a lifetime of healthful physical activity. This focus supports National Standard 5, which recognizes the value of physical activity for health, enjoyment, challenge, self-expression, and/or social interaction (SHAPE America 2014).

What about Dance and Gymnastics?

Our initial focus in the skill theme approach is on helping children develop and learn the fundamental movement skills. As children acquire these building blocks,

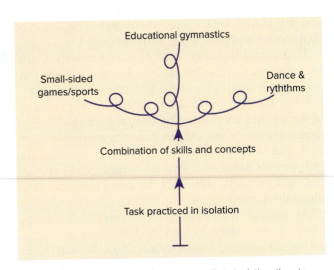

Figure 2.3 Skill themes are practiced initially in isolation, then in combination with other skills and concepts, leading to their use in games, dance and rhythms, and educational gymnastics.

they are placed into the contexts of dance and rhythms and educational gymnastics (and games) (Figure 2.3). It's important to understand that the purpose of dance and rhythms, educational gymnastics, and games extends beyond simply skill improvement. Dance is a form of expression by moving to rhythm alone or with others. Educational gymnastics is balance and weight transfers combined into smooth, repeatable sequences performed on the floor and/or on an apparatus to demonstrate strength, balance, and body control. Games are organized activities that require manipulative skills

©Hero Images/Image Source

The fundamental movement skill of balancing has many uses.

and are played for the enjoyment and satisfaction of cooperating and competing with others.

Dance and rhythms, educational gymnastics, and games require skills that are best learned initially outside these complex contexts. It's ineffective to always practice the skills in isolation. Therefore, the contexts of dance and rhythms, educational gymnastics, and games are interwoven throughout the movement concept and skill theme chapters (Parts 4 and 5). The chapters on dance and rhythms, educational gymnastics, and games (Chapters 29, 30, and 31, respectively) illustrate this technique.

An analogy with reading also illustrates this point. Most children learn to read in elementary school; as adults, they choose what they'll read. In the skill theme approach, we teach the fundamental movement skills that are thought to provide the foundation for a lifetime of enjoyable, hopefully regular, physical activity. The children might tell us they aren't interested in some skills now. But 20 years from now, who knows?

How Do Classroom Teachers Feel about the Skill Theme Approach?

Classroom teachers are positive about the skill theme approach because they can relate it directly to their work in the classroom and see positive learning implications for students. For example, there is an increasing recognition of the important link between physical activity and cognitive functioning (Ratey and Hagerman 2008). As suggested in their book *Spark*, there is an increasing body of evidence that physical activity has a number of positive influences on brain function in youth and adults. Among these positive influences is the correlation between physical activity and academic achievement. Castelli et al.

(2015, p. 4) indicate the following: "Long-term studies have demonstrated that increases in physical activity, resulting from greater time spent in physical education, were related to improved academic performance."

Classroom teachers also appreciate the fact that the skill theme approach accommodates the variation in abilities typical of any class of children (differentiated instruction). Many teachers also consider the program's deemphasis of competition a welcome alternative to those programs that constantly pit one team against another in games in which the score is kept. They feel not only that this is more consistent with the approaches they use in the classroom but also that it makes their jobs easier; the children don't come angrily into their rooms after physical education class, arguing about the scores or who cheated, for example.

How Do Middle (Junior) and High School Physical Education Teachers Feel about the Skill Theme Approach?

Clearly there are many views. Some middle school teachers are enthusiastically supportive, realizing the importance of ensuring that children maintain positive attitudes about physical activity. Their job is much harder if their students have been turned off to physical education. Interestingly, a number of middle school teachers have actually started focusing on skill themes in their programs in response to their students' poor movement skill development. These teachers realize it's extremely difficult to excite students about sports and lifetime physical activity if they have yet to acquire the basic fundamental movement or sports skills. The skill theme approach has no age or grade limits. It can be valuable for people of any age.

Summary

The skill theme approach describes both the content (what is taught) and the pedagogy (how it is taught) that are used in a developmentally appropriate program of physical education. This approach recognizes that age and grade level are inappropriate indicators of physical ability; therefore, lessons are designed to consider different abilities and interests. The Curriculum Diamond provides an overview of how content can be sequentially developed so that elementary school, middle school, and high school programs work together to provide a solid movement foundation for youngsters to attain the competence and confidence to remain physically active throughout a lifetime.

Initially the skill theme approach emphasizes the development of fundamental movement skills (e.g., throwing, balancing, striking). As the children progress in ability, the skill themes are taught in sports, games, dance, and gymnastics contexts. Because of the rapid changes in children's development, skill themes are revisited throughout the year rather than taught in units of several weeks. Concepts related to physical fitness and the cognitive and affective domains are interwoven throughout the lessons.

Reading Comprehension Questions

1. Why aren't games such as basketball and Duck, Duck, Goose included in this book?
2. In your own words, describe the skill theme approach. Use the Curriculum Diamond (Figure 2.2) as part of your explanation.
3. Four characteristics of the skill theme approach are listed in this chapter. In your opinion, which provides the most compelling reason for using a skill theme approach? Why?
4. When are children ready for organized games? Why is it incorrect to respond to this question by suggesting an age or grade level?
5. This chapter suggests that children should be taught that becoming skillful will probably require practicing at home. Write a brief explanation to the children for a physical education Web page that you might use to explain why they need to practice outside of physical education class if they want to become good at a sport or physical activity.
6. Health-related physical fitness is an important part of the skill theme approach, yet only one chapter addresses it. How can this be explained?
7. What is the Curriculum Diamond? How does it explain the progression of content in physical education during school years?
8. Do you think the skill theme approach should be used in middle schools? Why or why not?
9. As explained at the beginning of this chapter, some teachers' programs consist entirely of games. Use the content in this chapter to develop an argument as to why teaching only games is not in children's best interests.

References/Suggested Readings

Barnett, L. M., D. Stodden, K. Cohen, J. J. Smith, D. R. Lubans, M. Lenoir, S. Iivonen et al. 2016. Fundamental movement skills: An important focus. *Journal of Teaching in Physical Education* 35(3): 219–25.

Castelli, D. M., E. M. Glowacki, J. M. Barcelona, H. G. Calvert, and J. Hwang. 2015. *Active education: Growing evidence on physical activity and academic performance.* San Diego, CA: Active Living Research. www.activelivingresearch.org.

[CDC] Centers for Disease Control and Prevention. 2011. School health guidelines to promote healthy eating and physical activity. *Morbidity and Mortality Weekly Report* 60(5): 1–80.

Clark, J. E. 2007. On the problem of motor skill development. *Journal of Physical Education, Recreation & Dance* 78(5): 39–44.

Cooper, A. R., A. Goodman, A. S. Page, L. B. Sherar, D. W. Esliger, E. M. van Sluijs, L. B. Anderson, et al. 2015. Objectively measured physical activity and sedentary time in youth: The international children's accelerometry database (ICAD). *International Journal of Behavioral Nutrition and Physical Activity* 12: 113.

Gallahue, D. L., J. C. Ozmun, and J. Goodway. 2012. *Understanding motor development: Infants, children, adolescents, adults.* New York: McGraw-Hill.

Graham, G. 1987. Motor skill acquisition: An essential goal of physical education programs. *Journal of Physical Education, Recreation and Dance* 58(8): 44–48.

Graham, G., C. Hopple, M. Manross, and T. Sitzman. 1993. Novice and expert children's physical education teachers: Insights into their situational decision-making. *Journal of Teaching in Physical Education* 12(2): 197–214.

Hastie, P. A. 2017. Revisiting the National Physical Education Content Standards: What do we really know about our achievement of the physically educated/literate person. *Journal of Teaching in Physical Education*, 36:3–19.

Holt/Hale, S. 2015. The skill theme approach to physical education. In *Standards-based physical education curriculum development*, 3rd ed., ed. J. Lund and D. Tannehill. Burlington, MA: Jones & Bartlett.

Logan, S. W., L. E. Robinson, A. E. Wilson, and W. A. Lucas. 2012. Getting the fundamentals of movement: A meta analysis of the effectiveness of motor skill interventions in children. *Child: Care, Health and Development* 38: 305–15.

Logan, S. W., S. M. Ross, K. Chee, D. F. Stodden, and L. E. Robinson. 2017. Fundamental motor skills: A systematic review of terminology. *Journal of Sports Sciences* 36(7): 781–96.

Lund, J., and D. Tannehill. 2015. *Standards based physical education curriculum development.* 3rd ed. Burlington, MA: Jones & Bartlett.

Manross, M. 2000. Learning to throw in physical education class: What I learned from 4th and 5th graders: Part 3. *Teaching Elementary Physical Education* 11(3): 26–29.

Ratey, J. J., and E. Hagerman. 2008. *Spark: The revolutionary new science of exercise and the brain.* New York: Little, Brown.

Robinson, L. E., D. F. Stodden, L. M. Barnett, V. P. Lopes, S. W. Logan, L. P. Rodrigues, and E. D'Hondt. 2015. Motor competence and its effect on positive developmental trajectories of health. *Sports Medicine* 45(9): 1273–84.

[SHAPE America] Society of Health and Physical Educators. 2009. *Appropriate instructional practice guidelines,*

K-12: A side-by-side comparison. Reston, VA: SHAPE America.

[SHAPE America] Society of Health and Physical Educators. 2014. *National standards & grade-level outcomes for K-12 physical education*. Champaign, IL: Human Kinetics.

[SHAPE America and Voices for Healthy Kids] Society of Health and Physical Educators. 2016. *2016 Shape of the nation: Status of physical education in the USA*. Reston, VA: SHAPE America.

Stodden, D. F., J. Goodway, S. J. Langendorfer, M. A. Roberton, M. E. Rudisill, C. Garcia, and L. E. Garcia.

2008. A developmental perspective on the role of motor skill competence in physical activity: An emergent relationship. *Quest* 60: 290–306.

Tannehill, D. 2001. Using the NASPE content standards. *Journal of Teaching Physical Education, Recreation and Dance* 72(8): 19.

[USDHHS] U.S. Department of Health and Human Services. 1996. *Physical activity and health: A report of the Surgeon General*. Atlanta: Centers for Disease Control and Prevention, National Center for Chronic Disease Prevention and Health Promotion.

Skill Themes, Movement Concepts, and the National Standards

A physical education program for children which begins with an organized sport is analogous to a language arts program beginning with a Shakespearean sonnet.

—IRIS WELSH, STUDENT

Children are not little adults. Their responses to activity are quite different from those of adults. Activity programs should be planned with these differences in mind.

—ODED BAR-OR (1995)

Drawn by children at Monfort, Chappelow or Shawsheen Elementary Schools, Greeley, CO.
Courtesy of Lizzy Ginger; Tia Ziegler

Key Concepts

- Children need to become competent in basic movement skills if they are going to have the confidence to participate in and enjoy a variety of physical activities as teens and adults.

- In elementary school, the emphasis is placed on practicing the fundamental movement skills (i.e., the foundational skills of physical education), not on learning rules or the structures of sports.

- Skill themes are analogous to verbs (i.e., they are action words). They are subdivided into three categories: locomotor, nonmanipulative, and manipulative skills.

- Movement concepts are analogous to adverbs (i.e., they describe how an action is performed). They are also subdivided into three categories: space awareness, effort, and relationships.

- In the lower elementary grades, movement concepts are taught before the skill themes.

- The movement analysis framework "wheel" describes how the skill themes and movement concepts interact with one another.

- The "spirals" outline a developmentally appropriate progression for each of the skill themes.

- *Children Moving* aligns directly with the *National Standards & Grade-Level Outcomes for K-12 Physical Education* (SHAPE America 2014) as well as many state physical education standards.

> *Essentially, the notion is that these elements (fundamental motor skills) are learned in early life through the various activities performed (such as jumping, throwing, striking, and the like), and then when a new act is to be learned in later life, the student can piece together these elements in a more efficient way to achieve the new motor goal. The assumption is that by jumping over objects of various sizes, shapes, heights, etc., the student will have more effective "elements" for the performance of the next jumping tasks (e.g., the running long jump in high school).*
>
> —**RICHARD SCHMIDT**, "Schema Theory: Implications for Movement Education," (1977)

Our primary goal in the skill theme approach is to provide children with a degree of competence leading to the confidence that encourages them to become, and remain, physically active for a lifetime. Our intent is to help children gain enough skills to participate enjoyably in many activities, not just a few traditional team sports, and to avoid the abysmal failure and embarrassment that often result from a total lack of skill. By focusing on learning and practicing skills rather than on the rules or structure of a game or sport, we can dramatically increase the amount of practice the children actually receive, thereby heightening their opportunities to learn the fundamental movement skills that form the foundation for becoming lifetime movers. Equally important is how the skills are taught. The learning climate promoted in *Children Moving* is one of mastery through the use of meaningful, relevant learning experiences, not through "skill and drill."

Typically, children who are learning to read are taught first to recognize letters, then parts of words, then complete words, and finally sentences. Children who are studying mathematics learn to solve problems after they've grasped the basic functions of numbers and signs. Children learning to play a musical instrument typically study the scale before attempting a song. In physical education, however, all too often children are experiencing games, dances, or complex gymnastic stunts before they're able to adequately perform fundamental movement skills. Too often, children know the rules for a game or the formation of a dance, but they don't have the movement skills needed for successful and enjoyable participation. Our way of teaching children how to participate effectively in various activities is to focus on the development of the necessary movement skills. We call this approach teaching by skill themes.

One of the easiest ways to understand skill themes is to think of a popular sport. Let's pick softball. The major skills people use to play softball include throwing, catching, batting, and running. In another popular sport—basketball—throwing, catching, running, dribbling with hands, jumping and landing, and chasing and fleeing skills are used frequently. Obviously we could list a number of other sports and activities. The point is that some of the same skills—for example, throwing, catching, and running—are used in both sports, and in many more. Thus if children learn to throw and catch, for example, their odds of playing and enjoying a sport such as softball or basketball increase because they have a reasonable chance to succeed at that sport. We have termed these *skill themes* because they apply to many different sports and other forms of physical activity, although the way they are used (the context) differs from one sport to another. Table 3.1 lists various skill themes and indicates which sports emphasize them.

Table 3.1 Skill Themes Used in Sports*

Skill Themes	Basketball	Football	Dance	Golf	Hockey	Martial Arts	Rock Climbing	Soccer	Softball	Tennis	Track and Field	Gymnastics	Ultimate Frisbee	Volleyball
Traveling	×	×	×	×	×	×	×	×	×	×	×	×	×	×
Chasing, fleeing, dodging	×	×			×	×		×	×				×	
Jumping, landing	×	×	×			×	×	×	×	×	×	×	×	×
Balancing	×	×	×	×	×	×	×	×	×	×	×	×	×	×
Transferring weight	×	×	×	×	×	×	×	×	×	×	×	×	×	×
Rolling		×	×			×						×		×
Kicking		×	×			×		×						
Punting		×						×						
Throwing	×	×						×	×	×	×		×	×
Catching	×	×						×	×				×	
Volleying								×						×
Dribbling	×				×			×						
Striking with rackets										×				
Striking with golf clubs				×										
Striking with bats									×					
Striking with hockey sticks					×									

*This table is intended only to suggest how various skill themes are applied in sports contexts.

Characteristics of Themes

In music, a theme recurs in different parts of a song, sometimes in exactly the same way, at other times in a slightly different form. *The Random House Dictionary of the English Language* defines theme as "a short melodic subject from which variations are developed." In physical education, various movements can be thought of as a theme. Skill themes are initially practiced as fundamental movement skills and then in increasingly more complex contexts, with other skill themes and concepts, as the children become more skillful. Skill themes are the foundation or building blocks for successful and enjoyable participation in games, sports, gymnastics, dance, and other physical activities. By revisiting a movement—sometimes in the previous context and sometimes in a different one—we provide children with variations of a skill theme. These variations lead to proficiency as well as diversity. Jumping, for example, can be presented as jumping from an object—a box or a table—and landing softly. This movement can be revisited with a slight variation: jumping from an object and landing facing a different direction from the takeoff position. Jumping for distance or leaping in synchronization with the leap of a partner would be completely different, yet the theme would still be jumping. Jumping to catch a ball in football, softball, or basketball is also a variation on the theme of jumping.

Whenever possible, we point out to students the similarities in movements used in different contexts to enhance their cognitive understanding of the principles that underlie successful performance of a movement. This may result in transfer of learning from one skill to another and, later, one activity to another.

The instructor who teaches by themes can focus on helping children become skillful movers. Youngsters will have plenty of opportunities as they grow older to learn the rules, tactics, and cooperation associated with games, sports, dance, and gymnastics activities, but first, they must learn the basic movement skills needed for successful participation.

©Lars A. Niki

Try to bat the ball without hitting the cone is the challenge used by this child's physical educator.

set of dance steps may be embarrassed and frustrated, as may be the adult who is trying to learn to play tennis but cannot even hit the ball into the opponent's court. Our goal in the skill theme approach is to help youngsters become skillful adults who enjoy a variety of physical activities.

As children acquire the fundamental skills, the reflective teacher combines skill themes and movement concepts into the movement contexts we typically identify as games, gymnastics, and dance. The key word, however, is ready. We lead children to these experiences gradually rather than forcing them into adult settings prematurely. Let's use the batting skill theme as an example. In Chapter 27, we explain a variety of enjoyable ways children can practice the skill of batting without placing them in an adult-rules softball game. Consistently striking out in a softball game in front of your classmates is hardly conducive to wanting to play softball as an adult. Therefore, we have developed a sequence of batting learning experiences that gradually progress into small-sided batting games that also provide plenty of practice opportunities. We do the same for each of the other skill themes (Part 5).

Skill Themes and Movement Concepts

We hope by now you understand the rationale for the skill theme approach. In this section, two tables and two figures are especially important to a thorough understanding of the skill theme approach. The movement concept categories and components are listed in Table 3.2 and the skill theme categories, themes, and components in Table 3.3. These tables organize the

Many adults choose not to play tennis or swim or dance. They don't enjoy these activities because they don't possess the skills needed to participate successfully. An unskilled adult attempting to learn a complex

Table 3.2 Movement Concept Categories and Components

Movement Concept Categories	Movement Concepts	Components
Space Awareness (Chapter 14) (where the body moves)	Location	Self-space and general space
	Directions	Forward, backward; sideways (right and left); clockwise and counterclockwise
	Levels	Low, middle, and high
	Pathways	Straight, curved, and zigzag
	Extensions	Large, small; far, near
Effort (Chapter 15) (how the body moves)	Time	Fast, slow
	Force	Strong, light
	Flow	Bound and free; smooth and jerky
Relationships (Chapter 16) (of body parts, with objects, with people)	Of body parts	Round, narrow, wide, and twisted; symmetrical and nonsymmetrical
	With objects and/or people	Over/under; on/off; near/far; in front/behind, alongside; along, through; meeting/parting, surrounding, around
	With people	Leading/following; mirroring/matching; unison/contrast; alone in a mass, solo, partners, groups, between groups

*This table represents many of the movement concepts taught in elementary school physical education. It is not meant to be all-inclusive but to provide examples of movement concepts.

Table 3.3 Skill Theme Categories, Skill Themes, and Components*

Skill Theme Categories	Skill Themes	Sample Components
Locomotor	Traveling (Chapter 17)	Walking, running, hopping, leaping, sliding, galloping, and skipping • in general space • in pathways • in different directions • at different speeds • in bound and free flow • in games, sports, and gymnastics
Nonmanipulative	Chasing, Fleeing, and Dodging (Chapter 18)	Traveling to chase, flee, and dodge; dodging to avoid obstacles and people; chasing, fleeing, and dodging in games with others
	Bending, Stretching, Twisting, and Curling (Chapter 19)	Traveling and jumping while twisting, curling, and stretching; stretching to catch with a ball thrown by a partner while traveling
	Jumping and Landing (Chapter 20)	Jumping for distance and height; five basic jumping-and-landing patterns; jumping over obstacles; jumping rope; buoyant and yielding landings; jumping to throw and catch; partner jumping
	Balancing (Chapter 21)	Balancing on different bases of support; in different shapes; on benches; inverted balances; balancing sequences with other skill themes
	Transferring Weight and Rolling (Chapter 22)	Transferring weight from feet to hands, on and off equipment; traveling weight onto and off apparatus; transferring weight sequences Rolling forward and sideways; rolling at different speeds; transferring weight and rolling; rolling onto and off equipment; rolling sequences
Manipulative	Kicking and Punting (Chapter 23)	Kicking for distance; to targets; dribbling with feet; to a partner; one-on-one soccer; kicking in small-sided games Punting for distance; for accuracy; running and punting; in small-sided games
	Throwing and Catching (Chapter 24)	Throwing for distance; underhand, overhand, and sidearm; at targets; throwing with a partner; flying discs Catching from a self-toss; from a partner; while running; while jumping. In small-sided games
	Volleying and Dribbling (Chapter 25)	Dribbling in self-space and general space; at different levels; and traveling; and changing speeds, changing directions, in pathways, against a defender; in a small-sided game Striking balloons (and other objects) in the air with different body parts; over a net; partner volleying; modified volleyball
	Striking with Rackets and Paddles (Chapter 26)	Striking balloons and suspended balls; striking up, down, and at targets; striking at different levels; striking over a net; partner striking
	Striking with Long-Handled Implements (Chapter 27)	Striking with golf clubs, bats, and hockey sticks for distance and accuracy

*This table represents many of the skill themes taught in physical education. It is not meant to be all-inclusive but to provide examples of skill themes. The major source for this explanation of skill themes and movement concepts is from the work of Sheila Stanley, *Physical education: A movement orientation*, 2nd ed. (New York: McGraw-Hill, 1977). She analyzed and applied the work of Rudolf Laban for American physical educators.

content (fundamental skills and concepts) to be taught in physical education, not by sports, but by an analysis of movements used in most sports and physical activities. The tables also serve as a guide to be certain that we teach all the important movements and do not leave any out. The skill themes and movement concepts are defined and thoroughly explained in Parts 4 and 5. There are 3 movement concept chapters and 11 skill theme chapters.

The movement analysis framework, which has been termed "the wheel" (Figure 3.1), is intended to show how the skill themes and movement concepts interact

Fundamental movements such as running, jumping, skipping, sliding, catching, kicking, and striking are the basic components of the games, sports, and dances of our society. Children who possess inadequate motor skills are often relegated to a life of exclusion from the organized and free play experiences of their peers, and subsequently, to a lifetime of inactivity because of their frustrations in early movement behavior.

—VERN SEEFELDT, JOHN HAUBENSTRICKER, AND SAM REUSCHLEIN

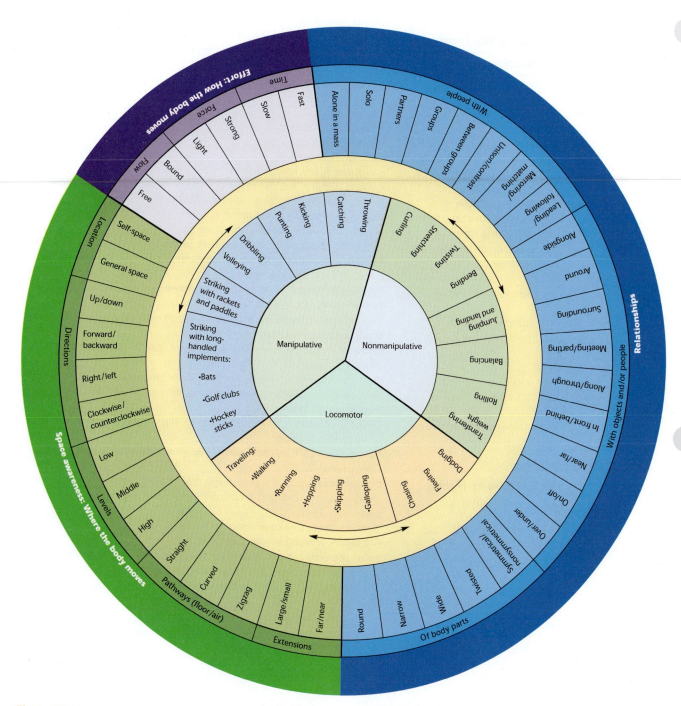

Figure 3.1 Movement analysis framework (wheel) depicting the interaction of movement concepts and skill themes. An interactive eWheel is located on http://www.mhhe.com/graham10e/eWheel.*

*Some movement analysis frameworks include the concept of space (direct and flexible) as a quality of movement. In our teaching, however, we use this concept so infrequently that we don't include it in our discussion of the qualities of movement.

with each other. The sample spiral (Figure 3.2) is an example of one of the developmentally appropriate progressions we have created for each of the 16 skill themes. (There are 16 progression spirals because some of the related skill themes are combined within the same chapter. Transferring weight and rolling are combined in Chapter 22, for example. Volleying and dribbling are combined in Chapter 25.)

Both the movement analysis framework and the progression development spirals are explained later in this

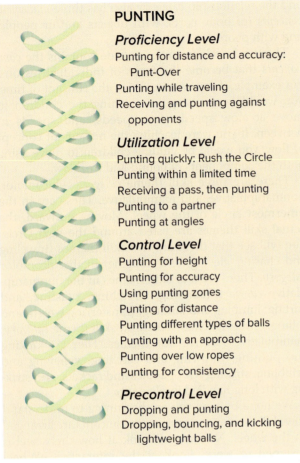

PUNTING

Proficiency Level
Punting for distance and accuracy:
    Punt-Over
Punting while traveling
Receiving and punting against
    opponents

Utilization Level
Punting quickly: Rush the Circle
Punting within a limited time
Receiving a pass, then punting
Punting to a partner
Punting at angles

Control Level
Punting for height
Punting for accuracy
Using punting zones
Punting for distance
Punting different types of balls
Punting with an approach
Punting over low ropes
Punting for consistency

Precontrol Level
Dropping and punting
Dropping, bouncing, and kicking
    lightweight balls

Figure 3.2 Progression spiral illustrating the contextual variations in which skill themes can be studied.

chapter. Obviously the content of our program consists of more than just skill themes. In fact, it's difficult to focus on a skill theme for long without introducing one or more movement concepts. The two terms, *skill themes* and *movement concepts*, differentiate the movements (skill themes) from the adverbs (movement concepts) used to modify or enrich the range and effectiveness of skill employment. Chapters 14–16 are devoted specifically to ideas and examples for teaching the movement concepts, whereas Chapters 17–27 do the same for skill themes. At this point, however, it is important to understand the differences between them.

The distinction between movement concepts and skill themes can be clarified by a comparison to grammar. Skill themes are always verbs—they're movements that can be performed. Movement concepts are always modifiers (adverbs)—they describe how a skill is to be performed. This distinction also clarifies how movement concepts are employed to embellish, enhance, or expand the quality of a movement. A verb by itself—strike, travel, roll—is typically less interesting than one that is modified by an adverb—strike hard, travel jerkily, roll smoothly. Skills can stand by themselves. You can roll or gallop or jump, but you can't low or high or under without moving. Concepts modify skills.

Skill themes perform three related functions.

1. They link the skills to the concepts, for example, fast running or slow running; balancing in a symmetrical or nonsymmetrical shape; striking a ball hard or easy.
2. They link one skill with another skill, for example, jumping and catching; running and kicking; twisting and dodging.
3. They are linked to dance, gymnastics, and games contexts.

Our initial focus with the lower elementary children (prekindergarten through grade 2) is on learning and understanding the movement concept vocabulary; for

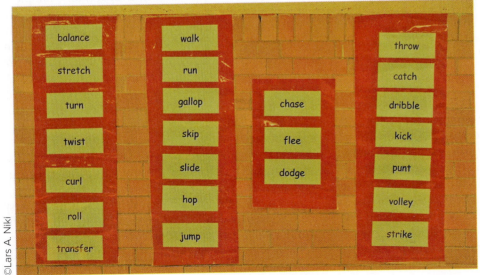

Children enjoy learning the vocabulary of the skill theme approach. This teacher has posted her skill themes on the gym wall.

this reason, the movement concepts are taught before the skill themes. We focus on movement concepts before skill themes because children in the lower grades spend a great deal of time studying vocabulary (learning new words), and many of the movement concepts can be part of this vocabulary. This is also the time when children truly enjoy the challenge of exploring, learning, and moving as they demonstrate their understanding of such movement concepts as symmetrical, zigzag, and twisted. We call this a "functional understanding" of the movement concept (i.e., cognitive and performance).

When the children are learning the movement concepts, they are also practicing the skill themes. As soon as the children begin to move, they are practicing one or more skill themes, even though they may not be thinking about it at the time. For example, if we ask children to skip in a curved pathway, they may be thinking about the curve, but they are also practicing skipping. If we ask them to land in a low level from a jump, they are also getting jumping and landing practice. In later grades, the teacher's focus will shift from the low level (movement concept) to providing cues for soft, safe landings—from the concept to the skill. The skill themes and movement concepts are constantly interacting as the children move—it is the emphasis of the teacher that changes.

The Wheel (Movement Analysis Framework)

The movement concepts and skill themes work together. In fact, one cannot teach a skill theme without including a movement concept, unless, of course, the children are just sitting and listening and not moving. Our goal, however, is to have children moving because this is the only way to effectively teach the movement concepts and the skill themes. Look closely at Figure 3.1, the wheel. (The interactive eWheel (http://www.mhhe.com/graham10e/eWheel) actually moves and will better help you understand our explanation. Locate it now.)

The interaction between the movement concepts and skill themes listed in Tables 3.2 and 3.3 is represented schematically by five concentric circles that make up the wheel. The outermost circle consists of three movement concept *categories*—space awareness, effort, and relationships. Each *category* consists of several *movement concepts* listed in the second circle from the outside. The *movement concept category* of space awareness, for example, consists of five *movement concepts*. They are location, directions, levels, pathways, and extensions. The effort movement concept category has three *movement concepts* (time, force, and flow),

and the relationship category also has three *movement concepts* (of body parts, with objects and/or people, and with people).

The third circle from the outside contains the *components* that become the focus of individual lessons. For example, if you were teaching the concept of time, you would be focusing on teaching the children to move at slow speeds, fast speeds, and speeds in between. If you were teaching the movement concept of flow, you would be guiding children to move using both the components of bound and free flow.

There are three skill theme *categories*—locomotor, nonmanipulative, and manipulative. These are in the innermost circle of the wheel. Moving outward, the actual skill themes are listed around the next circle. You will see that there are two skill themes (traveling and chasing, fleeing, and dodging) in the locomotor *category*. There are four skill themes in the nonmanipulative *category* (bending, stretching, twisting, and curling; jumping and landing; transferring weight and rolling; and balancing). The third skill theme *category*, manipulative, has five skill themes. They are kicking and punting, throwing and catching, volleying and dribbling, striking with paddles and rackets, and striking with long-handled implements.

We hope by now you are beginning to understand how skill themes and movement concepts are arranged on the wheel. Now we will look at how the wheel is designed to work. Look at the interactive eWheel (http://www.mhhe.com/graham10e/eWheel). You will see that the two innermost circles representing the skill themes are stationary. The three outer circles are connected to each other but can rotate around the two inner circles. The purpose of designing the wheel to rotate is to show that the same movement concept can be used to enhance the development of different skill themes. The concept of levels in space, for example, is useful for refining such skills as catching, striking, volleying, and balancing (e.g., catching at high level). The concept of fast and slow can be applied to the study of such skills as traveling, rolling, dribbling, transferring weight, and dodging (e.g., rolling at a slow speed). At times, some concepts blend with other concepts. For example, fast or slow as well as pathways may modify locomotor skills (e.g., galloping slowly forward in a zigzag pathway).

Do you understand now how the wheel works? If so that's great! If not, reread the previous paragraphs and, once again, refer to the interactive eWheel (http://www.mhhe.com/graham10e/eWheel). Once you grasp the concept behind the design of the wheel, you will understand the movement concept and skill theme chapters and are on your way to doing movement analyses for your students.

Progression Spiral

The progression spiral is much easier to understand than the wheel. As you no doubt understand, just learning the terminology for the movement concepts and the skill themes is not enough to begin actually teaching them to children. Subsequent chapters present explanations for each of the movement concepts and skill themes, along with numerous sample learning experiences (Chapters 14–27). In each of these chapters, we provide tasks and challenges (lesson ideas) in a progression from the easiest to the hardest, and from less to more complex. The content in each of the skill theme chapters is outlined in a figure we call a progression spiral (Figure 3.2). The spiral is intended to be read from the bottom to the top—that is, the easiest tasks are at the bottom, the hardest at the top. It also suggests that tasks may need to be retaught when, for example, it has been several months since the children have practiced that skill or it is the beginning of a school year.

Each line on the spiral corresponds to a section in the skill theme chapters. The lesson ideas are arranged in a progression from easy to hard. So, for example, if you were teaching a class that was predominantly at the control level, as explained in Chapter 5, you might want to teach the children how to punt for distance and/or punt for accuracy. (Chapter 23 contains lesson ideas for actually teaching children to punt accurately and for distance.) To make it easier for you to use the skill theme approach, all of the skill theme lesson ideas correspond directly (Chapters 17–27) to the progressions outlined in the spirals.

As you begin to plan using the learning experiences in the skill theme chapters, you will see how the movement concepts and skill themes work together. The movement concepts of fast and slow, for example, can be used to make a task more interesting or challenging. The skill theme of rolling or transferring weight can be made more difficult by challenging the children to move more slowly. But with a skill such as dribbling, which is easier to perform at a slower rate, the challenge "dribble faster" increases the complexity of the task. In short, there's no standard formula that can be used as a guide for varying the contexts in which all skill themes are studied. Each skill theme is different, as are the children. The 16 spirals in the skill theme chapters suggest a progression that will help you both understand and teach the skill themes effectively.

Notice in Figure 3.2 that the spirals do not suggest the length of time, or the number of lessons, to be spent studying a particular theme. In reflective teaching, as Chapter 4 details, these decisions are based on the frequency and length of classes, available equipment and facilities, class sizes, and characteristics of the students and the school. In other words, it would be impossible for us to use the same yearly and weekly sequence of lessons for every physical education program in the country unless they were all identical—which, as you know, they are certainly not!

Finally, the spirals provide a progression from the precontrol (beginner or novice) level up to the proficiency level (elite or highly skilled) (see Chapter 5).The movement concept and skill theme progressions in Parts 4 and 5 are based on our knowledge of the pertinent literature and on years of teaching experience. But you may find that a different ordering of the tasks (learning experiences) is more appropriate for a particular teaching situation. Each child, each class, each teaching environment differs from all others, and the reflective teacher adapts to these differences. We suggest you start with the learning experiences outlined in the content chapters (14–27) and then change and adapt your lessons and sequence based on your particular teaching situation.

The National Standards and the Skill Theme Approach

As indicated in Chapter 1, the *National Standards* provide the framework for what children should know and be able to do as a result of a highly effective physical education program. In this 10th edition of *Children Moving*, we attempt to show how our program fits with the content of the *National Standards & Grade-Level Outcomes for K-12 Physical Education* (SHAPE America 2014). We think this will be especially useful for teachers who are interested in revising their programs to reflect the content suggested in the *National Standards*. Before describing how *Children Moving* can be used as a guide to developing a program designed on the *National Standards*, it is important to understand the standards and the foundation on which they are based.

Background of *National Standards* Development

In the late 1980s, the National Association for Sport and Physical Education (NASPE) formed a blue-ribbon task force and asked its members to:

- Define a person who is "physically educated"
- Define "outcomes" and "benchmarks" that could serve as guidelines for constructing physical education program curriculums

The Outcomes Task Force worked on the project for more than five years; each year, at NASPE's national conference, physical educators from throughout the United States were invited to review and critique the work. The task force then revised its work based on these recommendations and presented it again the following year. Over several years, hundreds of physical educators reviewed the work of the task force, which, as a result, reflects the collective wisdom of much of the profession. The result of this work, published in 1992, was a document entitled *The Physically Educated Person* (NASPE 1992), which defined a physically educated person as an individual who:

- HAS learned skills necessary to perform a variety of physical activities
- IS physically fit
- DOES participate regularly in physical activity
- KNOWS the implications of and the benefits from involvement in physical activity
- VALUES physical activity and its contributions to a healthful lifestyle

Outcome statements were also developed for each of the five parts of the definition, along with benchmarks for kindergarten, second, fourth, sixth, eighth, tenth, and twelfth grades.

Using the same process, in 1995, NASPE built upon the foundation of the "Outcomes Project" to develop national content standards for physical education, including examples for assessment. The physical education content standards were especially important because they paralleled work that was also being done in other disciplines, such as mathematics, science, and geography. The standards were revised in 2004 (NASPE 2004) and again in 2014 (SHAPE America 2014). The 2014 revision included grade-level outcomes for each standard.

National Standards & Grade-Level Outcomes

The *National Standards* (SHAPE America 2014) describe the goal of physical education as a physically literate individual. *Children Moving* and its curriculum approach of educating the whole child (see Chapter 1, page 11) aligns with the *National Standards*. This alignment is illustrated in each of the standards:

Standard 1: "...demonstrates competency in a variety of motor skills and movement patterns." This standard focuses on the fundamental movement skills in locomotors, nonlocomotors, and manipulatives (e.g., striking, dribbling, volleying, transferring weight, balancing, running, sliding, skipping) that serve as the foundation for all physical education and physical activity. Standard 1 represents the learning domain that is unique to physical education, the psychomotor domain.

Standard 2: "...applies knowledge of concepts, principles, strategies and tactics related to movement and performance." This standard is a reminder of the importance of the cognitive learning domain in physical education. Recognition, demonstration, analysis, creativity, and application are cognitive skills in elementary physical education; they are benchmarks for Standard 2.

Standard 3: "...demonstrates the knowledge and skills to achieve and maintain a health-enhancing level of physical activity and fitness." The intent of this standard for children in elementary physical education is the awareness of the importance of healthy bodies and the ways to achieve and maintain good health. The standard focuses on knowledge of fitness, nutrition, and physical activity as well as developmentally appropriate assessment of health-related fitness.

Standard 4: "...exhibits responsible personal and social behavior that respects self and others." This standard focuses on the importance of the affective domain. Personal responsibility, working independently, respect for others in physical activity contexts, and working safely in physical activity settings are sample benchmarks. The affective domain plays a major role in students' learning in physical education and their participation in physical activity outside the school setting and beyond the years of elementary school. The affective domain, as is true for psychomotor and cognitive domains, must be built into the teacher's planning for expected student learning.

Standard 5: "...recognizes the value of physical activity for health, enjoyment, challenge, self-expression and/or social interaction." This standard identifies the reasons for participation in physical activity beyond the requirements imposed by the teacher. Enjoyment, challenge, confidence, success, health, and positive social interaction are benchmarks for Standard 5.

The grade-level outcomes for grades K–5 serve as benchmarks toward developing the mature pattern of the fundamental motor skills, understanding and applying movement concepts and fitness principles, and applying the affective concepts. By the end of elementary school physical education (grade 5) students are expected to:

- Demonstrate competence in fundamental motor skills and selected combinations of skills

- Use basic movement concepts in dance, gymnastics, and small-sided practice tasks
- Identify basic health-related fitness concepts
- Exhibit acceptance of self and others in physical activities
- Identify the benefits of a physically active lifestyle (SHAPE America 2014, p. 26)

Sample grade-level outcomes for Standards 1 and 2 are provided in Boxes 3-1 and 3-2.

It is important to remember that the standards are not intended as a prescribed set of goals or outcomes to be achieved by all physical education programs. The *National Standards* document is not a national curriculum! As detailed in Chapter 4, "Reflective Teaching," you will need to determine the goals of your program based on the specific characteristics of the schedule, the children, and the community—as well as your district and state standards. The suggested grade-level outcomes, for example, are only that—suggestions. The *National Standards* can be immensely helpful, however, because they represent the professional judgment of hundreds of physical education teachers and professors about the content of a quality physical education curriculum that provides the movement foundation for a lifetime of physical activity.

The *National Standards & Grade-Level Outcomes for K-12 Physical Education* (SHAPE America 2014) were written with a two- or three-day-a-week program (30-minute classes) in mind. For many the grade-level outcomes may appear as optimistic goals. Chapters 7–13 (Part 3: Active Teaching Skills) contain valuable information on maximizing instruction for student learning using deliberate practice, focused time on task, and student engagement. Faced with the challenge of one day a week for instructional physical education, the task will be a bit daunting as teachers will have to carefully select the outcomes they can truly accomplish in the amount of time they have allocated for physical education. The *National Standards* can also provide the foundation for a strong argument for more time in the school day for instructional physical education. This is needed more than ever as state and districts are beginning to hold physical education

---

Box 3-1

Sample Grade-Level Outcomes for National Standard 1

Dribbling/ball control with feet

- Taps a ball using the inside of the foot, sending it forward (kindergarten)
- Taps or dribbles a ball using the inside of the foot while walking in general space (grade 1)
- Dribbles with the feet in general space with control of ball and body (grade 2)
- Dribbles with the feet in general space at slow to moderate jogging speed with control of ball and body (grade 3)
- Dribbles with the feet in general space with control of ball and body while increasing and decreasing speed (grade 4)
- Combines foot dribbling with other skills in one-on-one practice tasks (grade 5)

Passing and receiving with feet

- *Developmentally appropriate outcomes first appear in grade 3 for this skill.*
- Passes and receives ball with the insides of the feet to a stationary partner, "giving" on reception before returning the pass (grade 3)

- Passes and receives ball with the insides of the feet to a moving partner in nondynamic environment (closed skills) (grade 4)
- Receives and passes a ball with the outsides and insides of the feet to a stationary partner, "giving" on reception before returning the pass (grade 4)
- Passes with the feet using a mature pattern as both partners travel (grade 5)
- Receives a pass with the feet using a mature pattern as both partners travel (grade 5)

Dribbling in combinations

- *Developmentally appropriate outcomes first appear in grade 4 for this skill.*
- Dribbles with feet in combination with other skills (e.g., passing, receiving, shooting) (grade 4)
- Dribbles with feet with mature pattern in a variety of small-sided game forms (grade 5)

Box 3-2

Sample Grade-Level Outcomes for National Standard 2: Movement Concepts

A more detailed description of each grade-level outcome, along with tasks and challenges to teach it, is included in the *Children Moving* chapter(s) listed below at the end of each outcome.

Kindergarten

- Differentiates between movement in personal (self-space) and general space (Chapter 14)
- Travels in 3 different pathways (Chapters 14, 17)

Grade 1

- Travels demonstrating low, middle, and high levels (Chapters 14, 17)
- Differentiates between fast and slow speeds and between strong and light force (Chapters 14, 15)
- Travels demonstrating a variety of relationships with objects (Chapters 16, 17)

Grade 2

- Combines shapes, levels, and pathways into simple travel, dance, and gymnastics sequences (Chapters 14, 16, 21, 22)

Grade 3

- Recognizes the concept of open spaces in a movement context (Chapters 14, 17)

Grade 4

- Applies the concept of open spaces to combination skills involving traveling (Chapters 14, 17, 25–27)
- Applies the concepts of direction and force when striking an object with a short-handled implement, sending it toward a target (Chapters 14, 15, 26)

Grade 5

- Analyzes movement situations and applies movement concepts in small-sided practice tasks in games environments, dance, and gymnastics (Chapters 14–17, 21, 22, 24–27)

---

teachers accountable for standards-based teaching and student learning. For those with a district supportive enough to schedule daily physical education, teachers will have the luxury of setting goals beyond that of the *National Standards*.

Since the *National Standards* were first published in 1995, a number of states have revised or developed state standards, many of them based on the *National Standards*. Go to the Web site for the Department of Education in your state to see if your state has revised or developed physical education standards. You may find it interesting to see how your state standards compare to the ones developed at the national level.

Skill Themes and the *National Standards*

The skill theme approach, as defined in *Children Moving*, is aligned with the *National Standards & Grade-Level Outcomes for K-12 Physical Education.* You will find references to the *National Standards* throughout the movement concept and skill theme chapters as well as

within the skill theme application chapters (28–31). Each movement concept chapter and each skill theme chapter contains sample grade-level outcomes and the standard reference for that skill or movement concept.

Children Moving is centered on meeting children where they are, providing developmentally appropriate tasks and challenges, and doing so with enjoyment and success for each child. The importance of elementary physical education cannot be overemphasized. The recognition of physical activity as a source of health, joy in movement, challenge, and success coupled with the fundamental movement skills of elementary physical education are the foundation for a lifetime of healthy, physical activity.

Catherine Ennis, in her address as the Alliance Scholar (2010), stated, "One of the most reliable predictors for lifelong physical activity is the power of early physical activity/physical education experiences."

Summary

Teaching by skill themes focuses on movement skill acquisition and knowledge of movement concepts. With quality instruction and frequent practice outside of the physical education class setting, the skilled child will eventually acquire the confidence and desire to be physically active throughout his or her lifetime. Skill themes are closely aligned with the *National Standards & Grade-Level Outcomes for K-12 Physical Education* (SHAPE America 2014). Games, sports, gymnastics, and dance typically require children to use combinations of movement skills and movement concepts that are developed only after a substantial amount of practice.

Teaching by themes also involves revisiting the same skills or concepts continually throughout the program at different times (distributed practice) and in different contexts. In preschool and the lower elementary grades, the focus is on developing a functional understanding, cognitive and performance, of the movement concepts (Chapters 14–16). When children have a functional understanding, the emphasis shifts to the skill themes (Chapters 17–27). The skill themes and movement concepts constantly interact, as depicted in the movement analysis framework (the wheel). The progression and learning experiences for each of the skill themes are outlined in the progression spirals in the skill theme chapters (17–27). The spirals are visual reminders that the child revisits each task to enhance skill acquisition and retention and that skills are best learned when they are presented in a progression.

Support for the skill theme approach can be found in four national documents, the *National Standards & Grade-Level Outcomes for K-12 Physical Education* (SHAPE America 2014); *Appropriate Instructional Practice Guidelines for Elementary School Physical Education* (SHAPE America 2009); *The Essential Component of Physical Education* (SHAPE America 2015); and *Opportunity to Learn Guidelines for Elementary, Middle and High School Physical Education* (SHAPE America 2010). Essentially, these sources recommend that physical education programs at the preschool and elementary school levels focus on helping children improve their fundamental movement skills. Cognitive and affective goals are interwoven throughout the program.

Reading Comprehension Questions

1. What do children need to learn in physical education before they're ready to play a game successfully and enjoyably? Why?

2. What is the difference between a movement concept and a skill theme?

3. In your own words, explain how the wheel works. Then briefly explain why it is important.

4. Find the dribbling progression spiral in Chapter 25. One of the progressions on the spiral is entitled "dribbling and looking." This refers to teaching children to look away from the ball when they are dribbling. On what page in the chapter are the tasks for teaching children to look away from the ball? Briefly summarize the two tasks that are described.

5. What three skill themes relate most directly to teaching dance? To teaching games? To teaching gymnastics? You may not use the same skill theme twice.

6. Select a team sport (or physical activity) you are familiar with. List skills that are needed to play the sport enjoyably. List three movement concepts that are also important for success in that sport.

7. Locate your state physical education standards at the Web site for your state's Department of Education. (If your state has not posted them, you can refer to the *National Standards*.) Find three examples of state (or national) standards for the elementary school grades that directly address the teaching of movement concepts or skill themes. Copy the standard (include the grade level and standard number) and indicate which skill theme or movement concept the standard addresses.

References/Suggested Readings

Bar-Or, O. 1995. Health benefits of physical activity during childhood and adolescence. In *President's Council on Physical Fitness and Sports Research Digest*. Washington, DC: President's Council on Physical Fitness and Sports.

Ennis, C. 2010. 2010 Alliance scholar lecture titled— On your own: Preparing students for a lifetime. *Journal of Physical Education, Recreation and Dance* 81(5): 17–22.

[NASPE] National Association for Sport and Physical Education. 1992. *The physically educated person*. Reston, VA: National Association for Sport and Physical Education.

[NASPE] National Association for Sport and Physical Education. 1995. *Moving into the future: National standards for physical education*. Reston, VA: National Association for Sport and Physical Education.

[NASPE] National Association for Sport and Physical Education. 2004. *Moving into the future: National standards for physical education*. 2nd ed. Reston, VA: National Association for Sport and Physical Education.

Schmidt, R. A. 1977. Schema theory: Implications for movement education. *Motor Skills: Theory into Practice* 2: 36–48.

[SHAPE America] Society of Health and Physical Educators. 2009. *Appropriate instructional practice guidelines for elementary school physical education*. Reston, VA: Champaign, IL: Human Kinetics.

[SHAPE America] Society of Health and Physical Educators. 2010. *Opportunity to learn guidelines for elementary, middle and high school physical education*. Champaign, IL: Human Kinetics.

[SHAPE America] Society of Health and Physical Educators. 2014. *National standards & grade-level outcomes for K-12 physical education*. Champaign, IL: Human Kinetics.

[SHAPE America] Society of Health and Physical Educators. 2015. *The essential components of physical education*. Champaign, IL: Human Kinetics.

Stanley, S. 1977. *Physical education: A movement orientation*. 2nd ed. New York: McGraw-Hill.

Becoming a Reflective Teacher

The three chapters in Part 2 introduce you to the concept of reflective teaching and the process of becoming a reflective teacher. Chapter 4, "Reflective Teaching," describes how teachers adapt their programs according to the particular characteristics of their school (for example, the number of days per week they teach physical education, the available facilities and equipment) and their children (for example, background, experience, type of community). The process of reflective teaching is contrasted with programs that assume all children have identical physical abilities and fail to adapt and change their programs to meet the needs of their students. Typically these programs consist primarily of games with little or no teacher instruction provided.

Chapter 5, "Determining Generic Levels of Skill Proficiency," introduces a system for analyzing the children's skills and abilities in a class in order to present content that is developmentally appropriate and beneficial in terms of learning. The generic levels of skill proficiency present a viable alternative to organizing the content by grade level or age.

Chapter 6, "Planning and Developing the Content," explains how reflective teachers plan their school years. The first three steps focus on long-term planning that answers the questions, "What do I teach and when?" The fourth step provides a practical, yet detailed, example of how to plan lessons. It demonstrates how to develop the content to match children's abilities by using the Reflective Planning Grid.

Reflective Teaching

The good teacher must relate his teaching to the world of his students as it is, not as he or she would like it to be.

—HERBERT FOSTER (1974)

No matter how much effort a teacher has put into individualizing tasks, there always seems to be a need to make tasks more appropriate for individuals or small groups within a class.

—JUDITH E. RINK (2014)

By Esmeralda Michelle Mejia

Ball

Drawn by children at Monfort, Chappelow or Shawsheen Elementary Schools, Greeley, CO. Courtesy of Lizzy Ginger; Tia Ziegler

Key Concepts

- The reflective teacher believes that students, classes, and teaching situations are different and develops lessons and the curriculum accordingly.
- The number of students in a class, frequency and length of classes, facilities, class sizes, equipment, behavior of the students, and characteristics of the school are all factors reflective teachers take into account as they develop their lessons and programs.
- The teacher's personal value system is the most important characteristic of a reflective teacher.
- Invariant teachers rarely reflect on their effectiveness, continuing to teach the same lessons and content year after year, ignoring the students' progress and interest.
- Reflective teachers are continually thinking about what they need to change, or do differently, to heighten their teaching and program effectiveness.

Chapters 1–3 introduced the purpose and characteristics of a quality physical education program, along with an overview of skill themes and concepts of movement. This short but important chapter also provides an overview—of reflective teaching and the reasons for reflective, as opposed to invariant, teaching (Table 4.1).

This chapter defines reflective teaching and why we believe it is so important for teachers today. One of the guiding concepts in education today is differentiation of instruction. This concept recognizes that all children are not identical and that teachers should attempt to vary their teaching, both what and how they teach, based on children's abilities. The authors of *Children Moving*, and many other respected educators, do not believe that a prepackaged curriculum can meet the needs and abilities of all children in a class. We want every child we teach to experience success, pleasure, and a sense of competence that leads to their becoming physically active for a lifetime. In order to do so, we differentiate our instruction—that is, we are reflective teachers who create quality programs of physical education that recognize one size does not fit all (SHAPE America 2009).

We know you agree that no two children are exactly alike. There are obvious physical differences and more subtle personality and individual differences. What is exciting to one child is boring to another. Some youngsters can accomplish a great deal on their own; other children require almost constant monitoring to make progress. This can be said about youth and adults too. Some may delight in the challenge and camaraderie of a team game, while others prefer the challenge and satisfaction of individual sports and activities.

Schools are also different. Administrators can be strict, stultifying, or supportive. Fellow teachers can be cooperative or competitive, helpful, or obstructive.

Table 4.1 Comparison of Reflective Teaching and Invariant Teaching

Variable	Reflective Teachers	Invariant Teachers
Planning	Adjust lesson plans to differences between classes and children	Use the same plan for each primary grade and the same plan for each intermediate grade
Progression within and between lessons	Base progression on such factors as youngsters' (1) rate and extent of improvement; (2) physical skill needs; (3) interest in a particular topic or activity	Base progression on such factors as (1) six-week units; (2) amount of material to be covered in a semester or year; (3) a predetermined formula for progression
Methodology	Vary the methodology according to such factors as (1) characteristics of children in the class; (2) purpose of the lesson; (3) ability of the children to accept responsibility	Employ the same methodology with all classes and hope that the children will eventually fulfill the teacher's expectations
Curriculum	Design curriculum for each unique class of children after examining the children to determine their abilities and needs	Use predetermined curricular content without considering such factors as children's ability, community influences, or children's interests
Equipment and facilities	Modify activities and lessons to available equipment and facilities	Teach activities and lessons that use available equipment and facilities
Discipline	Attempt to understand management problems and then seek the causes, modifying teaching procedure accordingly	Assume that the children are misbehaving and resort to punitive measures to modify individual and class behavior
Assessment	Regularly assess the children and seek constructive criticism about their teaching from children and colleagues	Assess sporadically and often base assessment on whether children liked the lesson, how long they remained interested, and how well they behaved

Gymnasiums, plentiful physical education equipment, adequate field space, and small class sizes are basic necessities in some elementary schools; other schools view such facilities as frills. Parents may be concerned, meddlesome, apathetic, helpful, or unavailable.

How is a teacher to succeed amid this diversity? We have no magical answers. But we are convinced that a prepackaged (linear) approach* to teaching is not effective, and so we encourage you to be reflective in your practice. The reflective teacher achieves success and professional satisfaction by differentiating instruction in an attempt to challenge both the high- and low-skilled children in a class. She also changes lessons from one class to another, recognizing that all third-grade classes, for example, are not identical.

What Is Reflective Teaching?

The practice of reflective teaching is recognizing that children are different—and doing something about it. It could also be called adapted teaching because the teacher adapts the content, and his teaching, to suit the needs of individual students and classes. Reflective teaching is directly related to the concept of developmentally and instructionally appropriate teaching, which acknowledges that students develop at different rates and stages (SHAPE America 2009). Invariant teaching, the opposite of reflective teaching, assumes that all children have identical abilities, interests, and level of physical fitness.

*Dwight Allen defined linear thinking as searching for the answer to a problem by investigating a single solution without considering feasible alternatives (Allen 1975).

The concept of reflective teaching is not new. In fact, the teachers in one-room schoolhouses were no doubt models of reflective teaching because they had to teach children of many ages in the same classroom. The results of attempting to teach prepackaged lessons without considering the unique characteristics of a class have been disastrous for both the children and many teachers. One can't help but wonder how many inactive, overweight, and obese people today were in physical education classes that had no lasting impact on their lifestyles because lessons were not designed to meet their needs.

In *Children Moving*, reflective teaching doesn't refer to any particular methodology or style of teaching; it refers to the many teaching skills employed by individuals who are respected as master teachers (Graham, Elliott, and Palmer 2016). The reflective teacher engages in reflective practice by designing and implementing an educational program congruent with the idiosyncrasies of a particular school situation. Invariant teaching is characterized by the use of one approach, and often identical content, in all teaching situations. Invariant teachers often rely on prescribed curriculums that provide the same lessons organized by grade level, thereby assuming that all children have the same abilities and that one school is virtually identical to another school.

The Need for Reflective Teaching

If all schools, classes, and youngsters were identical, there would be no need for reflective teaching. We would simply provide you with prepackaged lesson

Some teachers teach most of their lessons outdoors.

©Lars A. Niki

Figure 4.1 Interacting factors that contribute to the unique characteristics of each school.

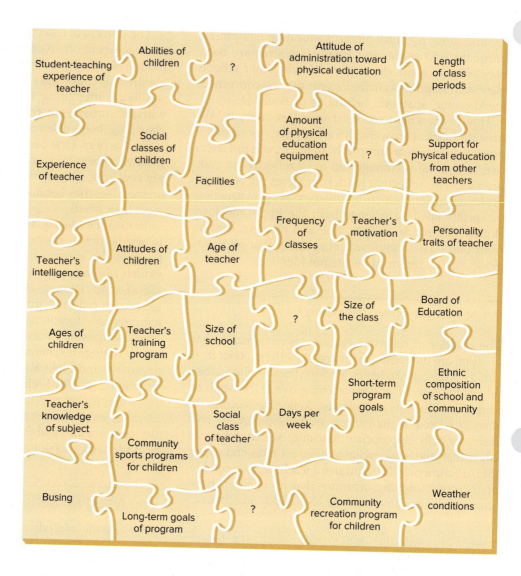

plans for each grade level, and you could follow them exactly. You know, however, that schools, programs, and youngsters are different. Figure 4.1 illustrates some of the obvious differences. Its puzzle shape indicates that teaching is a constant challenge as we attempt to fit the pieces together into a unified, consistent program that provides youngsters with the active learning experiences they need. Reflective teachers take these differences into account and continuously modify and change their teaching and curriculum based on the needs of the students at their school. We want to focus on six of these variables that are major factors in any program necessitating reflective teaching: values of the teacher, class size, the number of class sessions per week, facilities and equipment, student behavior, and the context of the school. Although they may seem obvious, it has been our experience that far too many invariant teachers fail to account for these variables in their teaching. We'll now discuss them in detail.

Values of the Teacher

Clearly one of the most important variables is the personal disposition (attitudes and beliefs) we, as teachers, bring to our teaching situation. Some physical education teachers, for example, are more interested in coaching than teaching—and their programs reflect a lack of planning and interest in high-quality physical education. Other physical education teachers are totally dedicated to their programs and spend countless hours planning new and interesting learning experiences, as well as volunteering time with children before and after school. Still other physical education teachers view physical education as merely a break for the children from the routine of the classroom, so their programs consist primarily of physical activity with virtually no purpose or emphasis on learning.

In some schools, physical education is also the classroom teacher's responsibility. Like physical education teachers, classroom teachers vary in their views of the purpose and importance of physical activity in children's lives. Some classroom teachers, for example, find time in their hectic schedules to develop programs for children that truly enhance the development of positive attitudes and learning, as suggested in Chapters 1 and 32. In contrast, other classroom teachers view physical education as a break for the children and themselves—and rely on traditional inappropriate activities such as kickball, dodgeball, and Duck, Duck, Goose.

Ideally, every classroom teacher or physical education teacher would appreciate the importance of physical education and physical activity for children and develop programs that are developmentally appropriate—and effective—for children. Realistically, however, there will always be some teachers who fall back on the ways things were done in the past rather than working to develop innovative programs. In addition to the teacher's values, a number of other variables contribute to the ease or difficulty of developing quality physical education programs.

Class Size

A variable that has particular impact on what a teacher is able to accomplish in physical education is the size of the classes. Physical education classes are all too often the largest classes in a school. A person doesn't need much teaching experience to realize that the number of students within a given class, other variables excluded, significantly dictates what a teacher can accomplish. Lessons that are possible with 25 children are difficult, if not impossible, with 100 children. Research indicates that, in these settings, students are at a disadvantage. With large classes, there is decreased

instructional time due to management issues and decreased practice opportunities (Hastie and Saunders 1991), as well as decreased ability of the teacher to provide individualized instruction (NASPE 2006). This is the primary reason it is recommended that physical education classes be the same size as in the classroom (SHAPE America 2015; USDHHS 2017).

For teachers to do more than provide directions to a mass of children, they must have opportunities to observe and analyze and give children feedback. The educational literature supports this viewpoint: "The more successful teachers did more tutorial teaching. They spoke to the class as a whole in order to provide structure and give general direction, but most of their actual instruction was given in small groups or to individuals" (Good, Biddle, and Brophy 1975, p. 70). Class size strongly influences the teaching approach that a given teacher can use to foster a successful educational experience.

For the reasons stated earlier, the authors of *Children Moving* assume that teachers have reasonable class sizes—30 or less. We also know this is unrealistic for many teachers. So what is a teacher to do if assigned 60 or even 90 children in a class? As described previously, negative consequences are associated with large class sizes including safety concerns, diminished practice opportunities, and decreased instructional time, among others (NASPE 2006). There are a number of resources available to combat these negative consequence (i.e., NASPE 2006). Here are a few suggestions of our own:

- **Maximize available equipment:** By utilizing as much equipment as is available, students' practice attempts can be maximized. This means that whenever possible, every student has a piece of equipment and there are no lines and/or large-sided games.

Some teachers teach in gymnasiumsthat are used only for physical education.

©Lars A. Niki

- Example 1: Give one ball of some type (or other equipment) per child and then change equipment during task so students can try other ball sizes (or different kind of equipment).
- Example 2: Have two students take turns in a task. For example, dribble 10 times with preferred hand and then hand the ball to your partner to do the same; run behind your partner as she dribbles in general space. On signal, change roles.

- **Utilize stations for practice:** Use stations to focus practice on a learning task, rotating groups after a specified time. For example, to practice overhand throwing, a series of stations can be created (1) throwing to wall targets (small, medium, large); (2) throwing with force to knock down bowling pins; (3) throwing a ball against a wall and catching the rebound; and (4) throwing and catching over a line with a partner. See Chapter 24 for even more throwing and catching learning tasks.
- **Set up multiple small-sided games:** Multiple, small-sided games, as recommended throughout the text, maximize practice attempts and activity time. Because teams are considerably smaller (e.g., team sizes of three or four students), students get more touches, more shots on goal, and repeated decision-making opportunities, and the games are much more active. See Chapter 31 for more information on games in the elementary physical education curriculum.
- **Use peer coaching/assessment:** By using a peer coaching strategy (see Chapter 12 for more information), students help one another to assess competence in performance of skills and demonstration of selected critical elements. For example, while working on dribbling with hands, one student can watch the other to see if the partner uses fingerpads, bends the knees, and has a staggered stance. To more fully tie assessment to instruction and learning, the partner can provide feedback to the performer to help him or her improve.
- **Recruit help:** Whenever possible, educate paraprofessionals, classroom teachers, and/or student assistants to "team teach," provide feedback, work with extremely high- or low-skilled students, keep students on task, and help with management of equipment and space. Because large classes are difficult to manage, recruit any help you can to provide students with a quality and safe learning experience.
- **Establish and maintaining the learning environment:** All of the above strategies require that you firmly establish an environment for learning to have an effective physical education program. Rules, routines, and protocols are hard enough to teach and

reinforce with a small class, but these difficulties become even more magnified when dealing with large groups. Without such strategies, there is little chance learning will occur.

Class Time and Sessions per Week

In addition to the teacher's values and the size of classes, another influential variable that must be considered is the amount of class time children have in physical education, including the number of class sessions per week. Children in some schools, for example, have instructional physical education only one day a week. Children in other schools have daily physical education. Obviously, children who have instructional physical education 180 days a year can learn significantly more than those who have physical education only 36 days a year (SHAPE America and Voices for Healthy Kids 2016; USDHHS 2017). The challenge for the teacher is to make the difficult decisions about what can be learned in one or two days a week so the children truly benefit from the program rather than simply being exposed to a variety of activities (Graham, Metzler, and Webster 1991; SHAPE America 2009). This also means that the teacher, or the district, will have to decide which state or national standards to exclude because of time constraints. An additional and sometimes problematic variable teachers must contend with is the length of class periods. In our experience, some teachers are asked to teach their classes for 50 minutes or even an hour, often to accommodate classroom teachers' extended planning periods. As authors of this text, we do not support this practice. The SHAPE America position on this is clear. The length of the daily class period should be appropriate to learners' needs and maturation levels, ideally 30 minutes (30 minutes maximum for K–2 and a maximum of 45 minutes per class in grades 3–5).

In schools where children don't have daily physical education, the classroom teacher can play a vital role in reinforcing what the specialist has taught—and vice versa. When the classroom teachers and the physical education specialist work together closely, the children reap the benefits.

Facilities and Equipment

A fourth variable is the adequacy of the facilities and equipment in a particular school. Established physical education programs often include adequate equipment and a reasonable solution to the use of indoor space during inclement weather. In contrast, fledgling physical education programs may lack equipment. In some schools, physical education classes are forced to use classrooms, cafeterias, or even hallways on rainy days.

Some teachers are masters of improvisation, but others struggle without adequate facilities and equipment. The teaching skills acquired during student teaching, when equipment and facilities were ideal, often must be adapted to less desirable conditions. You may find that there is only one ball per class instead of one ball per child. You may find yourself on a rainy afternoon teaching in a classroom instead of on a playground. Different environments call for different teaching skills.

> *At the heart of complexity in the gym is numbers. That the teacher is one and the learners are many is a fact of life which shapes every aspect of the teacher's experience. What many outsiders fail to appreciate is that an average class contains a lot of kids for one person to handle even if there were no intent to teach anything. This failure particularly is true of parents who often feel qualified as experts on child management because they deal more or less successfully with their own children in groups rarely exceeding three or four.*
>
> —**LARRY LOCKE**, The Ecology of the Gymnasium: What the Tourist Never Sees (1975)

So how do you accommodate all these situations? What if your equipment is limited and equipment budget is nonexistent? The following are some suggestions:

- **Facility limitations:** As a teacher, it is your responsibility to ensure your teaching space is a dedicated space and that the policy is respected and available at all times. There are times, however, when you may be forced to teach in an alternative space. Teaching in small spaces such as a classroom or hallway is limiting but still doable. When planning or modifying existing lessons, identify learning tasks that do not demand large spaces. For example, some individual practice like throwing and catching in self-space can be done in restricted spaces. Additionally, rhythmic and dance activities as well as small group tasks in which students create a movement or sport-related routine may be appropriate. Finally, if necessary, you can ask some children to be sideline peer coaches while others participate. After a period of time, give peer coaches the chance to provide feedback to those they were watching and

then switch roles. The bottom line is that when space is limited, you will have to be creative. Our challenge to you is to ensure that all students are engaged in meaningful tasks with ample opportunities to practice.

- **Equipment limitations:** Having enough equipment is essential to ensure all students can engage in learning tasks and maximize practice opportunities. If you are forced to justify why equipment is so important, you may explain that a ball in the hands of all students is no different than all students having a pencil in the classroom. If faced with insufficient equipment, first seek additional funding from your school or district. Often, physical education teachers receive a small yearly budget for equipment and other programmatic expenses. Next, inquire with your principal and/or parent–teacher organization about possible fundraising. Traditional fundraising such as fun runs and raffles may be one way to raise funds. More frequently, teachers are turning to crowdfunding (e.g., DonorsChoose.org, GoFundMe.com) to raise money online by creating a campaign for a project they would like to have funded (in this case, physical education equipment). In addition, you can approach local stores and businesses because they will often provide small grants to educational causes. If you have thoroughly exhausted all options of seeking funding for more equipment, the final way to address this problem is to become proficient at making your own. If possible, recruit parent volunteers to help. Throughout *Children Moving*, we have provided examples of how to make homemade equipment out of inexpensive everyday items (see Chapter 16 for hurdles; Chapter 18 for rumble rhumba [chasing, fleeing, dodging activity]; Chapter 21 for balance beam and bench and stilts; and Chapter 24 for yarn ball and plastic scoop). As you will see, with a little time and some inexpensive materials, you can create your own equipment! Note: Prior to constructing homemade equipment, we recommend you be certain that teacher-made equipment is permitted in your school and/or school district.

Student Behavior

Another variable that contributes to the need for reflective teaching is student behavior. The ability to manage children effectively is a major concern in education today among parents as well as teachers.

The ability to manage a class of children effectively is also one of the few teaching skills that educators agree is a prerequisite to successful teaching. A teacher must be able to create and maintain an appropriate environment if children are to learn. Some teachers are able to maintain desirable student behavior simply by glancing occasionally at certain children in a class. Other teachers spend most of their time trying to maintain order. We believe that specific teaching skills can be effectively employed to create and sustain an appropriate environment (see Chapters 7 and 8).

Unfortunately, many textbooks—and many teachers—underplay the role of maintaining appropriate behavior. These texts and teachers assume that a "good" teacher doesn't have discipline problems. Our experience suggests otherwise. During a teaching career, a teacher encounters many kinds of classes. Some will test the teacher's ability to maintain appropriate behavior; others are cooperative. Successful teachers are able to work effectively with both types of classes. See related chapters for strategies for preventing misbehavior (Chapter 7) and dealing with misbehavior (Chapter 8).

Context of the School

The last and equally important variable that supports the need for reflective teaching is the context of the school. Some schools today are populated predominantly by children in transient situations, many of whom will move before the end of the school year. An increasing number of children are from single-parent homes or families in which parents work outside the home and consequently are generally unavailable during the day or when the children return home after school. Rural schools continue to have children with needs different from those of children in suburban or inner-city schools. Moreover, it is typical today to have one or more children in a class for whom English is not their primary language, and it seems that more classes have more children with special needs than ever before. Each of these situations, as well as the many variations that have not been described, presents interesting challenges to teachers—challenges that have no standard answers. The one constant in all of these situations is that children need caring, dedicated teachers, perhaps more than ever.

Do I Want to Become a Reflective Teacher?

The first step to becoming a reflective teacher is believing that it is important to become a reflective, rather than invariant, one. This may be especially challenging for physical education majors who were athletes. Many

physical educators were athletes; consequently, we loved playing sports and frequently did very well in physical education classes. In fact, for many majors it was our best class. We really enjoyed physical education when it consisted of games, typically team sports, because we dominated the games with our friends and could hardly wait to play. The intent of *Children Moving*, however, is to convince you there is an alternative to programs based predominantly on team sports—these are programs that are meaningful and that encourage children of all skill levels to adopt a physically active lifestyle.

Can you recall many of your classmates in your physical education classes? Some were overweight, some were poorly skilled, some disliked competition, and some didn't enjoy physical activity in general. Now as a teacher you have responsibility for all of the children in your class—not only the athletes! What are you going to do for these youngsters who may not like sports and physical activity? Reflective teachers worry about these children: What can they do to provide interesting, enjoyable, beneficial learning experiences for them? The answer is that they will not teach as they did in the past because there are newer and better ways. The goal of *Children Moving* is to guide you to become a reflective teacher and deliver a new and improved physical education for all of the children in a class.

How Do I Become a Reflective Teacher?

How do you become a reflective teacher? Chapters 5, 6, 11, and 13 are designed to get you started on that journey.

Chapter 5 provides an alternative to grouping children by age or grade level. This will help you to plan lessons based on the children's abilities at your school and also differentiate your instruction. This is an important first step in becoming a reflective teacher.

Chapter 6 describes a planning process that will help you develop lessons (the content) that are not only meaningful but also beneficial so children will be physically active and, most important, will be developing the fundamental movement and sports skills that lead them to develop competence and confidence in their physical abilities. Reflective teaching involves planning and designing lessons that are enjoyable learning experiences. This is the opposite of "rolling out the ball" whereby teachers simply present activities that keep the children busy, happy, and good—with no learning intended. No single prepackaged curriculum or program works for all teachers in every school. If you accept this premise, you are well on your way to becoming a reflective teacher.

©Lars A. Niki

Reflective teachers are constantly observing their classes to determine the children's needs, interests, and abilities.

The next step in the process of becoming a reflective teacher is learning some of the techniques (systems) for reflecting on your teaching (Chapter 13) and observing student responses (Chapter 11) to determine how you are actually interacting with the children and whether your teaching is effective. One of the predominant characteristics of reflective teachers is that they are continually self-analyzing their teaching, asking themselves tough questions (Table 4.2) in order to improve. Being a reflective teacher involves a process of thoughtfully contemplating teaching practices and analyzing how something was taught and how the practice might be changed to result in better learning

outcomes. Reflective teachers have the ability to think critically as well as the ability to associate thought with action (Tsangaridou and O'Sullivan 1997). Reflective activities guide teachers' thinking before, during, and after instruction (Hall and Smith 2006) and inform both their day-to-day work with students as well as teaching over time (Tsangaridou and O'Sullivan 1997). The teachers don't teach the same lessons over and over, year after year. They change their lessons from class to class, day to day, and year to year based on their reflections about how and what might be improved.

An additional step in becoming a reflective teacher involves assessing student learning (see Chapter 12). Assessing for learning can help you to determine how well something was learned by students, providing you with additional information about your effectiveness. For example, you can assess fundamental movement skills using a variety of formal and informal tools. These tools can provide feedback to children, assess student learning, report progress to parents, and provide you, the teacher, with important information about individual children's needs and interests—all of which is important feedback that helps you to become a reflective teacher and informs future teaching. In Chapter 1, we provide indicators that can serve as a guide for determining what students are learning.

We wish that simply reading and understanding *Children Moving* would be enough to become a reflective teacher. It's not! Characteristics of reflective teachers take time and commitment (Table 4.3). If you have become a good athlete or an excellent musician or artist or made the dean's list every semester, you know how much time and hard work it takes to attain that

Table 4.2 Questions Reflective Teachers Ask

- What about my students, classes, and teaching situation is unique? Am I developing lessons and curriculum accordingly?
- To what extent did my students accomplish my lesson objectives? How do I know?
- What evidence do I have that my students are learning?
- To what extent are my students achieving my weekly and yearly learning goals? How do I know?
- To what extent are my students achieving the physical education *National Standards*? Are they achieving grade-level outcomes?
- What values guide my teaching? How does my program reflect those values?
- Is the class environment helping or hindering students' ability to learn?
- Do I treat all students equally?
- What are my biggest challenges, and how can I overcome them?
- What professional learning goals do I have? What professional development activities and resources can help me achieve those goals?

Table 4.3 Characteristics of Reflective Teachers

- Follow a cycle of describing and critiquing their teaching and setting goals
- Take into account the idiosyncrasies of schools
- Are committed to student learning and development
- Change teaching and curriculum based on the needs of students
- Plan and design lessons that are meaningful learning experiences
- Are committed to lifelong learning and professional development
- Are devoted to improved practice
- Seek advice, critique, and peer feedback
- Take responsibility for own actions rather than blaming children
- Are committed to own values
- Are open to experimentation and new ideas
- Devote time to thoughtfully contemplate their successes and areas that need improvement

level of achievement. Reflective teachers are no different. As you know by now, becoming an excellent teacher takes many, many hours of hard work. Just because a teacher has 10 or 15 years of teaching experience and a master's degree does not mean he or she has become an excellent teacher. The process of reflective teaching is no different. *Children Moving* will guide you in the process of beginning to become a reflective teacher. We hope you find your journey both enjoyable and worthwhile.

Summary

Six major variables necessitate the need for reflective teaching, or differentiated instruction: the values of the teacher, class size, the number of class sessions per week, facilities and equipment, student behavior, and the context of the school. The reflective teacher considers the characteristics of each class and the abilities of the individual students. A reflective teacher doesn't expect all children to respond in the same way or to achieve the same level of skill. Reflective teachers continually observe and analyze, a process that enables them to revise their expectations and adapt all the components of the program, thereby constantly improving the program's effectiveness. The reflective approach requires that teachers constantly and accurately monitor their teaching as they attempt to design and implement a physical education program for a given school. Reflective teachers also have a wealth of content knowledge that allows them to adapt and modify tasks for individuals of varying abilities. The process of becoming a reflective teacher takes time, practice, and a commitment to lifelong learning. *Children Moving* is designed to guide you in this process.

Reading Comprehension Questions

1. What is reflective teaching? What are its basic characteristics?
2. What does a linear approach to teaching mean? What is a prepackaged curriculum? How is it different from the skill theme approach?
3. Provide three examples of how class size influences the way a teacher teaches a lesson.
4. Provide an example of a teacher who "rolls out the ball." Contrast that teacher with a reflective teacher. What do they do differently in their planning, teaching, and assessment of their teaching?
5. In the previous two chapters, you have learned about skill themes and movement concepts. Explain the difference(s) between skill themes and games like Duck, Duck, Goose or elimination dodgeball.
6. In your own words, explain the major implication of reflective teaching, or differentiated instruction.

References/Suggested Readings

Allen, D. 1975. The future of education: Where do we go from here? *Journal of Teacher Education* 26: 41–45.

Foster, H. L. 1974. *Ribbin', jivin' and playin' the dozens: The unrecognized dilemma of inner-city schools.* Cambridge, MA: Ballinger.

Good, T. L., B. J. Biddle, and J. E. Brophy. 1975. *Teachers make a difference.* New York: Holt, Rinehart & Winston.

Graham, G., E. Elliot, and S. Palmer. 2016. *Teaching children and adolescents physical education: Becoming a master teacher.* 4th ed. Champaign, IL: Human Kinetics.

Graham, G., M. Metzler, and G. Webster. 1991. Specialist and classroom teacher effectiveness in children's physical education: A 3-year study [monograph]. *Journal of Teaching in Physical Education* 4: 321–426.

Hall, T. J., and M. A. Smith. 2006. Teacher planning, instruction and reflection: What we know about teacher cognitive processes. *Quest* 58: 424–42.

Hastie, P. A., and Sanders, J. E. 1991. Effects of class size and equipment availability on student involvement in physical education. *The Journal of Experimental Education* 59: 212–24.

Locke, L. F. 1975, Spring. The ecology of the gymnasium: What the tourist never sees. *Southern Association for Physical Education of College Women Proceedings*, 38–50.

[NASPE] National Association for Sport and Physical Education. 2006. *Teaching large class sizes in physical education: guidelines and strategies* [Guidance document]. Reston, VA: NASPE.

Rink, J. 2014. *Teaching physical education for learning*. 7th ed. New York: McGraw-Hill.

[SHAPE America] Society of Health and Physical Educators. 2009. *Appropriate instructional practice guidelines, K-12: A side-by-side comparison*. Reston, VA: SHAPE America.

[SHAPE America] Society of Health and Physical Educators. 2015. *The essential components of physical education*. Champaign, IL: Human Kinetics.

[SHAPE America and Voices for Healthy Kids] Society of Health and Physical Educators. 2016. *2016 Shape of the nation: Status of physical education in the USA*. Reston, VA: SHAPE America.

Tsangaridou, N., and M. O'Sullivan. 1997. The role of reflection in shaping physical education teachers' educational values and practices. *Journal of Teaching in Physical Education* 17: 2–25.

[USDHHS] U.S. Department of Health and Human Services. 2017. *School health index: A self-assessment and planning guide for elementary school*. Atlanta: Centers for Disease Control and Prevention. Available for free download from http://www.cdc.gov/HealthyYouth.

Determining Generic Levels of Skill Proficiency

Where parents have a voice in physical education programs, they usually insist that the curriculum includes the dances, games, and sports skills of their culture. At the elementary level these activities are often preceded by the fundamental skills that are combined into more complex tasks as age and skill levels increase. . . . Teachers are to concentrate on the process of learning by selecting the appropriate content for whatever level of development the child demonstrates.

—VERN SEEFELDT

by . Janette

Drawn by children at Monfort, Chappelow or Shawsheen Elementary Schools, Greeley, CO.
Courtesy of Lizzy Ginger; Tia Ziegler

Key Concepts

- The generic levels of skill proficiency (GLSP) provide a relatively quick and easy way to assess the abilities of entire classes of children.

- The GLSP apply to the skill themes, not the movement concepts.

- The GLSP serve as a guide to matching the difficulty of a task (activity) to the ability of the students so they can have success and yet still be challenged.

- At the precontrol level, the beginner or novice level, successful performances are typically accidents and are rarely repeated.

- At the control level, tasks require intense concentration if they are to be performed successfully. Learners at this level are easily distracted.

- At the utilization level, learners are ready to combine several skills together or practice in dynamic, unpredictable contexts.

- Proficiency level is the expert, or mastery, level.

- It is unreasonable to expect children to advance from the precontrol to the proficiency level in a skill theme if they practice that skill only during physical education classes.

- Adults can be at the precontrol level in skill themes they have had little or no opportunity to practice.

Think about a group of your friends or maybe a class you are teaching. If your friends or students were asked to dribble a ball with their feet through a general space, would they all be able to do it successfully? Would some, perhaps those on a soccer team, be much more proficient than others? Would some keep losing control of the ball?

You probably answered yes to the last two questions. Obviously age, or grade level, is not an accurate predictor of developmental level. If all fifth graders had identical fundamental movement skill abilities, this chapter would not be necessary. Typically, however, in a fifth-grade class, there is a wide range of abilities—and that range only increases with age. Therefore, as a reflective teacher, you want to design lessons that are both meaningful and developmentally appropriate for the classes you teach.

One of the major challenges of reflective teaching (Chapter 4) is matching a task (activity) to the child's ability. If a task is appropriate—that is, not too hard and not too easy—the child will typically be successful and

therefore remain interested, continue trying, and learn. If a task is too easy, however, the child will become bored and lose interest; if it is too hard, the child will want to do something else because of the frustration level. Matching tasks to abilities is complicated drastically by the fact that we don't teach one child at a time—we typically teach 25 or more in a class. And the range of abilities within any class is typically wide. Some of the children may never have tried an activity, whereas others may have been playing it at home after school or on a team for several years.

In writing this book, we knew from the outset that describing and organizing activities according to the children's grade level (or age) would be inadequate. We needed a classification system that would help us communicate with one another—and with you.

As we reviewed the literature, we came across a classification system developed by Sheila Stanley (1977), which we found to be descriptive and helpful in communicating the range of abilities related to a skill. She proposed four levels, which we have termed the generic levels of skill proficiency (GLSP): precontrol, control, utilization, and proficiency.

The term *generic* is synonymous with terms such as *universal*, *all-purpose*, and *covering a broad spectrum*. We thought it would be too difficult and confusing if we created a different classification system for each skill theme. Thus, we use the term *generic* to mean that the same classification system can be used to analyze youngsters' ability levels for all of the different skill themes. *Levels of skill proficiency* is the phrase we use to identify children's developmental level for each of the skill themes. We are not suggesting that the GLSP are precise, exact measures of motor ability. They are, however, immensely helpful as a way to observe a class of youngsters to quickly determine their overall ability and make an informed decision about which task is appropriate for the overall skill level of the class. The GLSP system also enables the teacher to assess individual youngsters quickly when attempting to manage an entire class.

We have organized and sequenced the content in the skill theme chapters by the GLSP. As you become familiar with these terms, we think you, too, will find them more descriptive and helpful than the beginner-to-advanced classifications that might have been used. We also hope you understand the connection between the GLSP and reflective teaching. The teacher who teaches as if all of her students have the same motor abilities is not only doing the children a disservice but also falling into the trap of boring some students and frustrating others. Before describing how we have used the GLSP throughout the text, we first need to define and describe each of the four skill levels.

Box 5-1

Observable Characteristics of the Generic Levels of Skill Proficiency

Precontrol Level

- Child is unable to repeat movements in succession; one attempt doesn't look like another attempt to perform the same movement.
- Child uses extraneous movements that are unnecessary for efficiently performing the skill.
- Child seems awkward and frequently doesn't even come close to performing the skill correctly.
- Correct performances are characterized more by surprise than by expectancy.
- When the child practices with a ball, the ball seems to control the child.

Control Level

- The child's movements appear less haphazard and seem to conform more to the child's intentions.
- Movements appear more consistent, and repetitions are somewhat alike.
- The child begins to perform the skill correctly more frequently.
- The child's attempt to combine one movement with another or perform the skill in relation to an unpredictable object or person is usually unsuccessful.
- Because the movement isn't automatic, the child needs to concentrate intensely on what he or she is doing.

Utilization Level

- The movement becomes more automatic and can be performed successfully with concentration.
- Even when the context of the task is varied (slightly at first), the child can still perform the movement successfully.
- The child has developed control of the skill in predictable situations and is beginning to move skillfully in unpredictable situations. The child can execute the skill the same way consistently.
- The child can use the skill in combination with other skills and still perform it appropriately.

Proficiency Level

- The skill has become almost automatic, and performances in a similar context appear almost identical.
- The child is able to focus on extraneous variables—an opponent, an unpredictable object, the flow of travel—and still perform the skill as intended.
- The movement often seems effortless as the child performs the skill with ease and seeming lack of attention.
- The movement can be performed successfully in a variety of planned and unplanned situations as the child appears to modify performance to meet the demands of the situation.

Identifying Generic Levels of Skill Proficiency

Observable characteristics of each generic level of skill proficiency are discussed below and listed in Box 5-1 (above).

Precontrol Level

The precontrol (beginner) level is characterized by lack of ability to either consciously control or intentionally replicate a movement. For example, a child at the precontrol level who is bouncing a ball spends more time chasing after the ball than bouncing it—the ball seems to control the child. A child who tries to do a forward roll may complete a revolution on a mat or may get stuck, not rolling at all or rolling half forward and half to the side and finishing flat on the back. A child's efforts to strike a ball with a racket are characterized by frequent misses, mishits, and an inefficient and inconsistent striking pattern. Successful skill performances are a surprise! Most preschool and kindergarten children are at the precontrol level. By the time children are in the first grade, however, you'll observe some of them entering the control level.

Control Level

The control (advanced beginner) level is characterized by less haphazard movements—the body appears to respond more accurately to the child's intentions. The child's movements often involve intense concentration because the movements are far from automatic. A movement that is repeated becomes increasingly uniform and efficient. At this level, a cartwheel the child performs is more or less identifiable as a cartwheel; the child is able to travel in a previously identified direction while briefly taking full weight on the hands. When the child tries to throw a ball at a target, the ball usually travels in the direction of the target.

Some children in lower elementary grades are at the control level. You'll begin to observe that a few children involved in certain youth sports programs are at the next level, the utilization level. This is true only for their sport, however. For example, children involved in after-school gymnastics programs may be approaching the utilization level in the skill themes of rolling or transferring weight, but they may be at the precontrol level for throwing and catching or kicking a ball.

Utilization Level

The utilization (intermediate) level is characterized by increasingly automatic movements. A child at this level is able to use a movement in a variety of ways because he or she doesn't need to think as much about how to execute the movement. Dribbling a ball in a game situation is appropriate for a child at the utilization level. When children at the previous level (control) try to dribble a ball, they spend more time chasing the ball than dribbling because they're unable to focus on dribbling a ball while trying to travel away from an opponent. A cartwheel, as one in a sequence of three movements, is also an appropriate task for a child at the utilization level.

As children get older, the gap between the skill levels widens. Children in the fourth and fifth grades who are involved in youth sports programs are often at the utilization level in the skill themes used in their sport but not necessarily used in other skills. In the same class, however, it's not uncommon to have children who have remained at the precontrol level, primarily because of their lack of activity beyond formally organized physical education classes.

Proficiency Level

The fourth level, proficiency (advanced), is characterized by somewhat automatic movements that begin to seem effortless. At this level, the child gains control of a specific movement and is challenged by the opportunities to employ that skill in changing environments that may require sudden and unpredictable movements (open skill). The challenge of repeating movements exactly and with ever-increasing degrees of quality (closed skill) is also appropriate for children at this level. Rarely are elementary school children at the proficiency level in a skill. In almost every instance, their proficiency is a result of their extensive involvement in after-school youth sports, dance, or gymnastics programs.

One Child, More than One Level

Now that you understand the four levels of skill proficiency, we can expand our use of the term *generic*. Once

again, our jobs as teachers would be much easier if every child had the same ability—not only within a grade but also for every skill. If this were so, we could, for example, merely observe a child kicking a ball at the utilization level and thereby determine that the child was also at the utilization level in throwing, balancing, and jumping and landing. As you know, however, this is not the case. A child may be at the utilization level in one skill and at the precontrol level in another. It's not uncommon for children in our classes to be skillful (utilization-level) throwers and catchers and be at the precontrol level in the nonmanipulative skills of rolling, balancing, and transferring weight. By generic, then, we mean that the terms *precontrol, control, utilization,* and *proficiency* are used to describe a child's ability in every skill we teach—we don't use a different set of terms to describe the skill level for balancing, for example, and still another set of terms to describe the skill level for volleying. The hypothetical example in Figure 5.1 illustrates two points: (1) the GLSP apply to all the skills we teach and (2) children are typically at different skill levels for different skills. Reflective teachers account for these differences in the way they plan their lessons (Chapter 6), establish the learning environment (Chapter 7), and teach the lessons (Chapter 9). The unreflective teacher assumes that all children have identical fundamental movement skills and abilities.

Figure 5.1 also suggests that age is not an accurate indicator of ability. If it were, all adults would be

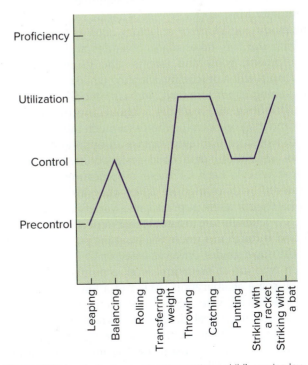

Figure 5.1 Hypothetical example representing a child's varying levels of proficiency in different skills.

skillful at striking with a racket, for example, and we know this isn't true. Fourth and fifth graders are often at the precontrol level when a new skill is introduced that they have never practiced. Generally, however, because of their physical maturation and previous experiences, they move from the precontrol level more rapidly than the primary-grade children (although there are always exceptions).

Using the Generic Levels of Skill Proficiency in Teaching

The generic levels of skill proficiency provide a broad guideline for answering two important questions for the reflective teacher:

1. What is the motor ability level of this class?
2. Which tasks and activities work best for a class at this GLSP?

Although there will be a range of skill levels within any class, we as reflective teachers make a judgment about the overall ability of the class. Then we modify the tasks for individuals using teaching by invitation and intratask variation, as discussed in Chapter 7.

Tasks that succeed with one third-grade class may need to be changed (made easier or harder) to meet the needs of the next third-grade class. The key is presenting tasks that are developmentally appropriate. For some children this may require increasing the difficulty, whereas for others, it may require decreasing the difficulty. Making tasks easier or harder can be achieved by modifying a variety of factors, such as the space in which the task takes place, obstacles and defenders, equipment, goals and targets, and group size. For example, when practicing dribbling while traveling and switching hands (control), an easier modification may be dribbling and walking without any obstacles or defenders (precontrol), whereas a much more complex task would be dribbling against an opponent one-on-one (utilization) or a child-designed invasion game (proficiency). Each of these modifications provides children with challenges when they are ready and holds their interest in practicing a variety of skills.

It is generally safe to assume that most children in preschool through first grade will be at the precontrol level. In the upper grades, however, we typically find a few children who are at precontrol level, a number at control level, some at utilization level, and a few, especially in middle school, who might be at proficiency level: the higher the grade level, the greater the range of skill levels within a class. The reflective teacher recognizes these differences and teaches accordingly. The unreflective teacher assumes that one third grade is identical to the next.

Note that we use the generic levels of skill proficiency to describe a youngster's proficiency for each skill theme—for example, kicking, jumping and landing, or striking a ball with a bat. The skill levels do not pertain to the movement concepts (Chapters 14–16) because the concepts aren't skills; they represent cognitive understanding expressed through versatile and efficient use of the skill themes. As you read further, this point will become clearer. For now, however, just remember that the four generic levels of skill proficiency apply to the skill themes only.

As reflective teachers we use the GLSP in two ways. First, we observe the students to determine their overall skill level. Second, we attempt to match the tasks to the skill level of the children in the class. For example, if we determine that the majority of the children in a class are at the precontrol level for the skill of kicking, we would not ask them to play a proficiency-level game such as Alley Soccer or Cone Soccer (Chapter 23). Instead, we would ask them to practice precontrol tasks, such as kicking a stationary ball from a standing position and then running to kick the ball.

Which Task?

As teachers gain experience in reflective teaching and learn to use the GLSP, they become able to assess the overall skill level of a class rather quickly and determine which tasks will be productive for that group (Graham et al. 1993; Housner and Griffey 1985). For those who are new to the skill theme approach, or perhaps new to a school, it will take time and experience to learn the tasks that work with different grade and ability levels. Veteran teachers who have been teaching by skill themes know which tasks will work—and which will not. Beginning teachers, in contrast, will learn with practice the tasks that are most effective and how to make them interesting and appealing to children of various generic levels. As you plan, especially when you start working with the skill theme approach, we recommend being prepared to deliver a series of 10 to 15 tasks in a lesson—not just 1 or 2! Extensive planning will also help you learn the progression of tasks for each skill theme and movement concept. The chapters on planning and observation techniques (Chapters 6 and 11) will also help you better understand how to plan for skill theme lessons—and when to use a task and when to change to a new one.

Finally, it is important to remember that there is no single, correct way to deliver the tasks in a lesson. Some teachers, for example, prefer to start at the precontrol level (for a class at the control level) and quickly progress up the spiral with a series of tasks that serve as a warm-up and review for the children. Others prefer to start with a task or activity that most closely matches that class's GLSP. If a task is too hard and children have high rates of failure and frustration, then a teacher who has planned well can move down the spiral to an easier task. That's why it is so important for the reflective teacher to plan a series of tasks rather than only one or two for a lesson.

How to Know if a Task Works

Chapter 11, "Observing Student Responses," explains in more detail how to know if a task works, but a quick overview of the process is helpful here. A task works when youngsters are provided numerous chances to be successful—and they want to keep doing the task. Tasks that are too hard or too easy lead to frustration or boredom. The GLSP will help you match tasks to the ability level of the majority of the class so that children are not frustrated or bored. This is why we did not organize the book by grade levels: There is such a wide range of variance among classes at the same grade level. As you increase your understanding of the skill theme approach, you will find it is relatively easy to change tasks and activities with classes.

When a class is required to play a sport or participate in a predesigned game—that is, a game designed with no knowledge of the class of children being taught—the teacher implicitly assumes that all the youngsters have the same abilities and interests. The response of a sixth-grade boy to an opinion poll about a "flag football" unit (Figure 5.2) provides one potent example of how some children feel when they are all required to play a sport that requires proficiency-level skills. Obviously this

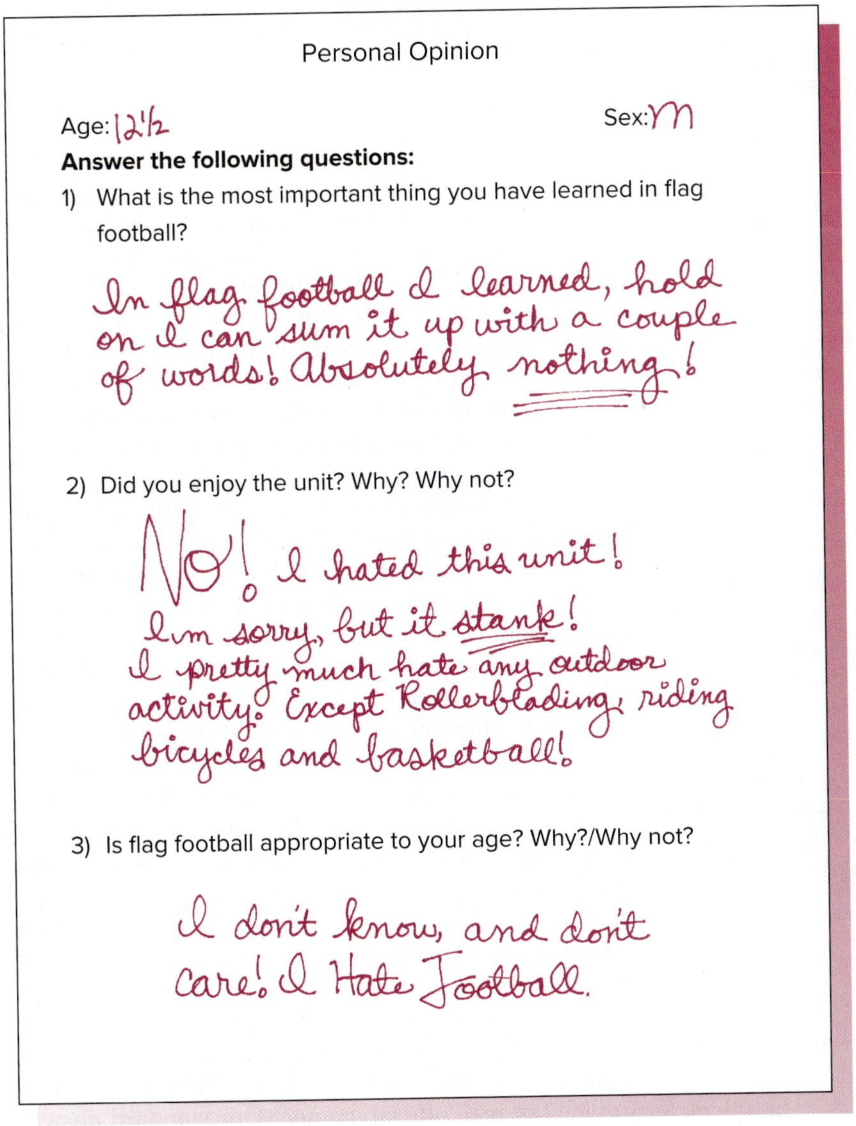

Figure 5.2 Sixth grader's evaluation of a flag football unit.

lesson (unit) was not taught by a reflective teacher. It also suggests why teaching the prerequisite skills for successful game playing, as opposed to playing games, is so important at the elementary school level—especially for those youngsters who have yet to reach the utilization or proficiency level.

> You are probably thinking the National Standards discussed in Chapter 3 and the GLSP are mutually exclusive; they cannot coexist in a curriculum for children. They do and they should. Grade-level outcomes are desired learning objectives (in this case, for a particular grade); GLSP, on the other hand, are a way of talking about the range of abilities related to a skill, and Children Moving organizes tasks by skill level not by grade. Therefore, children within any given grade are at precontrol, control, and utilization levels of a skill. We, as teachers, meet our students there and provide the tasks and challenges to help them achieve their maximum potential. Just like in math, language arts, and all other academic subjects, children are at different levels in physical education.

Insights about the Generic Levels of Skill Proficiency

Now that you're familiar with the four levels that constitute the GLSP, we want to suggest four insights that will enhance your understanding of the levels and help you apply them in your teaching situation.

Multiple Skill Levels in a Class

The first insight is that in the upper-elementary and middle school grades, you can expect to have children in the same class at three different levels: precontrol, control, and utilization. Your challenge as a reflective teacher is to determine the predominant skill level and then make adjustments for individuals through teaching by invitation or intratask variation (Chapter 7) and task sheets (Chapter 9) for example. In the preschool and lower grades, in contrast, many children will be at the precontrol and control levels—although there will always be exceptions.

Control Level in Two Days a Week

The second insight we can offer is that in programs of elementary school physical education in which children have physical education classes only once or twice a week, the children will reach the utilization level of most of the skill themes only if they do something outside of class (Graham, Metzler, and Webster 1991), such as with a parent or siblings or on an athletic team. Unfortunately, an increasing number of children today are not physically active after school and on weekends. In addition to the decline in physical activity beginning in the middle school years (Chapter 1), children who are less motor competent are less active (Barnett, Lai, et al. 2016; Logan et al. 2015), and being skilled as a child is associated with being more active (Barnett et al. 2008; Lopes et al. 2011) and fit (Barnett et al. 2008) into late childhood and adolescence. The implication, of course, is that it is not uncommon for a teacher to use control-level tasks for children in the fourth and fifth grades—because the majority of students haven't developed their skills beyond that level. If we develop lessons using utilization- and proficiency-level tasks, we end up frustrating these children and convincing them that physical activity is not enjoyable because they are so inept.

Proficiency Level Is Rare

Our third insight is that children at the proficiency level in a skill are the exception. Remember that the GLSP apply to skills, not ages. Thus anyone, regardless of age, can be at the precontrol level. The standards or criteria for each of the skill levels apply across the board to all skills and all ages. Consequently, we do not see many children at the proficiency level. In fact, it seems unlikely that many children can reach proficiency level simply by participating in a physical education program—unless that program is a quality, daily program. Typically children reach the proficiency level in a skill because they've been involved in an after-school sports program in which they practice the skill frequently or because a parent or older sister or brother is involved in a sport and the child consequently spends a lot of time practicing and receiving instruction in the backyard.

Overall, however, we do not observe children at proficiency level very often. For this reason, you will probably use the proficiency-level tasks we have listed in each of the chapters more as part of teaching by invitation and intratask variation (differentiated instruction) (Chapter 7) than with entire classes of children. This does not mean, of course, that some of the children don't want to perform the proficiency-level tasks, especially the skill themes used in popular games. Children who are new to the skill theme approach, particularly those in the upper-elementary and middle school grades, constantly ask the question, "When do we get to play the real 'official' game?" Our standard answer is, "At recess. At home. On the weekends." In time, as the children become accustomed to the skill theme approach and we're able to individualize the program to a greater extent, they no longer ask the question—at least, not as often.

Unfortunately, some teachers succumb to the pressure from the children to "play the game." In the long run, the children end up shortchanged, just as they do when their diet consists primarily of unhealthy snacks and fast food. Although it may not be as much fun (for some) as playing games such as kickball and dodgeball, a focus on learning and improving has the potential to help children eventually derive the benefits of regular involvement in physical activity (Barnett et al. 2008; Barnett, Stodden, et al. 2016; Holdfelder and Schott 2014; Malina 2001; Stodden et al. 2008). Failure to help children develop the prerequisite fundamental movement skills may mean that, as they age, children come to feel inadequate and incompetent in physical activity. Just as it's easier for parents to let their children sit in front of the television five or six hours a day, it's easier for teachers to let the children play kickball and dodgeball every day. But is this better for the children?

Assessment Using the GLSP?

As you will see in Chapter 12 on assessment, we do not suggest that the generic skill proficiency levels be used to assess children's progress in physical education. After reading this chapter, you can understand why. Change from one level to another (e.g., control to utilization) is primarily dependent on copious amounts of practice and experiences using the skill themes. Unfortunately, in too many programs of physical education, there is simply not enough time to reasonably expect children to progress from one skill level to another over a semester or even a year. For this reason, we assess what children can reasonably learn in the time allotted for physical education. Thus our final insight to conclude this chapter is that the GLSP are immensely helpful for determining the overall skill level of a class and the ability level of individual children. It seems unreasonable, however, to expect that we will see dramatic changes in skill level from year to year if children practice the skills only during physical education class. For this reason, we do not recommend that the GLSP be used to assess, or grade, individual students' progress.

Summary

Organizing curriculum by grade level or age is convenient. Yet because of the range of skills found at any grade level or age, these are inadequate indicators of children's skill levels. We have adopted the concept of generic levels of skill proficiency (GLSP). Assessing children's skills in terms of these levels is a basis for planning appropriate activities. The four generic levels of fundamental movement skill proficiency are (1) precontrol, (2) control, (3) utilization, and (4) proficiency.

Children at the precontrol level are unable to consciously control or replicate a particular movement. At the control level, the child's body appears to respond more accurately to the child's intentions, and movements become increasingly similar. Movements are even more automatic and reflexive at the utilization level; children can use a movement in a variety of contexts. At the proficiency level, the child has gained control of a movement and is challenged by the goal of repeating movements exactly or using movements effectively in dynamic, unpredictable situations.

The generic levels of skill proficiency are task related—that is, a child at the utilization level in one motor skill may be at the control level in another skill. Age and skill level are not necessarily related. The reflective teacher uses this information to plan enjoyable and effective lessons—rather than assuming that all children in a grade have identical physical abilities.

Reading Comprehension Questions

1. What is the purpose of the GLSP? How are they used?
2. In your own words, explain the differences between the four generic levels of skill proficiency.
3. What do we mean by generic?
4. Why isn't age, or grade level, an indicator of motor skill proficiency?
5. Pick a skill theme and describe how a reflective teacher would use the GLSP to help her make decisions about which tasks to include in a lesson. Contrast your explanation with how an unreflective teacher would teach a lesson.
6. Figure 5.1 shows a hypothetical example of a child's proficiency level at several skills. Use the following

form to create your own graph. Select 10 of the skill themes that represent your range of abilities. Graph your skill levels. Which skill themes do you need to work on most? Why are you less advanced at these skills than at the others? Did you rate yourself at the proficiency level for any of these skills? If so, why do you think you attained the proficiency level for that skill? Answer the same questions if you're at the precontrol level for any of the 10 skills you selected.

7. In Figure 5.2, a sixth-grade boy responds to three questions about a flag football unit. Why do you think he responded as he did? What do think his GLSP were for throwing, catching, chasing, and fleeing? What would you do if he were in your class to help him enjoy the unit?

References/Suggested Readings

Barnett, L., S. K. Lai, S. L. C. Veldman, L. L. Hardy, D. P. Cliff, P. J. Morgan, A. Zask, et al. 2016. Correlates of gross motor competence in children and adolescents: A systematic review and meta-analysis. *Sports Medicine* 46(11): 1663–88.

Barnett, L., P. Morgan, E. van Beurden, and J. Beard. 2008. Perceived sports competence mediates the relationship between childhood motor skill proficiency and adolescent physical activity and fitness. *International Journal of Behavioral Nutrition and Physical Activity* 5(40): 1–12.

Barnett, L., D. Stodden, A. D. Miller, K. E. Cohen, A. Laukkanen, J. J. Smith, D. Dudley, et al. 2016. Fundamental movement skills: An important focus. *Journal of Teaching in Physical Education* 35: 219–25.

Graham, G., C. Hopple, M. Manross, and T. Sitzman. 1993. Novice and experienced children's physical education teachers: Insights into their situational decision-making. *Journal of Teaching in Physical Education* 12(2): 197–214.

Graham, G., M. Metzler, and G. Webster. 1991. Specialist and classroom teacher effectiveness in children's physical education: A 3-year study [monograph]. *Journal of Teaching in Physical Education* 4: 321–426.

Holfelder, B., and N. Schott. 2014. Relationship of fundamental movement skills and physical activity in children and adolescents: A systematic review. *Psychology of Sport and Exercise* 15(4): 382–91.

Housner, L. D., and D. C. Griffey. 1985. Teacher cognition: Differences in planning and interactive decision making between experienced and inexperienced teachers. *Research Quarterly for Exercise and Sport* 56: 56–63.

Logan, S. W., E. K. Webster, N. Getchell, K. A. Pfeiffer, and L. E. Robinson. 2015. Relationship between fundamental motor skill competence and physical activity during childhood and adolescence: A systematic review. *Kinesiology Review* 4(4): 416–26.

Lopes, V. P., L. P. Rodrigues, J. A. R. Maia, and R. M. Malina. 2011. Motor coordination as predictor of physical activity in childhood. *Scandinavian Journal of Medicine and Science in Sports* 21(5): 663–69.

Malina, R. M. 2001. Adherence to physical activity from childhood to adulthood. *Quest* 53: 350.

Seefeldt, V. 1979. Developmental motor patterns: Implications for elementary school physical education. In *Psychology of motor behavior and sport,* ed. C. Nadeau, W. Halliwell, K. Newell, and C. Roberts. Champaign, IL: Human Kinetics.

Stanley, S. 1977. *Physical education: A movement orientation.* 2nd ed. New York: McGraw-Hill.

Stodden, D., J. Goodway, S. Langedorfer, M. Roberton, M. Rudisill, C. Garcia, and L. Garcia. 2008. A developmental perspective on the role of motor skill competence in physical activity. *Quest* 60: 290–306.

Planning

"Will you please tell me which way I ought to go from here?"
"That depends a good deal on where you want to get to," said the Cat.
"I don't care much where," said Alice.
"Then it doesn't matter which way you go," said the Cat.

—LEWIS CARROLL

If you want kids to learn to skip, teach them the essential components of skipping, let them practice skipping, and then assess how well they can skip.

—NASPE (2004, P. 3)

Drawn by children at Monfort, Chappelow or Shawsheen Elementary Schools, Greeley, CO.
Courtesy of Lizzy Ginger; Tia Ziegler

Key Concepts

- Reflective teachers constantly plan and revise their plans as they continue to strive to provide the most productive and meaningful learning experiences for children.

- Planning is divided into four steps in this chapter.

  - The first planning step is determining what you want students to learn over the entire program; this is the scope of the curriculum.

  - The second planning step is the development of learning indicators or benchmarks that allow reflective teachers to determine if the children are learning what is being taught.

  - The third planning step is to decide what you want students to learn each year of a program and the sequencing of the content of the program across and within each grade level.

  - The final planning step is the development of daily lesson plans that are interesting and beneficial to youngsters and achieve your objectives for the lesson.

- Ideally, lessons encourage students to be physically active during the majority of the lesson. Typically this occurs when children are able to be successful and consider the lesson fun.

- Just because a lesson is fun does not mean that it is a productive learning experience for children.

We want to begin this important chapter with two scenarios. The first is a story one of our grandchildren told her father. Savanna, who was age eight, had just started playing organized after-school soccer. This is the conversation she had with her dad on the way to her first after-school soccer practice.

"Dad, I know how to play soccer."

Her dad responded, "That's great. Where did you learn to play soccer?"

Savanna answered, "In PE."

On the way home after her first 90-minute practice, Savanna had another conversation with her Dad who has played a lot of soccer.

"Dad, can you help me with my soccer?"

He replied, "That would be great. But I thought you already learned to play soccer in PE?"

She responded, "No, Dad, we don't learn anything in PE. We just play."

The second scenario involves children from another school with whom we work. In their photo diaries regarding physical education are two snippets about their experiences in physical education:

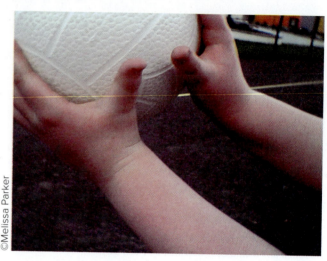

©Melissa Parker

"I learned that we have to shape our hands like a 'W' when catching a ball."

©Melissa Parker

"I learned that spread fingers help with dribbling."

The authors of *Children Moving* sincerely hope you are a teacher that produces results like those illustrated in the second scenario—a teacher from whom children learn, not just one who "does activities" in their physical education classes.

One of the basic premises on which *Children Moving* is based is that youngsters are learning the fundamental movement skills that provide the foundation for success in sports and physical activity. This chapter provides a detailed explanation of how teachers plan their programs so that youngsters actually leave the program having learned some, ideally many, of the fundamental movement skills. While there is not enough time in physical education to develop great athletes, it is possible for youngsters to learn the movement skills that lead to success and enjoyment for them throughout their lives. We constantly hear coaches talk about returning to the "fundamentals" with their athletes. The goal of *Children Moving* is to provide youngsters with these fundamentals.

Inappropriate planning has long-term implications. Many experts agree that a critical role of physical education in schools is to provide a variety of learning experiences that give children a broad foundation of movement abilities (Stodden et al. 2008). Children who are skillful in only a few activities, typically games, may be the products of programs characterized by inefficient planning. Instructors who don't plan are likely to teach only what they know well and what the children enjoy, which often results in an unbalanced program over the years.

Because planning is typically done during the teacher's own time rather than during school time, there are strong temptations to avoid it. It can be much more pleasant to watch television, go to a ball game, or just go to bed early. But planning, even though you may consider it as onerous as homework, is necessary.

The benefits of effective planning include classes that run more smoothly with less interruption and confusion; tasks that are interesting, enjoyable, and worthwhile; and, in some instances, less off-task behavior. In short, well-planned classes assist children in learning the concepts and skills being taught.

Reflective Planning

If all schools, all children, all facilities, all teachers, all communities, and all equipment were the same, we could simply provide you with a book of prepackaged lesson plans that would be successful with every class you teach, no matter the situation. As you know, however, that isn't the case. Reflective teachers plan lessons—and entire programs—that consider the various unique characteristics of their teaching situation.

The reflective planner considers many factors when trying to devise the best lessons possible under the circumstances. Planning can't be reduced to an exact formula, but certain factors will always influence lesson effectiveness. Each factor is important, and all interact to determine the teaching environment for which the reflective teacher must plan. As we described in Chapter 4, reflective teachers consider class size, frequency of class meetings, available equipment and facilities, personal characteristics of the children, and children's skill levels and interests in their teaching and planning.

©Ingram Publishing

Planning is an essential aspect of effective teaching

A Four-Step Planning Process

We ask, and attempt to answer, four questions in this chapter.

1. What do you want your students to learn over your entire program (often four to six years)?
2. What are along-the-way learning indicators or benchmarks to determine whether the children are learning what is being taught?
3. What do you want your students to learn each year they are in your program?
4. What do you want your students to learn in each lesson you teach?

This four-step planning process is called *backward design* or *design down* (Figure 6.1). It starts with the end—what you want your students to achieve as a result of your entire program (question 1)—and works down to what you want students to learn in each lesson (question 4). After you design from the top down, you teach from the bottom up. In other words, design down; teach up. In this chapter, we provide practical

- Learning Goals and content for the program

- Indicators of learning (benchmarks)

- Yearly plan and lesson progressions

- Daily lesson plans

Figure 6.1 Backward design: design down; teach up.

examples of each step as a way for you to get started. You may not use our examples exactly, but they provide a great place to start the process of planning.

An analogy may help explain the process. Imagine you and a friend are going on a trip. You are planning to drive several thousand miles to your final destination. To make the most of your trip, you will visit different places along the way. You would probably ask and answer questions similar to the four steps:

1. Where do we plan to end up? What do we plan to visit along the way?
2. What will we use as our indicators (or benchmarks) along the way to determine if the trip plan is working? How will we know we are there?
3. What is our action plan? How many days do we plan to stay in each location?
4. How will we organize each day?

Effective teachers ask, and answer, essentially these four questions as they plan their programs. The following sections describe (with examples) the planning process used by teachers using the skill theme approach. This process may appear complex, but, just as with a long journey, taking it step by step makes it much easier—and the examples we provide for each step should be very helpful.

Question 1: What Do You Want Students to Learn Over the Entire Program (Four to Six Years)?

The answer to this question (What do I want students to learn in my program?) is termed a curriculum scope. It is the "big picture" of what you intend for children as a result of being in your physical education program. While the answer to this question may at first seem simple, in reality, it is quite difficult. At this stage, you have to decide what you want students to learn over the entire time they are in your school and the content to be used to achieve that goal—every skill theme, every movement concept, and every fitness skill and concept. These decisions are based on the number of days per week children have physical education as well as the local needs and context. Most importantly, these decisions reflect what you want children to learn, not just what they "do" or are exposed to in physical education. Imagine that the children you teach live in a community where soccer or basketball is extremely popular.

- Will you devote a lot of your classes teaching the skills of basketball: dribbling with the hands, shooting (throwing), and guarding an opponent (relationship with a partner)?
- Will you spend a lot of time teaching soccer skills: kicking, dribbling with the feet, and moving in relation to others?
- Or will you devote relatively few lessons to these skills because you assume that many of the children you teach are already at the utilization or proficiency levels (Chapter 5) and therefore need to practice and learn skills for other sports and activities?

You may decide, or your district or state curriculum may suggest, that you should devote many lessons—or perhaps hardly any—to these skills. While the curriculum scope should be personalized for your situation, it should be related to district or state standards. It provides the long-term guide for what you want students to actually learn in your program. Though the tables in this chapter list content by skill theme or movement concept, you will also need to determine what your "big picture" learning outcomes for each skill theme or movement concept are. For example, by fifth grade, do you want students to be able to underhand throw and catch in a small-sided game? If so, then you will choose throwing and catching learning experiences over the years that lead to this outcome. If you are wondering

Understanding the Planning Language

Before we start, let's review a few terms that are important. Although they are all related to each other, they are also all different. Hopefully these definitions will let you see how they are aligned.

Standards—Standards define what students should know and be able to do at a given point in their education. For us, they are developed by the Society of Health and Physical Educators (SHAPE America) or state or local agencies and define what a student should know and is able to do as a result of a highly effective physical education program (SHAPE America 2014).

Grade-level outcomes—This is a term developed by SHAPE America to reflect what students should know and be able to do by the end of a given grade level. They provide a bridge between SHAPE America's *National Standards* and K–12 physical education curriculum development.

Learning indicators—Student learning indicators are benchmarks that can be used to determine if students are actually learning a skill and can demonstrate their learning through quality movement. These indicators or benchmarks are not designed to replace the *National Standards* (SHAPE America 2014), but instead serve as progress markers (indicators) of student learning toward some of those identified outcomes. We use the terms *learning indicator* and *benchmark synonymously*.

Objectives—Objectives describe how you will achieve the outcomes you have set forth. An educational objective states what the student will learn and be able to accomplish by the end of instruction. It describes a specific behavior that will lead to the desired goal. It is specific and measurable.

where to start with deciding these outcomes, the National Standards and Grade-Level Outcomes for K-12 Physical Education (SHAPE America 2014), especially the fifth-grade learning outcomes, will be quite useful. If we return to the trip analogy, this is really the hardest part—deciding where to go. The more specifically and precisely you can define the overall goals, the more focused your teaching will be.

Look at Tables 6.1 and 6.2. They provide a five- to six-year scope suggesting when to teach the movement concepts and skill themes as described in *Children Moving* that lead to the learning outcomes you have chosen for your program. (These examples are organized by grade levels to be consistent with the organization of SHAPE America's *National Standards* [2014]). The grade levels merely serve as a general indicator, however; the decisions about what and when to teach are based on observing the actual classes of children we teach. Table 6.1, for example, suggests that by the end of first grade, the children will have learned the concepts of self and general space, so these would not be the major focus of lessons in grades 2–5, although you would certainly review them. Table 6.2 suggests that throwing and catching would not be the major focus of lessons until grade 2. In what grade do the authors suggest that you begin teaching striking with bats, golf clubs, and hockey sticks?

Table 6.1 Sample of Movement Concept Scope and Sequence for Grades K–5 (Step 1 in Planning)

Movement Concept	K	1	2	3	4	5
Space Awareness						
Self-space	X	X				
General space	X	X	X			
Levels	X	X	X			
Directions	X	X	X			
Pathways	X	X	X			
Extensions			X	X		
Effort						
Time/speed	X	X	X	X	X	
Force			X	X	X	X
Flow			X	X	X	X
Relationships						
Body part identification	X					
Shapes	X	X	X			
Relationships with objects	X	X	X	X		
Relationships with people			X	X	X	X

Notes: This chart is intended only as an example. Reflective teachers will want to adapt this chart for their school.

X denotes that a movement concept is the major focus of lessons at a grade level. Concepts are studied at other grade levels but not as the primary focus of the lesson.

Table 6.2 Sample Skill Theme Scope for Grades K–5 (Step 1 in Planning)

Skill Theme	K	1	2	3	4	5
Traveling						
Walking	X	X				
Running	X	X				
Hopping	X	X	X			
Skipping	X	X	X			
Galloping	X	X	X			
Leaping	X	X	X	X		
Sliding	X	X	X	X		
Chasing, Fleeing, Dodging		X	X	X	X	X
Bending, Stretching, Twisting and Curling		X	X	X	X	
Jumping and Landing	X	X	X	X	X	X
Balancing	X	X	X	X	X	
Transferring Weight			X	X	X	X
Rolling	X	X	X	X	X	X
Kicking			X	X	X	X
Punting					X	X
Throwing			X	X	X	X
Catching			X	X	X	X
Volleying				X	X	X
Hand Dribbling			X	X	X	X
Foot Dribbling			X	X	X	X
Striking with Rackets			X	X	X	X
Striking with Long-Handled Implements						
Bats				X	X	X
Golf clubs				X	X	X
Hockey sticks				X	X	X
Fitness and Wellness Concepts		X	X	X	X	X

Notes: This chart is intended only as an example. Reflective teachers will want to adapt this chart for their school.

X denotes that a skill theme is the major focus of lessons at a grade level. Concepts are studied at other grade levels but not as the primary focus of the lesson.

In addition to the movement concepts and skill themes, you will notice that we suggest devoting a number of lessons every year to teaching fitness and wellness concepts (Table 6.2; see also Chapter 28). These concept lessons are in addition to the actual fitness learning experiences the students get in virtually every class we teach. Because we try to minimize waiting, instruction, and management time (Chapter 11), the students are moderately to vigorously active at least 50 percent of the time in every lesson we teach. However, although we strive to achieve high activity levels in each lesson, we also devote some lessons to teaching fitness and wellness concepts (Chapter 28).

As a reflective teacher, you will make changes to your "big picture" as you learn more about the children you are teaching, your program, and yourself

Less Is More

"Less is more" is a popular saying that refers to the fact that we often try to do more than we have time for. This is especially true in planning your curriculum. Many physical education programs expose children to a variety of motor skills and sports, but there is little, if any, learning that occurs as a result of this exposure. As you design your curriculum, keep this in mind. The classroom teacher easily describes what the children have learned in math or reading for that year. How will you respond if asked what the children have learned in your program? That response is quite different from simply explaining what you "did" in physical education that year.

as a teacher. You may also want to include additional topics. As you revise your scope, keep in mind that whatever you do it must be connected to state and district standards. This allows you to prove to your administrators what you are doing and that your curriculum aligns with current accepted practice. The point of developing a scope that is translated into a school year overview, however, is to determine what you want students to learn, and in which grades, during the years you are teaching the children.

Question 2: What Are Along-the-Way Learning Indicators or Benchmarks to Determine Whether the Children Are Learning What Is Being Taught?

The second step in the planning process is the development of benchmarks or indicators as spot checks to be sure children are learning what you want them to be learning. Please note that we use the terms *benchmarks* and *learning indicators* synonymously. These benchmarks allow for constant assessment of progress along the way to the big picture outcomes developed in Step 1. By developing these benchmarks, teachers don't wait until the fifth grade, for example, to assess what the children have learned (or not learned). They continually check to be sure the children are getting it before moving on and revisit areas that have not been clear to the children or areas in which they simply need additional time to practice.

The *National Standards* (SHAPE America 2014) document contains a list of sample grade-level outcomes that can be used as a guide to what students are expected to be learning in physical education programs. These grade-level outcomes provide checkpoints along the way, assuring us that we are on the right course in guiding youngsters in the process of becoming

physically active for a lifetime. However, these grade-level outcomes may not be specific enough for or aligned with your situation; therefore, we suggest you develop your own benchmarks or learning indicators representing your particular needs. We have provided an example of what these might look like in Table 1.4, but we encourage you to develop your own. There are plenty of examples to choose from—but the bottom line for the authors of *Children Moving* is that the students, when assessed, can explain, and hopefully demonstrate, what is being learned. If, using the example in Box 6-1, students can cite the cues of watch, reach, and pull and are able to catch a softly thrown self-tossed ball. The students have learned at least one of the fundamental movement skills that may lead to a lifetime of enjoyable participation in sports and physical activities such as softball, football, and frisbee.

Often the indicators contain the critical elements for various skills, and at other times, they are the use of the skill in a more complex situation (e.g., child-designed game). Thus, once a teacher makes the decision to spend a certain number of days on the skill of catching, for example, she will need to decide what the students are going to learn about catching—that is, the critical elements of catching or in what situation they want to see the skill used. Remember, students will not become proficiency-level catchers in one year, but they can learn one or more catching critical elements during a year. The skill theme chapters (17–27) provide critical elements to assist you in determining the objective(s) for your lessons. Chapter 12 will provide information about how to assess the Indicators you have chosen.

Table 6.3 provides one example of the cues and cue descriptors related to the critical elements for catching that will be emphasized from year to year or from control to proficiency generic level of skill proficiency (GLSP). Notice, too, that in grades 1–4 (or control through utilization) the cues focus on various critical elements of the skill of catching; however, at the proficiency level, the focus of the critical elements shifts to the use of the skill of catching in a dynamic situation. At this point, children have developed the skill, and they need to learn how to apply the skill. Assume that a teacher decides to teach using the five catching cues in Table 6.3 and also in Chapter 24, "Throwing and Catching." The teacher could then decide which critical elements to emphasize each year to serve as learning indicators of student progress. Accomplishment of the critical elements that these cues represent would provide a checkpoint to be sure that the children were actually remembering and applying the critical elements, which would assist them in becoming competent and confident catchers who, in fact, are able to catch in a variety of situations.

Table 6.3 Sample Progression of Cues and Cue Descriptors for Catching

Grade	GLSP	Cue (Cue Descriptor in Parentheses)
1	Control	Hands (Always use your hands, not your stomach or arms, to catch.)
2	Control	Watch, Reach, Pull (Watch the ball, reach for it, and pull it in.)
3	Control/ Utilization	Thumbs/Little Fingers (When you catch over your head, make sure your thumbs are together; if the catch is low, make sure your little fingers are together.)
4	Control/ Utilization	Ready Position (Position your body behind or under the ball, feet shoulder width apart, knees bent, and hands ready.)
5	Proficiency	Watch Passer, Then Ball (Watch the passer as you start to run, and then after the ball is thrown, track it all the way into your hands.)

Note: This does not suggest direct grade level alignment between generic levels of skill proficiency (GLSP) and grades but is provided as an example because teachers tend to plan by grade level.

In summary, the question we suggest you ask and answer for Step 2 of the planning process is this: "What are benchmarks or indicators of student learning that will allow me to know that students are learning?" For example, if a teacher wants students to know how to position their hands correctly to catch a ball above the waist, or below the waist, most children should be able to demonstrate this critical element correctly. If, however, most of them still cannot demonstrate the proper way to position their hands, then the teacher needs to reteach the skill so the students can eventually become successful throwers and catchers. Unfortunately, we observe far too many students who have been in physical education programs who have not learned to throw, catch, jump, or move in relation to others. We believe physical education should be an educational learning experience for all children—not just a few minutes to simply be physically active during the school day. This implies that although the benchmarks or indicators have been developed in Step 2, they appear in Step 3 and 4 planning as well.

Question 3: What Do You Want Your Students to Learn in a Given Year?

So once the decisions have been made about what you want your students to learn during their time in elementary school (the movement concepts and skill themes) and what will be the indicators of that learning, the next questions ask what you want them to learn during each school year, how it will be sequenced, and how many lessons it will take for students to learn the concepts and skills you plan to teach. These decisions are based on the learning indicators or benchmarks determined in Step 2 of this planning process, which were more than likely the grade-level outcomes designed to match the *National Standards* (SHAPE America 2014) or an adaptation of these for your school, district, or state. Now you must decide what content is to be taught and in what order. This yearly plan is also referred to as a pacing guide. In some schools and school districts, the pacing guide provides an overview of what is to be taught for a year and may indicate not only in what order the activities are to be taught, but also when in the school year. In this chapter, we have left these decisions to you. Table 6.4 provides an example a yearly overview or pacing guide for grades K, 2, and 4. In this example, the children have two lessons a week, about 72 days per year. If you look at the first line in the table, you will see that the teacher plans to spend six lessons for her kindergarten classes focused on establishing a learning environment

Table 6.4 Sample Yearly Overview of Number of Lessons for a Two-Day-a-Week Program: Grades K, 2, and 4 (Step 3 in Planning)

Concept/Theme/Activity	K	2	4
Establishing a Learning Environment	6	4	3
Space Awareness	10	4	2
Effort	4	4	3
Relationships	6	3	2
Traveling	10	3	1
Chasing, Fleeing, Dodging	3	5	3
Bending, Stretching, Twisting and Curling	0	3	2
Jumping and Landing	4	4	3
Rolling	2	4	4
Balancing	4	4	4
Transferring Weight	2	3	4
Kicking and Punting	4	4	4
Throwing and Catching	4	6	6
Volleying	0	2	4
Dribbling	1	2	3
Striking with Rackets	2	3	4
Striking with Hockey Sticks	0	1	2
Striking with Golf Clubs	0	1	2
Striking with Bats	0	1	2
Fitness/Wellness Concepts	5	7	9
Field Day and Other Events	5	4	5
Total Days per Year	72	72	72

Note: Numbers represent days per year that a concept theme will be the major focus of a lesson. Numbers are intended for discussion only; the overview will differ from teacher to teacher.

(Chapter 7), whereas this concept will be taught over four lessons with the second-grade classes and three lessons with the fourth-grade classes. In this example, the teacher plans to devote 10 lessons for the kindergarten classes on the movement concept of space awareness (Chapter 14) and only four lessons on effort concepts (Chapter 15). Do you agree with this?

So far, we have provided examples of long-term program goals or a scope, the development of benchmarks or learning indicators, and also a yearly overview or pacing guide. We hope these examples have been helpful. Now you might be saying to yourself, but how do I actually develop a pacing guide? Where do I begin? Those are good questions, and we have attempted to answer these questions by providing a detailed Appendix on planning at the end of this chapter. The Appendix (at page 87) provides a sample overview of a two-day-a-week program (72 days) for both lower and upper elementary grades. Each overview begins by providing hypothetical percentages and number of days a teacher might devote to the movement concepts and skill themes. Especially helpful for someone new to the skill theme approach, we then refer you to the chapter and pages in this book that are related to those topics for every lesson for the year.

So do yourself a favor. Turn to the Appendix at the end of this chapter and look at the examples we have provided. The first sections describe the percentage of the year we suggest focusing on each of the movement concepts and skill themes. Then we have outlined the day-by-day topics and the page numbers in the book that will help you get started planning your lessons. While these are just suggestions, they will hopefully provide an outline and a starting point for you.

Few, if any, teachers will be able to use this Appendix as written. If you have a one- or three-day-a-week program, for example, you will need to adapt the examples to fit your program. We have simply provided you a place to start.

If you look at the example in the Appendix for a two-day-a week program for lower grades, you will see that for each of the 36 weeks in the school year there are two lesson topics suggested for each week. So find week 9 in the Appendix. You will see that the first lesson of the week focuses on the basic jumping and landing patterns (Chapter 20, page 355). The second lesson of the week focuses on teaching the physical fitness concepts related to recommended amounts of physical activity (60 minutes a day) (Chapter 28). In the 32nd week of the school year, we suggest the first lesson focus on tasks related to teaching the children to throw and catch with a partner (Chapter 24, pages 484–499). The second lesson of the week is focused on teaching the children to strike a ball rebounding from a wall

with a racket or paddle (Chapter 26, page 537). This is because it is more engaging and skill development is enhanced if content is varied and revisited.

As you create your own pacing guide, it is important to keep in mind that the sequence of lessons developed is not arbitrary but carefully crafted to progressively achieve the learning indicator determined In Step 2. For example, if the learning indicator is to be able to travel forward, backward, and sideways using a different locomotor pattern with each change of direction, then the lessons chosen should focus on traveling using different locomotor patterns and directions, not traveling in different pathways. After teaching several lessons on a skill, you will also want to insert a mini-assessment task (see Chapter 12) to determine if the students are progressing toward the learning indicator as you hoped. Also remember that a pacing guide or yearly overview needs to be done for each grade level. Children are at different developmental levels; therefore, it is not appropriate to teach the same lesson to children in first and second grades or to those in fourth and fifth grades. Planning should be developmental and progressive across the grade levels. One size does not fit all!

We have provided a sample form (Figure 6.2) that may help you visualize your scope for the year. We have even known teachers who post their yearly planning calendar for their students. This also helps answer the often-asked question, "What are we doing in class today?" Planning for the year is very critical. And while the planning may not be that difficult, sticking to the plan can be. When realistically and appropriately developed, these yearly plans can provide direction and structure to teaching and help keep us "on the right track." However, they are not responsive to student learning needs, and if followed exactly, they may move too quickly or remain on content for a longer time than needed. This is the frustrating part—deciding when to stay with a content area and when to move on. Equally frustrating is that for every addition that is made, one day of teaching something else must be eliminated. To make this task easier, if the form in Figure 6.2 is created in a Word or Excel document, it is easier to revise your yearly plan. As a teacher, you will need to decide when to teach to the guide or the child.

You may be wondering why we have organized our scope and pacing guide the way we have. Actually, there are a number of good reasons—some of them based on the literature and others based on years and years of teaching children. The introduction to the Appendix provides a detailed explanation of our decisions (page 87). It is important to understand why we have organized the content the way we have for you to truly gain an understanding of the skill theme approach.

Week 1 M T W T F	Week 2 M T W T F	Week 3 M T W T F	Week 4 M T W T F	Week 5 M T W T F	Week 6 M T W T F
Week 7 M T W T F	Week 8 M T W T F	Week 9 M T W T F	Week 10 M T W T F	Week 11 M T W T F	Week 12 M T W T F
Week 13 M T W T F	Week 14 M T W T F	Week 15 M T W T F	Week 16 M T W T F	Week 17 M T W T F	Week 18 M T W T F
Week 19 M T W T F	Week 20 M T W T F	Week 21 M T W T F	Week 22 M T W T F	Week 23 M T W T F	Week 24 M T W T F
Week 25 M T W T F	Week 26 M T W T F	Week 27 M T W T F	Week 28 M T W T F	Week 29 M T W T F	Week 30 M T W T F
Week 31 M T W T F	Week 32 M T W T F	Week 33 M T W T F	Week 34 M T W T F	Week 35 M T W T F	Week 36 M T W T F

Figure 6.2 Yearly planning calendar.

Question 4: What Do You Want the Students to Learn in Each Lesson You Teach?

Once you have developed answers to the first three questions, the next one is "What do I want my students to learn in each lesson I teach?" If you thought the first three steps in the planning process were complicated, wait until you read about this step, planning daily lessons. We are going to show you a lesson planning format (Box 6-1) that we use to develop lessons in the skill theme approach adapted from the work of Judy Rink (2014). We call it the reflective planning grid. Before you start reading further, however, we want to provide an introduction that may help you understand why the format we suggest is actually less complicated than it may appear. Imagine that you have played a lot of volleyball, or tennis, or soccer. If you have, you could probably begin to teach the skills for those sports—you know a good progression, you know the critical elements that will help someone improve, and you also know some enjoyable tasks or mini-games that would

make your lessons more interesting to your students. This is how we suggest teachers plan using the reflective planning grid—develop a solid progression of tasks, highlight the cues that are used with your progression, and then develop learning experiences that the students will find interesting (tasks and challenges).

We can also tell you that if you start planning your lessons using the grid, it will take less and less time because you will remember the task progressions, cues, and challenges. We know veteran teachers who have been using the skill theme approach who have incredible lesson progressions in their head! They still plan, but it takes a lot less time than it did when they started planning using the reflective planning grid.

The purpose of this sample lesson is to work toward the suggested grade-level outcome for grade 5 stated in the *National Standards* for catching: "Catches a thrown ball above the head, at chest or waist level, and below the waist using a mature pattern in a non-dynamic environment (closed skills)" (SHAPE America 2014, p. 7). As you can see, we have selected only one of the

Box 6-1

Lesson Plan (Reflective Planning Grid) to Teach the Skill of Catching to a Control-Level Class

Class Name (Grade) _____ **Skill Level** Control

Lesson Length 30 minutes   10:20–10:50 a.m.

Number of Meetings per Week 2

Number of Students 25

Lesson Focus Catching

Objective(s): At the end of this lesson the children will be able to:
1. Catch a self-tossed ball by watching, reaching, and pulling the ball into their body by bending the elbows.
2. Accurately identify three cues for catching in a peer observation.
3. Work cooperatively with a partner by providing accurate feedback in a respectful manner on the catching cues.

Cues: Watch, reach, and pull

Materials/ Equipment 25 softball-size foam round balls that bounce, 25 beanbags; 25 scoops; 25 individual jump ropes

Instant Activity Find a rope and a space far away from others and start practicing your jumping tricks. Try to keep jumping until the music ends (*3–4 minutes*).

Set Induction What sports or games do you play, or want to play, that involve catching a ball? (*Children respond with sports like basketball, softball, football, playing catch with my friends, etc.*). Today we are going to practice catching so that you will be better when you play these sports on a team or in your backyard.

Content Development

Introduction

We are going to focus on catching cues. They are watching, reaching, and pulling. (*Demonstrate and then ask the children to show you "watching, reaching, and pulling" as they pretend to catch a ball. Check for understanding to see that they are watching, reaching, and pulling.*) When I say go, find a ball and find your own space spread throughout the gym. I will know you are ready when I see everyone in a space by themselves with the ball between their feet.

Page in CM	Task	Cue	Challenge	Organization/Safety
	(T) In your own space practice throwing and catching a ball to yourself.		(C) Each time you catch the ball say a letter of: • your first name • your last name • the street you live on	Be certain to observe the children stay in self-space.
	(T) You're going to practice catching this time so you can get used to catching a ball that's coming down toward you. In your own space, bounce the ball so it barely goes over your head, and then try to catch it as it comes down, before it hits the floor.	Watch, reach, pull	(C) Can you catch five in a row without a miss?	Be certain to observe the children stay in self-space.
	(T) If you can catch the ball six times in a row, bouncing it the way you have been, try bouncing it a little higher and still catching it using only your hands. If you have to use your body to catch the ball, you know you're bouncing the ball too high.	Watch, reach, pull		Be certain to observe the children stay in self-space.

Box 6-1 *(continued)*

Page in CM	Task	Cue	Challenge	Organization/Safety
	T This task is to give you more practice catching. In your own space, throw the ball up in the air and catch it. To begin, throw the object at about head level.	Watch, reach, pull	**C** How many catches can you make in a row that are about head high?	Be certain to observe the children stay in self-space.
	T Now that you're warmed up, practice throwing the object about arm's length above your head and catching it. This makes catching a little more difficult because there's more force involved.	Watch, reach, pull		Be certain to observe the children stay in self-space. Watch to see that the children are not throwing the ball too high to catch.
	T Once you're able to catch the object 10 times in a row using only your hands you're ready to throw it a little higher still, maybe 5 feet over your head. Always remember, you must still be able to catch with your hands at each level you throw to. If you can't, then you know you're throwing too high and need to bring the throw down a little.	Watch, reach, pull	**C** This time you are going to make a routine that you repeat over and over. The routine needs to contain five catches at different levels—some about head high and some higher. The pattern could be: head high, really high, medium high, really high, head high. Whatever you decide, you should be able to repeat the pattern three times.	Be certain to observe the children stay in self-space. Watch to see that children are not throwing the ball too high to catch.
	? For this task, you will need a partner. When I say "go," you should find someone with whom you can work productively. I will know you are ready when I see you seated together. Go. When I give the signal, one person in each group should come collect two peer coaching lists and a pencil. The two of you decide who is to throw and catch first, and the other person watches and makes an X in the box that says how your partner is catching. After five throws and catches, switch. When you are finished, make sure to talk to your partner about their throwing and give them one glow and one grow that help them throw well.	Watch, reach, pull		Each group should have an observation sheet similar to the ones in Figure 12.9 but with the cues of watch, reach, and pull. Be sure to observe the observers and provide feedback to them about what they are "seeing." Observe to see if partner groups are well spread apart

Box 6-1 *(continued)*

Page in CM	Task	Cue	Challenge	Organization/Safety
T	In your self-space, practice throwing the beanbag up with your hand and catching it in the scoop. To be a good catch, the beanbag must stay in the scoop and not bounce out.	Watch, reach, pull	**C** See how many catches you can make in 1 minute. This time, see if you can beat the score you had last time.	In the transition from the previous task, children will need to put their papers and pencils away, return the ball to the equipment location, and collect a beanbag and a scoop.

Closure

"Today we practiced catching. Can you show me what your hands and arms should do when you are trying to catch a ball? *(Check for understanding to see if the children are "reaching and giving" with their hands.)* Great! Now I want you to think about giving your partner feedback. Thumbs up if you gave your partner one glow and one grow; thumbs sideways if you sort of did it; and thumbs down if you didn't do it. Before our next lesson, I would like you to practice at

least 100 catches. You may do it alone with a ball or a beanbag or with a friend or maybe one of your parents. See you next class. We will practice catching with partners again."

Reflection/Insights/Comments

Use this space to write down your thoughts and insights about what worked, what didn't work, and future catching lessons.

----

critical elements for catching (watching, reaching, and pulling, which together we consider one critical element) on which to focus for this lesson. Why? Because in our experience, although it may be possible to accomplish two critical elements in one lesson, one is even more attainable. Accomplishing more than two elements is simply not realistic. The other critical elements may have previously been learned (however, in this case, these are the first ones), or we may focus on other elements (e.g., moving into position behind or under the ball) in another lesson. If our lesson is successful, however, by the end of the class, the students will be able to describe and demonstrate the critical element of watching, reaching, and pulling.

The first part of the reflective planning grid (lesson plan) (Box 6-1) consists of information related to the class(es) you teach—e.g., grade level, skill level of the class, time the class begins and ends, topic for the lesson (typically a skill theme or movement concept), an outline of the objective(s) for the lesson, and the materials/equipment you will need for the lesson. Although this may not seem necessary now, when you are teaching 6 or 8 or even 10 classes a day, it is immensely helpful, and it is even more important if you are a beginning teacher. We suggest beginning the lesson with an instant activity (Graham, Elliot, and Palmer 2016),

followed by communicating the purpose of the lesson (set induction or anticipatory set) and letting children know the intended lesson objectives as well as how they will know if they have achieved those objectives (success criteria). For example, for the catching lesson in Box 6-1, we might say, "Today we are going to work on catching. You will know when you have learned this when you can catch a ball you toss to yourself by reaching and pulling the ball to your chest." Some teachers present this to students as WALT (what we are learning today) and WILT (what I am looking for today). The next part of the plan, however, contains the actual grid used to guide the reflective teacher in developing lessons that vary from class to class based on the children's abilities and interests. The reflective planning grid consists of five parts organized into columns to make it easier to use in a dynamic teaching situation (Rink 2014). The first column in this example from Chapter 24 refers to the page number in *Children Moving* that contains the tasks, cues, and challenges that compose the lesson content. For the reflective planning grid in Box 6-1, we have chosen the skill theme of catching for a class in which most children are at the control level (pages 76–77).

The second column contains the tasks (learning experiences) for the lesson. The tasks are marked with the symbol 🅣, which will make it easier for you to locate them and see their progression. In Box 6-1, there are eight control-level tasks, one of which is also used as an assessment task, organized in a progression from easier to harder (pages 76–77). With some classes, the reflective teacher may use all of these tasks—and need even more. With other classes, the teacher may use only one or two of the tasks. Clearly this depends on the children in the classes and all of the other variables that make each class and child unique. We suggest that beginning teachers who are new to the skill theme approach plan more tasks than they think they will need for their lessons so they can progress based on student responses until they learn more about the abilities of different classes and understand more about content development. This planning format also allows you to use the same progression for different classes of the same grade level. This process of content development is also important when differentiating instruction for children of differing abilities (teaching by invitation and intratask variation; see Chapter 7) and when adapting the content for children with special needs (Chapter 10). Again, let us remind you that if you have played a sport, you already have a catching progression in mind and, no doubt, can add some additional tasks to the progression we suggest in this sample lesson plan. Keep in mind that the tasks you use must be developmentally appropriate and follow a clear progression. Assessment tasks are also included in this column and are marked with the assessment icon ❓.

The third column in the reflective planning grid contains the cues (short words for the critical elements) that the teacher has decided to reinforce during the lesson. Notice that the cue is in the same row as the task. This is both intentional and important because the cue needs to align with the task to be useful and effective. We will expand on this later in the chapter. The cues link directly to the lesson objectives. This is critical if the lesson is going to be an educational experience for the children. The cues also guide the teacher in providing specific, congruent feedback or developing refinement tasks, as explained in Chapter 7.

The fourth column in the reflective planning grid contains challenges. Challenges change the focus of the tasks on which children are working to encourage the children to continue practicing a task when their interest or attention begins to wane or allow them to "test" their learning. The challenges are marked in the movement concept and skill theme chapters (Chapters 14–27) with the symbol 🅒. Again, notice in Box 6-1 that the challenges are in the same row as the task and cue so the challenge aligns with the task the children are practicing. Challenges are useful for two reasons.

First, they provide opportunities for the children to apply the tasks in different contexts (e.g., successful repetitions, number done in a given period of time, repetition of a task). Second, as stated earlier, challenges also encourage children to continue practicing a task that they have yet to learn. All too often teachers make tasks harder before the children are ready, and this can be both discouraging and frustrating to some children in a class. Observation of students during a challenge task can help direct the teacher to move on or back up and revisit previous tasks.

The last column is a place to note any organization or safety reminders that are important not only for the lesson but for each task. Once again, these reminders are aligned in the same row with the tasks, cues, and challenges to help you remember these important parts of the lesson. Box 6-1 illustrates several examples of these reminders.

The closure, or conclusion, typically lasts no more than two or three minutes. The teacher calls the children together and quickly reviews the objectives (the learnable pieces) of the lesson that were stated at the beginning and emphasized throughout the class. As the sample lesson in Box 6-1 indicates, the teacher can phrase the closure in the form of questions. This is an especially important time to remind children of what has been emphasized throughout the class. It can also provide the teacher with an informal assessment about whether or not the children have attained the lesson objectives (see Chapter 12).

Effective closures typically have three characteristics: (1) they review the learning objectives of the day and the success criteria regarding what was learned, (2) they link what was taught in the lesson with past and future lessons (scaffolding), and (3) they suggest ways students can obtain more practice outside of the school setting.

Finally, in a perfect world, there would be time at the end of every lesson for a teacher to sit at his or her desk and reflect on the lesson just completed. Did I accomplish my objectives? Which tasks worked well? Which needed to be changed? What do I need to emphasize the next time I teach catching to this class? How far did the class get in the lesson? Unfortunately, this is not always the case, but when possible, it is really useful to record your thoughts about what worked, what didn't work, and what you might do next time you teach the lesson.

Hopefully you are beginning to understand how the planning process works. As you read the movement concept and skill theme chapters, we think the process will become even clearer because in each chapter there is a wealth of tasks, cues, and challenges from which to develop your lessons.

Planning Insights Gained from Years of Teaching Experience

In this section, we offer additional insights about planning. They are based on years of teaching experience and relate directly to the four steps we have outlined in the planning process. They provide insights we think you will find extremely useful as you develop your reflective planning skills. You might also call them lesson planning tips. They are important, and we think you will find them especially helpful for understanding the planning process we have outlined in this chapter and for gaining insights into the planning process.

Insights About Developing Lesson Objectives

As explained at the beginning of this chapter, lesson objectives are critical if the children are going to increase their understanding and skillfulness. Effective objectives state what we want the children to learn in the lesson rather than what they are to do. For example, stating that the children will throw and catch a ball in self-space is not an objective—it is a task. "The children will learn to catch a ball" is a goal. Unfortunately, this goal cannot be accomplished in a 30-minute lesson; it will take many lessons, perhaps thousands of practice catches, before a child can truly be able to catch a ball. Regrettably, there may not be enough time in the program for the children to actually catch a softly thrown ball, but if they have learned the critical elements, they have a much greater chance of learning to catch than if they have never learned them. If you look at the lesson objective in Box 6-1 that indicates students will be able to "Catch a self-tossed ball by watching, reaching, and pulling the ball into their body by bending the elbows," it contains some very specific and useful information. First, there is a behavior (always a verb) that describes what skill or concept the students are to learn. In this case, it is to "catch." Second, the conditions in which the learning is to be demonstrated are specified. In our example, it is a self-tossed ball. Last, the success criteria are provided. These criteria indicate how well we hope to see the children catch. For our objective, it is by "watching, reaching, and pulling the ball into their body by bending the elbows." So if the objective is written clearly, then it should guide the whole lesson. In this lesson, we would not be looking to see a child catch a football tossed by a partner or to catch the ball "any which way" 10 times, but to catch by "watching, reaching, and pulling the ball into their body by bending the elbows." Look at the objective written for the affective domain; can you find all the parts to it?

Insights About Task Development (Column Two)

Once the children have been provided with a starting task or activity, the reflective teacher observes the children to determine whether the task is too easy (the children are able to do it easily with no apparent challenge), too hard (the children are occasionally successful, but many are unable to do the task with success), or simply unproductive (the children just aren't benefiting [learning] from doing the task). In any of these cases, the teacher will want to change the task so more of the children can be successful.

Tasks that are "just right" allow children to succeed at the task about 80 percent of the time. The 80 percent success rate is a rough estimate, but it provides a guideline for determining the appropriateness of a task. High rates of success typically motivate children to keep trying and working at the task. Tasks that are too easy or too hard prompt off-task behavior or questions like, "When can we do something else?" "When do we get to play the game?"

Task progression, however, is not always about making a task harder. In some instances, you will want to make a task easier. The advantage of the reflective planning grid (Box 6-1) is that you can move up or down the task column (column 2) based on the children you are teaching. This provides a more dynamic way to think about the content. Veteran teachers have years of experience and are able to think about task progression without writing detailed lesson plans as suggested here. Engaging in the process we have described here, however, will help you develop a plethora of tasks that eventually you will remember and use dynamically when teaching your classes.

An analogy about moving is useful here. When you move to a town, for example, you probably rely a lot on a GPS (global positioning system; maps in the old days) or ask directions often. Once you have lived in that town for a few years, you rarely consult maps, the GPS, or others to get around town. The same is true for veteran teachers who spend a lot of time planning in their first few years—eventually they have a mental repertoire of effective tasks for teaching the movement concepts and skill themes.

Insights About Cues and Refinements (Column Three)

Once a task is judged to be appropriate (not too easy or too hard), the teacher can use cues or refinement tasks to help the children perform the skill more efficiently. The cues are short phrases used to help children focus on the critical elements. Providing cues is one of the most valuable roles a teacher can perform (Graham et al. 1993; 2014; Rink 2014). Cues help children understand how to perform a skill and shortcut the learning process as well as encourage the children to practice proper techniques. In the overhand throw for distance, for example, it is important that children learn to step with the foot opposite the throwing hand. When landing from a jump, it is important that the children learn to bend not only at the knees but also at the hips and ankles. These tips or cues help children learn skills more efficiently than they would by trial and error. The cues that reflect the critical elements are listed at the beginning of each series of tasks in the skill theme chapters (Chapters 17–27). In addition to helping the children learn the correct ways of performing a skill, emphasizing cues can also provide the children with a checklist of the important critical elements they will need when they decide to play a sport on their own outside of school.

During the actual lesson (using the example in Box 6-1), teachers will provide plenty of chances to practice catching, focusing on the cues of "watch, reach, and pull." This is done by demonstrating and providing individual feedback related to using the hands and arms appropriately to catch a ball or an object. During the lesson, the teacher will continually pause and remind the children of the cue they need to work on. Sometimes the teacher will demonstrate the critical element. Sometimes the teacher will point out other youngsters who are using the critical elements in their catching. As the children practice, the teacher will also move among them and provide specific congruent feedback (Chapters 7 and 11) about how well they are using the cues. The teacher will constantly remind individual children to watch, reach, and pull.

Besides just reminding children of the cues, the cues can also be rephrased as refinement tasks that actually ask the children to practice focusing on one aspect. Using throwing as an example, if the focus is on stepping with the opposite foot and the task has been throwing back and forth with a partner, the new task can be, "You are still going to throw and catch with your partner, but this time, really pay attention to stepping with the opposite foot." See Chapter 7 for more information on refinement tasks. Children who attend physical education class for an hour or less a week obviously don't have enough time to reach the utilization or proficiency level. We do know, however, that they can learn the critical elements, so at least they will recall how to perform a skill appropriately.

When you begin to use the information in the skill theme chapters, you will notice that no cues are provided with the tasks at the precontrol level of the GLSP

(Chapter 5). This is because youngsters at that level have had minimal experience with even attempting a given movement. We want them to first explore the skill until they have at least a general idea of how it feels and what is required to do it successfully (Schmidt and Wrisberg 2008). For example, if you have never attempted a movement, being told four or five cues will have little meaning and probably won't stick with you. Obviously we must emphasize safety, but explanation and demonstration of the critical elements can begin once youngsters have a basic understanding of the movement and are at the control level. At this point in the learning curve, they are often more receptive to learning the cues because they have discovered they are not adept at the skill and would like to know how to do it more efficiently and effectively.

You will also notice there is a progression of cues from the control to the utilization and then the proficiency level. This is because the movements are different at each level of the GLSP. For example, youngsters at the proficiency level in landing from a jump do not need to be told to "bend their knees"—they learned that when they were at the control level. Just as the tasks change for each of the GLSPs, so do the cues.

Each of the skill theme development chapters provides numerous cues that the children will find helpful for enhancing the quality of their movements. The challenge for you as a teacher is to select the cue, from the ones suggested in the chapters, that will be most helpful for your class. Much of this analysis is completed as part of the lesson planning when you develop the progression of tasks and the appropriate cues. Beware of the temptation to tell the children too much at once; present only one cue at a time! We want our children not only to hear the cues, but also to be able to recall and apply them.

Insights About Challenges (Applications) (Column Four)

Even when children are doing a task and succeeding at high rates, there comes a time when they become disinterested and are ready to move on to another task. The problem is that we are not always able to provide another task that is just a little bit harder. In some instances, a task is much harder, and if we ask the children to do this task before they are ready, many of the children will fail. Many challenges that will motivate the children to continue practicing are "invented" as part of the planning process. The important point to remember is that the task stays the same, but the challenge is designed to motivate the children to keep practicing that same task.

Let's take the example of batting. A logical progression from striking a ball from a batting tee is to strike a pitched ball (Chapter 27). Hitting a pitched ball is much more difficult for the children, especially at young ages when many children's throwing (pitching) skills are not yet refined. The right kind of challenge at the right time, however, will motivate the children to continue practicing batting from a tee. This will allow the teacher time to continue providing feedback about the way the children are (or aren't) stepping with the lead foot when they bat. The following list gives some examples of batting challenges. Note that all the tasks still require the children to keep batting from a tee, the task they had been working on before the teacher decided to provide a challenge.

- "Every time you bat the ball without hitting the tee with the bat, say a letter of your last name. Try to spell your whole name." (repetition challenge)
- "See how many times in a row you can hit the ball without hitting the tee or missing the ball." (keeping score challenge)
- "Try to hit the fence (wall) with the ball on a fly three times in a row." (repetition challenge)

These challenges do not substantively change the task; rather, they are designed to maintain the children's interest in that task by allowing them to "test out" the skill they have been practicing. In game-like settings, a challenge of keeping score, either cooperatively or competitively, would be a logical application for that task.

Some teachers find it easier than others to use challenges in their teaching. As we increase our understanding of how children at different ages think—and their sense of humor—it becomes easier to create challenges for them. Preschool children, for example, can be challenged simply by being asked to perform a task with a ball or hoop of a different color. Some upper elementary children enjoy the challenge of competing against a friend to see who can be more successful (keeping score). Others enjoy seeing if they can surpass their previous personal records (keeping score). We have provided a few examples of challenges in the subsequent chapters, but the best ones are those you create as you come to know the children you are teaching.

Insights About Additional Ideas (Content) for Lessons

The movement concepts and skill theme chapters (14–27) provide an excellent starting point for content development. Obviously, however, there are many other sources for lesson ideas, such as notes from classes, your own and others' observations, books (e.g.,

Holt/Hale and Hall, *Lesson Planning for Elementary Physical Education*, 2016) workshops, conferences, articles, and discussions with other teachers. The Internet is another great source. A myriad of Internet sites (e.g., PE Central, supportREALteachers.org, YouTube) have many excellent lesson ideas that are aligned with movement concepts and skill themes. Planning for lessons involves sifting through sources and then designing lessons to match the needs and characteristics of your students to help them learn the benchmarks developed in the previous step of the planning process. We've found few, if any, prepackaged lessons that worked for us as they supposedly worked for their authors. So instead of including specific lesson plans in *Children Moving* (with the exception of Box 6-1), we provide tasks for development to encourage you to develop your own plans.

Insights About Assessment

Every lesson needs some type of assessment plan to determine whether the students have achieved the learning objectives. Remember, though, as you teach that this does not always have to be a "formal" assessment. Challenges represent an informal assessment because you can observe how well the students are able to do a task. Observation of student use of the cues is another informal assessment. Feedback is another

The Kids Love It

One of the comments often heard from teachers whose goal is to keep youngsters busy, happy, and good is that the kids love the game or activity. Although it is certainly desirable for youngsters to enjoy an activity, it is not our sole criterion. For example, some children would love to eat ice cream or doughnuts or potato chips for every meal. Obviously, however, it would not be in these children's best interest if that was all they ate. The same is true for the classroom. There are many fun reading, math, and science games. But the successful teacher always evaluates these games or activities to be certain that if the children play them, they actually lead to better reading, more effective computing, or understanding of science concepts. So when we hear that youngsters love a game or an activity, we can't help but wonder: Are the children really learning something? Is the activity truly a learning experience? Should the fact that kids love it be the sole, or major, criterion to determine the success of a lesson? Our goal is to keep youngsters busy, happy, and good—but also learning! If they aren't learning, then what are we teaching them?

form of informal assessment, and when a teacher observes a skill and provides skill-specific congruent feedback, students are able to revise and improve their skills. If we look at the lesson plan example in Box 6-1, there is one formal assessment that is used to assess all three learning objectives. What is it? How many informal assessments can you find? Chapter 12 will provide more information about assessment.

Insights About Organization/Management/Safety (Column Five)

The fifth column of the planning grid entitled Organization/Safety provides the teacher with a place to write down and/or draw the different organizations and formats that will be used during a lesson. Although this may not be necessary for experienced teachers, it's very helpful for beginning teachers; it leads them to think through the organizational formats they might use during the lesson, thereby avoiding some of the problems that might occur—for example, when a teacher hasn't thought about how the children will move from throwing against a wall to finding a partner to throw and catch with. If not planned for carefully, these transitions can lead to wasted time, confusion, and even misbehavior.

Insights About Lesson Reflection

Lesson reflection answers two questions: What did students learn and how did I teach? The first question addresses to what extent the students achieved the learning objectives. The assessments used during a lesson should provide an answer to this question. A reflective teacher records the progress that a particular class, group, or individual makes during a lesson. An elementary school physical education specialist may teach 8 to 12 classes a day. Each group and each student will progress to a different degree and in a different way. A reflective teacher, whose approach takes these differences into consideration, will need notes on which to base the next day's (or week's) lessons.

You can write brief comments in a standard planning book or on index cards. Some teachers use tablets or cell phones to digitally record important thoughts from lessons. Notes summarizing what was accomplished during a lesson help you plan the next lessons. Ideally, the day's schedule will include 5 or 10 minutes between classes; you can use this time for recording observations and, if necessary, arranging equipment for the next class. Teachers who digitally keep track of their students' progress have the advantage of easily downloading the information into a computer for ease

of use and future reference. Whether you use note cards, a digital device, or some other technique, it will certainly help you plan more efficiently. What seems clear at 9 a.m. is often opaque by 4 p.m.

The second question reflection addresses is: How did I teach? This is a chance to make notes on what went well (and what did not) with respect to student learning, engagement, enjoyment, and classroom management. These types of reflection allow us to capitalize on our successes and not repeat our mistakes. See Chapter 13 for a multitude of options on which you might reflect.

Keeping Track of Your Lessons

We have suggested a lesson planning format that works for many teachers (Box 6-1). Certainly, however, changes can be made to our lesson plans. If you use the content development format of the planning grid (the five columns), it is relatively easy to add or delete content and continue to use the plans over a number of years.

A well-developed plan can be somewhat lengthy, especially for beginning teachers. For this reason, many teachers find it helpful to write a brief outline on a 5-by-8-inch card they carry with them during the lesson as a handy reminder.

Making Planning Enjoyable

Planning is hard work. It takes time and energy to plan effective lessons that are exciting and interesting to children. Teachers who fail to plan well are tempted to return to old standbys—kickball, dodgeball, and Four Square—that contribute minimally to children's learning in physical education.

You'll always be able to find something to do that is more interesting than planning lessons. So it's a good idea to devise ways to make planning easier and more fun. We've found the following ideas helpful:

- Set aside some time each day specifically for planning. Then you won't be constantly trying to find time to plan. Some people find that planning at school before they leave for home is effective; others prefer to arrive at school early to plan the day.
- Try to become excited about your plans. When you're excited about trying to present an idea in a new and interesting way, planning is fun, and you communicate your enthusiasm to your students. Reading books and journals, attending conferences, talking to colleagues, and searching the Internet are some ways you can find new and interesting ideas to incorporate into your plans. As you search available resources, be sure to screen for appropriate (and

inappropriate practices); remember you are looking for experiences that will lead to the acquisition of your learning objective—not something to occupy time. The caveat "less is more" always applies, so be sure to take something out for every new activity you add into your scope.

- Don't hesitate to experiment. The worst that can happen is that a lesson won't work as planned. When this happens, we tell the children we were trying a new idea and it didn't work. Children understand and sometimes make worthwhile suggestions about how the idea might be improved.

When you set aside appropriate amounts of time, discover new ideas, and attempt to make lessons exciting, planning becomes more enjoyable and your attitude toward teaching will be affected. Most of us experience uncertainty when beginning a lesson (or anything else) for which we're unprepared. When you've planned a lesson thoroughly, the assurance and enthusiasm you feel can be contagious.

Lesson Design

If children are to develop into skillful movers, they must do more than play games. Children need opportunities to practice skills in contexts that are meaningful to them. These meaningful experiences result in motor competence, include social interaction, are fun and challenging, and are personally relevant (Beni, Fletcher, and Ní Chróinín 2017). The teacher who can design interesting and exciting practice situations will rarely hear the question asked so often by highly skilled, unchallenged children: "When do we get to play a game?"

Motor Competence

Children want to be challenged and successful at the same time. The ideal task is difficult enough so the child can't do it as intended every time, yet easy enough so the child is successful much of the time. If small children try to shoot a basketball through a 10-foot-high basket, their success rate may be so low they'll quickly lose interest. If the same children are given options—for example, shooting at a basket 7 feet high or shooting through a hoop suspended from a pole—their interest will remain higher for longer periods, and their skills will therefore improve. In these lessons, tasks are developed through a planned sequence of extension, refinement, and application, and students receive massive amounts of feedback.

Lessons that result in motor competence contain maximum practice time. One of the clearest differences between more effective and less effective teachers is

that the students of more effective teachers actually spend more time practicing than do the children of less effective teachers (Rink 2014). The value of practice may seem obvious, yet practice is frequently neglected, particularly in teaching games. The number of practice trials a child receives is critical to what is learned. Therefore, the amount of equipment available and the organization of the lesson are important. When a class of 30 children practices a skill such as throwing or catching and they use only three or four balls, the children's skills will improve less than the skills of children whose teacher designs the same lesson with a ball for every two children in the class. When at all possible, we like to have some type of ball for every child. The key to this is recognizing that 30 of the same type of ball are not needed. For example, playground balls and plastic balls can be substituted for soccer balls or basketballs when learning to dribble. In addition, having students practice by themselves or with a partner is more effective than having them stand in line. Remember, not all children have learned to practice on their own. Making more equipment available doesn't guarantee increased practice time. In fact, we've observed instances in which the children in a class actually practiced more when there were only three or four balls available because most of the students in the class hadn't yet learned to work on their own.

Social Interaction

Students appreciate having voice and choice in their learning experiences as well as engaging with other students. This might be in the form of choosing their own partners or groups or simply working in partners. The social interaction allows students to learn from and with each other in a psychologically safe environment. Noise should always be at a "productive" level, but noise is good.

Enjoyable and Challenging Lessons

Many children, particularly younger ones, don't understand the need to practice to become more skillful. Children typically are interested only in the present and have little concern about future years. Thus, young children more easily accept and enjoy lessons with immediate meaning. For example, we wouldn't teach third graders how to turn on one foot (pivot) by having them perform a mass drill because such an exercise would have little meaning or interest to them. We might, however, have them jog in general space and instruct them, "Spin around on one foot when you hear the drum and then continue jogging." On the next drumbeat, we might say, "Pivot on the other foot" or "Spin in the opposite direction." Later, when the children are able to travel dribbling a ball, we might say, "Spin on the drumbeat while continuing to dribble a ball." We don't teach skills as if all children really want to learn the skill because they intend to play on a varsity team in high school—they don't.

Variety in a lesson also makes the lesson more enjoyable. We try to give children a number of related practice opportunities in a single lesson rather than having them practice the same skill the same way the entire lesson. The only way to accomplish this goal of providing variety is through extensive and thorough planning.

> One study (Graham et al. 1993) that compared student teachers with experienced teachers found that veteran teachers provided children with far fewer tasks than the novice teachers. The novices believed that they had to "get through all of the tasks in their plan." In contrast, the veteran teachers were focused on the children. If a task was "right," they stayed with it for long periods of time.

Relevant

Meaningfulness for students means recognizing the importance of what they are learning. They want to make explicit connections between physical education experiences and physical education outside of school, and this rarely happens (Parker et al. 2018). For teachers, this means that the sharing of learning outcomes and why they are important is crucial. This relevance may then be shared with parents and administrators.

Parting Thought

The planning process described in this chapter no doubt seems complex, time-consuming, and maybe even unnecessary. It's not! Think again about planning the trip mentioned at the beginning of the chapter. Time spent planning can heighten enjoyment dramatically. Being lost, confused, or in the wrong place at the wrong time is no fun; neither is a poorly planned lesson that is uninteresting, dominated by a few highly skilled children (unless, of course, you are one of the highly skilled), nor simply unproductive. If you want to become a highly successful teacher, it is going to take a lot of work—and the journey starts with planning.

The Relationship Between Planning and Content Development

Planning is the process of developing a progression of learning experiences that are productive, beneficial, and meaningful to the children. Reflective teachers use planning as a well-thought-out guide that provides a clear direction designed to accomplish the program's goals. Planning is typically done ahead of the lesson delivery before or after school, at home, or in the office at school.

Developing the content is the process of implementing the plan in the gym or on the playground. Essentially it is transferring the written plan to a series of learning experiences during the actual lesson. Rarely, however, do reflective teachers deliver lesson plans exactly as designed. Plans are meant to be dynamic and change according the GLSP in a particular class, students' interest on a given day, how quickly the children are grasping the content, and so on. One lesson rarely is identical to another lesson. The process of developing the content, therefore, makes lesson planning come to life as it evolves to cater to the unique children in a class.

Invariant teachers, in contrast, appear to make the assumption that "one size fits all." They teach virtually identical lessons, typically games, and provide little or no feedback and/or encouragement to the children they are teaching. It appears they are attempting to keep the children busy, happy, and good rather than providing worthwhile learning experiences for all children. Invariant teachers typically use an identical lesson plan for several grades, irrespective of the children's needs, interests, and skill levels. Reflective teachers, in contrast, develop the content by adapting the progression of tasks to the children in a given class. Rarely, if ever, do they teach identical lessons—even though the grade level may be same for three classes in a row.

Summary

Planning is a crucial part of the teaching process. Successful teachers plan effectively—not only their daily lessons but also the entire program, as well as each year of the program. Plans are guides, not cast in stone. As you learn more about the school, the children, and the context of the teaching situation, plans change!

This chapter asks and answers four questions: What will the students learn over the entire program? What are indicators of that learning? How will learning be sequenced in a given year? How will it be sequenced in each lesson? The tables and Box 6-1 in this chapter provide practical examples for the teacher to get started forming his or her own answers to these questions. The Appendix at the end of this chapter also provides examples of how to plan in the skill theme approach. The most detailed section of this chapter describes how to use a reflective planning grid for content development. It shows how teachers can develop skill progressions (tasks), teach critical elements with cues to help their students acquire the necessary skills, and create challenges to maintain the interest of the classes they teach. It concludes with insights about planning gained from years of teaching the skill theme approach.

Reading Comprehension Questions

1. What is meant by the term *reflective planning*? Think about your elementary school. Which contextual factors influenced the program and the way the teacher planned?
2. Explain in your own terms the four steps to planning that are outlined in *Children Moving*.
3. What might happen when a teacher does not bother to do Steps 1, 2, and 3 in the planning process and only plans day to day?
4. Tables 6.1 and 6.2 present sample scopes for the movement concepts and skill themes. In your own words, explain why some concepts and skills are not taught at various grade levels. Use specific concepts and skills in your explanation.
5. Using the skill theme of balance, complete Step 2 of the planning process. Develop five indicators of learning for rolling that would lead to the outcome of "Balances on different bases of support on apparatus, demonstrating levels and shapes" (SHAPE America 2014).
6. Using Table 6.3 as a guide, select first, third, or fifth grade, and do a yearly pacing guide for that grade.

Then write a brief analysis explaining what you changed from the grade before and after. For example, if you chose third grade, explain how your guide is different from those for second and fourth grades.
7. Use the guide for planning daily lessons (Box 6-1) to plan one of your own lessons. Use one of the skill theme chapters as a guide, but do not use the skills of throwing and catching. Include at least 10 tasks. Use the five-column reflective planning grid format described in this chapter.
8. Why is the development of clear objectives so important? Using a skill theme of something other than catching, develop a realistic objective for a control-level class.
9. Why should each lesson have an assessment plan?
10. Veteran teachers typically spend less time planning than do beginning teachers. Why might this be the case?
11. Explain how the concept "less is more" applies to developing a curriculum. What happens when a teacher attempts to jam too many skill themes into a year for the time allotted?

References/Suggested Readings

Beni, S., T. Fletcher, and D. Ní Chróinín. 2017. Meaningful experiences in physical education and youth sport. *Quest* 69(3): 291–312.

Graham, G., E. Elliot, and S. Palmer. 2016. *Teaching children and adolescents physical education.* 4th ed. Champaign, IL: Human Kinetics.

Graham, G., C. Hopple, M. Manross, and T. Sitzman. 1993. Novice and experienced children's physical education teachers: Insights into their situational decision-making. *Journal of Teaching in Physical Education* 12(2): 197–217.

Holt/Hale, S., and T. Hall. 2016. *Lesson planning for elementary physical education.* Champaign, IL: Human Kinetics.

[NASPE] National Association for Sport and Physical Education. 2004. *Moving into the future: National standards for physical education.* 2nd ed. Reston, VA: National Association for Sport and Physical Education.

Parker, M., A. MacPhail, M. O'Sullivan, D. Ní Chróinín, and E. McEvoy. 2018. Drawing' conclusions: Primary school children's construction of school physical education and physical activity opportunities outside of school. *European Physical Education Review* 24(4):449–466.

Rink, J. E. 2014. *Teaching physical education for learning.* 7th ed. New York, NY: McGraw-Hill.

Schmidt, R. A., and C. A. Wrisberg. 2008. *Motor learning and performance.* 4th ed. Champaign, IL: Human Kinetics.

[SHAPE America] Society of Health and Physical Educators. 2014. *National standards and grade-level outcomes for K-12 physical education.* Champaign, IL: Human Kinetics.

Stodden, D. F., J. D. Goodway, S. J. Langendorfer, M. A. Roberton, M. E. Rudisill, C. Garcia, and L.E. Garcia. 2008. A developmental perspective on the role of motor skill competence in physical activity. *Quest:* 290–306.

Sample School-Year Content Overviews (Pacing Guides)

Good teachers are good planners! They plan for the day, the school year, and the entire length of the program (e.g., kindergarten through fifth grade). If you are a new teacher or new to teaching by skill themes, we have provided two sample yearly overviews (pacing guides/ scopes and sequences) to help you get started planning your year(s).

The process of developing these overviews is described in detail earlier in this chapter.

One of the sample overviews in this Appendix is for a two-day-a-week program (72 lessons a year) for lower elementary grade (inexperienced) classes. The other sample overview is for a two-day-a-week (72 lessons a year) program for upper elementary (experienced) classes. It would be great if you could use these examples exactly as we wrote them. Unfortunately, some aspects, such as your schedule, equipment, or facilities, will not match up exactly with these overviews, so you will need to adapt these overviews. If, for example, your classes meet once a week, you will need to adapt the two-day-a-week outline to 36 lessons a year instead of 72, as in the sample overview. This is why we provide percentages in the overviews to aid with the adaptations you will need to make. We hope you will find these overviews to be a useful place to start outlining the content you will be teaching in a school year. The examples presented are for no particular grade; the number of days devoted to a particular skill may vary across grade levels as students progress upward in the spiral in their skill development.

As you study these overviews, keep these 12 important points in mind:

1. The content overviews show how to organize your school year using skill themes and movement and fitness concepts. We suggest they be used as starting points for developing your own yearly pacing guides or scopes and sequences.
2. In these examples, lower elementary (*inexperienced*) generally refers to K–2 classes and upper elementary (*experienced*) to grades 3–5.
3. The day-to-day content is intended to be the major focus of that day's lesson, but in many instances, other content will be taught during a lesson as well— for example, a review of a skill theme or concept from the previous day or a skill that needs to be worked on frequently but for short periods of time, such as jumping rope and transferring weight from feet to hands.
4. In both overviews in this Appendix, the first few lessons are devoted to establishing a learning environment, as outlined in Chapter 7. Several other lessons throughout the year are devoted to "reviewing" the learning environment. The period after winter or spring break, for instance, is often a good time to review the learning environment. Review days give you a chance to check the environment to determine if some areas, such as immediately stopping at the stop signal and paying careful attention when you are talking, need additional practice.
5. The sequencing of the skill themes and movement concepts takes typical weather patterns into account. Outdoor activities are grouped at the beginning and end of the school year, indoor activities toward the middle of the year. For the most part, the movement concepts are introduced early in the year and are revisited throughout the year when time permits.
6. We believe that it's not as effective to focus on a skill once a year and then never revisit it. Three lessons on the skill theme of rolling in February, for example, probably won't lead to the long-term learning of that skill, whereas three lessons—one each in October, February, and April—will provide a much higher success for student learning. That is why we organize the skill theme curriculum by skills and concepts, unlike traditional approaches that organize the physical education curriculum as a series of units.
7. Another advantage of distributing the lessons throughout the year, rather than teaching them as a single unit, is that you can essentially teach the same lesson again later in the school year. This is especially important for children at the precontrol level because the options to change tasks and activities without making them too difficult are limited when the children are first learning a skill.
8. When a skill theme is taught in the autumn, some of the children who were not developmentally ready in October may be ready in April. It's important to emphasize that the children will actually practice throwing in more classes than just the ones that

focus primarily on throwing. For example, the sessions dedicated to catching will typically offer many opportunities to throw.

9. To get you started, a major task is generally appropriate for the focus of a day's lesson. If you think the children will find a single task too strenuous or uninteresting, you may combine a major task from two different chapters. For example, you may combine the ideas under the heading Jumping a Turned Rope (Chapter 20) with the major task Traveling in Different Pathways (Chapter 17). This will give the children variety. Although most of our lessons focus on one major movement concept or skill theme, there's no reason not to focus on two themes or concepts in a single lesson, especially with the younger children who are at the precontrol and control levels (Chapter 5).

10. Fitness concepts (Chapter 28) are taught throughout the year approximately every four to five weeks in the two-day-a-week scope. Obviously they could be grouped differently, but this placement allows you to teach a concept or two and set aside time for the children to incorporate the concept into their lifestyle before you introduce another fitness concept. It also allows you to review and reinforce concepts throughout the year instead of lumping them into a block of lessons.

11. In our programs, time is allowed throughout the year for special events that take time away from teaching. (In most of the elementary schools in which we have taught, there are days when physical education must be missed because of field trips, holiday shows, assemblies, voting, picture days, etc.)

12. Notice that skill themes tend to be massed at the beginning (several days combined) and then distributed throughout the remainder of the year. Notice too that in the programs for the experienced classes, several days in a row are sometimes spent on a single skill theme. As children improve in skill proficiency, they tend to want to spend more days on the same skill because their success rate is much higher. When success rates are low, children seem to concentrate better when the skill themes are changed frequently and reviewed regularly.

Once you've written your yearly plan, use it as a guide and change it as often and as much as the particular situation requires. Write your outlines in pencil, leaving plenty of space for changes. As you gain in experience planning for skill themes, you will find that the process becomes easier and more predictable. But it will probably also always be changing. Again, we hope that you find these two sample overviews a good place to begin.

Sample Two-Day-a-Week Scope (72 Lessons) for Lower Elementary Classes

Topic of Lesson/Activity	Percentage of School Year[a]	Number of Days
Establishing a Learning Environment	4	3
Space Awareness	9	6
Effort	5	4
Relationships	5	4
Traveling	7	5
Chasing/Fleeing/Dodging	4	3
Jumping and Landing	5	4
Rolling	7	5
Balancing	5	4
Transferring Weight	5	4
Kicking and Punting	7	5
Throwing and Catching	7	5
Volleying	3	2
Dribbling	3	2
Striking with Rackets	4	3
Striking with Hockey Sticks	2	1
Striking with Golf Clubs	2	1
Striking with Bats	3	2
Fitness and Wellness	8	6
Field Day and Other Events	5	3
	100	72

[a]Percentages are approximate.

Note: This table does not match Table 6.4 on page 73. That is intentional so that adaptability of the skill theme approach is evident. Remember these are all just examples.

Sample Two-Day-a-Week Lesson Topics for Lower Elementary Classes (72 Days a Year)

Week	Chapter	Day	
1	7	1	Establishing an Environment for Learning (pp. 95–119)
	7	2	Establishing an Environment for Learning (cont.) (pp. 99–119)
2	14	1	Exploring Self-Space (p. 245)
	14	2	Exploring General Space (p. 246)
3	14	1	Traveling in Different Directions (p. 249)
	14	2	Traveling and Freezing at Different Levels (p. 251)
4	28	1	Teaching Physical Fitness, Physical Activity, and Wellness (pp. 597–623)
	24	2	Throwing at a Large Target (p. 474)
5	24	1	Catching a Rolling Ball (p. 474); Catching from a Skilled Thrower (p. 474)
	17	2	Traveling with Different Locomotor Patterns (p. 305): Sliding; Galloping; Hopping; Skipping (p. 306)
6	17	1	Performing Locomotor Sequences (p. 308)
	18	2	Traveling to Flee (p. 327); Fleeing from a Partner (p. 328)
7	18	1	Traveling to Dodge (p. 327); Dodging the Obstacles (p. 329)
	23	2	Kicking a Stationary Ball from a Stationary Position (p. 441)
8	23	1	Approaching a Stationary Ball and Kicking (p. 441); Kicking in the Air (p. 478)
	23	2	Dropping, Bouncing, and Kicking Lightweight Balls (p. 458); Dropping and Punting (p. 458)
9	20	1	Jumping and Landing: Basic Patterns (p. 360)
	28	2	Teaching Physical Fitness, Physical Activity, and Wellness (pp. 597–623)
10	25	1	Volleying Balloons in the Air (p. 504)
	25	2	Volleying a Ball Upward (Underhand Pattern) (p. 506)
11	25	1	Bouncing a Ball Down (Dribbling) Continuously (p. 521)
	25	2	Dribbling and Walking (p. 521)
12	15	1	Exploring Time (p. 262)
	15	2	Exploring Force (p. 268)
13	15	1	Traveling and Changing Force Qualities (p. 268)
	7	2	Establishing an Environment for Learning (pp. 95–119)
14	14	1	Exploring Pathways (p. 252)
	14	2	Exploring Extensions (p. 256)
15	17	1	Moving to Rhythms (p. 309)
	28	2	Teaching Physical Fitness, Physical Activity, and Wellness (pp. 597–623)
16	26	1	Striking Down; Striking Up (pp. 542, 543)
	26	2	Striking Up and Down (p. 543)
17	20	1	Jumping over Low Obstacles: Hoops (p. 362); Jumping over Low Obstacles: Hurdles (p. 362)
	20	2	Jumping a Turned Rope (p. 363); Jumping a Self-Turned Rope (p. 364)
18	16	1	Identifying Body Parts (p. 277); Balancing on Matching and Nonmatching Parts (p. 278)
	16	2	Traveling and Freezing in Different Body Shapes (p. 280)
19	28	1	Teaching Physical Fitness, Physical Activity, and Wellness (pp. 597–623)
	17	2	Leaping (p. 301)
20	16	1	Over, Under, Around, In Front Of, and Behind Concepts (p. 285)
	17	2	Locomotors and Rhythm: The Follow-Me Dance (p. 311)
21	22	1	Rocking on Different Body Parts (p. 418); Rocking to Match a Partner (p. 419)
	22	2	Rolling Sideways (p. 419); Rolling Forward (p. 422)
22		1	Special Event
	16	2	Matching (p. 288); Mirroring (p. 289); Matching and Mirroring (p. 290)
23	21	1	Balancing on Different Bases of Support (pp. 377, 378)
	21	2	Balancing in Different Body Shapes (pp. 378, 381)
24	22	1	Rolling in a Long, Narrow Position (Log Roll) (p. 419)
	22	2	Rocking Backward (p. 421)
25	22	1	Transferring Weight to Hands Momentarily (p. 404)
	22	2	Transferring Weight From Feet to Hands to Feet (p. 404)
26	24	1	Throwing Overhand (p. 476); Throwing Underhand (p. 476); Throwing Sidearm (p. 476)
	24	2	Throwing a Ball Against a Wall and Catching the Rebound (p. 484)

Sample Two-Day-a-Week Lesson Topics for Lower Elementary Classes (72 Days a Year)

Week	Chapter	Day	
27	21	1	Traveling on Low Gymnastics Equipment (p. 379)
	21	2	Balancing Sequence (p. 389)
28	15	1	Traveling and Flow (p. 269)
	22	2	Rolling After Jumping Off Equipment and Landing (p. 428)
29	22	1	Transferring Weight from Feet to Back with Rocking Action (p. 404)
	22	2	Transferring off Low Apparatus (Bench, Crate, or Low Table) (p. 406)
30	23	1	Kicking a Rolling Ball from a Stationary Position (p. 441); Kicking to a Partner (p. 453)
	23	2	Punting Different Types of Balls (p. 460)
31	28	1	Teaching Physical Fitness, Physical Activity, and Wellness (pp. 597–623)
	18	2	Dodging the Obstacles (p. 329)
32	24	1	Throwing and Catching with a Partner (p. 484)
	26	2	Striking a Ball Rebounding from a Wall (p. 552)
33	20	1	Jumping Far (p. 359); Jumping High (p. 359)
	27	2	Striking a Stationary Ball (p. 565); First Swings Golf (p. 590)
34	27	1	Striking to a Stationary Partner—Hockey
	27	2	Striking a Stationary Ball—Bats (p. 565)
35	28	1	Teaching Physical Fitness, Physical Activity, and Wellness (pp. 597–623)
	27	2	Striking a Pitched Ball—Bats (p. 584)
36		1	Field Day
		2	Field Day

Sample Two-Day-a-Week Scope for an Upper Elementary Class

Topic of Lesson/Activity	Percentage of School Year[a]	Number of Days
Establishing a Learning Environment	3	2
Space Awareness	3	2
Effort	5	4
Relationships	4	3
Traveling	4	3
Chasing/Fleeing/Dodging	4	3
Jumping and Landing	5	4
Rolling	7	5
Balancing	4	3
Transferring Weight	7	5
Kicking and Punting	7	5
Throwing and Catching	8	6
Volleying	5	4
Dribbling	4	3
Striking with Rackets	7	5
Striking with Hockey Sticks	3	2
Striking with Golf Clubs	3	2
Striking with Bats	3	2
Fitness and Wellness	8	6
Field Day and Other Events	4	3
	98	72

[a]Percentages are approximate.

Note: This table does not match Table 6.4 on page 73. That is intentional so that adaptability of the skill theme approach is evident. Remember these are all just examples.

Sample Two-Day-a-Week Lesson Topics for Upper Elementary Classes (72 Days a Year)

Week	Chapter	Day	
1	7	1	Establishing an Environment for Learning (pp. 95–119)
	7	2	Establishing an Environment for Learning (pp. 95–119)
2	14	1	Dodging in General Space w (p. 247)
	14	2	Combining Pathways, Levels, and Directions (p. 255)
3	22	1	Transferring Weight to Hands Momentarily (p. 404)
	22	2	Transferring Weight to Hands: Walking (p. 410)
4	23	1	Kicking to a Partner (p. 447)
	23	2	Keeping It Perfect: Zero, Zero (p. 450)
5	24	1	Throwing Overhand (p. 476); Throwing Underhand (p. 476); Throwing Sidearm (p. 476)
	24	2	Overhand Throw for Distance (p. 480)
6	18	1	Dodging Stationary Obstacles (p. 330); Dodging and Faking Moves to Avoid a Chaser (p. 331)
	18	2	Dodging and Faking Moves to Avoid a Chaser (p. 331)
7	23	1	Punting for Distance (p. 461)
	28	2	Teaching Physical Fitness, Physical Activity, and Wellness (pp. 597–623)
8	15	1	Combining Sport Skills and Time (p. 265)
	15	2	Using Imagery and Force (p. 268)
9	16	1	Creating Postcard Sculptures (p. 281)
	16	2	Creating Body Shapes in the Air (p. 281)
10	17	1	Performing Locomotor Sequences (p. 308)
	17	2	Traveling in Slow Motion: The Sports Dance (p. 313)
11	20	1	Jumping a Self-Turned Rope (p. 364)
	20	2	Jumping and Landing Task Sheet (p. 368)
12	22	1	Rolling after Jumping off Equipment and Landing (p. 428)
	22	2	Rolling and Traveling Quickly (p. 432)
13	25	1	Volleying a Ball Upward (Overhead Pattern) (p. 510)
	25	2	Volleying to a Partner (Overhead Pattern) (p. 511)
14	21	1	Performing Inverted Balances (p. 384)
	21	2	Balancing Symmetrically and Nonsymmetrically (p. 381)
15	16	1	Meeting and Parting in a Cooperative Group (p. 292)
	28	2	Teaching Physical Fitness, Physical Activity, and Wellness (pp. 597–623)
16	15	1	Following Flow Sentences (p. 270)
	15	2	Combining Time, Force, and Flow (p. 271)
17	22	1	Rolling over Low Hurdles; Rolling on Low Equipment (p. 432, p. 433)
	22	2	Rolling, Balancing, and Rolling (p. 431)
18	25	1	Dribbling and Traveling (p. 526)
	25	2	Dribbling Against an Opponent: One-on-One (p. 531)
19	26	1	Striking Backhand to the Wall) (p. 551)
	26	2	Striking a Ball Rebounding from a Wall (p. 552)
20	17	1	Shadowing a Partner's Travel (p. 316)
	28	2	Teaching Physical Fitness, Physical Activity, and Wellness (pp. 597–623)
21	20	1	Jumping to an Accented Beat (p. 371)
	22	2	Transferring Weight to Hands and Forming a Bridge (p. 410)
22	21	1	Traveling into and out of Balances by Rolling (p. 394); Moving out of and into Balances by Stretching, Curling and Twisting (p. 393)
	22	2	Rolling to Express an Idea (p. 431)
23	22	1	Transferring Weight onto Large Apparatus (p. 411)
	22	2	Combining Weight Transfer and Balances into Sequences on Mats and Apparatus (p. 415)
24	25	1	Volleying Game: Child-Designed (p. 513)
	25	2	Volleying with Different Body Parts while Traveling (p. 518)
25		1	Special Event
	28	2	Teaching Physical Fitness, Physical Activity, and Wellness (pp. 597–623)

Sample Two-Day-a-Week Lesson Topics for Upper Elementary Classes (72 Days a Year)

Week	Chapter	Day	
26	25	1	Dribble Tag (pp. 532–533)
	26	2	Hitting Cooperatively and Continuously with a Partner (pp. 553–554)
27	26	1	Striking Upward in a Dynamic Situation (p. 556)
	26	2	Team Striking across a Net (p. 558)
28	24	1	Throwing and Catching with a Partner (p. 484)
	24	2	Throwing and Catching While Traveling (p. 488)
29	27	1	Striking to Varying Distances—Golf (p. 591)
	27	2	Playing Hoop Golf (p. 592)
30	18	1	Dodging Semistationary Objects (p. 332)
	28	2	Teaching Physical Fitness, Physical Activity, and Wellness (pp. 597–623)
31	23	1	Dribble and Kick: Playing Soccer Golf (p. 452)
	23	2	Punting to a Partner (p. 463)
32	27	1	Traveling and Striking While Changing Pathways—Hockey (p. 570)
	27	2	Striking to a Stationary Partner—Hockey (p. 568)
33	24	1	Throwing for Distance and Accuracy (p. 491)
	28	2	Teaching Physical Fitness, Physical Activity, and Wellness (pp. 597–623)
34	24	1	Throwing and Catching in a Small-Sided Invasion Game (p. 496)
	20	2	Jumping to Catch (p. 368); Jumping to Throw (p. 370)
35	27	1	Striking a Pitched Ball—Bats (p. 586)
	27	2	One-Base Baseball (p. 588)
36		1	Field Day
		2	Field Day

Active Teaching Skills

Part 3 contains seven chapters describing many of the teaching skills reflective teachers use to help children learn and enjoy physical activity. Unlike Parts 4 and 5 that focus on the content (what to teach), the chapters in Part 3 focus on the teaching process, or pedagogy—how to teach.

Chapters 7 and 8 provide concrete examples related to creating a learning environment conducive to student learning. Chapter 7, "Establishing an Environment for Learning," describes many of the techniques teachers use to create positive attitudes toward physical education, ideas for fostering an atmosphere conducive to learning, and safety procedures for teaching inside and outside. This is a critical chapter. Successfully establishing an environment for learning allows students to spend more time learning and teachers to spend less time managing and dealing with off-task behavior.

Invariably, however, there will be some children who are off task, and Chapter 8, "Maintaining Appropriate Behavior," provides practical ideas for positively maintaining a productive environment while helping students learn to be responsible for their own behavior. Specific examples from actual teaching situations illustrate how to increase appropriate behavior, decrease inappropriate behavior, and maintain proper behavior. Additional techniques described in Chapter 8 include how to interact positively with children; how to work with them one on one; how to apply "punishment," such as time-outs and desists; and how to follow worthwhile reward systems, such as class rewards and tokens.

Chapter 9, "Instructional Approaches," provides an overview of the pedagogy of skill themes by describing a variety of different instructional techniques used to create active learning experiences for children. This chapter explains a number of approaches that go beyond direct interactive instruction to indirect instruction—including task sheets, stations, peer teaching, cooperative learning, guided discovery, and child-designed instruction. Each of these alternatives provides a more engaging way for children to learn and more fully addresses the cognitive and affective goals of our physical education classes. Links are made between the approaches suggested in the chapter to specific examples in Chapters 14–27.

Chapter 10, "Adapting the Content for Diverse Learners," provides an overview of the philosophy of inclusion and focuses on specific teaching strategies to help create an inclusive environment. One of the critical teaching skills for a reflective teacher is the ability to observe with understanding. For this reason, we dedicate an entire chapter to this process. Chapter 11, "Observing Student Responses," focuses on observing children's responses to movement tasks and includes a format for observing classes that includes safety, on-task behavior, and the movements of the entire class and individual children. Two observation techniques of back-to-the-wall and scanning are suggested as effective ways in which to observe.

Chapter 12, "Assessing Student Learning," helps answer the question, "Are my students learning what I want them to learn as a result of my teaching?" Designed as "assessment for learning" tasks, many of these techniques are ongoing (formative) rather than being a culminating experience at the end of a series of lessons or at the end of several years. The examples we use were designed by teachers and have been successfully used in their programs.

Chapter 13, "Reflecting on Teaching," provides practical techniques for analyzing the process of reflective teaching. It gives a cycle teachers can use to reflect on their own teaching. In a nutshell, Chapter 13 provides insights into the question, "How am I doing as a reflective teacher?"

Parts 4 and 5 (Chapters 14–27) focus on the content of the skill theme approach. These are important chapters, but the teaching process described in Chapters 7–13 is equally as critical. How we teach is just as important as what we teach. If attention is not paid to the pedagogy, there is less chance of providing worthwhile, enjoyable learning experiences for our students. In *Children Moving*, the content and the pedagogy are inextricably linked.

Establishing an Environment for Learning

A well run lesson that teaches nothing is just as useless as a chaotic lesson in which no academic work is possible.

—WALTER DOYLE

Drawn by children at Monfort, Chappelow or Shawsheen Elementary Schools, Greeley, CO.
Courtesy of Lizzy Ginger; Tia Ziegler

Key Concepts

- A learning environment are the conditions the teacher creates in a classroom that supports (or hinders) learning by the students.

- A learning environment consists of two components, a managerial component and an instructional component, both of which are necessary if physical education is to reach its full learning potential.

- The managerial component establishes the structures that allow the classroom to function effortlessly.

- The instructional component refers to the subject matter activities that allow students to learn physical education content.

- The development of a managerial component is a necessary, but not sufficient, condition for student learning.

- As part of the managerial component, reflective teachers develop protocols, including rules and routines that ensure smooth existence in the gymnasium and on the playground.

- Rules are general expectations for behavior that cover a wide variety of situations; routines are procedures for accomplishing specific managerial tasks within a class.

- Rules and routines are most effective when they reflect a positive environment while teaching children to be responsible for their own behavior.

- The instructional component includes creating purposely and progressively developed content, effective communication, focused feedback, and the accommodation of individual differences.

- Content development includes the use of tasks, cues, and challenges.

- The KISS principle, using one cue at a time, clear demonstrations, and pinpointing are all aspects of communication.

- Congruent feedback provides focused information to children about the skill they are practicing.

- Individual differences can be accommodated through the use of teaching by invitation and intratask variation.

- A major responsibility of every reflective teacher is to provide students with a physically and psychologically safe learning environment.

As we indicated in the opening chapters of the book, the goal of physical education is student learning and that requires purposeful teaching. As teachers, it is our responsibility to design and maintain an environment in which learning is supported and allowed to take place. We have to set the stage for student learning by making physical education a place that is warm and supportive and encourages student performance and achievement. This environment is a necessary, though not sufficient, condition for learning (Rink 2014). This means that without such an environment, there is little chance learning will occur; with it, learning is still not possible unless the instructional activities are carried out and appropriate curriculum is in place.

Establishing a learning environment involves two separate components, managerial and instructional, to place students in contact with—and to keep them in contact with—the subject matter at a high success rate for as long as possible. These components have been compared to systems, and similar to a smoothly operating piece of machinery, both must be present for the classroom to operate (Tousignant and Siedentop 1983). Regardless of the term used, both instructional and managerial structures must be present to establish an environment that has the potential for learning. One without the other is not adequate. You can manage without teaching, but you cannot teach without managing.

A component can be defined as a regular pattern of practices used to accomplish the class functions. The word cloud in Figure 7.1 indicates the multitude of learning environment aspects that need to be developed and maintained; it is obvious that this is an intricate task, but it is not magic. The managerial component refers to the non–subject-matter activities necessary for a class to run smoothly and efficiently over a period

©Melissa Parker

Figure 7.1 Learning environment word cloud.

of time. The instructional component refers to the subject-matter activities designed to see that children learn what is desired by participating in physical education. Both components need to be developed when establishing a learning environment. All too often, physical education teachers establish a managerial aspect (Mowling et al. 2004) but neglect to focus on an instructional aspect or component. This chapter and Chapter 8 are about the managerial components of the learning environment. This chapter plus Chapters 6, 9, 11, and 12 are about the instructional components of the learning environment.

For each of these components, certain teacher practices ensure that the component achieves what the teacher desires. A well-operating component, either managerial or instructional, establishes and maintains student responsibility for appropriate conduct, on-task engagement, and learning outcomes (see Chapter 6 and "The Instructional Component" section in this chapter). The practices that accomplish this are known as accountability measures (Hastie and Siedentop 2007). These accountability measures are so important that without them both the instructional and managerial components become dysfunctional (Doyle 1980). Traditional accountability measures in physical education include tests, grades, attendance, teacher reprimands, and punishment. These types of accountability measures are now thought to be largely inappropriate if student learning is the intended outcome of physical education. In fact, they undermine learning and communicate to the public that physical education has little to teach other than to dress and show up for class. This chapter introduces you to a variety of other teacher practices that serve as accountability measures in establishing the managerial and instructional components necessary for a smoothly running class in which learning occurs.

Although the development of a component sounds rigid and sterile, the type of component developed and how it is implemented reflect what we believe not only about physical education but also about education, children, and society. It mirrors what we feel is important about our school, our gymnasium, our students, and ourselves. All components must accomplish certain things—smooth and consistent gymnasium operation—yet it is how the component is put into action that says who we are and what we stand for. For example, a managerial component that is solely teacher developed and directed indicates a belief that student input or helping students learn to make decisions isn't important. On the other hand, the complete lack of a managerial component could indicate a teacher's abdication of all responsibility and a belief that it doesn't make any difference what we do (Ennis 1995).

However, components that seek student voice and help students learn to make decisions about managerial (noninstructional) situations and instructional (learning) situations indicate that we value students and have taken the responsibility not only to teach psychomotor content but also to teach the larger goals of personal and social responsibility (Dyson 2006; Parker et al. 2018; Parker and Stiehl 2015). The *National Standards* indicate that one of the goals of physical education is to develop individuals who exhibit responsible personal and social behavior that respects self and others (SHAPE America 2014). Although the classroom management literature relies a great deal on behavior management and business, where efficiency is paramount, there are educational models in which the development of responsibility and self-direction are important (Hellison 2011). In these models, although initial efficiency may be slightly compromised and the teacher must be willing to relinquish some control, students gradually move toward more independent learning and responsibility.

It is our belief that physical education is child centered and that students should develop increasing responsibility for their own behavior, attitudes, and learning. Therefore, the prevailing philosophy of this chapter is the development of components designed to accomplish the goals of self-directed learning and behavior. In other words, just like fitness and motor skill development, responsibility is part of the content with which students must stay in contact. See Box 7-1 for sample recommendations for establishing a learning environment from the Appropriate Practice Guidelines.

> *Classroom management helps run an effective classroom, but doesn't solve the social problems.*
>
> —**DON HELLISON**

Gymnasium Atmosphere

When the weather forecaster announces an impending low-pressure system, we know what it will feel like—heavy, humid, and often accompanied by rain or snow. Similarly, with high-pressure systems, we know to expect fair weather and dry air. The atmosphere of the gym is much the same except it is created by the teacher, not by weather systems. Regardless of the component—managerial or instructional—the atmosphere in the gym needs to be emotionally safe and positive. If this atmosphere is not created, then the remainder of this book is probably useless.

Box 7-1

Selected Appropriate and Inappropriate Physical Education Practices

Components: The Learning Environment and Instructional Strategies

Appropriate Practice

- Physical educators systematically plan for, develop, and maintain a positive learning environment focused on maximizing learning and participation, in an atmosphere of respect and support from the teacher and the peers of the child.
- The environment is supportive of all children, and promotes the development of a positive self-concept. Children are given chances to try, to fail, and to try again, free of criticism or harassment from the teacher or other students.
- Programs are designed to guide children to take responsibility for their own behavior and learning. Emphasis is on intrinsic, rather than extrinsic, incentives.
- Fair and consistent classroom management practices encourage student responsibility for positive behavior. Students are often included in the process of developing class rules/agreements.
- Bullying and inappropriate student remarks and behaviors are dealt with immediately and firmly.
- Physical educators make every effort possible to create a safe learning environment for students (e.g., safety considerations and plans are a part of every daily lesson plan). Routines and rules are developed with safety in mind.
- Activities are carefully selected to ensure they match the ability level of the students and are also safe for all of the students regardless of their ability level.
- Facilities and equipment are maintained and closely inspected daily for safety hazards (e.g., free of glass, proper ground cover under equipment).
- The physical educator creates an environment that is inclusive and supportive of all students regardless of their race, ethnic origin, gender, sexual orientation, religion, or physical ability. These differences are acknowledged, appreciated, and respected.
- All children (boys and girls, all skill levels) have equal opportunities for participation and interaction with the teacher (e.g., leadership, playing "skilled" positions, teacher feedback).
- All children, regardless of developmental level and ability, are challenged at an appropriate level.
- Both boys and girls are encouraged, supported, and socialized toward successful achievement in all of the content that is taught in physical education (e.g., dance is for everyone).

- Physical educators use gender-neutral language (e.g., students).
- Clear goals and objectives for student learning and performance are communicated to students, parents, and administrators.
- Physical educators form pairs, groups, and teams in ways that preserve the dignity and self-respect of every child (e.g., randomly, by fitness or skill level when necessary, or by a class system such as birthdays, squads, colors, numbers).

Inappropriate Practice

- The environment is not supportive or safe. As a result, some children feel embarrassed, humiliated, and generally uncomfortable in physical education class (e.g., teacher makes degrading or sarcastic remarks).
- Only highly skilled or physically fit children are viewed as successful learners. The teacher and peers overlook and/or ignore students if they are not highly skilled or physically fit.
- Children behave appropriately because they are fearful of receiving a poor grade or other punishment if they do not follow the teacher's rules.
- The rules are unclear and may vary from day to day.
- Verbal or nonverbal behavior that is hurtful to other children is overlooked and ignored.
- Teachers allow or ignore unsafe practices in their classes. Children are permitted to ignore the safety of others in the class (e.g., pushing, shoving, or tackling children in ball games) or use equipment unsafely (e.g., swinging bats in close proximity to others).
- Human target games (dodgeball) and/or drills that allow aggressive behaviors toward other students are permitted.
- No regular facility safety inspection occurs. Dangerous, broken, or outdated equipment is used.
- The physical education environment supports highly skilled children more fully than children who have less skill development (e.g., posters on display are predominantly of male professional athletes from the major sports).
- Teachers inadvertently promote exclusion by allowing student captains to pick teams or by arbitrarily separating teams by gender or skill level (e.g., popular or highly skilled students are chosen first and cliques are evident).

National Association for Sport and Physical Education, *Appropriate instructional practice guidelines for elementary school physical education.* 3rd ed., Reston, VA: National Association for Sport and Physical Education, 2009. Copyright ©2009 by SHAPE America. Reprinted with permission from SHAPE America - Society of Physical Educators, 1900 Association Drive, Reston, VA 20191, www.shapeamerica.org.

As discussed in Chapter 4, of all the teacher practices involved in establishing a positive learning environment, one of the most important pieces is also one of the least tangible and most easily compromised: teacher attitude or approach to teaching and children. This is essentially the translation of a teacher's beliefs into practice. The teacher's self-image and feelings about teaching, about physical education, and about children all influence atmosphere. The enthusiastic teacher conveys this attitude to the children and as a result heightens their enthusiasm for physical education. The teacher who views physical education as a time for learning communicates this feeling in a way that all the children adhere to certain criteria for behavior. Likewise, the teacher who believes that children are vessels to be molded and should be compliant with teacher expectations, whether they seem reasonable or not, communicates to children that they are not capable of making significant decisions.

Even though children's motivation for participation in physical education changes with age (Xiang, McBride, and Guan 2004), children at any age need to belong and feel competent, useful, potent, and optimistic in order to be motivated to learn. When those needs are met, people commit wholeheartedly to an endeavor (Sagor 2002). The study of physical activity settings has yielded similar findings (Curran and Standage 2017; Ward and Parker 2013). The teacher–student relationship is at the heart of this notion of class management/atmosphere that supports student learning.

In looking at thousands of teachers, Marzano and Marzano (2003) found three aspects contributed to the teacher–student relationship. First, teachers who had a positive relationship with youngsters displayed teacher dominance. While sounding negative, this is actually a positive trait that means teachers provide a clear purpose and strong guidance in content and behavior by establishing clear expectations and consequences as well as clear learning goals and the assertive behaviors to accomplish those goals. Second, appropriate levels of cooperation (characterized by strong feelings of membership, engagement, and commitment) were present in classrooms where real learning occurs. To create these levels of cooperation, the teacher provided students with flexible learning goals, took a personal interest in students, and used positive and equitable (not equal) classroom behaviors. Finally, the teacher–student relationship was enhanced by the teacher's awareness of high-need students (including those who were passive-aggressive, had attention problems, were perfectionists, or were socially inept). It is this atmosphere that must be created in the gym if we want all children to be attracted to being physically active for a lifetime.

It is our belief that few teachers would argue with the notion of creating an environment that empowers children; however, the act of doing it is difficult. Several strategies may help make your gym a place that attracts children to physical activity for a lifetime while helping them become self-directed, responsible learners.

1. *Change, challenge, choice.* The practices of change, challenge, and choice (Stiehl, Morris, and Sinclair 2008) can be employed as a way to differentiate instruction and to ensure the gymnasium is a place where all learners feel competent, useful, potent, optimistic, and empowered. Although slightly modified here, the premise of Stiehl and colleagues' work is that any aspect of an activity can (and should) be changed so the learner is allowed to be successful at the appropriate level. For example, equipment, space, or the task itself can be modified (see intratask variation examples later in this chapter). The challenges listed in Chapters 17–27 allow tasks to be adapted to more appropriately challenge all children. Choice empowers and intrinsically motivates children by allowing them input that meets their needs (Mowling et al. 2004). Choice can be offered in anything from the type of equipment used to how far apart partners stand. The technique of teaching by invitation provides a mechanism for allowing choice in activities. See Chapter 10 for additional examples of change, challenge, and choice in physical education.

2. *Catch children being good.* Positive reinforcement and praise need to dominate interactions with children. Unfortunately, the reverse is usually true. Subtle nagging statements such as "I am waiting for you to be quiet" and "Anytime now" are more often heard than "I like the way you came in and began your warm-up" or "Thanks for listening; it makes my job easier."

3. *People are not for hurting.* Children should be psychologically as well as physically safe in physical education. Hurting refers to everything from physical safety to inappropriate practices, such as games that pinpoint and demean (e.g., dodgeball and the like) to name-calling and bullying.

4. *Never use sarcasm.* As adults we have become used to sarcasm. Children take it literally. It has no place in physical education.

5. *There are no stupid questions.* As a friend of ours puts it, "It is OK not to know, but it is not OK to continue not knowing" (Stiehl 2011). The implication is that we need to make our gymnasiums places where children are free to ask questions.

6. *Physical education is for everyone.* Sports are for those who choose to participate in them. They are

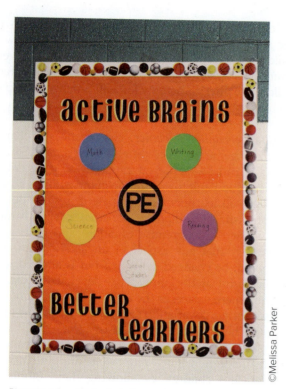

Physical education bulletin board.

©Melissa Parker

Box 7-2

Music

The use of music in physical education makes the environment more engaging while also serving as a stop/start signal and promoting physical activity.

Strategies for playing:

- A CD player
- A television or computer
- Docking stations for electronic devices. These stations allow you to connect your cell phone or tablet for projection.
- If you are lucky, there will be a built-in system in your teaching space.

Sources:

- Personal CDs and playlists (with or without music breaks)
- Music streaming (e.g., Amazon Prime, iTunes, Pandora, Deezer, YouTube, Spotify)

Whatever the source and the method of playing:

- Music should be mostly upbeat and a mix of electronic, pop, or dance beats.
- Music should be "clean." Listen to the lyrics carefully.
- A remote control to the system allows you to use the music effortlessly.
- Keep up with current children's movies as most have popular songs in them.

Think about letting children select the music or bring in their favorites (remember to review the music first); this is a great way to find new music.

usually dominated by the highly skilled and sometimes aggressive children. Physical education is an educational activity designed for every child of every skill level. This means multiple forms of equipment, multiple types of games at the same time, and intratask variation are all needed.

7. *Walk your talk.* We chose to be teachers. We are role models.

8. *Decorate.* For many, the gym is a scary place. Make your gym an attractive place to be—decorate the walls, paint with cheerful colors, keep the gym sparkling clean, make sure the lights are bright, and use music whenever possible (it is also a great stop/start signal; see Box 7-2). To make the gym more like other elementary school classrooms, add posters, pictures, student work, and bulletin boards. If these depict children of different races, genders, ethnic backgrounds, and disabilities engaging in physical activity, it helps children recognize that physical education and physical activity are for all. If pictures of only elite athletes, only boys, only the able-bodied, only one race, or only the fit are displayed, then this subtly reinforces that physical activity is only for certain groups of people.

It is wise to check yourself regarding these practices on a weekly basis to make sure you haven't slipped into an unproductive pattern.

When establishing the learning environment, the focus is on fostering acceptable behavior and creating an atmosphere appropriate for a physical education class. As in any class, some actions may be required to maintain the learning environment. However, an established, consistent, positive environment in the gymnasium and appropriate tasks go a long way in allowing students to know exactly what is expected of them and stimulate enthusiasm for learning. The remainder of this chapter deals with ways teachers have successfully developed both managerial and instructional components to establish a productive learning environment. Remember, a learning environment can't be maintained if it has not been established.

The Managerial Component

Some educators use the terms *management* and *discipline* synonymously; we don't. Developing the managerial component of a classroom environment is proactive; discipline is reactive. Discipline is required when a child's behavior is disruptive and the teacher needs to prevent the disruption from occurring again. The managerial component could be considered a "first base" skill because it establishes structures or protocols through which the physical education class becomes predictable and operates smoothly (Rink 2014; Tannehill, van der Mars, and MacPhail 2015). This component essentially consists of two aspects: creating the learning environment (this chapter) and maintaining it (Chapter 8). The creation involves the development of protocols, the rules, and routines that allow the gymnasium to function.

When they begin school, most children have few preconceptions about how a physical education learning environment will be structured. Within a short time, they learn to function according to the teacher's expectations. The managerial component establishes the limits for behavior and the teacher's expectations for the students. Because of our belief in children developing responsibility for themselves and our dislike for constantly feeling as if it is our job to control students, the managerial components we develop focus on establishing an appropriate learning environment and also on having students take more and more responsibility for it. If youngsters are allowed to develop unacceptable behavior in physical education class, the teacher will find it increasingly difficult to alter their behavior. Thus, it's crucial for teachers to establish an appropriate learning environment during their very first lessons with the students. How well they do this sets the tone for the remainder of the year. We've found the following techniques helpful in developing and holding students accountable for managerial components.

Developing Protocols

Research indicates that effective teachers develop gymnasium protocols that help their gyms run smoothly and minimize disruptions, thus maximizing students' learning time (Jones and Jones 2016). These protocols consist of both rules and routines. Rules identify general expectations for behavior that cover a variety of situations. Though rules are intended to address both acceptable and unacceptable behavior, they quite often focus on inappropriate behavior. A concept that some teachers have found useful in changing to a positive focus is explaining rules as guidelines to help children

examine their behavior and attitudes as they affect themselves and others (Jones and Jones 2016). Routines are procedures for accomplishing specific duties in a class. They are different from rules in that they usually refer to specific activities and are usually aimed at accomplishing tasks rather than forbidding behavior. Evidence has shown that effective teachers spend the first few days of the year teaching their classes protocols (Bohn, Roehrig, and Pressley 2004).

Protocols generally stay in effect for the school year (unless you find one that isn't working or discover that something has been neglected). It is frustrating and time-consuming to repeat the protocols for new students or for students who were absent when they were taught. Thus, we have found it valuable to digitally record the lessons at the beginning of the year when protocols and safety are presented and taught. When a new student joins the class, the recording can be used at school or at home to orient that student to your gymnasium protocols. The recording is also a useful resource to share classroom procedures with parents at parent–teacher meetings or, if needed, to document the teaching of rules and routines to a class. In addition, some teachers have made a pamphlet of protocols that can be shared with parents and new students. Still other teachers have included both protocols and safety information on the physical education page of the school Web site. These are also good ways to remind students of safety procedures.

Establishing Rules and Expectations That Reflect a Positive Environment

Establishing rules is more than providing the gymnasium "laws"; it also sets the general atmosphere of the gym and conveys the teacher's beliefs about control and responsibility. For example, if all the rules are developed by the teacher, are written as a series of don'ts, and are narrow and punitive, this sends the message that the teacher is the ultimate control figure and children are merely people to be controlled. However, if children provide input and the rules are guiding and broader, allowing children some part in the decision-making, then the message is that children are people learning to be responsible; they are capable of making decisions and have self-worth. These messages may appear subtle, but they are powerful to students. Therefore, our choice in the development of rules and routines is to be broad and guiding rather than narrow and restricting. They are essentially "ways of working" by which our classes have agreed to operate.

Children who understand the expectations within which they are to function are less likely to test the

Box 7-3

Responsibility Levels

Level I: Respecting the Rights and Feelings of Others

Self-control
The right to be included
The right to peaceful conflict resolution

Level II: Participation and Effort

Exploring effort
Trying new things
A personal definition of success

Level III: Self-Direction

On-task independence
Personal plan
Balancing current and future needs
"Striving against external forces"

Level IV: Caring about and Helping Others

Prerequisite interpersonal skills
Compassion
Contributing member of the community and beyond
Without rewards

Level V: Going Beyond

Being responsible at home and school, with friends
Positive role model

Source: D. Hellison, *Teaching responsibility through physical activity*, 3rd ed. (Champaign, IL: Human Kinetics, 2011).

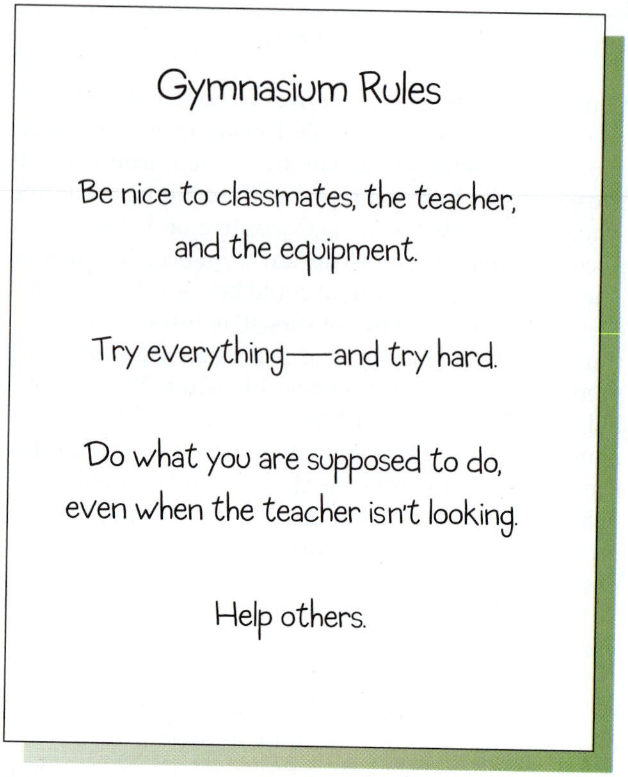

Gymnasium Rules

Be nice to classmates, the teacher, and the equipment.

Try everything—and try hard.

Do what you are supposed to do, even when the teacher isn't looking.

Help others.

Figure 7.2 Physical education bulletin board.

teacher's flexibility and more likely to cooperate. A few rules that the teacher states clearly and adheres to consistently can be helpful to everyone. One set of guidelines we have found to be effective—that helps children examine their behaviors and attitudes—is an adaptation of Hellison's five levels of responsibility (Hellison 2011; see Box 7-3). These guidelines are broad enough to encompass the aspects necessary for safe group survival in the gym while guiding students well beyond simple compliance into responsibility.

Figure 7.2 shows how these guidelines can be translated into class rules. A discussion of the guidelines can cover many things normally included in narrower rules. For example, respect for the rights and feelings of others can include all aspects of pushing, stopping, and looking when the teacher talks, being a good

sport, interrupting, use of equipment, and the like. The guideline of participation and effort is broad enough to include the whole idea of trying hard (even when you might not want to), giving 100 percent, and similar ideas. Interestingly enough, these two guidelines alone encompass most of the rules to which we are accustomed in the gymnasium. The third and fourth guidelines in Figure 7.2 provide an extension we consider important in our teaching. The third indicates that students should be able to work on their own, without the teacher's constant attention—a concept most of us relish. The fourth is one of our ultimate goals—that students care for and help each other. This can include actions as small as handing stray balls back to their owners or as broad as helping another student learn a skill.

Another way to present guidelines that encourage student responsibility is through the "five-finger contract" (Prouty and Panicucci 2007). In the five-finger contract, each finger represents a goal or guideline and the hand provides a mnemonic device for easy recall. While the guidelines may vary, the version of the five-finger contract that we use includes the goals of creating value for yourself; taking care of yourself; respecting others; committing to trying new things; and helping others. Figure 7.3 indicates how these constructs are translated into "kid-friendly language" and presented

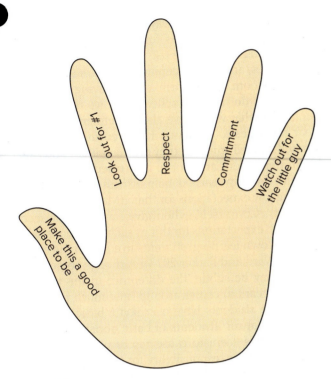

Figure 7.3 The five-finger contract.

in an instructionally friendly manner. Regardless of what values you choose or how they are presented, we have found that when we establish these types of guidelines and constantly adhere to them, students learn to manage themselves and develop the concepts of personal and social responsibility we desire as outcomes of our programs. With such a managerial component developed and in place, we find that we are "managing" less, have more time for teaching, and have more fun teaching because we do not need to behave like police officers.

Rules are necessary for group well-being and development. The picture on page 104 shows another set of gymnasium rules teachers have found successful in eliciting the learning environment they desire. You may wish to establish different rules; if so, the following general guidelines may help you:

- Explain why the rules are necessary. Children are far more cooperative with rules that make sense to them than with seemingly arbitrary regulations. In some cases, children can help make the necessary rules.
- State rules positively. Whenever possible, avoid using the words *don't*, *not*, and *no*. In essence, it is more productive to tell children what to do than what not to do.
- Keep the number of rules to a minimum. A good guide is to state no more than five rules.

- Post rules in an attractive fashion so they can be seen and read easily.
- Make sure the children understand the rules. To teach rules most efficiently, first describe and demonstrate the desired behavior, then have the children rehearse the correct behavior (this usually takes more than one rehearsal). Finally, provide feedback, especially the first time you ask the children to use a routine (the first days of school).
- Design, teach, post, and practice the consequences of breaking the rules.
- Especially in the beginning, prompt students toward appropriate behavior and reinforce appropriate behavior. Let students know when they've done something correctly.

One of the obvious questions, although students don't always ask it, is, "What happens when one of the rules is broken?" No matter how well we teach, some of the children will break some of the rules, so we find it helps at the outset of the year to describe the consequences for breaking a rule. These consequences are for relatively minor offenses; major offenses are discussed in Chapter 8.

The teacher needs to develop consequences appropriate to the particular teaching situation. Many teachers use a series of consequences similar to the following, which allow children to first take responsibility for their actions before the teacher does.

1. The first time a child violates a rule—for example, the child fails to stop and listen—give the child a verbal prompt.
2. The second time a child violates a rule in the same class period, ask if the child "needs to sit out for a while." The child's response to this question is usually amazingly honest, and the question places the responsibility on the child for his or her actions. To increase student reflection and responsibility, the child can reenter class when ready without consulting the teacher.
3. The third time a child violates a rule, tell the child to take a time-out. As in the previous step, the child may reenter class when he or she feels ready.
4. The fourth time a child violates the same rule, have the child sit out until a personal plan can be developed regarding his or her actions (see Chapter 8). This usually means the remainder of the class. Although sitting out the remainder of the class may seem a bit harsh, as teachers we need to be able to teach. A continually disruptive child takes our attention away from other children who deserve it just as much.

Be aware that some lapse in following rules may be minor or a nonproblem, whereas other actions are

Attractively posting classroom rules is an effective way to guide children's actions.

©Melissa Parker

major problems that can escalate. Be sure not to over-react to minor problems so children do not respect the actions taken. See Chapter 8 for further discussion of maintaining the learning environment.

As much as possible, the consequences for violating a rule should be noninterruptive. We try to deliver a consequence with a word or two and avoid interfering with the learning experiences of the rest of the class. One final comment about time-outs: They are effective when the children find the lesson interesting. If the lesson is uninteresting, dull, or inappropriate for a child, then the time-out becomes a reward rather than a consequence for off-task behavior.

Establishing Gymnasium Routines

Routines are protocols designed to help the gymnasium run smoothly and efficiently. Remember, routines are specific ways to accomplish certain tasks in a lesson; they should remain consistent as much as possible. Routines also reflect what we feel is important. Here are key areas in which physical education teachers find routines to be effective: entry to and exit from the

gymnasium/playground; ways to obtain, handle, and return equipment; signals for attention and starting and stopping activity; the use of space; boundaries for work spaces; and housekeeping activities such as going to the restroom, getting drinks, and leaving the room.

Routines do much to reflect what we think of students and what we believe about them and thus send clear messages to students. How routines are implemented can tell students they are competent and capable or dependent and not to be trusted. Teachers can actually develop learned helplessness in students by creating low expectations for them (Martinek and Griffin 1994). Conversely, when given and taught seemingly high expectations for things such as responsibility and their own learning, students lived up to the expectations (Ward and Parker 2013). Although some of the actions may be subtle, the difference in the two scenarios appears to center around how much perceived control the students have over some basic decisions. Routines that rob students of basic decisions or allow no alternative seem to cause resentment and let the students transfer responsibility for their actions to the teacher. Alternatively, routines that allow students some flexibility and decision making seem to empower them. Consider using some of the following suggestions as you develop routines for your classes.

Entering and Leaving the Gym We have found it beneficial to have a standardized way of entering and leaving the gym. It is helpful to have the classroom teacher bring students to the gym and to have a set routine when the students get to the gym. Some teachers have children sit on the center circle or line; others post an initial activity often called DIN (Do It Now; for example, an initial activity might consist of something as simple as finding a partner and moving around the space until the teacher says stop); still others have children in predetermined groups go to a predetermined part of the gym to warm up on their own. Children need to have something to do when they arrive or they will make something up themselves. Exiting should be the same as entering. Most schools require students to walk quietly in lines to and from places in the school. It is helpful if classroom teachers meet their classes in the gym for return to the classroom.

Stopping and Listening Skills In a successful learning environment, noise rarely exceeds a reasonable level that can be thought of as productive noise. Hollering, shrieking, and yelling, although appropriate at recess, are not appropriate in physical education. The children shouldn't be expected to be silent, but they should be able to hear a teacher speaking in a reasonable tone considerably below a shout.

One of the seemingly hardest routines to teach children in physical education is to stop activity quickly and listen to the teacher. When a teacher must spend time quieting the children so the entire class can hear an explanation or comment, the amount of time left for activities is decreased. Thus it's imperative that children learn to respond quickly and appropriately to the teacher's signal for quiet. We have seen teachers use a variety of signals, including dimming of the lights, verbal cues such as "freeze," turning music off and on, a hand drum or tambourine, or simply the raising of a hand. Regardless of the signal, it should be clear what the students are to do when the signal is given—hands on knees, eyes on teacher, equipment on floor, and the like. Listening games (Box 7-4) can be used to teach children to listen as they move and to respond quickly to the teacher's signals.

Equipment Getting and putting away equipment seem to be two of the biggest issues in class. We have

---

Box 7-4

Listening Games

While using movement concepts and skills as the physical activity, these listening games are management activities designed to help the children learn to stop and listen quickly. As you use them, do not single out or penalize children who are slow to respond. Embarrassment is counterproductive; you want children to enjoy exercise, not to think of it as unpleasant. Remember, learning management protocols takes the same practice as learning motor skills.

Stop and Go

Children travel in general space in a scattered formation. Once the children are able to (1) walk without touching others and (2) stay far away from others as they walk, you can begin to play Stop and Go. When you say "Stop," the children should stop and freeze instantly. When you say "Go," they should begin to travel again. Don't shout the signals—*speak* them so the children become accustomed to listening for your voice at a reasonable level. Vary the time of each movement segment, usually keeping the movement time to no more than about 10 seconds. This should be a very lively activity.

Hocus Pocus

One of the cleverest variations of Stop and Go we have seen recently was the use of the phrase *hocus pocus* by two student teachers, Jessica Segura and Cristian Sarmento. Whenever students were practicing and heard "hocus pocus," they responded with "time to focus," put their equipment on the floor, and put their hands on their knees and their eyes on the teacher. Youngsters seemed to love saying "time to focus," and the protocol worked like a charm.

Body Parts

This game focuses on the different body parts. Once the children have adjusted to Stop and Go, they enjoy the challenge of touching the floor with different body parts—elbow, seat, knee, wrist, waist, left hand, or right foot—as quickly as they can when you say "Stop."

Traveling

Once the children have learned to travel using different locomotor patterns, variations in these patterns are appropriate. Call out different ways of traveling—skipping, hopping, crab-walking, galloping—and challenge the children to change from one to another as rapidly as possible. You can increase the challenge of this game by combining traveling and the concept of direction—for example, gallop backward or hop to the right.

Shapes

This game can be played on a painted playground surface or in a gymnasium. Before class, draw circles, triangles, squares, etc., on the ground. The object is for the children to move as quickly as possible to the shape you name; for example, if you call out "circle," the children stand on a circle as quickly as possible. You can use colors instead of or in combination with shapes if the surface you're using is painted various colors. The terms you use will be determined by your pupils' knowledge of colors and shapes.

Numbers

In one version of this game, the children stop with the appropriate number of body parts touching the ground. For example, if you call out "three," the children should stop with three body parts touching the ground.

In a second version, the children stop in groups. The number the teacher calls determines the size of the group. This game is helpful when you want the children to form into groups of three, four, or five in a hurry.

Combinations

As children learn each variation, they find it challenging and fun to play several games at once. For example, you might call out a body part, a color, a locomotor pattern, or a number. Children thrive on increasingly difficult games.

Switch and Rotate

The purpose of this game is primarily to teach listening, but it's more appropriate for older children. The object of the game is to stay so close to a partner that when the teacher says "stop" and the players freeze, the follower can still touch the leader. When the teacher says "switch," the partners change roles, and the follower becomes the leader.

You can make this game more difficult by increasing the size of the group to three, then four, then five. The object of the game remains the same: Each child should be able to touch the person in front as soon as you say "Stop." When you add the challenge "Rotate," the leader goes to the end of the line and becomes a follower. Children find the challenge of listening and responding instantly while trying to remain close to the children

in front of them fascinating. You can make this game more challenging by varying the locomotor patterns—for example, from walking to skipping to hopping to galloping to running.

You might initially assign a criterion of five seconds as a reasonable amount of time for the children to stop and listen after they hear the stop signal. If the entire class stops and listens in five seconds or less, praise them. If they don't, explain that taking more than five seconds is too slow and have them practice again. Gradually raise the standard as the children become more proficient. The children often view these races against the clock as fun games and delight in the teacher's praise when they perform well. They also enjoy trying to beat their own records. This approach provides far more time for activity and instruction. As the children learn the value of spending less time on management tasks, you can eliminate these races against the clock. Teachers must be clear, concise, and to the point. As a general rule, once a class has begun, we try to keep our verbal explanations to less than one minute. Although this isn't always possible (or even appropriate), it does help to increase the children's willingness to stop and listen to us.

found several things to be helpful. Have equipment ready and available in various locations before class starts. For example, hula hoops create great storage areas for balls, but be sure to have multiple locations so all children are not going to one place to get equipment. It is also important for youngsters to walk rather than run and push to get equipment. The same is true for returning equipment at the end of activity; children

Spreading equipment out and providing equipment options are two routines that promote student responsibility.

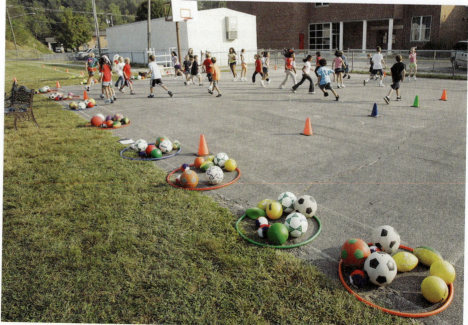

©Lars A. Niki

need to walk and place it in its spot—not shoot from the center of the gym. In the beginning, it may be useful to have selected groups of students—all those wearing red, for example—get equipment, and then have other groups go. The two least effective ways to distribute equipment are to hand it out individually and to have it all in one place.

Once children get equipment, they need to know what to do with it. Tell them, for example, "Walk, get a paddle and ball, carry it to your space, and wait for directions," or "Walk, get a ball, carry it to your space, and begin throwing and catching by yourself." As with entering the gym, if you don't tell them what to do, children will devise something to do with the equipment themselves, and it usually is not what you had in mind.

The final aspect of using equipment is what to do with it when the teacher is talking. Children, like adults, have a hard time holding on to equipment without playing with it. Many teachers will ask students to place the ball on the floor, to hold it like a pro under one elbow, or even to hold it on their heads. Regardless of the technique, children need to have something to do with the equipment when the teacher is talking.

Partners and Groups When choosing partners or teams, the more teachers choose partners for children, the more we disenfranchise them. It is important to have children learn how to appropriately choose their own partners. Box 7-5 has routines for choosing partners that have worked for us.

Other Routines Other helpful routines involve getting water, responding to accidents, using the bathroom, and dressing appropriately. Table 7.1 compares gymnasium routines that enable and don't enable

Box 7-5

Forming Partners or Groups

Though the days of having a class divide into two teams and play against each other are largely over in physical education, on many occasions children need to form partners or small groups. In some classes, the act of finding a partner creates many behavior problems. Children argue over who is going to be whose partner, other children are left out, the time used in deciding partners takes longer than the task itself, and then children want to change partners. The same problems occur, even more so, when dividing children into groups. We've found the following techniques helpful in avoiding such problems as much as possible.

Getting Partners

- Put a time limit on how long children can take to choose partners, such as "by the time I count from five to one, you should have your partner and be standing in your own space."
- Put restrictions on who may be partners—for example, "someone you've never worked with before," "the person sitting next to you," "the person who sits next to you in class," or "someone you know you can work with in a productive manner." A note here: children can understand the word *productive* if we teach it to them.
- Decide ahead of class who will be partners.
- Hand out color codes (pieces of paper, stickers, or marking-pen marks on the hand) at the beginning of class; the children who match up are partners.

Dividing into Groups

- Have children choose partners; then put one partner in one group and one in another. This works well for making groups equal.
- Assign each student a color or number (the number of colors or numbers equals the number of groups you desire) at the beginning of the year or month. When groups are to be formed, simply say, "Reds here," "Blues here," "Purples here," and "Greens here." (This is also an efficient way to take roll in your class.) Be sure to change colors or numbers by grading period so the groups are varied.
- Divide teams by certain generic characteristics, such as eye color, month of birth, number of siblings, or number of letters in first name.
- Divide groups ahead of time.
- Create a deck of cards (or shapes, letters, or numbers) that has the number of groups you desire. For example, if you want groups of four, configure the deck so you use four triangles, four circles, four squares, four stars, and four rectangles. Pass out the cards randomly and have the four that match become a group.

Whatever you do, don't take more than 60 seconds and, most important, don't alienate anyone. Under no circumstances should selecting partners or dividing children into groups be a popularity contest.

Table 7.1 Routines That Promote (and Don't Promote) Decision Making

Task	Promotes	Doesn't Promote
Getting equipment Entering the gymnasium	Spread equipment and have students walk to pick it up. Post initial activity; students begin to practice as soon as they enter.	Hand out equipment. Students line up, waiting for the teacher.
Choosing partners Dress Getting water/bathroom	Students choose partners with whom they can practice productively. Students choose appropriate clothing that allows them to participate freely. Students get a drink or use the restroom when they need it if no one else is at the drinking fountain or in the restroom.	Teacher assigns partners. Student wears uniforms. Drinking and/or restroom use is permitted only before or after class.

students to show responsibility. Any decisions we can help students learn to make on their own build independence, competence, self-worth, and confidence, thus reducing behavior problems. Taking away decisions students are capable of making fosters dependence and usually creates behavior problems. The key factor is first teaching students to make decisions competently. The net result of this instruction is that we as teachers are freed from trivial decisions that detract from our ability to teach—and we have a classroom that manages itself.

Getting Off to a Good Start

Typically, the first day a class meets, the teacher goes over the logistical and organizational rules and procedures she or he feels are essential for effective class functioning. Often, we've seen this done only in the first lesson via a lecture; the rules and procedures are never taught and never reviewed again unless something goes wrong.

> *Students don't need to be fearful of teachers to listen to them.*
>
> —**MARK MURDOCK**, practicum student, after his first time teaching sixth grade

It has become increasingly obvious how important the first few days of school are (Brooks 1985; Bohn, Roehrig, and Pressley 2004): The first days establish the environment for the entire year. The students learn what behavior and attitude are appropriate in the gymnasium and what will be expected of them in physical education. It is then that they learn the stated and unstated class rules. When a situation arises and is consistently treated the same way, the students know the teacher means what has been said. This establishes the behavior and attitude that will typify a class for the remainder of the year. We've found the following

suggestions helpful for getting off to a good start, and Figure 7.4 provides a checklist to ensure you're ready for the beginning of the school year. For those of you who are reading *Children Moving* and are about to begin a field experience, your beginning of the year is the first day you see your students. While you will not want to vary much from what your cooperating teacher does, you can use the same suggestions for letting students know that you know what goes on in the gym.

- *Ready the gym* Be certain that your gymnasium and materials are ready before the beginning of the year.
- *Plan protocols* Even if your plan is to have students provide input into the rules and routines of the gymnasium, decide before you meet your students what general rules (consequences) and routines are important and necessary for you. What is the general atmosphere you wish to create? In what ways can you guide students? Teachers who have the students decide on protocols often come prepared with generic guidelines (such as participation; treatment of others—students and teachers; safety; equipment) for operation of the gym. Students can then form specific rules within those guidelines. If you decide to develop the rules and consequences of the gym yourself, have them ready and posted before children arrive.
- *Plan beginning-of-school activities* Develop activities for the first few days of physical education that will involve students at a high success rate and have a whole-group focus (see Chapter 9). This gives you an opportunity to see who follows directions and to reinforce appropriate behavior and attitudes. Don't begin independent work until you are certain individuals know what is expected of them. Teach the rules of behavior and expected attitudes as well as classroom routines (e.g., what to do when arriving in class; how to take out, set up, and take down equipment; what to do in a fire drill). You can most easily do this by planning what the routines will be, designing situations that allow students to practice the routines, and teaching those routines in the gym. Spending time teaching behavior and attitudes

CHECKLIST FOR THE BEGINNING OF SCHOOL

Item	Check When Done	Notes
Are your teaching areas and equipment ready?		
Have you decided on your class protocols?		
Are you familiar with the parts of the school that you may use (halls, cafeteria, multi-purpose room, etc.) and any procedures associated with their use?		
Do you have complete class rosters for each class you teach?		
Do you have file information on your students, including any comments from previous teachers and information on health problems?		
Do you know if you have any students with disabilities who should be accommodated for in your instruction?		
Do you have an adequate amount of equipment for your students?		
Have you established the procedure for the arrival and departure of the students from the physical education area?		
Are the children's name tags ready? Do you have some blank ones for unexpected students?		
Do you have your first day's plan of activities?		
Do you have rainy-day activities planned?		
Have you inspected all facilities for safety issues?		
Do you have a letter ready to send home to the parents with information about the school year and expectations?		
Do you know how to obtain assistance from school staff members (e.g., school nurse, office personnel, and the custodians)?		

Figure 7.4 Checklist for the beginning of school.
Source: Adapted from C. Evertson, and E. Emmer, *Classroom management for elementary teachers*, 10th ed. (New York: Pearson, 2017).

at the beginning of the school year allows you to spend more time during the rest of the year teaching skills and much less time repeating what should already have become habit.

- *Communicating with parents* Many teachers find it valuable to communicate via a written newsletter or flyer the expectations of physical education class as well what to expect in terms of learning in the gym. The newsletter can include what themes will be taught and when, a bit about special events, the safety rules of the gym and playground, and how to contact you. Some teachers leave a place for comments on the flyer and request that a signed copy be returned.

- *Developing strategies for potential problems* Anticipate problems both in terms of content (e.g., what will be too hard for some students) or gymnasium routines (e.g., how students might potentially misunderstand a certain routine) and develop ways to prevent or reduce those problems.

- *Monitoring* In the early days, routinely check with students individually to determine how they're settling in and to gain other information relevant to the physical education and school setting.

- *Creating accountability* Develop procedures that help students learn to be responsible for their actions (Chapter 8) and work (Chapter 12).

School-Wide Programs

Many schools have adopted school-wide behavior management programs for all children in all disciplines. These programs, the most common of which is Positive Behavioral Interventions & Supports (PBIS), have as a focus positive behavior, rewarding children for positive behavior and acceptance of responsibility for that behavior. Behavioral expectations are positively stated, easy for the children to remember, and pertinent to the specific school setting. For additional information on PBIS, contact www.PBIS.org. If your school has such a program, it is important to adopt that program for physical education if it is going to be successful. Many schools and physical education programs have adapted the school logo as a way to make the expectations clear; the physical education teacher(s) and the students working together then develop specific guidelines that mesh with the school expectations. Figure 7.5 shows how one physical education program adapted school-level guidelines for physical education.

Chappelow Magnet School (the Cheetahs) developed PRIDE as the acronym for what was expected for all students in the school. At their school, Cheetah PRIDE stands for Personal Responsibility, Respect, Integrity, Determination, and Empathy.

To help the children better translate the abstract ideas into actions, specific behaviors were identified by letter.

P: I own my choices, words, and actions.

R: I honor myself, others, and my environment.

I: I am honest and make the right choices.

D: I try my best and don't give up.

E: I am kind and considerate.

In physical education, PRIDE was translated into the class rules of:

- Being responsible for yourself and your learning
- Respecting others and equipment
- Telling the truth and being honest during game play or any other movement activity
- Working hard by practicing tasks and not giving up
- Caring for others and being helpful

Figure 7.5 Cheetah PRIDE
Source: Tia Ziegler, Chappelow Elementary School, Greeley, CO.

Teaching Skills for Establishing the Managerial Aspects of the Learning Environment

The preceding sections emphasized the importance of a managerial component as well as the tasks necessary to create it. Effective teachers also use a number of generic teaching skills to help create and maintain a component. Such skills include teaching the protocols, setting performance standards, and maintaining consistency.

Teaching Protocols

When children are learning psychomotor skills, we commonly give them much practice; when they make mistakes, we provide feedback. We would never think about punishing a child who did not learn to throw correctly, especially after one try. The same is true with teaching rules and routines. For children to learn rules and routines, they should be taught just as you would teach content—using the same effective teaching skills. The following five aspects are some of the most important when teaching protocols.

1. *Describe, demonstrate, and expect acceptable behavior.* Use both words and actions to convey what specific behaviors are acceptable. For example, do not simply tell children you want them to "be good," but tell them what good means—for example, say thank you to others, walk to get equipment, put equipment down and listen when the teacher or others are talking, or walk around others to retrieve lost equipment. In addition, demonstrate what each behavior looks like. Many children will have a different idea than you do about what walking means. Setting performance standards helps define the atmosphere of the classroom and maintain safety.

2. *Practice the behaviors.* Practice helps children learn the appropriate behavior and at the same time allows you to see if the youngsters understand and can follow a procedure. Box 7-6 gives an example of a practice activity for rules and procedures. Note that the primary purpose of this activity is to help students learn the protocols of the gymnasium by performing a variety of activities. All the activities involve working together productively as a group, which focuses on the atmosphere of the gym itself.

3. *Provide feedback.* Protocols, just like motor skills, are learned, and children don't often get them right the first time. After students have successfully practiced the protocol for the first time, be sure to tell them they did it correctly and then praise them.

Teaching Protocols with Group Practice: Ring the Bell

Equipment

For an average-size class:

- Four sets of large cards, each with a protocol practice activity written on one side (see below). Each set of cards should be a different color.
- Four medium bells.
- Any equipment necessary to practice the card-activities.

Organization

After protocols have been explained and demonstrated, divide the class into four groups. Give each group a color to match the cards. All cards are spread out face down in the middle of the gym and mixed. When instructed, one member of each group retrieves a card for his or her group, takes it to the group, and they complete the activity. One member then returns to the middle, rings the cowbell, hands the card to the teacher, and retrieves another card. The activity continues until all cards have been completed.

Sample Card Activities

- At the regroup area, finger-spell your first name.
- Go get a drink of water. One at a time, please.
- Go to the blue neighborhood and do 10 push-ups of any kind.
- Go to the planning-time area (see Chapter 10) and review the rules with each other.
- Measure the length of the gym using your bodies. Lie down on the floor head-to-toe.
- Go to the bathroom pass area and show your group your favorite safe balance.
- Go to the red neighborhood, get a ball, and dribble it 15 times with your right hand and 15 times with your left hand.

Assessment

This would be an opportune time to check for understanding by using a student drawing or an exit slip (see Chapter 12) asking about one or two protocols.

Source: Adapted from material by Chet Bunting, Riverside Elementary School, Thornton, CO.

If improvement is needed, tell them exactly what is needed and practice again. Even after youngsters seem to know a protocol, be prepared to prompt and give feedback if they forget.

4. *Maintain consistency.* When establishing a classroom atmosphere, to avoid slippage (letting the children become lax as the year progresses), it's important that teachers be consistent in what they expect from one day to the next. Students learn best when the gymnasium is a predictable place to be. Rules and routines must be followed habitually. For example, if children are allowed to take out equipment mats by dragging them across the floor on one day, but on the next day four people are required to carry each mat, they receive mixed messages and consequently don't know what is expected of them and are confused. Therefore, after behaviors have been described and taught (performance standards set), the protocols practiced, and feedback given, you must be consistent with your actions if youngsters are to really understand your expectations.

5. *Teach with critical demandingness.* Finally, and *most* importantly, is a concept called critical demandingness (Graham, Elliott, and Palmer 2016).

Although this may seem like just another generic teaching skill, it's not. As suggested earlier, it answers the question, "Do you mean what you say?" Frankly, many of the excellent suggestions contained in this chapter, and the next, are irrelevant if, as a teacher, you don't mean what you say. As you know, or will quickly find out, your students will test you to see if you really mean what you say. When you give the stop signal, do you really mean stop or just slow down? When you say walk to get equipment, do you really mean walk or is a slow run okay?

Critical demandingness means that you set criteria for your expectations and then demand the criteria be followed. If you have a chance to observe veteran teachers, you will know in a very short amount of time if they are critically demanding. If, for example, they ask their students to stop and put their ball on the floor, do they really mean what they say—or are they just hoping their students will follow the direction? Teachers who are not critically demanding are constantly reminding, often nagging, their students to do what they ask. Are you going to be a critically demanding teacher or are you going to be a nagging teacher? The choice is up to you.

The Instructional Component

Although it is clear that effective managers set early and consistent standards and develop positive relationships with students (Cothran, Kulina, and Garrahy 2003), that is not enough. We must also teach so students can learn. Learning motor skills and fitness concepts is the unique goal of physical education. It guides our actions as teachers and directs student attention as well as participation and attitudes. The instructional component of the learning environment consists of subject-matter functions designed to see that children learn the intended content. Students are more likely to learn when expectations about learning are communicated. More learning occurs when students understand and value learning goals; when the task is appropriate and has a definite aim or focus; and when content is made personal, concrete, and familiar.

If students are to be held accountable for learning the expectations we have set, it is essential that they accomplish the task as intended. Accountability in a managerial component is clear: If a student is asked to walk but runs instead, he or she is asked to start over again and walk. Accountability also exists with motor performance, but the strategies differ. Typically we have used testing as the major accountability component for learning in physical education. Unfortunately, testing occurs infrequently and only at the end of a unit. Alternative assessment practices have helped alleviate that problem (see Chapter 12). Yet, to truly learn and understand, students need ongoing accountability components. Effective teachers utilize a variety of practices to create effective instructional components that keep students on task, focused, and motivated to improve their performance. Four concepts are foundational to creating an instructional environment primed for learning: content development (discussed in Chapter 6 and reinforced here), communication, feedback, and accommodating differences.

> *You haven't taught until students have learned.*
>
> —JOHN WOODEN

Content Development

Content development is the progression of learning tasks within a lesson that move children from less complex to more complex movement. (See Chapter 6 for a complete explanation of content development.) Varying the type of learning task builds student accountability for learning. In *Children Moving,* we use three types of learning experiences (adapted from Rink 2014). First are tasks (marked with a **T**). These tasks allow students to progress a skill to more complex situations. Second are the use of cues to refine the skill. These cues provide focus on the critical elements of a skill to make it successful. Last are challenges (marked with a **C**), which when used on a regular basis give students the opportunity to focus their work and informally assess their learning. Chapter 13, "Reflecting on Teaching," provides you with a way to determine how you are developing the content (see Figure 13.2). Although there is no magic number or mix, desirable task sequences consist of a more varied pattern that includes a mix of tasks that ask students to practice a skill, tasks that focus on the critical elements, and challenges that let children focus on using the skill. In other words, there is no formula that can be used for content development. It always depends on the abilities and interests of the class being taught—as well as the amount of time and effort the teacher has spent on planning interesting, enjoyable, and worthwhile lessons. In addition, it has been our finding that appropriate, challenging content eliminates about 90 percent of the potential behavior problems in class. We do know, however, that lessons that consist entirely of tasks without the use of and focus on critical elements do not result in student learning.

Communication

Effective teachers are good communicators. They provide clear and interesting explanations and descriptions so the children can easily understand the information. As you will see in the movement concept and skill theme chapters (Chapters 14–27), each section learning experience begins by providing the children with some information about how a particular task is to be done—for example, the equipment needed, the space in which the activity will occur, the rules, and whether the children will be working alone or with others. Ideally, the instructional part of the lesson is both brief and clear so the children can quickly begin practicing the starting task with few questions. When we provide this information, we also follow the KISS principle.

The KISS Principle The KISS principle (Keep It Short and Simple) is a good guideline to follow when talking to children. One trap teachers easily fall into is spending five or more minutes telling (and demonstrating) all they know about a skill or activity. There is a lot to tell the children—the problem is that the children can't possibly remember all that information when it is provided in a single minilecture. Think of a skill or exercise you know well. It would be easy for you to talk for five minutes, for example, on how to hit a ball with a bat or the correct way to do a crunch. The children won't remember all of this, however. If you don't believe it, try an experiment with one of your classes. Give them a minilecture. During the following class, use the Helping Murgatroid technique (see Chapter 12, Figure 12.4) to see what they actually are able to recall from your lecture. We believe you'll find that providing information in small bits throughout a lesson is more effective than long-winded explanations children don't remember. We try to limit our instruction to just what the children need to know—usually 30 to 60 seconds or less! Use the duration recording chart (see Chapter 13, Figure 13.5) to check how much time you actually spending talking and how much you talk at one time.

Demonstrations In addition to keeping our explanations brief and to the point, we also demonstrate whenever possible. This is helpful to children who are visual as opposed to auditory learners and to those learning a skill for the first time, and it's necessary for the increasing number of children in our classes who are English language learners. Demonstrations of motor skills need to be done correctly, and they must emphasize the part or parts the children need to pay attention to—the instep, the elbow, the shoulder, the hands—so children can clearly see how that part is to be used and how it fits into the total movement. This seems obvious, yet it is amazing to see how often teachers don't provide children with a demonstration or fail to demonstrate slowly enough or to emphasize a part so that the demonstration is just not helpful to children. If you digitally record some of your lessons, as we suggest in Chapter 13, and then use the demonstration checklist (see Chapter 13, Figure 13.6) to analyze your demonstrations, you will be able to ascertain quickly the effectiveness of your demonstrations.

Pinpointing There are times when we choose not to demonstrate or are unable to demonstrate a skill for the children. In these instances, pinpointing—inviting several children to do the demonstration—can be an effective technique (Graham et al. 2016). The children are encouraged when they see that their peers can demonstrate the skill or technique. When possible, we try to select two or more children to do the pinpointing; in this way, we avoid placing children who are uncomfortable performing in front of other children in a solo situation.

One Cue at a Time Learning cues also provide students with an instructional accountability mechanism. Cues are simply short phrases or words that focus the learner on the critical elements of the skill to be practiced. If for every task presented, the last thing the teacher did was to repeat the cue(s) for the task, many students would be highly focused. Major cues are provided at the beginning of each control-level through proficiency-level task in the skill theme chapters.

Generally we focus on one cue at a time in our instruction, demonstration, and pinpointing. For example, to a class of second graders, we might provide instruction and demonstrate the cue of stepping with the lead foot when batting (Chapter 27). We would then ask the children to continue the same task—batting off a tee against a wall or fence, for example—while we circulate and provide feedback.

If you can imagine this setting, you realize that the children may need several other cues. Some, for example, will not be swinging in a horizontal plane; some may not be swinging the bat appropriately on the backswing or following through. The problem, however, is that children at this age (and many adults, for that matter) can concentrate effectively on only one cue at a time. By focusing on one cue at a time, we heighten the chances that the children will learn this cue (Graham et al. 2016; Rink 2014). Once the children are actually using this cue—that is, when they are actually stepping with the lead foot as they swing—we move on to another cue. We may change the task, as suggested in the batting progression in Chapter 27, but the cue remains the same. Or in some cases, the cue remains the same for several different tasks.

Congruent Feedback

Providing specific congruent feedback about students' performance increases the accountability for learning. As the children practice a task, the teacher circulates among them, providing feedback. Again, there are many cues the teacher might provide in the form of feedback. However, we provide specific congruent feedback—that is, feedback directly related to the critical elements of the task and nothing else. If a teacher provides such feedback, student performance is then more directed and focused (Rink 2014). For example, during instruction, we might ask the children to think about stepping with the lead foot as they are batting; the feedback we provide, therefore, would be about how they are (or are not) stepping with the lead foot. We might say:

"Jackie, good lead step."

"Nick, don't forget to step into your swing."

"Verenda, remember to step with your lead foot."

"Tommy, way to step."

Interestingly, both the children and the teacher seem to benefit from this type of feedback. The children hear a consistent message and are able to recall and apply the cue. The teacher is able to focus quickly (Chapter 11) on a specific part of a movement while moving among the children rather than attempting to analyze all of the critical elements for every child's batting swing. The feedback analysis checklist (Figure 13.1 in Chapter 13) is one tool to help you analyze the type of feedback you provide to the children.

Accommodating Individual Differences

We have described a process for developing the content that enables children to truly learn and benefit from physical education lessons (Rink 2014). As you know, however, the process is made even more complicated by the fact that children in our classes have different skill levels and interests. Although we have no magic solutions, we do want to suggest two techniques that can help you to accommodate individual differences within a class—that is, to match the challenge of a task with the ability of the child (Csikszentmihalyi 2000; Graham et al. 2016). We have termed these two techniques, which are two ways to differentiate instruction, teaching by invitation and intratask variation.

Teaching by Invitation

One of the ways a teacher can adjust for individual differences is by inviting the children to decide some parameters of a given task. The teacher makes the statement to the entire class, and each child in the class then decides in which task he or she wants to participate. Teaching by invitation provides children with choice, which also increases student responsibility and ownership. The following are examples of teaching by invitation:

"You may want to continue dribbling in self-space, or you may want to begin dribbling and walking in general space."

"Working alone, or with a partner, design a sequence . . ."

"You may want to continue batting from the tee, or you may want to work with a partner, taking turns pitching a ball to each other."

"You may want to continue striking a ball with your paddle, or you may want to try striking a shuttlecock."

"You decide how far away you want to be from the goal when you kick."

"In groups of two or three, make up a game . . ."

If you use this technique, you will find that most of the children make intelligent decisions about the tasks in which they choose to participate. As in every instance, there will be a few children who, in your judgment, make questionable decisions. Overall, however, you will find your children will choose tasks that allow them to be successful—and yet tasks that are not too easy (Csikszentmihalyi 2000).

Intratask Variation

Teaching by invitation allows the children to make decisions about the task they prefer to work on. Intratask variation, by contrast, is a technique in which the teacher decides to extend a task for individuals or small groups in the class. The teacher bases this decision on specific knowledge of the children's abilities and interests. Typically, intratask variation is a rather private interaction between one or more children and the teacher, who makes a task easier or harder to better match the children's skill level. The following are examples of intratask variation:

"Eldridge, why don't you try striking a balloon instead of a ball?"

"José, you may want to practice dribbling behind your back and between your legs." (Other children are practicing dribbling and staying in self-space.)

"Gloria and Tanisha, why don't you two make up a partner sequence that has rolling and transferring weight in it." (Other children are practicing rolling in backward directions.)

"I would like the four of you to move over to the next field and make up a game that has kicking and dribbling with your feet in it." (Other children are practicing dribbling with their feet; these four have been playing soccer for several years and are skilled at kicking and dribbling with the feet. They move to the other field and quickly begin a two-against-two soccer game.)

Unfortunately, intratask variation is not a 100 percent guaranteed panacea that will allow you to adjust tasks satisfactorily to meet the needs of every child in a class. As with most teaching techniques, intratask variation is effective with some children in some classes some of the time. A teacher can heighten the potential success of intratask variation by explaining to the children, before using the technique, that sometimes during a lesson, various students will be asked to do different things. Understanding why this is being done—the children are already aware there is a wide range of skill levels in the class—will enable them to realize the teacher is not playing favorites but rather helping them benefit more from physical education class by adjusting tasks for children with differing abilities.

When using intratask variation, the teacher can also make the point that children at the higher skill levels—utilization and proficiency (Chapter 5)—have most likely acquired these skills because of the activities they pursue after school and on weekends. This also provides an excellent opportunity to explain that students at the utilization and proficiency levels for various skill themes have practiced those skills countless times in a variety of settings. In most physical education classes, there is just not enough practice time to attain the top two levels of the generic levels of skill proficiency (GLSP). This explanation will be especially helpful to those youngsters who may be under the mistaken impression that the more skilled youngsters in a class were born that way. They weren't! They have just had more practice.

Whatever the strategy, in order to learn, students must have a focus for the activity and be held accountable for realizing the focus. Without focus and accountability, students will lack motivation, will not learn the intended content, and will begin to behave inappropriately. This classroom learning can be achieved using multiple approaches (see Chapter 9), yet regardless of the approach, the key variables mentioned in this chapter need to be addressed.

Safety

Although teaching safety procedures could logically be included within the managerial component, it is so important that we have chosen to address it separately. We discuss it in generic terms here, but we also include specific safety aspects in each skill theme development chapter: These are coded with the safety icon ⚠.

A major responsibility of every physical education teacher is to provide students with a physically and psychologically safe learning environment (Tannehill et al. 2015). You as a teacher are entrusted with the safety of students in your class. The legal terminology is *in loco parentis*. In other words, when a child is with you, you act in place of the parent. The commonly accepted definition of this type of responsibility is that while a child is in a teacher's care, the teacher should act in a reasonable and responsible manner with respect to the child's welfare and safety. Reasonable behavior has been interpreted by the courts as what one would expect of a person with ordinary intelligence, ordinary perception, ordinary memory (Cotton and Wolohan 2016), and specified academic and professional credentials. This means that teachers are held

to the standard of the reasonably prudent "teacher" with all the pertinent credentials and experience this teacher possesses (that is, if teacher X has more than the basic knowledge, certifications, and so on, teacher X is held accountable for that knowledge). Teachers are held to the standard of the reasonably prudent teacher, not that of just any adult.

Elements of Negligence

When a teacher does not act in a reasonably prudent manner, negligence can occur. Negligence has four separate elements—duty, breach of duty, proximate cause, and injury—that all must be met to prove someone is liable.

Duty   The first element is established duty. This involves the relationship that exists between a teacher and students. By virtue of being a teacher, we have a duty to the students in our classes.

Breach of Duty   Duty requires that teachers maintain a certain standard of care regarding the students in their classes. A teacher is required (1) to anticipate foreseeable risk in any activity; (2) to take reasonable steps to prevent injury; (3) to provide a warning that risk is inherent in the activity; (4) to provide aid to the injured student; and (5) to prevent an increase in the severity of the injury. This standard of care is arrived at through expert testimony and other information that sets standards of practice. If an incident goes to court, the defendant's behavior will be compared to what the "reasonably prudent teacher" would have done in those circumstances to see if there was a breach of the standard of care either through an act of commission (something that was done) or an act of omission (not doing something that should have been done). This is a critical issue because all experts in a field may not always agree upon the accepted standard of care. For example, most would say that children should be warned and taught about the dangers of raising hockey sticks above the waist, but what about playing dodgeball as part of the physical education curriculum? Breach of duty, or of the standard of care, is the second element of negligence.

Proximate Cause   The third element of negligence is proximate cause, which means that the teacher's behavior was the cause of the injury. An example might involve a student who has a documented medical problem that precludes participation in certain activities. The teacher requires the student to participate anyway, and the student suffers an injury directly related to the medical problem. What the teacher did was the main factor in the injury.

Injury   Injury is the final element of negligence. This element requires that the injury must have occurred because of the breach of duty. For example, if a student falls from gymnastics equipment that has no mats under it and breaks a leg, an injury has occurred. If, however, a student falls under the same circumstances and no injury has occurred, then there is no case for negligence.

Areas in Which Negligence Might Occur

The four elements of negligence might occur in a variety of situations, but the three most common involve facilities and equipment, the conduct of the activity, and supervision.

Facilities and Equipment   Two major areas in which facilities and equipment are subject to negligent behavior are: (1) upkeep and general safety of the equipment and (2) facilities and the appropriateness of the equipment for the child. All students have the right to participate in a safe and developmentally appropriate environment. Keeping facilities and equipment safe and in "good working order" is the obvious aspect of this domain. Standards for equipment and facilities are available from most school districts as well as the Society of Health and Physical Educators (SHAPE America 2009). Grounds should be inspected regularly for potential hazards such as sprinkler heads, holes, rocks, and ants. If a facility or equipment needs attention, it can only be attended to if reported. Make sure the right people know what needs to be repaired and follow up on it. The less obvious aspect of this domain is that equipment should be matched to the child—that is, it should be developmentally appropriate. All equipment must be of the appropriate size and weight for the child. Thus, in one class you may have multiple types of balls or rackets available to children. For example, to ask most six-year-olds or beginners of any age to use a regulation bat is not appropriate.

Supervision   The teacher must be in the room or on the playground with the class and must be paying attention, and there must be enough supervisors for the participants present. This implies that you do not leave during class to do something else, even if it is to get equipment out of the equipment room. When present, teachers must actively observe the class (see Chapter 11) and be cognizant of what is occurring. If misbehavior, off-task behavior, or unsafe behavior exists, teachers have the obligation to respond to such behavior. Have all equipment out before class, and answer phone calls on breaks. In many schools, teachers going outdoors with children now carry walkie-talkies and/or cell phones for emergencies.

Conduct of Activities   The conduct of the activity may be the least obvious negligence area. Four aspects are important here: (1) how children are taught to perform the skill, including proper progression; (2) how they are instructed to use equipment; (3) what safety precautions the teacher takes; and (4) whether the inherent risk is explained to the children and whether emergency medical procedures and protocols are developed. The last two aspects of safety and risk are the two that are most often teachers' focus.

Safety precautions need to be stated as part of the general instructions to the children for every activity they undertake. These can be as simple as having students wait until everyone has thrown at a target before collecting the equipment and reminding them to walk around groups when collecting stray equipment; or safety instructions can be more formal, such as posting specific safety rules for activities that involve hockey sticks. Children and parents also need to know the risks involved in physical education classes. This can be done by sending communications home at the beginning of the year so parents can inform teachers of medical conditions of which they should be aware. General safety procedures can easily be taught at the beginning of the school year by incorporating them with other gymnasium rules and routines. These safety procedures must be explained and then taught and practiced.

We've found that special safety procedures that deal with specialized equipment or unique situations are most effectively taught at the time that situation arises. Again, the procedures shouldn't be glossed over; students should thoroughly understand them before you proceed. When specific safety rules are presented and taught, it is again a good time to digitally record the teaching—for students who may be absent, for those who tend to forget, or in case of legal action.

It's beneficial to explain why selected behaviors are inappropriate and why safety procedures are necessary. Explaining the possible harmful consequences of actions helps children understand the need for stated practices. As with all ongoing gymnasium rules, the consequences of breaking safety rules must be stated; they might easily be included in the general rules for behavior. The children need to understand that safety is their responsibility as well as the teacher's when activity begins. Student safety should be the first thing the teacher observes for when the children begin a task (see Chapter 11).

The first and second aspects regarding the conduct of activities—how children are taught to perform skills

and how they are taught to use equipment—are equally critical. First, children need to be taught the appropriate use of all equipment in class. For example, jump ropes are for jumping over and using as nets but not for slinging around the head as they are picked up. When equipment is not used appropriately, the risk of injury is far greater. It cannot be assumed that all children know the appropriate use of equipment.

Finally, all children are entitled to instruction that is appropriate. Proper task progressions are critically important to students' safety. A student must possess all the prerequisite skills before beginning a new task. A teacher who skips from the precontrol level to the proficiency level when students are still at the precontrol level, or from tasks to challenges without teaching critical cues, has not followed a proper progression. The teacher, in this case, is simply asking for safety and legal problems. Accurate records of lesson and unit plans allow teachers not only to establish proper progressions but also to document them. Directions should be clear and thorough to the point that students know exactly what they are to do and how, but not to the point of giving so much information that children are confused. Critical cues need to be provided for each task given, accompanied by an unambiguous demonstration.

Students need to behave safely in a safe environment. They also need to feel safe about what they are doing in class. Students who feel comfortable about what they are doing and are willing to participate fully by experiencing appropriate task progressions tend to behave safely because they are challenged by the task at hand yet feel able to accomplish it.

The authors of this book sincerely hope that you never have to face legal action regarding your teaching. If, however, you do face legal action, in addition to digitally recording your safety protocols, you will want to keep accurate and complete records of lesson and unit plans. This will allow you to document the fact that you have followed proper progressions. One of the authors of this book was asked to serve as an expert witness in a liability case involving a youngster who fell from a climbing rope. The only entry in the teacher's planning book was "climbing rope." There was no written indication that any safety protocols were followed. Needless to say, it would have been better if the teacher, in addition to writing that the children were going to be climbing a rope in class that day, would have indicated the safety protocols that were taught as part of the climbing rope lesson. It may not surprise you that some of the children in the class that day said safety was taught, whereas others said the teacher just said "Climb the rope." The case did not make it to court for several years, another good reason to maintain thorough written lessons.

This is a brief overview of some of the safety and legal issues teachers face. It is not intended as a compendium source. For more information, you may want to read *Law for Recreation and Sport Managers* (Cotton and Wolohan 2016). Be sure to check with your school district regarding its safety policies and procedures. As physical educators, we have always been conscious of safety, but in today's world of increasing legal action against teachers, we simply have to become more cautious and thorough in all that we do. To do anything less risks student injury as well as legal action.

Summary

Establishing a learning environment is essential if a teacher is to have an effective physical education program. The learning environment consists of two components: the managerial component and the instructional component. The managerial component involves all noninstructional activities, and the instructional component involves all activities designed to increase student learning. The teacher's attitude and beliefs permeate both components. The types of components that are set up are a direct reflection of the teacher's attitudes and beliefs about children, education, and physical education. Figure 7.6, which unscrambles the activities that were part of the word cloud at the beginning of this chapter, may help you to visualize the components of establishing a learning environment. Designing components that: (1) involve students in decision making, (2) view children as capable and able, and (3) are consistent with clear learning expectations and appropriate tasks usually creates an environment conducive to student learning and eliminates much off-task behavior.

Sample Web Sites

PE Central, supportREALteachers, and SHAPE America are physical education Web sites with a plethora of information on all aspects of physical education, including classroom management ideas. www.pecentral.org., supportrealteachers.org, and SHAPEAmerica.org.

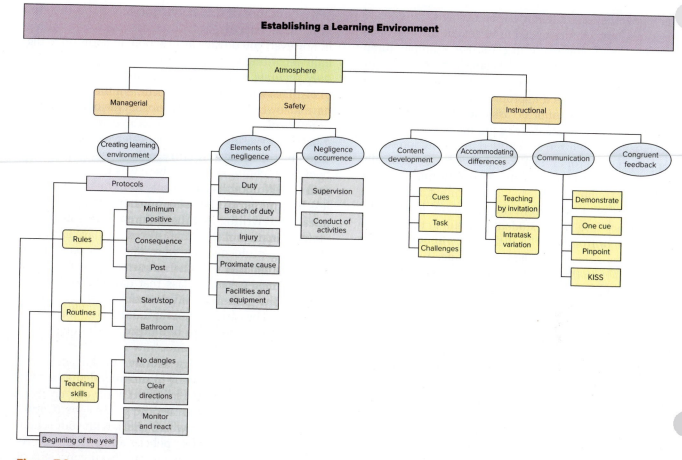

Figure 7.6 Establishing a learning environment.

Reading Comprehension Questions

1. What is meant by the following statement: "Management is a necessary, though not sufficient, condition for learning"?
2. What are the two major components in the establishment of a learning environment, and how do they differ from each other?
3. How does establishing a learning environment differ from discipline?
4. How do teachers' beliefs about children impact the learning environment?
5. What is the role of atmosphere in establishing a learning environment?
6. Describe and explain the three aspects that contribute to a productive teacher–student relationship. What are your thoughts on their importance and seemingly contradictory nature?
7. What are protocols? What two aspects make up protocols, and how do they differ?
8. What are three activities you can use to teach children to listen in a physical education environment?

9. List five guidelines for establishing rules of behavior in the gymnasium.
10. What four things can a teacher do to help students learn protocols?
11. Why are the first lessons of the year so important? List five suggestions for those lessons.
12. Identify and describe three aspects of teaching protocols.
13. Define developing the content, and explain why it is an important part of teaching physical education.
14. Why is providing cues an important teaching skill for physical education teachers? What might be the result when a teacher provides no cues or does so ineffectively?
15. As a teacher, do you think you are more likely to use teaching by invitation or intratask variation? Explain your answer.
16. What are the four aspects of negligence, and in what areas of teaching are they most likely to occur?

References/Suggested Readings

Bohn, C. M., A. D. Roehrig, and M. Pressley. 2004. The first days of school in the classrooms of two more effective and four less effective primary-grades teachers. *The Elementary School Journal* 104(4): 269–87.

Brooks, D. M. 1985. The first day of school. *Educational Leadership* 42(8): 76–78.

Cothran, D., P. Kulinna, and D. Garrahy. 2003. "This is kind of giving a secret away...": Students' perspectives on effective class management. *Teaching and Teacher Education* 19: 435–44.

Cotton, D. J., and J. T. Wolohan. 2016. *Law for recreation and sport managers.* 7th ed. Dubuque, IA: Kendall/Hunt.

Csikszentmihalyi, M. 2000. *Beyond boredom and anxiety: Experiencing flow in work and play.* San Francisco: Jossey-Bass.

Curran, T., and M. Standage. 2017. Psychological needs and the quality of students' engagement in physical education: Teachers as key facilitators. *Journal of Teaching in Physical Education* 36: 262–76.

Doyle, W. 1979. Making managerial decisions in classrooms. In *Classroom management: Seventy-eighth yearbook of the National Society for the Study of Education*, Part 2, ed. D. L. Duke. Chicago: University of Chicago Press.

Doyle, W. 1980. Student mediating responses in teaching effectiveness. Denton: North Texas State University. (ERIC Document Reproduction Service No. ED 187 698.)

Dyson, B. 2006. Students' perspectives of physical education. In *Handbook of physical education*, ed. D. Kirk, D., Macdonald, and M. O'Sullivan, 326–46. London: Sage.

Ennis, C. 1995. Teachers' responses to noncompliant students: The realities and consequences of a negotiated curriculum. *Teaching and Teacher Education* 11(5): 445–60.

Graham, G., E. Elliot, and S. Palmer. 2016. *Teaching children and adolescents physical education.* 4th ed. Champaign, IL: Human Kinetics.

Hastie, P., and D. Siedentop. 2007. The classroom ecology paradigm. In *Handbook of physical education*, ed. D. Kirk, D. Macdonald, and M. O'Sullivan, 214–25. London: Sage.

Hellison, D. 2011. *Teaching personal and social responsibility through physical activity.* 3rd ed. Champaign, IL: Human Kinetics.

Jones, V., and L. Jones. 2016. *Comprehensive classroom management: Creating positive learning environments and solving problems.* 11th ed. Boston: Pearson.

Martinek, T. & J. B. Griffin. 1994. Learned helplessness in physical education: A developmental study of causal attributions and task persistence. *Journal of Teaching in Physical Education* 13: 108–122.

Marzano, R. J., and J. S. Marzano. 2003. The key to classroom management. *Educational Leadership* 61(1): 6–13.

Mowling, C., K. Eider, S. Brock, and M. Rudisill. 2004. Student motivation in physical education. *Journal of Physical Education, Recreation and Dance* 75(6): 40–45.

Parker, M., A. MacPhail, M. O'Sullivan, D. Ní Chróinín, and E. McEvoy. 2018. Drawing' conclusions: Primary school children's construction of school physical education and physical activity opportunities outside of school. *European Physical Education Review* 24(4):449–466.

Parker, M., and J. Stiehl. 2015. Teaching personal and social responsibility. In *Standards based curriculum development*, 3rd ed., ed. D. Tannehill and J. Lund, 173–203. Boston: Jones & Bartlett.

Prouty, D., and J. Panicucci. 2007. *Adventure education: Theory and applications.* Champaign, IL: Human Kinetics.

Rink, J. 2014. *Teaching physical education for learning.* 7th ed. New York: McGraw-Hill.

Sagor, R. 2002. Lessons from skateboarders. *Educational Leadership* 60(1): 34–38.

[SHAPE America] Society of Health and Physical Education America. 2009. *Appropriate instructional practice guidelines for elementary school physical education.* 3rd ed. Reston, VA: SHAPE.

[SHAPE America] Society of Health and Physical Education America. 2014. *National standards & grade-level outcomes for K-12 physical education.* Reston, VA: SHAPE.

Stiehl, J. 2011. *Course outline SES 338: Teaching diverse populations.* Greeley, CO: University of Northern Colorado, School of Sport and Exercise Science.

Stiehl, J., G. S. Morris, and C. Sinclair. 2008. *Teaching physical activity: Change, challenge, choice.* Champaign, IL: Human Kinetics.

Tannehill, D., H. van der Mars, and A. MacPhail. 2015. *Building, delivering and sustaining effective physical education programs.* Sudbury, MA: Jones & Bartlett.

Tousignant, M., and D. Siedentop. 1983. The analysis of task structures in physical education. *Journal of Teaching in Physical Education* 3(1): 45–57.

Ward, S., and M. Parker. 2013. The voice of youth: Atmosphere in positive youth development program. *Physical Education and Sport Pedagogy* 18(5): 534–48.

Xiang, P., R. McBride, and J. Guan. 2004. Children's motivation in elementary physical education: A longitudinal study. *Research Quarterly for Exercise and Sport* 75(1): 71–80.

Maintaining Appropriate Behavior

The word *freedom* can never be uttered unless accompanied hand in hand with the word *responsibility*. It is kinder to keep the lid on the school for a start, lifting it little by little, simultaneously teaching responsibility, until the time comes when the lid can be cast entirely aside and only two conditions remain—freedom and responsibility.

—SYLVIA ASHTON WARNER

Drawn by children at Monfort, Chappelow or Shawsheen Elementary Schools, Greeley, CO.
Courtesy of Lizzy Ginger; Tia Ziegler

Key Concepts

- Maintaining the established learning environment is something that must be consciously cultivated.

- Appropriate behavior is not the mere absence of inappropriate behavior.

- If a learning environment is not effective, before blaming the students, assess your teaching behaviors.

- Three hierarchical aspects are paramount to maintaining a learning environment: increasing appropriate behavior, decreasing inappropriate behavior, and dealing with whole-class problems.

- Both proactive and reactive strategies can be used to increase appropriate behavior.

- Proactive strategies include positive interaction with children, prompting correct responses, and eliminating differential treatment of students.

- Behavior problems can be classified as a nonproblem, minor problem, major problem, or escalating problem.

- Ignoring inappropriate behavior when it is inconsequential or a nonproblem, using nonverbal interactions, and person-to-person dialogue are strategies that allow teachers to appropriately react to student behavior.

- To decrease inappropriate behavior, teachers can use desists, positive practice, time-outs, planning time, behavior contracts, and letters to parents, and as a last resort, they can involve the principal.

- Entire class behavior can be maintained by developing personal and social responsibility, class rewards, and token systems.

- A variety of teaching strategies can be used to maintain the class environment.

In the previous chapter, we explained a variety of effective techniques that teachers use to create successful learning environments so that their time can be spent actually teaching their classes rather than dealing with organizational issues and/or off-task behavior. You won't be surprised, however, to read that the techniques described in Chapter 8 aren't foolproof. Some children misbehave even when the teacher has done a great job practicing the protocols and doing everything she can to establish a positive learning environment. So what are some strategies used by teachers in dealing with misbehavior? That is the question we attempt to answer in Chapter 8.

Although we certainly don't have all the answers, we can share a number of techniques used by successful teachers to deal with misbehavior in physical education. We begin this chapter by describing strategies to prevent or minimize off-task behavior and then later suggest a number of strategies for actually dealing with misbehavior when it occurs—and it will.

Preventing Misbehavior

Consistently maintaining the environment designed for the class is second only to establishing it. Some call this discipline, but the word *discipline* has so many varied, and mostly negative, connotations that we have chosen to avoid it. Discipline most often implies punishing some type of inappropriate behavior. That, for us, is the last resort. From our viewpoint, establishing and maintaining a supportive learning environment is a more positive and appropriate perspective. We follow a positive approach to dealing with inappropriate behavior and attitudes that lets a teacher both create a positive atmosphere and teach students appropriate behavior for the gymnasium. In such a situation, the teacher's primary tasks are, first, to employ techniques that create the likelihood of appropriate behavior and, second, to use techniques that reduce inappropriate behavior.

We define appropriate behavior as student behavior consistent with the educational goals of a specific educational setting. Appropriate behavior is not the mere absence of inappropriate behavior; rather, it is a set of behaviors or actions. These positive behaviors or actions must replace the inappropriate behavior.

It's normal for all teachers to be concerned about how to hold students accountable for what they are supposed to do. Our work with beginning and veteran teachers, as well as our own teaching experiences, suggest that most teachers ask themselves questions about responding to student behavior. The difference between so-called good teachers and poor teachers is not their concern about holding children accountable—all teachers encounter deviant and disruptive behavior and must find ways of dealing with it. Rather, successful teachers are able to minimize the amount of time they devote to dealing with inappropriate behavior and do so in a largely positive manner.

Even the teacher who develops managerial and instructional components, establishes and explains rules of behavior, prompts and provides feedback for appropriate behavior, and teaches with a critical demandingness can't be sure that a class will perform as expected. In many classes, there will be some children who find it difficult to function in a school environment, not only in physical education, but in other classes as well. Occasionally an entire class has difficulty adhering to the established behavioral boundaries.

Whether it is one, several, or most of the children who are unable to abide by the rules, your first response might be to examine your performance as a teacher. When children react in unexpected ways, you may, upon reflection, find that their reactions are justified. Children are incredibly honest; two of the top three reasons they list for misbehavior are (1) the lesson was boring or (2) they didn't think they could do the tasks in the lesson, so they didn't try (Cothran and Kulinna 2007). A teacher may not want to know or believe that a lesson is a dud, but the children will let the teacher know. Occasionally it's the teacher's behavior, rather than the children's, that needs to be changed. As discussed in Chapter 4, becoming a reflective teacher requires that teachers are constantly monitoring their teaching and continually thinking about what needs to change or be done differently. For example, when children have problems with equipment or don't understand or hear the teacher's directions, they will participate at their own level, doing their own thing rather than asking for help. Likewise, if a task is too boring, too hard, or too easy, children will often change the task to meet their needs. Therefore, it doesn't look like the task that the teacher gave, and the children will be perceived as being off task.

If you determine that the lesson is appropriate and your performance as a teacher is satisfactory, you can then look for other causes for disruptive behavior. Try not to view disruptive behavior as a personal affront. A first step is to assess the behavior. Evertson and Emmer (2016) describe four possible categories of disruptive behavior: nonproblem, minor problem, major problem but limited in scope and effects, and escalating or spreading problem.

A nonproblem is any behavior for which an attempted reaction to it would consume too much energy, interrupt the lesson, and detract from the classroom atmosphere. A minor problem includes those things that run counter to classroom protocols but do not, when occurring infrequently, disrupt the class activities or seriously interfere with other students' learning. These behaviors are minor irritants as long as they are limited to a few students and are brief; we would not give them much attention except that, unattended, they might persist and spread. Not responding might cause an appearance of inconsistency and potentially undermine the management component, and student learning might be adversely affected. A major problem includes activities that interfere with others' learning. The occurrence may be limited to a single student or perhaps a few students not acting in concert. Major escalating problems constitute

Table 8.1 Levels of Management Issues

Level	Examples
Nonproblem	• Brief periods of inattention • Short pauses while working • Standing at the back of the group while others are sitting • A little talking while others are talking • Occasionally not immediately stopping on the signal
Minor Problem	• Excessive talking during group work • Running to get equipment after being asked to walk • Excessive playing with equipment when it should be held • Inappropriate language • Interrupting • Lying
Major Problem	• Constant movement around the space • Refusal to participate • Violation of school rules • Fighting • Unsafe actions
Major Escalating Problem	• Roaming around at will; leaving the space • Constant interference with others • Blatant refusal to cooperate

a threat to the learning environment. Table 8.1 lists examples of each type of problem.

Having assessed the behavior, you can deal with it in two phases: reacting appropriately in the short term and seeking to understand the cause in the long term. The remainder of this chapter is largely about short-term responses, as the behavior must be addressed before seeking a long-term solution. Once short-term behaviors are addressed, effective teachers will individually address long-term causes and solutions, if needed, to create a student-centered learning environment.

Comparing a referee's or an umpire's job with the teacher's need to hold children accountable places a teacher's job in perspective. Those referees whom players and coaches respect share the following characteristics: they're fair, consistent, accurate, and not emotionally involved. As teachers, we should keep these good characteristics in mind as we reflect on how to help children work within our guidelines. Although a referee's job is probably less enjoyable than a player's or coach's, it's an important aspect of organized sport. Similarly, maintaining the learning environment is an important role for a teacher. In physical education, as in sports, there will be violations and infractions.

Our goal is to help children become intrinsically motivated so they can learn the skills to become physically active. In some situations, this motivation will occur naturally, and thus few of the techniques described will be necessary. In other teaching situations, however, many of the techniques will be needed. In either case, the goal is to use fewer and fewer of these techniques so the children participate in physical education because they like it and feel it is valuable rather than because of an external reward or motivator. Our explanation of effective techniques for helping children work within our guidelines is divided into three steps: increasing appropriate behavior, decreasing inappropriate behavior, and maintaining whole-class appropriate behavior. Remember, your action as a teacher should match the magnitude of the problem. Overreacting will soon result in a negative class atmosphere and be similar to "crying wolf"—children will cease to respond. Underreacting creates an atmosphere of physical and psychological unsafety and nonlearning.

Increasing Appropriate Behavior

When behavior doesn't conform to the expectations established for the specific setting, a teacher's first strategy would likely be to increase appropriate behavior. Six techniques teachers have found useful for increasing appropriate behavior are positive interaction, eliminating differential treatment, prompting, ignoring inappropriate behavior, nonverbal teacher interactions, and person-to-person dialogue. Most of these techniques would be considered soft skills because they are noninvasive and subtle. Three of the techniques are proactive—that is, they are to be used in the absence of inappropriate behavior. The other three are reactive, to be used in response to inappropriate behavior.

Proactive Strategies

Teachers can use many techniques to increase the likelihood of students behaving appropriately. Many of these can be done proactively to increase the chances that appropriate behavior will prevail and that the atmosphere of the gymnasium remains positive.

Positive Interaction As discussed in Chapter 7, one of the most powerful things a teacher can do to create an environment where students want to be is to make the gymnasium a positive place. One of the most convincing ways to create a positive environment is to interact with students positively when they behave appropriately. In essence, this approach emphasizes the positive rather than the negative. Many children who are known throughout the school

as discipline problems have become accustomed to hearing nothing but negative comments about their behavior. Catching them in the act of doing something right and praising them for it can dramatically change their behavior.

But praise shouldn't be contrived and meaningless, offered with no genuine feeling, as is often the case. Give praise frequently but not so profusely that it seems trivial. And give it only when a child actually displays appropriate behavior. All children are capable of receiving some type of praise—catch them being good! Instead of waiting for problems to occur in order to prevent difficulties, teachers should strive to catch students being good to encourage positive behavior as it occurs.

This sounds like common sense, but research and our experiences have shown that this isn't the prevalent mode of operation in the gym. In 1984, Siedentop and Taggart wrote that "punitive and corrective interaction" were the most frequent forms of communication (p. 105). Almost 20 years later, it was found that although teachers espoused a positive form of classroom management, they relied almost exclusively on rewards and punishment (Cothran, Kulinna, and Garrahy 2003). Even today, little has changed. You can stand at many gymnasium doors and hear statements such as, "I'm waiting for you!" "*Ssshh!*" "Ben, whenever you sit down, we'll start," or "Kate, carry the ball." Although these statements aren't openly negative, they in fact reinforce certain children's inappropriate behavior and ignore the appropriate behavior of a large majority of students. They are what might be called nagging behaviors. The following list includes examples of positive verbal and nonverbal interactions. For an idea of how you're doing, have a student make a simple tally of your interactions or videotape a class and critique your own behavior.

Verbal Positive Statements	Nonverbal Positive Interactions
Good	High five
Terrific	Smiling
Right	Clapping
Nice job	Thumbs up
Way to go	Winking
That's it	Pat on the back
Thank you	Shaking hands
Great	Giving an OK sign
You did it this time	Fist bumping
Beautiful	
Excellent	
Nicely done	
OK	
All right	

Behavior problems are not as frequent when children have opportunities to respond with success and when their successes are acknowledged by teachers and peers (Park and Lynch 2014, p. 35).

	Name called	Reprimand	Positive Interaction
Juan	III	I	II
Sue			
Rich	II	I	I
Jesse			
Don	HHI IIII	IIII	HHI
Billie	I		I

Figure 8.1 Chart for identifying differential treatment of students.

Eliminating Differential Treatment Often a stranger can walk into a classroom and after a few minutes pick out the "discipline problems" or the "really good students" in a group of children he or she has never seen before. Frequently these are the children whose names the teacher is constantly calling out: "Rico, are you listening?" "Jade, sit down, please," or "Brady, that's great," "Jayla, you're awesome." It is not uncommon to see the same children singled out repeatedly. Typically they are masters of their craft—they know exactly how far they can go without actually being held accountable, or conversely, they know exactly what to do to gain the teacher's praise. Because they covet adult attention, these children persist in their behavior (and as long as we reinforce their behavior by acknowledging it, they become even more skilled at it). So, avoid singling out these children whenever possible.

Every person needs recognition. It is expressed cogently by the lad who says, "Mother, let's play darts. I'll throw the darts and you say 'Wonderful.'"

—DALE BAUGHMAN

One way to spot differential treatment of students in your classes is to audio-record a few lessons. This can be done by placing a digital audio recorder in the gymnasium, attached to your arm, or in a pocket. (This observation and analysis technique is discussed further in Chapter 13.) After you've recorded several lessons, listen and record the number of times you call each child's name and the number of reprimands as well as positive comments you give to individual children.

A simple way to record your tally is to use a copy of the class roster that has three columns to the right of the names (Figure 8.1). The first column is a tally for each time you call a child's name; the second column is a tally for each time you reprimand or interact negatively with a specific child; the third column is for tallying positive comments or interactions. After you complete your tallies, if you find that you single out the same few children and/or interact positively or negatively with a select few, you know you need to change your teaching behavior.

Prompting Prompting is a teacher behavior that reminds students what is expected of them. Some teachers find themselves prompting appropriate behavior only after inappropriate behavior has occurred. However, this is not the most effective way to use prompts. Prompts should be used as a positive tool as often as possible rather than as a negative interaction. For example, it is more beneficial to say, "Remember to walk as you go to pick up equipment," rather than "I told you to walk!" or even "Can't you remember by now that you are supposed to walk?" Used as in the first statement, prompting is a proactive response rather than a reactive response. Remember, many of the behaviors you want students to demonstrate are learned (just like fundamental movement skills), so initially you should prompt students frequently about what behavior is appropriate; later, you will probably need to prompt only when a new or different situation arises.

Talking to Equipment

A teacher recently shared with us a creative and effective way to prompt students toward appropriate use of equipment: talking to the equipment. When a youngster finds it hard to hold equipment still or place it on the floor, the instructor simply picks up the piece of equipment and directs the appropriate behavior and his or her comments toward the equipment. For example, the teacher might pick up the hockey stick and say, "I thought we agreed that you were supposed to be on the floor while I was talking. So that others can hear and I can talk, I really need you to be on the floor. Do you understand?" The teacher says the children think he is a bit crazy, but it works.

Reactive Approaches

Interacting positively, eliminating differential treatment, and prompting are all proactive strategies for increasing appropriate behavior and thus are a means of preventing inappropriate behavior before it happens. The three strategies that follow are reactive strategies designed to increase appropriate behavior. They are intended for use after the inappropriate behavior has occurred—as a means of reacting to it. Ignoring inappropriate behavior and using nonverbal interactions and person-to-person dialogue are strategies teachers can use as responses to inappropriate behavior; each is designed to increase appropriate behavior, especially when the problem is a nonproblem or minor problem.

Ignoring Inappropriate Behavior The opposite of emphasizing appropriate behavior with positive interactions is ignoring inappropriate behavior. Many of us find that praising appropriate behavior is hard, but ignoring inappropriate behavior is even more difficult. Inappropriate behavior can be ignored as a nonproblem when it meets the following three criteria:

1. It is of short duration and is not likely to spread or persist.
2. It is a minor deviation.
3. Reacting to it would interrupt a lesson or call attention to the behavior.

Student behaviors that could be ignored in a physical education setting include occasional calling out during discussions, brief whispering, short periods of inattentiveness or nonpractice, and occasional continuation of activity after the stop signal. Unless a behavior is harmful to other students, causes a safety problem, or seriously disrupts other students, reacting to it would consume too much of your energy, interrupt your lessons constantly, and detract from your classroom climate.

To be completely effective, teachers should ignore minor inappropriate behavior and simultaneously praise appropriate behavior. Yet, when we've become accustomed to saying, "Ssshh!" "Hurry up!" "I'm waiting for you to get quiet," or "Tommy!!!" it's not easy to change to phrases such as, "Tia was quiet when she heard the stop signal," "Terrific, you were ready to go in 10 seconds today," and "Jimmy, you showed thoughtfulness when you helped Dion up after he fell down." Such interactions, which can create appropriate behaviors in children, imply for many of us that the teacher is letting Tommy or the students who aren't yet quiet get away with inappropriate behavior. This is risky because the perceived implication is that our control is

in jeopardy. In reality, the teacher who ignores simple inappropriate behavior while praising appropriate behavior is teaching children what desired behavior is while creating an atmosphere that is warm and conducive to learning.

There's a subtle message about what merits attention in this scenario of praising appropriate behavior and ignoring inappropriate behavior. If a teacher instead used both sets of examples (praising appropriate behavior and reacting verbally to inappropriate behavior) described in the previous paragraph, the students would receive a message of confusion. Students would assume they could receive reinforcement and adult attention for either appropriate or inappropriate behavior.

For many of us, ignoring inappropriate behavior is uncomfortable and awkward. A good way to assess your skill in praising the good and ignoring the inappropriate is to audio-record your lessons and count the number of times you say something positive and the number of times you say something negative. Remember, even little things such as "Hurry up!" and "Ssshh!" count as negative interactions. Don't be surprised at what you first discover about your behavior; look at it as an opportunity to improve.

Nonverbal Teacher Interactions A number of simple nonverbal techniques are often sufficient to prompt appropriate student behavior when the behavior is a minor problem. Sometimes just the physical proximity of the teacher will solicit the desirable behavior from some students. For example, when giving directions or speaking to the class as a whole, the teacher merely stands near the student displaying inappropriate behavior. Another technique for increasing appropriate behavior is to borrow the equipment the student is using for purposes of demonstration. Finally, even less obvious actions often work. For example, simple eye contact or a signal, such as nodding the head, will redirect the student.

Person-to-Person Dialogue Another successful technique for increasing appropriate behavior with minor problems is the person-to-person dialogue. Arrange a time to meet with a child away from the class (though not immediately before or after). You might say to the child, "Robby, you don't seem to be enjoying our physical education class. I'd like you to come to my office after school today so that we can talk about it." The purpose of this meeting is to determine the reasons for the child's behavior in your class. This is not a time for a lecture; instead, it should be an open and honest conversation between teacher and student. We've found that a statement such as the following enables many children to begin a discussion of their concerns: "Robby, I'd like to talk to you about physical education class. Is there something I do that bothers you?"

This statement takes the focus off the child and places it on the teacher. Many children are quite candid about what's bothering them. Remember, this is a dialogue. Explaining to the child something about how and why you teach is constructive and often productive. Lecturing the child about behavior or threatening the child with future punishments is counterproductive. This dialogue is not teacher-to-child but person-to-person. Often the temptation to lecture, accuse, or blame a child is strong, but succumbing to this temptation is the quickest way to destroy rapport between student and teacher. If a child trusts you enough to talk candidly about personal concerns but you threaten or lecture, communication ceases. Many children—especially those who need individual attention the most—have been betrayed before, so they're likely to be

sensitive and wary. Use of teacher power in this situation reinforces a child's belief that teachers are untrustworthy and that being honest only gets him or her into more trouble.

Some children never want to participate in physical education class. A person-to-person dialogue is often helpful here, as is a conference with the child's other teachers. Some children may be afraid of participating in physical activity because they've already had unsatisfactory experiences at home or on the playground. Other children may have "issues" with classmates that are easily manifested in activity-oriented settings. Still others may be unmotivated and antisocial. Regardless, if a child has a legitimate reason, we respect the child and attempt to create a satisfactory alternative. Further, if a child is unmotivated and/or antisocial, person-to-person dialogue can act as a beginning point for seeking a solution to a problem that may be beyond physical education. Forcing a child to participate in physical education classes without first understanding the reason for the reluctance may not be in the child's best interests. Once you understand why a child is reluctant to participate, you can make an informed decision about the most appropriate action.

Decreasing Inappropriate Behavior

Although our first approach in dealing with inappropriate behavior is to attempt to increase appropriate behavior, this doesn't always work. At times, with major problems or with those behaviors that may escalate into major problems, a teacher must decrease inappropriate behavior. When this is necessary, the teacher should have a repertoire of strategies—often called hard skills because they are deliberate and obvious—available. Teachers in physical education have found the following techniques useful: positive practice, desists, working independently, time-outs, conflict resolution, behavior contracts, letters to parents, and involving the principal. Note that many of the techniques fit the psychological definition of the term *punishment*—they decrease the likelihood of an inappropriate behavior recurring by applying undesirable consequences to the behavior. To make these techniques effective, be sure that your class rules have first been established, taught, and learned. Afterward, punish the behavior and not the child; always maintain self-control without publicly confronting the student. Also, any action the teacher takes to decrease inappropriate behavior should be accompanied by actions to build appropriate behavior. Finally, it is in the best interest of the teacher to document incidents of both positive and negative behaviors. Evidence can go a long way when communicating with

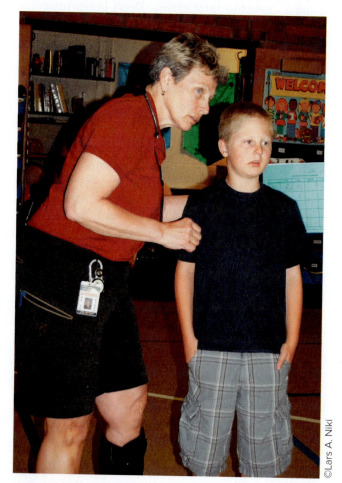

©Lars A. Niki

Person-to-person dialogue allows a teacher to know students individually.

students, parents, or administrators (see Chapter 12, Figure 12.18, for a sample affective rubric).

Nowhere in our discussion will you find strategies that advocate physical exercise as a technique to reduce inappropriate behavior. Physical activity (sit-ups, push-ups, running laps, etc.) should never be used as a technique to hold children accountable for their behavior. Using physical activity as punishment is counterproductive to what we want to happen as a result of physical education (SHAPE America 2009a, 2009b). Our goal is for children to acquire the skills and desire to be physically active for a lifetime. Using physical activity as punishment may temporarily reduce the off-task behavior being punished, but the long-term result is often the reduction of any participation in the physical activity used as punishment. Instead of learning to love activity, children will hate activity because of its association with punishment. Following are techniques that can be used to react to inappropriate behavior in an attempt to reduce and eliminate it.

Positive Practice

Positive practice is a technique that requires the student, group, or class to practice the acceptable or desired behavior after the demonstration of an inappropriate behavior. For example, students are asked to walk and get equipment, but they run instead. Most of us would remind them to walk or ignore the behavior.

An acceptable way to have them learn to walk is positive practice. Stop the students and have them go back to where they started and repeat the activity of getting equipment—this time walking. You may even have them repeat it several times. Do this every time students run when you say "walk," and soon they will learn to walk.

Desists

Sometimes it is impossible to ignore inappropriate behavior, especially when safety is an issue. When that is the case, one of the most common and useful ways to react to the behavior is with a desist, a verbal statement that tells a child to stop doing something. Using desists effectively can result in behavior change. In his seminal work, Kounin (1970) established several conditions that must be present for a desist to be effective:

- A desist must be clear. "Ellen, stop doing that" isn't enough. The desist must contain exact information about what the student is doing wrong. For example, "Ellen, stop hitting the basketball with the tennis racket" is clear and specific. The student knows exactly what she is doing wrong.
- A desist must be firm. Firmness is the degree to which the teacher follows through on the desist, making sure the student knows that the teacher means what was said. Moving a bit closer to the student, momentarily looking the student in the eyes, and keeping a straight face when delivering the desist all communicate the teacher's firmness.
- A desist must be well timed. The behavior must desist immediately before it's allowed to spread to other students and before a child forgets what was done.
- A desist must be appropriately targeted. It must be directed at the original offender, not a second or third party.
- A desist must not be harsh. Rough desists may upset children or make them defensive and usually aren't effective. Firmness doesn't mean harshness or punitiveness; it is simply meaning what you say.

Working Independently Away from the Group

A step used by some teachers to address inappropriate behavior before resorting to a time-out may be to have students work independently away from the rest of the class. In this way, the student is not totally removed from the environment. Instead, the student is placed at the edge of the activity space, away from the immediate class. This strategy is particularly appealing because it addresses the inappropriate behavior but keeps the

---

Alternatives to Physical Activity as Punishment

The position statement *Using Physical Activity as Punishment and/or Behavior Management* (SHAPE America 2009b, p. 3) suggests the following actions as suitable alternatives to using physical activity as punishment:

- Include students in establishing expectations and outcomes early in the year, and review those expectations and outcomes frequently.
- Include students in meaningful discussions about goals and how to reach them.
- Be consistent with enforcing behavioral expectations within the learning environment.
- Practice and reward compliance with rules and outcomes.
- Offer positive feedback and catch students doing things right.
- Don't reinforce negative behavior by drawing attention to it.
- Hold students accountable for misbehavior.
- Develop efficient routines that keep students involved in learning tasks.
- Wait for students to be attentive before providing directions.

student actively engaged in the learning task. If the student has maintained nondisruptive behavior for a specific amount of time, the teacher may ask the student whether he or she understands the particular misbehavior in question and if the student is ready to join the class.

Time-outs

A time-out is much like a penalty box in hockey. However, unlike the penalty box, our use of time-outs is designed to help children take responsibility for their own behavior and thus may differ slightly from what you have been accustomed to. During a time-out, a child, either through choice or at the teacher's request, withdraws from class until ready to return and function according to the class rules. When ready to return to class, the child simply rejoins the activity. Teach the time-out procedure with all other procedures at the beginning of the year so you can subsequently give a time-out as a standard penalty without disrupting the rest of the class. Here are some other considerations for effective use of time-outs:

- The student must find physical education enjoyable; if not, the time-out may be a reward instead of a punishment.
- The time-out area should be a clearly designated place where social contact with classmates isn't possible.
- To make time-outs designed to enhance student responsibility and decision making, we advocate a four-step progressive approach. The first time a student displays a behavior that might result in a time-out, prompt him or her toward what is appropriate. The second time, ask if the student needs a time-out. (Some children are amazingly honest here.) If they elect to go to time-out, they can return when ready. The third step in the sequence is, "You need a time-out." Once again, students can return when they are ready. The fourth step is not only, "You need a time-out," but the student needs to stay there until a conversation between the teacher and the child can take place.

Some teachers have developed a version of time-out that allows students to reflect on their behavior. In these situations, students react in written format to what they did and what they should do. Younger students may draw their time-out reflections, and the teacher then writes what the drawing means when talking to the child (Figure 8.2a); older students often write theirs (Figure 8.2b). While this strategy removes

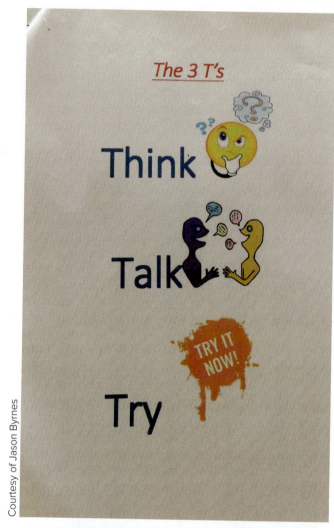

Courtesy of Jason Byrnes

Think, Talk, Try allows children to work out conflicts for themselves

the child from activity for a longer amount of time, the result is that the child rarely ends up in time-out again.

Conflict Resolution Strategies

A variety of conflict resolution strategies with application to physical education exist, including planning time, talking bench, and conflict corner (Landers 2014). Each is a peer-directed alternative to time-outs designed for inappropriate behavior involving two students interacting with one another. When students sit alone, as in a time-out, they do not have the opportunity to discuss or resolve their problems. Conflict resolution strategies, by contrast, give students who do not demonstrate appropriate behavior a chance to resolve their conflict. When students find themselves in a conflict with others in the class, they can make their way

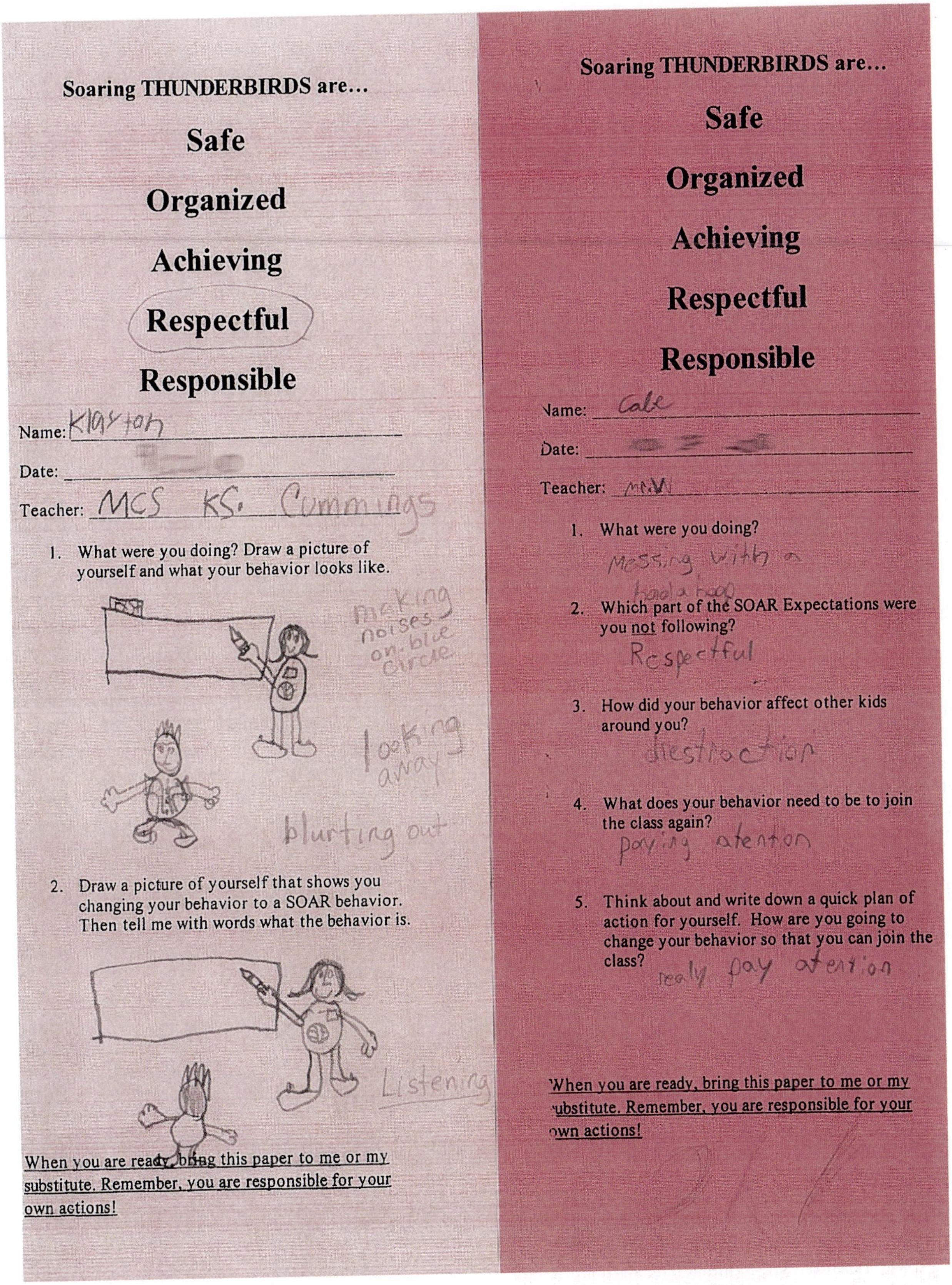

Soaring THUNDERBIRDS are...

Safe

Organized

Achieving

(**Respectful**)

Responsible

Name: Klaxton

Date: _____

Teacher: MCS   KS. Cummings

1. What were you doing? Draw a picture of yourself and what your behavior looks like.

making noises on blue circle

looking away

blurting out

2. Draw a picture of yourself that shows you changing your behavior to a SOAR behavior. Then tell me with words what the behavior is.

Listening

When you are ready, bring this paper to me or my substitute. Remember, you are responsible for your own actions!

Soaring THUNDERBIRDS are...

Safe

Organized

Achieving

Respectful

Responsible

Name: Cale

Date: _____

Teacher: Mr.W

1. What were you doing?
   Messing with a hoola hoop

2. Which part of the SOAR Expectations were you not following?
   Respectful

3. How did your behavior affect other kids around you?
   diestroction

4. What does your behavior need to be to join the class again?
   paying atention

5. Think about and write down a quick plan of action for yourself. How are you going to change your behavior so that you can join the class?
   really pay atention

When you are ready, bring this paper to me or my substitute. Remember, you are responsible for your own actions!

Figure 8.2 (a) Left: Time-out reflection form for lower grades. (b) Right: Time-out reflection form for upper grades.
Karla Drury, Shawsheen Elementary School, Greeley, CO. Used with permission.

Possible Cues and Questions for Conflict Resolution

The problem in our own words . . .

When and where the problem took place . . .

Strategies we used to try to avoid the problem . . .

Our behavior affected others by . . .

What we will do to prevent the problem from occurring again . . .

Follow-up actions we will take now . . .

This should happen if the problem occurs again . . .

to a predesignated area of the gymnasium, where they are required to sit together and develop a resolution. One of the most effective strategies we have seen used to structure the conflict resolution is the use of the "Three T's" (Byrne 2018; Cothran 2001). In this situation, the conflict resolution space contains a bench (or two chairs) and an egg timer. When the children go to the space, they turn over the egg timer for one minute of *thinking* time about the event that has occurred (no talking allowed); then they engage in one minute of *talking* time with each other about what happened. This is followed by developing a clear practical commitment from both children to *try* to do something differently so as to lessen the likelihood of this dispute ever happening again. There must be a plan before the children rejoin the lesson.

Be aware that, as with any educational strategy, students need to be taught how to use conflict resolution strategies effectively. Cues and questions (Box 8-1) can be posted on the wall or on a written sheet similar to the ones used in time-out to prompt students toward appropriate behavior (Figures 8.2a and 8.2b). Students can then read and review the prompts to assess the nature of their behavior and develop an alternative. Essentially, this process places the responsibility of conflict resolution on the students As with any new technique, learning to do it takes time, but the result is a class that cooperates more and students who learn to resolve their differences.

Behavior Contracts

Have you ever tried to lose weight by making a "deal" with yourself or by rewarding yourself at the end of losing so many pounds? The same is true with some isolated children in your class: They need a written "deal"

with the teacher as a prompt to make things happen. A behavior contract provides that. It is a written agreement between a student and the teacher regarding behavior in the physical education setting. Although it may seem like overkill, a contract can be done quietly, simply, and privately to provide some students with the necessary focus to enjoy physical education and allow others to enjoy it.

The contract includes a statement of the desired behavior, the conditions (how much, for how long), and the rewards that will be earned if the behavior and the conditions are met. When using a behavior contract, remember that students must have a role in defining all three aspects of the contract: behavior, conditions, and rewards. After all three have been agreed upon, it is important that both parties (sometimes a third party as a witness) sign the agreement. The student should be made aware of the importance of the agreement and, just as the teacher does, view it as a formal agreement, not to be taken lightly. Figure 8.3 gives an example of a behavior contract with one student.

Communication to Parents

Desists, time-outs, planning time, and behavior contracts work with some children but not with others. When a child continues to misbehave and present problems, a written report to the parents can be effective in obtaining that child's cooperation. But this technique should be used only after other approaches have proved unsuccessful.

The written report lists specific behaviors (Figure 8.4). The child is to have the report signed by a parent and then is to return it to you. The report is usually followed by improvements in behavior. When that occurs, send home another report, as soon as possible, that enumerates the improvements as clearly as the earlier report catalogued the violations. This second report congratulates the child on improved behavior and, like the first one, requires a parent's signature.

Catch Them Being Good and Tell Someone

Better yet, phone, text, or e-mail a parent at the end of the school day when the child has had a "really good day." Remember that for some children, small steps mean a lot. Send the text or make the call after the parent has arrived home. You will be amazed at the reaction from parents when they receive a positive message. You will be even more amazed at the change in the child's behavior as a result of the positive communication to the parent.

Figure 8.3 Typical behavior contract.

BEHAVIOR CONTRACT

Kim Thomas and Mr. Diller agree that the following plan will be in effect for the next two weeks.

Starting date _____ Ending date _____

Kim will

1. Not interrupt other students' work by trying to knock their equipment away

2. Not disturb class by talking while the teacher is talking

3. Participate in all activities and try hard to improve her skills in throwing

Mr. Diller will

1. Give Kim individual help on throwing

2. Count one point for each day that Kim meets the three points stated above

3. Let Kim help with the physical education equipment for one week if she earns five points during the two weeks of the contract

Signed _____

_____

_____

Figure 8.3 Typical behavior contract.

Written reports to parents should not be used only as a measure to decrease inappropriate behavior. The teachers of St. Andrew's Episcopal School in Austin, Texas, found that a "good" letter (Figure 8.5) was one of their most effective strategies for increasing support for the program and generating goodwill with parents (D. Lambdin, personal communication, July 1991). In the St. Andrew's program, a "good" letter was sent home with every deserving student during one marking period each year. The response from parents was gratifying. Many parents commented on how wonderful it was that teachers took time to let them know about good behavior.

Involving the Principal

On rare occasions, you as the teacher may need to discuss a child's inappropriate behavior with the principal. The decision, however, should not be taken lightly. You may wish to initially seek advice from other, more experienced teachers because they likely have successfully dealt with similar situations. Additionally, you may also choose to seek your principal's advice because they serve as a critical resource for beginning teachers. When meeting with other teachers or the principal, explain the situation and seek advice in devising a plan for addressing the behavior on your own. Only when

ELEMENTARY SCHOOL
PHYSICAL EDUCATION BEHAVIOR REPORT

NAME _____ DATE _____

Educational research has consistently shown that when a teacher spends class time managing discipline problems, less teaching and student learning occur. Disruptive behavior, therefore, is a primary reason for poor student achievement.

We regret to inform you that your child exhibited the following misbehavior during physical education class today:

_____ Fought with others	_____ Refused to participate
_____ Argued with others	_____ Was lazy; had no hustle or energy
_____ Mistreated equipment	_____ Was late to class
_____ Disrupted the work of others	_____ Was disruptive in hallway
_____ Was discourteous to others	_____ Was continually off-task; did not follow teacher's directions
_____ Frequently clowned, acting foolish and silly	_____ Spoke using inappropriate language
_____ Talked while teacher was talking	_____ Did not listen to teacher

Teacher's Comments: _____

_____

_____

Please discuss today's incident with your youngster. We are concerned about the harm your child's behavior is causing himself/herself and his/her classmates. We will keep you informed of your child's behavioral progress during the coming weeks.

Thank you for your cooperation.

TEACHER _____

PARENT'S SIGNATURE _____

Figure 8.4 Behavior report for parents.

you've tried every other possible technique to deal with behavior detrimental to the child and his or her classmates should you take steps to send a student to the principal to explain his or her actions.

Maintaining Appropriate Behavior in Entire Classes

The scene: May in the Southeast, a fourth-grade class with a student teacher conducting the lesson and two cooperating teachers observing. The setting: An old school with no air-conditioning and all the windows open in the second-floor gym. The unit: Throwing and catching. The equipment: Beanbags. The task: Some version of throw-and-catch with a partner. The result: The students thought the better task would be to throw the beanbags out the windows to see if they could hit the sidewalk below. The larger result: The teacher was befuddled, unnerved, and demoralized. (This is a true story from one of the five authors of this book!)

The moral of the story: All teachers at some time experience entire classes that test their ability to maintain the preferred learning environment. At this point,

Figure 8.5 "Good" letter for parents.

ELEMENTARY SCHOOL
PHYSICAL EDUCATION BEHAVIOR REPORT

Name _____ Date _____

Educational research has shown that when a teacher spends class time managing discipline problems, less teaching and less learning occur. Therefore, when disruptive behavior is nonexistent in a class situation, greater student achievement is likely to result.

We are glad to inform you that _____*(child's name)*_____ consistently exhibits the following exemplary behaviors in physical education class:

_____ Listens to the teacher   _____ Is courteous to others

_____ Is on-task, following   _____ Treats equipment with
directions   care

_____ Is eager to participate   _____ Plays safely

Your child is doing a wonderful-terrific-dynamite job in physical education and we are proud of him/her. You are to be commended for preparing your youngster to function so well in school. We are more effective teachers because of your efforts.

Thank you for your cooperation.

TEACHER _____

---

two things can happen. Either you can write the class off as "bad" (it was tempting) and resign yourself to the role of a police officer trying to keep control of a group or you can assume the role of a teacher and guide and try to find a mutually acceptable solution to the problem.

In this section we offer three approaches. The first and second, class rewards and individual rewards, are clearly behaviorally oriented and designed to remedy the problem and then find out why it existed. They are for use when nothing else seems to work. The last approach, developing personal and social responsibility, is a more detailed reiteration of establishing a learning environment and brings us back to where we started in Chapter 7. Although we are not advocating that developing personal and social responsibility is a management system, we include this approach again because its use results in children who are active learners and capable partners in their educational experiences (Hellison 2011; Parker and Stiehl 2015; Stork and Sanders 2002). The personal-and-social-responsibility approach promotes children as competent decision makers, and as such, "management" becomes almost a nonissue.

Reward Systems

Rewards can reduce inappropriate behavior and help build a positive climate. The improvement occurs because children are attracted to the rewards and thus direct their behavior toward appropriate behavior and away from inappropriate behavior. If you decide to implement a reward system, consider the following guidelines:

- Check your school and district policies to see if any rewards are prohibited. For example, parties with food are not allowed in some schools, and others restrict off-campus trips. Avoid use of candy or other unhealthy treats that may contradict a healthy active lifestyle.
- Make sure the rewards are attractive to the students. Successful rewards to be earned in physical education have included public recognition (name boards, photo boards, names in school newsletter), extra physical education time, free-choice time (at the end of class or the end of the week), special privileges (helping the teacher with other classes or before school), field trips, equipment use (borrowing equipment to use at home and on weekends), and t-shirts. Regardless of what reward is established, its effectiveness is based on the children having had a part in the decision. The easiest way to do this is to ask them.
- The rewards should target the behavior you are after. If you want children to stop activity and listen when asked, then the rewards should be for those specific behaviors.
- Design a reward system in which it is not too difficult to achieve the reward (this will frustrate students) or too easy (this will lose their attention).
- Make record keeping easy so your system does not create an enormous amount of paperwork.

One caution regarding reward systems: Research is fairly clear that extrinsic rewards can reduce intrinsic motivation (Deci, Koestner, and Ryan 1999; Wang, 2017). That is, if students work only for the reward, they will not be motivated to continue that same behavior when the reward is withdrawn. When using reward systems, be thoughtful about their use. No purpose is served by rewarding activities that are already motivating to students. With any reward system, the goal is to eventually withdraw the reward and have student behavior remain appropriate. Thus, when creating a reward system, also develop strategies for its eventual nonuse—for example, increasingly longer times or increasingly more displays of appropriate behavior before receiving rewards.

Two reward systems, one for a class and one for individuals, are described below.

Class Rewards   With class rewards, the whole class has the opportunity to earn rewards for abiding by the class rules. The first step is to establish a reward. When an entire class does well for a day (week, month), it receives the reward. For example, if a class consistently does better than the performance standards established for management tasks over a given period of time, it receives a poster or banner to display in its room. Some teachers provide a reward for a "class of the week." We prefer, however, that rewards not be exclusionary. Every class should be able to earn a reward every week. Competition should be limited to the class against a standard, not the class against other classes.

Token Systems   Time-out penalizes disruptive behavior; a token system rewards desirable behavior. A token system is a program with academic, organizational, or managerial outcomes accompanied by a system in which students can earn "tokens" that can be exchanged for various rewards (Siedentop and Tannehill 2000). The intent is to reward appropriate behavior and thereby encourage all children to behave appropriately.

The teacher initially explains to the class that a particular rule or procedure is being violated or not being accomplished as efficiently as possible. In doing this, the teacher must clearly define the behaviors to be improved. After the behaviors have been defined, rewards must be developed. This is best done with the students' input by having them rank the rewards the teacher has offered according to their desirability. The higher the ranking, the more the students will be motivated by the reward; the lower the ranking, the greater the probability it won't do much to encourage children to change their behavior.

Once the behavior has been specified and the rewards agreed upon, it must be decided how many tokens it will take to earn a certain reward. For example, five minutes of free time at the end of class might cost 3 tokens, whereas a t-shirt might cost 50 tokens. Just as in a store, different merchandise costs different amounts; if you don't have the money (tokens), you can't buy the reward. It is also important to specify ahead of time when the tokens can be redeemed—for example, only on Fridays.

After all aspects of the token system are in place, the project begins. For example, the teacher explains that some students aren't stopping and listening as soon as they hear the signal. Beginning today, the teacher will check off on a class list the names of the students who don't stop and listen within five seconds after the signal is given. Students who have less than five checks during class will earn one token.

As the project progresses, in an effort to get classes off the token system, the teacher gradually increases the number of tokens it takes to receive a reward and/or increases the length of time between token redemptions. Once children have learned to abide by the rules that are vital for the successful functioning of a large group, the token system becomes unnecessary.

Developing Personal and Social Responsibility

Because physical education largely focuses on the development of motor skills and fitness, teachers often ignore social and personal development—the very thing usually needed when an entire class seems unable to respond appropriately. Hellison (2011) states that it is usually assumed that students will be under control and that cooperation will automatically result in stability. As we know, such bliss does not occur automatically.

Personal and social responsibility involves much more. In a basic sense, the concept can be defined as "personal acceptance of being answerable for our conduct concerning others, our surroundings, and ourselves" (Parker and Stiehl 2015, p. 175). Although these attributes occur naturally to some extent, to develop fully and appropriately, they must be learned just like a motor skill. Thus, they must be taught and practiced at the developmentally appropriate time and with developmentally appropriate opportunities (Brustad and Parker 2005). There is much debate about whether teaching responsibility is curriculum (what we teach) or instruction (how we teach). Regardless, the basic premises involve including all children; inviting and making use of student input; providing choice; having students practice making choices; allowing for reflection; and being student centered (Parker and Stiehl 2015). Don Hellison is the most widely known advocate for developing personal and social responsibility. In his book *Teaching Responsibility through Physical Activity* (Hellison 2011), he provides field-tested instructional strategies for fostering responsibility through physical activity (curriculum). In terms of instruction, he offers students guidelines for their behavior, outlines expectations, and invites greater participation in learning. Regarding curriculum, he identifies personal and social responsibility in terms of principles or goals: respect for the rights and feelings of others, participation and effort, self-direction, helping others, and leadership. These goals are then presented in a hierarchy of levels that represent an informal progression.

These ideas, the philosophy underlying the establishment of a learning environment presented in Chapter 7, are presented here specifically for use with classes that have a hard time accepting responsibility for their own actions. This approach is not a quick fix for class problems but rather a shift in thinking and action that permeates all activities in class. It is a philosophical approach to teaching that places the focus on creating personal and social responsibility using physical activity as the medium for all that is done. For many youngsters, this type of empowerment shifts their focus from one of fighting "the system" to actively becoming part of creating a system that works.

Through the interaction of teaching and responsibility content, students begin to develop more responsibility for themselves and their classmates' well-being. The description given here is not sufficient to implement the social responsibility model. If you are interested in implementing this approach, please see Hellison's 2011 text, *Teaching Responsibility through Physical Activity*, or the Parker and Stiehl (2015) chapter "Personal and Social Responsibility" in *Standards-Based Physical Education Curriculum Development*.

Corporal Punishment

Corporal punishment, or physically hitting a child, is against the law in 31 states (Gunderson Center for Effective Discipline 2017) and in many school systems (check with yours). The authors of this text strongly believe there are more appropriate and effective strategies for addressing misbehavior. Using this type of punishment only proves to children that physically striking another person is a legitimate alternative when no other course of action appears effective.

Teaching Skills to Maintain a Productive Learning Environment

Near the end of Chapter 7, we talked about various teaching skills that could be used to help establish a learning environment (e.g., defining and demonstrating the desired behavior, practicing the behavior, providing feedback). Several other skills can be employed to help maintain the environment as well. One major reason beginning teachers struggle with classroom management is that they are so preoccupied with other things they simply do not see the inappropriate behavior, or if they do see it, they aren't quite sure how to approach it. The following strategies are useful in monitoring and reacting (or not reacting) to student behavior, allowing you to be consistent in what you do.

- Keep movement patterns unpredictable. Vary the way you circulate through the class during activity. Stand in various places in the gym when you give directions or speak to the whole class. In our experience, many teachers always "talk" from the same place—for example, next to the sound system.
- Scan the class frequently to "catch students being good" and pinpoint the appropriate behavior. For example, "I like the way Nikko is holding the equipment." To scan, stop and quickly look across the class in a predetermined direction, usually right to left, at regular intervals.
- Make sure all students can see and hear you. Practice giving instructions in situations where you face the distractions, not the students—for example, students face away from the sun or other groups. Make sure you can see all students before you start.
- Provide clear and concise directions, and repeat them at least once for clarity; then ask for questions to check for understanding. For example, after providing the direction, "Walk, choose a ball or beanbag to use to practice tossing and catching, and carry it to your self-space. I will know you are ready when I see you standing in your space, holding the equipment," ask a student what he or she is supposed to do and have the student repeat it back to you.
- Separate the organization aspects of directions from the content aspects (Rink 2014). For example, for a throwing-and-catching task, you might say, "When I say 'Go,' each of you should walk, pick up a ball, and find a space on a poly spot. I will know you are ready when I see each of you on your own spot with the ball at your feet." After this organizational aspect is accomplished, then add the content: "On the signal,

we will practice throwing to the wall. As you throw, concentrate on stepping forward on the opposite foot. Does everyone understand? Ready. Begin." By separating organization from content, children are able to clearly focus on the different parts of the task.
- Maintain the quality of appearing to have eyes in the back of your head or, as some call it, "with-it-ness" (Kounin 1970).
- Attend to two tasks simultaneously. Decades ago, Kounin (1970) called this skill "overlapping"; today the language could easily be "multitasking." For example, you should be able to provide feedback to one group practicing their self-designed game while at the same time being aware that one child has left the gym to use the restroom.
- Avoid dangles or issues left in midair (Kounin 1970). Statements or directions left unfinished tend to confuse students. Not knowing what to do, they make up what they think may be an appropriate response.
- Avoid flip-flopping (terminating one activity, starting another, and returning to the first) (Kounin 1970).
- Use targeting, or direct your interactions toward the appropriate students.
- Display the skill of timing. As a general rule, the shorter the lag time between student action and teacher behavior, the better. If, when a class is practicing balancing and rolling, you see a student push another student off-balance, effective timing means reacting immediately to the incident rather than waiting to see if the student is pushed to the floor again.

If you practice these techniques consistently and regularly, the functioning of the gymnasium is more likely to progress in a manner that enhances learning. Inappropriate behavior problems, although they won't vanish, will be curtailed.

Summary

The key to maintaining a learning environment is the presence of appropriate behavior that supports the educational goals of the specific situation. During the time needed to establish a learning environment, behavior inappropriate for the setting may occur. When it does, the teacher should first make certain that the lesson plans are pedagogically sound. If they are, then focus on the students' behavior. It's important to understand that problems with inappropriate behavior are normal; all teachers will encounter some children who are off task.

There are two phases to managing inappropriate behavior: the immediate (short-term) response to the situation and the long-term strategy. The latter involves recognizing the need to prevent recurrence of the behavior by finding out what triggered it and developing ways of helping students learn more constructive means for dealing with inappropriate behavior. Short-term techniques give a teacher practical skills to use instantly when undesirable behavior occurs. Only after the teacher has acquired and consistently used these techniques with positive results is she or he comfortable with addressing the long-term aspects of inappropriate behavior. The techniques are simply a way of dealing with the immediate inappropriate behavior; as a learning environment is developed and students accept the responsibility for their own behavior, such techniques should no longer be needed and can gradually be phased out.

When inappropriate behavior first occurs, the teacher should use the techniques for increasing appropriate behavior: positive interaction, eliminating differential treatment, prompting, ignoring inappropriate behavior, nonverbal teacher interactions, and person-to-person dialogue. When teachers find it necessary to decrease inappropriate behavior, successful techniques include positive practice, desists, time-outs, planning time, behavior contracts, letters to parents, and involving the principal. Remember, strategies to reduce inappropriate behavior should always be accompanied by techniques to increase appropriate behavior. At no time should physical activity or hitting a child be used as a punishment. Techniques for refocusing an entire class that is off task include class rewards, token systems, and incorporating a system for developing student responsibility. Monitoring and reacting strategies can be used to help maintain an environment conducive to learning.

Reading Comprehension Questions

1. What should your first step be when most of the students in your class are misbehaving? Why?
2. Why have we chosen not to use the word *discipline*?
3. What does it mean when we say that appropriate behavior is not the mere absence of inappropriate behavior?
4. What are the different types of problems that may occur in a class? Why is it important to differentiate the types of problems?
5. What is the first strategy for maintaining an effective learning environment in the gymnasium? What techniques can be used to accomplish this goal?
6. Why are positive interactions with students so important, especially at the beginning of the year?
7. When should you ignore inappropriate behavior?
8. What does differential treatment of children mean? How can you determine whether you are doing this?
9. What is the major point to remember in a person-to-person dialogue with a student?
10. What is the second strategy for handling inappropriate behavior in the gymnasium? What techniques can you use to accomplish this goal?
11. What are the characteristics of an effective desist?
12. What is a time-out? What points should you remember when using a time-out? When is a time-out not effective? How does planning time differ from a time-out?
13. When is a letter to parents useful? What should you include in the letter?
14. What is one strategy for dealing with an entire class that isn't able to work productively?
15. Why should physical activity not be used as punishment?
16. Why should many of the techniques discussed in this chapter not be used as the school year progresses?
17. Explain the relationship between the development of personal and social responsibility and management.

References/Suggested Readings

Brustad, R., and M. Parker. 2005. Enhancing positive youth development through physical activity. *Psychologica* 39: 75–93.

Byrne, J. 2018. *Strategies to manage conflict and behaviour during PE*. Presentation at the Irish Primary Physical Education Association, Galway, Ireland.

Cothran, D. 2001. The three T's of conflict resolution. *Teaching Elementary Physical Education* 12: 20–21.

Cothran, D., and P. Kulinna. 2007. Students' reports of misbehavior in physical education. *Research Quarterly for Exercise and Sport* 78: 216–24.

Cothran, D., P. Kulinna, and D. Garrahy. 2003. "This is kind of giving a secret away...": Students' perspectives on effective classroom management. *Teaching and Teacher Education* 19: 435–44.

Deci, E. L., R. Koestner, and R. M. Ryan. 1999. A meta-analytic review of experiments examining the effects of extrinsic rewards on intrinsic motivation. *Psychological Bulletin* 125: 627–68.

Evertson, C., and E. T. Emmer. 2016. *Classroom management for elementary teachers*. 10th ed. London: Pearson.

Gunderson Health System. 2017. Gunderson Center for Effective Discipline. http://www.gundersenhealth.org/ncptc/center-for-effective-discipline/.

Hellison, D. 2011. *Teaching responsibility through physical activity*. 3rd ed. Champaign, IL: Human Kinetics.

Kounin, J. 1970. *Discipline and group management in classrooms.* New York: Holt, Rinehart & Winston.

Landers, B. 2014. The conflict corner [Blog post]. https://www.thepespecialist.com/how-to-stop-tattle-tailing-with-a-conflict-corner/.

Park, H. L., and S. A. Lynch. 2014. Evidence-based practices for addressing classroom behaviour problems. *Young Exceptional Children* 17(3): 33–47.

Parker, M., and J. Stiehl. 2015. Personal and social responsibility. In *Standards-based physical education curriculum,* 3rd ed., ed. J. Lund and D. Tannehill, pp. 172–203. Sudbury, MA: Jones & Bartlett.

Rink, J. 2014. *Teaching physical education for learning.* 7th ed. New York: McGraw-Hill.

[SHAPE America] Society of Health and Physical Educators. 2009a. *Using physical activity as punishment and/or behavior management* [Position statement]. Reston, VA: SHAPE America.

[SHAPE America] Society of Health and Physical Educators. 2009b. *Appropriate instructional practice guidelines, K-12: A side-by-side comparison.* Reston, VA: SHAPE America.

Siedentop, D., and A. Taggart. 1984. Behavior analysis in physical education and sport. In *Focus on behavior analysis in education,* ed. W. Heward, T. Heron, B. Hill, and J. Trap-Porter. Columbus, OH: Merrill.

Siedentop, D., and D. Tannehill. 2000. *Developing teaching skills in physical education.* 4th ed. New York: McGraw-Hill.

Stork, S., and S. Sanders. 2002. Why can't students just do as they're told?! An exploration of incorrect responses. *Journal of Teaching in Physical Education* 21(2): 208–28.

Wang, J. C. K. 2017. Maximizing student motivation in physical education: A self-determination theory perspective. In *Routledge handbook of physical education pedagogies,* ed. C. D. Ennis, pp. 594–606. New York: Routledge.

Instructional Approaches

I am convinced that specific methodologies are used because of what the teacher believes about children and the process of education, not because of what he believes about course content.

—KATE BARRETT (1973)

by Gyeongmin

Key Concepts

- Instructional approaches indicate how content is delivered to students.

- The instructional approaches presented in this chapter range from direct to indirect instruction, and they are all designed to move students toward being more independent learners.

- When using the interactive teaching approach, the teacher influences the students' responses by telling them what to do, showing them how to practice, and directing their practice.

- The instructional approach of task teaching involves different students (often individually or in pairs) practicing different tasks at the same time.

- In peer-teaching approaches, the teacher designs and communicates the task, and students assume the roles of providing feedback and assessing.

- Guided discovery instructional approaches, either convergent or divergent, are designed to let students think and solve problems.

- In cooperative learning approaches, group interdependence and individual responsibility are promoted without compromising the integrity of motor skill learning.

- Child-designed instruction, in the form of child-designed tasks or contracts, allows children to structure their own learning.

Skill themes are most often referred to as a curricular model (Lund and Tannehill 2015), yet skill themes also embrace certain pedagogies, or ways of teaching. In this book, instructional approaches are referred to as planned interactions between the teacher and the students designed to result in the accomplishment of chosen learning outcomes (Byra 2006). Three aspects distinguish one approach from another: (1) the actions and decisions the teacher makes; (2) the actions and decisions the student makes; and (3) the objectives that the student–teacher relationship accomplishes (Mosston and Ashworth 2008). In other words, instructional approaches define the different ways a teacher organizes for instruction, rather than what is taught (Rink 2014). This chapter focuses on six instructional approaches—interactive teaching, task teaching, guided discovery, peer teaching, cooperative learning, and child-designed instruction—that we have found to be most useful in teaching elementary school physical education. Each approach is unique in the way that content is delivered to the students and, at times, in its organizational format.

Direct versus Indirect Instruction

How content is delivered to students reflects the degree to which children are involved in the decision making that takes place in a lesson. This is often referred to as the directness of instruction. Simply put, in direct instruction, the teacher makes most of the decisions, whereas in indirect instruction, the students share more of the decisions with the teacher.

It is easiest to view the directness of instruction as a continuum of direct to indirect. At the direct end of the continuum, the class environment involves highly active teaching; focused, goal-oriented, academic learning; structured learning activities; immediate, academically oriented feedback; and student accountability (Rink 2014). Research in education and physical education has indicated that students are more likely to learn specific content when direct instruction is used (Byra 2006).

On the other hand, indirect instruction often enhances what is known as constructivist learning and is characterized by content being presented holistically and expanding the students' role in the learning process so their thinking, feelings, and interactions are built in. In indirect instruction, individual student abilities, interests, and needs receive more attention. Indirect instruction may foster children's self-responsibility (Chen 2001) and lead to more transfer of skills and the development of problem-solving abilities and other cognitive skills (Rink 2014) and affective goals. These skills, such as interaction skills, cooperation, positive interdependence, and inquiry skills (Byra 2006), result in more meaningful learning (Beni, Flecther, and Ní Chróinín 2017).

The obvious questions are, "Do I use direct or indirect instruction?" "Which is best?" The answer is, "It all depends." Effective teachers should be able to use both direct and indirect instruction based on a number of variables. The teacher's beliefs about the ultimate purpose of education and the lesson goal should play a vital part in the type of instruction used in a class, yet both must be tempered by other aspects.

The six approaches outlined in this chapter range from direct to indirect, serving the dual purpose of delivering the content of physical education effectively and moving children toward becoming more responsible for their own learning and interactions with others.

Here is Edward Bear, coming downstairs now, bump, bump, bump, on the back of his head, behind Christopher Robin. It is, as far as he knows, the only way of coming downstairs, but sometimes he feels that there really is another way, if only he could stop bumping for a moment and think of it.

—**A.A. MILNE**, Winnie the Pooh (1926)

Instructional Approaches

In the following section, we identify six instructional approaches we have found useful in teaching skill themes. Table 9.1 outlines the approaches and the characteristics of each. The arrow on the left-hand side of the table indicates how "direct" an approach is; the more direct the approach, the more decisions a teacher makes and the fewer decisions the students make. Alternatively, the more indirect the approach, more decisions are made by students and the fewer made by teachers. As a teacher moves from direct to indirect approaches, the teaching skills become more advanced.

Interactive Teaching

Interactive teaching, often referred to as direct instruction, is by far the most common (and probably easiest) approach used in physical education classes. In an effort not to confuse the notion of the directness of instruction with the name of a teaching approach, we have chosen to use the term *interactive teaching* (Rink 2014). Interactive teaching is in the top left-hand corner of Table 9.1; thus, it is a very direct style of instruction. In interactive teaching, the teacher guides the students' responses by telling them what to do, showing them how to practice, and then managing their practice. Students usually work as a whole class or in small groups. As children practice, the teacher evaluates what they are doing and provides more instruction. Each teacher decision (instruction) is based on

the responses the students give to the previous task. (The ability to observe movement responses and make an instantaneous decision about the next task is a difficult skill to develop. Reflective teachers will use the observation strategies suggested in Chapter 13 to help hone this important skill.) The teacher communicates the content and controls the pacing of the lesson. Usually the entire class practices the same task or a variation of that task.

Interactive teaching is effective when your goal is to have students learn a specific skill and perform it correctly in a specific manner, for example, a roll in a forward direction that stays round throughout. At this point, interactive teaching would be an appropriate instructional choice—some children might learn the correct way of rolling without your assistance, but many would not. However, interactive teaching is not an appropriate approach for children who are at the precontrol level of skill development and are not developmentally ready to produce a mature skill pattern. These children need to explore a skill (see the guided discovery section that follows).

Let's look at another example. If you want children to learn to use opposition when they throw overhand, you'll need to give them plenty of practice opportunities and feedback to be certain they step with the opposite foot before moving on to another aspect of the overhand throw. If you don't require the children to practice stepping with the opposite foot until the movement is overlearned, then they will quickly forget the concept of opposition once the task changes. Then you'll find yourself continually reminding them, "Step

Table 9.1 Characteristics of Six Instructional Approaches

Instructional Approach	Goal	Teacher Skills	Student Characteristics	Content	Context
Interactive teaching	Efficient skill learning	Clarity	Control-level learners; new students	Specific skills	Whole class
Task teaching	Skill learning + independence	Ability to monitor multifaceted environment	Independent working skills	Already learned skills; self-assessment; product-oriented tasks	Large spaces
Peer teaching	Skill learning + cooperation	Active monitoring	Independent working skills	Simple, clear cues; limited performance	Large spaces Large groups
Guided discovery	Skill learning + transfer; problem solving	Questioning	Precontrol-level learners All learners with new content	Exploration Concept learning	Whole class
Cooperative learning	Skill learning + group interdependence; individual responsibility	Ability to design meaningful tasks	Independent working skills	Complex sequences; basic skills	Groups
Child-designed instruction	Skill learning + self-responsibility	Ability to guide and monitor	Ability to use time wisely; independent working skills	Application of learned skills	Groups

Direct ↑ Indirect

with the opposite foot when you throw." This is where interactive teaching works best. It allows you to teach a skill so that it is learned correctly.

Interactive teaching works well for beginning teachers or teachers who haven't worked with a group of students for a long while. Once the teacher has established a productive learning environment, teaching by invitation or intratask variation (Chapter 7) is helpful for changing the tasks to meet individual students' needs within the interactive approach. This strategy also requires less time for organization than the other approaches, an important consideration for teachers who meet with their students only once or twice a week.

Interactive teaching utilizes all the components of effective teaching, but five are particularly important.

- Initially the teacher gives the student a clear idea of what is to be learned. The teacher or a student correctly demonstrates the skill and identifies the important critical elements of the skill. For example, the teacher who is focusing on landing from a jump emphasizes in the demonstration that for a soft, quiet landing, the ankles, hips, and knees must be flexed on landing. The teacher then provides tasks focusing on one cue at a time.
- The second aspect is to give explanations and instructions clearly and repeat the cues often. At the end of a lesson, we often ask the children to repeat the cues so we know whether we've been effective. The students' answers to the question, "What are

the important things to remember when you're trying to land softly and quietly from a jump?" will tell you whether the children have really remembered your teaching cues related to soft, quiet landings.
- Next, the teacher gives specific feedback. In our example, the children now practice flexing their knees, hips, and ankles on landing; the teacher specifically provides them with feedback on how well they're flexing their knees, hips, and ankles. Once the children have the big idea—soft, quiet landings— the teacher helps them land softly and quietly by structuring appropriate tasks and giving them information about how well they perform. The teacher proceeds in small steps but at a brisk pace.
- One of the most important and obvious factors in interactive teaching is often overlooked. Children need considerable opportunities for practice if they're actually going to learn to land softly and quietly. For this reason, we always try to structure the learning situation so the children have plenty of practice. Most of the time we're able to arrange the environment so the children rarely, if ever, have to wait. We try to ensure all the children are active at least 50 percent of the lesson, and more when possible.
- High success rates are also important for learning, especially when learning the basic skills. We provide tasks that allow children to be successful about 80 percent of the time. This motivates the children and allows them to grasp one skill before moving on to the next level. If children can't land softly and

Using the interactive teaching approach, this teacher can effectively communicate specific content to the class as a whole.

©Barbara Adamcik

quietly when they jump from the floor, for example, then obviously they won't be able to land effectively when they jump from a bench or a wooden box.

Each of these components is developed and explained in more detail in Chapter 7. The first six tasks in Box 6-1 in Chapter 6 are an example of interactive teaching.

Task Teaching

As we move down the left-hand column of Table 9.1, task teaching is the first "less direct" instructional approach as it allows different students to practice different tasks at the same time. This approach is often called station teaching. In our approach, task teaching includes both stations and task sheets. With either option, different students practice different, specified tasks, often at their own pace and gauging their performance against predesigned criteria throughout the lesson.

Stations provide several activity areas (or learning centers) in the teaching space, each with a different task, through which students rotate during the class. See Figure 9.1 for an example of arrangement of stations that could be used to practice a variety of balancing skills during one lesson. The sequence for Striking at High and Low Targets in Chapter 26 (page 547) is another example of tasks that might be used at stations.

Task sheets provide another task-teaching option that allows children to practice at their own pace. Each child is given a task sheet (Figure 9.2), which contains a progression of activities and criteria for completion. After successfully completing each task, the student records it on the task sheet with that day's date and then asks the teacher, a parent, another student, or an older child to observe the accomplishment and sign the sheet. Initially we have entire classes work on the same task sheet at the same time. As children learn to use task sheets, we let them pick from task sheets on several different skill themes. One way to use task sheets is to develop multiple task sheets for each generic level of proficiency for each skill theme and store them in a box with file dividers. Students can then choose task cards at the appropriate level of skill proficiency (C. Galvan, personal communication, 2011). Figure 9.3 provides an example of task cards for the skill theme of striking with rackets and paddles at several levels.

One advantage of the task-teaching approach is that it allows you to set up areas that don't require students to wait in line for turns, thus making up for limitations in space and equipment. If, for example, in a balance unit you have a limited number of balance boards and balance beams, you can design tasks for each piece of equipment and have students rotate among the stations. Task-teaching instructional approaches also work well when children have to be spread out over a large space and verbal communication is difficult.

With task teaching, children won't all be involved in the same activity simultaneously; they and you need to be ready to have more than one activity happening at the same time. Efficient task teaching demands complex organizational and managerial skills on the

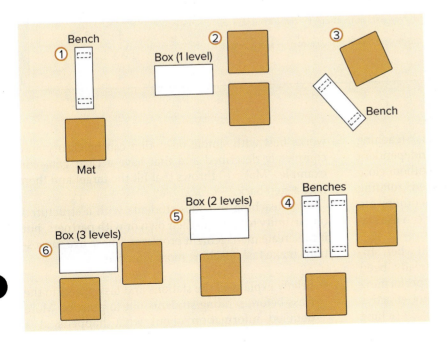

Figure 9.1 Arrangement of stations (learning centers) in the teaching space.

Figure 9.2 Task sheet.
Jeremy Hayes, University of
Northern Colorado. Used with
permission.

THROWING AND CATCHING TASK SHEET

Directions: This task sheet lists 20 tasks. Some are easy. Some are very hard. When you get to a task you cannot do, that is the one on which to spend time practicing. Don't worry about other classmates. Just try to practice so you can improve. I will help you as you practice. You may do this as partners, in a group, or by yourself. When you can do a task, write your initials beside it. For the tasks with an asterisk (*), ask the teacher to see it as well.

Your Name _____

Initials:

1. *_____ I can throw using "**Point, step, and throw**" 10 times.

2. _____ I can throw so a moving target (a classmate) can catch.

3. _____ I can throw to a target on the wall 4 times.

4. _____ I can do 10 sit-ups.

5. _____ I can throw at a target on the wall while moving.

6. *_____ I can throw 10 times to a partner.

7. _____ I can tell Mr. Hayes when my birthday is.

8. *_____ I can throw a ball off of the wall and catch it 5 times.

9. _____ I can catch a ball one handed 8 times.

10. _____ I can hit a target on the wall 7 out of 10 times.

11. _____ I can hit a target on the wall from far away 3 times.

12. _____ I can throw and hit a poster on the wall 2 times in a row.

13. _____ I can give Mr. Hayes a high-five.

14. _____ I can toss and catch a scarf in the air 20 times.

15. _____ I can do 20 jumping jacks.

16. *_____ I can catch above my head 10 times.

17. _____ I can catch below my waist 10 times.

18. _____ I can skip across the gym 2 times.

19. _____ I can throw and catch just below the ceiling 4 times in a row.

20. _____ Create your own challenge (write it in space below):

©kali9/Getty Images

teacher's part. To benefit from the task-teaching approach, students need to have good independent working skills and to be able to function without close teacher supervision. Stopping when asked, rotating systematically, and not interfering with others are skills students need to practice before they can use stations effectively.

A task instructional approach works well when students are practicing skills that have already been taught, are doing self-assessment, or are performing product-oriented tasks. The approach is not effective for introducing new or complex skills. Task teaching works best with simple tasks that can be clearly and completely described and that have a clear goal—for example, "Make 10 throws that hit the target and then take a step back."

Task teaching provides students with a structured opportunity to work on their own or with partners, but it can create management problems. These five suggestions make task teaching more effective.

- Briefly explain all the stations and task sheets to the class before sending students out to practice. More detailed information about what happens at a

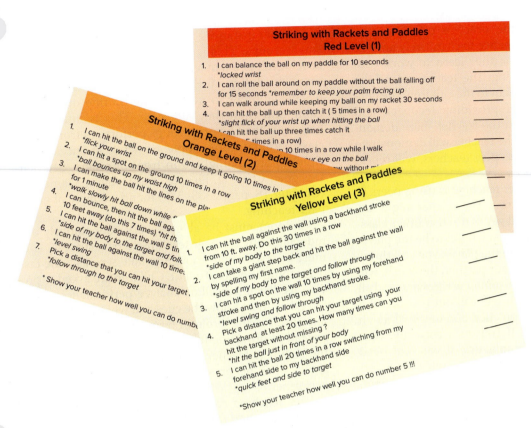

Figure 9.3 Task cards by skill level. Christine Galvan, California State University, Long Beach.

Striking with Rackets and Paddles
Red Level (1)

1. I can balance the ball on my paddle for 10 seconds
   *locked wrist
2. I can roll the ball around on my paddle without the ball falling off
   for 15 seconds *remember to keep your palm facing up
3. I can walk around while keeping my balll on my racket 30 seconds
4. I can hit the ball up then catch it (5 times in a row)
   *slight flick of your wrist up when hitting the ball
   I can hit the ball up three times catch it
   5 times in a row)
   10 times in a row while I walk
   ur eye on the ball
   ow without mi

Striking with Rackets and Paddles
Orange Level (2)

1. I can hit the ball on the ground and keep it going
   *flick your wrist
2. I can hit a spot on the ground 10 times in a row
   *ball bounces up my waist high
3. I can make the ball hit the lines on the pla
   for 1 minute
4. I can bounce, then hit the ball aga
   *walk slowly hit ball down while
5. 10 feet away (do this 7 times) *hit th
   I can hit the ball against the wall 5 tin
   *side of my body to the target and follc
6. I can hit the ball against the wall 10 times
   *level swing
7. Pick a distance that you can hit your target
   *follow through to the target

* Show your teacher how well you can do numb

Striking with Rackets and Paddles
Yellow Level (3)

1. I can hit the ball against the wall using a backhand stroke
   from 10 ft. away. Do this 30 times in a row
   *side of my body to the target
2. I can take a giant step back and hit the ball against the wall
   by spelling my first name.
   *side of my body to the target and follow through
3. I can hit a spot on the wall 10 times by using my forehand
   stroke and then by using my backhand stroke.
   *level swing and follow through
4. Pick a distance that you can hit your target using your
   backhand at least 20 times. How many times can you
   hit the target without missing ?
   *hit the ball just in front of your body
5. I can hit the ball 20 times in a row switching from my
   forehand side to my backhand side
   *quick feet and side to target

   *Show your teacher how well you can do number 5 !!!

station can be provided through posters with bullet points or pictures or information on tablets or other digital devices at each station. Tell the children what they are supposed to do and, if they are to have activities verified, who is to do the verification (teacher or another student).

- The structure of stations or task sheets may vary. Some teachers use written directions that provide options for the various skill levels, and children can choose at which level they will practice. For example, at a fitness station, there may be the choice between skipping rope for 15 seconds with two feet; skipping rope for 15 seconds with the right foot and then 15 seconds with the left foot; or skipping rope as fast as you can for 20 seconds. The options at a station might also involve having the choice of different equipment. See Figure 9.3 for an example of task cards that provide for varying levels of ability.
- Make sure the managerial aspects are explicit. Designate the areas in which activities are to occur or where specific stations are located. Design, explain, and teach a rotation system between stations or areas. We initially have children change stations on a signal. Once children are able to function using this strategy, they can be allowed to choose the stations at which they'd like to work (although we usually limit the number of students at any one area or station). Eventually students can rotate from one station to another at their own pace. Post the necessary cues and directions at each station or practice area. This technique substantially reduces the time spent in providing additional instruction.
- Move around the room and check with students frequently. The role of the teacher is not to sit and watch but to observe, evaluate, and provide feedback.
- Start slowly, with only a few (maybe three) stations or a small task sheet (maybe five items) at the end of the lesson. In our experience, children enjoy working on task sheets and in stations, especially as a culminating activity, but they need guidance if this approach is going to succeed for them and you.

Peer Teaching

Task teaching provides children with initial opportunities to work independently of the teacher. Peer teaching takes this a step further. This instructional approach uses peers teamed in pairs or small groups to actively teach one another. Peer teaching provides an indirect experience that meets multiple educational goals: It provides an effective medium for children to learn a skill—they receive multiple practice opportunities, plentiful feedback, and a chance to cognitively analyze skill—and at the same time, they learn to work with each other. In peer teaching, the teacher plans the tasks and communicates them to the children; the children assume the roles of providing feedback and assessing. The children and the teacher share demonstration of the skill. Often the teacher will demonstrate initially and the children, as peer teachers, will repeat the demonstration as necessary.

A simple example of peer teaching is using peers to help teach the overhand throw. The teacher might say, "For this next task, you will get to teach another classmate how to throw. Each of you will get to be the player and the coach. When you are the player, you will throw five times against the wall. Your partner, the coach, will have a card with a picture of someone throwing and all the cues labeled. The coach will call out one cue at a time to you. Then you will practice, and they will watch to see if you do the cue. If you do it correctly, your coach will give you a 'thumbs-up'; if you still need some practice, your coach will tell you what to correct for the next throw. And then you get to practice again. After every five throws, change roles. This is how it will look and sound." At this point the teacher demonstrates the entire task while providing sample feedback to the thrower. Figure 9.4 gives an example of a coach's card for the overhand throw. We know one elementary teacher who uses iPod Touches to do the same thing, except in this instance one student films another and then the partners talk about the performance and make suggestions to each to other.

In other instances, peer teaching can be used with small groups. This is especially useful when groups have developed dance, gymnastics, or jump rope routines or designed their own games. One group teaches another to perform the routine or play the game and then they alternate. This is much more beneficial than having groups perform in front of the class because more people are active at once and no children are spotlighted in front of others. See Self-Designed Chasing, Fleeing, and Dodging Game task (Chapter 18, pages 338–339) for an example of group peer teaching.

Children must be able to work cooperatively and independently for peer teaching to be a success. They must be responsible enough to take seriously the task of teaching another student. Children are asked to provide feedback as well as analyze performance; therefore, they must know the cues and what the skill looks like. The teacher's role in terms of feedback changes; instead of providing feedback to the child performing the skill, the teacher provides feedback to the coach about what he or she is seeing and saying to the performer.

Peer teaching can work with any content, but it works best when the skills are simple, there are clear criteria for observation, and the performance is limited and easily measured. For example, peer teaching works well with basic skills but is much more difficult with dynamic and tactical skills. Children thoroughly enjoy being the teacher, but because teaching requires analysis of a skill, students must be able to both observe the skill and provide feedback—something

---

Help your partner learn to throw!!!
The three cues on which we are focusing today are:

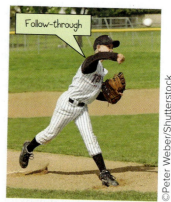

You should "coach" your partner using one cue at a time. For example, have your partner use the first five throws making sure their arm is way back. Then when they throw the second five throws make sure that they step with the opposite foot. On the last five throws focus on the follow-through. When you are done help each other decide what you need to practice more.

Figure 9.4 Peer Teaching Task Card.

©Barbara Adamcik

Peer teaching provides the opportunity for children to analyze and teach a skill while learning to work with others.

the teacher can help them learn through her or his presentation of the task.

For peer teaching to be an effective instructional approach, follow several key points:

- The skill should be simple, the cues for observation clear, and the performance easily measured.
- Post the cues either on the wall or on individual cue cards so the peer teachers can remember them.
- Children need to have the skills of giving and receiving feedback from others. We have found it useful to demonstrate and role-play what this looks like and sounds like.
- Start small. You might consider including one peer-teaching task in a lesson and then expand.

> *Teaching was easy. All you did was tell them and they did it.*
>
> —Fourth grader after teaching a self-designed game to another group

Guided Discovery

The fourth instructional approach is guided discovery. Guided discovery is designed to facilitate children's critical thinking, as reflected in their movement responses, and to let them solve problems rather than copy the teacher's or another student's correct performance. Guided discovery also enhances student interest and motivation (Chen 2001). In this student-centered

approach, the teacher typically gives the task by asking questions. The teacher most often describes how the task will be practiced and some way to measure success, but exactly how to perform the task is left to the child to explore and interpret. For example, the teacher may say, "From your spot on the floor, try to kick the ball to the wall both in the air and on the ground." The child knows how to practice (from the spot on the floor, kick) and a little about success (to the wall, in the air, and on the ground), but the rest is left up to the child. Guided discovery really serves as an umbrella for two different types of discovery: convergent and divergent. One asks children to find a single answer to a task, whereas the other asks children to find multiple answers to a task.

Convergent Inquiry

Convergent inquiry encourages children to discover the same answer(s) to a series of questions the teacher asks. The teacher guides the children toward one or more correct answers. This approach has been successfully adapted to teaching game skills and strategies, and it is the fundamental principle underlying teaching games for understanding or the tactical approach to teaching games (Mitchell, Oslin, and Griffin 2013). Mosston and Ashworth (2008) suggested that children can discover ideas, similarities, dissimilarities, principles (governing rules), order or system, a particular physical activity or movement, how, why, limits (the dimensions of "how much," "how fast"), and other elements. When we want children to learn one of these elements, we often use the discovery approach to increase their involvement.

The following sequence illustrating Mosston and Ashworth's (2008, pp. 157–58) classic slanty rope technique is a very good example of convergent inquiry encouraging children to find ways to avoid eliminating others from activity.

Step 1: Ask two children to hold a rope for high jumping. Invariably they will hold the rope horizontally at a given height (for example, at hip level).

Step 2: Ask the group to jump over. Before they do so, you might want to ask the rope holders to decrease the height so that everybody can be successful.

Step 3: After everyone has cleared the height, you ask, "What shall we do now?" "Raise it!" "Raise it!" is the answer—always! (The success of the first jump motivates all to continue.)

Step 4: Ask the rope holders to raise the rope just a bit. The jumping is resumed.

Step 5: "Now what?" "Raise it!" the children will respond.

Step 6: Raising the rope two or three more times will create a new situation, a new reality. Some children will not be able to clear the height. In traditional situations, these children will be eliminated from the jumping, and only some will continue; there will be a constantly diminishing number of active participants. The realization of individual differences becomes real; the design for opportunity for all has not yet come about.

Step 7: Stop the jumping and ask the group, "What can we do with the rope so that nobody will be eliminated?" Usually one or two of the following solutions are proposed by the children: (a) Hold the rope higher at the two ends and let the rope dip in the center. (b) Slant the rope! Hold the rope high at one end and low at the other.

The effectiveness of convergent inquiry is largely dependent on the questions the teacher asks. We offer three suggestions for making the questions work successfully.

1. Formulate in advance the questions to be asked so you can determine the correct sequence of questions that will lead children to the answer you desire.
2. Ask questions in relatively small steps rather than spanning too large of a gap.
3. Wait for an answer (even 10 to 15 seconds; count to yourself) rather than becoming impatient and giving the answer. If you wait for an answer, children will really start to think and thus the learning becomes more meaningful and personal.

The Throwing to a Moving Target sequence in Chapter 24 (page 491) is an example of convergent inquiry used to teach the concepts of throwing to an open space and leading a receiver.

Divergent Inquiry

In divergent inquiry, the teacher outlines a problem and then challenges the children to find many answers. This technique encourages children to find movement alternatives. When using a divergent approach, every child will not exhibit the same movement response to a task. For example, in response to the task of, "Find three different inverted balances," one child may balance with her hands and feet on the mat and down in a piked position, another child may have his head and hands and one foot on the mat with the other foot in the air, and yet another child might do a handstand. A typical divergent question will always ask for diversity: "Find at least three different ways to travel under the hoop (supported on cones) and at least three different ways to travel over the hoop."

In the divergent inquiry approach, the teacher must be careful not to impose personal values on the children's responses. The emphasis is on obtaining a variety of responses, not a single answer. For this reason, Mosston and Ashworth (2008) warned of two verbal behavior patterns to avoid when using divergent inquiry. "You can do better than that" in response to a child's movement indicates that the teacher doesn't really value the response or that the teacher has a particular response in mind. Another counterproductive verbal behavior is a statement such as, "Stop. Everyone watch Penny." After Penny finishes her movement, the teacher says, "Terrific, Penny." This teacher behavior, although perhaps innocent, suggests to students that there's a right answer and therefore encourages the children to find a correct answer (convergent) rather than searching for a variety of alternatives, which is the goal of divergent inquiry.

In contrast, two productive verbal behaviors might include such statements as:

"Now that you have found two ways, try to make the third one quite different."

"Stop. Everyone watch this half of the class. Good! Now, let's watch the other half. Great."

These two statements allow the teacher to provide feedback while encouraging creativity and diversity of responses.

We have found the following points helpful in our use of divergent inquiry:

- Provide feedback that encourages exploration and problem solving rather than a single right answer (see the Mosston and Ashworth examples above) and be willing to accept different responses.
- Structure questions (tasks) that challenge children in small, sequential steps. These questions are based on a detailed knowledge of the content and knowing what should come next.
- Become a master at providing children with prompts that encourage them to keep practicing by trying different ways or looking for different solutions.
- When demonstrations are used, provide multiple demonstrations of different answers to the task. If a single demonstration is used, children are likely to copy it.

The Jumping to Form a Body Shape During Flight sequence in Chapter 20 (page 365) is an example of divergent inquiry.

We've found guided discovery especially helpful for encouraging children to think on their own to discover new and different approaches to performing skills and to solve questions related to teamwork and strategy. Guided discovery is also important for those children who aren't developmentally ready to learn a mature version of a skill and simply need opportunities to explore the movement. It is often the strategy we use at the precontrol level when students are exploring a new skill. It provides children a chance to try things without a specific focus or direction.

> *Teachers have to learn how to provide transitions for their pupils. It is not possible for most young people to make choices after five or six years of being told what to do every minute they are in school. It is equally hard for them to share resources, help other students, or decide what they want to learn after years of being expected to hoard, compete, and conform. Transitional situations often have to be provided. Some students need workbooks for a while; others want to memorize times tables or have weekly spelling tests. Young people are no different from adults. When faced with new possibilities they want something old and predictable to hold onto while risking new freedom. Inexperienced teachers often make the mistake of tearing down the traditional attitudes their students have been conditioned to depend upon before the students have time to develop alternative ways of learning and dealing with school. In their impatience they become cruel to students who do not change fast enough or who resist change altogether. One just cannot legislate compassion or freedom. Teaching as a craft involves understanding how people learn; as an art it involves a sensitive balance between presenting and advocating things you believe and stepping away and encouraging your students to make their own sense of your passion and commitment.*
>
> —**HERBERT KOHL**, *On Teaching* (1976)

Cooperative Learning

Toward the indirect end of the instructional approaches continuum is cooperative learning. Cooperative learning is a small group instructional approach designed to promote group interdependence and individual responsibility while teaching content. The principles underlying the use of cooperative learning are a respect for all students, confidence in their potential for success, and a belief that learning is a social process (Dyson and Casey 2016). There are three common cooperative learning formats: pairs-check, jigsaw, and co-op (Kagan 1990).

In pairs-check, children are in groups of four with two partner-pairs in each group. Each pair practices a task, teaching each other as in peer teaching. The two pairs then get together to assess each other to see if they are achieving the same outcomes, to provide further feedback, and to practice. For example, the pairs-check strategy could be used to teach dribbling with the hands. After the initial task is given, each pair works together, focusing on using the finger pads, having the knees bent, and keeping the hand on top of the ball. Then, when both members of a single pair think they have mastered the task, they come together to check the other pair. In this sense, pairs-check is much like peer teaching.

In the jigsaw format, children are usually in "home" groups of three or four. Each child becomes an expert on one aspect of a skill or task by working with the children who are experts from other groups. Children then return to their home group and teach their group their piece of the skill. The jigsaw format can be used quite effectively to teach activities with multiple parts and simultaneously develop interdependence.

For example, the jigsaw approach could be used when creating a simple dance routine in involving traveling, balance, and space concepts. The class is divided into home groups of four. At the beginning of class, four stations are set up—one on traveling, incorporating different levels; one with traveling in different pathways; one with twists and turns; and another with balances with different extensions. One person from each home group goes to each station and designs a sequence with her group to meet the criteria at the station. Each child then returns to his home group as an expert on that sequence and teaches it to the group. The group then puts the sequences in order to form their dance.

Co-op is a cooperative learning format in which small groups create a project with many components (Dyson and Casey 2016). Each small group is responsible for one component of the larger project. The co-op format can be used to have children create a dance sequence in which several elements are to be portrayed. For example, in the dance depicting African American heritage described in Chapter 29 (page 643), one group might develop the concept of slavery, another the concept of freedom, another the concept of strength as a people, another dispersal, another gathering, and another respect. Each group would then bring their piece to the full dance.

Cooperative learning works equally well with children who have highly developed responsibility skills and with children who need to learn to work together. Research shows that cooperative learning has affective as well as cognitive benefits (Dyson and Casey 2016).

However, to achieve such benefits, the teacher's role must change from the interactive teaching used in structured approaches to facilitation and indirect teaching. First, the teacher must be skilled in designing tasks that are meaningful to children. Second, the teacher's role regarding demonstrations and feedback shifts. As in divergent inquiry, multiple demonstrations of possible responses are needed. Feedback initially takes the form of helping groups work together to solve group issues and to answer the task, followed by skill feedback once the groups have designed their response.

Cooperative learning strategies provide a chance for skill learning and teaching responsibility. There is however a word of caution here. The goal of skill learning should not be sacrificed when using cooperative learning activities. The primary purpose of some cooperative learning activities, especially from adventure education, is group development and problem solving. These activities have their place and are often fun; however, they do not teach the primary content of physical education. For cooperative learning to be a viable part of physical education, it needs to integrate psychomotor, cognitive, and personal-social responsibility goals. It must provide what Rink (2014) calls a rich learning experience. The cooperative learning activity must teach a psychomotor goal while addressing the other goals.

For teachers who want to successfully use cooperative learning approaches, structure is essential. Six important guidelines help provide structure that allows student direction (Dyson 2002; Mills 2002).

- First, make sure you know the academic and social goals of what you want to accomplish through the cooperative learning task and communicate those goals.
- Second, groups need to remain small.
- Third, teach the children the roles they will need in the group. For example, if students need to provide feedback to others, teach them what feedback to provide.
- Fourth, design an assessment or accountability system (see Chapter 12) so the children are responsible for the end result or product as well as the process and there is closure to the task.
- Fifth, students need to learn how to communicate with each other. In other words, it is not enough to be able to provide feedback; they must learn how to deliver it so others hear it and it is not hurtful.
- Finally, cooperative learning takes time. Like any instructional format that calls for problem solving and student input, allow ample time for the children to work through the process of the task. Groups should remain together long enough to establish a working relationship.

Posting instructions for child designed instruction allows children to take more responsibility for their work and increases time spent in activity.

©Barbara Adamcik

Child-Designed Instruction

The last instructional approach we use is child-designed instruction. These approaches are student-centered, indirect approaches that allow the child to be the center of the learning activities. In these strategies, the teacher serves as a guide or mentor.

Child-designed instructional approaches allow children to actively take the major responsibility for their learning. When used with careful planning and patience, these approaches empower children. Children become engaged and most often design activities appropriate to their level of development. We are committed to children designing their own experiences, although this is not always easy and is often messy. There are several child-designed strategies; child-designed tasks and contracts are the two we use most often. Although older elementary students are fully capable of designing personal contracts, with structure, the use of child-designed tasks such as game, routines, and obstacle courses can begin with seven-year-olds.

To function productively with a child-designed approach, children need to be highly motivated and self-directed and have the skills to work independently. They need to be knowledgeable about using the time and materials available to them. The teacher must be skilled in designing the initial task and then must let the students work on their own, making their own decisions and mistakes. This is very hard for many of us to do. Child-designed strategies work well after the basic skill has been learned. They are especially useful with dynamic situations, when children are at different skill levels, and as event tasks after children have practiced a skill or several combinations of skills for a while.

Child-designed games or routines ask students to create their own "game" or "routine" within certain parameters. The game, dance, or gymnastics task is based on the skill theme being studied and allows students to apply what they have learned in a setting that matches their interests and abilities. Figure 9.5 provides an example of a checklist used with control-level children to guide their creation of an obstacle course reflecting what was learned while dribbling with the feet in different speeds, with different pathways, while avoiding an object, and passing to a target. See the Child-Designed Racket Games task in Chapter 26 (page 560) for an example of a child-designed game. See Chapters 29, 30, and 31 for explicit details about how to develop child-designed activities in dance, gymnastics, and games contexts.

As children become accustomed to working on their own, the teacher can use independent contracting to make instruction more personal. A teacher who uses independent contracting is saying to the students,

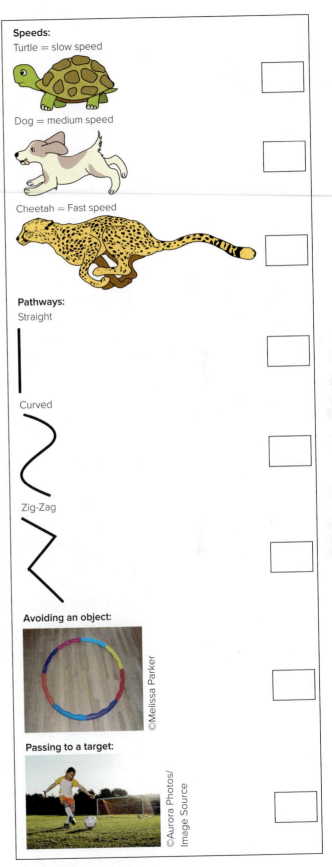

Figure 9.5 Checklist for child-designed obstacle course.
Jen Morse and Jesse Sirio, University of Northern Colorado. Used with permission.

Figure 9.6 Individual contract.
Tia Ziegler, Chappelow K-8
Magnet School, Evans, CO.
Used with permission.

PE Class Contract

Name_____ Contract for_____, 2018

Goal for the day:

_____

_____

Things I will do to accomplish goal_____

_____

Time Allowed	Activity/Task	Equipment	Partner (if working with one)

Self Check:
Points Earned in Class_____/ 10 (5—in-class participation, 5—showing Respect)
Explain:

Comments:
1) How do you know you accomplished your goal or didn't accomplish it?

2) What do you need to work on during the next class?

Teacher Check:
Points Earned in Class_____/ 10 (5—in-class participation, 5—showing Respect)
Explain:

"I trust you to make intelligent and responsible decisions about what you need to practice." We've used the written contract illustrated in Figure 9.6. Each child writes down the skill or activity she or he will be practicing or playing, the goal to be achieved, the time to be spent practicing each activity, and (when appropriate) the name of a practice partner. Recognizing the dynamic nature of a physical education class, we let the children change their contracts during class, provided they write down all changes. We encourage the children to save time by coming to physical education class with their contracts already completed for that day. In the final few minutes of a class, we ask the children to evaluate their accomplishments for that day.

Contracts can be used in physical education classes in a variety of ways. When you first use independent contracting, restrict each child to a single skill theme or even a certain aspect of the skill theme or unit. For example, some teachers have used contracts as a culminating activity to let students decide how they want to complete their learning on a specific topic. The sequence Throwing for Distance and Accuracy in Chapter 24 (page 491) is an example of a modified contract.

For teachers who want to try to incorporate child-designed approaches in their teaching but aren't sure where to begin, we have found the following suggestions to be helpful.

- Use moderation and structure as the keys to success. Give specific directions. The results can be disastrous if you simply say, "Make up your own game; it has to include throwing and catching," or "Write a contract about what to do in physical education." We know from experience. Try to give children more specific instructions for designing activities that include the exact focus of the activity and what the final product is to be, such as:

  "Design beginning and ending movements for the balance, roll, balance sequence you've been practicing."

  "You've been practicing five movements: leaping, spinning, sinking, exploding, and freezing. Use them in a sequence that flows together smoothly."

  "We've been practicing dribbling for the past few lessons and will continue to do so for another week. Design a contract that tells what you will do each day for the first five minutes of class to practice your dribbling skills."

- Provide the managerial aspects of the task, such as how large the space can be and where; when the task should be completed; how long before they should be practicing; the maximum and minimum number of people in the group; and the equipment available.

- Check with groups often to see how they are doing (especially those who seem to be having a difficult time getting started). Move around the area. Ask questions about their activity. Prompt.

- Provide feedback while resisting telling children how to practice. Teacher responses to child-designed activities need to encourage children to stay on task while at the same time provide reinforcement for the students' decisions.

- Allow enough time. Designing instruction takes time. We usually find that it takes the majority of a lesson (and sometimes two lessons) for children to design and implement self-designed activities.

- Find ways for children to be accountable for what they are doing. A variety of assessment options—such as exit slips that ask students to explain their creation (Chapter 12), reflection on the process of the development in journals (Chapter 12), or teaching their game or routine to another group—allows children to be accountable for the learning process. These options also let children think about how much effort they put into accomplishing their independent tasks. (See Chapter 15 for more options.)

I recently walked into a large multipurpose room full of 30 second graders. As I sat to watch, I noticed that six very diverse activities were taking place: striking with hockey sticks in a game situation, doing pull-ups, jumping rope, shooting at targets, wall climbing, and jumping and landing using a vaulting horse. The teacher was walking around from group to group talking to the children, offering feedback and encouragement, but no instructions or managerial directions. At this point, I started to look more closely. All the children were active and on task. The noise level was productive; there was no screaming or yelling. Children were moving from activity to activity as they saw fit. Some were recording scores on wall charts. The teacher was never asked to make the decisions of a referee in the game. Children calmly retrieved stray equipment without interfering with other activities or sending the mob to chase a stray ball. These were seven-year-olds. I then asked the teacher how this situation came to be. His response: "I taught them at the beginning of the year the rules for Fridays (the designated day for choice activities), and we practiced."

Choosing the "Right" Instructional Approach

We started this chapter with a question about knowing which approach is the right one. The answer is "It all depends." The goals of the lesson, the teacher's skill and preference, the students' characteristics, the nature of the content, and the context in which the teaching is taking place (Tannehill, van der Mars, and MacPhail 2015) all affect the selection of an instructional approach.

Goals of the lesson. After selecting the learning objectives for the lesson, you need to think about the various instructional activities you will use to engage students with the material to support them in meeting the objectives. For example, if your goal is for students to work cooperatively to accomplish a task, you will most likely select an indirect instructional approach. Whereas, if you are working with beginners learning the fundamental motor skill of throwing, a more direct approach may be more appropriate.

Your skills and preference.   Your teaching skills, as well as your personal preferences, should be a major factor, although not a controlling factor, in the instructional approach you choose to use. Your comfort zone is a legitimate ingredient in how you choose to deliver content to the children. This is not to say you shouldn't ever stretch your limits, but teachers generally are more effective when they are using strategies that fit them. As teachers grow and develop, they acquire new ideas and see a need for new approaches to accomplish the goals they have set for their classes.

Students' characteristics.   The characteristics of the children in your classes have a significant impact on the instructional approach you choose. How much responsibility is the class ready for? How many decisions are the students capable of sharing? Will the lesson fail if the students are allowed to choose among several activities? These are some of the other considerations a teacher must take into account. For example, if the teacher believes students should be responsible for their own decisions and should direct their own learning, then direct instruction might seem to be contradictory to the teacher's goals. But for children who have never been given the responsibility to make decisions about their own learning or have never been taught any self-direction, a child-designed program would most likely lead to chaos. Instead, the teacher might use direct instruction while giving children limited or structured choices, thus teaching them how to make responsible decisions.

Nature of the content.   Different content may lend itself to different instructional approaches. When you are teaching a basic skill, a direct instructional strategy may be the most effective. When the children are asked to design complex routines and sequences, a child-designed or guided discovery strategy may be more effective.

Context.   The environment or context in which the learning is occurring is an additional factor that influences the instructional approach used. This is especially true of facilities and equipment. If a task or lesson requires students to be spread out over a large space (such as a field), making it difficult to provide continuous feedback to and maintain verbal communication with the children, a task-teaching strategy may be appropriate. When safety is a paramount issue, as in a first experience with large apparatus in gymnastics, direct instruction may be more appropriate.

To accommodate the goals of the lesson, your skills and preferences, student characteristics, the content of the lesson, and the context, it is often useful to use more than one approach in a lesson or combine approaches. For example, a review of the previous lesson could be accomplished using stations and then new content could be taught using interactive teaching. Alternatively, the throwing and catching task sheet on page 144 combines the use of divergent inquiry with task teaching. Ultimately the approach should be based on what is best for fostering the children's learning. One approach is better than the other only for a particular situation.

Regardless of the instructional approach used, it is important to carefully observe the children's responses to the task and make your next decision as a teacher based on what you observed. For example, suppose that while using the direct approach you have the children focus on dribbling using their finger pads, and you observe they are not doing that. The next step is to stop and redirect the task to the use of finger pads. However, if you're using a peer-teaching approach to teach the same skill and the children are not using their finger pads, you would refocus the peer teachers on what to look for. In any case, careful observation of how children are responding to the task should guide your response and feedback to them.

To become a skillful teacher in all six instructional approaches is quite difficult and takes a lot of time to practice. Although some of the indirect approaches at first appear easy, in reality they are difficult. Designing meaningful learning experiences for all students is complex. Yet, the use of indirect approaches takes children to a different place—one that has them become the artists of their own learning

---

Summary

An instructional approach can be defined as planned interactions between the teacher and the students designed to result in accomplishing a specific set of learning outcomes. The uniqueness of each instructional approach revolves around the extent to which students are involved in the decision making that takes place in a lesson. The six instructional approaches (summarized in Table 9.1) range from direct to indirect instruction.

The interactive approach is effective when students are to learn a specific skill technique. A task-teaching approach is helpful when having students practice a skill they have already learned. Peer teaching fosters cooperation and provides repeated practice and feedback for children. The guided discovery approaches stimulate thinking and students' involvement on a cognitive level. Cooperative learning develops group-relation skills, as well as stimulating cognitive involvement. Child-designed approaches encourage creativity and inventiveness; they involve children in creating their own learning experiences.

Each approach has its strengths, and each requires different student and teacher skills. Which strategy to select depends on the teacher's goals. One of the challenges reflective teachers face is analyzing both their students' and their own needs and skills and matching them with the goals of the lesson. Ideally, over a period of weeks, both the teacher and the children learn to work effectively, no matter which instructional strategy is selected.

Regardless of the approach used, the progression of the learning experience is always based on the students' response to the task they were given. Thus, the ability of the teacher to observe (Chapter 11) is critical.

Reading Comprehension Questions

1. What is the implication of the quote from Kate Barrett on the opening page of the chapter? How does it relate to the content of this chapter?
2. What is an instructional approach? How does the concept of direct or indirect instruction relate to instructional approaches? Explain the differences among the six instructional approaches presented in this chapter.
3. What criteria might the teacher use in selecting a particular instructional approach for use with a class?
4. Using the skill of punting, give examples of convergent and divergent inquiry, written in the actual form in which they would be stated.
5. Select a skill theme from one of the skill theme chapters (Chapters 17–27) and develop a task sheet similar to the one in Figure 9.2. Include at least six different tasks, ranging from precontrol through utilization levels.

6. Why do we say that an interactive approach may not be the best for children who are not developmentally ready?
7. Using the skills of throwing and catching against a defense, design a task sequence using the jigsaw cooperative learning strategy.
8. What strategies can a teacher employ to begin to use child-designed approaches for instruction? Give an example of how one strategy might be developed for a group of 11- or 12-year-olds.
9. How can different instructional approaches be used to help students meet various national standards for physical education?

References/Suggested Readings

Barrett, K. 1973. I wish I could fly: A philosophy in motion. In *Contemporary philosophy of physical education and athletics*, ed. R. Cobb and P. Lepley, 3–18. Columbus, OH: Merrill.

Beni, S., T. Fletcher, and D. Ní Chróinín. 2017. Meaningful experiences in physical education and youth sport. *Quest* 69(3): 291–312.

Byra, M. 2006. Teaching styles and inclusive pedagogies. In *The handbook of physical education*, ed. D. Kirk, D. Macdonald, and M. O'Sullivan, 449–66. Thousand Oaks, CA: Sage.

Chen, W. 2001. Description of an expert teacher's constructivist-oriented teaching: Engaging students' critical thinking in creative dance. *Research Quarterly for Exercise and Sport* 72: 366–75.

Dyson, B. 2002. The implementation of cooperative learning in an elementary physical education program. *Journal of Teaching in Physical Education* 22: 69–88.

Dyson, B., and A. Casey. 2016. *Cooperative learning in physical education and physical activity. A practical introduction*. New York: Routledge.

Hall, T., and B. McCullick. 2002. Discover, design, and invent: Divergent production. *Teaching Elementary Physical Education* 13(2): 22–24.

Kagan, S. 1990. The structural approach to cooperative learning. *Educational Leadership* 47(4): 12–16.

Lund, J., and D. Tannehill. 2015. *Standards based physical education curriculum development*. 3rd ed. Sudbury, MA: Jones & Bartlett.

Mills, B. 2002. *Enhancing learning—and more!—through cooperative learning. Idea Paper #38*. Manhattan, KS: The IDEA Center.

Milne, A. A. 1926. *Winnie the pooh*. New York: Dutton.

Mitchell, S., J. Oslin, and L. L. Griffin. 2013. *Teaching sport concepts and skills*. 3rd ed. Champaign, IL: Human Kinetics.

Mosston, M., and S. Ashworth. 2008. *Teaching physical education*. 1st online ed. Sara Ashworth. https://www.spectrumofteachingstyles.org/pdfs/ebook/Teaching_Physical_Edu_1st_Online_old.pdf

Rink, J. 2014. *Teaching physical education for learning*. 7th ed. New York: McGraw-Hill.

[SHAPE America] Society of Health and Physical Educators. 2014. *National standards & grade-level outcomes for K-12 physical education*. Champaign, IL: Human Kinetics.

Tannehill, D., H. van der Mars, and A. MacPhail. 2015. *Building, delivering and sustaining effective physical education programs*. Sudbury, MA: Jones & Bartlett.

Adapting the Content for Diverse Learners

Every student can learn, just not on the same day, or in the same way.

—John Evans

If a child can't learn the way we teach, maybe we should teach the way they learn.

—Ignacio Estrada

©Dillon Patton

Key Concepts

- With the diversity of schoolchildren in the United States (and other countries), physical education teachers must be prepared to provide a quality physical education experience to students with a wide variety of abilities, needs, and interests.

- Inclusion is the philosophy that diverse learners—including those with differences in mental, social, and physical abilities, skill levels, fitness levels, gender, culture, language, religion, socioeconomic status, and physical characteristics—are able to learn and to develop skills in the regular physical education program.

- It is physical education teachers' responsibility to learn about the unique needs of each diverse learner and the implications for physical education.

- With modifications in teaching and curriculum, the teacher can challenge all students in ways that provide maximum opportunities for learning and development of each child's personal potential.

- Physical education is a direct, required service for all children identified under the Individuals with Disabilities Education Act (IDEA) of 1990 (reauthorized in 2004 and 2014).

- The physical education teacher is a critical member of the Individualized Education Program Team and should be in attendance at all meetings that involve students he or she teaches in physical education.

- Zero exclusion and zero failure is the standard for all children in physical education.

An adapted physical education specialist once shared that Children Moving is the perfect book for making instructional decisions when teaching a diverse population. The philosophy of child-centered physical education is evident in Children Moving through the use of the generic levels of skill proficiency (Chapter 5 and in all skill theme chapters), the variety of instructional approaches (Chapter 9), and the ideas of intratask variation and teaching by invitation (Chapter 7).

As a group of second graders enters the gym for class on the first day of school, Mrs. Thomas, the physical education teacher, notices one child rolling his wheelchair through the door and hears two other children speaking an unfamiliar language. She has already been informed that two students in the class, Jacob and Kashonda, have autism. Mrs. Thomas's heart begins to beat a little faster; even though she has several years of teaching experience, she feels a rush of self-doubt and begins to question her ability to meet the needs of all her students.

Although this may seem unusual as you read this text, it is more common now than ever before to find physical education classes with increasingly diverse groups of students. *Diversity* is typically defined as the differences that exist among people. Some identifiers that may represent the diversity in your classes are represented in Figure 10.1.

Finding ways to meet the needs of all students in physical education can bring both joy and challenge for everyone involved. To make a difference, we must commit ourselves to providing a physical education experience in which *all* children can be successful. This chapter provides strategies to help physical education teachers meet the needs of the increasingly diverse population of children entering our schools. Our goal is for *all* students to experience a sense of empowerment and competence in physical education that leads to lifetime participation in physical activity.

Inclusion as a Philosophy

Inclusion is based on a philosophy and belief that a separate education is not an equal education. Traditionally, in terms of physical education, inclusion has meant that students with disabilities are placed in the regular physical education setting. However, to better represent the wide variety of student abilities, needs, and interests resulting from the increased diversity of schoolchildren, and because teachers today are faced with more than teaching children with special needs, we have expanded our philosophy of inclusion. It is time to support, not just include, diverse learners, in all their variety of forms, through a broadened conceptualization of inclusion.

Inclusive education is essential for our society to function as a real modern society removing the final barrier to rights for equality & shared value of difference.

—ELLY CHAPPLE

Inclusion is a philosophy that all children can learn and all children want to learn. In an inclusive physical education environment, the question is not whether children can develop skills, but *how* they can develop skills and how we as teachers can foster the development of those skills. Inclusion identifies and cultivates each student's unique abilities, recognizing that all children do better when the emphasis is on strengths. Discovering children's abilities and helping them learn what they are

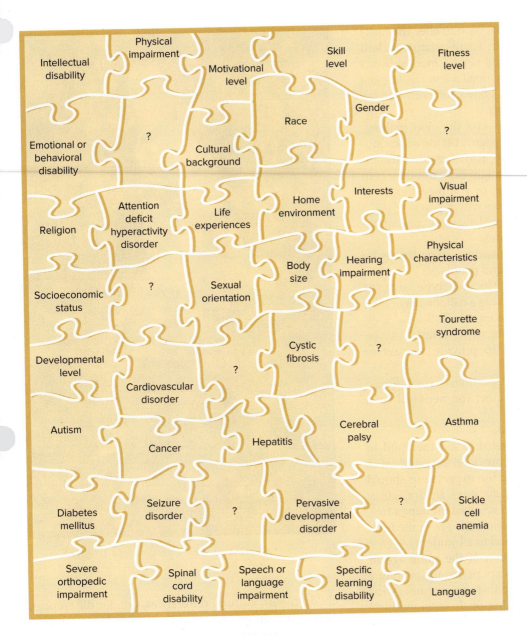

Figure 10.1 The unique makeup of students in our schools may include all the factors in this puzzle and perhaps additional ones.

good at is critical to their success. The emphasis, therefore, is on each individual's strengths and abilities.

An inclusive environment involves teachers creating a healthy learning climate in which all children feel physically and emotionally safe, successful, motivated, accepted, and valued. It is an environment where positive behaviors are modeled and interaction opportunities occur daily. It is an opportunity for friendships to develop across diverse lines. It is a place free from anxiety, a place where put-downs are not allowed and acceptance is the norm.

Physical education programs that include diverse learners have the same basic goals as any other quality program. However, strategies are used to support program goals while considering participant needs,

interests, abilities, and skill and fitness levels. These strategies include the following:

- Lesson objectives are written with reasonable expectations for all learners. Lesson objectives may be the same for all children, altered slightly for a few individuals, or completely different for one individual.
- Task progressions are altered based on skill, cognition, or social/emotional abilities.
  - The generic levels of skill proficiency (GLSP) in each of the skill theme chapters will aid in making task decisions.
  - Students are challenged at their level by varying the task for individuals. Intratask variation (page 114) is a technique in which the teacher

makes an instructional decision to alter the tasks based on individual or small-group student needs. Some children may need a more difficult task, whereas others may need a less challenging task. Intratask variation allows for both success and challenge.

- Students are included in task decision making. Teaching by invitation (page 114) provides student choice, which may also increase student autonomy. An example might be, "You may continue striking to the wall, or you may choose to attempt consecutive strikes with a partner."
- Self-testing or cooperative challenges are emphasized over competitive ones.
- Modifications are made in learning experiences by altering equipment, space, and people.
  - Equipment options may include type, size, or weight. For example, striking a balloon may result in more success than striking a ball.
  - The space or area for practicing a task may be increased or decreased to provide success or challenge.
  - The options of individual, partner, or small-group tasks may be varied to meet the needs of each child.
- Support services are utilized.
  - An assistant may be needed to aid the child in learning. If an assistant is provided for a student or teacher in the classroom, the expectation should be the same in physical education. In fact, safety may make the addition of an assistant imperative. This individual may also allow the physical education teacher to better attend to all students.
  - Peer tutoring with children of the same age or older can be a positive experience for everyone involved. Be sure to alternate the peer tutors so as not to impede the learning of these individuals (see Chapter 9).

> *Inclusive education is essential and should be at the heart of initial teacher training.*
>
> **—SARAH LACHLANN**

Inclusion begins with a teacher willing to accept all children; a teacher open and responsive to individuals and the unique needs of each; a teacher who celebrates children's strengths and adjusts, accommodates, and modifies to provide maximum learning for each child. The better informed we are about the diversity of our children, the better we will be able to teach each child.

Diversity in your school, beyond children with disabilities, will most likely include overweight children;

©Barbara Adamcik

The individualization of instruction leads to success for all children.

children with cultural differences, gender differences, or religious differences; and children living in poverty. Following are specific implications for inclusive teaching in regard to each of these.

Overweight Children

As mentioned in Chapter 28, childhood obesity rates in the United States have reached epidemic proportions. Today's youth are considered the most inactive generation in history. Physical education teachers can help overweight children build healthy bodies and establish healthy lifestyles by teaching them ways to include physical activity in their daily lives. Physical educators can play an important role in the treatment and prevention of overweight children by giving them the skills and confidence they need to participate in physical activity for a lifetime and by educating children about the importance of health-related fitness and wellness concepts as outlined in Chapter 28.

Specific implications for teaching overweight children include the following:

- Allow children to set individual goals related to their own skill and fitness improvement.
- Emphasize self-improvement and personal best instead of comparing children to each other. Create opportunities to document and celebrate success.
- Create a psychologically safe climate where all children are accepted. Be observant of any teasing or bullying behaviors. Avoid learning experiences that emphasize winning or comparing scores. Learning experiences that emphasize personal goal setting and improvement should be used instead.
- Provide opportunities for success by providing choices within tasks. For children to persist at a task, they must feel competent and confident in their ability to reach a specific goal (self-efficacy).
- Keep all or most children active at the same time so no one feels pressure to perform alone in front of peers (spotlighting individuals); overweight children often have low skill levels and would consider this humiliating.
- Use short bouts of high-intensity activity throughout the class period. Knowing the higher level of intensity will not last long can help motivate less fit children. Overweight children may participate longer in low-intensity learning experiences. Duration should be stressed over intensity.
- Modify activities so students have choices related to intensity.
- Provide frequent guidance and encouragement during the lesson.
- Use heart rate monitors with older students to help them determine when they reach their target heart rate (THR) zone. Overweight students often push themselves well beyond the THR, thinking this is what exercise feels like, when in reality they can get the full benefits of exercise by participating at a much lower and thus more comfortable intensity level.
- Help children develop the knowledge, attitudes, and skills they need to adopt and maintain physically active lifestyles.
- Emphasize enjoyable participation in a variety of physical activities before, during, and after school.

Overweight and obese children were not as common when most of us were in elementary school. As discussed in Chapter 28, there are many contributing variables to this new culture. As physical educators, we have the opportunity to be one of the variables for positive change. Embrace these children and help build their skills, self-esteem, knowledge of healthy choices, and love for physical activity. For a generation that is not expected to live as long as their parents, we have to make a difference—for their present and their future.

Cultural Differences

Culture serves as the fabric of one's being and includes language, beliefs, attitudes, and patterns of communication (Tiedt and Tiedt 1990). Schools are more culturally and linguistically diverse than ever before. A monolingual, English-speaking physical education teacher is increasingly likely to face the challenge of teaching young children whose languages and backgrounds are completely unfamiliar (Harrison, Russell, and Burden 2010). Often in this situation even the most well-meaning educators inadvertently reinforce children's conflicting feelings about fitting into the majority culture. Effective teachers are culturally responsible and are open to embracing students from all cultural backgrounds. To become more culturally responsive and reflective teachers (Chapter 4), we must use the cultural knowledge, prior experiences, and learning style preferences of children from diverse cultures to make learning more appropriate and effective for them. Culturally responsive teaching is teaching to and through the strengths of these students (Gay 2000).

Specific implications for teaching children from different cultures include the following:

- Incorporate the language and culture of all students into the school program. You may want to place posters in the gym written in two languages.
- Accept the differences without overlooking the similarities between children of diverse cultures.
- Be informed; educate yourself about the culture of your students. This may include traditions, communication styles, or social values of several diverse cultures. For example, some in Native American and Asian cultures believe direct eye contact is a sign of disrespect, and in other cultures, encroachment on personal space is not polite. Share your culture. Build trust.
- Learn students' names; pronounce them correctly in their native language.
- Challenge yourself to learn and use greetings in many languages, and never hesitate to ask children how to say basic expressions.
- Interact with all children and provide feedback to all. Have someone conduct an interaction checklist during one or more of your classes (Figure 13.3, page 229). You may be inadvertently overlooking a particular culture of children.

- Become aware of the children's learning styles. Some cultures use more visual cues, whereas others prefer tactile or auditory cues for learning. Physical education offers many opportunities for explanation and demonstration of skills. Peer teaching (Chapter 9) allows children to assist each other in learning.
- Be sure that all instructional materials include perspectives from different cultural groups rather than just the majority group within the class. Use materials that represent diverse cultural groups.
- Use the rich heritage of games, sports, and other forms of physical activity that has evolved from cultures throughout the world to highlight unique contributions.
- Invite parents to come to physical education classes to see what their child is learning. Send home a letter introducing yourself to parents. Remember, many parents do not read English. For example, in many regions of the United States, it is best to send home materials in English and Spanish (this is required in some school districts). Seek out resources in the school district to help with translation of materials.

To effectively build a culturally responsive environment, we as teachers of physical education must value the richness of diversity in our gymnasiums, in our classrooms, and on our playgrounds. We must foster positive attitudes toward diversity in our classes and promote an environment in which all children can be successful. The goal of inclusion is not to make differences invisible, but to create a classroom, a gymnasium, and a society in which all children and their families feel welcomed and valued (Sapon-Shevin 2008).

Gender Equity

In 1972, the United States Congress passed Title IX of the Education Amendments, mandating gender equity in all educational institutions receiving federal funding. One of the intentions of Title IX was to provide equal opportunity for physical education instruction to all students. Title IX may have started the process of providing gender equity, but we are still far from ensuring an equitable learning environment or equal opportunities for boys and girls in our classes. When the curriculum is identified as for boys (e.g., football, hockey, martial arts) or girls (e.g., dance, gymnastics) rather than for all, when boys demonstrate skills more often than girls and their questions are more frequently answered, when push-ups are labeled as either boy or girl push-ups, gender bias exists in our gymnasiums.

Many teachers treat children differently based on gender without even realizing it. To develop gender fairness, physical education teachers must create an environment in which all children feel safe to explore and develop their abilities in whatever venue of physical activity they choose. Title IX provided the foundation for change, but we as teachers are the key to assuring its implementation.

Specific implications for teaching for gender equity include the following:

- Use inclusive language, such as "player-to-player defense," "straight-leg push-ups," "modified push-ups" (rather than "boy push-ups" and "girl push-ups"), and "you all" rather than "you guys."
- Ask equal numbers of boys and girls to demonstrate skills, help with equipment, and answer questions in class.
- Interact with all students and provide an equal amount of quality feedback to boys and girls.
- Be sure that all instructional materials equally represent both girls and boys. Use pictures and media representative of male and female athletes, dancers, and gymnasts.
- Use newsletters, bulletin boards, and Web pages to help advertise after-school sport, dance, and gymnastics opportunities for both boys and girls.
- Ask the classroom teachers and others supervising recess to encourage coed play.
- Group students using a mixture of boys and girls. Do not have students participate in small-group tasks with boys versus girls.
- When grouping students, having them obtain or put away equipment, and asking them to line up at the end of class, do not do so by gender. Use birth date, number of pets, color of clothing, favorite foods, or other categories.

Although tremendous progress has been made, the gender gap still exists. In reality, many teachers and parents, some cultures and religions, and the media do little to encourage girls to participate in sports. Physical activity for girls still tends to be encouraged in the form of gymnastics, dance, or cheerleading. Leading sport television stations limit coverage of women's sports, thereby providing few role models for young girls. It is not surprising that the physical activity gap increases with age. It is our responsibility as physical education teachers to provide the foundational movement skills to both boys and girls to be physically active. Our responsibility is to encourage and motivate *all* students to be involved in physical activity, in and out of school.

Religious Differences

The First Amendment to the U.S. Constitution granted freedom of religion to all people more than 200 years ago. Today parents from diverse religious backgrounds entrust the education of their children to the teachers in public schools. Therefore, it is important for schools to be places where religion and religious conviction are treated with fairness and respect. Public schools uphold the First Amendment when they protect the religious liberty rights of students of all faiths or none. Because of the confusion that has surrounded the topic of religion in public schools throughout the years, this is perhaps easier said than done.

Specific implications for teaching children from different religions include the following:

- Work closely with parents and community members to know, understand, and appreciate religious differences.
- Excuse children who object to lesson content on the grounds of religious beliefs.
- Allow children whose dress reflects their religious views or modesty to wear such clothing. While dress requirements are typically not a part of elementary physical education, one should be informed. For example, Muslim girls should be allowed to wear a hijab over their hair and long pants under their shorts, and Sikh boys should be allowed to wear turbans.
- Make modifications or allow nonparticipation for students who observe rules regulating physical contact and modesty such as holding hands in a dance.
- Respect differences in holiday celebrations. Special lessons prepared for the observance of holidays occurring during the school year such as Halloween, Thanksgiving, Valentine's Day, and St. Patrick's Day may not match the religious beliefs of all children.

Overall, teaching children in one of the most religiously diverse countries in the world requires additional planning, communication, and flexibility. We are not suggesting that you change your religious views or even completely understand the religious views of others, but as a reflective teacher, you will need to take the time to learn about and respect religious differences. Keep in mind that religion deals with an individual's beliefs. While one religion may be dominant in a specific culture, do not assume everyone in that culture is of the same religion. For example, if you were to visit Israel, you would assume that Jewish is both a race and religion. You would be correct in the assumption, but what you would also learn is that everyone who is Jewish by race does not embrace the religion and that there are many people who are Jewish in religion but not in race.

Children Living in Poverty

The ever-widening gap between socioeconomic levels in the United States has resulted in a tremendously large group of children living at or near the poverty level. Approximately 44 percent of all public school children are eligible for free or reduced lunch (NCES 2018). When an individual school has 40 percent or more of students on free or reduced lunch, it is considered a poverty school. These schools have access to Title I funds for schoolwide programs designed to upgrade their entire educational programs to improve achievement for all students, particularly the lowest-achieving students. For some families, the poverty is situational, created by a loss of job, divorce, illness, death, or other variables beyond the control of the children or parents in the family. For other families, the poverty is generational, existing for such a long period of time that neither the children nor the adults in the family have ever known nonpoverty conditions. Children of poverty live in apartments, in houses, in shelters, on the streets, and in automobiles. They live with single parents, with multiple families, and with no parents. They exist in all ethnic groups. What they have in common is poverty—an existence below that necessary for meeting the basic needs of food, clothing, and shelter, an existence void of the basic components of wellness.

Children living in poverty:

- Have higher rates of lead poisoning
- Have poorer vision and poorer oral hygiene
- Have more asthma and more exposure to smoke
- Have poorer nutrition and less adequate pediatric care
- Go to bed hungry or ill fed more often
- Have families who relocate more frequently and must change schools several times within a single year
- Have less access to adults who can read to them or talk to them in intellectually stimulating, enriching ways

The social class differences in academic potential exist by the time children are three years old. Children living in poverty enter kindergarten with academic delays and cognitive experiential deficiencies. Many come to us with developmental delays and motor deficiencies.

Implications for teaching children living in poverty are the same as for all children:

- Provide physically, emotionally safe environments for learning.
- Assure that each child feels loved and worthy. In physical education, shoes can be provided for children in need.
- Provide hope for a significant future.

We must believe that all children are capable of success and empower them with the tools for success—in physical education, in the classroom, and beyond their years in school—and believe in their ability to achieve success.

It is important that teachers are sensitive to the diversity of home environments. Not everyone comes from a traditional family. You will also teach children whose family structure may be defined in any of the following ways: foster care, adopted, parents of the same sexual orientation (e.g., two mothers or two fathers), or single-parent homes. Children in these defined households should have the same opportunity to lead a healthy and happy life as those in a traditional family.

Children with Disabilities, Impairments, and Disorders

People with disabilities are the largest minority group in the United States (Block 2017), and with the inclusion approach, you will most likely have two or three students with a disability, impairment, or disorder in every class. Each child with a disability, impairment, or disorder has unique needs; successful inclusion, participation, and learning are our goals for each child.

Children with disabilities tend to be less physically active than children without disabilities. This is due to a number of factors: the nature of the disability itself, overprotective parents, and a lack of recreational and play facilities accessible for those with disabilities. Yet physical activity is extremely important for children with disabilities for many of the same reasons that it is for all children. Physical activity opportunities provide the chance to apply and enhance skill development. In a physical activity environment, social skills are learned and practiced, and self-confidence for social interaction is enhanced. Through physical activity, fitness is improved. Better fitness brings increased muscle tone for those prone to being less mobile; and muscle tone brings better posture, more control of manipulatives, and thus increased independence.

Many children with disabilities can participate in the regular fitness assessment program. However, for some boys and girls, modifications in assessment will be necessary. Box 10-1 provides information relative to fitness assessments designed especially for students with disabilities.

Efforts to keep students with disabilities from being ignored or discriminated against in our schools or in our society started decades ago. In the early 1970s, there were 46 right-to-education lawsuits that led to the Rehabilitation Act of 1973 (Section 504) and Public Law 94-142 (The Education for All Handicapped Children Act of 1975). Public Law 94-142 was replaced with the Individuals with Disabilities Education Act

Box 10-1

Physical Fitness Test Package for Students with Disabilities

Additional information concerning specific physical fitness assessment for students with disabilities may be obtained from the following source:

Brockport Physical Fitness Test Manual (2014), 2nd edition by J. Winnick and F. Short.
Human Kinetics
P.O. Box 5076
Champaign, IL 61825-5075
www.humankinetics.com

(IDEA) of 1990, 2004, and 2014. Schools are accountable to requirements of both IDEA and Section 504.

IDEA guarantees all children with disabilities from ages 3 to 21 a free and appropriate education and includes physical education as a direct service—one that must be provided for all students. IDEA further states that placement should be in the least restrictive environment and, to the maximum extent appropriate,

Avoid Using these Inappropriate Descriptors

- "Afflicted" - negative term suggesting hopelessness
- "Confined" to a wheelchair - people are not imprisoned in wheelchairs
- "Crippled" - implies someone who is pitiful and unable to do anything
- "Deaf and Dumb" & "deaf-mute" - outdated terms
- "Gimp" - once referred to someone who walked with a limp
- "Poor" - describes a lack of money or someone to be pitied
- "Retard" & "retarded" - medical diagnosis
- "Spastic" - lack of coordination due to physical/neurological impairments
- "Suffering" - implies that the disability causes constant pain
- "Unfortunate" - implies unlucky or unsuccessful
- "Victim" - is a person sacrificed by an uncontrollable force or person

Shared by a young adult paraplegic athlete who wishes to remain anonymous.

children with disabilities are to be educated together with children without disabilities. Over the years, this has translated to a philosophy of inclusion. With few exceptions, most children in America now attend physical education with their homeroom class.

Section 504 obligates school districts to identify, evaluate, and extend to every qualified student with a disability the right to a free and appropriate education. It is an equal opportunity law that may include modifications to learning, accommodations and accessibility, specialized instruction, and related aids (Winnick and Porretta 2017). Some students you teach may meet requirements for Section 504 but not for IDEA, but all children who qualify under IDEA receive Section 504 accommodations (several resources have been listed at the end of the chapter for additional information on IDEA and Section 504.)

Individualized Education Program

If a child qualifies under IDEA, an individualized education program (IEP) must be created and implemented. The appropriate education—both placement and curriculum—for each student with disabilities is determined by an IEP Team. The team is composed of all those involved in providing an appropriate education for the child: the classroom teacher, special educators (physical education), parents, and professionals from related services. Following an educational assessment by the school psychologist and other professionals as needed, the IEP Team designs the educational program for the child, identifies support services needed and services to be secured from outside agencies, and establishes the educational goals to be attained within the given school year.

Because physical education is a direct service for all children with disabilities, the physical education teacher is a vital member of the IEP Team. As a member of the team, the physical education specialist provides information about how the identified disability will affect the child's performance in the existing program of physical education; the child's performance in physical fitness and basic motor skills and patterns of physical education; and the support services needed to meet this child's unique needs and facilitate maximum learning in physical education. It is the *responsibility* of the physical education professional to attend the IEP meeting and provide input for each child with disabilities.

During the IEP Team meeting, short- and long-term goals are written for all areas of the child's learning, including physical education, and the environment most conducive to meeting those goals is identified. As the physical education professional on the team, your input is needed to establish the short- and long-term goals relative to physical education and to identify the environment most conducive to meeting those goals. Physical education options may include full inclusion, inclusion with a teacher assistant, or remedial physical education in addition to the regular program.

For some students with disabilities, full participation in physical education is possible; for those students, the IEP will not address physical education. For other students, full participation is possible with support services, that is, personnel and/or specific equipment. If an educational assistant is needed for safety or to aid in the learning experience, the physical education teacher should recommend this addition during the IEP Team meeting. For other students, the development of skills for successful participation will require modification within the physical education curriculum, such as an alternative when a lesson is not appropriate or is contraindicated. This alternative may be participation in another physical education class or work on a short-term physical education goal from the IEP within the class setting. Remedial physical education is another placement option to *accompany* inclusion. For some children with disabilities, this small-group physical education class can provide the "extra" practice they need beyond their general physical education class. For these children, the remedial physical education class provides the environment for learning the basic skills of physical education that will enable them to participate successfully in the gymnasium and on the playground.

Implementing the IEP

After the IEP has been written, it is the responsibility of all teachers working with the child with disabilities to implement what is written in the program. It is the responsibility of the physical education teacher to design instruction and to modify both teaching and curriculum to meet the short- and long-term goals written for physical education within the environment deemed least restrictive by the IEP.

Whether the IEP specifies full inclusion, inclusion with support services, or inclusion plus a remedial program, you cannot be content with letting the child with disabilities serve only as the scorekeeper, control the music, or turn the jump rope for others. *Zero exclusion* (Weber 2009) is the basic concept of physical education for all children with disabilities. Our task is to design the program to develop each child's skills in gymnastics, games, and dance and to provide opportunities for these students to reach the goals established for them.

Adaptations in tasks will permit any child to participate, to achieve, and to develop skills commensurate with personal ability. A good adaptation promotes interaction with other students, does not draw attention to the student, provides maximum participation, and provides a safe physical and emotional learning environment. With an understanding of basic concepts, an awareness of the children's needs, and knowledge of how to adapt the environment and the curriculum, the teacher can create an enabling environment for children with special needs. Children with disabilities can best learn in an elementary physical education environment that promotes individual response and fosters performance at the individual's skill level. In this environment, the teacher observes, reflects, and teaches to each child's strengths and needs.

Disabilities, impairments, and disorders include visual and hearing impairments; a number of physical disabilities; health-related disorders; emotional, behavioral, and social disorders; and intellectual and learning disabilities. It would be impossible in one chapter to inform you about every disability, disorder, or impairment you may encounter as a teacher. The luxury of the Internet permits us to search and learn this information (use reliable Web sites ending in .org or .gov). It is your responsibility as a teacher to read and learn about all of the characteristics of children who have a disability, impairment, or disorder. However, beyond the characteristics you may find on a reliable Web site or in a quality book, communicating with classroom teachers and parents or guardians is crucial to learning about the child's specific needs and strengths.

Natural Proportions

During the early days of mainstreaming, children with disabilities were often grouped together and placed in one general physical education class, resulting in the class increasing in number by as many as 5 to 10 children with special needs. "Natural proportions" is the recommended principle to match the philosophy of inclusion and maximize learning for all students (Block 2017). The principle of natural proportions means the normal ratio of persons with disabilities will be the guideline for the placement of children with disabilities in general classes. With approximately 10 to 15 percent of the school-age population having disabilities, a general elementary physical education class of 20 to 25 youngsters would have 2 to 3 children with disabilities. The principle of natural proportions creates a physical education environment that promotes success and positive experiences for all children.

Following are general implications for teaching students with physical disabilities, cognitive disabilities, emotional and behavioral disorders, social interaction disorders, visual and hearing impairments, and common health-related disorders. Each disability, impairment, or disorder is unique to a child.

Physical Disabilities

Physical disabilities include conditions resulting in orthopedic impairments, such as cerebral palsy and

Task and equipment adaptations can allow all children to experience success.

©Barbara Adamcik

spina bifida, the crippling diseases of arthritis and muscular dystrophy, permanent loss of limbs, and the temporary disabilities caused by fractures. Other related health factors that can mean limited or restricted learning experiences in physical education include hemophilia, severe burns, congenital heart defects, and respiratory disorders.

Each child with a physical disability has different physical and motor capabilities, so the learning goals must be designed to meet individual needs. The child's physical education program will include two aspects: (1) learning experiences to meet specific needs and develop motor skills and (2) any adaptations in the regular program of physical education. The following procedure is recommended when planning the program for children with physical disabilities:

1. Identify the child's clinical condition.
2. Determine what learning experiences would be contraindicated based on medical recommendation.
3. Determine functional motor skills needed.
4. Plan learning experiences that will develop desired motor skills.
5. Adapt the physical education environment and equipment as needed to provide the program.

It's important to remember that the program should be designed in consultation with a physician and a physical therapist. As teachers of physical education, we aren't expected to make a clinical diagnosis or to prescribe a program of individualized remedial exercises without the assistance of trained medical professionals.

General implications for teaching children with physical disabilities include the following:

- Emphasize duration of tasks over intensity.
- Observe safety concerns and assure special equipment is available for any needed body support.
- Incorporate balance tasks (static and/or dynamic) when possible.
- Include weight-bearing, muscular strength, and flexibility tasks. Consult the student's physical therapist for specific exercises.
- Adapt equipment and space in tasks (e.g., use larger, softer balls or larger targets, decrease the distance).
- Learn how to best interact with the child (Box 10-2).
- Request an educational assistant when needed for safety.

Intellectual Disabilities

Children with intellectual disabilities and specific learning disabilities have cognitive limitations. The term *intellectual disabilities* refers to intellectual functioning that is significantly below average,

©Barbara Adamcik

With help from an educational assistant, this child participates successfully in the physical education program

accompanied by deficits in adaptive behavior. Children with intellectual disabilities have problems of maturation, learning, and/or social adjustment, which, to different degrees, result in a degree of independence or social responsibility lower than that expected for their age. These characteristics manifest themselves during the early developmental periods of life. A *specific learning* disability is a disorder in one or more of the basic processes involved in understanding or using language. According to the U.S. Department of Health and Human Services, the disability may manifest itself as an imperfect ability to listen, think, speak, write, spell, or do mathematical calculations. Children with learning disabilities have normal intelligence but, unlike other children, are unable to perform academically within the normal IQ range. Children with learning disabilities are typically characterized by hyperactive behavior, short attention span, impulsiveness, poor self-concept, and often a delay in play development.

The physical skills of children with cognitive limitations will be no different than the variety within any class; the difficulties center around comprehending written and verbal instructions and staying focused on tasks. Typically there is a Section 504 accommodation for longer time in taking tests, creating shorter tests,

Box 10-2

Interacting with Children with Disabilities

- Act naturally. Relax and be yourself.
- Be courteous, not condescending. Talk as you would to any child until you are told to do otherwise. It is better to "talk up" to someone than to talk down.
- Don't feel as if everything you have to say needs to be funny or light. Serious topics are welcomed.
- Talk to the child, not to the attendant, parent, or teacher.
- It is fine to use phrases such as, "I have to run now" to a child in a wheelchair, or "I see" to a child who is blind.
- Avoid simple yes/no questions. They make for dull, one-sided conversation—for anyone! Instead, ask about family, friends, and activities. Don't ask, "Did you enjoy the circus?" but rather, "What did you see at the circus?" and "Tell me about the elephants."
- Be considerate and patient of the extra time it might take for the child to respond or to finish a task.
- Yes, touching is okay. Holding hands, hugging, or a pat on the back is appropriate if it is something you would do with any child. A pat on the head is typically considered a condescending gesture. Appropriateness is the key. Keep in mind that some children are too affectionate and need to learn proper social interaction.

- Offer assistance, but wait until it is accepted *before* you help.
- Be careful not to be overprotective. Do not allow other children to be overprotective.
- A child with a disability can misbehave just like any other child. Don't let yourself become so tolerant that you allow clearly unacceptable behavior.
- Establish eye contact. This may mean sitting down, kneeling, or moving to one side (if the child cannot look straight ahead). Avoid standing behind the wheelchair and talking. Many children rely on facial cues, gestures, and clear hearing to understand all that you are saying.
- Keep conversation about a child's wheelchair to a minimum, not because it is insulting (it isn't), but because often it is all people find to talk about (e.g., "I bet you can zoom around in that thing! I wish I had one. How fast does it go? Can I ride? How long do the batteries last?"). A little wheelchair talk is okay, but move to other topics that are more interesting to the child.
- Do not move a child's wheelchair or other mobility device out of reach without his or her permission.

Source: Adapted from Dave Taylor, *Project Active Newsletter* 12(1), 1991.

---

and/or reading the questions to the child. Be sure to check with the classroom teacher or consult the child's school records for any IEP or Section 504 modifications or accommodations.

General implications for teaching children with intellectual disabilities include the following:

- Keep verbal directions to a minimum; when possible, use both visual and verbal instructions.
- Communicate in a direct, simple, and meaningful manner.
- Structure the environment for focus on tasks and a minimum of distractions.
- Maintain a routine so the child knows what to expect.
- Provide repetition of experiences for overlearning.
- Break tasks into simpler, smaller steps.
- Present the lesson in short segments; restate the task at regular intervals.
- Reinforce strengths with frequent praise; minimize weaknesses.
- Engage the child in conversation. Ask questions; encourage a response.

- Be an attentive listener; listen when the child speaks.
- Do not pretend to understand if you do not.
- Create opportunities for cooperative learning experiences that actively involve the child.
- Recognize achievements; share them with the whole class so they can appreciate and share in the child's accomplishment.
- Encourage verbal expression of feelings.
- End the lesson with a brief relaxation period.

Atlantoaxial Subluxation

A number of children with Down syndrome have a condition called *atlantoaxial subluxation*, a maladjustment of the cervical vertebrae in the neck. Because of the possibility of serious injury, people with atlantoaxial subluxation should not participate in any activities that place stress on the head and neck muscles. Down syndrome children with atlantoaxial subluxation should not be actively involved in inverted balances, rolling activities, or other gymnastics actions that could place stress on the head and neck.

Emotional and Behavioral Disorders

In increasing numbers, children come to us with behavior disabilities, including children with emotional or behavioral disorders or who are hyperactive, distractive, aggressive, impulsive, or socially challenged. Some may have been diagnosed with attention deficit disorder (ADD) or attention deficit hyperactivity disorder (ADHD). Children classified as having an emotional or behavioral disorder have deficiencies in at least one of the following: characteristics that facilitate learning, characteristics that promote interpersonal relationships, and characteristics that foster appropriate behavior under normal conditions. What classifies children with these disorders is the persistence of the behavior, its severity, and its adverse effects on educational performance.

General implications for teaching children with emotional or behavioral disorders include the following:

- Provide a sense of order, structure, routine, and dependability in the learning environment.
- Teach the child that verbal responses to frustration and conflict are acceptable but that physical aggression is not.
- Make it clear to the child that he or she is accepted even when the behavior is unacceptable.
- Establish short-range, achievable goals geared to the child's current level of functioning.
- Convey your expectations through your conduct and consistent messages.
- Avoid overreacting to extreme behavior; an emotional response from the teacher is counterproductive.
- Remember, what works for one child with emotional or behavioral disorders may not work for another.
- Avoid competition; create opportunities for cooperative learning experiences.
- Communicate with the classroom teacher to be informed of "how the day is going."
- Request an educational assistant if needed.

Social Interaction Disorders

Children with social interaction disorders or pervasive developmental disorders include those with autism, Asperger syndrome, and Rett syndrome. Although each disorder has its unique characteristics and varying degrees of severity, common to all are severe impairment of communication and/or social interaction skills and the presence of repetitive behaviors. These children may appear extremely shy or often withdrawn into their own world. The indoor and outdoor environments of physical education can be a nightmare with loud sounds, an abundance of visual stimuli, and constantly changing activity. Often the recourse for these children is to withdraw to the inner world of self-movement (stimming) and self-talk or to wander aimlessly. Motor skills are often below the level of their peers.

General implications for teaching children with social interaction disorders include the following:

- Keep verbal directions to a minimum; visual cues and one-on-one demonstrations are valuable.
- Structure the environment for focus on tasks and a minimum of distractions.
- Maintain a routine so the child knows what to expect.

©Barbara Adamcik

Physical activity is just as exciting to children with disabilities as it is for those without disabilities.

- Encourage but do not require partner tasks; individuals may have one peer they trust.
- Use sensorimotor tasks (e.g., jumping on a mini-trampoline, crawling through a tunnel, rolling down an incline mat, using balls of different sizes and textures, using music).
- Request an educational assistant if needed.

Visual Impairments

The two categories of visual impairment are blindness and partial sight. Impairments range from blindness to blurred/distorted vision, tunnel vision, and the ability to see out of the corners of the eyes only. Children with partial sight may be able to adapt to the physical education environment with the exception of tracking moving objects at a high speed. Catching and striking skills may be below those of most children.

General implications for teaching children with severe visual impairments include the following:

- Include learning experiences that focus attention on other sensory abilities (e.g., tactile, auditory), spatial awareness, and mobility.
- Add balance tasks when possible.
- Use auditory cues.
- Include mobility training of the environment.
- Use manual guidance accompanied by verbal directions.
- Provide specific and immediate feedback (knowledge of results may not exist).
- Avoid learning experiences that involve throwing and catching with fast speed and travel.
- Avoid learning experiences that include striking a moving object. For stationary striking, use larger, bright-colored objects.
- Use an educational assistant or peer teacher to assist with the manual guidance and verbal feedback.
- Keep the outdoor teaching area and the gymnasium well organized and consistent.
- Ensure the gymnasium is well lit to help the child with residual vision.
- Provide tactile markings on the floor as a reference for teaching stations, the center for teacher directions, water fountains, etc.
- Use helpful equipment or devices (e.g., brightly colored balls and objects for children with limited vision, sponge and foam balls for safety, and sound-emitting devices on equipment for tracking and to denote location).
- Provide a large gymnastics mat to serve as "personal space" for safety.
- Always identify yourself and others in the group and inform the individual when you are walking away.

Ron, a child blind since birth, was attending general physical education where the class was studying balance—balance on different bases of support and balance in inverted positions (Chapter 21). Ron was working independently in the space defined by the boundaries of his gymnastics mat. Suddenly he cried aloud; the entire class stopped and turned in his direction. Nothing was wrong; Ron was experiencing for the first time the change in body position and perception that accompanies being balanced in an inverted position on the hands only. Ron apologized for disturbing the class, and activity continued. During sharing time at the end of the class, Ron shared his feelings of the experience and his enthusiasm for more gymnastics.

Hearing Impairments

The term *hearing impairment* refers to hearing loss that can range from mild to profound. The disability includes those who have trouble hearing normal speech and those who can't understand even amplified speech. Most individuals have some level of hearing and are able to understand speech with the help of amplification or by hearing combined with watching the speaker's lips, facial expressions, and gestures.

General implications for teaching children with severe hearing impairments include the following:

- Adapting the equipment or environment, as a rule, won't be necessary.
- Position yourself so the child with a serious hearing impairment can read your lips; be conscious of not turning your back when speaking; and be close enough for lip reading.
- Face the sun when outdoors so that the hearing-impaired child doesn't have to face the sun.
- Allow the hearing-impaired child to move freely in the teaching environment so he or she can always be in the best position for hearing.
- Demonstrate skills both visually and manually; don't rely on verbal directions alone.
- Remember, the hearing-impaired child can't read lips or hear a whistle across the playing field or gymnasium; accompany the auditory sound with large hand signals.
- Learn the basic sign language needed for communication.
- Include balance tasks for those with balance problems and vertigo due to damage to the inner ear.
- Do not speak when writing on the board or doing a demonstration. If you do, repeat what was said facing the student.

We strongly recommend a course in sign language for teachers with hearing-impaired children in their classroom or gymnasium. Think of how much better a child with a hearing impairment will feel when greeted on the first day of physical education by a teacher she or he can communicate with!

Health-Related Disorders

Although not normally thought of as physical disabilities, several other health-related disorders can affect a child's full participation in physical education. You will probably have children with health disorders that will impact their participation in physical education; these disorders may include juvenile arthritis, asthma, diabetes, heart defects, sickle-cell anemia, severe burns, cancer, hepatitis, epilepsy or seizure disorders, Tourette syndrome, allergies that require EpiPens, and respiratory disorders. It is extremely important that the physical educator review health records early in the school year, making note of any conditions that require monitoring and/or temporary adaptations. Another good practice is to send a note home with all students at the first of the year asking parents or guardians to share any health concerns. Open communication with the child's parents, rapport with the child, and an understanding of the particular disorder and its effects will result in maximum participation for the child as well as increased trust among you, the parents, and—most important—the child. Asthma and diabetes mellitus are the most common health-related disorders in schools today.

Asthma   Children are being affected in increasing numbers by asthma, an allergic reaction that results in wheezing, coughing, tightening of the airways, and accumulation of mucus in the bronchial tubes. An asthmatic attack can be triggered by allergens, upper respiratory infections, or even robust laughing. The most common conditions we see in physical education are reactions to changes in the weather (especially cold weather) and to strenuous exercise (e.g., the distance run for fitness assessment).

Asthma is a serious health problem for millions of children. Failure to attend to the condition can result in serious and sometimes life-threatening consequences for the child.

The following suggestions are helpful in ensuring maximum, healthy participation for children with asthma:

- Know how to recognize an episode (wheezing, excessive coughing, difficulty talking).

- Encourage students to inform you if they are having a difficult day with their asthma or had a rough, sleepless night from coughing.
- Check on the child regularly during class if the learning experiences are highly aerobic or if the child reports concerns for the day.
- Use a peer buddy system to help alert you to concerns.
- Ask the child to bring an inhaler to physical education class. Be aware that inhalers are stimulants, may raise the heart rate, and can affect behavior.
- Encourage water breaks; hydration is important and should be encouraged.
- Consult with the parents of children with serious asthmatic conditions for any special safeguards or procedures.

Diabetes Mellitus   Another health disorder that necessitates our attention is diabetes mellitus, a condition affecting the body's ability to process, store, and use glucose. Basically, the disease prevents your body from properly using the energy from the food you eat. Type 1 (insulin-dependent) diabetes is the most serious and affects more children. Type 2 diabetes (insulin resistance combined with insulin deficiency), also known as lifestyle diabetes, was once diagnosed only in adults but is becoming more common in children. Although we may experience only a few children with diabetes in our years of teaching, the child with diabetes requires the teacher to have a thorough understanding of the disorder, an awareness of the warning signs of low blood sugar, and the knowledge to initiate immediate emergency procedures. For children with type 1 diabetes, a serious condition known as hypoglycemia or low blood sugar can result in a coma without immediate attention. Too much sugar in the blood is called "hyperglycemia" (high blood sugar).

The following suggestions are helpful in ensuring maximum, healthy participation for children with diabetes:

- First, take advantage of available training in your school district or community.
- Recognize the symptoms of hypoglycemia (e.g., shaking, sweats, irrational, moody, tired) and hyperglycemia (e.g., increased urination, tired, thirsty).
- Reinforce self-awareness and health responsibility. A child should be taught to make the diabetes fit into his or her daily life. Although this is the role of doctors and parents, teachers can reinforce this behavior.
- Encourage daily physical activity. Diet and exercise go hand in hand for quality of life.
- Teach the movement skills, wellness, and fitness concepts to prolong quality of life.

Handling Body Fluids

Working with young children will result in an occasional "accident" on your gym floor. Young children and special needs students sometimes do not stop activity quick enough to make it to the restroom. It is inevitable that someone will also have an upset stomach and vomit. A bloody nose, scrape, or cut, although rare, does occur.

Be cautious because you have no way of knowing the health risks involved in coming into contact with any body fluids. Follow these suggestions:

1. Try not to draw attention to the child.
2. Mark the contaminated area with cones or chairs.
3. Call or send for the custodian.
4. If the child is bleeding. Do not touch the blood. If you need to assist the child, take time to put on rubber gloves. For a nose bleed, ask the student to squeeze his or her nose as if something stinks. When bleeding stops, send the child to the restroom to wash his or her face and hands with soap and water. Contact the custodian for clean-up. Know and use universal precautions for handling blood.
5. Send the child to the school nurse when necessary.
6. Complete all necessary school forms; coordinate with the school nurse for a note home informing the parent(s) of cuts, bloody nose, or upset stomach. *A text, e-mail, or phone call later that evening means the world to the child and to the parents.*

- Check on the child regularly during class.
- Use a peer buddy system to help alert you to concerns.
- Keep snacks or juice readily available.

Creating an Inclusive Environment

Inclusion does not come without challenges in physical education. With large class sizes, lack of preparation or

Coordination with Classroom Teacher

One of the keys to successful inclusion of children with disabilities is to promote the acceptance of those children by their peers. Many children have never been around children with disabilities and are hesitant about beginning conversations with them or engaging in activity. The physical education teacher should coordinate efforts with the classroom teacher to orient the class to the nature of the child's disability, its correct name, any limitations it imposes, and the child's potential for maximum participation in physical education.

knowledge of how to relate and teach certain populations, the desire to provide some students more attention than others, and lack of time to collaborate with other teachers or specialists, some teachers struggle with creating an inclusive environment. Even with a strong belief in the philosophy of inclusion, initial attempts at implementation are often accompanied with feelings of apprehension. Can I meet the needs of children with disabilities? Can I meet the needs of all the children in my class? In addition to the implications for teaching children shared in the previous sections, the following strategies will assist in implementing inclusion:

- **Prepare yourself**
  - Learn everything you can about your students. Do your research. Search the Internet; the search will be limited only by the time you can devote to the learning. Use quality Web sites (ending in .org or .gov).
  - Get to know the families. Invite the parents or guardians to school to observe a physical education class. Keep an open line of communication with parents and guardians.
  - Find out if your school district has a committee on adapted physical education (CAPE) or a district consultant. If not, form a support group of other physical educators in your district.
  - The better informed you are, the better you will be at meeting the needs of a diverse population.
- **Prepare the class**
  - Discuss the disability or uniqueness of some individuals in general terms with the class. Explain in age-appropriate terms.
  - Tell the class about the child—his or her likes and dislikes, his or her strengths and abilities. Discuss things the class can do to help the child in physical education. Encourage children to assist when needed but not to be overprotective or condescending.
  - Bring in guest speakers from the community to aid in helping you and students to learn about a specific disability or culture.
  - Emphasize your expectations for a positive emotional learning environment; no put-downs and no bullying
  - Teach children what has been termed *cultural dexterity*, acknowledging the differences among us and then embracing those differences. We are all not the same; that is a positive. Focus on the similarities, but do not deny the differences.
- **Become an *active* member of the IEP Team**
  - You are the expert in terms of the child's motor functioning and skill level. You are the key in the

design of goals for motor development and appropriate placement for the child. You are critical to the discussion of assistance needed for the child in physical education.

- Request educational assistants, paraprofessionals, or volunteers to aid with safety and learning.
  - Determine their existing knowledge and experience.
  - Offer to educate them specifically on what you need for them to do.
  - Conduct a professional development for them.
  - Inform them of your routines and expectations.
  - Do not assume they know the physical education content or safety protocols; inform them.
  - Although they know the student, you know the content and the adaptations needed.
- Provide written plans for assistants, paraprofessionals, or volunteers. Provide them with a skill progression for the day. Use visuals when possible.
- **Plan for success**
  - Make sure all facilities are accessible to all students (e.g., restroom, water fountain).
  - Make sure the physical environment is safe for all students.
  - When planning, make modifications as needed for individuals in each class.
  - Include ongoing reflection and regular assessment in your program.
  - Provide a motivating atmosphere for success.
  - Emphasize the strengths and abilities of each individual.
  - Use inclusive language.

Most important, remember that inclusion is a philosophy that reflects a belief that all children, regardless of abilities or disabilities, should be educated within the same environment (Block 2017). It is a physical education environment where each and every child has his or her needs met. It is an environment where all children are accepted and all are valued, an environment in which we design, adapt, and modify experiences on a daily basis to maximize individual learning. To be an effective teacher in a diverse setting, you must first become aware of your biases. Then, take the steps to move beyond your biases so you will value diversity and be culturally responsive to the needs, interests, and abilities of *all* of the children you teach. It is time to support, not just include, diverse learners, in all their various forms.

> *Inclusive education is essential because not being included means you are excluded!*
>
> **—RK TENACIOUS**

A Final Thought

If we are to become teachers of all children—children of diversity, children with disabilities—we must be aware of and move beyond our individual biases, beyond our preconceived expectations of students and their potential (Timken 2005). We must value the richness of diversity and be responsive to the cultures, needs, interests, and abilities of the children we teach. We must know our students and know them well.

As we strive to provide maximum opportunities for learning and development of personal potential in all children, may the following student request be our inspiration:

Please, my teacher, open up your . . .
> *Heart* to *care* ever more deeply for us;
>
> *mind* to *think* ever more creatively about ways of helping us learn;
>
> *mouth* to *seek* fresh ideas and feedback (including from us!); and
>
> *classroom* to *join* colleagues and parents in a thriving community
>
> where as teacher, parents and children together
>
> we strive to reach our potential.
>
> *okay?*

—*Ronald F. Ferguson, August 2003*

Summary

Diversity in the United States is steadily increasing. Diversity is defined as differences that exist among people. Cultural dexterity is recognizing the differences and embracing the differences. It is time to support diverse learners through a broadened conceptualization of inclusion that goes beyond accommodating students with special needs. Physical education teachers must be prepared to teach all students, including those with differences in mental and physical ability, skill level, fitness level, gender, culture, language, socioeconomic status, physical characteristics, and so on. Preparation begins with educating ourselves about the child's unique needs through extensive reading, as well as communicating with qualified professionals, parents, and community members.

Inclusion does not mean sitting on the sidelines keeping score. Inclusion involves teachers creating a healthy learning climate where all children feel safe, successful, motivated, and connected to others. When learning objectives and tasks do not meet these basic needs of all learners, modifications must be made.

When working with diverse students, it is important to know that integrating children with special needs into regular educational settings is not a choice for teachers and administrators. Teachers are accountable to requirements of both the IDEA and Section 504 legislations that guarantee each child with a disability a free and appropriate education in the least restrictive environment. IDEA requires that an IEP Team determine the placement that constitutes the least restrictive environment. Inclusion is considered the least restrictive

environment unless the nature or the severity of the disability is such that the use of supplementary aids and services cannot be achieved in a satisfactory way.

The child's educational program, including annual goals, support services, and any special services, is written into the IEP. The IEP includes physical education as a direct service for all children with disabilities. It is the physical education teacher's responsibility to provide input to the child's IEP by attending the IEP Team meetings.

We need to educate all children concerning individual differences and to orient them to the world of diversity. By promoting the acceptance of all individuals and presenting a curriculum that focuses on the development of skills commensurate with ability, we can promote the acceptance of all children as contributing members of physical education classes. "Zero exclusion and zero failure" is the standard for all children in physical education; nothing less is acceptable.

Reading Comprehension Questions

1. Define diversity and provide three specific examples of diversity in physical education.
2. Explain the term *inclusion*.
3. Explain what culturally responsive teaching is. Provide two specific examples of things a physical educator might do to become a more culturally responsive teacher.
4. Describe three ways a teacher can create a more gender-equitable environment.
5. Explain the purpose(s) or reason(s) for modifying learning experiences.
6. What is the Individuals with Disabilities Education Act? What is its impact on physical education?
7. What is an individualized education program (IEP)? What does it include?
8. What is an IEP Team? What is its function? Who serves on the team?
9. What is the role of the physical education teacher as a member of the IEP Team?
10. Why is planning so important for inclusion of a child with disabilities in physical education?
11. Choose one physically disabling condition and explain its implications for physical education. Discuss the adaptations involved in physical education for this child—adaptations for the child, adaptations for the whole class, and adaptations for the teacher.

References/Suggested Readings

American Association for Physical Activity and Recreation. 2003. *Physical education for infants, children, and youth with disabilities: A position statement.* Reston, VA: American Association for Physical Activity and Recreation.

[AOA] American Obesity Association. 2010. Childhood overweight. www.obesity.org (accessed August 25, 2010).

Association for Supervision and Curriculum Development. 2003. Teaching all students. *Educational Leadership* 61(2).

Auxier, D., J. Pyfer, L. Zittel, and K. Roth. 2010. *Principles and methods of adapted physical education and recreation.* New York: McGraw-Hill.

Block, M. E. 2017. *A teacher's guide to including students with disabilities in general physical education.* 4th ed. Baltimore: Brookes.

Cruz, L. M., and S. C. Peterson. 2011. Teaching diverse students: How to avoid marginalizing difference. *Journal of Physical Education, Recreation and Dance* 82(6): 21–28.

Gay, G. 2000. *Culturally responsive teaching: Theory, research, and practice.* New York: Teachers College Press.

Harrison, L., R. L. Russell, and J. Burden. 2010. Physical education teachers' cultural competency. *Journal of Teaching in Physical Education* 29(2): 184–96.

Hovart, M., L. Kelly, M. Block, and R. Croce. 2019. *Developmental and adapted physical activity assessment.* 2nd ed. Champaign, IL: Human Kinetics Publishing.

Kahan, D. 2003. Religious boundaries in public school physical activity settings (law review). *Journal of Physical Education, Recreation and Dance* 74(1): 11–13.

Meece, J. L., and B. Kurtz-Costes. 2001. The schooling of ethnic minority children and youth. *Educational Psychologist* 36(1): 1–7

Napper-Owen, G. E. 1994. Equality in the elementary gymnasium. *Strategies* 8(3): 23–26.

[NCES] National Center of Educational Statistics. 2018. *Digest of educational statistics.* Washington, DC: U.S. Department of Education. http://www.NCES.ed.gov (accessed May 30, 2018).

Sapon-Shevin, M. 2008. Learning in an inclusive community. *Educational Leadership* 66(1): 49–53.

Sherrill, C. 2004. *Adapted physical activity, recreation, and sport.* 6th ed. New York: McGraw-Hill.

Stephens, T. L., L. Silliman-French, L. Kinnison, and R. French. 2010. Implementation of a response-to-intervention system in general physical education. *Journal of Physical Education, Recreation and Dance* 81(9): 47–53.

Taylor, D. 1991. *Project Active Newsletter* 12(1).

Tiedt, P. L., and I. M. Tredt. 1990. *Multicultural teaching: A handbook of activities, information, and resources.* Boston: Allyn & Bacon.

Timken, G. L. 2005. Teaching all kids: Valuing students through culturally responsive and inclusive practice. In *Standards-based physical education curriculum development,* ed. J. Lund and D. Tannehill, 78–97. Boston: Jones & Bartlett.

Tipps, C. R. 2006. Kids at hope: All children are capable of success—No exceptions! *Journal of Physical Education, Recreation and Dance* 77(1): 24–26.

Tomlinson, C. A. 2003. Deciding to teach them all. *Educational Leadership* 61(2): 7–11.

Weber, M. C. 2009. Special education law: Challenges old and new. *Phi Delta Kappan* 90(10): 728–32.

Winnick. J. P., and F. X. Short. 2014. *Brockport physical fitness test manual.* 2nd ed. Champaign, IL: Human Kinetics.

Winnick, J. P., and D. Porretta. 2017. *Adapted physical education and sport.* 6th ed. Champaign, IL: Human Kinetics.

Reflecting on Student Responses

It is vital for a teacher to observe children, whatever the subject or situation. It is through observation that the successful teacher assesses the moods, attributes, needs, and potential of individuals and groups.

—E. MAULDON AND J. LAYSON

Drawn by children at Monfort, Chappelow or Shawsheen Elementary Schools, Greeley, CO.
Courtesy of Lizzy Ginger; Tia Ziegler; Karla Drury

Key Concepts

- Reflective teachers are effective observers.
- If every student or class was identical, observation would not be necessary!
- Accurately observing classes of students in a physical activity setting is a pedagogical skill acquired through practice and experience.
- Teachers must continually examine their classes to be certain they are, and remain, safe.

ocke (1975) provided the following description of a two-minute segment of a class of 34 fourth-grade students:

Teacher is working one-on-one with a student who has an obvious neurological deficit. She wants him to sit on a beam and lift his feet from the floor. Her verbal behaviors fall into categories of reinforcement, instruction, feedback, and encouragement. She gives hands-on manual assistance. Nearby two boys are perched on the uneven bars and are keeping a group of girls off. Teacher visually monitors the situation but continues to work on the beam. At the far end of the gym a large mat propped up so that students can roll down it from a table top is slowly slipping nearer to the edge. Teacher visually monitors this but continues work on the beam. Teacher answers three individual inquiries addressed by passing students but continues as before. She glances at a group now playing follow-the-leader over the horse (this is off-task behavior) but as she does a student enters and indicates he left his milk money the previous period. Teacher nods him to the nearby office to retrieve the money and leaves the beam to stand near the uneven bars. The boys climb down at once. Teacher calls to a student to secure the slipping mat. Notes that the intruder, milk money now in hand, has paused to interact with two girls in the class and, monitoring him, moves quickly to the horse to begin a series of provocative questions designed to reestablish task focus.

After painting this picture of the complexity of teaching, Locke aptly reminds us:

That was only 120 seconds out of the 17,000 the teacher spent that day in active instruction. A great deal of detail was unobserved or unrecorded over those two minutes, and nothing in the record reflected the invisible train of thought in the teacher's mind.

That scenario provides us with glimpses of establishing a learning environment (e.g., much student choice and independence in activities); maintaining the

environment (e.g., standing near students who are off task); and developing content (e.g., providing reinforcement, instruction, feedback). It also reminds us once again of the complexity of teaching physical education. To become a reflective (and effective) teacher who meets your students' needs, it is essential you see and are then able to react to your students' responses, both behavioral responses and responses to learning tasks—while you are teaching. (Locke had the luxury of sitting on the sidelines and seeing when he wrote this!) There are multiple reasons to observe (and reflect) in the gym. In *Children Moving*, we have chosen to focus on two that we deem most important—observing the children's movement responses and observing teacher actions related to effective teaching. Although we treat these as two separate and distinct skills serving two different purposes, they are inextricably related to each other. There are effective teaching skills not related to observing children's movement, yet the ability to be an effective (and reflective) teacher without observing children's movement is impossible. Rink (2014) most poignantly communicates this when she indicates that the teaching cycle of teacher task, to children's movement response, to subsequent teacher task is at the heart of the learning process. Without acute and accurate observation of the children's movement responses, it is impossible to create appropriate follow-up tasks. In this chapter, we address reflecting on student responses to those practices; in Chapter 13, we look at observing your actions as a teacher. But, before you can reflect and respond, you have to be able to see what the children are actually doing—and that's not easy or automatic!

Be gentle with yourself. Don't be disappointed initially if, in the relative tranquility after you've finished teaching, you find that you made some apparently obvious errors. Observation appears easy to the spectator, but the complexity of teaching and observing movement can be fully appreciated only when one assumes the role of the teacher. In time and with practice, you'll become increasingly satisfied with your ability to observe and analyze movement.

This chapter on observation is one of the most important chapters in the book—perhaps the most important. Why? Observe a class of students playing a sport such as softball and watch the individual students. Do you see how many of them are unable to throw or catch or bat the ball? And yet the teacher continues to play the game as if all of the students in the class have the necessary skills to play softball successfully and enjoyably. Often, they don't—and we wonder what the teacher of that class is actually looking at. Is the teacher observing the students? Doesn't the teacher see that many of the students need to practice the skills rather than be in a game situation—especially one where score is being kept?

In our opinion, this is one of the main reasons that so many middle and high school students get turned off to sports—because they don't have the skills they need. And yet the teachers aren't seeing them; they are not observing their classes as defined in this chapter. Now the concept may seem easy—observe to see what the students are able or not able to do and then adapt the lesson content accordingly. As you will see, however, truly observing your students is a complex process that we attempt to describe in detail in this chapter.

The process of observation can be divided into two aspects: what to observe and how to observe.

- **What to observe:** This aspect includes four categories: safety, on-task behavior, class movement patterns, and individual movement patterns.
- *How to observe:* Observational techniques are generic, regardless of what is observed; they include positioning, knowing what to look for, and having an observational strategy.

The remainder of this chapter introduces you to these two aspects of observation.

What to Observe

When teaching physical education, a teacher is constantly bombarded by seemingly hundreds of ideas in just a few seconds. Thus, we've provided a procedure that we've found valuable for observing and understanding all that goes on in our classes. Because teaching is so complex, it's important that a teacher knows what to look for in a particular lesson before conducting the lesson itself. This requires planning. When we don't plan, we often find it difficult to decide what to observe during a lesson, so our lessons lack focus or direction. It's almost as if we were just doing things with children rather than actually teaching with clear learning outcomes. For this reason, when we plan, we divide our observation into four categories: (1) safety, (2) on-task behavior, (3) class movement patterns, and (4) individual movement patterns.

Safety

For obvious reasons, safety is the first aspect to observe, but what makes a safe environment? The elements are usually included in class protocols—not interfering

with others, following directions, and so on. You must identify what each aspect of safety looks like. For example, what does not interfering with others look like if you have asked students to "throw and catch with a partner in a space that matches your abilities"? What would be the first safety aspect to observe? For us, it would be, "Are the students spread out so they do not interfere with each other?" In other words, are partners not throwing across another group of partners, and do they have enough space between groups? For a different task, to "jump over a low hurdle, make a wide shape in the air, land, and roll," our first observation for safety might be to make sure that the students are actually landing before they roll rather than diving over the hurdle. At the same time, we might check the following: Is only one student on a mat at a time? Is there enough space between the mats? Are students pushing each other?

As a teacher, your first and constant attention must always be directed toward the children's safety. Whenever you observe an unsafe situation, remember that safety must always take priority over everything else going on in the lesson. If you have stated a task in such a way that the children are responding unsafely, stop the class and restate the task. If equipment is unsafe or being used unwisely, stop the class to make the use of the equipment safe. We also teach the children about safety so they're able to understand and develop a respect for potential hazards they may encounter if they aren't careful. Initially, we explain the reasons for our safety procedures to enable children to better understand and make intelligent decisions about their own safety. That's not enough, however. We need to constantly be aware of unsafe conditions. Following are several safety precautions we always keep in mind as we observe the classes. Some of these precautions are also described in Chapter 7 and in respective skill theme chapters.

- It is essential that children work independently without pushing, shoving, tripping, or otherwise interfering with other children.
- A working knowledge of self-space is obligatory. Children must work in a space a safe distance from others. When they get too close—for example, when striking with rackets—we stop the lesson and make them adjust their space.
- Depending on the surface, our children work in tennis shoes or barefoot. We don't allow stockinged feet, especially on hardwood or tile floors because they're so slippery. Children enjoy sliding, but this is a definite hazard.
- In lessons on skill themes, such as rolling, transferring weight, and balance (educational gymnastics

context), we don't allow "I Dare You" and "Follow the Leader" games or touching and pushing.

- In lessons in which gymnastics apparatus is being used, we allow only one child on the equipment at a time unless otherwise indicated. This condition might change once the learning environment has been effectively established.

Legal liability is an increasing concern for teachers, particularly physical education teachers. We strongly encourage you to teach safety rules similar to those just described and to include the rules in the written lesson plan so they're part of a permanent record in the unfortunate event you have to document safety precautions. Most of these safety rules should be taught in the first few weeks of school (Chapter 7) and then be reinforced throughout the year. Again, as you observe, make sure safety is constantly the forefront of your focus.

On-Task Behavior

Once you've determined that the environment is safe, your next focus is to decide whether children are on task. Are they actually doing what you asked them to do? For example, if you asked your class to throw and catch with a stationary partner, are they doing so? Or are they throwing to a moving partner across the space? For the rolling task described earlier, this would again include whether students are jumping, landing, and rolling. (This is both a safety and an on-task focus because being off task here is unsafe.) Are students remaining at their own mats or traveling around the room? Are they simply rolling and forgetting to jump? Are they jumping but without wide body shapes? If so, these are off-task behaviors, and you need to attend to them immediately. Stop the lesson!

There are three reasons why children may be off task:

1. The children are trying to perform the task, but it was stated unclearly. You must restate the task.
2. The task may not be appropriate. It could be too hard or too easy. If it's too easy, many children will become bored and thus off task. If it's too hard, many children will become frustrated and thus off task. Determining the students' success rate is one way to check the difficulty of the task. A guideline for the right success rate is 80 percent—in other words, the students you observe should be successful 80 percent of the time. Figure 11.1 provides an example of an observation sheet that can be used to assess task difficulty. Success at this point is defined as the use of the proper cues or the efficiency of the skills, not the result of the skill. For example, when

watching a child throw, we would watch to see if the critical elements were used, not if the ball hit the target. In situations in which the task is too hard or too easy, or was not stated clearly, children will most often make up their own task. Rarely will young children come to the teacher and say, "Teacher, the task is too hard," or "Teacher, I didn't understand."

> When students are "off task," our first response should be to ask, "What's the task?"
>
> —ALFIE KOHN (1996, P. 19)

3. The children haven't yet learned to be on task. If so, you'll need to practice the appropriate behavior in physical education class. It is impossible to teach without first managing (Chapter 7). The time spent on management is well worth it later when your class is running smoothly. If you don't spend time on management early, you will find yourself constantly managing later. As the old saying goes, "An ounce of prevention is worth a pound of cure."

The reality of teaching, unfortunately, is that often a class has one or two children who tend to be off task more than others. What do you do with them? After all, their behavior interferes with your right to teach and other youngsters' right to learn. Refer to Chapters 7 and 8 for ideas about working with these students.

Class Movement Patterns

When you've determined the class is working safely and on task, begin observing the movement patterns of the entire class to see how students are accomplishing the task. (Constantly be on the alert, however, for unsafe and off-task situations.) The observation of class movement patterns shifts the focus of the observation from "Are the students simply on task?" to the quality of students' skill. Yet, how do we decide what to look for in terms of skill? The easiest way to observe is to start with one cue (reflecting a critical element) and observe to see if the students are using that cue correctly. If they are, then move to another cue. If the majority of the class is not using the cue correctly, then you want to stay with that cue, rather than switching to a different cue. For example, the rolling forward (see Chapter 22; page 422) cues of "Hands, Lean, Hike, Look, Tip" help students learn and understand the critical elements for how to do a forward roll (see Box 22-2). The task is fairly controlled, so the observation is simplified. As you plan lessons, identify specific critical elements for the skill being taught and the cues you

Figure 11.1 Practice attempts recording sheet.

Practice Attempts Recording Sheet

Teacher: _____ Date: _____ Content: _____

Lesson Starting/Ending Time: _____ _____

Students: 1._____ 2._____ 3._____

4._____ 5._____ 6._____

Charting Instructions: Note each task and record the number of practice attempts provided (choose two students to observe for each task and record their total practice attempts). Indicate successful (efficient) tries by circling the tally marks for that try.

Task	# of Skill Attempts	Totals (attempts/successful attempts)
1.	Student 1:	
	Student 2:	
2.	Student 3:	
	Student 4:	
3.	Student 5:	
	Student 6:	
4.	Student 1:	
	Student 2:	
5.	Student 3:	
	Student 4:	

Totals (Student 1)

a. # of attempts (all tasks) 5 _____
b. # of successful attempts (all tasks) 5 _____
c. % of attempts successful 5 _____
d. Rate of attempts per minute (# of attempts/# of minutes) _____

Totals (Student 2)* (Total attempts for all students in the same manner.)

e. # of attempts (all tasks) 5 _____
f. # of successful attempts (all tasks) 5 _____
g. % of attempts successful 5 _____
h. Rate of attempts per minute (# of attempts/# of minutes) _____

will use (in the skill theme chapters, these are identified at the beginning of every task). Remember you will focus on those cues one at a time.

Based on your observation of the class, you'll make one of four decisions according to what you observe the majority of the children doing. Your choices are to (1) leave the task the same and let the students continue practicing, (2) change the task by increasing or decreasing the complexity, (3) refine the task to focus on quality, or (4) present a challenge to the children if you decide to modify the task in anyway. Chapter 6 discusses the three content development decisions in detail. We mention them here to emphasize that these decisions need to be based on what you observe, not on an arbitrary time allotment that doesn't take into account, for example, children's abilities and interests.

As part of making the decision, ask yourself if the task is really helping the students learn what they need to know (Rink 2003). If, for example, your lesson goal is to guide children to use "strong muscles" and "stretch your legs" when transferring weight onto their hands and bringing their feet to the floor in the same place, then you will want to be sure that the way the children have understood and are practicing the tasks is really leading to the use and understanding of those cues. If, after you observe your students enjoying success with this task and effectively demonstrating the cues (strong muscles and stretch your legs), it is time to make the task more complex. To make this task more difficult, you may ask students to transfer their weight from their feet to their hands to travel across the mat. In this case, the decision to move to a more complex task was based on your observation with a focus on performing the cues with quality. As if observing the children's responses was not difficult enough, the appropriate teacher response to what is seen is even harder—especially with a class of 30 children.

Let's take another example. Say that for this lesson you've decided your second graders need practice throwing overhand and your goal is to begin to teach four characteristics of a mature throw. You select a series of tasks from Chapter 24. You also decide that your critical element for this lesson will be the use of opposition—that is, that the children learn to step with the foot opposite their throwing arm. Once you've defined the task and explained the critical element ("Throw the ball as hard as you can against the wall. Remember to step with the foot on the other side of your body from your throwing arm"), you observe to see which children are using opposition and which ones aren't. If you observe that most of the children aren't using opposition, stop the class and provide a refinement task to focus on the cue of step with the

opposite foot (e.g., "This time, as you throw the ball as hard as you can, I really want to see you step forward with the opposite foot"). You may also demonstrate the correct performance yourself or pinpoint as models several children who are using opposition. Then the children can return to their practice. Be sure to observe the children's responses to determine whether they are performing as the cue indicates. Remember, the cue (step with the opposite foot) is what you actually expect the children to learn in this lesson. This cycle of teacher task/student response/teacher observation and decision about subsequent task is the heart of teaching for student learning in physical education (Rink 2014). Without the ability to observe astutely, it is impossible to teach for student learning.

We encourage observing class movement patterns before observing individual movement patterns because, by working with individuals too early, the teacher may lose focus on the entire class. We've seen this happen frequently with beginning teachers. The teacher becomes so involved helping an individual child that he or she loses focus on the entire class and may suddenly look up to find that a number of children are off task or that an unsafe condition has developed. This is not to suggest that teachers shouldn't work with children individually—we certainly should and do. But teachers must make sure they don't become so involved with one child that they forget to concentrate on the whole class. As Locke's vignette at the beginning of the chapter suggests, doing so is a real challenge.

Individual Movement Patterns

Teaching children individually is something we try to do as teachers. Obviously, however, it's not an easy job. Chapter 7 describes two instructional techniques for working with individuals: teaching by invitation and intratask variation. The use of these approaches involves the ability to observe individuals and yet maintain the focus on the entire class.

When we work with individuals, we use essentially the same process we use for the entire class. We differentiate instruction by varying the task for different children (intratask variation). If you ever have an opportunity to watch a skilled teacher, you'll see that this teacher is constantly using intratask variation as he or she travels from child to child while remaining conscious of the entire class, safety, and on-task behavior. Now you can better understand why it's so important to spend time establishing a learning environment at the beginning of the year.

Recently I observed a teacher attempting to teach a child how to run and kick a stationary ball. The child was unable to adjust her run to enable herself to arrive at the ball in a proper kicking position. After each unsuccessful attempt (the ball barely moved, and the child almost appeared to step on the ball rather than kick it), the teacher would say to the child, "No, that's not it!" The child knew she had failed as she watched the ball erratically dribble away from her foot, and yet the teacher offered no prescription for improvement. Rather than stating results the student can readily observe, the successful instructor offers a prescription for practice—that is, a cue.

When presented separately, the four aspects or categories of observation—safety, on-task behavior, class movement patterns, and individual movement patterns—seem simple and easy to follow. When teaching, however, a teacher is rarely able to focus on any one aspect at a time. As Locke's vignette suggests, the teacher must concentrate simultaneously on the four aspects. To aid in your observation, Figure 11.2 provides a flow chart of the questions we use to guide our observation of classes. Note that the arrows between the questions go both ways, indicating that the observation focus isn't linear, but that there's a constant interplay between the questions. Note, too, that this observation may all happen within 60 seconds! Remember, whenever a new task is given, always start over with the first two questions: Are the children working safely, and are they on task?

How to Observe

Once you have decided what you want and need to observe, the next step is actually observing so that you see. As we indicated earlier, observation is a learned skill that can improve with practice. Bird watching provides an apt analogy here. Non-bird watchers who see a bird might think, "There is a big bird." Novice bird watchers will say, "There is a big bird with a white head and dark body." Intermediate bird watchers, with binoculars, might note a large bird with a dark body, white head, and white on the tail. An expert, with binoculars, will identify the bird as a bald eagle. It takes practice to become an expert observer, but the result is rich and detailed information about what you have seen and hence where to proceed. Two techniques are helpful in learning to observe with insight (Rink 2014):

1. Positioning
2. Having a strategy for observing

Positioning

Positioning in the gym or on the playground is essential. To return to the bird-watching analogy, if you are standing behind a tree, you might not be able to see the bird at all; if you are standing behind the bird, you might only see the tail; and if you are standing too close, you might frighten the bird. Thus, positioning is important from three perspectives: being able to see, being able to see important aspects, and how you affect the learners' performance (Rink 2014).

First, for safety purposes, never spend long in a position where you are unable to observe all the

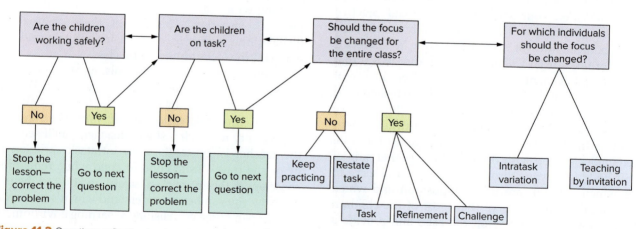

Figure 11.2 Questions reflective teachers use to guide the observation of students.

students in your class. While there are a variety of techniques useful in facilitating the observation of the whole class, we have found the back-to-the-wall or 90/90 (being able to see 90 percent of the students 90 percent of time) technique to be the most useful for seeing all students. Using this technique, the teacher stands outside the area in which the children are working so she or he can see the entire class. From a legal perspective, this allows for direct supervision. When the teacher enters the middle of an instructional area, he or she is unable to see part of the class (Figure 11.3) and should consequently limit the time spent in the middle. The ability to observe all that is going on, particularly with classes that are difficult to manage, is important both for effective classroom management and for comprehensive observation. Once the teacher is sure that a class is capable of working without constant monitoring, he or she can reduce the use of the back-to-the-wall technique, except when using it to observe the whole class.

Second, your position must allow you to see the critical elements of the skill on which the lesson is focused. For example, if your lesson is focused on absorbing weight through the back of the head and shoulders and keeping the body round while rolling forward, the logical observation point would be from the child's side. If observing from the back, you would not be able to see the critical elements you were looking for. When teaching, be sure to choose observation positions that permit you to see what you need to see.

Finally, whether we like to admit it or not, where you stand affects children's performance. Older children tend not to work in the area immediately around where the teacher is standing, and younger children cling to the teacher. So if you always stand in the same place to give directions or observe, some children will always be where you do not have a clear view of them. Thus, to be able to see better and increase on-task behavior, you should constantly move around the space and refrain from having one position that becomes your home base from which you always give directions or talk to the class.

> *The first time I taught the whole class [26 children], I had a great deal of trouble seeing individuals in the class. All I saw, no matter how hard I tried, was a mass of individuals. I couldn't see individual performances.*
>
> —**FRAN MCGILLAN** (as a junior in college)

Strategies

Even though a teacher is in a position to observe, has planned ahead, and knows what to observe, it doesn't

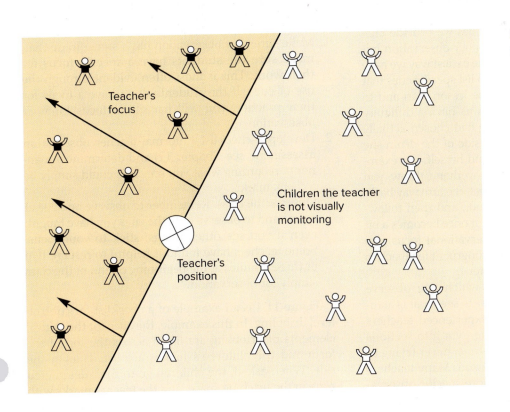

Figure 11.3 Ineffective teacher position for observation.

Teacher's focus

Children the teacher is not visually monitoring

Teacher's position

mean he is observing effectively. It's not unusual to become so focused on the movement or behavior of a particular individual or group that the teacher becomes oblivious to other children within the class. The two strategies of scanning and limited selection are presented here to help you observe.

Scanning   We encourage teachers to focus initially on using the scanning technique to observe safety, on-task behavior, and class and individual movement patterns. In scanning, the teacher uses a left-to-right sweep to glance at an entire class in just a few seconds and accurately assess how all the children are working. For example, if you want to determine the number of children who are actively practicing a given movement, you could quickly observe the class from left to right, counting as you scan. By comparing the number practicing a particular movement with the total number of children in the class, you can rapidly (in no more than 15 seconds) assess the way the class is working.

Limited Selection   The technique of limited selection allows you to observe only certain aspects at one time. There are three ways in which we accomplish this: (1) limiting what we look at; (2) limiting the area in which we observe; and (3) limiting the number of students to observe.

First, limiting what you are looking for suggests that you only observe selected items at one time. We have found that limiting our observation to one cue at a time (just like limiting the number of cues we provide children at one time) not only focuses our observation but also focuses the learners as well. The easiest way we have found to accomplish this focus is to list specific cues that are the focus of your lesson on the lesson plan and to stick to them. One teacher who was having difficulty remaining faithful to the cues she had chosen actually wrote them on her hand or the inside of the drum she used as a stop/start signal to remind herself. For example, if students are practicing the overhand throw, you might first watch for side to the target, the arm way back, then stepping with the opposite foot, and then follow-through. Trying to observe all cues at once becomes a bit overwhelming. Limiting your observational focus also makes it easier to provide specific congruent feedback to the students, as described in Chapter 7.

Second, limiting the area in which you observe intently may initially make it easier to see what is actually happening. The way many experienced teachers use this technique is to divide the gym into sections and observe only one section at a time, never trying to observe all sections during one lesson. Many teachers use this idea when making the more specific observations that lead to written records. To limit the

observation area, they observe only one part of the gym, making sure the same students are always in the same section of the gym. For example, one teacher we know uses color-coded neighborhoods (or zones); all students are assigned a neighborhood. At various times, he will ask students to go to their neighborhood to practice (not always during observation). That way he knows exactly which children are in what area. Another teacher has her students in specific quadrants of the gym for the initial activity of the lesson, and that is when she does her observation.

Finally, similar to limiting the area in which you observe is limiting the number of students you observe intently at any given time. This simply means that you observe only a few representative students. The easiest way to limit the number of students observed while getting a representative idea of what is occurring is to choose students of different skill levels to observe and have them act as your barometer for the lesson. To do this, choose three to five students of varying skill levels prior to class; throughout that class, observe those students first to get a feel for what is occurring. (It has been fairly well substantiated that three to five students of varying skill levels are representative of the entire class.) The next time the class meets, choose three to five different students. You may want to record or mark in your records the date you observe each student until you have rotated through the entire class.

The following are some helpful hints to make the most of your observations:

1. Make sure your observation has a focus. To do that, make sure the students have a specific focus for their work. This is most often evident through the use of cues. If the students don't have a focus for their practice, you will have little focus for your observation.
2. Develop a checklist (informal teacher observation assessment; see Chapter 12) and determine a manner of recording what you see. This could simply be a check mark.
3. Observe the class. Remember to observe one cue at a time and to observe only the cues you have taught, even if you see other things; stick to your focus. Some teachers have found it helpful to reserve two or three minutes at the beginning or end of the class simply for observation.

Figure 11.4 is an example of a checklist for control-level dribbling. In this example, the cues for the critical elements of dribbling are listed across the top of the form and the children's names are listed down the side. When asked, the children go to their designated zone in the teaching space, and the teacher marks with a checkmark whether the child demonstrated the cue.

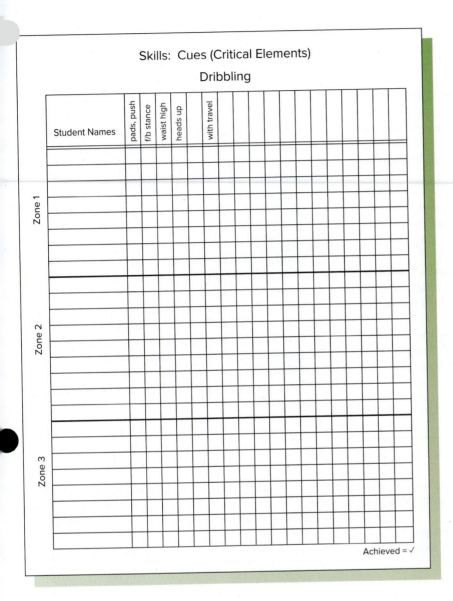

Figure 11.4 Sample of a blank checklist for observing skill.

To make the observation more efficient, some teachers will only mark the children who have not received the developing stage. The information gathered from observing student responses to your teaching serves a myriad of informal and formal assessment purposes. It is useful for planning future instruction, either adding additional cues or revisiting previous ones. It also provides information about where to begin when skill themes are revisited. Fundamentally, it provides information regarding student learning (see Chapter 12).

Summary

Observing—the ability to see with understanding—is a crucial skill for the reflective teacher. Successful observation can be learned and involves knowing what and how to observe. What to observe includes, first, safety, followed by on-task behavior, class movement patterns, and individual movement patterns. Although presented hierarchically, these four aspects continually interact with each other and may all be observed within a 60-second time frame. How to observe involves the positioning of the teacher, knowing what to look for, and observational strategies. Teacher positioning influences what a teacher is able to see, whom the teacher is able to see, and how the student performs a task. The teacher's knowledge of content affects the accuracy of what he or she is able to see. Two strategies, scanning and limited selection, aid teachers as they attempt to observe learners' movement responses.

Reading Comprehension Questions

1. In reflective teaching, what is the purpose of observation of student responses?
2. Why is observation in physical education so difficult?
3. In your own words, explain the key aspects of safety for which a reflective teacher watches.
4. What does off-task behavior look like? Give three examples you remember from your physical education classes.
5. Imagine you are teaching children to kick a ball to a partner. Briefly describe what you might observe that would cause you to change the task to make it easier or harder.
6. In the same imaginary situation as the question above, describe what you might observe that would cause you to provide a refinement task rather than move to a more difficult task.
7. Again, assuming the same teaching situation, describe what you might observe that would cause you to provide a kicking challenge rather than changing the task or using a refinement task.
8. If observing is the process of seeing clearly, what is the best position for observing the placement of the nonkicking foot when kicking a stationary ball? Why? The use of finger pads while dribbling? Why? Contact with the ball in striking with hockey sticks? Why? Tightness of muscles in balancing? Why?
9. How can a teacher avoid having children's performance affected by her or his position in class?
10. For the skill of dribbling with the feet in general space, what focus would you have as a teacher?
11. If observing the cue of wide base of support while balancing, what are the three ways a teacher can limit his or her observation as described in this chapter?

References/Suggested Readings

Kohn, A. 1996. *Beyond discipline: From compliance to community.* Alexandria, VA: Association for Supervision and Curriculum Development.

Locke, L. F. 1975, Spring. The ecology of the gymnasium: What the tourist never sees. In *Southern Association of Physical Education for College Women Proceedings.*

Mauldon, E., and J. Layson. 1965. *Teaching gymnastics.* London: MacDonald & Evans.

Rink, J. E. 2003. Effective instruction in physical education. In *Student learning in physical education,* 2nd ed., ed. S. Silverman and C. Ennis, 165–86. Champaign, IL: Human Kinetics.

Rink, J. E. 2014. *Teaching physical education for learning.* 7th ed. New York: McGraw-Hill.

Assessing Student Learning

Student assessment is the gathering of evidence about student achievement and making inferences about student progress based on that evidence.

—SHAPE AMERICA (2015)

You haven't taught until they've learned.

—JOHN WOODEN

Drawn by children at Monfort, Chappelow or Shawsheen Elementary Schools, Greeley, CO. Courtesy of Lizzy Ginger; Tia Ziegler.

Key Concepts

- Assessment is the gathering and collection of information framed by how that information is used.

- Two of the most common ways of classifying assessment are as: assessment for learning and assessment of learning.

- Assessment for learning shares the following characteristics: it is linked directly to instruction; it views the student as the primary client; it is meaningful; it happens as part of instruction; and students know what they are supposed to learn ahead of time.

- Teacher observation, exit slips, student journals, homework, peer observation, self-assessment, event tasks, video and digital analysis, student drawings and displays, and student portfolios are all viable assessment for learning items in physical education classes.

- Holistic or analytic rubrics are used to distribute assessment criteria to students and subsequently evaluate student performance.

- Assessment should occur in cognitive, affective, and psychomotor domains of learning.

- Assessment of learning is used to confirm what students have learned by comparing achievement against a class-, district-, or nationwide benchmark or standard.

- When assessment of learning is reported to parents, they should be made aware of what students have learned in physical education and where students are with respect to essential learning.

In this chapter, we use many terms specific to assessment, so we thought it might be helpful to explain these before we begin. Study the terms carefully because they are related to, but different from, each other.

Assessment for Learning—Positions assessment as an integral part of the teaching and learning process in ways that allow teachers to make inferences about children's learning and can include both formative and summative elements. Teachers use the results of these assessments to modify and improve teaching techniques during an instructional period.

Assessment of Learning—Used to confirm what students have learned by comparing achievement against a class, district, or nationwide benchmark or standard. It is summative. At times, this is referred to as assessment for accountability.

Summative Assessments—Used to evaluate student learning at the conclusion of a specific instructional period—typically at the end of a unit, course, semester, or school year. These can be assessments for learning or of learning.

Formative Assessments—Ongoing evaluations of student learning that are typically administered multiple times during a unit, course, or program.

Formal Assessments—Systematic, preplanned assessments that allow teachers to measure how well a student has mastered learning outcomes.

Informal assessments—Used to gather information that can be used to make judgements about children's learning using means other than standardized instruments.

This chapter is divided into four sections. The first section introduces the concept of assessing for learning or assessing what we are teaching in our lessons—often and regularly. The second section describes a process teachers follow to adapt or create assessments based on standards. The third section provides 14 examples of practical, frequently used assessments for learning. The final section deals with reporting the results of assessment.

Assessment for Learning

Many of us can vividly remember fitness tests in the fall and spring, with a few cognitive tests on rules and history thrown in during the year. But are isolated fitness scores and rules and history what we really want students to learn from our classes? Are the age-old ways of measuring that knowledge really the best ways? Assessment can be defined as the gathering and collection of information framed by how that information is used (Hay 2006). Assessment information can be used in two ways: assessment for learning and assessment of learning (Hay 2006). Both serve a distinct and powerful purpose. It is important to understand how they relate to each other and enhance teaching and learning.

Although the two ways of using assessment information are not distinctly separate, they are different and serve different purposes. Assessment of learning, often linked to assessment for accountability, is used to confirm what students have learned by comparing achievement against a class, district, or nationwide benchmark or standard. It is often thought of as large-scale standardized testing. This type of assessment has become more commonplace within the current educational reform movement and the passage of legislation such as Race to the Top (2009) and Every Student Succeeds Act (2015), often resulting in state-mandated assessment exams. Yet, other than fitness testing in some states, there is little of this type of assessment in physical education. Assessment of learning or account-ability also takes the form of summative assessment at defined key points during a unit of work. It can be used to plan future learning goals and provide evidence of achievement to the wider community, including parents, educators, the students themselves, and outside groups (State of New South Wales 2012).

Alternatively, assessment for learning (AfL) positions assessment as an integral part of the teaching and learning process that allows teachers to make inferences about children's learning (Black and Wiliam 2018). It is about contextually relevant or meaningful tasks that develop higher-order knowledge and skills that can be transferred outside the classroom setting (Hay 2006). Assessment for learning focuses on the learner and assumes that assessment should provide feedback to the learner. In short, you assess what you teach every day in your lessons. It can be both formative and summative (Black and Wiliam 2018).

Children Moving endorses assessment for learning, and this kind of assessment is very different from the kind of assessment most of us remember. Assessment for learning is more teacher friendly and student friendly. It is essentially a child being able to demonstrate, in context, the learning outcomes or goals you planned for the child to achieve. It reflects what was taught and how well it was learned. This idea of assessment contains several key essential pieces: what was learned; how well it was learned; and in what context the demonstration of learning took place.

Understanding Assessment for Learning

Let's explore these ideas a bit further. The idea of demonstrating what was learned implies that the student completes some type of performance that others can evaluate. How well something is learned implies that the student's performance is evaluated against preset criteria that are known ahead of time. This performance with its evaluation criteria takes place in an authentic or real setting. Finally, the performance, the criteria, and the setting should directly reflect a previously identified goal to be achieved. In other words, a teacher assesses what is taught, and what is taught should reflect the learning goals for students. These assessments are tied directly to the objectives of the lesson plans described in Chapter 6.

A subtle but important aspect here is the "reflection of a previously identified goal" (these goals could be learning indicators, benchmarks, grade-level outcomes, or lesson objectives). The important piece is that before designing any assessment item, it is essential to know what you want students to learn and how that learning

contributes to the overall goal of children's physical education—becoming physically active for a lifetime. Assessment without a linked purpose is no better than no assessment at all. The key is that the assessments are designed to contribute to a child's learning—not just isolated events that have no personal meaning or relevance.

An example may help. Physical Education Standard 1 indicates that in order for a person to be physically active for a lifetime, he or she should demonstrate competency in a variety of motor skills and movement patterns (SHAPE America 2014). One of the grade 3 sample grade-level outcomes for dribbling presented by SHAPE America (2014) is: "Dribbles and travels in general space at slow to moderate jogging speed, with control of ball and body." A possible demonstration of the ability to dribble and travel in general space would be to have the children perform the task of dribbling and traveling (see Chapter 25, page 526). This would be the focus of several lessons and written in the lesson objectives (Chapter 6). The preset criteria for determining how well this ability was learned might be: (1) maintains dribble; (2) avoids contact with others; (3) hand a little behind the ball; and (4) moves at a jog. Students would be considered "accomplished" if they could meet all four criteria, "almost there" if three of the criteria were accomplished, and "still working on it" if they could accomplish only one or two of the criteria. To use a "real" context, the whole class might perform the task while the teacher walks around with a checklist evaluating the criteria. This assessment might occur over several lessons as the teacher observes the children.

> *Authentic assessment strikes me as being quite interesting. The reason for this involves my current experiences as an eighth-grade basketball coach. When choosing players for the team during tryouts, I evaluated players mostly on drills. However, I have realized that while they do quite well during drills, many of them do not utilize these skills in a game situation. Next time, I believe I will use much scrimmage time to evaluate my players.*
>
> —**ANDY BARRY,** sophomore physical education major and first-year basketball coach

Although assessment for learning has many distinctions that separate it from traditional assessment (e.g., fitness tests, written knowledge tests, skill tests), we have elected to focus on five characteristics:

1. Assessment and instruction are linked.
2. Assessment is learner centered.
3. Assessment is an ongoing part of teaching, not an end or an afterthought.

4. Assessment comprises meaningful tasks performed in context.
5. The criteria for assessment are known in advance.

These ideas for assessment for learning are supported by *Appropriate Instructional Practice Guidelines, K-12: A Side-by-Side Comparison*, from the Society of Health and Physical Educators (SHAPE America 2009; see Box 12-1).

Linking of Assessment and Instruction

Within AfL, the teacher devises classroom learning experiences and tasks to provide evidence of learning. As such assessment is part of the whole learning process.

Box 12-1

Appropriate and Inappropriate Physical Education Practices

Component: Assessment

Appropriate Practice

- Formative and summative assessments are an ongoing and an integral part of the learning process for all students, including students with disabilities.
- Physical educators systematically teach and assess all domains (cognitive, affective, and physical) using a variety of assessment techniques.
- Assessments include clearly defined criteria, which are articulated to children as part of instruction prior to the assessment (e.g., a rubric is provided and explained during instruction).

Inappropriate Practice

- Assessment is rare and random and only occurs in the context of grading.
- Teachers only assess physical fitness.
- Assessments are not clearly defined and/or do not relate to program goals or objectives.
- Children are not sure what exactly is being tested/measured. They are not clear about what they are expected to do or know.
- Assessment is not multifaceted but addresses only a single performance score on fitness.

SHAPE, *Appropriate instructional practice guidelines, K-12: A side-by-side com-parison*. Reston, VA: Author, 2009. Copyright ©2009 by SHAPE America. Reprinted with permission from SHAPE America - Society of Physical Educators, 1900 Association Drive, Reston, VA 20191, www.shapeamerica.org.

It allows children and teachers not only to see that something has been learned but also to actually demonstrate it. This is critical to effective teaching. It also changes the relationship between teachers and students, as well as student outcomes. It addresses how we teach, as well as student achievement. It is said that if assessment and teaching are done well, the student should not know the difference between the two. It may be like the Friday night basketball game: Is the game an assessment of what was learned in practice during the week, or is it just another activity in which to participate?

Assessment Is Learner Centered

How many times have you been told that the purpose of a midterm exam is to help you as a student? It is much like being told that a punishment hurts your parents more than it hurts you. It may be true in your parents' or teachers' minds, but it is rarely true for you.

Assessment for learning strives to view the child or student as the person who benefits most from the assessment (remember, assessment is supposed to be a learning experience). First and foremost, assessments should provide feedback to the students that they can use and make sense of. (Failing a midterm, without feedback, simply tells you that you failed—maybe you didn't guess well, you did not study, the teacher didn't ask the questions you knew, or others did better than you did—it doesn't tell you how well you know something.) What would happen if a teacher provided many little checks before a test that let you know how you were doing but that weren't recorded as part of your final grade? Assessment for learning is laden with those little checks. What this also means is that assessment is not grading. The primary purpose of assessment for learning is to give students information they can use to enhance learning. The secondary use of assessment for learning is for reporting or grading purposes. This view of assessment requires us to change our thinking about assessment that has been ingrained in our minds our entire educational careers.

> *Because the student is the primary client of all assessment, assessment should be designed to improve performance, not just monitor it.*
>
> —**GRANT WIGGINS,** *Assessing Student PERFORMANCE (1993)*

Assessment Is an Ongoing Process

The third characteristic of assessment for learning is that it is an ongoing process. Have you have been in a physical education or other class in which assessment was done only as a midterm and/or a final exam. This is called summative assessment. It is also an example of assessment for accountability, which is not necessarily bad, except when it is the only assessment used. Did the results of these summative exams provide you, as a student, useful information you were able to use to improve your skill or knowledge? Probably not. Assessment for learning, as opposed to midterm and final exam testing, is an ongoing process. It includes both formative and summative tasks. It is a means to an end, not an end in itself. This aspect makes assessment for learning largely formative (or ongoing)—not always used for grading but brimming with feedback. Summative assessment (at the end of a term, for example) is part of assessment for learning, but it is done only after an immense amount of formative feedback. In assessment for learning, summative assessments can be considered celebrations of learning where children are given the opportunity to uniquely display all they have learned, often assessing all three learning domains simultaneously. Assessment for learning, then, is a planned part of the ongoing route to student learning. It should provide meaningful feedback to the learner on an ongoing basis—not only as a final exam.

Assessment Comprises Meaningful Tasks

There once was a student who was a Division I varsity soccer player. The university at which he played allowed students to "test out" of activity courses if they showed a proficiency level of skill. Proficiency was demonstrated by a series of skills tests. One of the skills tests for soccer involved kicking a ball to a wall from a certain distance a certain number of times in an allotted amount of time. The soccer player failed the skills test twice. On the third and final attempt, he failed again. As he left, he turned and said, "I can play soccer—come watch me on the field—but this has nothing to do with soccer." Today he is a professional soccer player.

That scenario is telling. The fourth characteristic of assessment for learning is to make it more meaningful and relevant. Ideally, assessment should provide students with information that will fuel their interests and move their learning forward (Wiliam 2011). A good assessment model supports students' desire to learn and improve. Assessment for learning employs tasks that make sense, are in context, and are real to the students. Assessment for learning does not ask children to demonstrate skills in situations that don't relate to what they are supposed to be learning. These real contexts may be contrived or natural, but they are as close to the actual situation in which the skill is used

as possible. In other words, no more wall volleying in volleyball (since when do you get to use the wall in a volleyball game?).

Criteria for Assessment Are Known in Advance

How often have you wondered what was going to be on a test? How would you feel if you knew ahead of time what material you were going to be assessed on so you didn't have to guess what you were supposed to learn? Assessment for learning provides children with the assessment criteria (in the form of scoring rubrics) before they actually start the learning or assessment. These rubrics indicate not only what is to be learned, but how well it is to be learned. Some teachers present this to students as WALT (what we are learning today) and WILT (what I am looking for today) at the beginning of every lesson.

Making It Work

We hope by now you have a clearer understanding of assessment for learning. We realize all this sounds wonderful (especially if you are a college student and can get your instructors to accept it). Yet the larger question remains: How do we do this type of assessment? Below we have provided some suggestions about making AfL work. We hope these suggestions will enable you to make assessment for learning not only happen but also work the way it should as part of learning. As you will see, it links directly to planning in Chapter 6 because assessments ask and answer the questions, "Where do we want to go?" and "How do we know if we are getting there?" Here are four suggestions to make assessment for learning succeed.

1. We know that, by now, we are beginning to sound like a broken record, but the key to all assessment (and teaching) is being clear about what you want students to learn—at all levels. Although discussed in Chapter 6, it bears repeating here, the first thing you need to do is to determine what it is that you want students to learn and what that looks like at various points in time. These points in time could be the end of a series of lessons based on a skill theme or within one particular lesson. The SHAPE America *National Standards & Grade-Level Outcomes for K-12 Physical Education* (2014) provide broad guidelines for learning at each grade level; in Chapter 1, we provided some specific sample learning indicators developed for skill themes (see Table 1.4). Figure 12.1 gives another example of one school district's grade-level learning indicators for

JUMPING AND LANDING PERFORMANCE INDICATORS

By the end of fifth grade students should be able to:

- Enter a long rope; jump continuously while changing levels, shape or direction and exit.
- Turn an individual rope and jump efficiently and effectively with single and/or double bounces incorporating simple tricks.
- Efficiently and effectively combine balance, weight transfer or roll, and locomotor movements into a rhythmic sequence with intentional changes of direction, speed, level and pathway, with choice of objects and/or music.
- Efficiently and effectively combine balance, weight transfer or roll, and locomotor movements into a sequence on equipment with changes of level and direction.
- Efficiently and effectively jump off equipment with turns, shapes, and different directions in the air and land safely on both feet.

By the end of fourth grade students should be able to:

- Enter, jump continuously, and exit a long jump rope.
- Turn an individual rope (individual freestyle) and jump efficiently and effectively with single and/or double bounces.
- Combine balance, weight transfer or roll, and locomotor movements (to include jumping) into a sequence with intentional changes in direction, speed, level, and pathway with choice of objects and/or music.
- Combine balance, weight transfer or roll, and locomotor movements (to include jumping) into a sequence on equipment with changes in level and direction.
- Efficiently and effectively jump with turns, shapes, and directions in the air over a low object (6–12 inches) and land safely with one and two foot landings.

By the end of third grade:

- Successfully enter a turning long jump rope and jump.
- Turn an individual jump (individual freestyle) rope and jump continuously forward and backward.
- Combine balance, weight transfer or roll, and locomotor movements (to include jumping) into a sequence using different speeds, levels and pathways.
- Efficiently and effectively jump using turns, shapes, and different directions in the air.

By the end of second grade students should be able to:

- Jump starting from a stationary position in a long jump rope.
- Turn individual jump rope overhead with multiple jumps.
- Efficiently and effectively jump and land using different body shapes and different directions in the air.

By the end of first grade students should be able to:

- Turn individual jump rope overhead with one successful jump.
- Jump and land using the five basic jumps.

Figure 12.1 Sample district learning indicators: Jumping and landing.
Source: Weld Co. District 6 Schools, Greeley, CO.

the skill theme of jumping and landing. Regardless of which indicators you choose, a series of lesson objectives are then developed to address each desired benchmark or indicator.

2. The assessment instruments should match what it is you want students to learn. After you have decided what you want students to learn, then you need to decide on how you will assess that learning. You might adapt existing assessments, or develop your own assessment methods, strategies, and criteria for use in judging student learning. This requires the use of assessment items that allow students to demonstrate what they have learned using criteria that have meaning to the children. The next two

sections of this chapter, "What Has Been Learned? Selecting Assessment Options" and "Assessing How Well Something Was Learned," provide multiple assessment examples you can adopt and/or adapt for assessing the progress your students are making toward your program outcomes.

3. Teach to the test! Lesson content should lead to what you want students to learn and the assessment chosen. At this point you need to decide on the lesson content progressions you will teach to guide your students toward attaining the selected outcomes. The skill theme and movement concept chapters in *Children Moving* (Chapters 14–27) provide content progressions designed to guide children toward meeting the outcomes you select. The assessment items you have chosen will become embedded in the lesson content you have chosen. If you are truly looking at "for learning," these assessments may occur in the middle of a lesson or at the beginning of a second or third lesson. Importantly, they may well not be at end of the lesson. In the skill theme chapters (Chapters 14–27), you will notice that assessment suggestions are inserted in various places using ❓.

4. The important thing to remember is that AfL is part of instruction. In many instances, children will not even know a task is being used as an assessment. See the task of Rolling Using Different Directions and Speeds (page 427) in Chapter 22 for an example of how a task in a lesson can also be an assessment item.

I recently listened to and watched a teacher give an assessment task to two different classes. In the first class, the teacher said, "Now we are going to do a peer assessment; your partner is going to see how well you can dribble." The partners proceeded with their peer observations as the evaluators. The students visibly tensed up and became silent. The peer observer said little to the student who was dribbling and felt awkward in marking a student "down." During the second class, the teacher said, "Now your partner is going to help you learn to dribble even better. They are going to watch you and then give you some hints about what you did really well and one thing on which to work. Then you get to practice again." The same checklist was used, but the observing partner was coached to observe and then provide feedback that would help the dribbling partner get better. The tension in the previous lesson did not exist, and there was much teaching going on within the peer groups.
Bottom line: Don't call it assessment!

Assessment is just like instruction; in fact, assessment for learning is part of instruction. It needs a plan to guide the process and to give direction and focus to the various assessment pieces. A variety of options exist. Although the topics of deciding on the goal and content as well as developing and teaching instructional progressions are dealt with elsewhere in this text, they are mentioned here to reinforce how assessment is linked to instruction. For learning to occur in physical education outcomes, assessment and instruction need to be aligned with each other. In a cyclical fashion, each informs the other. The remainder of this chapter provides options for selecting and developing assessment items that meaningfully assess student learning (the "how to and in what context to assess" piece) and how to develop the criteria for use in judging student performance (the "how well" piece). We also provide suggestions about what to do with the results.

What Has Been Learned? Selecting Assessment Options

Now that we have outlined the theory underpinning assessment for learning, in this section we are going to provide 14 assessment examples that reflective teachers use to assess their children's progress. The first three examples, challenges and checking for understanding, are often used in every lesson taught. The next 11 assessments are more structured and typically aren't used as often.

Informal Assessments

Challenges Many instructional tasks are actually informal assessments. For example, throughout the skill theme chapters, challenge tasks are presented as part of the progression of tasks. Recall from Chapters 6 and 7 that challenges keep the children practicing a task without making the task more difficult. The challenges provide the teacher, and the children, with informal assessments about their progress. Although these tasks are designed primarily to maintain interest and focus, they also serve as a minicheck on how well a child is progressing toward a goal. The challenge task of "See how many times in a row you can hit the ball without hitting the tee or missing the ball" provides children, as well as the teacher, with feedback. If most of the class can hit the ball only once or twice, the teacher knows she or he needs to provide more practice before moving on. Likewise, if most of the class is successful with continuous hits and an individual student can hit the ball only once or twice, the teacher knows she or he needs to work with that student.

Students can also measure their ability to hit in the same manner.

Checks for Understanding   Many of the assessments embedded in the skill theme and movement concept chapters (Chapters 14–27) are cognitive checks for understanding. These questions ask children to show their understanding of a particular aspect of the lesson that has been taught. For example, the assessment of locomotor actions provided on page 403 of Chapter 22 would allow the teacher to informally ascertain whether children understood the differences among skipping, jumping, and hopping. These checks for understanding can be in the form of quick questions to the entire class at different points in the lesson and may call for verbal or physical answers, a show of hands, or a simple thumbs-up or thumbs-down. In the movement concept and skill theme chapters these checks are untitled and indicated by the ❓.

Feedback   Skill-specific congruent feedback (Chapters 7 and 13) also provides an informal assessment. When you observe a child's movement response and provide detailed feedback to the child about their performance, it is an assessment that provides feedback and enhances learning. Take, for example, the child who is practicing "Rolling in a Long, Narrow Position (Log Roll)" (Chapter 22, page 419) and the teacher notices that the child's legs are floppy and apart as he rolls. If the feedback to the child says, "Great job on keeping your arms over your head; next time try to keep your legs tight together as you roll," there has been a mini-assessment of student learning and the student has Information to Improve his performance.

Formal Assessments

The assessment options that follow are more formal assessments. Our purpose in these assessments is to see what students have learned: Are they on the road to their goal, or have they achieved their goal? Of the multitude of assessment options available, we outline 11 here that are designed to provide feedback to the teacher as well as the student. These are broader than the challenges and the checks for understanding, often assessing the cognitive domain (knowledge base) and affective domain (values and feelings), as well as the psychomotor domain. With the exception of the student journal, these assessment options can provide either formative assessment to students or a summative product that can be scored for reporting. In the skill theme chapters, we include suggestions (identified with the assessment icon ❓) as to when these assessments might be used. The examples show how we

make assessment part of our daily teaching, not a separate entity at the end of a unit. Although we focus on a limited number of assessment options here, many more are available. We hope these suggestions will allow you to develop other options specific to your situation. When you find an assessment option that really works, we invite you to share it with us.

There are two key points to remember as you choose or design any assessment option: (1) you cannot assess content if you didn't teach it and (2) you can't assess without a goal. The first point, to teach before assessing, is largely self-explanatory—children have to have been taught precisely what you want to assess, or the assessment won't yield information that promotes student learning. The second point, to assess with a goal, essentially says that your assessment needs to match the learning objectives identified in your lesson plan (Chapter 6). For example, an outcome for throwing and catching at the control level might be to demonstrate the skill in an isolated situation. When performance moves toward combining skills and skill performance in dynamic situations (utilization/proficiency), the skill will be assessed in an environment more closely resembling the actual environment in which the skill will be used. A goal might be to throw and catch with a partner while on the move by demonstrating leading the partner at an appropriate distance. Assessment should be done in a context appropriate to the skill and assess aspects of the goal being taught—the use of throwing to lead a partner. This assumes the skill of throwing has already been mastered and assessed. Skill themes develop from the simple to the complex, or from the mastery of basic skills, to combinations of skills, to the use of skills in a more complex and dynamic environment. Assessment should follow the same guidelines. Assessments at the early control level should assess the elements critical to the mature pattern in an isolated situation. As children progress to later control and early utilization levels, assessment will focus on the use of the skill in a variety of contexts and combinations. Later, utilization and proficiency-level assessments will focus on the use of the skill in changing environments. In addition, at each level of skill development, cognitive understanding needs to be assessed, as does the affective dimension of our work.

Teacher Observation

Teacher observation is the most common form of assessment used in physical education classes. It is generally employed to assess psychomotor performance but can be applied to the affective domains as well. It is highly appropriate for assessing the

Figure 12.2 Teacher observation checklist.

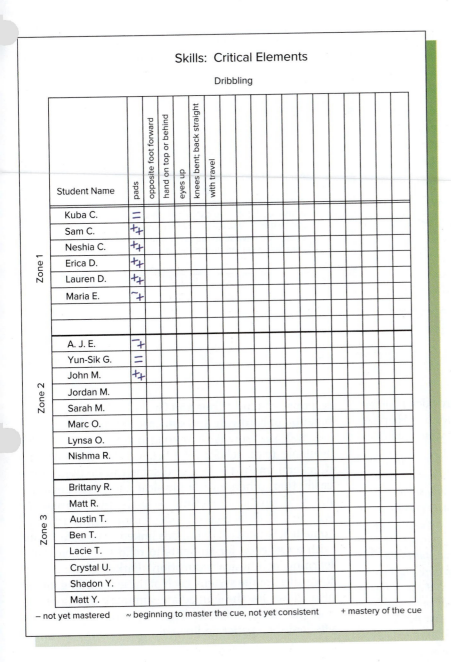

Skills: Critical Elements

Dribbling

	pads	opposite foot forward	hand on top or behind	eyes up	knees bent; back straight	with travel												
Student Name																		
Kuba C.	=																	
Sam C.	++																	
Neshia C.	++																	
Erica D.	++																	
Lauren D.	++																	
Maria E.	~+																	
A. J. E.	~+																	
Yun-Sik G.	=																	
John M.	++																	
Jordan M.																		
Sarah M.																		
Marc O.																		
Lynsa O.																		
Nishma R.																		
Brittany R.																		
Matt R.																		
Austin T.																		
Ben T.																		
Lacie T.																		
Crystal U.																		
Shadon Y.																		
Matt Y.																		

Zone 1 / Zone 2 / Zone 3

− not yet mastered   ~ beginning to master the cue, not yet consistent   + mastery of the cue

acquisition of critical elements of skill that together form a mature motor pattern. Figure 12.2 shows a teacher checklist used to assess the critical elements of dribbling. (Suggestions for designing and using such checklists are included in Chapter 11, "Reflecting on Student Responses.") The key factors involved in designing checklists that yield the information you want are identifying the critical elements and designing the checklist so that it is usable. A final hint for using checklists is to observe one critical element at a time. Just as we teach children by using one cue at a time, we should observe one critical element at a time.

Exit (or Entrance) Slips

Exit slips are short written pieces given at the end (or beginning) of a lesson and designed to assess cognitive (Standard 2; SHAPE America 2014) and affective (personal-social) (Standard 4, SHAPE America 2014) goals. They are developed to assess learning outcomes specific to the lesson just taught. The slips, often printed on half pieces of paper, contain one to three questions or ask the student to write in some form about specific learning cues or affective goals for the lesson (Figure 12.3).

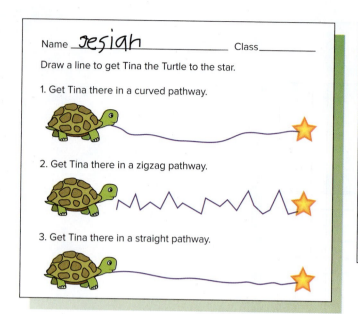

Figure 12.3 Exit slips.

Source: Schroeder, Dani, Devine, Elizabeth, Deputy, Grace and Hoffman, Kaily. University of Northern Colorado.

The Helping Murgatroid technique provides another format for exit slips. Following is how we use Helping Murgatroid; modify the instructions to fit your situation:

The lesson is being taught in a multipurpose room that becomes a cafeteria from 11:30 a.m. to 1:00 p.m. On one side of the room, lunch tables are permanently set up. Before beginning the lesson, the teacher places pencils and pieces of paper on the lunch tables, enough for each child in the upcoming class. The lesson begins as normal. At some point, the teacher stops the lesson and says to the children, "Remember several weeks ago we were practicing throwing? What I want you to do now is sit at one of the lunch tables so that you each have a piece of paper and a pencil. Then I want you to write a note to your friend Murgatroid. Murgatroid is not a very good thrower. List five things that might help Murgatroid become a better thrower. As soon as you are finished, you can return to the other side of the gym and continue working on your jumping-and-landing sequence."

Figure 12.4 provides three examples of Helping Murgatroid written by fifth graders. Which set of responses would you be satisfied with if you were the teacher? The entire process of exit slips takes less than five minutes, but it can be enormously helpful in assessing what the children remember from past lessons.

One of the issues with exit slips is the collation of information and all of the papers involved (not to mention the environmental impact). Recent technology may have solved this problem for teachers. Classroom response systems (Chng and Gurvitch 2018) are a combination of hardware and software that facilitate teaching and assessment. A myriad of these systems are available (e.g., "clickers," Plickers, Poll Everywhere, iClickers), many for free, and some can be used more easily than others in the physical education environment to provide real-time assessment information without children feeling self-conscious. Alternatively, some teachers have used iPods linked to Google forms with a QR code for students to reflect on their daily learning in physical education (Parker et al. 2017). Regardless of the system, each of these recording forms also allows for the immediate summary of responses and the storage of data. They are more useable and efficient than paper and pencil.

Student Journals

Student journals, like diaries, are written records of participation, results, responses, feelings, perceptions, or reflections about actual happenings or outcomes. Student journals provide a wonderful opportunity to assess the affective domain (Standards 4 and 5; SHAPE America 2014) of our teaching (Cutforth and Parker 1996). Students can be asked simply to write down their feelings (Figure 12.5), or they can be asked to respond to structured questions to assess more specific goals (Figure 12.6).

Remember, journals are personal (Figure 12.7), their purpose is for students to reflect on their feelings,

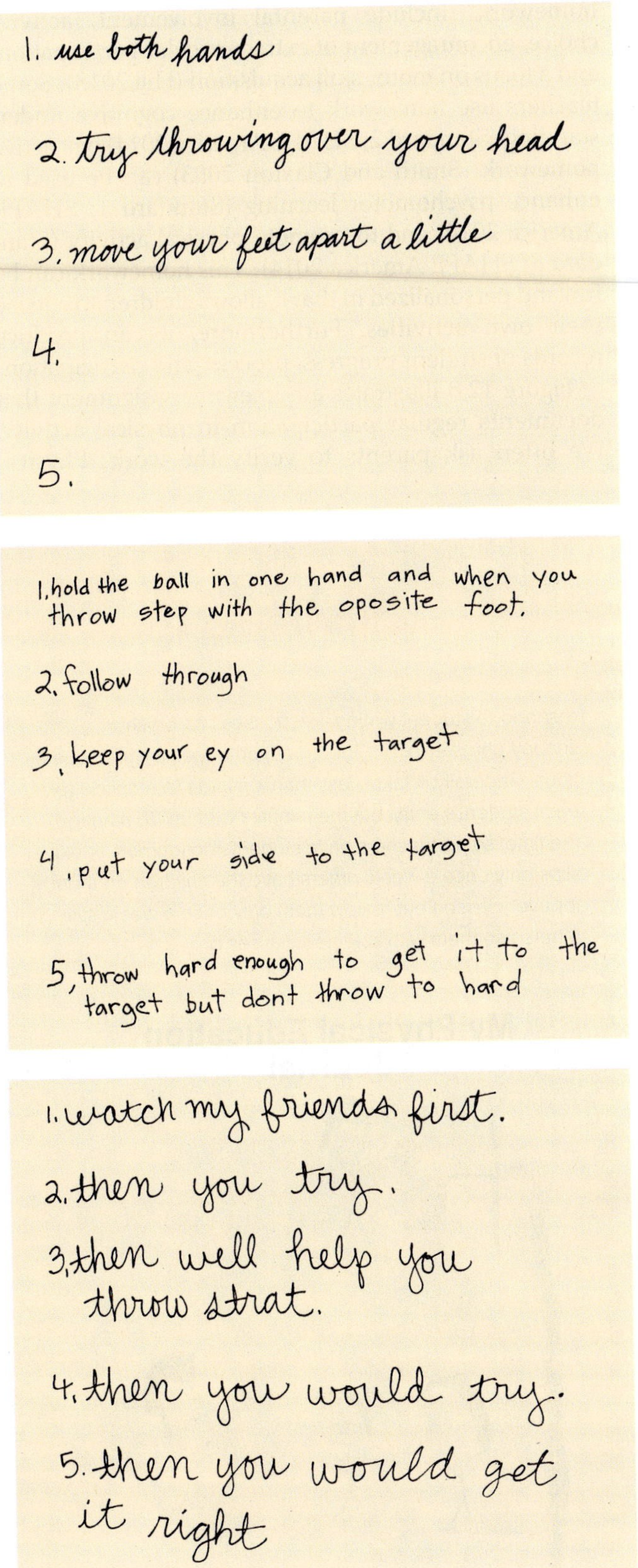

1. use both hands

2. try throwing over your head

3. move your feet apart a little

4.

5.

1. hold the ball in one hand and when you throw step with the oposite foot.

2. follow through

3. keep your ey on the target

4. put your side to the target

5. throw hard enough to get it to the target but dont throw to hard

1. watch my friends first.

2. then you try.

3. then well help you throw strat.

4. then you would try.

5. then you would get it right

Figure 12.4 Sample fifth-grade responses to the question, "What would you suggest to help Murgatroid become a better overhand thrower?"

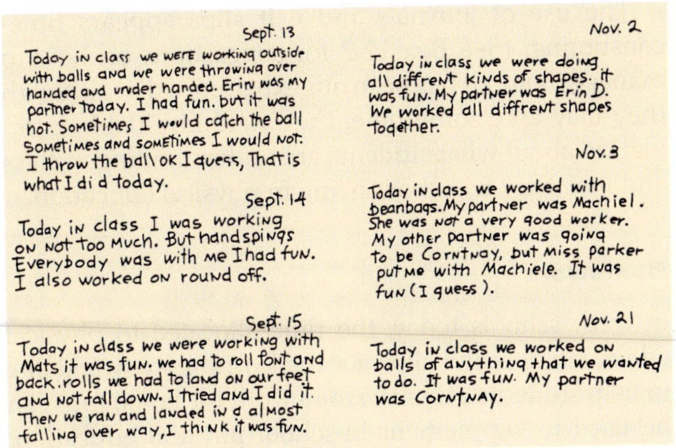

Sept. 13
Today in class we were working outside with balls and we were throwing over handed and under handed. Erin was my partner today. I had fun. but it was not. Sometimes I would catch the ball sometimes and sometimes I would not. I throw the ball ok I guess, That is what I did today.

Sept. 14
Today in class I was working on not too much. But handsprings Everybody was with me I had fun. I also worked on round off.

Sept. 15
Today in class we were working with Mats it was fun. we had to roll font and back. rolls we had to land on our feet and not fall down. I tried and I did it. Then we ran and landed in a almost falling over way, I think it was fun.

Nov. 2
Today in class we were doing all different kinds of shapes. it was fun. My partner was Erin D. We worked all different shapes together.

Nov. 3
Today in class we worked with beanbags. My partner was Machiel. She was not a very good worker. My other partner was going to be Corntnay, but miss parker put me with Machiele. It was fun (I guess).

Nov. 21
Today in class we worked on balls of anything that we wanted to do. It was fun. My partner was Corntnay.

Figure 12.5 Fourth-grade child's class journal.

growth, frustrations, joys, and successes regarding physical activity and physical education (Figures 12.5 and 12.6). Students must feel safe in doing that. One sure way to stifle students' honesty and reflectivity is to grade journals. This is one assessment piece used almost solely as a nongraded assessment. The purpose of journals is to give students a venue for writing honestly and freely.

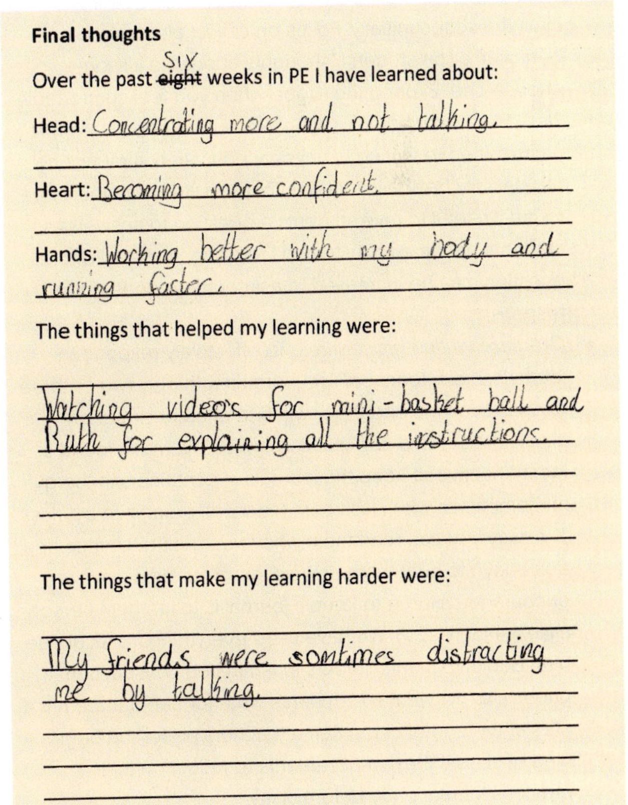

Final thoughts

Over the past ~~eight~~ six weeks in PE I have learned about:

Head: Concentrating more and not talking.

Heart: Becoming more confident.

Hands: Working better with my body and running faster.

The things that helped my learning were:

Watching video's for mini-basket ball and Ruth for explaining all the instructions.

The things that make my learning harder were:

My friends were somtimes distracting me by talking.

Figure 12.6 Fifth-grade student structured journal.

The use of journals and exit slips appears time-consuming. (See Box 12-2 for suggestions on how to manage them.) It has been our experience that although they may take some time, they yield invaluable information about what students are understanding in class and how they feel about being in physical education.

Homework

In most schools today, the time allocated to physical education does not allow for the learning we would like to help students achieve. Homework (or home fun) can be used to supplement in-school physical education. Essentially, homework is work a student completes outside physical education class. Characteristics of "active homework" include parental involvement, activity choice, encouragement of extracurricular participation, and a focus on motor skill acquisition (Hill 2018). Some teachers use homework to enhance cognitive understanding (Standard 2; SHAPE America 2014); yet active homework (Smith and Claxton 2003) can be used to enhance psychomotor learning (Standard 1; SHAPE America 2014) and to promote physical activity (Standard 3; SHAPE America 2014). This homework can be fun and personalized in that it allows children to choose their own activities. Furthermore, it can produce records of student progress, process, and participation.

Figure 12.8 illustrates a homework assignment that documents regular participation in physical activity. We often ask parents to verify the work. Physical

---

Box 12-2

Managing Journals and Written Exit Slips

From the teacher's perspective, managing journals and exit slips is the key to their success (or lack of it). Four guidelines may help:

- *Determine the major purpose of the journal or exit slip.* Limit the scope initially. Focus on critical elements, on behavior, or on students' thoughts about the lesson—choose one. Expand the scope when you feel comfortable.

- *Decide on a format for writing.* Because students are not accustomed to writing in physical education, their writing may initially be shallow and unfocused. We have therefore found it useful to give students a question to answer. As students become accustomed to writing, the level of the question may be increased to ask for more open-ended responses.

- *Organize writing procedures.* To effectively respond to journals, many teachers use journals with only two or three classes at a time and then switch to another group of classes at the end of a marking period. We have found it most effective to keep the journals in containers in the gym (or sometimes with classroom teachers) organized by class. This way you can read them when you get the chance and don't have to hunt them down. One of the best ways to encourage children to keep a journal is to let them personalize it (Figure 12.7). We have used everything from college blue books to manila folders to laminated construction paper. Usually we have students write for about three minutes at the end of class. Some teachers prefer the beginning of class if they want students to reflect on their previous journal entry before class.

- *Read and respond.* One key aspect of journals and exit slips is providing feedback to students. Teachers need to respond to student writing. Responses can be short, snappy phrases (e.g., "Good job!") or longer, probing questions. Generally, it takes less than a minute to respond to each student's entry, but the minutes add up. To manage the time, some teachers have students do journals or exit slips only once a week; others have the children do them for every lesson but review them only once a week; still others use them with selected classes only.

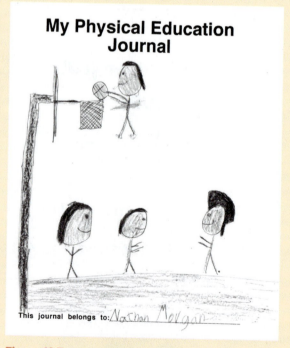

Figure 12.7 Personalized second-grade journal cover.

After School/Weekends

Activities

Jump Rope

Skating

Jogging

Soccer

Basketball

Hockey

Baseball

Sledding

Skiing

Dancing

Gymnastics

Biking

Other (_____)

_____
Parent Signature

Date: ___/___/___

Instructions:

1. When an activity is completed for at least 20 minutes, write in which day the activity was done in the box. Use the letters M, T, W, R, F, S or Su. (more than 20 minutes still only counts as one activity credit).

2. Have your parents sign and date the record, and bring it to school.

Figure 12.8 Homework assignment: fitness.
Source: M. Parker et al., Super active kids: A health related fitness program. In *Health and fitness through physical education*, ed. R. Pate and R. Hohn, 155–63. Champaign, IL: Human Kinetics, 1994.

education homework is similar to reports of reading done at home, and we have found homework to be quite useful, especially in terms of fitness or activity participation.

Peer Observation

Peer observation of students by other students can be used to assess competence in performance of skills and demonstration of selected critical elements (Standard 1; SHAPE America 2014) as well as cognitive understanding of what the demonstration of a selected cue looks like (Standard 2; SHAPE America 2014). Peer observation is easily built into tasks by asking students to work as partners and to provide each other with selected feedback regarding performance. For example, while working on dribbling with the hands,

one student can watch the other to see if the partner uses the finger pads, bends the knees, and has a staggered stance. To more fully tie assessment to instruction and learning, the partner can provide feedback (Standard 4; SHAPE America 2014) to the performer to help him or her improve. On a more formal basis, students can record their observations for later use by the teacher.

Children enjoy peer observations (and peer teaching), but a few key points help make the task more successful. First, define the critical element clearly enough so the partner can observe and comment. Second, structure the task so the children observe only one critical element at a time. Remember, doing peer observation requires practice and independent learning skills (see Chapter 9). Start small and simply. Figure 12.9 provides examples of peer assessments for

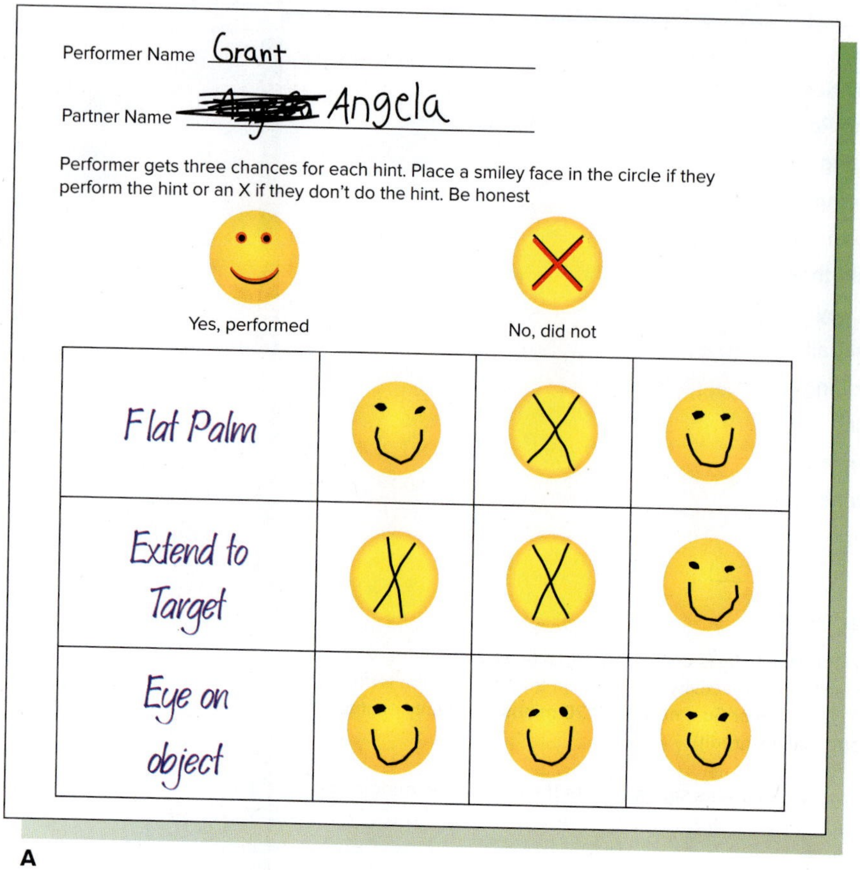

Performer Name _Grant_

Partner Name _~~Angela~~ Angela_

Performer gets three chances for each hint. Place a smiley face in the circle if they perform the hint or an X if they don't do the hint. Be honest

Yes, performed   No, did not

Flat Palm	☺	✗	☺
Extend to Target	✗	✗	☺
Eye on object	☺	☺	☺

A

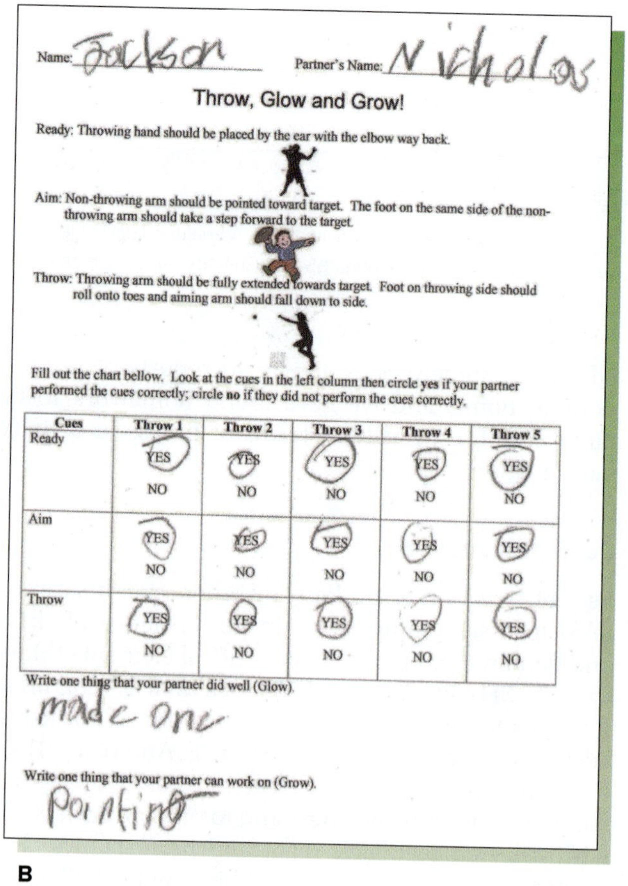

Name: _Jackson_   Partner's Name: _Nicholas_

Throw, Glow and Grow!

Ready: Throwing hand should be placed by the ear with the elbow way back.

Aim: Non-throwing arm should be pointed toward target. The foot on the same side of the non-throwing arm should take a step forward to the target.

Throw: Throwing arm should be fully extended towards target. Foot on throwing side should roll onto toes and aiming arm should fall down to side.

Fill out the chart bellow. Look at the cues in the left column then circle yes if your partner performed the cues correctly; circle **no** if they did not perform the cues correctly.

Cues	Throw 1	Throw 2	Throw 3	Throw 4	Throw 5
Ready	YES / NO	YES / NO	YES / NO	YES / NO	YES / NO
Aim	YES / NO	YES / NO	YES / NO	YES / NO	YES / NO
Throw	YES / NO	YES / NO	YES / NO	YES / NO	YES / NO

Write one thing that your partner did well (Glow).

made one

Write one thing that your partner can work on (Grow).

Pointing

B

Figure 12.9 (a) First-grade striking with hands observation sheet. (b) Partner evaluation of throwing (fourth grade).
Source: Schroeder, Dani, Devine, Elizabeth, Deputy, Grace and Hoffman, Kaily. University of Northern Colorado.

Peers can provide meaningful and relevant feedback to each other.

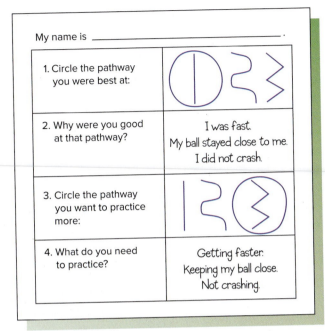

Figure 12.10 Example of a student self-assessment.
Source: Sirio, Jesse and Morse, Jen. University of Northern Colorado.

striking with the hands (first grade) and for throwing (fourth grade).

Self-Assessment

Self-assessments can be used to assess psychomotor (Standard 1; SHAPE America 2014), cognitive (Standard 2; SHAPE America 2014), and affective (Standards 4 and 5; SHAPE America 2014) aspects of children's work. Although peer and teacher observations are useful tools for assessment of the critical elements, self-assessments provide a unique opportunity to evaluate larger components or application of a skill or the beginning use of a skill. For example, in the case of learning to dribble, we might ask children if they could dribble using the preferred hand, the nonpreferred hand, while walking, while traveling at a jog,

without a defensive player, and with a defensive player. Figure 12.10 provides an example of a self-assessment designed to ask questions like these.

Self-assessments may be used at the end of a series of lessons on one skill theme to have students assess their achievement. Alternatively, the self-assessment may be used throughout a series of lesson as each of the critical elements is introduced and practiced; each individual assessment is dated and provides a record of the child's achievement of the various critical elements. In this instance, self-assessment would be an extension of a task sheet (Figure 9.2). Regardless of when self-assessment is used, children need to have ample opportunity to practice the various components before completing it. If it is used at the end, children should have a chance for a brief practice period before completing the assessment.

Another version of self-assessment that can be used with older children is a self-rating scale (Figure 12.11). The self-rating scale contains the same skill categories as the self-assessment, but the rating scale provides students an opportunity to assess themselves on a numerical scale. The key to this is providing descriptors for the numbers on the rating scale so children can anchor their self-assessments on clear criteria. Self-rating scales can be appropriately used for assessment before teaching as well as after.

Self-assessments can also provide a glimpse into children's feelings and attitudes. Some children's

Figure 12.11 Example of a student self-rating scale.

Dribbling and Pivoting Self-Rating

Name: _____   Homeroom: _____   Date: _____

| | | | | | | | | | | |
|1|2|3|4|5|6|7|8|9|10|

1 – 3   I still need to practice this skill.
4 – 6   I am pretty good at this skill.
7 – 8   I am very good at this skill.
9 – 10 This is my best skill.
* This is my favorite skill.

	Rating	Comments
1. Dribbling with preferred hand		
2. Dribbling with other hand		
3. Dribbling while walking		
4. Dribbling while jogging		
5. Dribbling at full speed		
6. Dribbling against a cone		
7. Dribbling against a passive defense		
8. Dribbling against an active defense		
9. Dribbling without breaking stride		
10. Dribbling while keeping head up		
11. Dribbling in a game situation		

You may add comments if you wish.

Teacher Comments:

ratings may be significantly higher or lower than the teacher's observations. At this point, the self-assessment becomes an opportune place to begin discussions with individual children. Another option is to ask children directly on self-observations how they feel about performing certain skills.

Some teachers often voice concerns about children's honesty when doing self-assessments and peer assessments. We have found that children are incredibly honest when assessing their own and others' skills (they especially take the assessment of others very seriously). Some children may initially inflate scores, but if self-assessments are a regular part of instruction and children become aware of their role in the evaluation process and of the purposes of assessment, inflation is short lived.

Event Tasks

Event tasks are tasks that can be completed in one class period or a portion of it. The task is designed broadly enough so there are multiple solutions.

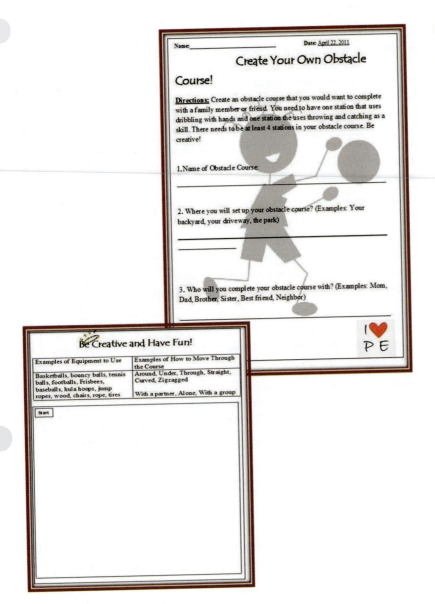

Figure 12.12 Self-designed obstacle course.
Source: Schroeder, Dani and Devine, Elizabeth.
University of Northern Colorado.

The task might be entirely psychomotor (Standard 1; SHAPE America 2014), or it may include cognitive (Standard 2; SHAPE America 2014) and affective (Standards 4 and 5; SHAPE America 2014) aspects as well. Event tasks that we use frequently are self-designed games (see Chapter 31), or self-designed obstacle courses or gymnastics and dance routines (Figure 12.12). Other tasks might be having students design a presentation for a parent–teacher conference on the skills they have been learning, or having them prepare to make a presentation to younger students on the critical pieces of a skill. Figure 12.13 shows an example of a role play used as an event task. The success of event tasks depends on the attractiveness of the task (whether it captures children's attention) and the structure the teacher provides. Event tasks require independent and group working skills. See Chapter 9 for ways to determine when children and teachers might be ready use those skills.

Digital Recordings

Although not common in all schools, taking digital videos and pictures is becoming easier with flip cameras, smartphones, iPads, and digital cameras and can provide a final, permanent product for gymnastics sequences, dances, or self-designed games. These formats can also let students display their knowledge and

Directions: Find a group of 2 or 3 with whom you can work productively; choose one scenario card. Read your card, you will have 15 minutes to develop a role play that solves the problem on your card. When you think you are ready, I will videotape your role play. Remember, all group members must be involved in the skit; all critical elements must be explained/demonstrated; and the quality of the presentation must be first-rate—memorized, practiced, and done without prompting.

Omar is having trouble playing catch with his buds during recess. He is so scared of being hit by the ball that he turns his head whenever someone is throwing him the ball. Omar is embarrassed and ready to quit the game. How would you encourage Omar to keep playing and improve his ability to catch?

You are a group of firefighters called to a fire at an apartment building. Several small children are trapped inside and will have to jump. Absent-minded Alfred forgot to make sure the landing net was on the fire truck, so it looks like everyone is going to have to catch the children. The chief needs to instruct everyone how to catch so the children can be rescued safely.

April is having trouble throwing to her partner and is getting upset. As her partner, you want to make her feel better. You also want to help her throw better. What tip did you learn in PE that you can tell to help April throw better? What will you say to April to encourage her?

Bernice is playing flag football during physical education class and she cannot seem to catch the ball! Every time the quarterback throws to her, the football bounces off her hands. What tip did you learn in your PE class that could help Bernice? Why would you tell Bernice that it is important to keep trying?

Vladimir has just moved to the United States from Russia and is a new student to the class. Not only does he not speak English, but he has never been taught to throw overhand. You and your group must teach him to throw overhand and to try to hit a wall target. Remember, Vladimir doesn't understand English.

Figure 12.13 Example of role play used as an event task. (Note: The individual circled scenarios should be written on separate cards.)
Source: Adapted and expanded from PE Central by Segura, Jessica and Sarmento, Cristian. University of Northern Colorado.

skill with respect to critical aspects of a skill. One possible task is to have students video record or take pictures of each other performing a certain skill and then analyze the critical elements for that skill. Likewise, students can video record each other and provide "color" commentary (ongoing narrative as in sports announcing) regarding the performance. Another video recording assessment might require students to develop an infomercial about a certain skill or fitness activity. Before using any form of digital recording be sure to check school policy.

For video/digital analysis to be successful, the criteria (scoring rubric; see page 206) for the task must be made explicit and a sufficient amount of time must be allotted. When they know what they are looking for, children love to watch themselves. It is initially helpful to limit the length of the video to less than 10 seconds and provide children with checklists (see Figure 12.2) or observation cards (see Figure 12.9) to guide their observations. Some teachers have also used apps such as iSwing to record in slow motion while limiting recording time (Parker et al. 2017). Children may also

combine video analysis with homework, thereby eliminating the need for multiple playback units.

A word of caution when using cell phones to record in physical education class. If used, be sure that all images are deleted before students leave the gymnasium so that they cannot be posted on social media or used to bully other children. Also check school rules regarding the use of cell phones. While they may be most readily available recording device, they may also represent the greatest risk.

Technology and Assessment

Current technology is changing at such a rapid pace that what we write now may well be out of date before this edition is published. Regardless of the medium, when used for observation and tracking of activity in physical education, technology provides instant learning for both teachers and students. As an example, heart rate monitors and pedometers provide immediate information on physical activity levels. Flip cameras, digital still cameras, and child friendly video cameras allow children and teachers to instantly view skill responses and produce permanent products that can be analyzed and shared with parents. One teacher we know uses a flip camera on a daily basis to record several children's responses in physical education; each night (while he is watching television), he sends two or three clips to parents about their child's progress. These technologies are now both relatively inexpensive and easy to use. A word of caution: Technology should always be used to enhance learning; it is a means to an end, not an end itself.

Student Drawings

Children love to draw, and we have found drawing to be one of the most rewarding assessment tools. The options for student drawing are endless. Children can be asked to draw about themselves, what a sequence looks like, what a skill looks like, or what they liked best. Figure 12.14 shows a student drawing used as an assessment piece demonstrating the understanding of a critical element. We also hope you have enjoyed the drawings of the children at the beginning of each chapter and hope you have wondered, as we have, what each child is trying to say about physical education. Sometimes it is obvious, and sometimes it is not—especially when the child is at the precontrol level of drawing.

Figure 12.14 Second grader's drawing assessing the critical element of using the shoelaces to kick.

Source: Drawn by children at Monfort, Chappelow or Shawsheen Elementary Schools, Greeley, CO. Courtesy of Lizzy Ginger; Tia Ziegler

Student Displays

Student displays are public displays of student work that communicate what the children have learned (Standard 2; SHAPE America 2014) or value (Standard 5; SHAPE America 2014). These displays can take a variety of forms, from posters on which students have drawn a person displaying a skill and have labeled the cues, to photographs, to bulletin boards, to maps of where they pursue physical activity.

Portfolios

Portfolios not only measure current achievement but also monitor and report students' achievement over time. They are systematic collections of student work over time that show progress, achievement, and effort in one or more areas of learning (Melograno 2006). They may assess one or multiple learning indicators or standards and relate to a single unit, an entire school year, or students' whole elementary careers. Portfolios can be likened to a trophy case of a child's accomplishments. Portfolios are powerful because they help students learn about their learning (Davies 2000). They provide an opportunity for students to share the responsibility for collecting proof of their learning. In addition, they provide a rich resource for reporting to both teachers and parents.

The first consideration with a portfolio is its purpose. It is quite difficult to select items without a sense of purpose. Common purposes include keeping track of progress, providing students a way to assess their own accomplishments, and determining the extent to which learning objectives have been achieved. For example, if one of the purposes of your physical education class is helping students practice a healthy lifestyle, their portfolios might include various pieces that attest to their knowledge of fitness, activities they do to stay fit, and indications of how they value fitness. Many products of the assessment options discussed in this chapter could be included in a portfolio. For example, a fitness portfolio might include some of the following artifacts: results of a health-related fitness test given at the beginning of the school year; goals set as a result of that test; activities in which the student participated to achieve the goals set; weekly homework sheets that document physical activity; a written fitness report; results of a fitness test later in the year; an indication of how well personal goals were met; and, finally, goals for the summer. The teacher may specify some items in the portfolio, but because the portfolio is a personal record, the student should be allowed and encouraged to decide which items will most strongly "make the case."

A portfolio communicates more when the reader knows why pieces have been chosen for inclusion. When children are including certain pieces, they might use categories such as "my best work," "the hardest skill I can do now," and "my most improved skill." By having criteria regarding the inclusion of items, students understand better what they are to learn and how to talk about it. Thus, portfolios serve as a powerful link from instruction and assessment to learning.

The development and use of portfolios seem intimidating. Davies (2000) has the following suggestions for beginning portfolio work with children:

- Maintain a clear purpose.
- Keep the portfolio process simple. Start small.
- Remember, there is no one best way to do portfolios. Decide what is right for you and your situation.
- Include more than written work. Video or digital analysis is helpful here.
- Ask children to explain and record why they chose each piece of work.
- Ensure that children have involvement and ownership. Portfolios document their learning.

Some teachers have "portfolio days" on which students share their portfolios with parents in lieu of the traditional parent–teacher conference.

Assessing How Well Something Was Learned

Not all assessment items will (or need to) be scored. Any of the assessment options listed previously could be done with students and simply used to provide feedback to them. For example, the observer or teacher could give the student the peer check in Figure 12.9 with some feedback that the child needs to practice this aspect more. But some items do need to be scored for children and teachers to know to what extent the goal has been achieved. To return to our trip analogy used in Chapter 6, did we get to our destination? Or just some place along the way? Remember, though, that what is assessed must match the task, what was taught, and what was expected to be learned.

Rubrics (evaluation matrices) describe varying levels of quality or achievement for a specific task. Their purpose is to guide students in the expectations for their learning, provide informative feedback about the extent to which work met the expectations, and give detailed assessment of the final product. Because rubrics ultimately guide learning, they should be shared with students in advance so students are aware of the expectations. The development of rubrics takes time, but the results make learning expectations clear, provide feedback, and support learning and the development of skills and understanding. Essentially they provide the success criteria for the task.

Writing Rubrics

There are three components to a rubric: (1) the criteria, or essential components to be assessed; (2) the steps of quality, or the rating scale; and (3) the descriptors that illustrate how each of the steps is related to the criteria.

1. *Criteria* The criteria match those asked for in a task. They are the essential elements determined necessary to achieve the specified goal. It is not necessary or feasible to include every possible element, so select ones appropriate for the level of development. For example, at the control level, the essential elements might be the critical cues of the mature motor pattern; at the proficiency level, essential elements would be the use of a variety of skills in a game situation. For students, this can often be translated into "what counts."

2. *Quality* The steps of quality, or the rating scale, identify various levels of the standard that might be achieved or various levels of competence. These can be thought of as steps or stops along the way to the final goal. These steps can be called by a variety of names—for example: 1, 2, 3, 4; "excellent," "above average," "needs improvement," "incomplete"; Junior Olympian, Bronze Medal, Silver Medal, Gold Medal; Little League, Minor League, Major League, Coach. Regardless of the scale used, it must distinguish one level of achievement from another.

3. *Descriptors* The last aspect of a rubric, descriptors, illustrates, or describes what the quality looks like at each level for each criterion. This is the aspect that lets children know specifically what is expected. The scale usually contains three to four levels each representing different levels of achievement and how much information you want to collect. For example in a four-point rubric, a four would represent what a student does who exceeds expectations; a three would indicate the desired level of achievement; a two the low end of achievement; and a one still developing or not achieving at the desired level of achievement. Using our travel analogy in Chapter 6 let's say you chose to travel by plane. One criterion might be getting on the correct plane. Driving down the correct highway. The possible scale or steps might be the following: a four would equal checking in at the counter, going to the right gate, giving the ticket to the gate agent, and getting on the right plane before the boarding process was complete; a three would equal going to the correct

Game Creation Rubric

	3 POINTS	2 POINTS	1 POINT
Describe how to play your game	Game is well described so that you could hand your sheet to someone and they could play your game.	Game description is a little confusing and needs a little more explanation.	No game description.
Rules for the game	2–3 rules are clearly written that make sense for the game.	Only 1 rule is written and makes sense for the game.	No rules are written.
Keep Score	There is an easy scoring system used that gives points for dribbling.	Scoring system is used but it is hard to follow.	No scoring system is used.
Draw a picture	Picture clearly shows how to set up and play the game.	Picture is unclear on how to set up or play the game.	No picture is drawn.
Cue / movement Examples: (eyes up) / (start/stop)	At least one learned cue or movement is included in the game.	An incorrect cue or movement is used.	No cue or movement is used.

Total Score: _____/ 15 points

Figure 12.15 Example of an analytic rubric.
Source: Schiemer, S. *Assessment strategies for elementary physical education.* Champaign, IL: Human Kinetics, 2000.

gate, giving the ticket to the gate agent, getting on the right plane, but not checking in at the ticket counter; a two would equal giving the ticket to the gate agent and getting on the right plane , but forgetting to check in at the ticket counter and going to the wrong gate first; a one would equal not getting on the right plane.

Figure 12.15 illustrates a rubric written for the creation of a child-designed game using the same format. These rubrics are called analytic rubrics, as performance is analyzed with respect to pieces of the whole. Analytic rubrics are time-consuming but provide invaluable information for the teacher and the student (Schiemer 2000).

Rubrics can also be holistic. Holistic rubrics assess children's performance as a whole. They combine a variety of essential performance elements to determine an overall level of achievement. The result is then reflected in a single score. Holistic rubrics are easier to use and are effective in assessing large numbers of students. They use the same set of components as analytic rubrics, but all descriptors for a certain level are listed together; to achieve that level, the student must accomplish all aspects of the criteria at the level indicated. A holistic rubric for the trip above might be: 4 = getting on the right plane, getting off the plane at the destination, arriving at your hotel, acquiring tickets for a jazz concert In town, and attending the concert; 3 = getting on the right plane, getting off at your destination, and

Figure 12.16 Teacher assessment checklist for throwing and catching role play (Figure 12.13).

Role Playing Assessment Form

Names of Group Members: Group Score: _____

1. _____

2. _____

Scenario/Skill: _____

Scoring Rubric

4. All critical elements of the skill are clearly explained/demonstrated
   All group members are active participants in scene
   Top-notch, professional presentation—ready for Broadway!

3. Most critical elements of the skill are clearly explained/demonstrated
   All group members are active participants in scene
   Top-notch amateur presentation—ready for center stage!

2. Some critical elements of the skill are clearly explained/demonstrated
   Most group members are active participants in scene
   Top-notch school presentation—ready for local cable TV!

1. Few critical elements of the skill are clearly explained/demonstrated
   Some group members are active participants in scene
   Could be a top-notch presentation—practicing for a school assembly!

getting to your hotel, but being unable to get tickets to the concert; 2 = getting on the right plane and getting off at your destination, but being unable to figure out how to get tickets to the concert; 1 = not getting on the right plane or any plane. As you can see, this assessment looks at the whole process of getting to the Bears game, not just the one aspect of getting on the right plane. Figure 12.16 illustrates a holistic rubric for the throwing and catching role play.

Regardless of the type of rubric chosen, here are some strategies to make designing them easier:

- Look at models of well-written rubrics. In the beginning, you want to adopt or adapt rubrics that others have used.
- If you are going to develop your own rubrics, start with content areas in which you have the most expertise.
- List the criteria; then relist and relist them until they don't overlap and they indicate the learning you want to see achieved.

- Have a friend review your rubric.
- Revise the draft. Be ready to write and rewrite. Creating good rubrics takes time.
- Try out the rubric with one class.
- Revise again.

Rubrics take time (and patience), but the end result clarifies student learning and your teaching. The time is well spent.

Assessing All Three Domains

We do not teach only motor skills and fitness. For us, there are clear affective and cognitive goals in our programs. Therefore, we must also assess those goals. The examples provided in the previous section include assessment ideas in all three domains. Assessments for motor skills and fitness include homework and peer observation. Assessment of the affective domain can occur in the form of student journals or a teacher checklist (Figure 12.17). The affective domain can be a

	Respect	Self-Directed	Participation	Comments
Alicia				
Bersava				
Juan				
Miguel				
Natalia				
Jasmine				
Daisy				

Level 4 = Always   Level 3 = Mostly   Level 2 = Sometimes   Level 1 = Rarely

Rubric

Description of Cues	
Respect	Listens to others; encourages others; willingly works with anyone in class; does not disrupt the learning environment
Self-Directed	Returns equipment, stays on task (even when the teacher is not looking)
Participation	Maintains a positive attitude throughout all activities: tries new things without complaining and saying "I can't"

Figure 12.17 Teacher observation affective checklist and rubric. *Source:* Adapted from Easter, Jeanette and Sassano, Carla. University of Northern Colorado.

bit tricky to assess—remember, if you want to assess something, there must be a goal, and it must be taught. Therefore, if you have affective goals, they need to be clear to students—for example, using the fingers of the hand to represent various expected responsibilities in class. Figure 12.18 provides an exit slip used to assess knowledge of the expected class responsibilities and then to have students' self-assess and goal set. The cognitive domain can be assessed through exit slips (e.g., Helping Murgatroid) or simply by checking for understanding with questions during class. The move to assessment for learning has provided teachers with noninvasive, instructional ways to assess all three domains.

Fitness Assessments

In Chapter 28, we discuss in depth the use of fitness assessments in physical education. We encourage you to refer to that chapter when conducting fitness assessments. The assessment of fitness should follow the same guidelines as all other learning in physical education. The potential downfall of fitness scores is that, although they are easy to collect and report, often they are not an indication of learning in physical education. As with other types of assessment, we must have taught the content of fitness with clear goals throughout the physical education program; must have used

multiple formative assessments along the way; and must have provided much activity and practice. Otherwise, fitness reporting does not provide an indication of achievement in physical education. Readers sometimes think we are "anti-fitness" due to the stand we take on formal exercises/calisthenics and fitness testing for children. We believe very strongly in personal health-related fitness for children; we also believe in fitness as a process and as a product of quality physical education programs.

A Word about Assessing Movement Concepts

As you might have noticed, our discussion of assessment has largely focused on skill themes. Some might ask, "What about assessing movement concepts?" If you remember, movement concepts are always performed with a skill theme; therefore, it is difficult to physically separate the skill from the concept. You will find some assessment options in the movement concept chapters, but they are largely cognitive. Cognitive understanding of the concepts (and skills) precedes application of the concepts in children's movement. Early assessment of the concepts, therefore, centers on cognitive understanding—for example, checking the class for understanding; asking for partner-to-partner recall (two students sharing key points of the lesson with each other); or using exit slips. As movement

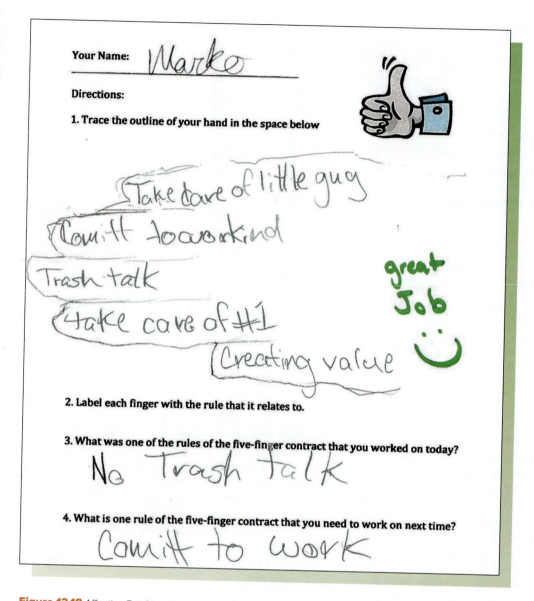

Your Name: Marko

Directions:

1. Trace the outline of your hand in the space below

> Take care of little guy
>
> Comitt to working
>
> Trash talk
>
> take care of #1
>
> Creating value

great Job :)

2. Label each finger with the rule that it relates to.

3. What was one of the rules of the five-finger contract that you worked on today?

No Trash Talk

4. What is one rule of the five-finger contract that you need to work on next time?

Comitt to work

Figure 12.18 Affective Exit Slips. (*continued*)
Sources: Adapted from Crisman, Emily and Hagen, Justin University of Northern Colorado. University of Northern Colorado and Reliford, Jioni.

skills develop, concepts and skills are used in combination—for example, striking to send a ball to the right or left; using easy force for the drop shot; or free-flow rolling in gymnastics. While it is hard to separate the understanding of a concept from the ability to do the skill, the use and understanding of concepts can be assessed when there is a reasonable level of achievement with the skill. For example, if a child can travel at a medium speed without difficulty, the assessment of the use of pathways and changes of direction would be reasonable. However, if the child was asked to dribble a ball at the same time and the child's skill with dribbling was at the control level, you would not be able to discern the nonuse of pathways from the lack of skill in dribbling.

Assessment of Students with Disabilities

Assessment for learning offers the teacher a unique opportunity to provide feedback and guidance to the child with disabilities. Experts (Block, Lieberman, and Connor-Kuntz 1998) have strongly suggested the use of assessment for learning for children with disabilities to counteract the pitfalls of traditional assessment with them. They contend that traditional assessment is misused for determining individualized education

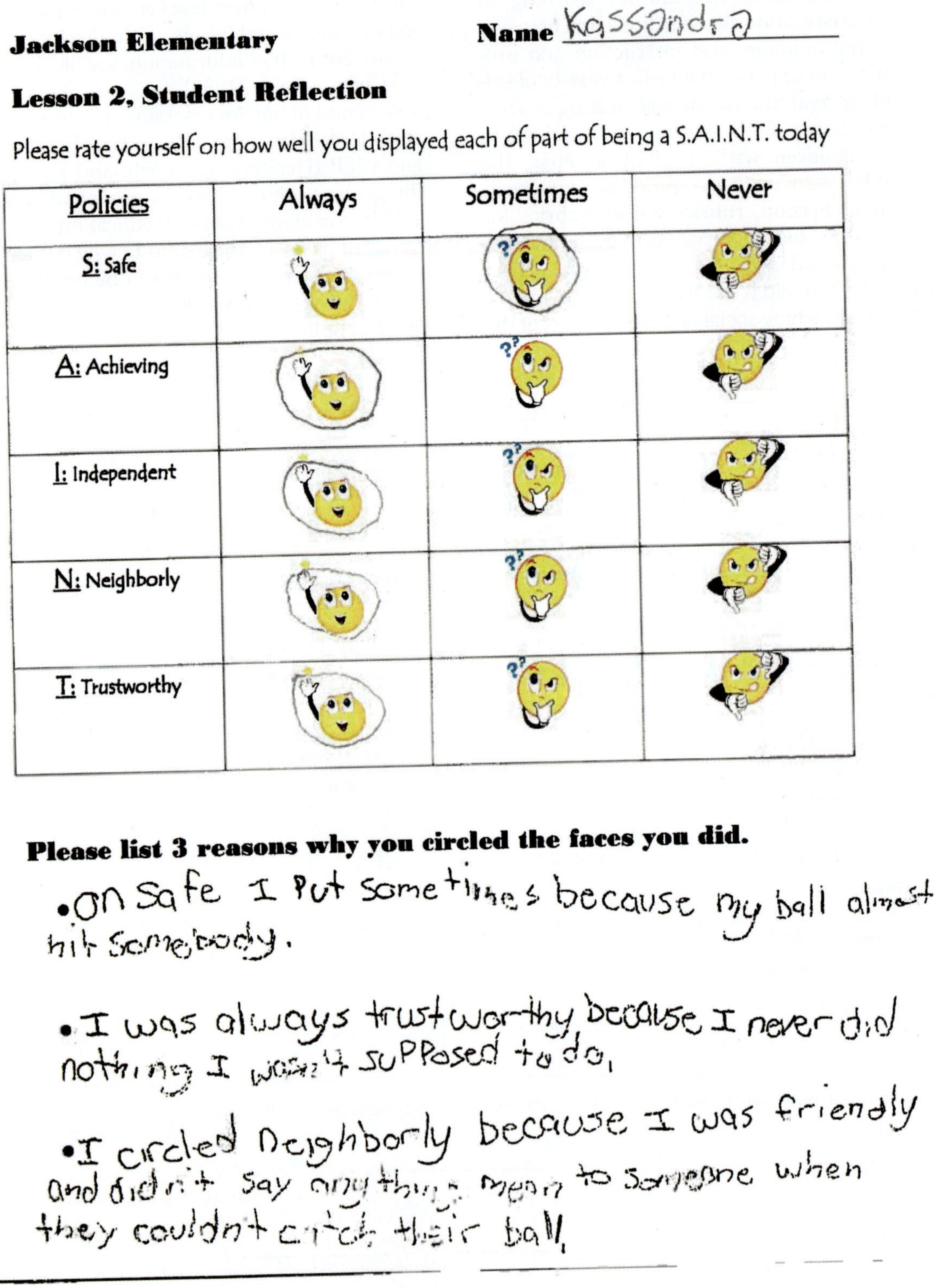

Jackson Elementary

Name Kassandra

Lesson 2, Student Reflection

Please rate yourself on how well you displayed each of part of being a S.A.I.N.T. today

Policies	Always	Sometimes	Never
S: Safe			
A: Achieving			
I: Independent			
N: Neighborly			
T: Trustworthy			

Please list 3 reasons why you circled the faces you did.

• On Safe I put sometimes because my ball almost hit somebody.

• I was always trustworthy because I never did nothing I wasn't supposed to do,

• I circled neighborly because I was friendly and didn't say anything mean to someone when they couldn't catch their ball.

Figure 12.18 (continued)

programs (IEPs) because it has no functional relevance, doesn't help determine instructional techniques, may be inaccurate, and doesn't communicate much to parents. They claim that assessment for learning in adapted physical education allows a direct link between assessment, programming, and instruction and promotes measurement of performance in a variety of settings, including real-life functional settings. They suggest using rubrics with certain modifications to accommodate children with disabilities. First, the rubric should be extended to accommodate more levels of development. Second, rubrics within rubrics (or analytic rubrics) should be designed to accommodate specific goals included in the IEP, such as social behavior. For example, if a child is in a gymnastics unit, items can be added that include social behavior as part of the

gymnastics rubric. Third, children with more severe problems may need individual rubrics. Alternative assessment, especially with the use of appropriate rubrics, may well help teachers more fully and appropriately include children with disabilities in their classes. For further information, see Block, Lieberman, and Connor-Kuntz (1998).

A second option for assessing students with disabilities is to develop a grading contract based on the student's IEP (Henderson, French, and Kinnison 2001). The grading contract lists the goals and objectives the child is to achieve in physical education. The student is evaluated based on the extent to which these goals are achieved. The objectives should be graduated so they lead to the desired goal. See Figure 12.19 for an example of a grading contract.

Annual Goals	Specific Educational Services Needed	Present Level of Performance	Person Delivering Service
Goal 1. Trevor will improve abdominal strength.	Special physical education consultant services.	Performs eight bent-leg sit-ups with assistance.	Morgan Stewart, special physical educator
Goal 2. Trevor will improve throwing skills.	Special physical education consultant services.	With a tennis ball, Trevor hits a 2'x2' target five feet away on 2 of 10 trials.	Morgan Stewart, special physical educator

Short-Term Objectives	Date Completed	Special Instructional Methods and/or Materials	Grade
Goal 1. Objectives			
1. In the gym, with assistance, Trevor will perform 10 bent-leg sit-ups.	10-21-18	mat; social praise; a performance graph	C
2. In the gym, without assistance, Trevor will perform eight bent-leg sit-ups.	11-7-18	same	B
3. In the gym, without assistance, Trevor will perform 25 bent-leg sit-ups.	Progressing; can do 21	same	A
Goal 2. Objectives			
1. With a tennis ball, Trevor will hit a 2'x2' target 5 feet away on 6 of 10 trials.	11-14-18	tennis ball and target	C
2. With a tennis ball, Trevor will hit a 2'x2' target 10 feet away on 6 of 10 trials.	11-21-18	same	B
3. With a tennis ball, Trevor will hit a 2'x2' target 20 feet away on 8 of 10 trials.	12-10-18	same	A

SIGNATURES AND TITLES OF APPROPRIATE TEAM MEMBERS: (Signatures indicate approval of this IEP)

_____   _____   _____
(Parent)   (Teacher)   (Administrator/Supervisor)

Figure 12.19 Sample grading contract.

Source: H. Henderson, R. French, and L. Kinnison, Reporting grades for students with disabilities in general physical education, *Journal of Physical Education, Recreation and Dance* 72, no. 6 (2001): 50–55.

What to Do with the Results of Assessment, or Standards-Based Summarizing and Reporting Progress

At some point, teachers are required to summarize and report children's progress to parents and others. This summative evaluation and assessment of learning provides parents and children with an indication of what the child has learned and where he or she is with respect to essential learning in physical education. It also provides teachers with information about their program—what has been accomplished and what needs to be worked on. For physical education teachers, reporting has always been nothing short of a nightmare; however, if you have designed and collected information on an ongoing basis, these systems should allow you to report that information to parents. The two systems presented here are standards-based reporting systems because they provide both parents and children with a meaningful indication of what is being taught in physical education as well as what their child has learned.

Standards-based report cards differ from traditional report cards in that they link the learning in physical education directly to the established goals. For example, instead of simply indicating the subject area of physical education and place for a grade, they indicate the specific learning standards and/or performance outcomes on which children have been working for the marking period. This new approach is more accurate because it measures each student against a stated set of criteria instead of against each other or subjective criteria. Instead of letter grades, students receive marks that show how well they have mastered selected skills or critical elements of skills. The marks might show whether the student is advanced, basic, or below basic for each expected outcome, or they might be numbers representing whether students meet, exceed, or approach the expected outcome. Children usually get separate comments for work habits, participation, and the like (see the Approach to Learning section in Figure 12.21), which are important for parents to keep tabs on even if these characteristics aren't included in the assessment of the student's academic skills. Two different reporting systems are presented as examples of standards-based report cards.

Standards-Based Reporting   A standards-based student progress report should be designed to provide targeted feedback in relation to student progress toward *National Standards* for K–12 physical education (SHAPE America 2014). As an example, SHAPE America (2016) provides a standards-based report card

template (Figure 12.20) to be customized so that teachers can adjust it to meet their requirements in a variety of situations.

Fargo Report Card   The system designed for use by Fargo, North Dakota (Figure 12.21) schools provides the standard with learning outcomes addressed underneath the standard. For this system, the report card remains the same for the entire school year with non-addressed performance outcomes marked out. The assessment key clearly provides a qualitative description of the extent to which the outcome was met, whereas the approach to learning indicators relay important feedback about a child's approach to school that can impact learning.

Similarities   Both of these reporting systems involve multiple assessments—at least two and sometimes more—for each theme studied. Often the assessments include at least one teacher observation of critical elements of the skill, one event task, and one self-assessment. Although the reliability of self-assessments is often questioned, teachers using these types of systems found that student self-assessment was not only accurate and honest but also increased student learning while integrating instruction and assessment. The assumption is that when children think about their own learning, they attend more carefully to that learning. In addition, self-assessment helps teachers—even though they may have kept lots of records—find the time, energy, and ability to assess each child more accurately. Note that none of these systems reported student learning as "grades" per se: The teachers found that "grades" did not communicate much to the parents or the students.

Grading

Standards-based report cards make grades a thing of the past. To be honest, even though we have advocated for no grades for more than 25 years, we never thought we would be able to make that statement. To many, assessment and grading are synonymous. In reality, there are subtle but significant differences between the two. Assessment involves how teachers find out what students know and can do in relation to the standards or learning goal. Grading, on the other hand, involves procedures for compiling data so an evaluation can be made for reporting to parents or others. The report systems we have shown report progress and achievement, linking the content to standards and reporting student progress toward achieving the standard. We think that grades without an indication of what the standard is do not communicate meaningful

Standards-Based Physical Education Student Progress Report
Elementary School Example

Student Information

Student Name:	Caroline Carter	Classroom Teacher:	Jones
Grade:	2	School Year:	2015-2016

Evaluation Key

3 = Excellent: Student exceeds grade-level expectations.

2 = Competent: Student meets grade-level expectations.

1 = Needs Improvement: Student needs more practice to meet grade-level expectations.

NA = Not assessed.

National Standards for K-12 Physical Education	Assessment Tools	Assessment Scores, by Grading Term		
		Term 1	Term 2	Term 3
Standard 1. The physically literate individual demonstrates competency in a variety of motor skills and movement patterns.				
Skips using a mature pattern (S1.E1.2)	Structured observation/video in a variety of settings	2	3	3
Demonstrates 4 of the 5 critical elements for jumping & landing in a horizontal plane using a variety of 1- and 2-foot take-off and landings (S1.E3.2)	Identification assessment, peer feedback, video-capture teacher feedback	2	3	3
Balances in an inverted position with stillness and supportive base. (S1.E7.2b)	Group-supported balance demonstration, station demonstrations (peer and teacher), with video check	NA	2	2
Dribbles using the preferred hand while walking in general space (S1.E17.2b)	Group practice, peer feedback, game-like practice popsicle stick feedback from teacher	NA	2	2
Jumps a self-turned rope consecutively forward and backward with a mature pattern. (S1.E27.2a)	Video analysis by teacher	2	3	3

© 2016, SHAPE America – Society of Health and Physical Educators ● www.shapeamerica.org
1900 Association Drive, Reston, VA 20191 ● 800.213.7193 ● membership@shapeamerica.org

Figure 12.20 Standards-Based Physical Education Student Progress Report (SHAPE America 2016). (*continued*)

Throws underhand using a mature pattern. (S1.E13.2)	Partner feedback, peer checklist	NA	2	3
Standard 2. The physically literate individual applies knowledge of concepts, principles, strategies and tactics related to movement and performance.		**Term 1**	**Term 2**	**Term 3**
Combines locomotor skills in general space to a rhythm. (S2.E1.2)	Call-and-response teacher observation, teacher-led progressions to music, partner patterns	2	2	3
Standard 3. The physically literate individual demonstrates the knowledge and skills to achieve and maintain a health-enhancing level of physical activity and fitness.		**Term 1**	**Term 2**	**Term 3**
Actively engages in physical education class in response to instruction and practice. (S3.E2.2)	Ongoing feedback using a classroom management app	3	3	3
Standard 4. The physically literate individual exhibits responsible personal and social behavior that respects self and others.		**Term 1**	**Term 2**	**Term 3**
Accepts responsibility for class protocols with behavior and performance actions. (S4.E2.2)	Ongoing feedback using a classroom management app	2	2	3
Recognizes the role of rules and etiquette in teacher-designed physical activities (S4.E5.2)	Ongoing feedback using a classroom management app	2	3	3
Standard 5. The physically literate individual recognizes the value of physical activity for health, enjoyment, challenge, self-expression and/or social interaction.		**Term 1**	**Term 2**	**Term 3**
Recognizes the value of "good health balance." (S5.E1.2) (Refer to S3. E6.2)	Calcium word-search homework, Grade 2 body book entry, sock monkey adoption assignment (home)	2	3	N/A

Sample teacher notes on student assessments by grading term
Term 1: Participates with enthusiasm, yet distracts others from learning.
Term 2: Listens well and works/plays well with others.
Term 3: Takes responsibility for learning.

Figure 12.20 (continued)

FIFTH GRADE APPROACH TO LEARNING

APPROACH TO LEARNING—Collaboration	1st	2nd	3rd
Follows class and school rules			
Follows directions			
Respects self, others, and property			
Accepts responsibilty for actions			
Participates in classroom activities			
Works cooperatively in groups			
Works independently to complete classwork			
Uses time appropriately			
Completes homework on time			
Produces and maintains quality work/writes legibly			
Keeps material organized			

	1st	2nd	3rd
Your child's absences/tardies negatively affect your child's progress. (Yes/No)			

FIFTH GRADE LANGUAGE ARTS STANDARDS

READING: LITERATURE—Critical Thinking	1st	2nd	3rd
Key Ideas and Details			
Craft and Structure			
Integration of Knowledge and Ideas			
Range of Reading and Level of Text Complexity			

READING: INFORMATIONAL TEXT—Critical Thinking	1st	2nd	3rd
Key Ideas and Details			
Craft and Structure			
Integration of Knowledge and Ideas			
Range of Reading and Level of Text Complexity			

READING: FOUNDATIONAL SKILLS—Critical Thinking	1st	2nd	3rd
Phonics and Word Recognition			
Fluency			

WRITING—Communication	1st	2nd	3rd
Text Types and Purposes			
Production and Distribution of Writing			
Research to Build and Present Knowledge			

SPEAKING AND LISTENING—Communication	1st	2nd	3rd
Comprehension and Collaboration			
Presentation of Knowledge and Ideas			

LANGUAGE—Communication	1st	2nd	3rd
Conventions of Standard English			
Knowledge of Language			
Vocabulary Acquisition and Use			

FIFTH GRADE MATH STANDARDS

OPERATIONS AND ALGEBRAIC THINKING—Critical Thinking	1st	2nd	3rd
Write and interpret numerical expressions			
Analyze patterns and relationships			

NUMBER AND OPERATIONS IN BASE TEN—Critical Thinking	1st	2nd	3rd
Understand the place value system			
Perform operations with multi-digit whole numbers and with decimals to hundredths			

NUMBER AND OPERATIONS—FRACTIONS—Critical Thinking	1st	2nd	3rd
Use equivalent fractions as a strategy to add and subtract fractions			
Apply and extend previous understandings of multiplication and division to multiply and divide fractions			

MEASUREMENT AND DATA—Critical Thinking	1st	2nd	3rd
Convert like measurement units within a given measurement system			
Represent and interpret data			
Geometric measurement: understand concepts of volume and relate volume to multiplication and to addition			

GEOMETRY—Critical Thinking	1st	2nd	3rd
Graph points on the coordinate plane to solve real-world and mathematical problems			
Classify two-dimensional figures into categories based on their properties			

SCIENCE—Critical Thinking	1st	2nd	3rd
Life Science			
Earth & Space Science			
Physical Science			
Engineering & Design			

SOCIAL STUDIES—Critical Thinking	1st	2nd	3rd
Understands important historical events			
Understands economic concepts			
Understands concepts related to government and citizenship			
Understands and applies geography concepts			

Figure 12.21 Fargo North Dakota Schools - Fifth Grade Report Card (*continued*)
©Fargo North Dakota Public Schools. All rights reserved. Used with permission.

VISUAL ARTS	1st	2nd	3rd
CREATING: Student is able to generate artistic ideas, develop, refine, and complete artistic work—Creativity			
Create grade-level appropriate artistic works using multiple techniques			
PRESENTING: Student is able to select, analyze, and share artworks—Communication			
Select, analyze, and share artworks for a specific purpose			
RESPONDING: Student is able to discuss art made by themselves and others—Critical Thinking			
Respond to art using grade level art vocabulary			
CONNECTING: Students create art related to personal experience and or cultural traditions—Communication			
Visually communicate for a specific purpose			
APPROACH TO LEARNING—Collaboration			
Demonstrates respect for art, people and art materials			

MUSIC	1st	2nd	3rd
CREATING: Student is able to create, improve, and share musical works/ideas—Creativity			
Create grade-level appropriate musical works for a specific purpose using rhythms, melodies and simple accompaniment patterns			
PERFORMING: Student is able to rehearse, refine, and perform musical works—Communication			
Selects and sings a diatonic melody in tune with accurate rhythm			
Selects and performs musical patterns on an instrument with accurate rhythm			
Reads a diatonic melody			
Reads grade-level rhythms			
RESPONDING: Student is able to evaluate and respond to musical works—Critical Thinking			
Explains how a variety of factors influence personal response to music using grade-level vocabulary			
APPROACH TO LEARNING—Collaboration			
Displays a positive attitude and follows directions during music			

PHYSICAL EDUCATION	1st	2nd	3rd
Standard 1: Demonstrates competency in a variety of motor skills and movement patterns			
Throws overhand demonstrating all five critical elements along with accuracy			
Catches a ball above the head, at chest or waist level with all five critical elements			
Strikes an object consecutively, using a short-handled implement, in a cooperative game environment			
Standard 2: Applies knowledge of concepts, principles, strategies and tactics related to movement and performance.			
Recognizes offensive and defensive strategies needed for different games and sports situations			
Standard 3: Demonstrates the knowledge and skills to achieve and maintain health-enhancing level of physical activity and fitness			
Participates in moderate to vigorous physical activity			
Analyzes results of fitness assessment, comparing results with fitness components for good health			
Standard 4: Exhibits responsible personal and social behavior that respects self and others—Collaboration			
Applies rules and procedures during Physical activities (safety, equipment, following directions) and shows respect for self and others			

KEYBOARDING—Communication	1st	2nd	3rd
Words per minute and accuracy			
Grade 5 End of Year Goal: 25-29 WPM and 90%+ Accuracy			

Figure 12.21 (continued)

This report is a standards-based Progress Report to give you a clear message of what your child knows, is able to do and what s/he still needs to learn in relation to state standards.

APPROACH TO LEARNING ASSESSMENT KEY:

C - Consistently demonstrates this approach to learning.

I - Inconsistently demonstrates this approach to learning.

R - Rarely demonstrates this approach to learning. Academic progress is affected.

* - Modifications/Accommodations

STANDARDS PROGRESS REPORT ASSESSMENT KEY:

5: Exceeds grade-level standards.
   The student exceeds grade-level standards. A "5" indicates the student is:
   • consistently exceeding grade-level standards and has advanced understanding.
   • demonstrating academically superior skills in that specific area.
   • performing above grade-level and is nearing proficiency towards the next grade-level's standards.

4: Meets grade-level standards.
   The student consistently demonstrates mastery the current grade-level standards. A "4" indicates the student is:
   • meeting grade-level standards and has proficient understanding.
   • right on track with our high academic expectations.

3: Making adequate progress toward grade-level standards.
   The student frequently demonstrates mastery of current grade-level standards. A "3" indicates the student is:
   • making adequate progress toward mastery of the grade-level standards.
   • not yet mastering the grade-level standards completely and consistently.

2: Making minimal progress toward grade standards.
   The student demonstrates a beginning understanding of the current grade-level standards. A "2" indicates the student is:
   • making minimal progress toward mastery of the grade-level standards.
   • needing extra help or time to develop the concept or skill.

1: Not meeting grade-level standards.
   The student does not demonstrate mastery of the previous grade-level standards. A "1" means the student is:
   • working below grade-level and receiving instructional intervention(s).

Figure 12.21 (*continued*)

information to parents or others. After all, what does an "A" say about what a child can do or has learned? We would much rather provide information that can be used as feedback and guidance.

We realize, however, that some school districts require you to grade. If that is the case, we first recommend specifying as clearly as possible what each grade means in relation to the standard (as on rubrics). Then assess exactly the same thing as specified. Translate your scales from the rubrics into grades and report to parents. For example, Fargo's rating scale of 1 to 5 is directly linked to the achievement of the suggested grade level outcomes for the standard. Remember, though, as with all assessment, there should be many assessment opportunities and options. Grades should be a result of all of these. If possible, we suggest reporting progress and achievement in ways that are the most meaningful. Grades rarely indicate such. Box 12-3 indicates appropriate and inappropriate assessment and grading practices.

Finding the Time for Assessment

Time has always been an issue in physical education. One concern many physical education teachers voice is that these assessment for learning options take time (and we have little time as it is in physical education).

In recent years it has become increasingly obvious to us that physical education programs limited to one or two days a week have less impact on children than daily physical education programs. That is true, but it has also become clear that what is not assessed is not valued (Rink and Mitchell 2002). Indeed, the marginalized status of physical education can, in part, be attributed to the lack of assessment (Hay 2006). Thus, to some extent, the future of physical education may lie in how well we can document what students learn in our classes. Remember, assessment for learning links instruction and assessment by providing meaningful learning tasks. Well-designed assessment tasks thus enhance learning.

The development of assessment items, like good teaching, takes time. No instructor who teaches several hundred children each week—as many physical education instructors do—has time to use all the assessment techniques described in this chapter. But a reflective teacher is aware of these techniques and uses them with different classes for different purposes. Perhaps you'll have one class at a time keeping logs. And you may be able to send only one written report a year to parents.

Select from the various assessment techniques those that are most appropriate; each technique provides a different type of information. For example, journals provide fascinating insights into how children are

Box 12-3

Appropriate and Inappropriate Physical Education Practices

Components: Test Procedures and Grading

Appropriate Practice

- Test results are shared privately with children and their parents/guardians as a tool for developing personal goals and strategies for developing and improving skills and health-related fitness.
- Physical educators provide regular reports of student progress to students, parents, and/or guardians using a variety of continuous, formative evaluations and assessments (e.g., heart rate monitor printouts, pedometer step sheets, skill assessments, knowledge tests, portfolios).
- Grades in physical education are based on thoughtful identified components that are aligned with course goals and national standards.
- Students know the component criteria included in their grade and the rationale for each.

Inappropriate Practice

- Individual scores are publically posted where comparisons are made between student scores.
- Parents/guardians never receive information about program content and their child's progress beyond a letter grade on a report card.
- Grades are based on a single opportunity to perform; formative assessment is not used (e.g., children receive a grade in physical education based on their scores on a standardized fitness test or the number of times they can continually jump rope).
- Teachers use subjective measures to assign grades (e.g., grades are based solely on effort, participation, and/or attitude).

SHAPE America. *Appropriate instructional practice guidelines, K-12: A side-by-side comparison.* Reston, VA: SHAPE America, 2009. Copyright ©2009 by SHAPE America. Reprinted with permission from SHAPE America - Society of Physical Educators, 1900 Association Drive, Reston, VA 20191, www.shapeamerica.org.

progressing in designing their own games or dances, but a checklist would be far less appropriate for that purpose. In contrast, a checklist is useful for assessing children's individual abilities in a new situation—for example, for a class of kindergarten children or during a teacher's first year in a new school. To simplify that process, we encourage you to use examples you find here and to modify examples you find elsewhere.

PE Central (www.pecentral.org/) and SuportREAL-teachers.org (https://www.supportrealteachers.org/) are wonderful sources of possible assessment items.

Even when you narrow the assessment options to be used with your classes, time can still be an issue. For example, it's counterproductive to assess one child while the others stand in line waiting their turn. There are several ways to minimize the waiting time for children during assessment:

- Set up stations or learning centers (Chapter 9). Stay at one of the stations, and use that as the assessment station. If you plan to do this, be certain the children are familiar with the other stations so you can devote most of your time to helping with the assessments rather than explaining procedures at the other stations.
- Ask the classroom teacher (or another teacher, paraprofessional, parent, or high school student) to help with the class. The assistant can either help some children while you work with the others or supervise most of the class while you work with a few children at a time.
- Video record the children so you can make your judgments about skill levels and progress during your planning time or after school.
- Use a digital voice recorder as you teach, and use the class list as a guide for observing each child; record your comments about the child's ability level and improvement as you move about.
- Divide the gym into sections, and have students begin each day in a home section that is consistent. Design the first task children are to do as an assessment task—for example, "Dribble with your dominant hand using the cues we have practiced." Using a teacher observation checklist, observe one or two groups each day until you have observed all children.

The recent surge of tablet assessment programs you can use to download results into desktop computers makes assessment much less time consuming. Many programs allow you to record "on the spot" children's scores and the results of assessment tasks and then enter them automatically into various record-keeping programs. These programs and computers have become much more affordable, accessible, and user friendly. This information changes on almost a daily basis, but we suggest you check *Using Technology in Physical Education* (Mohnsen 2012) or *Digital Technologies in Youth Physical Activity, Physical Education and Sport* (Casey, Goodyear, and Armour 2017) or your district's technology department for more information on these programs.

Handheld tablets (e.g., iPads, Netbooks) have revolutionized assessment practices because of the reduction of paperwork and increased efficiency they provide. As indicated, however, in the Chapter 28 box, "Technology in Fitness/Wellness Education" (page 613), even though we encourage the use of technology to enhance your physical education program, do not confuse the increased use of technology with effective teaching.

Although it may not be possible for children to reach utilization or proficiency level in a skill such as throwing in the limited time allotted to physical education, it is realistic to expect that children can at least learn the critical elements for the points we emphasize in our programs. Although that is not totally satisfactory, it does represent progress. It is encouraging to realize that even though all the children in our program are not throwing at the utilization level, they do know how to throw correctly if, and when, they choose to throw on their own. The time issue will not go away, but it is our belief that the use of time for assessment is well worth the investment. The information gathered from and provided by assessment is critical to children's learning, to instructional decisions that meet the child's needs, and to the design and maybe even to the retention of the program. The assessment movement has aligned goals and evaluation with instruction. They are no longer separate entities but pieces of the same puzzle. Assessment is an ongoing process that occurs in every lesson, simply by the nature of the tasks students do. Assessment is instruction. Assessment is simply teaching well.

Summary

Assessment can be defined as determining whether and to what extent a student can demonstrate, in context, his or her understanding and ability relative to identified standards of learning. This definition alludes to three critical elements: (1) a performance of learning, (2) in a real setting, (3) against previously set success criteria.

Assessment also provides a direct measure of teaching effectiveness. No longer is assessment an end-of-the-unit thing; now it is an ongoing process that happens on a daily basis in physical education classes. This type of assessment is known as assessment for learning; it is directly linked with instruction, not separated from it. In this way, instruction and assessment inform the whole learning process.

Many assessment for learning options exist. The formal ones we have chosen to focus on include journals, exit slips, homework, peer observation, event tasks, video/digital analysis, student drawings, student displays, teacher observation, self-assessment, and portfolios. These assessment options can provide feedback to children, assess student learning, report progress to parents, and discover individual children's needs and interests. Standards-based report cards to children's parents are the preferred mode of reporting student progress whenever feasible.

Reading Comprehension Questions

1. What is assessment for learning? How does it differ from assessment of learning and traditional assessment modes?
2. What are the purposes of assessment in physical education?
3. What does it mean to tie assessment to instruction and the whole learning process?
4. What are five options available for assessment for learning?
5. What is the purpose of having children keep a journal? How does the journal differ from the other assessment options?
6. What are scoring rubrics? How do they work?
7. What is the difference between assessment and grading? Why should grades be obsolete in physical education?
8. What is a standards-based report card? Provide an argument for using that type of report card as opposed to a traditional report card. Prepare your argument as if you were to present it to the superintendent.
9. Explain why assessment is necessary in children's physical education.

References/Suggested Readings

Black, P., and D. Wiliam. 2018. Classroom assessment and pedagogy. *Assessment in Education: Principles, Policy & Practice*, DOI: 10.1080/0969594X.2018.1441807.

Block, M., L. Lieberman, and F. Connor-Kuntz. 1998. Authentic assessment in adapted physical education. *Journal of Physical Education, Recreation and Dance* 69(3): 48–55.

Casey, A., V. Goodyear, and K. Armour (Eds.). *Digital technologies in youth physical activity, physical education and sport: Pedagogical cases.* London: Routledge.

Chng, L., and R. Gurvitch. 2018. Using plickers as an assessment tool in health and physical education settings. *Journal of Physical Education Recreation and Dance* 89(2): 19–25.

Cutforth, N., and M. Parker. 1996. Promoting affective development in physical education: The value of journal writing. *Journal of Physical Education, Recreation and Dance* 67(7): 19–23.

Davies, A. 2000. Seeing the results for yourself: A portfolio primer. *Classroom Leadership* 3(5): 4–5.

Every Student Succeeds Act. 2015. S. 1177-114th Congress. Retrieved from www.govtrack.us/congress/bills/114/s1177

Hay, P. J. 2006. Assessment for learning in physical education. In *The handbook of physical education*, ed. D. Kirk, D. Macdonald, and M. O'Sullivan, 312–25. Thousand Oaks, CA: Sage.

Hill, K. 2018. Homework In physical education? A review of physical education homework literature. *Journal of Physical education, Recreation, and Dance* 89(5): 58–63.

Henderson, H., R. French, and L. Kinnison. 2001. Reporting grades for students with disabilities in general physical education. *Journal of Physical Education, Recreation and Dance* 72(6): 50–55.

Lambert, L. 2007. *Standards based assessment of student learning: A comprehensive approach.* 2nd ed. Reston, VA: National Association for Sport and Physical Education.

Melograno, V. J. 2006. *Professional and student portfolios for physical education.* Champaign, IL: Human Kinetics.

Mohnsen, B. 2012. *Using technology in physical education.* 8th ed. Cerritos, CA: Bonnie's Fitware, Inc.

Parker, M., J. Morrison, K. Patton, M. Stellino, C. Hinchion, and K. Hall. 2017. Jamie: "I couldn't teach without technology": A teacher and student learning journey. In *Digital Technologies in Youth Physical Activity, Physical Education and Sport: Pedagogical cases*, ed. A. Casey, V. Goodyear, and K. Armour, 31–47. London: Routledge.

Parker, M., T. Steen, J. Whitehead, C. Pemberton, and B. Entzion. 1994. Super active kids: A health related fitness program. In *Health and fitness through physical education*, ed. R. Pate and R. Hohn, 155–63. Champaign, IL: Human Kinetics.

Race to the Top. (2009). *Race to the Top Program executive summary.* Washington, DC: Department of Education. Retrieved from https://www2.ed.gov/programs/racetothetop/executive-summary.pdf

Rink, J., and M. Mitchell. 2002. High stakes assessment: A journey into unknown territory. *Quest* 54(3): 205–23.

Schiemer, S. 2000. *Assessment strategies for elementary physical education.* Champaign, IL: Human Kinetics.

[SHAPE America] Society of Health and Physical Educators. 2009. *Appropriate instructional practice guidelines, K-12: A side-by-side comparison.* Reston, VA: SHAPE America.

[SHAPE America] Society of Health and Physical Educators. 2014. *National standards and grade-level outcomes for K-12 physical education.* Champaign, IL: Human Kinetics.

[SHAPE America] Society of Health and Physical Educators. 2015. *The essential components of physical education.* Reston, VA: SHAPE America.

[SHAPE America] Society of Health and Physical Educators. 2016. *Standards-based physical education student progress report: Introduction & guidance on usage.* Reston, VA: SHAPE America.

Smith, M. A., and D. B. Claxton. 2003. Using active homework in physical education. *Journal of Physical Education, Recreation and Dance* 75(5): 28–32.

State of New South Wales. 2012. *NSW syllabus.* Sydney: Board of Studies New South Wales.

Wiggins, G. 1993. *Assessing student performance.* San Francisco: Jossey-Bass.

Wiliam, D. 2011. What is assessment for learning? *Studies in Educational Evaluation* 37: 3–14.

Reflecting on Teaching

Of all the things teachers undertake, the most important, it seems to me, is doing the thinking of teaching or the reflecting about the complexities of their work. . . . Learning is continuous as reflective teachers engage in the work of thinking and doing. . . . In this way, learning is central to teaching.

—ANNA RICHERT

We do not learn from experience; we learn from reflecting on experience.

—JOHN DEWEY

Courtesy Children at Monfort Elementary School, Greeley, CO

Key Concepts

- Reflection on teaching is an essential aspect of continual growth as a teacher.
- Reflective teachers follow a cycle of describing teaching, critiquing teaching, and setting goals.
- Regular self-reflection on teaching allows teachers to describe their teaching and determine more specific information to gather.
- Systematic observation allows reflective teachers to critique their teaching by obtaining clear and detailed information about various effective teaching aspects.
- Systematic observation techniques include unassisted and assisted techniques.
- Collecting information on feedback and lesson content development are unassisted techniques.
- Assisted techniques that provide more observable information include such things as information on interaction patterns with students, the quantity of practice opportunities the students have, feedback, the use of time in class, and the clarity of demonstrations.
- Goal setting provides reflective teachers with a mechanism to determine if there are changes to teaching.
- Professional learning communities allow teachers to reflect on teaching learning environments with the support of others.

Quite simply, the practice of reflective teaching requires reflection. One implication of Chapter 4, "Reflective Teaching," is that teaching is an incredibly complex activity, requiring teachers to actively reflect on the circumstances of their teaching environment. As we teach, a variety of influences must be considered, including our experience as a teacher, the facilities in which we work, the frequency of our class meetings, the number of students in our classes, children's attitudes toward physical education, our beliefs as a teacher, and the like. It is one thing to understand the environment in which you teach but quite another to actually adjust your teaching to that environment. In Chapter 11, we talked about reflecting on student responses to your teaching; in this chapter, we address reflecting on your teaching. Both are in an effort to promote student learning.

As teachers we have the responsibility to choose the content to teach, determine how to deliver it meaningfully, and deliver it to meet all learners' needs. In addition, we must effectively interact with children, administrators, parents, custodians, and other teachers. We have to comfort the fearful child and assure concerned parents. What is more, we inspire hope, coax curiosity, and celebrate success (Richert 1995). This list of "jobs" could go on and on, and as Locke (1975) indicates, it represents only a portion of what is necessary to do the work of good teaching. Yet our job doesn't end here. Reflective teachers share the ownership of the teaching and learning process.

Some have asked us why we even include this chapter on reflecting on teaching in *Children Moving*. It is precisely because this continuing to wonder, worry, and reflect on what is happening in their gymnasiums and classrooms and on their playgrounds is what separates effective from ineffective teachers. Effective teachers are reflective teachers who learn by inquiring into their practice. They not only think about their experiences in order to make sense of them but also analyze specific aspects of teaching and student learning (Lorson, Goodway, and Hovatter 2007). When faced with a situation for which there is no easy or certain answer, they engage in reflective inquiry. They gather as much information as possible about a situation that puzzles them and then scrutinize the information to determine how they will act in the future. Most often this process is informal—we all engage in it to some extent to answer the millions of questions we encounter daily in our work—but occasionally the process is more formal. Either way, the constant and ongoing process of reflection on teaching provides the basis for learning in teaching. It is this process of learning in teaching that allows teachers to differentiate instruction (see Chapter 4). Reflective teachers work to improve their students' learning by improving their teaching throughout their careers. Unfortunately, reflection and inquiry into teaching are left largely to the individual teacher. The notion that, upon certification, a teacher knows all there is to know about how and what to teach and requires little, if any, assistance is quickly being discredited (Stroot 2001). In its place is growing acceptance of the belief that teachers can benefit from reflection, guidance, and assistance if they are going to progress in their teaching. If you are fortunate, your school district provides induction and ongoing mentoring programs coupled with continuing professional development. Some school districts may allow novice teachers to be paired with veteran teachers, or they may even make it a requirement. These mentors enhance the likelihood that new teachers will be provided assistance in reflecting on teaching. Increasingly, as it becomes apparent that teacher growth and change are part of a lifelong process requiring constant support, school districts are also arranging for ongoing reflection and development opportunities throughout the teaching years in the form of learning communities (Darling-Hammond and Richardson 2009).

Regardless of the support, reflection begins with the teacher. Good reflection is cyclical. It involves a description of your teaching, a critique of your teaching performance, and setting goals to continue to develop your teaching skills throughout your career (SHAPE America 2009). This chapter provides strategies and techniques for thinking about the extent to which your teaching is a reflective practice. This allows you to make teaching congruent with your beliefs about school, children, physical education, effective teaching, and learning environments as well as meet the needs of children in your school. This will allow you to "see" yourself through self-reflection, systematic observation, and support groups.

> *Although written in 1975, the seminal work by Larry Locke describing the ecology of the gymnasium still holds true today in many schools:*
>
> *Elementary school physical education teachers have been observed who clocked as little as three and a half minutes of significant face-to-face contact with other adults between the hours of 7:30 a.m. and 4:30 p.m. The teacher can be psychologically alone in a densely populated world. The physical (architectural) isolation of the gym located away from the political heartland of the school and the social isolation of the physical educator role, which may make the teacher peripheral to the real business of the school, both seem to sustain and intensify the feelings of isolation. Teaching physical education in some schools is a lonely job, awash in an endless sea of children.*
>
> —**LARRY LOCKE**, "The Ecology of the Gymnasium: What the Tourist Never Sees" (1975)

Self-Reflection: Describing Your Teaching

Continuous reflection regarding one's knowledge, beliefs, instructional practices, and teaching effectiveness is essential to ongoing professional growth (Banville and Rikard 2001; Housner 1996). Self-reflection allows a teacher to thoughtfully describe and contemplate the struggles and successes encountered in teaching (Stroot and Whipple 2003). Self-reflection is best accomplished as an ongoing and purposeful process that creates a permanent product of your thoughts. Most often this is through a written journal or digital audio log. Regardless of how self-reflection is accomplished, there are two keys to its success. First, be consistent with it. Set a time frame for self-reflection. It

might be daily, biweekly, or weekly. Yet, regardless of the time period you choose, do it consistently. Second, whether your reflection is written or verbal, review it periodically. These reflections often lead teachers to identify concerns and begin to think about how to reduce problems and enhance the learning environment. When specific concerns are identified or interests arise, systematic observation can be employed to obtain more formal and reliable information.

Systematic Observation: Critiquing Your Teaching

Consistent self-reflection allows us to determine points of exploration about our teaching; systematic observation allows us to obtain more objective information about those points. Systematic observation is the orderly and focused collection of specific and defined information about teaching. Again, in view of the usual lack of assistance teachers receive, many techniques we include in this chapter can be carried out on your own or with the assistance of another teacher, digital recordings, or an untrained observer.

Getting Started

Regardless of who is collecting the information about your teaching, the most important aspect is deciding what teaching action to look at or target. Although it may seem as if we are stating the obvious, we have seen more than one teacher collect information about his or her teaching without having a clear purpose. Remember, your focus should be on creating a learning environment that is meaningful for *all* children. The targets you choose may stem directly from your self-reflection or from the variables that have been shown to be related to effective teaching. Box 13-1 enumerates some of the actions, gleaned from research on teaching, of effective teachers. In Chapter 7, we stated that establishing a learning environment is a necessary but not sufficient condition for student learning and that the class environment indicates what you believe about children and physical education. Therefore, if nothing else seems to fit, determining whether you have set up a learning environment and what that environment is like may be a good place to start. The checklists in Box 13-2 can help you decide what to look for, based on your questions about teaching.

Unassisted Techniques

You can learn much about your teaching without relying on others for observation, interpretation, or

Box 13-1

Actions of Effective Teachers

Research has shown that effective teachers—whether classroom or physical education teachers—share similar behaviors. Effective teachers:

- Give students time to learn by devoting a high percentage of time to the academic subject.
- Communicate high, yet realistic, expectations for students.
- Establish routines and organizational structures that lead to a positive classroom management climate.
- Present meaningful and challenging tasks in which students are highly successful.
- Move the class forward with determined direction.
- Communicate the content clearly and hold students accountable for completing tasks.
- Assess students' skill progress closely and change practice to fit students' needs.
- Communicate warmth through clear, enthusiastic presentations.

Source: B. Cusimano, P. Darst, and H. van der Mars, Improving your teaching through self-evaluation, *Strategies*, 7, no. 8 (1993): 28.

Box 13-2

Determining What to Observe

If you're having problems with inappropriate student behavior, select one or more of the following:

- Look at your plans for potential breakdowns.
- Transcribe all your instructions to the class, and check for clarity. Did you know what was supposed to happen? Did you mix the organizational and content portions of your instruction?
- Digitally record a lesson to reflect on your use of time. Was there an extreme amount of management time? Waiting time?
- Record your feedback. Did you handle inappropriate behavior promptly and consistently, or did you nag often?

To check the atmosphere of your class, do one or more of the following:

- Tally your feedback. Was there a large percentage of negative feedback?
- Check student interaction patterns. Did you favor one group over another?
- To assess the instructional environment, select from the following:
  - Check your task development. Did you disperse challenges throughout the lesson or only at the end?
  - Assess each student's practice opportunities. Did children have lots of practice chances?
  - Check the general use of class time.
  - Tally feedback with specific attention to skill feedback.
  - Evaluate the quality of the demonstrations provided to your class.

analysis. Unassisted analysis techniques for analyzing your teaching performance involve either audio or digital recording. Audio recording can easily be done by placing a recorder (or your cell phone) in a pocket. Digital recording using a wireless microphone will lend itself to gathering even more information (without a wireless microphone, the noise in the gym makes it almost impossible to hear the conversations between teacher and children). The children quickly become accustomed to the recording device, and before long, they forget about it.

You can gain a wealth of information from listening to your teaching. For example, you can learn the answers to such important questions as:

- What percentage of a lesson did I spend talking to the entire class? To groups? To individuals?
- Are my verbal comments clear? Do I repeat myself frequently?
- What percentage of my comments to the children is positive? Negative? Neutral? Do I nag the children?
- Do I interact with many children in a class? Or do I focus on just a few, constantly calling their names? Do my comments focus on skill or behavior?
- How do I develop the lesson content?

You can answer these and many other questions by making audio recordings. Finding the answers involves defining what you want to assess, listening to the recording, tallying the number of times each behavior occurs or recording the length of time something occurs, and then determining percentages. We often use these kinds of recordings to analyze the feedback we give to students and how we develop content with individual classes.

Feedback Analysis   Feedback, the information the teacher provides to individual or small groups of children about the quality of their movement or behavior, based on observation, is one teaching aspect on which you can reflect from an audio or digital recording. The

Teacher Feedback

Teacher: _____   Date: _____

Grade/Activity: _____   # of Pupils: _____

Start time: _____ End time: _____ Elapsed time: _____

FEEDBACK	BEHAVIOR FEEDBACK		SKILL FEEDBACK						
	Praise	Scold	Positive	Corrective	Negative	Congruent	Incongruent	Total	Rate/Minute
Specific									
General									
Total									
Rate/Minute									

Rate/Minute ____ ____ ____ ____ ____ ____ ____ ____ ____ ____
COMMENTS:

Figure 13.1 Teacher feedback form.

teacher feedback form (Figure 13.1) allows you to examine your feedback by tallying each comment you make to children. Depending on the lesson and your interest, you may simply want to total the amount and type of feedback you give. You may also want to determine which children receive your feedback—and what type of feedback they receive. If you want to probe the total feedback you give to children, simply tally each statement, placing it in one of the feedback categories shown in Figure 13.1 and defined below. (You may want to use all these categories, or just one or two.)

Your first choice of feedback type is specific versus general feedback. Specific feedback has to do with either the child's skill or the child's behavior. If the feedback is specific, the next step is to determine whether it is about skill (movement) or behavior. Then, ask yourself whether the child to whom the comments were provided would perceive them as positive, corrective, or negative. However, if there is no

way for the child to tell (based just on your statement) whether your comment is about skill or behavior, the feedback is general. "Good" is probably the most common general feedback statement heard in physical education lessons, followed closely by "Okay." In addition, you may want to determine whether the feedback was congruent or incongruent with the lesson cues—specifically, with what you asked the children to think about when you last gave instruction. Congruent feedback relates directly to the cues you said immediately before the children began their task. Incongruent feedback, in contrast, might be about something the children were never told or hadn't been reminded of for several weeks. (Note that if you code congruent/incongruent feedback, it will be a "double tally" in a row. One for positive, corrective, or negative, and one for congruent/incongruent.) This sounds complicated, but as the process is broken down, it will become easier.

Assume, for instance, the children are practicing striking with paddles (Chapter 26), and the teacher is focusing on teaching them to turn their sides to the target so they can swing more efficiently. "Side to target" is said right before they begin the task. The following are some examples of feedback and the way each statement would be coded on the teacher feedback form in Figure 13.1:

- "Marilyn, that swing was great! You really turned your side to the target." (specific, skill, positive, congruent)
- "Terrific." (general, positive)
- "Mark, remember to keep your eye on the ball." (specific, skill, corrective, incongruent)
- "Ayana, stay in your own space." (specific, behavior, scold)
- "Kakki, way to keep your side to the target." (specific, skill, positive, congruent)
- "Good side, Rosie." (specific, skill, positive, congruent)
- "Kevin, that's wrong." (general, negative)
- "Side, Anthony." (specific, skill, corrective, congruent)
- "Juan, you are facing the target; don't do that." (specific, skill, negative, congruent)

When you tally your various feedback statements, you will have a profile that lets you know what type of feedback you tend to give. In addition, you can determine a feedback rate per minute by dividing the total number of statements into the elapsed time to find out how much feedback you give. While the information on the types of feedback necessary is mixed (Rink 2003), a good pattern to strive for is skill-specific, corrective, and congruent feedback to enhance learning, and positive behavior feedback to promote an appropriate environment. Don't worry if your pattern doesn't initially appear as you would like it to be; after all, anything we do takes practice. The good news is that adjusting feedback is relatively easy.

Lesson Content   Another useful type of information you can collect for reflection is how content is developed in your lesson. As described in Chapter 6, there are three categories of information you may wish to collect regarding your lessons: the tasks you give the children, the refinements students are asked to practice, and the challenges you offer. The tasks are what you actually ask the students to do, such as dribbling a ball in self-space or bouncing a ball while traveling in general space. Refinements are tasks that focus specifically on a particular cue to help children perform the skill more efficiently. In the case of teaching dribbling, refinement

tasks might be "This time, as you practice your dribbling, concentrate on using your finger pads" or "With this next task, be sure to bend your knees as you dribble." Refinement tasks always seek to improve the quality of the student performance. The cues that might be the focus of refinement tasks are listed at the beginning of each task segment in the skill theme chapters. Finally, challenges shift the focus to using the skill in a more demanding or testing situation. These are most often self-testing, cooperative, or competitive situations.

Figure 13.2 shows a graph you can use to determine how content is developed in a lesson. Before filling in the graph, listen to your recording and write down, in order, every movement experience presented during the lesson, categorizing each as a task, refinement, or challenge. (For this project, record only tasks, refinements, or challenges given to the entire class, not feedback or suggestions given to individual students.)

After you have labeled the tasks, refinements, and challenges, plot them on the graph in the order in which they occurred. Once you have finished, you will have a picture of how your lesson progressed. Although there is no perfect pattern of content development, a good rule of thumb is that the graph should reflect a zigzag pattern and not steps. The use of tasks, refinements, and challenges should be mixed across the lesson rather than task, task, task, challenge. This mix allows children to progressively develop their skills while staying motivated and focused.

Assisted Techniques

Assisted observation techniques provide information that cannot be obtained by the unassisted techniques described earlier. Assisted techniques involve the use of another person to help collect observation information about your teaching. Potential "observers" are colleagues who are willing to help you assess your teaching performance, mature responsible students (it is a great activity for a student who might not be able to participate), or volunteer parents or administrators (builds great support for your program). The techniques presented here allow you to gain more detailed information about practice opportunities and feedback, to determine how time was used during the class, and to assess the quality of the demonstrations given to the children. The four assisted techniques that follow can provide a great deal of information about the class learning environment.

Interaction Patterns   It's important to interact, verbally or nonverbally, with each child during each

CONTENT DEVELOPMENT

TEACHER: _____ DATE: _____ GRADE: _____ NO. OF STUDENTS: _____

DIRECTIONS: Write down, in order, the statements made to the entire class about motor skills. At times you may need to leave out a few words, but try to get down the intent of the statement. After the lesson is over, classify each statement as a task, refinement, or challenge, and then graph the statements in the order they occurred. Use the back of the sheet if necessary.

1.

2.

3.

4.

5.

6.

7.

8.

9.

10.

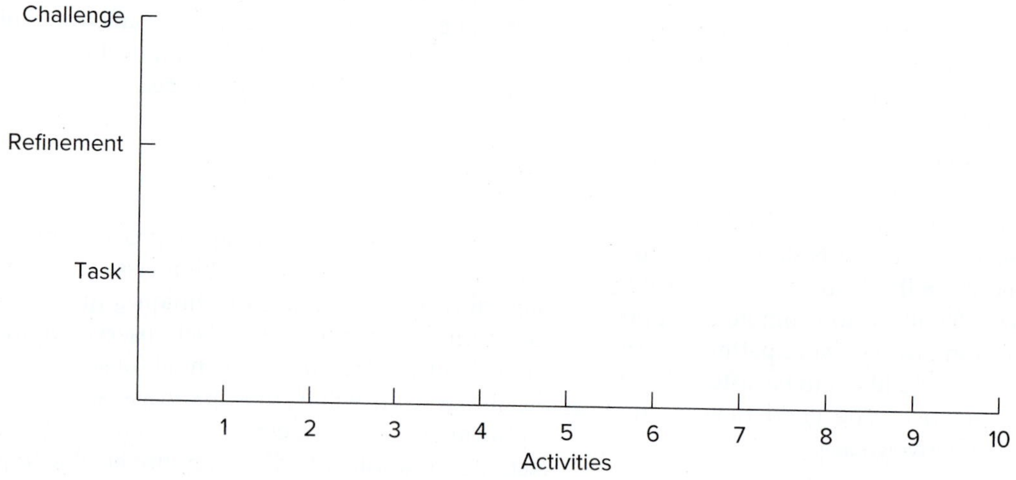

Definitions:
  Tasks: Activities that present the skill to be practiced
  Refinements: Task that focus on a particular cue or the quality of the movement
  Challenges: Self-testing, cooperative or competitive experiences

Analysis: Number of tasks, cues, or challenges/Total number of activities = %
  _____ % tasks
  _____ % refinements
  _____ % challenges

Figure 13.2 Content development graph.

Figure 13.3 Interaction checklist.

INTERACTION CHECKLIST

Date: _____

Teacher: _____ Observer: _____

Start Time: _____ End Time: _____

Student's Name	Talked To	Made Eye Contact	Nodded Approval	Total
		Types of Interaction		
Nick	||				3
Tom	|||				4
Carlos	||				2
Naomi					1
Abbey	|||||		||	7
Total Interactions	12	2	3	17

COMMENTS:

lesson. You can use an interaction checklist (Figure 13.3) to obtain information about your interaction patterns with an entire class.

Make certain the observer knows the names of all the children in the class (this is great observation for a child to do). Give the observer a checklist on which you've listed the names of the entire class. The observer can then make a tally, in the appropriate column, across from the name of each child you talk to, touch, or smile at during one class period. At the conclusion of the lesson, you can use the completed checklist to analyze your interaction patterns and determine if there is differential treatment of children.

On another level, you may be able to determine whether there's a disparity in your interactions with different groups of children. Are you interacting more with the most-skilled children than with the least-skilled ones? Are you interacting with boys more than girls? Are you interacting with one race or ethnicity more than the others? Or do the interaction patterns indicate some other distribution of attention? For example, identify a most-skilled and a least-skilled group—each group should include about 25 percent of the class. From an analysis of the interactions with each group and a comparison of these two interaction patterns, you determine the group to whom you are devoting more time.

Practice Opportunities Effective teachers give children plenty of practice opportunities. One way to indirectly assess the number of practice opportunities students are getting in a class is to ask a peer or student to record the number of practices for selected

Figure 13.4 Practice opportunities checklist.

Teacher _____ Observer _____

Date _____

Theme of Lesson _____

OBSERVATIONAL DATA

Practice Opportunities

Name of Child	ROLL	CATCH	KICK	THROW

students (Figure 13.4). You may want to select the children to be observed, or the observer can select several children to observe. This technique works best when the lesson focuses on discrete skills—such as rolls, catches, or kicks—that can be written on the form before the lesson.

Duration Recording System Duration recording allows you to reflect on how you use time in your physical education class. It provides a look at what students are actually doing and for how long. This system divides the use of class time into four categories: activity time, instruction time, management time, and waiting time. The total amount of time, in minutes and seconds, is determined for each of the four categories, allowing the teacher to see how the class spent its time.

Minutes and seconds can be converted into percentages so you can compare one lesson with another.

The duration recording form (Figure 13.5) contains five time bars, each representing 7 minutes, marked off in 15-second increments. The form defines the codes the peer assistant should use to report what is happening: A for activity, I for instruction, M for management, and W for waiting. The peer assistant records the exact time the lesson begins—the time at which the children enter the gym or playground. (Alternatively, you can use a digital video of the lesson to reflect on how you use time in your lesson.) From that moment until the end of the lesson, the peer assistant, using a clock that allows for the determination of seconds, marks the time bars to reflect what is happening in the class. When there is a change in student behavior, the

Figure 13.5 Duration recording form.

DURATION RECORDING—LEARNING TIME ANALYSIS

Teacher: _____ Grade/Activity: _____
Coder: _____ Date: _____ # of Students: _____
Start time: _____ End time: _____ Elapsed time: _____

TIMELINE

1	2	3	4	5	6	7

`A | I | A | - | - | A | - | - | I | - | - | A | - | - | - | - | - | W | - | - | I | - | - | -`

8	9	10	11	12	13	14

`A | - | - | - | - | - | - | - | M | - | - | A | - | - | - | M | - | - | - | A | - | - |`

15	16	17	18	19	20	21

22	23	24	25	26	27	28

29	30	31	32	33	34	35

Codes: Activity = A   Instruction = I   Management = M   Waiting = W

Time Analysis: No. of intervals × 15 seconds = _56 × 15 = 840_ (total lesson time in seconds)

Total Lesson Time

A = _33 × 15 = 495/840 = 59%_   M = _8 × 15 = 120/840 = 14%_

I = _12 × 15 = 180/840 = 21%_   W = _3 × 15 = 45/840 = 5%_

Note: Percentages don't equal 100 due to rounding.

COMMENTS:

©Barbara Adamcik

During instructional time, the opportunity to learn is present, but the students aren't active.

Waiting time can include the minutes when students are waiting in line for their turn.

©Lars A. Niki

assistant indicates the change by writing the appropriate letter in the next space on the bar. At the end of the lesson, the time is recorded. The peer assistant uses the definitions and examples in Table 13.1 as guides to accurate coding. It is important to remember to code what 51 percent (or more than half) of the students are doing and to code what is happening for the majority of the segment. So, if only 10 of 25 students are active or if 15 students are active but only for 5 seconds of the 15-second segment, a W would be recorded (if the students are waiting for a turn).

After the lesson, the information on the duration recording form can be used to calculate what percentage of class time was spent in each category. The following procedure should be used: Determine the total number of 15-second intervals recorded in the lesson. Then determine the number of 15-second intervals for each of the four time categories. Next, divide each number by the total number of seconds for the lesson. The result is the percentage of time in each category.

In the beginning, the peer assistant may be uncertain about how to code a particular event. This is not uncommon when one is learning to use any type of analysis system. The assistant should make a decision and then code other such events the same way. That will enable you to compare a succession of lessons to determine what progress you're making.

Table 13.1 Coding Guide for the Duration Recording System

Category	Definition	Examples
Activity time	Time when most students (51 percent or more) are involved with physical movement consistent with the goals of the particular lesson.	Practicing a skill; designing a game, dance, or gymnastic sequence; participating in a group or individual game; providing assistance for a partner.
Instruction	Time when students have an opportunity to learn. They may be receiving verbal and nonverbal information. Most students (51 percent or more) are engaged in cognitive activity about the lesson focus.	Listening to a lecture, watching the teacher or another student demonstrate a skill, participating in a class discussion, answering teacher's questions.
Management	Time when the opportunity to learn is *not* present. Most students (51 percent or more) are involved in activities only indirectly related to the class learning activity. There is no instruction, demonstration, or practice.	Changing activities, forming groups, listening for roll call, getting out or putting away equipment, getting into line.
Waiting	Time not defined by the other three categories.	Waiting for class to begin, or waiting for instruction to resume when it has been interrupted by another teacher, student messenger, parent, principal, or public address system; waiting in line for a turn.

During activity time, the children are involved in movement that is consistent with the teacher's goals.

There are no hard-and-fast rules as to how time should be distributed within a lesson; however, a major consideration is the focus of the lesson. If the focus is learning a motor skill, the majority of the time in a lesson (more than 50 percent) should be spent practicing the skill. If students are waiting or listening, they are not able to practice. There is a bit of a catch here—there may be such a thing as too much practice time. If there is no instruction, it may be an indication that students are not receiving the information they need to practice correctly. Thus, more than 70 percent practice time may be an indicator that the lesson is simply a physical activity session and not physical education.

Demonstration Checklist   Observers can also help reflect on your demonstrations. Most young students are visual learners; therefore, the demonstrations you give them often influence their skill responses as well as their ability to perform a task the way you designed it. Accurate demonstrations are vital to task clarity. By analyzing your demonstrations using the demonstration checklist in Figure 13.6, you can determine if your

The time taken to retrieve equipment is considered management.

Demonstration Checklist

Teacher: _____ Observer: _____ Date: _____ Time: _____

Grade: _____ Class Size: _____ Content: _____

DIRECTIONS: Answer the following questions "yes" or "no" based on the instructor's demonstration of the skills.

Components	Task 1	Task 2	Task 3
1. Was the whole skill/action shown early in the demonstration?			
2. Was the skill/action performed at correct (full) speed?			
3. Was the skill performed at more than one angle?			
4. Was a student used to demonstrate the skill (if practical)?			
5. Did the demonstration use the same organizational format that is required for practicing/using the skill?			
6. Were the major common errors (nonexamples) shown?			
7. Were the essential, accurate cues to the performance verbalized?			
8. Were the cues emphasized more than once?			
9. Was noncritical information left out?			
10. Was a check for understanding done?			
11. Do you think students were able to form an accurate mental image of the skill/action as a result of the demonstration?			
12. Was information provided that showed why the skill should be performed as it was demonstrated?			
13. Was the demonstration done in a location similar to where students will perform the skill/action?			

COMMENTS (reference specific comments by number):

Figure 13.6 Demonstration checklist.

demonstrations are enhancing the clarity of your instruction and your students' skill. If after analyzing the information from the form you discover that the demonstration was not performed correctly, it could explain why some students were off task.

Making Sense of It All: Combining and Adapting Techniques and Setting Goals

Many observation systems have been developed to help reflect on the teaching performance of physical education teachers. The preceding examples have all focused on "standard" effective teaching constructs that promote student learning; many would call this "technical" reflection. As presented, they may or may not fit your

needs. Feel free to adjust them to make the technique or tool useful for your teaching situation. You can develop your own coding instrument based on your environment and particular needs. For most of the questions you want to ask about your teaching, you can develop similar, uncomplicated systems that will give you the specific information you want to know. The secret to developing such systems is to define the behavior (what you want to observe or listen to) very precisely so you can tell when it does and doesn't happen. It doesn't help very much to say, "I want to find out if I was clear when I talked to students"; you need to define what "clear" means to you. It could mean that students didn't have to ask you questions about how to do a task after you gave it; it could mean you didn't mumble and slur your words when you gave a task; or it could mean you didn't have to turn the audio device up to high to be able to hear yourself. Whatever it is, define it, and then try to assess it by listening to your recording.

After obtaining data about his or her teaching performance, the reflective teacher reflects on the information, draws conclusions, sets goals, and engages in reflective practice. The improvement can be measured over a period of weeks or months. For example, you may want to set a goal of interacting at least once with every child in the class or to have at least 80 percent of your comments positive. As you set goals, be gentle with yourself; set reasonable and progressive goals. If your feedback was at a rate of 0.25 per minute the first week, increasing to a rate of 2.0 per minute the next week may be unreasonable. When you listen to the recording after a class, you'll learn whether you've achieved your goal. Remember, what is measured or how it is measured is less important than the continuing effort to systematically assess and improve your teaching performance. Relying on your subjective judgment ("I think I'm getting better") or that of a colleague ("That lesson looked good") is not nearly as effective as collecting and analyzing relatively objective data you can refer back to in a few days, months, or even years.

Being Observed

Because many of us are reluctant to be observed while we teach, it may be less threatening to begin your assessment process with the unassisted techniques. When you've progressed to the point where you desire information that can only be gathered by outside eyes, be thoughtful about whom you ask to observe you. We've found it easier and more comfortable to use a colleague who is a nonjudgmental friend, someone to whom you're willing to expose both your good points and weaknesses, someone you can trust. For most of us, it takes a while to build up to this point—take it slowly.

Always remember you're obtaining this information to help improve your teaching. The information is yours to do with as you wish; no one else needs to see it unless you want them to. When viewed this way, assessing your teaching performance can be interesting and challenging, not threatening.

Professional Learning Communities

The techniques described for reflecting on one's teaching practices are effective approaches to improving performance. But successful teaching is more than using specific teaching behaviors in predetermined ways. Teaching can never be totally reduced to specific

formulas of behavior that guarantee success for all teachers with all classes (Glickman, Gordon, and Ross-Gordon 2014). However, systematic observation can help answer some questions and provide information that can influence a teacher's success. Other questions require careful thought and analysis, and they cannot be answered through self-reflection or solely by systematic observation. Sometimes we need to sit down with colleagues who will listen carefully and help us understand a particular situation. This is what professional learning communities (PLCs) do. Teachers form PLCs to build relationships that allow them to learn from and with each other. These communities are based on trust, collegiality, and a desire to learn; within them, individuals share their concerns, questions, dreams, and hopes about themselves as teachers (Parker, Patton, and Tannehill 2012).

If you're not careful, teaching can be a lonely and difficult profession; the importance of a community in which to reflect cannot be overestimated. As a poster depicting an exhausted teacher at the end of an obviously difficult day reminds us: "No one ever said teaching was going to be easy." When your teaching isn't going well, or when you've had a spectacular day, a support group can provide comfort and encouragement or share your excitement. It's reassuring to have a stable group of colleagues who'll listen carefully, verbally applaud your successes, and help you dissect your concerns. For those of us in physical education, it is important to seek out those PLCs that are discipline or content specific (Patton and Parker 2015). Often PLCs are established at the school level, and these can be beneficial for physical education teachers to stay connected to the mission and current initiatives of the school. The most beneficial PLCs, in terms of learning, for physical education teachers, however, may be at the district level. In this case, it may be necessary for the physical education teachers within a district to request a full or half professional development day for physical education teachers only. Most teachers occasionally complain about teaching conditions, parents, administrators, or fellow teachers. We all have our down days. Within a PLC, however, complaining is inappropriate because it's often toxic and tends to contaminate others' thinking. PLCs are designed to enhance teaching and learning by empowering teachers as learners.

Teaching will never be an exact, predictable science. There will always be an art to teaching effectively. Self-reflection, systematic observation techniques, and support groups are three approaches to improving both teaching performance and one's personal satisfaction and enthusiasm for teaching; combined, they may lead to reflection that goes beyond the technical to the critical analyses of what happens in teaching.

Summary

Reflective teaching is a developmental process, and because effective teaching involves learning, it is a continuous, lifelong process. Teachers who want to become more effective invoke a reflective cycle that includes describing teaching, critiquing teaching, and setting goals to guide their thinking about teaching.

Describing teaching through self-reflection involves the thoughtful contemplation of the act of teaching. It usually results in a permanent product much like a diary or journal. Systematic observation can be used to gather an orderly and focused collection of specific and defined information to critique teaching. It can be classified into unassisted and assisted techniques. Goal setting allows reflective teachers to determine whether they are making changes to their practices that enhance student learning.

A valuable aid in the teacher reflective process is a PLC, or professional learning community. These groups, made up of fellow teachers, can provide not only comfort and encouragement but also an environment in which teachers learn from and with each other. When a group of peers actively listen to each other's questions and help clarify each other's thoughts, the teaching skills and knowledge of all the members are improved.

Reading Comprehension Questions

1. Why is this chapter included in *Children Moving*? What is the value of self-reflection?
2. What is a reflection cycle? What three aspects are included in it?
3. What purpose does self-reflection serve in the reflective cycle?
4. How does systematic observation allow a reflective teacher to critique his or her teaching? Identify two systematic observation techniques you can use by yourself. What information can you obtain from each technique?
5. What type of content development pattern would you deem optimal in your teaching situation? How could you use the content development form to compare what actually happens to your desired pattern? What various types of feedback can be determined from recording teacher feedback? What goals would you set if student learning was the focus of your teaching?
6. What kind of analysis can you make from student–teacher interactions?
7. What is duration recording? What categories does it contain? How is each category defined? How does a duration recording system work?
8. Why is the use of systematic observation without a clear purpose of improving teaching to improve student learning counterproductive?
9. What is the key to goal setting?
10. What are professional learning communities? What is their value?

References/Suggested Readings

Banville, D., and Rikard, L. 2001. Observational tools for teacher reflection. *Journal of Physical Education, Recreation, and Dance* 72(4): 46–49.

Cusimano, B., P. Darst, and H. van der Mars. 1993, October. Improving your teaching through self-evaluation. *Strategies* 7(8): 26–29.

Darling-Hammond, L., and N. Richardson. 2009. Teacher learning: What matters? *Educational Leadership* 66(5), 46–53.

Glickman, C., S. Gordon, and J. Ross-Gordon. 2014. *Supervision and instructional leadership: A developmental approach.* 9th ed. Upper Saddle River, NJ: Pearson.

Housner, L. 1996. Innovation and change in physical education. In *Student learning in physical education: Applying research to enhance instruction*, ed. S. Silverman and C. Ennis, 367–89. Champaign, IL: Human Kinetics.

Locke, L. F. 1975, Spring. The ecology of the gymnasium: What the tourist never sees. *Southern Association of Physical Education for College Women Proceedings* 38–50.

Lorson, K., J. Goodway, and R. Hovatter. 2007. Using goal-directed reflection to make reflection more meaningful. *Journal of Physical Education, Recreation, and Dance* 78(4): 42–47.

Richert, A. 1995. Introduction. In *Teachers who teach teachers: Reflections on teacher educations*, ed. T. Russell and F. Korthagen, 1–7. London: Falmer Press.

Parker, M., K. Patton, and D. Tannehill. 2012. Mapping the landscape of Irish physical education professional development. *Irish Educational Studies Journal* 31(3): 311–27.

Patton, K., and M. Parker. 2015. "I learned more at lunchtime": Guideposts for reimagining professional development. *Journal of Physical Education, Recreation and Dance* 86(1): 23–29.

Rink, J. 2003. Effective instruction in physical education. In *Student learning in physical education: Applying research to enhance instruction*, 2nd ed., ed. S. Silverman and C. Ennis, 165–86. Champaign, IL: Human Kinetics.

Stroot, S. 2001. Once I graduate, am I an expert? *Teaching Elementary Physical Education* 12(2): 18–20.

Stroot, S., and C. Whipple. 2003. Organizational socialization: Factors impacting beginning teachers. In *Student learning in physical education: Applying research to enhance instruction*, 2nd ed., ed. S. Silverman and C. Ennis, 311–28. Champaign, IL: Human Kinetics.

Movement Concepts Development

The three chapters in Part 4 explain the movement concept categories of space awareness (Chapter 14), effort (Chapter 15), and relationships (Chapter 16) and present ideas for teaching them to children. Because these are concepts rather than actual skills, *levels of skill proficiency are not discussed.* As children study space awareness, effort, and relationships, they learn to demonstrate, through movement, their understanding of the meaning of each concept. You will find many learning experiences for each of the concepts. As a reflective teacher, you will want to make decisions about which tasks will best meet your students' needs and assist them in gaining a functional understanding of the concepts. The range of learning experiences suggested provides a breadth of experiences related to each concept. Once children have acquired this functional understanding, the concept is used primarily as a subfocus—or an adverb—to enhance the range and quality of skill development that result from the study of the various skill themes (Part 5).

Suggested tasks are designated with the symbol **T**; challenges are designated with the symbol **C**; tasks and challenges were described in Chapter 6. In addition, you will also find suggested assessments within the movement concept chapters and in Chapter 12 to help you determine how well the children are understanding the concepts.

When teaching the movement concepts, it's easy to forget that the purpose is to have the children actually *know* what each concept means. Imagine that one of us is going to teach a class of your second graders. Before teaching, we might ask whether your children know the space awareness concepts. If you say yes, we would assume the children can show movement of body parts and total body in self-space and/or general space when asked to do so. Or we would assume the children can travel in straight, curved, and zigzag pathways and that they can move body parts at high, medium, and low levels. "Knowing" doesn't mean the concepts were taught; knowing means the children are able to show their understanding through their movement. In other words, the children have *functional understanding.*

Space Awareness

cody

Drawn by Children at Monfort, Chappelow or Shawsheen Elementary Schools, Greeley, CO.
Courtesy of Lizzy Ginger; Tia Ziegler

Key Concepts

- Movement concepts expand the range and enrich the quality of skills in physical education.

- Movement concept categories include space awareness (location, directions, levels, pathways, extensions); effort (time, force, flow); and relationships (of body parts, with objects, with people).

- Learning experiences in the concepts chapters are designed to help children attain a functional understanding (cognitive and performance) of the concepts.

- Children need a wide breadth of experiences with each concept to achieve functional understanding.

- When movement concepts are introduced to children, the focus of the lesson is on the concept; the movement (skill) is secondary to the concept.

- Concepts become modifiers to skills as children move to higher levels of performance.

- Levels of skill proficiency are not included for movement concepts; they are concepts to be understood, not skills to be mastered.

- Once children understand a movement concept, it can be used in combination with other concepts and in combination with skills.

- A functional understanding of concepts must be attained before the concepts can be used in skill themes.

Box 14-1

Space Awareness in the *National Standards & Grade Level Outcomes for Physical Education*

The movement concept of Space Awareness is referenced in the National Standards & Grade Level Outcomes (SHAPE America, 2014) under Standard 2: "…Applies knowledge of concepts, principles, strategies and tactics related to movement and performance." The intent of the standard is facilitation of learners' ability to use cognitive information to understand and enhance motor skill acquisition and performance. At the lower-elementary level, emphasis is placed on establishing a movement vocabulary and demonstrating a basic understanding of the concepts. At the upper-elementary level, emphasis is placed on applying the concepts in dance, educational gymnastics, and game environments.

Sample grade-level outcomes from the National Standards* include:

- Differentiates between self and general space (K)
- Travels in 3 different pathways (K)
- Travels demonstrating low, middle, and high levels (1)
- Combines shapes, levels, and pathways into simple sequences (2)
- Recognizes the concept of open spaces (3)
- Applies the concept of open spaces (4)
- Applies simple strategies & tactics in chasing and fleeing activities (3)
- Applies simple offensive and defensive strategies & tactics in chasing and fleeing activities (4)
- Combines concepts and skills in practice tasks, gymnastics, and dance environments (4)
- Combines spatial concepts with locomotors and nonlocomotors in game, dance, and gymnastics environments (5)
- Applies basic offensive and defensive strategies & tactics in invasion and net/wall small sided practice tasks (5)
- Analyzes and applies movement concepts in game, dance, and gymnastics environments (5)

*Suggested grade-level outcomes for student learning

National Standards & Grade-Level Outcomes for K–12 Physical Education (SHAPE America 2014).

All movement occurs in space. Because children who develop a keen space sense will be better able to move safely as they travel through physical education environments, it's beneficial to focus on the concept of space awareness at the beginning of the physical education program.

Children can be made aware of the different aspects of space and then challenged to think about spatial considerations as they engage in game, gymnastics, and dance experiences. As children move their bodies in different ways through varying spatial conditions, they begin to feel and understand space in new ways. As relationships between the body and space become clear, adeptness at controlling movements in functional or expressive physical education activities is enhanced. For example, children learn to maneuver across a large span of climbing equipment, traveling around, over, and under other youngsters without bumping any of them or losing control of their own movements. See Box 14-1 for linkages between the movement concept of Space Awareness and the

Recall from earlier chapters that the movement analysis framework consists of both movement concepts and skill themes. Space awareness—where the body moves—is one of the three categories of movement concepts (Chapter 3, Table 3.2). The space awareness categories are shaded in the movement analysis

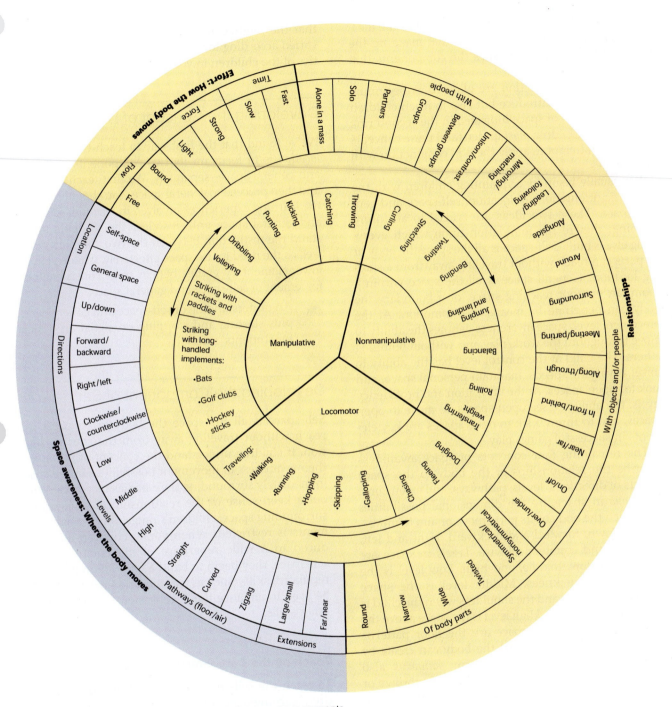

Figure 14.1 Movement analysis framework: space awareness concepts.

framework wheel (Figure 14.1). The position of space awareness on the wheel indicates it is a movement concept or modifier. In other words, it describes how a skill is to be performed as opposed to stating what skill is to be performed.

The space awareness section of the wheel is divided into five subcategories that delineate various concepts of space: location, directions, levels, pathways, and extensions. In turn, each of these concepts is further divided into specific components that are the working or teachable aspects of space awareness. For example, the location concept is divided into the components of general space and self-space. Study Figure 14.1 to determine all the subdivisions for each of the separate aspects of space. It helps to think of the three outermost portions of the wheel as three levels of the same idea. The first level, or outside ring, describes the idea, the second ring gives the concepts that make up the idea, and the third ring defines the components that are found in each concept.

Activities in this section are planned as beginning tasks, not only to introduce but also to teach children the five concepts of space indicated in the second ring of the wheel. Children *must* understand these concepts before they attempt to apply them in conjunction with skill themes.

We usually begin by acquainting children with the two basic orientations of location: self-space and general space. These two ideas are crucial to all future learning; they're the foundation upon which everything else is built. Self-space is all the space the body or its parts can reach without traveling away from a starting location. General space is all the space within a room, an outdoor teaching space, or a boundary the body can penetrate by means of locomotion. At the precontrol level, space awareness denotes the ability to move throughout the work/play area without bumping others. The child at the control level has the ability to travel at varying speeds, maintain personal space, and look for open spaces. At the utilization and proficiency levels, the ability to see open spaces, to move to open spaces, and to throw/kick to open spaces are key elements in successful games play.

The remaining four concepts of space awareness describe the relationships of the body to the space aspects of directions, levels, pathways, and extensions. *Directions* in space are the dimensional possibilities into which the body or its parts move or aim to move—up and down, forward and backward, right and left, clockwise and counterclockwise. *Levels* in space are divided into low, middle, and high. Low level is the space below the knees. Middle level is the space between the knees and the shoulders when the child is in a standing position. High level is the space above the shoulders. *Pathways* in space are the floor patterns (straight, curved, and zigzag) the body can create by traveling through space. The term *pathways* also denotes the possible floor or air patterns of a thrown or struck object—for example, the arched flight of a basketball set shot or the straight path of a line drive in softball.

The concept *extensions* includes the size of movements of the body or its parts in space (for example, small arm circles or large arm circles) and the distances from the center of the body the parts reach to carry out a movement. The tennis serve a skilled player performs is a far extension, whereas the tennis serve a beginner executes is often much closer to the body.

The ideas for developing each space awareness concept are stated in direct terms. Remember, though, that the method used to study each concept can be varied according to your purposes and the characteristics of the children in your class (see Chapter 9).

Developing the Concept of Location

We've found that the best way to teach the concept of *location* is to focus on its two components—self-space and general space—separately. We first teach self-space and then proceed to general space. You should repeat all the learning experiences involved in teaching self-space and general space until it's clear the students understand the distinction between the two components, as well as the need to use space effectively. Children in the lower-elementary grades benefit from consistent reinforcement of self-space and general space.

 An understanding of self-space and general space plus starting and stopping on signal are crucial for students' safety.

Developing the Component of Self-Space

Self-space is all the space the body or its parts can reach without traveling away from the starting location. If children understand the concept of self-space, their awareness of movement possibilities in the space immediately surrounding their bodies increases. Without a keen sense of the relationship of self-space to surrounding space, children's range of potential movements is restricted. When young children are introduced to a wide repertoire of movement skills in self-space, they begin to build a foundation of nonmanipulative skills (such as twisting and turning) that can be used to enhance the development of concepts and other skills.

Teaching the Component of Self-Space

To teach the self-space component, we give the children learning experiences they can accomplish in one location, without traveling. The absence of locomotion enhances kinesthetic awareness of stretching, curling, twisting, and swinging movements and builds the children's movement vocabularies.

An analogy such as the idea of staying on your island is helpful as children learn the concept of self-space. Even with the best analogies in the world, it's sometimes difficult for children, both young and old, to understand the idea of self-space. When this happens, we use hoops, spots, ropes shaped into circles, or X's marked on the floor to help children differentiate and remember what their self-space really looks like. As soon as children demonstrate a functional understanding (both cognitive and performance) of self-space, we remove the props.

Each individual is surrounded by a self-space as he or she travels in general space—the possible movements into space immediately surrounding the body will be the same regardless of location. However, children will understand this idea most easily if they learn it while remaining stationary. Staying in one location will clarify for the children the difference between the movements possible in the space immediately surrounding the body and the movements possible when the body travels through general space.

Learning Experiences Leading to Movement Concept Understanding

Exploring Self-Space

Setting: Children scattered throughout general space

Tasks/Challenges:

T While standing in a place all by yourself, not traveling anywhere else, move your arms in as many places as possible around your body. Pretend that you're on an island in the middle of shark-infested waters and that all your friends are on islands of their own. You can't reach your friends on their islands, and they can't reach you. You're stranded.

T This time, while in a place by yourself, move your legs all around you. Try places that you think are difficult to get to, like behind you or way out to the side; come very close to falling off your island.

This young boy, appropriately challenged, is enthralled with the prospect of exploring space.

T Once you think you're very good with moving your arms and legs without leaving the space you're in, choose other body parts you can move without leaving your space. Use body parts you think would be really difficult to move around in your space without moving your whole body from your island. Explore your whole island.

The area that you've just explored is called *self-space*; it's like your own island or armor that travels with you wherever you go. Your self-space belongs to you, and no one else is allowed in it unless you let them. Remember, too, that you're not allowed in anyone else's self-space unless they invite you.

Curling, Stretching, and Twisting in Self-Space

Setting: Children scattered throughout general space

Tasks/Challenges:

T While staying in self-space, where you can't touch anyone else, curl your body up very tightly so you look like a little ball. Now that you're curled up, begin to stretch, ever so slowly, until you're stretched as tall and wide as possible. As you stretch, remember that you can't leave your own space. You're in your own birdcage. Slowly stretch just one arm, then the other arm. Slowly stretch only one leg, then the other leg. Don't forget to stretch your fingers and toes while you are in self-space.

T Pretend you're trying to reach the cookie jar on a shelf at the very top of your cage. Stretch as tall as you can to get it. Now, just as you have two cookies in your hand, your mother walks in. Sink very quickly back to the floor and make yourself very small in order to hide.

T This time, a big spider is on the floor of the cage, near your feet. Stretch tall; you're trying to reach the top rungs of your cage to pull yourself up out of the spider's way. Now the spider climbs to the top; shrink slowly to get away from the spider.

T Now that you've practiced your stretching and curling actions, you're going to add twisting actions to them. You want to twist your whole body, not just one part. To start, make believe the cookie jar is on the very back of the shelf, behind two boxes; as you stretch, twist your body so you can get to the cookie jar.

T Stretch toward the top of the birdcage (as you did to get away from the spider). Now pretend that suddenly you have an itch in the middle of your back. Hold on to the top of the cage with one hand and try to scratch your back with your other hand.

(T) Pretend you have an itch in the middle of your back that is impossible to reach. Twist your body in different directions as you attempt to reach the itch. Stretch, curl, and twist body parts in self-space to scratch the itch.

(C) See how many body parts you can stretch in self-space. How many different ways can you curl without moving from your self-space? Isolate different body parts for twisting in self-space.

Moving the Whole Body in Self-Space

Setting: Children scattered throughout general space

Tasks/Challenges:

(T) So far, all you've done in self-space is curl, stretch, and twist; you haven't really moved your whole body using any kind of specific movement. This time, let's practice walking in place, in self-space. Remember, you can't go anywhere off your island or out of your birdcage—that's all the area you have.

Other actions to practice in self-space: hopping, jumping, and turning slowly like a music box dancer.

Developing the Component of General Space

General space is all the space within a room or boundary into which an individual can move by traveling away from the original starting location (self-space).

We help the children learn different ways of traveling safely through general space by providing appropriate movement tasks. Once the children are able to travel safely (without bumping or losing control) in general space, they're ready to experience more complex tasks that include several concepts in combination, such as speed, pathways, and directions. Manipulating balls as one travels through general space is an even more difficult challenge.

Teaching the Component of General Space

The learning experiences in this section are designed to help children learn to travel safely and efficiently through general space. You can increase the complexity of the activities by focusing on the concepts of speed, pathways, and directions and on the manipulation of objects through general space. Traveling in general space is an excellent warm-up activity you can use

each day; it also provides additional opportunities for practice of the various locomotor skills.

Learning Experiences Leading to Movement Concept Understanding

Exploring General Space

Setting: Children scattered throughout general space

Tasks/Challenges:

(T) Find a space by yourself within the boundaries of our work area. I'll know you're ready when I see you standing very still in a space where you can't touch anyone else. When I say "Go," begin to walk around the room, trying not to come near anyone else and at the same time not leaving any empty spaces in the room. On signal (*verbal signal or drumbeat*), stop very quickly right where you are. When you stop, you shouldn't be able to touch anyone else.

This area that you just moved in is called *general space*; it's all the space available for you to move in. As you move in general space, your self-space goes with you, like a bubble that surrounds you, so you're protected.

(T) Let's try the same activity again, but this time move a little faster through general space. Remember, as you move and when you stop, you shouldn't be able to touch anyone else.

(!) Increase the speed only when you observe that the children are able to travel without bumping into one another; for some classes, this will take several days. Always start slowly.

(T) This time, instead of walking through general space, you're going to jog (or skip, hop, gallop, etc.) through general space. Remember, always stay as far away from other people as you can. Think about visiting different places in the area, such as the corners and the middle of the area.

After you give the stop signal, you can further enhance concept development by giving the children feedback, for example:

- *Praise youngsters who stop in isolated areas.*
- *Praise youngsters who stop quickly and safely.*
- *Point out congested or vacant spaces.*
- *Praise youngsters who've avoided collisions by traveling defensively.*

(?) Pretend you have one foot glued to the ground with sticky chewing gum; wave your arms up and down, all around. Is this movement in self-space or general space? Now travel waving your arms as you go, up and down, all around. Is this movement in self-space or general space?

Open Spaces

Setting: Children scattered throughout general space

Tasks/Challenges:

🅣 Travel throughout general space, constantly moving to an open space. When you arrive at that open space, quickly move to another one when someone invades your open space or you see a second or a third open space.

🅣 Travel throughout general space looking for an open space. When you see an open space, pretend you are throwing a ball to that space; then quickly travel to that space to "catch" the ball. Look for another open space, "throw," and travel again.

🅣 Travel throughout general space looking for an open space. Each time you travel to an open space, claim that space as your own by calling "Yes." Then quickly move to a new open space.

Reducing the Size of the General Space

Setting: Children scattered throughout general space facing the teacher, who is positioned at the edge of the general space. All the children will be moving within the boundaries. When you want the space to become smaller, take a step or two toward the center of the general space—the idea is an entire wall moving forward at one time.

Tasks/Challenges:

🅣 Spread out and find a space by yourself. On the signal, begin to travel on your feet in general space, not touching anyone else. The difficult part this time will be that I'm going to keep making your space smaller as you move. For me to do that, you must always stay in front of me; I'll keep moving forward until your general space is very small.

Reducing the Size of General Space and Changing Speed

Setting: Children divided into two groups in a reduced amount of general space as in the previous learning experiences

Tasks/Challenges:

🅣 Let's move within this reduced amount of space as if we were in a crowded city. We will begin walking at a moderate speed to avoid bumping others on the crowded streets. On signal, increase the speed of your walking as if you were in rush-hour traffic. Remember, no collisions.

🅣 Now move very slowly because the area is congested. Increase your speed again.

🅣 Group 1, stand very still in your self-space. You are the tall buildings in the city; you may be tall and wide or just tall. Group 2, walk throughout the general space without bumping other walkers or the buildings. Listen for the signal to increase or decrease your speed. (*Switch the groups after 30 seconds.*)

Dodging in General Space

Setting: Children divided into two groups: half the children on one side of the work area, half on the other side

Tasks/Challenges:

🅣 Let's practice our moving in general space in a game. The object of the game is for both groups to

Spatial awareness is critical to working safely in group situations.

©Lars A. Niki

get to the other side of the area without touching anyone else. The difficult part is that both groups will be moving at the same time. Remember, all of you in both groups are trying to switch sides without touching anyone else. I'll watch very carefully to see if I can find anyone touching.

T Now, instead of walking, you're going to gallop (*or skip, hop, jump, etc.*) to the other side.

⚠ Permit children to travel at fast speeds, such as running, only after they have mastered stopping on signal and moving with no collisions.

Traveling Over, Under, and Around Obstacles in General Space

Setting: Small obstacles (hoops and ropes on the floor or suspended between crates or cones, milk crates, and low benches) spread out in various places around the area

Tasks/Challenges:

T Travel around the space without touching any piece of equipment or any other person. You may go over, under, or around any of the obstacles, but don't touch anyone or anything. Remember, if someone else is at a piece of equipment, go on to another one; don't wait in line.

? *Teacher Observation:* Functional understanding of self-space and general space

Show me your self-space/your personal space within the boundaries of our movement area.

Now, travel throughout general space; on signal, stop in your self-space

Criteria for Assessment

Developing

> Unable to demonstrate an understanding of self-space in relation to others

> Unable to differentiate between self-space and general space

Competent

> Demonstrates an understanding of self-space and general space

> Demonstrates differentiation of movement in self-space and in general space

Proficient

> Demonstrates understanding of self-space when combined with travel

> Demonstrates self-space and general space, maintaining body control and avoiding collisions

Adapted from PE Metrics SHAPE America (2018).

Space Awareness Obstacle Course

Setting: Jump ropes, wands, hoops, yardsticks, crates, and similar small equipment placed around the edge of the work area

Tasks/Challenges:

T Today you are going to design an obstacle course for our traveling in general space. What is an obstacle course? Right; it's an area to travel through without bumping into things or going outside the boundaries. Select two or three pieces of the small equipment, and place them on the floor; you may wish to place them so they are touching or so they

These youngsters understand both extensions and levels as they meet and part.

©Lars A. Niki

connect with the equipment of the person working next to you. (*Allow two to three minutes for the children to construct the obstacle course.*)

Walk throughout general space, avoiding the obstacles placed on the floor; travel without touching the equipment or any other person.

Travel in a way other than walking.

If the children have been introduced to the concept of pathways, they can design the obstacle course to show straight, curved, and zigzag pathways. Their travel can then be a combination of different locomotors and pathways—for example, walk the straight pathways, gallop the curved pathways, and jump as you travel the zigzag pathways.

Developing the Concept of Directions

Directions in space are the dimensional possibilities into which the body or its parts move or aim to move—up and down, right and left, forward and backward, clockwise and counterclockwise. There is no universally correct direction; direction is a function of the body's orientation in space. Forward and backward, for example, depend on the way a person is facing rather than a location in a room. Left and right refer to the respective sides of the body, not a certain wall or location in a gymnasium. Because the direction components of right and left (sideways) and clockwise and counterclockwise require cognitive as well as physical maturation for correct execution, it's not uncommon to find that children learn the directions forward and backward and up and down before they learn the directions right and left and clockwise and counterclockwise.

Teaching the Concept of Directions

The learning experiences in this section provide ideas for helping children understand the components of direction—forward and backward, up and down, sideways (right and left), clockwise and counterclockwise. As the children become more capable, the complexity of the tasks is increased—the children are challenged to combine two or more direction components and to move in different directions in relation to objects or people.

Learning Experiences Leading to Movement Concept Understanding

Traveling in Different Directions

Setting: Children scattered throughout general space

Tasks/Challenges:

🅣 On the signal, walk as you usually walk, with the front of your body going first. This direction is called *forward*.

🅣 This time, walk with your back going first. This direction is called *backward*. For safety reasons, you need to look over your shoulder to see where you're going.

🅣 Now move with one side of your body going first. This direction is called *sideways*. You can move to either your right or left side. Let's practice both ways. First, move with your right side going first. When you hear the drumbeat (*if you don't have a drum, use a metal can, a baby rattle, or a party noisemaker*), change so your left side goes first.

🅣 Skip forward, walk slowly backward, slide from side to side like an ice-skater, and jump up and down as though you were on a pogo stick or a trampoline.

Moving Clockwise and Counterclockwise

Setting: Children scattered throughout general space

Tasks/Challenges:

Rotation describes movement in a clockwise or counterclockwise direction. When we want children to turn, spin, or pivot, using the terms right and left is inaccurate. Instead, the terms clockwise and counterclockwise indicate the appropriate direction in which to move. These movements later transfer to many games/sports, dance, and gymnastics experiences.

🅣 How many of you have ever seen a clock with "hands" that move around the numbers in a circle? Before digital clocks, this is how they looked. (Show an illustration of a clock if there is not one on the wall.) Look down at the floor. Imagine there's a clock on the floor in front of you. Slowly turn around, turning in the direction the hands on the clock move. This direction is called clockwise. Now turn in the other direction. This direction is called counterclockwise.

🅣 Now practice the different directions some more. See if you can spin clockwise on one foot. Now change and spin counterclockwise on the same foot.

🅣 Swing your arms in the direction you want to spin, and see if you can spin all the way around before you stop. Swinging your arms will help you spin farther. Remember to swing in the direction you want to go.

🅣 In a seated position, raise your feet, and try spinning clockwise. Now spin counterclockwise.

❓ Is it easier to spin in a clockwise or a counterclockwise direction? Why do you think so? Find a partner. One of you spin or jump and turn while the other watches. See if your partner can tell you whether you were spinning (turning) in a clockwise or a counterclockwise direction. Now watch as your partner spins (turns).

T This time try jumping. Everyone face a wall; jump and turn clockwise so you are facing the wall to your right. Now jump and turn counterclockwise facing the same direction where you started. This time, jump and turn clockwise, facing the wall behind you. Yes, that is more difficult; it is a 1/2 turn. Reverse and face the same way you started using a counterclockwise jump. Staying in your self-space, jump and turn as far as you can, making sure you bend your knees to land in a balanced position. You may be able to jump with a full turn, landing where you started.

T Practice turning clockwise and counterclockwise when you jump. Can you turn farther in one direction than the other?

T Now you're going to try something different. Travel in general space. When you hear one drumbeat, spin in a clockwise direction and keep traveling. When you hear two drumbeats, spin in a counterclockwise direction and keep traveling. If you hear three drumbeats, change the way you're traveling— for example, from a skip to a slide. Do you think you can remember all this? Let's see!

You can also teach and reinforce clockwise and counterclockwise when working with several of the skill themes by having the children dribble in a clockwise or counterclockwise direction, for example, or push a puck with a hockey stick in both directions.

Exploring Directions

Setting: Children scattered throughout general space

Tasks/Challenges:

T In your self-space, point with the body part named in the direction that I call out. (You can continue the list with any body part.)

With your foot, point forward.
With your elbow, point backward.
With your hip, point to the left.
With your left foot, point to the right.
With one finger, point up.
With your thumb, point down.

As you point, make sure the direction you're pointing to is very clear—so I could easily tell which way to go if you were pointing out a direction to me.

? The above task would make an excellent assessment.

Changing Directions on Signal

Setting: Children scattered throughout general space

Tasks/Challenges:

T Now that you know the directions, move a little faster when you practice them, and mix them all up. On the signal, begin to travel in general space in a forward direction. After that, each time you hear the signal, change the direction you're moving in. For example, if you start out moving in a forward direction, the first time you hear the signal, change to a sideways direction; the next time you hear the signal, change to a backward direction; and the next time, change back to a sideways direction. Remember, make your directions very clear.

While the children are waiting for the signal, have them think about how they're going to change direction.

T This time, change not only the direction of your travel but also the locomotor movement you use— for example, gallop forward, walk backward, or slide to the right.

T This time the changes of direction are going to be a bit more difficult. They'll be in code. One beat of the drum means forward. Two beats of the drum mean sideways. Three beats of the drum mean backward. Spread out in general space in a space by yourself. When you hear the beat of the drum, begin to travel in the direction indicated by the code. When you hear the next beat of the drum, change and travel in the direction that it indicates. Listen very carefully to the drumbeats because I might try to trick you.

Turning While Moving in Different Directions

Setting: Children positioned around the perimeters of the gymnasium, facing the walls

Tasks/Challenges:

T Spread out around the outside of the room and face the wall. When you hear the drumbeat, begin to travel around the space by using a sideways sliding pattern. As the drum beats again, turn, without stopping, to face the inside of the room—keep sliding. Each time the drum beats, change the way you're facing, and continue moving sideways. When you do this, I'm looking for turns that are smooth and slides that don't stop as you turn.

Developing the Concept of Levels

Levels are the horizontal layers in space where the body or its parts are positioned or can move.

Low level is the space below the knees, close to the floor. A stamp or twist of the foot is an action at a low level. Crawling, creeping, and rolling are locomotor actions performed at a low level.

Middle level is the space between low level and high level—the area between the knees and shoulders. Catching a thrown ball, for example, typically occurs in middle level.

High level is the space above the shoulders, toward the ceiling or the sky. Although one can't move the whole body into high level, actions such as stretching the arms up high or standing on the balls of the feet bring body parts into a high level. A jump can take much of the upper body into a high level, while part of the body remains at a middle or low level because of the pull of gravity.

Teaching the Concept of Levels

The learning experiences in this section give children movement challenges that help them learn to move the body, body parts, and objects into different levels in space.

Learning Experiences Leading to Movement Concept Understanding

Traveling and Freezing at Different Levels

Setting: Children scattered throughout general space

Tasks/Challenges:

🅣 Spread out and find a space by yourself. On signal, begin to travel in general space. When you hear the drumbeat, stop where you are, with your whole body at a low level.

🅣 This time, travel, and on the signal, stop with your body at low level and a body part at high level. Make it very clear which part is at a high level. Remember, if your body is at a low level, the full extension of a free body part places it at a high level in relation to the rest of your body.

🅣 This time, when you stop, stop with your body at a middle level. Remember, a low level means below your knees, a middle level is from about your knees to your shoulders, and a high level is above your shoulders.

Traveling with Body Parts at Different Levels

Setting: Children scattered throughout general space

Tasks/Challenges:

🅣 Travel around general space with as many of your body parts as possible at a low level. Remember, your body parts should always be at a low level when you're traveling, not just when you freeze. Be sure and look for open space as you travel. Even at a low level, you should be able to maintain your self-space when traveling in general space.

🅣 As you travel this time, try to have as many body parts as possible at a middle level. Remember, it isn't possible to have all body parts at a middle level as you travel because your feet always have to be on the floor, but have as many parts as possible at a middle level and none at a high level.

🅣 This time as you travel, have as many parts as possible at a high level. This activity is harder than the other two, so be very careful that all possible body parts are at a high level.

❓ Show me hands at high level, middle level, low level.

Young children enjoy exploring body parts at different levels in self-space (e.g., feet, elbows, and nose, as well as combinations of levels, such as one foot low, one foot high).

Rising and Sinking to Create Different Levels

Setting: Children scattered throughout general space

Tasks/Challenges:

🅣 Find a space by yourself, and get into a low position you like. I'm going to beat the drum very slowly eight times. As I beat the drum, rise very slowly to the eight beats until you attain a position of stillness with as many body parts as possible at a high level. Remember, rise slowly. But also remember you have only eight beats in which to get to a high level, so judge your movement so you get there in time. After you've reached your high position, on the next eight beats slowly sink back to your low position. The sequence then goes like this: a low position; eight beats to get to a high, still position; eight beats to return to your low position. Let's try it.

Traveling While Rising and Sinking

Setting: Children scattered throughout general space

Tasks/Challenges:

🅣 As you travel around the space this time, I'll give you drumbeats to guide your actions. The drumbeats will be in counts of four, with the accent on the first beat. Start by traveling at a middle level. On the accented first beat, quickly jump and stretch into a high level and then immediately return to a middle level of travel until the next accented beat. Your movement should look like this: travel middle, jump high, travel middle, jump high, travel middle, and so on. Make your jump very clear and as high as possible and your travel at a middle level very clear. I should be able to easily tell the difference between the two levels.

Developing the Concept of Pathways

A pathway is an imaginary design that the body or its parts creates when moving through space along the floor or through the air. A pathway is also the trail of an object (a ball or hockey puck) as it travels from one player to another or toward a goal.

At first, young children may have difficulty understanding the concept of pathways in space. However, a class of young children can become enthralled with the process of discovering and experimenting with the many pathways the body can travel. A teacher can plan experiences that enable youngsters to recognize pathways and to effectively use knowledge of pathways to improve control of travel. For instance, even very young children can come to understand that a curved or zigzag pathway is effective for avoiding collisions when traveling through a crowd.

Teaching the Concept of Pathways

Children learn to travel in straight, zigzag, and curved pathways, and in combinations of these pathways, by experiencing the activities in this section. More difficult learning experiences involve manipulating various objects in pathways and traveling in relation to others along various pathways.

Learning Experiences Leading to Movement Concept Understanding

Exploring Pathways

Setting: Markings drawn on the board similar to those shown in Figure 14.2; one beaded or cloth rope per child; children scattered throughout general space

Tasks/Challenges:

- **T** Today you're going to learn about pathways. A line that doesn't turn or twist and is always straight is called a *straight pathway*. A line that circles around is called a curved pathway. A semicircle is a *curved pathway*. A line that looks like a lot of Zs put together is a *zigzag pathway*. Now find a space and

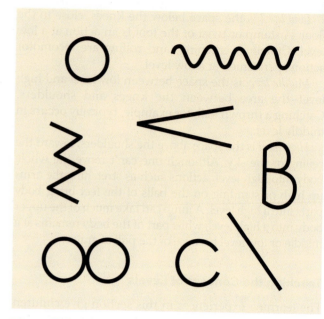

Figure 14.2 Pathways drawn on the board

using your jump rope make the pathway that I draw on the board (see Figure 14.2 for examples). Travel the pathway walking next to your rope; be able to tell me what kind of pathway it is when I ask you.

- **T** This time as you travel, change your direction, sometimes going forward beside your rope pathway, sometimes sideways, and sometimes backward. Try out all directions on your pathway.

- **T** Now change the way that you travel along your pathway. Sometimes you may want to hop, sometimes slide sideways, sometimes crawl. Find at least four different ways you can travel along your pathway.

- **C** Now we are going to travel pathways without the ropes. When I call out a pathway, travel the pathway pretending there is paint on your feet that marks the pathway on the floor. Let's start with walking a straight pathway; try walking backward in a straight pathway. Skip or gallop in a curved pathway. Pretend you are a bird and extend your arms as you glide in curved pathways. Finally, slide sideways, leaving your footprints in a zigzag pathway.

Using Pathway Maps

Setting: A card, similar to the ones shown in Figure 14.3, for each child

Figure 14.3 Pathway cards.

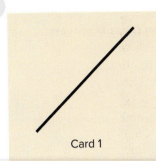

Card 1

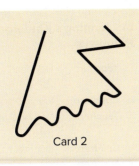

Card 2

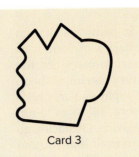

Card 3

Figure 14.3 Pathway cards.

Tasks/Challenges:

T Take a card and find a space by yourself. Travel on your feet and follow the pathway indicated on your card. Pretend your card is a map showing the route to take to get to a new place. Keep practicing your pathway until you're very sure it's just like the one on the card and you can do it the best you can. Be able to tell me the name of the pathway you're following whenever I ask you.

T Now trade cards with someone else and practice that pathway until you think it's perfect.

C In a group of three or four, you are going on a pathway expedition. The first person will draw a pathway card from the card pile. Return to your group and lead them on this expedition. When you get to your final destination, pass the card to the person behind you. That person will trade the card for a new one and lead the group on the next expedition. As the leader, you can decide the locomotor skill you want to use, or you can be creative and pretend you are going through mud or going up a steep mountain. When you are the leader, be creative but always be able to tell me the pathway.

Designing Pathways

Setting: Children scattered throughout general space

Tasks/Challenges:

T Pick a spot on the wall across the room from you. Remember where your spot is, and in your mind, plan a pathway that will take you from where you are now to that spot. Think about it a long time so you can remember it when you start to move. When I give the signal, travel along your made-up pathway until you get to the spot you've picked out. Stop when you get there. On the next signal, travel back to the place you started from, following the same pathway you took coming over. This is similar to following a path through the woods: You can't go off the path or you'll get lost.

T Now I am *not* going to give you the signal anymore. Practice your pathway on your own until you have memorized it and can repeat it exactly every time.

? *Student Drawing.* Asking children to draw the various pathways and label them would be an easy way to assess their understanding.

Creating Follow-the-Leader Pathways

Setting: Sets of partners scattered throughout general space

Tasks/Challenges:

T Find a partner and stand in a space together. I'll know that you're ready when I see each of you standing quietly in your space. Decide which of you is going to be the leader. On the signal, the leader travels a pathway to somewhere else in the room and stops. The follower then moves along the same pathway the leader took until the follower catches up with the leader. The leader and follower switch places. The secret is for the follower to watch the leader very closely. In the beginning, the leader should not make up difficult pathways. Followers, remember to copy the leaders' pathways exactly.

? Have each child create a pathway sequence using one straight, one curved, and one zigzag pathway in any order they choose. After they create their pathway sequences, they will draw them on paper, creating their unique design. After the child creates, practices, and memorizes the pathway sequence, a peer can watch for correct execution and order, thus assessing understanding of pathways.

Traveling Pathways and Obstacles

Setting: Half the class positioned throughout general space, the other half around the perimeter of the space

Tasks/Challenges:

T Now you're going to travel in pathways that go around, over, and under obstacles in your way. Always remember that your classmates are the obstacles, so you have to be very careful of them. You can't touch anyone else. People who are obstacles must remember to stay very still so as to not interfere with anyone who's moving. Obstacles, go find a position in a space by yourself that you can hold still. It can be any position you like—a bridge, a statue, or a balance. Just remember you must be able to hold still. Those of you on the side of the space, pick a point on the other side of the room and plan a pathway to get there. Remember, your pathway can go over, under, or around any of the obstacles. Think about it and really make it different from anything you've done before.

Give the children a few seconds to plan their pathway and the obstacles time to select their position.

On the signal, follow your pathway to the point you picked on the other side of the room. Stop when you get to the point you picked. On the next signal, try to retrace your pathway until you get back to your starting position.

Obstacles and travelers change roles and repeat.

C Each of you will now create a pathway sequence. Find a starting point and make a beginning pose at a high, middle, or low level. Create a sequence that includes all of the pathways as you travel around, over, and under the obstacles. You may travel using any locomotor skills (hop, gallop, skip, etc.) and directions (forward, backward, sideway, clockwise, counterclockwise, up and down). End your sequence by freezing in a different level than your start. Retrace your pathway back to the start. Practice your pathway sequence until you hear the signal to stop. Remember, avoid running into other travelers as you cross the space. Always have a clear beginning and ending to your pathway sequence.

When all have completed their pathway sequences, have the students switch places and perform their sequence.

? *You can enhance this challenge by asking children who are the obstacles to observe one person and do a peer assessment. The criteria may simply be to observe for all three pathways.*

Following-the-Dots Pathways

Setting: A pencil plus a card with dots randomly plotted on it for each child; spots on the floor in a pattern similar to that of the dots on the card

Mr. Jenning's Kindergarten Class Discovers Pathways

Teacher:	Boys and girls! How did we get to the physical education space today?
Children:	We walked!
Teacher:	Yes! And what parts of our bodies did we use?
Children:	Our feet . . . our legs.
Teacher:	You got it! Tell me, did we leave a trail behind us? Any footprints on the floor?
Children:	No! (*Loud and laughing*)
Teacher:	I don't see any either. But what if your shoes were muddy. Would we have left a trail?
Children:	Yes! But Mrs. Farmer (*the principal*) sure would be mad!
Teacher:	I think she would be, too! But if we did leave muddy footprints from your classroom all the way to the physical education space, what would our path look like?
Children:	Long . . . Messy . . . we go by the library.
Teacher:	I think you're all right. I have an idea. . . . Let's look at the whiteboard. Here's your room way over here, and this is where the physical education space is. Look at our pathway. Although we didn't leave any real footprints, we did follow a path. We follow this same pathway each time we come to the physical education space. Tell me, is our path just one straight line, or did we make any turns?
Children:	We turned when we came out of the room. At the library.
Teacher:	You are sharp today. Can you think of any other pathways you follow each day?
Children:	We go to lunch . . . walk to school . . . down to the playground.
Teacher:	We follow a lot of pathways each day. Let's see if we can have some fun with pathways today. Pick a spot somewhere on the outside edge of the room (for example, a brick, a picture), and when I say "Go," stand up and walk in a straight line to your spot and freeze. Here we go!

Tasks/Challenges:

T Connect the dots on your card to form any design you like. After you've finished connecting the dots, follow the path you drew from one spot to the other. Make sure you know the type of pathway you've designed because I might ask you.

T Now trade maps with someone else. Follow that person's map. Decide if that pathway is different from yours and if so, how is it different?

Combining Pathways, Levels, and Directions

Setting: A task sheet, similar to that in Figure 14.4, for each child

Tasks/Challenges:

C This activity lets you combine pathways, levels, and directions. It's also a good way to test yourself. When you're finished, I'll come and check you out. You may use a friend to help you if you want extra help.

? *Self-Assessment.* The task sheet in Figure 14.4 would make an excellent self-assessment.

Name _____ Teacher _____			
Pathways, Levels, and Directions Task Sheet			
Challenge	I am good	I need more practice	Please watch me
I can travel forward in a straight pathway.			
I can travel backward in a straight pathway.			
I can travel sideways in a straight pathway.			
I can travel forward in a curved pathway.			
I can travel backward in a curved pathway.			
I can travel forward in a zigzag pathway.			
I can travel sideways in a zigzag pathway.			
I can travel forward at a low level and in a curved pathway.			
I can travel backward at a high level and in a straight pathway.			
I can travel sideways at a middle level and in a zigzag pathway.			
I can travel backward at a middle level and a curved pathway.			
I can travel*			
I can travel			
I can travel			
* Make up three more ways you can travel and add them above.			

Figure 14.4 Task sheet for pathways, levels, and directions.

Developing the Concept of Extensions in Space

Extensions in space are best understood as two separate possibilities. First, extensions are spatial relationships of body parts to the entire body. Body extremities can be held in close to the body, as in a curl, or they can be opened up, as in a stretch. Extensions are also the size of movements in space. Movements with extremities held close to the body are *small movements*, such as putting a golf ball; those with the extremities extended or opened up are *large movements*, such as driving a golf ball.

Teaching the Concept of Extensions in Space

The concept of extensions is taught through learning experiences that give children a functional understanding of the differences between large and small, as well as near and far, extensions (movements).

Learning Experiences Leading to Movement Concept Understanding

Exploring Extensions

Setting: Children scattered throughout general space

Tasks/Challenges:

🅣 Find a space by yourself. With your hands, explore all the space close to your body. Remember to not reach very far from your body; this is an extension near your body. We call it a *near* extension.

🅣 Now, without leaving your self-space, explore all the space that is far away from your body. Try to reach as far as you can without leaving your space. Remember, explore above and behind as well as in front of you. This is called an extension that is far away from your body. We call it a *far* extension.

Traveling and Extensions

Setting: Children scattered throughout general space

Tasks/Challenges:

🅣 Travel around the room. When you hear the drumbeat, stop in a position where your body reaches as far into space as possible. Be very sure that all possible body parts are as far away from the center of your body as you can get them.

🅣 This time as you travel, when you hear the drumbeat, stop with all body parts as close to your body

as possible. Remember, keep all your body parts as close to yourself as you can.

🅣 Now try traveling with change. When you hear the drumbeat, jump high into the air, extending your arms and legs as far away from your body as possible. When you land, hold a position very still, with all body parts very close to the center of your body. Really try to make a clear difference between the far and near extensions.

Changing from One Extension to Another

Setting: Children scattered throughout general space

Tasks/Challenges:

🅣 Find a space by yourself, and get into a tight position you like. I'll beat the drum six times, in slow beats. On the first six beats, gradually extend all body parts far away from your body. On the next six beats, slowly move to your tight, curled position. The movement then goes like this: first a tight, curled position; on six beats, slowly move to a spread-out position; on the next six beats, slowly move back to a near extension. Try to make your extensions very clear. We'll practice this task a number of times so you can work on doing your best.

Using Extensions and Imagery

Setting: Children scattered throughout general space

Tasks/Challenges:

🅣 As you travel around general space, pretend you're carrying an object you don't want anyone to see or that you're trying to hide or protect something, such as a baby bird, a million-dollar jewel, or a lot of money. As you walk, think very carefully about how you would actually carry the object you've chosen.

🅣 Now, instead of having an object you want to hide, you have one you're proud of and want to show off—maybe a trophy you just won. How would you carry it? Go!

🅣 In your own space, pretend you are passing a soccer ball to someone right next to you. Now, you are the goalie and need to punt the ball far down the field.

❓ In which activity did you use a near or small extension? In which activity did you use a large or far extension?

To create this group balance, these youngsters need to understand personal space, extensions, and levels.

©Barbara Adamcik

Applying the Space Awareness Concepts

Location (self-space and general space) is often the appropriate beginning concept for children who have had little experience in formal physical education classes. One of the important skills children need to develop early is the ability to occupy an area or to travel in an area while maintaining awareness of others. An understanding of self-space and general space is helpful when learning these skills.

The concepts of directions, levels, and pathways are usually introduced after children have developed the ability to differentiate self-space from general space. Until the children actually acquire a functional understanding of directions, levels, and pathways, the observational focus is primarily on the concept rather than on correct performance of a particular skill. For example, if you ask the children to throw so that the ball starts off at a high level, you're less interested in the actual mechanics of throwing than in the child's ability to release the ball at a high level. Once you're confident that the children are able to apply the concepts, you can focus more on appropriate skill technique.

Most children take a longer time to grasp right and left, air pathways, and extensions. Thus, it's wise to introduce the other concepts and components to children before focusing on these.

The ability to understand the notion of right and left is related to cognitive maturation. Some children will need more time and more practice opportunities than others to master left and right. Many children easily acquire cognitive understanding of the concepts of extensions and air pathways for objects, but most require a certain degree of skill before they can express these ideas in movements. Children with immature throwing and kicking patterns, for example, have difficulty propelling objects so they travel in different (but intended) air pathways. Children with immature striking or catching patterns are unable to consistently catch or strike an object far from or near to the body.

There's no universally successful sequence for introducing these concepts and their components. The reflective teacher uses all available information and makes judgments about the most appropriate time, sequence, and duration for introducing and studying the concepts of space awareness and the application of the concepts to specific skill-practice situations.

Reading Comprehension Questions

1. What is the primary reason for focusing on space awareness at the beginning of a physical education program?
2. What does the term *space awareness* mean? What are the characteristics of someone who is "aware of space"?
3. Why is space awareness so important for children at the precontrol and control levels?
4. Why is an understanding of open spaces important for utilization and proficiency movers?
5. What directions in space are studied in this program? Why do children find some directions more difficult than others to understand?
6. Distinguish the three levels of space from each other.

7. List the three types of pathways an individual might travel. Give an example of when each is used.

8. Give two examples of a far extension and two examples of a near extension.

9. Why do we have children study self-space while stationary rather than traveling?

10. What does it look like when children are able to travel safely in general space?

11. Using the movement analysis eWheel (http://www.mhhe.com/graham10e/eWheel), manipulate it to show space awareness in relation to locomotor, manipulative, and nonmanipulative skills. Identify two skills for each category that space awareness can modify, and write a sample task for each.

References/Suggested Readings

Holt/Hale, S., and Hall, T. 2016. *Lesson planning for elementary physical education*. Champaign, IL: Human Kinetics,

[SHAPE America] Society of Health and Physical Educators. 2014. *National standards & grade-level outcomes for K-12 physical education*. Champaign, IL: Human Kinetics.

[SHAPE America] Society of Health and Physical Educators. 2018. *PE metrics: Assessing student performance using the national standards & grade-level outcomes for K-12 physical education*. 3rd ed. Champaign, IL: Human Kinetics.

Effort

Drawn by children at Monfort, Chappelow or Shawsheen ElementarySchools, Greeley, CO.
Courtesy of Lizzy Ginger; Tia Ziegler

This chapter explains and provides multiple learning experiences for the movement concept category of effort. (See Table 3.2 in Chapter 3 for a full listing of the movement concepts taught in elementary school physical education.) Remember, we first provide experiences for children to attain a functional understanding of the movement concepts. When they have this understanding, the concepts are then used to enhance the skill themes—adverbs to enrich action verbs.

Too often teachers make no conscious, planned attempt to help children understand the effort concepts of time, force, and flow and the application of these concepts to specific skills.* Many teachers don't feel comfortable teaching these concepts, which are vague and abstract. It is not like teaching a child to strike a ball with a paddle, in which the objective of striking is obvious and the result easily perceived. Despite many teachers' hesitancy to undertake teaching effort concepts, there is agreement that an applied understanding of these concepts is essential in skill development, from beginning through advanced levels. See Box 15-1 for linkages between the movement concepts of Effort and the *National Standards & Grade-Level Outcomes for K–12 Physical Education* (SHAPE America 2014).

Whereas space awareness defined where the body moves, the effort concepts define how the body moves. The category is divided into three concepts—time, force, and flow—that are defined by observable characteristics that can be taught to children. Figure 15.1 conceptualizes this idea and puts it into perspective with the other movement concepts and skill themes. The effort category is in the shaded portion of the framework. The outside ring identifies the category, the second ring identifies the concepts, and the third ring defines the three components.

We begin to teach effort concepts to children by providing experiences to help them understand the contrasts of fast-slow, strong-light, and bound-free. Once the children have grasped the differences between the extremes, we focus on the concepts as they apply to specific skills (such as throwing, striking, and transferring weight) and in different situations (for example, to assist in the expression of an idea or to accomplish a particular strategy). As children become more skillful, we focus on the degrees among the extremes. To illustrate, initially we might ask children to travel rapidly and slowly. As children develop the ability to differentiate between the extremes, we focus more on the

---

*Some movement analysis frameworks include direct and flexible space as effort qualities of movement. In our teaching, however, we use them so infrequently we've chosen not to include them in the discussion of the qualities of movement.

Box 15-1

Effort in the *National Standards & Grade-Level Outcomes for K–12 Physical Education*

The movement concept of Effort is referenced in the *National Standards & Grade-Level Outcomes for K–12 Physical Education* (SHAPE America 2014) under Standard 2: "Applies knowledge of concepts, principles, strategies and tactics related to movement and performance." The intent of the standard is facilitation of learners' ability to use cognitive information to understand and enhance motor skill acquisition and performance. At the lower-elementary level, emphasis is placed on establishing a movement vocabulary and demonstrating a basic understanding of the concepts. At the upper-elementary level, emphasis is placed on applying the concepts in dance, educational gymnastics, and game environments.

Sample grade-level outcomes from the *National Standards** include:

- Differentiates between fast and slow speeds (1)
- Differentiates between strong and light force (1)
- Varies time and force with gradual increases and decreases (2)
- Applies the movement concepts of speed, endurance, and pacing for running (4)
- Applies the concepts of direction and force when striking an object with a short-handled implement sending it toward a designated target (4)
- Analyzes movement situations and applies movement concepts (force, speed) in small-sided practice tasks in game environments, dance, and gymnastics (5)

*Suggested grade-level outcomes for student learning.

---

movement possibilities that occur between the extremes—faster, slower, accelerating, decelerating, sudden changes of speed. Highly skilled (proficiency level) movers have developed an internalized, reflexive knowledge of the proper amount and degree of time, force, and flow. They're able to adjust the quality of movements in relation to the demands of a situation—harder or softer, faster or slower, bound or free.

Many learning experiences in this chapter use imagery to help children distinguish among different concepts of effort. It's important to keep in mind that the focus is on the movement qualities of the various images rather than on the images themselves. For example, when we say, "Move like a hippo," we're not asking the children to pretend to be hippos; we're using this task to help the children envision a slow,

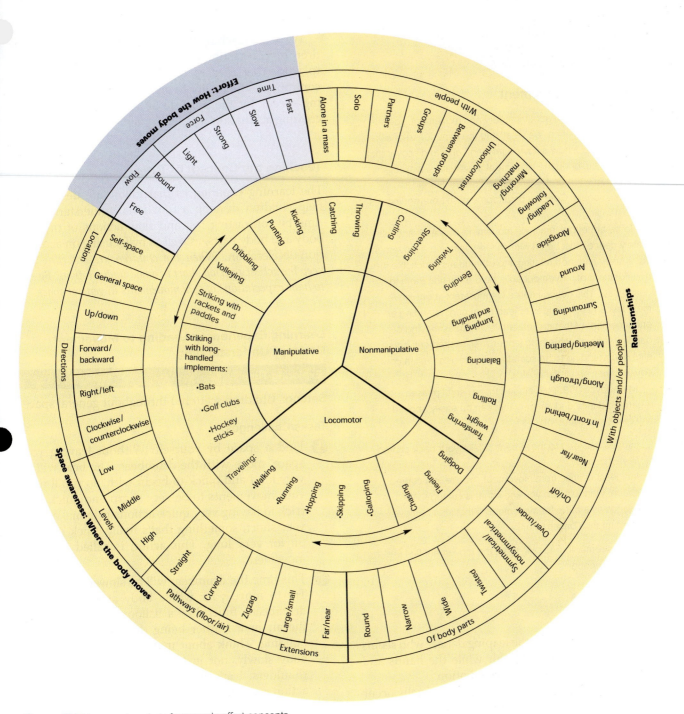

Figure 15.1 Movement analysis framework: effort concepts.

lumbering movement. Box 15-2 and Chapter 29 contain additional information about the appropriate use of imagery in teaching movement.

Developing the Concept of Time

Time to a young child is the tick-tock of a grandfather clock, the cuckoo clock on the wall, or the numbers racing by on a digital timepiece. When spoken of in relation to movement, time is fast—being able to run like the wind; being the fastest in the class; zip, dash, zoom.

In physical education, speed is often the measure of success; therefore, children often have difficulty comprehending slowness and seeing the importance of this rate of movement in their actions. Yet the performer executing a walkover on the balance beam grasps the

Box 15-2

Imagery and Movement

Much has been said about imagery and movement, specifically related to dance. We've all had the experience of asking children to "show a flower growing," only to discover that instead of exploring the movement possibilities available, the children were pretending to be flowers. Herein lies the pitfall of imagery: Concept development isn't pretending; it's understanding.

To be beneficial, teaching movement concepts and ultimately dance must begin with children learning a movement vocabulary and then relating it to other ideas (much like the development of movement skills before relating them to game play). This notion implies we must talk about movement first and use images to lead to an understanding or enhancement of that movement. It precludes moving or dancing "about" something (anger, fear, excitement, horses, etc.) or pretending to be something (a piece of fruit, a cowboy, a flower, an airplane, etc.).

Mary Joyce (1993) developed three useful phases regarding dance and imagery that can be easily applied to any creative movement:

1. Images that lead to movement: "Make your back curved like a banana."
2. Images that arise from movement: "You're in a curved shape. What else do you know that is curved?"
3. Images as a basis for movement: "What kind of movement might a banana do?"

Always remember to talk about the movement first and the image second.

We begin teaching the concept of time to young children by contrasting extremes. Gradually we advance to work that focuses on degrees of speed along a continuum—the ability to execute movements at varying speeds for the purpose of adapting, changing, or creating a situation.

Teaching the Concept of Time

The learning experiences that follow are designed to help children develop a functional understanding of time by contrasting fast and slow actions of the total body and body parts, as well as by focusing on acceleration-deceleration. *When the children are traveling fast, keep the activity period short to avoid undue fatigue. Be sure to have expectations of safe movements in general space.*

Learning Experiences Leading to Movement Concept Understanding

Exploring Time

Setting: Children scattered throughout general space

Tasks/Challenges:

Ⓣ Find a space by yourself. Without leaving your space, move with the drumbeat. The beat will be very loud and quick to begin with, so you'll want your movements to be very sharp and quick. The trick to having very quick actions is to make them very short; something that's really quick can't go on for very long. This action is called a *sudden* movement.

Ⓣ This time the drumbeat will be slower and longer. Try to move your whole body as slowly as the drumbeats, much like a balloon floating through the air or a feather being dropped from a high building. Think about moving every part of your body slowly, not just your arms but your head, shoulders, back, stomach, legs, everything. This action is called a *sustained* movement.

Using Different Speeds in Self-Space

Setting: Children scattered throughout general space

Tasks/Challenges:

Ⓣ In a space by yourself, bring your hands together very slowly, as if to catch an insect that might try to fly away. At the very last moment before your hands are going to touch, quickly separate them as if you're surprised to find out that the insect is a bee. When you do your slow movements, remember to

idea of slowness, as does the leaping dancer who seems to remain suspended in the air while the hands and arms express a certain feeling or emotion.

Changes in the timing of a movement usually occur without forethought as children adapt to different situations—speeding up or slowing down to maintain possession, to avoid being tagged, to get in open space and receive a pass. Many movements and specific skills dictate the rate of movement. A handspring is done quickly, but a back walkover is performed slowly. In some movements, the child is free to assess a situation and then perform a skill at the best rate. For example, a movement executed quickly in dance or gymnastics elicits feelings of power and speed; the same movement executed slowly expresses the ultimate in control.

These young children are enjoying the sensation of running—a fast movement.

©Barbara Adamcik

make them very slow but to always keep your hands moving; make your quick movements so quick that they're like flashes of lightning.

T Let's try those movements five more times. You can bring your hands together any way you want as long as you do so slowly, and then quickly take them away any way you want. Remember, make your slow and quick movements as clear as they can be. Five times. Go.

T Now, on your own, find other body parts you can bring together slowly and then quickly pull apart. Try to find at least three combinations. Practice each movement so the difference between fast and slow is very clear.

This activity is more difficult than it sounds because it asks for extremes of a movement. You can have children practice this activity over and over; always ask for faster and slower actions than the children previously exhibited.

Moving at Different Speeds

Setting: Children scattered throughout general space

Tasks/Challenges:

T On the signal, move as fast as you can, but remain in self-space; on the next signal, freeze in a balanced position that you can hold very still. Remember, try to go as fast as you can, but you must be able to stop on the signal without falling over.

©Lars A. Niki

Slowness is necessary for travel at low level.

Ⓣ Now, on the start signal, move as slowly as you can in self-space. Try to move very slowly, but always keep moving. On the stop signal, freeze in a balanced position. Remember, stay in your self-space.

Ⓣ Your first movement was at a fast speed; your second, at a slow speed. Could you tell the difference? Again, you're going to practice both fast and slow speeds. Try to make the movements very clear so I can really tell the difference between them. As you move, I'll call out "Fast" or "Slow," and you change your speed accordingly. If I call out "Slow," move very slowly, and if I call out "Fast," move fast. Listen very carefully because I might try to trick you. Make your fast really fast and your slow really slow.

Once the children demonstrate an understanding of speed in self-space, you can transfer these same tasks to traveling in general space.

Traveling and Freezing by Using Changes in Time

Setting: Children scattered throughout general space

Tasks/Challenges:

Ⓣ This time, begin your traveling with a quick explosion of speed, and keep going at a fast speed; then freeze very quickly in a balanced position. The movement should be like this: Begin really fast as if you've been shot out of a cannon; then move fast as if you're running from someone; then freeze quickly as if someone has surprised you and you can't move. Make each segment of your traveling very clear so that I can tell when you change from one part to the other. I'll give you the start signal; then you're on your own.

Ⓣ Now that you've practiced sudden starts, traveling fast, and then freezing, you're going to make up a sequence using those speeds. Choose one sudden-start, fast-travel, and freeze position you really like, and practice it until you can do it smoothly and with control. Each of the three parts should be very clear and very different from one another. After you think the sequence is really good, practice it three more times. Remember, start and end in the same place each time. Your three movements should look the same every time, as if they had been recorded.

Ⓣ Now begin very slowly, as a car does on a cold morning. As you warm up, gradually increase your speed until you're moving fast. Then freeze suddenly. The sequence should look like this: a slow

start, a gradual increase to fast speed, then a freeze. This is different from your last traveling action, so make that difference very clear.

Ⓒ Now make up a sequence that includes a slow start that gradually increases to a fast speed and suddenly freezes. Practice the sequence until you're ready to show someone else, who, after seeing it, should be able to tell you what the three parts were.

Children often equate slowness with heavy, jerky, stiff actions rather than with graceful movement. Examples of animals with slow, graceful movements can be useful here. Box 15-3 also contains hints for helping children learn to design movement sequences.

Box 15-3

Designing Sequences

Following are several tips we've found helpful when beginning to have children design sequences.

- It takes time.
- Structure the sequence into a simple form that is easily remembered—for example, a starting shape, a middle moving phase based on a specific aspect of movement, an ending shape.
- Practice the starting and ending shapes separately before adding the middle movement.
- Initially, provide a beginning signal, some time to practice (20–25 seconds), and then an ending signal.
- During the first stages, prompt the children during the movement aspect about exactly what movements need to be included (change of level, speed, etc.).
- Have children repeat their sequence several times. The middle movement aspect may vary slightly each time, but the beginning and end should remain constant.
- Hold the children accountable for what they've created—for example, divide the class in half and have them present their sequence to their half; present their sequence to another person; or write it down.

As the children's ability to design sequences increases, you can gradually relax some of these guidelines, but we've found these steps useful for both the students and the teacher when children first begin to create movement sequences.

Source: Adapted from Mary Joyce, *First steps in teaching creative dance to children,* 3rd ed. (Palo Alto, CA: Mayfield, 1993).

Combining Imagery and Time

Setting: Children scattered throughout general space

Tasks/Challenges:

T This time you're going to practice traveling the way different things move—fast or slow. Remember, you aren't really trying to act like the things you're pretending to be; you're just trying to move at the speed they move. Let's practice one movement. On the signal, move as a turtle would move. Think carefully about it—a turtle moves very slowly. Now try moving as fast as a rabbit. Go really quickly.

T How does a well-tuned race car move? Let's try to go as fast as a race car can. There's only one thing different about this race car: It goes so fast it can't make any noise. Go as fast as a silent race car. Change your race car to an old junky car trying to go uphill; the car is really tired and old, so remember that it goes very slowly.

Some classes enjoy and can accept the responsibility for making the sounds of race cars and noisy old cars. Use your judgment about whether to encourage the sounds, which can be either productive or detrimental, depending on the circumstances.

T Now pretend the carnival is in town and you're going to go with your friends tonight to ride all the rides and eat all your favorite foods. How excited are you? Really let your excitement show as you go home from school. Try it. Now, instead of going to the carnival, you're going home, and you know you'll be in trouble because your mom told you not to take anymore cookies from the cookie jar, and you got caught taking the last two.

T You're the fastest sprinter in the Olympics and you're in the starting blocks waiting for the gun to go off. Go. Now you're a distance runner just about to start a 10-mile race; you have a long way to go, and you don't want to wear yourself out.

T You're a mouse running from a cat. Now you're a hippopotamus with a full stomach trying to move.

? *Show me fast movement with your fingers. Show me slow movement with your fingers. Show me slow jogging, fast running.*

Differentiating Among Time Words

Setting: Children scattered throughout general space

Tasks/Challenges:

T Show me the differences between the words *dash, waddle, dart,* and *crawl.* First, dash. Go. Now, waddle. Go. Now, dart. Go. Next, crawl. Remember, change speeds with each word so the speeds are very clear.

T Let's try them again. Listen very carefully because I'm going to start calling them out faster, and you'll have to change quickly from one to the other.

Other pairs of words can be used to elicit changes in time: creep/explode, pop/sneak, gallop/totter, slither/stride. See Box 15-4 for additional action words that can be used in teaching the various effort concepts.

Combining Sport Skills and Time

Setting: Children scattered throughout general space

Tasks/Challenges:

T Before beginning, I want you to think of your favorite sports person. Be sure you can tell me who it is when I ask because this is important. After you decide who your favorite person is, choose one action she or he performs that you really like. For example, if you choose a famous football quarterback, you might pick "throwing the bomb" as your favorite action. Think carefully to pick your person and action.

T Now, on the signal, you'll perform the action you chose as if it were on video set at a fast speed—in a fast motion instead of slow motion. Repeat your fast-motion action four times, each time making the motion faster.

T Now do the same action as if it were in slow motion, just like instant replays. Make sure there's a clear difference between your fast and slow motions. I should be able to tell just from watching which motions are fast and which ones are slow.

T Repeat the same action in the speed someone would see you performing it. We will call this regular speed.

C Now choose a different sport action from the one you previously performed. Practice that action in regular, fast, and slow motion. Demonstrate your sport skill in the three speeds for a partner to observe. Your partner should be able to name the sport and the order of the speeds in which you performed the skill. Your partner should give you a thumbs up if you were able to correctly demonstrate the three speeds in your performance.

Continually Changing in Time While Traveling

Setting: Children scattered throughout general space

Tasks/Challenges:

T As you're standing in your self-space, pick a point across the room you want to focus on. All the traveling you do will be directed toward that point.

Box 15-4

Action Words

When you're teaching the effort concepts, action words help elicit many of the responses desired. For the exercise to be productive as well as exciting, students need to have more than a few common words repeated over and over. Here are some possibilities.

Single Action Words

Traveling Actions

Run	Hop	Creep
Dash	Skate	Sneak
Dart	Jump	Slither
Skip	Bounce	Crawl
Gallop	Slide	Step
Stamp	Kick	Stride
Whirl	Spin	Shuffle
Waddle	Totter	

Nontraveling Actions

Flick	Squeeze	Contract	Dangle
Jerk	Compress	Fold	Jab
Twitch	Explode	Splatter	Slash
Writhe	Spread	Punch	Chop
Stab	Tense	Pull	Saw
Grip	Relax	Press	Drip
Release	Push	Lower	Drag

Stopping Actions

Pause	Collapse
Stop	Slide
Freeze	Flop
Anchor	Crumble

Sinking Actions

Melt	Spin	Screw
Flop	Turn	Hammer
Drop	Slink	Spread
Collapse	Squash	Deflate
Pounce	Shrink	Crumple

Rising Actions

Evaporate	Spin	Swell
Float	Pop	Inflate
Rise	Grow	Lift
Turn	Blossom	Gyrate

Vibratory Actions

Shake	Wriggle
Rattle	Squirm
Vibrate	Snake
Whisk	
Tumble	

Sentences of Action Words

Run—freeze—skip	Slither—inflate—explode	Rise (turn)—twitch—skip
Dart—collapse—pop	Squeeze—jump—release	Gallop—stamp—screw
Grow—spin—deflate	Creep—pounce—explode	Jump—freeze—jab
Writhe—jerk—pop	Skip—pause—flop	Chop—whirl—slash

Descriptive Words (for use with action words)

Droopy	Excited	Light	Springy	Spikey	Square
Tired	Heavy	Tense	Carefree	Sharp	Angular
Happy	Strong	Floppy	Carefully	Rounded	Curvy
Greedy	Loving	Gentle	Fierce	Soft	Hard
Prickly	Spongy	Big	Small	Enormous	Tiny
Bubbling	Nervous	Unsure	Confident	Bold	Afraid

Nonsense Words

Snickersnack	Spelunk	Krinkle	Blump
Gallumph	Brip	Siczac	Crickcrock
Cavort	Bruttle-brattle	Swoosh	Snap-crackle
Flip-flop	Achoo	Kerumph	Wheezey
Grunch	Hic-up	Squizzog	

Source: David Docherty, *Education through the dance experience* (Bellingham, WA: Educational Designs and Consultants, 1975). Used with permission from the author.

On the signal, slowly begin to travel around the point you've chosen, much like a lion stalking its prey. Gradually increase your speed so you're traveling at your maximum speed. Just before you reach the spot you've chosen, slow down, slowly circle, and then suddenly pounce. The differences in the speeds at which you travel should be very clear. Thus, your sequence should go like this: Pick a point to focus on, start slowly circling toward that point, gradually pick up speed until you're going really fast, then gradually slow down and suddenly pounce toward your spot.

C Now that you have the idea, pick a new spot and practice your circling routine five times so it's very good. Try to make it the best you can because we're going to show some of them to the class. Slow should be really slow, fast really fast, and the pounce as quick as lightning.

To help clarify this activity, choose three or four children who are successfully completing it to demonstrate (they can all demonstrate at the same time). Reinforce the notions of gradually increasing speed and the sudden contrast of the pounce.

T Now we are going to learn two new words: accelerate and decelerate. What do you think they mean? If you said speed up and slow down, you are right! Standing in self-space, pretend you are now old enough to drive. Start by backing slowly out of your driveway or parking place at home. Travel slowly as you leave your neighborhood. Increase your speed when you turn onto a main road. You are coming up on the interstate. As you merge with traffic, accelerate into a fast speed. Coming off the interstate, you will decelerate just a little to return to a main road. Slow down even more as you return to your neighborhood, and finally, decelerate as you park the car. You are going to be a great driver!

Developing the Concept of Force

Force is the contrast of muscular tensions. The extremes are strong and light, but there are obvious degrees between the extremes. Just as *speed* to a young child is "as fast as you can go," *force* often means trying to bat a ball as hard as possible, whether the situation calls for a bunt or an outfield placement. A preschooler is likely to use the same degree of force to throw a ball 3 feet as to throw it 10 yards.

We usually introduce the concept of force by combining it with a skill that has been developed to the control level, preferably to the utilization level. For example, think of the child at a precontrol level who is learning to strike a moving ball. The youngster is so fully concentrating attention on making contact with the ball that the concept of force is an unnecessary and probably confusing thought. Hard and easy hits can come later, once the child is able to hit a ball consistently.

After children have a functional understanding of force, it is then studied in combination with skills. The application of force for throwing and kicking leads to a mature pattern of the skill; the ability to throw, strike, and kick purposely with strong or light force is practiced in combination with the skills at the control and utilization levels.

A dancer exemplifies the qualities of strong and light movement while expressing aggression, strength, and power; the gymnast exemplifies the qualities in floor and apparatus routines while combining firm and fine actions and balancing in a demonstration of muscular control and strength.

©Lars A. Niki

Young children's attempts at strong shapes show a beginning understanding of the concept of force.

Teaching the Concept of Force

This section provides suggestions for helping children to understand the concept of force. The learning experiences presented help youngsters develop a functional understanding of the strong (firm) and light (fine) actions of body parts and of the entire body. *Actions of concentrated movement and muscular tensions are very tiring; keep the activity periods short.*

Learning Experiences Leading to Movement Concept Understanding

Exploring Force

Setting: Children scattered throughout general space

Tasks/Challenges:

T In your own space, with your whole body, make a statue that shows how strong you are. (A strong force is also called "heavy" or "firm.") Now practice the activity again, but think about making every muscle in your body strong, even your head, neck, stomach, back, hands, and feet.

T Now make a statue that is very light, such as a ghost would be. Your statue should be so light it would blow away if a strong wind came along. This is called a light force. Try a light shape again, such as a leaf floating through the wind.

T When I beat the drum, change from a strong to a light statue and then back.

Traveling and Changing Force Qualities

Setting: Children scattered throughout general space

Tasks/Challenges:

T This time you're going to travel around the whole space. But as you travel, try to be as strong as you can be. You're an indestructible and all-powerful force; make all your body parts strong.

T Now, as you travel, make yourself as light as can be, just as if you were floating away. All your muscles should be loose, not tight at all; make your entire body light.

Using Imagery and Force

Setting: Children scattered throughout general space

Tasks/Challenges:

T This time you're going to use different images you know to help you understand the force qualities. On the signal, think of yourself as a stick of butter left out on a hot day. All day long you sit in the hot sun, all weak and melted. Then suddenly someone puts you in the refrigerator, and in a little while you feel strong and solid again. Remember, make it clear with your whole body what it's like to be weak, and then make it clear with your whole body when you're strong again.

The imagery sequences you design provide experiences in extreme contrasts. Focus on the degrees along the continuum (the subtle changes) in conjunction with the actual skill, such as jumping and landing or balancing.

? ***Exit Slip.*** This is an appropriate time to use an exit slip to check students' understanding of the concept of force.

Showing Contrasts of Force

Setting: Children scattered throughout general space

Tasks/Challenges:

T Now you're going to show the force differences in your movements. On the signal I'll call out an idea; you show me what the idea looks like by moving either strong or light. Make it very clear which you are: strong or light.

Young children often equate the concept of strong force with the concept of size. Be careful not to pair all imagery examples as such—big-firm or small-fine. Ideas:

1. ***Frosty the Snowman.*** You're going to show the life of Frosty the Snowman. First, you're a single snowflake falling through the air; then you're several snowflakes that are beginning to stick together to make a shape; now you're the solid, sturdy snowman that can't be knocked over; and finally, you're the snowman melting slowly as the sun comes out.

2. ***Punch/flick.*** Now we're going to use words to help us tell the difference between strong and light movements. The first two words are *punch* and *flick*. I'll give you a story, and you make the movements that go with it. One movement should be strong, the other light. Make each movement very clear. Pretending that you're a boxer, punch your opponent as hard as you can. Now, just flick a fly off your mother's freshly baked chocolate cake.

3. ***Creep/pounce.*** The words *creep* and *pounce* can help us learn strong and light movements. Let's try it. You're playing hide-and-seek; creep very quietly from your hiding place so no one will see or hear you. Now, you're creeping up to catch your runaway kitten. You've found her and are

ready to pounce and grab her before she runs away again. Ready, pounce. Oops, you missed.

? Which movement was strong and which was light?

4. *Sneak/scare.* This time you're going to show light and strong actions when I use the words *sneak* and *scare*. Let's pretend your brother has a note from his girlfriend. You want to know what it says, so you sneak up behind him to find out. You can't read over his shoulder, so you figure if you scare him, he'll drop the note and run. Go. You need to sneak, then scare.

5. *Float/collapse.* Have you ever seen a hang glider? It's like a big kite that floats through the air, but a person is floating with it, just as if he or she were attached to a kite. You're now a hang glider sailing over the mountains. Go. Oh, no—all the wind suddenly died; your hang glider is crashing to the ground. You just collapse as you hit the ground.

6. *Glide/stomp.* You're a very good skater, and today you go rollerblading. You are gliding along, having a grand time. Now something sticks to your skate; you don't fall, but you have to stomp your skate really hard to try to get the object off. Clearly show the difference between your light and strong movements.

7. *Raindrop/thunderstorm.* You're a raindrop in a gentle spring rain that makes all the flowers bloom and the grass turn its brightest green. Now you're a raindrop in a bad summer thunderstorm—you know, a storm where the wind blows so hard you think the trees will fall down and the sky turns very dark. Remember, make it very clear which raindrop is strong and which one is light.

8. *Friends/foes.* Now you're going to show strong and light as you greet your friend and then as you meet an enemy. Pretend you're walking down the street and see an old friend. How would you greet him or her? Now move as if you've just seen the biggest bully in the school. How would you greet him or her?

? Which force was light? Which one was strong?

9. *Ant/rock.* Imagine what an ant trying to lift a rock feels like. Try hard; you're the only hope of the rock getting off the ground. Now you're a strong person trying to lift the same rock the ant lifted. How are your actions different?

10. *Olympic weight lifter.* You're an Olympic weight lifter going for the gold medal; this is the heaviest weight you've ever lifted. As you pretend, remember to keep your entire body strong. Even show in your face that you're strong. Now

you're lifting a five-pound bag of flour. How easy is it for you? Make your whole body light as you show this action. All your muscles should be loose as if they're hardly being used at all.

Developing the Concept of Flow

Watch a very young child running down a hill. The actions are unstoppable, almost out of control, until the child reaches the bottom. A batter's swing at a baseball, the smash a tennis player executes, a gymnast's giant swing on the high bar—all these are examples of *free flow* in movement. It seems that the performer is lost in the movement; the movement, not the performer, seems to control the situation.

Bound actions are stoppable, cautious, and restrained. The performer is in control at all times. Pushing a heavy object, traveling a zigzag pathway while trying to stay within boundaries, and executing a slow cartwheel with a pause for a handstand before traveling on are all examples of *bound flow*.

Teaching the Concept of Flow

This section provides learning experiences designed to help children understand and demonstrate the difference between free flow and bound flow. The tasks and challenges encompass a variety of movements important for both skill performance and safety. *Music can greatly enhance the feel of bound and free flow.*

Learning Experiences Leading to Movement Concept Understanding

Traveling and Flow

Setting: Children scattered throughout general space

Tasks/Challenges:

T On the signal, travel around the room and pause the instant you hear the stop signal. I'm really looking for stops that happen suddenly, without you taking any extra steps. Freeze in your tracks. This kind of movement—jerky and with lots of stops—is said to have *bound flow*. In other words, it doesn't flow very smoothly.

Children tend to anticipate the teacher's signals. Make stop signals close together and frequent so this activity will be successful.

T This time as you travel around the space, pretend you're completely free, like an eagle soaring high, or a really happy person who has no cares in

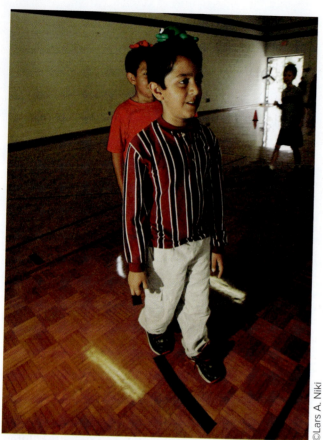

To elicit bound flow, the teacher challenged these children to travel while balancing beanbags on their heads.

©Lars A. Niki

the world. Make your traveling seem as if it has no end; it could just keep going and going. This type of movement is said to have *free flow*; it doesn't stop, much like a balloon or cloud floating in the air.

Eliciting Flow Qualities

Setting: Children scattered throughout general space

Tasks/Challenges:

T This time I'm going to give you some actions to help you practice bound flow. Pretend to do each action I tell you, always showing the bound flow of what you're doing. Remember, bound flow can be stopped and is generally slow and sometimes jerky.

1. Press the floor with your hands and feet as you move. Make sure you keep a bound flow throughout the whole motion.
2. Pretend you're pushing a heavy box.
3. Now carry a glass of milk that is too full without spilling any of it.
4. Pretend as if you're pulling from the bottom of a well a full bucket of water on a pulley.

T Now I'll give you some actions that require free flow. Free flow can be more difficult than bound flow, so really concentrate on making your movements seem as if they could go on forever. Make it very clear these are free movements and unstoppable.

1. Pretend to flick away a fly.
2. This time you're really upset with your brother. Slash your arms through the air to show how really angry you are.
3. You're cooking bacon on the stove, and the grease starts to splatter; jerk your head and arms away so you won't get burned.

T This next action will combine free and bound flow. Raise your arm high above your head with bound flow, stoppable at any moment. Let your arm fall freely downward in an unstoppable action.

? Which movement is unstoppable—bound or free? Which movement is stoppable at any time—bound or free?

? *Student Display.* Flow is a difficult concept for students to understand. A useful assessment is having children bring in magazine pictures that illustrate the various qualities in action and then creating a student display labeling the qualities.

Following Flow Sentences

Setting: Children scattered throughout general space

Tasks/Challenges:

T On the board are a number of sentences. The first one says, "Walk, run, jump." On the signal, begin to travel, using the sentence as your guide. The words are clear; the commas mean to pause or hesitate, and the periods mean to stop. Make it very clear where your pauses are and when you stop. Repeat the action of the sentence three times.

Other possible sentences: "Walk, sneak, pounce." "Leap, stomp, twist." "Creep, hop, flop."

T What you just did was an example of bound flow. Now you're going to turn the same thing into free flow. This time, on the signal, you're going to follow the same sentences but without the punctuation marks—in other words, no commas and no periods or no pauses or stops. You'll start at the beginning of the sentence and keep going all the way through; no one should know when you're going to change to the next action. Your action should just flow smoothly, one action leading to the next. When you get to the end of a sentence, just start over again. On the signal, let's start with the first sentence.

Children enjoy using interpretations of different punctuation marks, such as the exclamation point and question mark, as different ending shapes.

C Now that you're so good at the sentences, you're going to make up one of your own. On the board is a list of words. (Such words as walk, shrink, gallop, skip, explode, jump, roll, and hop are good to use.) Choose three of the words and make your sentence. Put punctuation in because punctuation is the key to when you stop or pause. Practice your sentence five times with the punctuation in it; then practice it five times without punctuation. Practice it very carefully because we'll show some of the sentences to the class. It should be obvious when the punctuation is and isn't in the sentence.

Practicing Flow Sequences

Setting: Children scattered throughout general space

Tasks/Challenges:

T This time, there are two columns of words on the board but no punctuation. You're going to join the words together to make a sequence. The first column of words reads *melt, inflate, slither, shrink*. On the signal, practice the words in the order you see them. It is your choice when to change from one word to the next. Go.

Now, do the second column of words: *jump, spin, stride, pop*.

? Which sequence gave you a bound feeling? Which one a free feeling?

C Now go back and practice each sequence three times, making it very clear each time which one is bound and which one is free.

Using Flow for Movement Conversations

Setting: Children with partners, scattered throughout general space

Tasks/Challenges:

Children beginning sequence work often need guidance in restricting the length of the sequence; generally, two or three actions are appropriate for the initial sequence.

T Now you're going to work with and talk to your partner. The only catch is that neither of you can use your voice to talk. You're going to talk with your body. One of you needs to be bound flow and the other one free flow; go ahead and decide that now. Ready? This is how you'll talk: The partner who is bound flow will talk about being grounded and not being allowed to go outside and play; the partner who is free flow will talk about how wonderful it is to roam and explore and run up and down the hills in the neighborhood; in other words, what it's like to be free. Now, one of you start; with your body, talk about your aspect. Keep your sentence very short. As you move, your partner listens or watches. After you make your statement, stop; your partner then answers with a statement, and you listen. When your partner finishes, you again provide an answer. The whole conversation should go back and forth until each of you has moved five times.

C After you've completed the conversation once, go back and practice it twice more so that it's very clear who is free flow and who is bound flow. I know this is a bit hard to understand, so let me go over it one more time. You and your partner are going to talk about bound and free flow with your body actions, not your voices. Just as in any conversation, it's a give and take situation. One of you will make a short body action sentence, and then the other one will answer. Each of you gets to talk five times, and then it ends. After you've finished once, go back and practice two more times. Remember, two people can't talk at once, so listen when your partner is talking. "Still" is the word.

It really helps to find at least one twosome (ideally more) doing the conversation correctly and have them demonstrate. Be patient; the task will take time if the children are to really develop their conversations. Children should switch roles after sufficient time to practice the other aspect of flow.

Combining Time, Force, and Flow

Setting: Children scattered throughout general space

Tasks/Challenges:

T The task sheet (Figure 15.2) for today will allow you to practice combining the concepts of time, force, and flow. After you practice each challenge so you feel it's as clear as you can make it, find a friend to watch you. If the friend feels you've done the challenge correctly, she or he signs her or his name in the blank; if not, you'll have to go back and practice some more. I'll walk around the class, and at any time, I can ask you to show me any challenge you've marked off. If you have any questions, ask me.

? *Self-Assessment.* The task sheet in Figure 15.2 could easily serve as a self-assessment of the effort concepts by changing "Observer" to "I still need practice" or "I'm good" or "Please watch me."

Figure 15.2 Task sheet for time, force, and flow.

Name _____ Teacher_____

Time, Force, and Flow Task Sheet

Date	Observer	Challenge
		Find three body parts that you can move at a slow speed.
		Find three body parts (different from the ones in the first challenge) that you can move at a fast speed.
		Find four ways to move while showing free and light qualities.
		Find two movements that you can first make strong and slow and then make light and fast.
		Find any movement you want that combines two aspects of the effort concept (**time:** fast-slow, **force:** strong-light, **flow:** bound-free). After you finish, write down your movements and the concepts they included.

Movement   Concept

_____   _____

_____   _____

_____   _____

_____   _____

See Chapter 12 for more information on developing student self-assessments.

Applying the Effort Concepts

We focus on concepts until the children have learned the basic terminology related to the effort qualities of movement. When the children are able to accurately demonstrate the differences between the extremes of each concept, we no longer focus on the concept. Instead, we focus on how the concept relates to the performance of a particular skill: fast dribble, fluid roll, or light gallop. We want the children to learn the effort concepts so they can apply the concepts to actual skill-learning situations.

The ability to use degrees of movement qualities distinguishes the inept performer from the skilled one, the sloppy movement from the polished one. An individual can learn to execute the basic requirements of a cartwheel, for example, so it can be recognized as a cartwheel. But when that cartwheel is executed in a ragged, uneven, uncontrolled manner, it is clearly and easily distinguishable from a cartwheel performed by an experienced, trained gymnast. We teach children to apply the qualities of movement to their skill performances to help them become skillful movers.

Generally, the concept of time (fast-slow) is easier for children to grasp than either the concept of force (strong-light) or the concept of flow (bound-free). For this reason, you may need to focus more on force and flow than on time. Time can be studied as an applied concept—fast and slow skips, rolling fast and rolling slowly, accelerated and decelerated change of levels—before force or flow. The difference is that in teaching a concept, our observational focus is primarily on the children's ability to understand and apply the effort concepts. In contrast, when we use a concept as a subfocus, we know the children already understand the concept from previous lessons, and therefore, our teaching focus is primarily on the skill and how it can be executed by using varying movements.

Reading Comprehension Questions

1. How is a movement performed at fast speed different from the same movement performed at slow speed?
2. How is a movement executed with strong force different from the same movement performed with light force?
3. How is a movement performed with bound flow different from the same movement performed with free flow?
4. Initially, the extremes, rather than the degrees, of the effort concepts are emphasized. Why?
5. When is slowness an important concept? List several movements.
6. What does the term *acceleration-deceleration* mean? Answer by using examples from the text or from your own experiences.
7. What does focusing on the movement quality of an image rather than on the image itself mean? This statement will help you: "Imagine the floor is covered with peanut butter 6 inches deep." Why is this focus important?
8. When do you change from focusing on the effort concept to focusing on how the concept relates to the performance of a particular skill?
9. What is the purpose of teaching children to apply the qualities of movement to their skill performances?
10. Using the movement analysis eWheel (http://www .mhhe.com/graham10e/eWheel), manipulate the wheel to show an effort concept in relation to locomotor, manipulative, and nonmanipulative skills. Identify two skills for each category that an effort concept can modify, and write a sample task for each.

References/Suggested Readings

Joyce, M. 1993. *First steps in teaching creative dance to children.* 3rd ed. Palo Alto, CA: McGraw-Hill.

[SHAPE America] Society of Health and Physical Educators. 2014. *National standards & grade-level outcomes for K-12 physical education.* Champaign, IL: Human Kinetics.

Relationships

Relationships is the third, and last, of the three movement concept chapters. This chapter focuses on the myriad relationships in our lives. The first part of the chapter emphasizes the relationship of one body part to another. These categories are typically taught to young children as they begin to learn the names of body parts and how they work with each other to form balances and shapes. They also learn about traveling on a variety of body parts.

The second part of the chapter focuses on ideas for teaching the relationship with different objects as they travel over, under, around, and through benches and hoops in a variety of ways. We understand that concepts such as along, close to, and far away may be new to young children. For example, the concept of matching parts in a balance can be a real test for the young child to figure out which parts match and which do not. There are numerous suggestions in this chapter for teaching young children these concepts.

The final section of the chapter, relationships with people, is far more difficult to learn. These relationship concepts are emphasized throughout the school years and throughout adulthood, albeit in different contexts. If you watch a high school or college team sport, for example, a major emphasis is continually on maintaining a relationship with others—those on your own team and your opponents too. Are you familiar with "Xs" and "Os," the shorthand coaches use to diagram plays in team sports? Using these letters, the coach is trying to tell the team where players need to be in relationship to others on the team.

Initially, as you will see, we start teaching children to work alone in a mass (working within a group without interfering with others) and gradually progress to working with groups and eventually between groups. Working with others in groups (teams) to design a dance or gymnastics sequence, however, is not an easy process to learn as you well know. The relationship between groups (as in basketball or soccer) is even more complicated and difficult to learn. This is why we wait until the children are ready for the relationship concepts of working with groups. If you are an experienced teacher, you understand that some children find it very difficult to share with others and work as a team—one of the many challenges of teaching.

The concept of relationships is important not only in physical education classes but also in everyday life. Driving to and from work in an automobile, maneuvering through an aisle crowded with people in a supermarket, or walking in a crowd—all these activities involve complex, dynamic relationships. And each relationship involves several contextual variables (bodies, body parts, and objects) in simultaneous interaction.

Figure 16.1 revisits the wheel (movement analysis framework) introduced in Chapter 3 (Figure 3.1) and emphasizes the relationship concepts. Notice that almost half of the movement concept categories on the wheel are in relationships.

As explained at the beginning of this chapter, we typically begin with the simplest relationships for children to understand—the self-relationships. Because so many young children are still at the "I" stage, the initial lessons focus on naming and identifying body parts and their relationship to one another, followed by body part shapes. As the children develop a functional understanding of the relationships between body parts, we shift the emphasis to moving in relation to different objects and to one another. In the lower-elementary grades, however, some of these concepts will simply be a review for the children, and therefore, the lessons can progress more rapidly. The third category of concepts, relationships with others, is typically combined with the study of other concepts and skill themes. Initially, the focus is on working with partners; when the children develop the social and physical maturity needed to collaborate with three or four others, we're able to include tasks that require them to work in groups.

When teaching the relationship concepts, it's easy to forget that the purpose is to have the children actually understand and be able to demonstrate each of the relationship concepts. Imagine someone came to your school to teach a class of your second graders. Before teaching, she might ask whether your children have been taught the relationship concepts. If you say yes, she would assume, for example, that the children can demonstrate the difference between a symmetrical shape and a nonsymmetrical shape when asked to do so. "Knowing" doesn't mean the concepts were taught; knowing means the children can demonstrate their understanding through their movements. In other words, the children have a functional understanding—they are able to demonstrate the concepts. The visiting teacher might quickly review these symmetrical and nonsymmetrical shapes and then begin to focus on using these shapes as children travel and stop and in balances.

Developing the Concept of the Relationships of Body Parts

Before children can focus on the relationships between body parts, they need to be able to identify specific body parts. Thus, it's essential for each child to acquire a functional vocabulary of body part names. Examples

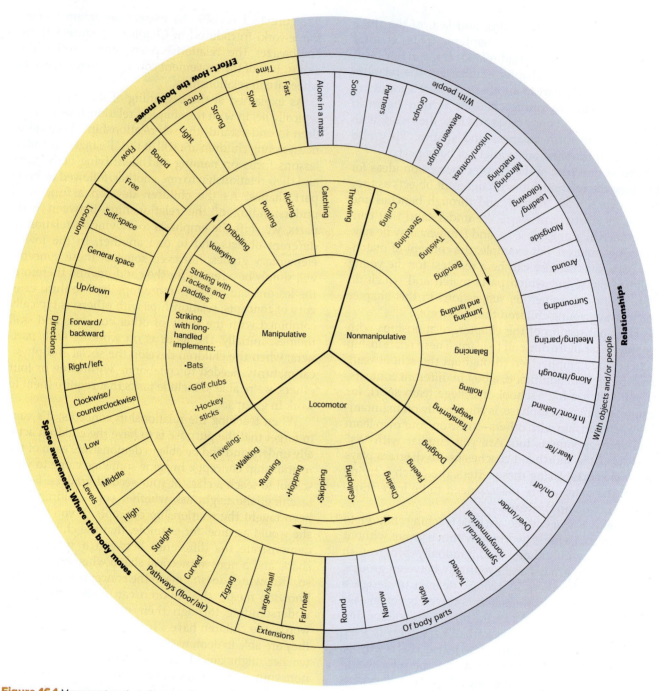

Figure 16.1 Movement analysis framework: relationship concepts.

of tasks that can be used in teaching this vocabulary include:

- Point to the ceiling with the elbow (knee, nose).
- Touch the floor with the wrist (waist, stomach).
- Travel around the room, and on the signal, stop and touch heels (shoulders, heads) with another person.

Once the children have learned the names of the body parts, lessons focus on making shapes (round,

narrow, wide, twisted, symmetrical, and nonsymmetrical) and using body parts in relation to one another. For example, we might ask children to:

- Travel and stop in a twisted shape.
- Change slowly from a symmetrical to a nonsymmetrical shape.
- Make a wide shape during a jump.
- Try to find three different ways to get their feet higher than their heads.

Teaching the Concept of the Relationships of Body Parts

This initial section provides learning experiences for teaching children to identify and use different body parts and how different body parts can relate to one another. Tasks for teaching the concepts of various body shapes and body part shapes also are presented. You can use any body parts for the tasks and challenges given here, but with the tasks that require balancing, be careful not to use parts that will elicit balances that may be too complex for some students. For example, when using parts such as the hands, make it clear that other parts can be used in conjunction with them.

Learning Experiences Leading to Movement Concept Understanding

Identifying Body Parts

Setting: Children in self-space, on a spot, or on an X on the floor

Tasks/Challenges:

T I'm going to call out different body parts. Touch the body parts I call out as quickly as possible when you hear them. Remember, pay close attention to what I'm saying because I may start to go faster or try to trick you. Ready? Remember, touch each body part as I call it out.

Body parts might include nose, arm, chin, ankle, ear, foot, elbow, temple, wrist, neck, shoulder, eyebrow, eye, teeth, cheek, leg, forehead, knee, thumb, mouth, side, hip, lip, or earlobe.

C This time you're going to play a game with finding body parts, similar to Simon Says, except you don't have to sit out if you miss. Here's how to play. I'll call out, "Simon says to touch your toes," and you'll touch your toes. But if I don't say "Simon says," then you aren't supposed to do it. So, if I just say, "Touch your toes," you aren't supposed to touch your toes because Simon didn't say to do it. Pay attention because the game will start to go very quickly. Remember, I'm watching to see if you touch the right parts and how quickly you can do it.

T This time, instead of just touching a body part as I name it, you'll have to touch whatever hand I call out to the different body parts I call out. This activity will be harder because you'll have to remember which is your right and which is your left. For example, if I say, "Right hand to left knee," touch your right hand to your left knee. Try to do this as quickly as possible, but be careful in deciding what body parts to use. Just to help you out, let's review right and left. Raise your right hand. (Check to see that students are correct.) Ready? Let's try it. If this is new to the children, you may want to provide each of them with a thick rubber band around the right wrist, a sticker, or some other technique, to help them distinguish their right hand from their left hand.

Body part directions can include left hand to right knee, right hand to left elbow, left hand to left shoulder, right hand to left knee, left hand to left foot, or right elbow to left knee.

T This time, instead of touching your hands to different body parts, you're going to touch two different body parts together. For example, I'll call out "Knee to elbow," and you'll touch your knee to your elbow. You'll have to think hard on this one. Ready? I'm looking to see if you can get the correct different parts together.

Possible body part combinations include knee to elbow, hands to waist, head to knees, foot to shoulder, knee to foot, elbow to wrist, and back of wrist to back of knee.

These young children explore the various ways their arm can move in relationship to their bodies.

©Barbara Adamcik

Freezing on Different Body Parts

Setting: Children scattered in general space

Tasks/Challenges:

T When I say "Go," you're going to walk around in general space. When you hear the stop signal, touch the body part I call out to the floor. So, if I call out "Elbow" as you stop, touch your elbow to the floor. As you move, be very careful to not run into others and be sure to stay in a space by yourself, so you don't touch anyone when you're trying to touch different body parts to the floor. This activity will start to go very fast, so touch the parts to the floor as quickly as possible, and make it very clear which part is touching the floor.

Body parts can include arm, ankle, foot, leg, side, and hip. For more challenge, change from walking to running, sliding, skipping, galloping, etc.

T When you travel this time, instead of touching body parts to the floor, touch the body parts I call out to the same parts of another person. So, if I call out "Heels," stop, touch your heels to the heels of one other person, and then freeze. As you do this, make the touching parts very clear; don't just stand beside the other person. To be safe, make sure as you touch that you stop first and then touch easily so no one gets hurt. The idea is to quickly and easily touch and then be ready to go again. Ready?

Body parts can include wrist, shoulder, forehead, knee, thumb, arm, ankle, foot, elbow, leg, side, or back. Note: This activity can start out slowly, but to really challenge children, the pace should be speeded up considerably.

Traveling on Different Body Parts

Setting: Children scattered in general space

Tasks/Challenges:

T This time, instead of balancing on different body parts, you're going to travel on different body parts. What body parts do we usually travel on? Let's start with the feet just to get warmed up. Make sure to travel in all the space and to stay on your feet. Let's start by walking.

T Now try something a little different: the hands and feet. Remember to travel with your hands and feet both touching the floor at some time. Ready? Try to travel and use as much of the general space as possible. Be sure to move to open spaces away from others.

T This time you're going to make up your own way of traveling using different body parts (not your feet).

As you do this, make sure that I can tell from just looking at you what body parts you're using for traveling; you should be using different body parts to move around the room. Be very careful to watch where you're going and not touch anyone else.

Ways of traveling can include crawl, roll, scoot on seat, etc.

Balancing on Matching and Nonmatching Parts

Setting: Each child in a personal space

Tasks/Challenges:

T This time, instead of balancing on a certain number of parts, you're going to balance on parts that are alike and parts that are different. Parts that are alike are called matching parts. What parts do you have that are matching or alike? *(Children respond "Hands," "Feet," etc.)* Good; let's try to balance on some of those parts. First let's try an easy one: the feet. Now, how about the knees? Think up one of your own. Make sure that the parts you use are matching parts. For safety reasons, avoid balancing on hands.

T Now pick one set of matching parts; make up a balance you like and practice it. Be sure you know the name of the matching parts you're balancing on because I'll come around and ask some of you, just to make sure.

T This time you're going to balance on different parts. Different parts are parts that don't match each other; they aren't alike. What are some possible combinations of different parts? *(Children respond "Knee and elbow," "Back and hands," etc.)* Let's try some. First, try the seat and the feet. Now try the shoulders and the elbows. What about the knees and the elbows? Now, make up one combination on your own.

C Now pick one set of different parts and make up your own balance. Be sure the different parts you're using are very clear because I might ask you what they are.

Round, Narrow, Wide, and Twisted Body Shapes

Setting: Each child in self-space

Tasks/Challenges:

T Today you're going to learn about different shapes you can make with your bodies. Everyone find a self-space so you can't touch anyone else. The first shape you're going to make is a pretzel. All of you try to make a pretzel out of your body; hold very still. This shape is called a twisted shape.

T Now make a different twisted shape on your own. As you do so, make sure your whole body is twisted, not just your arms and legs. Try to twist your spine, too. For each new shape, try to hold very still like a statue.

T The next shape is curled. Try to make your whole body look like a ball or like the letter "O." This is called a round shape.

T Now try to make up a different round shape by yourself. Make sure your whole body is making the round shape and that it is very round. Remember, round things have no bumps in them.

T This time you're going to make a pencil shape. All of your body parts are close to your trunk. This is called a narrow shape.

T Find another narrow shape by yourself. Pretend as if you are hiding behind a door and do not want to be found.

T What do you think the opposite of narrow is? *Wide*, right. Now make your body as wide as possible. Extend your body parts away from your trunk.

T Try another wide shape by yourself. Remember, get as wide as possible, as if you were trying to stop someone from getting around you.

C This time pick your favorite kind of shape, and make it, holding it very still. I'm going to come around and guess which type of shape it is, so make your shape as clear as possible. Your shape should be wide, narrow, round, or twisted.

T Things are going to be a little harder this time. Staying in your own space, you're going to make a wide shape. Then, when I give the signal, change your wide shape to a narrow shape, and hold it very still. The difference between the wide and narrow shape should be very clear. Make a wide shape and hold it. Now change that wide shape to a narrow shape.

T Try it again—another wide shape; change to a narrow shape.

T Now, a third.

C This time, pick the shape you liked the most and practice it until it changes very easily from wide to narrow. Work on it until it's your best and both shapes are very clear.

T You thought the last task was hard? This one is even harder! Think you can do it? You're going to change from a twisted shape to a round shape. So make your twisted shape. Got it? On the signal, change that twisted shape to a round shape.

T Now, let's try a different twisted to round shape. Go.

©Lars A. Niki

Freeze in a low, wide shape.

T And a third twisted to round shape. Make sure your twisted shape is really twisted, and your round shape is very round. I should be able to easily tell the difference.

C Now, pick your favorite round and twisted shape. Practice your favorite one so your move from twisted to round is smooth (not jerky) and your shapes are so clear the principal could easily tell the difference if she walked in.

Changing from One Body Shape to Another

Setting: Children in self-space moving to a drumbeat

Tasks/Challenges:

T You'll really need to be in a good self-space for this activity, so make sure you're as far away from everyone else as you can be. Again you're going to change from one shape to another, but I'm going to give you drumbeats to help (some children may find the analogy of a flower opening when the sun comes out helpful for this task). You're going to move from a round shape to a wide shape, but instead of just doing it on your own, you'll have six drumbeats to get from the round shape to the wide shape, and then six beats to get back to your round shape. Listen now while I give you the drumbeats. Does everyone understand? You'll start in a round shape and, on the six beats of the drum, slowly open to a wide shape. You'll hold your wide shape very still, and then on the next six beats of the drum, you'll return to your round shape. Let's try it. Find your round shape.

T Let's try it again; this time find different round and wide shapes.

T Now, let's do a third set of shapes.

C You're now going to practice one set of shapes four more times so you can make it really good. Pick your favorite shapes. Remember as you move to make each shape very clear, and make sure the movement goes with the drumbeats.

Pinpoint two or three children who are succeeding with the activity, and ask them if they'd like to show it to the class.

T You're going to make the shapes a little different this time. Instead of opening up on six beats and closing on six, you're going to open up on one quick beat and then close slowly on six. So the sequence will now go like this: Start in a round shape; on the drumbeat, quickly open up to a wide shape, and hold it still; then on the next six drumbeats, slowly return to your round shape. Remember, open from the round to the wide shape very, very quickly, as if you were a flash of lightning.

C Now practice your favorite shapes four times. Remember the first shape is made quickly and the second is performed slowly. Also be sure to make your round and wide shapes very clear. To look really good, remember to hold the beginning and the end very still so we all know when you started and when you finished.

Traveling and Freezing in Different Body Shapes

Setting: Children traveling in general space

Tasks/Challenges:

T Instead of making shapes in your self-space, this time you're going to travel around the space and on the signal stop and quickly make the shape I call out. For example, if you're traveling and I call out "Twisted," on the signal, make a twisted shape. As you make your shapes, be sure they're very clear so I can easily tell what they are. As you travel, be careful of your classmates.

T Now, as you stop to make your shape, try to do it as quickly as possible, almost as if you just froze in that shape when you stopped. Remember, frozen shapes don't fall over.

Making Symmetrical and Nonsymmetrical Shapes

Setting: Children in self-space

Tasks/Challenges:

T You've already learned about wide, narrow, round, and twisted shapes. This time you're going to

learn about two different kinds of shapes. The words describing these shapes may be new, so listen carefully. First, find a body shape that looks exactly alike on both sides of your body; in other words, if you were divided in half, both sides of you would look alike. This is called a symmetrical shape.

T Try making a symmetrical shape. Remember, both sides of your body must look exactly alike.

T Now find a shape in which the two sides of your body don't look alike. In other words, if you were cut in half, each side would have a different shape. We call this a nonsymmetrical shape.

T Make another nonsymmetrical shape. Remember, both sides must be different.

T Since you now know the difference between symmetrical and nonsymmetrical, let's find three more balances of each shape. First do symmetrical; remember, both sides are alike. When I beat the drum, change from one symmetrical shape to the next one. Try to make each of your balances very clear so I can tell without thinking what kind of shape it is.

T Now do nonsymmetrical shapes. Find three more nonsymmetrical shapes. Try to make the sides of your body as different as possible so no one could possibly confuse your shape with a symmetrical one. Change each time you hear the drumbeat.

C Once you've found three more nonsymmetrical shapes, practice your favorite one five extra times so you can show it to the whole class. (Half the class demonstrates their favorite nonsymmetrical shape, and then the other half shows their favorite nonsymmetrical shape.)

? *Event Task.* This would be an appropriate time to use an event task to determine if students are able to make different body shapes. A possible task might be the following:

You and a partner are going to make up a routine. It will consist of three shapes. In each of the shapes, you and your partner should match—you should look exactly alike. Here are three shapes:

1. Symmetrical, narrow shape
2. Twisted shape
3. Nonsymmetrical wide shape

Start with the first shape and hold it for three seconds (crocodiles, elephants, hamburgers, your city or state). When I say change (or beat the drum), change to the second shape. Hold it for three seconds, and then change to the third shape and hold that one for three seconds.

It is important to determine children's understanding of relationships. Either of the following ideas will allow you to do that rather quickly:

- *Exit slip.* Ask children to draw a symmetrical shape and a nonsymmetrical shape.
- *Homework.* Ask children to find an example of a shape (e.g., wide, narrow, round, or twisted) in a magazine, newspaper, or online. Have them cut out or print the shape and label it.

Creating Postcard Sculptures

Setting: Museum postcards of statues, one postcard for every child. Photos laminated from magazines or the Internet can also be used for this task so children are clear on the terms *statue* or *sculpture*. Children love to play the roles of statues and sculptors but tend to get silly during this activity. Remind them they need to respect their partners. Also caution them to place others only in shapes they can hold without too much difficulty so no one gets hurt. This may not work for some of your classes if they have yet to learn to work successfully with a partner.

Tasks/Challenges:

(T) You're going to pretend you're sculptors who are creating great statues. To do this you'll need a partner. When I say "Go," find a partner, and sit beside him or her. I'll know you're ready when I see everyone seated beside a partner. Each set of partners has two postcards (photos) of statues; you're going to form each other into these statues. Decide which partner will be the sculptor first; the other partner is a ball of clay in a round shape in low level. The sculptor then decides which statue to make the partner into. First, form the statue by gently guiding your partner (the ball of clay) into the shape just as it is on the card. Remember, balls of clay cannot talk, so you need to guide them into the shape you want, not tell them.

Once you are satisfied with your sculpture, if it's symmetrical, change it to nonsymmetrical; if it's nonsymmetrical, make it symmetrical. Mold each statue very carefully, and be sure you can tell me which statue is symmetrical and which is nonsymmetrical. After you make your statue, trade places with your partner; now you will become the ball of clay and your partner will become the sculptor.

(T) This time you're going to design your own statues. You'll still need your partner. Go ahead and decide which of you is to be the sculptor and the ball of clay first. Make your first statue symmetrical. The statue stays "frozen" until the signal. At the signal, move to someone else's statue and redesign it to suit yourself.

On the next signal, move to another new statue and redesign it. Keep doing this until you're told to change. When you hear the change signal, find your partner, and now you will become the ball of clay.

Let's practice once. Form your partner into a symmetrical statue. (Allow at least one minute.) Now, move to another statue and remake it, still into a symmetrical shape. Do you have the hang of it? (*Select several children for demonstration.*) Go to the next statue.

(T) Now trade places with the statue you've just made. The activity changes a little this time; you're going to create nonsymmetrical statues. Ready? Without moving to a new place, form a nonsymmetrical statue out of your partner.

(T) Change to a new statue, and then change this statue to a nonsymmetrical shape. Remember: Nonsymmetrical means that both sides of the body are very different from each other.

(T) Change one more time. Make this your best statue yet.

With a digital camera (e.g., iPad or cell phone), the postcard sculptures are excellent photo opportunities. They also can be used on a bulletin board with actual sculpture photographs next to them. This project can be especially interesting in combination with the study of European countries.

Creating Body Shapes in the Air

Setting: Boxes, benches, and/or low beams with mats set up around the space. (*Figure 16.2 shows a typical equipment setup.*)

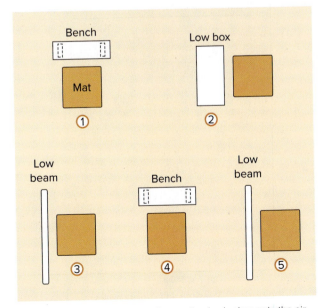

Figure 16.2 Equipment set up for creating body shapes in the air.

Tasks/Challenges:

T Now you're going to combine all the different kinds of body shapes you've practiced so far. What you're going to do may be hard, but it'll be fun. Remember, as you work, all the rules for gymnastics apply. (See Chapters 7 and 8 for establishing and maintaining a learning environment and Chapter 30 for the rules of a gymnastics environment.) Three or four of you will be at a piece of equipment at once. One at a time, you'll each jump off the equipment and make a shape in the air. Each time you jump, try to make that shape in the air. Let's start with a wide shape. Make sure you land on your feet after the jump and don't crash to the ground.

After a while, change to narrow, twisted, round, symmetrical, and nonsymmetrical shapes.

T Now that you've been through all the shapes separately, you may practice them in any order you wish. Make the shapes so clear that I don't have to ask you what they are. Remember to land on your feet.

? *Self-assessment.* The task sheet in Figure 16.3 is a useful self-assessment.

Name _____ Teacher _____

Relationships Task Sheet

Challenge	I am good	I need more practice	Please watch me
I can make a wide shape with my body			
I can make a narrow shape with my body			
I can make a round shape with my body			
I can make a twisted shape with my body			
I can make a symmetrical shape with my body			
I can make a nonsymmetrical shape with my body			
I can jump off equipment and make a wide shape in the air			
I can jump off equipment and make a narrow shape in the air			
I can jump off equipment and make a round shape in the air			
I can jump off equipment and make a twisted shape in the air			
I can jump off equipment and make a symmetrical shape in the air			
I can jump off equipment and make a nonsymmetrical shape in the air			
*I can			
*I can			

Figure 16.3 Task sheet for relationships.

*Create another challenging movement that represents a relationship (of body parts, with objects and/or people)

Developing the Concept of the Relationships with Objects

Some concepts are studied in relation to objects; others have more meaning when they're practiced in relation to people. The concepts of *on* and *off*, *along*, *through*, *over*, *under*, *around*, and *surrounding* apply primarily to relationships with objects. The concepts of *near* and *far*, *in front*, *behind*, and *alongside* are generally studied as person-to-person relationships. Because objects are more predictable (less dynamic) than children, however, we first focus on the concept of relationships with objects and then on relationships with people.

Children frequently identify a lesson by the equipment used in the lesson rather than the movement concept. For example, after a lesson in which hoops were used to study the concepts of traveling over, under, and through, children might say, "Hey, that was fun! Are we going to play with hoops again tomorrow?" In time, however, children begin to understand and use the terminology we use. For instance, a child might say, "It's easier to go over and under the hoop than to go through the hoop."

Within the context of a game or a dance lesson, specific terms are classified as objects. In dance, for example, wands, streamers, newspapers, or scarves are considered objects. Goals, boundaries, nets, and targets are objects with which the child learns relationship concepts within a game context. See Box 16-1 for linkages between the movement concept of relationships and the National Standards and Grade-Level Outcomes for K–12 Physical Education (SHAPE America 2014).

Teaching the Concept of the Relationships with Objects

The learning experiences in this section are designed to enhance the children's awareness of and ability to function effectively in relation to some of the objects (equipment) used in a variety of physical activity contexts.

Learning Experiences Leading to Movement Concept Understanding

Traveling Over, Close to, Far Away, Inside

Setting: A rope for each child

Tasks/Challenges:

T To warm up, travel over your rope stretched in a straight, narrow shape. As you travel, make sure you actually go over the rope, not around it.

Box 16-1

Relationships in the *National Standards and Grade Level Outcomes for K–12 Physical Education*

The movement concept of relationships is referenced in the *National Standards and Grade-Level Outcomes for K–12 Physical Education* (SHAPE America 2014) under Standard 1, "Demonstrates competency in a variety of motor skills and movement patterns," as well as Standard 2, "Applies knowledge of concepts, principles, strategies and tactics related to movement and performance." The intent of these standards is facilitation of learners' ability to perform fundamental motor skills and movement patterns as well as use cognitive information to understand and enhance motor skill acquisition and performance. At the lower-elementary level, emphasis is placed on establishing a movement vocabulary and demonstrating a basic understanding of the concepts. At the upper-elementary level, emphasis is placed on applying the concepts in dance, educational gymnastics, and game environments.

Sample grade-level outcomes from the *National Standards** include:

- Combines locomotor skills and movement concepts (levels, shapes, extensions, pathways, force, time, flow) to create and perform a dance with a partner (4)
- Combines locomotor skills and movement concepts (levels, shapes, extensions, pathways, force, time, flow) to create and perform a dance with a group (5)
- Travels demonstrating a variety of relationships with objects (e.g., over, under, around, through) (1)

*Suggested grade-level outcomes for student learning.

T This time as you travel over your rope, try to stay as close to it as possible. This may mean you travel at a low level. Try to keep as much of your body as possible close to the rope, not just one body part.

T Now, instead of being close to the rope, try to have as many body parts as possible as far away from the rope as possible. Only the parts that are really used to support your body should be near the rope. Make sure your whole body is as far away as possible, not just the upper parts of your body.

T The activity is a little harder now. Start on the outside of your rope, put your weight down on your hands inside the circle made with a rope, and then continue to travel over it. Make sure you shift your weight to your hands inside the rope at some point.

(T) These are all relationships your body can have to equipment or other people. We can go over things, we can be close to things, we can be far away from things, or we can go inside things. Practice all four of these relationships on your own: over, close to, far away, and inside. See if you can find three different ways to do each relationship—for example, three different ways to go over your rope. Be sure you know which concept you're practicing, because I'll come around and ask you.

If you say you're going to come around and ask the children questions or see their work, do it! Otherwise, the children may soon stop believing you.

Traveling Over, Under, Close to, and Far Away from Equipment

Setting: A rope inserted into two cones so the middle is 12–18 inches off the ground (or high enough for children to fit under), hurdle, or other object that the children can travel over and under (Figure 16.4)—one for each child in the class, scattered throughout the space

Tasks/Challenges:

(T) To begin, travel *over* the rope (hurdle) any way you can; you can jump or use your hands and feet. Whatever you do, make sure you can land on your feet on the other side without falling down. This is called going over an object. Sometimes when we try to go over an object, we accidently go around the side of it. Make very, very sure you really do go over and not around.

(T) Now, instead of going over the hurdle, you're going to go under it. This will be hard because the hurdle (rope) isn't very far off the ground. You'll really have to get low. Try to do it without touching the hurdle.

(T) Now, let's try going under in different ways. Sometimes go under feet first, sometimes head first, sometimes on your back, and sometimes on your stomach. Be careful; always know where your body is, even those parts that you can't see.

(T) One more activity. This time you're going to put part of your weight on your hands and bring your feet down in different places around the hurdle. To begin, bring your feet down very close to the hurdle. You may take your feet across the hurdle or simply leave them on one side; whatever you do, be sure your feet come down close to the hurdle.

(T) Now try bringing your feet down far away from the hurdle. Make sure that every time your feet touch the floor, they're far away from the rope.

(T) Now, as you work, your feet can be close to the hurdle or far away, but sometimes have your feet land close to each other, sometimes spread far apart from each other. Be able to tell me if your feet are close together or far apart when I ask you. Remember, close together means almost so close that nothing could get between, and far apart means spread out so much that a person could crawl through.

Onto/Off Concepts

Setting: Low boxes or benches, scattered throughout the space

Tasks/Challenges:

(T) You're now going to learn two more types of relationships: *onto* and *off*. I think you probably already know what these two concepts mean, but let's practice them just to make sure. Find at least three different ways to get onto and three different ways to get off your piece of equipment. I'm really

Figure 16.4 Construction of hurdles. Hurdles can be made from plastic bleach or milk jugs and rolled newspaper held together with masking tape.

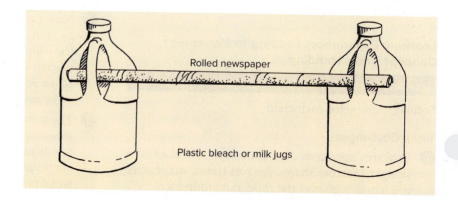

Rolled newspaper

Plastic bleach or milk jugs

looking for very different ways to get onto and off the equipment—as long as they are safe and you are being careful (Figure 16.2).

C After you find three different ways, practice your favorite way four extra times, so that you can show it to the class. Make it really special.

T I'm going to make the activity a little harder this time by combining different types of relationships. When I say "Go," each of you get a hoop and place it on the floor beside your box. Travel into the hoop before you travel onto and off the box or bench. So your sequence will involve three different relationships: into, on, and off. Find three different ways to do this. Make them very different from each other. Go.

Pinpoint several children who are doing the activity correctly or have found very creative ways to accomplish the activity to demonstrate their actions for the rest of the class. Be sure to use a variety of students so the rest of the class has a number of different creative ideas to base their work on.

T Now you're going to make up a sequence of the relationships you practiced with the box and hoop. You must include the concepts of *off, onto,* and *into* in your sequence. You can start with any of the three. Once you find a sequence you really like, practice it until you can do it from memory and it looks the same each time.

Over, Under, Around, In Front Of, and Behind Concepts

Setting: A streamer, such as one used in rhythmic gymnastics, for each child; index cards and pencils. (You can make streamers from 2-inch-wide crepe paper or from surveyors' tape cut into 4- to 10-foot lengths.)

Tasks/Challenges:

T Just to warm up, practice moving your streamer anywhere around your body. Remember, always try to keep the streamer in the air. To do this, you'll have to keep the streamer moving all the time; you can't let it stop, or it'll touch the floor.

T Now that you know how to keep the streamer in the air, try to make it go over, under, around, in front of, and behind different body parts, such as your head, legs, and trunk. (*You will ask the children to do these one at a time—e.g., over, then under, then around.*) Try to keep the streamer moving at all times.

T Now you're going to pretend you're Olympic rhythmical gymnasts. Make up a sequence in which your streamer goes over, under, around, in front of,

and behind two different body parts—for example, over your head and over an arm. After you make up a sequence you like, practice it until it looks the same each time and you can do it from memory. It's very important that you remember exactly what you did because we're going to do something really special with it. It may help to say each concept out loud as you do your sequence.

T Do you remember your sequence? Now you're going to write it down on a card and exchange the card with a friend. Your friend will try to do your sequence, and you will try to do your friend's sequence just by reading the directions on the card, so make it very clear which parts you went over, under, around, in front of, and behind.

C Now practice your friend's sequence until you think you've learned it perfectly. When you think you're ready, ask your friend to watch you do the sequence. In a few minutes I'll ask for volunteers to show routines that clearly have all five of these concepts.

This series of learning experiences is also very good for developing the concept of free flow (smooth rather than jerky, halting movements). You will find it works best to gradually combine the concepts—for example, over, then under, then over and under together, and so on.

Traveling on Equipment

Setting: Low balance beams or benches on the floor set up around the room

Tasks/Challenges:

T So far, we've practiced the relationships of on, off, over, in front of, *under, around,* and *behind.* Now we're going to learn to move while *on* equipment. At your piece of equipment, each of you, one at a time, should travel on the beam or bench by walking. Make sure you travel from one end of the beam or bench to the other. This relationship means being on a piece of equipment and traveling from one part of it to another.

If it's easy for you to walk on the beam, try some other ways. Try a slide. If you need help keeping your balance, spread your arms out to either side.

As children progress with learning how to travel on equipment, you can increase the complexity of the learning experiences by changing the locomotor pattern required for traveling. Patterns can include hopping, skipping, running, or fun movements like waddling. Before you change the pattern, be sure the children are able to advance safely to the next pattern. In other words, don't have them run on the balance beam before they can keep their balance at a fast walk.

T This time, we're going to be funny by combining two different relationships while you travel along the bench. Have some of your weight on the bench and some on the floor. For example, have one hand and foot on the bench and one hand and foot on the floor, or have both your feet on the bench and both your hands on the floor. The idea is to place part of your weight on the equipment and part on the floor. Make sure I can tell where your weight really is.

C Make up one way you like to travel with part of your weight on the floor and part on the bench, and practice it so you can show the class. Try to give your movement a name.

Traveling Through Obstacles

Setting: Hoops on foam supports

Tasks/Challenges:

T So far, we have practiced traveling over, under, around, in front of, behind, and along. Now we are going to practice traveling *through* obstacles. Look around the area. You will see hoops standing up straight on foam supports. See if you can travel through the hoops without touching the sides. Start going through at a slow speed. If that is easy, gradually go through at a faster speed.

T If you can travel through the obstacle without knocking it down or touching it at a fast speed, then try going through it in a backward direction—slowly at first and then faster and faster.

Moving in relationship to a rolling hoop is a fascinating challenge for the skilled child.

C See if you can go through the hoop three times without touching it in a forward direction at a fast speed. See if you can travel through three times in a backward direction without touching the obstacle.

T This game is called rolling hoops. You may work alone or with a partner. The object is to travel through a rolling hoop without touching it so the hoop keeps rolling after you travel through it. If you work with a partner, ask your partner to roll the hoop slowly or to make it spin by throwing it so the hoop spins back to the thrower. Try to go through the hoop when it changes direction and starts back to the thrower.

⚠ (*Remind children of safety expectations; i.e., avoid collisions, try to stay on feet*)

❓ **Teacher Observation.** The following task might be used with a teacher observation to assess children's ability to use the concepts of *over, into, out of, around,* and *along.*

I am going to ask you to travel in relationship to a hoop and do five things.

1. Travel over the hoop. (It's okay if you just travel over part of the hoop.)
2. Travel into the hoop.
3. Travel out of the hoop.
4. Travel around the hoop.
5. Travel along the hoop

I will call out each relationship. Don't start the next one until I ask you to change. Sometimes you will keep moving. Sometimes you will stop after the movement is done.

Can you travel through the hoop without touching it?

Remember, cognitive understanding precedes the ability to perform. If children are having difficulty "doing" the concepts, you may want to assess their cognitive understanding. For example, can they verbally or on an exit slip explain the difference between around *and* along?

Going Over and Under the Obstacle Course

Setting: An obstacle course made by placing elastic or regular ropes at various heights around the room. Chairs, volleyball standards, and benches can be used to anchor the ropes.

Tasks/Challenges:

(T) You can see that the whole room is now a giant maze. Your task is to go through the maze by going over or under the ropes. Everyone can move at once, but be sure to not touch anyone else as you find your way through the maze. You can start at different places on the maze, but everyone needs to move in the same direction.

(T) Now that you've gone through the maze at least once, I'm going to make the activity harder. This time, try to go over some of the high ropes that you went under, and go under some of the low ropes that you went over. Be very careful not to touch anyone else, and try not to touch the ropes.

(C) This will take a lot of concentration—pretend the ropes are a maze of lasers that will sound an alarm if you touch them.

This is a good initial activity because you can set it up before class and then have the children help you take it down if you don't want to use it for the entire class. Children really enjoy this activity.

Developing the Concept of the Relationships with People

The third category in relationships is relationships with others. As stated at the beginning of the chapter, this is the hardest type of relationship to learn and is one that is truly important throughout a lifetime. When teaching youngsters about relationships with people, we focus on five related relationships: alone in a mass, solo, partners, groups, and between groups. These relationships can occur in a variety of ways: Each child dribbles a ball in general space (alone in a mass); one child demonstrates a sequence before an entire class (solo); a child mirrors or matches the movement of a partner or partners; children meet or part in a dance with a group to express an idea (groups); and

individuals work with others as a team to accomplish a task against another team (between groups).

Alone in a Mass

We use the term *alone in a mass* to describe those times when all children move simultaneously, with no intent of observing one another. It's frequently seen in lessons that use a problem solving or guided discovery approach (Chapter 9). The children are indirectly relating to one another as they move throughout general space. In contrast to a solo relationship (explained in the next section), the children practice independently, even though they're surrounded by classmates. A child is experiencing the relationship concept alone in a mass when dribbling his or her own ball through general space or when an entire class is running simultaneously to a predetermined location.

Solo

A solo relationship exists between an individual and an audience. Examples are the pitcher on a baseball team, a featured performer in a ballet, and a gymnast—or a child who is being pinpointed by a teacher (Chapter 7). Because some children experience unpleasant pressure or tension when they're the center of attention, we make solo performances voluntary rather than mandatory. This is particularly important for the poorly skilled child, who often feels increased tension and pressure when asked to perform in front of an audience. For this reason, we always try to pinpoint two or more children simultaneously (Chapter 7). Some children, however, enjoy the challenge of solo performances and actually seem to do better when watched by a group. The feeling experienced when moving and being observed by others is an interesting phenomenon and one we want children to explore but in a safe, nonthreatening environment. Laughing at or negatively criticizing the other children's performances is not tolerated!

Partners

Most elementary school children will be able to work cooperatively with a partner to explore different relationships. In every class, however, there may be a few children who are not yet developmentally ready to cooperate with a partner—especially if you are asking them to share equipment. Examples of partner relationships include two dancers moving in synchronization, two people paddling a canoe, and two synchronized swimmers performing a routine together. Relationship concepts introduced as children work with partners (or groups) include:

- Meeting and parting—traveling toward or away from a partner
- Unison and contrast—both partners intentionally do the same thing (unison), or they intentionally do the same thing in different ways (contrast)
- Leading and following—one partner leads; the other follows
- Matching—partners are side by side and attempt to duplicate one another's movements instantaneously (to make the same movement at the same time)
- Mirroring—partners face one another and form the reverse reproduction of the partner's movements, as if looking in a mirror

Groups

Group cooperative relationships occur when more than two children work together for a common purpose. These relationships include children working together to express an emotion in dance, to design a game or a sequence, or as a team trying to keep a ball from touching the floor but without catching it.

As the size of the group increases, so, too, does the complexity of the relationship. A partner relationship involves being aware of one other child; a successful group relationship necessitates an awareness of two or more children. The difficulty of decision making also increases proportionately with the size of the group. The concepts of meeting and parting, unison and contrast, and leading and following all become increasingly challenging as the size of a group increases. Group relationships are typically focused on in game situations—for example, a play in basketball, spacing on a soccer field. When coaches are drawing their Xs and Os, they are describing group relationships.

Between Groups

A between-group relationship occurs when two or more children relate to two or more children. It's the most complex of relationships because it involves not only being aware of one's own group but also having a responsibility to relate to another group. This relationship is extremely challenging, as demonstrated by the wide appeal of sports that match one team against another. We keep intergroup relationships small (two to three on a side) and try to allow choices about whether or not to participate in an intergroup relationship.

Between-group relationships can be competitive (working with a group to outmaneuver another group) or collaborative (two groups striving for a common goal). We suggest beginning with collaborative relationships and later providing children the opportunity to choose competitive activities.

Teaching the Concept of the Relationships with People

The following learning experiences are designed to improve children's ability to function successfully with other individuals and groups in a variety of situations.

Learning Experiences Leading to Movement Concept Understanding

Matching

Setting: Partners in a self-space

Working with a partner increases the fun of an activity for many children.

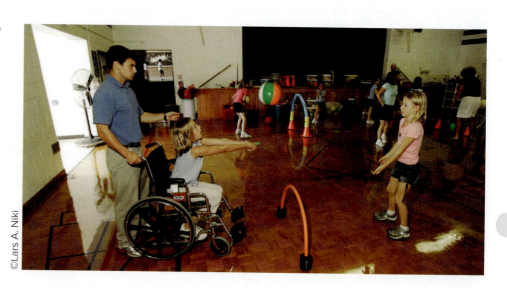

©Lars A. Niki

Tasks/Challenges:

T Stand alongside a partner. Partner 1 should make a symmetrical shape, and partner 2 should try to copy it exactly. Try to make the shapes so alike that you look like twins. Hold your shape for two alligators (count one alligator, two alligator) so your partner can match exactly.

T Now it's partner 2's turn to make a symmetrical shape, and partner 1 should match it. Be sure to hold your shape still so your partner can match it. When I say go, partner 2 will make a nonsymmetrical shape.

T It's partner 1's turn again. Partner 1 will now make three different shapes, holding each one still so your partner can match you before moving on to the next shape. Try to make some shapes symmetrical and some nonsymmetrical. After making three different shapes, partners should change places, with partner 2 now making the shapes while partner 1 copies them. Work hard to make the shapes exactly alike.

Leading and Following

Setting: Partners traveling in general space

Tasks/Challenges:

T Now you're going to play Follow the Leader. On the signal, partner 1 leads by walking; partner 2 follows. When I beat the drum, you both stop, and the follower, partner 2, matches the leader, partner 1. Be sure to follow and match exactly what your partner does. Be sure when you're the leader that you walk at a speed where your partner can keep up—don't go too fast. When you hear my signal, stop, and I will let you know when to switch the leader and the follower.

T Now instead of walking, the leader is going to gallop (or skip, hop, jump, etc.). On my signal, we will switch the leader and follower.

T This time, choose another way to travel, and when you are the leader, try using different pathways (see Chapter 17 for additional pathway experiences). Remember, we can travel in straight, curved, and zigzag pathways.

⚠ Permit children to travel at fast speeds, such as running, only after they have mastered stopping on signal, moving in general space with no collisions, and successfully transitioning from leader to follower.

Traveling and Matching

Setting: Partners traveling in general space

Tasks/Challenges:

T Now you'll perform matching actions while traveling instead of being still. With your partner, make up five different ways you can travel and then perform the movements side by side at the exact same time, as if you're both part of a marching band that does everything alike. Skipping and hopping are two of the ways you might want to try. Practice doing the movements together so you do them at exactly the same time. It may help to count to yourselves as you move. When I beat the drum, switch to a different way of traveling (e.g., from skipping to hopping).

Mirroring

Setting: Partners in a self-space

Tasks/Challenges:

T This time you're going to try something a little different. Face your partner; partner 1 will be the leader and partner 2 the follower. The leader will make a statue using one of the shapes we learned earlier (wide, narrow, round, or twisted), and the

©Lars A. Niki

Children try to mirror their partner as they make nonsymmetrical balances.

follower will then make the same balance, only opposite. For example, if partner 1 uses her right arm to do something, partner 2 uses his left arm—just like looking in a mirror. Make five statues, and then trade places. Hold each statue for two elephants (count one elephant, two elephants) before moving to the next statue. Work very hard to make every part of the statue the exact opposite of what you see. These types of actions are called *mirroring* actions because it is like looking in a mirror.

Matching and Mirroring

Setting: Partners in a self-space

Tasks/Challenges:

🅣 This activity tests how well you understand the difference between mirroring and matching. With your partner, make a matching statue. On the signal, change that statue so you mirror each other.

It helps to have two partners who are doing the activity correctly pinpoint it for the class so you are sure they understand the task.

🅣 With your partner, now try to find three more statues that you can change from matching to mirroring. I'm going to come around as you practice and ask to see at least one of your combinations, so be sure you know the difference. If you have questions, ask now.

🅣 This time, the activity will be harder. Instead of copying a still statue your partner makes, you're going to mirror your partner's movements. It will be just like looking in a mirror when you brush your hair. Remember, this is still in your own space and there's no traveling. So if your partner moves his or her left arm down, you move your right arm down. Make four moves and change leaders. This is hard. Think about it.

🅣 This time, try to tell a story with your mirroring actions, such as a baby first seeing herself in the mirror, a woman putting on her makeup, or a man shaving. Practice your story until you can do it the same way three times in a row. Then we'll have the class try to guess what you're saying.

Traveling Alongside/Following

Setting: Traveling in general space with a partner

Tasks/Challenges:

🅣 In many of our other lessons you were practicing another type of relationship when you followed your partner around the space: leading and following.

Now let's try traveling alongside (next to) your partner. One person is still the leader and the other the follower, but you both move as if you were a team of horses: beside each other. Switch leaders when I give the signal. This activity is harder than leading and following, so you have to watch very closely what your partner does. Start out with slow walking, and you can get faster gradually. Once you get the hang of it, try to find fun, different ways to travel.

🅣 Now try to speed it up a little. Watch carefully. Try to follow exactly.

The leader must be aware of the follower's capabilities so that the leader challenges the partner but doesn't frustrate the partner with movements that are too difficult.

Following with a Group

Setting: Traveling in general space with a group

Tasks/Challenges:

🅣 This time, you're going to try another type of following: from behind, with four or five of you in a group. The first person in line is the first leader

©Lars A. Niki

Children try to match each other's rocking motions.

and leads the group all over the room. Start with walking. Then when you hear the drum (or tambourine), the first person goes to the end of the line, and the second person becomes the leader and travels in a different way—for example, if the first leader hops, the second leader might gallop; this change continues until everyone has had a chance to lead. The activity is just like Follow the Leader. Remember, no touching. Can your group come up with five different ways to travel? Can you add different pathways, levels, or directions to your travel?

T This time you're going to make the activity even harder. I'm not going to give you the signal to change anymore. Your group will have to make up its own change signal—maybe a hand clap or a whistle. You'll start as you did before, with the first person leading. Then at some time, the second person in line will give the change signal and at the same time start traveling a new way. When this happens, the whole line starts to follow the new leader, and the old leader goes to the back of the line. The hard part is that you're going to do this without stopping the movement; try to always keep moving. Keep going until everyone has had a chance to be the leader. Remember, the second person in line always gives the change signal.

Meeting/Parting

Setting: Partners working in self-space and general space

Tasks/Challenges:

T Now you're going to work with partners again. Find a different partner. First you and your new partner are going to work only with your hands while sitting in a self-space, facing each other. Very slowly, try to bring your hands as close to your partner's as you can without touching them. As soon as your hands are close, pull them as far away as you can without moving your body.

T This relationship is called *meeting and parting*. To make it a little easier, I'm going to give you a drumbeat to go by. On the six slow counts of the drum, bring your hands as close as possible without touching them, and freeze. Then, on the sudden loud beat, quickly pull your hands as far away as possible, as if you don't want them to touch poison.

T Now try meeting and parting with your whole body. Stand up and move a few feet apart. Use the six slow drumbeats to walk as close together as

possible without touching, and then freeze. On the sudden beat, quickly move back to where you started. The secret is to walk away quickly, as if you were a flash of lightning, and then freeze very still.

T The task will be harder this time. You'll still have the same partner, but you will be traveling around the room without your partner. When you hear the drumbeat, quickly come toward your partner and freeze very close to each other in a matching shape, just for a few seconds, and then begin your traveling again. Do this every time you hear the signal. The secret is to always know where your partner is. Maintain eye contact but also watch for others.

T This time, as you and your partner meet on the sound of the signal, come together as if you're greeting a friend you haven't seen in a long time; then, as you get right up to each other, you realize that you really don't know the person and quickly move away. It could be really funny.

Forming Cooperative and Collaborative Relationships

Setting: Groups of four traveling and throwing and catching balls or beanbags in a large space. The tasks work well if a lined field (such as a football field) is available and the children can follow the lines as guides. The tasks also assume that the children are at least at the control level of catching

Tasks/Challenges:

T So far, all our relationships with people involved how we moved with those people. In your group of three, you're going to travel in a line spread out across the field (gym) toward the other side. As you travel, throw the ball (beanbag) back and forth to each other, always trying to stay the same distance apart. Imagine a marching band moving across the field but throwing a ball as they move. The secret is that the receivers move slightly ahead of but not toward the passers, and the passers throw the ball ahead of the receivers so they don't have to stop walking to catch it. This type of relationship is called a *cooperative relationship* because everybody has to work together to make it work.

When children begin to work with others in collaborative and competitive situations involving a manipulative skill (e.g., throwing and catching), the skill level tends to deteriorate briefly if they're concentrating on the relationship. This should be expected and explained.

T Now you're going to change the cooperative relationship a little. You're still going to work with your group of three to move the ball across the field (gym) while staying the same distance apart,

but one person is going to try to steal the ball while it is in the air coming toward you. It will be really hard to resist the temptation to go close to your own players to try to help them, but remember you have two goals: to stay away from your teammates and to not let the other person steal the ball. It really does help to stay away from the other people on your team.

This is called a collaborative relationship because you have to work with the people on your team to keep the other person from getting the ball. Let me give you a few more hints on how to make such a relationship work really well. First, when it's your turn to receive the ball, move slightly in front of the passer so the passer can easily throw the ball to you. Second, pass before the defender gets close to you; when you're free to pass, don't wait until the defender is so close that you're forced to pass.

You may want to make the choice of having a defender optional because for some children it will be enough of a challenge to try to throw, catch, and travel at the same time with a defender.

Meeting and Parting in a Cooperative Group

Setting: Groups of three or four in general space

Tasks/Challenges:

 This time, instead of meeting and parting with a partner, you're going to meet and part with a small group. Your group forms a group shape (e.g., circle, square, triangle). Remember, be close but not touching. Then on the signal, suddenly leave, as if you're in a hurry, but take only a few steps and then freeze into a shape you like. On the next signal, slowly come back to your group and form the same group shape with which you started. To repeat, start with a group shape; on the signal, quickly leave and form a shape of your own; and then on the next signal, return to the first group shape—almost as if someone was playing a movie forward, backward, forward, backward.

Ⓒ Let's work on this activity with one series you really like. Practice it so it works out the same each time. This will involve hard thinking. It may help to count your steps so you know exactly how far to move. It also helps not to laugh too much. Who knows, you could be stars!

Performing Solo

Setting: Groups of six, each group with a foam ball and markers to define an area for each group; pencil and paper for each child

Tasks/Challenges:

Ⓣ You're going to play several small tag games—only six people in a group. Start with two people as taggers. When you get tagged, do not sit out, but become a tagger, so in the end there will be many taggers and one person in the middle. When you finish one game, just start another one. The last two players left in the middle are the first taggers in the next game. Remember, think about what it's like to be left in the middle.

After the youngsters have played the game, you have an excellent opportunity to briefly discuss the feelings of being in a solo relationship when each child is the center of attention. Point out that some people (probably the highly skilled) like being solo, but others (probably the less skilled) prefer to not be solo.

Applying the Concept of Relationships

The concept of relationships with objects and people is a beginning theme in the dance and gymnastics areas as the children are taught the concepts of *over, under, around, through, along,* and *onto.* This is explained further in Chapters 29 and 30. At this time, however, focus is on whether the child understands the concept rather than on how she is doing the skill. For example, you could observe whether a child was actually jumping symmetrically over a hurdle rather than whether she was crossing without knocking it over or using correct form. Once you're sure the child understands the concept, then in later grades you will focus on the critical elements related to successful jumping. Once a particular concept has been learned, it can also be used for expressive purposes in dance.

We don't introduce the concept of relationships with objects in the games area until children have reached at least the control level for the manipulative skills (e.g., throwing, kicking) (Chapter 5). Children must learn to manipulate objects alone before they can reasonably be expected to manipulate them in relation to objects or people. If children are given tasks involving manipulative skills and relationships too early, they become frustrated.

The concept of relationships with others is the last concept we introduce. Socially, children enjoy working near other children at a very young age (parallel play), but often physically and cognitively, they aren't able to function effectively in relationship to others. For example, children at the precontrol level don't possess enough skill to be able to consistently work with a partner throwing and catching a ball. Therefore, it's best not to address relationships with others as a concept

until the children's fundamental movement skills are adequate and they've matured enough socially so their abilities are enhanced when they work with other children. There are no magical ages or times for introducing the different relationship concepts. Each teacher must reflect on information about the environment, the children, the skill, and personal ability to determine the best time for introducing the concept of relationships. Typically, however, the concepts are introduced in the early elementary grades and then revisited when the children are practicing various skill themes.

Competition

We were not sure where to discuss competition within the skill theme approach, so we chose to place it at the end of the relationship chapter because most competitive situations involve relationships—between individuals, partners, or groups. The Society of Health and Physical Educators (SHAPE America 2009) suggests that requiring students to compete in games in which there are "winners and losers" is an inappropriate practice for elementary school physical education, especially when there are rewards for winning and losing in class games. Traditionally, however, physical education classes have consisted of a plethora of team sports, especially at the secondary level.

We are not opposed to competition! We are, however, opposed to requiring children to compete in games against their will. When children, or adults for that matter, choose not to compete, it is often because they do not have the prerequisite skills (are at the precontrol or control level) or prefer not to be placed in situations that are potentially humiliating or embarrassing. This is hard for many to understand, especially physical education majors, many of whom were highly skilled athletes and thrive on competitive situations. An emphasis on winning creates an intense emotional involvement that can produce disturbing feelings in some children.

In the skill theme approach, if competition is involved, it is often deemphasized by the teacher, and you will not find games pitting one half of a class against another. However, you will find many ideas for small-sided games and opportunities for children to design their own games (Chapter 31). When children play small-sided games, they have a choice to keep score or not. (We often find they intend to keep score but forget to do so after a few minutes into the game.) In the skill theme approach, we try to help children to understand that it's acceptable to choose not to keep score.

Finally, we need to realize there are many opportunities for children to participate in competitive situations outside of physical education. By the time they are in third grade, many have already been on softball, basketball, soccer, or swim teams, or have participated in other types of competitive situations. Thus, competition is not new for most youngsters. When teachers can help children to place competition in perspective and understand the strong feelings associated with winning and losing, they need to do so. The major purpose of the skill theme approach, however, is to encourage children to develop movement skill proficiency and positive attitudes toward physical activity. Although some youngsters thrive in competitive situations, others do not. For this reason, in the skill theme approach, we present competition as a choice, not as a requirement.

Reading Comprehension Questions

1. List three tasks you might use when teaching children each of the three relationship categories in this chapter—body parts, relationships with objects, and relationships with people (total of nine tasks).

2. What does the term *functional understanding* mean?

3. Today you made symmetrical and nonsymmetrical shapes when you were in class, studying, or eating lunch. Briefly describe what you were doing when you made your symmetrical shapes and when you made your nonsymmetrical shapes. For example, "When I was taking a nap I was in a . . ."

4. We recommend that you teach the concept of relationships with objects before teaching relationships with people. Why?

5. Briefly describe one example of when you prefer to be in a solo relationship as defined in this chapter. Then describe one example when you prefer not to be in a solo relationship.

6. We recommend that solo performances and intergroup experiences be voluntary, not required. Why?

7. Explain the difference between mirroring and matching. Use one example from the book and one example from something you did yesterday.
8. Pick a team sport with which you are familiar. Use the eWheel (http://www.mhhe.com/graham10e/eWheel) (movement analysis framework) (Figure 16.1) to indicate how five of the 22 relationship concepts are used when playing that game at a high school or college level.
9. The last section in this chapter is titled "Competition." Do you agree or disagree with it? Why?

References/Suggested Readings

[SHAPE America] Society of Health and Physical Educators. 2009. *Appropriate instructional practice guidelines, K-12: A side-by-side comparison.* Reston, VA: SHAPE America.

[SHAPE America] Society of Health and Physical Educators. 2014. National standards and grade-level outcomes for K-12 physical education. Champaign, IL: Human Kinetics.

Skill Theme Development

Courtesy Children at Monfort, Chappelow or Shawsheen Elementary Schools, Greeley, CO

Chapters 17 to 27 discuss the content of the skill themes we focus on in our physical education programs. Each chapter begins with an introduction to the skill theme; the introduction includes a discussion of the skill theme's characteristics and how the theme can be applied to teaching children. It's tempting to skip the introduction and get to the actual lesson ideas, but we recommend that you carefully read the introduction so you'll be able to adapt the skill theme to your particular needs. Obviously, you'll change some of the ideas; an understanding of the skill as taught to children will help you make these adaptations.

Each skill theme chapter is arranged in a logical progression, from precontrol through proficiency levels as explained in Chapter 5. Precontrol experiences are designed for exploration of the skill; experiences at the control, utilization, and proficiency levels are designed to lead youngsters in the skill development of the particular theme. This progression is accompanied by what we call a progression spiral, which outlines the content of each skill theme. Each line in the spiral corresponds to a section in the chapter that explains how to develop that idea. The progressions are presented as a series of tasks and challenges (not lessons) that you will be able to develop based on the skill level and abilities of your students.

The skill theme chapters are based on the generic levels of skill development, not on chronological age or grade-level progressions. While many of the tasks and challenges in a skill theme may be successfully completed at the precontrol or control levels in elementary school, that will not be true at the utilization or proficiency levels where children are asked to apply the skill in more complex contexts. Therefore, practice at these levels will need to continue in middle school and even into high school physical education. The development of competency requires time and deliberate practice of skills; placing students into physical activity situations before the competent skill base is developed results in failure and frustration, which will likely not lead to a lifetime of physical activity.

Each series of tasks begins by describing the space and equipment you will need. At the precontrol level, children are encouraged to explore movements, and therefore, cues are not provided. At the next three generic skill levels, however, cues are provided before the actual task(s). In parentheses next to each cue are phrases to further define the cues. You are reminded that it is probably most effective to focus on only one of these cues at a time (see Chapter 7, page 95). The reason we provide several at the beginning of the series of tasks is to allow you to observe your children to determine which cue will be the most appropriate for them. Sometimes when children progress to a more advanced level of the skill, you will find cues within the tasks. When this occurs, the cue is in bold print. The idea is for the teacher to refine the quality of the skill and place the student's focus on the cue.

Following the cues are one or more suggested tasks (designated with the symbol **T**) and also challenges (designated with the symbol **C**). As you recall, tasks and challenges were described in Chapter 6. In addition, you will find suggested assessments (Chapter 12) to help you determine how well the children are understanding the concepts and skills you are teaching.

We encourage you to adapt the suggested progressions and implied methodologies to suit your students' needs and your teaching goals. Our suggestions are certainly not prescriptions. Reflect on your situation and your students, and design the curriculum for your children.

Key Concepts

- Skill themes are fundamental movements modified into more specialized patterns that become increasingly complex as the students develop skillfulness.

- Skill themes include: manipulative (kicking and punting; throwing and catching; volleying and dribbling; striking with rackets, paddles, and long-handled implements); nonmanipulative (rolling, balancing, transferring weight, jumping and landing, stretching, curling, bending and twisting); and locomotor skills (traveling, chasing, fleeing, and dodging).

- Learning experiences in the skill theme chapters are designed to assist children in moving from precontrol to control to utilization to proficiency levels of skill.

- Children need multiple and recurring experiences with each skill to become competent movers.

- When skill themes are introduced, the initial tasks allow children to explore the skill (precontrol). Tasks then focus on helping children produce the correct skill in non-changing environments (control). This is followed by combining skills in dynamic situations (utilization), and finally the use of skills in a variety of changing environments (proficiency).

- It is only after the skill can be produced consistently that it is made more complex with the addition of movement concepts.

- As children gain increasing competency with skills, the skills are applied in educational gymnastics, dance, and game contexts.

Traveling

Drawn by children at Monfort, Chappelow or Shawsheen Elementary Schools, Greeley, CO.
Courtesy of Lizzy Ginger; Tia Ziegler.

Children are first capable of changing the location of their bodies at about three months of age, when they turn over from their backs onto their stomachs. Unless developmentally delayed, they'll soon begin to crawl and then creep. At about one year, they'll take their first step. And by the time they enter preschool, they'll exhibit relatively mature walking patterns. While many children enter kindergarten with the ability to walk, run, gallop, and skip, the locomotor patterns may not be at a mature, efficient level of execution. Practice of these skills, along with appropriate cues, will assure children are progressing toward efficient locomotor patterns.

Most children attain a mature walking pattern through experience. Verbal cues from the teacher, plus modeling the correct pattern, will help children with inefficiencies. Continued deviations (e.g., toes turned out or in) signal the need for a thorough physical examination by a pediatrician.

Similarly, it's important to ascertain how many students can perform the fundamental locomotor skills that emerge from the walk-run pattern: hopping, skipping, galloping, sliding, and leaping. Young children need much practice of each locomotor skill when introduced, and they also need distributed practice throughout the lower-elementary grades. Young children inexperienced in different locomotor skills may not be able to give the correct locomotor response to a verbal command because they often lack cognitive understanding rather than motor performance. We've found that modeling is the best way for young children to learn these skills; the children follow the example of the teacher and other children who've mastered the skill. It's also important to name the locomotor skill each time you or others demonstrate it to the children.

By the end of second grade, it is reasonable to expect that most children will be able to execute the locomotor skills of hopping, sliding, galloping, and skipping in response to a verbal command. This expectation implies that children recognize the word and the action it represents and that they've mastered the skill. After mastery of the locomotor skills, learning experiences for traveling center on combining locomotor skills with movement concepts in educational gymnastics, dance, and games and recognizing the locomotor skill and its use within each of those contexts. See Box 17-1 for linkages between the skill theme of traveling and the *National Standards & Grade-Level Outcomes for K–12 Physical Education* (SHAPE America 2014).

Fundamental Locomotor Skills

The locomotor skills of walking, hopping, skipping, galloping, sliding, running, and leaping are presented below with a listing of the critical elements for each.

Box 17-1

Traveling in the *National Standards & Grade-Level Outcomes for K–12 Physical Education*

The skill theme of traveling is referenced in the *National Standards & Grade-Level Outcomes for K–12 Physical Education* (SHAPE America 2014) under Standard 1: "Demonstrates competency in a variety of motor skills and movement patterns." The intent of the standard is developing the fundamental skills needed to enjoy participation in physical activities, with the mastery of movement fundamentals as the foundation for continued skill acquisition.

Sample grade-level outcomes from the *National Standards** include:

- Performs locomotor skills while maintaining balance (K)
- Hops, gallops, jogs, and slides using a mature pattern (1)
- Skips using a mature pattern (2)
- Runs with a mature pattern (2)
- Leaps using a mature pattern (3)
- Uses various locomotor skills in a variety of small-sided practice tasks, dance, and educational gymnastics experiences (4)
- Demonstrates mature patterns of locomotor skills in dynamic small-sided practice tasks, gymnastics, and dance (5)

Additional grade-level outcomes for traveling and locomotor skills specific to educational dance and gymnastics can be found in Chapters 29 and 30, respectively.

The skill theme of traveling is also referenced in Standard 2: "Applies knowledge of concepts, principles, strategies and tactics related to movement and performance." The intent of the standard is facilitation of learners' ability to use cognitive information to understand and enhance motor skill acquisition and performance.

*Suggested grade-level outcomes for student learning.

These critical elements will be helpful as you observe the particular locomotor skill, provide individual feedback for assistance, and select appropriate learning experiences for the children performing that locomotor skill. Illustrations of "correct" patterns for the locomotor movements can be found in Boxes 17-2 through 17-7. You may notice the skill of jumping is not included in the following descriptions. Although jumping is considered a locomotor skill if used for travel, the primary use of the skill is for height or distance. For that reason, we have devoted an entire chapter to jumping and landing (Chapter 20).

Box 17-2

Critical Elements: Hopping Pattern

One to one

Lift knee

Lift arms

Body stays erect

Momentarily airborne

©Derek Sine&Van Tucker

Walking

Walking is a process of alternately losing balance and recovering it while moving forward in an upright position.

- While moving forward, the body should display minimum up-and-down or side-to-side movement.
- The arms and legs move in opposition.
- A mature walking pattern looks smooth and is accomplished easily.

Most school-age children have a mature walking pattern unless developmentally delayed. The teacher's first task is to evaluate traveling performance to ensure that any youngster who exhibits severely immature or inefficient patterns will receive remedial assistance. When assessing the walking pattern of young children, look for the following inefficiencies:

- Bouncy walk—too much vertical push
- Excessive swing of the arms away from the sides
- No arm swing
- Feet held too close together so the entire body looks jerky as the child walks
- Feet held too far apart—duck walk
- Toes turned out
- Toes turned in—pigeon-toed
- Walking on toes or balls of feet
- Head too far forward—body leaning forward before the lead foot touches the ground

Hopping

The hop is a springing action from one foot, in any direction, to a landing on the same foot (Box 17-2). The knee seldom straightens fully; the work of the ankle joint is primarily what accomplishes the push into the air and the absorption of the landing shock.

The critical elements for hopping are:

- Take off on one foot and land on the same foot
- Knee of nonlanding leg is bent and lifted
- Momentarily airborne
- Arms push up and down (to lift and for balance)
- Body stays erect

Skipping

The skip is a combination of a step and a hop, first on one foot and then on the other foot (Box 17-3). The pattern has the alternation and opposition of the walk plus the same-sided one-foot hop. The skip has an uneven rhythm.

The critical elements for skipping are:

- Feet alternate lead in a rhythmical pattern
- Arms move in opposition to feet
- Step and hop on one foot and then on the other foot
- Arms swing as leg lifts on hopping action
- Momentarily airborne

Box 17-3

Critical Elements: Skipping Pattern

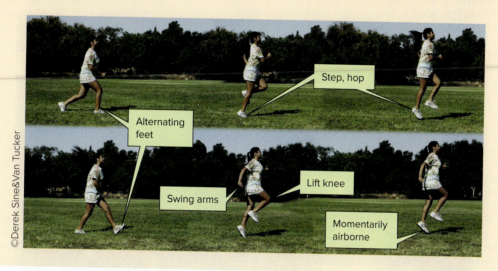

Step, hop

Alternating feet

Swing arms

Lift knee

Momentarily airborne

©Derek Sine&Van Tucker

Galloping

The gallop is an exaggerated slide in a forward direction (Box 17-4). The lead leg lifts and bends and then thrusts forward to support the weight. The rear foot quickly closes to replace the supporting leg as the lead leg springs up into its lifted and bent position. The rhythm is uneven, the same as that of a slide.

The critical elements of galloping are:

- Hips (torso) facing forward in direction of travel
- Travel in a forward direction with a smooth, rhythmical action on the balls of the feet
- Momentarily airborne (no foot drag)
- Demonstrates lead leg step-close action without crossover
- Arms in front, bent slightly

Sliding

A slide is similar to a gallop but in a sideways direction (Box 17-5). The lead step is quickly followed by the free foot closing to replace the supporting foot. The lead foot quickly springs from the floor into a direction of intended travel. The weight is primarily on the balls of the feet. The sequence is repeated for the desired distance. The movement has an uneven rhythm: step-close, step-close, step-close.

The critical elements for sliding are:

- Travel in a sideways direction with a smooth, rhythmical action on the balls of the feet

- Demonstrates lead leg step-close action without crossover
- Hips (torso) facing forward while side clearly faces direction of travel
- Momentarily airborne (no foot drag)
- Arms are lifted by the sides

Running

During the earliest stage of running (at about 24 months), a child's new speed produces precarious balance. The child makes exaggerated leg movements. In particular, the knee of the recovery leg swings outward and then around and forward in preparation for the support phase. This knee action is accompanied by the foot of the recovery leg toeing out. These exaggerated movements gradually disappear as the legs become longer and stronger.

Most school-age youngsters are able to run at a relatively fast speed and are fairly successful at changing direction while running. In a mature running pattern (observed when the children are attempting to run at maximum velocity), each leg goes through a support phase and a recovery phase, and the full sequence produces two periods of nonsupport (Box 17-6). We have found that some children need instruction and ample practice opportunities running at maximum speed to develop the mature running pattern. The critical elements for running are:

- Toes point forward
- Feet land heel to toes

Box 17-4

Critical Elements: Galloping Pattern

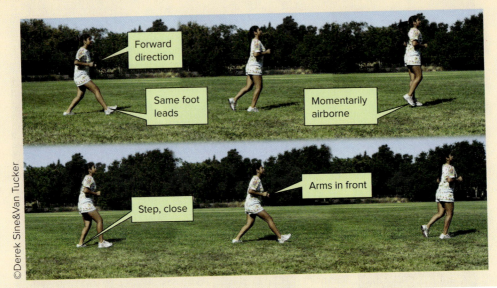

©Derek Sine&Van Tucker

- Trunk leans slightly forward
- Arm-leg opposition throughout running action
- Arm swing is forward-backward pumping action (no crossing of the midline)

Leaping

A leap is an extension of a run—greater force is used to produce a higher dimension than a run (Box 17-7). A one-foot takeoff propels the body upward to a landing

Box 17-5

Critical Elements: Sliding Pattern

©Derek Sine&Van Tucker

Box 17-6

Critical Elements: Running Pattern

©Derek Sine&Van Tucker

Box 17-7

Critical Elements: Leaping Pattern

©Derek Sine&Van Tucker

on the opposite foot. Arm opposition is the same as for the run. There's an emphasis on body and arm extension for height or for distance. Upon touching the floor, the landing leg bends to absorb the force of the body and continues with the run (run, leap, run action).

The critical elements for leaping are:

- Takeoff is on one foot, propelling body upward and landing on the opposite foot
- Legs extend for height and distance
- Arms extend for height and balance
- Knee bends to absorb force on landing
- Continue the run

Young children love to move; they run, jump, leap, hop, skip: They move! Children run in games at recess; they chase, dodge, and flee for the pure joy of movement. They run, slide, leap, and jump in basketball, soccer, and football. They gallop, skip, jump, and leap in dance. They run, jump, and leap in gymnastics. The skills of traveling are critical for children's success in dance, gymnastics, and games. The progression spiral shows the development of the skill theme of traveling at the precontrol, control, utilization, and proficiency levels.

Precontrol Level (GLSP): Experiences for Exploration

Activities at the precontrol level are designed to introduce children to the fundamental locomotor patterns and help them explore the skill of traveling. Children learn to travel without bumping others; they experience traveling with different locomotor movements and traveling on body parts other than their feet. A functional understanding of space awareness (Chapter 14) is a prerequisite for traveling skills.

Traveling in General Space

Setting: Children scattered throughout general space

Tasks/Challenges:

T On the signal, travel any way you wish in general space. Control your speed to avoid colliding with others, and stop without falling when you hear the drum.

T Change to a different way to travel. Some of you are hopping; some are galloping; most are running. Travel throughout general space any way except running. Watch out for others as you travel to avoid collisions

T See how many different ways you can travel on your feet, sometimes traveling on one foot, sometimes on two feet, sometimes on one foot and then the other.

C Show me three different ways you can travel on your feet.

Traveling with Different Locomotor Movements

Setting: Children scattered throughout general space

Tasks/Challenges:

T When we explored different ways to travel, some of you were hopping, some were walking, some were galloping. Let's explore the different locomotor skills as we travel in general space. Travel throughout general space with your favorite locomotor movement; I will name the ones I see: walking, running, galloping. . . .

T Travel throughout general space with a hop, staying on one foot. Switch to the other foot after several hops so you will not become tired and lose your balance.

T Travel throughout general space with a jump, two feet to two feet. Make some of your jumps small and low, some of them long, some of them high in the air.

T Travel throughout general space with a gallop, with one foot always staying in front of the other. Can you gallop backward?

T Travel throughout general space with a run, always looking for the open spaces. Remember, stop on the signal without falling down.

Thus far, you have traveled by hopping, jumping, galloping, and running; you were already very good at walking. Of those five locomotor actions, choose your favorite three and practice them as if you were going to teach them to someone who does not know how to do them—perfection!

Traveling in Different Ways

Setting: Children scattered throughout general space

Tasks/Challenges:

T Travel throughout general space on two feet. On the signal, change the way you are traveling, yet remain on your feet.

C How many different ways can you travel on your feet?

T Travel throughout general space on two feet and two hands; travel forward, backward, and sideways on your feet and hands.

T Travel throughout general space on body parts other than your feet. How many different combinations of body parts can you use for travel?

Traveling with Imagery

Setting: Children scattered throughout general space

Tasks/Challenges:

T Travel throughout general space like a rabbit, jumping from two feet to two feet; travel like a frog, jumping from pad to pad.

T Travel throughout general space, walking as if in sticky mud or a sea of peanut butter.

T Walk like a robot. March like a soldier.

T Travel throughout general space like a large elephant. Will your steps be heavy or light?

T Travel like a tall giraffe with your head above the clouds.

T Run quietly like deer through the forest.

T Slither like a snake. Crawl like an inchworm, then like a snail.

Traveling Through Rope Pathways

Setting: An obstacle course of markers and ropes on the floor to form varying pathways of different widths for travel (Figure 17.1)

Tasks/Challenges:

T On the signal, travel around the markers and between the rope boundaries without touching them. Try to finish with a perfect score—no touches.

T Repeat the course using a different locomotor movement.

C Challenge yourself to travel throughout the obstacle course three times with no collisions with others or the items in the course.

Figure 17.1 Rope pathways as an obstacle course.

Traveling Among Wide and Narrow Shapes

Setting: Children with partners, scattered throughout general space

Tasks/Challenges:

Ⓣ Stand in your self-space, stretching in all directions to be sure you have a clear self-space; it is not important that you be near your partner. Partners A, stand in your self-space, extending your arms and legs to make a very large, wide shape. Partners B, travel throughout general space with any locomotor pattern you wish; avoid touching anyone traveling or a stationary wide shape. *Have partners switch roles after 30 seconds of travel.*

Ⓣ Partners B, stand in your self-space with a tall, narrow shape. Partners A, run throughout general space with no collisions; always look for open spaces as you travel. Switch roles after 30 seconds.

Control Level (GLSP): Learning Experiences Leading to Skill Development

Control-level experiences are designed to help children master the basic locomotor skills and expand their traveling abilities. The teacher's attention now changes to using the critical elements and modeling the correct form. Mastery of the basic locomotor skills is the primary focus for beginning control-level experiences.

Following mastery of the locomotors, the learning experiences focus on using different traveling patterns with movement concepts, traveling rhythmically and traveling expressively to create new dances.

A note about cues: *Although several cues are listed for many of the learning experiences, it's important to focus on only one cue at a time. This way, the children can really concentrate on that cue. Once you provide feedback to the children and observe that most have learned a cue, it's time to focus on another one.*

Traveling with Different Locomotor Patterns

Setting: Children scattered throughout general space

Cues	
Heads Up	(Keep your head up and eyes forward for good balance and to avoid collisions with others.)
Balanced Stops	(Spread your feet apart and lower your hips slightly to maintain your balance when you stop.)

Tasks/Challenges:

Ⓣ On signal, travel any way you wish in general space. Avoid colliding with others, and stop without falling when you hear the signal.

These children are enjoying traveling at a low level.

©Barbara Adamcik

When teaching the locomotor skills, include demonstrations by the teacher or a skilled student. Watch for fatigue as children tire easily when practicing locomotors.

Hopping

Cues	
One to One	(Up and down on one foot/the same foot.)
Arms Out	(Keep your arms out for good balance.)
Up, Up, Light, Light	(Make light, quick actions as you hop.)

Tasks/Challenges:

(T) Hop on one foot in self-space. Hop on the other foot.

(T) Hop on one foot as you travel in general space. Hop on the other foot.

(T) Hop on one foot five times, and then hop on your other foot five times. Continue to alternate hopping on your right foot and then your left foot until you hear the signal to stop.

Skipping

Cues	
Step, Hop	(Step forward on one foot and then hop on the same foot with an uneven rhythm.)
Lift Your Knees	(Lift your knees, swing your arms . . . step, hop.)
Keep the Rhythm	(Keep moving; don't stop.)

A clap, drumbeat, or music with the uneven rhythm will be helpful to the children.

Tasks/Challenges:

(T) Now that you can hop, you are ready to try skipping. Earlier we tried hopping five times on one foot and then changing to the other foot. The skip is a step and hop on one foot that immediately changes to a step and hop on the other foot without stopping. Try it in slow motion. That is, step with your right foot and then hop with your right foot. Step left and then hop left.

(T) Skip throughout general space until you hear the signal to stop.

(T) Find a partner and try skipping together. *Matching a student who is having difficulty with a successful skipper often helps the child having difficulty with skipping to establish the rhythm that can lead to success.*

Developmentally, some children may first be able to skip on only one side of the body before alternating sides and performing the mature skipping pattern.

Galloping

Cues	
Same Foot Forward	(Keep the same foot in front as you gallop.)
Step, Chase	(The back foot tries to catch the front foot with each step . . . but never does.)
Spring, Spring	(Make light, "springy" actions as you travel.)

Tasks/Challenges:

(T) On the signal, gallop in general space, keeping the same foot in front throughout the action.

(T) Now lead with the other foot as you gallop.

(C) Can you change the lead foot without stopping the gallop? Try five gallops with your right foot in front and then switch to five gallops with your left foot. Continue until you hear the signal to stop.

Avoid using imagery such as "gallop like a horse." This typically results in hands held as if holding the reins and a crossover step instead of the correct movement of step-close.

Sliding

Cues	
Side Leads	(Point your shoulder in the direction you travel.)
Step, Chase	(One foot tries to catch the other foot with each step . . . but never does.)
Spring, Spring	(Make light, "springy" actions as you travel.)

Task/Challenges:

(T) Raise your right arm and point toward the far side of the blacktop (gymnasium). On the signal, use a slide to travel across the area. When your left foot almost touches your right foot, step again quickly to the side with your right foot. Keep the slide

moving as you travel—no stopping. Now, repeat pointing with your left arm.

T Keep your right arm raised and slide sideways as you travel through general space. Repeat with your left arm. Now try both left and right foot leading without arms pointing.

C Can you change the lead foot without stopping the slide? Try five slides with your right foot leading and then switch to five slides with your left foot leading. Continue until you hear the signal to stop.

T Slide across the area like a dancer, arms extended to the side and your body stretched upward as you travel with a light bouncy step.

T Slide like a basketball player with your knees bent, hips lowered, and arms extended in front.

Running

Setting: Children scattered throughout general space outdoors. Markers forming a large rectangular area.

Cue	
Light on Your Feet	(Make light, buoyant landings for quick steps.)

Tasks/Challenges:

T Now that you can move without bumping others and stop on signal, try running throughout general space. Cover as much area as you can. Be sure your entire foot contacts the ground, not just your toes.

T Find a personal space anywhere on the outside of the marked boundaries. Run as fast as you can the length of the rectangular boundaries. Jog, or run slower, the width of the boundaries. Travel around the area until you hear the signal to stop (2 or 3 minutes). If you get tired, you may elect to walk. *Giving children the opportunity to run full speed will provide the chance to observe for the mature running pattern.*

Leaping

Cues	
One to One	(Take off on one foot and land on the other foot, continuing into a run.)
Soft Landings	(Bend your knee and hip as you land for a cushioned landing.)
Arms Up . . . Stretch	(Lift your arms; stretch your arms and legs as you leap.)

Tasks/Challenges:

T We did leaping when we worked on jumping and landing. Who can remember what a leap is? Right, it's taking off on one foot and landing on the other, with the body airborne between the takeoff and landing. Travel in general space by running. After running three steps, leap high in the air, and when you land, continue to run. Your travel will be this: Run, run, run, leap; run, run, run, leap. Remember to land softly by bending your knee.

T Repeat the task focusing on extending your legs and arms on each leap.

⚠ When children are running and leaping, a reminder for sufficient space and awareness of others is important to avoid airborne and landing collisions.

? *Teacher Observation of Locomotor Skills*

Arrange stations for student practice of various skills with one station set aside for assessment. At the assessment station, students will be asked to travel through general space demonstrating the locomotor skills named by the teacher (e.g., hop, gallop, skip, slide) for approximately 15 to 20 seconds. The teacher will observe for the critical elements of the skill and mark on a checklist. This assessment will inform the teacher of the critical elements for which the child needs feedback and practice.

? *Event Task: Dance of Locomotors*

Students will perform a "Dance of Locomotors" in which they travel in different ways through general space. Students will be asked to create a dance with four different locomotor skills, a beginning pose and an ending pose. Students are scattered in general space and asked to show their beginning poses. On the signal (music starting or teacher command), the students are to travel in the first movement pattern selected. Upon hearing a designated signal from the teacher, students will change to the next locomotor, continuing until all four locomotors have been performed. On the last signal, the students demonstrate their ending poses. Repeat the dance. The teacher should encourage creative modes of travel.

Criteria for Assessment

a. Demonstrates at least three different locomotors.
b. Demonstrates smooth transitions between the locomotors.
c. Exhibits a beginning and ending pose/shape.

Adapted from NASPE 1995.

Traveling to Open Spaces

Setting: Children scattered throughout general space

Cues	
Heads Up	(Keep your head up for good balance and to avoid collisions with others.)
Balanced Stops	(Spread your feet apart and lower your hips slightly to maintain your balance when you stop.)

Tasks/Challenges:

T In your self-space, look around the work space. Do you see open spaces that no one has taken as his or her space? On the signal, run to that open space. When you arrive, stop and look for another open space; run to that space.

T Travel throughout general space, always looking for the open spaces. This time you will only pause at an open space long enough to see your next open space.

C I will time you for 60 seconds of travel. Your task is to travel throughout general space always looking for and moving to open spaces with no collisions.

Performing Locomotor Sequences

Setting: Index cards with a sequence of locomotor movements written on them—for example, "Walk, hop, gallop"—one sequence card per child

Cues	
Heads Up	(Keep your head up for good balance and to avoid collisions with others.)
Pause and Go	(Pause momentarily; then continue your locomotor movement.)
Balanced Stops	(Spread your feet apart and lower your hips slightly to maintain your balance when you stop.)

Tasks/Challenges:

T Think of your favorite locomotor movement that you've practiced. On signal, use that movement to travel in general space. I should be able to identify the locomotor movement by watching you travel.

T There are cards spread around the wall. When I say "Go," get a card and bring it back to your space. Read your card. Each card contains a movement sentence: three locomotor movements separated by commas. What does a comma mean in your reading? Right—pause. After each locomotor movement, you'll pause. Your sequence will be travel, pause; travel, pause; travel, stop. Practice your movement sentence until you can do it the same way three times. Find someone near you and exchange cards.

Traveling in general space lets children practice finding open spaces.

©Lars A. Niki

Children whose reading level reflects ways to end a sentence enjoy stopping with an image of a period, an exclamation, or a question mark.

? *The above task easily becomes an assessment by including measurable criteria. Specifics for development of criteria and rubrics can be found in Chapter 12, "Assessing Student Learning."*

Moving to Rhythms

Setting: Children scattered throughout general space

Cues	
Heads Up	(Keep your head up for good balance and to avoid collisions with others.)
Pause and Go	(Pause momentarily; then continue your locomotor movement.)

Tasks/Challenges:

T Listen to the drumbeat. I'll beat a cadence of one, two, three, four, and then you'll clap the same. Listen. (Beat drum four times in even rhythm.) Now clap. Walking and running are both even rhythms. Let's try again. Listen; then clap.

T Let's walk the rhythm of the beat. Listen to the speed. (Beat four times in even rhythm, slowly.) Ready? Walk as I beat the drum. Clap as you walk.

T You'll need to walk more quickly or slowly now, depending on the beat of the drum. I'll pause between each segment so you can hear the change in tempo.

T Now run to the beat of the drum. It's an even rhythm but a faster speed. Be sure you listen for the beat. Ready, go.

Traveling with Music

Setting: Children scattered throughout general space; music with appropriate even and uneven beats for different locomotor movements; hoops, one per child, at the edge of the space

Cues	
Heads Up	(Keep your head up for good balance and to avoid collisions with others.)
Balanced Stops	(Spread your feet apart and lower your hips slightly to maintain your balance when you stop.)

Tasks/Challenges:

T Walk, skip, gallop, or hop throughout general space without touching anyone else. Remember, you may have to move to the right or left to avoid bumping into someone else. When I give the signal, stop quickly with both your feet on the floor.

T I've selected music for each of our locomotor movements. The first is for skipping. Listen to the beat. Is it an even or uneven rhythm? Right, skipping is an uneven rhythm. Begin skipping when you hear the music. Stop when the music stops.

T Now listen to the music for the gallop; it's also uneven. (Pause, play music.) Ready? Gallop.

T The music for hopping is short and quick. Clap the rhythm. Is it even or uneven? Hop on one foot to the music.

T I've saved your favorite locomotor movement until last. What is it? Running. Run quietly so you'll hear the music stop.

Children tend to practice with only their favorite locomotor skill when the task is open. We find it helps to specify each skill in addition to "your choice" or "your favorite."

C This is a game like musical chairs, except that you are never out. When the music begins, travel throughout general space using the traveling action that I call out. When the music stops, find a space inside a hoop as quickly as possible. Each time, I will remove some of the hoops. The trick is that someone must be in every hoop, but any number of people can be inside the hoops as the number of hoops decreases.

Traveling an Obstacle Course

Setting: An obstacle course using any of the following: hoops, bamboo poles, ropes, low beams, aerobic steps, mini hurdles, and other items (Figure 17.2)

Cues	
Heads Up	(Keep your head up for good balance and to avoid collisions with others.)
Pause, Look, Go	(Pause momentarily to avoid others who are also moving.)

Tasks/Challenges:

T You've worked on various locomotor skills and on moving with control. Using a combination of a hop, skip, gallop, leap, walk, and slide, move through the obstacle course without touching other people or the obstacles.

Figure 17.2 An obstacle course.

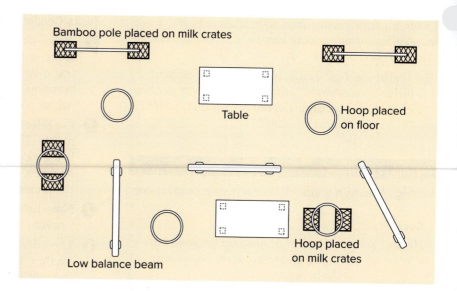

Bamboo pole placed on milk crates

Table

Hoop placed on floor

Hoop placed on milk crates

Low balance beam

Traveling in Different Directions

Setting: Children scattered throughout general space

Cues	
Heads Up	(Keep your head up for good balance and to avoid collisions with others.)
Hips over Feet	(Keep your body centered over your feet for good balance and quick changes of direction.)

Tasks/Challenges:

T You have learned six directions. Let's name them together: forward, backward, right, left, up, and down. This time as you walk, gallop, skip, or hop, change directions as you travel.

T Begin walking forward. On the signal, change directions and walk backward. Exaggerate your movements so you look like a toy soldier or robot.

T On the signal, skip in a forward direction. When you hear the drum, slow your speed, and skip to the side or backward. Take only a few skips; then continue skipping forward.

T Pretend you're going to draw a square with one foot. Hop forward, backward, to the right, and to the left to draw your square.

C This time, we will really see how well you can travel in different directions. I will call out a traveling action and a number. If the number is even, travel forward; if it is odd, travel backward.

⚠ Traveling backward can be dangerous if students try to move quickly. Encourage lowering of the body and slower movements for control when traveling backward. Running backward should be discouraged.

Remember do this last task only with students who know the difference between odd and even numbers.

Skip and Balance Dance

Setting: Children scattered throughout general space; Music of Seven Jumps (Shenanigans: Dance Music for Children, Level 1)

Cues	
Heads Up	(Keep your head up for good balance and to avoid collisions with others.)
Hips over Feet	(Keep your body centered over your feet for good balance and quick changes of direction.)

Tasks/Challenges:

T When the music begins, travel in general space skipping to the beat of the music. When the music stops, you will hear one clear beat; on that signal, stop and balance on one foot. When the music begins again, return to skipping. The music will stop with two individual beats; when you hear these beats, balance on one foot, and then the other foot. Begin skipping again with the music. Each time the music stops, I will call out a different balance to add to your previous balances.

The progression of "Seven Jumps" includes seven balances, each one added to the previous.

They include:

>*one foot;*
>
>*one foot, other foot*
>
>*one foot, other foot, one knee*
>
>*one foot, other foot, one knee, other knee*
>
>*one foot, other foot, one knee, other knee, one elbow*
>
>*one foot, other foot, one knee, other knee, one elbow, other elbow*
>
>*one foot, other foot, one knee, other knee, one elbow, other elbow, head*

This combination of travel and balances is the ingredients of the folk dance "Seven Jumps." You may choose other locomotor skills for travel to the beat as well as different balances or body shapes.

T In a small group of four, six, or eight persons, repeat the "Seven Jumps" dance traveling in a circle. For the first part, you will skip eight times in a clockwise direction. After the first balance, you will skip eight times in a counterclockwise direction. Continue alternating clockwise and counterclockwise.

C In your small group of four, six, or eight persons, use a combination of skips and balances to create your own version of "Seven Jumps." Practice with your group until you are ready to show the dance to another group or to the whole class.

Traveling in Different Pathways

Setting: Children scattered throughout general space

Cues	
Heads Up	(Keep your head up for good balance and to avoid collisions with others.)
Hips over Feet	(Keep your body centered over your feet for good balance with changes in direction and/or pathways.)

Tasks/Challenges:

T Earlier you learned three different pathways. Who remembers what they were? That's right: straight, curved, and zigzag. This time, change your pathway as you travel. Begin by walking in a straight pathway. On the signal, change to a curved pathway. Exaggerate your movements so the pathway is really quite curved.

T This time, practice traveling in a zigzag pathway. Remember, zigzag looks like the letter Z; make really sharp angles.

T Hop in a straight pathway.

T Skip in a curved pathway.

T Slide sideways in a zigzag pathway.

T Run and leap in a straight pathway.

T On the signal, begin traveling in a straight pathway. You may use any form of traveling you wish. When you hear the signal, change to another pathway. The next time you hear the drum, change your pathway again. On each pathway change, use a different locomotor pattern.

C This will be a test of how well you can travel using the different pathways. The game is like Follow the Leader. When I say "Go," find a partner whose skill in traveling is about the same as yours. Stand one behind the other. Leader, you are to travel using any traveling action you like and as many different pathways as possible. The follower will try to copy your every move. But don't make it so hard that your follower can't possibly keep up with you. Make it fun. When you hear the signal, you must be able to stop without falling over or touching each other.

Locomotors and Rhythm: The Follow-Me Dance

Setting: Instrumental music with a strong and distinct 4/4 beat; children scattered throughout general space, facing the teacher

Cues	
Heads Up	(Keep your head up for good balance and to avoid collisions with others.)
Hips over Feet	(Keep your body centered over your feet for good balance and quick changes of direction.)
Balanced Stops	(Spread your feet apart and lower your hips slightly to maintain your balance when you stop.)

Tasks/Challenges:

T We're going to practice our locomotor skills today; we'll combine the skills of traveling and keeping the beat in self-space. This is called Follow Me. Spread throughout general space, facing me. I'll move to the right, the left, forward, and backward. You'll mirror my direction. So if I go left, you go right; if I go forward, you go backward. I'll hop, jump, gallop, slide, walk, and move in other ways. After each locomotor phrase, you'll stop in

self-space and do such things as touch your hands to your heels, nod your head forward and backward, cross your knees as in a Charleston, and so on. You only need to watch and follow me.

Keep all movements in a count of eight—for example, two slides to the right and two slides to the left (eight counts of step/close); touch hands to knees in a crisscross motion eight times to the music; gallop forward two times and backward two times (eight counts of step/close); clap hands in time to the music for eight counts.

The Locomotors, Directions, and Pathways Dance

Setting: Children scattered throughout general space. Later, divide class into groups of five to eight persons; paper and pencil for each group.

Cues	
Heads Up	(Keep your head up for good balance and to avoid collisions with others.)
Hips over Feet	(Keep your body centered over your feet for good balance with changes in direction and/or pathways.)

Tasks/Challenges:

🇹 You have practiced hopping, skipping, galloping, sliding, leaping, and running. You have traveled in different directions and pathways. Now, we are going to combine a couple of movements. Walk forward four times (right, left, right, left). Now, slide sideways to the right two times touching your left toe on the second slide (slide, close, slide, touch). Reverse and go the left (slide close, slide, touch). Repeat the movement several times until you can go right from the walk sequence into the slide, close, slide, touch sequences. The final challenge is to keep the movement going. In other words, go from the left slide step directly into the walk and keep repeating it.

🇹 Make a group with five to eight people. Form a circle by joining hands and taking three steps backward as you drop hands. Your group is going to synchronize your movements. What does that mean? If you said, "Move together," you are correct. One person needs to volunteer to be the leader. The leader's role is to count down when to start ("One, two, three, go.") and everyone takes the first step with the right foot. You may find it helpful if the leader says each step. The task is to repeat the above actions as a group.

🇨 Now it is your turn. In your group, combine two or three locomotor movements with directions and pathways to create a dance. You will need to decide:

- The amount of space you'll need.
- The formation you want to dance (side by side, in a circle, one behind the other, etc.). *A demonstration of formations will be helpful here.*
- Which locomotor movements you want to perform and with what directions and pathways.

When you have created your dance, record it on paper, and practice it several times; then we will watch them. The criteria for observation will be correct execution of the locomotors, cooperative work with your group, and creative ideas in the dance.

❓ *Event Tasks.* Children's dance projects can serve as events tasks and provide excellent assessments of student learning. *See Chapter 12 for establishing criteria and designing rubrics.*

Traveling Using Different Directions, Levels, Pathways, and Locations

Setting: Several sets of task cards: one set that names single locomotor actions (e.g., walk, run, or hop); a second set that names different directions; a third set that names different levels; a fourth set that names different locations (general and self-space); and a final set that names different pathways. It is helpful to color-code the different sets.

Cues	
Heads Up	(Keep your head up for good balance and to avoid collisions with others.)
Hips over Feet	(Keep your body centered over your feet for good balance with changes in direction and/or pathways.)

Tasks/Challenges:

🇹 Choose a card from each color (stack) and return to your self-space. You are going to travel using the directions on the cards you have. For example, if your cards say "Walk," "Backward," "Low," "Straight," and "General Space," you walk backward at a low level in a straight pathway in general space.

🇹 This time, change one card of the same color with the person next to you. Now move according to the new directions.

The combinations here are endless. You could trade as many cards as you like until the children have practiced a multitude of combinations.

C With the last set of cards that you have, practice the action until you think it is so clear that anyone could figure it out just by watching you. (Give children time to practice.) Now, when I say "Go," choose a partner whom you can work with well. Go. Show your partner your sequence, and see whether he or she can guess what your cards said. Now, switch: Watch your partner's sequence, and you guess.

? *Peer Assessment.* Sharing sequences with partners can be an excellent peer assessment. *See Chapter 12 for establishing criteria and designing rubrics.*

Changing Speeds to Music

Setting: Recordings of music with increasing and decreasing speeds; children scattered throughout general space

Cues	
Heads Up	(Keep your head up for good balance and to avoid collisions with others.)
Speed Check	(Slow your speed slightly to avoid others.)
Balanced Stops	(Spread your feet apart and lower your hips slightly to maintain your balance when you stop.)

Tasks/Challenges:

T Listen to the music; it will start slowly and gradually increase in speed to a faster tempo. Do you think you can run with a gradual increase and decrease in your speed? Match your running speed with the music. Begin slowly, and gradually increase to your fastest speed; as the music begins to slow, decrease your speed to a jogging pace.

Traveling with Changes in Speed: A Dance of Water, Steam, and Ice

Setting: Children scattered throughout general space

Cues	
Pause and Go	(Pause between actions to express changes.)
Exaggerate	(Exaggerate movements and shapes for expression.)

Tasks/Challenges:

T Let's think about how water changes form as the temperature changes. At normal temperature, water is a liquid whose molecules are moving at a medium speed. As the temperature increases, the water molecules move faster and faster until the water is transformed into steam. As the temperature decreases, the molecules move more and more slowly until they finally freeze, forming ice.

Traveling while manipulating an object is used in a game setting.

©Lars A. Niki

Let's put this story into a creative dance. As I tell the story, you'll travel with changes in speed as the molecules increase their speed, decrease their speed, and freeze.

Traveling in Slow-Motion: The Sports Dance

Setting: Children scattered throughout general space

Cues	
Pause and Go	(Pause between actions to expression changes.)
Exaggerate	(Exaggerate movements and shapes for expression.)

Tasks/Challenges:

T Think about how the players move when a film is shown in slow motion or when the sports announcer replays a special segment from a game. I want each of you to think of your favorite moment in a sport. Is it when the quarterback breaks away to run for a touchdown, or was it when you scored the winning soccer goal? Perhaps it was the throw of the javelin at the Olympics or the relay team running at the track meet. Decide what kind of locomotor movement would portray your favorite moment. Combine your movements as in a slow-motion replay. How would you begin—in what position? How will the replay end? Practice the segment until you can do it three times the same way, just like a replay. Remember, it is slow motion.

C Find a partner and teach each other your sports dance. After you teach, the two of you can select one and perform it together.

Other ideas for creative dance and travel include walking through a thick jungle, walking through a completely dark and haunted house, walking on the ledge of a 10-story building, traveling across a high wire on a windy day, or traveling during a strong windstorm.

Combination Locomotors

Locomotors are essential to almost all movement forms. All dances are combinations of locomotor skills and nonlocomotor body actions. Child-designed gymnastics sequences are often inclusive of travel, balance, and weight transfer (Chapters 21 and 22). Combinations of locomotor movements are used in game and sport skills (e.g., dribbling a soccer ball in general space, catching on the move, moving sideways, and striking a ball with a racquet), as illustrated in many learning experiences in Chapters 18 to 27.

Utilization Level (GLSP): Learning Experiences Leading to Skill Development

At the utilization level, children combine travel with other skills and concepts in preparation for their application in the contexts of educational gymnastics, dance, and games. Most of the tasks focus on traveling with a variety of movement concepts and traveling with partners and in small group situations (e.g., matching traveling pathways with a partner, maintaining position beside or behind a partner while traveling and changing speeds, and the exaggeration of actions for expressive movements).

Traveling with a Partner: Matching Pathways

Setting: Sets of partners scattered throughout general space

Cue	
Heads Up	(Keep your head up for good balance and to avoid collisions with others.)

Tasks/Challenges:

T Stand back to back with a partner. When I say "Go," each partner travels in the direction he or she is facing. That is, each of you travels away from your partner. When you hear the drum, stop, turn around, and return to your partner with the exact pattern and locomotor movements you used before (Figure 17.3). Return at the same speed you used to travel away from your partner.

T Earlier you learned there are three pathways. (See Chapter 14, "Space Awareness.") All patterns are made up of those pathways or combinations of those pathways. This time as you travel away from your partner, be aware of the pathways you use. On your return, copy the same pathways.

Stand beside your partner. This time as you travel, use a slide to move away from your partner. Remember, return using the same pathway.

Select a partner, and decide who is to be the first leader. When the follower says "Go," the leader travels across the field with a combination of straight, curved, and zigzag pathways. When the leader stops, the follower then travels the same pattern. The other partner then designs the pattern. (For tips on helping children learn to design floor patterns for dance, see Box 17-8.)

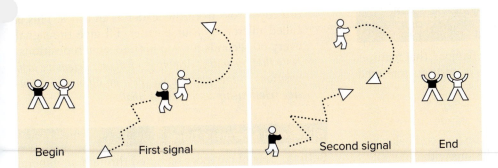

Figure 17.3 Traveling in pathways away from and toward a partner.

Begin   First signal   Second signal   End

Designing Floor Patterns for Dance

The floor patterns created in dance experiences and the locomotor movements used are important components of creative dance. The patterns created as the dancer moves can tell a story, set a mood, or portray an idea. The various ways of travel used in dance and the patterns created aren't accidental; they're planned and carefully designed. When designing the travel pattern of a dance, teacher and children can focus upon the following concerns:

- What idea stimulated the dance? Was it a music selection? An action movie? A wiggly snake?
- What qualities are inherent in the theme of the dance or the music selection? Is the tempo slow, moderate, or fast? Is the rhythm even or uneven? Is the music harmonious? Vibrant? Mellow?
- What pathway best expresses the feelings or emotions you sense? Advancing, attacking? Retreating? Collapsing? Gathering? Departing? Wavy? Angular, jagged?

It's a good idea to have the children keep notes and diagram their pathways as they design them, for several reasons. First, they will clearly visualize what the floor pattern looks like and be better able to evaluate its suitability for the dance. Second, children usually use several classes to put together a completed dance and often fail to remember ideas they had in earlier classes. Third, when children finish a dance, they can add the written work to their portfolios.

It's often beneficial to post several examples of pathways around the room on the walls, to give children an idea of what's expected. Another effective teaching aid is to post drawings of locomotor skills and positions of stillness that the children have experienced. Rather than trying to diagram a sequence from memory, youngsters can look at these posters and select movements to incorporate along their floor patterns.

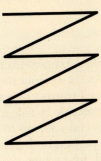

Zigzag path   Straight path

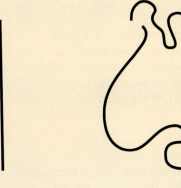

Curved path

Traveling with a Partner: Copying Locomotors and Directions

Setting: Music, such as "Dueling Banjos," that features copy phrases, AB, AB design; sets of partners scattered throughout general space

Cue	
Heads Up	(Keep your head up for good balance and to avoid collisions with others.)

Tasks/Challenges:

T Earlier this year, you practiced traveling with a partner, copying pathways. This time you will copy not only pathways with your partner, but also locomotors and directions in a dance called "The Copy Cat." For your beginning, you may choose to stand beside or behind your partner. Partner A will travel away from partner B as the first phrase of music plays; partner B will then travel with the exact pattern and locomotor. The dance continues as one partner leads and the other copies. Listen to the phrases of the music to time the length of your travel.

C You and your partner decide on your four favorite travel moves from the previous task. Practice them until you have memorized your unique "Copy Cat" dance.

? *Event Task.* Creative dance projects provide event tasks that are excellent assessments of children's work. The above task could easily be made into an event task by having students write out their dance and perform it for someone else.

Traveling with a Partner: Changing Speed and Direction

Setting: Sets of partners scattered throughout general space

Cues	
Heads Up	(Keep your head up for good balance and to avoid collisions with others.)
On Your Toes	(Keep your weight on the balls of your feet for quickness.)

Tasks/Challenges:

T Stand facing a partner approximately 3 feet apart: One of you is the leader; the other is the follower. The leader slides to the right or left, changing directions quickly. The follower tries to stay

directly across from the leader at all times. This is called mirroring your partner. I'll give the signal every 60 seconds for you both to switch positions. *Note that by adding dribbling a ball and defensive arm positions to this pattern, we form an offensive–defensive relationship used in basketball.*

Shadowing a Partner's Travel

Setting: Sets of partners scattered throughout general space

Cues	
Heads Up	(Keep your head up for good balance and to avoid collisions with others.)
On Your Toes	(Keep your weight on the balls of your feet for quickness.)

Tasks/Challenges:

T Choose a partner whose speed and ability to change directions are very similar to yours. Partner 1 stands approximately 2 feet behind partner 2. When I say "Go," partner 2 travels quickly, changing directions with sharp turns to the right and to the left; partner 1 attempts to stay within an arm's distance at all times. When you hear the drumbeat, stop without colliding or losing your balance. Partner 1 now stands in front, ready to be the new leader. Keep your eyes on your partner's waist when you're the follower.

Meeting and Parting While Traveling with a Partner

Setting: Sets of partners scattered throughout general space

Cue	
Heads Up	(Keep your head up for good balance and to avoid collisions with others.)

Tasks/Challenges:

T This task is called Leapin' Lizards. On the signal, you are to travel throughout the general space. On the cue "Leapin' Lizards," find a partner as quickly as possible, travel side by side for a few steps, then leap in unison and split up to continue traveling using the new pattern I call out. The next time you hear the signal, find a new partner, travel and do two leaps, then split to travel in a new way. We will continue until the number of leaps gets to five.

(T) This time, instead of partners, find a group of three whenever you hear the cue. Make sure all of you leap at the same time. With a larger group, it is harder to coordinate your leaps. It might help if one person calls out, "One, two, three, leap."

Performing Rhythmical Patterns

Setting: Hoops, one per child, scattered throughout general space

> **Cues**
>
> **Heads Up**   (Keep your head up for good balance.)
> **Soft Landings** (Bend your knees for a soft landing.)

Tasks/Challenges:

(T) Jump in and out of your hoop with a four-four rhythm: two jumps in, two jumps out, or three jumps in, one jump out. You may jump forward and back or side to side. Maintain an even tempo by clapping the four counts as you jump.

I'll clap the rhythm I want you to use for your jumps: one, two, three, four. Let's all clap the rhythm together before we begin our jumps. (Group practices with teacher as leader.)

(C) Practice until you can match the rhythm three times with no mistakes.

(T) Try your jumping pattern in and out of the hoop with the music. Remember, you may choose a three-one or a two-two pattern in and out.

Cultural Dances

Cultural dances are an important part of our heritage. The dances are combinations of locomotor movements—combinations into specific steps, changes in directions, and partner/group formations. Collaborate with the classroom teacher to integrate cultural dance with social studies themes. See Chapter 29, "Teaching Educational Dance," for the teaching of simple cultural dance experiences in elementary school physical education.

Traveling to Tell a Story: The Fountain of Youth Dance

Setting: Children scattered throughout general space

> **Cue**
>
> **Exaggerate** (Exaggerate your actions and gestures for expression.)

Tasks/Challenges:

(T) Using combinations of locomotor movements, body language, and gestures, tell the story of a very old person who discovers the Fountain of Youth. Let me set the stage for you. A very old person is walking down the street. The person feels weary, tired, without enough energy to hold his or her head high. While walking down the street, the oldster sees a bottle in a gutter. An examination of the bottle reveals the words "Fountain of Youth Juice." Puzzled, hesitant, yet desperate, the oldster takes a drink and then a few more. The transformation begins. The old person is changed into an ecstatic youth who dances merrily down the street. Think of the following as you prepare your dance:

What type of movements would the old person use? Jerky or smooth? Slow or fast?
What body posture and what hand gestures would the old person assume?
How would the oldster approach the bottle?
Would the transformation occur quickly or be rather slowly executed?
How would you contrast the oldster's movements with those of the ecstatic youth: type of travel, speed, level, gestures?

Dance that tells a story can easily become only pantomime. Children will need guidance in avoiding exactly replicating gestures and shapes, using more total-body movement and space.

Traveling in Bound and Free Flow

Setting: Children scattered throughout general space

> **Cues**
>
> **Exaggerate** (Exaggerate your actions and gestures for expression.)
> **Free Flow**   (Unstoppable from beginning to end.)
> **Bound Flow** (Jerky; stoppable at any moment.)

Tasks/Challenges:

(T) Here are two additional ideas for short dance phrases based on imaginary situations. First, a rag doll comes to life for a brief time. One interpretation is that the rag doll slowly comes to life with jerky, uncoordinated (bound) movements, falls over, and has trouble gaining control and balance; the doll gradually improves and is then running and leaping, turning in the air (free), and enjoying life. Then the doll suddenly stops, slowly walks back to the starting location, sits and sighs, freezes, and is a doll once again.

T Second, a balloon filled with helium escapes from the hands of its owner, floats across the sky, leaks, and falls back to earth.

These types of dance experiences are often short phrases, culminating the practice of travel patterns. Discuss with children the travel qualities and movement concepts (space awareness and effort) appropriate for each activity. Each dance should have a clear beginning, rise to a climax, and then wind down to a conclusion.

Proficiency Level (GLSP): Learning Experiences Leading to Skill Development

At the proficiency level, learning experiences are designed to encourage youngsters to use their travel skills and knowledge of travel patterns in combination with other skills to design and perform dances, gymnastics routines, and basic strategic game maneuvers.

In games, they use effective travel skills and strategic pathways, reacting quickly to a batted ball by charging forward, to the left or right, to collect a ground ball and throw accurately to a teammate; using fakes and quick changes of direction to lose an opponent while dribbling; running a planned pass pattern to receive a ball a teammate throws. See Chapters 23–27.

In educational gymnastics, they combine travel patterns with the skills of jumping and landing, balancing, and transferring weight to create sequences on the floor and on apparatus. See Chapters 19–22.

In dance, experiences become increasingly complex with movement concepts, combinations of locomotor patterns, and use of space, shapes, and nonlocomotor actions.

Tasks are more complex at the proficiency level, typically requiring children to coordinate several movements simultaneously in a dynamic context.

Traveling with Shapes and Actions: A Story Without Words

Setting: Class divided into groups of six to eight. Each group is subdivided into two groups to represent the "tribes."

Tasks/Challenges:

T Dance can be a story without words. You're going to tell the story of primitive tribes through shapes and actions. (Show children cave drawings of tribal dances.) Use your imagination as you look at the drawings. How do you think these people lived? What was their work? What was home like for them—did they have a home? Now let's put your ideas into movement terms. At what level would the people move? Would their movements be flowing or sustained, jerky or smooth?

Your dance will tell the story of two primitive tribes. Part 1 of your dance will show how the people live as a group. Show through your movements and gestures the life of a person in a primitive tribe. Part 2 of your dance will portray the two tribes discovering each other, their fear of the unknown, and their battle to defend their territory. Part 2 includes each group beginning with the movements portraying preparation for battle. The battle will consist of approach, attack (with no contact), and a retreat.

The following questions will help you design your movements for this dance story:

- Will your travel be fast or slow when preparing for battle, approaching the enemy, retreating from the battle?
- How can your gestures best represent the punching, jabbing, kicking, slashing actions of battle?
- Will your travel be low, with angular actions, or high and smooth?
- As you retreat from battle, how will your travel show caution, fear, injury?

Body Shapes and Group Travel: A Study in Form

Setting: Class divided into groups of six to eight. Each group is subdivided into two groups, A and B.

Tasks/Challenges:

T Dance doesn't always tell a story. Sometimes dance is a study in form—the shapes we can make with our bodies, the spatial patterns we create as a group. Group A will represent tradition. Use your body shapes and group travel to show the characteristics of tradition—for example, a firm, solid shape, such as a square group, formed by identical and simultaneous group movements; use of a small amount of space; and firm, sustained quality—control at all times.

Group B will represent the forces of change. The characteristics of change include individualized shapes, travel in different directions, use of a large amount of space, and a variety of movements. Working together as a group, design a dance that combines at least five shapes and three locomotor patterns to portray the characteristics of your group.

When we look at the tradition group (A), we should see oneness, sturdiness, caution; the shapes and actions of the change group (B) should portray individuality, risk taking, and freedom.

Event Tasks. Children's dance projects can serve as events tasks and provide excellent assessments of student learning. *See Chapter 12 for establishing criteria and designing rubrics.*

Performing Rhythmical Patterns: Jump Bands/Aerobic Tinikling

Setting: Set of jump bands per four students (Figure 17.4). This activity is a more active version of the original version from the Philippines where bamboo poles are used.

Tasks/Challenges:

Ⓣ Practice clapping eight times to my 4/4 rhythm. Listen carefully, are you on beat? Try hopping this eight-count sequence to the beat: left, left, right, right, left, left, right, right.

Ⓣ Jump bands is a rhythmical activity we are going to try today. It involves coordinated hopping and jumping actions with three or four people. Let's get the feel of jumping with the bands. Two students, called the band jumpers, start by standing and facing each other. Place the bands around your ankles and slowly back away until you feel a slight tension in the band. Stand with your feet together. This foot position is called "in." Practice coordinating your jumps with two beats with feet together and then two beats with feet apart. This straddle foot position is called "out." As you work, you may want to say "in, in, out, out." Repeat until you can coordinate 16 beats. *Take one step toward the other band jumper to safely remove the bands.* Change places so the other two students can practice as the band jumpers. Continue practicing until all four people feel comfortable in the role of band jumpers. When waiting your turn to use the bands, practice the "in, in, out, out " in your self-space.

Ⓣ You are ready to add the center jumpers. The center jumpers will always jump opposite the pattern of the band jumpers. In the starting position, with feet together, two students assume the role of band jumpers practiced in the previous task. On your start signal, you will jump the in, in, out, out pattern. The center jumper will stand facing one band jumper with the bands to his right. Hop on the left foot twice outside the bands followed by two hops on the right foot inside the bands (Figure 17.5). Each center jumper attempts the hops for eight counts (out, out, in, in, out, out, in, in). If successful, on your second attempt, repeat the sequence for 16 counts. The success of this task depends on

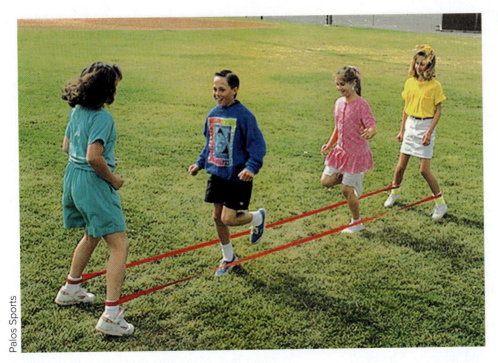

Figure 17.4 Jump bands/aerobic tinikling

Palos Sports

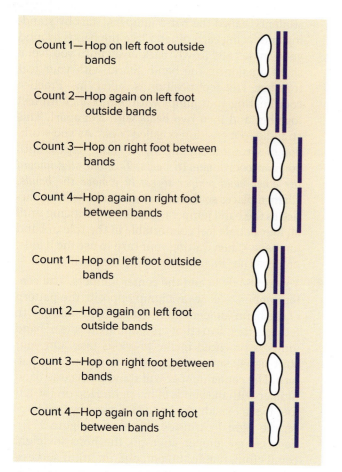

Figure 17.5 Jump bands/aerobic tinikling: basic hop pattern.

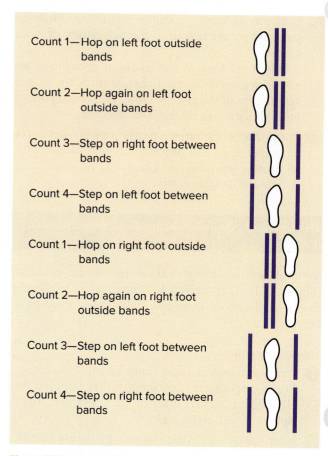

Figure 17.6 Jump bands/aerobic tinikling: advanced hop pattern.

the band jumpers and the center jumper coordinating the movement. Communication may be the key to your success. Band jumpers and center jumpers change roles after two attempts each.

T If you are comfortable with the pattern, try a double-step hop pattern (Figure 17.6). Begin by practicing the pattern without the bands. Everyone try: left, left, right, left, right, right, left, right. After everyone in your group has the pattern, try it with the bands. Start on the outside (facing a band jumper with the band to the right). The pattern for the band jumpers is still in, in, out, out. The center jumper pattern is: out left foot, left foot; in right foot, left foot; out (on the right-side band) right foot, right foot; and in left foot, right foot (Figure 17.6). Each center jumper attempts the eight counts. If successful, on your second attempt, repeat the sequence for 16 counts. Band jumpers and center jumpers change roles after two attempts each.

T The next pattern is a two-foot jump pattern. As before, the center jumper will start on the left side of the bands facing the band jumpers. The band

jumpers will repeat the same pattern as before: in, in, out, out. The pattern for the center jumper is using a two-foot jump: out, out, in, in, out, out, in, in. Everyone practice this two-foot jump pattern without the bands first. Just like the hop pattern, start to the left out, out, in, in, and transfer to the right side out, out, in, in. When you are ready, try it with the bands. After eight jumps, allow the other center jumper to try. After everyone has had a turn, try a little more challenging two-foot pattern: out, out, in, in, straddle, straddle, in, in. The straddle is landing one foot on either side of the band (Figure 17.7). You may want to practice this pattern without the bands.

C Select the pattern you like best and practice until you can perform the eight-count pattern four consecutive times (32 counts) without any mistakes.

T You are ready for doubles. Try one of the patterns with two people in the middle.

C See if your group can create a new pattern with a four-four beat. Make sure everyone is in the role of

Figure 17.7 Jump bands/aerobic tinikling: double jump pattern.

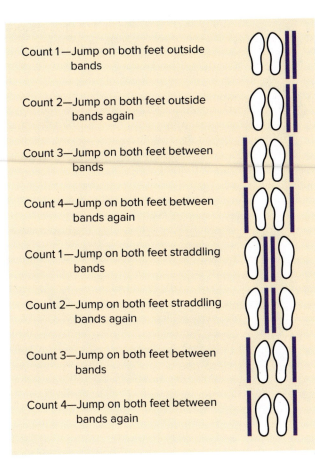

Count 1—Jump on both feet outside bands

Count 2—Jump on both feet outside bands again

Count 3—Jump on both feet between bands

Count 4—Jump on both feet between bands again

Count 1—Jump on both feet straddling bands

Count 2—Jump on both feet straddling bands again

Count 3—Jump on both feet between bands

Count 4—Jump on both feet between bands again

both center jumper and band jumper. You can do singles or doubles.

 Remind students to always take one step toward the other band jumper to safely remove the bands.

Aerobic tinikling, the use of jump bands, has become very popular and adds more activity to traditional tinikling. Many Web sites have videos demonstrating this rhythmical activity. Options include various jumps, turns, traveling across multiple bands, adding additional center jumpers, and use of current music. The American Heart Association has created jump band skill cards.

Traveling in Games and Sports

The ability to travel in games is often what separates the skilled player from the average player. Many children can throw and catch accurately and with control while they're stationary, but they regress to a precontrol level when travel is added. Thus, traveling is an important part of the utilization and proficiency sections of the games skills chapters. Games-related tasks that incorporate traveling are discussed in Chapter 18, "Chasing, Fleeing, and Dodging," as well as all manipulative skill theme chapters (Chapters 23–27).

Traveling in Gymnastics

Traveling in gymnastics supplies the buildup of force necessary for step and spring takeoffs when transferring weight on mats and onto equipment. The floor patterns the travel creates form an important component of educational gymnastics routines (Figure 17.8). Travel in relation to gymnastics is discussed in Chapters 20, 21, and 22.

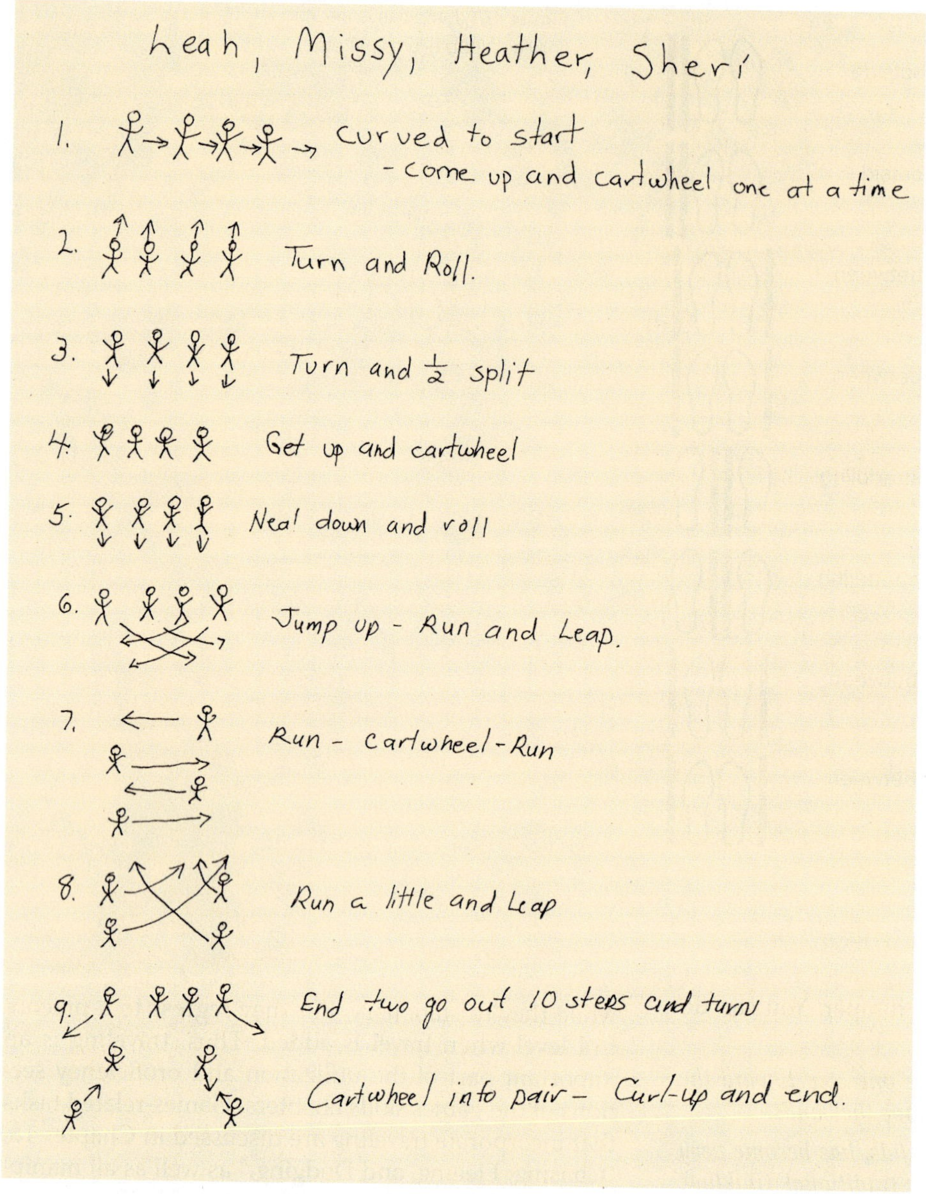

Figure 17.8 Children's travel patterns in gymnastics.

Reading Comprehension Questions

1. What components of traveling are taught in a program of physical education for children?
2. List the fundamental locomotor skills. Why are these skills important for children?
3. Describe a mature running pattern. Do all children have mature running patterns? Do all adults? Explain.
4. What are the differences between a hop, a leap, and a jump?
5. What are the similarities between a slide and a gallop?
6. Describe how travel is studied at the proficiency level in games, gymnastics, and dance.

References/Suggested Readings

Bennett, J. P., and P. C. Riemer. 2006. *Rhythmic activities and dance.* 2nd ed. Champaign, IL: Human Kinetics.

Cone, T. P., and S. L. Cone. 2012. *Teaching children dance.* 3rd ed. Champaign, IL: Human Kinetics.

Holt/Hale, S., and T. Hall. 2016. *Lesson planning for elementary physical education: Meeting the national standards and grade-level outcomes.* Champaign, IL: Human Kinetics,

[NASPE] National Association for Sport and Physical Education. 1995. *Moving into the future: National standards for physical education.* St. Louis, MO: Mosby.

[SHAPE America] Society of Health and Physical Educators. 2014. *National standards & grade-level outcomes for K-12 physical education.* Champaign, IL: Human Kinetics.

Chasing, Fleeing, and Dodging

Drawn by children at Monfort, Chappelow or Shawsheen Elementary Schools, Greeley, CO. Courtesy of Lizzy Ginger; Tia Ziegler.

Since ancient times, children have delighted in countless chasing, fleeing, and dodging games. These games all challenge a child to evade a chasing player through dodging and fleeing. Such sports as basketball, hockey, soccer, rugby, and football are simply more elaborate forms of these games using the same elements. Physical education programs can build on the innate pleasure children experience from playing these games. Often within the context of games and sometimes dance, a teacher can help youngsters develop chasing, fleeing, and dodging skills (see our skill progression development on this page).

Experience suggests that it's best to focus on chasing, fleeing, and dodging skills after children have developed a working understanding of space awareness concepts and have mastered fundamental traveling skills. In reality, chasing, fleeing, and dodging are an advanced mixture of traveling skills combined with the refined use of effort, space, and relationship concepts and often requiring the manipulation of an object. Therefore, the use of chasing, fleeing, and dodging will often appear in the traveling chapter (Chapter 17) and the manipulative skill themes chapters (Chapters 23–27). In this chapter, our purpose is to focus on the skills in some isolation before applying them in more complex situations.

Chasing, fleeing, and dodging tasks and learning experiences using these skills are best played outdoors in grassy areas (for safety) with limited and clear boundaries (to facilitate skill development). Refer to Box 18-1 for linkages between the skill theme of

Skill Theme Development Sequence

Chasing, Fleeing, Dodging

Proficiency Level

Self-designed chasing, fleeing, and dodging game
Dodging while manipulating an object in an invasion gamelike situation
Using team strategy for chasing, fleeing, and dodging in an invasion gamelike situation
Dodging in a target gamelike situation
Dodging in a gamelike situation
Chasing and fleeing in an invasion gamelike situation
Chasing and dodging simultaneously
Dodging while maintaining possession of an object
Child-designed dance
Continual fleeing and chasing with a large group

Utilization Level

Dodging while manipulating an object
Dodging in a dynamic situation
Dodging and chasing one person in a mass
Dodging limited movement obstacles
Dodging and faking moves to avoid a chaser
Dodging stationary obstacles

Control Level

Fleeing a chaser
Overtaking a fleeing person
Dodging with quick changes of speed: Darting
Dodging the obstacles
Fleeing from a partner
Dodging and tagging in a small space
Dodging in response to a signal

Precontrol Level

Make-believe chase
Traveling to dodge
Traveling to flee
Moving obstacles

Box 18-1

Chasing, Fleeing, and Dodging in the *National Standards and Grade-Level Outcomes for K–12 Physical Education*

The skill theme of chasing, fleeing, and dodging is referenced in the *National Standards & Grade-Level Outcomes for K–12 Physical Education* (SHAPE America 2014) under Standard 2: "Applies knowledge of concepts, principles, strategies, and tactics related to movement and performance." The intent of the standard is facilitation of learners' ability to use cognitive information to understand and enhance motor skill acquisition and performance.

Sample grade-level outcomes from the *National Standards** include:

- Applies simple strategies and tactics in chasing activities (3)
- Applies simple strategies in fleeing activities (3)
- Applies simple offensive strategies and tactics in chasing and fleeing activities (4)
- Applies simple defensive strategies and tactics in chasing and fleeing activities (4)

*Suggested grade-level outcomes for student learning.

chasing, fleeing, and dodging and *National Standards & Grade-Level Outcomes for K–12 Physical Education* (SHAPE America 2014).

Chasing

Chasing is traveling quickly to overtake or tag a fleeing person. In many learning experiences, the fleeing player is given a head start and allowed time to run away before the chaser can begin traveling. The fleeing player tries to avoid being caught or tagged. Thus the chaser needs to be able to run at full speed and to react quickly to changes in the direction of the fleeing player's travel.

Fleeing

Fleeing may be considered the antithesis of chasing as it involves traveling quickly away from a pursuing person or object. In most chasing, fleeing, and dodging learning experiences, the fleeing person tries to keep as much distance as possible between himself or herself and the chaser. When the pursuer does close in, the fleeing person uses any maneuver possible to avoid being tagged—the fleeing person dodges, changes direction quickly, or runs full speed. This continual demand on the fleeing person to react quickly to emerging, uncertain situations is what makes tag games thrilling for children.

Dodging

Dodging is the skill of quickly moving the body in a direction other than the original line of movement. This includes any maneuver a person undertakes to avoid being touched by a chasing person. Dodging may occur while a person is fleeing or stationary. Effective dodging actions include quick fakes, twisting, and changes of direction.

Levels of Skill Proficiency

We've found that most school-age children are familiar with a variety of tag and dodging games. But some youngsters whose chasing, fleeing, and dodging skills are at the precontrol or control level of proficiency have limited success participating in these activities; that is, although many children can chase, flee, and dodge, they can't perform these skills effectively in dynamic situations. In a game of tag, for instance, the child doing the chasing is often unable to overtake or tag any of the fleeing players and quickly tires of playing the game.

Many utilization and proficiency-level learning experiences incorporate dynamic and often gamelike tasks in the development of chasing, fleeing, and dodging skills. Because of the nature of the skills themselves, the use of dynamic gamelike activities may be more prevalent here than with other skill themes, and the tasks may initially look and sound more like "traditional" games. Look closely beyond the name. All the learning experiences involve small-sided groups in reduced spaces and are designed to help children develop and subsequently apply the skills of chasing, fleeing, and dodging. The tasks should be used as an integral part of the lesson, after the prerequisite skills are developed, not just as an activity to do. As noted, many of these experiences involve the use of groups. The groups recommended here are of small sizes and can usually be designed by having children form their own groups. See Box 7-4 (in Chapter 7) for tips on partner and group formation.

Children are inherently attracted to chasing, fleeing, and dodging, and it is easy for us and the children to get caught up in the excitement and lose sight of the quality of the movement. They can't continue these intense activities for long periods without tiring, which is almost always accompanied by a deterioration in quality. A quick search on the Internet also shows that many schools and districts have banned chasing games during recess and free time because of associated problems—most often safety. Issues noted include excessive contact when tagging as well as frequent arguments among students. Rather than establishing and maintaining firm rules about these behaviors, many administrators have found it easier to eliminate them altogether. These issues reinforce the need for clear safety guidelines in physical education class.

A note about dodgeball, which was actually included in the first edition of *Children Moving*. Over the past 30 years, our knowledge of child growth and development has expanded exponentially, and as a result, practices have changed. Consequently, we eliminated all dodgeball activities from the development of dodging skills. A number of factors influenced this decision. From a psychological perspective, we believe that throwing an object at another person, with the intent of hitting the person, subtly supports violence and goes against all that we know and believe about appropriate practice (SHAPE America 2017; see Boxes 18-2 and 18-3). From a safety standpoint, the risk of detached retinas, as well as other serious head injuries, is extreme in dodgeball (regardless of the type of ball used). From a transfer perspective, we know of no

Dodgeball Is Not an Appropriate Physical Education Activity

SHAPE America's position statement takes a clear stance that dodgeball is not an appropriate activity because "it does not support a positive climate, the application of appropriate social behaviors or the goals of physical education" (2017, p. 1). SHAPE America conveys that the traditional form of dodgeball, in which the primary goal is to eliminate opponents by hitting them with a ball, is not consistent with the goal of creating and maintaining a positive learning environment and, in doing so, subverts the primary purpose of physical education.

SHAPE America – Society of Health and Physical Educators, *Dodgeball is not an appropriate physical education activity [position statement]*. Reston, VA: Author, 2017. Copyright ©2017 by SHAPE America. Reprinted with permission from SHAPE America - Society of Physical Educators, 1900 Association Drive, Reston, VA 20191, www.shapeamerica.org.

sport that utilizes the skill of throwing at a human being. From a legal perspective, many states have already banned dodgeball from schools (check yours).

If you are a skilled player reading this book, you are probably thinking, "I loved dodgeball" and that it was "really fun." For you it was because you were the skilled player. If you were less confident in your skillfulness,

Dodgeball in *Appropriate Instructional Practice Guidelines for Elementary School Physical Education*

Appropriate Instructional Practice Guidelines for Elementary School Physical Education, under the safety aspect of the learning environment, identifies dodgeball as an inappropriate practice. Their statement, "Human target games (dodgeball) and/or drills that allow aggressive behavior to other students are permitted," **reflects what should not happen in physical education classes.** The appropriate practice is, "Activities are selected carefully to ensure that they match students' ability and are safe for all students, regardless of ability level."

SHAPE America – Society of Health and Physical Educators, *Appropriate instructional practice guidelines, K-12: A side-by-side comparison*. Reston, VA: Author, 2009. Copyright ©2009 by SHAPE America. Reprinted with permission from SHAPE America - Society of Physical Educators, 1900 Association Drive, Reston, VA 20191, www.shapeamerica.org.

you are probably joyous that it has been eliminated. It is important to remember that physical education is for all students, not just the skilled. There are aspects of dodgeball that more successful students like, such as the intrigue, the fast pace, and the challenge. As authors of this text, however, we are adamant that dodgeball should be replaced all together instead of simply being modified. Common modifications include using softer balls and allowing eliminated players back into the game (SHAPE America 2017). Despite these modifications, the fact remains that students are purposefully hitting others with an object. No matter of modification alters this fact. Therefore, in this chapter, we offer numerous alternative learning experiences that, we feel, are much more effective at developing chasing, fleeing, and dodging skills.

Precontrol Level (GLSP): Experiences for Exploration

In school situations in which preschool youngsters' opportunities to play with other children are limited, a teacher may need to provide precontrol-level chasing, fleeing, and dodging tasks. These experiences are designed to help children explore the skills of chasing, fleeing, and dodging in simple situations, such as:

- Running as fast as possible from one location to another
- Traveling around a room and changing the direction of travel quickly when on signal
- When a signal is given, quickly performing a designated dodging maneuver
- Running as fast as possible away from a partner; on the signal, running quickly toward a partner

Before beginning any practice with this theme, children should be at the control level of traveling and have had ample practice with space awareness.

⚠️ When working with chasing, fleeing, and dodging tasks that involve a finish line, be certain the line is far away from any obstructions. This precaution allows the children to run through the finish line at full speed safely.

Moving Obstacles

Setting: Children scattered in general space

Tasks/Challenges:

Ⓣ On the signal, travel in general space. Make sure you look up so you can avoid collisions with others.

Ⓣ This time, make your travel faster but still avoid others.

Have half the children move to one side of the room and half to the other.

T On the signal, both lines will try to walk to the opposite side of the room without touching anyone else. (If children are easily succeeding with the task, just make the space smaller.)

T This time, travel with three body parts touching the floor. Still no touching.

T Now you will cross the space using different levels. Everyone who has blue eyes will travel with his or her body parts high in the air; those with brown eyes should travel at a low level; those with green or gray eyes, at a medium level.

T This time you can choose any way you wish to travel, but go at a medium speed.

T Try jogging or running, if you feel ready.

C You have 10 points to start; subtract 1 point for every collision. Try to end with all 10 points.

Begin slowly. Have children walk. Gradually increase speed as you observe the children traveling competently and without collisions.

⚠️ Because of the exciting nature of chasing, fleeing, and dodging activities, children's speed tends to increase, sometimes to unsafe levels. Monitor the speed of activities, always reminding children that they must be able to stop and change directions without falling. They should be able to tag someone without pushing.

Traveling to Flee

Setting: All children spread out in a space (an outside grassy space is best) about 20 yards by 20 yards

Tasks/Challenges:

T You've all played games in which you had to run away from someone who was chasing you. This time you are going to have an imaginary chaser. On the signal, practice fleeing from your chaser by walking very quickly. On the next signal, stop. Remember, everyone is moving, so look up.

T This time, practice fleeing your chaser by running.

C How fast can you move to get away from your chaser?

Traveling to Dodge

Setting: Spots or markers spread out on the floor as obstacles

Tasks/Challenges:

T On the signal, travel around the general space without touching anyone else or any of the objects on the floor. Be sure to keep your head up so you can avoid collisions.

C How many different ways can you find to avoid the obstacles?

T This time, try to go as fast as you can with no collisions and avoiding all the objects.

Make-Believe Chase

Setting: Children spread out in general space

Tasks/Challenges:

T For this task, you will have a make-believe partner. On the signal, try to catch your make-believe partner. Your partner is very quick, so you will really have to work hard to catch him or her. Remember, everyone is chasing, so look up to avoid collisions.

T This time, you will chase your dog, which got off its leash. You want to catch your dog before it gets to the street.

? What are the differences among chasing, fleeing, and dodging?

Control Level (GLSP): Learning Experiences Leading to Skill Development

Children who can competently perform a variety of quick, dodging maneuvers while running fast are at the control level. Challenging control-level learning experiences have children keep their eyes focused on a target child and react quickly to that child's movements by chasing, fleeing from, or dodging the target child. Such tasks include:

- Staying as close as possible to a fleeing, dodging partner
- Chasing after a person who has been given a slight head start and is fleeing
- Trying to run across a field while dodging one or more chasers

These learning experiences are designed to allow children to practice chasing, fleeing, and dodging in relatively static situations. Often chasing, fleeing, and dodging are combined with only a single other variable.

A note about cues: Although several cues are listed for many of the learning experiences, it's important to focus on only one cue at a time. This way, the children can concentrate on that cue only. Once you provide feedback to the children and observe that most have learned a cue, it's time to focus on another one.

Dodging in Response to a Signal

Setting: Children scattered in general space

Cues	
Fake	(Step/lean one way; go the other.)
Split Second	(Make your moves quicker than the speed of light.)

Tasks/Challenges:

T Now you're going to become really sneaky. As you travel throughout the general space, pretend you are going in one direction and then quickly change and go in a different direction when you hear the signal.

T This time, whenever you hear the signal, try not to let anyone know which direction you'll travel; try to fake them out by looking one way and stepping the other.

T Now, instead of me giving you the signal, you'll fake on your own. Whenever you come to another person, pretend you're going to go one way, but go another. Really try to confuse the other person so he or she doesn't know where you'll be going. Make your move quickly once you decide which way you're going.

C See if you can travel and dodge for 20 seconds without colliding with anyone.

Dodging and Tagging in a Small Space

Setting: Partners in a square about 5 feet by 5 feet, each with a flag or scarf tucked in the back of the waistband or on a flag belt

Cues	
Split Second	(Make your moves quicker than the speed of light.)
Jump and Twist	(Use little jumps and twists to dodge.)

Tasks/Challenges:

T Staying within your space, your task is to try and pull the scarf from your partner's waistband. Remember you cannot hold onto your scarf. If you are able to pull it; give it back and start again.

C I will time you for two minutes. See how many times you can capture your partner's flag.

©Lars A. Niki

Practicing dodging moves with a partner would be an appropriate control-level task.

Fleeing from a Partner

Setting: Partners about 10 feet apart; spots might be useful to mark starting positions

Cue	
Split Second	(Make your moves quicker than the speed of light.)

Tasks/Challenges:

T Face your partner. On the signal, walk slowly toward each other until you are as close as you can be without touching. Then, quickly jump back as if you're scared, and walk backward to your starting position, keeping a close watch on your partner.

T This time, you're going to do the activity a little differently because you seldom would move slowly to get away from someone. Try to move a little quicker and faster as you flee or go away from your partner. Just remember: Don't go so fast that you fall down.

T Now, instead of walking away from your partner, try jogging.

Dodging the Obstacles

Setting: Low- and medium-height height cones placed around the room as obstacles

Cues

Split Second	(Make your moves quicker than the speed of light.)
Fake	(Step/lean one way; go the other.)

Tasks/Challenges:

T On the signal, travel around the general space without touching anyone else or any of the obstacles on the floor. Everything is poison. Be sure to watch for other people as well as the objects.

T This time, try to move through the area a little faster.

C I will time you for 30 seconds. See if you can travel for that long with no touches.

Children never seem to tire of this task, regardless of their skill level. As the children's skill levels increase, decrease the space between obstacles or use more obstacles to increase the complexity of the task.

Dodging with Quick Changes of Speed: Darting

Setting: Children scattered in general space

Cues

Fake	(Step/lean one way; go the other.)
Split Second	(Make your moves quicker than the speed of light.)
Dart	(Use quick changes of speed to move away from others.)

Tasks/Challenges:

T This is very similar to what you practiced before. Travel around in the general space. When you come close to someone, get as close as possible, and then quickly dodge away and look for another person to approach. There should be a clear burst of speed as you dodge away from the person—as if you're trying to escape. Remember, watch out for others.

T Dodging with speed as you did is called darting. This time practice getting as close to the person you approach as you can before quickly darting away. Make the dart very clear.

C Practice until you can make five darts in a row without having to stop.

Overtaking a Fleeing Person

Setting: Partners scattered in general space one in front of the other

Cues

Chaser	
Watch the Hips	(Watch the hips of the runner to tell his or her next move.)
Runner	
Split Second	(Make your moves quicker than the speed of light.)
Change Direction	(Use changes of direction to avoid the chaser.)

Tasks/Challenges:

T In this task you are going to try and catch your partner, who has a head start. On the first signal, the front partner darts away from the back partner. After 2 seconds, another signal will sound and the second partner, who has remained still, chases after the first partner, trying to tag him or her before I signal in 10 seconds. For the next round, switch places. You must always stay inside the boundaries. So the activity goes like this: Stand together. On the first signal, partner 1 takes off running. On the second signal, partner 2 takes off and tries to catch partner 1 before I blow the whistle in 10 seconds.

T Let's go again. Remember, never give up, even if the runner keeps getting away. See if you can use all the moves you know.

This task is appropriate when the children have learned to travel in general space without bumping into one another. Initially, children can perform this task more easily (and safely) in large areas because they're able to focus more on their partners and less on avoiding other children.

? *Exit Slip.* This is an appropriate time to use an exit slip (Chapter 12) to assess whether the children know the difference among chasing, fleeing, and dodging and the cues associated with each.

Fleeing a Chaser

Setting: Five people in a group *(see Figure 18.1 for setup)*

Cues

Fleers	
Split Second	(Make your moves quicker than the speed of light.)
Fake	(Step/lean one way; go the other.)
Dart	(Use quick changes of speed to avoid the chaser.)
Chaser	
Watch the Hips	(Watch the hips of the runner to tell his or her next move.)

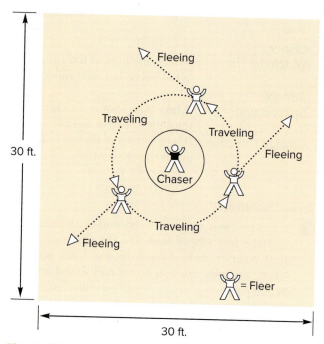

Figure 18.1 Setup for fleeing a chaser.

©Barbara Adamcik

Fleeing a chaser always provides a challenge for youngsters.

Tasks/Challenges:

T This task is designed to let you practice fleeing from a chaser. There will be five people in a group—one chaser and four fleers. The chaser, who is in the middle circle in a squat position, tells the fleers how to travel. The fleers then travel inside the box and not in the center circle. When the chaser gets to his or her feet, all the fleers run toward the outside of the square, trying not to get tagged. A fleer who is tagged helps the chaser the next time. When all the fleers are caught, the last fleer caught becomes the new chaser. Chasers, be sure to change the traveling action each time.

⚠ *This task requires multiple groups playing at once; be sure there is ample space between groups so the fleeing children do not disrupt others. Mark the boundaries clearly.*

❓ *Teacher Observation.* Each of the preceding tasks is an opportune place for teacher observation of the use of critical cues for skills of chasing, fleeing, and dodging before moving on to more dynamic settings. See Chapters 11 and 12 for the development of observation checklists and assessment items.

Utilization Level (GLSP): Learning Experiences Leading to Skill Development

When children can effectively flee a chasing person and can dodge quickly and accurately to avoid others' swift, darting movements, they're ready for utilization-level experiences. Now the youngsters'

chasing, fleeing, and dodging skills enable them to enjoy testing their abilities in ever-changing and complex environments. Challenging learning experiences include the following:

- The players of one group flee and/or dodge the players of an opposing group while controlling an object (such as a football, flying disc, or basketball).

- One group chases the members of an opposing group, but instead of fleeing their chasers, that group tries to run past and dodge the chasing group without being touched. Children at the utilization level are ready to test their skills in increasingly complex and sometimes gamelike situations. In these experiences, children will have to fake and dodge quickly in reaction to the deceptive movements of others.

A note about cues: Although several cues are listed for many of the learning experiences, it's important to focus on only one cue at a time. That way, the children can really concentrate on that cue. Once you provide feedback to the children and observe that most have learned a cue, it's time to focus on another one.

Dodging Stationary Obstacles

Setting: Groups of six: three taggers, three dodgers, each group with a space about 10 feet by 20 feet; spots on the floor to indicate where the taggers are to stand

Cues

Split Second	(Make your moves quicker than the speed of light.)
Fake	(Step/lean one way; go the other.)

Tasks/Challenges:

🇹 This task will give you a chance to practice your dodging skills. Three people in each group are taggers and the others are dodgers. Taggers stand with both feet on a spot. The dodgers start on one side of the space and try to get to the other side of the space without being tagged. After five runs, switch places. If you get tagged, try to figure out how to avoid being tagged the next time.

🇹 Now the activity gets a little harder. If you're tagged, you must freeze right where you're tagged and become a tagger. Dodgers, this will get really hard at the end, so be on your toes.

❓ *Video/Digital Analysis.* Digitally recording students chasing, fleeing, and dodging in this activity would be an appropriate way to assess their use of chasing, fleeing, and dodging in a more complex situation. Students can review the recording with a partner to assess themselves in relation to the cues.

Dodging and Faking Moves to Avoid a Chaser

Setting: Groups of six, each with a space about the size of a quarter of a basketball court

Cues

Dodgers	
Split Second	(Make your moves quicker than the speed of light.)
Fake	(Step/lean one way; go the other.)
Dart/Change Direction	(Use quick changes of speed and direction to avoid the chaser.)
Chasers	
Watch the Hips	(Watch the hips of the runner to tell his or her next move.)
Teamwork	(Decide your plan for catching together.)

Tasks/Challenges:

🇹 This chasing-and-dodging task will really make you work hard. You can't be slow; if you are, you'll be caught. Make sure you know where your boundaries are. Two people will start out as chasers—you decide who they'll be. The other four are dodgers.

On the signal, the chasers have 1 minute to try to catch all the runners. If tagged, a dodger has to freeze and then count to 10 out loud before starting to run again. The object is for the chasers to catch all the dodgers at the same time. After the first minute, change chasers and play again. Remember, the chasers have to try to catch everyone, and no one can go outside the boundaries.

After several rounds of dodging and chasing, allow the children to have a "team meeting" to develop one strategy for chasing and one for dodging that will allow them more success.

⚠️ When children tag one another, they can be quite rough, sometimes knocking others over. Here are two rules that have helped us: (1) A tag is only a touch, not a slap or hit. (2) All tags must be on the shoulders or below.

Dodging Limited Movement Obstacles

Setting: Class divided into groups of about six to eight, with each group in a clearly defined space about 20 feet by 20 feet; tape or spots on the floor approximately an arm's length apart to designate where the members of one group must place their feet (Figure 18.2)

Cues

Split Second	(Make your moves quicker than the speed of light.)
Fake	(Step/lean one way; go the other.)
Jump and Twist	(Use little jumps and twists to dodge.)
Tagger	
Watch the Hips	(Watch the hips of the runner to tell his or her next move.)

Tasks/Challenges:

🇹 To do this activity, half of your group will be taggers, and you must stand on the marks on the floor. One foot must always stay on the mark; you can move the other foot to reach in different directions. The other half of you are dodgers. You'll begin at one side of your space and try to travel through the taggers without being touched. After the dodgers make it to the other side of the space, and everyone is ready, go again, and keep trying to get through the taggers until you hear the stop signal. On the stop signal, switch places.

🇹 This time, things are going to be a little harder for the taggers. Instead of just tagging the dodgers, the taggers have to tag the left knees of the dodgers with their right hands.

Figure 18.2 Setup for dodging limited movement obstacles.

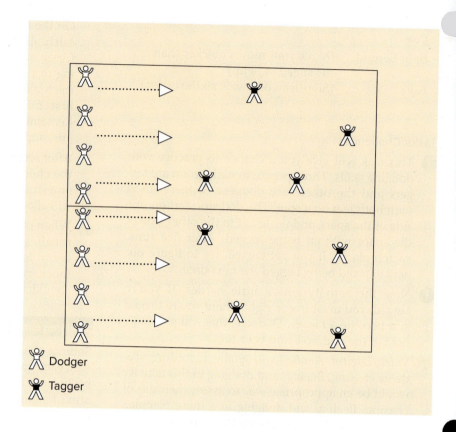

☖ Dodger

☗ Tagger

You can change these directions to several combinations of body parts—for example, right hand–right knee; left hand–right knee; left hand–right elbow.

🅣 This time, let's make it harder for the dodgers. Taggers can now move one foot to tag. The other foot has to be on the mark.

Dodging and Chasing One Person in a Mass

Setting: Partners spread apart on a field (the space should be small enough to challenge the dodgers, but not so large as to prevent to chasers from tagging)

Cues	
Dodgers	
Split Second	(Make your moves quicker than the speed of light.)
Fake	(Step/lean one way; go the other.)
Dart/Change Direction	(Use quick changes of speed and direction to avoid the chaser.)
Chasers	
Watch the Hips	(Watch the hips of the runner to tell his or her next move.)

Tasks/Challenges:

🅣 For this task, you and your partner are on opposite teams. One of you is a chaser; the other one is a dodger. On the signal, the chasers will spread out inside the boundaries, and the dodgers will line up on one side of the field. On the next signal, the dodgers will try to get to the other side of the field without being touched by their partners, the taggers. The trick is that each dodger can be tagged only by his or her partner. When the dodgers get to the other side, they return to the starting line by going around the outside of the field and continue to travel across the space until they hear the stop signal. On the stop signal, trade places with your partners.

🅣 This time I'm going to decrease the space to half the size it was. Ready? Go again.

🅒 Can you stay untagged until the signal sounds?

❓ *Peer Observation.* This would be an appropriate opportunity for a peer observation assessment. Two sets of partners could be paired. One set would participate and the other set would observe. The observers would have an index card with the cues listed and a space for names and would assess whether the participants used the cues. After five tries, the observers and participants would switch places. See Chapter 12 for the development of peer observation checklists and scoring rubrics.

Bombardment

In some school yards we've observed classes of children playing a game popularly called Bombardment, Killer, or Murder Ball. As these names imply, the game can be dangerous. Typically, a class is divided into two teams, with a middle line separating each team. Each team throws a hard ball in an attempt to strike players on the opposing team; the teams often throw from close range and toward an unsuspecting child. We don't support this activity. There are many other dodging-type experiences you can plan that are safer, allow more children to participate, and are more apt to result in skill development.

Dodging in a Dynamic Situation

Setting: Groups of 10: 8 runners and 2 chasers; a space about 30 feet by 30 feet, preferably grass

Cues

Dodgers

Split Second	(Make your moves quicker than the speed of light.)
Fake	(Step/lean one way; go the other.)
Dart/Change Direction	(Use quick changes of speed and direction to avoid the chaser.)
Twist, Stretch, Jump	(Twist, stretch, and jump to dodge.)
Chasers	
Watch the Hips	(Watch the hips of the runner to tell his or her next move.)
Teamwork	(Decide your plan for catching together.)

Tasks/Challenges:

Ⓣ This is a tag activity. The object, if you are a tagger, is to tag the runners on the named body part or, if you're a runner, to avoid being tagged on the named body part. Chasers, try to touch the runners on the body part I call out. Any runners you tag must freeze. The tagged runners can be unfrozen if they're tagged by a free runner on a body part other than the tagged part. The taggers will have 1 minute to try to catch all the runners. At the end of 1 minute, start again with two new taggers. You must stay inside your boundaries. "Shoulders"—Go.

Dodging While Manipulating an Object

Setting: Multiple circle areas about 10 feet in diameter marked off on the floor or the pavement; two or three children occupying each circle, one of whom is trying to take the ball away

Children should be at the utilization level in dribbling before attempting this task.

Cues

Dodgers

Fake	(Step/lean one way; go the other.)
Dart/Change Direction	(Use quick changes of speed and direction to avoid the chaser.)

Tasks/Challenges:

Ⓣ The object of this task is to dribble a ball while protecting it from someone else. Here's how it works. Each of you in your circle will be dribbling a ball. There will be one defender trying to take the ball away from you. As you dribble, try to use fakes and changes of speed to get away from the defender. If your ball gets knocked out, just go get it and start again.

Proficiency Level (GLSP): Learning Experiences Leading to Skill Development

Children at the proficiency level are ready to use their skillful chasing, fleeing, and dodging abilities in a variety of complex and ever-changing, gamelike and dance situations. Both the chasers and the fleeing, dodging players are skilled. At times, the chaser gets the target; at other times, the fleeing, dodging player escapes. Advanced chasing, fleeing, and dodging skills are evident in invasion (see Chapter 31 for more on invasion-type games) situations such as the following:

- A player in a running invasion game darts quickly past the defense, dodging around the players who are chasing him.
- A player in a foot dribble invasion activity advances the ball past a defensive player by faking one way and then traveling quickly in the opposite direction.
- A defensive player in a running invasion game runs 20 to 30 yards to overtake an offensive runner heading for a score.
- In a hand dribbling invasion game, a player races down court to score, although a defensive player is chasing right behind.

In elementary school settings, children at the proficiency level enjoy playing teacher- and student-designed games and dances in which chasing, fleeing, and dodging are the primary movements. Although some learning experiences are included here, when children are at the proficiency level of chasing, fleeing, and dodging, they are in actuality using those skills in combination with manipulative skills. Thus, appropriate tasks would also be gamelike proficiency-level manipulative activities in which chasing, fleeing, and dodging skills lend the strategic dynamics to the game. See proficiency-level tasks in the manipulative skill theme chapters (Chapters 23–27).

A note about cues at the proficiency level: At the proficiency level, tasks are more complex, typically requiring children to coordinate several movements simultaneously in a dynamic context. A list of cues is provided to assist the children in being more successful in the learning experience. The challenge for the teacher is in determining which cue will be most beneficial for each child—and when. Thus, careful observation and critical reflection become very important as you watch the children move and then decide which cue will be the most helpful to move each learner to a higher skill level.

Child-Designed Dance

Setting: Children in groups of three to five, in a space about 10 feet by 10 feet

Cues	
Dart/Change Direction	(Use quick changes of speed and direction to avoid others.)

Tasks/Challenges:

C For this task, your group will get to make up your own dance. The theme of the dance should be about being fearful. You can design your own plot. Be sure to include chasing, fleeing, and dodging movements to indicate your feelings. As with all dances, your dance should contain a clear beginning, a middle, and an end. (See Chapter 29 regarding more ideas on child-designed dance.)

? *Video/Digital Analysis.* The completion of the dance provides a perfect opportunity to digitally record the dance, and then the group can analyze how and where the use of chasing, fleeing, and dodging communicated the theme of fearfulness.

Continual Fleeing and Chasing with a Large Group

Setting: Children scattered throughout the space: three taggers (with colored armbands); the rest, dodgers
Note: The complexity of this task—as with most chasing, fleeing, and dodging tasks—can be increased or decreased by increasing or decreasing the space available or changing the size of the group. Smaller groups and smaller spaces increase the difficulty for the dodgers; larger groups and larger spaces increase the difficulty for the chasers.

Cues	
Dodgers	
Split Second	(Make your moves quicker than the speed of light.)
Fake	(Step/lean one way; go the other.)
Dart/Change Direction	(Use quick changes of speed and direction to avoid the chaser.)
Chasers	
Watch the Hips	(Watch the hips of the runner to tell his or her next move.)
Teamwork	(Decide your plan for catching together.)

Tasks/Challenges:

T This task is very much like freeze tag, except that when you are tagged, you must freeze with your legs wide apart and your hands clasped to your head. You can then be "freed" by any free player crawling through your legs. There will be three taggers, each with a colored armband.

Note: It is virtually impossible for the taggers to catch all the dodgers, so set a time for play (e.g., 1 to 2 minutes) and switch taggers.

? How did you use teamwork to catch the runners?

Dodging While Maintaining Possession of an Object

Setting: For each child, a scarf in the waistband or flag belt; first put partners in a space about 10 feet by 10 feet and then alone using the space approximately the size of the entire gym

Dodgers	
Split Second	(Make your moves quicker than the speed of light.)
Fake	(Step/lean one way; go the other.)
Jump and Twist	(Use little jumps and twists to dodge.)
Chasers	
Watch the Hips	(Watch the hips of the runner to tell his or her next move.)

Tasks/Challenges:

T For this task, you will need a scarf tucked in your waistband. You and your partner should find a space where you are not close to other groups. When I say "Go," you will try to snatch the scarf from your partner without having yours snatched. If you snatch the scarf, simply give it back to your partner. The other rules are (1) you can't protect your scarf with your hands and (2) you can't touch your partner. Remember, stay in your own space.

T This time we will add chasing to the task. When you pull your partner's scarf, toss it in the air and move quickly away. When the partner picks up the scarf and puts it back into his or her waistband, the partner begins chasing the runner. When caught, stop and play again.

T This time the task becomes harder. You now can travel over the entire space and try to snatch anyone's scarf If you snatch a scarf, this time you hold on to it. The same rules of (1) not protecting your scarf with your hands and (2) not touching anyone still apply.

C How many points can you get? Score one point for each scarf you snatch; subtract five points if yours is taken.

In many primitive tribal games, the tribes believed that the chaser was evil, magic, or diseased and that the chaser's touch was contagious. Although today's games are a far cry from fleeing possible death, one has a hard time believing otherwise when observing the intensity and all-out effort children display when fleeing a chaser!

Chasing and Dodging Simultaneously

Setting: Start with partners in a space about 5 feet by 5 feet; then increase the group size to about six and the space to about 20 feet by 20 feet; enough flag belts or scarves (of two colors) for all the youngsters

Cues

Dodgers

Split Second	(Make your moves quicker than the speed of light.)
Fake	(Step/lean one way; go the other.)
Dart/Change Direction	(Use quick changes of speed and direction to avoid the chaser.)

Chasers

Watch the Hips	(Watch the hips of the runner to tell his or her next move.)

Tasks/Challenges:

T Each partner should have on a flag belt or scarf tucked into his or her waist. In your space, your task will be to try to grab the flag from your partner. If you grab it, give it back and start again. Remember, you cannot protect your flag with your hands, and you cannot touch the other person.

T In this task, all other players are your opponents. The object is to snatch the flag from another

player's belt without losing your own flag and while staying within the designated boundaries. If your flag is pulled off, another player can put it back on and you can keep playing. You can't put your own flag back on. You will really need to watch all the other players and move to stay out of their way. Remember all the turning, twisting, and jumping dodges.

C How many points can you accumulate? Score one point for every flag you take; subtract three points for every time your flag is taken.

T Now form a group of six. Each group of six should divide into two groups of three, with each group having a different-colored flag belt. Find a space about 20 feet by 20 feet. You will now work as a team, and your task is to try and grab the flags of the other group. If you get them all, return them and start over again.

Chasing and Fleeing in an Invasion Gamelike Situation

Setting: Small groups of four to six, each with a ball; enough flag belts or scarves (of two colors) for all the youngsters; a space about 20 yards by 10 yards

Cues

Offense

Toward Goal	(Always move toward your goal.)
Fake	(Step/lean one way; go the other.)
Dart/Change Direction	(Use quick changes of speed and direction to avoid the chaser.)

Defense

Watch the Hips	(Watch the hips of the runner to tell his or her next move.)
Teamwork	(Decide your plan for catching together.)

Tasks/Challenges:

C One group will start with the ball. On the signal, a player on the group with the ball (group 1) tries to pass or run the ball from its goal line to the other group's goal line without the ball touching the ground or group 2 grabbing the flag of the player with the ball. If a flag is grabbed, the ball touches the ground, or the goal line is crossed, the other group gets the ball.

? *Video/Digital Analysis.* The above task, with established criteria and a rubric, provides a wonderful opportunity for digital analysis of the use of the critical elements in a dynamic situation. Each group could do its own analysis.

Dodging in a Gamelike Situation

Setting: A large marked-off area containing hoops as safety bases (Figure 18.3); groups of no more than five

Cues	
Dodgers	
Split Second	(Make your moves quicker than the speed of light.)
Fake	(Step/lean one way; go the other.)
Dart/Change Direction	(Use quick changes of speed and direction to avoid the chaser.)
Chasers	
Watch the Hips	(Watch the hips of the runner to tell his or her next move.)
Teamwork	(Decide your plan for catching together.)

Tasks/Challenges:

T The object of this task is for a group of runners to cross the space without being touched by the other group, who are taggers. The runners begin at one end of the space; the taggers begin at the other end. On the signal, the runners try to cross the space without being tagged; the taggers try to stop any runners from getting across the space. The runners are safe—can't be tagged—when they're in any of the hoops. The runners have about 1 minute to cross the space. After two turns, you'll switch places. The safety bases will help, but use them wisely—only as a last resort when you're about to be tagged. Don't just stand in them the whole time.

? You have used teamwork before to catch runners. How does the teamwork in this game differ? What teamwork strategies did you use here?

Figure 18.3 Setup for dodging in a gamelike situation.

Invasion gamelike experiences involve constant chasing and fleeing.

©Barbara Adamcik

Dodging in a Target Gamelike Situation

Setting: A marked-off square playing area initially about 10 feet by 10 feet and later about 20 feet by 20 feet with a hoop in its center and a beanbag inside the hoop (Figure 18.4); first in partners and then in groups of about five. Note: Before beginning this task, children should be at the utilization level of throwing and catching.

Cues

Offense

Split Second	(Make your moves quicker than the speed of light.)
Fake	(Step/lean one way; go the other.)
Dart/Change Direction	(Use quick changes of speed and direction to avoid the chaser.)
Heads and Shoulders Up	(As you bend to retrieve an object, be sure to keep your head and shoulders up and to bend at the knees.)

Defense

Watch the Hips	(Watch the hips of the runner to tell his or her next move.)

Tasks/Challenges:

🔵 To begin this task, you and your partner will need one hoop and one beanbag in a space about 10 feet by 10 feet. Place the beanbag inside the hoop. One of you will be offense and the other, defense. Do you remember what offense and defense are? The defensive player will try to protect the beanbag from the offensive player, who is trying to grab it out of the hoop. No one can step inside the hoop. If the offense gets it, just put it back in the hoop and start again. I will tell you when to change roles.

⚠️ This is a task children love, but much attention needs to be paid to their keeping their heads and shoulders up as they try to retrieve the beanbag. If children are dodging with their heads down, the likelihood increases that heads will collide.

🔵 The task now gets harder. There are now four offensive players and one defensive player. Make your square a little bigger and be sure to mark your boundaries. The object stays the same—try to get the beanbag or protect it. I will tell you when to switch positions.

🔵 Now we will make a game of it. On the signal, the offense will have 2 minutes in which to retrieve the beanbag from inside the hoop and get it to the outside of the square without being touched by the defense. If the offense gets the beanbag to the outside or the 2-minute limit is reached, play starts over again, and a new defender tries to protect the treasure. No one can go inside the hoop.

❓ *Event Task.* A likely assessment option would be to have each group write out the strategy the members plan to use in the game. After the game is over, they can analyze how well it worked and what they will need to practice next time to be more effective. This plan can then serve as the initial activity in the next lesson.

Using Team Strategy for Chasing, Fleeing, and Dodging in an Invasion Gamelike Situation

Setting: Groups of eight, four players in each group, each group with matching colored flags of a different color from those of the opposing group; a flag belt with two flags on it for each group member

Cues

Dodgers

Split Second	(Make your moves quicker than the speed of light.)
Fake	(Step/lean one way; go the other.)
Dart/Change Direction	(Use quick changes of speed and direction to avoid the chaser.)

Chasers

Watch the Hips	(Watch the hips of the runner to tell his or her next move.)
Teamwork	(Decide your plan for catching together.)

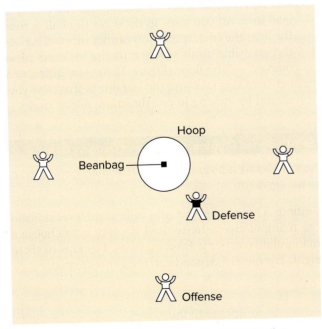

Figure 18.4 Setup for dodging in a target gamelike situation.

Tasks/Challenges:

C The object of this task is to see how many of the other group's flags you can get without losing your own. One group begins at each end of the space. On the signal, both teams move into the playing area, and each group tries to snatch as many flags as possible from the other group's belts while preventing the other group from stealing their own flags. On the next signal, all play stops, and the teams return to their sidelines and count how many flags they were able to steal.

? *Journal.* For a journal entry at this point, you might ask children how they feel about their chasing, fleeing, and dodging abilities.

Dodging While Manipulating an Object in an Invasion Gamelike Situation

Setting: This activity requires utilization-level skills in the manipulative activity you choose to use. It can be done with virtually any manipulative skill; the most common are dribbling and passing with the hands or feet, throwing and catching, or striking with a hockey stick. Whatever skill you choose, you will need one ball per group and appropriate other equipment. Even-numbered groups of six to eight.

Cues	
Offense	
Split Second	(Make your moves quicker than the speed of light.)
Fake	(Step/lean one way; go the other.)
Dart/Change Direction	(Use quick changes of speed and direction to avoid the chaser.)
Defense	
Watch the Hips	(Watch the hips of the runner to tell his or her next move.)
Teamwork	(Decide your plan for catching together.)
Play the Ball	(Force the pass by playing the ball first.)

Tasks/Challenges:

T This task is like Keep-Away. There will be equal numbers on each group. You must clearly mark your boundaries, which can be no larger than half a basketball court. The object is for your group to keep the ball away from the other group. Here are the rules:

1. A ball can be stolen only on a pass; it cannot be taken when someone else has control of it.

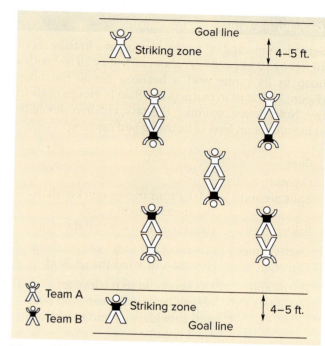

Figure 18.5 Goal line for Dodging While Manipulating an Object in an Invasion Gamelike Situation.

2. No one can hold onto the ball longer than 5 seconds before passing it.
3. There can be no direct hand-offs; the ball must be passed.
4. If the ball goes out of bounds, it belongs to the other group.

C We are going to change the game a little this time. You will keep your same groups, but each group will be trying to score by getting the ball across a goal line. All you have to do is get the ball across the line; the trick is that you cannot throw it across the goal line until you are in the striking zone marked on the floor (Figure 18.5). The difference between this task and the last one is that now you should be moving in one direction, not all over.

Self-Designed Chasing, Fleeing, and Dodging Game

Note: This task is an example of a student-designed instructional approach.

Setting: This activity requires utilization-level skills in the manipulative activity used if youngsters choose a manipulative activity. Even-numbered groups of six to eight. Equipment depends on the game created.

Cues	
Appropriate to the game	

Tasks/Challenges:

C Today you're going to combine all that you've practiced into a game. You'll make up your games yourselves. In your groups, make up a game that involves chasing, fleeing, and dodging. You can use equipment or not; it's your choice. You can have whatever rules you want as long as you include these three:

1. The game must involve chasing, fleeing, and dodging.
2. Everyone in your group must be playing at the same time.
3. You cannot throw an object at another person.

In other words, nobody sits out and waits for a turn, and no one gets hit. Remember, groups of no more than six; chasing, fleeing, and dodging; and everybody plays. Go.

T After you've made up your rules and started to play your game, make sure you know your rules so you can tell somebody else how to play your game. At the end of class, I'll ask you to write down your game.

? *Event Task.* An appropriate assessment task at this point would be to have children write down how to play their games and then share the games with others. See Chapter 12 for more assessment examples.

Reading Comprehension Questions

1. List the differences among chasing, fleeing, and dodging.
2. Describe three effective dodging movements.
3. What are the characteristics of each of the four levels of skill proficiency for chasing, fleeing, and dodging?
4. Rank the following tasks by placing the number 1 in front of the easiest (most basic), the number 2 in front of the next more difficult level, and so on.
   ( ) A defensive player in a football-type game pursues an offensive runner.
   ( ) You travel around the room. On a signal, you change directions as quickly as possible.
   ( ) You stay as close as you can to your partner, who'll try to get away from you.
   ( ) One group chases the members of an opposing group.
5. What is a fake? Give several examples of when a fake might be used.
6. Why do you use large areas when introducing the chasing, fleeing, and dodging skills?
7. Why have we eliminated dodgeball from the development of dodging skills?
8. What are some important cues to give when you're teaching fleeing? List at least three.
9. When a child is tagged during a tag game, what is one alternative to eliminating the child until a new game begins?
10. Killer (also called Bombardment) is a game that has been played for years in elementary schools. What is our reason for not recommending it?
11. What are two strategies for offense and two for defense that apply when chasing, fleeing, and dodging while manipulating an object? How might you teach them?

References/Suggested Readings

[SHAPE America] Society of Health and Physical Educators. 2009. *Appropriate instructional practice guidelines, K–12: A side-by-side comparison.* Reston, VA: SHAPE America. Available at http://www.shapeamerica.org/standards/guidelines/opportunity.cfm.

[SHAPE America] Society of Health and Physical Educators. 2014. *National standards & grade-level outcomes for K-12 physical education.* Champaign, IL: Human Kinetics.

[SHAPE America] Society of Health and Physical Educators. 2017. *Dodgeball is not an appropriate physical education activity* [position statement]. Reston, VA: SHAPE America.

Bending, Stretching, Curling, and Twisting

By Meghan Wampler

The professional baseball player hitting a line drive across third base, the high school swimmer performing a pike dive, the college basketball player reaching the extra inch to gain possession of the rebound, the ballet dancer leaping as he travels across the stage, the Olympic gymnast performing an aerial roll, the rock climber reaching for the next hold—all are executing skills from a foundation of body actions—twisting, bending, stretching, and curling. The skills of stretching, curling, bending, and twisting are the core of advanced movements in gymnastics, dance, and sports. See Box 19-1 for linkages between stretching, curling, bending, and twisting and the *National Standards & Grade-Level Outcomes for K–12 Physical Education* (SHAPE America 2014).

The ability to integrate stretching, curling, bending, and twisting in the execution of the skill often delineates the difference between the average and the proficient athlete. We begin teaching the difference between

these body actions with young children and, throughout our program, combine them with other skill themes to enhance the quality of their movement. The definitions of each action follow.

- *Stretching* is the extension of body parts away from the trunk and/or the stretching of the trunk itself.
- *Bending* is the creation of angles of body parts and/or the trunk to produce a pike position of the trunk or angles of body parts.
- *Twisting* is the rotation of the trunk or body parts around a stationary axis. Arms, legs, the head, and the trunk can perform the twisting action.
- *Curling* involves the spine. The trunk can curl; body parts cannot. The spine can curl forward into a tight curved shape, slightly to either side, or even backward.

When children are introduced to the body actions of stretching, curling, twisting, and bending, they explore the action in isolation, e.g., stretching in self-space at different levels, sometimes slowly, sometimes quickly. Exploring each of the actions in isolation is then followed by the addition of traveling and combining the action with other skill themes, such as stretching to catch a ball at high level. After mastery of the action in combination with other skills and concepts, the student is ready for the dynamic environments of games/sports, gymnastics, and dance that require quick decisions regarding which body action is appropriate and the ability to execute the action correctly. The progression spiral shows bending, stretching, curling, and twisting at each level of skill development, from precontrol to proficiency.

Box 19-1

Stretching, Curling, Bending, and Twisting in the *National Standards & Grade-Level Outcomes for K–12 Physical Education*

The body actions of stretching, curling, bending, and twisting are referenced in the *National Standards & Grade-Level Outcomes for K–12 Physical Education* (SHAPE America 2014) under Standard 1: "Demonstrates competency in a variety of motor skills and movement patterns." The intent of the standard is developing the fundamental skills needed to enjoy participation in physical activities, with the mastery of movement fundamentals as the foundation for continued skill acquisition.

Sample grade-level outcomes from the *National Standards** include:

- Contrasts the actions of curling and stretching (K)
- Demonstrates twisting, curling, bending, and stretching actions (1)
- Differentiates among twisting, curling, bending, and stretching actions (2)
- Moves into and out of gymnastics balances with curling, twisting, and stretching actions (3)
- Moves into and out of balances on apparatus with curling, twisting, and stretching actions (4)
- Performs curling, twisting, and stretching actions with correct application in dance, gymnastics, and small-sided practices tasks in game environments (5)

* Suggested grade-level outcomes for student learning.

Precontrol Level (GLSP): Experiences for Exploration

Experiences at the precontrol level are designed to introduce children to stretching, bending, curling, and twisting. As children explore the body actions, they become aware of the difference between each of the actions and the correct vocabulary for each action.

Stretching in Self-Space

Setting: Children scattered throughout general space

Tasks/Challenges:

🅣 In your self-space, explore stretching body parts as far as possible. Stretch your legs, your arms, your fingers, and your toes.

🅣 While standing, stretch your entire body, even your trunk, at as high a level as possible. Now try high and wide; really stretch.

Skill Theme Development Progression

Progression Spiral— Bending, Stretching, Twisting, Curling

Proficiency

In combination with other skill themes in complex and dynamic game, dance, and gymnastics settings

Utilization

Stretching, curling, bending, and twisting against multiple opponents

Stretching, curling, bending, and twisting against an opponent

Stretching to catch against an opponent

Stretch, catch, release

Stretching to catch with a partner while traveling

Transferring weight to hands and forming a bridge

Transferring weight onto hands and twisting

Control

Balancing on apparatus with body actions

Stretching, curling, and twisting into weight transfers

Twisting for placement when batting

Twisting while striking a tossed ball

Twisting while striking with a bat

Twisting to catch a ball with a partner

Stretching for the jump ball

Stretching to catch a ball with a partner

Catching with a stretch and curl

Performing jumping sequences with bending, twisting, curling, and twisting

A dance of bending, stretching, twisting and curling

Jumping over while stretching, bending and twisting

Jumping off while stretching and twisting

Bending, stretching, twisting, curling in mime

Balancing with bends, stretches, twists, and curls

Precontrol

Stretching and curling

Stretching, body shapes, and locomotion

Twisting in self-space

Bending body parts

Curling to roll like a ball

Curling in self-space

Stretching in self-space

T Let's try the same stretching action while at a low level. Try it sitting and then try the same stretch lying flat on the floor.

Curling in Self-Space

Setting: A mat for every child or two, or a large grassy space; children positioned so they will not rock into each other (Figure 22.5, page 418)

Tasks/Challenges:

T In your self-space, curl like a playground ball, a roly-poly bug, or the letter C.

T Explore curling while lying on the floor. How many different ways can you curl? What body part is always involved in the curling action? Right, the spine is always involved in the curling action.

T Sitting in your self-space, explore curling—forward with arms and legs tucked tightly to the trunk. Can you curl to the side? Arch the spine slowly backward? Which direction is best for the curling action? Right, curling is a forward action of the spine.

Standing in your self-space, slowly curl the spine forward being careful not to lose your balance. Remember, curl the spine so I can see the curve when I look at you. Now explore curling to the side and ever so slowly backward. That one is very difficult.

T On your mat, try to find as many ways as possible to curl your body so it is round. Three different ways would be good. If I make a circle with my arms (*demonstrate*), is my body curled? If you said no, you are correct. Remember, the spine has to curl.

Curling to Roll Like a Ball

Setting: A mat for every child or two, or a large grassy space; children positioned so that they do not roll into each other

Tasks/Challenges:

T Can you make your body like a ball? How many ways can your ball move around in your self-space? Remember, only round balls roll.

Bending Body Parts

Setting: Children scattered throughout general space

Tasks/Challenges:

T Explore bending body parts while in your self-space. How many body parts can bend? Fingers,

wrists, elbows, knees, ankles. Create very sharp angles as you bend body parts.

Ⓣ Create contrasting shapes as you bend opposite body parts, for example, bending the fingers of your left hand versus fingers of your right hand or your left arm versus your right arm. I will play some music as you create your Dance of Bending Parts.

Ⓣ Standing in your self-space, bend forward at the waist, creating a 90-degree angle with your body. This is called the *pike position* in gymnastics and in diving.

Twisting in Self-Space

Setting: Children scattered throughout general space

Tasks/Challenges:

Ⓣ Stand in your self-space with your feet "stuck" to the floor. Rotate your trunk clockwise without moving your feet. This is a twisting action. Now twist the trunk counterclockwise. Remember, keep your feet firmly planted—no movement.

Ⓣ Extend your arms outward to the side. Rotate your arms in a forward motion. Rotate them in a backward motion. Twist one arm forward and the other backward; reverse the twisting action. Cross your arms in front of you. Is this a twisting action? No, the body part must rotate for the twisting action.

Ⓣ Sitting in your self-space, twist one leg toward the body. Twist both legs inward. Twist both legs outward. What body parts can twist? Arms, legs, and trunk. Remember one part is stuck like glue; it remains still while other parts perform the twisting/rotating action.

Ⓣ Sitting or lying down in your self-space, begin to twist different body parts until you look like a pretzel. How many different body parts can you twist? Create a really unique pretzel. When everyone has completed their twisting, we will freeze in a Portrait of Pretzels. Ready? Begin.

Stretching, Body Shapes, and Locomotion

Setting: Children with partners, scattered throughout general space

Tasks/Challenges:

Ⓣ Stand in your self-space, stretching in all directions to be sure you have a clear self-space; it is not

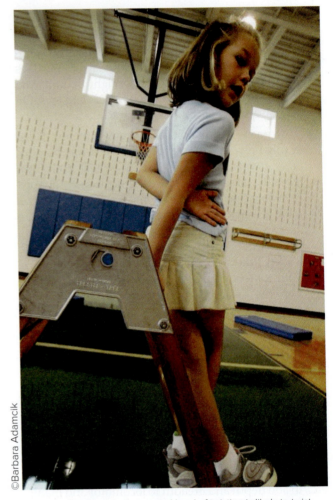
©Barbara Adamcik

A child at the precontrol or control level of twisting is likely to twist body parts without twisting the torso.

important that you be near your partner. Partners A, stand in your self-space, stretching your arms to make a very large, wide shape. Partners B, travel throughout general space with any locomotor pattern you wish; avoid touching anyone traveling or standing in a wide shape.

Have partners switch travel and stationary activities after 1 or 2 minutes of travel.

Ⓣ Partners B, stand in your self-space twisting to form a tall, narrow shape. Partners A, run throughout general space with no collisions; always look for open spaces as you travel.

Switch roles after about 30 seconds.

Stretching and Curling

Setting: Children scattered throughout general space

Tasks/Challenges:

T In your self-space, bring your arms and legs close to your body, curling into a tight ball. On the eight-count signal, slowly stretch your arms and legs away from your body. On the eighth count, you should be fully extended, even fingers and toes. On signal, quickly curl the body back into a tight ball.

T How many of you have ever seen a tiny bug called a roly-poly? What special thing does this bug do? Yes, it curls into a tight ball to protect itself from possible danger. When everything is safe, the roly-poly bug uncurls and stretches out, ready to crawl. That is exactly what you are going to do. Pretend to be roly-poly bugs crawling in general space. When I enter your self-space, quickly curl into a tight ball. When I move away, stretch your arms, your legs, your total body, and begin moving again. Remember, the curling action is quick; the stretching action is a slow extension.

Control Level (GLSP): Learning Experiences Leading to Skill Development

Bending, stretching, curling, and twisting actions are used in combination with other skills in dance, gymnastics, and game environments. Once the children have a functional understanding of bending, stretching, curling, and twisting, these skills are combined with balancing, traveling, catching, jumping, striking, etc., to add depth and breadth to locomotor and manipulative skills. The tasks and challenges at the control level provide the learning experiences to begin the development of these combinations.

A note about cues: *Although several cues are listed for many of the learning experiences, it's important to focus on only one cue at a time. This way, the children can really concentrate on that cue. Once you provide feedback to the children and observe that most have learned a cue, it's time to focus on another one.*

Balancing with Bends, Stretches, Twists, and Curls

Setting: Children scattered in self-space with sufficient mat space to work safely

Cues:	
Stillness	(No wiggles, no wobbles. Hold the balance very still.)
Extend	(Extend body parts with tight muscles.)
Curl the Spine	(Curve the spine forward, to the right, to the left.)

Sharp Angles	(Bend body parts, bend at the waist for clear, sharp angles.)
Pretzels	(Twist the trunk, the legs, the arms, and the neck.)

Tasks/Challenges:

T Standing on one foot, stretch the free leg and both arms to create a balance.

T Sitting on your mat, stretch body parts to create a balance. Create balances on different bases of support by stretching free body parts.

T Create balances by curling your spine. How many different bases of support can you use for curling into balances?

T Create balances by twisting the trunk and/or body parts. See how many different ways you can twist into balances.

T Standing on your mat, bend forward, creating a 90-degree angle with your body. Using this balance as the beginning, create balances by twisting, curling, and stretching.

C Create a four-part sequence by stretching into balances. Remember, hold each balance very still for 3 seconds before stretching into the next one. (Repeat with curling, bending, twisting action.)

C You have really created a large number of balances today by stretching, curling, bending, and twisting. Of all the balances you have completed today, choose one that shows stretching into the balance, one that shows curling into the balance, one for the

Through using both stretching and bending, this balance is both stable and unique.

©Barbara Adamcik

twisting action, and one for bending. Remember, I am watching for the action; the balance is the ending of the stretching, bending, etc.

Bending, Stretching, Twisting, and Curling in Mime

Setting: Children scattered in general space

Cues

Extend	(Extend body parts with tight muscles.)
Curl the spine	(Curve the spine forward, to the right, to the left.)
Sharp Angles	(Bend body parts, bend at the waist for clear, sharp angles.)
Pretzels	(Twist the trunk, the legs, the arms, and the neck.)

Tasks/Challenges:

T Have you ever seen a mime? They tell a story without ever speaking; in fact, they never speak. They use their bodies to convey emotions and express feelings. Today we are going to use the body actions of stretching, curling, twisting, and bending to express feelings, to tell a story. You may travel, but only a short distance in relation to your "spot," your chosen self-space. Begin with bending, stretching, curling, and twisting, really exaggerating the action. The music will set the tempo for the movements.

C After you have explored a variety of stretching, twisting, curling, and bending actions, think of an emotion you wish to express (for example, sad, happy, eager, frustrated, excited) or a simple story of two to three sentences you wish to convey. Now combine the actions to complete that sequence. When you are ready, you may be the Mime on the Street Corner.

Jumping Off While Stretching and Twisting

Setting: Children scattered throughout general space. Various pieces of equipment: low tables, boxes, benches, low balance beams, step aerobics boxes, and boxes (stuffed with newspaper or packing materials and taped closed so they will support a child's weight) positioned throughout general space, with sufficient room between for children to work safely.

⚠ This task is taught in conjunction with jumping and landing (Chapter 20). The body must return to ready position for a balanced landing.

Generating the force to take the body upward is a more advanced jump than jumping off. Therefore, the progression of twisting, curling, bending, and stretching with jumping is jumping off, jumping over, and then jumping for height.

Cues

Extend	(Extend body parts with tight muscles.)
Pretzels	(Twist the trunk, the legs, the arms, and the neck.)

Tasks/Challenges:

T Jump off your equipment, and stretch while you're in the air. A stretch shape means your arms and legs are away from your body—and you can be narrow or wide. Remember, make all the parts of your body stretched, not just one part. Practice your stretch until it's as stretched as it can be. Remember to control the jumps and actions so you have safe landings on your feet. Stick as if you have glue on your feet.

T This time, you're going to jump off the equipment and twist while in the air. You may choose to twist body parts or your total body.

C Now try twisting your entire body while in the air. Practice your shape until it's as twisted as it can be. Your body should look like a pretzel.

Jumping Over While Stretching, Bending and Twisting

Setting: Children scattered throughout general space, each with a rope stretched on the floor

Cues

Extend	(Extend body parts with tight muscles.)
Sharp Angles	(Bend body parts, bend at the waist for clear, sharp angles.)
Pretzels	(Twist the trunk, the legs, the arms, and the neck.)

Tasks/Challenges:

T Jump over your rope, and stretch while you're in the air. A stretch shape means your arms and legs are away from your body—and you can be narrow or wide. Remember, make all the parts of your

body stretched, not just one part. Practice your stretch until it's as stretched as it can be. Explore different stretched shapes.

T This time you're going to jump using twists in the air. You may choose to twist body parts or your total body. A twist means that you will make your body like a pretzel. Practice your shape until it's as twisted as it can be. Explore more twisted shapes.

⚠ Remind children they need to be able to land on their feet and not "crash" after doing twists in the air.

T This time, you're going to learn some harder moves. First, you're going to make bent shapes with body parts in the air. A bent shape has sharp angles like this. (*Be sure to demonstrate here.*) At your rope, practice making body parts bent while you are in the air. Make some silly-looking shapes with your bending.

C Create five more jumps with bent parts.

T This time you're going to jump while curling your body. In a curled jump, your body has a C shape. Remember, absorb force when you land by bending your knees.

C Approach your rope with three to four running steps. Now try your jumps with stretching, twisting, and bending in the air before landing safely. Remember, body parts bend; total body or body parts stretch and twist.

⚠ Students should attempt running and jumping with different body actions while airborne, only after they have demonstrated safe landings in self-space and over their ropes—absorbing the force by bending the knees and landing in a balanced position without falling forward.

A Dance of Stretching, Bending, Twisting, and Curling

Setting: Partners scattered in general space

Cues	
Extend	(Extend body parts with tight muscles.)
Curl the Spine	(Curve the spine forward, to the right, to the left.)
Sharp Angles	(Bend body parts, bend at the waist for clear, sharp angles.)
Pretzels	(Twist the trunk, the legs, the arms, and the neck.)

Tasks/Challenges:

T Begin your dance facing your partner. The movements of your dance will be opposites; for

example, if partner A stretches to the left, partner B will stretch to the opposite side. If partner B stretches high in the air, partner A will stretch arms toward the floor. If partner A bends arms and fingers inward, partner B will bend arms and fingers outward. One curls to the right; one curls to the left. One twists clockwise, one twists counterclockwise. Explore the possibilities of stretching, curling, twisting, and bending. Begin facing your partner, and then try standing side by side or one behind the other. Use the bending, stretching, curling, and twisting actions we have practiced to create a dance of Opposite Matches.

T When you are comfortable with creating opposites that match in body action, vary the speed of the movement—sometimes slowly, sometimes very quickly.

C Now for the really difficult part: Can you create a sequence of four opposite matches that are timed exactly together?

Performing Jumping Sequences with Bending, Twisting, Curling, and Stretching

Setting: Note cards with various bending, twisting, curling, and stretching sequences written on them, with each sequence containing at least four body actions; children scattered throughout general space, each with a sequence card

Cues	
Extend	(Extend body parts with tight muscles.)
Curl the Spine	(Curve the spine forward, to the right, to the left.)
Sharp Angles	(Bend body parts, bend at the waist for clear, sharp angles.)
Pretzels	(Twist the trunk, the legs, the arms, and the neck.)

Tasks/Challenges:

T On your card are listed four body actions. You're going to make up a sequence of jumps that shows those body actions in the air. To do this, you'll first travel a bit and then jump, showing the first body action; then you'll travel again and jump and show the second body action listed; you'll travel again and jump using the third body action; you'll travel one more time and jump showing the last body action. Your sequence should be like this: Travel, jump; travel, jump; travel, jump; travel, jump, freeze. Repeat the sequence enough times so you

can do it the same way each time. Memorize it. When it's memorized, show the sequence to a friend. Remember, use buoyant landings between jumps and a yielding landing after your last jump. (*See Chapter 20.*)

Catching with a Stretch and Curl

Setting: Children scattered in general space, each with a ball for catching

Cues:	
Extend	(Reach toward the ceiling/sky as you stretch to catch.)
Reach and Pull	(Reach to catch the ball, then pull it in as the body curls around it.)

Tasks/Challenges:

T In your self-space, toss the ball above your head, stretch to catch the ball, and then curl around the ball as if protecting an opponent from getting the ball. Toss the ball higher so you must really stretch to catch. Don't forget the curl.

T Stand approximately 6 to 8 feet from the wall. Toss the ball to the wall and jump to catch it high above your head. Stretch your arms really high.

Stretching to Catch a Ball with a Partner

Setting: Children with partners, sufficient space to throw and catch; a variety of balls for catching

Cues:	
Reach and Pull	(Reach to catch the ball, then pull it to your belly button.)
Extend	(Reach toward the ceiling/sky as you stretch to catch.)

Tasks/Challenges:

T Stand approximately 10 feet from your partner. Toss the ball above your partner's head, just out of reach so the person must jump to catch. Catching partner, stretch your arms really high toward the ceiling to catch the ball. Remember, pull the ball in toward the body as if protecting it.

T Toss the ball to your partner's side so he or she must stretch to catch. Catcher, keep one foot firmly planted as you extend to the opposite side to catch. Let's make it easy. Catcher, keep your left foot still;

extend to your right side for the catch. Thrower, toss the ball to your partner's right side, just beyond the person's reach so he or she must extend for the catch. After five tosses, switch the toss to the opposite side.

T When you are successful at the stretch and catch, the thrower will mix up the throws, some to your left side and some to your right side. Don't forget to switch position so each person is the catcher and each is the thrower.

T Pretend you are the second baseperson in the softball game. Keep one foot firmly planted "on the base" and stretch to catch—high, to the right, to the left. Maybe even stretch at low level!

T Try the stretch and catch with different types of balls of different shapes and sizes—football, softball, basketball—stretching to catch will be important in each game or sport.

©Barbara Adamcik

This youngster uses complete stretching of the body to catch.

Stretching for the Jump Ball

Setting: Class divided into groups of three, each person in the group approximately the same height

Cues	
Extend	(Stretch really high toward the ceiling/sky as you reach to tap the ball.)

Tasks/Challenges:

Ⓣ Partners A and B stand facing each other, approximately 6 inches apart; partner C is going to toss the ball above your heads, beyond your reach like the referee in a basketball game. Jump high in the air, and extend your arm really high to tap the ball as if sending it to a teammate. Remember, tap the ball; don't catch it. You are trying to jump higher and stretch farther than your partner. After five tries, switch positions so the next person is the referee tossing the ball.

Twisting to Catch a Ball with a Partner

Setting: Partners scattered in general space with sufficient space for travel, a variety of balls for catching

Cues	
Over the Shoulder	(Look backward over your shoulder to see the ball.)

Tasks/Challenges:

Ⓣ Stand beside your partner. Partner A, with the ball, will give the signal for partner B to begin running away from the starting position. When partner A hears the special signal, he or she will twist the head, looking back over the shoulder, to catch the ball. Continue travel to the opposite side of the gymnasium/playing area. Hint: In the beginning, partner A will tell you which shoulder he or she is going to throw to so you will know which way to twist.

Ⓣ When you are successful at twisting, catching, and continuing your travel, the throwing partner will no longer tell you in advance which way to twist. That will be determined by which shoulder the ball is traveling toward. Remember, it is a twisting action, not a full turn.

Twisting While Striking with a Bat

Setting: Class divided into groups of three (batter, pitcher, outfielder) with sufficient space for striking a ball; five whiffle balls, a plastic bat, and a batting tee for each group

Cues	
Watch the Ball	(Watch the ball until your bat makes contact.)
Twist the Trunk	(Twist your upper body to send the ball to left field [right-handed batter].)
	(Twist your upper body to send the ball to right field [left-handed batter].)

Tasks/Challenges:

Ⓣ Partner A in position for batting. Remember the things we learned when striking with a bat, such as position of the feet and grip of the bat. On signal, strike the ball, sending it far into the "outfield" where partner C is standing. Partner B will be positioned in the pitcher's position. Partner C, the outfielder, retrieves the ball and returns it to partner B. After five hits, partner B goes to the batting position, partner C to the pitcher position, and partner A to the outfield. Remember, wait for the signal for batting. Hint: I will know everyone is ready when I see each batter and each fielder in position. Switch positions after five hits.

Twisting While Striking a Tossed Ball

Setting: Class divided into groups of three (batter, pitcher, outfielder) with sufficient space for striking a ball; five whiffle balls and a bat for each group

Cues	
Watch the Ball	(Watch the ball until your bat makes contact.)
Twist the Trunk	(Twist your upper body to send the ball to left field [right-handed batter].)
	(Twist your upper body to send the ball to right field [left-handed batter].)

Tasks/Challenges:

Ⓣ Partner A is in position for batting, partner B is in position as the pitcher, and partner C is in the outfield. Partner A, remember all the cues we learned for successful striking. Partner B, toss the ball underhanded for a successful hit. Partner C, be ready to catch or retrieve the ball after the hit.

(T) Your challenge is to strike the ball so it travels to the outfield—even for a homerun. Remember, wait for the signal for batting and retrieving. After five hits, we will rotate positions so everyone practices as the batter, the pitcher, and the outfielder.

Striking a ball with a bat requires twisting actions at the beginning and end of the swing.

©Barbara Adamcik

Twisting for Placement When Batting

Setting: Class divided into groups of three (batter, pitcher, outfielder) with sufficient space for striking a ball; five whiffle balls, a bat, and batting tee for each group

Cues	
Watch the Ball	(Watch the ball until your bat makes contact.)
Ready Twist	(Twist your upper body in preparation for hitting the ball.)
Twist the Trunk	(Twist your upper body to send the ball to left field [right-handed batter].)
	(Twist your upper body to send the ball to right field [left-handed batter].)

Tasks/Challenges:

(T) Partner A is in position for batting, partner B is in position as the pitcher, and partner C is in the outfield. Partner A, focus on the cues for successful striking. Partner B and partner C will be ready to catch or retrieve the ball after you hit. Partner A will be batting off the tee. This will allow you to concentrate fully on the direction of the hit. Your challenge is to strike the ball so it travels to the outfield—even for a homerun. Practice hitting the ball so it travels straight forward over the pitcher, sometimes to the left of the pitcher and sometimes to the right. Remember, wait for signal for batting and retrieving. After five hits, we will rotate positions so everyone practices as the batter, the pitcher, and the outfielder.

(T) When you are successful at sending the ball forward and to the right and left, tell your partners where you are going to hit the ball before you hit it. What is the difference in the twisting action for hitting forward and hitting to the right or left field?

(T) When you are ready, you may have partner B toss the ball to you for the hit. (Repeat the tasks with a partner tossing the ball.)

(?) How many of you were successful at sending the ball to both the right and left of the pitcher? What is the key for successful placement?

Stretching, Curling, and Twisting into Weight Transfers

Setting: Small mats and/or carpet squares scattered throughout general space

Cues	
Extend	(Extend body parts with tight muscles.)
Curl the Spine	(Curve the spine forward, to the right, to the left.)
Pretzels	(Twist the trunk, the legs, the arms, and the neck.)

Tasks/Challenges:

(T) Balance on one foot. Bend at the waist, extending your arms forward and your free leg backward. Stretch your arms forward until you are off balance; then transfer your weight to your hands and next to your curled back to roll forward out of the balance.

(!) Children should demonstrate a mastery of rolling forward with a rounded back before they attempt this task.

(T) Balance on your knees and one hand. Extend your free arm under your body, twisting your trunk until your weight transfers to your shoulder and new bases of support. Twist gently into the new balance.

(T) Balance in a shoulder stand with your weight on your shoulders, upper arms, and head, stretching

These girls demonstrate the result of curling to form a partner balance.

your legs toward the ceiling. Twist your legs and trunk, bringing your feet to the mat behind you in a new balance.

T Balance on your chosen base of support. Twist until you are momentarily off balance; transfer your weight onto a new base of support.

T Balance on your chosen base again. Use different stretching, curling, and twisting actions to transfer onto new bases of support.

Balancing on Apparatus with Body Actions

Setting: Variety of gymnastics equipment (tables, benches, beams) with sufficient mats and space for children to work safely

Cues	
Stillness	(No wiggles, no wobbles. Hold the balance very still.)
Extend	(Extend body parts with tight muscles.)
Curl the Spine	(Curve the spine forward, backward, to the right, to the left.)
Sharp Angles	(Bend body parts, bend at the waist for clear, sharp angles.)
Pretzels	(Twist the trunk, the legs, the arms, and the neck.)

Tasks/Challenges:

T Remember when we worked on balances that followed stretching, twisting, bending, and curling?

Today we are going to try stretching, twisting, bending, and curling into balances on equipment. You may choose to be on the bench (beam, table) or to be partially supported by the bench, i.e., on the mat beside the bench. Explore the actions we practiced earlier of stretching into a balance. Some of the balances may be easier on or beside the equipment; some may be more difficult. Remember, slowly stretch into the balance. (Repeat for each of the body actions.)

Depending on the length of time between balancing on the mats and the equipment, you may need to repeat each of the above tasks.

⚠ *Emphasize safety, body control, and stillness.*

Utilization Level (GLSP): Learning Experiences Leading to Skill Development

Bending, stretching, curling, and twisting actions are used in combination with other skills in dance, gymnastics, and game environments. At the utilization level, these skills and combinations of skills are now experienced and developed in the unpredictable environment of game situations, in gymnastics routines, and in the choreography of dance.

A note about cues: *Although several cues are listed for many of the learning experiences, it's important to focus on only one cue at a time. That way, the children can really concentrate on that cue. Once you provide feedback to the children and observe that most have learned a cue, it's time to focus on another one.*

Transferring Weight to Hands and Twisting

Setting: Large gymnastics mats throughout general space, with sufficient room for children to work safely on transfers

Cues	
Pretzels	(Twist the trunk, the legs, the arms, and the neck.)

Tasks/Challenges:

T How many of you have seen a clock with "hands" that move around the numbers in a circle? Before digital clocks, this is how they looked. (Show an illustration of a clock if there is not one on the wall.) Look down at the floor. Imagine there's a clock on the floor in front of you. Place your feet at 6 o'clock. Transfer your weight to your hands in the middle of the "clock" and twist your body slightly to the right landing at 5 o'clock. Repeat to the left and land at 7 o'clock.

T Now, add a little more twist to try and land at 3 or 9 o'clock. Remember to land safely on your feet.

C If successful, try to twist beyond 3 or 9 o'clock. How close to 12 o'clock can you safely land? This amount of twisting may require you to move your hands during the weight transfer.

Transferring Weight to Hands and Forming a Bridge

Setting: Large gymnastics mats throughout general space

Cues	
Curl the Spine	(Curve the spine forward, backward, to the right, to the left.)
Strong Muscles	(Strong arms and shoulders for supporting weight on hands.)
Tight Muscles	(Tighten the abdominals for control.)

Tasks/Challenges:

T Using a step action, transfer your weight to your hands with sufficient force to continue the forward motion. Your feet should remain in the step-like stance as they move upward over your hands. Just before your feet contact the floor, bring them together, and bend your knees slightly. You will then balance in a bridge with your feet and hands supporting your weight. Keep your legs in the step-like stance throughout the transfer.

T As your feet contact the surface, push with your hands to continue your transfer to a standing position. This transfer without a pause is a walkover.

⚠ Assure that students have the upper body strength to hold weight on two hands in a balanced positioned before attempting this task.

Stretching to Catch with a Partner While Traveling

Setting: Partner scattered throughout general space, a variety of balls for catching

Cues	
Reach and Pull	(Reach to catch the ball, then pull it in as the body curls around it.)
Open Spaces	(Open spaces for the catcher.)

Tasks/Challenges:

T You and your partner will be traveling throughout general space, avoiding collisions with others. Throw the ball to your partner so it is above his or her head, just out of reach. Catcher, stretch high in the air for the catch, travel, and then throw to your partner. Remember, you are both traveling; all throws must be above the head so the catcher is stretched.

Stretch, Catch, Release

Setting: Partners scattered throughout general space; a variety of balls for catching

Cues	
Reach and Pull	(Reach to catch the ball, pull it in to the body, then release for the throw.)
Control	(Gain control of the ball and body before the throw.)
Open Spaces	(Open spaces for the catcher.)

Tasks/Challenges:

T This time when you and your partner are traveling, throwing, and catching, you will receive the ball at high level, travel 1-2-3-4-5, and then throw to your partner. This is a pretty quick release; don't forget to pull the ball into the body before you throw.

T Can you reduce the count to 1-2-3 and then release the ball for the throw? Remember, the throw must reach your partner at high level.

T In a game situation, the count for the throw will vary, sometimes more, sometimes less, often determined by the position of your partner. Travel and throw to an "open" partner. Receiver, remember open spaces for a good catch.

Stretching to Catch Against an Opponent

Setting: Class divided into groups of three, with a variety of balls for catching.

⚠ Sufficient space for children to travel safely.

Cues	
Receiver	(Open spaces for catching.)
Thrower	(High-level throws to stretch partner.)
Be Aware	(Be aware of others traveling, throwing, and catching.)

Tasks/Challenges:

T Partners A and B will be traveling and throwing to each other. Partner C will be trying to intercept the throw to gain possession of the ball. If partner C successfully makes an interception, return the ball to partners A and B; I will give the signal for changing positions in 30 seconds or so.

T Remember, the throw and catch must be at high level—stretch for the catch. Increase the distance of your throws. Change the speed of your traveling.

Stretching, Curling, Bending, and Twisting Against an Opponent

Setting: Class divided into groups of three, with a variety of balls for catching. Sufficient space for children to travel safely.

Cues	
Receiver	(Open spaces for catching.)
Be Aware	(Be aware of others traveling, throwing, and catching.)

Tasks/Challenges:

T Thus far, we have focused on stretching to catch and stretching to intercept the ball. Now we will put stretching, curling, twisting, and bending into a game. Partners A and B will be traveling and throwing to each other. Partner C will be the defensive player trying to intercept the throw to gain possession of the ball. If partner C successfully makes an interception, return the ball to partners A and B; I will give the signal for changing positions in 30 seconds or so. The throw can now be at high level, to the side, or even at low level. Receiver, you must now be ready to stretch, to twist, or even to bend for the catch. Receiver, remember to curl momentarily to protect the ball before traveling.

T Increase the distance of your throws. Change the speed of your traveling. Use fakes and quick moves to try and trick the defensive player.

Stretching, Curling, Bending, and Twisting Against Multiple Opponents

Setting: Class divided into groups of four, with a variety of balls for catching

⚠ Sufficient space for children to travel safely.

Cues	
Receiver	(Open spaces for catching.)
Be Aware	(Be aware of others traveling, throwing, and catching.)

Tasks/Challenges:

C Today we are going to use all the skills we have learned of throwing and catching while traveling, combined with stretching, bending, twisting, and curling in a game of two versus two, an old-fashioned game of Keep-Away. We call it an old-fashioned game because your parents probably played this game at recess when they were in elementary school. However, they were not as skilled as you; they had not learned the actions for stretching, twisting, bending, and curling, and how to use them in the game.

T Your game will be two partners throwing and catching (offense) and two partners trying to intercept (defense). Receiver, look for the open space and move quickly to receive the pass. Interceptors, try to close the open space. Remember to momentarily curl the body and bend the arms to pull the ball close after the catch. This curling and bending action allows you to protect the ball while locating your "teammate" in an open space. If you are successful at an interception, give the ball back to the offense; I will give the signal for the switch of offense and defense.

? *After a couple of switches, with teams being both offense and defense, pull the class together to discuss the body actions used in combination with the throwing and catching. Guided self-assessment works really well and moves the game to a higher level of play.*

Proficiency Level (GLSP): Learning Experiences Leading to Skill Development

You will not find a series of proficiency-level tasks for bending, stretching, twisting, and curling in this chapter; we do not teach these skills at this level in our physical education programs. The actions of bending, stretching, curling, and twisting for the highly skilled are best pursued in programs out of school, e.g., gymnastic clubs, youth sports, and ballet or yoga classes.

Reading Comprehension Questions

1. Use your own terms, not the ones at the beginning of the chapter, to distinguish between the actions of bending, stretching, curling, and twisting.
2. Young children often cross their arms and/or legs and think they are twisting. What would you say to help them understand the concept of twisting?
3. Make a table that has four rows and four columns. Label the columns *bending, stretching, twisting,* and *curling*. Pick four activities, or sports, you like and list them in the four rows. Then indicate how bending, stretching, twisting, and curling (the columns) are used in each the sports or activities you have listed (the rows).
4. Why are proficiency-level tasks not included for bending, stretching, twisting, and curling?
5. Imagine a parent asks you why you are teaching bending, stretching, twisting, and curling in your program. Write the response you might give in 25 words or less.

Reference/Suggested Reading

[SHAPE America] Society of Health and Physical Educators. 2014. *National standards & grade-level outcomes for K-12 physical education*. Champaign, IL: Human Kinetics.

Jumping and Landing

Christopher Whi

Jumping is a movement skill in which the body propels itself off the floor or apparatus into a momentary period of flight. As an isolated maneuver or in combination with other basic patterns, jumping—particularly the flight phase, when the body is unsupported in the air—is a fascinating body action.

There are many jumping patterns (see below). A basic two feet to two feet jump can be a form of locomotion, or it can be performed in self-space with no locomotor action. Other locomotor terms related to jumping include hopping (one foot to the same foot) and leaping (combining a run with a jump from one foot, landing on the other foot). Beyond locomotion, a jump is performed for one of two reasons: (1) to raise the body vertically (straight up) for height or (2) to raise the body with a forward momentum to travel over a distance. Children who learn to jump effectively for height and distance are prepared for a multitude of game, dance, and gymnastics experiences in which the performer needs to be a skilled jumper. Young children enjoy jumping just for the sensation of the body in flight; they jump for distance and for height. Thus, we begin with children learning the basic types of jumps and landing safely from jumps. Once children are capable of jumping and landing safely, they are ready for jumping in combination with other skills. See Box 20-1 for linkages of the skill theme of jumping and landing to the *National Standards & Grade-Level Outcomes for K–12 Physical Education (SHAPE America 2014).*

Fundamental Jumping Patterns

Wickstrom (1983) suggested that children are developmentally capable of performing a jumping action when they're approximately 24 months old. He described the types of jumps preschool children achieve in terms of progressive difficulty:

Jump down from one foot to the other

Jump up from two feet to two feet

Jump down from two feet to two feet

Run and jump from one foot to the other

Jump forward from two feet to two feet

Jump down from one foot to two feet

Run and jump forward from one foot to two feet

Jump over object from two feet to two feet

Jump from one foot to same foot rhythmically (hop)

It's safe to assume that within an average class of young children, some will be incapable of performing

---

Box 20-1

Jumping and Landing in the *National Standards & Grade-Level Outcomes for K–12 Physical Education*

Jumping and landing are referenced in the *National Standards & Grade-Level Outcomes for K–12 Physical Education* (SHAPE America 2014) under Standard 1: "Demonstrates competency in a variety of motor skills and movement patterns." The intent of the standard is developing the fundamental skills needed to enjoy participation in physical activities, with the mastery of movement fundamentals as the foundation for continued skill acquisition.

Sample grade-level outcomes from the *National Standards** include:

- Performs jumping and landing actions with balance (K)
- Demonstrates 2 of the 5 critical elements for jumping and landing in a horizontal plane using two-foot takeoffs and landings in a vertical plane (1)
- Demonstrates 4 of the 5 critical elements for jumping and landing in a horizontal plane using a variety of takeoffs and landings and in a vertical plane (2)
- Jumps and lands in the horizontal plane/in the vertical plane using a mature pattern (3)
- Uses spring-and-step takeoffs and landings specific to gymnastics (4)
- Combines jumping and landing patterns with locomotor and manipulative skills in dance, gymnastics, and small-sided practice tasks in game environments (5)

*Suggested grade-level outcomes for student learning.

---

one or more of these jumping tasks. Initial observations will probably reveal a wide range of jumping abilities. Typically, kindergarten students are at the precontrol level. Their jumps usually achieve little height or distance, and they jump on two feet to ensure they maintain their balance. Children at this level seem to be jumping merely to enjoy the sensation of momentarily losing contact with the ground and the challenge of maintaining balance upon landing. A teacher can build on this natural fascination by providing learning experiences that progressively lead children toward the mature performance of jumping and landing in different dance, game, and gymnastics situations.

The basketball player with mastery of jumping for height secures the rebound from a missed shot or a pass from a teammate. The football player with that extra inch on the jump receives the pass or captures the interception. The split-step in tennis, the jump-stop in basketball, and the preparatory two-one jump prior to the spike in volleyball all stem from mastery of the basic patterns of jumping. The two-foot takeoff in preparation for vaulting, aerials, and mounts onto gymnastics apparatus; the dancer suspended in flight; the elite basketball player who appears suspended in time following a leap—all are executing skills from the theme of jumping and landing. See our progression spiral on page 358 for the development of jumping and landing from precontrol to proficiency levels.

The fundamental jumping pattern consists of the following five basic variations:

1. Two-foot takeoff to a one-foot landing
2. Two-foot takeoff to a two-foot landing
3. One-foot takeoff to a landing on the same foot (hop)
4. One-foot takeoff to a landing on the other foot (leap)
5. One-foot takeoff to a two-foot landing

However, the specific actions of the body in performing a jump vary according to the purpose or intention—for example, jumping to catch or jumping to dismount from apparatus.

When we begin to focus on jumping, we have children think of the skill as three successive phases:

1. **Takeoff:** Actions of the body as it's propelled off the ground

2. **Flight:** Actions of the body while it's off the ground and in the air
3. **Landing:** Actions of the body as it reestablishes contact with the ground

The photo sequences in Boxes 20-2 and 20-3 show the critical elements for the takeoff, flight, and landing phases of jumping and landing. Box 20-2 illustrates the correct form for jumping for height; Box 20-3 shows the correct form for jumping for distance. It is important that the teacher is familiar with the critical elements needed for quality instruction, demonstration, and observation of the skill. Throughout the chapter are sample cues (short phrases or words summarizing these critical elements). Ideally, if the cue is the last thing a teacher repeats before sending the students to practice, the learner will be cognitively focused on the critical elements.

Critical elements for jumping and landing for height (vertical plane) include:

- Arms extend back; hips, knees, and ankles bend in preparation for jumping action
- Arms extend upward as body propels upward
- Body extends and stretches upward while in flight
- Hips, knees, and ankles bend on landing
- Shoulders, knees, and ankles align for balance on landing

Box 20-2

Critical Elements: Jumping for Height

©Derek Sine & Van Tucker

Arms back, knees bent

Arms extend upward

Extend body-stretch

Hips, knees, ankles bend

Shoulders, knees, ankles align

Box 20-3

Critical Elements: Jumping for Distance

Arms back, knees bent

Arms extend forward

Extend body

Arms forward

Hips, knees, ankles bend on landing

©Derek Sine & Van Tucker

Critical elements for jumping and landing for distance (horizontal plane) include:

- Arms extend back; hips, knees, and ankles bend in preparation for jumping action
- Arms extend forward as body propels forward
- Body extends and stretches slightly upward while in flight
- Hips, knees, and ankles bend on landing
- Shoulders, knees, and ankles align for balance on landing

In the beginning, we have children focus on the takeoff and the landing phases of jumping. As they experiment with different takeoff and landing combinations, they begin to sense which takeoff procedures result in the highest jumps as opposed to which result in the longest jumps.

Children find that actions of the legs, arms, torso, and head during the flight phase influence the trajectory of the jump. They come to recognize the unique giving action of the ankles, knees, and hips in absorbing the shock of landing. Actions during the flight phase of jumping are introduced only after children can achieve momentary suspension of the body in flight and have control of their bodies for balanced landings. A mature pattern of jumping and landing signals children are now ready for combining jumping with other skills and maneuvers while in the air. As is true with the learning of each new skill, guided practice is extremely important—practice that often extends beyond elementary physical education into middle school physical education and the specific jumping skills for sports, gymnastics, and dance.

Precontrol Level (GLSP): Experiences for Exploration

The following learning experiences are designed for exploration of jumping. Through these tasks and challenges, children will begin to discover different types of jumps as well as jumps that take them high and jumps that take them far.

Jumping and Landing: Exploring Different Patterns

Setting: Ropes (one per child) placed around the edge of the teaching area.

Skill Theme Development Sequence

Jumping and Landing

Proficiency Level

Jumping hurdles
Jumping, dancing, and imagery
Jumping as part of a dance creation
Jumping with a springboard
Jumping with a partner to match actions
Jumping with a partner to mirror actions

Utilization Level

Jumping to an accented beat
Throwing and catching while jumping
Jumping on a bench
Jumping to throw
Jumping to catch

Control Level

Jumping and landing task sheet
Jump, Squash, TaDa
Jumping on and off equipment using buoyant
    and yielding landings
Jumping over equipment using buoyant landings
Performing jumping sequences and making
    body shapes
Traveling, jumping, and body shapes
Jumping to form a body shape during flight
Jumping using buoyant and yielding landings
Jumping a self-turned rope
Jumping a turned rope
Jumping in rhythmical sequences
Jumping rhythmically
Jumping over low obstacles: hurdles
Jumping over low obstacles: hoops
Jumping for height
Jumping for distance
Jumping and landing: basic patterns

Precontrol Level

Jumping over a swinging rope
Jumping high
Jumping far
Jumping and landing: exploring different patterns

Tasks/Challenges:

🅣 At the edge of our working space are ropes. Select a rope and place it in a straight line in your self-space. Jump over the rope, and land on the other side without falling down.

©Lars A. Niki

Young children are challenged by the task of propelling the body off the ground for a momentary period of being airborne.

🅣 Explore different ways to jump over your rope, sometimes taking off on one foot and landing on two, sometimes taking off on two feet and landing on two.

🅣 What other ways can you jump over the rope? *Look for options children discover and add suggestions as needed (e.g., hop, jump sideways, jump backward).*

⚠ It is important to stress from the beginning that children land on their feet when jumping, not fall to the floor when they land.

🅣 Jump high in the air as you travel over your rope.

⚠ Before having children jump for distance, conduct a safety check to be sure each child has sufficient space for landing safely after the jump, with no collisions with another child.

Running and jumping combine skill and spatial awareness.

©Lars A. Niki

Tasks/Challenges:

(T) Place your rope on the floor away from others. Jump over your rope, landing as far from your rope as possible. Try the two feet to two feet jump. Next, try the one foot to two feet jump.

(T) Place your piece of masking tape on the floor. Lie down with your feet touching the tape, and place the rope by the top of your head. If you have trouble, ask a friend to help. The distance from the rope to the tape is how tall you are. Standing behind your rope, try to jump your height. How close can you come to your piece of tape?

(⚠) Remember, land on your feet.

(C) Can you jump even farther than your height?

Jumping High

Setting: Streamers hung at various heights from a rope stretched along the work area (portable volleyball standards work well as supports for the stretched rope)

Tasks/Challenges:

(T) Jump to see if you can touch the streamers hanging from the rope.

(T) Run and jump to touch the streamers.

(⚠) Conduct a safety check to be sure each child has sufficient space for running, jumping, and landing safety, with no collisions with another child.

Jumping over a Swinging Rope

Setting: Class divided into groups of threes, each group with a "long" rope

Tasks/Challenges:

(T) In your groups of three, you are going to take turns jumping over a swinging rope. Two of you will gently swing the rope side to side while the third person jumps. The secret is to time your jumps; jump as the rope swings toward you. After five jumps, trade places.

(C) Practice for 10 jumps without a mistake.

Control Level (GLSP): Learning Experiences Leading to Skill Development

At the control level, we encourage children to practice both long and high jumps until their landings are balanced and controlled with the goal being a mature pattern of jumping and landing. Children begin to explore the flight phase of the jump; they discover the world of

(T) Arrange your rope in a shape different from a straight line—for example, a circle or a rectangle. How many ways can you find to jump into the shape and out the other side?

Jumping Far

Setting: Ropes (one per child) placed around the edge of the teaching area; strips of masking tape (one per child) on the wall

jumping rope. They are challenged with jumping and landing as they relate to dance, gymnastics, and game skills.

A note about cues: *Although several cues are listed for many of the learning experiences, it's important to focus on only one cue at a time. This way, the children can really concentrate on that cue. Once you provide feedback to the children and observe that most have learned a cue, it's time to focus on another one.*

Jumping and Landing: Basic Patterns

Setting: Ropes (one per child) placed around the edge of the teaching area

Cue	
Squash	(Bend your knees to absorb the force and maintain balance when you land.)

Tasks/Challenges:

T When we first worked on jumping, you explored different ways to jump over your rope—just for fun. Place your rope in a straight line on the floor; choose three of your favorites from those different types of jumps and practice jumping over your rope, landing each time in a balanced position without falling down. Bend your knees when you land so your landings are very quiet.

T Jump over your rope, taking off on two feet and landing on two feet.

T Position yourself approximately 10 feet from your rope. Approach your rope with a series of running steps; jump over your rope, taking off on one foot and landing on two feet.

⚠ Teach the children to conduct a safety check before they begin any jumping that involves an approach to assure sufficient space for landing safely with no collisions.

T Using a series of running steps to approach your rope, take off on one foot and land on the opposite foot on the other side of your rope. Taking off on one foot and landing on the opposite foot is called a leap. For the leap, instead of the squash landing, continue with a few quick, running steps before you stop.

T Change the shape of your rope from a straight line to a circle, rectangle, or triangle. Standing just outside the rope shape, take off on one foot and jump inside your shape, landing on the same foot. What locomotor action did you just do with this jump? A hop. Hop into and out of your rope.

? Peer and/or teacher observation of the different jumping patterns would be beneficial at this point. *Review Chapter 12 for specific examples of assessments.*

Jumping at high level varies as children practice the skill.

©Lars A. Niki

Jumping for Distance

Setting: Ropes (one per child) placed around the edge of the work area; large color/panel gymnastics mats; strips of masking tape (one per child) on the wall

Cues	
Knees Bent/ Swing Back	(Bend your knees and swing your arms back to prepare for the takeoff.)
Swing Forward	(Swing your arms forcefully forward for maximum distance.)
Squash	(Bend your knees to absorb the force and maintain balance when you land.)

Tasks/Challenges:

T Stand beside and at one end of your rope, making sure you are not close enough to land on your rope. Bend your knees and swing your arms in preparation for the jump. Taking off on two feet and landing on two, jump forward as far as you can. You may be able to jump the full length of your rope.

T Remember when you practiced jumping your height by placing a piece of masking tape on the floor at the place of your feet and your rope on the floor the distance from your feet to your head? Try that jump again, taking off on two feet and landing on two feet. If you jump farther than your height, move the tape to where your heels first land.

T Standing at one end of the mat, jump as far as you can toward the other end of the mat. Count your score by the number of panels you jumped over. **Remember, bend your knees and swing your arms in preparation for the jump; then swing your arms forward for a really far jump.** Keeping your arms stretched forward will also keep you from falling backward when you land! *Mark feet or meters on the mat, allowing students to measure the distance of the jumps.*

The three tasks above work well in station format for practice of the two-foot to two-foot jumping for distance.

? Teacher Observation of Jumping and Landing: Horizontal Plane (Jumping for distance)

Perform three forward jumps for distance, using a two-foot takeoff and a two-foot landing.

Sample Criteria for Assessment Rubric:

Developing: Demonstrates 4 or less of the critical elements* in 2 or 3 attempts.

Competent: Demonstrates all 5 critical elements in 2 of 3 attempts

Proficient: Demonstrates all 5 critical elements in all 3 attempts

*See critical elements on page 356.

Adapted from PE Metrics (2018).

You can complete this assessment easily in station setup. Refer to Chapter 12, "Assessing Student Learning," for the use of rubrics as assessment.

Jumping for Height

Setting: Balloons suspended at various heights from a stretched rope; milk crates or low boxes (packed firmly with newspaper) positioned around the room, with sufficient mats for safety (place mats in front of and behind equipment to prevent sliding of boxes and crates)

Cues	
Knees Bent/ Swing Back	(Bend your knees and swing your arms back to prepare for the takeoff.)
Swing Upward	(Swing your arms upward for good height.)
Squash	(Bend your knees to absorb the force and maintain balance when you land.)

Tasks/Challenges:

T Scatter throughout general space and jump high in the air, returning to the floor in your same self-space. Take off on two feet and land on two feet.

T Jump high in the air, taking off on two feet and landing on two feet. Swing your arms upward; this will help you jump higher.

T Positioned around the work area are milk crates or boxes stuffed with newspaper. Large gymnastics mats are in front of and behind the crates or boxes. Standing on the box or crate, jump high in the air and land on two feet on the mat in front of the box or crate. **Remember, swing your arms upward, reaching for the sky, to gain maximum height on your jump**.

T Jog throughout general space; on the signal, jump high in the air by taking off on one foot and landing on the opposite foot. This is the leap we practiced earlier; swing your arms upward as you jump to stay airborne as long as possible. Continue your jog.

(T) Positioned around the work area are balloons suspended from stretched ropes. Using a two-foot takeoff and a two-foot landing, jump to touch the balloons like a basketball player trying to tap the ball on the jump.

(T) Approach the balloon with a series of running steps using a one-foot takeoff and a two-foot landing to jump for the balloon. Which type of jump gives you more height: a two-foot takeoff or a one-foot takeoff? A standing jump or a running approach to the jump?

(?) Jumping and Landing: Vertical Plane (Jumping for Height)

Perform three upward jumps, using a two-foot takeoff and a two-foot landing

Sample Criteria for Assessment Rubric:

Developing: Demonstrates 4 or less of the critical elements* in 2 or 3 attempts.

Competent: Demonstrates all 5 critical elements in 2 of 3 attempts

Proficient: Demonstrates all 5 critical elements in all 3 attempts

*See critical elements on page 357.

Adapted from PE Metrics (2018).

You can complete this assessment easily in station setup. Refer to Chapter 12, "Assessing Student Learning," for the use of rubrics as assessment.

Jumping over Low Obstacles: Hoops

Setting: Hoops (one per child) scattered throughout the teaching area

Cues	
Knees Bent/ Swing Back	(Bend your knees and swing your arms back to prepare for the takeoff.)
Swing Upward	(Swing your arms upward for good height.)
Swing Forward	(Swing your arms forcefully forward for maximum distance.)
Squash	(Bend your knees to absorb the force and maintain balance when you land.)

Tasks/Challenges:

(T) Jump over your hoop. As your feet touch the ground, freeze your body perfectly still; this means you must bend your ankles, knees, and hips as

you land. **Think of your feet sinking into the floor as if the floor were a sponge.**

(C) Practice jumping over your hoop with two-foot takeoffs and landings until you can land without falling three times in a row. Can you then do the same three perfect landings with a one-foot takeoff and a two-foot landing?

(T) Travel throughout general space, leaping over hoops. **Remember to extend your arms up for good height as you leap.**

Jumping over Low Obstacles: Hurdles

Setting: One hurdle (cones and rolled newspaper or rope) per child

Cues	
Knees Bent/ Swing Back	(Bend your knees and swing your arms back to prepare for the takeoff.)
Swing Upward	(Swing your arms upward for good height.)
Squash	(Bend your knees to absorb the force and maintain balance when you land.)

Tasks/Challenges:

(T) Standing just behind your hurdle, jump over it using a two-foot takeoff and a two-foot landing. Try to be really high when you cross the top—**push with your toes; reach for the sky.**

(T) Now as you jump over the hurdle, try to use the different types of jumps you have learned. Try the easiest ones first and then the most difficult ones.

(C) Practice each jump until you can do it three times with a soft landing and without touching the crosspiece.

(T) Stand approximately 6 feet behind your hurdle. Approach the hurdle with quick, running steps. Jump over your hurdle using a one-foot takeoff and a two-foot landing.

(T) When you can clear the hurdle without touching the crossbar and land without falling down, approach the bar with quick, running steps. Jump over the bar using a one-foot takeoff and then land on the opposite foot; continue with a few quick, running steps before you stop. Wow! You look ready for the Olympics.

In conjunction with these tasks, you may want to add the following: Jumping Over While Stretching, Bending, and Twisting and Jumping Off While Stretching and Twisting (page 345).

Jumping Rhythmically

Setting: Children scattered throughout general space; a recording of the sounds of tools and machines

Cues

Spring, Spring	(Quick, springy landings for the fast beat.)
High Jumps, Full Squash	(Full squash following the high jumps.)
Heads Up	(Keep your head and shoulders up for good balance.)

Tasks/Challenges:

T Standing in your personal space, jump while keeping beat with the drum. You'll have to listen carefully because the drumbeat will change at different times. **To do this without losing the beat, take little jumps so your feet barely leave the floor.** In other words, you'll be almost bouncing on your toes.

For the next task, play music with the sounds of tools and machines. (Children enjoy electronic/synthesizer music.)

T This time, instead of a drumbeat, you'll hear the sounds of different machines and tools you're familiar with. Staying in your self-space, take little jumps, keeping time with the tool and machine sounds you hear. The sounds will change often, so be alert, and take little bouncy jumps on your toes.

T Again, the drumbeat will guide your jumps. As you hear the slow beat, take big, high jumps. When you hear the quick beat, take small jumps. This maneuver involves careful listening, so be prepared to change at any time. Make sure your jumps are clearly big on the slow beats and really little on the fast beats; adjust the height of your jump for fast (low) and slow (high).

The folk dance "Jump Jim Joe" is an excellent activity for the practice of rhythmical jumping. Young children enjoy the repetitive nature of the jumping in the dance.

Jumping in Rhythmical Sequences

Setting: Children scattered throughout general space

Cues

Heads Up	(Keep your head and shoulders up for good balance.)
Swing Upward	(Swing your arms upward for good height.)
Spring, Squash	(Springy landings to continue travel; full squash to stop.)

Tasks/Challenges:

T This time, you're going to travel and then jump and travel again, always keeping the same rhythm. To begin, you'll all practice the same travel jump pattern, which will go like this: Run, run, run, leap/run, run, run, leap. As you move, all of you will say together, "Run, run, run, leap," so you can stay together. Let's practice saying that and keeping the same tempo before beginning to move. (Practice saying the phrase in tempo.) As you jump and run this time, remember to stay with the voices; everyone should be jumping at the same time if you're all together.

T Now instead of saying the phrase, you're going to clap it as you go. You'll have to remember what to do on your own.

C Now that you can follow the phrase I designed for you, you're going to work in a group of three or four, make up your own phrase, and follow it. Your phrase should contain three traveling actions followed by one jumping pattern. You should repeat the sequence three times before coming to a stop. Practice the whole thing until you think it's the best you can do. As you begin, it helps to say to yourself what you're supposed to be doing, just as you did in the previous activity. When you think you know it, try clapping instead of saying it. When you're really good, practice doing it with no noise at all. Remember: three traveling actions followed by one jumping action, repeated three times. Keep the same rhythm throughout each part of the sequence. The key with your group is good communication. *(Pinpoint several groups who've created an interesting sequence—they don't have to be the most skilled children in the class.)*

Jumping a Turned Rope

Setting: Class divided into groups of two or three, each group with one long rope. If the children are in groups of two, attach one end of the rope to a post, pole, or chair. Mark (tape) a box on the floor at the center of the rope for the jumper and an X on the floor where the turner or turners stand.

Cues

Jumpers

Heads Up	(Keep your head and shoulders up for good balance.)
Jump, Jump	(Small, springy jumps with very little height.)

Turners

One, Two, Three	(Swing the rope back and forth before the first swing over the head, counting "One, two, three"; this will help the jumper be ready.)
Smooth Turns	(Turn the rope with large, smooth swings.)

Tasks/Challenges:

T At your ropes, two people will practice turning a long rope. Turn large smooth swings. You and your partner will need to communicate to coordinate the movement. After 10 turns, allow the other person to turn. As a fun assessment, I will travel through the gym and jump into your rope, jump two or three times, and then run out. You pass the test if you can turn high enough and smooth enough for me to jump.

T At your ropes, two people will turn and one person will try to jump. Jumpers should try to stay in the boxes marked on the floor as you jump. After 10 jumps, trade positions.

T When you can successfully jump the rope by starting in the middle, try to start from the outside: run in and jump. Turners: Turn the rope so it turns toward the jumper—the front-door approach. Jumpers: Start your run as soon as the rope touches the floor. Jump 10 times and run out.

C Create a new rhyme as you jump the long rope. *Record the children's rhymes in a booklet of "Jump Rope Rhymes."*

Jumping a Self-Turned Rope

Setting: Ropes of different lengths so each child has a personal rope of the proper length

Cues	
Heads Up	(Keep your head and shoulders up for good balance.)
Jump, Jump	(Small, springy jumps with very little height.)

Tasks/Challenges:

T Place both handles in one hand and practice turning the rope using your wrist. Then try jumping to the rhythm of your turn. You can do a single jump or a double jump to help you find the beat. Repeat with the other hand.

T Practice jumping your rope by turning it over your head. Some of you will find that jumping forward is easier; others will find that jumping the rope as it turns backward is easier. Be sure you try jumping both ways.

T If you're having trouble, bring the rope over your head, stop it on the floor in front of your feet, and then jump over the rope. As you become successful, go a little faster, and don't let the rope stop so much. As you practice, you will find yourself stopping the rope less.

T When you become successful at jumping in one direction (forward or backward) without missing, try jumping in the other direction.

C Set a goal for yourself of the number of jumps you want to make without a mistake.

T Try jumping with the different types of jumps we have learned—two feet to two feet, one foot to the same foot, two feet to one foot, and so forth.

Jumping a self-turned rope can be difficult for some students. Revisiting rope jumping and encouraging out-of-class practice will help.

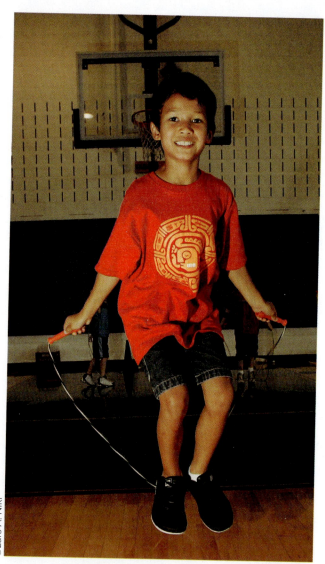

©Lars A. Niki

Jumping rope is a favorite children's pastime.

Jumping Using Buoyant and Yielding Landings

Setting: Children scattered throughout general space; paper and pencil available outside the work area

Cues

Swing Upward	(Swing your arms upward for good height.)
Heads Up	(Keep your head and shoulders up for good balance.)
Yielding Landings	(Bend your knees to absorb the force when you land, as if sinking into the floor.)
Buoyant Landings	(Bend your knees as you land; then spring up quickly.)

Tasks/Challenges:

T Jump three times in a row on two feet, pausing between each jump. This is called a yielding landing.

T This time, jump three times in a row using a two-foot takeoff and a two-foot landing without pausing between each jump. This is a buoyant landing. **Spring up quickly after each jump.**

T Now, jump twice in a row, the first time with a buoyant landing and the second time with a yielding landing. Make sure your landings are clearly different so I can tell which one you're doing simply by watching.

T This time on the signal, jump high, turn in the air, land balanced, and freeze. Again, use yielding landings.

T Now, jump high, turn in the air, and after landing safely on two feet, collapse to the floor, curl, and freeze. **Remember, use your arms to help you turn in the air.**

T Try this one: Jump high, turn in the air, and upon landing, collapse to the floor, curl, and freeze for an instant—and then quickly resume traveling. Make your moves very smooth so they really go together and you know exactly what you're doing and what comes next. Use your arms to help you get up in the air. Strive for a yielding landing.

C So far I've made up all your jumping and traveling patterns. On your piece of paper, write down a jumping and traveling pattern that you would like to do yourself. After you've written it down, practice it until it goes smoothly and you know it by heart. Make sure you always begin and end in the same place, which is one way you know you're doing the same thing each time. I should be able to tell what you're doing and the type of landing by watching you. If I can't, I'll ask you.

©Lars A. Niki

The sensation of jumping delights young children.

Jumping to Form a Body Shape During Flight

See Chapter 16 to review body shapes.

Setting: Children scattered throughout general space, each with a hurdle or a rope in a shape on the floor

Cues

Swing Upward	(Swing your arms upward for good height.)
Heads Up	(Keep your head and shoulders up for good balance.)
Yielding Landings	(Bend your knees to absorb the force when you land, as if sinking into the floor.)

Tasks/Challenges:

T Jump over your equipment and form a narrow body shape while you're in the air. A narrow body shape is very thin. Remember, make all the parts of your body narrow, not just one part. Practice your shape until it's as narrow as it can be.

C Now think of five more narrow body shapes you can make while you're in the air. Practice all the shapes until they're the best you can do. I'll come and ask each of you to show me your best shape, so be ready. **Remember not to fall over on your landings; your feet should stick as if you had glue on them. What kind of landings will you need?**

T This time you're going to jump using wide body shapes in the air. A wide shape is very big and spread out, like a wall. **Remember as you jump to make your whole body wide in the air by stretching your arms and legs outward from your body.** Practice your shape until it's as wide as it can be.

⚠ Feet need to return to shoulder width for a safe landing; remind the children not to land with the legs stretched in a wide shape.

C Now that you know what a wide shape is, think of five more wide shapes you can make when you jump. Let them be really different, even weird. Practice all the shapes until they're the best you can do. I'm going to ask some of you to show your wide shapes, so work hard.

Pinpoint several children who are using wide shapes.

T This time, you're going to learn some new names for body shapes. First, you're going to make symmetrical shapes in the air. A symmetrical shape looks exactly alike on both sides. For example, if I were to cut you in half from head to toe, you would look the same on each side. At your equipment, practice making a symmetrical shape in the air. Be sure the two sides of your body look exactly alike.

C Create five more symmetrical shapes with your jumps.

T This time you're going to do nonsymmetrical jumps. In a nonsymmetrical jump, the two sides of your body look really different. So if I were to cut you in half, one arm might be up in the air and the other one out to the side, or one leg might be going forward and the other one backward. In other words, one side shouldn't look like the other one. In your space, create a nonsymmetrical jump. **Remember, absorb force when you land by bending your knees.**

C Create five nonsymmetrical jumps you can do in the air.

T Try to do wide symmetrical jumps. Find three you really like, and practice them.

T Now try to find three narrow symmetrical jumps. After you do that, find three wide nonsymmetrical jumps and three narrow nonsymmetrical jumps. I'm going to ask some of you to show your jumps to the class, so make them the best that they can be.

T Approach your hurdle or rope shape with a series of running steps. Jump in the air, making a wide shape. **Land in a balanced position without falling down.**

T Try your other shapes in the air combined with your short running approach.

⚠ Students should attempt running, jumping, and making shapes while airborne only after they have demonstrated safe landings in self-space—absorbing the force by bending the knees and landing in a balanced position without falling forward.

Traveling, Jumping, and Body Shapes

Setting: Children scattered throughout general space

Cues	
Swing Upward	(Swing your arms upward for good height.)
Heads Up	(Keep your head and shoulders up for good balance.)
Buoyant Landings	(Bend your knees as you land; then spring up quickly.)

Tasks/Challenges:

T As you travel around the room, make the kind of jump I've called out each time you hear the drumbeat. The jump may simply be wide, or it may be narrow and nonsymmetrical. I will call out the kind of jump before I say "go." We'll use buoyant landings so we can be ready to travel again. Remember, make your shapes as clear as you possibly can.

Performing Jumping Sequences and Making Body Shapes

Setting: Note cards with various body-shape sequences written on them, with each sequence containing at least four different body shapes (e.g., wide; wide symmetrical; narrow nonsymmetrical; narrow); children scattered throughout general space, each with a sequence card

Cues

Swing Upward	(Swing your arms upward for good height.)
Heads Up	(Keep your head and shoulders up for good balance.)
Buoyant Landings	(Bend your knees as you land; then spring up quickly.)
Yielding Landings	(Bend your knees to absorb the force when you land, as if sinking into the floor.)

Tasks/Challenges:

T On your card are listed four body shapes. You're going to make up a sequence of jumps that shows those body shapes in the air. To do this, you'll first travel a bit and then jump, showing the first body shape; then you'll travel again and jump and show the second body shape listed; you'll travel again and jump using the third body shape; you'll travel one more time and jump showing the last body shape. So your sequence should be like this: Travel, jump; travel, jump; travel, jump; travel, jump, freeze. Repeat the sequence enough times so you can do it the same way each time. Memorize it. When it's memorized, show the sequence to a friend. **Remember, use buoyant landings between jumps and a yielding landing after your last jump.**

Jumping over Equipment Using Buoyant Landings

Setting: Pairs of hurdles around the room, spaced so children can jump the first and then the second hurdle

Cues

Heads Up	(Keep your head and shoulders up for good balance.)
Buoyant Landings	(Bend your knees as you land; then spring up quickly.)
Yielding Landings	(Bend your knees to absorb the force when you land, as if sinking into the floor.)

Tasks/Challenges:

T Earlier in our work, you practiced taking off on one foot and landing on the opposite foot, as in a leap. This is the action you use to clear a hurdle. Approach the first hurdle with quick, running steps; jump over the first hurdle with the one-foot to one-foot action; use a buoyant landing to continue your travel and jump over the second hurdle.

C Practice this task until you seem to just pop over the first and then the second hurdle.

Jumping On and Off Equipment Using Buoyant and Yielding Landings

Setting: Boxes packed firmly with newspaper, low benches, milk crates, and other low equipment positioned around the room, with sufficient mats for safety (place mats around equipment to prevent sliding of boxes and crates)

Cues

Heads Up	(Keep your head and shoulders up for good balance.)
Buoyant Landings	(Bend your knees as you land; then spring up quickly.)
Yielding Landings	(Bend your knees to absorb the force when you land, as if sinking into the floor.)

Tasks/Challenges:

T Jump onto a piece of equipment, and use a buoyant landing to quickly spring off with another jump to the floor. **You should barely touch the equipment before you are off again and back to the floor, almost as if you were on a springboard—no stopping between jumps.**

T This time, jump onto the piece of equipment using a yielding landing, hold still on top of the equipment a couple of seconds, and then jump to the floor with another yielding landing. **Remember, on this jump, your knees should really bend, and you should be able to hold still when you finish.**

T Try jumping onto the equipment with the different jumps we have learned—two feet to two feet, one foot to two feet, and so on. Sometimes use a buoyant landing on the equipment so you can quickly jump off; sometimes use a yielding landing on the equipment, pausing before you jump off. Always use a yielding landing on two feet when you jump off the equipment to the floor.

? Which landing is used for a quick, springy action to continue movement? Which landing is used for landing and holding still?

Jump, Squash, TaDa

Setting: Low benches, low balance beam, folded mats positioned throughout general space; children divided into groups for stations

Cues

Swing Upward	(Swing your arms upward for good height.)
Heads Up	(Keep your head and shoulders up for good balance.)
Squash	(Bend your knees to absorb the force and maintain balance when you land.)

Tasks/Challenges:

🔵T Have you ever watched gymnasts perform a stunt and then extend their arms high above their heads? Why do you think they do this movement? They do it to regain balance and proper body alignment after the gymnastics action. In the cartoon *Calvin and Hobbes*, Calvin called this recovery the "TaDa" of gymnastics, the recovery to a balanced position no matter what has happened during the movement. Let's add that action to our jumping and landing work today. Jump from your mat (bench, beam) with a two-foot takeoff and a two-foot landing. Jump for maximum height, squash into a balanced position, then stretch your body upward, extending your arms to the sky as you say "TaDa."

🔵T Jump off your mat (bench, beam) with a quarter turn in the air. Land in a balanced position; recover with a full extension. **Don't forget the TaDa!**

🔵T When a friend gives you a thumbs-up for a good landing on your quarter turn, you may want to try a one-half turn. Practice turning your body clockwise and counterclockwise.

🔵T Jump off the mat (bench, beam), make a shape in the air, land in a balanced position, and recover with a full gymnastics extension.

🔵T Combine jumping off the low equipment, landing, and rolling in a gymnastics sequence; finish your sequence by returning to a standing TaDa.

⚠️ Use the previous task only if children have mastered rolling from Chapter 22 or in combination with work from that chapter. Emphasize a safe landing before rolling.

See Chapter 22 for additional combination tasks, as well as for transferring off low apparatus.

Jumping and Landing Task Sheet

Setting: A jumping and landing task sheet (similar to the example in Figure 20.1) for each child

Cues

Heads Up	(Keep your head and shoulders up for good balance.)

Swing Upward	(Swing your arms upward for good height on the jump.)
Buoyant Landings	(Bend your knees as you land, then spring up quickly.)
Yielding Landings	(Bend your knees to absorb the force when you land, as if sinking into the floor.)
Swing Forward	(Swing your arms forcefully forward for maximum distance.)

Select cues appropriate to the tasks on the sheet (e.g., jumping forward, jumping upward, jumping and continuing action, jumping/landing with a stop of movement).

Tasks/Challenges:

🔵C This task sheet lets you test the jumping skills you've practiced so far. Whenever you've practiced a challenge and think you can do it correctly, ask a friend to watch you. If your friend thinks you've done the challenge well, the friend signs her or his name on the sheet next to the challenge.

Utilization Level (GLSP): Learning Experiences Leading to Skill Development

Experiences at the utilization level provide contexts in which children use jumping and landing in combination with other movements. They are challenged to combine jumping with throwing and catching in both static and dynamic situations. They combine jumping and landing with the gymnastics skills of balancing and transferring weight. They explore the complexity of rhythm with accented beats.

A note about cues: *Although several cues are listed for many of the learning experiences, it's important to focus on only one cue at a time. This way, the children can really concentrate on that cue. Once you provide feedback to the children and observe that most have learned a cue, it's time to focus on another one.*

Jumping to Catch

Setting: Sets of partners with beanbags, plastic balls, foam footballs, tennis balls

Cues

Swing Upward	(Swing your arms upward for a full extension and added height on the jump.)
Yielding Landings	(Bend your knees to absorb the force when you land, as if sinking into the floor.)

Figure 20.1 Task sheet for jumping and landing.

Name _____	Teacher _____

Jumping Task Sheet

Observer	Challenge
	I can jump starting on two feet and landing on two feet.
	I can jump from two feet to one foot.
	I can jump from one foot to the other foot.
	I can hop from one foot to the same foot.
	I can jump from one foot to two feet.
	I can jump, turn in the air, and land without falling.
	I can jump off a box and land without falling.
	I can jump off a box, turn in the air, and land without falling.
	I can run and jump over a hurdle and land without falling.
	I can turn a jump rope myself and jump 15 times without missing.
	I can
	I can
	I can

Tasks/Challenges:

C In pairs, scatter throughout general space. See how many times you can jump and catch without a mistake; count your score only if you catch the ball before you land. After three trials, switch thrower and catcher.

T When the task becomes easy for you and your partner, try throwing the ball so your partner has to reach to the left or to the right to make the catch.

T Throw the ball so your partner is forced off the ground to catch it; this means you have to throw the ball to a point above where the catch will actually be made. This is a high-level catch—feet off the floor, arms extended above the head.

Throwers: It helps to pick a spot on the wall (tree, telephone pole) above and behind your partner to aim at.

T Try both one- and two-foot takeoffs.

T Switch with your partner after five throws. You are now the catcher; your partner will throw the ball above your head, so you must jump for the catch.

T When you are confident throwing and catching while jumping, you and your partner can add a new element—traveling. Practice running, jumping, and catching in the air. For the two of you to do this task well, your partner will need to make a good throw. At first, run and jump from right to left; then, run and jump from left to right.

T When you are able to make at least three catches in a row, run away from the thrower—that is, start close to and run away from your partner, as you might in a football game.

Jumping to Throw

Setting: Sets of partners with whiffle balls, tennis balls, footballs

Cues	
Vertical Jumps	(Jump upward, not outward, to throw.)
Yielding Landings	(Bend your knees to absorb the force when you land, as if sinking into the floor.)

Catching at a high level combines jumping and stretching.

©Barbara Adamcik

Tasks/Challenges:

T Pick a target, such as a target on the wall (or a basketball backstop, a hoop, or a stationary partner). Jump and throw the ball to the target.

T When you hit the target five times in a row, move farther away from the target. It counts as a successful throw only if you hit the target and make your throw while in the air.

T As this task gets easier, try running, jumping, and throwing to the target.

Jumping on a Bench

Setting: Low benches scattered throughout the work area

Cue	
Squash	(Bend your knees to absorb the force and maintain balance when you land.)

Tasks/Challenges:

T You will work one at a time on the bench. Travel to the middle of the bench; jump upward, taking off on one foot and landing on two feet on the bench. **Focus your eyes on the end of the bench.**

T When you're able to do this task several times without falling off, practice landing on only one foot. Hold your balance on the bench before your other foot comes down on the bench. Try to hold your balance for 2 or 3 seconds.

C Design a sequence along the bench that includes at least two different jumps. For example, hop on one foot along the bench, jump and turn so you land facing the opposite direction, and travel back to the start using small leaps. At first, your jumps won't be very high, but as you get better, you'll want to make them higher. Practice your sequence until you can do it three times in a row without falling off.

When you observe that children are competent and comfortable with different types of jumps on the bench, they may progress to low and medium balance beams. This is an excellent opportunity for intratask variation.

Throwing and Catching While Jumping

Setting: A court, its boundaries marked with a rope or a net (size of court is determined by space available; the larger the court, the more difficult the game)

©Barbara Adamcik
©Barbara Adamcik

The skill of jumping is important to success in games, dance, and gymnastics.

Jumping onto a bench challenges utilization-level children.

Cues

Buoyant Landings	(Bend your knees as you land; then spring up quickly—to throw or travel.)
Yielding Landings	(Bend your knees to absorb the force, and sink into a balanced position.)

Tasks/Challenges:

🄲 The game you're going to play will give you a chance to practice throwing and catching while jumping. The object is to have the ball touch the floor on the opposite side of the net. Here are the rules:

1. There are three players on a team.
2. There is one team on each side of the rope (or net).

3. A player must be off the floor when the ball is thrown or caught.
4. At least two players on your team must touch the ball before it is thrown back over the rope (net).
5. Points are scored when the ball lands out of bounds, the ball hits the floor inbounds, or a player throws or catches the ball while that player's feet are touching the ground.

This game can also be played cooperatively: Both teams work together to see how many times the ball can cross the rope or net without breaking any of the rules. A point is scored each time the ball crosses the net. A good score to aim for is 10 throws in a row over the net without breaking a rule.

Jumping to an Accented Beat

Setting: Children scattered throughout general space, each with a hoop

Cue	
Buoyant Landings	(Bend your knees; then spring up quickly to travel.)

Tasks/Challenges:

T When I beat the drum, jump into and out of your hoop each time you hear the drumbeat.

T Now take off on two feet, and land on two feet. As the drumbeat gets faster, be ready to jump by having your knees bent and your arms flexed. Try to land on only the balls of your feet, which means your heels won't touch the ground.

T Take off on one foot, and land on the same foot.

T Try to keep up with the beat—it's going to get faster and faster. When one leg gets tired, change to the other leg.

T Listen as I beat the drum. The first beat is louder than the others. This is called an accented beat. Use one- or two-foot takeoffs and landings, but jump on only the accented beat. The first beat will be accented; the next three beats will be unaccented.

Proficiency Level (GLSP): Learning Experiences Leading to Skill Development

At the proficiency level, dynamic dance, game, and gymnastics experiences are designed to help youngsters use, refine, and enjoy their jumping abilities. At this level children almost always jump in relation to objects or other people (or both) and use jumping for both expressive and functional purposes. Jumping is now infused into the skill themes of games. It is an integral part of gymnastics routines, both with and without apparatus. It is a major component of all styles of dance and a key element in choreography.

A note about cues at the proficiency level: *At the proficiency level, tasks are more complex, typically requiring children to coordinate several movements simultaneously in a dynamic context. A list of cues is provided to assist the children in being more successful in the learning experience. The challenge for the teacher is in determining which cue will be most beneficial for each child—and when. Thus, careful observation and critical reflection become very important as you watch the children move and then decide which cue will be the most helpful to move each learner to a higher skill level.*

Jumping with a Partner to Mirror Actions

Setting: Children with partners and sufficient space for safe movement

Cues	
Heads Up	(Keep your head and shoulders up for good balance.)
Yielding Landings	(Bend your knees to absorb the force, and sink into a balanced position.)
Buoyant Landings	(Bend your knees as you land; then spring up quickly.)

Tasks/Challenges:

T You and your partner are going to mirror each other's jumps. Mirroring means you face each other and copy the other's movements, as if you were looking in a mirror. Therefore, if your partner uses the left arm, you'll use your right arm. To start, decide which of you will be the first leader. The leader makes up the first jump and shows it to the partner. Then you both face each other and do that jump at the same time, mirroring each other exactly. This task will be hard at first because you'll have to take off at the same time, jump the same height, and do everything exactly together. Start with some easy jumps and then go to harder ones. Each person takes three turns as leader and then switches. Again, make your jumps look like a reflection of your partner's. **Don't forget: Yielding and buoyant landings will be part of the mirror action.**

Pinpoint several pairs who are mirroring jumps accurately.

T As you get better at mirroring your partner, you may want to include such actions as gesturing in the air, turning in the air, making shapes in the air, or rolling after landing. **This will really take a lot of work; you will need to communicate.**

Jumping with a Partner to Match Actions

Setting: Children with partners and sufficient space for safe movement

Cues	
Travel, Jumps, and Landings	(Everything must match your partner—travel, jumps, and landings.)
Heads Up	(Keep your head and shoulders up for good balance.)

Tasks/Challenges:

T Now that you've become very good at mirroring a partner's actions and jumps, you're going to try matching jumps side by side. Matching means you do the same thing at the same time; thus, if you use your right leg, then your partner must also use the right leg. Again, decide which of you will be the first leader. The leader demonstrates; the two of you then match jumps. Take three turns as leader, and then switch. Start with easy jumps. **Counting will help you match starting each jump.**

C Once you've become quite good at matching jumps with your partner, try this: Travel a short distance together, and then, at a set point, do matching jumps in the air. This task will be hard. You must pick a starting point, count exactly how many steps you'll travel before you jump, and then jump and land. First, by yourself, practice the traveling by itself and then the jump by itself; then, combine the traveling and jumping. Finally, try to do the task with your partner. The sequence is this: Travel, jump, land, freeze—all movements exactly matching those of your partner. You two should look like twins.

T To the sequence you just made up, add a second traveling action and a second jump.

Jumping with a Springboard

Setting: Springboards positioned throughout the work space with sufficient large mats for safe landings

Cues	
Push	(Push hard with your feet and legs as you contact the board.)
Swing Upward	(Swing your arms upward for good height.)
Squash	(Bend your knees and spread your feet for a stable, soft landing.)

Tasks/Challenges:

T Using the nearest springboard, run and jump, using a two-foot landing/takeoff on the board; spring up high and land on two feet on the mat.

T As you become good at going off the springboard and landing without falling over, add a half turn in the air as you jump so you end up facing the place where you started. **Remember, bend your knees and spread your feet apart when you land.**

T When you're able to do this task, try a complete 360-degree turn in the air before you land. To get all the way around, you'll have to throw your arms up and around in the direction you want to turn.

Jumping as Part of a Dance Creation

Setting: Children divided into small groups, no more than four per group

Cues	
Individual cues as needed	

Tasks/Challenges:

C Now you're going to use jumps to make up a dance. The main actions of the dance will all use different jumps. First, think of a theme for your dance, such as a battle scene. If you use that idea, your jumps will contain such gestures as punching, slashing, jabbing, protecting, and retreating.

As a group, think of what you want your dance to say. Once you've decided the theme, try to put together a series of jumps that express that idea. You'll be using your jumps and other movements to tell a story. It may be that you all move at the same time, or that two of you move and then the other two move. Your dance needs to have a definite beginning and a definite ending, with at least six different jumps in the middle. Try to make the dance look really professional. This will take a while to do; I'll be available to help each group as you work. Toward the end of class, we'll show the dances to the rest of the class.

Jumping, Dancing, and Imagery

Setting: Children divided into small groups, no more than four per group

Cues	
Individual cues as needed	

Tasks/Challenges:

T Jumps can be used to create a dance about the things around you (the flight of a bird, leaves in the wind, etc.). This time, you're going to create a dance that uses one of these things as its main idea. Jumps will communicate that idea to your audience. You must decide in your group what natural thing you would like to communicate in a dance using jumps.

After you've decided, begin to develop your dance, keeping the following ideas in mind:

- The actions you're demonstrating should clearly portray your theme.
- The starting location of each person should be clear.
- The dance should rise to a climax and then wind down to a conclusion.

- The jumps and gestures you're using to communicate your ideas should be the most effective ones you can create.
- The pathways used in the dance should be clear.

At the end of class, you may show your dance to the class.

Jumping Hurdles

Setting: A series of hurdles set up throughout the work area, with sufficient space between for children to run between, jumping over each; stopwatches at starting line (optional)

Cues

Foot to Foot	(Opposite: one foot to the other foot.)
Extend	(Front leg upward and forward.)
Heads Up	(Keep your head and shoulders up for good balance.)

Tasks/Challenges:

T In this activity, you'll be *hurdling*, which is sprinting over barriers, called hurdles, placed along the way. Begin behind the first hurdle, and run to the end of the line of hurdles. Each time you come to a hurdle, jump it and keep going. Run to the end of the line, come back to the first hurdle, and start again. Start your jump *before* you reach the hurdle by extending your front leg upward and forward. Try to get over the hurdles by barely clearing them rather than jumping really high over them. You need a horizontal rather than a high vertical jump for hurdles.

Use low barriers at first so youngsters can focus on proper technique without worrying about clearing the obstacles. Once children begin to exhibit quality hurdling actions, you can gradually increase the height of the barriers to meet the individual jumping ability Milk crates spread apart with bamboo poles or ropes supported between them are satisfactory barriers.

C As you feel you're getting better at hurdling, time yourself and see if you can improve. You can use one of the stopwatches available at the starting line of each row of hurdles.

Reading Comprehension Questions

1. Name the two basic reasons for performing jumps.
2. What are the three phases of a jump?
3. List in order of difficulty the different takeoff and landing patterns for jumping.
4. What does a precontrol jump look like?
5. How does jumping and landing differ at each of the generic levels of skill proficiency?
6. What is the focus of the jumping and landing learning experiences for the control and proficiency levels?
7. Describe a low obstacle children can safely practice jumping over.
8. What is the difference between a buoyant landing and a yielding landing?
9. Describe a sequence for teaching young children to jump rope.
10. Describe how jumping is used in (1) gymnastics, (2) games/sports, and (3) dance. Give a specific example of jumping in each of these content areas.

References/Suggested Readings

Holt/Hale, S., and T. Hall. 2016. *Lesson planning for elementary physical education: Meeting the National Standards & Grade-Level Outcomes.* Champaign, IL: Human Kinetics,

[SHAPE America] Society of Health and Physical Educators. 2018. *PE metrics: Assessing student performance using the national standards and grade-level outcomes for K-12 physical education.* 3rd ed. Champaign, IL: Human Kinetics.

[SHAPE America] Society of Health and Physical Educators. 2014. *National standards & grade-level outcomes for K-12 physical education.* Champaign, IL: Human Kinetics.

Wickstrom, R. L. 1983. *Fundamental motor patterns.* 3rd ed. Philadelphia: Lea & Febiger.

Balancing

Drawn by children at Monfort, Chappelow or Shawsheen Elementary Schools, Greeley, CO.
Courtesy of Lizzy Ginger; Tia Ziegler.

Merriam Webster's Collegiate Dictionary defines *balance* as "stability produced by even distribution of weight on each side of the vertical axis" and as "an aesthetically pleasing integration of elements." There's no extraneous motion, no flagrant waving of arms to maintain position, no near topple or wobble from side to side. The center of gravity is clearly over the base of support.

The elementary school child attempting to do a headstand, walk a beam, ride a skateboard, or use in-line skates encounters different types of static and dynamic balance challenges. Among the key teaching concepts in providing balance experiences are the following:

- It's easier to balance over a wide base of support than a narrow base.
- The center of gravity should be aligned over the base of support for stationary balance (Figure 21.1).
- Extensions to one side of the body beyond the base of support necessitate extensions in the opposite direction for counterbalance.

Static balance involves maintaining a desired shape in a stationary position; gymnastics balances, headstands, and handstands are examples. Dynamic balance involves maintaining an on-balance position while moving, starting, or stopping. Dynamic balance occurs in weight transference, jumping, throwing, catching, and all forms of travel. Balance as a concept is discussed in Chapters 17, 20, 22, and 24 as it applies to learning specific skills. See Box 21-1 for linkages of the skill theme of balancing to the *National Standards & Grade-Level Outcomes for K–12 Physical Education* (SHAPE America 2014).

Box 21-1

Balancing in the *National Standards & Grade-Level Outcomes for K–12 Physical Education*

The skill of balancing is referenced in the *National Standards& Grade-Level Outcomes for K–12 Physical Education* (SHAPE America 2014) under Standard 1: "Demonstrates competency in a variety of motor skills and movement patterns." The intent of the standard is developing the fundamental skills needed to enjoy participation in physical activities, with the mastery of movement fundamentals as the foundation for continued skill acquisition.

Sample grade-level outcomes from the *National Standards** include:

- Maintains momentary stillness on different bases of support (K)
- Maintains stillness on different bases of support with different body shapes (2)
- Balances on different bases of support, combining levels and shapes (3)
- Balances in an inverted position with stillness and supportive base (3)
- Balances on different bases of support, demonstrating muscular tension and extensions of free body parts (3)
- Balances on different bases of support on apparatus, demonstrating levels and shapes (4)
- Combines balance and transferring weight in a gymnastics sequence or dance with a partner (5)

*Suggested grade-level outcomes for student learning.

Figure 21.1 Center of gravity over base of support.

Young children sporadically achieve balance; it's often more coincidental than intentional. The very young child attempting to stand upright, the toddler taking those first steps, the youngsters in our classes challenging themselves as they attempt new balance experiences—all are attempting to master stability, i.e., balance. The balance is momentary as the child calls out, "Watch me" and immediately loses balance. The momentary balance is the incentive for continued practice, both for the beginner and the advanced; the momentary mastery provides both the reward and the challenge.

The skill theme of balance must be taught in a safe environment. (See Chapter 30 for the establishment of procedures for working on gymnastics skills, working with and alongside others, as well as on apparatus.) With the establishment of procedures for activity, the selection of developmentally appropriate tasks, and the use of intratask variation, the skill theme of balance provides challenging experiences for all children.

We tend to think of balance as a gymnastics skill, and although it is extremely important in gymnastics, balance is also an important skill for everyday activities as well as dance, games, and sports. Carrying a lunch tray loaded with food through a crowded school cafeteria, maintaining a firm hold on the family dog while walking on an icy street, and walking down a flight of stairs with a heavy backpack are all tasks that require balance. The seemingly effortless execution of a punt, the heading of the soccer ball, the dodging of a tag in baseball, the twists and turns of skateboarding, and the aerials of snowboarding all require a solid foundation of balance and its continued application into sports. Balance does not reach completion with maintaining a headstand for three seconds. The study of balance continues into middle school and high school physical education. The progression spiral for the skill theme of balance at the precontrol, control, utilization, and proficiency levels of skill development is found on this page.

Precontrol Level (GLSP): Experiences for Exploration

Tasks at the precontrol level are designed to provide exploration of the concept of balance. As children explore the concept of balance, they begin to maintain simple stationary balances and to stop in balanced positions while traveling. The beginning balance tasks work well on a grassy surface or floor. If available, small individual mats are beneficial.

Balancing on Different Bases of Support

Setting: Children scattered throughout general space (small mats are optional)

Tasks/Challenges:

(T) Your base of support is the body parts holding you in the balance. Show me a balance with one foot as your base of support and try to hold very still. Now, explore balances on different bases of support on your mat. See how many body parts can be bases of support. Hold each balance as you count to yourself 3 seconds: "one thousand one, one thousand two. . . ."

(T) Try different combinations of body parts as you create your balances.

(T) Let's list all the body parts you've used as bases of support for your balances. *(List on board or flip chart as students give responses.)* Do you see some body parts listed as bases of support that you didn't try? Take a few minutes to try all the combinations.

(!) Some children will watch others in class, often the more skilled students, and attempt to copy their balances. This can result in injury to the less skilled. Individual feedback and a reminder to the class of what the teacher is looking for alleviate this potential problem.

(T) Now I'll name the body parts I want to be the bases of support. First, two hands and two feet. Be creative in your balance. Although you're all using the same base of support, the gymnastics balances may be very different.

Additional exploration: two feet and one hand, two hands and one foot, knees and elbows, stomach, and base of spine. Encourage creativity by asking for second and third balances with the same base of support. Children love the cognitive engagement.

(!) Sometimes children attempt to balance on body parts that aren't appropriate for supporting weight. Don't let youngsters balance in unsafe positions that could result in stress or injury. You may choose to leave out the head in a balance until direct and specific instruction is provided.

(C) Balance on your favorite bases of support, holding the balance very still. Let's pretend I am going to take a photo of the balance—no wiggles, no wobbles.

(?) *Exit Slip.* Young children enjoy labeling on a large stick figure the body parts that can serve as bases of support. *Refer to Chapter 12, "Assessing Student Learning," for the use of exit slips in physical education.*

Balancing on a Wide Base of Support

Setting: Children scattered throughout general space (small mats are optional)

Tasks/Challenges:

(T) Create a four-part balance on your hands and lower legs; have your hands under your shoulders and your legs approximately the same distance apart as the width of your hips. This wide base of support creates a very stable balance.

(T) Move your hands toward each other and your legs toward each other until they touch. Do you feel stable now? Could I push you over?

(T) Explore the concept of wide to narrow balances with different bases of support: hands and feet, knees and elbows.

Balancing in Different Body Shapes

Setting: Children scattered throughout general space (small mats are optional)

Tasks/Challenges:

(T) Create a gymnastics balance on a wide base of support. Create a wide body shape by extending free body parts outward from your trunk (free body parts are those you're not using as bases of support).

(T) Create a narrow-shape gymnastics balance on your base of spine—extend free body parts long and thin like a piece of spaghetti.

(T) Create a curled-shape gymnastics balance on your chosen base of support. Free body parts can be tucked close to the body, or they may be added to the curled shape by bending them in the curve.

(T) Create a twisted-shape gymnastics balance. Use your two feet as your base of support and twist your body like a pretzel.

Traveling and Stopping in Balanced Positions

Setting: Children scattered throughout general space

Tasks/Challenges:

(T) Travel through general space any way you choose. On the signal, stop and create a gymnastics balance with two feet and two hands touching the floor.

Additional exploration: two feet and one hand, base of spine, two knees and one hand.

(T) Travel again, but this time balance on three body parts when you hear the signal. Think which three parts you're going to use before traveling. Ready? Go.

Additional exploration: four body parts, five body parts, two body parts.

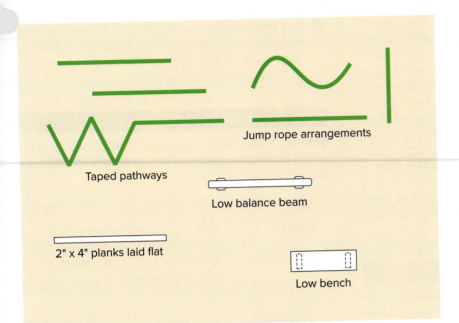

Taped pathways

Jump rope arrangements

Low balance beam

2" x 4" planks laid flat

Low bench

Figure 21.2 Equipment arrangement for traveling.*

* Prior to constructing homemade equipment we recommend you be certain that teacher-made equipment is permitted in your school and/or school district.

Traveling on Low Gymnastics Equipment

Setting: Low balance beams; 2-by-4-inch planks; low, narrow benches, mats as needed for safety; tape pathways arranged on the floor (Figure 21.2)

Tasks/Challenges:

T Travel on the different pieces of equipment without losing your balance and falling off.

Additional exploration: travel backward; travel with your arms above your head; walk with a beanbag on your head.

Balancing on Boards

Setting: Square, rectangle, and circular balance boards arranged as a station for the study of balance (Figure 21.3)

Tasks/Challenges:

T Balance on a balance board without falling off or letting the edges of the board touch the ground. You may want a partner to stand in front of the balance board to help when you first step up; place your hands on the partner's shoulders for support.

T Explore standing with your feet shoulder-width apart and with your feet close together. Which gives you better balance on the board?

Control Level (GLSP): Learning Experiences Leading to Skill Development

Learning experiences at the control level focus on maintaining the stillness and control of a balance.

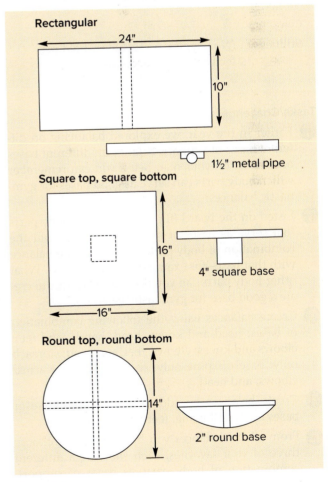

Rectangular

24"

10"

1½" metal pipe

Square top, square bottom

16"

16"

4" square base

Round top, round bottom

14"

2" round base

Figure 21.3 Construction of balance boards of various shapes.*

* Prior to constructing homemade equipment we recommend you be certain that teacher-made equipment is permitted in your school and/ or school district.

Children balance on increasingly smaller bases of support while holding the body in inverted positions and in stationary balances on apparatus. These experiences begin to provide the ingredients for a movement repertoire of balances that may be included in sequences involving traveling and other balances. Several tasks explored at the precontrol level will be repeated at the control level, with the focus on refinement cues.

A note about cues: *Although several cues are listed for many of the learning experiences, it's important to focus on only one cue at a time. This way, the children can really concentrate on that cue. Once you provide feedback to the children and observe that most have learned a cue, it's time to focus on another one.*

Balancing on Different Bases of Support

Setting: Small mats scattered throughout general space with sufficient room between them for children to work without bumping others

Cue

Stillness   (No wiggles, no wobbles—hold perfectly still for 3 seconds.)

Tasks/Challenges:

T Earlier in the year, we explored balancing on different bases of support. Balance on different bases of support on your mat. See if you can remember which body parts can serve as good bases for gymnastic balances.

T Listed on the board (flip chart) are the body parts that serve as bases of support. I will call out the combination of body parts; you create the balance with that base—for example, feet and hands. What other body parts can you use with your feet to create a good base for gymnastic balances?

T Create balances using the following combination of bases: head and knees; head, hands, and feet; elbows and knees; elbows, feet, and head; stomach only; base of spine only; shoulders, upper arms/elbows, and head.

T Create balances by adding your chosen base or bases to the following: feet and elbows.

C From all the balances you have practiced, choose three of your favorites, each showing a different combination of body parts as bases of support. Practice until you can hold each balance for 3 seconds without moving or losing your balance. When you are ready, show your balances to a partner, who will give you a thumbs-up if you hold the balance stationary for 3 seconds.

? *The above challenge easily becomes an assessment by including measurable criteria. Specifics for development of criteria and rubrics can be found in Chapter 12, "Assessing Student Learning."*

Tightening the Gymnastics Muscles

Setting: Small mats scattered throughout general space, with sufficient room between them for children to work safely

Cues

Stillness   (No wiggles, no wobbles—hold perfectly still for 3 seconds.)

Tight Muscles (Muscular tension is the key to holding the balance.)

Tasks/Challenges:

T Balance on your favorite base of support, holding the balance very still. Tighten the muscles of the body parts supporting your balance to maintain stillness.

T Balance on a different base of support. Tighten the muscles of the free body parts to hold a stretched or curled shape very still.

T Assume your favorite balance position. See if you can tighten the muscles without changing the appearance of your balance. You should look the same but feel the tightening inside.

C Continue to practice your balances with a focus on tightening the muscles without changing the appearance of the balance. As I walk by you, I should feel the tightness in the extended arm or leg if I touch you.

This tightening of the muscles is a key factor in holding the balance very still without extraneous movement and in maintaining the position.

Counterbalance

Setting: Small mats scattered throughout general space, with sufficient room between them for children to work safely

Cues

Stillness   (No wiggles, no wobbles for 3 seconds.)

Tight Muscles (Muscular tension is the key to holding the balance.)

Extensions   (Extend free body parts for stability in your balance.)

Tasks/Challenges:

T Balance on one foot. Extend your arms and free leg, holding the balance very stationary. Repeat the balance, extending the arms but not the leg. Which balance is easier to maintain? Right, the one with arms and free leg extended in opposite directions. This is the concept of counterbalance. Extensions to one side of the body necessitate extensions in the opposite direction.

T Balance on your base of spine. Extend free body parts to one side only; repeat with the extension in the opposite direction.

T Explore balances on different bases of support, extending your body parts in different directions from your body for counterbalance. In conjunction with these tasks, you may want to add the following: Balancing with Bends, Stretches, Twists, and Curls (page 344).

Balancing Symmetrically and Nonsymmetrically

Setting: Small mats scattered throughout general space, with sufficient room between them for children to work safely

Cues	
Tight Muscles	(Muscular tension is the key to holding the balance.)
Extensions	(Extend free body parts for stability in your balance.)
Smooth Transitions	(Move slowly from one balance to the next for a smooth transition.)

Tasks/Challenges:

T Balance on your base of spine, with arms and legs extended outward. Create exactly the same shape on both sides of your body. This is called a symmetrical shape; both sides of the body look the same.

T Keeping the same base of support, change your free body parts, still creating a symmetrical shape.

T Balance on your chosen base of support. Create a symmetrical shape. Now change to a nonsymmetrical shape—the sides look different—while balanced on that same base.

T Balance on your shoulders, back of head, and arms. Create a symmetrical shape with your legs. Change to a nonsymmetrical shape and then back to a symmetrical one.

T Repeat this three-part symmetrical, nonsymmetrical, symmetrical sequence; slowly change your legs

into the different shapes. This smoothness in transition is an important component of gymnastics.

? *Peer Observation*

Students are asked to work on balancing on different bases of support (e.g., two hands and one foot, hands and knees, headstand). Students should balance in four different positions, two using symmetrical shapes, and two using asymmetrical (nonsymmetrical) shapes. Students are asked to draw their favorite symmetrical and asymmetrical balances on paper, labeling S and A, respectively. Students now select a partner who will observe their balances and then indicate on the paper: (1) if the drawn figures were labeled correctly and (2) if the balances were held still for 3 seconds.

Criteria for Assessment

a. Completes four balances—two symmetrical and two asymmetrical (nonsymmetrical)
b. Correctly labels balances S and A.
c. Maintains stillness in balance for 3 seconds.
d. Observer correctly assesses the appropriateness of the labels and the extent to which the performer was still.

NASPE (1995, p. 19)

Balancing in Different Body Shapes

Setting: Small mats scattered throughout general space, with sufficient room between them for children to work safely

Cues	
Tight Muscles	(Muscular tension is the key to holding the balance.)
Extensions	(Extend free body parts for stability in your balance.)
Smooth Transitions	(Move slowly from one balance to the next for a smooth transition.)

Tasks/Challenges:

T Remember when we explored basic body shapes for physical education? Who can name the four shapes? Wide, curled, twisted, narrow—that's right. Let's create balances that show each of those shapes. Now that you have learned to balance on different bases of support, try to have a different base of support for each of your balances.

T Let's focus on wide-shape balances. Create wide-shape balances with different bases of support. Remember, extensions of arms and legs away from the body create wide shapes.

C I'm going to put on some background music for a few minutes. Create three balances that show wide

©Barbara Adamcik

©Barbara Adamcik

These youngsters maintain stillness in symmetrical and nonsymmetrical balances.

shapes; each balance is to have a different base of support. Challenge yourself with a level of difficulty that tests your skills. When the music stops, we will look at the balances.

T Now let's create gymnastics balances that show narrow shapes. Remember, we create narrow-shape balances by holding body parts close to each other. How many different narrow balances can you create?

T Create a narrow balance on your base of spine. **Stretch your legs and arms to counterbalance.**

T Create two new narrow balances, one at a low level, the other at medium level.

T You can create a curled (round) shape by curling your spine forward or arching your spine backward. Free body parts may be tucked close to the body, or they may be added to the curled image by bending in the curve. Create a curled gymnastics balance on your chosen base of support.

T Create a curled-shape gymnastics balance in which the spine curls forward; slowly change into a curled-shape balance with your spine arched backward.

T Stand in a balanced position, with both feet as bases of support for your weight. Create a twisted shape by turning your body to the right or the left without moving your feet. Now balance, using your left foot and the lower portion of your right leg as bases of support. Create a twisted shape from this base.

T Create twisted shapes by rotating your trunk, arms, legs, neck, ankles, and wrists while balanced on different bases of support.

T Balance on three body parts. Create a twisted shape by rotating free body parts—for example, arms, legs, trunk, neck. Create two more twisted-shape balances on various bases of support.

C Think of all the balances you have created today. They represent four shapes: wide, narrow, curled, and twisted. Review the balances you did; choose your favorite balance for each shape. On each signal, show me your favorite wide-, narrow-, curled-, and twisted-shape balance. **Concentrate on holding each perfectly still and moving smoothly from balance to balance.**

? *Peer Observation.* Peer observation of body shapes and balances would be appropriate here. A possible task would be to have students, using stick figures, draw each of the four balances, one representing each of the four shapes. Have them label the body shape of each figure, then exchange papers with a neighbor, who will be the "gymnastics judge" (Figure 21.4).

Figure 21.4 Student balance drawings and peer assessment results.

Refer to Chapter 12, "Assessing Student Learning," for the use of peer observation as assessment.

C Working in groups of four, create a balance statue in which each person partially supports another. Each person should represent one of the four basic shapes: wide, narrow, curled, and twisted. After you make the body-shape statue, convert it to a movable monster by moving as a unit in either self-space or general space.

Balances and Shapes: The Gymnastics Dance

Setting: Children scattered throughout general space, in groups of four to six students

Cues	
Tight Muscles	(Muscular tension is the key to holding the balance.)
Extensions	(Extend free body parts for stability in your balance.)
Smooth Transitions	(Move slowly from one balance to the next for a smooth transition.)

Tasks/Challenges:

T Let's create a gymnastics dance that focuses on body shapes and balance. Select one person in your group to form a statue by holding a gymnastics balance with a wide base of support. You will need to hold your wide balance as others come and go.

T Each person in the group will add to the statue by making a wide, narrow, curled, or twisted shape. When I touch you, move slowly toward the "statue," connect by touching the statue with one body part, and then make a wide, narrow, curled, or twisted shape. (Move among the children, touching individuals to move to the central statue; continue until everyone in the group has added to the statue by touching the first person and making a shape.) That looks really good; the shapes are clear, and the balances are stationary.

T On signal (drumbeat, tambourine), begin to move slowly from the original wide-shape balance that was the first one created without disturbing others in the group. Use a locomotor movement or a turning action to move from the group.

T As I touch you, move slowly back into the large balance statue, with clear shapes and stillness in your balance. On signal, move away again, forming an individual statue by yourself with a different base of support and different shape from the one you used before. (Remember a touch to move toward the main statue, a signal to move away.)

Performing Inverted Balances

Setting: Small mats scattered throughout general space, with sufficient room between them for children to work safely

Cues	
Tight Muscles	(Tighten your abdominal muscles to hold the inverted balance—stretch toward the sky!)
Equal Weight	(Take weight equally on all body parts that are bases of support.)

Tasks/Challenges:

T An inverted balance is when your head is lower than most of your body. Balance with your head and two feet as your base of support.

⚠ When performing an inverted balance involving the head, it's important to distribute the body weight equally among all body parts serving as the base of support.

T When performing these inverted balances, concentrate on taking your weight equally on the following bases:

- Head and knees
- Head, hands, and two feet
- Head, hands, and one foot
- Elbows, feet, and head
- Back of head, shoulders, and arms

T Balance on your head and hands, with your knees resting on your elbows (Figure 21.5). The secret to remember here is to make a triangle with your head and two hands. Keep the triangle in place; moving your hands will take you off-balance. *Use a*

Figure 21.5 Inverted balance on head and hands.

Figure 21.6 Other inverted balances.

student to demonstrate while you share the "secret" (see Figure 21.5).

T Explore other inverted balances that you can safely hold for 3 seconds (Figure 21.6).

Alignment of Body Parts

Setting: Small mats scattered throughout general space, with sufficient room between them for children to work safely

Cues	
Tight Muscles	(Tighten your abdominal muscles to hold the inverted balance—stretch toward the sky!)
Alignment	(Toes over knees, over hips, over shoulders to form a straight line.)

Tasks/Challenges:

T Repeat your balance on head and hands with knees resting on elbows. **Concentrate on tightening your abdominal muscles to align your hips over your shoulders.**

T Balance on your head and hands, with your trunk and legs extended toward the ceiling. Form a triangular base with your weight equally distributed on your head and hands. Stretch your body like a straight line, aligning hips over shoulders, feet over

hips. Pretend your toes are attached by a string to the ceiling. Stretch and keep those muscles tight.

⚠ Teach children to roll safely out of an off-balance head-and-hands position by pushing with the hands, tucking the chin, and curling the back.

Spotting

The question of spotting—physically assisting a child with a skill—often arises with gymnastics. Spotting is seldom used in educational gymnastics because it often encourages or forces children to attempt a skill before they are ready. See Chapter 30 for a more complete discussion on the use of spotting.

Doing Kickups

Setting: Large gymnastics mats and/or small mats that will not slip, scattered throughout general space, with sufficient room between them for children to work safely

Cues	
Tight Muscles	(Tighten your abdominal muscles to hold the inverted balance—stretch toward the sky!)
Alignment	(Toes over knees, over hips, over shoulders to form a straight line.)

Tasks/Challenges:

T Place one foot in front of the other (front-back stance); lean forward, and place your hands on the floor shoulder-width apart, fingers pointing forward. Using your back leg as a lever, kick your leg upward so your weight is supported on your hands only. Each time try to kick a little higher.

C Practice counting seconds as you balance on your hands.

With practice, the success rate for balancing on hands is very high, but practice must be massed and distributed.

⚠ Teach the children to come safely out of an off-balance weight-on-hands position by twisting the trunk slightly to bring the feet down in a new place.

Traveling and Stopping in Balanced Positions

Setting: Children scattered throughout general space

Cues	
Stillness	(Hold your balance perfectly still—no wiggles, no wobbles.)
Tight Muscles	(Muscular tension is the key to holding the balance.)
Extensions	(Extend free body parts for stability in your balance.)

Tasks/Challenges:

T We worked earlier on traveling through general space and creating a gymnastics balance when we stopped. Let's review those skills: Travel through general space any way you choose. On the signal, stop and create a gymnastics balance with two hands and one foot touching the floor.

T This time, change your way of traveling. If you ran before, skip or gallop through general space. On the signal, stop and create a balance with *four body parts* as bases of support. Think of the four parts you will choose before traveling.

T Repeat the travel, stop, balance sequence with different combinations of body parts as bases of support and different ways to travel.

C Remember the balance you created with four bases of support? Think of the balance you created with two bases. Now you are going to make a sequence of two travels and two stationary balances. Your sequence will be this: Travel, stop, and balance on four bases; travel, stop, and balance on two bases of support. I'll give the signal for travel each time. You will decide the ways you are going to travel;

use the balances you just practiced. We will practice several times so you can repeat the travel, balance sequence exactly the same way each time.

C After you have completed your two-part sequence and feel good about your travel and balances, create a larger sequence by adding other ways to travel and additional balances—for example, three bases, five bases. How about going from five bases of support to one base, with travel between the balances? Remember, there are ways to travel other than on your feet

? *The above challenge easily becomes an assessment by including measurable criteria. Specifics for development of criteria and rubrics can be found in Chapter 12, "Assessing Student Learning."*

Stationary Balances on Equipment

Setting: Various pieces of gymnastics apparatus arranged throughout general space: low tables, boxes firmly stuffed with newspaper, benches, climbing frames, low balance beams. *(See Figures 21.7 and 21.8 for plans for constructing balance beams and balance benches.)*

Cues	
Stillness	(Hold your balance perfectly still—no wiggles, no wobbles.)
Tight Muscles	(Muscular tension is the key to holding the balance.)
Extensions	(Extend free body parts for stability in your balance.)

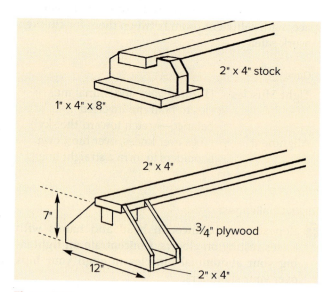

Figure 21.7 Construction of a balance beam.*

* Prior to constructing homemade equipment we recommend you be certain that teacher-made equipment is permitted in your school and/or school district.

Maintaining stillness while balancing on different body parts is important before balancing on equipment.

⚠ Extended edges and bases/supports of gymnastics apparatus sometimes need extra padding to assure safety and prevention of injury.

Tasks/Challenges:

🅣 Earlier in the year, we explored traveling safely on gymnastics equipment. Select the piece of apparatus you want to begin working on; spend a few

minutes exploring the apparatus until you are comfortable on this new surface and height. Travel forward and backward on the apparatus. Try some of the balances you did on the floor/mat surface on the apparatus.

🅣 Perform your balances at different places on the apparatus: on the top, near one end, in the middle, on a low rung, underneath. Try some balances

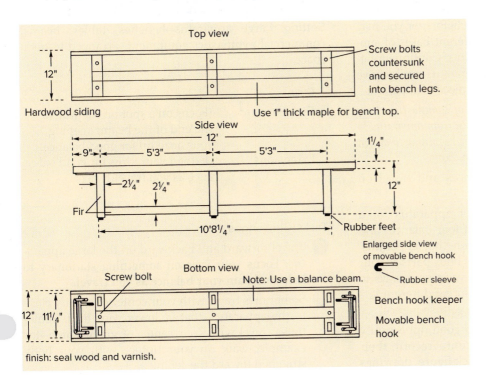

Figure 21.8 Construction of a balance bench.*

*Prior to constructing homemade equipment we recommend you be certain that teacher-made equipment is permitted in your school and/or school district.

©Lars A. Niki

Figure 21.9 Noninverted hands-only balances on apparatus.

with a combination of bases on the floor and on the apparatus.

🅣 Balance on your hands only on the low bench, low beam, or crate. The chart on the wall (Figure 21.9) will provide examples of balances that do not require you to be inverted when you balance hands-only on the equipment.

🅣 Create a balance on the apparatus; then move slowly to another part of the apparatus for your second balance. Can you create a combination of travel and three different balances?

🅣 After you create three balances on the first piece of apparatus, move to another piece of gymnastics apparatus and create balances on that one. You may be able to repeat balances from before, or you may need to create balances on different bases of support to suit the different apparatus. Continue rotating to the various pieces of apparatus until you've created three balances on each piece of apparatus.

When children first begin this type of gymnastics, they may not be able to move independently from apparatus to apparatus. We have found it best in the beginning to assign the children to groups and rotate the stations.

🅣 Create combinations of balances and travel on each of the pieces of apparatus.

🅣 Choose your favorite piece of apparatus for a sequence. Create a sequence of four balances and four different ways to travel on that apparatus. Select different combinations of body parts as your bases of support, and be creative in your ways to travel on the apparatus. Don't forget different levels and directions as you create your sequence.

❓ *Portfolio.* Sequences provide a good opportunity for portfolio use. Have students record their sequences on paper using stick-figure drawings and writing; place the sequences in their portfolios. Make sure you let students know you will return to this work later in the year, possibly when you work on approaches and dismounts from apparatus.

⚠ Permit the children to attempt balances on apparatus only after they can safely hold the balances for 3 to 5 seconds on the floor or mats.

In conjunction with these tasks, you may want to add the following: Balancing on Apparatus with Body Actions (page 350).

Traveling on Large Apparatus

Setting: Large apparatus—benches, tables, beams, commercial gymnastics equipment—arranged in open space

Cues	
Eyes Forward	(Focus on a spot on the wall or the end of the beam, keeping your head up for good balance.)
Extensions	(Extend your arms for good balance as you travel.)

Tasks/Challenges:

🅣 Travel forward and backward on the large apparatus. **Focus your eyes on something stationary to help maintain your balance as you travel.**

🅣 Sometimes travel with your center of gravity close to the apparatus—that is, lower your hips. Sometimes travel with your center of gravity high—for example, walk on your tiptoes with your body stretched toward the ceiling.

T Walk forward the length of the beam or bench; make a half turn, and walk forward again. The secret to the turn is to take your weight on the balls of your feet and then pivot and quickly drop your heels so they make contact with the beam.

T Practice turning both clockwise and counterclockwise while traveling forward and backward.

T Walk to the center of the apparatus and lower your hips into a squat position. Execute your turn in this low-level position.

T If you are comfortable rolling on the mats, try rolling slowly forward across the apparatus. **Pretend you are executing the skill in slow motion; tighten your abdominal muscles for control.**

⚠ Students should perform rolling on apparatus only after demonstrating mastery of the rolls on the floor or mats.

C Perform the tasks on each piece of apparatus.

T Add changes in directions and levels to your locomotors on the apparatus.

Traveling While Balanced

Setting: Large apparatus—benches, tables, beams, commercial gymnastics equipment—arranged in open space

Cues	
Eyes Forward	(Remember to focus your eyes on something stationary when you travel.)
Extensions	(Extend your arms for good balance when doing your locomotors.)

Tasks/Challenges:

T Travel on the apparatus using a series of gallops, hops, or skipping steps. You'll probably want very little height when you perform these skills on the apparatus.

T Travel across the apparatus on four body parts.

Balancing Sequence

Setting: Large apparatus—benches, tables, beams, commercial gymnastics equipment—arranged in open space

Cues	
Eyes Forward	(Remember to focus your eyes on something stationary when you travel.)
Smooth Transitions	(Move smoothly between balances and travels.)

Note: Individuals, sometimes classes, may need reminders of earlier cues—for example, Stillness, Extensions, Tight Muscles.

Tasks/Challenges:

T Remember those balances you created on apparatus earlier in the year? You recorded them on paper and placed them in your portfolios. We are now going to revisit that lesson to create a sequence of

Traveling on equipment while balanced requires concentration.

©Barbara Adamcik

traveling and balancing on your favorite piece of apparatus. Your task will be to design a sequence of traveling and balancing on one piece of equipment. You will choose either sequence A or sequence B.

Sequence A: Create a sequence of traveling combined with balancing on different bases of support. Your sequence must contain three balances with different bases and at least two travels.

Sequence B: Create a sequence of traveling combined with balancing in the basic body shapes. Your sequence must contain the four basic shapes—wide, narrow, curled, twisted—and at least three travels.

Practice your sequence on the floor and then on the apparatus. When you have the sequence memorized, let a friend watch it to see if:

- The bases of support are clear.
- The balances are stationary.
- The travels are smooth.

T You have refined your sequence nicely, with a friend giving pointers. Now we need to add the beginning shape and the ending of the sequence. Begin your sequence on the apparatus positioned in what you wish to be your starting shape. The beginning shape you choose will be determined by your first action: travel or balance. Think of the level you need, and the direction, as well as the shape.

T Now that you have a beginning shape, let's focus on the ending of your sequence. Earlier in the year, we studied jumping and landing—jumping for height and landing safely. We will review those skills, and then you can select the type of jump/land action with which you want to end your sequence. *Review jumping off apparatus (Chapter 20) with the children, emphasizing safe landings and body shapes in the air.*

C On the assignment table, you will find the forms for sequence A or B. The paper is divided into four parts: beginning shape, travel and balances, dismount, and ending shape. Using stick figures to represent your balances, write or draw your sequence, remembering the number of balances needed for the sequence. When you can repeat the sequence without referring to your paper, ask a friend to watch it.

? *Peer Observation.* Your friend will be your "refinement coach," giving you pointers to make your sequence even better. The "coach" will observe your sequence for the following cues: stillness (3 seconds for each balance with no wiggles, no wobbles); tight muscles (muscular tension that holds body parts perfectly still); extensions

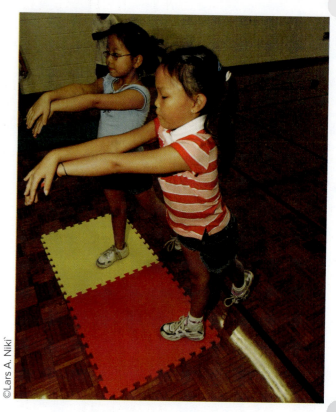

©Lars A. Niki

At the control level, youngsters are challenged to create matching nonsymmetrical balances.

(pointed toes, stretched arms and legs). After the friend watches your "dress rehearsal," come to me for your final assessment.

? *Event Task.* The above task can easily become an event task assessment of children's work. *Specifics for development of event tasks can be found in Chapter 12, "Assessing Student Learning."*

Balancing on Stilts

Setting: Several stations in general space at which children can experience/practice dynamic balance; tin can stilts (see Figure 21.10 for instructions for making them) at some of the stations; wooden stilts (see Figure 21.11) at others; markers placed around the general space

Cue	
Heads Up	(Eyes focused forward, shoulders erect.)

Children first experiencing this type of dynamic balance can develop confidence on tin can stilts before progressing to regular stilts.

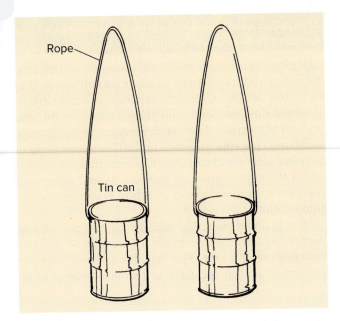

Figure 21.10 Construction of tin can stilts from discarded rope and large cans from the school cafeteria. To create, (1) cut two holes in the top sides of the cans and (2) string rope through the holes and tie it together inside each can. To use the stilts, children put each foot on a can and pull on the rope with their hands.*

* Prior to constructing homemade equipment we recommend you be certain that teacher-made equipment is permitted in your school and/ or school district.

🅣 Walk forward on the tin can stilts. You'll have to take smaller steps than you would when walking normally.

🅣 Walk backward.

🅣 Walk around the markers.

🅣 After you've mastered walking on the tin can stilts, you're ready for the higher wooden stilts. It's easier to mount the stilts from an elevated position, such as from a step or chair.

🅣 Walk forward, backward, and sideways.

🅣 Walk around the markers.

🅣 Shift your weight to one stilt; lift your other leg, and swing it around.

Balance Boards

Setting: Balance boards set up as one of several stations at which children can experience static and dynamic balance

Cues	
Heads Up	(Eyes focused forward, shoulders erect.)
Extensions	(Extend arms to the sides for good balance.)

Tasks/Challenges:

🅣 Remember when we did balances on boards earlier in the year? You practiced balancing on the different boards and learned that a wide base of support—feet shoulder-width apart—created a more stable balance on the boards, as in all balances. Practice your balance skills on the boards. Try to maintain your balance, without partner support, for several seconds.

*Prior to constructing homemade equipment we recommend you be certain that teacher-made equipment is permitted in your school and/or school district.

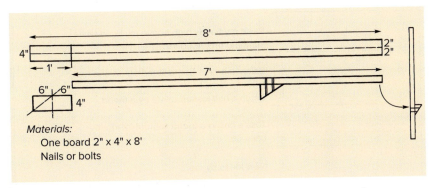

Materials:
One board 2" x 4" x 8'
Nails or bolts

Figure 21.11 Construction of wooden stilts. (Each board makes one set of stilts.)*
Directions:
1. Cut 12 inches from one end of the board.
2. Cut the 12-inch board in half.
3. Cut the 6-inch board diagonally in half for the steps.
4. Cut the remaining 7-foot board lengthwise to make two 2-inch by 7-foot poles.
5. Nail or bolt the steps to the poles.

(T) When you can stand on the board for 5 seconds without the support of your partner and without losing your balance, you're ready to try the tasks written on the chart:

1. Slowly move your arms above your head. What happens to your center of gravity? (Right—it moves upward.)
2. Slowly move from a standing to a squat or low-curl position. Which is more stable? Why is the low position more stable? (When working on large apparatus, remember that we're better balanced when the center of gravity is low.)
3. Catch a ball thrown by your partner; toss the ball to your partner.

(?) *Write additional tasks on flip charts or task cards near the balance board. Balance board activities can also be recorded on a task sheet (see Figure 21.12).*

Utilization Level (GLSP): Learning Experiences Leading to Skill Development

Learning experiences at the utilization level combine balancing and transferring weight for a contrast in stillness and action. Children experience balancing in dynamic environments and transferring weight into and out of balances. Gymnastics sequences that involve skills and concepts, transfers and stillness, are particularly important and valuable. Children make decisions about the combination of movements and select and invent ways for one balance or action to move smoothly into another.

A note about cues: *Although several cues are listed for many of the learning experiences, it's important to focus on only one cue at a time. This way, the children can really concentrate on that cue. Once you provide feedback to the*

Figure 21.12 Task sheet for balance board activities. Younger children enjoy drawing the smile face for completed tasks; older children can record the date of successful completion.

Name___*Melissa*___

Homeroom ___*4b*___

Balance Board Task Sheet

Draw a smile face beside those activities you can successfully complete.

I am able to:

___(☺)___ Balance on the board standing on two feet

___(☺)___ Sit in a balance position on the board

_____ Change from a standing to a sitting position on the board without losing balance

_____ Raise my hands high above my head while standing on the board

_____ Balance on the board standing on one foot

_____ Catch a ball tossed to me by a friend

_____ Toss a ball to a friend without losing my balance

New ideas by me:

_____ *clap my hands 3 times*

_____

_____

children and observe that most have learned a cue, it's time to focus on another one.

Balancing on Crates

Setting: Milk crates and boxes (stuffed with newspaper or packing materials and taped closed so they will support a child's weight) positioned throughout general space, with sufficient mats surrounding them and room between for children to work safely

Cues	
Tight Muscles	(Muscular tension is the key to holding the balance.)
Extensions	(Extend free body parts for balance/counterbalance.)
Alignment	(Position yourself over your base of support or extend free body parts for counterbalance.)

Tasks/Challenges:

T In our previous work on balance, you explored balancing on different bases of support and in different shapes. You practiced holding balances stationary while performing them on mats, on low equipment, and on large apparatus. Review your balances on different bases of support on the crate or box. Many of the balances that were easy for you to perform on the mat or the low equipment will be more difficult on the crate or box because of the added height and the size of the surface.

T Create a series of balances without ever leaving the surface of the crate or box. Transferring from one balance to the next will now be a major part of the sequence.

T Create a sequence of balances on your crate or box that includes an approach to the crate, a transfer onto the crate, a series of balances on the crate, and a dismount from the crate. You may choose to focus on either bases of support or different shapes.

Select tasks from Chapter 22, "Transferring Weight and Rolling," for a review of approaches to and dismounts from low equipment.

T Select a partner to work with for a sequence on the crates. Explore matching symmetrical and nonsymmetrical balances on the crates or boxes. You may choose to work side by side to match shapes, or face to face to mirror shapes.

C Design a partner sequence of symmetrical and nonsymmetrical balances on the crates or boxes. Your sequence must contain the following:

- Three symmetrical and two nonsymmetrical balances
- A minimum of three different bases of support
- An approach to the crates or boxes and a dismount followed by ending shape

Your sequence should represent a double image. Not only will your balances match those of your partner but also the transitions between them will be the same action and the same speed.

? *Digital Recording* The children's sequences provide an excellent means of assessing their gymnastics skills. A possible idea is to have partners digitally record their completed sequence. Both partners can then evaluate the sequence using the criteria discussed in class. After the initial evaluation, children may make changes in the sequence. *Refer to Chapter 12, "Assessing Student Learning," for examples of digital recording analysis and assessment.*

Moving out of and into Balances by Stretching, Curling, and Twisting

Setting: Sufficient mats for children to work safely without bumping others as they practice

Cues	
Smooth Transitions	(Move smoothly through the transition from balance to balance.)

Tasks/Challenges:

T Balance on a very narrow base of support. Stretch your free body parts in one direction away from the base. At the moment of moving off balance, transfer your weight to a new base of support.

T Balance on one foot. Stretch forward until you are off balance; transfer your weight to your hands and feet in a new balance.

T Balance on favorite bases of support. Extend free body parts with a stretching action to move into a new balance.

T Balance on your head and hands with knees on elbows as in a three-point stand or tripod. Push with your hands, tuck your head, and curl your back to roll out of the balance. Make a new stationary balance after the rolling action.

T Explore curling your spine to roll out of different balances until you find three balances in which you can use the curling action to get out of and into a new balance.

Extensions provide aesthetic appeal as well as good balances.

©Lars A. Niki

Ⓣ Balance on the base of your spine only, as in a V-seat. After you have held the balance very still, twist your trunk until the action moves you off balance and into a new balance with a different base of support.

Ⓣ Balance on two hands and one foot, with the free leg extended. Twist your trunk and the free leg until you transfer to a new balance on hands and feet.

Ⓒ Practice balances with different bases of support and moving out of the balance by stretching, curling, or twisting. When you are comfortable with one of each, put them together in a sequence as follows: balance, stretching action into new balance, curling action into new balance, twisting action into new balance. Your sequence will include four stationary balances and three transitions. Practice until you have quality balances and smooth transitions.

❓ *The above challenge easily becomes an assessment by including measurable criteria. You may wish to digitally record the sequences to evaluate and/or show to the students. Specifics for development of criteria and rubrics can be found in Chapter 12, "Assessing Student Learning."*

Additional balances with stretching, curling, and twisting actions can be found in Chapter 22, "Transferring Weight and Rolling."

Traveling into and out of Balances by Rolling

Setting: Sufficient mats for children to balance and roll without bumping into others as they practice

Cues

Stillness and Action	(Remember to hold your balance perfectly still for 3 seconds; then move smoothly through the rolling action.)
Rounded Body	(Keep your back round and your chin tucked for a good roll.)
Narrow and Tight	(Arms extended over your head, tight abdominal muscles, and lead with hips.)

Tasks/Challenges:

Ⓣ Balance on two hands and two feet in a narrow body shape; hold for 3 seconds, and then roll sideways using a log roll. **Remember to extend arms over your head and lead with your hips.**

Ⓣ Rock backward into a shoulder stand; hold the balance for 3 seconds, and then roll using either a forward or backward shoulder roll.

Traveling into and out of balances with rolling should be attempted only after children have mastered forward rolls and shoulder rolls.

Ⓣ Balance in a headstand for 3 seconds; then, press with your hands, and roll forward.

Ⓣ Balance with your weight on your hands, slowly lower yourself to the mat, and roll forward. **Remember to tuck your chin and curl your back.**

Ⓣ Transfer your weight from your feet to your hands; pause in the handstand; then make a quarter turn, and transfer your weight back to your feet.

Ⓒ Connect two balances using a rolling action as a transition. You will need to think about what balances can be easily connected with a roll and what rolling action is best for the transition. You are creating a balance, roll, balance sequence.

Ⓒ Challenge yourself by creating two more sequences.

❓ *The above challenge easily becomes an assessment by including measurable criteria. Specifics for development of criteria and rubrics can be found in Chapter 12, "Assessing Student Learning."*

Performing Inverted Balances on Equipment

Setting: Boxes or crates, benches, and/or low tables arranged for balancing, with sufficient mats around them for children to work safely

Cues	
Tight Muscles	(Remember to tighten the abdominal muscles plus free body parts for stillness in your balances.)
Alignment	(Position yourself over your base of support or extend free body parts for counterbalance.)

Tasks/Challenges:

T Balancing in an inverted position on a piece of apparatus is quite different from balancing on the mats or the floor. The position of your hands is often quite different, and the surface is much smaller. Perform the balances until you are quite comfortable and skilled with them on the low equipment before you attempt them on the higher, more narrow apparatus (Figure 21.13).

T Balance on your shoulders, back of your head, and arms. Stretch your legs upward.

T Balance on your head, two hands, and one foot.

T Balance on your head and hands in a tripod position.

T Balance on your head and hands with your legs extended toward the ceiling.

T Balance on your hands only in an inverted balance.

T While balanced on your hands only, turn slightly, and bring your feet down to the floor beside the beam, bench, or crate. This is the safety skill you will need when you become overbalanced.

T Perform your inverted balance on the larger pieces of apparatus—vaulting box, balance beam, climbing frames.

⚠ Inverted balances on apparatus should be attempted only after children show mastery of the balances on the floor or mats. Always have a mat area available for children to use to practice before performing their balances on apparatus.

⚠ Position yourself at the station where children are doing inverted balances; be sure you maintain a visual scan of the entire class.

Performing Sequences That Combine Stationary Balances and Traveling on Mats

Setting: A floor gymnastics area designed using available mats

Cues	
Stillness in Balances	(Tighten the muscles to hold the balance very still.)
Smooth Transitions	(Make transitions between balances very smooth, whether they're fast or slow.)
Extensions	(Extend free body parts for aesthetic appeal as well as good balance.)
Alignment	(Position yourself over your base of support or extend free body parts for counterbalance.)

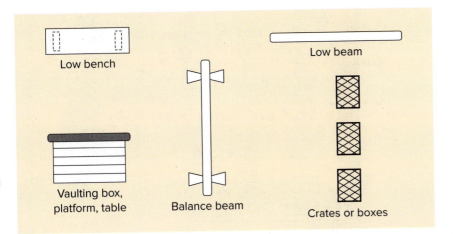

Figure 21.13 Low equipment for inverted balances.

Tasks/Challenges:

T Create a sequence that combines stationary balances and travel. As with an Olympic-style gymnastics routine, design your sequence to cover the length of the mat, as well as each corner. Your sequence must include the following:

- A minimum of six balances, each with a different base of support
- A minimum of three travels, with a change in direction and level
- At least two inverted balances
- A beginning and an ending shape

T Add contrasts in time of actions—some fast, some slow—and changes in force—some powerful movements, some delicate—to add interest to your sequence.

C Tomorrow we're going to practice the routines to music. If you like, bring a recording of music from home, or you may select from those we have. You will then practice your routine with the music until you can repeat it three times exactly the same way. (*See Figure 21.14 for an example of a routine.*)

? Gymnastics routines are excellent projects for assessment of children's gymnastic skills and their understanding of the critical cues. *Refer to Chapter 12, "Assessing Student Learning," for guidelines for developing criteria and rubrics.*

Proficiency Level (GLSP): Learning Experiences Leading to Skill Development

At the proficiency level, balance is studied on the floor and on various pieces of apparatus in combination with movement concepts to express contrast in power, stillness, and excitement in sequences. Children are encouraged to perfect the flow of their movements from one position to another and to develop their use of focus and full extensions.

A note about cues: At the proficiency level, tasks are more complex, typically requiring children to coordinate several movements simultaneously in a dynamic context. A list of cues is provided to assist the children in being more successful in the learning experience. The challenge for the teacher is in determining which cue will be most beneficial for each child—and when. Thus, careful observation and critical reflection become very important as you watch the children move and then decide which cue will be the most helpful to move each learner to a higher skill level.

Figure 21.14 Child's sequence to music, showing use of rolling; weight transfer; balance; and concepts of narrow, wide, curled, and directions.

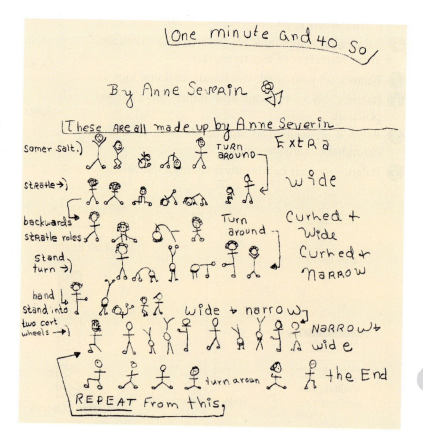

Balancing While Supporting the Weight of a Partner

Setting: Sufficient mats for children to work safely without bumping others

Cues	
Wide Base	(A wide base of support provides greater stability.)
Extensions	(Extensions beyond the line of gravity require extensions in the opposite direction for counterbalance.)

Tasks/Challenges:

🅣 Working with your partner, create a balance that shows one wide and one narrow shape. You and your partner must be helping each other by partially supporting each other's weight.

🅣 Create different balances with your partner in which you are partially supporting each other's weight. If you and your partner are not the same weight, which of you will be the supporting partner?

Partners of similar size enjoy experimenting with each being the base for the balances and/or equally supporting each other. If partners are not the same weight, assist the children in understanding the important role of the base partner.

🅣 Create a balance in which the base partner is supporting the weight of the top partner, who is in an inverted position.

⚠️ *Base partner:* Your bases of support—for example, your arms and legs—should be no farther apart than the width of your hips and shoulders. *Top partner:* Make sure you put your weight over your partner's arms and hips, never in the middle of the back, which is unsupported.

🅒 Create two new balances supporting your partner's weight (Figure 21.15). You will need to make decisions based on the weight of both partners: Will you partially support each other, or will one of you totally support the other? Draw your two balances on a sheet of paper, and post them at the partner balance center.

Balancing on Hanging Ropes

Setting: Hanging ropes with sufficient mats below for children to work safely

Figure 21.15 Student-created balances supporting a partner.

<table>
<tr><td colspan="2">

Cue

Tight Muscles   (Tighten your muscles to support body weight and maintain balance on ropes.)
</td></tr>
</table>

Tasks/Challenges:

T On a hanging rope, support your weight with both hands, then your hands and legs, and finally one hand. Create each of the basic shapes—wide, narrow, curled, twisted—with your free body parts (Figure 21.16). Perform your balances on the hanging ropes with your head upward.

T Create a series of symmetrical and nonsymmetrical shapes while supporting your weight on the rope.

⚠ Permit inverted balances on the hanging ropes at low height and only for children with sufficient upper-arm/shoulder strength.

Transferring Off Equipment with Weight on Hands

Setting: Gymnastics apparatus positioned throughout general space, with sufficient mats for children to work safely

Cues

Alignment	(Feet over hips, over shoulders, over hands for a straight-line weight on hands.)
Tight Muscles	(Muscular tension is the key to holding the balance.)

Tasks/Challenges:

T Balance momentarily on your hands on the apparatus, make a quarter turn, and then transfer your weight from your hands to your feet on the mat. **Remember the cues for safety as you land.**

T Practice this skill on the floor and on the low apparatus to be sure you can turn to the right or to the left.

⚠ Be sure students have mastered this skill on the floor or mats and on low apparatus before they attempt it on higher, narrower apparatus.

Performing Apparatus Sequences That Combine Stationary Balances and Traveling with Movement Concepts

Setting: Gymnastics apparatus positioned throughout general space, with sufficient mats and spacing for children to work safely

Cues

Individual cues as needed

Tasks/Challenges:

C Select a piece of equipment that will be your choice for your final gymnastics project. Your assignment will be to design a sequence combining stationary balances and travel in relation to that piece of apparatus. The sequence must include the following:

1. An approach to the apparatus and a mount onto the apparatus
2. A series of stationary balances and travels on the apparatus

Figure 21.16 Head-up balances on hanging ropes.

timed it with your music, show it to a friend and then to me. We will digitally record the sequence for inclusion in your portfolio.

C Select a grouping of three to four pieces of gymnastics apparatus for your final project. Design a sequence that combines stationary balances and travel in relation to each piece of apparatus, as well as travel between the pieces of apparatus. The sequence must include the following:

1. An approach to the first pieces of apparatus and a mount onto the apparatus
2. A series of stationary balances and travels on the apparatus
3. A dismount from the apparatus
4. Travel to the next piece of apparatus
5. A series of balances and travels on that apparatus
6. A repeat of Steps 4 and 5 until you have visited each of the three (or four) pieces of apparatus in the grouping
7. A dismount and ending shape

Remember, excitement and interest are added to your sequence with changes and contrasts in movement concepts. (See listing above.) Also, grouping the apparatus and traveling between them frees the inner spirit for creativity, as dance and gymnastics are combined for your final project.

? *Portfolio. It is good to provide portfolio opportunities as an option for students. As an example, you might tell students the following: Practice your sequence as if you were preparing for a gymnastics competition or a recital. When you have completed and timed it with your music, show it to a friend and then to me. If you wish, we will then digitally record the sequence for inclusion in your portfolio as your self-expression in gymnastics. Refer to Chapter 12, "Assessing Student Learning," for the use of portfolios for assessment in physical education.*

Balances can be performed alone, with a partner, or in a group.

3. A dismount and ending shape from the apparatus

You can add excitement and interest to your sequence with:

- Contrasts in fast and slow actions
- Turning, twisting, curling actions
- Changes in levels and directions
- Combinations of slow, controlled movements and quick, sharp movements
- Inverted balances and actions

Practice your sequence as if you were preparing for the Olympics. When you have completed and

Reading Comprehension Questions

1. In your own words, define *balancing*. Be sure to include the meanings of *base of support* and *center of gravity*.
2. Draw or diagram (stick figures are best) the three key teaching concepts that are emphasized in providing balance experiences.
3. What is the difference between a static balance and a dynamic balance?
4. What are the characteristics of balancing for each of the skill levels? For example, what does a precontrol-level balance look like?
5. List three concepts or skills typically used as subthemes with balance.
6. Why are muscular tension, counterbalance, and alignment of body parts important in teaching gymnastics for children?

©Barbara Adamcik

7. List five different pieces of equipment that children can use to practice balancing. Include a task you might use with each piece of equipment.

8. Educational gymnastics does not require Olympic-style apparatus. List or diagram four pieces of non-Olympic gymnastics equipment that can be used for balancing. List three tasks for your balance study on the equipment.

9. What does *inverted balance* mean?

10. Why are jumping and landing studied in conjunction with balances on apparatus?

11. How is transfer of weight typically combined with balancing to present challenging tasks to children at the utilization and proficiency levels?

References/Suggested Readings

Holt/Hale, S., and T. Hall. 2016. *Lesson planning for elementary physical education: Meeting the national standards and grade-level outcomes.* Champaign, IL: Human Kinetics.

[NASPE] National Association for Sport and Physical Education. 1995. *Moving into the future: National standards for physical education.* St. Louis, MO: Mosby.

[SHAPE America] Society of Health and Physical Educators. 2014. *National standards & grade-level outcomes for K-12 physical education.* Champaign, IL: Human Kinetics.

Transferring Weight and Rolling

Courtesy Children at Monfort Elementary School, Greeley, CO.

Transferring Weight

To travel—walking, running, leaping, rolling, stepping, springing, sliding—is to transfer weight on hands, on feet, on different body parts. The infant creeping on trunk and elbows is transferring weight, as is the toddler shifting weight from side to side during the beginning phase of walking unassisted, the gymnast performing a walkover, the Russian dancer executing a series of rapid mule kicks, the athlete poised to shift her weight to fake an opponent, and the dancer collapsing to the floor in an expression of grace and control. Locomotion is transfer of weight.

The most common form of transferring weight is from foot to foot. In its simplest form, this is walking. At an advanced level—and when combined with the stretching, curling, and twisting actions of layouts and with full-body twists—it demands extraordinary kinesthetic awareness, muscular strength, and control. While we have chosen to develop transferring weight and rolling separately in this chapter, rolling is simply one form of transferring weight, and often the two ideas are developed simultaneously. See Box 22-1 for linkages of the skill theme of transferring weight to the *National Standards & Grade-Level Outcomes for K–12 Physical Education* (SHAPE America 2014).

Young children come to us with control of their bodies in the basic forms of locomotion, i.e., transferring weight. They are fascinated with exploring transferring weight in different ways, e.g., on their hands, on their backs, stretched, curled, and twisted. This fascination with the skill of transferring weight leads to a world of exciting challenges as children defy gravity and gain control of their bodies. Our task as teachers is to capture this fascination with the skill and lead the children to higher levels of skill development, expanding the child's realm of possibilities while maintaining safety. The progression in our teaching of gymnastics is from mats on the floor to low apparatus with a large surface to higher apparatus with a narrow surface.

The skill theme of transferring weight must be taught in a safe environment. (See Chapter 30 for the establishment of procedures for working on gymnastics skills, working with and alongside others, as well as working on apparatus.) With the establishment of procedures for activity, the selection of developmentally appropriate tasks, and the use of inter- and intratask variation, the skill theme of transferring weight provides exciting, challenging learning experiences for all children.

While transferring weight is inherent in all forms of locomotion and therefore a component of all skill themes, we have chosen to focus this chapter on transferring weight as it applies to gymnastics. Children are

---

Box 22-1

The Skill of Transferring Weight and Rolling in the *National Standards & Grade-Level Outcomes for K–12 Physical Education*

Transferring weight and rolling are referenced in the *National Standards & Grade-Level Outcomes for K–12 Physical Education* (SHAPE America 2014) under Standard 1: "Demonstrates competency in a variety of motor skills and movement patterns." The intent of the standard is developing the fundamental skills needed to enjoy participation in physical activities, with the mastery of movement fundamentals as the foundation for continued skill acquisition.

Sample grade-level outcomes from the *National Standards** include:

- Rolls sideways in a narrow body shape (K)
- Transfers weight from one body part to another in self-space in dance and gymnastics environments (1)
- Rolls with either a narrow or curled body shape (1)
- Transfers weight from feet to different body parts/bases of support for balance and/or travel (2)
- Rolls in different directions with either a narrow or curled body shape (2)
- Transfers weight from feet to hands for momentary weight support (3)
- Transfers weight from feet to hands, varying speed and using large extensions (4)
- Transfers weight in gymnastics and dance environments (5)

*Suggested grade-level outcomes for student learning.

---

fascinated with the challenge of transferring weight, balancing on the head, and walking on hands with twists and turns. Gymnasts expand those skills with round-offs; aerials; vaulting; transfers while on large apparatus; and dismounts with twisting, curling, and stretching actions while in flight. Olympic gymnasts build upon the transference skills with increased time in flight and more complex combinations of twisting, curling, and twisting actions on mats and apparatus. At this level, transferring weight, balance, and dance come together to create routines in hopes of the "Perfect 10."

Our progression spiral on page 403 presents the full spectrum of transferring weight, from the precontrol level to the proficiency level of skill development. Bending, stretching, curling, and twisting actions (Chapter 19) should be taught as a prerequisite to transferring weight tasks.

Skill Theme Development Progression

Transferring Weight

Proficiency Level

Club gymnastics
Olympic-style transfers

Utilization Level

Combining weight transfer and balances into sequences on
    mats and apparatus
Combining skills on mats
Transferring weight on bars
Transferring weight to hands on low apparatus
Transferring weight along apparatus
Transferring weight over apparatus (vaulting box)
Transferring weight onto bars (parallel bars, climbing frame)
Transferring weight to head and hands on apparatus (box,
    beam, table)
Transferring weight onto large apparatus
Transferring weight to hands and forming a bridge
Transferring weight to hands and twisting
Transferring weight to hands: walking

Control Level

Transferring weight to hands by stepping: cartwheels
Maintaining transfer from feet to hands
Transferring onto low apparatus
Traveling over low apparatus
Making spring/step takeoffs with sequences
Transferring off low apparatus (benches, crates,
    or low tables)
Performing spring/step takeoffs onto crates and/or benches
Performing spring/step takeoffs
Transfers with stretching, curling, and twisting
Transferring weight from feet to back with a rocking action
Transferring weight from feet to hands to feet

Precontrol Level

Transferring weight onto and off equipment
Transferring weight to hands momentarily
Transferring weight with a rocking action
Locomotor actions

Precontrol Level (GLSP): Experiences for Exploration

Tasks at the precontrol level are designed for the exploration of transferring weight to different body parts and in relation to gymnastics equipment. Through this exploration, children will begin to develop an awareness of the body parts best suited for transferring weight and control of their bodies as they transfer weight in different ways.

Locomotor Actions

Setting: Children scattered throughout general space

Tasks/Challenges:

- Ⓣ All locomotor movements are actions of transferring weight. When you walk, hop, skip, or gallop, you transfer your weight from foot to foot. Let's review some of the locomotor movements. Travel throughout general space with a skip or gallop.

- Ⓣ Travel with a jump—two feet to two feet.

- Ⓣ Hop on one foot. Do you transfer weight to different body parts when you hop? No, you move on one foot only.

Additional exploration:

- Ⓣ Travel and jump high in the air like a basketball player.

- Ⓣ Travel and jump over a brook; a large, flat rock; a puddle. This jump is sometimes called a leap—taking off on one foot and landing on the other.

- Ⓣ Explore other ways to travel throughout general space, transferring weight from foot to foot; twirl, spin, slide....

- Ⓣ Explore traveling on body parts other than your feet: slither, crawl, walk like a crab....

- ❓ When you skip, you transfer weight from what body part to what body part? When you jump, you transfer from what to what? What is the difference between a jump and a hop?

Transferring Weight with a Rocking Action

Setting: Individual mats throughout general space, with sufficient room between them for children to work safely

Tasks/Challenges:

- Ⓣ Squat on your feet with your back rounded like an egg. Transfer your weight from your feet to your back with a rocking action.

- Ⓣ Transfer your weight from your feet to your rounded back and return to your feet with the rocking action.

- Ⓣ Give the rocking action a little extra effort, transferring your weight from feet to rounded back, to feet, and then returning to a standing position.

Transferring Weight to Hands Momentarily

Setting: Large gymnastics mats and/or small mats that will not slide as children transfer weight, scattered throughout general space

Tasks/Challenges:

T Transfer your weight from your feet to your hands to your feet, momentarily taking your weight on your hands only.

Wedge mats or folded or rolled mats may be easier for children just beginning to take weight on their hands and/or for those uncomfortable with transfer from standing position to mat on floor.

Transferring Weight onto and off Equipment

Setting: Low gymnastics equipment—benches, tables, balance beams, and so on—scattered throughout general space

⚠ Carefully examine all equipment to be used for gymnastics in elementary school physical education. Extended edges of gymnastics equipment and bases/supports of apparatus sometimes need extra padding to assure safety and prevention of injury for children.

Tasks/Challenges:

The focus for exploration of equipment at the precontrol level is safety—getting on and off equipment with personal safety and without creating an unsafe situation for others.

Control Level (GLSP): Learning Experiences Leading to Skill Development

Tasks at the control level are designed to help children transfer their weight to specific body parts—feet to back, to hands, to head and hands—as they balance, as they travel, and in relation to gymnastics apparatus. Control of their bodies, i.e., safety throughout the weight transfer, is the goal at the control level.

A note about cues: *Although several cues are listed for many of the learning experiences, it's important to focus on only one cue at a time. This way, the children can really concentrate on that cue. Once you provide feedback to the children and observe that most have learned a cue, it's time to focus on another one.*

Transferring Weight from Feet to Hands to Feet

Setting: Lines marked or taped on the floor; children scattered throughout general space

Cues

Strong Muscles	(Strong arms and shoulders—no collapse.)
Stretch Your Legs	(Extend your legs upward—stretch to the sky.)

Tasks/Challenges:

T When we were exploring transferring weight, you practiced taking your weight on your hands and bringing your feet to the floor at the same place. Practice taking your weight on your hands and bringing your feet down safely (Figure 22.1) at a new place—to the right or the left of their original place.

T Now you are going to transfer your weight from your feet to your hands to travel across your line. Stand on one side of your line, transfer your weight to your hands, and bring your feet down on the other side. You will travel across the line by transferring your weight from feet to hands to feet.

You may want to begin in a squat position with your feet on the floor and your hands on the other side of the line, or relatively close to your feet. Transfer your weight to your hands and bring your feet down a short distance away—just over the line.

C When you are comfortable taking your weight on your hands for a longer time and you are landing safely, kick your legs higher in the air to remain on your hands even longer.

T Stand at the side of your line, in a front-back stance. Extend your arms upward. Step forward with your lead foot, and transfer your weight to your hands. Bring your feet to the floor on the opposite side of your line. If you stretch your trunk and legs as you transfer your weight to one hand and then the other, you will begin to do a cartwheel (Figure 22.1).

Transferring Weight from Feet to Back with a Rocking Action

Setting: Large or small mats that will not slide, scattered throughout general space

Cues

Rounded Back	(Curl your back and body for all rocking skills.)

Tasks/Challenges:

T Transfer your weight from your feet to your back with a rocking action. Always return to your feet (Figure 22.1).

Figure 22.1 Transfer of weight from feet to other body parts.

Transfers with Stretching, Curling, and Twisting

Setting: Large or small mats that will not slide scattered throughout general space

Cues	
Smooth Transitions	(Move smoothly through the transition from balance to off balance to balance.)
Tight Muscles	(Tighten your abdominal muscles as you transfer weight for control of the action.

Tasks/Challenges:

T Balance on one foot. Bend at the waist, extending your arms forward and your free leg backward. Stretch your arms forward until you are off balance; then transfer your weight to your hands and one foot for a new balance.

T Balance on your knees and one hand. Extend your free arm under your body, twisting your trunk until your weight transfers to your shoulder and new bases of support. Twist gently into the new balance.

T Balance in a shoulder stand with your weight on your shoulders, upper arms, and head, stretching your legs toward the ceiling. Twist your legs and trunk, bringing your feet to the mat behind you in a new balance.

T Balance on your chosen base of support. Twist until you are momentarily off balance; transfer your weight onto a new base of support.

T Balance on your chosen base again. Use different stretching, curling, and twisting actions to transfer onto new bases of support.

Performing Spring/Step Takeoffs

Before practicing spring and step takeoffs in weight transfer, children should be at the control level of jumping and landing (Chapter 20).

Setting: Large gymnastics mats throughout general space

Cues

Heads Up	(Keep your head and shoulders erect for a balanced landing.)
Soft Landings	(Bend your knees on landing to absorb the force.)

Tasks/Challenges:

Ⓣ Approach your gymnastics mat from a distance of 10 to 12 feet. Just before you reach the mat, use a two-foot takeoff to spring high in the air; land softly in the center of the mat. The spring takeoff in gymnastics is very similar to the approach on the diving board.

The spring takeoff is used for gymnastics skills requiring power—for example, mounts onto beams and parallel bars, handsprings, and vaulting. It is a jump for height; that is why the arms are extended upward. It is also the takeoff used for a basketball jump ball or rebound.

Ⓣ Approach the mat, spring off your two feet, make a quarter turn, and land in a balanced position. Now try the turn in the opposite direction.

Ⓣ When you are comfortable with the quarter turn, try a half turn. Remember, practice both clockwise and counterclockwise turns.

Ⓣ Approach the mat from the distance of 10 to 12 feet. Using a step takeoff, land on your two feet in the center of the mat.

The step takeoff is the takeoff used for gymnastics skills requiring slow control. Who can give some examples of those? Right, walkovers and cartwheels. It is also the takeoff needed for a layup in basketball.

Performing Spring/Step Takeoffs onto Crates and/or Benches

Setting: Milk crates positioned against large gymnastics mats

⚠ Place the crates against mats to prevent them from sliding.

⚠ If there is any danger of crates sliding during the activity, have partners work together with one holding the crate steady as the other practices transfers onto the crate.

Cues

Heads Up	(Keep your head and shoulders erect for a balanced landing.)
Easy On	(Slowly absorb weight on crate—with control.)

Tasks/Challenges:

Ⓣ Approach the crate or bench from a distance of 10 to 15 feet. Using either a spring or a step takeoff, land in a balanced position on the crate.

Ⓒ Practice each takeoff until you can transfer your weight onto the crate or bench in a balanced position three times.

Ⓣ Approach the crate or bench, use a spring takeoff, and transfer your weight to your feet and hands on the crate or bench.

Ⓣ Approach the crate or bench, use a step takeoff, and transfer your weight momentarily to your hands only on the crate or bench. Remember, strong arms for weight on hands.

Transferring off Low Apparatus (Benches, Crates, or Low Tables)

Setting: Benches, crates, and/or low tables surrounded by mats and positioned throughout general space

⚠ Place the crates against mats to prevent them from sliding.

⚠ If there is any danger of crates sliding during the activity, have partners work together with one holding the crate steady as the other practices transfers off the crate.

Cues

Soft Landings	(Bend your knees on landing to absorb the force.)

Tasks/Challenges:

Ⓣ Transfer your weight off the equipment with a jump. Make a wide body shape by extending your arms and legs while in the air. Land in a balanced position on two feet on the mat. **Keep your head and shoulders up as you jump.**

Ⓣ Transfer off with a jump, making curled, narrow, and twisted shapes while in the air, and then each time land in your balanced position. Remember, the body returns to ready position for a balanced landing.

Ⓣ Transfer off with a jump, turning in the air so you land facing in a different direction. Remember, twist your shoulders in the direction you wish to turn.

T When you are comfortable with a quarter turn, try to execute a half turn in the air so you land facing in a different direction.

Revisit/review "Jumping to Form a Body Shape During Flight" in Chapter 20 (page 365) for additional tasks. Although specific tasks for transferring weight with large apparatus aren't listed until the utilization level, children at the precontrol and control levels need exploration time on large apparatus to become familiar with the equipment and to gain confidence moving on it.

Making Spring/Step Takeoffs with Sequences

Setting: Benches, crates, and/or low tables surrounded by mats

Cues	
Soft Landings	(Absorb the force; land softly on and off the equipment.)
Smooth Transitions	(Move with control from balance, to transfer, to balance....)
Rounded Back	(Remember, a curled body with chin tucked for all rolls.)

Children should be able to tell you the critical elements for the skills and demonstrate the individual skills before combining skills in sequences.

Tasks/Challenges:

T Approach the bench (crate, table) and use either a step or a spring takeoff to transfer onto it.

Decide what body parts are going to serve as your first bases of support before you begin; this will determine whether you use a step or a spring takeoff.

T Create a series of four balances by transferring your weight to different body parts on the bench (crate, table).

Review "Balancing on Different Bases of Support" (page 377–378), "Balancing in Different Body Shapes" (page 378), and "Balancing Symmetrically and Nonsymmetrically" (page 381) in Chapter 21.

T Transfer off the bench (crate, table) in one of the following ways: (1) jumping and turning, (2) jumping and making a shape while in the air, or (3) using a transfer that you have created.

C Combine the above into a gymnastics sequence that includes: (1) a beginning shape; (2) an approach to and on the gymnastics equipment (mount); (3) a series of four balances; (4) transfer off the equipment (dismount); and finally, (5) an ending shape.

⚠ Have the student tell you if the transfer off the low apparatus includes inversion or weight on hands; if so, be sure the student demonstrates mastery on the floor or mats before attempting a transfer off the low apparatus.

Traveling over Low Apparatus

Setting: Milk crates, benches, low tables, hurdles, and milk-jug/rolled-newspaper or dowel-rod "hurdles" throughout general space (Figure 22.2)

Figure 22.2 Equipment setups for transfer of weight when traveling over low apparatus.

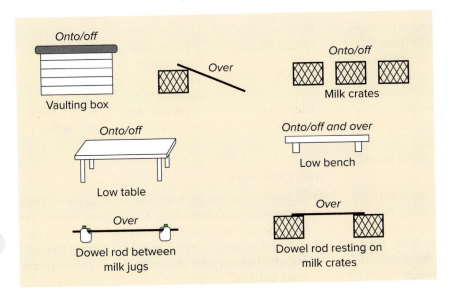

Onto/off — Vaulting box

Over

Onto/off — Milk crates

Onto/off — Low table

Onto/off and over — Low bench

Over — Dowel rod between milk jugs

Over — Dowel rod resting on milk crates

Cues

Strong Muscles	(Strong arms and shoulders—no collapse.)
Stretch Your Legs	(Extend your legs upward—stretch to the sky.)

Tasks/Challenges:

T Travel over the various pieces of low equipment by transferring your weight from your feet to your hands to your feet. At the hurdles with the newspaper or dowel rods, place your hands on the mat on the other side of the hurdle or rod, and then transfer your weight over, landing on your feet. At the benches and milk crates, place your hands on the equipment, take your weight on your hands only, and land on your feet on the opposite side of the equipment.

T As you become comfortable taking your weight on your hands, kick higher toward the ceiling, stretching your legs and trunk.

Transferring onto Low Apparatus

Setting: Benches, crates, and/or low tables surrounded by mats in general space

Cues

Strong Muscles	(Strong arms and shoulders for transfer onto hands.)
Soft Landings	(Absorb the force on feet and/or hands and lower body gently onto apparatus.)

Tasks/Challenges:

T Use the benches (crates, low tables) to practice transferring your weight onto equipment. Transfer your weight from your feet to your hands on the equipment by springing off your two feet and landing on your hands and feet. Take your weight momentarily on your hands, then softly lower to your feet; don't jump onto the equipment.

T Using your spring takeoff, transfer your weight to your hands and knees on the apparatus. Yes, you still take your weight momentarily on your hands only.

T Use a front-back stance and step into the transfer, momentarily taking your weight on your hands only on the equipment, then lowering your total body onto additional body parts. Be sure your hands are firmly planted on the equipment so you won't slip when you transfer to hands-only.

©Barbara Adamcik

Traveling over, under, and through apparatus builds youngsters' skills in transferring weight to a variety of body parts as well as their comfort with the equipment.

Maintaining Transfer from Feet to Hands

Setting: Large gymnastics mats scattered throughout general space, with sufficient room between them for children to work safely

Cues

Strong Muscles	(Strong arms and shoulders to take weight on hands.)
Stretch to the Sky	(Stretch your trunk and legs upward.)
Alignment	(Feet over hips, over shoulders, over hands—in a straight line.)

Tasks/Challenges:

T Transfer your weight from your feet to your hands to your feet, momentarily taking your weight on your hands only. Reach downward, not forward, with your hands. **Stretch your legs toward the ceiling and tighten your stomach muscles to maintain your balance.**

You may want to begin in a squat position with your hands and feet touching the floor. Transfer your weight to your hands by kicking your feet in the air.

Use a step action to transfer your weight to your hands; try to have your shoulders directly over your hands when you kick your legs up.

T When you are comfortable with your feet being just a few inches off the floor, begin to kick your feet higher in the air.

C Practice until you can balance for 3 seconds on your hands. Transfer your weight back to your feet in their original position each time.

⚠ Teach children in the practice stages of taking weight on hands to twist the trunk, doing a quarter turn and bringing feet down to the floor safely, if they begin to overbalance. This prevents falling on the back in the event of an overbalance.

? *Journal.* This is an opportune time to have children record in their journals the date on which they successfully took their weight on their hands for 3 seconds. Have them describe the feeling of "weight on hands." *Refer to Chapter 12, "Assessing Student Learning," for the use of journals in physical education.*

This student practices transferring off apparatus, taking weight on hands.

©Barbara Adamcik

Transferring Weight to Hands by Stepping: Cartwheels

Setting: Large gymnastics mats throughout general space, with sufficient room between them for children to work safely

Cues	
Strong Muscles	(Strong arms and shoulders to take weight on hands.)
Stretch	(Stretch your trunk and legs toward the sky—legs straight.)

Tasks/Challenges:

T Using a step action, alternate transferring your weight to your feet and to your hands, returning to your feet in a step action, as in a cartwheel. Your weight transfers momentarily from one foot to the other foot, to one hand, to the other hand, to the foot, to the other foot.

T Experiment with beginning the cartwheel by facing the mat or by standing sideways with one shoulder toward the mat. You may choose either starting position.

T As you feel comfortable with the foot-foot-hand-hand-foot-foot transfer, try to make a straight pathway with your feet and hands along the mat.

T Practice leading first with your right and then with your left side so you can do a cartwheel in either direction.

C Practice until you can perform your cartwheel in a straight line three times.

? *Portfolio.* Achievements in weight transference are exciting for children. When they can perform a cartwheel in a straight line, with legs fully stretched in the air, have a partner assess the skill. Have them record the date on a gymnastics checklist in their portfolios. *Refer to Chapter 12, "Assessing Student Learning," for guidelines on assessment.*

T Transfer your weight to your hands, as in the cartwheel. While you are balanced in the inverted position, bring your feet together, twist a half turn, and bring your feet down quickly to face in the opposite direction; this is a round-off.

Children won't master gymnastics tasks in only one or two 30-minute lessons. A station format plus revisitation (see Chapter 9) provides opportunities for distributed practice of skills.

Utilization Level (GLSP): Learning Experiences Leading to Skill Development

Children at the utilization level of transferring weight learn to transfer their weight to their hands for longer

Transfer of weight, combined with balance and apparatus, is a utilization level task.

©Barbara Adamcik

periods of time and in combinations with stretching, curling, and twisting actions. Tasks are designed to teach children to transfer weight onto, over, and off large apparatus. The tasks also emphasize the development of more complex sequences involving transferring weight.

A note about cues: *Although several cues are listed for many of the learning experiences, it's important to focus on only one cue at a time. This way, the children can really concentrate on that cue. Once you provide feedback to the children and observe that most have learned a cue, it's time to focus on another one.*

Transferring Weight to Hands: Walking

Setting: Large gymnastics mats throughout general space, with sufficient room between them for children to work safely on transfers

Cues	
Strong Muscles	(Strong arms and shoulders for weight on hands.)
Stretch	(Stretch your trunk and legs toward the sky—legs straight.)
Alignment	(Feet over hips, over shoulders, over hands—in a straight line.)

Tasks/Challenges:

🔵 When you are confident and comfortable balancing on your hands for 3 seconds, try walking on your hands.

⚠️ Children should attempt walking on their hands only if they have sufficient upper-body strength to support weight in the inverted position for several seconds and can move into and out of a balance on their hands only with control.

Transferring Weight to Hands and Twisting

Setting: Large gymnastics mats throughout general space, with sufficient room between them for children to work safely on transfers

Cues	
Strong Muscles	(Strong arms and shoulders for weight on hands.)
Stretch	(Stretch your trunk and legs toward the sky—legs straight.)
Alignment	(Feet over hips, over shoulders, over hands—in a straight line.)

Tasks/Challenges:

🔵 Transfer your weight to your hands, twist your body a half turn, and bring your feet to the floor so you are facing in the opposite direction.

🔵 While balanced on your hands, slowly walk on your hands a half turn to face in the opposite direction.

Transferring Weight to Hands and Forming a Bridge

Setting: Large gymnastics mats throughout general space

Cues	
Strong Muscles	(Strong arms and shoulders for supporting weight on hands.)
Tight Muscles	(Tighten the abdominals for control.)
Extend	(Stretch from your fingertips to your toes as you transfer from feet to hands to feet.)

Tasks/Challenges:

🔵 Using a step action, transfer your weight to your hands with sufficient force to continue the forward motion. Your feet should remain in the step-like stance as they move upward over your hands. Just before your feet contact the floor, bring them together, and bend your knees slightly. You will then balance in a "bridge" with your feet and hands supporting your weight.

Keep your legs in the step-like stance throughout the transfer.

T As your feet contact the surface, push with your hands to continue your transfer to a standing position. This transfer without a pause is a walkover.

Transferring Weight onto Large Apparatus

Setting: Large apparatus—benches, tables, vaulting boxes, balance beams, parallel bars, large climbing frames—placed around the gym. *Many transfers at the utilization and proficiency levels of transferring weight are specific to particular pieces of apparatus; the name of the apparatus appears in parentheses following the task.*

Cues	
Heads Up	(Keep your head and shoulders erect as you approach the apparatus.)
Soft Landings	(Absorb the force on your feet and/or hands and lower your body slowly to the apparatus.)

Tasks/Challenges:

T Transferring weight onto large apparatus in gymnastics usually includes an approach to build momentum, a spring or step takeoff, and the transfer onto the apparatus. Approach the apparatus from about 15 feet. Using a spring takeoff, transfer your weight from your feet on the floor to your feet and hands on the apparatus (box, beam, table).

T Transfer your weight to your feet and hands with your body curled in a tuck position. *(Demonstrate.)*

T Transfer your weight to your feet and hands with legs extended in a straddle position. *(Demonstrate.)*

T Transfer your weight to your feet and hands in a "wolf" position: one knee bent, one leg straight (Figure 22.3). *(Demonstrate.)*

T Approach the apparatus from the sides as well as the front. Practice both spring and step takeoffs to transfer your weight to various body parts on the apparatus.

Many of the control-level tasks for transferring weight onto and off low apparatus can be repeated for large apparatus. This is good practice because it enables children to adjust comfortably to the increased height and narrower surface of large apparatus.

Figure 22.3 Tuck, wolf, and straddle positions on large apparatus following spring takeoffs.

Transferring Weight to Head and Hands on Apparatus (Box, Beam, Table)

Setting: Large apparatus placed throughout general space, with sufficient mats for children to work safely

Cues	
Heads Up	(Keep your head and shoulders erect as you approach the apparatus.)
Strong Muscles	(Strong arm and shoulder muscles to support weight on the apparatus.)
Soft Landings	(Absorb the force on your feet and/or hands and lower your body slowly to the apparatus.)

Tasks/Challenges:

T Approach the apparatus and use a spring takeoff to transfer your weight to your hands and head on the apparatus. Push hard with your legs on the takeoff for sufficient height and time for the transfer, taking your weight first on your hands only and then gently, with control, on your head and hands.

⚠ Have the children approach the box, beam, or table from the end rather than the side for this transfer to head and hands. This allows sufficient space for rolling across the apparatus if they overbalance.

⚠ Teach the children to roll slowly across the apparatus if they overbalance on the head-and-hands transfer; teach them to transfer weight back to their feet on the floor if they do not have sufficient push to move into the inverted position on the apparatus.

Transferring Weight onto Bars (Parallel Bars, Climbing Frame)

Setting: Large apparatus placed throughout general space, with sufficient mats surrounding for safety

Cues	
Heads Up	(Keep your head and shoulders erect as you approach the apparatus.)
Strong Muscles	(Strong arm and shoulder muscles to support weight on the apparatus.)
Soft Landings	(Absorb the force on your feet and/or hands and lower your body slowly to the apparatus.)

Tasks/Challenges:

T Standing under the apparatus, use a spring takeoff to transfer your weight to your hands on a high bar. Hanging on the bar, pull up with your arms as you swing your legs over a lower bar and balance in a sitting position.

T Approach the apparatus with a series of steps. Using a spring takeoff, grasp the bar with your hands and jump up. Push really hard with your arms to lift your body above the bar; balance with your hands and upper thighs on the bar. Swing a leg over the bar so you can straddle the bar.

T Approach the apparatus with a series of steps. As you step under the bar, grasp it with your hands, and kick your rear leg forcefully upward to bring your hips to the bar. Keeping your arms bent and pulling your body close to the bar, assume a pike position by bending at the hips. The momentum of the leg kick will cause your body to circle the bar. Balance on your hands and upper thighs on the bar.

C You have now practiced jumping into a hip mount and doing a hip circle with the body in a pike position. Practice these skills until you master them.

? Add these to your gymnastics checklist in your portfolio.

T Approach the apparatus from the back, front, and side; practice both spring and step takeoffs to transfer your weight to various body parts on the apparatus.

Transferring Weight over Apparatus (Vaulting Box)

Setting: Vaulting boxes, with sufficient mats for safety, in general space

Cues	
Heads Up	(Keep your head and shoulders erect as you approach the apparatus.)
Strong Muscles	(Strong arm and shoulder muscles to support weight on the apparatus.)
Soft Landings	(Bend your knees for a controlled landing.)

Tasks/Challenges:

⚠ Position yourself at the vaulting station when children are transferring weight over the apparatus. As a spotter, you should not help the children perform the skill, but you can help prevent serious injury from a fall. Because spotting techniques differ for each skill, you should consult a gymnastics text or certified gymnastics coach before attempting to spot students in specific gymnastics tasks.

Ⓣ Approach the vaulting box with light running steps, keeping your weight on the balls of your feet. Using a spring takeoff, plant your hands firmly on the box, shoulder-width apart. Travel over the vaulting box, landing on your two feet on the mat.

Ⓣ Now transfer over the box by placing your hands shoulder-width apart on the apparatus, bringing your legs up between your arms in a tuck or curled position. Pause momentarily on the box in this curled shape; then jump forward to the mat.

Ⓣ Push harder with your hands this time to bring your body into a curled position, and push yourself over the box without pausing in the tuck position on top of the box.

⚠ Children should attempt vaulting over the box with a curled, straddle, or wolf vault only after they have mastered transferring onto the apparatus with these techniques.

Ⓣ Transfer over the vaulting box by bringing your feet and legs together, stretched to one side, as you cross over the box. Place your hands shoulder-width apart on the box, and shift your weight to

one hand as you swing your legs over the box. Push off from the vaulting box with the supporting hand, landing on two feet with your back to the vaulting box. This is called *a flank* vault. That spring takeoff we practiced earlier becomes increasingly important as you work on mounts onto and transfers over large apparatus.

Ⓣ Transfer your weight onto the vaulting box in a wide shape by placing your hands shoulder-width apart and stretching your legs to either side of the box, supporting your weight momentarily on your feet and hands. From a standing position on the vaulting box, transfer your weight to your feet by jumping to the mat. You will need a really strong takeoff to gain the height for this transfer.

Ⓣ Transfer your weight over the vaulting box by taking your weight on your hands, shoulder-width apart, and bringing your feet over the box in the stretched, wide shape. Keep your head and shoulders erect to prevent losing your balance. This is called a *straddle* vault. *Do not attempt this vault without the spotter (teacher or qualified adult) at the station.*

⚠ Always have the children tell you which vault they are attempting and whether they are stopping on top or transferring over before they begin their approach. This allows you to be ready for the proper spotting of that skill.

Transfer of weight on low equipment precedes the use of high equipment.

©Barbara Adamcik

Transferring Weight Along Apparatus

Setting: Stationary bar, tables and benches of various heights, vaulting boxes, balance beam, a stage

Many of the gymnastics skills learned on the floor and on low equipment can also be performed on large apparatus. Before children try them on a large apparatus, they should review the skills on the floor or mats, then on the low equipment, concentrating on the skill and its critical elements.

Transferring Weight to Hands on Low Apparatus

Setting: Tape lines on the gym floor, with sufficient space between them for children to work safely; low benches surrounded by mats

Cues

Strong Muscles	(Strong arms and shoulders to take weight on hands.)
Stretch	(Stretch your trunk and legs toward the sky—legs straight.)
Muscular Tension	(Maintain tension through arms, trunk, and legs for full extension—stretched for cartwheels, arched for walkovers.)

Tasks/Challenges:

T Practice a cartwheel on a tape line on the floor until you can do it perfectly three times. Now transfer your weight from your feet to your hands in a cartwheel on the low bench.

Teaching by invitation or intratask variation (Chapter 6) is very effective when working with transferring weight on apparatus. Permit only those children who are clearly ready to do so to practice inverted weight transference along apparatus.

T Transfer your weight from your feet to your hands, slowly execute a half turn, and bring your feet down on the apparatus surface facing the opposite direction.

⚠ Teach children to push with their hands to move the body away from the bench and to transfer weight to their feet on the floor if they feel off balance or unable to complete the transfer after inverting.

C Create three ways to transfer your weight while moving along the apparatus. Consider changes in levels and directions of travel. Diagram and/or describe your transfers on paper. Show your three transfers to a friend; ask the friend to give you pointers to make your transfers even better.

❓ *Peer Observation.* Children working together, as in the preceding task, can be an excellent type of assessment. *Refer to Chapter 12, "Assessing Student Learning," for more information on peer assessment.*

Transferring Weight on Bars

Setting: Parallel bars and/or large climbing frame, with sufficient mats surrounding

Cues

Strong Grip	(Maintain a strong grip on the bars to work safely.)
Strong Muscles	(Strong arm and shoulder muscles to maintain control on the bars.)

Tasks/Challenges:

T Transfer your weight to different body parts as you move from bar to bar on the parallels or other climbing apparatus. Make some of your transfers very slowly; make others very quickly.

T Circle the bar with your body curled, in a pike position.

T Use twisting actions to move your body off balance and into the transfer.

Combining Skills on Mats

Setting: Large gymnastics mats in general space, with sufficient room between them for children to work safely

Cues

Individual cues as needed

Tasks/Challenges:

T Travel the length of your mat, transferring your weight from your feet to other body parts, in various combinations to create a sequence. For example:

- Perform slow movements and then very quick movements for contrast.
- Do movements that show strength and then movements that demonstrate slowness and smooth control.
- Perform twisting, turning actions—for example, a round-off, weight on your hands, a 360-degree turn on your hands.
- Travel the length of your mat, combining a balance, a jump, a roll, and a hands/feet action.

- Travel the length of your mat, transferring your weight from your feet to your hands, followed by a roll and an ending balance.

⚠ Include rolling as an option for children only if rolling has been taught as a prerequisite and children have demonstrated mastery of the roll selected for their sequences.

Combining Weight Transfer and Balances into Sequences on Mats and Apparatus

Setting: Large and small gymnastics apparatus, the large apparatus positioned in general space

Tasks/Challenges:

❓ *Gymnastics routines on mats and apparatus are combinations of weight transfers and balance. Children at the utilization and proficiency levels of balance and weight transfer are ready for sequences involving combinations of skills and travel. Figure 22.4 gives an example of an assignment, plus guidelines for completing it.*

Figure 22.4 Sample assignment for utilization- or proficiency-level weight-transfer and balance sequence.

Name ————————————————

Final Project: Gymnastics

Grade 5: (a) mat sequence, (b) equipment sequence

Alone; with a partner: mirror, side by side

1. Beginning
   A. Approach:
      distance, starting point, pathway
      walk, run, leap, roll, walkover, cartwheel
      other ————————————————————
   B. Takeoff:
      spring, step
2. Development of sequence: Mix in any order for interest.
   A. Balances:
      minimum of four body shapes/four different bases of support
   B. Actions:
      minimum of three
      stretch, curl, twist, turn
   C. Transfers:
      movement
      feet to hand, back, head/hands
      (headstands, cartwheels, rolls, etc.)
   D. Inversion:
      minimum of two
3. Ending shape or dismount
   A. Music selection: ninety seconds
   B. On back side of page, list the progression of section 2; illustrate it if you wish.

❓ *Event Task*

As the final project in gymnastics, students are to design a 90-second routine for either mats or apparatus. They may choose to work alone or with a partner; the partner relationship may be mirror or side by side. The routine must include an approach, development, and ending shape or dismount. The development portion of the routine must include the following: a minimum of four balances of different shapes and bases of support, a minimum of three locomotor and/or nonlocomotor actions, weight transfer, and at least two inversions. The selection of music for the routine is a student decision. The routine is to be diagrammed or written on paper and practiced until the sequence is memorized in its entirety. The routine will be digitally recorded for inclusion in student portfolios.

Criteria for Assessment

a. Routine includes all necessary components: approach, balances, weight transfers, inversion, dismount (ending shape).
b. Routine matches music in length.
c. Demonstrates changes in tempo in routine.
d. Selects balances and weight transfers that can be correctly performed (i.e., skills matched to personal gymnastic ability).
e. Maintains stillness in balances.
f. Displays creativity in routine design.
g. Transitions between movements are smooth.

NASPE (1995, pp. 47–48)

Proficiency Level (GLSP): Learning Experiences Leading to Skill Development

Tasks at the proficiency level focus on increasing the horizontal and/or vertical distance of the weight transfer, as well as the intricate maneuvers (twisting and curling actions) that the body and its parts perform as weight is transferred from and received by different body parts. Examples include hands-only vaulting; performing stretching and twisting actions while airborne; and dismounting from apparatus by transferring weight from hands to feet combined with aerial twists, turns, and curls.

Activities at this level use specific gymnastics equipment and more closely resemble Olympic-style stunts. These skills are most often learned through club gymnastics. We do not teach them to the total class because very few children attain this level of performance. For those children who are ready to learn these skills or already proficient in these tasks, we provide individual teaching or coaching (see Chapter 30).

Rolling

Rolling is a specialized act of transferring weight to adjacent body parts around a central axis. Children find the sensations of rolling—dizziness, loss of perception, and not knowing where they are or how they'll finish a roll—intriguing and perplexing. So children love to roll. As they become adept at rolling, the fascination of traveling upside down is augmented by the pleasure of being able to roll in different directions and at various speeds. Whether recovering after falling off a skateboard or bicycle or participating in formal gymnastics settings, children who master the skill theme of rolling are able to participate comfortably and safely in activities that involve being off balance and falling because they possess sufficient recovery techniques. In physical education classes, rolling is generally dealt with in a gymnastics context, as transference of weight provides children a fluid way to connect different balancing actions and to change direction and/or speed in a dynamic, unpredictable situation. In addition, safety through rolling is introduced early to help children avoid crashing to the floor when they lose their balance. In dance and games, rolling is dealt with briefly to increase the children's range of movement and to enhance expressive abilities (see the progression spiral on page 417).

You will notice that no proficiency-level skills or back rolls over the neck are included in the progression spiral for rolling. Children proficient in rolling enjoy rolling backward, rolling over high equipment, and aerial rolls. They also combine rolling as a means of weight transfer between various forms of balance and other forms of weight transference. At this level, children are capable of difficult and sophisticated rolls, but because of safety considerations, the teacher's skills, equipment requirements, and the student–teacher ratio of physical education classes, we do not teach them. Such rolls as back rolls; dive rolls; rolls along high, narrow equipment; and rolls from aerial positions are better left to club gymnastics.

It is important that the teacher is familiar with the critical elements needed for quality instruction, demonstration, and observation of the skill. Throughout the chapter are sample cues (short phrases or words summarizing these critical elements). Ideally, if the cue is the last thing a teacher repeats before sending the students to practice, the learner will be cognitively focused on the critical elements.

The critical elements for forward rolling are:

- Crouched position; back in C shape.
- Head tucked.
- Hips raised.

Skill Theme Development Progression

Rolling

Proficiency Level

Club gymnastics

Utilization Level

Catching, throwing, and rolling
Rolling and striking
Rolling to meet and part
Rolling and balancing on equipment
Rolling onto low equipment
Rolling while throwing, and catching
Rolling to express an idea
Rolling, balancing, and rolling
Traveling and rolling between pieces of equipment
Rolling off low equipment
Rolling on low equipment
Rolling over low hurdles
Rolling, jumping, and traveling in relationship to others
Rolling and traveling quickly

Control Level

Rolling while traveling, jumping, and landing
Rolling, levels, directions, and jumping
Rolling after jumping over equipment and landing
Rolling after jumping from different heights
Rolling after jumping for height and landing
Rolling after jumping off equipment and landing
Rolling using different directions and speeds
Linking rolls
Rolling from different directions and positions
Rolling in different directions
Back shoulder roll
Rolling at different speeds
Rolling from different positions
Rocking backward over the shoulders
Rolling forward
Rolling over
Forward straddle roll
Rocking backward
Forward shoulder roll
Rolling sideways on different body parts
Rolling in a long, narrow position (log roll)
Rocking to match a partner

Precontrol Level

Curling to roll
Rolling sideways
Rocking on different body parts
Making curled shapes

- Hands to mat. The arms and hands receive the body evenly at the beginning of the roll so the child does not roll to one side.
- Head slides through as the weight shifts from the hands to the upper back.
- The body stays tight throughout the roll.
- Roll ends on the feet. The feet are parallel on landing, not crossed.

The photo sequences in Box 22-2 shows critical elements for rolling. Please note that these critical elements and the cues used to aid student learning will change depending on the type of roll a child is learning.

As with any weight-bearing activity, it is critical to carefully consider each child's physical maturity and skill. Before they're ready to attempt forward rolls, children *must be able to support their body weight with their arms.* We believe that children should not be forced to do any specific roll. We are especially concerned about asking children to do traditional rolls when they haven't yet developed the strength they need to protect themselves from back and neck injuries. Thus, we have provided illustrations of the hand and body positions for a variety of rolls and eliminated backward rolls from the tasks provided.

Finally, while children love the sensation of rolling, it is an activity that cannot be done for extended periods. In an effort to maintain the quality of the skill and to prevent off-task behavior because children are too dizzy, we have often found it more productive to focus on rolling for only part of a lesson. Thus, especially in the early stages of rolling, children are able to recover between practices of rolling.

When introducing the skill of rolling, we prefer to have one mat for each child. When we don't have a mat for each child, we use as many mats as possible. We've found that a good ground rule for any rolling situation is to have only one child at a time on the mat. This does not mean the other children must stand in line and wait; they can stand around the mat and roll, in turn, as soon as the mat is empty. (See Figure 22.5 for a class setup that maximizes rolling opportunities for each child.) Sometimes we set up learning centers to prevent long waits in line. Grassy areas can also serve as appropriate areas for practicing rolling. When children roll on or over equipment, we make sure the surrounding area is covered with mats. When teaching rolling, it is especially important to employ the back-to-the-wall observational technique discussed in Chapter 11.

Precontrol Level (GLSP): Experiences for Exploration

The precontrol level of rolling is characterized by exploration of various ways in which the body is able to

Box 22-2

Key Observation Points: Rolling Pattern

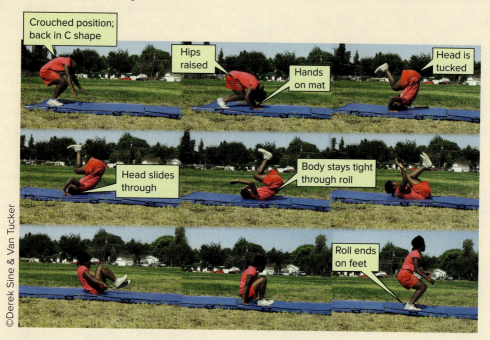

Crouched position; back in C shape

Hips raised

Hands on mat

Head is tucked

Head slides through

Body stays tight through roll

Roll ends on feet

©Derek Sine & Van Tucker

be round. This exploration includes rocking actions from the head to feet on the back and stomach. At this level, children are challenged when asked to perform actions such as rocking back and forth like a rocking chair or rolling in a stretched position like a log. Rocking in a ball-like position, in preparation for rolling, is also explored at this level. When a child first begins to roll, the arms and hands are of little use. The child may get over, but the whole body usually uncurls in the middle of the roll, and the child lands sitting down.

Making Curled Shapes

Setting: A mat, space on a mat, or a grassy area for each child; children positioned so they will not rock into each other (Figure 22.5)

Tasks/Challenges:

Ⓣ On your mat, try to find as many ways as possible to curl your body so it is round. Three different ways would be good.

Rocking on Different Body Parts

Setting: A mat, space on a mat, or a a grassy area for each child; children positioned so they will not rock into each other

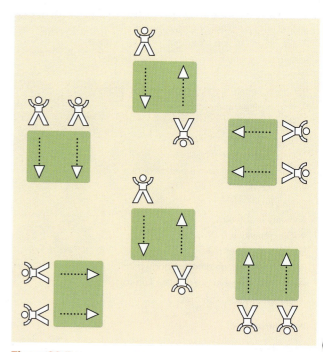

Figure 22.5 Mat positions that minimize the likelihood children will rock or roll into each other.

Tasks/Challenges:

T In self-space, you're going to pretend to be a rocking horse. But this rocking horse can do special things. First, you want to find out what it is like to rock on your back. To rock on your back, you must make your back round because flat things can't rock.

T Now your special rocking horse is going to try to rock on its stomach. Remember, make your stomach round so you can rock smoothly.

T Now you are going to try to do what no rocking horse has ever done: You are going to try to rock on your side. Can you make your side round? Try it.

T Your rocking horse is just getting warmed up, so let's see if it can go faster. See if you can rock so fast on your back that it takes you up to your feet.

T Now see if you can keep rocking on your back without stopping, almost as if you can't stop. If it helps, use your hands and arms.

Rolling Sideways

Setting: A mat for every child or two or a large grassy space; children positioned so they do not roll into each other

Tasks/Challenges:

T Now we are going to try something different: rolling sideways like a log. Try to roll slow and fast.

T Can you find another way to roll sideways? Maybe like an egg?

Curling to Roll

Setting: A mat for every child or two or a large grassy space; children positioned so they do not roll into each other

Tasks/Challenges:

T Can you make your body like a ball? How many ways can your ball move around your space? Remember, only round balls roll.

Rolling and Equipment

Many people are hesitant to teach gymnastics due to a perceived lack of equipment. Many people are hesitant to teaching rolling due to a perceived lack of mats. The surface needed for most fundamental rolling activities only needs to be large enough to cushion the head and upper back.

Control Level (GLSP): Learning Experiences Leading to Skill Development

At the control level, children become capable of controlling their bodies while rolling. They learn to roll in different directions using their arms and hands to push while the body stays curled and from different positions so they're able to perform other movements safely and use rolling as a response to a fall. Children also practice rolling as a conclusion to jumping and landing. Emphasis at this level is on control and the ability to roll in various situations.

A note about cues: *Although several cues are listed for many of the learning experiences, it's important to focus on only one cue at a time. This way, the children can really concentrate on that cue. Once you provide feedback to the children and observe that most have learned a cue, it's time to focus on another one.*

Rocking to Match a Partner

Setting: Partners side by side on a mat or in a grassy area, with enough space between them so that they do not hit each other

Cue	
C Bodies	(Curve your body like the letter C to rock.)

Tasks/Challenges:

T To warm up a bit, practice rocking back and forth on your mat. See if you can make your rocks very smooth.

T This time you are going to play a game called Twin Rockers. You and your partner will be side by side. On the signal, you'll start to rock on your back. The challenge is to rock the same way and at the same time as your partner so you look like twins.

T This time, rock on your stomach.

C Now see if you and your partner can develop two other Twin Rockers. Practice them until you can do them so they match exactly.

Rolling in a Long, Narrow Position (Log Roll)

Setting: A mat (no larger than 4 feet by 6 feet) for every child or two or a large, grassy space; children positioned so they do not roll into each other

Cues	
Stretch Arms	(Stretch your arms above your head.)
Straight Body	(Straighten your body.)
Feet Together	(Bring your feet tight together.)

Tasks/Challenges:

T On your mat, make your body long and skinny with your arms over your head. You could call this a log or pencil. See if you can roll to the right and to the left in this position. Practice until you can go both ways just as smoothly.

T This time try to make your log roll go in a straight line, still keeping your body position. Try to go from one end of your mat to the other without rolling off.

T Try changing the speed of your log roll: Sometimes roll slowly as if you were rolling on flat land and sometimes move quickly as if rolling downhill.

T If you feel comfortable doing your roll with your hands over your head, try to do it with your arms at your sides.

C Try to make a sequence of rolls in this narrow position—for example, one slow to the right, two quickly to the left, one slow to the right, and then repeat the sequence. Be sure to stay in your space or on your mat.

? *Portfolio* Children can write their sequences out, date them, and include them in their portfolios as an assessment task.

Rolling Sideways on Different Body Parts

Setting: A mat for every child or two or a large grassy space; children positioned so that they do not roll into each other

Cues	
C Bodies	(Curve your body like the letter C to roll.)
Hold Knees	(Hold your knees tight, either from the outside or from the inside out; *see* Figure 22.6.)

Figure 22.6 Arm positions for keeping ankles and knees tight while rolling sideways on different body parts.

Tasks/Challenges:

T This time try to roll sideways like an egg in a curled position. Practice rolling this egg in different directions—sometimes left, sometimes right.

T Try rolling on different body parts—shoulder, back, even upper legs.

T In your space or on your mat, practice using the egg roll to travel. Can you roll around the whole space?

T Roll at different speeds around your space or mat.

Forward Shoulder Roll

Setting: A mat for every child or two or a large grassy space; children positioned so they do not roll into each other

Cues	
Drop	(Drop one shoulder to the mat.)
Tuck	(Tuck the elbow and knee of the dropped shoulder under.)
Roll	(Roll over.)

Tasks/Challenges:

T This time we are going to roll over a shoulder. To do that, you need to start on your hands and knees, drop one shoulder to the mat, tuck your elbow and knee under your body, and roll over. Your roll should take you back up to your hands and knees. *(Demonstrate the roll.)* Let's all do it together this first time. Ready? Hands and knees, drop, tuck, roll. Good. (See Figure 22.7.)

T Practice the roll on your own. **Say the cues out loud as you go to help you remember the process.** Do one roll across your mat, get up, and try another one. You know you are really good when you can come up to your hands and knees each time.

T Once you feel comfortable rolling in one direction, try dropping the other shoulder and rolling that way.

C See if you can do three rolls in each direction that stay round throughout the whole roll.

T If you feel really good about rolling on your shoulder from your hands and knees, you may want to try it from a squatting position. The cues are the same; just the starting position changes. *(If this task is worded in this way, it is "teaching by invitation," allowing children to progress at their own speed. See Chapter 7 for more about this concept.)*

Figure 22.7 Forward shoulder roll.

? *Children's Drawing.* This would be a wonderful time to use children's drawings of rocking and rolling to assess their knowledge of the critical elements. *See Chapter 12 for the development of children's drawings as assessment items.*

⚠ Forward rolls should always be optional for children; insisting that students perform specific rolls can result in serious neck injuries.

Rocking Backward

Setting: Each child with a space at a mat or in a large grassy area; children positioned so they do not roll into one another; music conducive to rocking and an audio device

Cues	
C Back	(Curve your back like the letter C.)
Tuck	(Tuck your chin to your chest.)
Round Body	(Pull your knees to your chest, tuck your chin, and hold.)

Tasks/Challenges:

T Remember when we explored rocking horses and did Twin Rockers? This time we are going to try a back rocker. Start by squatting down with your back to the mat, place your fingers on the floor, slowly transfer your weight backward to the mat, and, as your back reaches the mat, tuck your chin in, bring your knees to your chest, wrap your arms around them, and rock backward until your head touches the mat. Rock forward to your starting position. Watch me as I show you. *(Demonstrate.)* Squat, lower, tuck, knees, rock.

T Practice the back rocker on your own. Don't ever go over your head. See how smoothly you can make the rock.

T As you rock, try to come back up to your feet at the end. What does it take to do this?

C See if you can keep your back rocker going for as long as I play the music. *(Play music in increasingly longer intervals, beginning with about 5 to 10 seconds.)*

? What does it look like when body parts are round? Show me.

Forward Straddle Roll

Setting: Small or large mats that will not slide, scattered throughout general space, with sufficient room for children to work safely

Cues	
Feet Wide Apart	(Your feet should make a wide shape with hands firmly on the mat.)
Lean and Tuck	(Tuck head through legs as weight shifts forward.)
C Back	(The back stays curled throughout the roll.)

The straddle roll, with feet wide apart, places students in a position with the head close to the mat; the wider the legs, the closer the head is to the mat. We have found the straddle roll reduces the fear of the tuck position, which some children have.

T Standing at the end of your mat, spread your legs wide apart in a straddle position.

Place your hands firmly on the mat positioned between your feet. Lean forward and tuck your chin, lower your body to the mat, and roll forward across the mat.

T Explore rolling with different ending shapes: wide, narrow, curled.

Rolling Over

Setting: Each child with a space at a mat or in a large grassy area; children positioned so they do not roll into one another

Cues

Hands   (Your hands should be on the floor on the outside of your knees.)

Lean   (Lean forward.)

Hike   (Hike your bottom up high into the air.)

Look   (Look back through your legs.)

Tip   (Tip over; place the top of your shoulders on the mat.)

⚠ Never force children to do a specific roll. Some may still prefer to roll over their shoulder at this point. If so, we place the emphasis on being round and staying in control. Gradually, we encourage children to move to positions higher than their hands and knees—for example, squatting—and to start the roll from there.

Tasks/Challenges:

Ⓣ Now we are going to try rolling forward. This roll goes over your head. To do it, begin in a squat position, lean forward, hike your seat up in the air, look through your legs, and tip over. Everyone watch me do it once. *(Demonstrate.)* Now, let's do it together on the cues: Hands, lean, hike, look, tip.

Ⓣ Now practice on your own. **Say the cues as you roll so you don't forget them.** Practice once across your mat. Get up and go again.

Ⓒ See if you can do three rolls that stay round all the way.

Ⓣ When you can stay round all the way through the roll, you may want to try to return to a standing position after the roll. The starting position is the same.

Rolling Forward

Cues

C Back   (Round your back like the letter C.)

Tuck   (Tuck your chin to your chest.)

Hike   (Hike your bottom up high into the air.)

Push   (Push off with your legs and make sure your weight is on your arms so your shoulders and back touch the mat in a very controlled way.)

Note to teachers: These cues vary slightly from the previous ones. They all are designed to elicit the critical elements of the roll. Use what works for your students!

Bubble Gum = Head Down

Getting children to keep their heads down is often difficult when they are first learning to roll. Two hints we have seen used are asking children to think of bubble gum connecting their chin and chest or having children hold a beanbag with their chin to their chest. Both ideas work.

❓ Have children touch the back of their heads with their hand so you know they can distinguish between the back and top of their heads.

⚠ Children should not be forced to roll over their heads if they cannot support their body weight with their hands or are uncomfortable with the roll.

Tasks/Challenges:

Ⓣ Now we are going to try a forward roll. Squat down at your mat and place your hands on the mat just to the outside of your knees. Make your back really round like the letter C. Tuck your chin all the way down to your chest. Hike your bottom way up in the air. Push with your arms and roll. The top of your head should not touch the mat. Imagine there is paint on the top of your head; try not to get any on the mat. Watch me while I show you how it will look. *(Demonstrate.)* Practice once with me all together as we say the steps: Hands (Figure 22.8), C, tuck, hike, push, and roll.

⚠ Some children may be more comfortable doing a shoulder roll. Encourage them to concentrate on roundness and tucking, while gradually trying to get them to raise their starting position farther off the ground to kneeling or squatting.

Point of Contact

There is some debate regarding the point of contact on the forward roll. Some prefer the shoulders and back; others indicate the back of the head. In our research, we have found both. (We advocate the shoulders.) Regardless of which point of contact is used, several key points ensure the safety of the skill: (1) the weight is held by the arms, not the neck and head; (2) the body parts are in a round position and stay that way throughout the roll; and (3) the transference of weight occurs under control so there is no sudden crunching of weight onto any body part.

Figure 22.8 Hand positions on forward roll.

Inclined Surfaces

For many children, it is easier to learn to roll forward on an inclined surface. To do this, use a wedge mat approximately 10 inches high at the top tapering to 2 inches high at the bottom, and at least 30 inches long and 18 inches wide. You will need a box for children to stand on at the top of the mat. With this task, be sure that children start their rolls from a squatting position. The cues remain the same.

Ⓣ Now practice on your own. Do one roll, get up, and start again. Roll straight across the mat. Say the cues aloud as you practice so you won't forget them.

Ⓒ See if you can do three forward rolls that stay round from beginning to end. Remember, stop, and reset yourself between the rolls.

Ⓣ If you feel really good about your forward roll, try to come up to your feet at the end.

Back Rolls

As we indicated earlier, back rolls over the head and neck have been removed from this edition of *Children Moving*. Our rationale is largely based on safety. Beginners often will put their full body weight onto their head and neck when attempting a back roll. They do it because they are either too weak, too inexperienced, or simply do not know any better. This situation is basically a neck injury waiting to happen. We still include backward rocking and back shoulder rolls as these do not place the same strain on the neck. However, do all backward rolling activities with extreme caution.

Ⓒ See if you can do five forward rolls that the Olympic judges would give a "10."

❓ What parts of your body have to be round to roll forward? Show me.

❓ *Peer Observation.* After successfully completing a forward roll, a friend could then observe the roll. That person should then record the date and initial the roll on a gymnastics checklist in children's portfolios. *Refer to Chapter 12, "Assessing Student Learning," for more on the use of peer observation for assessment in physical education.*

Rocking Backward over the Shoulders

Setting: Each child with a space at a mat or in a large grassy area; children positioned so they do not roll into one another

Cues	
C Back	(Round your back like the letter C.)
Hands Behind Head	(Clasp your hands behind your head with your elbows sticking out to the sides; *see* Figure 22.9)

Tasks/Challenges:

Ⓣ Start by squatting down with your back to the mat; clasp your hands behind your head with your elbows out as far as possible; slowly transfer your weight backward to the mat; as your back slowly reaches the mat, tuck your chin in, bring your knees to your chest, and rock backward as far as possible until your weight is on your elbows. Rock

Smaller mats are adequate for introducing children to rolling; larger mats can be used for rolling in sequences and in relation to apparatus.

©Barbara Adamcik

forward to your starting position. Watch me as I show you. *(Demonstrate.)* Practice it once with me: Squat, clasp, lower, tuck, knees, rock.

Rolling from Different Positions

Setting: Each child with a space to roll on a mat or grassy area

Cues	
Round Body	(Round your back and tuck your chin for a good roll.)
Strong Muscles	(Use strong arms and shoulders to transfer weight slowly to the roll.)

Tasks/Challenges:

T So far you have started your rolls from a low position, close to the mat and a straddle position that was a bit higher. Now we are going to practice the

straddle position again. Stand behind your mat with your feet wide apart; stretch your hands to the ceiling. Now put your hands on the mat almost between your feet (don't reach forward), tuck your chin to your chest, and roll forward. You will land sitting down. As with all rolls, keep your back rounded. Let's practice one together as we say the steps out loud: feet apart, stretch arms, hands on mat, tuck chin, slowly roll.

T Practice the straddle roll on your own until you can do it slowly and smoothly.

T Now that you can roll from the squatting position and the straddle position, see if you can find other positions from which to roll. You may want to try your knees, standing, one leg, and one arm. **Each time, remember to use strong muscles to lower slowly to the mat.** Try to find four different starting positions.

C Choose the starting position you like most. See if you can do four rolls from that position that stay rounded, and lower slowly to the mat. When you think you can, ask a friend to watch you and give a thumbs-up for each roll that you do correctly.

Rolling at Different Speeds

Setting: Each child with a space to roll on a mat or grassy area without rolling into each other

Cues	
Round Body	(Round your back and tuck your chin and knees for a good roll.)
Arms	(Your arms are your brakes and accelerator for these rolls.)

Figure 22.9 Handclasp position for rocking over the shoulders.

Tasks/Challenges:

T Do you remember when you worked on traveling at different speeds? Now you are going to roll at different speeds. Sometimes you will roll fast, sometimes you will roll slowly, and sometimes you will roll at a medium speed. Now practice doing rolls at different speeds. Your speed should be so clear that I can tell which speed it is just by watching. I shouldn't have to ask you.

C Now I am really going to give you a challenge. I'll call out a speed, and you roll at that speed. I'll be watching to see if you really roll at the speed I call out.

Back Shoulder Roll

Setting: Each child with a space at a mat or in a large grassy area; children positioned so they do not roll into one another

Cues	
Round Body	(Round your back and tuck your chin and knees for a good roll.)
Arm to Side	(Keep the arm of the shoulder you are going to roll over out to the side of your body.)
Head to Side	(Tuck your head to one side as you go over.)

Tasks/Challenges:

T We are going to try rolling backward over a shoulder with our hands on the mat to push. Watch me as I show you what it looks like. *(Demonstrate.)* Squat with your back to the mat with your hands on the floor in front of you, push with your hands and rock backward to the mat, bring the arm of the shoulder you are going to roll over out to the side of your body and the other arm back over your head, tuck your head to one side, push with your arms, and roll over that shoulder. Let's practice one together as we say the steps: Squat, hands in front, push and rock back, arm to side, tuck head, roll (Figure 22.10).

T Now practice the back shoulder roll on your own, **each time saying the steps so you do not forget them.**

T When you feel good about going over one shoulder, try to tuck your head the other way and go over that shoulder.

C Try to do four backward shoulder rolls that stay round all the way through. When you think you can do it, raise your hand and ask me to come watch, or have a friend watch.

? What parts of your body have to be round to roll backward over your shoulder? Show me.

? *Peer Observation.* This task works well as a peer observation opportunity, even with young children, provided the cues are simple and clear. It also gives children an opportunity to take responsibility for helping someone else learn. See Figure 22.11 for a sample peer observation sheet.

Rolling in Different Directions

Setting: Multiple large mats scattered around the area with ample space between them; each child with a space at a mat

Cues	
Round Body	(Round your back and tuck your chin and knees for a good roll.)
Three Directions	(Make sure you roll backward, sideways, and forward.)
Feet	(Make sure at the end of your roll you come to your feet.)

Figure 22.10 Head and hand positions for back shoulder roll.

Figure 22.11 Peer Observation for Back Shoulder Roll.

My Name is: _____	I Watched: _____	
	_____	
Did your partner say the cues?	Yes 👍	Needs Help 👎
Did your partner use Mickey Mouse ears?	Yes 👍	Needs Help 👎
Did your partner keep a tight ball?	Yes 👍	Needs Help 👎
Did your partner push with his or her arms?	Yes 👍	Needs Help 👎

Tasks/Challenges:

Ⓣ You have practiced rolls that went sideways and forward and back shoulder rolls. Now you are going to put all three together. Practice rolls from all three directions—one roll at a time. Remember as you work that only one of you rolls on the mat at a time; however, as soon as the person ahead of you finishes, you can roll. I shouldn't see anyone standing in line, just rolling from all places around the mat.

Ⓣ This time I am going to add one more thing to what I would like to see. Each time you roll, try to end up on your feet, not your knees or your seat.

Ⓣ Decide which roll is the hardest for you to do. Practice that roll until you feel it is as good as your others.

Rolling from Different Directions and Positions

Setting: Each child with a space on a mat or grassy area to roll

Cues	
Round Body	(Round your back and tuck your chin and knees for a good roll.)
Strong Muscles	(Use strong arms and shoulders to transfer weight slowly to the roll.)
Feet	(Make sure at the end of your roll you come to your feet.)

Tasks/Challenges:

T We are going to combine two things you have done: rolling in different directions and rolling from different positions. There are many combinations. You can use any version of forward, forward shoulder, backward shoulder, and sideways rolls you want. Why not start by rolling forward from a standing position?

T Next roll backward over your shoulder from a sitting position.

T Now roll sideways from a squatting position.

T On your own, practice as many ways to roll as you can think of. You should always be able to tell me the direction of your roll and the position you are starting from.

C Now that you've practiced on your own, find three different direction/position combinations you like, and practice them until they are very smooth and flowing. Be able to tell me what position and direction you are using.

? *Exit Slip.* This would be an appropriate time to use an exit slip (see Chapter 12) that asks the children to record the three combinations of rolls used and react to the difficulty they had in making the sequence flow together.

Multiple Rolls

⚠ Having children do multiple (more than two) rolls in a row is not helpful—and can be dangerous. When more than two rolls are asked for in a sequence, some other movement or a balance should come between each roll.

Linking Rolls

Setting: A large mat or a soft grassy space for each child to roll, or multiple large mats scattered around the area with ample space in between them

Cues

Round Body	(Round your back and tuck your chin and knees for a good roll.)
Strong Muscles	(Use strong arms and shoulders to control your body from one roll to the next.)
Smooth Transfer	(Pause between rolls.)

Tasks/Challenges:

T Now you get a chance to do what you have wanted to do for a long time: more than one roll at a time.

First, practice by doing two forward rolls in a row. When you can do two smoothly, balance, and try two more. To make the links look good, the transfer between rolls should be smooth. To make it smooth, pause for a second and then go into your next roll. Use only a pause, not a stop.

T When you feel comfortable doing two forward rolls or two forward shoulder rolls, try two backward shoulder rolls.

T Try sideways rolls: one, then a pause, then two.

T This time we are going to put together a sequence of three different rolls. For starters, try forward, sideways, forward. There should be one pause or balance in your sequence.

C Now make up your own sequence. It should have three or four rolls, with pauses after each roll, and two directions. When you can do your sequence really well, ask a friend to watch. See if your partner can name the sequence of rolls. Then watch your partner's sequence and name the rolls.

Rolling Using Different Directions and Speeds

Setting: Each child with a space on a mat or grassy area to roll; two bags—one containing index cards with a speed category on each card and the other containing index cards with a direction on each card; the number of cards in each bag should equal or exceed the number of children in the class; paper and pencil for each child

Cues

Round Body	(Round your back and tuck your chin and knees for a good roll.)
Arms	(Your arms are your brakes and accelerator.)

Tasks/Challenges:

T Here's another combination—directions and speeds. This means, for example, that sometimes you will use a back shoulder roll at a fast speed and sometimes at a slow speed. Practice on your own using all three speeds—fast, medium, and slow—combined with all three directions—forward, backward shoulder, sideways. That makes nine different ways you can roll; practice all of them.

T Now you are going to draw your speeds and directions out of a bag. On the signal, one at a time come and draw one card from each bag. One card will have a direction on it, and the other card will have a speed on it. The two cards together will give you the direction and speed you are to practice.

T Now for the hardest rolling task yet. Imagine you are in the Olympics and you are going to do a rolling sequence that combines directions and speeds. Let's start with this sequence: forward, fast; pause, backward shoulder, slow; forward, fast. The sequence is written on the board in case you forget.

C Now make up your own combination. Practice it until it flows together well. When you finish, write it down. You can use the example on the board as a guide to tell you how to write it. Practice your combination three more times.

? *Portfolio.* The previous task can be used as an assessment task by having children record the sequence as an entry in their portfolios. This is also an opportune time to use a live or digitally recorded teacher/peer observation checklist to assess the critical elements of rolling.

Rolling After Jumping Off Equipment and Landing

Setting: A low box, milk crate, or low step aerobics platform placed against every mat the children are using for rolling

You can sometimes get milk crates from the local dairy. Low boxes can be made by filling soft-drink cases (24-can size) with flat newspapers and taping the outside of the boxes shut securely. Place crates, boxes, or platforms against the mat so they won't slide. If you are still worried about crates sliding, children can work in partners with one partner holding the crate and the other one jumping.*

Cues	
Jump, Land, Roll	(Jump; land on your feet; pause then roll.)
Strong Muscles	(Use strong muscles to lower slowly to the roll.)
Round Body	(Round your back and tuck your chin and knees for a good roll.)

The cues for the following tasks focus largely on rolling, not on jumping and landing. This assumes children have already mastered jumping and landing. If they crash when they land or do not use soft landings, you will want to revisit jumping and landing (Chapter 20) before progressing.

**Prior to constructing equipment, we recommend you check with school administration to be certain that district policy permits homemade equipment.*

⚠ The first observation you need to make after children begin this task is whether they are landing on their feet before they roll. Quite often, children begin dive-rolling here. If they do, stop the task immediately, and refocus or provide another demonstration that shows the correct way.

Tasks/Challenges:

T You're now going to jump off a box (crate), land with your knees bending as your feet contact the floor, and then roll. There's a box (crate) at the end of your mat. One at a time, jump off the box (crate), land on your feet, take a little pause, and then roll. Go slowly at first until you get the hang of it. Always be sure to land on your feet. The next person can go as soon as the person in front gets off the mat. Don't rush, but go quickly.

⚠ Make sure children jump up, not out. When they jump out, they push against the box or crate, sending it sliding across the floor, which causes them to fall.

T It's getting harder. This time, change the direction of your jump. Sometimes jump backward, sometimes sideways, and sometimes forward; then roll in any direction you want. If you aren't sure about jumping backward, just try stepping off until you get used to it.

T We're going to change the activity again. This time, you'll still jump off in different directions, but you'll roll in the same direction as the jump. So if you jump sideways, you roll sideways; if you jump forward, you roll forward.

? What does it mean to land before you roll?

Rolling After Jumping for Height and Landing

Setting: A low box or milk crate placed against every mat the children are using for rolling

Cues	
Jump, Land, Roll	(Jump, land on feet with knees bending on contact with the floor, pause, then roll.)
Strong Muscles	(Use strong muscles to lower slowly to the roll.)
Round Body	(Round your back and tuck your chin and knees for a good roll.)
Feet	(Make sure at the end of your roll you come to your feet.)

Tasks/Challenges:

T This time, instead of changing directions, you're going to practice jumping higher off the boxes (crates), still landing, and rolling. Do you remember when we worked on jumping? What do you do to make your jump go higher? To warm up, just practice jumping high off the box (crate) and landing on your feet. If you fall on the landing, you know you're jumping too high.

T Now add a roll after your jump and landing. Everything should be in control. If you're falling on your landing or crashing into your roll, you'll know you're jumping too high. Try it: High jump, land, and roll.

T So far, most of what I've been seeing are jumps, lands, and rolls in forward directions. Go back and add different directions to your high jumps.

Jumping backward from the equipment is difficult for some children as well as scary. Have the youngsters first step backward if they're hesitant or fearful.

⚠ Permit children to jump backward only to a height they can control when they land. They should be able to land on their feet, balanced, absorbing their weight.

Rolling After Jumping from Different Heights

Setting: Boxes and benches of varying heights at stations around the room (Figure 22.12); arrows pointing from station to station on the floor; children in groups of four; mats at each station

Cues	
Jump, Land, Roll	(Jump, land on your feet with knees bending on contact with the floor, pause, then roll.)
Strong Muscles	(Use strong muscles to lower slowly to the roll.)
Round Body	(Round your back and tuck your chin and knees for a good roll.)

Tasks/Challenges:

T We're working at stations for this task, which will give you practice jumping from objects of different heights. This is how the activity works. There will be four of you at each station. On the signal, you'll begin to practice jumping, landing, and rolling from the equipment at your station. On the next signal, stop, rotate to the station the arrow on the floor points to, and then start all over again. Remember, you're practicing jumping, landing, and rolling from the equipment that's at your station.

Rolling After Jumping over Equipment and Landing

Setting: A hurdle set up at the end of each mat; see Chapter 16 (Figure 16.4) for hurdle construction details

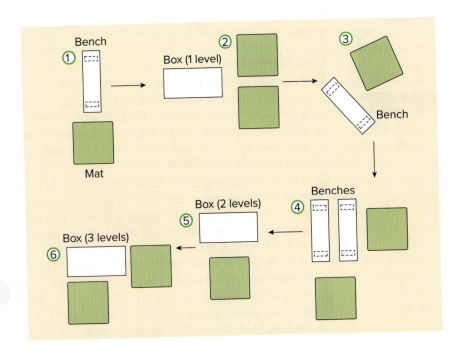

Figure 22.12 Stations to facilitate jumping from different heights, landing, and rolling.

Cues

Jump, Land, Roll	(Jump, land on your feet with knees bending on contact with the floor, pause, then roll.)
Strong Muscles	(Use strong muscles to lower slowly to the roll.)
Round Body	(Round your back and tuck your chin and knees for a good roll.)

⚠️ The hurdle should be only as high as children are able to jump over without difficulty and land in control (see Chapter 20). The hurdle should be an obstacle to cross, not a challenge to jump. Our hurdles are no higher than about 8 to 12 inches and may be as low as 3 to 4 inches.

Tasks/Challenges:

Ⓣ Your task now is to jump over the hurdle, land, and roll. Remember, just as in jumping off objects, you must land on your feet before you roll.

Ⓣ This time, change the direction of your jump. Sometimes try to jump sideways and backward as well as forward.

Ⓣ Now change the direction of your roll after the jump to match the direction of the jump. So if you jump backward, roll backward over your shoulder. **Controlled jumps and round rolls are our goal.**

Ⓣ You can also change the speed of the jump and of the roll. This time, practice mixing up the speeds of the jump and roll. In other words, you might mix a slow-motion jump with a fast roll or combine a fast jump and a fast roll. Make whatever speeds you use very clear.

❓ What does it mean to have controlled jumps? What do they look like?

Rolling, Levels, Directions, and Jumping

Setting: A jumping and rolling space for each child and several spaces that include boxes; a task sheet (Figure 22.13) for each child

Cues

Jump, Land, Roll	(Jump, land on your feet with knees bending on contact with the floor, pause, then roll.)
Strong Muscles	(Use strong muscles to lower slowly to the roll.)
Round Body	(Round your back and tuck your chin and knees for a good roll.)

Tasks/Challenges:

Ⓒ Today I'll give you the chance to test yourself and see how well you can do the rolls you've been practicing. I'll also give you time to practice the rolls that have been hardest for you. Each of you has a task sheet. Your challenge is to do all the tasks on the sheet. When you think you can do something well, have a friend watch you; if the friend thinks you did the challenge correctly, the friend puts his or her initials on the sheet. The area has been set up so there's space to practice each challenge. Remember, at the stations with boxes, there should be only two people at the station at one time.

❓ *Self-assessment.* This task can serve as a self-assessment and/or peer assessment. When completed, it can be included in the child's portfolio. See Chapter 9 for information on developing task sheets.

Rolling While Traveling, Jumping, and Landing

Setting: Mats spread throughout general space with sufficient space between for travel. Groups of three or four at each mat.

Cues

Jump, Land, Roll	(Jump, land on your feet with your knees bending on contact with the floor, pause, then roll.)
Strong Muscles	(Use strong muscles to lower slowly to the roll.)
Round Body	(Round your back and tuck your chin and knees for a good roll.)

Tasks/Challenges:

Ⓣ Now you're going to use only the mats, but you're going to jump, land, and roll at your mats all on your own. Practice jumping, landing, and rolling in different directions at your mat. Remember, you can start or end at any place around the mat, so there should be no lines.

Ⓣ This time, begin to travel around the outside of the mat. When the mat is empty, take a little jump, land, and roll. You'll almost be jumping from a moving position, but not quite. You'll travel, jump, pause, and roll, so you really come to a short stop before you roll. If you crash, you're going too fast. There should only be one person on the mat at a time.

Ⓣ Here's a new challenge. Instead of just jumping this time, try jumping over the corners of the mat; then, land and roll. Remember, practice all the different

Figure 22.13 Task sheet for Rolling

Name ————————— Teacher —————————

Rolling Task Sheet

Friend's Check-off	Challenge
	I can roll forward, coming up to my feet.
	I can roll sideways, coming up to my feet.
	I can roll backwards over my shoulder, coming to my feet.
	I can jump, land, and roll forward.
	I can jump, land, and roll sideways.
	I can jump land, and roll backwards over my shoulder.
	I can jump over an obstacle, land, and roll, coming back to my feet.
	I can jump, land, change directions, and roll.
	I can jump, twist in the air, land, and roll without falling down.
	I can jump off a box, land, and roll without falling down.
	I can jump off a box in different directions, land, and roll.
	I can jump off a low box, make different body shapes in the air, land, and roll.
	I can jump off a box, twist in the air, land, and roll without falling down.
	I can . . . (make up your own sequence)

jumps you learned: one foot to the other, one to the same, two to one, one to two, and two to two.

T Now I'll challenge you even further. As you jump the corners of the mat, add a twist or turn in the air before you land. You still have to land on your feet before you roll.

Utilization Level (GLSP): Learning Experiences Leading to Skill Development

At the utilization level, children no longer focus on rolling as an isolated skill but concentrate on using rolling for other purposes. Children develop the ability to combine rolling with manipulative skills, such as catching and throwing and as an expressive form. Much of their rolling at this level is directed toward its use as a form of weight transfer between balances. In addition, rolling is used to transfer weight onto, from, and over large apparatus.

At this level, because rolling is most often used not as an isolated skill but as an act of weight transference, many tasks at the utilization level of rolling are included in the earlier weight transference section of this chapter. When that occurs, reference is provided. In addition, many of the cues focus on the use of the skill rather than the skill itself.

A note about cues: *Although several cues are listed for many of the learning experiences, it's important to focus on only one cue at a time. This way, the children can really concentrate on that cue. Once you provide feedback to the children and observe that most have learned a cue, it's time to focus on another one.*

Rolling and Traveling Quickly

Setting: Mats spread out throughout the space; three or four children at a mat

Cues	
Jump, Land, Roll	(Jump, land on your feet with your knees bending on contact with the floor, pause, then roll.)
Strong Muscles	(Use strong muscles to lower slowly to the roll.)
Round Body	(Round your back and tuck your chin and knees for a good roll.)

1. If students are not able to safely decide who is to roll when, specify the order in which they'll roll before they begin.
2. This is an exhausting task; if children are really doing it well, they usually can't continue it for a long time.

Tasks/Challenges:

T This activity is called Busy Mat. It'll really give you a workout, so get ready. The object of the game is to have someone always rolling on the mat while the others are traveling around the outside of the mat. As soon as one person finishes rolling, another person should start. The timing should be split-second. Everyone should always be moving, either on the outside by jumping and landing or on the mat by rolling. Let's do a practice round.

Rolling, Jumping, and Traveling in Relationship to Others

Setting: Mats spread out throughout the space; three or four children at a mat

Cues	
Off Balance	(Be slightly off balance toward the mat as you land.)
Strong Muscles	(Use strong arms and shoulders to smoothly lower to the roll.)
Round Body	(Round your back and tuck your chin and knees for a good roll.)

Tasks/Challenges:

T Now you're going to practice making your jumps, landings, and rolls more professional. We could call them touch-and-go rolls. So far you've been coming to a clear stop after landing and before rolling. Now you're going to roll with no hesitation. Your feet should barely touch the floor before you're into the roll. Your roll just flows, but your feet still have to hit the floor before you roll. To do this, you'll really have to bend your knees on landing, let your arms absorb your weight, and make sure your shoulders are round.

T Practice making your jumps so you land a little off balance right before you move into a roll. You are trying to make it as smooth as possible, as if to save yourself from crashing. No stopping—touch and go.

T Make sure you sometimes change the direction of your land and roll, making it sideways as well as forward, and still keeping your touch-and-go actions.

Aerial Rolls

Because of safety considerations, the student–teacher ratio, the varied student skill level, and the high skill level required to teach and spot aerial rolls, we feel that they are best left to the private setting. To explain this to the students who are capable of such tasks, we simply say that we don't have the facilities to practice the rolls and don't want to encourage the children who aren't ready to try them. The more skilled students can instead use physical education class for refining their skills or helping others. We do not advocate teaching aerial or dive rolls in physical education classes.

Rolling over Low Hurdles

Setting: A low hurdle at each mat

⚠ The height of the hurdle should be low enough so children can put their hands on the ground on the other side with no effort. Hurdles may be as low as 3 to 4 inches and no higher than 10 to 12 inches. Hands must be on the floor before the feet leave the floor.

Cues	
Strong Muscles	(Use strong arms and shoulders to slowly lower into the roll.)
Round Body	(Round your back and tuck your chin and knees for a good roll.)
Hands on Floor	(Start with your hands on the floor on the other side of the hurdle.)

Tasks/Challenges:

T Place your hands on the mat on the other side of the hurdle and try to roll over the hurdle without touching it. **You will really need to raise your bottom in the air and push off with your legs. Remember, tuck your head to keep your body round. As you do this, make sure you're arms really give when your feet leave the floor. Giving with your arms a little as you push off helps you let yourself down slowly.**

Rolling on Low Equipment

⚠ Rolling on equipment should be introduced only after children have mastered rolling on the floor or mats.

Setting: Low, wide benches around the room with mats under them

⚠ At this point, the equipment should be low and wide, not more than 18 inches off the floor.

Cues	
Round Back	(Round your back and tuck your chin and knees for a good roll.)
Control	(Tight muscles, slow-motion action for control throughout the roll.)

Tasks/Challenges:

T At your piece of equipment, get on it in any way you like, and practice rolling on the top of it, lengthwise; then get off in any way you like. Although this position is very different from the one you use for rolling on mats, it provides a steady base on equipment. Tuck your head and slowly roll forward on the equipment. If you fall off a lot, you may want to go to a wider piece of equipment.

T As you practice now, try to make your rolls very smooth.

C Now you're going to make up a sequence using all you've practiced. First figure out how you want to get on the equipment; you don't have to get on by rolling. When you're on the equipment, roll along the equipment, get off any way, and roll after your dismount. The sequence will go like this: Get on, roll along, get off, roll on the mat. Practice on your own until your sequence looks the same each time you do it.

Practice your sequence three more times just to make sure it's really in your memory. When you finish, write it down (Figure 22.14).

Rolling off Low Equipment

Setting: Low boxes and benches, scattered throughout the space; mats around and under each piece of equipment. Children must be able to reach the mat from the equipment.

Cues	
Round Body	(Keep your back round and tuck your chin and knees for a good roll.)
Strong Muscles	(Use strong arms and shoulders to lower slowly into the roll.)
Feet	(Make sure at the end of your roll you come to your feet.)

Tasks/Challenges:

T Assume a kneeling position at the end of your piece of equipment, place your hands on the mat, slowly lower your weight to the mat, and roll forward.

T Once you feel comfortable with one piece of equipment, try another one.

Brian P.
Bench
Walk on-roll forwards
Slide off and roll backwards over my shoulder

Figure 22.14 Child's rolling sequence.

⚠️ This task should be preceded by the task of rolling over low hurdles. To do this activity safely, children must be able to absorb their body weight with their arms.

❓ What is the key to rolling off equipment safely?

Traveling and Rolling Between Pieces of Equipment

Setting: Two pieces of low, wide equipment placed about 2 feet apart at each station; mats under, around, and between all equipment

Cues	
Round Body	(Keep your body round and tuck your chin and knees for a good roll.)
Control	(Use tight, strong muscles to roll slowly.)
Feet	(Make sure at the end of your roll you come to your feet.)

Tasks/Challenges:

🔵T This next activity is similar to others you have done. As you can see, there are two pieces of equipment at each station. Your task now is to get on the first piece of equipment, roll one way on it, travel to the second piece of equipment without touching the floor, roll a different way on the equipment, jump to get off, and roll on the mat. The sequence goes like this: Get on, roll, travel across, roll another way, jump off, roll. Practice these ideas.

🔵C Now pick one sequence you really like, and practice it until it's smooth and fluid. There should be no breaks, and you shouldn't have to stop and think about what comes next. Make sure you land on your feet after you jump off and before you roll.

❓ *Video/Digital Analysis.* As children develop sequences using selected skills, the videotaping of their sequences provides an excellent opportunity for videotaped assessment. As children watch the video for the first time, have them write down the moves they used to develop the sequence. When they watch for the second time, have them assess their execution of those skills in relation to the critical cues.

Rolling, Balancing, and Rolling

(See also Traveling into and out of Balances by Rolling on page 394 of Chapter 21, "Balancing.")

Setting: Mats around the room large enough for children to roll and balance

Cues	
Round Body	(Keep your body round and tuck your chin and knees for a good roll.)
Control	(Tight, strong muscles to roll slowly.)

Tasks/Challenges:

🔵T You worked on balancing before; now you're going to combine balancing and rolling. At your mat, practice rolling forward into a symmetrical balance. Try to roll right into the balance so there's no pause between the roll and the balance.

🔵T This time try to focus on the connection between the roll and the balance. Continue practicing focusing on rolling right into the balance, with no stop, no pause.

🔵T Most of you are balancing on very stable body parts, such as knees and hands. This time, try some body parts that aren't quite so stable and see if you can still balance.

🔵T Now try rolls from different directions—backward over your shoulder and sideways—and still roll straight into the balance. Hold the balance still. **Shifting some of your weight backward, just as you balance, might make balancing a little easier.**

Rolling to Express an Idea

Setting: A soft, grassy area; children in pairs

Cue	
Round Body	(Keep your back round and tuck your chin and knees for a good roll.)

Tasks/Challenges:

🔵C This time you're going to roll to express an idea. You're going to pretend and tell a story by rolling. The first thing you're going to tell is "being scared." Here's how it works. Your partner will come close to you and pretend to scare you, without using words. You're so scared that you fall down and roll backward over your shoulder trying to get away. Make sure your roll really shows that you're afraid; it should be a very stiff roll. After two turns, switch places with your partner.

🔵C You're going to tell a desert story this time. Have any of you seen those old Westerns on television where tumbleweeds go blowing across the desert, with nothing stopping them? Well, you're going to be a tumbleweed, just blowing and rolling all over the desert. Remember, a tumbleweed is loose and bouncy as the wind just bumps it along.

T Instead of being a loose piece of tumbleweed, this time you're going to be a seed. The wind is blowing you all over; you're bouncing all around. Suddenly, the wind stops and you sprout roots and start to grow. When you start to grow, remember the ideas we talked about earlier about rising and spreading. Your sequence goes like this: The wind blows you around, the wind stops, you send out roots and grow into a big tree or flower.

Rolling While Throwing and Catching

Setting: A soft grassy area (or if done inside, a very large mat [like a wrestling mat] or a space completely covered with smaller mats); children in pairs; a variety of objects (beanbags, flying discs, balls) for each set of partners to throw and catch

Cues	
Tuck Shoulder	(Tuck your shoulder so it is round.)
Round Body	(Round your back and tuck your chin and knees for a good roll.)

Tasks/Challenges:

T With your partner, throw and catch the beanbag. Throw so your partner has to really stretch to catch the beanbag. Remember, to make your partner stretch, you really have to throw to a point away from your partner.

T Now that you're stretching to catch, as soon as you catch the beanbag, roll in the direction you had to stretch to catch the beanbag. Keep the beanbag in your hand as you roll. Remember the whole sequence: Stretch to catch, catch, and then roll.

T Now, for just a little while, practice throwing and catching the beanbag to yourself. Throw to yourself so you have to jump to catch the beanbag in an off-balance position and then roll to break the fall from being off balance. The hardest part is throwing so that you force yourself to be in an off-balance position.

T Now go back to working with your partner. Try the same task. Throw so your partner has to first catch the beanbag in an off-balance position and then roll after catching it. Catchers make sure you're really off balance and have to roll to recover your

balance or so you won't be hurt. Throwers, really force the catchers off balance when they catch.

T Once you feel comfortable with a beanbag, try using another object, such as a flying disc or a ball.

Successful throwing and catching with partners depends on throwers' ability to force the catchers to be off balance or to move to catch. Before exposing children to these ideas, make sure they're at the utilization level of throwing and catching.

Spotting

The question of spotting—physically assisting a child with a skill—often arises with gymnastics programs. While the skill of spotting can be taught and learned, it isn't used often in educational gymnastics programs as it often encourages or forces children to attempt a skill before they are ready. See Chapter 30 for a more complete discussion on the use of spotting.

Rolling onto Low Equipment

Setting: Benches or low boxes with mats surrounding them

Cues	
Round Body	(Round your back and tuck your chin and knees for a good roll.)
Control	(Tight muscles, slow-motion action for control throughout the roll.)

Tasks/Challenges:

T Use a roll to get onto your piece of equipment. Stand at the end of the equipment. **Place your thumbs and the sides of your palms on the top of the equipment and your hands and fingers on the sides of the equipment;** then slowly lower into a forward roll to get on to the equipment. Get off in any way you like.

T Now I'm going to add to your task. Roll onto the equipment, travel any way you want while on the equipment, jump to get off, land, and roll. Again, make sure you're actually using a roll to get onto the equipment.

Rolling and Balancing on Equipment

Setting: Benches and beams spread throughout the room, with mats surrounding all the equipment

Cues

Round Body	(Round your back and tuck your chin and knees for a good roll.)
Control	(Tight muscles, slow-motion action for control throughout the roll.)
Stillness	(Keep balances motionless.)

Tasks/Challenges:

Ⓣ At your equipment, practice mounting the equipment, balancing on it, rolling out of the balance, and dismounting. Make sure your rolls out of the balances are going in the direction that seems natural for the balance, not necessarily the easiest way for you.

Ⓣ Now, keep the same balances, but for each balance find at least one more roll, going in a different direction than the first roll. Thus, you should have two rolls out of each balance, each roll going in a different direction.

Ⓒ See if you can develop five balances and rolls you can do so they are smooth and round.

❓ *Student Display.* A fun assessment project at the utilization level is for students to develop a poster or bulletin board that displays how rolling is used in sports other than gymnastics. *See Chapter 12 for the development of scoring rubrics to accompany such a project.*

Rolling to Meet and Part

Setting: Groups of five; a large grassy area or wrestling mats

Cues

Smoothness	(Make your rolls flow smoothly into and out of each other.)
Planned Pauses	(Be sure any stops in your routine are on purpose.)

Tasks/Challenges:

Ⓣ You're going to work with the idea of meeting and parting. There will be five people in each group. Start by spreading apart from one another and coming together by traveling on your feet. When you get together, make any group shape you want and hold it still for a few seconds. Next, each of you leaves your group by rolling away and freezing in a shape by yourself. You need to plan your rolls so all of you come together at the same time to form the group shape, and you know exactly when to roll away.

Ⓒ Practice your routine until you can repeat it three times in a row, always doing it the same way. When you've done that, we will show the routines to the rest of the class.

❓ *Video/Digital Analysis.* Digitally recording routines provides an excellent assessment option for seeing if children can both use the rolling cues and incorporate them with smoothness to express an idea. Either teachers or peers could use a checklist to assess the tape.

Rolling and Striking

Setting: A large grassy area; a plastic ball or training volleyball or the like for each person; children by themselves initially and then in pairs

Cues

Tuck Shoulder	(Tuck your shoulder so it is rounded.)
Round Body	(Round your back and tuck your chin and knees for a good roll.)

Tasks/Challenges:

Ⓣ In a space by yourself, strike a plastic ball with any body part so you fall off balance when you strike and have to roll in the direction that you're falling. Make sure you really strike the ball before you roll, and roll in the direction you're falling, not some other direction.

Ⓣ Try to strike the ball so you have to roll in directions other than forward, such as sideways.

Ⓣ Now work with a partner. The partner throws the ball to you; you try to strike the ball back to your partner, roll, and be ready for the next throw. The thrower should always throw the ball so the striker really has to reach for it. After five strikes, change places.

Catching, Throwing, and Rolling

Setting: A large grassy area; partners; one ball or beanbag per pair

Cues

Tuck Shoulder	(Tuck your shoulder so it is rounded.)
Round Body	(Round your back and tuck your chin and knees for a good roll.)

Tasks/Challenges:

T This is a really tough task. Your partner will throw you a ball so you have to stretch and roll to catch it. Your job is to try to throw the ball back to your partner as you begin the roll. Remember, you must throw as you begin the roll, not after you've rolled. A bit of a hint here: A forward shoulder roll really works best here. After five times, switch places.

other movements. Because of time limitations, equipment requirements, safety aspects, and the normal student–teacher ratio, we do not teach rolling skills at this level. However, if you have students who have progressed to this level and enjoy the sensation these types of movements produce, encourage them to pursue out-of-school gymnastics clubs. These organizations allow children to increase their skill level beyond what we can do in a class setting.

Proficiency Level: Learning Experiences Leading to Skill Development

At the proficiency level, children enjoy aerial rolls that defy gravity and intricate combinations of rolls with

Reading Comprehension Questions

1. List several examples of weight transfer.
2. What is the most common example of weight transfer?
3. Children at the precontrol, control, utilization, and proficiency levels are ready for what types of weight-transfer experiences?
4. Which relationship concepts are typically used as a subfocus in the study of weight transfer?
5. What does the question "Do the feet come down with control?" mean?
6. What are weight-transfer tasks at the utilization level designed to do?
7. What is the difference between a spring takeoff and a step takeoff? What is the purpose of each in gymnastics?
8. Define rolling and rocking.
9. How is rolling used in dance and in games?
10. In what way is rolling a safety skill?
11. What are the characteristics of rolling for each of the four skill levels? For example, what does a control-level roll look like?
12. What is our position on spotting? Why?
13. Identify three key safety points you would observe when teaching rolling.
14. Why don't we advocate teaching backward over the head and neck or aerial rolls in physical education class?

References/Suggested Readings

Holt /Hale, S., and T. Hall. 2016. *Lesson planning for elementary physical education: Meeting the National Standards & Grade-level Outcomes*. Champaign, IL: Human Kinetics.

[NASPE] National Association for Sport and Physical Education. 1995. *Moving into the future: National standards for physical education*. St. Louis, MO: Mosby.

[SHAPE America] Society of Health and Physical Educators. 2014. *National standards & grade-level outcomes for K-12 physical education*. Champaign, IL: Human Kinetics.

Kicking and Punting

Drawn by children at Monfort, Chappelow or Shawsheen Elementary Schools, Greeley, CO. Courtesy of Lizzy Ginger; Tia Ziegler.

A young boy kicking a stone along the sidewalk as he walks home from school, a neighborhood game of kick the can, kickball on the school playground at recess, an aspiring athlete practicing the soccer (futbol) dribble, and the professional punter—all are executing a similar movement: the kick. This movement requires accuracy, body control, point of contact, force, and direction. Some children seem to perform the kick with intense concentration; others, effortlessly.

We try to give children a variety of opportunities to practice kicking so they'll develop a foundation of kicking skills they can use in different situations. For young children, the challenge is simply making contact with the ball; at the advanced level, the challenge is participation in dynamic group activities combining the skill of kicking with other skills and movement concepts. See Box 23-1 for linkages of the skill theme of kicking and punting to the *National Standards & Grade-Level Outcomes for K–12 Physical Education* (SHAPE America 2014).

Box 23-1

Kicking and Punting in the *National Standards & Grade-Level Outcomes for K–12 Physical Education*

Kicking and punting are referenced in the *National Standards & Grade-Level Outcomes for K–12 Physical Education* (SHAPE America 2014) under Standard 1: "Demonstrates competency in a variety of motor skills and movement patterns." The intent of the standard is developing the fundamental skills needed to enjoy participation in physical activities, with the mastery of movement fundamentals as the foundation for continued skill acquisition.

Sample grade-level outcomes from the *National Standards** include:

- Kicks a stationary ball from a stationary position, demonstrating two of the five critical elements of a mature pattern (K)
- Approaches a stationary ball and kicks it forward, demonstrating two of the five critical elements of a mature pattern (1)
- Uses a continuous running approach and kicks a moving ball, demonstrating three of the five critical elements of a mature pattern (2)
- Uses a continuous running approach and intentionally performs a kick along the ground and a kick in the air, demonstrating four of the five critical elements of a mature pattern for each (3)
- Uses a continuous running approach and kicks a stationary ball for accuracy (3)
- Kicks along the ground and in the air, and punts using mature patterns (4)
- Demonstrates mature patterns of kicking and punting in small-sided practice task environments (5)

* Suggested grade-level outcomes for student learning.

Skill Theme Development Progression

Kicking

Proficiency Level

Playing Cone Soccer
Playing Alley Soccer
Playing Soccer Keep-Away
Playing Mini Soccer
Kicking at a moving target
Kicking at small stationary targets

Utilization Level

Playing two-on-one soccer
Passing to a partner in general space
Kicking to a traveling partner
Kicking to a partner from various angles
Dribble and kick: playing soccer golf
Playing one-on-one soccer
Traveling and kicking for a goal
Performing a continuous dribble and change of direction
Changing directions: dribble

Control Level

Dribble: control of ball and body
Dribbling around stationary obstacles
Dribble: Traveling in pathways
Dribble: Starting and stopping
Dribbling the ball along the ground
Kicking/passing to a partner
Kicking to targets
Kicking at low targets
Kicking a rolling ball from a running approach
Kicking a rolling ball from a stationary position
Kicking to a distance zone
Kicking for distance along the ground and in the air
Kicking in the air
Kicking on the ground

Precontrol Level

Tap/dribble the ball
Approaching a stationary ball and kicking
Kicking a stationary ball from a stationary position

Kicking

Children come to us with a range of kicking abilities. Some have been involved in youth sports at a very early age; some come from families where outdoor play activities have provided rich experiences in manipulative skills. The following critical elements of kicking for distance (or force) will assist you in the selection of appropriate tasks for children as you observe their kicking:

- Nonkicking foot lands alongside the ball following a step-hop action
- Contact the ball with shoelaces (top of foot) for kicking action
- Contact with the ball is made directly **behind** center of ball (kicking along the ground) *or* directly **below** center of ball (kicking in the air)
- Arms extend for balance and trunk leans back slightly
- Follow through with kicking leg extending forward and upward toward target

The photo sequence in Box 23-2 illustrates these critical elements for kicking a ball into the air. It is important that the teacher is familiar with the critical elements needed for quality instruction, demonstration, and observation of the skill. Throughout the chapter, sample cues (short phrases or words summarizing these critical elements) are provided. Ideally, if the cue is the last thing the teacher repeats before sending the students to practice, learners are cognitively focused on the critical elements.

Whether involved in a kickball game at recess, a pick-up game of soccer in the neighborhood, or being selected as the punter for the high school football team, the skills of kicking and punting are important for successful physical activity within and beyond the school day. The skills of dribbling with feet and all its combinations (passing, shooting for the goal, etc.) are in the sport of soccer from beginning to advanced levels. The punt increases in accuracy, distance, and placement as the youngster advances from mastery of the skill to punting in football, rugby, and soccer. The entire

Box 23-2

Critical Elements: Kicking a Stationary Ball in the Air

Arms extend forward

Foot placement alongside ball

Contact slightly below center

Contact with shoelaces

Slight backward lean of trunk

Follow through

©Derek Sine & Van Tucker

spectrum of kicking experiences, from precontrol through proficiency, is represented in our progression spiral on page 439. The tasks are stated in terms that imply a direct approach (see Chapter 9), but teachers are encouraged to vary the approach according to the purpose of the lesson and the characteristics of the class. Many of the kicking tasks and challenges are best taught outdoors. If you teach the skill of dribbling indoors, a slightly deflated ball is best for control.

Precontrol Level (GLSP): Experiences for Exploration

For children at the precontrol level, kicking tasks are designed to provide opportunities for exploration with both the right and left foot as children explore dominance. Many of the tasks and challenges are designed to elicit force, which aids the student in developing a mature kicking pattern. Dribbling tasks involve gentle taps using the inside of each foot.

Kicking a Stationary Ball from a Stationary Position

Setting: A variety of plastic, foam, and rubber balls for kicking, placed around the gymnasium approximately 10 feet from the wall; sufficient spacing between students for safety (Figure 23.1).

Tasks/Challenges:

Ⓣ Place the foot you want to kick with behind the ball. Place your nonkicking foot beside the ball. Kick the ball really hard so it travels to the wall.

Ⓒ Practice until you can kick the ball three times in a row to the wall. Success equals foot contacting the ball, and ball contacting the wall.

Ⓣ Practice kicking with one foot and then with the other foot.

Ⓣ Practice kicking the ball, making it go sometimes along the ground, sometimes in the air.

❓ What determines whether the ball travels along the ground or in the air?

Approaching a Stationary Ball and Kicking

Setting: Balls for kicking, placed around the gymnasium approximately 10 feet from the wall (Figure 23.1)

Tasks/Challenges:

Ⓣ Stand 3 to 4 feet behind the kicking ball. Approach the ball and kick it forward to the wall.

Ⓣ Try again, kicking the ball as hard as you can.

Ⓣ Alternate kicking with your right foot and your left foot so you will be skilled at using either foot. Which foot is your favorite?

Ⓒ Practice until you can successfully approach and kick to the wall three times. Success equals foot contacting the ball, and ball contacting the wall.

Tap/Dribble the Ball

Setting: Children scattered throughout general space, each with a foam ball

Tasks/Challenges:

Ⓣ Gently tap the ball from one foot to the other, using the inside of your foot. Keep one foot on the ground at all times.

Ⓣ Walk through general space, tapping the ball from foot to foot—left, right, left, right—as you go. Keep the ball between your feet throughout the travel.

Ⓣ Walk through general space, tapping the ball slightly in front of you from foot to foot, avoiding collisions with others. This means you must control for the tap and control for no collisions.

Figure 23.1 Arrangement for the approach and kick of a stationary ball.

After a couple of years, the 8 1/2-inch inexpensive plastic balls become partially deflated. These half-life plastic balls are excellent for kicking, especially indoors. We mark them with a large K so children know which balls are for kicking and which are for other skills. Playground balls can also be partially deflated for beginning practice and for use indoors.

Control Level (GLSP): Learning Experiences Leading to Skill Development

At the control level, children focus on consistently contacting the ball, with a goal of a mature kicking pattern. Experiences begin with kicking for distance (force) and then progress to accuracy, kicking in different directions, and partner relationships. Most children will establish a foot preference. With some tasks and challenges, we encourage practicing with both feet as the skill is needed in some game/sport situations.

A note about cues: *Although several cues are listed for many of the learning experiences, it's important to focus on only one cue at a time. This way, the children can really concentrate on that cue. Once you provide feedback to the children and observe that most have learned a cue, it's time to focus on another one.*

Kicking on the Ground

Setting: A variety of balls for kicking—foam, plastic, rubber—placed around the gymnasium approximately 10 feet from the wall (see Figure 23.1); if space is limited, place students with a partner to alternate kicks

Cues	
Shoelaces	(Contact the ball with the top of your foot—not your toes.)
Behind the Ball	(Contact the ball directly behind center for travel forward at a low level.)
Beside the Ball	(Nonkicking foot lands beside the ball.)

Tasks/Challenges:

T When we were exploring kicking, you kicked balls that were positioned on the ground by placing your kicking foot behind the ball and your nonkicking foot beside the ball. Try a few kicks to the wall from this starting position.

T Try this kick again and focus on the shoelaces contacting the center of the ball.

T Kick the ball hard so it hits the wall with enough force to rebound back to you.

Place a series of 2-inch tape markers on the walls of the gym approximately 3 feet above the floor.

T Kick the ball so it hits the wall below the tape line. Remember, contact the ball directly behind center so it will travel at a low level.

T Practice your kicking with both your right and your left foot. In game situations, you need to be skilled with both feet.

C Practice kicking with each foot until you can kick three times in a row with each foot, with the ball contacting the wall below the tape line.

T Assume a starting position 5 to 6 feet behind and slightly to the side of the ball. Approach the ball for the kick. The cues are the same; nonkicking foot lands beside the ball and contact with shoelaces behind the ball.

T The balls for kicking are scattered around the edge of the gymnasium. Begin traveling in general space, avoiding collisions with others or the balls on the floor. On the signal, approach the ball nearest you and kick it low toward the wall. Quickly retrieve the ball you kicked and place it 10 to 12 feet from the wall. You are now ready to move again. Ready? Travel in general space. Remember to listen for the signal to kick.

? *Exit Slip.* This would be an excellent time for an exit slip to assess student understanding of one or two of the cues emphasized for kicking. The exit slip might be a drawing of a shoe with directions for the child to circle the part of the foot that should be used for contact on the ball; a verbal statement, "shoelaces" versus "toes," to a partner or the teacher; or a whisper to the teacher as each child exits the gymnasium.

Kicking in the Air

Setting: A variety of balls for kicking—foam, plastic, rubber—placed around the gymnasium approximately 10 feet from the wall (see Figure 23.1); if space is limited place students with a partner to alternate kicks; tape on the wall approximately 3 feet from the ground

Cues	
Step-Hop	(Step-hop on your nonkicking leg to complete a running approach.)
Beside the Ball	(Nonkicking foot lands beside the ball.)
Shoelaces	(Contact the ball with the top of your foot—not your toes.)
Under the Ball	(Contact the ball below center for travel upward through the air.)

Tasks/Challenges:

T Earlier we practiced kicking the ball low with a running approach. Try a few kicks with each foot. Focus on the nonkicking foot landing beside the ball and contact with shoelaces behind the ball.

T Assume a starting position 5 to 6 feet behind and slightly to the side of the ball. Approach the ball for the kick; take a small hop on your nonkicking leg, landing beside the ball. At the same time, contact the ball below center so it will travel upward. *(Demonstrate or ask a child to demonstrate the step-hop action.)*

T Practice your kicking with the step-hop, sending the ball through the air so it contacts the wall above the tape line.

C Practice kicking through the air until you can successfully complete the aerial kick five times.

? Tell the person next to you the difference between the follow-through for a kick through the air compared to that for a kick along the ground. If you said that the kicking leg goes higher for a kick through the air, you are correct.

Kicking for Distance Along the Ground and in the Air

Setting: Balls for kicking placed in a large circle in an open field space (Figure 23.2); children positioned inside the circle, facing outward. If space is limited or you are concerned about fatigue, organize students with a partner to alternate kicks.

Cues	
Step-Hop	(Step-hop on your nonkicking leg to complete a running approach.)
Beside the Ball	(Nonkicking foot lands beside the ball.)
Shoelaces	(Contact the ball with the top of your foot—not your toes.)
Behind the Ball	(Contact the ball directly behind center for travel at a low level, along the ground.)
Under the Ball	(Contact the ball below center for travel upward through the air.)

Tasks/Challenges:

T Stand inside the circle, just behind a ball, facing away from the center of the circle. You are going to review kicking along the ground and in the air. There's enough room for you to kick as far as you wish. Practice your first series of kicks standing just behind the ball—no running approach. Kick the ball so it travels along the ground at low level. After you kick, retrieve the ball and quickly bring it back to your starting place for the next kick.

The skill of kicking improves with practice.

©Lars A. Niki

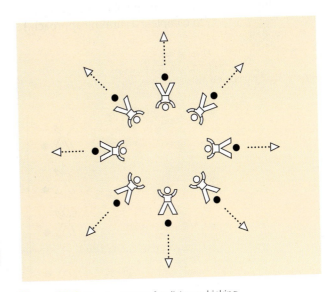

Figure 23.2 Circular pattern for distance kicking.

T Now kick the ball with your nonpreferred foot. Does the ball travel as far?

T Kick the ball with your preferred foot, sending it through the air. Remember, stand just behind the ball for the kick.

? What is the key for sending the ball along the ground? In the air? Where on the foot do you make contact for each kick? How is the follow-through different?

T Place the ball on the ground, and take three or four steps back from the ball. Approach the ball with three or four running steps, and then alternate kicking the ball along the ground (and in the air) as far as you can. Don't forget the step-hop on the nonkicking leg as you make contact.

C Practice kicking both along the ground and through the air. Challenge yourself to kick farther each time. Can you attain that distance both along the ground and in the air?

C Play a game of Call Ball with a partner. The partner calls high or low, and you respond with your kick. Can you intentionally kick high or low?

Using different-colored balls or numbering the balls 1, 2, 3, 4, and so forth, eliminates confusion about which ball belongs to which child.

Kicking to a Distance Zone

Setting: Markers placed at 10-foot intervals across the playground, numbered consecutively so the children can see the numbers from the kicking line (Figure 23.3), one ball for each child

Cues	
Step-Hop	(Step-hop on your nonkicking leg to complete a running approach.)

Beside the Ball	(Nonkicking foot lands beside the ball.)
Shoelaces	(Contact the ball with the top of your foot—not your toes.)
Under the Ball	(Contact the ball below center for travel upward through the air.)

Tasks/Challenges:

T Place the ball you are going to use at the kicking line. Approach the ball from about 5 to 6 feet and slightly to the side of the ball. Kick the ball so it travels as far as possible through the air. Note the number of the zone in which the ball first contacts the ground. Kick five times, trying to improve your distance.

C Try to kick the ball so it lands in the same zone three times in a row.

Kicking a Rolling Ball from a Stationary Position

Setting: Partners positioned 10 to 12 feet from each other, each pair with a ball for kicking

Cues	
Shoelaces	(Contact the ball with the top of your foot—not your toes.)
Behind the Ball	(Contact the ball directly behind center for travel at a low level.)
Under the Ball	(Contact the ball below center for travel through the air.)
Watch the Ball	(Focus on the ball until the ball leaves your foot.)

Figure 23.3 Numbered distance zones.

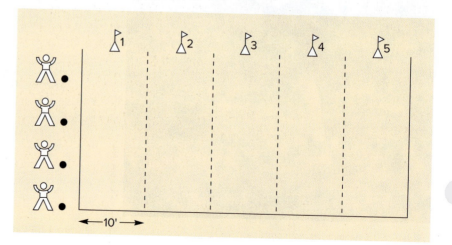

Tasks/Challenges:

T Partner 1: Roll the ball along the ground to partner 2. Partner 2: Kick the ball so it travels back to partner 1. Kick so the ball stays on the ground and only hard enough for the ball to travel the distance to your partner.

T Practice the kick along the ground with both your right foot and your left foot. **Focus on the timing of the kick as the ball rolls to you.**

T Practice the kick through the air to your partner. Sometimes in game situations you want to kick along the ground; sometimes you need to kick in the air.

C Practice until you can kick the ball along the ground five times to your partner so your partner does not have to move from self-space to retrieve the ball—five times with the left foot, five times with the right.

C Can you meet the challenge of kicking the ball through the air so your partner does not have to move to retrieve it? Give it a try!

Kicking a Rolling Ball from a Running Approach

Setting: Groups of four: one kicker (player 1), one roller (player 2), and two fielders (players 3 and 4); tape on the floor to mark "home plate"

Cues	
Shoelaces	(Contact the ball with the top of your foot—not your toes.)
Under the Ball	(Contact the ball below center for travel through the air.)
Watch the Ball	(Focus on the ball until the ball leaves your foot.)

Tasks/Challenges:

T Player 2: Roll the ball along the ground to "home plate." Player 1 is positioned two to three steps behind "home plate." Player 1: Use a running approach to kick the ball high and to the fielders. Try to kick as close to the fielders as you can. Players 3 and 4: Catch or collect the ball and return it to the roller. Rotate positions after four kicks.

T Practice the kick with both your right foot and your left foot. **Focus on the timing of the kick as the ball rolls to you.**

C Can you meet the challenge of kicking the ball through the air so the fielders do not have to move more than one step to retrieve it? Give it a try!

Kicking at Low Targets

Setting: Large targets on the wall at low level; free-standing targets placed 4 to 5 feet from the wall (Figure 23.4); a variety of plastic, foam, and rubber balls for kicking

Cues	
Point with toes	(Point your nonkicking toes toward your target.)
Inside of foot	(Swing your kicking foot and contact the ball with the inside of your foot.)
Behind the Ball	(Contact the ball directly behind center for travel at a low level, along the ground.)
Watch the Ball	(Focus on the ball, not the target, until the ball leaves your foot.)

Tasks/Challenges:

T Stand beside your kicking ball. Kick the ball toward the target, trying to hit it.

T Practice kicking at the different types of targets. Which is your favorite? Which is your best for accuracy?

C Choose your favorite target; stand 8 feet away from the target and kick. When you can hit the target two times in a row, take a giant step backward and try from that distance.

Kicking to Targets

Setting: A series of targets of different heights arranged throughout the gymnasium (Figure 23.5); a variety of balls for kicking

Cues	
Shoelaces	(Contact the ball with the top of your foot—not your toes.)
Under the Ball	(Contact the ball below the center for travel upward through the air.)
Behind the Ball	(Contact the ball directly behind center for travel at a low level, along the ground.)
Watch the Ball	(Focus on the ball, not the target, until the ball leaves your foot.)

Tasks/Challenges:

T Spaced around the gym are targets for kicking— suspended hoops to kick through, cones to kick

Figure 23.4 Target arrangement for kicking at low targets.

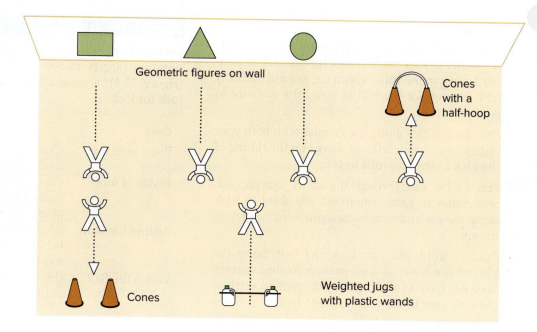

between and to hit, ropes hung between chairs for kicking over, tape squares on the wall as targets.

I'll assign you to a station; at that station, practice kicking at the target. Place the ball at the kicking line. Approach the kicking line with two or three steps before you make contact. After your turn, retrieve the ball and return to your group to wait your next turn. Continue practicing at your station until the signal is given to change to another

kicking station. You may need to adjust your force when you're kicking to hit a target. You may choose to move closer than the kicking line I have marked, or you may want to move back a step or two.

At the hoops, kick the ball through the circle. At the large and small cones, kick the ball hard enough to make the cone fall over. At the rope between the chairs and the rope stretched between the standards, kick the ball so it travels over the rope.

Figure 23.5 Targets for kicking.

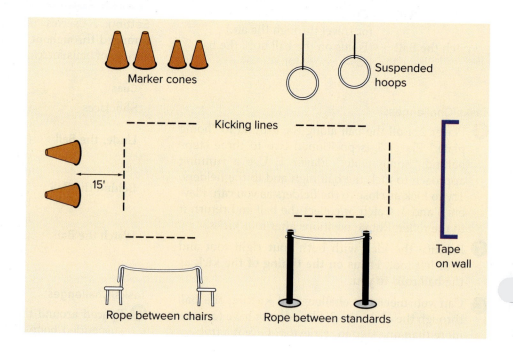

At the goals, kick the ball along the ground between the cones. At the tape square, kick the ball so it touches the wall inside the square.

Cones or tape marks on the wall can serve as goals. Vary the width of the goal according to individual abilities.

? *Peer Observation.* Station practice provides an opportune time for peer observation of cues. Designate one station, for example, cones to kick between, and have partners observe each other kicking for travel along the ground. When partners are observing for a cue, such as contact behind the ball or on shoelaces, remind the observers of their focus; accuracy of the kick is not what is being assessed. *See Chapter 12, "Assessing Student Learning," for development and recording of peer observation.*

Kicking/Passing to a Partner

Setting: Partners facing each other, 15 to 20 feet apart, each pair with a ball for kicking; two markers available for each set of partners

Cues

Sender

Point with Toes	(Point your nonkicking toes toward your target.)
Inside Foot, Not Toes	(Kick the ball with the inside of your foot, not with your toes.)
Behind the Ball	(Contact the ball directly behind center for travel at low level, along the ground.)
Watch the Ball	(Focus on the ball, not your partner, as you kick and as you receive.)

Receiver

Trap/Control	(Gain control of the ball by rotating your nonsupport leg outward/knee slightly bent, raising the nonsupport foot off the ground/toes up, and giving slightly to absorb the motion of the ball.)

Tasks/Challenges:

T Using the inside of your foot, pass the ball along the ground (or floor) to your partner, so he or she can gain control of the ball without moving from

self-space. This is called control trapping the ball. To trap, rotate the nonsupport leg outward with knee slightly bent, raise the foot off the ground with toes up, and give slightly to absorb the force of the traveling ball.

T Practice sending and receiving—kicking and trapping—with your partner. Always gain control of (trap) the ball before kicking it back to your partner. Practice the kick with both your right foot and with your left foot.

C Practice until you can kick five times to your partner so he or she can trap without moving from self-space.

C When you are comfortable with your skill and can kick accurately five times, take a large step backward and repeat the task. Practice at different distances to determine your maximum distance for accuracy with your partner.

T Place two markers between you and your partner. Using the inside of your foot, pass the ball through the markers to your partner. After trapping the ball, the partner will return the ball with a pass. If you and your partner can make 10 successful kicks and traps without missing, then both of you move back two giant steps and practice from there. Make good passes so your partner does not have to move to trap the ball.

C This time we'll play a game called One Step. Each time both you and your partner make a pass through the markers with a successful trap, both of you move back one giant step. If you miss, you both move toward each other one giant step. Determine the distance where you and your partner can accurately kick through the markers and to your partner.

C Return to where you and your partner started in the above task and add a new challenge. This is called Two Touch. You will pass the ball to your partner who will receive with one touch and return to you with the next touch. You will also receive one touch and pass on second touch. Remember give on the reception, control the ball, and return the pass. If successful, you may increase your distance by two giant steps. **Watch the ball, not your partner.**

Dribbling the Ball along the Ground

Setting: Children scattered throughout general space, with one ball per child for kicking (slightly deflated playground or soccer balls; plastic or foam balls); listening position is one foot resting on top of the ball (trap/stop)

Cues

Tap, Tap	(Gently tap the ball so it stays within 3 to 4 feet of you at all times.)
Inside of Foot	(Tap the ball with the inside of your foot—left and right.)
Open Spaces	(Look for open spaces as you travel.)
Trap/Stop	(Gain control of your ball by placing one foot on top.)

Tasks/Challenges:

Ⓣ When we were exploring kicking, you practiced tapping the ball between your feet, inside to inside. Practice that skill of gently tapping back and forth. Remember, keep one foot on the ground at all times.

Ⓣ On the signal, begin walking through general space, tapping the ball with the inside of your foot. Alternate tapping on your right foot and then your left foot; turn your feet out like a duck. When you hear the signal, gain control of your ball and place one foot on top (trap/stop).

Ⓣ On the signal, begin walking in general space, tapping the ball in the soccer dribble. Try to travel and tap with alternate feet and without letting the ball get away from you or colliding with another person. The ball should always be within one or two steps of you. Ready? Tap, tap . . . open spaces.

Ⓒ Now dribble in general space. See if you can keep it up for 30 seconds without colliding ball to ball or person to person.

As the children improve, you can increase the time to 45 seconds and then to 1 minute.

Ⓣ Begin walking in general space, dribbling the soccer ball as you go. Gradually increase your speed to a slow jog, keeping the ball within 3 to 4 feet of you at all times. Increase and decrease the speed of your travel, adjusting the force of your dribble as you increase and decrease the speed and as you approach others. When you hear the signal to stop, place one foot on top of the ball (trap/stop).

Ⓒ I will time you again for a 30-second dribble. Challenge yourself to dribble at your personal maximum speed—with control of the ball and your body.

Ⓒ We will now play a game called Perfect 10. You will begin with 10 points, and the goal is to keep as many points as you can. The game will last for 1 minute. If your ball touches another ball, a

person, a wall, or an object in the gym, you lose 1 point. Additionally, you must show control of your ball (trap/stop) within 3 seconds of the stop signal or you lose another point. Go at your best speed for control. We will start with a goal of 8 points remaining.

Ⓒ What are some strategies you used to keep your points? We will go one more time, and your goal is to improve your score.

❓ *Teacher Observation.* Teacher observation of critical elements in a dynamic, noncompetitive setting is important at this point. *See Chapters 11 and 12 for teacher observation examples.*

Dribble: Starting and Stopping

Setting: Children scattered throughout general space, each with a ball for kicking

Cues

Tap, Tap	(Gently tap the ball so it stays within 3 to 4 feet of you at all times.)
Inside of Foot	(Tap the ball with the inside of your foot—left and right.)
Trap/Stop	(Gain control of your ball by placing one foot on top.)

Tasks/Challenges:

Ⓣ Begin dribbling in general space. When you hear the signal, quickly trap the ball. Maintain a balanced, ready position (weight centered over support leg) so you can move again quickly. Ready? Begin.

This activity provides practice in stopping the ball quickly. Frequent signals will be needed: 10 seconds of dribbling, stop; 30 seconds of dribbling, stop. . . .

Ⓣ Travel through general space, dribbling as you go. Each time you meet another person, trap the ball quickly, execute a quarter turn, and continue dribbling. The ability to stop and start quickly is an important offensive skill that helps you maintain control of the ball and avoid your opponents.

Ⓒ Test your dribbling and trapping skills with this 2-minute activity: On the signal, begin dribbling in general space. Each time you hear the drum or meet another person, trap the ball, execute a quarter turn, and continue dribbling. Your goal is to stop-start for 2 minutes without losing control of the ball or bumping another person or ball. The signal at the end of the 2 minutes will be a double drumbeat. Look for the open spaces.

Dribble: Traveling in Pathways

Setting: Children scattered throughout general space, each with a ball for kicking

Cues	
Tap, Tap	(Gently tap the ball so it stays within 3 to 4 feet of you at all times.)
Inside/Outside	(Use both the inside of your foot and the outside of your foot—left and right—to tap the soccer ball.)

Tasks/Challenges:

T Dribble the ball along the ground, traveling in a combination of straight, curved, and zigzag pathways. Travel at a speed you can control—no collisions, no loss of the ball. Be sure to travel all the pathways. I should be able to identify the pathway you are traveling.

T As you dribble the different pathways, you begin to discover that the inside of the foot is perhaps not always the best surface to use for the dribble. Practice the dribble with the outside of your foot as well as the inside. **Keep the tap gentle—with control.**

Dribbling Around Stationary Obstacles

Setting: Markers positioned throughout general space; a kicking ball for each child

Cues	
Tap, Tap	(Gently tap the ball so it stays within 3 to 4 feet of you at all times.)
Inside/Outside	(Use both the inside of your foot and the outside of your foot—left and right—to tap the soccer ball.)
Heads Up	(Keep your head up to avoid collisions—people, obstacles, soccer balls.)

Tasks/Challenges:

T Dribble the ball throughout general space, alternating contact with your right foot and your left foot. Avoid bumping into the markers with either the ball or your body. Travel in zigzag and curved

pathways to avoid the obstacles. Your visual range must now include the ball you're dribbling, other people, the balls they're using, and the obstacles.

T Dribble in general space. Each time you approach an obstacle, trap the ball, execute a quarter turn to either the right or the left, and continue dribbling.

T Vary the speed of your travel—sometimes approach a marker very quickly, sometimes slowly.

T Dribble in general space. As you near a marker, tap the ball gently with the inside of your right foot, passing the ball to the left of the marker. Quickly continue the dribble.

T Dribble in general space. As you near a marker, tap the ball gently with the inside of your left foot, passing the ball to the right of the marker.

T Dribble in general space. As you near the marker, tap the ball gently with the outside of your right foot, passing the ball to the right of the marker.

T Dribble in general space. As you near a marker, tap the ball gently with the outside of your left foot, passing the ball to the left of the marker.

C This time as you practice dribbling, trapping, and turning, pretend you have 100 points. If the ball you are dribbling contacts a marker, subtract 10 points from your score. If you have a collision with another person, subtract 25 points. Try to complete your practice with 100 points!

Dribble: Control of Ball and Body

Setting: Markers positioned throughout general space; a kicking ball for each child

Cues	
Tap, Tap	(Gently tap the ball so it stays within 3 to 4 feet of you at all times.)
Inside/Outside	(Use both the inside of your foot and the outside of your foot—left and right—to tap the soccer ball.)
Heads Up	(Keep your head up to avoid collisions—people, obstacles, soccer balls.)

Tasks/Challenges:

C Thus far in our dribble study, you've practiced dribbling with control, trapping the ball, avoiding obstacles, changing the speed of your travel, traveling in different pathways and tapping the ball to

Kicking a moving ball requires visual focus and concentration.

©Barbara Adamcik

the right or the left to change directions. The game of Keeping It Perfect: Zero, Zero will give you a chance to test these skills.

Each of you has a perfect score of zero. The object of the game is to still have the perfect score at the end of the 2 minutes of activity. On the signal, begin to dribble in general space. You may travel at any speed you choose, increasing and decreasing your speed as you wish. When you hear the drum, trap the ball quickly; I'll give a verbal "Go" for you to continue.

You earn negative points if you:

- Don't trap/stop the ball within 2 seconds of the drumbeat (–1)
- Bump into another person or the ball they're dribbling (–1)
- Bump into a marker (–1)

The key is control. Ready? Go.

You can use this activity to focus on specific skills. For example, in the first 2 minutes, children are to travel in general space (control); in the second 2 minutes, they are to travel in each area of the gymnasium (speed); in the third 2 minutes, they are to zigzag around as many markers as possible (passing, accuracy).

At the end of each 2 minutes, stop, rest, and calculate your scores. Remember, a perfect score is zero.

Utilization Level (GLSP): Learning Experiences Leading to Skill Development

At the utilization level, experiences are designed for combining and applying kicking skills in unpredictable

situations of increasing complexity. Performing skills on the move and in relation to an opponent are important challenges. A great degree of accuracy and control is the goal at this level.

A note about cues: *Although several cues are listed for many of the learning experiences, it's important to focus on only one cue at a time. This way, the children can really concentrate on that cue. Once you provide feedback to the children and observe that most have learned a cue, it's time to focus on another one.*

Changing Directions: Dribble

Setting: Children scattered throughout general space, each with a ball for kicking

Cues	
Tap, Tap	(Gently tap the ball so it is always within your control—no more than 3 to 4 feet from you—even with increased speed.)
Middle of Ball	(Contact directly behind the middle of the ball, using the insides, outsides, and heels of your feet for the dribble.)

Tasks/Challenges:

T Begin traveling in general space, tapping the ball 3 to 4 feet in front of you as you go. When you are comfortable with your control of the dribble, tap the ball ahead of you, run quickly beyond the ball, tap it gently with your heel, quickly turn, and continue the dribble. Be sure you run beyond the ball to tap the front of it; contact on top of the ball will cause you to fall.

Performing a Continuous Dribble and Change of Direction

Setting: Children scattered throughout general space

Cues	
Tap/Tap	(Tap the ball with control so it stays within 3 to 4 feet of you at all times.)
Inside/Outside/Heels of Feet	(Tap the ball with different parts of your feet as you dribble.)
Heads Up	(Keep your head up to avoid collisions—people, soccer balls.)

Tasks/Challenges:

T You learned to change the direction of the ball by tapping it to the right or left with the inside or outside of your foot. And you just learned one method of changing direction front to back. Travel within the boundaries of our work area using changes of direction to avoid contact with others and to avoid crossing the outside boundaries. Your task is continuous dribbling. Ready? Begin.

T Approach a boundary quickly; use the heel tap to change the direction of the dribble at the last moment to prevent crossing the boundary.

T Purposely approach some other students; use a pass to the right or left to avoid contact with them.

C Challenge yourself by increasing your speed to the maximum rate you can travel with a controlled dribble and frequent changes of direction.

? *Self-assessment/digital recording.* As children begin combining skills, digitally recording their practice provides an excellent opportunity for self-assessment. Have them watch the recording and code the number of skills they included in their practice, for example, inside of foot, outside of foot, tapping with heel. As they watch the second time, have them assess their execution of those skills relative to the cues.

| **Traveling and Kicking for a Goal** |

Setting: Hoops scattered throughout general space; cones for goals (Figure 23.6), one ball per child

Cues	
Behind the Ball	(Contact the ball directly behind center for travel along the ground.)

Gentle Taps/ Hard Kicks	(Gently tap the ball for the dribble; kick hard for the goal.)

Tasks/Challenges:

T Travel at your own speed and dribble the ball while avoiding obstacles and other people. On the signal, travel quickly to an open space, and kick for the goal. Retrieve the ball; begin dribbling again, listening for the signal to kick for the goal.

T Practice dribbling around obstacles and kicking for the goal on your own; I won't give the signal for the kick.

| **Playing One-on-One Soccer** |

Setting: Sets of partners in general space; kicking balls; cones for goals

Cues	
Gentle Taps/ Hard Kicks	(Gently tap the ball for the dribble; kick hard for the goal.)
Heads Up	(Keep your head up to avoid collisions—people, soccer balls.)
Inside/Outside/ Heels of Feet	(Tap the ball with different parts of your feet as you travel.)
Offense	(Open Spaces . . . Look for Them, Move to Them)
Defense	(Trap or Tap to Gain Possession)

©Lars A. Niki

Dribbling in open space allows children to focus on kicking and their relationship to others.

Figure 23.6 Set-up for traveling and kicking for a goal.

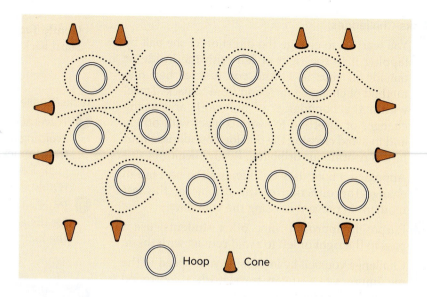

Hoop   Cone

Tasks/Challenges:

(T) Select a partner whose dribble skills are very similar to your skills. Cooperatively decide the boundaries for your area; a small area provides more practice. Partner 1 begins to travel and dribble the soccer ball within that area; partner 2 attempts to gain possession of the ball by using the feet to trap the ball or tap it away. Follow these rules:

1. Contact the ball, not the person.
2. Gain possession of the ball; don't kick it away.
3. If you gain possession of the ball, begin your dribble as the offensive player; your partner will be the defense.

If partners are unmatched in skill, give a signal for the change from offense to defense. That is, each time partner 2 gains possession of the ball, that person will give it back to partner 1, who continues to dribble until the signal to switch positions is given.

(T) Within your area, set up two cones as a goal. Partner 1 will dribble until within scoring range (10 to 12 feet of the goal) and then kick for the goal. Partner 2 will attempt to gain possession of the ball using the feet only. After each kick for the goal, switch positions.

(C) You may want to design a game using the skills of the soccer dribble and kicking for the goal. Work cooperatively with your partner to decide the rules of the game, scoring, and boundaries. Can you think of a name for your game? (See Chapter 31.)

Dribble and Kick: Playing Soccer Golf

Setting: Obstacle course arrangement (Figure 23.7); a kicking ball for each child

Figure 23.7 Soccer Golf course arrangement.

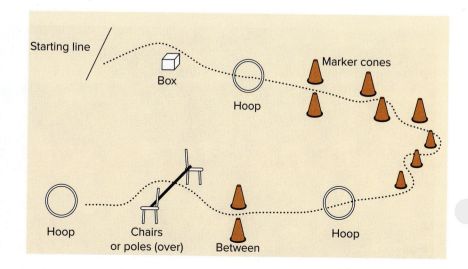

Starting line

Box

Hoop

Marker cones

Hoop

Chairs
or poles (over)

Between

Hoop

Cues

Behind the Ball   (Contact the ball directly behind center for travel along the ground.)

Under the Ball   (Contact the ball slightly below center for travel upward through the air.)

Gentle Taps/ Hard Kicks   (Gently tap the ball for the dribble; kick hard for the goal.)

Tasks/Challenges:

C The game of Soccer Golf involves the skills of dribbling in pathways, kicking for a goal, and kicking over a low height. The playground is arranged as a golf course. Your task is to complete the course with the fewest number of kicks. There are boxes to dribble around, cones to zigzag, hoops to kick through, poles to kick over and a final hoop to kick into. Count your kicks as you proceed through the course. When you finish the course, begin again, trying to lower your score.

To decrease waiting time, have the children begin at different holes on the course rather than having everyone start at the first hole.

Kicking to a Partner from Various Angles

Setting: Partners positioned 15 to 20 feet from each other, each pair with a kicking ball

Cues

Point with Toes   (Point your nonkicking toes toward your target.)

Behind the Ball   (Contact the ball directly behind center for travel along the ground.)

Foot, Not Toes   (Kick the ball with the inside or the outside of your foot, not with your toes.)

Kick Hard   (Kick the ball with enough force to send it to your partner.)

Trap/Control   (Gain control of the ball by rotating the leg outward/knees slightly bent, raising the foot/ toes up, giving to absorb the force.)

Tasks/Challenges:

T Review the skill of kicking along the ground (the floor) so your partner can trap the ball without moving (passing with your feet). When you are comfortable with the pass, take three to four steps to the right so you are at an angle to your partner. Kick the ball from this position so it travels directly to your partner. Kick with the inside of your right foot and the outside of your left foot until you can kick four out of five times directly to your partner with each foot.

T Move to the left three to four steps from your original position. Pass the ball to your partner from this angle. Practice the kick with the inside of your left foot and the outside of your right foot. Then practice with the outside of your left foot and the inside of your right foot.

T Position yourself at different angles in relation to your partner, and practice passing to your partner from these positions. The ability to kick at different angles is important in passing the ball to teammates and in kicking for a goal in games.

Kicking to a Traveling Partner

Setting: Sets of partners at one end of the playing field (gymnasium) approximately 15 feet from each other; one partner with the ball for kicking (Figure 23.8). If space allows have more than one set of partners traveling at the same time.

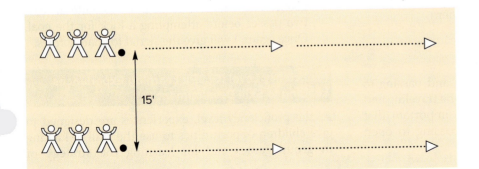

Figure 23.8 Kicking to a traveling partner.

Cues

Behind the Ball	(Contact the ball directly behind center for travel along the ground.)
Inside of Foot	(Kick the ball with the inside of your foot, not with your toes.)
Kick Hard	(Kick the ball with enough force to send it to your partner.)
Sender	
Ahead of Partner	(Kick just beyond your partner.)
Receiver	
On the Move	(Don't stop and wait for the ball. Receive, dribble, and pass.)

Tasks/Challenges:

Ⓣ Travel the length of the playing field (gymnasium) passing the ball to each other as you travel. Remember, pass to your partner while you are on the move; don't stop to execute the kick.

Ⓣ Pass the ball *ahead* of your partner so he or she can continue traveling, rather than having to stop to receive the pass.

The second set of partners may begin their travel/pass when the partners in front of them are one-third the distance of the field (gymnasium), or you may signal when each set of partners is to begin traveling.

Passing to a Partner in General Space

Setting: Sets of partners in general space, each set with a ball for kicking

Cues

Heads Up	(Keep your head up to avoid collisions—people, soccer balls.)
Pass at an Angle	(Use the inside/outside of your feet [right/left] to send the ball to your partner.)
Pass to the Open Space	(Kick the ball to the open space ahead of your partner.)

Tasks/Challenges:

Ⓣ Travel in general space, dribbling and passing to your partner. All other players will be traveling and passing at the same time, so it is important that you be aware of others and of passing to open spaces. Ready? Begin.

Ⓣ Challenge yourself always to pass the ball ahead of your partner—to the open space. If you are successful, your partner will never have to stop to receive the pass.

Ⓒ Try for five successful completions: open space, partner on the move.

Playing Two-on-One Soccer

Setting: Groups of three in general space; cones for goals; balls for kicking

Cues

Pass at an Angle	(Use the inside/outside of your feet [right/left] to send the ball to your partner.)
Pass to the Open Space	(Kick the ball to the open space ahead of your partner.)
Gentle Taps/ Hard Kicks	(Gently tap the ball for the dribble; kick hard to pass and to make a goal.)

Tasks/Challenges:

Ⓒ Form groups of three; two of you will be offensive players, and one of you will be a defensive player. The two offensive players will dribble and pass to each other within the boundaries of your soccer area. The offensive pair will try and maintain possession for 2 minutes. The defensive player will attempt to gain possession of the ball by intercepting passes or tapping the ball away on the dribble. Defense scores a point for each possession gain. At the end of each 2 minutes, I will give the signal for the defensive player to rotate to offense and one offensive player to rotate to defense, thus changing the two-on-one teams.

Ⓒ This time we will add goals so the offense can score. The offensive team will have possession of the ball for 2 minutes. See how many goals you can score within that interval; remember, there is no goalie! The offensive team must execute at least two passes before attempting a kick for the goal. Once again, I will give the signal to change roles.

Proficiency Level (GLSP): Learning Experiences Leading to Skill Development

At the proficiency level, experiences are designed to give children opportunities to use the skill of kicking in group games and for learning the strategy of

offensive/defensive participation. Children play self-designed games, or the teacher chooses the games. These games involve relationships made increasingly complex by the number of players and types of strategies required.

A note about cues: At the proficiency level, tasks are more complex, typically requiring children to coordinate several movements simultaneously in a dynamic context. A list of cues is provided to assist the children in being more successful in the learning experience. The challenge for the teacher is in determining which cue will be most beneficial for each child—and when. Thus, careful observation and critical reflection become very important as you watch the children move and then decide which cue will be the most helpful to move each learner to a higher skill level.

Angles and Open Spaces

Kicking (passing) at angles and kicking (passing) to the open space are two of the most critical skills for game play. They provide the bridge between skill mastery in a static situation and successful skill execution in a dynamic environment.

Kicking at Small Stationary Targets

Setting: Sets of cones 6 feet apart to serve as goals; a line for kicking 15 to 20 feet from each target (Figure 23.9)

Cues

Individual cues as needed

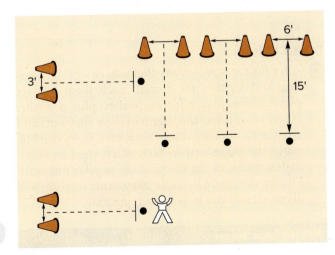

Figure 23.9 Kicking at small targets.

Tasks/Challenges:

T Each person will have 10 kicks at the goal; mentally record your personal score. After each person has kicked 10 times, move the cones closer together until they are 3 feet apart. Now kick 10 times at this target. Compare this score with your score for the 6-foot target.

T Position yourself at an angle facing the target. Repeat the tasks, kicking at an angle rather than in a direct line to the target. Compare your scores to your direct-line kicks.

C Set a personal goal for successful kicks. Practice to meet that goal for both direct and angle kicks.

T Repeat the above tasks using a dribble approach.

? *Teacher Observation.* At the utilization and proficiency levels, children's kicking should show mature patterns as well as accuracy. Checklists for recording accuracy scores can also include analysis of errors and correction cues. *See Chapter 12, "Assessing Student Learning," for the development of observation checklists.*

Kicking at a Moving Target

Setting: Sets of partners in general space (outdoors), each set with a ball for kicking and hoop for rolling (outdoor blacktop/asphalt area)

Cue

Ahead of the Target (Kick the ball to the open space just beyond the moving target.)

Tasks/Challenges:

T Partner 1 rolls the hoop along the ground. Partner 2, approximately 10 to 12 feet away, kicks the ball at the moving target, attempting to kick the ball through the hoop. After five tries, partners change places.

This learning experience reinforces kicking to the open space and kicking at angles, which were introduced earlier. Remind children to kick the ball to the space where the hoop will be, not to the space where the hoop is when they execute the kick, thus reinforcing the concepts of angle and open-space target!

Playing Mini Soccer

Setting: Markers as boundaries; children in groups of four, six, or eight

Cues

Offensive

Pass at an Angle to Teammates	(Use the inside/outside of your feet [right/left] to send the ball to your partner.)
Pass to Open Space	(Pass ahead of the receiver.)
Body Between Ball and Opponent	(Keep your body between the ball and the defender at all times; quickly switch the dribble to the outside foot.)
Defensive	
Tap or Trap	(Attempt to gain control of the ball by tapping away or trapping it.)

Tasks/Challenges:

Ⓒ With your group, design a game of Mini Soccer using the skills we have been practicing. Cooperatively decide the rules, scoring, and the boundaries. I will place only one limitation on the game: Each member of the offensive team must dribble the ball before making a kick for the goal.

❓ *Journal.* After children are involved in a dynamic kicking/dribbling situation involving combining of skills, have them reflect on their play with a journal entry. *See Chapter 12, "Assessing Student Learning," for journal entry guidelines.*

Playing Soccer Keep-Away

Setting: Children in teams of three to six; large open space

Cues

Offensive

Pass at an Angle to Teammates	(Use the inside/outside of your feet [right/left] to send the ball to your partner.)
Pass at an Open Space	(Pass ahead of the receiver.)
Body Between Ball and Opponent	(Keep your body between the ball and opponent)
Defensive	
Close the Open Spaces	(Move quickly to close the open spaces.)

Tasks/Challenges:

Ⓒ The object of Soccer Keep-Away is to keep the ball away from your opponents using dribbling and

passing skills you have been practicing. There is no kicking for the goal, only passing and dribbling in the game. To begin the game, one person throws the ball (two hands, overhead) in from the sideline. Play continues with the ball being dribbled and passed as the other team attempts to gain possession by trapping, intercepting, or gaining control of the dribble. At the end of each 3 minutes of play, I will signal for the other team to execute the throw-in to begin a new game.

Alley Soccer and Cone Soccer (below) are proficiency-level games that demand combinations of skills. Because it is rare for all the students in a class to be ready for this type of game at the same time, some children will benefit from practicing different types of kicking while others are playing the game (see Chapter 31).

Playing Alley Soccer

Setting: A playing field divided into five equal alleys (Figure 23.10); cones for goals 6 feet apart at each end of the field; six-member teams

Cues

Offensive

Pass at an Angle to Teammates	(Use the inside/outside of your feet [right/left] to send the ball to your partner.)
Pass to Open Space	(Pass ahead of the receiver.)
Body Between Ball and Opponent	(Keep your body between the ball and the defender at all times; quickly switch the dribble to the outside foot.)
Defensive	
Close the Open Spaces	(Move quickly to close the open spaces.)

Tasks/Challenges:

Ⓒ Alley Soccer is an activity that uses dribbling, passing, and kicking for a goal. Each team has six players—one player for each alley plus a goalie. Players may travel the length of their alley but can't cross into another alley. Your task is to dribble, avoid the opponent in your alley, pass to teammates, and kick for the goal. At regular intervals, I'll give the signal to rotate alleys; this rotation will allow each of you to play each position.

Playing Cone Soccer

Setting: A large cone placed at either end of the playing area with a circle (spray paint or marking dust)

Figure 23.10 Alley Soccer.

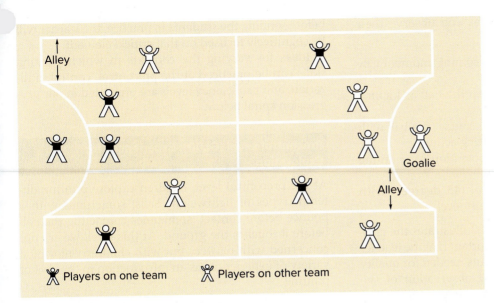

Figure 23.10 Alley Soccer.

Alley

Goalie

Alley

🏃 Players on one team   🏃 Players on other team

10 feet in diameter surrounding each cone (Figure 23.11); teams of two to six members

Cues	
Offensive	
Kick at an Angle to Teammates	(Use the inside/outside of your feet [right/left] to send the ball to your partner.)
Pass at an Open Space	(Pass ahead of the receiver.)
Gentle Taps to Dribble/Hard Kicks to the Target	
Body Between Ball and Opponent	(Keep your body between the ball and the defender at all times; quickly switch the dribble to the outside foot.)
Defensive	
Close the Open Spaces	(Move quickly to close the open spaces.)

Tasks/Challenges:

Ⓒ Cone Soccer emphasizes dribbling, passing, and kicking for accuracy. The object of the game is to kick the ball, knock over the other team's cone, and protect your own cone. No one is allowed inside the circle to kick or to defend. If one team makes body contact, the other team gets a free kick on the spot; everyone must be 3 feet away for the free kick. Points can be awarded for contacting the cone and points doubled if the cone falls over.

A good way to form teams for equal skill is to ask children to select a partner and then place the selected partners on opposite teams. We have found when given this choice, children select partners with very similar skill to their own, i.e., highly skilled with highly skilled, etc.

Punting

Punting is a form of kicking: A ball is released from the hands and kicked while it is in the air. This is a difficult skill for children to master. Because the punt involves a complex coordination of body movements—moving the body forward, dropping the ball accurately, and kicking it before it reaches the ground—we have found it best to introduce the punt after children have practiced other types of kicking.

When children first try to punt, they toss the ball up and then "kick" it with a knee or leg rather than the foot. We give children at the precontrol level round, lightweight balls and balloons, challenging them to contact the "ball" with the foot before it touches the ground. As children advance in their ability to punt, they are challenged with accuracy and placement, as well as dynamic situations such as might occur in soccer (futbol), football, or rugby. The following critical elements of punting will assist you in the selection of

← 10' →   ← 10' →

Figure 23.11 Cone Soccer. Dimensions of the playing area may be adjusted to the size of the available area and the number of players.

appropriate tasks for children as you observe their punting:

- Use a step-hop approach, becoming momentarily airborne
- Arms extend forward and drop the ball as kicking leg moves forward
- Kicking leg and foot extend to contact the ball with shoelaces (top of foot) for punting action
- Trunk leans backward in preparation for punting action
- Contact is made at knee level (45 degrees) with follow-through just beyond waist level

The photo sequence in Box 23-3 illustrates the critical elements for punting. It is important that the teacher is familiar with the critical elements needed for quality instruction, demonstration, and observation of the skill. Throughout the chapter are sample cues (short phrases or words summarizing these critical elements). Ideally, if the cue is the last thing the teacher repeats

before sending the students to practice, the learner will be cognitively focused on that critical element.

Ideas for varying the contexts in which punting skills can be practiced at the precontrol, control, utilization, and proficiency levels are presented in our progression spiral below.

Precontrol Level (GLSP): Experiences for Exploration

At the precontrol level, children explore punting different types of lightweight balls, sometimes with a bounce before contact, sometimes contacting the ball before it touches the ground. At this level, we are not concerned with mastery but with children enjoying a variety of experiences as an introduction to the skill of punting.

Dropping, Bouncing, and Kicking Lightweight Balls

Setting: Lightweight balls (plastic, foam) that bounce, positioned around the perimeter of the gym (one ball for each child), approximately 15 feet from the wall

Tasks/Challenges:

T Drop the ball to the floor. After the first bounce, contact the ball with your shoelaces, sending it to the wall.

T Try the kick with your right foot and with your left foot to determine which is your preferred foot.

C With your preferred foot, drop and kick the ball after the bounce. Repeat several times to determine your personal best.

Skill Theme Development Progression

Punting

Proficiency Level

Punting for distance and accuracy: Punt-Over
Punting while traveling
Receiving and punting against opponents

Utilization Level

Punting quickly: Rush the Circle
Punting within a limited time
Receiving a pass, then punting
Punting to a partner
Punting at angles

Control Level

Punting for height
Punting for accuracy
Using punting zones
Punting for distance
Punting different types of balls
Punting with an approach
Punting over low ropes
Punting for consistency

Precontrol Level

Dropping and punting
Dropping, bouncing, and kicking lightweight balls

©Lars A. Niki

The skill of kicking improves with practice.

Box 23-3

Critical Elements: Punting

Step, hop, punt

Drop ball, not toss

Slight backward lean of trunk

Contact at 45-degree angle with foot extended

Extend kicking leg, follow through

©Derek Sine & Van Tucker

Dropping and Punting

Setting: Kicking balls (plastic, foam) positioned around the perimeter of the gym (one ball for each child), approximately 15 feet from the wall

Tasks/Challenges:

T Stand behind the kicking line, holding the ball in both hands. Drop the ball and kick it to the wall, making contact before the ball touches the floor. This drop-kick action is called a punt.

Children who are having difficulty with the drop-kick action can benefit from practicing punting with a balloon. This helps them understand the concept of dropping—rather than tossing—the object to be punted.

Control Level (GLSP): Learning Experiences Leading to Skill Development

At the control level, children need experiences to develop consistency in contacting the ball for the punt, with the goal of a mature punting pattern. After children can consistently make contact, they are provided

opportunities to punt different types of balls, to increase distance on the punt, and to improve accuracy.

A note about cues: Although several cues are listed for many of the learning experiences, it's important to focus on only one cue at a time. This way, the children can really concentrate on that cue. Once you provide feedback to the children and observe that most have learned a cue, it's time to focus on another one.

Punting for Consistency

Setting: Lightweight balls for each child placed around the perimeter of the gym, approximately 20 feet from the wall

Cues	
Shoelaces	(Contact the ball with the top of your foot—not your toes.)
Eyes on the Ball	(Watch the ball until it contacts your foot.)
Drop	(Drop the ball for the punt; don't toss it upward.)

Tasks/Challenges:

T When we worked on punting earlier, you punted just for fun. Sometimes the ball went through the air, sometimes backward over your head, and sometimes nowhere! Today we will begin to practice punting so we can consistently kick the ball forward through the air. Stand behind the ball, holding it in both your hands at waist level. Take a small step on your nonkicking leg, and then extend your kicking foot forward. Lean over and drop the ball as the kicking leg moves forward. We are not actually kicking here but practicing making contact with the top of your foot.

T Now you will actually punt the ball. Punt the ball lightly five times. How many times did you contact the ball before it touched the floor (ground)? Continue your practice of sets of five attempting to make three or more contacts. You are not trying to punt it really high yet, just high enough for travel through the air.

T Good, you are now consistently contacting the ball before it touches the floor (ground). Now let's focus on the ball consistently traveling forward when you punt. Continue your practice with sets of five punts; mentally record how many times in each set you are successful at punting with your shoelaces and sending the ball forward to the wall.

Punting over Low Ropes

Setting: Ropes suspended between standards or across chairs at a height of 4 to 6 feet; lightweight balls for punting; sets of partners on opposite sides of the rope

Cues	
Extend	(Extend your foot to contact the ball with your shoelaces, point your toes.)
Eyes on the Ball	(Watch the ball until it contacts your foot.)
Drop	(Drop the ball for the punt; don't toss it upward.)

Tasks/Challenges:

T Stand approximately 10 feet behind the rope. Punt the ball so it travels over the rope. Your partner will retrieve the ball and punt from the opposite side of the rope.

C Give yourself a point each time you are successful at punting the ball over the rope. How many combined points can you and your partner make out of 10 trials?

? *Teacher Observation.* Before children incorporate skills into dynamic situations, observation of critical elements is very important. A teacher observation checklist is useful here.

Punting with an Approach

Setting: Lightweight balls for punting, placed around the perimeter of the gym, approximately 20 feet from the wall. *If indoor space is not sufficient for this task, move the class outside and punt away from the circle; see Figure 23.2.*

Cues	
Nonstop Approach	(Take a few running steps; then punt without stopping your forward momentum.)
Step-Hop	(Make your last step before contact a step-hop on your nonkicking leg so you'll be airborne for the punt.)

Tasks/Challenges:

T Take a series of quick steps forward. As your kicking leg moves back to front for the contact with the ball, hop slightly on your supporting leg so you are actually airborne for the contact. Quickly straighten your kicking leg at the moment of contact. (*Demonstrate or ask a child to demonstrate the step-hop action.*)

T Continue to practice the approach and punt. As you become more comfortable with the step-hop action, you will probably want to lean slightly backward as you kick to counterbalance the forceful swing of your kicking leg.

C Practice until you can punt successfully three times in a row. When I watch your punting action, I should see the following:

1. A series of quick steps
2. Your body airborne for contact
3. The ball being dropped, not tossed
4. The top of your foot (your shoelaces) extended and making contact with the ball

Punting Different Types of Balls

Setting: A variety of youth-size balls for punting—plastic, foam, rubber, footballs, rugby balls—placed around an outdoor teaching area

Cues

Extend	(Extend your foot to contact the ball with your shoelaces, not your toes.)
Eyes on the Ball	(Watch the ball until it contacts your foot.)
Drop	(Drop the ball for the punt; don't toss it upward.)
Step-Hop	(Make your last step before contact a step-hop on your nonkicking leg so you'll be airborne for the punt.)

Tasks/Challenges:

T Scattered around the practice area are punting balls of different types and sizes. Practice punting with each type of ball using your running approach and airborne action for the kick.

C Practice with each type of ball until you can punt successfully three out of five times.

T Select a football or rugby ball for punting. What is very different about this ball? Yes, all the others are round. Hold the ball with one end facing the direction in which the ball is to travel; all your other actions are the same as for punting other types of balls. Compare how well you're able to punt the football or rugby ball with your success with the other types of balls.

When footballs are added to the selection, some children may want to practice punting only with the footballs; encourage the children to practice punting with each type of ball.

Punting for Distance

Setting: A variety of balls for punting; colored jugs for use as markers; children positioned at one end of an outdoor practice area

Cues

Step-Hop	(Make your last step before contact a step-hop on your nonkicking leg so you'll be airborne for the punt.)
Extend and Connect Low	(Extend your foot and your kicking leg, making contact at knee level [45 degrees] with follow-through just beyond waist level.)
Kick Hard	(Kick hard to send the ball really far.)

Tasks/Challenges:

T Take a series of running steps, and punt the ball as far as possible. Place a colored jug at the spot where the ball first touches the ground, and then try to punt beyond that spot. Remember, making the ball travel at a 45-degree angle when you punt it gives you the best distance. **To achieve that angle, extend your foot and contact the ball at or below knee level.**

C Continue to practice your punting, trying to extend your distance with each punt. Each time you better your distance, move your marker to that spot. **Straightening your kicking leg when you contact the ball will increase your power for distance.**

When a new factor (distance) is added, children may modify their kicking patterns. Some may need verbal cues as they practice.

Using Punting Zones

Setting: Colored tape, spray paint, markers, or colored streamers to mark a series of target zones, each approximately 15 feet in length (Figure 23.12); a variety of balls for punting (target zones may be numbered, color-coded, or named for states, professional teams, etc.)

Cues

Extend	(Extend your foot and your kicking leg for a really good punt.)
Step-Hop	(Make your last step before contact a step-hop on your nonkicking leg so you'll be airborne for the punt.)
Nonstop Approach	(Take a few running steps; then punt without stopping your forward momentum.)

Tasks/Challenges:

T Approach the kicking line with a series of running steps; punt the ball for maximum distance. Mentally note the zone the ball first lands in. Retrieve the ball and be ready for another turn.

T Try to increase your distance each time.

A key component in punting for distance is practice. Keeping the same distances and codes (colors, names) for zones permits children to check themselves against their best during previous lessons.

Figure 23.12 Punting zones.

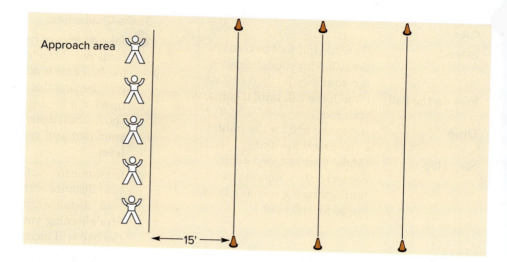

Approach area

←—— 15' ——→

Punting for Accuracy

Setting: Colored tape, spray paint, markers, or colored streamers to mark a series of target zones, each approximately 15 feet in length (see Figure 23.12); a variety of balls for punting

Cues	
Extend	(Extend your foot and your kicking leg for a really good punt.)
Step-Hop	(Make your last step before contact a step-hop so you'll be airborne for the punt.)
Hard Kick, Soft Kick	(Use a hard kick for maximum distance, a soft kick for shorter distances.)

Tasks/Challenges:

T We previously used the target zones in punting for distance. Now we will use them to focus on accuracy—making the ball land within a particular area. Practice punting with a running approach to review the skill and to determine the zone that is your best distance. Try to punt the ball consistently to that zone.

C Punt the ball five times attempting to make it land within the same zone each time.

T Punt the ball so it lands within the first target zone. To do that you must adjust the amount of force behind the kick.

T Choose a zone midway between the first target zone and your best distance. Punt the ball so it lands within that target zone.

C Select three zones as your targets. Practice until you can successfully punt three out of five balls into each of those zones.

T Repeat the process for your three selected zones using each type of ball—foam, deflated rubber, soccer ball, football. Compare your accuracy with the different types of balls.

Being able to adjust force to kick a shorter distance is an important punting skill for playing games and one that does not come easily for children. Encourage them to select zones of varying distances, not just their maximum.

Punting for Height

Setting: Colored tape, spray paint, markers, or colored streamers to mark a series of target zones, each approximately 15 feet in length (see Figure 23.12); a variety of balls for punting

Cues	
Under the Ball	(Contact the ball below center to send it upward and forward.)
Eyes on the Ball	(Watch the ball until it contacts your foot.)
Kick Hard	(Make a firm step-hop and swing of leg for good height.)

Tasks/Challenges:

T Sometimes in a game you want the ball to travel in a high aerial path rather than at a 45-degree angle so you can adjust the forward distance of the punt. What did we learn earlier about contacting a ball to send it upward rather than forward? Right, contact must be made directly underneath the ball for travel upward. You will also get more height on the punt if you contact the ball a little higher, then follow-through to just beyond waist level. Take a series of small steps, then punt the ball so it travels as high as possible.

T Punt the ball high in the air; see if you can catch it before it touches the ground.

⚠ Because of the hazard of running to catch while looking up, this task must be done in a large outdoor field space. If such a space is not available, some children can practice punting for height while others practice punting for distance.

T Select one of the first three target zones as your target area. Punt the ball so it travels in a high aerial path to that zone.

Children highly skilled in punting for accuracy will enjoy the challenge of targets. Subdividing the zones into three mini-zones works well for this. Placing a colored marker in each mini-zone denotes the target areas.

? What makes the difference between the ball traveling in a very high aerial path versus a 45-degree angle for distance?

Utilization Level (GLSP): Learning Experiences Leading to Skill Development

At the utilization level, we provide punting experiences in dynamic situations. This encourages children to use punting skills in combination with other factors, such as time and accuracy. To stress relationships with a partner, focus on punting so a partner can catch the ball or on punting shortly after receiving a pass from a partner.

A note about cues: Although several cues are listed for many of the learning experiences, it's important to focus on only one cue at a time. This way, the children can really concentrate on that cue. Once you provide feedback to the children and observe that most have learned a cue, it's time to focus on another one.

Punting at Angles

Setting: Spray paint, marker dust, or markers to designate target zones divided by width and length (Figure 23.13); lightweight balls for punting

Cues	
Extend to Target	(Extend your kicking foot and leg toward the target, to the right or left.)

Individuals and/or classes may need reminders of earlier cues (e.g., Eyes on the Ball, Drop, Step-Hop).

Tasks/Challenges:

T Practice punting into the different target zones—to the right and to the left of where you're standing.

T Select a target zone and practice until you can consistently punt the ball into that zone. Then select a zone on the opposite side.

C Practice until you can select a target zone, tell a partner which one you've chosen, and then punt three out of five balls into that zone. How about five out of five?

Punting to a Partner

Setting: Colored tape, spray paint, cones, or streamers to mark target zones, each approximately 15 feet long; partners, each pair with a lightweight ball for punting (Figure 23.14)

Cues	
Eyes on the Ball	(Watch the ball—not your partner—until it contacts your foot.)
Step-Hop	(Make your last step before contact a step-hop so you'll be airborne for the punt.)
Adjust	(Adjust your power to match the distance your partner is from you.)

Tasks/Challenges:

T Using the target zones as a measure of distance, tell your partner where to stand for the two of you to punt to each other; choose a distance at which both of you have been successful. Punt the ball so your partner can catch it without moving more than a couple of steps.

T Punt so your partner can catch without moving from self-space.

T From behind the kicking line, practice punting to your partner in each of the target zones: near/far, right/left angles.

T Punt some balls high and lofty; punt others at a 45-degree angle.

Receiving a Pass, Then Punting

Setting: Partners scattered throughout general space in an outdoor area; a variety of youth-sized balls for punting—playground balls, soccer balls, footballs, rugby balls

Cues	
Eyes on the Ball	(Watch the ball, not your partner.)
Step-Hop-Punt	(Take a couple of steps only; then punt.)

Figure 23.13 Punting at angles.

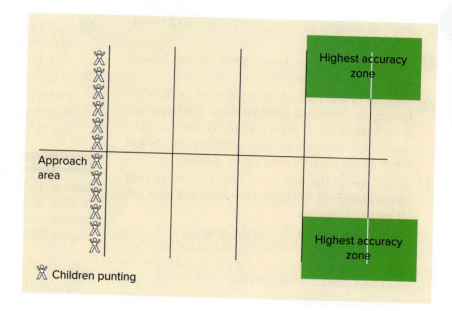

Figure 23.14 Punting to a partner.

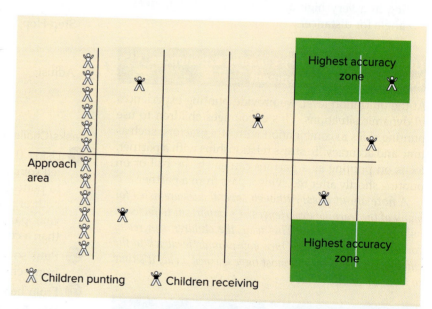

Tasks/Challenges:

T Select a partner with whom you can work well independently. Separate to a distance at which you can both throw and catch successfully. Partner 1 throws the ball to partner 2; partner 2 receives the ball and then quickly takes a couple of steps and punts the ball across the playing field. Your goal is to punt as quickly, yet correctly, as possible. Alternate positions as passer and punter.

⚠ With children throwing, catching, and punting, space awareness can be a safety factor. Organize this activity with all passes and punts traveling in the same direction—across the playing area or end to end, not in multiple directions.

Punting Within a Limited Time

Setting: Partners scattered throughout general space in an outdoor area; a variety of youth-sized balls for punting—playground balls, soccer balls, footballs, rugby balls

Cues	
Eyes on the Ball	(Watch the ball, not your partner.)
Step-Hop-Punt	(Take a couple of steps only; then punt.)

Tasks/Challenges:

T Partner 2 throws the ball to partner 1. As soon as partner 1 receives the pass, partner 2 begins to count "one alligator, two alligators, three alligators." After receiving the pass, partner 1 punts it across the playing field as quickly as possible, trying to complete the punt before partner 2 counts "three alligators." Partner 1 retrieves the ball and switches positions with partner 2. Follow all the proper steps, even though you're punting quickly.

Punting Quickly: Rush the Circle

Setting: A spray-paint or marker-dust circle drawn on a field, with a diameter of 10 feet or larger, and a passing line approximately 15 feet from the edge of the circle (Figure 23.15); children with partners; a variety of youth-sized balls for punting—playground balls, soccer balls, footballs, rugby balls

Cues	
Eyes on the Ball	(Watch the ball, not your partner.)
Step-Hop-Punt	(Take a couple of steps only; then punt.)

Tasks/Challenges:

T Select a partner whose throwing and catching skills are similar to yours. The punter will be positioned inside the circle; the passer will be approximately 20 feet away, behind the passing line. The passer throws the ball from behind the passing line. When the punter receives the catch, the passer runs toward the circle, trying to reach the circle before the punter can kick the ball. The punter punts the ball as quickly as possible when he or she receives the pass. In other words, the punter tries to punt the ball before the passer reaches the circle.

? *Digital Recording.* It would be beneficial to digitally record a game situation containing a punt

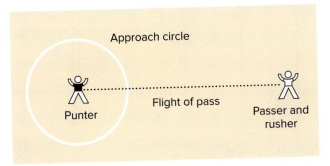

Figure 23.15 Punting quickly: Rush the circle.

with added pressure. Use self-analysis or peer analysis of the punt. To structure the observation, provide the children with lead questions: Was the punt as well executed as it was when you were not rushed by a partner? What makes the difference? Should there be a difference in the execution? What cue do you consider most critical for success in this situation? Why?

At this level of punting and kicking combined with throwing and catching, some children will enjoy developing point systems and minigames for each task. Others will continue to enjoy practicing the skill in the dynamic environment.

Proficiency Level (GLSP): Learning Experiences Leading to Skill Development

Punting experiences at the proficiency level lead to the ability to punt accurately and for distance in dynamic and unpredictable situations. The relationships are more complex. Emphasis is on punting while traveling and on working with others in game situations.

A note about cues: At the proficiency level, tasks are more complex, typically requiring children to coordinate several movements simultaneously in a dynamic context. A list of cues is provided to assist the children in being more successful in the learning experience. The challenge for the teacher is in determining which cue will be most beneficial for each child—and when. Thus, careful observation and critical reflection become very important as you watch the children move and then decide which cue will be the most helpful to move each learner to a higher skill level.

Receiving and Punting Against Opponents

Setting: Groups of three, each group with a ball for punting

Cues	
Eyes on the Ball	(Watch the ball—not your opponent))
Individual cues as needed	

Tasks/Challenges:

T Working in groups of three, two partners will assume the offensive positions of passer and punter. The other player will be the defense, attempting to block the punt. *Offense:* Partner 1 (the passer) throws the ball to partner 2 (the punter) from a distance of about 20 feet. Partner 2 punts the ball down the playing field. *Defense:* Rush the punter, starting from the 20-foot distance at which the passer is standing, to tag the punter before the punter releases the kick. You can't begin the rush until the punter receives the pass.

Alternate positions until each person has been the punter, the passer, and the defense.

Punting While Traveling

Setting: Spray paint, marker dust, or markers to indicate distance zones approximately 15 feet in length; a variety of balls for punting

Cues	
Nonstop Approach	(Take a few running steps; then punt without stopping your forward momentum.)
Step-Hop	(Make your last step before contact a step-hop on your nonkicking leg so you'll be airborne for the punt, even with a longer approach.)

Tasks/Challenges:

T Run with the ball the distance to two target zones, then quickly punt the ball. Focus on accuracy of contacting the ball for forward travel.

T Focus on making the ball land accurately in a specific zone.

T Focus on punting for maximum distance.

Punting for Distance and Accuracy: Punt Over

Setting: Spray paint or markers to indicate target zones, approximately 10 feet in length; teams of four or six players; a choice of youth-sized football, soccer ball, rugby ball, or playground ball for each team

Cues
Individual cues as needed

Tasks/Challenges:

C The object of the game Punt-Over is to punt the ball over your opponents so it lands in the end zone. You can play it in groups of four or six. Here are the basic rules:

1. Play begins with the punting team in their first zone; one person punts the ball toward the opposite end zone.
2. If the opponents catch the ball, they advance forward one zone before they punt.
3. If the opponents retrieve the ball short of the end zone, they punt from that spot.
4. The game consists of alternate punts; the number of points awarded for landing in the end zone corresponds to the zone from which the ball was punted (Figure 23.16).

The groups decide cooperatively:

1. If the defensive team catches the ball on the punt, can they run to the opposite end zone to score?
2. Can members of the opposite team rush the punter after the punter has received the pass?

Figure 23.16 Punting for distance and accuracy: Punt-Over.

Reading Comprehension Questions

1. What is the difference between a kick and a punt?
2. What is a mature kicking pattern? What is a mature punting pattern?
3. What kicking tasks lead to the development of a mature kicking pattern?
4. Describe appropriate kicking tasks for each of the four levels of skill proficiency.
5. At the precontrol level, why do we suggest using different-colored balls or numbering the balls?
6. Where does a child's foot need to be to contact the ball so it travels into the air? Along the ground?
7. What experiences do children have at each of the four skill levels when they're learning to punt a ball?
8. What is the outcome when contact is made too soon in a punt? What happens when contact is made too late?
9. List the kicking skills needed for success in soccer.

References/Suggested Readings

Holt/Hale, S., and T. Hall. 2016. *Lesson planning for elementary physical education: Meeting the national standards and grade-level outcomes.* Champaign, IL: Human Kinetics,

[SHAPE America] Society of Health and Physical Educators. 2014. *National standards & grade-level outcomes for K-12 physical education.* Champaign, IL: Human Kinetics,

Throwing and Catching

Drawn by children at Monfort, Chappelow or Shawsheen Elementary Schools, Greeley, CO. Courtesy of Lizzy Ginger; Tia Ziegler.

Throwing and catching go together just as nicely as soup and a sandwich. The two skills, however, are opposite in movement focus and unusually difficult for young children to master. It is important that they master these skills, however, as they are necessary for enjoyable participation in neighborhood games and backyard catch as well as possible participation in sports like softball, team handball, basketball, and ultimate Frisbee, to name a few.

Although throwing and catching are complementary, we've learned that children have limited success in combining throwing and catching in game situations unless each skill has been given specific attention and developed in appropriate practice situations. It is important that the teacher be certain children can throw and catch with relative success before progressing to the utilization and proficiency levels. Learning experiences at those levels—throwing to a running partner or trying to prevent an opponent from catching a ball—require mature throwing and catching skills. Too often teachers neglect catching, feeling it isn't that important. But as anyone who has ever watched a professional baseball game knows, catching is a skill that often determines whether a game is won or lost. Refer to Box 24-1 for

---

Box 24-1

Throwing and Catching in the *National Standards & Grade-Level Outcomes for K–12 Physical Education*

Throwing and catching are referenced in the *National Standards & Grade-Level Outcomes for K–12 Physical Education* (SHAPE America 2014) under Standard 1: "Demonstrates competency in a variety of motor skills and movement patterns." The intent of the standard is developing the fundamental skills needed to enjoy participation in physical activities, with the mastery of movement fundamentals as the foundation for continued skill acquisition.

Sample grade-level outcomes for throwing from the *National Standards** include:

- Throws underhand with opposite foot forward (K)
- Throws underhand demonstrating two of the five critical elements of a mature pattern (1)
- Throws underhand using a mature pattern (2)
- Throws overhand demonstrating two of the five critical elements of a mature pattern (2)
- Throws overhand demonstrating three of the five critical elements of a mature pattern, in nondynamic environments (closed skills) for distance and/or force (3)
- Throws underhand to a partner or target with reasonable accuracy (3)
- Throws overhand using a mature pattern in nondynamic environments (4)
- Throws overhand to a partner or at a target with accuracy at a reasonable distance (4)
- Throws to a moving partner with reasonable accuracy in a nondynamic environment (4)
- Throws underhand (and overhand) using a mature pattern in nondynamic environments with different sizes and types of objects (different sizes and types of balls) (5)
- Throws underhand and overhand to a large target with accuracy (5)
- Throws with accuracy, both partners moving (5)
- Throws with reasonable accuracy in dynamic, small-sided practice tasks (5)

- Combines traveling with throwing and catching in teacher- and/or student-designed small-sided practice-tasks environments (4)
- Combines manipulative skills and traveling for execution to a target (5)

Sample grade-level outcomes for catching from the *National Standards** include:

- Drops a ball and catches it before it bounces twice (K)
- Catches a large ball tossed by a skilled thrower (K)
- Catches a soft object from a self-toss before it bounces (1)
- Catches various sizes of balls self-tossed or tossed by a skilled thrower (1)
- Catches a self-tossed or well-thrown ball with hands, not cradling against the body (2)
- Catches a gently tossed hand-size ball from a partner, demonstrating four of the five critical elements of a mature pattern (3)
- Catches a thrown ball above the head, at chest or waist level, and below the waist using a mature pattern in a nondynamic environment (closed skill) (4)
- Catches a batted ball above the head, at chest or waist level, and along the ground using a mature pattern in a nondynamic environment (5)
- Catches with accuracy, both partners moving (5)
- Catches with reasonable accuracy in dynamic, small-sided practice tasks (5)

Throwing and catching are also referenced in Standard 2: "Applies knowledge of concepts, principles, strategies and tactics related to movement and performance." The intent of the standard is facilitation of learners' ability to use cognitive information to understand and enhance motor skill acquisition and performance.

*Suggested grade-level outcomes for student learning.

Source: Society of Health and Physical Educators, *National Standards & Grade-Level Outcomes for K-12 Physical Education.* Champaign, IL: Human Kinetics, 2014. Copyright ©2014 by SHAPE America. Reprinted with permission from SHAPE America - Society of Physical Educators, 1900 Association Drive, Reston, VA 20191, www.shapeamerica.org.

linkages of the skill theme of throwing and catching to the *National Standards & Grade-Level Outcomes for K–12 Physical Education* (SHAPE America 2014).

Throwing

Throwing is a basic movement pattern performed to propel an object away from the body. Although throwing style (overhand, underhand, sidearm) and purpose may vary, the basic pattern and some critical elements are similar.

When we begin to focus on throwing, we have children think of it in three phases: preparation, execution, and follow-through. The preparation phase builds momentum for the throw; the execution is the actual release of the object; and the follow-through is to maintain control and balance while using up the momentum of the throw.

It is important that the teacher is familiar with the critical elements needed for quality instruction, demonstration, and observation of the skill. Throughout the chapter are sample cues (short phrases or words

summarizing these critical elements). Ideally, if the cue is the last thing a teacher repeats before sending the students to practice, the learner will be cognitively focused on the critical elements.

The photo sequence in Box 24-2 shows the critical elements for the overhand throw.

The critical elements for throwing are:

Throwing underhand

- Face target in preparation for throwing action
- Arm back in preparation for throwing action
- Step with opposite foot as throwing arm moves forward
- Release ball between knee and waist level
- Follow through to target

Throwing overhand

- Side to target in preparation for throwing action
- Arm back and extended, and elbow at approximately shoulder height in preparation for action
- Step with opposite foot as throwing arm moves forward; elbow leads

---

Box 24-2

Critical Elements: Throwing

©Derek Sine & Van Tucker

- Hip and spine rotate to initiate throw and as throwing action is executed
- Follow through toward target and across body

In the elementary school setting, a wide range of throwing abilities among a class will be observed. To initially assess children's generic level of skill proficiency (Chapter 5), it is best to ask them to throw hand-sized objects, such as fleece balls or yarn balls, hard to open space or the wall. At this point, the teacher can observe for significant developmental characteristics. After making an overall assessment of the students' development in throwing, there is a basis for structuring appropriate instructional tasks for the class as a whole and designing intratask variations (Chapter 9) for those who might benefit from them.

(See our progression spiral for throwing and catching learning experiences below.)

When children begin throwing at a target or a partner (often at the control level), they focus primarily on hitting a target and regress to inefficient throwing patterns. What they are actually doing is using a pattern that allows them to be accurate—a pattern in which they control as many segments as possible and thus use as few body parts as possible. They have adapted their skill level to the task. Asking children to use a mature throwing pattern when throwing at a close or small target is an inappropriate request for the task. Generally, longer throws in an open field or hard throws to a large target elicit mature throwing patterns. Therefore, it is a good idea to teach throwing for distance or force before throwing for accuracy.

Skill Theme Development Sequence

Throwing and Catching

Proficiency Level

Throwing and catching while using simple offense and defense in a small-sided invasion game
Throwing, catching, and dribbling in a small-sided invasion game
Throwing and catching with a football in a small-sided invasion game
Throwing and catching with a flying disc in a small-sided invasion game
Throwing and catching in a small-sided keep-away type invasion game
Throwing at a stationary object while being defended
Throwing and catching in a small-sided invasion game
Throwing to avoid a defender
Throwing and catching in a field, run, and score game-like situation
Throwing and catching a flying disc in different places around the body with a partner

Utilization Level

Throwing while in the air
Catching to throw quickly to a target
Catching to throw quickly to a partner
Throwing flying discs at targets
Throwing at a target from different distances
Throwing for distance and accuracy
Throwing to a moving target
Throwing to make a partner move to catch
Throwing on the move
Throwing and catching different objects
Throwing and catching while traveling
Moving to catch
Catching at different levels

Control Level

Catching off a bounce
Throwing and catching over a net with a partner
Throwing and catching with a partner
Throwing a ball against a wall and catching the rebound
Catching off the fly

Skill Theme Development Sequence

Throwing and Catching (continued)

Control Level (continued)

Catching with a scoop
Throwing and catching a flying disc
Throwing backhand to a target
Throwing to high targets
Throwing underhand to targets: hoops
Throwing underhand to low targets
Throwing overhand at a low stationary target
Throwing overhand at a high stationary target
Overhand throwing for distance
Throwing underhand for distance (varying force)
Catching in different places around the body
Throwing an object to different levels and catching it
Bouncing a ball to self and catching it
All three throwing patterns: over, under, and side
Throwing sidearm
Throwing overhand
Throwing underhand

Precontrol Level

Tossing to self and catching
Drop–Catch
Catching from a skilled thrower
Catching a rolling ball
Throwing at a large target
Throwing a yarn ball against the wall

Catching

Catching is the receiving and controlling of an object by the body or its parts. Initially, a young child's reaction to an oncoming object is to fend it off, to protect self—often by using the whole body rather than the arms and hands. Typically, a ball bounces against the young child's chest as the remainder of the body scrambles to surround it and still maintain equilibrium.

Children's catching abilities, like their throwing skills, vary immensely. Until children can catch on a consistent basis in static situations, they generally have an easier time and experience more success when soft, textured, relatively large balls are used. Initially, the teacher who plans learning sessions in which young children use such as objects as beanbags, foam balls, or yarn balls can observe for the developmental characteristics of catching. (See the photo sequence for catching in Box 24-3 as a guide.) To determine children's generic level of skill proficiency in catching, have them catch a soft, larger-sized object that is thrown easily and consistently.

The critical elements for catching are:

- Extend arms outward to reach for ball
  - Thumbs in for catch above waist
  - Thumbs out for catch at or below waist
- Watch the ball all the way into the hands
- Catch with hands only; no cradling against the body
- Pull the ball into the body as the catch is made
- Curl the body slightly around the ball (specific only to certain catches)

The progression spiral for throwing and catching (page 472) has learning experiences the teacher can expand while leading children from the precontrol to the proficiency level. Initially, children need experiences that let them explore the whole action of catching—trying to accurately manipulate their arms and hands into a position to receive an object. At this level, it is important to note that children are often also at the precontrol level of throwing and thus have difficulty throwing an object accurately to themselves or to a partner, and an inaccurate throw is difficult to catch. Consequently, we have found it helpful to find ways to

Box 24-3

Critical Elements: Catching

©Derek Sine & Van Tucker

Watch   Reach   Pull

---

minimize throwing inaccuracy. We often teach the skill of throwing before catching. More skilled throwers, such as older children or parents and grandparents serving as teacher aides, can gently and accurately throw a ball to children whose throwing skills are still inconsistent. Another option would be the teacher positioned at a station throwing to the children while other students are engaged in various throwing and catching stations.

Precontrol Level (GLSP): Experiences for Exploration

For children at the precontrol level, the tasks are designed to provide exploration of a multitude of throwing and catching experiences. Many of the throwing experiences are designed to elicit distance throws, which force children to use a more mature throwing pattern. With catching, emphasis is placed on catching throws made directly to the child and on throwing in static situations, to enable success.

Throwing a Yarn Ball Against the Wall

Setting: Spots about 15 feet from the wall, one spot for each child; one yarn ball per child (*see Figure 24.1 for construction of a yarn ball*)

Tasks/Challenges:

T Throw the ball against the wall as hard as you can. Use the hand you hold your pencil with.

C Practice until you can hit the wall three times in a row.

T Practice throwing the ball with your other hand— the one you do not hold your pencil with.

T Now using your favorite hand, see how many different ways you can throw—sometimes overhand, sometimes underhand, and sometimes from the side of your body.

T This time move three steps farther away from the wall and try to hit the wall using the different throws.

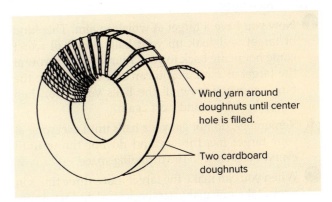

Wind yarn around doughnuts until center hole is filled.

Two cardboard doughnuts

Figure 24.1 Construction of a yarn ball.*
1. Cut two "doughnuts"—rings made from cardboard—with a diameter 1 inch larger than you want the diameter of the yarn ball to be. The center hole of each doughnut should be about 1 inch in diameter.
2. Cut several 10-foot lengths of yarn. Rug yarn is excellent, but any heavy yarn will do. A 1-ounce skein will make two 3-inch balls.
3. Place one doughnut on top of the other. Wind yarn around each doughnut (through the hole and around the circle) until the cardboard is covered and each hole is full of yarn.
4. Slip scissors between the doughnuts at the outer edge and cut the yarn all the way around.
5. Slip nylon string between the doughnuts, making a circle around the yarn in the middle. Pull tight and then make a strong knot.
6. Pull the doughnuts off and fluff the ball. You can trim any longer strands of yarn to make a smoother, rounder ball.

*Prior to constructing equipment, we recommend you check with school administration to be certain that district policy permits home-made equipment.

Move back to your first spot and try to throw a different way than you threw the first time. Practice that throw about 15 times.

For children at the precontrol level, the emphasis is on providing many throwing experiences. Varying the context too early (for example, placing children in game-like situations) causes children to use immature throwing patterns in an attempt to achieve the called-for results. Throwing experiences at the precontrol level may be used to help children determine dominant hand for throwing. For some children, the dominant side with manipulative activities may be different than for writing.

Beanbags and Throwing

Beanbags are an age-old, inexpensive, developmentally appropriate object for children to use in learning to throw. There is just one problem—some children soon learn that if they grab the beanbag by the corner it can easily be slung, harder, faster, and for greater distance. However, this throw is unsafe. One solution is to have children "cup" the beanbag in their hand. It allows for the continued use of beanbags in an appropriate manner.

Throwing at a Large Target

Setting: Several large targets suspended in various places around the room; several balls or beanbags for each child; spaces marked on the floor about 10 feet from each target for four children to throw at each target. (For the large targets, old sheets work well. Attach the top of the sheet to a broom or dowel stick, and weight the bottom with heavy washers. Attach a rope to both ends of the rod at the top of the sheet, and then hang the rope from basketball goals or rafters.)

Tasks/Challenges:

Now you have a target at which to aim. This kind of target will soak up your ball; your ball won't come bouncing back to you. Your job is to throw at the target as hard as you can and try to make the target move. Throw all the balls you have, then bring them back and start again.

Remember, do not get your balls until everyone at your target has thrown and do not throw until everyone is back to the throwing space.

When you can make the target move three times in a row, take one giant step backward and try again.

Move back to your starting position, and try to make the target move by throwing with your other hand.

When you can make the target move three times, take a giant step backward and try again.

Targets for Throwing

A student teacher once embellished Throwing at a Large Target (above) with his own creativeness. It was October, so on the target he painted the school, a full moon, corn stalks, and other autumn scenes. The children certainly threw hard to try to hit the target once there was a little colored paint and a semblance of a drawing at which to aim! You don't have to be an artist—a little tempera/poster paint, a little imagination, and a good story to tell the children are all that it takes.

Catching a Rolling Ball

Setting: Partners about 5 feet apart; one large plastic or rubber ball per pair

Tasks/Challenges:

With your partner, you're going to practice catching the ball. You should be seated facing each other, with your legs like a V. One of you rolls the ball to the other, and the other one of you catches it with your hands. The second partner then rolls the ball back to the first partner.

When the two of you can make five catches in a row, both of you should move backward a little and try again.

See if the two of you can make 10 catches without missing.

Catching from a Skilled Thrower

Setting: A skilled thrower (older students, classroom teacher, parents, or grandparents) partnered with each child; one light, medium- to large-sized ball per pair

This activity is a wonderful way to directly involve others in the physical education program. It serves as a great public relations activity. If you are in a setting where this option is not available, use throwing and catching stations with the teacher at one station throwing the ball.

Tasks/Challenges:

For this task you have a "big" partner. You and your partner will stand about 4 to 5 feet apart in your own space. Your big partner will throw the ball to you so you can practice catching. When you catch the ball, throw it back to your big partner so he or she can throw it to you again.

After you can make five catches in a row from your partner, take one giant step backward. When you can make five more catches, take another giant step backward.

Young children use extreme concentration to catch.

©Barbara Adamcik

Drop–Catch

Setting: A folded gymnastics mat for every pair of partners (if mats are not available, benches or the bottom rows of bleachers also work); one light, medium- to large-sized ball per pair

Tasks/Challenges:

T This is a fun task. One partner will stand on the folded mat or on the bottom bleacher and hold the ball in his or her hands with the arms straight out from his or her body. The other partner will stand

close so his or her hands and arms can be under the ball. The partner on the mat/bleacher then drops the ball, and the other partner catches it. After five turns, switch places.

C Say one letter of your name every time you catch. See if you can spell your name before missing.

Tossing to Self and Catching

Setting: Self-space; a yarn ball, beanbag, or light-weight ball for every child

Tasks/Challenges:

T In a space by yourself, you're going to practice tossing and catching by yourself. Toss the ball (beanbag) very close to your body, close enough so the ball (beanbag) doesn't go very high over your head or very far out from your stomach. Catch it.

T When you can toss and catch the ball (beanbag) five times in a row, keeping it very close to your body, then toss it just a little farther away and see if you can still catch it.

C This is your challenge for the day. See if you can toss and catch the ball (beanbag) 10 times in a row without moving more than one step from your space.

Control Level (GLSP): Learning Experiences Leading to Skill Development

Children at the control level still need practice developing mature throwing and catching patterns, yet they are also ready to focus on more complex learning experiences that still allow them to throw and catch in static situations. Therefore, we expose children to various contexts so they use throwing actions in different but relatively static situations that are designed to help children learn to throw for accuracy and with varying degrees of force and to throw a variety of objects.

Children at the control level of catching need opportunities to develop the skills used when catching with two hands, one hand (both right and left), on either side of the body, and at various levels. For example, they are challenged by catching at different levels, catching at different places around their bodies, and using one or two hands to catch.

A note about cues: Although several cues are listed for many of the learning experiences, it's important to focus on only one cue at a time. This way, the children can really concentrate on that cue. Once you provide feedback to the children and observe that most have learned a cue, it's time to focus on another one.

Throwing Underhand

Setting: Tape marks or spots on the floor about 15 feet from the wall; one ball per child

Cues	
Face Wall	(Your body should be looking at the wall.)
Arm Way Back	(Your throwing arm should come back behind your seat.)
Step with Opposite Foot	(Step forward on the foot opposite the hand you are using to throw.)
Follow Through	(Make your arm follow your throw straight to the wall.)

Make sure to demonstrate the throw.

Some children have a hard time remembering which foot to step with to achieve opposition. To help these children, place an old wrist sweatband around the appropriate foot as a reminder to step with the opposite foot. You can also use a large loose-fitting rubber band; some teachers have children take off one shoe to illustrate this point.

Tasks/Challenges:

T You have a big target today: the wall. The throw we are going to use is called an *underhand throw.* Standing on your spot, practice throwing underhand to the wall.

T Move back three steps and practice again.

T Move back to your first spot, and this time you will underhand throw as if you are bowling. That is right, the ball will roll all the way to the wall. **Bend your knees a little more so the ball rolls smoothly.**

T Again, move back, and try that smooth roll.

Throwing Overhand

Setting: Tape marks or spots on the floor about 15 feet from the wall; one ball per child; children alone at first and later with a partner

Cues	
Side to Target	(Make sure the side of your body away from the hand you are throwing with is toward the wall; if you were to walk straight ahead, you would walk along the wall, not toward it.)
Arm Way Back	(Bring your throwing arm way back so your elbow is almost

above your ear and your hand is behind your head.)

Step with Opposite Foot	(Step forward on the foot opposite the hand you are using to throw with.)
Follow Through	(After you throw, make your arm follow the ball. Your hand should end up almost at your knee.)

Tip: It is useful to demonstrate these cues. After the children understand them, it is easy to reduce them to one-word cues: Side, Arm, Step, Follow. Remember to focus on only one cue at a time.

Tasks/Challenges:

T At your own mark, practice throwing at the wall. Throw the ball overhand as hard as you can. **Remember, in an overhand throw, your arm comes above your shoulder.**

T Move three steps farther away from the wall and practice overhand throwing.

C This time you will have a partner, who is your coach. You throw four times, with your favorite hand, and your partner will tell you if you used each of the cues: Side, Arm, Step, Follow. (*Teachers, remember to call out one cue only, allowing both the thrower and the coach to focus on that one cue.*) The partner gives you a thumbs-up if you demonstrated the cue or a thumbs-down if you didn't. After all four throws, if you had any thumbs-down from your coach, the coach tells you which part to practice, and you practice that two times. Then switch places.

? *Peer Assessment.* Although informal, the challenge listed above is a peer assessment (see Chapter 12).

Throwing Sidearm

Setting: Tape marks or spots on the floor about 15 feet from the wall; one ball per child

Cues	
Side to Target	(Make sure the side of your body away from the hand you are throwing with is toward the wall; if you were to walk straight ahead, you would walk alongside the wall, not toward it.)
Arm Way Back	(Your throwing arm should come back sideways, behind your back.)
Step with	(Step forward on the foot

| Opposite Foot | opposite the hand you are using to throw.) |
| Follow Through | (Make your arm follow your throw across your body.) |

Tasks/Challenges:

T Now you are going to try another throw. Instead of throwing overhand or underhand, you are going to throw from the side. This is called a *sidearm throw.* To do this, bring your arm away from the side of your body and throw from a middle level. (*Be sure to demonstrate this throw.*) You would use this type of throw with a flying disc. Remember, it's not a fling. **Release the ball just as your hand faces straight at the wall.**

T After you can hit the wall eight times in a row, move back one giant step. Try again.

? Which way should your body face when you are throwing overhand? Underhand? Sidearm?

All Three Throwing Patterns: Over, Under, and Side

Setting: Tape marks or spots on the floor about 15 feet from the wall; one ball per child

Cues	
Face Wall/Side to Wall	(Remember, depending upon your throw, your body should be looking straight at the wall or be turned sideways to it.)
Arm Way Back	(Your throwing arm should come way back behind your back, head, or seat depending upon the throw.)
Step with Opposite Foot	(Step forward on the foot opposite the hand you are using to throw.)
Follow Through	(Follow your throw.)

Tasks/Challenges:

T Now that you know the names for the three different kinds of throws, you're going to practice the throws on your own. You can practice them in any order you want, but make sure you practice each one at least 15 times.

T Here's some more practice. Pick out the throw you're having the most trouble with. Practice only that throw until you can hit the wall 10 times in a row. After you can hit the wall 10 times with the

throw you found the most difficult, pick another throw you're having trouble with, and practice it until you can hit the wall 10 times in a row.

T When you can hit the wall 10 times in a row with all three throws, take three giant steps backward and try again.

? *Exit Slip.* This would be a good time to include a Helping Murgatroid (see Chapter 12) exit slip that has children explain to Murgatroid how to throw correctly.

Bouncing a Ball to Self and Catching It

Setting: Self-space; a playground ball (or tennis ball if you want to increase the complexity of the task) for each child

Cues	
Hands	(Always use your hands—not your arms or stomach—to catch.)
Watch the Ball	(Your eyes should be on the ball. You should see the ball as it comes into your hands.)

©Lars A. Niki

At the control level, remind youngsters to concentrate on the catching cues: Watch the Ball, Reach, Pull It In.

Tasks/Challenges:

T You're going to practice catching this time so you can get used to catching a ball that's coming down toward you. In your own space, bounce the playground ball (tennis ball) so it barely goes over your head, and try to catch it as it comes down, before it hits the floor.

T If you can catch the ball six times in a row, bouncing it the way you have been, try bouncing it a little higher and still catching it using only your hands. If you have to use your body to catch the ball, you know you're bouncing the ball too high.

Throwing an Object to Different Levels and Catching It

Setting: Self-space; a beanbag or yarn ball for each child

Cues	
Watch the Ball	(Keep your eyes on the ball; see it come into your hands.)
Reach	(Reach to meet the ball; don't wait for it to come to your hands.)
Pull It In	(Pull the ball toward you so your catches are soft and quiet; give with the ball.)
Thumbs/ Little Fingers	(When you catch over your head, make sure your thumbs are together; if the catch is low, make sure your little fingers are together.)

Tasks/Challenges:

T This task is to give you more practice catching. In your own space, throw the beanbag (yarn ball) up in the air and catch it. To warm up, throw the object at about head level.

T Now that you're warmed up, practice throwing the object about arm's length above your head and catching it. This makes catching a little more difficult because there's more force involved.

T Once you're able to catch the object 10 times in a row using soft, quiet catches, you're ready to throw it a little higher still, maybe 5 feet over your head. Always remember, you must still be able to catch quietly at each level you throw to. If you can't, then you know you're throwing too high and need to bring the throw down a little.

Catching in Different Places Around the Body

Setting: Self-space; a beanbag or yarn ball for each child

Cues	
Watch the Ball	(Keep your eyes on the ball; see it come into your hands.)
Reach	(Reach to meet the ball; don't wait for it to come to your hands.)
Pull It In	(Pull the ball toward you so your catches are soft and quiet; give with the ball.)

Tasks/Challenges:

T You practiced catching an object that goes to different heights; now you're going to practice catching an object that goes to different places around your body. Standing in your own space, throw the beanbag (yarn ball) so you have to reach in different places around your body to catch it. This may mean catching it to the sides sometimes or behind your head. See how many different places you can find to catch the beanbag (ball) from without leaving your self-space.

C Most of us don't like to practice places that are really hard. This time as you practice, pick out two places that you tried to catch and had the hardest time with. Practice those two places until you can catch the beanbag (yarn ball) four out of five times.

T This time practice your same catches in new places around your body. **Always try to make sure the catches are as quiet as possible.**

T Now that you have practiced catching at different places, try to use only one hand for the catch. You will need this skill for our next task.

T I'm going to make this task a little harder still. It's easy to catch the beanbag (ball) when it's fairly close to your body, but now I want you to practice

Staying in Self-Space and Catching

While many tasks ask that youngsters throw and catch in self-space, if they are pushing themselves to really accomplish the task, the balls and beanbags will often force them out of their self-space. This is the nature of the task and necessary for skill development, so it is important that they be taught how to retrieve objects when they enter someone else's space and to return to their space to resume practice.

©Lars A. Niki

Intratask variation can be used to adjust the catching task to different children's skill levels.

children all facing the same way in a line; each pair with about four beanbags, yarn balls, or tennis balls (outdoors only); four objects (spots or cones) for use as markers per pair

Cues	
Face Forward	(Your body should be looking the direction you throw.)
Arm Way Back	(Your throwing arm should come back behind your seat.)
Step with Opposite Foot	(Step forward on the opposite foot at the same time you throw.)
Follow Through	(Make your arm follows your throw straight to the target)

Tasks/Challenges:

T You're going to practice throwing for different distances using an underhand throw. One of you will start as the thrower and the other one will be the "marker." The thrower stands near the end line of the space, and the "marker" is in the open area in front. For this task, the marker only needs one cone or spot. The thrower throws one beanbag (ball) and the marker moves to that spot and places the spot or cone there. The thrower then throws the remaining beanbags (balls) with the "marker" moving each time the throw goes farther. Each time, try to beat your last throw. After you've thrown all the beanbags (balls) you have, trade places with your partner. (*If using beanbags, remind children to cup them in their hand rather than slinging them from the corner.*)

T This time you are going to attempt to adjust your distance by changing the amount of force you use. Sometimes use a lot of force, sometimes not very much force. Your partner will not need to mark these. Each time, make sure you step and follow through, no matter what amount of force you use. After all four throws, help your partner collect the balls and trade places.

C Now you're going to play an accuracy game. Your partner will need four markers. First, throw the ball as far as possible; your partner will place a marker where the ball (beanbag) fell. Your partner will now place another marker half way between you and the far marker. Try to throw the remaining balls as close to that marker as you can. Collect the balls (beanbags) you threw. Before you change places with your partner, try one more super challenge. Place another marker between the two existing markers. Place the last marker halfway

catching the beanbag (ball) so you have to reach to catch it. Really stretch so you feel you're almost going to fall over. It helps to think of keeping one foot glued in place all the time. You stretch from that glued foot—the foot can't move. This is a time you will want to use one hand to catch.

T As you're stretching to catch, don't forget to keep trying to catch in different places. So the task should be like this: Stretch and reach to catch in different places around your body.

The child's success with the previous tasks depends a great deal on the child's ability to throw so she or he has to stretch. It helps to practice stretching without the throw or simply throwing away from the body. If the students are catching without full extension away from the body, the reason may be the throw.

In conjunction with these tasks you may want to add the following: Catching with a Stretch and Curl, Stretching to Catch a Ball with a Partner, Stretching for the Jump Ball, and Twisting to Catch a Ball with a Partner (Chapter 19, pages 347–348).

Throwing Underhand for Distance (Varying the Force)

Setting: Partners; outdoors on a large field so children can work safely, or spread on one side of the gym;

between you and the closest marker. You now have four targets. Throw your first ball to the closest target. The second ball to the next one and continue. After your last throw, collect the balls and try one more time. Now, pick up all of the balls and markers and change roles with your partner.

Overhand Throwing for Distance

Setting: Partners in a large outdoor field, each pair with a bucket of about 10 tennis balls; beanbags to mark where the balls land. (You can often get old tennis balls from parents who play tennis. Send parents a note at the beginning of the year asking tennis players to save old tennis balls; collect them regularly. It doesn't take long to accumulate more balls than you need.)

Cues	
Side to Target	(Turn your hips and upper body toward your throwing hand when you pull it back in preparation to throw.)
Arm Way Back	(Pull your throwing arm way back before you begin the throw.)
Step	(Step forward on the foot opposite the hand throwing the ball.)
Follow Through	(Follow through toward the target, ending at your knees.)

Tasks/Challenges:

T You're going to practice throwing long distances—like playing the outfield in baseball. Throw each tennis ball as far as you can. With the beanbags, your partner will mark your farthest throw and collect the balls. Each time, try to beat your last throw. After you've thrown all the balls you have, trade places with your partner.

Throwing Overhand at a High Stationary Target

Setting: Targets about 5 or 6 feet high on the wall, one for each student (hoops, large paper archery targets, or drawings on a 4×4 foot paper/poster make good targets); a spot for each child (to help maintain their spacing); a ball for each child

When drawing targets at which children will throw, we do not draw faces on the targets. Putting faces on targets subtly reinforces the idea of throwing at people, a violent concept we do not support in physical education programs.

Cues	
Eyes on Target	(Your eyes should be on the target all the time.)
Side, Arm, Step, Follow	(Don't forget the cues for throwing—always use them.)

Tasks/Challenges:

T This time you're going to throw at targets. You'll have to keep your eyes on the target. Each of you has a target in your own space. See how often you can hit it.

T When you can hit your target three times in a row, take a giant step backward and try from that distance.

This same task can be changed for underhand throwing by lowering the targets to 2 to 3 feet from the floor. The second cue would change from Side to Face, Arm, Step, Follow.

More Targets for Throwing

Two student teachers came up with a great target for Throwing Overhand at a Stationary Target. They partially filled self-tie plastic kitchen trash bags with old aluminum cans. On the outside of each bag they drew a target and then inserted a coat hanger in the top of each bag, closed it, taped it for reinforcement, and hung each one from various things in the gym. The children loved it—the targets were big and made noise when they were hit. The cleanup was much simpler than with plates, more than one child could work at a target, and the targets were reusable.

Throwing Overhand at a Low Stationary Target

Setting: Partners, one ball per pair; institutional food cans or other objects stacked on benches or three to five plastic bowling pins to form a target for each pair; spots as starting points

Children love this activity because of the noise. Beware of the noise level of the cans, especially if you have a tile floor.

Cues	
Eyes on Target	(Your eyes should be on the target all the time.)
Side, Arm, Step, Follow	(Always use the throwing cues.)

asks/Challenges:

T With a partner, you're going to practice throwing at the tin cans stacked in front of you. Stand behind your spot as you throw. To start, one of you is the thrower, one of you the stacker. The stacker stands far enough behind the cans so as not to get hit if the thrower hits the cans but close enough to pick them up quickly if they topple. After six throws, trade places. The secret is in the stacking: the faster you stack, the faster the game goes.

T If you can knock the cans over two times in a row, move your spot back three giant steps and try throwing from the new distance.

Throwing for Accuracy

When practicing throwing at targets, we always try to have a throwing area for each child, group, or pair of partners to maximize the number of throwing opportunities. When accuracy is added to any manipulative action, the critical elements of the skill may be lost as children strive to hit the target. Therefore, we use several strategies to increase the likelihood of retaining the critical elements. First, we use large targets that are almost impossible to miss. Second, increasing the distance to the target increases the likelihood of using the critical elements. Third, during the learning experiences, remember to reinforce the critical elements through the use of cues and refinement tasks.

Throwing Underhand to Low Targets

Setting: Partners, each with a target on the floor (such as several 2-liter plastic bottles, weighted with sand or dirt, or three to five plastic bowling pins) and a 4- to 6-inch playground ball

Cues	
Eyes on Target	(Your eyes should be on the target all the time.)
Face, Arm, Step, Follow	(Don't forget the cues for throwing—always use them.)

Tasks/Challenges:

T With a partner, you're going to practice throwing at targets on the ground by using an underhand throw that rolls along the floor. One of you is the setter; the other is the bowler. Using an underhand throw, roll the ball and try to knock the pins over. The setter will set the pins up again and roll the ball back to you. This is like bowling. After five turns, trade places.

T If you knock the pins over twice in a row, move one giant step back and try again.

Throwing Underhand to Targets: Hoops

Setting: Partners with a hoop (on the floor between them) and a beanbag for each pair. Tape marks on the floor at various places around the hoop.

Cues	
Eyes on Target	(Your eyes should be on the target all the time.)
Face, Arm, Step, Follow	(Don't forget the cues for throwing—always use them.)

Throwing at a large target challenges youngsters at the control level.

Tasks/Challenges:

Ⓣ This time you're going to practice throwing so your beanbag lands in the hoop that's in the middle of your space on the floor. Throw the beanbag so it lands inside the hoop. Move one giant step back each time the beanbag lands in the hoop. Your partner will collect the beanbag and throw it back to you. After five throws, switch places. **Remember, the best way to do this is to throw underhand.**

Ⓒ A game you can play is called Around the World. Start in one place and try to hit the hoop. If you hit the hoop from that place, move to the next spot, and try to hit the hoop from there. You can keep adding new spots to throw from as you get better.

Throwing to High Targets

Setting: Partners, with a ball for each pair; ropes with hoops attached strung across the space (Figure 24.2) at different heights as targets: some at chest height, others above the heads

Cues	
Eyes on Target	(Your eyes should be on the target all the time.)
Side, Arm, Step, Follow	(Don't forget the cues for throwing—always use them.)

Tasks/Challenges:

Ⓣ You're going to be aiming at a high target or goal—the hoops. This task will give you good practice for basketball later. Decide how far away from your goal you want to stand. Use your overhand throw for this task.

Ⓒ This time you're going to test yourself. Pick a place to stand, and see how many throws in a row you can put through the hoop. When you make 8 out of 10 goals, move to a new spot and try for 8 out of 10 goals again.

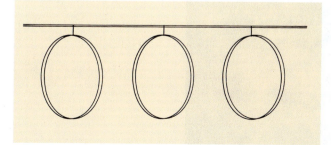

Figure 24.2 Hoops suspended from rope as targets.

Throwing Backhand to a Target

Setting: Individuals or partners; sticks (similar to horseshoe stakes) in the ground and plastic deck rings for each child

Cues	
Eyes on Target	(Your eyes should be on the target all the time.)
Throwing Side to Target	(The side of the arm you throw with should be facing the target.)
Arm Way Across Body	(Instead of bringing it to the back, bring the arm you throw with way across your body.)
Step with Same Foot	(This is one of the few times you step toward the target with the foot on the same side as the arm you're throwing with.)
Follow Through	(Make your arm follow your throw toward the target.)

Tasks/Challenges:

Ⓣ Try to throw the ring so it goes over your stick. This activity is a little different from anything you've done before, so start very close. The throwing action is also different; instead of throwing overhand or underhand, you're actually throwing sort of backward—sidearm using a flick of your wrist away from your body toward the stick. (*The teacher or a skilled child should demonstrate the throw.*)

Ⓣ If you can ring the stick six times in a row from where you're standing, move back a couple of steps and try it again.

Throwing and Catching a Flying Disc

Setting: Partners; one flying disc per pair

Cues	
Throwing	
Eyes on Target	(Your eyes should be on the target all the time.)
Throwing Side to Target	(The side of the arm you throw with should be facing the target.)
Arm Way Across Body	(Instead of bringing it to the back, bring the arm you throw with way across your body.)
Step with Same Foot	(This is one of the few times you step toward the target with the foot on the same the arm you're throwing with.)

Follow Through	(Make your arm follow your throw toward the target.)
Catching	
Watch the Disc	(Keep your eyes on the disc; see it come into your hands.)
Reach	(Reach to meet the disc; don't wait for it to come to your hands.)
Alligator Hands	(Catch the disc with one hand under the disc and one on top; clasp hands together like an alligator chomp.)

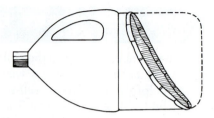

Figure 24.3 Plastic scoop. You can make scoops for throwing and catching by cutting the end and part of the side from large plastic jugs that have grip-type handles. For protection, place tape over the cut edges.*

*Prior to constructing equipment, we recommend you check with school administration to be certain that district policy permits home-made equipment.

Tasks/Challenges:

T Now you get to practice throwing a flying disc. The action involved is similar to the one you just did with the ring: a flick of the wrist to make the flying disc fly. *(A demonstration is essential here.)* Practice throwing the flying disc to the wall. Don't worry about aiming—just try to throw to the wall in front of you. You'll know you're getting better when the flying disc flies flat (not tilted) each time you throw it. Take turns with your partner. When you see the disc is going straight, back up a few steps.

T Practice throwing and catching the flying disc with your partner. Start off close together, and slowly move farther apart as you improve.

Catching with a Scoop

Setting: Individuals alone at first, and then partners; a plastic scoop (Figure 24.3) and beanbag for each child

Cues	
Watch the Bag	(Keep your eyes on the bag; see it come into your hands.)
Reach	(Reach to meet the bag; don't wait for it to come to your scoop.)
Pull It In	(Pull the scoop toward you so your catches are soft and quiet—give with the bag.)

Tasks/Challenges:

T In your self-space, practice throwing the beanbag up with your hand and catching it in the scoop. To be a good catch, the beanbag must stay in the scoop and not bounce out.

T Now your partner will throw the beanbag to you, and you'll catch it with the scoop. The partner

shouldn't be very far away to begin. After seven throws, trade places.

T The way you reach and pull in with the scoop as you catch the beanbag has changed a little now that a partner is throwing to you. **Instead of reaching up and pulling down, as you did when you caught from a throw you made yourself, you have to reach out and pull back.**

? Why is it so important to "watch, reach, and pull it in" when catching with a scoop?

Catching off the Fly

Setting: Large space; groups of three or four; one playground ball and one beanbag per group

Cues	
Watch, Reach, Pull	(Watch the ball, reach for it, and pull it in.)
Get Behind	(As the beanbag comes toward you, position your body so you are behind the beanbag, not to the side of it.)

Tasks/Challenges:

T This task could be called Catching a Flying Beanbag. We are going to practice catching a beanbag on a hop. This is like baseball players catching a baseball on a bounce. To do this, one person puts the beanbag on the ball and drops the ball. *(A demonstration would be good here.)* When the beanbag "flies" off the ball, the closest person to it catches it. Switch "droppers" after five turns.

C How many flying beanbags can you catch in a row?

Throwing a Ball Against a Wall and Catching the Rebound

Setting: A wall with enough space so the children can spread out and not be in each other's way as they throw; spots as helpful reminders of self-space; one tennis ball per child; a line on the wall 3 feet above ground and one on the ground 10 feet from the wall

Cues

Throwing

Eyes on Target	(Your eyes should be on the target all the time.)
Side, Arm, Step, Follow	(Don't forget the cues for throwing—always use them.)

Catching

Watch, Reach, Pull	(Watch the ball, reach for it, and pull it in.)
Get Behind	(As the ball bounces off the wall, position your body so you're behind the ball, not to the side of it.)
Thumbs/Little Fingers	(When you catch over your head, make sure your thumbs are together; if the catch is low, make sure your little fingers are together.)

Tasks/Challenges:

T At your spot, throw the ball against the wall, let it bounce on the ground on the return, and catch it.

T As you practice this time, try to catch the ball at stomach or chest level.

T As you practice now, sometimes throw the ball hard and sometimes soft so you have to move forward and backward to catch it.

T To make it a little harder, now try to catch the ball without letting it bounce.

T Now throw from behind the line on the ground so the ball hits the wall above the line on the wall. Catch the ball as it rebounds before it hits the ground. Give it a try.

C We'll make a game out of it this time. I'll time you for 1 minute. Count to yourself how many times you can hit the wall above the line and catch the ball in the air on the rebound. Remember the number because we'll do it again so you can try to improve your score.

Throwing and Catching with a Partner

Setting: Partners about 10 feet apart; one ball (varying the object used to throw and catch increases or decreases the complexity of this task) per pair

Cues

Throwing

Eyes on Target	(Your eyes should be on the target all the time.)
Face, Arm, Step, Follow	(Don't forget the cues for throwing—always use them.)

Catching

Watch, Reach, Pull	(Watch the ball, reach for it, and pull it in.)
Ready position	(Position your body behind the ball, feet shoulder width apart, knees bent, and hands ready.)
Thumbs/Little Fingers	(When you catch over your head, make sure your thumbs are together; if the catch is low, make sure your little fingers are together.)

Tasks/Challenges:

T Throw the ball so your partner doesn't have to move to catch it. You'll probably want to start with an underhand throw.

T If you and your partner can make 10 throws and catches from the place where you are now without missing, then both of you move back two giant steps and practice from there. Do the same thing as before: Make good throws so your partner doesn't have to move more than a step in either direction to catch.

T Try to make sympathetic throws. These are throws that have enough force to get to your partner but are not so strong your partner can't catch them.

C From wherever you are standing, see how many throws and catches you can make without a miss. To count, the ball must be caught, not just batted back to your partner.

C This time we'll play a game called One Step, which goes like this: Each time you and your partner make a catch, both of you move back one giant step; if you miss, you both move toward each other one giant step.

T Change and use an overhand throw. First, just practice back and forth. When you can make 10 in a row, move back two giant steps.

If children are relatively close to one another, don't expect mature throwing patterns. As the distance between the partners increases, you should start observing more mature patterns.

Baseball Gloves

A baseball glove is an implement that can be used to catch an object, but generally we prefer not to use gloves in our program. When children bring their own gloves to school, there are problems. Many children prefer to not share their gloves with children who don't have gloves. We also have a hard time justifying the expense of purchasing gloves for a physical education program. In the schools we've taught in, we've always wanted other equipment that needs to be purchased and is more important than baseball gloves. However, if you do have some gloves, you may want to create a task teaching experience (see Chapter 9) that provides for the use of gloves.

? *Event Task:* Have the students pretend that Sophie recently enrolled in your school. She knows nothing about catching a ball. Students are asked to explain what Sophie needs to know to catch a ball thrown to her from the front at about chest height. Instruct the students to imagine themselves practicing with Sophie and providing feedback after each attempted catch. Have them imagine looking for critical elements (ready position, hand and arm position, eye contact, and pull it in.)

Adapted from Moving into the Future: National Standards for Physical Education (NASPE 1995, p. 21).

Throwing and Catching over a Net with a Partner

Setting: Partners; nets or ropes between two chairs at various heights, enough for one per pair; beanbags and yarn balls

Cues

Throwing

Eyes on Target	(Your eyes should be on the target all the time.)
Face, Arm, Step, Follow	(Don't forget the cues for throwing—always use them.)

Catching

Watch, Reach, Pull	(Watch the ball, reach for it, and pull it in.)
Ready Position	(Position your body behind the ball, feet shoulder width apart, knees bent, and hands ready.)
Thumbs/ Little Fingers	(When you catch over your head, make sure your thumbs are together; if the catch is low, make sure your little fingers are together.)

Tasks/Challenges:

T With your partner, choose a net (rope) that you want to practice throwing and catching over and a beanbag or a yarn ball. After you've chosen your net (rope), begin throwing underhand and catching. Try to throw so the throw has an arch on it and your partner doesn't have to move more than one step in either direction to catch the beanbag or ball.

C See how many throws and catches you and your partner can make without missing. Watch the object closely. Use sympathetic throws.

T If you are really good with the underhand throws over the net, change to overhand throws.

C With your partner make a goal for how many overhand throws and catches you can do without missing? Can you make your goal?

Catching off a Bounce

Setting: Partners, each pair with a playground ball and a bench or table

Cues

Throwing

Eyes on Target and Bench (Table)	(Your eyes should see your partner and the bench [table] at the same time—they are both targets.)

Catching

Watch, Reach, Pull	(Watch the ball, reach for it, and pull it in.)
Ready Position	(Position your body behind the ball, feet shoulder width apart, knees bent, and hands ready.)

Thumbs/Little Fingers	(When you catch over your head, make sure your thumbs are together; if the catch is low, make sure your little fingers are together.)

Tasks/Challenges:

T Let's call this Bench Bounce Catch. You will need to bounce the ball on your side of the bench (table) so it travels over the bench (table) and your partner catches it. Your partner shouldn't have to move more than one step in either direction to catch the ball. Remember, the ball should bounce on the floor on your side of the bench, not on the bench itself.

T As you bounce the ball over the bench (table), sometimes bounce it with one hand and sometimes with two hands.

C Try to keep the ball going back and forth as long as you can, using the bounce throw over the bench (table). To do this, you will have to remember your quick feet. Remember, this is a throw and catch, not a volley across the bench.

Accommodating Different Skill Levels

Teachers often ask, "How do I accommodate different skill levels in one class?" More specifically, "How do I do this with little equipment?" We've found the best way is to vary the major task using intratask variation or teaching by invitation for individual children according to their needs (see Chapter 7 for more on these concepts). Often you can reduce or increase the complexity of the task without substantially changing the equipment used.

Consider the task of throwing a ball to a partner so the partner is fully extended to catch. You can reduce the complexity of this task by changing the equipment from a ball to a beanbag or by having the partner use an outstretched arm as the target. Then, by changing the task so the throw forces the partner to take a step to catch the ball, you increase the complexity of the same task.

You can make such changes by moving from group to group, observing, and modifying accordingly. In this way, the entire class is then practicing variations of the same task.

Utilization Level: Learning Experiences Leading to Skill Development

Once the children are able to perform smooth throwing and catching actions in a variety of static contexts,

they're ready for utilization-level experiences. At this level, children are given tasks that encourage refinement of skills and begin to use the skills in dynamic, unpredictable situations. Throwing tasks at the utilization level are designed to help children learn to throw while traveling, to throw accurately at moving targets, and to jump to throw. Catching experiences include catching while traveling, while in the air, and in game-like activities that require the ability to catch while moving in relationship to various objects and/or people.

A note about cues: *Although several cues are listed for many of the learning experiences, it's important to focus on only one cue at a time. This way, the children can really*

At the utilization level, children profit from stretching and/or jumping to catch.

©Lars A. Niki

concentrate on that cue. Once you provide feedback to the children and observe that most have learned a cue, it's time to focus on another one.

Catching at Different Levels

Setting: Self-space; a 7- to 8.5-inch playground ball for each child; a beanbag or yarn ball for each child

Cues	
Watch, Reach, Pull	(Watch the ball, reach for it, and pull it in.)
Thumbs/Little Fingers	(When you catch over your head, make sure your thumbs are together; if the catch is low, make sure your little fingers are together.)

Tasks/Challenges:

T In your own space, toss the ball about two feet above your head and catch it at middle level. Sometimes toss it where it comes straight down, and other times, toss it where you have to reach forward to catch it.

T Toss the ball again about two feet above your head, but this time stretch your arms and reach to catch it at a high level. Catch it before it drops to your head. Toss it a little bit higher and continue to practice this high-level catch. If you are having trouble catching it, you may be tossing it too high. *How can you get higher to catch? If you said jump, you are correct.* The secret to a jump and catch is in the timing of your jump. Practice a few times trying to jump at just the right time. Pretend as if you are pulling down a rebound in basketball.

C How many high-level catches can you make in a row? You decide if you want to add the jump.

T This next task may be harder. Toss the ball just above your head, let it bounce one time and then catch it at a low level, below your knees and as close to the floor as possible. Stand up each time you throw, and remember to toss the ball just above your head. After you catch three in a row, try to catch the ball at a low level before the bounce. A low-level catch really requires you to watch the ball all the way to your hands.

T This will be the hardest task yet—you are going to catch at different levels while moving. Start out by walking; on the first toss, catch the ball at a high level; on the second toss, catch it at a medium level; and on the third toss, catch the ball at a low level. The trick is to never stop moving so you are really catching on the move. Always remember to watch out for others. Keep practicing each time, catching at a different level until you hear the signal to stop.

C Now that you have become quite good at this, your challenge is to make a routine that involves catching at different levels on the move. Your routine must include two catches at each of the levels. It should have a clear starting point and a clear ending. Practice until you can do your routine twice in a row with no mistakes.

Moving to Catch

Setting: Individuals in self-space with a lot of extra space around each one; one ball per person

Cues	
Throwing	
Away, But Close	(Throw away from your body so that you have to move, but don't throw so far that you can't catch the ball.)
Catching	
Under or Behind Ball	(Move to a position that puts you under or behind the ball, not to the side)
Watch, Reach, Pull	(As always, watch the ball, reach for it, and pull it in.)

Tasks/Challenges:

T You're going to practice throwing so you have to move to catch. Each of you has to be in your own self-space with much space around you so you don't run into others. To begin, toss the ball so you have to move just one step to catch it—put the ball just barely out of your reach. This is a skill often used in football and basketball.

T Practice throwing and catching in all places around your body: forward, backward, and sideways.

T I see some people catching at the same place; try to catch at different places, especially toward the back of your body.

Setting: A large area (a full-size gymnasium or, preferably, outdoors in a large, open space)

Tasks/Challenges:

T This task will take a lot of concentration on your part, not only to catch the ball, but to make sure you do not run into or hurt others. It's fun, but it must be done with a great deal of safety. You practiced moving one or two steps to catch the ball; now you are going to practice moving a long way to catch. Throw the ball away from you so you have to move several steps to catch it. Make the catch; then throw again so you have to move to catch the ball. Your throws should always be catchable. In other words, don't throw so far that there is absolutely no way that you could possibly catch the ball. Start out with throws that make you move only a few steps, and then try longer throws. **Remember, if at all possible, you should be under or behind the ball when you catch it.**

T After each successful catch, see if you can throw the ball a little farther the next time. In other words, see how far you can really move to make the catch.

? *Teacher Observation.* This would be an excellent time to use a teacher observation checklist (digital-recording or live) of the critical catching elements developed at the control level. You know real learning has occurred if the children are able to catch in the dynamic situations of the utilization level using the cues.

©Lars A. Niki

Throwing and catching different objects increase children's physical activity options.

Throwing and Catching While Traveling

Setting: Individuals in self-space with a lot of extra space around each one; one ball or beanbag per person

Cues

No Stopping	(Both the throws and the catches should be on the move, with no stops.)
Throwing	
Away, But Not Too Far	(Throw away from your body so that you have to move, but not so far that you can't catch the ball.)
Catching	
Under or Behind Ball	(Move to a position that puts you under or behind the ball, not to the side.)
Watch, Reach, Pull	(As always, watch the ball, reach for it, and pull it in.)

Tasks/Challenges:

T You practiced throwing that made you move to catch, but you were standing still when you threw. Now you are going to throw and catch while moving. To begin, toss the ball into the air and catch it while you walk around the space. You must be very careful while you do this and use two sets of eyes: one to watch the ball and one to watch out for other people so you don't run into them.

⚠ Mastery of space awareness—moving in relation to others—is a prerequisite to this activity.

T If you can catch the ball almost all the time when you are walking and throwing and catching, try slowly jogging as you travel. Always watch closely so you don't collide with others.

Throwing and Catching Different Objects

Setting: A large outdoor space; partners; a variety of objects for throwing and catching (five or six of the following: junior-size footballs, foam footballs, junior-size rugby balls, lacrosse sticks and balls, scoops and balls, junior basketballs, flying discs, soft-coated softballs, etc.)

Note: This task is an example of both task teaching and divergent inquiry instructional approaches. See Chapter 9 for more ideas on these approaches.

Cues

Throwing	
Eyes on Target	(Your eyes should be on the target all the time.)

Face (or Side), Arm, Step, Follow	(Don't forget the cues for throwing—always use them.)
Catching Watch, Reach, Pull	(Watch the ball, reach for it, and pull it in.)
Ready position	(Position your body behind the ball, feet shoulder width apart, knees bent, and hands ready.)

throwing performance using a checklist provided by the teacher.

Criteria for Assessment
a. Recognizes difference in various types of throws.
b. Compares and contrasts throwing of different objects for different purposes.
c. Analyzes personal throwing skills accurately.

Adapted from NASPE (1995).

Lacrosse Sticks

The use of small lacrosse sticks is an exciting way to extend the skill theme of throwing and catching. Virtually all tasks in this chapter could be repeated with lacrosse sticks. The cues for the static throw would be:

Throw
Dominant (throwing) hand at the top of the stick; nondominant hand at bottom of stick
Nonthrowing shoulder toward target; throwing hand above shoulder
Step forward on opposite foot
Follow-through across body

Catch
Watch the ball into the pocket
Reach for the ball
Give or cradle the ball to reduce force

Tasks/Challenges:

T Today we have a variety of pieces of equipment to throw and catch. Many games and sports require good throwing and catching skills to be successful, yet some of the ways the object is thrown are different. You and your partner select a piece of equipment and attempt 20 total throws. After 20 throws, return your equipment and select another option. You will find that each piece of equipment is a little different to throw and catch. Explore a few minutes and then ask me for help if you need it.

You may wish to demonstrate with each piece of equipment before the students begin.

T Try some of the equipment again, but this time, explore underhand, overhand, and sidearm throws. Try five of each before attempting the same task with another piece of equipment.

C Now that you have explored several types of objects to throw, choose your favorite object. With your partner, design a two-person task that lets you practice the skill of throwing and catching with your favorite object. The task needs to include lots of chances to throw and catch and should be one that you enjoy doing.

C This last task asks you to solve problems about throwing and catching using a task sheet (Figure 24.4). Find a partner with whom you can work well, get one task sheet for the two of you, and a pencil. Start to work!

? *Self-Assessment/Checklist.* Following a period of working on throwing different types of objects (flying discs, footballs, deck tennis rings, with lacrosse sticks, with scoops, rugby balls, softballs, basketballs, etc.), students are asked to identify the objects they have thrown and the types of throwing patterns they have used with these objects. They are also asked to do a self-assessment of their

Throwing on the Move

Setting: A large space; partners; relatively large, stationary targets (a hoop hanging from a basket, a tire hanging from a tree, a target placed on a backstop) for each pair; one ball or beanbag per pair

Cues	
Straight Pathway	(The ball should travel in a straight pathway, not curved or arched.)
No Stopping	(The throws should be on the move, with no stops.)

Tasks/Challenges:

T With a partner, you're going to practice throwing at a target while running. Run across in front of your target, and try to throw the ball through or into your target. Your partner will give the ball back to you so you can throw again. After four throws, trade places.

T Sometimes when people perform this task, they tend to run, stop, and then throw. **What you really want to be doing is throwing as you run, so the**

Figure 24.4 Problem solving throwing and catching task sheet.

Source: Adapted from C. Chatoupis, C. 2018. Engaging students in designing movement: The divergent discovery style of teaching, *Journal of Physical Education, Recreation and Dance*, 89(3), 29–33

Solve the problems!!

Names: _____ and _____

Skill Theme: Throwing and Catching

We have practiced throwing and catching many times over the past few weeks. Now, with a partner, you have the chance to solve some problems with throwing and catching. One of you is Partner 1 and the other Partner 2. Try to find solutions to the problems below and write your answers in the spaces provided. The solutions you come up with should be new ones to you. Get a ball, find a space in gym, and start solving! You have 30 minutes.

Problem	Solution 1	Solution 2	Solution 3
1. Partner 1 stands about 3 feet away from Partner 2. Find three ways to pass the ball to each other without the ball touching the ground.			
2. Solve the same problem as in #1, but this time find three ways to do while moving forward.			
3. Solve the same problem as in #1, but this time choose a different object to throw.			
Teacher Feedback:			

throw just seems to flow out of the run and you **keep running afterward.** This time, have your partner watch you closely as you run and throw. Your partner's task is to tell you whether you stop and throw or throw on the run. Sometimes it is hard to feel what we are actually doing; partners make good observers.

Throwing to Make a Partner Move to Catch

Setting: A large space; partners; one ball or beanbag per pair

Cues

Throwing
Throw Beyond (Throw beyond your partner. Pick a spot just beyond your partner and aim for it.)

Catching
React Quickly (As soon as the ball leaves the thrower's hand, move to the spot to catch.)

Watch, Reach, Pull (Watch the ball, reach for it, and pull it in.)

Tasks/Challenges:

T With your partner, throw back and forth so your partner has to stretch or move a few steps to catch. The idea is not to make your partner miss but to force your partner to really stretch or move to catch so he or she can practice difficult catches.

In conjunction with these tasks, you may want to add the following: Stretching to Catch with a Partner While Traveling; Stretch, Catch, Release; Stretching to Catch Against an Opponent; Stretching, Curling, Bending, and Twisting Against an Opponent; and Stretching, Curling, Bending, and Twisting Against Multiple Opponents (Chapter 19, pages 351–352).

? *Event Task.* Students are to design a game of throwing and catching for one or two persons to play that requires the catching partner to move to catch. The game must include a throwing skill that makes the partner move to catch. Students write a description of the game so other students can play the game. They are also asked to describe at least two strategies that are needed to be successful in the game.

Criteria for Assessment
a. Game incorporates use of throwing skills that require the partner to move to catch.
b. Description of game adequately identifies needed skills and rules of the game.
c. Description accurately explains at least two strategies for success.

Adapted from NASPE (1995, p. 35).

Throwing to a Moving Target

Setting: A large space; partners; one ball per pair

Cues	
Throwing	
Lead the Receiver	(Throw to an open space just in front of the catcher.)
Catching	
Know Where to Go	(Know where the throw is supposed to go and run toward that spot.)
Watch Passer, Then Ball	(Watch the passer as you start to run, and then after the ball is thrown, track it all the way into your hands.)

Tasks/Challenges:

This task is an example of a convergent guided discovery instructional approach (see Chapter 9).

T We are going to practice throwing the ball to your partner, who is moving. Your ultimate goal is to throw so your partner doesn't have to stop moving or turn around to catch the ball. The thrower should remain still; the catcher jogs away from the thrower. After six tries, trade places.

? Call the class together and ask where the ball should be so the catcher can keep moving. There will be multiple responses that include: to them and in front of them.

T Let's practice again. This time try to throw the ball to the receiver. Take five turns and trade places.

? Gather the class. How did that work? Could the catcher catch without having to stop? The answer is almost always no. What should we do? Throw the ball in front of the catcher.

T This time try to throw the ball in front of the catcher. After five tries, switch places.

? Ask the class, Was the catcher able to catch without stopping? Usual answer: Sometimes. Why? Our timing was off. Sometimes it went in front, and sometimes it didn't. How could we help that? Throw to a place in front of the catcher that both of us decide on.)

T This time practice throwing to a place the two of you decide on. Seven times each and switch.

? How did that work?

T Instead of your partner running away from you, change so your partner is running across in front of you. **As before, you still throw the ball to a space in front of the runner; the runner is simply coming from a different direction.** Decide ahead of time where you are going to try to give the runner the ball.

? A similar line of questioning can be used here, if needed.

T There's one more way to practice this idea. This time the runner must be coming toward the thrower. **Again, target a space in front of the runner so the runner doesn't have to stop and turn around to catch the ball.**

T Until now, each set of partners decided where the catch was to be made. Now practice without deciding ahead of time where you'll throw the ball. This means the thrower will have to be very accurate with the throws, and the catcher will have to be always on the alert to catch the ball whenever and wherever it goes.

Throwing for Distance and Accuracy

Setting: A large space; partners; one ball per pair

Cues	
Watch the Target	(Look at your partner the whole time.)

| Side, Arm, Step, Follow | (For long throws you really have to do all of these.) |
| Almost Straight | (The ball should travel in a pathway that is almost halfway between the ground and straight up in the air—at about a 45-degree angle.) |

Tasks/Challenges:

T The object of this task is to practice throwing and catching accurately to someone far away. You and your partner need to start throwing about 10 yards apart. Throw so your partner doesn't have to move to catch the ball. You want the ball to go straight to your partner.

T If you can throw successfully 10 times to your partner 10 yards away, each of you back up two giant steps and try again. Each time you can successfully make 10 throws, back up another two giant steps. Try to find your maximum distance.

? *Exit Slip.* This is a wonderful place to use an exit slip that asks each group of partners to evaluate their throwing and catching and plan an initial activity for the next class that will let students practice what they need to work on.

©Barbara Adamcik

Shooting a basketball is a version of throwing at a target.

Shooting Baskets

In addition to throwing and catching in relation to others, the game of basketball involves a specific type of throwing at a target—shooting a basket. When children are first learning the skill of shooting baskets, the following cues will be helpful:

Preparation

- Keep eyes focused on the goal.
- Bend the knees.
- Keep elbows close to the body, not extended outward from the body.
- Place hands behind the ball, fingers (not palms) touching the ball.

Release

- Push the ball upward from the chest toward the basket.
- Extend legs as arms extend toward the target.
- Arch the ball upward and over the front rim of the basket.

Throwing at a Target from Different Distances

Setting: A large space; stationary targets in various places (against baseball backstops, trees, or playground apparatus) around the space

Cues	
Watch the Target	(Look at the target the whole time.)
Side, Arm, Step, Follow	(For long throws you really have to do all of these.)

| Almost Straight | (The ball should travel in a pathway that is almost halfway between the ground and straight up in the air—at about a 45-degree angle.) |

Tasks/Challenges:

T The task is now to try to hit the target from far away. Start close enough so you know you can hit the target. When you hit it three times, back up about five steps and throw again. After five successful throws, back up again.

C See how far you can get and still hit the target.

C See how many throws out of 10 you can make right to the target.

Throwing Flying Discs at Targets

Setting: A flying disc for each student; a flying disc golf course: Use hoops tied between two chairs or hoops suspended from trees as targets. The distance and angle of the targets from the starting lines can vary, depending on the amount of space available and the skill of the students. Trees, playground apparatus, fences, or backstops can be used as obstacles to throw over and around.

Cues	
Watch Target	(Always look at the target.)
Throwing Side to Target	(The side of the arm you throw with should be facing the target.)
Arm Way Across Body	(Instead of bringing it to the back, bring the arm you throw with way across your body.)
Step with Same Foot	(This is one of the few times that you step toward the target with the foot on the same side as the arm you're throwing with.)
Follow Through	(Make your arm follow your throw toward the target.)

Tasks/Challenges:

C The name of this game could be Disc Golf. The object is to throw the disc for distance, and often around obstacles, eventually placing it through a

target hoop. You want to use as few throws as possible. Here are the rules:

1. All players make their first throw from behind the starting line.
2. Players make the second throw and all throws after that from the landing spot of the previous throw. Players are allowed to take one step in throwing.
3. Players count how many throws were needed to place the disc through the hoop.

Catching to Throw Quickly to a Partner

Setting: Partners; one ball or beanbag per pair

Cues	
Move and Face	(Move toward the approaching ball and begin to face the direction you are to throw.) *It is helpful to demonstrate this cue.*
Flow	(The catch and the throw should flow together; simply move directly into the throw.)

Tasks/Challenges:

T Sometimes it is necessary to throw very quickly after you catch the ball, much as baseball players do when they are trying to make a double play. With your partner you are going to practice throwing quickly after catching. Your partner will throw the ball to you; you throw it back as quickly as possible, like a hot potato. The throw to your partner needs to be accurate as well as quick. To begin, one of you practices quick throws; the other one simply makes the first throw and is a target. After seven throws, switch places.

T Repeat the task with the partner starting the task throwing the ball sometimes really high (like a pop-fly in baseball or softball) and sometimes throwing so the catching partner has to move right or left a little for a successful catch.

T When most of the throws go directly to your partner, back up a few steps and try the task again.

T This time we are going to repeat the task with a slight change. Your partner will roll the ball to you; you catch it and quickly throw it back. After five rolls, switch places. When you find you are quite good at this, you may want to make the roll a little faster.

T Now try rolling the ball to either side of your partner. Again, change places after five turns.

T Now, to make the task even harder, try to catch the ball with one hand and throw it with the same hand.

This is almost as if you don't really want to hold the ball—as if you need to get rid of the ball quickly. You may want to use a softer ball for this task.

In conjunction with these tasks, you may want to add the following: Jumping to Catch and Jumping to Throw (Chapter 20, pages 368–370).

Catching to Throw Quickly to a Target

Setting: Partners; fairly large (2-by-2-feet) targets spread around the area

Cues	
Move and Face	(Move toward the approaching ball and begin to face the direction you are to throw.) *It is helpful to demonstrate this cue.*
Flow	(The catch and the throw should flow together; simply move directly into the throw.)

Tasks/Challenges:

T With your partner, you're going to practice catching and throwing quickly to a target. This skill is used, for example, in the game of team handball. Your partner throws you the ball; you catch it and quickly throw it to the target. You're trying for a quick throw so no one can block your shot. After six times, switch places.

C See how many times out of 10 you can hit the target. **Remember, quick throws only**; ones that stop don't count. Your partner is the judge.

Many of the throwing and catching skills at the utilization level can be transformed into game-like situations for children. Some children at this level enjoy practicing in non-game contexts, whereas others are interested in practicing only if the skill is used in a game-like situation. Generally, these are the children who continually want to know, "When do we get to play the game?"

Throwing While in the Air

Setting: A large grassy space; partners; one ball or beanbag per group; partners initially and then groups of four

Cues	
Face Target	(When you are in the air, your upper body should be facing the target.)
Follow	(Follow through to the target.)

Throw in Air	(Be in the air when you throw; don't jump, land, and then throw.)

Tasks/Challenges:

T Sometimes when you throw, you need to be in the air. This type of throwing is harder than throwing when you're on the ground. To start, run a few steps, jump in the air, and throw the ball to your partner while you're in the air. Make the throw as accurate as possible.

T Often when people practice this task they aren't in the air when they think they are. Sometimes people run, throw, and then jump; sometimes they run, jump, land, and then throw. It's hard to tell exactly what you're doing without some help. So for this experience, you will need to join another set of partners. One set of partners will observe very carefully to see if throwers are really in the air as they throw. For now, the extra partners take the place of the teacher—the observers should tell you exactly what they saw. After eight throws, switch throwers and observers, but not before feedback is given to the first set of throwers.

In conjunction with these tasks, you may want to add the following: Throwing and Catching While Jumping (Chapter 20, page 370–371).

Proficiency Level: Learning Experiences Leading to Skill Development

Children are at the proficiency level of throwing and catching when they are able to throw and catch effectively in unpredictable, dynamic contexts. They are ready to practice throwing and catching as it's used in the relatively complex and changing environments in combination with other skills in game-like situations. Experiences at the proficiency level include throwing and catching in relation to an opponent who attempts to prevent the throw or the catch. These tasks foster development of consistent degrees of accuracy and distance in throwing. Children learn to catch a variety of objects while traveling rapidly and suddenly changing direction and level.

Many of the learning experiences at the proficiency level resemble traditional games. Yet they are designed to enhance skill development. Thus they are all intended to be played in small groups with multiple games being played at once. They are not meant to be played with large groups, for if we played with large groups, many students would be waiting and not participating. Strategies for achieving maximum activity in game settings are included in Chapter 31.

A note about cues: *At the proficiency level, tasks are more complex, typically requiring children to coordinate*

several movements simultaneously in a dynamic context. A list of cues is provided to assist the children in being more successful in the learning experiences. The challenge is in determining which cue will be most beneficial for each child—and when. Thus, careful observation and critical reflection become very important as you watch the children move and then decide which cue will be the most helpful to move each learner to a higher level.

Throwing and Catching a Flying Disc in Different Places Around the Body with a Partner

Setting: A large space; partners; one flying disc per pair

Cues
Catching
Behind and Under (Move so you are behind and under the disc when you catch it.)
Watch, Reach, Pull (Watch the disc, reach for it, and pull it in to your body.)
Alligator Hands (Catch the disc with one hand under the disc and one on top; clasp hands together like an alligator chomp)
Throwing
Throw Away (Pick a spot just barely out of your partner's reach and aim for it.)

Tasks/Challenges:

C The object of this activity is to throw the flying disc so your partner has to stretch to catch it. The scoring is this: If the flying disc is caught, that counts as one point. If the body is stretched a long way while reaching to catch the flying disc, that counts as three points. I'm going to throw a few to Mary. Let's watch to see how many points she'll get for each of her catches. (*Select a skilled catcher and throw, or have someone else throw the flying disc so the catcher has to stretch to make the catch.*)

C You may want to change the way you score the game. You can work together to see how many points you can make; or you may want to play against your partner. Remember, though, you'll have to make good throws if your partner is going to have a chance.

Throwing and Catching in a Field, Run, and Score Game-like Situation

Setting: Two teams, four players each; four bases as in baseball; one ball

Cues
Watch Target (Your eyes should always watch the target. This time it is the catcher's chest.)
Move and Face (Move toward the approaching ball and begin to face the direction you are to throw.)
Flow (The catch and the throw should flow together; simply move directly into the throw.)

Tasks/Challenges:

C The object in this situation is to throw a ball around the bases twice before a runner can circle the bases once. Here are the rules:

1. The fielding team places a player at each base—first, second, third, and home plate.
2. The player at home plate (the catcher) begins with the ball. On the signal, two runners try to run the bases before the fielders throw the ball to each base twice.
3. If the runners travel the bases before the fielders throw and catch the ball twice, they score a run. If all the fielders throw and catch twice before the runners circle the bases, it's an out.
4. After three outs or when all runners have had a chance to run the bases twice, the teams switch roles.

Adjust the distance between the bases according to the throwers' ability and the runners' speed. For safety, place hoops for the throwers just within the base pathway.

A Thematic Approach to Games

Almond (1986) proposed a thematic approach to classifying games that is now used in Tactical Games approach (Griffin, Mitchell, and Oslin, 2013). The approach, which classifies games according to conditions, goals, and tactics used to play the game versus individual sports, parallels the notion of skill themes, and we have chosen to use it here. Striking and fielding games involve games in which an object is struck into a space defended by players with accuracy and force so the striker can run between two points. Invasion games involve two groups invading the other's space to score, and net/wall games include those activities that require striking an object into court space so an opponent cannot return it. We have chosen to use these designations as they allow more options for youngsters without "trapping" them (or us) into preconceived notions of traditional games and allow for more conceptual transfer.

Throwing to Avoid a Defender

Setting: A 15-by-15-foot space; groups of three; one ball or beanbag per group

Cues	
Throwing	
Lead the Receiver	(Throw to an open space just in front of the catcher.)
Quick	(Make your throw quickly, as soon as you know the receiver is open.)
Catching	
Move to Open Space	(Move to a space that is at an angle from the thrower.)
Watch Passer, Then Ball	(Watch the passer as you start to run, and then after the ball is thrown, track it all the way into your hands.)
Intercepting	
Hips	(To tell where a person is going to move, watch the hips or the belly button.)
Play the Ball	(Always go after the person with the ball—to force the person to pass it.)

It is very helpful to children to demonstrate the concept of moving away from the thrower at an angle of about 45 degrees (Figure 24.5).

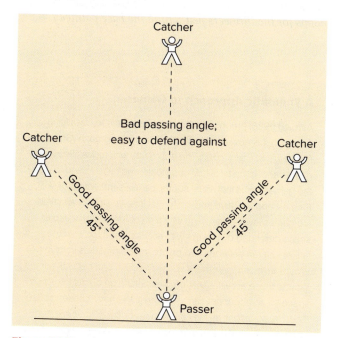

Figure 24.5 Passing angles for throwing against a defense.

Tip: When playing against a defense, the concept of catching changes to being able to catch while outmaneuvering the opponent. We assume that children at this point have mastered space awareness and dodging. The ability to move to an open space at an angle (approximately 45 degrees) away from the thrower is initially very difficult to understand. To get students to move away from the passer at an appropriate angle, a skilled soccer coach once provided these cues: See the Passer, See the Ball, See as Much of the Field as Possible. You may want to try using them.

Tasks/Challenges:

T In this task, you'll practice throwing to someone against a defense. One of you is the thrower, one is the receiver, and the other one is the interceptor. Thrower, your job is to get the ball to the receiver. **Use quick moves and get rid of the ball when you have a chance. Receiver, move to an open space to catch the ball. Interceptor, make them throw the ball, but don't forget that you are not allowed to touch the receiver or the thrower.** After five throws, change places.

? What is one strategy you can use to throw successfully when being defended? What can the catcher do to be successful in catching? What can you do to intercept the ball?

Throwing and Catching in a Small-Sided Invasion Game

Setting: Self-determined space; four markers for each group; groups of three; one ball

Cues	
Throwing	
Lead the Receiver	(Throw to an open space just in front of the catcher.)
Quick	(Make your throw quickly, as soon as you know the receiver is open.)
Catching	
Move to Open Space	(Move to a space that is at an angle from the thrower.)
Watch Passer, Then Ball	(Watch the passer as you start to run, and then after the ball is thrown, track it all the way into your hands.)
Intercepting	
Hips	(To tell where a person is going to move, watch the hips or the belly button.)
Play the Ball	(Always go after the person with the ball—to force the person to pass it.)

must be able to throw the football into the other team's goal area); teams of two; a (foam) junior-size football. (Note: A foam football is easier to catch, but it is more difficult to throw. Use the type of football most suited to the needs of your students.)

Cues

Throwing

Lead the Receiver	(Throw to an open space just in front of the catcher.)
Quick	(Make your throw quickly, as soon as you know the receiver is open.)

Catching

Move to Open Space	(Move to a space that is at an angle from the thrower.)
Watch Passer, Then Ball	(Watch the passer as you start to run, and then after the ball is thrown track it all the way into your hands.)

Intercepting

Hips	(To tell where a person is going to move, watch the hips or the belly button.)
Play the Ball	(Always go after the person with the ball—to force the person to pass it.)

Tasks/Challenges:

Ⓒ This football game has just throwing and catching, no running with the football. You and your partner are a team. You try to throw the ball to your partner, who's being defended by someone on the other team. Here are the rules:

1. Each team has four chances to throw and catch the ball in an attempt to move the ball from their goal line to the opposing team's goal area.

2. When on offense, one player is the thrower. He or she may not move forward. The thrower tries to accurately throw the ball downfield to her or his teammate, the receiver.

3. When on defense, one player tries to stay with the receiver to deflect or intercept the ball. The other player remains at the location where the play starts. That player counts aloud, "One alligator, two alligators," up to "five alligators," and then rushes the thrower, trying to touch the thrower or block the thrower's pass.

4. A play is over when the ball touches the ground or when a defensive player touches the offensive player who has possession of the ball.

Throwing, Catching, and Dribbling in a Small-Sided Invasion Game

Setting: A large open space (*see* Figure 24.8 *for setup*); teams of three or four; a 5-inch foam or playground ball

Cues

Throwing

Lead the Receiver	(Throw to an open space just in front of the catcher.)
Quick	(Make your throw quickly, as soon as you know the receiver is open.)

Catching

Move to Open Space	(Move to a space that is at an angle from the thrower.)
Watch Passer, Then Ball	(Watch the passer as you start to run, and then after the ball is thrown, track it all the way into your hands.)

Intercepting

Hips	(To tell where a person is going to move, watch the hips or the belly button.)
Play the Ball	(Always go after the person with the ball—to force the person to pass it.)

Tasks/Challenges:

Ⓒ This game is a little like soccer because there's a goalie, but you throw the ball rather than kick it. The object is to throw the ball through the other team's goal. Here are the rules:

1. Players must stay out of the semicircle.

Figure 24.8 Setup for throwing, catching, and dribbling in a small-sided invasion game. Goals can be made of stacked tires; semicircles can be spray-painted on the ground.

2. The goalie must stay in the semicircle. She or he tries to collect the ball to prevent it from going through the goal.

3. A player who has the ball can bounce it, pass it to a teammate, or throw it toward the goal. Once a player stops bouncing the ball, he or she must pass or shoot it; she or he can no longer dribble it.

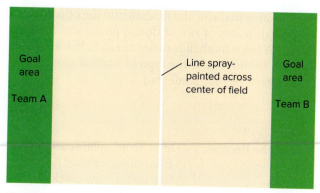

Figure 24.9 Setup for throwing and catching while using simple offense and defense in a small-sided invasion game. Adjust the dimensions of the field according to the children's ability.

Throwing and Catching While Using Simple Offense and Defense in a Small-Sided Invasion Game

Setting: A large open space (*see* Figure 24.9 *for setup*); teams of three; any type of ball; markers

Cues

Throwing
Lead the Receiver (Throw to an open space just in front of the catcher.)
Quick (Make your throw quickly as soon as you know the receiver is open.)

Catching
Move to Open Space (Move to a space that is at an angle from the thrower.)
Watch Passer, Then Ball (Watch the passer as you start to run, and then after the ball is thrown, track it all the way into your hands.)

Intercepting
Hips (To tell where a person is going to move, watch the hips or the belly button.)
Play the Ball (Always go after the person with the ball—to force the person to pass it.)

Tasks/Challenges:

Ⓒ This game is a little like football. The object is to pass a ball to someone on your team who's in the other team's goal area. It helps to decide the type of pathways the receivers will be running before each play: straight, curved, or zigzag. Here are the rules:

1. The quarterback must remain behind the line marked across the middle of the field. No defensive player may cross the line.
2. The offensive team has three plays or attempts to have successful pass completions. Then the teams switch roles.
3. A point is scored each time a receiver catches the ball. Two points are scored when a receiver catches the ball in the end zone.
4. After each play, the ball is again placed at midfield.
5. No player may purposely bump or block another.
6. All players rotate to different positions after each play.

Reading Comprehension Questions

1. Name the three styles of throwing. What type of task encourages children to practice overhand throws?
2. What does hip and spine rotation mean when throwing a ball?
3. What issues exist when children begin to throw at targets? Design a task that will alleviate the issues created by throwing at a target and illicit a mature throw.
4. What does throwing in a static context mean? Describe an example of a task that includes throwing in a static context and an example of a task that includes throwing in a dynamic context.
5. Why do we focus on throwing before catching?
6. Name two characteristics of an individual at the utilization level in catching.
7. What does tracking a ball mean? How can a teacher tell if a child is tracking a ball appropriately?
8. Rank the following tasks by placing the number 1 in front of the easiest (most basic) task, the number 2 in front of the next more difficult task, and so on.

   ( ) Throw and catch while using simple offense and defense in a small-sided invasion game.

(   ) Toss up a beanbag and try to catch it with a plastic scoop.

(   ) While running, throw a ball to a partner who's also running.

(   ) Toss a yarn ball high in the air so you have to travel to catch it.

(   ) Throw and catch with a partner.

9. What four cues do we use to remind children about the correct way of throwing a ball overhand? Explain the meaning of each cue.

10. What three cues do we use to remind children about the correct way of catching a ball? Explain the meaning of each cue.

References/Suggested Readings

Almond, L. 1986. Reflecting on themes: A games classification. In *Rethinking games teaching*, ed. R. Thorpe, D. Bunker, and L. Almond, 71–72. Loughborough, England: University of Technology.

Chatoupis, C. 2018. Engaging students in designing movement: The divergent discovery style of teaching, *Journal of Physical Education, Recreation and Dance* 89(3): 29–33.

Griffin, L., S. Mitchell, and J. Oslin. 2013. *Teaching sports concepts and skills: A tactical games approach.* 3rd ed. Champaign, IL: Human Kinetics.

Holt /Hale, S., and T. Hall. 2016. *Lesson planning for elementary physical education: Meeting the National Standards & Grade-level Outcomes.* Champaign, IL: Human Kinetics.

[NASPE] National Association for Sport and Physical Education. 1995. *Moving into the future: National standards for physical education.* St. Louis, MO: Mosby.

[SHAPE America] Society of Health and Physical Educators. 2014. *National standards & grade-level outcomes for K-12 physical education.* Champaign, IL: Human Kinetics.

Young, D. B., and J. Langdon. 2011. *Moving to success.* Greenville, SC: DBY Publications.

Volleying and Dribbling

The word *volley* brings images of a high net, two teams, and the sport of volleyball, but the skill of volleying is much broader, as proved constantly by children's creative games. Games designed by youngsters, games of different cultures, and innovative equipment have opened our eyes as teachers to volley-birds, foot bags, bamboo balls, and balzacs, as well as to Don't Bounce Count, Power, and Hand Bumping (page 514). For our purposes, we define *volleying* as striking or giving impetus to an object by using a variety of body parts—for example, hands, arms, or knees. Dribbling is a subdivision of volleying. Although our discussion here is divided into two separate sections—volleying and dribbling with hands—when teaching, you may choose to develop dribbling and volleying together. Volleying and dribbling are almost exclusively game skills used in such sports as soccer, volleyball, handball, basketball, and speedball.

Volleying

Children at the precontrol level of volleying are still struggling to achieve the hand–eye coordination required to contact a ball. They are rarely able to intentionally direct the flight of a ball when contact is made. Therefore, at this level, we provide a variety of experiences for the exploration of volleying—balloons and lightweight balls to maximize visual tracking and success.

As the children are able to continuously strike the ball, challenges are presented with overhead and underhand patterns, volleying with different body parts, and volleying in a variety of contexts. Our goal is two-fold: a mature pattern of volleying and expanding the repertoire of volleying skills for children, e.g., low nets, high nets, handball, four-square, foot bags, bamboo balls, and volleyball.

Give a child a ball, balloon, a volleybird, or a foot bag, and they begin to bounce it on the ground or floor. If it will not bounce, they immediately begin to volley in the air—sometimes upward, sometimes forward—with the hand, the head, the thigh, and the foot. Thus, volleying is the skill of striking with a body part; dribbling and kicking are forms of volleying. For our purposes, dribbling and volleying are separated within this chapter. See Box 25-1 for linkages of the skill theme of volleying to the *National Standards & Grade-Level Outcomes for K–12 Physical Education* (SHAPE America 2014).

Efficient striking patterns are generally the last of the fundamental manipulative patterns to develop because of the fine perceptual and motor adjustments the child must make. Once the child does begin to

---

Box 25-1

Volleying in the *National Standards & Grade-Level Outcomes for K–12 Physical Education*

Volleying is referenced in the *National Standards & Grade-Level Outcomes for K–12 Physical Education* (SHAPE America 2014) under Standard 1: "Demonstrates competency in a variety of motor skills and movement patterns." The intent of the standard is developing the fundamental skills needed to enjoy participation in physical activities, with the mastery of movement fundamentals as the foundation for continued skill acquisition.

Sample grade-level outcomes from the *National Standards** include:

Volley, underhand

- Volleys a lightweight object (balloon), sending it upward (K)
- Volleys an object with an open palm, sending it upward (1)
- Volleys an object upward with consecutive hits (2)
- Volleys an object with an underhand or sidearm striking pattern, sending it forward over a net, to the wall or over a line to a partner, while demonstrating four of the five critical elements of a mature pattern (3)
- Volleys underhand using a mature pattern in a dynamic environment (e.g., 2 Square, 4 Square, handball) (4)
- Applies skill (5)

Volley, overhead (Developmentally appropriate outcomes first appear in grade 4)

- Volleys a ball with a two-hand overhead pattern, sending it upward, demonstrating four of the five critical elements of a mature pattern (4)
- Volleys a ball using a two-hand pattern, sending it upward to a target (5)

*Suggested grade-level outcomes for student learning.

---

strike an object, the range of possible activities is enormous. Our progression spiral for volleying (page 504) indicates learning experiences at various levels, from precontrol through proficiency. The text ideas include suggestions for children at the different levels and a range of learning experiences within each level, stated directly. Remember, though, we encourage you to modify the suggested organizational structure to satisfy your objectives (see Chapter 9).

It is important that the teacher is familiar with the critical elements needed for quality instruction, demonstration, and observation of the skill. Throughout

Skill Theme Development Progression

Volleying

Proficiency Level

Volleying game: Modified Teacher Designed Game

Volleying in a line formation

Striking downward with force

Volleying with different body parts while traveling

Utilization Level

Volleying over a high net (underhand pattern)

Volleying three-on-three

Volleying continuously to a partner

Volleying over a high net (overhead pattern)

Volleying to the wall—varying levels, force, and body position

Volleying with a volleybird

Volleying from head to foot: Aerial Soccer

Volleying with the foot

Volleying a ball continuously with different body parts

Volleying game: child-designed

Control Level

Obstacle-Course Volley

Volleying with a bounce

Cooperative volleys (overhead pattern)

Volleying to a partner (overhead pattern)

Volleying a ball upward (overhead pattern)

Volleying to the wall (overhead pattern)

Volleying over a low net (underhand pattern)

Volleying for direction and accuracy: Four Square, Two Square

Volleying for force and angle (underhand pattern)

Volleying a ball to a partner (underhand pattern)

Volleying a ball to the wall (underhand pattern)

Volleying a ball upward with the forearms

Volleying a ball upward (underhand pattern)

Volleying a ball noncontinuously with different body parts

Precontrol Level

Volleying lightweight objects

Volleying with different body parts

Volleying a balloon forward

Volleying balloons in the air

Critical elements for the underhand volley include:

- Face the target in preparation for the volley
- Opposite foot forward
- Flat surface for contact
- Contact the ball/object between knee and waist level
- Follow through upward and to the target

Critical elements for the overhead volley include:

- Body aligned and positioned under the ball
- Knees, arms, and ankles bent in preparation for the volley
- Hands rounded; thumbs and first fingers make triangle (without touching) in preparation
- Ball contacts fingerpads only; wrists stay firm
- Arms extend upward on contact; follow through toward target

Precontrol Level (GLSP): Experiences for Exploration

At the precontrol level, children need a variety of learning experiences involving the skill of volleying. As with all skills involving sending and/or receiving an object, they will need to watch the object as it approaches (and contacts) the hand or body part used for the volley. At this exploration level, variety is the focus; contact is the measure of success.

Volleying Balloons in the Air

Setting: Children scattered throughout general space, each with an inflated balloon

Tasks/Challenges:

T Volley the balloon in the air, staying in your self-space.

T Strike the balloon upward with your open palm so it stays in the air. Try to keep the balloon from touching the floor.

T Strike the balloon high above your head. Practice striking with both your right and your left hand so you will be equally good with each hand.

C See if you can volley the balloon 10 times without letting it touch the floor.

C As you volley in the self-space, say one letter of the alphabet for each volley. Can you get to Z?

Volleying a Balloon Forward

Setting: Children scattered throughout general space, each with an inflated balloon

---

the chapter are sample cues (short phrases or words summarizing these critical elements). Ideally, if the cue is the last thing a teacher repeats before sending the students to practice, the learner will be cognitively focused on the critical elements.

Volleying an object requires visual tracking.

Tasks/Challenges:

T Strike your balloon in the air so it travels forward as you walk through general space.

T Strike your balloon so it travels forward as you walk in curved pathways. Can you travel in zigzag pathways as you volley the balloon?

C Travel across the gymnasium (blacktop area) as you volley the balloon forward. Can you complete your volley/travel without letting the balloon touch the ground?

? Where on the balloon is contact made for it to travel upward? Where is contact made for the balloon to travel forward?

Volleying with Different Body Parts

Setting: Children scattered throughout general space, each with an inflated balloon

Tasks/Challenges:

T Keep the balloon in the air by striking it with different body parts. How many different body parts can you use to volley the balloon upward?

T Volley the balloon upward by striking it with your head, then your hand. Try a combination of hand, elbow, head. Try alternate volleys from foot to hand.

C Count how many times you can volley the balloon before it touches the floor. Don't use the same body part two times in a row.

T Let's try a combination of more than two body parts. Volley the balloon with these body parts: hand, head, knee, elbow.

C Make your own combination of volleys using different body parts. You may choose a two-, three-, or four-body-part sequence.

Volleying Lightweight Objects

Setting: Children scattered throughout general space; a variety of lightweight objects for exploration of the volley—beach balls, lightweight plastic balls, balloons, foam balls, and so forth

Tasks/Challenges:

T You have been exploring volleying with balloons—striking them upward in self-space and forward while walking slowly through general space. Now we will try the volley with different types of lightweight balls. Select the ball (or balloon) of your choice and volley it upward in your self-space. On the signal, you will exchange that ball or balloon for a different type (rotate each 2 to 3 minutes until the children have volleyed with each type of ball or balloon).

As children become more skilled, they enjoy volleying with a small group.

T When you begin to volley with some of the balls, you may wish to let the ball bounce after each volley; the skill then becomes "volley, bounce, volley, bounce. . . ." Remember, strike the ball upward when you volley.

T Let's try one more exploration: This time the sequence will be "volley, bounce, catch; volley, bounce, catch. . . ." Are you discovering that some types of balls are better for the volley; that some require volley, bounce; and that others require volley, bounce, catch?

T Count the number of times you can volley the ball or balloon before it touches the ground. Repeat the task for a second trial; remember to count your score. After two tries, switch to a different type of ball or a balloon. Which did you like best? Which one was easiest? Which gave you the highest score?

C Choose your favorite type of ball or balloon to volley. Choose your type of volley: continuous volley; volley, bounce, volley, bounce; or volley, bounce, catch. See how many times you can complete your volley sequence without a mistake.

Volleying with Lightweight Objects

At the precontrol and control levels, volleying tasks and challenges are best done with larger, lightweight objects, such as beach balls, balloons, or inexpensive plastic balls. They float slowly, providing more time for visual tracking. This allows children time to move under the object and volley it without the fear that accompanies heavier objects.

Most equipment companies have also developed a large lightweight volleyball that provides an excellent progression from the very lightweight objects. These "trainer" balls are lighter in weight and larger, yet their flight is true; children at the utilization and proficiency levels of volleying are challenged by the trainers. None of these objects works outside well on windy days, however.

Control Level (GLSP): Learning Experiences Leading to Skill Development

At the control level, children learn an underhand and an overhead volley. They volley with different body parts, volley in relation to other people, and volley with a variety of objects. Children at this level still find that it helps to let the ball bounce between volleys so they can gain control of the volley; they will eliminate the bounce when they are ready to do so.

A note about cues: *Although several cues are listed for many of the learning experiences, it's important to focus on only one cue at a time. This way, the children can really concentrate on that cue. Once you provide feedback to the children and observe that most have learned a cue, it's time to focus on another one.*

Volleying a Ball Noncontinuously with Different Body Parts

Setting: Children scattered throughout general space, each with a lightweight ball (beach ball, foam ball, plastic ball)

Cues	
Flat Surface	(Keep the striking surface—your leg, foot, hand—as flat as possible for contact.)
Extend to Target	(Extend upward as you contact the ball.)

Tasks/Challenges:

T Strike the ball upward with different body parts: foot, elbow, upper thigh, shoulder, head, hand. Catch the ball after each volley.

T Of the body parts you used for the volley, which parts can provide a flat surface for the volley? This time as you volley the ball upward, contact the ball with the flattest surface possible—foot, upper thigh, hand. Where is the contact surface for a head volley?

C Practice until you can do three single volleys, with a catch after each, without moving from your self-space. Practice with your foot, thigh, hand, head.

T Try your body-part volleys with a beach ball, a foam ball, or a plastic ball. When you are comfortable with the upward volley, you may wish to try the skill with a playground ball or soccer ball.

Volleying a Ball Upward (Underhand Pattern)

Setting: Children scattered throughout general space, each with a beach ball, a foam ball, or an 8-inch plastic ball

Cues	
Flat Surface	(Extend your hand with your palm flat, like a pancake.)
Extend to Target	(Extend your hand upward on contact.)
Quick Feet	(Move your feet quickly to always be in position to volley the ball upward.)

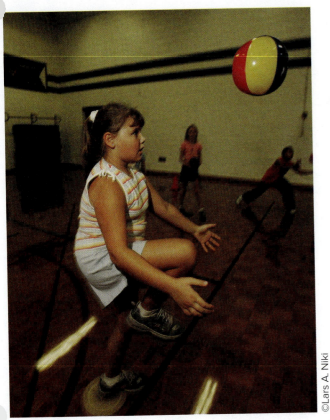

This youngster experiments with using the flat surface of the thigh to volley.

©Lars A. Niki

Tasks/Challenges:

T Strike the ball with your hand, palm flat, so it travels directly upward. Where on the ball will you need to make contact if you want the ball to travel in a straight pathway upward?

T Volley the ball directly upward so you can catch it without moving from your self-space.

T Volley the ball directly upward a distance of 4 to 5 feet above your head.

C Practice until you can do this underhand volley five times, never leaving your space.

T Volley the ball upward continuously. Move your feet quickly to always be in position directly under the ball.

C Record your personal best for today by counting the number of consecutive volleys you can complete without a mistake.

? *Peer Observation.* This is an excellent time for a peer observation of critical elements, for example, "flat surface for volley," "quick feet to be in position under the ball." Peer assessment can also include verbal recall of cues and peer feedback for improvement. *See Chapter 12, "Assessing Student Learning," for development of peer observations.*

Volleying a Ball Upward with the Forearms

Setting: Children scattered throughout general space, each with a lightweight ball (e.g., a beach ball, a foam ball, or an 8-inch plastic ball)

Cues	
Flat Surface	(Extend your arms forward, forearms together, to create a flat surface.)
Extend to Target	(Extend your arms upward on contact.)
Quick Feet	(Move your feet quickly to always be in position to volley the ball upward.)

Tasks/Challenges:

T Toss the ball slightly upward. Quickly extend your arms, bringing your forearms together to form a flat surface. Volley the ball upward above your head so it returns to you. Catch the ball after each volley. In volleyball, this is called a *bump*.

T Toss the ball, and then volley (bump) it upward two times before you catch it again.

C How many volleys (bumps) can you do without a mistake?

Volleying a Ball to the Wall (Underhand Pattern)

Setting: Children spaced around the perimeter of the gymnasium, facing the wall at a distance of about 6 feet; a lightweight plastic ball for each child

Cues	
Flat Surface	(Keep your palm flat, like a pancake.)
Extend to Target	(Extend your legs, body, striking arm toward the wall.)
Quick Feet	(Move your feet quickly to always be in position behind the ball.)

Tasks/Challenges:

T Bounce the ball one time, then strike it with your open palm, underhand volley, so it travels to the wall. As the ball rebounds from the wall, let it bounce one time and then catch it (Figure 25.1). **Where on the ball do you need to make contact for it to travel forward to the wall? Right, slightly below center and behind the ball.**

Select two children who are using the correct pattern to demonstrate for the class.

Figure 25.1 Underhand striking pattern.
1. Hold ball in one hand, with feet in front-back stance.
2. Let ball bounce once. Bring hitting arm back so it's ready to hit.
3. As ball bounces back, hit it from underneath with open palm and with body extending forward.

Ⓒ Practice until you can execute the drop-hit-bounce pattern three times. Remember, catch after each sequence.

Ⓣ Using the underhand action, strike the ball with your open palm so the ball contacts the wall 3 to 4 feet above the floor. Continue the volley after each bounce. The pattern will be this: volley, bounce; volley, bounce. . . . The ball will not always come back exactly to you; **move your feet quickly to be in position to extend toward the target as you volley.**

Ⓒ Count the number of volleys you can make without a mistake. A mistake is two bounces on the rebound or a volley that hits the ceiling.

Ⓣ Practice the volley with each hand. When the ball comes to your right side, contact it with your right hand; when it rebounds to your left side, use your left hand.

Ⓣ You have been practicing volleying to the wall by yourself. Now you are going to add a partner. The rules are the same, except after you volley the ball, your partner will take the next hit. You will be alternating volleys. **Now your quick feet will really be important!**

Ⓒ See how many times you and your partner can volley without missing.

❓ *Peer Observation.* Partner work provides an opportune time for children to observe/assess the critical elements—for example, Flat Surface, Extend to Target. *See Chapter 12 for development of peer assessments.*

Volleying to a Partner (Underhand Pattern)

Setting: Sets of partners scattered throughout general space; tape line on floor between each set; a lightweight plastic ball or playground ball

---

Cues

Flat Surface	(Keep your palm flat, like a pancake.)
Extend to Target	(Extend your legs, body, striking arm toward the target.)
Quick Feet	(Move your feet quickly to always be in position behind the ball.)

Tasks/Challenges:

Ⓣ You'll be practicing underhand hits with your partner. Stand approximately 3 feet from the tape line and face your partner across the line. Using the underhand action, strike the ball so it crosses the line and bounces on the other side. Your partner will then volley the ball back to you so it bounces on your side.

Ⓣ Practice striking the ball with each hand so you will be skilled with your right and your left hand.

Ⓒ Cooperate with your partner to see how many times you can strike the ball back and forth over the line. Set a personal goal for your volleys over the line.

Volleying for Force and Angle (Underhand Pattern)

Setting: Children with partners and one lightweight ball or playground ball for each group; place two tape X's (12"in length) on floor between the partners about 10 feet apart; students stand behind an "X" facing the partner (Figure 25.2)

Figure 25.2 Setup for Volleying for Force and Angle.

Cues

Flat Surface	(Keep your palm flat, like a pancake.)
Extend to Target	(Extend your legs, body, striking arm toward the target.)
Control	(Adjust your force to control the volley.)

Tasks/Challenges:

T You have been practicing the underhand volley, striking the ball to the wall and over a line. Today you will practice striking the ball to send it to a partner; however, the ball must bounce on or near the "X" in front of your partner! Remember, we are practicing the underhand pattern; that is the skill you must use in your game.

Volley the ball only after it bounces at the "X" in front of you. You will need to explore how much force is needed for this volley. A perfect volley comes at an angle to your partner about middle level.

C See how many times you can keep the ball going without missing.

Volleying for Direction and Accuracy: Four Square, Two Square

Setting: Children's choice: Some children in groups of four (Four Square); others in groups of two (Two Square); squares marked off on the floor for the games (Figure 25.3)

Cues

Flat Surface	(Keep your palm flat, like a pancake.)
Extend to Target	(Extend your legs, body, striking arm toward the target.)
Quick Feet	(Move your feet quickly to always be in position behind the ball.)

Tasks/Challenges:

T Stand outside your assigned square. Serve the ball by dropping it and hitting it underhand after the bounce. The server can hit the ball to any of the other three courts (Four Square). The player receiving the ball must keep it in play by striking the ball with an underhand hit to any square. Play continues until one player fails to return the ball or commits a fault. Faults include hitting the ball sidearm or overhand, stepping in another square to play the ball, catching the ball, and letting the ball touch any part of the body other than the hands. After each mistake, rotate positions and servers. (Use two squares for a two-person game.)

C Play your game cooperatively by counting the number of volleys made by your group before a mistake. Hit the ball so the person will be in the best position to contact it.

C Play the game competitively by changing force and angles of travel for the ball; however, the volley must be underhand—no sides, no overs. **The receiver will really need quick feet to move into position for the volley.**

? *Teacher Observation.* Game play provides an excellent setting for teacher observation of critical elements in dynamic situations, that is, alternative assessment. *See Chapter 11, "Reflecting on Student Responses," and Chapter 12, "Assessing Student Learning," for examples.*

Volleying over a Low Net (Underhand Pattern)

Setting: Partners; nets at varying heights (lower standard nets or improvise nets from ropes [Figure 25.4]) throughout the gym; one lightweight ball or playground ball for each pair

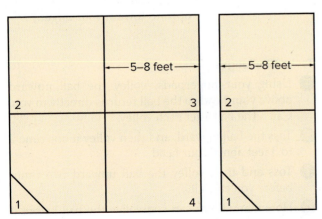

Figure 25.3 Four Square and Two Square courts.

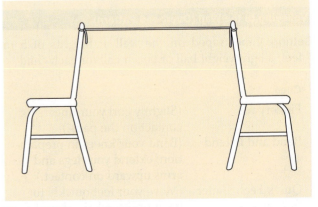

Figure 25.4 Construction of a net. Suspend a rope between two chairs.

Cues

Flat Surface	(Keep your palm flat, like a pancake.)
Extend to Target	(Extend your legs, body, striking arm toward the target.)
Quick Feet	(Move your feet quickly to always be in position behind the ball.)

Tasks/Challenges:

T You have practiced the underhand volley against the wall and over a line on the floor. Now you are ready to use the same skill to send the ball over a net to a partner. The server bounces the ball one time and then sends it over the net with the underhand volley. The partner returns the volley *after the ball bounces one time*.

C When you are ready, keep a collective score of how many volleys you and your partner can do before making a mistake.

T Slant your net from high to low, and repeat the skill, volleying the ball over the net at differing heights.

T Practice varying the force and the angles at which you volley the ball to your partner. Remember, the ball must bounce one time on each side before the contact.

C Based on your scores from the collective game, set a personal goal and see if you and your partner can attain that goal for the underhand volley over the net. Remember, volley the ball so your partner will always be in the best position for the return.

C Challenge your partner to a competitive game of volleys over the net. Add to the challenge with changes in force and angles; however, the hit must be the underhand volley you have practiced.

Volleying to the Wall (Overhead Pattern)

Setting: Lines taped on the wall at heights of 5 to 7 feet; a lightweight ball or beach ball for each child

Cues

Fingerpads	(Slightly curl your fingers for contact on the pads.)
Bend and Extend	(Bend your knees in preparation; extend your legs and arms upward on contact.)
Quick Feet, Under the Ball	(Move your feet quickly to be in position behind and under the ball for contact.)

Tasks/Challenges:

T Stand approximately 4 feet from the wall at the tape height you choose. Toss the ball slightly in front and above your head, then volley it to the wall with both hands. Catch the ball after the volley and begin again.

Select two children who are contacting the ball with their fingerpads and using their legs for the force of the volley to demonstrate the key concepts of the skill. Point out the critical elements to the children as they are demonstrated.

C Practice until you can execute three overhead volleys to the wall without catching the ball or letting it drop below the tape line.

C Count the number of volleys you can hit to the wall above the tape line. Remember, the volley must be with two hands; don't catch the ball.

? *Peer Observation.* As with all skills, the continued use of the critical elements is crucial to success in dynamic situations. A peer observation assessment of critical elements with appropriate feedback for improvement would be useful here.

Volleying a Ball Upward (Overhead Pattern)

Setting: Children scattered throughout general space, each with either a beach ball or a lightweight plastic ball

Cues

Fingerpads	(Slightly curl your fingers for contact on the pads.)
Quick Feet, Under the Ball	(Move your feet quickly to be in position under the ball.)
Bend and Extend	(Bend the knees and arms in preparation; on contact, extend the legs and extend arms upward toward your target.)

Tasks/Challenges:

T Using your fingerpads, volley the ball upward above your head so the ball returns directly to you. Catch the ball after each volley.

T Toss the ball upward, and then volley it one time 2 to 3 feet above your head.

T Toss and then volley the ball upward two times before you catch it.

C How many times can you volley the ball before it touches the ground?

Volleying to a Partner (Overhead Pattern)

Setting: Sets of partners scattered throughout general space; one lightweight ball for each set of partners

Cues	
Fingerpads	(Slightly curl your fingers for contact on the pads.)
Quick Feet, Under the Ball	(Move your feet quickly to be in position under the ball.)
Bend and Extend	(Bend the knees and arms in preparation; on contact, extend the legs and extend arms upward toward your target.)

Tasks/Challenges:

Ⓣ Stand 3 to 4 feet from your partner. Partner 1, toss the ball to your partner at a high level (above your partner's head). Partner 2 volley the ball back to your partner. Partner 1, catch the ball and repeat the task. After three attempts, switch positions for tossing and volleying.

Ⓣ Using the same overhead skill, volley the ball back and forth to your partner. Each of you gets two hits for your turn: Volley the ball first to yourself for control and then to your partner.

Ⓣ When you are comfortable with two volleys for your turn, try doing the task with only one volley each.

Ⓒ On the signal, begin your partner volleys. I will time you for 30 seconds. Try to continue without a mistake for the entire time . . . and beyond!

Cooperative Volleys (Overhead Pattern)

Setting: Groups of four or five children (the smaller the group, the more participation/practice of the skill each child gets); a lightweight ball (or a volleyball trainer—a larger, lightweight volleyball) for each group

Cues	
Fingerpads	(Slightly curl your fingers for contact on the pads.)
Quick Feet, Under the Ball	(Move your feet quickly to be in position under the ball.)
Bend and Extend	(Bend the knees and arms in preparation; on contact, extend the legs and extend arms upward toward your target.)

Tasks/Challenges:

Ⓣ The object of the game Keep It Up is to see how many times your group can volley the ball before it touches the ground. There are only two rules: A player cannot hit the ball twice in a row, and the hit must be the overhead volley. Practice several times.

Ⓒ Continue your cooperative volleys with your group. This time count your group volleys, calling out the volley number as you contact the ball.

Ⓣ This time as your group plays Keep It Up, be sure each person in the group does a volley before anyone takes a second turn.

Ⓒ As a group, set a goal for the number of volleys you wish to attain, and then play the game to see if you can reach that number without a mistake.

❓ *Teacher Observation.* Cooperative games provide an opportune time for teacher observation of critical elements. *See Chapters 11 and 12 for development of teacher observation assessments.*

Volleying with a Bounce

Setting: Children in groups of equal numbers (three or four per group) on either side of a low net; a lightweight ball that will bounce

Cues	
Quick Feet, Under the Ball	(Move your feet quickly to be in position under the ball.)

Tasks/Challenges:

Ⓒ A player begins the game by bouncing the ball one time and striking it over the net with the underhand volley action. The receiving side may let the ball bounce one time before hitting it back (or may volley the ball with no bounce). Only one bounce is permitted before the ball is volleyed back over the net; however, any number of players may volley the ball before it crosses the net. You may volley with any body part that you choose. The serving team scores a point when the receiving team fails to return the ball over the net within bounds or when the ball bounces more than one time.

Obstacle-Course Volley

Setting: Prior setup. (See Figure 25.5 for an example of a volley obstacle course.) Tasks in the obstacle course can require a student to use a number of different volleying skills. It may be helpful to provide a number of different objects to volley in order to allow for differences in skill development.

Tasks/Challenges:

Ⓣ Work your way through the course, following the instructions at each station.

Figure 25.5 Setup for Obstacle-Course Volley.

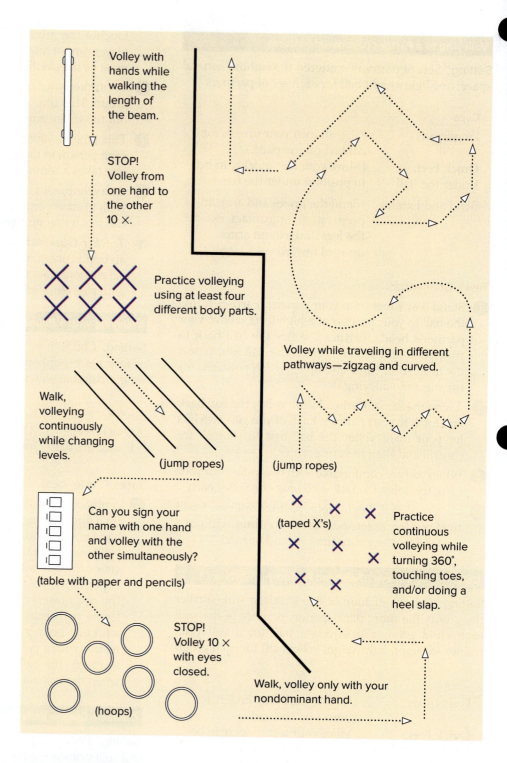

Volley with hands while walking the length of the beam.

STOP! Volley from one hand to the other 10 ×.

Practice volleying using at least four different body parts.

Volley while traveling in different pathways—zigzag and curved.

Walk, volleying continuously while changing levels.

(jump ropes)   (jump ropes)

Can you sign your name with one hand and volley with the other simultaneously?

(table with paper and pencils)

(taped X's)   Practice continuous volleying while turning 360°, touching toes, and/or doing a heel slap.

STOP! Volley 10 × with eyes closed.

Walk, volley only with your nondominant hand.

(hoops)

For continuing skill development in volleying, children must develop consistency and accuracy. They should be able to use various body parts to volley and move in relationship to other people and objects. Strategic placement skills in a relatively stable situation are developed at the utilization level.

A note about cues: *Although several cues are listed for many of the learning experiences, it's important to focus on only one cue at a time. This way, the children can really concentrate on that cue. Once you provide feedback to the children and observe that most have learned a cue, it's time to focus on another one.*

Volleying Game: Child-Designed

Setting: A variety of lightweight balls; paper and pencils for children to record their games

Cues

Flat Surface	(Keep your palms flat, like a pancake.)
Extend to Target	(Extend your legs, body, striking arm toward the target.)
Quick Feet, Under the Ball	(Move your feet quickly to be in position under the ball.)

Tasks/Challenges:

C Earlier in our work you practiced striking the ball against the wall and over a line using the underhand volley—striking with an open palm. You are very good at that volley. Today you will use that skill in a game situation. Your task is to design an original game for two partners or a small group to provide practice of the underhand volley in a dynamic, on-the-move situation. You can design your game so it can be played against the wall or over a line on the floor. **Remember, the focus is the underhand volley; your game must use that skill.** You will need to decide the following:

- Will your game be against the wall or over a line?
- Will the game be cooperative or competitive?
- Will you keep score?
- How does a player score a point?
- Will the game be played with a partner or in a small group?
- What are the boundaries?
- What are the rules?

Record your game on a piece of paper so you can refer to it later and others in the class can learn how to play it. You may give your game a name if you wish (Figure 25.6).

Children not experienced in designing games will need more direction from the teacher and fewer opportunities to make decisions; for example, the teacher decides whether the game is against the wall or over a line and whether the game is cooperative or competitive. See Chapter 31 for more on child-designed games.

Volleying a Ball Continuously with Different Body Parts

Setting: Children scattered throughout general space, each with an object suitable for the volley—plastic ball, soccer ball, playground ball, foot bag

Cues

Flat Surface	(Keep the body part as flat as possible for contact.)
Bend and Extend	(Bend your knees to be in position for the volley; extend upward on contact.)
Quick Feet, Under the Ball	(Move your feet quickly to be in position under the ball.)

Tasks/Challenges:

T Volley the ball (foot bag) from your thigh to your foot by striking it with your upper thigh and then with the top of your foot. Catch the ball (foot bag) after the volley from your foot.

T Practice with your right leg and foot as well as with your left. You want to be equally skilled with both.

T Now choose any three body parts to keep the ball (foot bag) going. See if you can keep it going from part to part without letting it touch the ground. You may choose to repeat the same body part; for example, foot, thigh, foot.

C This time you are going to see how well you can use different body parts for consecutive volleys. Choose the three body parts with which you like to volley. Try to keep the ball (foot bag) going with your three parts. Can you keep it going for 15 seconds? Thirty seconds? Sixty seconds?

⚠ Children should not volley with the head. While some equipment may be safe, students may be inclined to try the skill with a heavier ball. Many youth soccer leagues have removed the option of heading.

What Is a Foot Bag?

A very popular game that has made a resurgence in the past few years is foot bag. Foot bags are small leather-covered (or crocheted) beanbag-type balls. The game requires a great deal of skill but delights children and adults for hours. Children at the utilization and proficiency levels will enjoy using a foot bag at times instead of a ball. Foot bags are relatively inexpensive and are great on the playground or field trips.

Volleying with the Foot

Setting: Children scattered throughout general space, with access to beach balls, plastic balls, and/or playground balls

Cue

Flat Surface	(Make the inside, outside, top of your foot as flat as possible for the contact.)

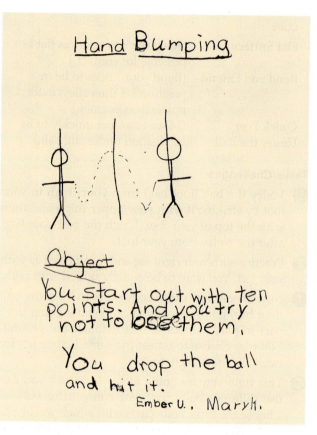

Hand Bumping

Object

You start out with ten points. And you try not to lose them.

You drop the ball and hit it.

Ember U., Maryh.

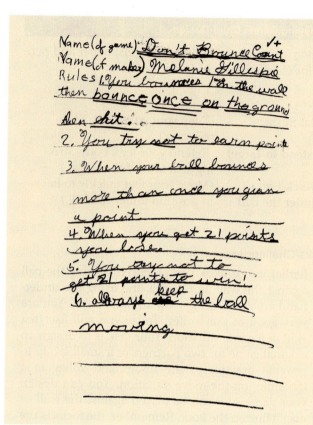

Name (of game): Don't Bounce Count ✓+
Name (of maker): Melanie Gillespie
Rules: 1. You bounces 1 on the wall then **bounce once** on the ground then **hit** it.
2. You try not to earn points
3. When your ball bounces more than once you gian a point
4. When you get 21 points you lose.
5. You try not to get 21 points to win!
6. always keep the ball moving

Figure 25.6 Child-designed games over a line (Hand Bumping) and against the wall (Don't Bounce Count; Pomer).

Pomer

John Davis Peter Wiegand

We hit agensts the Wall.
and let the Ball Bonch
One nch. and the ather Parson
hits it Agent the Wall

Tasks/Challenges:

T Volley the beach ball with your foot, keeping the ball in the air for several contacts. Use the inside, outside, and top of your foot and your heel to send the ball upward.

T If consecutive volleys with the beach ball are easy, try the plastic or the playground ball.

C On the signal, begin your foot volley. I'll give the count each 10 seconds; keep the ball in the air as long as possible.

Volleying from Head to Foot: Aerial Soccer

Setting: Children scattered throughout general space, small lightweight ball

Cues	
Flat Surface	(Make the foot surface as flat as possible for the contact.)
Quick Feet	(Move your feet quickly to always be in position for a good volley.)

Tasks/Challenges:

T Practice your skills of foot volleys, aerial kicks, and foot-to-thigh volleys with the ball.

C When you feel comfortable with the individual skills of Aerial Soccer and can keep the ball aloft for at least 10 seconds, you can play a game of Aerial Soccer with a partner or in a small group. The ball must stay aloft at all times. You will need to decide the following:

- Is the game to be cooperative or competitive?
- How many will be in the group? (Not more than six—three-on-three.)
- Will you play in self-space or travel in general space?
- What boundaries do you need?

Volleying with a Volleybird

Volleybirds are flat-bottomed shuttlecocks that have been used in Taiwan for centuries. The volleybirds are volleyed with different body parts, including hands, thighs, the instep of the foot, and the inside and outside of the foot. The volleybirds are flat bottomed, so they can also be caught on different body parts. Young children find these relatively slow moving and brightly colored "birds" very attractive.

Setting: Children scattered in general space, each with a volleybird

Cues	
Flat Surface	(Make your hand, thigh, foot surface as flat as possible for the contact.)
Quick Feet	(Move your feet quickly to always be in position for the volley—under the volleybird.)

Tasks/Challenges:

T Try to continually strike the volleybird before it touches the ground. Start with one hand; then try your other hand. Other body parts you can use are your thigh, the instep of your foot, or the inside or outside of your foot.

C See how many times in a row you can strike the volleybird.

C Make up a sequence that uses three different body parts. See if you can repeat the sequence without a miss.

Striking to the Wall—Varying Levels, Force, and Body Position

Setting: Lines marked on the wall at heights of 3 and 7 feet; a variety of balls for a combination of volleying and bouncing (plastic balls, playground balls)

Cues	
Flat Surface	(Flat/open palm for contact.)
Extend to Target	(Extend your legs, striking arm, and body toward the target.)
Quick Feet	(Move your feet quickly into position for the volley.)

Tasks/Challenges:

T Strike the ball to the wall between the 3- and 7-foot tape marks so the ball contacts the wall at different levels. Strike the ball so it sometimes hits the wall at a high level, just below the 7-foot mark, and sometimes at a low level, just above the 3-foot mark.

T Vary your striking action; sometimes use an underhand strike, sometimes an overhead one.

T Vary the amount of force you use when hitting the ball. Sometimes hit the ball hard so it rebounds far from the wall; sometimes use just enough force to get the ball within the tape zones. How will the ball rebound this time? Right—close to the wall.

T Strike the ball from different positions in relation to your body. Contact the ball while it's high over your head, close to the floor, on your right side, on your left side. Being able to contact the ball from different positions is important in game situations when you don't always have enough time to get in position.

C With a partner, play handball. Your target is the area between the 3- and 7-foot tape marks. Try to strike the plastic (playground) ball to the wall so your partner can't return the shot. Challenge your partner to a game of 15 points.

Each time you select a partner, both of you should agree on the rules, including the outside boundaries, type of hits, how to keep score, and number of bounces permitted on the rebound. Possible rules include alternating hits and hitting the ball to a certain space on the wall.

C With a group of two or four, play Hand Corner Ball. (See Figure 25.7 for court setup.) The rules are these:

1. It can be a singles or a doubles game.
2. You serve by dropping the ball and underhand volleying it against the wall.
3. The ball must contact the wall above the 18-inch line and rebound back into one of the three activity zones.
4. Volleying alternates between teams. In doubles play, it also alternates between players. So, if player 1 on team A serves and player 1 on team B returns it, player 2 on team A takes the next volley.

Cornerball

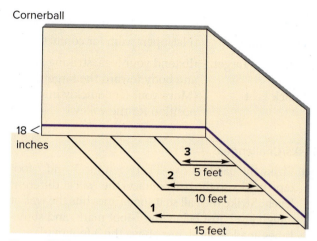

Figure 25.7 Setup for Hand Corner Ball.

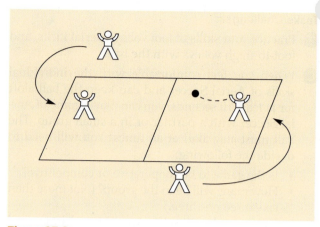

Figure 25.8 Two-person running volley.

5. If a team is unable to return the ball, the other team earns the number of points of the zone in which the ball landed.

6. A game is 15 points.

? *Digital Analysis.* Game play at the utilization and proficiency levels provides an excellent opportunity for videotaping or digital picture analysis of performance and student self-assessment. Students assess themselves in authentic settings in relation to the cues with skills performed in dynamic environments.

Volleying over a High Net (Overhead Pattern)

Setting: Nets at a no greater than 7-foot height; a variety of beach balls, 8-inch plastic balls, and volleyball trainers

Cues	
Fingerpads	(Slightly curl your fingers for contact on the pads.)
Quick Feet, Under the Ball	(Move your feet quickly to be in position under the ball.)
Bend and Extend	(Bend the knees and arms in preparation; on contact, extend the legs and extend arms upward toward your target.)

Tasks/Challenges:

T Select a partner; stand on either side of the net, and face each other. Partner 1 tosses the ball over the net; partner 2 volleys the ball back over the net to partner 1 with the two-hand overhead hit. Partner 1 catches the ball and then tosses again. After 10 tries, partner 2 tosses, and partner 1 volleys.

T Volley the ball so your partner can catch it without moving from self-space.

T For this task, you will need four people, two on each side of the net. One of you will be on the court, and the other waits behind the end line. The activity is almost the same as the last one, with one exception: After you hit the ball, you run off the court, and the person behind comes up to return the shot. Then, that person runs off the court, and you come back on (Figure 25.8). The activity goes very quickly, so you must be ready to move as soon as your partner hits the ball. The task is still: toss, volley, catch. The difference is you must be in position quickly.

Volleying Continuously to a Partner

Setting: Nets at no greater than 7-foot height; a variety of beach balls, 8-inch plastic balls, and volleyball trainers

Cues	
Fingerpads	(Slightly curl your fingers for contact on the pads.)
Quick Feet, Under the Ball	(Move your feet quickly to be in position under the ball.)
Bend and Extend	(Bend the knees and arms in preparation; on contact, extend the legs and extend arms upward toward your target.)

Tasks/Challenges:

T Partner 1 tosses the ball slightly above the head, then volleys the ball over the net to partner 2. Partner 2 volleys the ball back over the net. Continue to volley, using the overhead volley for balls at a high level.

C Set a personal best goal with your partner. See if you can attain that goal. Give your partner your best volley each time.

Volleying Three-on-Three

Setting: Children in groups of six, with three on each side of the net (Figure 25.9)

Cues	
Fingerpads	(Slightly curl your fingers for contact on the pads.)
Quick Feet, Under the Ball	(Move your feet quickly to be in position under the ball.)
Bend and Extend	(Bend the knees and arms in preparation; on contact, extend the legs and extend arms upward toward your target.)

Tasks/Challenges:

T Use only the overhand volley to hit the ball in the air three times on your side of the net. On the third contact, volley the ball over the net to the other team. Each team volleys the ball three times, sending it over the net on the third hit. A different player makes each one of the three hits.

T Rotate positions, so you hit the ball from different places.

C Work cooperatively to keep the ball in the air as long as possible. Remember: three hits per side, one hit per person.

C Challenge the other team to a three-on-three game. Rather than cooperating to keep the ball in the air, use strategies to outscore the other team. Rather than just hitting the ball over the net, direct it to a certain location; vary the amount of force on the volley, sometimes sending it just over the net, sometimes sending it deep into the court. A point is scored when the ball hits the floor or lands out of bounds.

Volleying over a High Net (Underhand Pattern)

Setting: Lines marked on the wall 7 feet from the floor; nets at a no greater than 7-foot height; plastic balls and volleyball trainers

Cues	
Watch the Ball	(Watch the ball until the striking arm contacts it.)
Extend to Target	(Extend the striking arm toward the target—over the net.)

Tasks/Challenges:

T You learned the underhand action of striking the ball with your open palm, swinging your arm forward/backward, stepping forward on your opposite foot, and contacting the ball slightly below center and back. Now you're going to modify that skill slightly for the underhand action of a serve. Stand 10 to 15 feet from the wall; serve the ball to the wall; your target is the area just above the 7-foot tape line. For this skill, the ball will not bounce first. You will be striking the ball directly from your hand. *(Demonstrate)*

Distance from the wall/net for the service is determined by the children's skill; modify the distance for success, gradually increasing the challenge.

T I'll walk around and observe the underhand action of your serve. When it's correct and you feel successful, select a partner for practice over the net. Partner 1 stands 10 to 15 feet from the net and serves the ball over the net. Partner 2 retrieves the ball and then serves it back over the net.

T After you feel successful serving over the net, your partner will select a position on the court and stand in that spot. Serve the ball away from your partner so your partner can't catch the ball without moving from self-space.

The last task may seem a bit backward from "what has always been done." It is. When children begin by "serving" to a partner, they tend to do the same thing in a game situation—the exact opposite response from the one required. This way, we get them to practice serving to an open space early on.

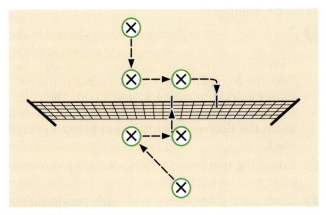

Figure 25.9 Three-on-three volleys: two patterns.

Proficiency Level (GLSP): Learning Experiences Leading to Skill Development

Children at the proficiency level should be able to move consistently and accurately in relation to others and to react effectively to increasingly dynamic and unpredictable situations. They can simultaneously focus on volleying and on the game activity around them.

A note about cues: *At the proficiency level, tasks are more complex, typically requiring children to coordinate several movements simultaneously in a dynamic context. A list of cues is provided to assist the children in being more successful in the learning experience. The challenge for the teacher is in determining which cue will be most beneficial for each child—and when. Thus, careful observation and critical reflection become very important as you watch the children move and then decide which cue will be the most helpful to move each learner to a higher skill level.*

Volleying with Different Body Parts While Traveling

Setting: A variety of lightweight balls: 8-inch plastic, foam, volleyball trainers

Cue	
Quick Feet	(Move your feet quickly to always be in position to volley the ball.)

Tasks/Challenges:

- (T) Travel the length of the gym, volleying the ball with different body parts as you go. Don't catch the ball at any time, and don't let it touch the floor.
- (T) Select a partner. Travel throughout general space, volleying the ball back and forth with different body parts. Both of you should always be moving.
- (T) This time as you travel and volley with your partner, vary the level of the volley—sometimes high, sometimes middle level. **Remember, Flat Surface, Quick Feet.**

Striking Downward with Force

Setting: Tape lines on the wall at about 7 and 2 feet from the floor; a variety of lightweight balls for individual practice

Cues	
Quick Feet	(Move your feet quickly to always be in position to volley the ball; transfer your weight forward as you volley.)
Up, Up, Up, Down Soft, Soft, Soft, Hard!	(Volley the ball up, up, up, down; soft, soft, soft, hard.)

Tasks/Challenges:

- (T) Standing 10 to 12 feet from the wall, begin volleying the ball between the tape lines, using the underhand pattern; you may or may not include a bounce with the volleys. After several volleys, strike the ball on top so it travels downward to the wall, contacting the wall just above the 2-foot tape line. Contact the ball with your hand slightly cupped. *(Demonstrate.)*
- (T) Practice a pattern of three underhand volleys followed by a downward hit with force.
- (C) Challenge a partner to a handball game against the wall. Throughout the game, use a combination of forceful downward hits and underhand volleys.
- (C) Challenge the same partner to a competitive Two Square game over a line. Use the forceful downward striking to create situations that move your partner/opponent out of position, making a good return more difficult.

Volleying in a Line Formation

Setting: Tape marks on the wall at a height of about 7 feet; groups of four, each in a line formation facing the wall and 3 to 4 feet from it; a variety of lightweight balls (8-inch plastic, foam balls, volleyball trainers)

Cues	
Fingerpads	(Slightly curl your fingers for contact on the pads.)
Quick Feet, Under the Ball	(Move your feet quickly to be in position under the ball.)
Bend and Extend	(Bend the knees and arms in preparation; on contact, extend the legs and extend arms upward toward your target.)

Tasks/Challenges:

- (T) The first person in your line volleys the ball to the wall so it contacts the wall above the tape line; then that person moves quickly to the back of the line. The second person volleys the ball to the wall, moves quickly to the back, and so on. The objective is to keep the volley going. Don't let the ball touch the floor or touch the wall below the tape mark.
- (C) Count the number of volleys your team can complete without a mistake.
- (T) Continue the line volley, with each person calling "mine" just before he or she contacts the ball.

T Remaining in your group of four, face another group, with approximately 10 feet between the two leaders. Team members line up behind the leaders. One leader tosses the ball to the leader of the other team; that leader then volleys the ball back and quickly moves to the end of the line. This game is very similar to the volley against the wall: Each person volleys and then moves to the end of the line. The objective is to keep the volley going between the teams. *Remember, two hands for the volleys.*

C How many times can you "volley the line" without the ball touching the floor? You may have to include volleying with other body parts to keep it going.

Volleying Game: Modified Teacher-Designed Game

Setting: Teams of four or six, depending on space available *(place an equal number of children with comparable skills on each team; the size of the court and the height of the net are determined by the players' skill)*, a beach ball, plastic ball, or oversized volleyball trainer

Cues	
Quick Feet	(Always keep on the move to be in position for the volley.)
Bend and Extend	(Bend the knees and arms in preparation; extend the arms, legs, and body toward the target on contact.)
Offense	
Open Space	(Hit to the open space.)
Defense	
Ready	(Bent knees, ready hands.)

Tasks/Challenges:

C The game begins with a serve from the back boundary line; you will have two chances to serve the ball successfully over the net. In a regulation volleyball game, the ball may be hit only three times on a side; we'll decide as a class if we want three hits per side or unlimited. *(Discuss; vote.)* Getting unlimited hits per side increases the volley practice and the overall physical engagement in the game. Here are the guidelines for play:

1. You can contact the ball only one time and then someone else must volley the ball before you volley again.
2. You receive a point whenever the other team misses. If a team is serving when they miss, then the serve goes to the other team.

3. A serve that touches the net is no good; a ball in play is good even though it touches the net.
4. Although this is not an official rule, try to use the skills you learned, such as the two-hand volley. Use one hand only for the serve.

The purpose of the game today is to practice the overhead skills of volleying we have learned. We will rotate positions so everyone plays each spot on the court. There may be times you have to strike with other body parts to keep the ball going.

Dribbling

Give children balls that bounce and what happens? More often than not, they bounce them. *Dribbling* is striking or bouncing downward, generally with the hands. An important skill theme to develop, dribbling most often leads to participation in the traditional sport of basketball whether in recreational pick-up games or more organized competition. Dribbling also plays a prominent role in team handball, speedball, Gaelic football, and netball. Yet, because its possible uses are endless, we focus on it as one aspect of volleying (or striking) rather than as a sport-specific skill. Children enjoy working with bouncing and dribbling skills and will spend many hours practicing the finest details. Remember, though, that dribbling, as a skill—like volleying upward—is one of the last fundamental skills to develop because it requires fine hand–eye coordination and the control of two objects that do not come to rest. Our progression spiral for dribbling appears on page 520. Dribbling a ball on the floor or ground, as in soccer, could have been included in this chapter, but because it's also a kicking skill, we have included it with kicking and punting in Chapter 23. Refer to Box 25-2 for linkages of the skill theme of dribbling to the *National Standards & Grade-Level Outcomes for K–12 Physical Education* (SHAPE America 2014).

It is important that the teacher is familiar with the critical elements needed for quality instruction, demonstration, and observation of the skill. Throughout the chapter are sample cues (short phrases or words summarizing these critical elements). Ideally, if the cue is the last thing a teacher repeats before sending the students to practice, the learner will be cognitively focused on the critical elements.

The critical elements for stationary dribbling in self-space are:

- Knees bent
- Opposite foot forward
- Firm contact with fingerpads (not the fingertips); push, don't slap, the ball
- Contact on top of ball

Skill Theme Development Progression

Dribbling

Proficiency Level

Child-designed invasion games
Dribble/Pass Keep-Away
Dribbling and throwing at a target
Child-designed dribbling/passing routines
Maintaining possession while dribbling and passing
Dribbling while dodging
Dribble Tag
Dribbling against opponents: Stationary defenders

Utilization Level

Dribbling against an opponent: One-on-one
Dribbling and passing with a partner
Dribbling around stationary obstacles in limited space
Dribbling around stationary obstacles in general space
Dribbling while stopping, starting, and turning (pivots
    and fakes)
Mirroring and matching while dribbling
Dribbling in different pathways
Dribbling in general space while changing directions
Dribbling and changing speed of travel

Control Level

Dribbling, traveling, and switching hands
Dribbling and traveling
Dribbling while changing directions in self-space
Dribbling in different places around the body while
    stationary
Dribbling with the body in different positions
Dribbling while switching hands
Dribbling and looking
Dribbling at different levels
Continuous dribbling
Dribbling in self-space

Precontrol Level

Dribbling and walking
Bouncing a ball down (dribbling) continuously
Bouncing a ball down and catching it

- Eyes looking forward, not down at the ball
- Height of dribble at middle level

Figure 25.10 shows the correct hand and body position for stationary dribbling. Please note these critical elements and the cues used to aid student learning will change slightly for dribbling while moving.

Precontrol Level (GLSP): Experiences for the Exploration

For children at the precontrol level, tasks are designed to provide opportunities for exploration of striking down repeatedly while maintaining control. We first want children to strike a ball down repeatedly without losing the ball from self-space. When the children are able to do this, we add tasks that encourage limited dribbling while walking. Relatively light balls—8-inch rubber playground balls or rubber basketballs—that bounce true (i.e., they aren't lopsided) are best for introducing children to dribbling. Be careful when inflating balls: Too much air equals too much bounce for control.

Bouncing a Ball Down and Catching It

Setting: Children scattered in general space, each with a ball

Tasks/Challenges:

Ⓣ Bounce the ball down in front of you so it comes straight back up. Catch it when it gets to about middle level.

©Barbara Adamcik

It is difficult for children at the precontrol level to dribble continuously.

Box 25-2

Dribbling in the *National Standards & Grade-Level Outcomes for K–12 Physical Education*

Dribbling is referenced in the *National Standards & Grade-Level Outcomes for K–12 Physical Education* (SHAPE America 2014) under Standard 1: "Demonstrates competency in a variety of motor skills and movement patterns." The intent of the standard is developing the fundamental skills needed to enjoy participation in physical activities, with the mastery of movement fundamentals as the foundation for continued skill acquisition.

Sample grade-level outcomes from the *National Standards** include:

- Dribbles a ball with one hand, attempting the second contact (K)
- Dribbles continuously in self-space using the preferred hand (1)
- Dribbles in self-space with preferred hand demonstrating a mature pattern (2)
- Dribbles using the preferred hand while walking in general space (2)
- Dribbles and travels in general space at slow to moderate jogging speed, with control of ball and body (3)
- Dribbles in self- space with both the preferred and the nonpreferred hands using a mature pattern (4)
- Dribbles in general space with control of ball and body while increasing and decreasing speed (4)
- Dribbles with hands or feet in combination with other skills (e.g., passing, receiving, shooting) (4)

- Combines traveling with the manipulative skills of dribbling, throwing, catching, and striking in teacher- and/ or student-designed small-sided practice-task environments (4)
- Combines hand dribbling with other skills during one-on-one practice tasks (5)

Dribbles with hands or feet with mature patterns in a variety of small-sided game forms (5)

- Combines manipulative skills and traveling for execution to a target (e.g., scoring in soccer, hockey, and basketball) (5)
- Dribbling is also referenced under Standard 2. "Applies knowledge of concepts, principles, strategies and tactics related to movement and performance." The intent of this standard is facilitation of a child's ability to use cognitive information to understand and enhance motor skill acquisition and performance.

Sample grade-level outcomes from the National Standards* include:

- Applies the concept of open spaces to combination skills involving traveling (e.g., dribbling and traveling) (4)
- Dribbles in general space with changes in direction and speed (4)

*Suggested grade-level outcomes for student learning.

T Try bouncing the ball with two hands.

T Now try bouncing with one hand.

T Try bouncing with the other hand.

Bouncing a Ball Down (Dribbling) Continuously

Setting: Children scattered in general space, each with a ball

Tasks/Challenges:

T Try bouncing the ball with both hands so it keeps going for three times in a row. This bounce that keeps going is called a dribble.

T Try dribbling the ball with one hand. If it starts to get away from you, catch it, and start over again.

T Now try the other hand.

C Can you bounce five times in a row?

T Try changing from one hand to the other.

Dribbling and Walking

Setting: Children scattered in general space, each with a ball

Tasks/Challenges:

T Bounce the ball with two hands and catch as you take three slow steps forward. Stop and then go again.

T Try bouncing the ball with one hand while you take three slow steps forward. Stop and then go again.

C See if you can take five steps without losing the ball.

Control Level (GLSP): Learning Experiences Leading to Skill Development

At the control level, children begin with experiences in self-space that are similar to those at the precontrol level but focus on the critical elements of the skill. Learning experiences provide opportunities to learn to dribble in different places around the body and then progress to dribbling and traveling while varying both direction and pathway. In all experiences, children are encouraged to use both the preferred and nonpreferred hands.

A note about cues: *Although several cues are listed for many of the learning experiences, it's important to focus on only one cue at a time. This way, the children can really concentrate on that cue. Once you provide feedback to the children and observe that most have learned a cue, it's time to focus on another one.*

Dribbling in Self-Space

Setting: Children scattered throughout general space, each with a ball

Cues

Fingerpads	(Use the fingerpads, not fingertips.) (*Demonstrate*)
Knees Bent	(Bend the knees slightly.)
Push, Push	(Push to the floor, snap the wrist at the end)
Opposite Foot	(Opposite foot slightly forward; see Figure 25.10.)

Tasks/Challenges:

T Dribble the ball with one hand.

T Dribble the ball with the other hand.

C Count the number of times you can dribble without losing control.

T On the signal, begin dribbling with one hand. Continue dribbling until the signal is given to stop.

Figure 25.10 Correct hand and body position for dribbling a ball.

Have children repeat each task with their nonpreferred hand throughout all levels of the skill. The proficient dribbler is equally skilled with each hand.

Continuous Dribbling

Setting: Children scattered in general space, each with a ball (either a smaller basketball or a playground ball)

Cues

Fingerpads	(Use the finger pads, not fingertips.)
Knees Bent	(Bend the knees slightly.)
Push, Push	(Push to the floor, snap the wrist at the end.)
Opposite Foot	(Opposite foot of the dribbling hand should be slightly forward.)

Tasks/Challenges:

T Remember when you bounced a ball down so it came back up to you and then pushed it down again so the bounce continued? This continuous bounce is called a dribble. Practice dribbling now.

C Practice until you can dribble the ball five times without losing control of it.

C Say one letter of the alphabet for each time you dribble. Can you get to Z?

Tip: Children tend to dribble either with the whole palm or with the ends of the fingers. Besides using the term fingerpads, we have also found it useful to put chalk or tape on the fingerpads to help children learn the correct part of their fingers to use.

? Point to which parts of your fingers are used for dribbling.

? *Student Drawing.* Students are provided with a drawing of a handprint and are asked to color the portion of the hand used in mature dribbling. Students may also be asked to draw an entire person dribbling to show the overall critical elements of this movement task.

Criteria for Assessment

a. Correctly identifies position of hand used in mature dribbling.

b. Identifies the critical elements of dribbling.

NASPE (1995, pp. 20–21)

Dribbling at Different Levels

Setting: Children scattered throughout general space, each with a ball

Cues

Knees Bent	(Bend the knees slightly.)
Push, Push	(Push hard to the floor; snap the wrist at the end.)
Hand on Top of Ball	(Make sure your hand touches the ball almost on its top.)

Tip: The preceding cues focus on the skill of dribbling. At the same time, it is necessary to check to see if children are also dribbling at the appropriate level. The cues would then change to high, middle, and low.

Tasks/Challenges:

🅣 Staying in self-space, dribble the ball with your preferred hand. Continue dribbling until you hear the signal to stop.

🅣 Dribble the ball at a low level so it bounces only to your knees. Keep your body in a standing position; don't kneel or squat to the floor.

🅣 Dribble the ball so it rebounds to a level between your waist and your knees. This middle-level dribble is the one most often used in games. We will probably practice this the most often.

🅣 This time try to dribble really high so the ball comes up to your shoulders.

🅣 On the signal, begin dribbling the ball at waist level. When you hear the drumbeat, change to dribbling at a low level. On the next beat, change to a high level. Then on the final beat, go back to a middle level. Stay in your self-space.

❓ At which level was it easiest to control the ball? Which was the hardest?

Dribbling and Looking

Setting: Children scattered in general space, alone at first and later with partners, each child with a ball for dribbling

Cue

Look Up	(Eyes looking forward, not down at the ball.)

Tasks/Challenges:

🅣 Begin dribbling the ball, then raise your head and continue dribbling without looking at the ball. You may want to find a spot on the wall to look at to help you look up. Just glance down at the ball sometimes to check on it. Your peripheral vision enables you to look straight ahead and still see the ball. Your peripheral vision is your ability to see things at the edges of your field of vision and straight ahead at the same time. This is extremely important in a game involving dribbling.

🅣 For this task, you will need a partner, and each one of you will need a ball. Face your partner; decide which one of you will be the first leader. The leader starts dribbling at any level he or she wants; the partner must follow by dribbling at any other level than the level at which the leader is dribbling. For example, if the leader is dribbling at a high level, the partner can dribble at a low or a middle level. The leader can change levels after three dribbles at the same level. Use quick changes of level to try to fake your partner. When you hear the signal (about 30 seconds), change leaders.

Dribbling at the precontrol and control levels requires an awareness of space.

©Lars A. Niki

? *Peer Observation.* Dribbling at the control level readily lends itself to peer assessment. Check cards (index cards with the cues listed) can be used. The observer calls out how the partner is to dribble (e.g., low and right-handed) and then checks off the cues that are used. Any combination of movement concepts can be combined with dribbling. *See Chapter 12 for examples of peer observation cards.*

Dribbling While Switching Hands

Setting: Children scattered in general space, each with a ball for dribbling

Cue	
Hand to Side of Ball	(Keep your hand a little behind and to the outside of the ball.)

Tasks/Challenges:

T Begin dribbling with your preferred hand. After several dribbles, switch to the other hand and continue dribbling. Don't catch the ball; simply switch from dribbling with one hand to dribbling with the other.

T Begin dribbling with your preferred hand. Dribble five times, and then switch to your other hand. Continue to switch after five dribbles per hand. **One change here from the regular dribbling hints: Instead of having your hand directly on top of the ball, it is helpful to push the ball from the side when you want to change dribbling hands.**

T On the signal, begin dribbling with your preferred hand. Each time you hear the drumbeat, switch hands. Continue to dribble and switch hands on each drumbeat until you hear the signal to stop. **Don't forget to switch the feet for opposite foot forward.**

C See if you can dribble continuously, switching hands for 1 minute without losing control.

? When switching hands while dribbling, why does your hand position on the ball need to change?

Dribbling with the Body in Different Positions

Setting: Children scattered in general space, each with a ball for dribbling

Cues	
Push, Push	(Push hard to the floor; snap the wrist at the end.)
Ball: Side and Front	(Keep the ball a little in front of your body and out to the side.)

Tasks/Challenges:

T Assume a kneeling position. Balance on one knee and one foot, with your body at a low level. Dribble with one hand while you maintain the balanced position.

T Dribble while in a squat or tuck position, balanced on both feet at a low level.

T Balance in different positions, dribbling with one hand. Create three different positions in which you can dribble with either your right or left hand.

T Begin dribbling in a standing position. Continue to dribble as you change your position to a low level—a kneeling or squatting position. Continue changing body positions while maintaining the dribble.

Choose several children to demonstrate the combinations of body positions they assume while dribbling.

C This time you get to develop a dribbling routine. Using the three balance positions you developed before; create a sequence or routine that moves from one balance position to another all the time maintaining your dribble. After you can connect all the balances, develop a beginning and ending to your routine.

Dribbling in Different Places Around the Body While Stationary

Setting: Children scattered in general space, each with a ball for dribbling

Cues	
Ball Close to Body	(Ball close to body, within half an arm's length.)
Push, Push	(Push hard to the floor; snap the wrist at the end.)

Tasks/Challenges:

T Standing in self-space, dribble the ball in different places around your body: on your right, on your left, behind your legs. **As you dribble, remember to keep the ball close to your body.**

T Begin dribbling with your right hand; after several dribbles, bounce the ball under your right leg from back to front, and continue the dribble with your left hand. **The hand position will be like that for switching hands, a little to the side of the ball.**

T Practice the skill from right to left and from left to right until you can execute it in both directions.

T Dribble the ball directly in front of your body; bounce the ball between your legs from front to back. **You will need to twist your body to recover the dribble in the back.**

T Can you dribble the ball from back to front?

C Put together a dribbling sequence of all the ways you can dribble in self-space: in front, to the side, in back, around your body, between your legs. Remember, change levels as you go and to find different positions balanced on different parts.

? *Exit Slip.* This might be a good time to include an exit slip to assess students' knowledge of different positions, places around the body, and levels, as well as a self-assessment of skill. A possible exit slip could ask children to write out the dribbling sequence they performed, indicating which positions were easy and which they will want to practice in the future.

Dribbling with control requires concentration.

©Barbara Adamcik

Dribble While Changing Directions in Self-Space

Setting: Children arranged in a scattered formation, about 3 to 4 feet apart, all facing the same direction (Figure 25.11); teacher at the front of the group, facing the children

Cues	
Hand Position	(Moving to the side, your hand is on the side; moving forward, hand behind; moving backward, hand in front.)
Step-Close	(Moving sideways, step-close in a sideways direction without crossing your feet.)

Tasks/Challenges:

T Begin dribbling in self-space, keeping your head up, eyes focused on me. On the first signal, I'll point to your left; dribble with your right hand as you sidestep to your left. When you hear the next signal, stop your travel but continue to dribble. I'll then point forward; travel backward as you dribble. Stop on the signal. Each time the signal is given, change the direction of your travel: right, left, forward, backward. The hand positions we used before are important here.

Children need both verbal and visual directional signs as well as audible signals (via drumbeat or noise maker) for change of directions. The children will mirror your visual cues.

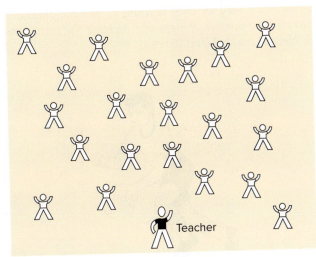

Figure 25.11 Formation for practicing dribbling and moving in directions the teacher suggests.

Dribbling and Traveling

Setting: Children scattered throughout general space, each with a ball

Cue	
Hand Position	(Contact behind rather than on top of ball.)
Front and Side	(Ball in front and to the side of the body)

Note: When the focus of the task is shifted to dribbling while traveling, the cues also shift (see Figure 25.12). The two slightly altered critical elements are:

- Contact behind rather than on top of the ball
- Ball in front and to the side of the body

The critical elements that remain the same as for stationary dribbling are:

- Knees bent
- Firm contact with fingerpads (not the fingertips); push, don't slap, the ball
- Eyes looking forward, not down at the ball
- Height of dribble at middle level

Tasks/Challenges:

T This time start dribbling in self-space. After a few dribbles, take four steps; then stop and dribble three times in self-space; then take four more steps; then stop and dribble three times. Keep traveling in general space like this until you hear the stop signal. **As you dribble, push the ball slightly forward.**

Tip: This task works well when children are first learning to travel and dribble because they are able to regain control of the ball if they are close to losing it. You can gradually increase the number of steps and decrease the stationary dribbles as the skill level increases.

Figure 25.12 Hand and ball position for dribbling while traveling.

T Begin dribbling and walking in general space. When you hear the drumbeat, stop in self-space and continue dribbling. The second drumbeat is the signal to travel again. The pattern is this: drumbeat, travel with dribble, drumbeat, stop with continued dribble....

C Each of you has 100 points. On the signal, begin traveling in general space. If you lose control of the ball, subtract 10 points; if you collide with another person, subtract 25 points. I'll time you for 60 seconds; try to keep all 100 points. Ready? Begin.

Another way to do the challenge is to have it as "Keep it Zero." Each person has no points, and you add points rather than subtract. It works well if children's subtraction skills aren't as developed as their addition skills.

? *Teacher Observation.* At this point, when children are beginning to combine skills and practice them in more dynamic situations, it is appropriate to use a teacher checklist or observation to assess youngsters' continued use of the critical elements.

Dribbling, Traveling, and Switching Hands

Setting: Children scattered in general space, each with a ball for dribbling

Cues	
Hand Position	(Contact behind and a little to the outside of ball.)
Head Up, Look Forward	(Eyes looking forward, not down at the ball.

Tasks/Challenges:

T Start dribbling with your preferred hand while walking. On the signal, without stopping, change the dribbling to the other hand and keep walking.

T Begin dribbling in general space; each time you meet someone, switch hands, and continue to travel and dribble.

? We have now practiced three different hand positions on the ball. Where should your hand be for stationary dribbling? Where should it be for dribbling while traveling? Where should it be for switching from one hand to the other?

Utilization Level (GLSP): Learning Experiences Leading to Skill Development

At the utilization level, tasks and challenges focus on traveling while dribbling and on incorporating traveling into dynamic game-like situations by combining the skills of throwing, catching, dodging, and dribbling; the complexity of the dribbling is increased by providing children with situations in which they must dribble with either hand, without looking at the ball.

A note about cues: *Although several cues are listed for many of the learning experiences, it's important to focus on only one cue at a time. This way, the children can really concentrate on that cue. Once you provide feedback to the children and observe that most have learned a cue, it's time to focus on another one.*

Dribbling and Changing Speed of Travel

Setting: Children scattered in general space (alone at first and later with partners), each child with a ball

Cues	
Head up, look forward	(Eyes looking forward, not down at the ball.))
Ball Low	(Dribble the ball only as high as your waist.)

Tip: You may also need to refocus on speeds here. If so, the cues would be fast, medium, and slow. (See Chapter 14.)

Tasks/Challenges:

T Travel throughout general space, maintaining a controlled dribble at all times. Travel sometimes very fast, sometimes slowly.

T Begin moving through general space with a slow, steady walk. As you're dribbling, focus your eyes on a spot on the floor 15 to 20 feet away. Without stopping your dribble, move as quickly as possible to that spot. When you arrive, stop your travel but continue dribbling. Visually choose another spot and repeat the sequence. The ability to change speeds and maintain a continuous dribble is a very important offensive skill in basketball.

T This time as you travel, practice quickly changing the speed of your dribble as you travel to your chosen point. It will be as if you have almost invisible stops and starts along the way. Slow down and speed up, changing the speed of travel in mid-dribble.

T Stand beside a partner whose dribbling skill is very similar to yours. Partner 1 begins the travel/dribble throughout space, changing from fast to slow speeds at will. Partner 2 attempts to stay beside partner 1 at all times. Both of you will dribble continuously. When the signal is given, rest for 10 seconds. Then partner 2 becomes the leader.

C Now practice your movement with your partner so that you are like twins moving around the room.

See if you can move while perfectly matching each other all the time.

Dribbling in General Space While Changing Directions

Setting: Children scattered throughout general space, each with a ball for dribbling. Markers scattered throughout the space.

Cues	
Hand Position	(Moving to the side, your hand is on the side; moving forward, hand behind; moving backward, hand in front.)
Step-Close	(Moving sideways, step-close in a sideways direction without crossing your feet.)

Tasks/Challenges:

T Dribble throughout general space; whenever you come to a marker, change the direction of your travel: sometimes travel forward, sometimes backward, sometimes to the right, sometimes to the left. Travel slowly when you first begin the travel/dribble with a change of direction. Maintain the dribble during all your direction changes; don't stop and start again. The hand positions we used before are important here. If you want to go to the side, your hand is on the side; to go forward, hand behind; to go backward, hand in front.

Traveling backward and dribbling isn't easy because the ball must move toward the body and often hits the feet. Children should develop this direction last and should be made aware of the difficulty of dribbling backward.

T Begin dribbling in general space, traveling in a forward direction. Each time you hear the drumbeat, quickly change the direction of your travel and continue the travel/dribble.

Dribbling in Different Pathways

Setting: Children scattered in general space (alone at first, then with a partner), each with a ball. (Note: if you notice children having difficulty adhering to pathways, try taping pathways on the floor as a visual cue.)

Cues	
Ball Close	(Ball close to your body, within half an arm's length.)
Ball on Outside	(Keep the ball on the outside of the curve or zigzag, the wide side.) (Demonstrate; see Figure 25.13.)

Figure 25.13 Dribbling in a curved or zigzag pathway.

Tasks/Challenges:

T Now try dribbling curved pathways. **If you curve to the left, dribble with your right hand; if you curve to the right, dribble with your left hand. Always keep the ball on the outside of the curve.**

Figure 25.14 A child's dribbling pathway map.

T This time travel/dribble throughout general space, quickly moving from side to side in a zigzag pathway. Make sure the ball changes hands each time you move from side to side.

T This time start your travel in a straight pathway as you dribble. Each time you meet another person or hear the drum, turn quickly to your right or left and continue to travel/dribble in a straight pathway.

T You will still start your travel/dribble in a straight pathway. But on the signal, now quickly zigzag to miss an imaginary opponent and then continue dribbling in a straight pathway.

T Stand approximately 3 feet behind a partner; each of you has a basketball (playground ball). Partner 1 (in front) travels/dribbles throughout general space, changing pathways. Partner 2 (in back) follows staying about 3 feet behind the lead partner at all times. Switch leaders on the signal.

C Design a traveling/dribbling strategy to move from the center of the gym (or outside blacktop) to the end line. Design the strategy using combinations of pathways to outsmart imaginary opponents. Practice the traveling/dribbling strategy until you can do it three times exactly the same way. After you are done, draw and write out your strategy (Figure 25.14).

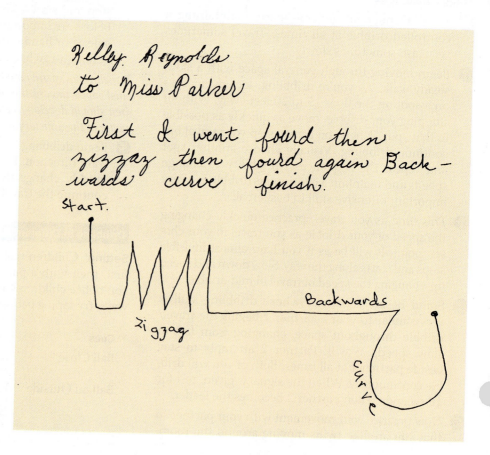

💬 If I were to place three opponents in your way, could you still execute your plan?

Setting: The gym set up with four or more "vacation spots" around the space. Each vacation spot should be designated with a large cone, a laminated picture of the vacation spot (e.g., Rocky Mountains #1, Disney World #2, Statue of Liberty #3, Joshua Tree National Park #4) and envelopes for each group with tasks in them. For example:

Envelope #1: Make up a name for your group that you all agree on!

Envelope #2: Make up a group cheer that you all agree on. At your final vacation spot, you have to shout your group cheer as loudly as possible. Example: *1, 2, 3, Go Tigers! Give me a T, give me an I, give me a G, give me an E, give me an R, give me an S! What's that spell? TIGERS!*

Envelope #3: Introduce yourself and your group name to the teacher! Example: Hi! My name is _____. Our group name is _____.

Envelope #4: Write down one nice thing about somebody in your group on a note card.

Children in four or more groups (note that the number of groups and the number of vacation spots should be the same). Number groups 1 through 4.

ⓒ Your group is going on a vacation around the United States. Each group will start at the vacation spot that matches your group number. Your group must dribble with your hands using curved or zig-zag pathways to get to the next vacation spot. Each group member must use the same pathway to reach the vacation spot, and you must follow the person in front of you. Once you have arrived at your new vacation spot, find the envelope with your group number on it, open the envelope, and follow the directions found inside the envelope. Before your group can continue to the next vacation spot, you will need to complete the directions found in your group's envelope and draw the pathway your group is going to use to get to the next vacation spot. Your group must travel over the star in the middle of the map before reaching your next vacation spot.

(This task was created by Jerod Dean and Brian Gerwig, University of Northern Colorado, Greeley, Colorado.)

💬 *Event Task.* The above task can easily be used as a formative or summative assessment.

Mirroring and Matching While Dribbling

(See Chapter 16, "Relationships," for a discussion of mirroring and matching.)

Setting: Partners of approximately the same skill level facing each other about 3 to 4 feet apart

Cues	
Mirroring	(Like looking in a mirror.)
Matching	(Use the same hand.)
Head Up, Look Forward	(Eyes looking forward, not down at the ball.)

Tasks/Challenges:

Ⓣ Face your partner. The partner whose name comes first in the alphabet is the first leader. The leader starts dribbling, and the follower has to mirror the actions of the leader. Remember, mirroring is like looking in a mirror. If your partner uses the left hand, you use your right hand. Don't make it too hard on your partner; you want them to be successful. On the signal (about 45 seconds), change leaders.

Ⓣ Now that you have gotten to be so good, try matching your partner's actions. Matching is harder than mirroring when you're facing your partner. Remember, if your partner works with the left hand, you will use your left hand.

Ⓣ This one is really hard. The leader can now travel in general space. The follower must try to copy exactly what the leader does. This is matching again.

Dribbling While Stopping, Starting, and Turning (Pivots and Fakes)

Setting: Children scattered in general space, each with a ball

Cues	
Ball Close	(Ball close to your body, within half an arm's length.)
Forward–Backward Stance	(Opposite forward when you stop.)

Tasks/Challenges:

Ⓣ Standing in your own space, we are first going to practice pivoting without the ball. To do this, stand in a forward–backward stance with your opposite foot forward (the foot opposite your preferred dribbling hand). The opposite foot is your pivot foot. **To pivot, you would spin (as if squashing a bug) on the opposite foot while stepping forward or backward with your preferred foot.** In your space, practice each of these until you can do them smoothly.

T Now we are going to combine dribbling and pivoting. Again in your own space, begin by dribbling the ball with your preferred hand. Keep dribbling and practice turning forward as you pivot, all the time maintaining the dribble. **As you pivot, the ball will change to your nonpreferred hand.**

T Now practice turning backward as you pivot while maintaining the dribble. **As you pivot, the ball will change to your nonpreferred hand.**

T Begin dribbling in general space. Travel slowly at first, and then gradually increase your speed until you are moving at a medium speed while maintaining your dribble. On the signal, quickly stop both your travel and the dribble.

T Begin dribbling throughout general space. On the signal, stop quickly in a forward–backward stance, maintaining the dribble. Pivot turning backward; turn on the ball of your foot. Continue your travel/dribble. **Remember, the ball changes hands as you turn.**

T This time try to turn forward to pivot when you stop.

C As you are moving, I will call out forward or backward. See if you can pivot in the called direction each time.

T Choose a point across the gym. Begin dribbling in general space, moving toward your point. Every time you come to a line on the floor, stop, fake as if you are going to change pathways, and keep going. **To use a fake, come to a stop, quickly take a step with one foot as if you are going to change pathways, and then keep going in the same pathway.** It may be easier if you pretend there is an imaginary defender in your way who you have to get around. When you reach your point, choose another one and keep going.

T This time, as you travel to your point, sometimes fake and sometimes change pathways. **Remember, in a game, you are trying to outsmart a defender.**

Dribbling Around Stationary Obstacles in General Space

Setting: Cones placed randomly (not in a line) throughout general space (spots do not work well because children can travel over them) with varying space between the cones (place some 3 feet apart, others 5 to 6 feet apart)

Cue	
Cone, Body, Ball,	(Protect the ball by putting your body between the cone and the ball.)

Tasks/Challenges:

T Travel/dribble throughout general space, dribbling around the obstacles keeping your body between the ball and the obstacles. Make sure to change hands so the outside hand will be the one dribbling when you pass an obstacle.

C See if you can dribble 60 seconds without bumping into an obstacle or another person or losing control of the ball. See how many obstacles you can pass in the 60 seconds. **Remember, Head Up, Look Forward.**

Dribbling Around Stationary Obstacles in Limited Space

Setting: The floor or blacktop divided into a series of alleys with colored tape; children in groups, one group per alley

Cue	
Person, Body, Ball,	(Protect the ball by putting your body between the person and the ball.)

Tasks/Challenges:

T One person in your group will be the dribbler; that person will stand at the end of the alley. The others in your group should arrange themselves in a zig-zag obstacle pattern in your alley (Figure 25.15). The dribbler attempts to dribble the length of the alley, avoiding the obstacles and staying within the side boundaries. The obstacles try to gain possession of the ball. Obstacles can stretch and pivot, but one foot must remain glued in place at all times. Obstacles can touch only the ball, not the dribbler.

The difficulty of this task can be increased or decreased by adjusting the width of the alley or by changing the alley to a square and spreading the obstacles out. Always begin with larger spaces so the dribbler has the advantage.

Dribbling and Passing with a Partner

Setting: Partners, at one side of the gymnasium or blacktop; one partner with a basketball for dribbling and passing

Cues	
Receiver Slightly Ahead of Passer	(Receiver about four or five steps ahead of the passer.)
Lead Receiver	(Pass to the open space just in front of the receiver.)
No Stopping	(Both the passer and the receiver should be moving.)
Smooth Transitions	(Dribble and pass; Catch and dribble—one motion.)

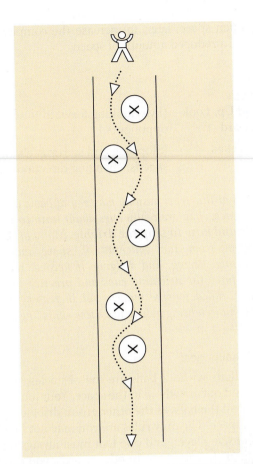

Figure 25.15 Dribbling around stationary obstacles in general space.

Tasks/Challenges:

NOTE: *Before beginning this task, children should have gained competence in throwing and catching on the move and to a moving partner (see Chapter 24).*

T To start, we are going to dribble and pass to a stationary partner. You and your partner should be facing each other about 20 feet apart. One of you will take about five dribbles moving toward your partner. After the fifth dribble, pass the ball to your partner without stopping your dribble. **The trick is as soon as the ball reaches the top of the dribble, put two hands on it and pass. The ball should never stop in your hands.** After five tries, switch dribblers and passers.

T This time the object of this task is to practice passing while moving forward. You and your partner are traveling in the same direction. Your job is to move across the space to the other line. Partner 1 will dribble three or four times and then pass to partner 2, who has been traveling forward. Partner 2 receives the pass, dribbles as he or she travels forward, and then passes back to partner 1. Partners continue to travel/dribble the length of the

space. With this task both the passer and the receiver should always be moving to the other side; never stop moving forward. To really make the action smooth pick up the ball to pass in one motion without having to stop and receive the ball from the pass to the dribble in one motion.

Setting: Partners about 15 feet apart, scattered throughout general space, each pair with a ball

Tasks/Challenges:

T On the signal, begin traveling, dribbling, and passing to your partner. (*Allow about 2 minutes of activity, and then rest for 10 seconds. Repeat.*)

Dribbling Against an Opponent: One-on-One

Before beginning tasks that involve offense and defense, students should be skilled with the space awareness and dodging tasks that ask them to use the offensive and defensive skills of moving into open space; avoiding other persons; and using fakes, stops and starts, pivots, and other avoidance skills without manipulating equipment. (See Chapter 14, "Space Awareness," and Chapter 18, "Chasing, Fleeing, and Dodging.") Children need to have polished these skills before they are asked to use them while manipulating equipment.

One key to this task—and to other initial tasks involving offense and defense—is to clearly define the boundaries of the space the students are to use. A small space gives an advantage to the defense; a large space provides an offensive advantage. Similarly, a long, narrow space gives the advantage to the defense; a wider space helps the offense. Initial tasks should generally favor the offense.

Setting: Partners facing each other scattered throughout general space, each pair with a ball. One begins as an offensive player and the other a defensive player.

Cues	
Offense	
Head Up, Eyes on defense	(Eyes looking forward on defense.)
Move to Goal	(Always move to your goal.)
Ball, Body, Shield, Defense	(Body between ball and defense; nondribbling arm curled to shield from opponent.)
Defense	
Body Between Offense and Goal	(Body between offense and goal, face the opponent. l.)
Watch Hips	(Watch the offensive players hips.)
Give Space	(Two to three feet away from the offense.)

Tasks/Challenges:

🔵 Select a partner who dribbles while traveling as well as or slightly better than you do. Select a make-believe point across the space that will be your goal. On the signal, partner 1 begins dribbling while traveling toward the make-believe goal; partner 2 (facing partner 1) attempts to gain possession of the ball by tapping it away. Neither partner should foul the other by bumping, pushing away, nor reaching in. Partner 1 attempts to keep possession of the ball for 30 seconds; if partner 2 gets the ball, he or she gives it back. At the end of 30 seconds, partner 2 will dribble and partner 1 will try to take the ball away. Begin.

❓ *Digital Recording.* If the previous task is digitally recorded through still pictures or motion, and coupled with a self-assessment of the use of the critical elements, youngsters start to understand how the skills are used and developed in dynamic, changing situations. Students could be provided with a self-assessment checklist and view the recording with their partner to analyze "film" as coaches do.

Proficiency Level (GLSP): Learning Experiences Leading to Skill Development

Children at the proficiency level seem to dribble without thinking about it; dribbling seems to be almost automatic. They're able to change direction, speed, and pathway at will. They're challenged by situations that involve other children as partners or as opponents who make the situation increasingly unpredictable. They enjoy dribbling in larger groups with more complex relationships and the excitement of strategy development.

A note about cues: *At the proficiency level, tasks are more complex, typically requiring children to coordinate several movements simultaneously in a dynamic context. A list of cues is provided to assist the children in being more successful in the learning experiences. The challenge is in determining which cue will be most beneficial for each child—and when. Thus, careful observation and critical reflection become very important as you watch the children move and then decide which cue will be the most helpful to move each learner to a higher level.*

Dribbling Against Opponents: Stationary Defenders

Setting: Children divided into two equal groups, one group with playground balls for dribbling; initially, a fairly open space; later, to increase the complexity of the task, a reduced amount of space

Cues	
Offense	
Head Up, Look Forward	(Eyes looking forward to see opponents.)
Use Fakes	(Stopping and starting, changing speeds, changing directions.)

*The cues at this level assume mastery of basic dribbling skills; hence, they are really cues about **how to use the dribble and how to stop the dribble.** Many of the cues are taken from the concepts of space awareness and chasing, fleeing, and dodging. If needed, return to and reinforce the dribbling cues and practice the basic offensive and defensive moves, but increasingly move toward children being able to use these skills in game-like situations.*

Tasks/Challenges:

🔵 Students without balls are the obstacles; you can spread out anywhere in the space. Your job is to try to steal the balls as the other group dribbles across the space. The only rules are you may not touch an offensive player, and one foot must always remain "glued" to your spot. In other words, you can step with one foot, but you cannot move from your spot. On the signal, the offense will begin dribbling from one end line and try to get to the other side without losing the ball. If the defense (the obstacles) gets a ball, just give it back. We'll trade places after three tries.

When the activity is a game situation with competing skills, it is best if you ask children to form groups with those "whose skill levels are about the same as theirs," or if you divide the children into groups so that groups have relatively equal skill levels.

Dribble Tag

Setting: Each child with a playground ball for dribbling; two or three children designated "it" wearing identifying jerseys if possible

Cues	
Head Up, Look Forward	(Eyes looking forward to see opponents.)
Use Fakes	(Stopping and starting, changing speeds, changing directions.)

Tasks/Challenges:

C On the signal, everyone with a ball will begin dribbling in general space. The players who are "it" will try to tag you as you're traveling and dribbling. You're caught if:

1. You're tagged by an "it."
2. You lose control of the ball.

If you're caught, stand and hold the ball above your head. You'll be free to travel if a player who is dribbling touches you. Each 2 minutes, we'll rest for 10 seconds while I choose new people to be "it."

A way to make this activity more complex is to have the taggers not have to dribble. This small change calls for a significant increase in dribbling skills and more closely resembles basketball game-like activities. Just remember the heightened level of dribbling skill needed.

Dribbling While Dodging

Setting: Children, each with a basketball or a playground ball and a flag tucked in the waist

Cues	
Head Up, Look Forward	(Eyes looking forward to see opponents.)
Use Fakes	(Stopping and starting, changing speeds, changing directions.)
Ball, Body, Shield, Defense	(Body between ball and defense; nondribbling arm curled to shield from opponent.)

Tasks/Challenges:

C You will need a partner of about your same ability level for this task. You will need to establish clear boundaries for your area, about 10 feet square. Start by facing each other and dribbling. The object is to keep dribbling and pull your partner's flag. See how many times you can pull your partner's flag in 2 minutes.

? What is one hint for not losing control of the ball in this activity?

Maintaining Possession While Dribbling and Passing

Setting: A clearly defined space (the complexity of the task is increased or decreased depending upon the size of the space; initially, a larger space gives the advantage to the offense); groups of three

Cues	
Offense	
Receiver Moves to An Open Space	(Move to an open space at an angle to the passer.) (See Chapter 24 for a detailed explanation of this cue.)
Lead the Receiver	(Pass the ball to the open space just in front of the receiver.)
Defense	
Go After the Ball	(Pressure person with ball.)
Hustle	(Move quickly when the ball is passed.)

Tasks/Challenges:

T Working in your group of three, two of you will dribble and pass while the third player tries to steal the ball. We'll rotate the interceptor every 2 minutes. Remember, you must either be dribbling or passing the ball. You may not hold it; no touching. Be sure to stay in your boundaries.

Child-Designed Dribbling/Passing Routines

This task is an example of a child-designed instructional approach. See Chapter 9 for more ideas on child-designed tasks.

Setting: Groups of four to six; a space about 15 feet square; any number of basketballs; music and audio device (optional)

Cues	
	The cues for this task are dependent upon what you want students to include in the routine. Some possibilities:
Pathways	(In your routine be sure to include at least two different pathways: straight, curved, zigzag.)
Dribbling	(The dribbling part of your routine needs to include different levels of dribbling and dribbling in different places around the body.)

Tasks/Challenges:

C Put together a series of dribbling and passing skills in a fancy routine—kind of like a basketball warm-up drill. Design the floor pattern, ways to travel, individual tricks, and partner or group skills. In your routine, be sure to include at least two different pathways: straight, curved, zigzag. The dribbling part of your routine needs to include different levels of dribbling and dribbling in different places around the body. Your routine might also include passing. Practice your routine until you have it memorized and in time with the music.

? *Digital Analysis.* Routines such as this are good places to use digital recordings for observation and assessment. The digital recording also adds incentive for students to perform well and do their best. Remember, design your scoring rubrics ahead of time so students know what is expected of their performance. *See Chapter 12 for guidance in designing rubrics.*

Dribbling and Throwing at a Target

Setting: Four-foot-square targets marked with colored tape on the walls of the gym, approximately 7 feet above the floor; each child with a ball at first, then later with partners and a shared ball

Cues

| No Stopping | (Dribble and throw without stopping.) |
| Watch the Target | (Eyes on the target.) |

Tasks/Challenges:

T Beginning at the center of the gymnasium, travel/dribble toward the target on the wall. When you're within 12 feet of the target, throw the ball, trying to hit the wall within the target square. Collect the ball, quickly move to the side, and return to middle of the space.

T Select a partner who will serve as defense. Partner 1 dribbles toward the wall and attempts to score by hitting the target; partner 2 tries to gain possession of the ball on the dribble or block the throw to the target. Change partner roles after each try.

T Practice the dribble/target activity with an offensive partner. Combine dribbling and passing to a partner as you travel toward the target. Alternate the throw to the target between partners.

? *Event Task.* By having partners join with another set of partners for a two-on-two game of dribbling, passing, and throwing at a target, you can create a child-designed game to be used as an event task. *(See Chapter 12 for creating a scoring rubric to use with child-designed games. See Chapter 31 for information on child-designed games.)*

Tip: Place targets around the walls as space allows. Place targets on both sides and on end walls to provide maximum activity.

Dribble/Pass Keep-Away

Setting: Groups of four in a space about one-quarter the size of a basketball court (or smaller)

Cues

Offense

Don't Pass Until the Defense Commits	(Until the defense plays defense on you, no need to pass.)
Receiver Moves to an Open Space	(Move to an open space at an angle to the passer.)
Defense	
First Player Ball; Second Player Receiver	(Defend person with the ball first; then the receiver.)
Go After the Ball	(Pressure player with ball.)

Tasks/Challenges:

T In your group, two of you will dribble and pass while the other two try to gain possession of the ball either by intercepting the pass or by stealing the ball on the dribble. Remember, on defense, you cannot touch the other player. When you walk, you must dribble the basketball.

Child-Designed Invasion Game

This task is an example of a child-designed instructional approach. See Chapter 31 for more ideas on child-designed games.

Setting: Groups of no more than three; half-court or short basketball court with lowered baskets

Cues

Offense

Don't Pass Until the Defense Commits	(Until the defense plays defense on you, there is no need to pass)
Receiver Move to an Open Space	(Move to an open space at an angle to the passer.)
Defense	
Go After Ball	(Pressure the player with the ball.)
Ball, Body, Basket	(Keep your body between the basket and the offensive player.)
Hustle Back	(After a score, run back down the court.)

Tasks/Challenges:

Ⓒ If you are comfortable with your skills of dribbling, passing, and throwing at a target, you may want to play a small-group game that involves shooting at a target. The maximum number of players on a team is three. The one rule I have is that every player must touch the ball before a shot is made. Match the skills on your team so the game will be a challenge for everyone; it's no fun if the score is a runaway.

❓ *Event Task.* At this point, it is helpful to have students think about their skill as well as doing it. Before beginning team play, have students think of all the skills needed for being successful in an invasion game–type situation: spatial awareness, throwing, catching, traveling, dodging, dribbling, shooting at a target. Within each group, discuss what a person needs to be able to do with each skill to be successful in basketball.

Reading Comprehension Questions

1. Discuss the difference between volleying and dribbling.
2. Name four body parts that can be used to volley a ball.
3. What is the primary focus of the tasks at the precontrol level of volleying? What is the teacher trying to accomplish before moving on to the control level?
4. List four different types of balls that can be used to practice volleying at the precontrol level.
5. What does the phrase "strike the ball with a level body part" mean? What does the phrase "meeting the ball" mean?
6. Rank the following tasks by placing the number 1 in front of the easiest (most basic) task, the number 2 in front of the next more difficult task, and so on.
   ( ) Volleying a ball to different levels
   ( ) Volleying a ball with two hands
   ( ) Volleying a ball to outwit an opponent
   ( ) Volleying a balloon
   ( ) Volleying a ball to a partner
7. Explain the meaning of the phrase "the location of the hit determines the direction of travel."
8. Give two examples of dynamic and unpredictable situations related to the skill of volleying.
9. What characterizes each of the four skill levels of dribbling?
10. What does it mean to keep one's hands firm and flexible as opposed to flat and stiff when dribbling?
11. How can you teach a child to use the fingerpads while dribbling?
12. How do the cues for dribbling change when traveling is added to the skill?
13. How does the size of the space affect dribbling skills that are used in offensive and defensive situations?
14. How do the cues for dribbling and volleying change at the proficiency level?

References/Suggested Readings

Holt/Hale, S., and T. Hall. 2016. *Lesson planning for elementary physical education: Meeting the National Standards & Grade-level Outcomes*. Champaign, IL: Human Kinetics.

[NASPE] National Association for Sport and Physical Education. 1995. *Moving into the future: National standards for physical education*. St. Louis, MO: Mosby.

[SHAPE America] Society of Health and Physical Educators. 2014. *National standards & grade-level outcomes for K-12 physical education*. Champaign, IL: Human Kinetics.

Striking with Rackets and Paddles

Ello Rumann

Tennis, racquetball, badminton, table tennis, pickleball, and squash—what do they all have in common? They are all activities in which people can participate for a lifetime, and they all stem from the skill theme of striking with a racket or paddle. Participation in lifelong physical activity requires both confidence and competence in the activity to be performed. Mastery of striking with rackets and paddles helps develop skills that provide a viable option for youth and adults to be physically active for a lifetime.

Yet, striking with rackets and paddles, as well as striking with long-handled implements (Chapter 27), is one of the last skills that children develop. There are three basic reasons: (1) children don't refine or develop visual tracking until the later elementary school years, (2) hand–eye coordination at greater distances from the body is more difficult, and (3) most often in striking situations with rackets and paddles, there are two objects in motion at once—the paddle and the object being struck.

Striking with these implements, however, is a skill children enjoy and can be taught at younger ages with a few simple equipment modifications. Because of the complexities of striking, we teach the skill of striking with rackets and paddles after children have been introduced to the skill of striking with body parts, specifically the hand (see Chapter 25). Because the difficulty of striking with an implement increases with the length of the implement, we teach the sidearm pattern of striking with rackets and paddles before striking with long-handled implements in a horizontal plane (Chapter 27). If you are teaching in a program where children only have physical education once or twice a week, mastery of the skill theme of striking with rackets and paddles may be acquired at the control level, but children will still need practice at these levels as well as utilization and proficiency levels in middle school before being introduced to the regulation games associated with them. If children do not achieve mastery at the utilization and proficiency levels before introduction to the sport, they will be unsuccessful when they have to use the skill in dynamic situations and thus likely to end their participation in activities that involve striking with rackets and paddles. The end result is that activities that involve striking with rackets and paddles will be eliminated from their list of possibilities of being physically active for a lifetime.

Children learning to strike with a racket or paddle must coordinate many familiar skills into new ones. They must learn to accurately toss or drop the object to be contacted, visually track the object while they're traveling to an appropriate location, and contact the object at exactly the right moment. And simultaneously, they must adjust to the weight and length of the

Skill Theme Development Progression

Striking with Rackets and Paddles

Proficiency Level

Child-designed racket games
Group striking across a net
Team striking across a net
Aerial striking over a net
Partner striking across a net
Striking to and from different places
Striking at angles to two walls with a partner
Striking to one wall with a partner

Utilization Level

Striking upward in a dynamic situation
Striking in various aerial pathways in dynamic situations
Striking continuously upward with a group
Striking overhead over a net
Striking overhead
Striking to different places around a partner
Hitting cooperatively and continuously with a partner
Hitting from different places

Control Level

Striking a ball rebounding from a wall
Striking continuously over and through a target
Striking backhand to the wall
Striking an object to send it over a net
Striking through a target
Striking to different places
Striking at high and low targets
Striking forehand to the wall
Striking underhand to hoops (varying the distance)
Striking underhand for distance (varying the force)
Striking underhand to wall targets
Striking to self on both sides of the body
Striking up, down, and underhand forward
Striking underhand against a wall
Striking up and down
Striking up
Striking down

Precontrol Level

Upward bound
Hit the wall
Striking a suspended ball
Balloon strike (lightweight paddle)
Paddle balance

Box 26-1

Critical Elements: Striking Forehand with Rackets and Paddles

Side to Target

Racket Back

Step on opposite foot

Swing low to high

Swing Through

Coil/Uncoil

Follow Through High

©Derek Sine & Van Tucker

implement. A successful striker must coordinate all these variables.

It is important that the teacher is familiar with the critical elements needed for quality instruction, demonstration, and observation of the skill. Throughout the chapter are sample cues (short phrases or words summarizing these critical elements). Ideally, if the cue is the last thing a teacher repeats before sending the students to practice, the learner will be cognitively focused on the critical elements.

The photo sequence in Box 26-1 shows the critical elements for sidearm striking (forehand) with rackets and paddles. Below are the critical elements for both the underhand and sidearm (forehand) strike.

The critical elements for striking are:

Striking underhand

- Face target in preparation for striking action
- Arm back in preparation for striking action
- Step with opposite foot or transfer weight from back to front foot
- Paddle face flat; slanted toward target
- Follow through to target

Striking sidearm (forehand)

- Side to target
- Racket back in preparation for striking
- Step on opposite foot as contact is made
- Paddle face flat; slanted toward target

- Swing racket or paddle low to high with firm wrist
- Follow through toward target and across shoulder

Our skill theme progression presents ideas for developing the skill of striking with rackets and paddles from the precontrol through the proficiency levels. Refer to Box 26-2 for linkages of the skill theme of striking with rackets and paddles to the *National Standards & Grade-Level Outcomes for K–12 Physical Education* (SHAPE America 2014).

Precontrol Level (GLSP): Experiences for Exploration

Children at the precontrol level struggle just to make contact between the implement and the object and are truly excited when they do—regardless of where the object goes. At this level, we provide exploratory learning experiences using short-handled, lightweight implements to contact balls, shuttlecocks, and other objects. These objects are often suspended from ropes at various heights to make the task easier.

We recommend balloons at the precontrol level because the flight of a balloon is longer and slower than that of a ball, and the child therefore has more time for visual tracking. Heavier balloons, although a bit more expensive, are more durable than inexpensive,

Striking with Rackets and Paddles in the *National Standards & Grade-Level Outcomes for K–12 Physical Education*

Striking with short-handled implements, rackets, and paddles is referenced in the *National Standards & Grade-Level Outcomes for K–12 Physical Education* (SHAPE America 2014) under Standard 1: "Demonstrates competency in a variety of motor skills and movement patterns." The intent of the standard is developing the fundamental skills needed to enjoy participation in physical activities, with the mastery of movement fundamentals as the foundation for continued skill acquisition.

Sample grade-level outcomes from the *National Standards** include:

- Strikes a lightweight object with a paddle or short-handled racket (K)
- Strikes a ball with a short-handled implement, sending it upward (1)
- Strikes an object with a short-handled implement, using consecutive hits (2)
- Strikes an object with a short-handled implement, sending it forward over a low net or to a wall (3)
- Strikes an object with a short-handled implement while demonstrating three of the five critical elements of a mature pattern (3)
- Strikes an object with a short-handled implement while demonstrating a mature pattern (4)
- Strikes an object with a short-handled implement, alternating hits with a partner over a low net or against a wall (4)
- Strikes an object consecutively, with a partner, using a short-handled implement, over a net or against a wall, in either a competitive or cooperative game environment (5)

Striking with rackets and paddles is also referenced under Standard 2. "Applies knowledge of concepts, principles, strategies and tactics related to movement and performance." The intent of this standard is facilitation of a child's ability to use cognitive information to understand and enhance motor skill acquisition and performance.

*Suggested grade-level outcomes for student learning.

lightweight balloons. They also tend to be less erratic during flight and consequently are easier for children to strike successfully. Before using balloons, be sure to check with your school about any latex restrictions that may be in place.

⚠ Striking is one skill theme in which safety plays an important role. Be sure to include wrist strings or guards on all rackets and paddles (and have children use them) and provide ample space for children to strike and move safely around one another.

Paddle Balance

Setting: A paddle and a balloon, beanbag, and ball for each child. *Foam paddles are best because they are lightweight and easy to control.*

Tasks/Challenges:

Ⓣ You're going to practice a new skill now. Try to balance the balloon on the paddle. **As you do this, try to keep the balloon in the middle of the paddle.**

©Lars A. Niki

This young girl is practicing balancing a ball on a paddle as a prerequisite to striking.

(T) If you are having a little trouble with the balloon on the paddle, you may want to try balancing a beanbag on the paddle.

(T) The balloon was fairly easy to balance, but this time we are going to make the task a little harder. Instead of a balloon, try to balance a ball on your paddle. Try to keep the ball on your paddle as long as you can.

(T) If you are really good at keeping the ball on your paddle so it doesn't fall off very often, try rolling the ball around on the paddle while still keeping it on the paddle. At times you will really have to do some fast work to keep the ball on the paddle.

(C) I will time you. See if you can keep your object on the paddle for 15 seconds. Ready? Go.

(T) This time we are going to try something even harder. Choose the object you like best. Try to walk around just in your self-space and balance the object on your paddle at the same time.

Volleybirds or petecas (badminton shuttlecocks with flat bottoms; see Chapter 25) also work well with children at the precontrol level. The youngsters learn to keep the paddle flat as they walk around carrying the volleybird or peteca on the paddle.

Balloon Strike (Lightweight Paddle)

Setting: A nylon-hose (Figure 26.1) or foam paddle and a balloon for each child; a spot or other way of defining self-space for each child. When children first begin striking balloons with paddles, tie the balloon with string to the paddle handle. This saves much chasing time and makes it easier for the children to remain in self-space.

Tasks/Challenges:

(T) In your space with your paddle and balloon, strike the balloon up in the air. Do one hit, then catch, and start again. Find out how to make the balloon go in the air.

(T) Now try to strike the balloon more than once—maybe twice—then catch.

(C) How many times can you strike the balloon, keeping it in the air without missing it or moving from your space? Five would be a really good number.

(T) So far, you've tried to stay still in your own space while you were striking the balloon. This time try to move a few steps while striking. It might be good to try and take two steps, then stop, and then take two steps again

(T) Now we are going to try to walk in general space while striking the balloon. Go slowly and look where you are going so you don't hit others. To be safe, the balloon should be close to you.

Striking a Suspended Ball

Setting: A ball suspended from a string (Figure 26.2) and a paddle for each child; for the first task, suspend the balls above shoulder height; place spots or other markings on the floor behind each ball

Tasks/Challenges:

(T) In your space, you have a ball hanging from a string. Try to strike the ball forward while standing on your spot. After each strike, be sure to stop the ball before you try to hit it again.

Setting: Balls lowered to waist height; spots moved to a position beside the suspended balls

Tasks/Challenges:

(T) Things have changed a little this time. Now your spot is beside the ball. Again, try to strike the ball from your spot so it travels straight forward—as in baseball. Be sure to stop the ball after each hit.

Figure 26.1 Construction of nylon-hose paddles. Lightweight paddles can be made from old coat hangers, nylon socks (or stockings), and tape.*

*Prior to constructing equipment we recommend you check with school administration to be certain that district policy permits homemade equipment.

C You have been striking the ball fairly well. This time, if you strike the ball well, yell, "Whacko!" If you miss, just start again.

At this point, children should be striking on their preferred side. When the children begin to strike consistently, challenge them to strike on the opposite side of their bodies (for example, backhand).

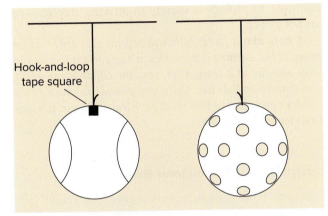

Hook-and-loop tape square

Figure 26.2 Suspending balls on strings. Glue a hook-and-loop tape square to a string and another to a tennis ball to enable the ball to drop from the string when the ball is struck, or knot string or elastic into the holes of a plastic whiffle ball. Balls can be hung from climbing apparatus, from traveling rings, and between vertical game standards, and they can be attached to walls in the corners of the gym.*

*Prior to constructing equipment, we recommend you check with school administration to be certain that district policy permits home-made equipment.

> *At the park, I noticed a girl named Sarah. Her older brothers were busy playing street hockey and tennis (on the tennis courts). She was about six and, being ignored by her brothers, was in her own world. The boys had left a tennis racket and a ball lying aside. She picked them up, held the racket somewhere in the middle of the handle, and began to try to hit the ball. It took four tries before she even made contact, and the ball rolled away into the grass. It didn't matter; you could tell by the smile on her face that she was delighted. She ran after the ball, picked it up and (after a few attempts) hit it again, and was again off to chase it. Her game took her on a journey all over the park and continued for 20 minutes or so. Then she proudly walked over to her mother and declared, "I can play tennis!"*

Hit the Wall

Setting: A foam or wooden paddle and a high-density foam ball or volleybird for each child; spots on the floor about 5 feet away from the wall to identify self-space

Tasks/Challenges:

T At your spot, strike the ball so it travels to the wall. Just try for one hit at a time. Remember, if the ball goes away from you, collect it and bring it back to your spot before striking again.

T Try hitting the ball on both sides of your body.

C Try for five single hits; if you can do five, try seven.

Equipment Modifications

Visual tracking is a skill that is not refined until the later elementary grades; therefore, striking, unless modified, is a difficult skill theme for children. A few simple equipment modifications allow young children to experience success in tracking. The use of large, slow-moving, easy-to-see objects, such as balloons or beach balls, makes tracking easier. The use of lightweight, short-handled, easily maneuverable rackets compensates for the developing hand–eye coordination and limited arm strength and endurance. The basic guideline to follow is that the equipment should not hamper the movement pattern; if it does, modify the equipment.

Upward Bound

Setting: A wooden, foam, or plexiglass paddle (Figure 26.3); a shuttlecock or volleybird and a light-weight ball; a spot or some way to define self-space for each child

Tasks/Challenges:

T This time try striking the shuttlecock (volleybird) upward. Drop the object and try to strike it so it goes straight up.

T Once you are comfortable with one hit, try to hit the shuttlecock (volleybird) more than once before catching it.

Paddles and Safety

Although wooden and plexiglass paddles are very good for learning to strike, they do present a safety problem. Paddles made of foam—with both short and long handles—are available. We prefer foam paddles whenever the children are working in close spaces or in groups.

C Try to hit the shuttlecock (volleybird) four times in a row.

T Trade in your shuttlecock (volleybird) for a ball. Try to hit the ball up in the air. **Remember, one hit and catch it; then hit again.**

T Try to strike the ball up more than once—maybe twice—and then catch it.

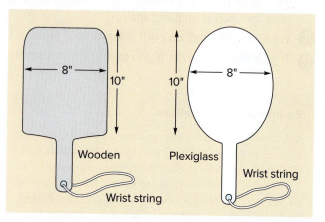

Figure 26.3 Construction of short-handled paddles. Short-handled paddles can be cut with a jigsaw from 1/2-inch finished plywood or from 1/4-inch plexiglass. Sand plywood edges until they're smooth, and wrap the handles with fiberglass tape.*Each paddle should have a wrist string for safety.*

*Prior to constructing equipment, we recommend you check with school administration to be certain that district policy permits home-made equipment.

Control Level (GLSP): Learning Experiences Leading to Skill Development

When children are able to strike a ball consistently in precontrol-level contexts, they're ready for control-level experiences, which include contacting a rebounding ball a number of times in succession, sending the object in a desired direction, and varying the force of the contact. Learning experiences at this level are designed to help children go beyond just contacting the ball. Children now learn to control the direction, force, and aerial pathway of an object. One of the first cues we give children when beginning striking tasks is "watch the ball." This is hard for many youngsters because so much else is going on around them. To help children focus on the ball, paint a bright dot or letter on it, and direct their concentration toward that mark.

At the control level, we also familiarize children to a variety of striking implements and to objects with various surfaces, lengths, and types and degrees of bounce,

including table tennis paddles, racquetball rackets, paddleball paddles, badminton and crossminton rackets, short-handled tennis rackets, paddleballs, foam tennis balls, tennis balls, racquetballs, rubber balls, shuttlecocks, petecas, speeders (the shuttlecock for speed badminton or crossminton that is more heavily weighted), and table tennis balls. This allows teachers to help children choose the equipment that best meets their needs. We also introduce children to the sidearm pattern. (At the utilization and proficiency levels, we continue to provide a variety of striking implements and objects.)

A note about cues: Although several cues are listed for many of the learning experiences, it's important to focus on only one cue at a time. This way, the children can really concentrate on that cue. Once you provide feedback to the children and observe that most have learned a cue, it's time to focus on another one.

High Density Foam Tennis Balls

Recently equipment companies have developed a high density foam tennis ball. These balls come in a variety of sizes—some slightly larger than a regular tennis ball—and have a density that facilitates striking. We have found they are more effective for use with rackets and paddles than dead tennis balls.

Striking Down

Setting: A wooden paddle, a dead tennis ball or foam ball, and a self-space for each child

Cues	
Flat Paddle	(Keep your paddle flat as a board.)
Watch the Ball	(Keep your eyes on the ball all the time.) *It's helpful to paint a dot on the ball so children have something on which to focus.*

Tasks/Challenges:

T In your own space, strike the ball down with your paddle. See if you can keep it going without a miss. **Remember, if the ball starts to get away, just catch it and start over again.**

T Once you can keep the ball going five times or more in a row without leaving your space, see if you can strike the ball so it stays below your waist.

C How many down strikes can you get in a row without having to leave your self-space? These strikes don't have to be below your waist. Ready? Go.

Striking Up

Setting: A wooden paddle, a dead tennis ball or a foam ball, and self-space for each child

Cues	
Flat Paddle	(Keep your paddle flat as a board.)
Stiff Wrist	(Keep your wrist tight; don't let it flop around.)
Watch the Ball	(Keep your eyes on the ball all the time.) *It's helpful to paint a dot on the ball so children have something on which to focus.*

Tasks/Challenges:

T Now let's see if you can stay in your self-space and keep the ball going, but hit it up so it doesn't touch the floor. If you need to let it bounce every so often to gain control, that is okay.

T Can you hit the ball up so it goes above your head every time and still stay in self-space?

C Every time the paddle hits the ball, say one letter of your name. Can you spell your first name? Your last name? Your best friend's name? **Remember, each time you miss, you have to start spelling the word over again.**

? Show me what a flat paddle looks like.

Striking Up and Down

Setting: A foam or wooden paddle, a dead tennis ball or a foam ball, and self-space for each child

Cues	
Flat Paddle	(Keep your paddle flat as a board.)
Stiff Wrist	(Keep your wrist tight; don't let it flop around.)
Watch the Ball	(Keep your eyes on the ball all the time.)

Tasks/Challenges:

T Now let's see if you can still stay in self-space and keep the ball going. One time bounce it off the floor, and the next time, hit it into the air.

C Let's make up a sequence. For example, your sequence might be: up once, down once, up twice, down twice, up three times, down three times, and then start over. Practice until you can do your sequence two times in a row.

T This time make your self-space a bit larger. Can you hit the ball up and down while walking around your slightly bigger self-space—without losing control of the ball?

C Try to do your sequence while you walk around in self-space.

T If that was easy, you might want to try skipping, or sliding, or galloping in your bigger self-space as you strike the ball.

Even the youngest children are fascinated with striking.

©Lars A. Niki

T This time it becomes harder. We are going to walk in general space while striking the ball. Walk very slowly while you continue to strike the ball. For safety, be sure to look where you are going. If you think you are going to lose control of the ball, stand still for a second and catch the ball or let it bounce on the floor until you get control back; then keep going. If you do lose your ball, walk and pick it up, and start again.

⚠ When children begin moving and striking simultaneously, they tend to concentrate so much on the striking they forget to watch out for others and for rolling balls. Besides reminding them to watch out, conduct these tasks in the largest possible space, preferably outdoors.

💬 *Student Drawing.* This would be a great time to have students draw a picture of themselves striking up and striking down to assess their knowledge of the critical elements of flat paddle and stiff wrist.

Modifying the Task

The difficulty of all striking tasks can be increased or decreased by changing the object being struck. We most often start with shuttlecocks or volleybirds and progress to foam balls and dead tennis balls or high-density foam tennis balls. We tend to stay away from "live" tennis balls because they encourage children to "hit hard" rather than use the correct pattern and move to receive the ball. Adjust the equipment for each task as appropriate for your children.

Striking Underhand Against a Wall

Setting: A shuttlecock, a foam ball or a dead tennis ball, and a paddle for each child; children about 5 feet

from the wall, with spots to remind them of their self-space and distance from the wall.

Cues	
Paddle Way Back	(Start the paddle back behind your hips.)
Opposite Foot	(Just as in throwing, step forward on the foot opposite the arm you are using to strike.)
Slanted Paddle	(For this hit, keep the paddle face flat, but slant it just slightly toward the ceiling so the ball will go to the wall.)

The slight angle (slant) of the paddle face is critical here. It is helpful to demonstrate the subtle difference between it and a flat paddle and what the skill looks like.

Tasks/Challenges:

T Facing the wall and at your own spot, drop the shuttlecock and try to strike it so it goes straight ahead—forward toward the wall. **This strike is a little like an underhand throw—you are actually striking the shuttlecock from slightly underneath, not from the side.**

T Now trade in your shuttlecock for a ball. This will be a little harder, but it's the same idea. Try to strike the ball with the paddle so it goes straight forward toward the wall. You may want to let the ball bounce first before you hit it. Remember, just one hit at a time. Drop, hit, catch—then go again.

T Practice until you can hit the ball so it travels to the wall five times.

C Ask the person beside you to watch you strike the ball. Your neighbor will give you a point if you step

By allowing children the choice of striking implement and type of object to strike, children are able to adapt the task to their ability.

©Lars A. Niki

forward on the opposite foot as you hit. You'll get a second point if you swing the paddle underhand, not sidearm or overhead. Practice with your neighbor watching for a few minutes; then watch your neighbor.

? *Peer Observation.* The preceding task could easily be turned into a peer assessment of critical elements by using a peer observation card. Remember to encourage peer observers to focus on only one cue at a time. See Figure 12.9 page 200.

Striking Up, Down, and Underhand Forward

Setting: Four stations set up (see Figure 26.4), with children divided equally among the stations; at stations 1 and 3, foam balls or dead tennis balls and paddles for every child; at station 2, balloons and paddles for each child; at station 4, yarn balls and paddles for each child, as well as seven hoops in a cloverleaf pattern for each pair

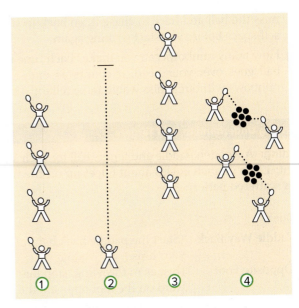

Figure 26.4 Station setup for ups, downs, and forwards.

Cues	
Stations 1, 2, and 3	
Flat Paddle	(Keep your paddle flat as a board.)
Stiff Wrist	(Keep your wrist tight; don't let it flop around.)
Watch the Ball	(Keep your eyes on the ball all the time.)
Station 4	
Paddle Way Back	(Start the paddle back behind your hips.)
Opposite Foot	(Just as in throwing, step forward on the foot opposite the arm you are using to strike.)
Slanted Paddle	(For this hit, keep the paddle face flat, but slant it just slightly toward the ceiling so the ball will go to the hoops.)

Tasks/Challenges:

T The stations today provide a chance to practice all the striking we have been doing. Some are just practice tasks; others are challenges. Do your best. Change on the signal.

Station 1: How many downward hits can you do with no mistakes? Count them.

Station 2: Travel across the gym, striking the balloon upward as you go.

Station 3: Can you do five single upward hits without moving from self-space? Try continuous hits.

Station 4: Strike the ball so it travels forward and lands in a hoop. Each time you are successful, increase your distance by taking one giant step backward. One partner can strike and the other can collect the balls. Switch every five strikes.

? *Self-Assessment.* The preceding task could easily be turned into a self-assessment by having children record on cards how they did at each station.

Striking to Self on Both Sides of the Body

Setting: A wooden or foam paddle, a dead tennis ball or foam ball, and a self-space for each child

Cues	
Flat Paddle	(Keep your paddle flat as a board.)
Stiff Wrist	(Keep your wrist tight, don't let it flop around.)
Watch the Ball	(Keep your eyes on the ball at all times.)

Tasks/Challenges:

T In tennis, racquetball, pickleball, or badminton, players use both sides of the paddle. Let's try this. Keep hitting the ball up. Try to hit the ball with one side of the paddle, then the other.

T If that is easy, see if you can use both sides of the paddle and both sides of the body. Try to not always strike the ball when it is right in front of you.

T Can you make a rainbow with the ball? Hit it on one side of your body and then the other so the ball travels in a rainbow shape. Remember, if you miss the ball and have to chase it, go back to your self-space before you start striking again.

C How many rainbows can you make? Each time the ball goes over your head, it counts as one. Five rainbows without a miss would be excellent!

Striking Underhand to Wall Targets

Setting: A wooden paddle and tennis ball for each student; 12- to 20-inch circles about 6 feet up on the wall in a scattered pattern

Cues	
Paddle Way Back	(Start the paddle back behind your hips.)
Opposite Foot	(Just as in throwing, step forward on the foot opposite the arm you are using to strike.)
Slanted Paddle	(For this hit, keep the paddle face flat, but slant it just slightly toward the ceiling so the ball will go to the wall.)

Tasks/Challenges:

T Find a spot about 10 feet from the wall in front of a circle. Strike the ball to the wall, trying to hit the circle. Remember, this is a back-to-front swing—like an underhand throw. **If you are doing it correctly, your arm will almost brush your hip on the way forward.**

T For the next five hits, freeze your follow-through. **Check to see if you have the opposite foot forward and your arm extended, with the racket face slanted slightly toward the ceiling.**

C When you think you can do five perfect hits with opposition and slanted racket facing the target, raise your hand and I will come to observe or a friend can observe for you.

T Try to send the ball to the wall so it touches within 2 to 3 inches of the target.

C You come that close.

T Take a giant step backward. Strike the ball so it contacts the wall at the height of the target.

T When you are successful in hitting the target six times, take another giant step backward.

T Move back to your first space closest to the wall. See if you can use an underhand strike to make the ball drop just in front of the wall.

T When you can successfully drop the shot just in front of the wall, take a giant step backward and try the drop shot from the longer distance.

C Pick your favorite distance. Count how many times you can hit the target without a mistake. How many times can you drop the ball just in front of the wall?

? How does the paddle face differ when striking to the wall from when striking up or down?

Striking Underhand for Distance (Varying the Force)

Setting: Outdoors on a large field (so children can work safely without hitting one another); children all facing the same way, either in a line or away from the center of a circle; a paddle and a variety of objects to strike for each child; one marker for each child

Cues	
Opposite Foot	(Just as in throwing, step forward on the foot opposite the arm you are using to strike.)
Slanted Paddle	(Keep the paddle face flat, but slant it slightly toward the ceiling. s)
Low to High	(Follow through low to high.)

Tasks/Challenges:

T Standing on the line, all facing the same direction so you won't hit anyone else, practice striking the objects, changing the amount of force you use for hitting. Sometimes use a lot of force, sometimes not very much force. Each time, make sure you use the proper underarm swing and follow through, no matter what amount of force you use. Use up all your objects and then go collect them.

C This time you're going to play a game with yourself. First, strike an object as far as possible. Take a marker and mark the place where your object fell. Be sure you can see the mark from the striking line. Now try to hit an object to halfway between the striking line and your far object. Practice until you feel as if you've really figured out just exactly the right amount of force to use. Then see if you can hit the middle spot three times in a row.

T After you've done this task three times in a row, hit another object as far as you can, mark it, and try the same thing all over again.

Striking Underhand to Hoops (Varying the Distance)

Setting: Partners; a wooden paddle and a variety of objects to hit for each child; a hoop to serve as a target for each pair

Cues	
Opposite Foot	(Just as in throwing, step forward on the foot opposite the arm you are using to strike.)
Slanted Paddle	(For this hit, keep the paddle face flat, but slant it just slightly toward the ceiling so the ball will go to the target. Use less slant for longer hits.)
Low to High	(Follow through low to high.)

Tasks/Challenges:

T Place your hoop on the ground. One partner will be the hitter; the other, the catcher. The hitter strikes the object so it lands in the hoop—that is, it hits the target. First, stay close, and then after you can hit the target three times, move back a few steps and try again. Your partner will keep the objects from going all over the place. After you take six hits, switch places with your partner for six hits and then switch back.

C Now you're going to make a game out of striking into hoops. Place three hoops on the floor, one about 3 feet away from you, one 6 feet away, and one 10 feet away. One partner will try to strike so the object lands in each hoop; the other partner will collect the object after the hits. Then the partners switch places. You can make up any other rules you wish, but you both need to practice striking into all three hoops.

? *Teacher or Student Observation.* This task lends itself well to a teacher or student observation checklist on the use of the critical elements for striking at various distances. *See Chapter 12 for the development of checklists.*

Striking Forehand to the Wall

Setting: A paddle and ball for each child; marks or spots to define self-space; large Xs placed about 3 feet high on the wall in front of each space

Cues	
Slanted Paddle	(Keep your paddle slanted slightly upward.)
Stiff Wrist	(Keep your wrist tight; don't let it flop around.)
Side to Wall	(Keep to the wall the side opposite the arm you're using to hit.)
Opposite Foot	(Just as in throwing, step forward on the foot opposite the arm you are using to strike.)

An additional cue sometimes needed with the sidearm pattern is to keep the elbow away from the side. We use that cue as necessary with individuals or groups of children.

Tasks/Challenges:

T Until now you have used an underhand pattern to strike the ball. Now we are going to learn a new pattern: the sidearm pattern, similar to what is used in tennis and racquetball. **This time your side is to the wall and your paddle is flat.** This is called the forehand, and you will use the forehand grip (see later Figure 26.7). Practice striking the ball to the wall from a mark on the floor using the sidearm pattern. Remember, these are single hits—drop, hit, and catch, and go again.

T Practice until you can hit the ball so it travels to the wall five times.

T After you can hit the wall five times, take one giant step backward and try from that distance. When you can hit the wall five times, move backward again.

T Return to your first spot and try to hit the X on the wall in front of your space. When you can make five hits, move backward again.

C Pick your favorite distance. How many times can you hit the target without missing?

With the forehand and backhand grips, we demonstrate the grip before the task, observe the children's grips as they practice, and provide feedback as necessary. We do not spend a lot of time teaching the grip.

Striking at High and Low Targets

Setting: A paddle and a ball for each child; four stations (see Figure 26.5 for set up). At stations 1 and 2: spots marked on the floor about 6 and 10 feet from the wall; targets on the wall in front of each space about 3 feet high. At station 3: spots marked on the floor about 10 feet from the wall; targets on the wall about 6 feet high (see Figure 26.6). At station 4: hoops on the floor against the wall; spots marked in various places around the hoops about 3, 6, 10, and 15 feet away. Targets at all stations should be large so that they are easy to hit and do not cause the child to sacrifice form for accuracy. *This sequence of learning experiences is an example of task teaching.*

Cues	
Paddle Face	(Keep your paddle slanted slightly upward.)
Stiff Wrist	(Keep your wrist tight; don't let it flop around.)
Watch the Ball	(Keep your eyes on the ball all the time. Watch it hit the paddle.)
Opposite Foot	(Step forward on the opposite foot.)

Task/Challenges:

T You have practiced both underhand and sidearm striking patterns. You can use them both, but one is better for some things, and the other is better for other things. The underhand pattern works best when you want to send the ball to high places or make it drop low. The sidearm pattern works when you want the ball to go in a more straightforward route. Now you will get a chance to mix them up. At each station you will have to decide which striking pattern is best to use. See if you can figure out each station.

Station 1: Using an underhand strike, try to hit the target as many times as you can. When you hit the target six times, move backward to the next mark.

Station 2: Try to hit the target with a side-armed pattern. What is the highest number of times you can hit the wall from each spot?

Station 3: Choose whatever striking pattern you wish, pick out one X on the target, and see if you can hit it five times; then choose another X, and another, and finally the last X. When you can hit all of them five times, move backward one step.

Station 4: From each of the marks on the floor, see if you can drop the ball into the hoop.

? *Exit Slip.* It would be appropriate here to use an exit slip to assess the children's understanding of the various striking patterns, their cues, and their uses. *See Chapter 12 for examples.*

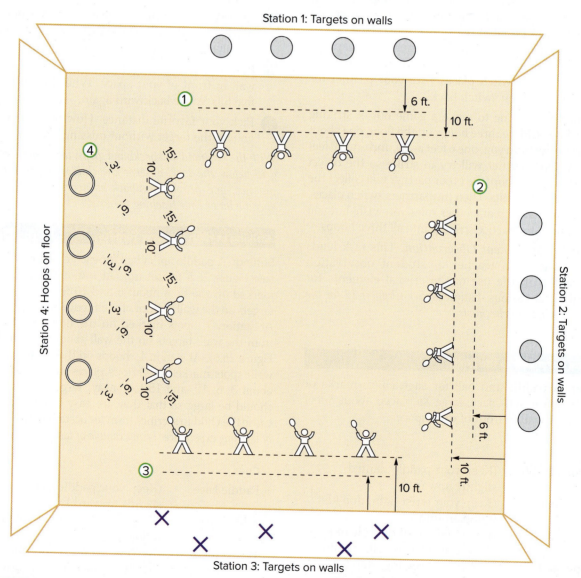

Figure 26.5 Station setup for striking at high and low targets.

Targets on walls

6 ft. | 10 ft.

③

Figure 26.6 Target design for striking at high and low targets, station 3. *The Xs on the wall should be large enough to be hit easily.*

Accuracy and Form

Form and force always precede accuracy. Tasks that require children to strike to a target (accuracy) should only occur after form has been developed. When targets are used, they should be large so that children do not modify the form they have developed. Just look at many people's second serve in tennis and you will understand!

Striking to Different Places

Setting: A paddle and a ball for each child; marks or spots to define self-space; large Xs about 3 feet high on the wall in front of each space

Cues	
Paddle Face	(Keep your paddle slanted slightly upward.)
Low to High	(Follow through low to high.)
Watch the Ball	(Keep your eyes on the ball all the time. Watch it hit the paddle.)
Opposite Foot	(Just as in throwing, step forward on the foot opposite the arm you are using to strike.)

Tasks/Challenges:

Ⓣ This time, instead of trying to hit the X, pretend the target is your opponent. Try to hit a space about 2 feet to the right of the X. Practice until you can hit your space six times. You can use an underhand or a sidearm pattern.

Ⓣ Now practice trying to hit a space to the left of the X. Again, practice until you can hit the space six times.

Ⓣ This time, practice doing one hit to the right, the next hit to the left, and the next hit to the X. See if you can repeat your pattern five times.

Ⓒ Ask the person next to you to be your partner. You will call out where you are going to hit before the strike. Your partner gives a thumbs-up if you hit where you called out or a thumbs-down if you didn't. After eight hits, trade places.

❓ *Peer Observation.* The previous task is a great peer observation assessment task. *See Chapter 12 for more information on peer assessments.*

Auditory Feedback

Place a metal gong, small bells, loose plastic jugs, or similar sound-producing objects on a wall as targets. Young children enjoy the auditory feedback when contact is made.

Striking Through a Target

Setting: A hoop suspended at about shoulder height for each group of two; a paddle for each child; one ball per group

Cues	
Paddle Face	(Keep your paddle slanted slightly upward.)
Watch Ball/ Watch Target	(Keep your eyes on the ball all the time: See it hit the paddle; see it go to the target. Watch the target out of the corner of your eye.)
Opposite Foot	(Step forward on the opposite foot.)

Tasks/Challenges:

Ⓣ At your hoop, one of you will bounce the ball on the floor and then try to strike it through the hoop. The partner will catch the ball and return it to the striker. After 10 strikes, change places.

Ⓣ Now that you've practiced by first letting the ball bounce, try it without letting the ball bounce. In

Striking learning experiences require well-defined spaces.

©Lars A. Niki

other words, just drop the ball, hit it before it hits the ground, and try to make it go through the hoop.

C Since you are so good at this, why don't we make it a game? How many hits in a row can you and your partner combined get?

Striking an Object to Send It over a Net

Setting: A net (or a rope between two chairs) about 2 to 3 feet high for each group of partners (later groups of three); a paddle for each child; one ball per group

⚠ When striking with a partner, children tend to forget their own space and often unknowingly encroach on the space of other groups, risking collisions. Therefore, for this task and all tasks that involve striking to a partner, have children clearly define their space with lines or spots.

Cues	
Paddle Face	(Keep your paddle slanted slightly upward.)
Watch Ball/ Watch Target	(Keep your eyes on the ball all the time: See it hit the paddle; see it go to the target. Watch the target out of the corner of your eye.)
Opposite Foot	(Step forward on the opposite foot for the forehand.)

Tasks/Challenges:

T With one partner on either side of the net, partner 1 strikes the ball across the net. Partner 2, instead of

hitting the ball back, will catch it and throw it back to partner 1. After 10 hits, change roles. Bounce the ball on the floor once before you hit it across the net.

T This time, use two different striking patterns to hit the ball across the net: forehand swing and underhand swing. Take 10 practices with one swing, and then switch; take 10 practices with another swing, and then switch. Ready? Two different ways of striking, 10 practices each.

C You can practice any way of striking you want this time, but instead of standing in one place, your partner will stand in a different place each time; hit toward your partner. As before, your partner will toss the ball back to you, but each time, he or she will move to a different location. How many of the 10 can you hit within arm's reach of your partner? Ten tries each, then switch.

T Now we are going to change this up a bit. You will need three people in your group; one will be the hitter, one the tosser, and one the catcher. The tosser and catcher will be on one side of the net and the hitter on the other. The tosser will toss the ball over the net so that it bounces on the forehand side and just in front of the hitter. The hitter will then strike the ball back toward the catcher who is at the back of the space. After seven hits, rotate: hitter to catcher; catcher to tosser; and tosser to hitter. After seven more hits, rotate again. *(Demonstrate this task so children know what it looks like.)*

Many teachers hesitate to teach striking over nets due to a lack of equipment. A simple solution so children in every group have their own net to work over is to suspend a rope between two chairs. This way you can set up nets of different heights and lengths at various places around the space. Let children set up their "own nets" in their "own space" for increased responsibility and more effective use of space.

Striking Backhand to the Wall

Setting: Partners; a paddle and a ball for each child; marks or spots to define self-space; large Xs placed about 3 feet high on the wall in front of each space

Cues	
Flat Paddle	(Keep your paddle flat toward the wall all the time.)
Stiff Wrist	(Keep your wrist tight; don't let it flop around.)
Watch the Ball	(Keep your eyes on the ball all the time. Watch it hit the paddle.)
Same Foot/ Same Shoulder	(Just as in throwing a flying disc, step forward on the same foot. The shoulder of the arm you are using to strike should be toward the wall.)

Tasks/Challenges:

T This is also a sidearm pattern, but from the other side of your body. In tennis, it is called the backhand, and you will use the backhand grip (Figure 26.7). It is the same as the forehand, except the side of your body with the striking arm is to the wall, and you step forward on the same foot as your striking arm. You reach across your body to hit. With a partner, find a space at the wall; one partner will drop the ball, while the other one

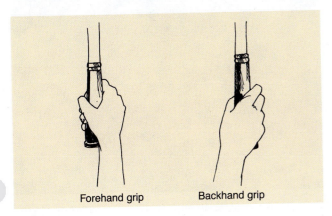

Forehand grip   Backhand grip

Figure 26.7 Examples of forehand and backhand grips.

strikes and hits to the wall after the bounce. After every five hits, switch roles. (*Demonstrate this because the partner needs to drop the ball so the hitting partner can hit backhand and so children understand the safety implications.*)

T By yourself now, start with a strike on the forehand side and hit so the ball comes to your backhand. After that, try to hit on the backhand side as much as you can. Let the ball bounce before striking it back to the wall. You may catch it and start over each time or hit continuously.

T Practice until you can hit the ball so it travels to the wall five times.

T After you can hit the wall five times, take one giant step backward and try from that distance. When you can hit the wall five times, move backward again.

T Return to your first spot, and try to hit the X on the wall in front of your space. When you can make five hits, move backward again.

C Pick your favorite distance. How many times can you hit the target without missing?

Note: The same progression used for underhand and forehand striking can be added here.

Striking Continuously Over and Through a Target

Setting: A hoop, hoop stand, two paddles, and a ball for each set of partners

Cues	
Quick Feet	(As the ball returns, you want to be behind it and a little to the side. You will have to move quickly to get there.)
Watch the Ball	(Keep your eyes on the ball all the time. See it hit the paddle; see it go over the hoop.)
Bend Knees	(Bend your knees and contact the ball at waist height.)

Tasks/Challenges:

C Now you'll play a game with your partner using all you have learned. Set up the hoop on the hoop stand on the center line of your area. Hit the ball back and forth over the hoop, letting the ball bounce on your side before hitting it back. After five hits over the hoop, the receiver must hit the ball through the hoop so it goes to the partner's side. If the hit through the hoop is good, play continues for another five "overs" and one "through." If the "through" is not good, the five "overs" start over again.

Striking a Ball Rebounding from a Wall

Setting: Wall space, with a line marked about 3 feet up the wall and a line marked on the ground 6 to 8 feet from the wall; a paddle and a ball for each child

Cues	
Quick Feet	(As the ball returns, you want to be behind it and a little to the side. You will have to move quickly to get there.)
Watch the Ball	(Keep your eyes on the ball all the time. See it hit the paddle; see it go to the wall.)
Bend Knees	(Bend your knees and contact the ball at waist height.)

Tasks/Challenges:

T Now you're going to have a chance to strike the ball against a wall. In your space, about 6 feet from the wall, practice striking the ball against the wall with a forehand strike and the forehand grip (Figure 26.7). **When you hit the ball, you should be slightly behind and about an arm's length to the side of the ball.**

C Here comes the challenge. See how many times you can strike the ball against the wall and let the ball bounce only once before hitting it again. If you miss, just start counting over.

T Now the activity will be a little harder for you. Hit the ball to different places on the wall, always

Striking Safely

To be accomplished both safely and effectively, striking activities require a great deal of space. Unfortunately, many indoor facilities in elementary schools don't have such spaces available. If this is true at your school and there aren't any outdoor alternatives, you can have two activities going simultaneously in the space available. Some children can carry out striking activities against the walls while other children carry out activities that require less space, such as balancing or weight transference, in the center of the space or on a stage area.

trying to be ready to hit it when it comes back to you. **In other words, you'll have to figure out where the ball is coming when it bounces off the wall and be behind it so you can hit it again. Remember, hit different places on the wall.**

C This time, the challenge is really hard. You need to see how many times in a row you can hit the ball above the line on the wall. The ball can bounce only once on the ground between hits. Ready? Go.

T This time, we are going to do the same thing, but really work on swinging low to high and following through. But there are some rules. First, the ball must land behind the line marked on the ground; second, you're allowed only one bounce to hit the ball back.

⚠ When allowing children to strike the ball continuously, make sure they are spread far apart and clearly understand the rules for retrieving a ball that has gone into another person's space.

? When do you use a forehand grip and swing? A backhand grip and swing?

©Barbara Adamcik

Children at the control level benefit from striking a ball rebounding from the wall.

Utilization Level (GLSP): Learning Experiences Leading to Skill Development

Children at the utilization level are able to contact a ball repeatedly without a miss (bouncing it up or down with a paddle or racket) and send a ball or other object various distances and in different directions. Experiences at this level enable children to strike with an implement, not as an invariant skill, but in dynamic environments that involve partners and striking from different positions in relation to the body. These children are now ready to apply striking skills in dynamic situations, such as moving into various positions to contact an object at different places around the body and returning shots to a partner.

A note about cues: *Although several cues are listed for many of the learning experiences, it's important to focus on only one cue at a time. This way, the children can really concentrate on that cue. Once you provide feedback to the children and observe that most have learned a cue, it's time to focus on another one.*

Hitting from Different Places

Setting: A space about 10 feet by 10 feet; partners, each with a paddle; two balls per group

Cues

Watch the Ball	(Keep your eyes on the ball all the time. See it hit the paddle; see your partner hit it.)
Bend Knees	(Bend your knees and contact the ball at waist height.)
Side to Target	(Whether you strike forehand or backhand, your side should face your partner.)
Get Home	(Return to a position in the center and near the back of your space after each hit. It will take quick feet to get there.)

Tasks/Challenges:

Ⓣ This time, your partner is going to throw rather than hit to you. Partner 1 will throw the ball to partner 2 so it bounces once before it reaches partner 2. Partner 2—the hitting partner—then tries to hit the ball straight back to partner 1—the thrower—regardless of where the ball has been sent. Partner 1 then catches the ball and throws to a new place. After 10 throws, switch places. The first time, always throw the ball to your partner's forehand side. The next time, always throw it to your partner's backhand side.

Ⓣ This time, don't let your partner know to which side you're going to throw the ball. **Hitters, as soon as you see the ball leave the thrower's hand, adjust your position so you can return the ball.** Throw 10 times, and change.

In the beginning stages of striking a ball sent by a partner, children benefit from having the ball tossed consistently to their preferred or nonpreferred side. This way they can progress to adjusting the preparatory stage according to the direction of the oncoming ball.

❓ *Peer Observation.* This is an excellent time for a student observation of the critical elements practiced at the control level. True learning occurs when children can use the cues correctly in dynamic, unpredictable situations. *See Chapter 12 for assessment examples.*

Hitting Cooperatively and Continuously with a Partner

Setting: A space about 10 feet by 10 feet; partners, each with a paddle and one ball

Cues

Get Home	(Return to a position in the center and near the back of your space after each hit. It will take quick feet to get there.)
Watch the Ball	(Keep your eyes on the ball all the time. See it hit the paddle; see your partner hit it.)
Bend Knees	(Bend your knees and contact the ball at waist height.)

Tasks/Challenges:

Ⓣ With your partner, in a space by yourselves, see if you can strike the ball back and forth to each other. The ball should bounce in the middle, but remember to get ready to hit the ball again after each hit.

Ⓒ Set a personal-best goal with your partner for the number of hits you can get without missing. See if you can attain your goal. Give your partner your best hit each time.

Ⓣ Make sure you and your partner practice hitting on both sides of your body.

Tip: The preceding task can be used with any of the striking patterns or a combination of patterns. You may need to remind children about the cue differences for sidearm and underhand striking.

❓ Where is home position when hitting with a partner?

Striking to Different Places Around a Partner

Setting: A space about 10 feet by 20 feet for each set of partners; two paddles and a ball

Cues	
Get Home	(Return to a position in the center and near the back of your space after each hit. It will take quick feet to get there.)
Watch the Ball	(Keep your eyes on the ball all the time. See it hit the paddle; see your partner hit it.)
Low to High	(Follow through low to high in the direction you want the ball to go.)

Tasks/Challenges:

🔵 With your partner, strike the ball back and forth, each time hitting to the alternate side of your partner's body. In other words, once you will hit to your partner's left and the next time to your partner's right. Try to keep the ball going for as long as possible. (*Have skilled students demonstrate what it looks like to hit to alternate sides.*)

🔵 As you practice now, see how long you can keep the ball going, while making your partner move to return the ball.

Striking Overhead

Setting: A wall space, with a line marked on the wall about 3 feet from the floor, a spot marked on the ground about 10 feet from the wall, and a paddle and a ball for each child

Cues	
Toss	(Toss the ball just barely above the top of the paddle.)
Reach and Stretch	(When you hit the ball, reach and stretch as high as possible.)
Flat and Down	(Your paddle should be flat and facing slightly downward and forward as you strike the ball.)

Demonstrate the skill of striking overhead.

Tasks/Challenges:

🔵 Stand on your spot, about 10 feet from the wall. Toss the ball higher than your racket can reach in the air and then stretch to hit the ball when it's at its highest point. In other words, throw the ball up, and when it reaches the very top of the throw—the point where it won't go up any farther and hasn't started to come down—hit it so it goes against the wall. Don't try to hit the ball back when it bounces off the wall; just catch it and start over.

🔵 Now that you've caught on to this idea, try to make the ball go down so it hits the wall near the line, about 3 feet above the floor. **To make it go down like that, the face of your racket must point slightly down as you hit the ball. Give it a try. Remember, watch the ball contact the racket so you can see what you're doing.**

🔵 This time, try to strike overhead again, but have the ball strike the wall just above the line. **Watch your racket contact the ball so you can tell which direction your racket face is pointed.**

❓ *Exit Slip or Self-Assessment.* After this task, an exit slip or self-assessment would be an appropriate way to see how students feel about their ability to strike in overhead fashion. Questions on an exit slip might include a recall of the cues or a Helping Murgatroid question. A self-assessment might ask how well they did with each of the cues. *See Chapter 12 for further information on both of these techniques.*

Striking Overhead over a Net

Setting: Balls, a paddle, and a net 2 to 3 feet high for each set of partners

Cues	
Toss	(Toss the ball just barely above the top of the paddle.)
Reach and Stretch	(When you hit the ball, reach and stretch as high as possible.)
Flat and Down	(Your paddle should be flat and facing slightly down and forward as you strike the ball.)

Tasks/Challenges:

🔵 You're going to practice hitting overhead again. Stand at the back of your court area, with your partner on the other side of the net. The partner with a paddle and some balls throws a ball in the air just above her or his reach, including the reach of the paddle, and then hits the ball down and over the net. This is like a tennis serve, only everything is smaller. The nonhitting partner should collect all the balls as they're hit. After 10 times, switch places.

T As you begin to hit more balls over the net and in the court, start to try to hit the ball a little harder. But don't attempt this until you can get 10 hits in a row over the net and into the court.

⚠ Whenever children are striking over a net, always have them clearly define the boundaries of their striking area so they don't interfere with others.

Striking Continuously Upward with a Group

Setting: Groups of three; a paddle for each player; one ball for each group

Cues	
Flat Paddle	(Keep your paddle flat as a board.)
Watch Ball/ Watch Players	(Always watch the ball. Watch the other players and the space out of the corner of your eye.)
Quick Feet	(It will take quick feet to get behind and under the ball.)

Tasks/Challenges:

T You need to clearly define the boundaries of your space; the three of you should be approximately 8 to 10 feet apart. Your task is to keep the ball moving by striking it to each player without losing control. Bounces are allowed if you want them, but you do not have to use them. There is no set order in which you have to hit.

C See how long you can keep the ball going without losing control.

Setting: Groups of three, each group with one ball, three paddles, and five hoops; a space (see Figure 26.8 for set up)

Tasks/Challenges:

C This is a game that will let you practice striking in the air. The person in the center hoop begins by striking the ball in the air to a person in one of the other hoops. That person receives the ball, strikes it twice to himself or herself, and sends it back to the middle person, who also has to strike it twice

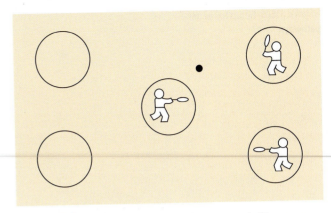

Figure 26.8 Setup for striking continuously upward with a group.

before sending it to the other outside person. That outside person has to strike three times to himself, before sending it back to the middle, where it is struck three times. This continues until the middle person has to strike seven times to himself or herself. Just to make it harder, the outside people, after striking the ball, have to move to one of the empty hoops. If anyone misses, the whole group starts over again. We will change middle hitters after seven hits or 3 minutes.

Striking in Various Aerial Pathways in Dynamic Situations

Setting: Different-colored pieces of yarn suspended one above the other—at 3 feet, 6 feet, and 10 feet—for use as nets (Figure 26.9); partners, each with a paddle; one shuttlecock, volleybird, or peteca per group

Cues	
Slanted Paddle	(Keep your paddle slanted slightly upward.)
Low to High	(Follow through low to high toward the string you are trying to go over.)
Get Home	(After each hit, move back to your center back position to get ready to hit again.)

Tasks/Challenges:

T Using a shuttlecock (volleybird) and an underarm swing, try to make the object go over the lowest piece of yarn. After five tries, switch with your partner.

T Now try the middle piece of yarn. Do this five times each, then switch.

Figure 26.9 Setup for aerial pathways.

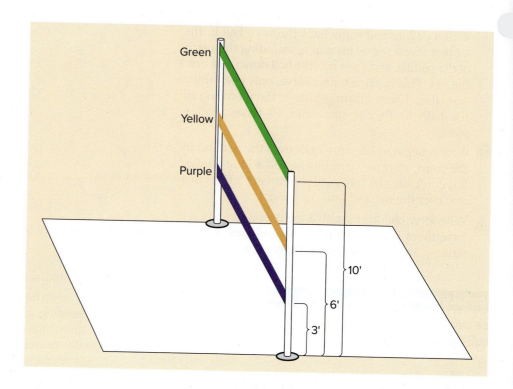

T Now the highest piece. For this one, you're really going to have to use a big underarm swing to get the object over the net.

C This task will be difficult. Try to keep the shuttlecock (volleybird) going with your partner, but this time, on the first hit, make it go over the low piece of yarn; on the next hit, make it go over the middle piece; on the third hit, make it go over the top piece. Then start over and reverse the order. Practice until you can do the sequence one time all the way through.

Striking Upward in a Dynamic Situation

Setting: Group of up to five people, each with a paddle; one ball per group

Cues	
Flat Paddle	(Keep your paddle flat as a board.)
Watch Ball/ Watch Players	(Always watch the ball; watch the other players and the space out of the corner of your eye.)
Quick Feet	(It will take quick feet to get behind and under the ball.)

Tasks/Challenges:

C You are going to strike in a game-like situation. Here are the rules:

1. One person stands in the middle of a circle.
2. The person in the middle hits the ball with a paddle straight up in the air and calls out the name of another person in the group.
3. The person whose name is called out must run to the middle of the circle, hit the ball up in the air before it bounces, and call out another student's name.
4. The caller takes the place of the person whose name was called out.

⚠ This is an exciting task for youngsters, and they often lose track of where they are in space. Constant safety reminders may be necessary.

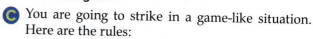

The type of racket used can increase the complexity of any striking situation. A light, short-handled racket is the easiest for a child to master; a heavy, long-handled racket is the most difficult. As children begin to master the skills of striking with rackets, we gradually change the type of racket used to make the task more difficult.

Proficiency Level (GLSP): Learning Experiences Leading to Skill Development

When the children have attained the proficiency level, they demonstrate a mature pattern of striking: the ability to control both body and implement while traveling and to select the most effective type of striking when responding to a partner.

Experiences at this level encourage children to enjoy the challenge of striking with short-handled implements in game-like situations. These experiences involve partner or opponent relationships, spatial strategy, and the varied use of effort qualities. Because of the game-like nature of the tasks, it can be quite tricky to keep them developmentally appropriate, especially in terms of active participation for all children. There are several solutions here. Set up multiple courts around the gym. The courts may be odd sizes, but they should allow for maximum participation. Another option is to have stations, several that offer game-like challenges and several that have practice opportunities that require less setup and space. Finally, you could have peer assessment opportunities in which half the members of a small group will play and half will observe; then switch. Regardless of the solution, please remember that game-like challenges should be appropriate for all children. See Chapter 31 for more information on game options in physical education.

A note about cues: At the proficiency level, tasks are more complex, typically requiring children to coordinate several movements simultaneously in a dynamic context. A list of cues is provided to assist the children in being more successful in the learning experiences. The challenge is in determining which cue will be most beneficial for each child—and when. Thus, careful observation and critical reflection become very important as you watch the children move and then decide which cue will be the most helpful to move each learner to a higher level.

Striking to One Wall with a Partner

Setting: Two children per group, each with a paddle; one ball per group; court (see the set up in Figure 26.10)

Cues	
Get Home	(Return to a position in the center and near the back of your space after each hit.)
Watch the Ball	(Keep your eyes on the ball all the time. See it hit the paddle; see it hit the wall; see your partner hit it.)

Mix 'Em Up	(It's time to use all your different strikes: to different spots on the wall and soft and hard strikes.)

Tasks/Challenges:

C The objective of this task is to hit the ball against a wall so your opponent is unable to return it. Here are the rules:

1. You may score only when you serve.
2. The ball may be returned either after one bounce or before the bounce.
3. To make your partner miss, you must use placement, not force. All shots should be of a force that is playable.

The courts are marked on the floor. To start play, partner 1 serves the ball against the wall, and partner 2 tries to return it. Each time partner 1 hits the ball, partner 2 tries to return it. You can play cooperatively—seeing how long you can keep the rally going—or competitively—accumulating points when you make your opponent miss. The choice is yours.

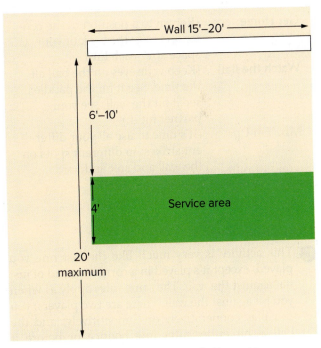

Figure 26.10 Setup for striking to one wall with a partner.

Striking at Angles to Two Walls with a Partner

Setting: Two people per group, each with a paddle; one ball per court; court (see the set up in Figure 26.11)

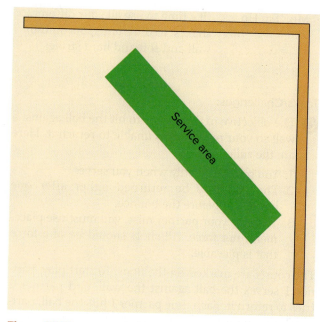

Figure 26.11 Setup for striking at angles to two walls with a partner.

Cues	
Get Home	(Return to a position in the center and near the back of your space after each hit.)
Watch the Ball	(Keep your eyes on the ball all the time. See it hit the paddle; see it hit the wall; see your partner hit it.)
Mix 'Em Up	(It's time to use all your different strikes: to different spots on the wall and soft and hard strikes.)

Tasks/Challenges:

Ⓒ This activity is very much like the last one you played, except it's played in a corner instead of just flat against the wall. The same rules apply as when you hit against the wall: There are two players; you can play cooperatively or competitively; and the ball is hit either after one bounce or before it bounces. The ball placement should cause someone to miss, not the force of the shot. Go ahead and get used to playing in the corner.

For a more advanced game of striking at angles to two walls with a partner, see Striking to the Wall—Varying Levels, Force, and Body Position in Chapter 25 (page 515).

Striking to and from Different Places

Setting: Four square courts, each about 15 by 15 feet, labeled A, B, C, and D; groups of four students, with paddles and a ball

Cues	
Ready Position	(Keep your weight on the balls of your feet, with your knees slightly bent.)
Paddle in Front	(To be ready, hold your paddle in front of your body about waist high.)
Back of Square	(Stay near the back of the square so you can move forward.)

Tasks/Challenges:

Ⓒ This task is like Four Square. Here's how it works:

1. Square A starts the game.
2. You must hit the ball to another square.
3. The ball can't be hit to the person who hit it to you.
4. You must hit the ball after its first bounce.
5. The person who misses the ball goes to square D, and everyone else moves up a square.
6. All strikes must be underhand.

Partner Striking Across a Net

Setting: Partners; a low net on a surface that allows the ball to bounce, with a marked-off court at each net area for each pair

Cues	
Get Home	(Return to a position in the center and near the back of your space after each hit.)
Watch the Ball	(Keep your eyes on the ball all the time. See it hit the paddle; see your partner hit it.)
Mix 'Em Up	(It's time to use all your different strikes: to different spots on the court and soft and hard strikes.)

Tasks/Challenges:

Ⓒ The objective of this game is to send the ball over the net so it bounces within the court, and the opponent hits the ball before it bounces twice. Here are the rules:

1. Play begins with an overhead strike behind the end line.

2. The ball can bounce no more than once on each side of the net.
3. You may hit the ball before it bounces.
4. The ball cannot be hit so hard it is unreturnable.

You may or may not keep score; the choice is yours. If you decide to keep score, decide before you start to play how you'll do so.

Aerial Striking over a Net

Setting: Solid rackets, paddles, or badminton or crossminton rackets; shuttlecocks, tennis balls, or volleybirds; one net (between children's shoulder and head height) for each set of partners; a marked-off court at each net with a serving line (Figure 26.12)

Cues

Get Home	(Return to a position in the center and near the back of your space after each hit.)
Watch the Ball	(Keep your eyes on the ball all the time. See it hit the paddle; see your partner hit it.)
Mix 'Em Up	(It's time to use all your different strikes: to different spots on the court and soft and hard strikes.)

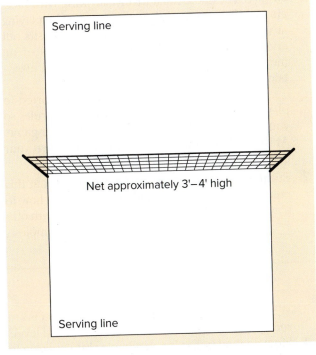

Figure 26.12 Court setup for aerial net games.

Tasks/Challenges:

Ⓒ The objective of this aerial net game is to send the object over the net so the opponent can return it before it touches the floor. Here are the rules:

1. Play begins with an underhand strike behind the serve line.
2. Aerial strikes continue until the object touches the floor or goes out of bounds.
3. If you like, you can make up your own way of changing serves and keeping points.

Aerial net games using a shuttlecock can be played with regular tambourines, with old ones that are discarded from rhythm bands because the jingles have been lost, or with tambourines with rubberized heads. Children enjoy the sound made when the shuttlecock strikes the tambourine.

Team Striking Across a Net

Setting: Groups of four with foam tennis balls, paddles, and a net; a court of four equal squares, with a net running down the center

Cues

Get Home	(Return to a position in the center and near the back of your space after each hit.)
Watch the Ball	(Keep your eyes on the ball all the time. See it hit the paddle; see your opponents hit it.)
Mix 'Em Up	(It's time to use all your different strikes: to different spots on the court and soft and hard strikes.)
Cover Space	(You want to block all the space on the court. One player usually plays near the net, and one back. When one moves, the other must adjust.)

Tasks/Challenges:

Ⓒ This task is like a miniversion of tennis or pickleball doubles. Here's how you play:

1. There are two people on each team.
2. Team A serves underhand and diagonally to team B.
3. The two teams hit the ball back and forth across the net until one team misses.
4. When the team serving misses, the other team takes over serving.
5. When the receiving team misses, the serving team keeps serving.

6. The serve always begins in the back right-hand corner behind the line, alternates to the back left-hand corner on every consecutive serve, and then back to the right.

7. The ball may be hit before it bounces or after one bounce.

8. The ball cannot be hit so hard that it is not returnable.

? *Homework.* At this point in learning to strike, you might give children a homework assignment to observe a tennis match in person or on television and analyze how one player uses the strategies of getting home, watching the ball, mixing up shots, and covering space.

Group Striking Across a Net

Setting: Groups of six, with badminton or crossminton rackets or paddles, shuttlecocks or speeders, and a net

Cues	
Quick Feet	(Move quickly to get behind and under the shuttlecock.)
Close to Net	(One player should be close to the net for the last hit.)
Get Home	(After each hit, move back to your position on the court so the space is covered.)

Tasks/Challenges:

C You're going to strike across a net with a team. Here are the rules:

1. There are three players on each side.
2. A player near the back of the court serves underhand to the other side of the net. The opponents hit the shuttlecock twice on their side of the net and then return it over the net.
3. The shuttlecock must be hit twice by two different players on each side of the net before it's returned.
4. The shuttlecock must be hit before it touches the ground.

5. When the serving team misses, the other team scores.

6. Keep score any way you want or not at all.

⚠ The preceding activity is an enjoyable game, but the use of long-handled rackets requires enough room to allow children to strike without hitting each other. Play the game in a space at least the size of a regulation volleyball court.

Child-Designed Racket Games

This task is an example of a child-designed instructional approach. See Chapters 9 and 31 for more ideas on child-designed tasks and games.

Setting: Depends on the game; groups of four or fewer, each child with an appropriate racket or paddle of choice

Cues
Appropriate to the game

Tasks/Challenges:

C Today you're going to combine all that you've practiced into a game. You'll make up your games yourselves. In your groups, make up a game that involves striking with a racket. You can have whatever rules you want as long as you include these two: (1) The game must involve striking with rackets and (2) everyone in your group must be playing at the same time. In other words, nobody sits out and waits for a turn. Remember, groups of no more than four, striking with rackets, and everybody plays. Go.

After you've made up your rules and started to play your game, make sure you know your rules so you can tell somebody else how to play your game. At the end of class, I'll ask you to write down your game.

? *Event Task.* An appropriate assessment task at this point would be to have children write down how to play their games and then share the games with others. See Chapter 12 for more assessment examples.

Reading Comprehension Questions

1. Why is striking with rackets or paddles one of the last and most difficult skills to develop?
2. Students at the precontrol level benefit from striking an object suspended from a string. Describe three different ways to suspend objects.

3. What types of striking implements and objects are recommended for students at the precontrol level?
4. How does a teacher know when a child is ready to be challenged to strike the ball on the opposite side of the body (i.e., backhand)?

5. Describe the position of a child's arms and feet when the child is striking with a racket or paddle.

6. What characterizes each of the four generic levels of skill proficiency of striking with rackets and paddles?

7. What does a flat paddle look like? What does a slanted paddle face look like? What happens when an object is struck with a paddle held in each position?

8. What does it look like when children run around the ball instead of striking the ball on the opposite side of the body? Describe a task that would help them learn to not run around the ball.

9. A child swings a racket so it remains at waist level throughout the swing. What direction does the ball travel if the child strikes the ball too early in the swing? Too late in the swing?

10. Design six tasks related to striking with rackets or paddles. Rank them in order from the easiest to the hardest. Be certain to include at least one task from each skill level. Use a different striking implement or object for each task.

11. Name the major safety cue regarding striking.

References/Suggested Readings

Holt/Hale, S., and T. Hall. 2016. *Lesson planning for elementary physical education: Meeting the national standards & grade-level outcomes*. Champaign, IL: Human Kinetics.

[SHAPE America] Society of Health and Physical Educators. 2014. *National standards & grade-level outcomes for K-12 physical education*. Champaign, IL: Human Kinetics.

Striking with Long-Handled Implements

By Lindy Mutter

Drawn by children at Monfort, Chappelow or Shawsheen Elementary Schools, Greeley, CO.
Courtesy of Lizzy Ginger; Tia Ziegler.

The skill theme of striking is used in many games—from backyard softball to baseball, golf, cricket, and hockey. We have divided striking into various skill themes: kicking and punting, volleying and dribbling, striking with rackets and paddles, and striking with long-handled implements. While this division allows us to cover in some detail the gamut of striking activities, the basic purpose in all striking is the same—giving impetus to an object with a hit, punch, or tap—although often the specific motion and the equipment differ.

Like transferring weight and rolling, and volleying and dribbling, we have subdivided striking learning experiences in this chapter to more fully cover the striking tasks that use long-handled implements. In three separate sections, this chapter focuses on one striking action that uses swings in a horizontal plane (batting) and two striking actions that use vertical (hockey-type and golf-type actions) planes. The implements used to accomplish these swings vary from softball and cricket bats to hockey sticks to golf clubs to Pilo-Polo sticks—yet all have the underlying challenge of coordinating hands and eyes when striking with a long implement. Because vertical and horizontal swings have distinctive characteristics, critical elements for each are presented separately. Both swings involve striking away from the body, but the motor skills differ in relation to the purpose of the task.

We don't introduce children to striking with long-handled implements so they'll become experts at golf, baseball, or hockey. We provide children opportunities to practice striking patterns they're likely to use in a variety of contexts throughout their lives. This rationale can be fully appreciated when watching an adult trying to strike with a long-handled implement. If that individual has had no previous experience with a particular striking pattern, the results can be disastrous. Frustration will result, and ultimately the person may abandon the sport. Our emphasis is on giving children a variety of movement opportunities rather than on perfecting the technical aspects of a particular swing. Specific opportunities to refine and perfect different swings are provided at the secondary level or in private instruction.

Striking with long-handled implements is referenced in the National Standards & Grade-Level Outcomes for K–12 Physical Education. (SHAPE America 2014) (see Box 27-1).

Most long-handled implements are designed for adults. Because children aren't "regulation size," they find it difficult to manipulate implements of official size, length, and weight, so we use lightweight plastic implements in our programs, or we make implements that match the sizes of the children. This prevents the

Box 27-1

Striking with Long-Handled Implements in the *National Standards & Grade-Level Outcomes for K–12 Physical Education*

Striking with long-handled implements is referenced in the *National Standards & Grade-Level Outcomes for K–12 Physical Education* (SHAPE America 2014) under Standard 1: "Demonstrates competency in a variety of motor skills and movement patterns." The intent of the standard is developing the fundamental skills needed to enjoy participation in physical activities, with the mastery of movement fundamentals as the foundation for continued skill acquisition. (Developmentally appropriate outcomes for long-handled implements first appear in grade 2.)

Sample grade-level outcomes from the *National Standards** include:

- Strikes a ball off a tee or cone with a bat using correct grip and side orientation/proper body orientation (2)
- Strikes a ball with a long-handled implement sending it forward, while using the proper grip for the implement (3)
- Strikes an object with a long-handled implement while demonstrating three of the five critical elements of a mature pattern for the implement (4)
- Strikes a pitched ball with a bat using a mature pattern (5)
- Combines striking with a long-handled implement with receiving and traveling skills in a small-sided game (5)

Striking with long-handled implements is also referenced under Standard 2: "Applies knowledge of concepts, principles, strategies, and tactics related to movement and performance." The intent of this standard is facilitation of a child's ability to use cognitive information to understand and enhance motor skill acquisition and performance.

*Suggested grade-level outcomes for student learning.

children from learning poor habits when they try to use equipment that is too heavy or too long. The equipment should never inhibit the mature striking pattern.

Generally, striking is the last fundamental motor pattern learned because of the complexity of the hand–eye coordination involved. Within this skill theme, there are also multiple levels of complexity. Actions that require striking a stationary ball (as in golf) are easier than actions that require the striking of a moving object (as in hockey). Both of these actions are less complex than striking a pitched ball with a bat. In the latter action, both objects are moving and never come to rest. In all cases, children may possess a mature striking pattern before they're able to consistently make contact with the ball.

Striking with Long-Handled Implements—Hockey Sticks

Think about it: Where would you find adults (or children for that matter) striking with a hockey stick–type implement except in hockey? What about polo? Pilo Polo? Roller hockey? Croquet? All these activities require an object on the ground to be struck with a stick, and there are sure to be many more. Because the striking possibilities are endless, we focus on it as a generic skill rather than as a sport-specific skill. Our progression spiral for striking with a hockey stick appears on page 564. Striking with a golf club could have been included with striking with a hockey stick, but due to its specialized nature, we have included it in a separate section later in this chapter.

A swing with a hockey stick–type implement uses an underhand swinging pattern because in many ways it resembles the movement used to throw a ball underhand. The underhand swing developed in this chapter is one that would be used for the short passes (10 yards or less) that children would use in physical education experiences.

The critical elements for striking with a long implement (passing or shooting a goal with a hockey stick) are:

- Grip is with hands apart, with preferred hand about halfway down the shaft of the stick; nonpreferred hand on the top; thumbs of both hands face down
- Stance is shoulder width apart with opposite foot slightly forward
- Body orientation is facing the target
- Hip and upper body coil and twist as stick is taken about a foot back from puck or ball
- Hip and upper body uncoil and strike hockey puck (or ball), and step is made with the opposite foot

The swing we have developed is a shortened hockey-type swing. We have chosen not to develop fuller swings for long passes that might be used in hockey-type activities played in large spaces because the space available in physical education is not conducive to this striking pattern and may not be safe. Numerous implements can be substituted for hockey sticks (see the "Implements for Underhand Striking" box, page 566). See our skill theme progression for striking with hockey sticks for skill development ideas from precontrol through proficiency levels.

Skill Theme Development Progression

Striking with Long-Handled Implements—Hockey

Proficiency Level

Small-sided hockey invasion game
Keep-Away
Striking to dodge an opponent

Utilization Level

Two-on-one hockey
Keeping It Moving
Passing and receiving on the move
Striking from a stationary position to a
     moving target
One-on-one hockey
Traveling and striking for a goal
Pathways, speeds, and directions
Performing a continuous dribble with changes
     in direction and speed
Striking to small targets

Control Level

Striking while dodging stationary obstacles
Traveling and striking while changing pathways
Traveling and changing speeds
Traveling, stopping, and controlling the ball
Traveling slowly while striking a ball
Striking to a stationary partner
Striking toward a target (Around the World)
Striking to targets
Striking a stationary ball on the ground

Precontrol Level

Traveling slowly while striking a ball
Striking (dribbling) a ball in self-space
Striking a stationary ball

Before the children begin swinging bats, golf clubs, or hockey sticks, you will need to define clear zones and spaces where the swing may occur—and where it cannot. Use ropes, cones, hoops, and other equipment to provide a hitting zone (that is, an area for *each child* clearly defined by ropes or cones or spray paint if you are outside). For striking with bats and golf clubs, you will also need to define a "no-enter zone" so the children who are not swinging do not accidentally run into a bat or golf club. It is also important to teach children that when they hear the phrase "safety check" they should check around them to make they are in their own space. Chapter 7 becomes very important here—the children need to listen and follow your instructions so that no one gets injured.

Precontrol Level (GLSP): Experiences for Exploration

Learning experiences at the precontrol level ask children to explore all varieties of striking with long-handled implements. At this level, a chopping, downward swing is typical for any striking pattern. Children struggle just to make contact between the ball and the striking instrument. Therefore, we give children tasks and challenges that let them explore striking with the added length that comes with hockey sticks—and the greater demands that length places on their hand–eye coordination. Due to the difficulty of the skill, tasks are developed using large objects to be struck. Children explore striking stationary objects, and they begin to develop the ability to control a ball while traveling.

All learning experiences at this level need to be done with balls of various sizes. For beginners, yarn balls or large plastic balls are easier because they're larger and/or don't roll as fast as other balls. For tasks that involve traveling, plastic pucks are easier to control initially if the lesson is being taught on a smooth wood or tile floor.

Striking a Stationary Ball

Setting: Preferably a large indoor space (but can be adapted for an outdoor space if the surface is hard and there is a fence to stop the ball); plastic floor hockey stick for each child (short-handled and long-handled street hockey sticks are not appropriate); a variety of foam and plastic balls and pucks; each child in his or her individual striking zone defined by ropes or markers, facing a wall or an object that will block the ball

Tasks/Challenges:

T Stand behind your ball and strike it so it travels to the wall. Hit it hard so it goes all the way to the wall. Make sure to stop the ball when it comes back before you hit it again.

C Practice until you can hit the wall three times in a row.

T Practice hitting from both sides of your body. Each time, try to make the ball go to the wall.

T Trade in the ball for another kind of ball. Try all the different things with your new piece of equipment.

C Practice until you can get the ball or puck to the wall three times.

Safety with Hockey Sticks

There is much concern over the use of hockey sticks and the teaching of related skills in elementary school. With the increased popularity of street and ice hockey, hockey sticks are being raised above the shoulders on both the backswing and the follow-through. Because elementary school physical education classes are usually crowded (due to numbers or space), raised hockey sticks can cause injuries. We've successfully reduced the chance of such injuries **by not letting youngsters raise their hockey sticks higher than their waists on any stroke.** One way to help children with this is to tell them the backswing should not be more than a foot and the stick should scrape the floor just behind the puck or ball. This restriction doesn't significantly alter the striking action. A trick to getting children to keep the follow-through low is to have them "roll" their wrists as they follow through. *(A demonstration of rolling the wrists may be needed.)*

Striking (Dribbling) a Ball in Self-Space

Setting: Children in self-space, each with a hoop, a hockey stick, and a foam, yarn, or plastic ball

Tasks/Challenges:

T For this task, the ball is in the hoop and you are on the outside of the hoop, use the hockey stick to gently move the ball around in as many ways as possible.

T On the signal, begin striking the ball with little taps inside your hoop and keep striking until you hear the signal to stop. Remember, stay in your own space. Do not travel.

C I will time you for 15 seconds. Try to keep your strikes going for the whole time.

Traveling Slowly While Striking a Ball

Setting: A hockey stick and a foam or plastic ball or puck for each child

Tasks/Challenges:

T This time, instead of staying in your own space, you are going to travel in general space. We will begin by walking short distances, tapping the ball as you did in self-space. To start, you are only going to take four steps with taps; then stop, count to two, and go again. It is like this: four taps, stop, count to two, four taps, stop, count to two. The ball must always be very close to your stick.

T Now travel on your own, walking and tapping the ball as you go. If you think you are losing control, stop and count to two and start again.

(T) This time as you are walking, try to avoid running into others. This means you will have to keep the ball very close and look up every once in a while to check for others.

Implements for Underhand Striking

Although we have associated hockey with tasks that use an underhand striking action, other sports also use the underhand swing pattern. Several striking implements may be substituted for hockey sticks or golf clubs; many times, these alternatives may be more appropriate. Pilo-Polo sticks are lighter and softer than hockey sticks. Short-handled broomball sticks provide a wider striking surface but unfortunately are available only in certain areas of the country. Substitution of either of these implements not only may reduce the complexity of the task but also can take the focus away from a single sport.

Control Level (GLSP): Learning Experiences Leading to Skill Development

At the control level, children begin to develop mature striking patterns that are used in increasingly complex contexts. They can be challenged with tasks that require them to include one or two other variables besides striking, such as traveling while striking or tapping an object along the ground combined with changing direction and/or speed.

A note about cues: *Although several cues are listed for many of the learning experiences, it's important to focus on only one cue at a time. This way, the children can really concentrate on that cue. Once you provide feedback to the children and observe that most have learned a cue, it's time to focus on another one.*

Striking a Stationary Ball on the Ground

Setting: Preferably a large indoor space (but can be adapted for an outdoor space with a hard surface and a fence to stop the ball); a plastic floor hockey stick (short-handled or long-handled street hockey sticks aren't appropriate) and a plastic or foam ball for each child; each child in his or her individual striking zones defined by ropes or cones, facing a wall or an object that will block the ball; at least 5 feet between children

Cues

Hands Apart	(Keep top hand at top of stick and favorite hand part way down.)
Face the Target	(Be sure to face the target throughout the swing.)
Sweep Low	(Swing the stick backward and forward sweeping the stick to make contact with the ball.)

Tasks/Challenges:

(T) When we explored striking with hockey sticks, you practiced hitting the ball to the wall by standing behind it and having it travel on the ground. Now we get to do that again. Practice striking the ball, standing behind it, so it travels to the wall.

(T) We are going to practice the same swing, but we are now going to use a hockey grip (Figure 27.1); start the backswing below your knees and end below your knees. An easy way to help it end below your knees is to turn your wrists over on the follow-through. This is called a short swing.

(T) Using the short swing, strike the ball to the wall with enough force so it comes back to you. **The secret to force is to step with the opposite foot at the same time you swing.**

(C) Practice striking the ball against the wall until you can hit the wall three times in a row and have the ball come back to you.

(T) Most of you have been hitting the ball from the preferred side of your body. That is called your *forehand*. This time we are going to practice hitting the ball from the nonpreferred side of your body. You don't change your hands; instead you use the back side of the stick to do it. Try to hit the ball to the wall this way.

(T) Practice hitting the ball hard enough so it rebounds back to you.

(C) Again, try for three hits in a row that are hard enough so the ball comes back to you.

Figure 27.1 Hockey stick grip.

Striking to Targets

Setting: Plastic hockey stick or other implement and a foam or plastic ball for each child; in front of each child, a target on the floor next to the wall marked with cones or spots about 4 feet apart and tape marks on the floor in front of each target at about 6 feet, 10 feet, and 12 feet; each child in his or her individual striking zone defined by markers

Cues	
Step	(Step forward on the opposite [front] foot.)
Watch the Ball	(Keep your eyes on the ball all the time.)
Face the Target	(Be sure to face the target throughout the swing.)
Follow Through	(Follow through toward the target with your stick.)

Tasks/Challenges:

T Starting from behind the ball at the closest mark, try to strike the ball so it goes between the two markers.

T Practice sending the ball between the markers from your forehand and backhand sides.

C Practice striking until you can hit the ball between the markers five times from each side. Remember, stop the ball each time it comes back to you before hitting it again.

T When you can hit the target five times in a row without missing from the closest mark, move back to the next mark. When you can hit the target from that spot five times without missing, move back

again. If you hit the target four times and then miss, start your counting over. Practice from both the forehand and backhand sides.

⚠ With this task, make sure that students are spread well apart, that they stop the ball completely on its return, and that they retrieve a ball in front of others only when no one is striking.

Striking Toward a Target (Around the World)

Setting: Targets (made with two markers), with five tape marks in a semicircle on the floor in front of each; three or fewer students per target; a hockey stick or other striking implement and ball or puck for each child *Note: This task is also appropriate as one of a series of stations.*

Cues	
Watch the Ball	(Keep your eyes on the ball until it leaves your stick.)
Face the Target	(Be sure to face the target throughout the swing.)
Step	(Step toward the target on the opposite [front] foot.)
Follow Through	(Follow through toward the target with your stick.)

Tasks/Challenges:

T This time, the striking is going to be like a game. Have you ever played Around the World in basketball? This game is going to be Around the World in striking. As you see, there are five tape marks on the floor in front of you. You must hit the ball through the target from each tape mark. Strike from behind the ball. You can start on either side.

Passing to a partner is a task appropriate at the control level.

©Lars A. Niki

T When you make it through once, go back and hit from each mark using the backhand strike.

? *Teacher Observation.* This task lends itself easily to a teacher observation of the critical elements for striking with hockey sticks. *See Chapter 12 for the development of a teacher observation checklist.*

Striking to a Stationary Partner

Setting: Partners about 6 to 7 feet apart, each with a hockey stick; one ball or puck per group; each striking zone defined by ropes or markers

Cues	
Sending	
Watch the Ball	(Keep your eyes on the ball all the time.)
Face the Target	(Be sure to face the target throughout the swing.)
Step	(Step forward on the opposite foot.)
Follow Through	(Follow through toward your partner with your stick.)
Receiving	
Give	(Relax your grip and move your stick back a little just as the ball hits your stick, to absorb the force.)

Tasks/Challenges:

T Strike the ball (puck) back and forth to your partner. Hit straight to your partner so she or he doesn't have to move. The task works like this: you hit the ball to your partner; your partner stops the ball completely still and then hits it back. Remember, strike easily so your partner is able to stop the ball, and when you are the partner receiving, you need to absorb the force of the ball (puck) by relaxing your grip and moving the stick back a little to stop it. *A demonstration is helpful here.*

T Before you practiced hitting the ball (puck) to different places. Now you're going to do that with your partner, and your partner's stick is going to be a target at which you will aim. The partner who is to receive the ball will put his or her hockey stick out in one place and tap it twice; the partner hitting the ball will use the stick as a target and aim toward the stick. Remember, stop the ball every time before returning it. Change roles each time.

C With your partner, see how many times you can hit the ball (puck) back and forth without a miss.

Remember, you must stop the ball before you return it to your partner. If you miss, just start counting all over. If you get to 10, let me know.

T After you hit the ball (puck) successfully to your partner 10 times and your partner is able to stop the ball, move back two steps each and start again. When you're successful 10 times in a row, move back again.

T This will make it a little harder: Move back to your close position. After you pass the ball this time, move to a new space and stand still. The receiver must control the ball (puck), look to see where you are, and then pass. Each time after someone passes, move to a new space, stop, and then receive the ball.

C Now see how many times you can keep this up without missing.

We have observed children trying to curve the blades of hockey sticks. Having the children keep the blade straight ensures two things: (1) The puck (ball) has a greater chance of staying on the floor and (2) your hockey sticks last a lot longer.

Traveling Slowly While Striking a Ball

Setting: A hockey stick and a ball or puck for each child

Cues	
Light Taps	(Use light taps to keep the ball close to your stick.)
Hands Apart	(Move your hands 8 to 10 inches apart to control the ball better.)
Both Sides of Stick	(Use both sides of the stick to dribble around the obstacle.)

Tasks/Challenges:

T Before, we practiced moving around the entire space while striking a ball with the hockey stick. Let's practice again—this is called dribbling or stick-handling. To begin, go slowly. Your task is to travel in general space while striking the ball and not touching anyone else.

T This time as you travel, I'm going to hold up different numbers of fingers. Tell me how many fingers I'm holding up. You'll have to look often because I'll change the number of fingers often and try to trick you.

C You have 50 points. Your task is to keep all your points. Move around the room dribbling the ball. Every time you lose the ball, subtract 5 points. See how many points you have at the stop signal.

©Lars A. Niki

Traveling, stopping, and controlling an object with a hockey stick take an acute awareness of others.

Traveling, Stopping, and Controlling the Ball

Setting: A plastic hockey stick and a ball for each child

Cues	
Light Taps	(Use light taps to keep the ball close to your stick.)
Hands Apart	(Move your hands 8 to 10 inches apart to control the ball better.)

Tasks/Challenges:

🅣 Before, you practiced traveling around the room keeping the ball close to you. This time, you're going to do the same thing, but with something added. Whenever you hear the signal, stop the ball, using only your stick, and wait for the signal to go again.

🅣 This time, try going a little faster and doing the same thing. Move around in general space, striking the ball with your hockey stick. On the signal, stop the ball and wait for the "Go" signal. I'll know you can really do this if I always see the ball close to the stick and all the balls stopped on the signal.

🅣 Now I am going to change the task a little. Again, you should move around striking the ball. But this time, on the signal, instead of stopping the ball, stand still and keep moving the ball in your self-space until you hear the signal to travel again. This is called controlling the ball. You'll know you're really good at this when, as soon as you hear the

signal, you can stop and start moving the ball in your self-space without first having to chase the ball across the room.

🅒 This time, the stopping will be like a game. When I say "Stop," I'll start counting backward from 10. When all the balls have stopped, I'll stop counting. Your goal is to get me to stop counting before I get to zero.

🅒 You're going to play a little game with the stopping this time. Every time you come near another person, stop or control the ball and then start again. It's as if you don't want anyone to come near your ball, so you are going to protect it—and the only way you can protect it is by controlling it in your self-space or stopping it.

❓ Why should you control the ball or puck before you send it back? What do you have to do to control it?

Traveling and Changing Speeds

Setting: A striking implement and a ball or puck for each child

Cues	
Light Taps	(Use light taps to keep the ball close to your stick.)
Hands Apart	(Move your hands 8 to 10 inches apart to control the ball better.)
Both Sides of Stick	(Use both sides of the stick to dribble around the obstacle.)

Tasks/Challenges:

🅣 One of the important things in games that use dribbling or stick-handling is the ability to change the speed at which you are traveling while you dribble. Travel in general space going at a slow speed. Now try a fast speed. Can you find speed that is a medium speed?

🅣 This time I will call out speeds as you travel. See if you can match every speed I call out.

🅣 This time change your speed as you go. It should be easy for me to tell which speed you are using.

🅣 Now you will practice using different speeds with a partner. It is like follow the leader. You will follow a partner, dribbling in general space. The first partner starts and travels, changing the speed of the travel often. The second partner follows, always trying to travel at the same speed as the first partner. On the signal, switch places.

Traveling and Striking While Changing Pathways

Setting: A hockey stick and ball or puck for each child; various pathways (the more, the better) taped or marked on the floor

Cues	
Light Taps	(Use light taps to keep the ball close to your stick.)
Hands Apart	(Move your hands 8 to 10 inches apart to control the ball better.)
Both Sides of Stick	(Use both sides of the stick to dribble around the obstacle.)

Tasks/Challenges:

T You're going to practice something new this time: changes in pathways. Do you remember pathways: straight, curved, and zigzag? Again, you're going to move around the entire space, but whenever you come to a pathway on the floor, try to follow it exactly. Once you finish one pathway, travel to another and follow it. As you follow the pathways, be sure you're striking the ball, not pushing it along.

T Something very different happens when you follow a zigzag pathway. What is it? That's right—you have to move your stick from one side of the ball to the other, like moving the ball in self-space to keep control of it. Practice zigzag pathways on your own. Remember, every time you come to a zig or a zag, you have to move your stick to the other side of the ball.

T This time, we are going to practice striking while traveling in different pathways with a partner. You're going to play follow the leader. The leader travels in different pathways—curved, straight, and zigzag—as the follower tries to stay close behind, copying the exact pathways the leader makes. Leaders: As you begin, make easy pathways. The object is not to lose your partner but to practice striking while traveling in different pathways. On the signal, change positions as leaders and followers.

T This time, the following is going to be a little harder. Instead of staying right behind the leader, the follower is going to watch while the leader moves in a short pathway sequence. When the leader stops and freezes, the follower moves, copying the pathway of the leader until she or he catches up with the leader. When the follower catches up, the leader takes off again. This is a bit like a game of cat and mouse: Just as soon as you think you've caught someone, the person slips

away again. As you move, remember that the purpose of this task is to practice different pathways, so include them in your movements. After five turns as a leader, switch places.

C This is the real pathway test. By yourself, make up a sequence of traveling and striking that involves four changes of pathways. Practice your sequence until you can do it from memory three times without stopping. Each time the sequence should look the same. Then we'll all share the sequences.

? *Student Drawing.* This task creates a perfect opportunity for student drawings. Have youngsters draw the pathway sequence and label the pathways used.

Striking While Dodging Stationary Obstacles

Setting: An obstacle course of cones and hoops or other equipment throughout general space; a hockey stick and a ball for each child

Cues	
Light Taps	(Use light taps to keep the ball close to your stick.)
Both Sides of Stick	(Use both sides of the stick to dribble around the obstacle.)
Look Up	(Look up as you travel so you can see the obstacles.)

Tasks/Challenges:

T You've traveled while dodging objects. This time, you're going to travel and dodge objects while dribbling a ball with a hockey stick. Your task is to travel throughout the space, dribbling the ball with the hockey stick. Try not to let the ball get away from you. Don't touch any of the obstacles or other people. Freeze on the signal and have the ball with you.

T As practice for looking up, we're going to play the counting game again. I'll keep holding up a different number of fingers, and you tell me how many I'm holding up while you're striking the ball around the space.

T This time we are going to dribble in general space, and each time you come to an obstacle, control the ball, execute a quarter turn to the right or left, and continue dribbling.

T You've all been going at fairly slow speeds. This isn't always good in game situations, so you're going to practice going at different speeds. Sometimes approach an obstacle very quickly, sometimes slowly. Make the change clear. The rules are still the same: No touching, and you must be able to stop on the signal and have the ball with you.

T Dribble in general space. As you near an obstacle, dribble past the obstacle; sometimes going to the right and sometimes going to the left.

C This time as you practice dodging, pretend you have 100 points. If the ball you are dribbling touches a cone, subtract 10 points from your score. If you contact another person, subtract 25 points; if the ball you are dribbling contacts the cone or another person subtract 10 points. Try to complete your practice with 100 points!

Utilization Level (GLSP): Learning Experiences Leading to Skill Development

At the utilization level, children are able to control a ball in the space around them and strike consistently with the appropriate striking pattern. We challenge them to use their striking skills in more dynamic and unpredictable situations.

A note about cues: *Although several cues are listed for many of the learning experiences, it's important to focus on only one cue at a time. This way, the children can really concentrate on that cue. Once you provide feedback to the children and observe that most have learned a cue, it's time to focus on another one.*

Striking to Small Targets

Setting: Six pins (2-liter soft-drink bottles or light-weight plastic bowling pins), a ball, and a hockey stick for every two children; a marked lane leading away from the pins for a bowling alley

Cues	
Eyes on Target	(Watch the target at all times.)
Step	(Step forward on the opposite foot.)
Follow Through	(Follow through toward the target with your stick.)

Tasks/Challenges:

C This game is called Hockey Bowl. Your task is to strike the ball from behind the line and see how many pins you can knock down. Your partner stands near the pins and rolls the ball back to you after each strike. After three hits, or when all the pins have been knocked down (whichever happens first), trade places.

T The first time you can knock down all the pins three times in a row, move back three steps, and try it again. If you still want to make the task harder, take away some of the pins so you have a smaller target.

Performing a Continuous Dribble with Changes in Direction and Speed

Setting: Children scattered throughout general space, each with a hockey stick and ball

Cues	
Light Taps	(Use light taps to keep the ball close to your stick.)
Both Sides of Stick	(Use both sides of the stick to dribble when you go around an obstacle.)
Heads Up	(Look up to avoid collisions.)

Tasks/Challenges:

T You learned to change the direction of the ball by dribbling it to your right and left with both sides of the stick. Travel within general space, using changes of direction to avoid collisions with others. Your task is continuous dribbling.

T This time as you change direction, also change your speed. To begin, with the first change of direction accelerate, or go faster, after you make the change of direction.

T Try the same thing again, but with the change of direction, decelerate, or go slower.

T Now you choose: sometimes accelerate; sometimes decelerate.

T Dribble as close as you can to another person without touching him or her and quickly use a move to the right or left to dodge him or her.

T Gradually increase the speed of your travel to determine the maximum rate you can travel with a controlled dribble and frequent changes of direction.

A while ago I was at a party where the hosts set up a croquet game. Adults and children alike were intrigued, and, bingo, I realized: This is a striking game! Do you remember it? Croquet is a fun activity to add to physical education class as a special treat and ties together the ideas of striking at targets and varying force and distance really well. No croquet sets, you say? You'll be amazed how many families have croquet sets at home that they're willing to let you use (or sometimes even give to you). I just acquired an antique croquet set that was on its way to Goodwill. Give croquet a try sometime!

Pathways, Speeds, and Directions

Note: This task is an example of a task teaching instructional approach. See Chapter 9 for more ideas on task teaching ideas.

Setting: A hockey stick and ball for each child

Cues	
Light Taps	(Use light taps to keep the ball close to your stick.)
Both Sides of Stick	(Use both sides of the stick to dribble when you go around an obstacle.)
Heads Up	(Look up to avoid collisions.)

Figure 27.2 Task sheet for striking with hockey sticks.

Tasks/Challenges:

Ⓒ This is a self-testing task. The task sheet (Figure 27.2) lets you assess your traveling and striking in different directions, pathways, and speeds. Practice the tasks one by one. When you think you can do a task well, have a partner watch you. If your partner thinks you did the task successfully, the partner signs the sheet. I'll check to see how you're progressing.

❓ *Peer Observation.* The preceding challenge is a wonderful peer observation assessment. With the date recorded, it provides an indication of when students accomplished the skill.

Name _____ Class _____

Task Sheet for Striking with Hockey Sticks

Observer's Name	Task
	I can strike a ball with a hockey stick in a straight pathway, keeping the ball close to the stick.
	I can strike a ball with a hockey stick in a curved pathway, keeping the ball close to the stick.
	I can strike a ball with a hockey stick in a zigzag pathway, keeping the ball close to the stick.
	I can strike a ball with a hockey stick around four cones set up about four feet apart, keeping the ball close to the stick.
	I can strike a ball with a hockey stick through the cones while running, keeping the ball close to the stick.
	I can strike a ball with a hockey stick while traveling sideways.
	I can make up a sequence including two pathways, two changes in speed, and two different directions. I have written my sequence below.
	Sequence:

Traveling and Striking for a Goal

Setting: Cones scattered throughout general space; markers for multiple goals around the outside boundary; a hockey stick and ball for each child

Cues	
Face Target	(Be sure to face the target throughout the swing.)
Light Taps/ Hard Strikes	(Light taps to dribble the ball; strike hard at the goal.)
Follow Through	(Follow through toward the goal with your stick.)

Tasks/Challenges:

Ⓣ Travel at your own speed and dribble the ball while avoiding the obstacles and other people. On the signal, travel quickly toward an open space, and strike for the goal. Retrieve your ball; begin dribbling again, listening for the signal to strike for the goal.

Ⓣ Practice dribbling around the obstacles and striking for the goal on your own; I won't give the signal.

One-on-One Hockey

Setting: Partners in general space, each with hockey sticks, a ball, and markers for a goal

It's a challenge to try to keep the puck away from a partner while dribbling it.

©Barbara Adamcik

Cues	
Light Taps/ Hard Strikes	(Light taps to dribble the ball; strike hard at the goal.)
Heads Up	(Look up to avoid collisions.)
Dodges	(Use stopping/starting, both sides of the stick, and turns to avoid your partner.)

Tasks/Challenges:

Ⓣ Select a partner whose dribbling skill is about the same as yours. Cooperatively decide the boundaries for your area; a small area provides more practice. One of you begins to dribble the ball within the area; the other one tries to gain possession of the ball by using the stick to steal the ball. Follow these rules:

1. You can only contact the ball, not the person.
2. Be sure to gain possession of the ball; don't slap it away.
3. If you gain possession, begin dribbling as the offensive player; your partner is now defense.

If partners are unmatched in skill, provide a signal to change from offense to defense. Players stay on offense or defense until they hear the signal.

❓ When playing one-on-one hockey, how can you steal the ball and not hit the other player's legs with the hockey stick?

Ⓣ Within your area, set up two markers as a goal. The first partner will dribble until within scoring range (10 to 12 feet) and then shoot for a goal. The second partner will attempt to gain possession of the ball, using only the stick. After each strike for goal, switch positions.

Ⓒ Design your own game using the skills of stick-handling and shooting for the goal. Work with your partner to decide the rules of the game, scoring, and boundaries. Can you think of a name for your game? (See Chapter 31 for more ideas on child-designed games.)

❓ *Peer Observation.* After students have a chance to play their one-on-one games for a while, a peer observation would be appropriate. Have another pair of partners observe for the use of the cues of Light Taps/ Hard Strikes, Heads Up, and Dodges. Direct the students to observe one cue at a time. After a designated time, the observers and players switch roles.

Striking from a Stationary Position to a Moving Target

Setting: Partners, each pair with two hockey sticks and a ball; a large enough space (about 10 feet by 10 yards) to send and receive the ball on the run

Cues

Lead Receiver	(Pass the ball to an open space in front of the receiver.)
Angles	(Your receiver should always be to the side and in front of you.)
Heads Up	(Always look up so you can see where your receiver is.)

Tasks/Challenges:

T You practiced striking the ball to a partner before, but then you were always standing still. When you're in a real game, how often are you able to pass to a partner who is standing still? Not very often. You're going to practice striking to a partner who is moving. One of you will be the passer, and the other the receiver. The passer stands still and the receiver starts to run downfield, away from the passer at an angle. When the receiver is about 5 yards away, the passer sends the ball. The receiver should collect the ball on the run and then keep going for a few more steps before returning back to the starting position. Take five turns, and then switch roles.

T You've been passing to the same side so far. Now try passing to the other side so the receiver has to receive with the backhand. This will seem awkward at first, but stick with it. Pass five times, and then switch.

Passing and Receiving on the Move

Setting: A large, outdoor area; children in pairs, with one ball for each pair and a hockey stick for each child

Cues

Lead Receiver	(Pass the ball to an open space in front of the receiver.)
Angles	(Your receiver should always be to the side and in front of you.)
Heads Up	(Always look up so you can see where your receiver is.)

Tasks/Challenges:

T Travel in the same direction as your partner, side by side, about 20 feet apart. As you're traveling, pass the ball back and forth using the hockey stick. The key is that you both must always be moving forward. When you get to the end of your area, turn around and come back.

T Now travel with your partner in general space, dribbling and passing. All the other players will be doing the same thing, so it's important that you are aware of others and of passing to open spaces. Go.

C Challenge yourself to always pass the ball ahead of your partner—to the open space. If you are successful, your partner will never have to stop to receive the pass. Try for five successful completions: open space, no stopping.

Keeping It Moving

Setting: Four markers in a space 5 yards by 5 yards; three or four children per group, each with a hockey stick, and a ball or puck for the group

Cues

Lead Receiver	(Pass the ball to an open space in front of the receiver.)
Angles	(Your receiver should always be to the side of and in front of you.)
Heads Up	(Always look up so you can see where your receiver is.)

Tasks/Challenges:

C This time you're going to play a game called Keeping It Moving. One person begins by passing the ball to another player. That player passes it to someone else, and so on. The object is to never let the ball stop moving and never let it go out of bounds.

Two-on-One Hockey

Setting: Children in groups of three, each group with sticks, a ball, and cones to use as goals

Cues

Offense	
Lead Receiver	(Strike the ball to an open space ahead of your receiver.)
Light Taps/ Hard Strikes	(Light taps to dribble the ball; strike hard at the goal.)
Angles	(The receiver should be in an open space at an angle to and in front of the passer.)
Defense	
Play the Ball	(Make your first move to the player with the ball.)

Tasks/Challenges:

C In your group, two of you will be the offensive players, and one will be the defensive player. The two offensive players will pass and dribble to each other within the boundaries of your area. The defensive player will attempt to gain possession of the ball by intercepting passes or tapping the ball away on the dribble.

Each team will have possession of the ball for 2 minutes. See how many goals you can score in that time. The offensive team must execute at least two passes before attempting a goal.

Proficiency Level (GLSP): Learning Experiences Leading to Skill Development

When children reach the proficiency level, many possess mature striking patterns, and striking becomes a skill that can be used in complex, unpredictable, game-like and game-playing situations. Children are now able to incorporate previous experiences into situations that involve strategic and split-second decisions. At this level, children are given situations that facilitate development of the ability to strike with implements while focusing on the tactics and outcome of the action and on their skill. Cues are focused on the use of the skill rather than on the skill itself.

As with other skill themes, at the proficiency level, many appropriate learning experiences call for the use of striking skills in game-like and game-playing situations. It can be quite tricky to keep these tasks and challenges developmentally appropriate, especially in terms of active participation for all children. There are several solutions here. One is to set up multiple playing areas around the space. Another option is to have stations, several of which offer game-like challenges and others which provide practice opportunities that are more invariant requiring less space and setup. Finally, you could have peer assessment opportunities; within small groups, half will play and half observe, and then they switch. Regardless of the solution, all game-type learning experiences should be appropriate for all children. See Chapter 31 for more information on game options in physical education.

A note about cues: *At the proficiency level, tasks are more complex, typically requiring children to coordinate several movements simultaneously in a dynamic context. A list of cues is provided to assist the children in being more successful in the learning experiences. The challenge is in determining which cue will be most beneficial for each child—and when. Thus, careful observation and critical reflection become very important as you watch the children move and then decide which cue will be the most helpful to move each learner to a higher level.*

Important points for the following activities: Before beginning tasks that involve offense and defense, students should be skilled in the space awareness and dodging tasks that ask them to master the offensive and defensive skills of moving into open space; avoiding other persons; and using fakes, stops and starts, pivots, and other avoidance skills without manipulating equipment. (See Chapter 14, "Space Awareness," and Chapter 18, "Chasing, Fleeing, and Dodging.") Children need to have mastered these skills before they are asked to use them while manipulating equipment.

One key to these tasks—and to other initial tasks involving offense and defense—is to clearly define the boundaries of the space the students are to use. A small space gives an advantage to the defense; a large space provides an offensive advantage. Similarly, a long, narrow space gives the advantage to the defense; a wider space helps the offense. Initial tasks generally favor the offense.

Striking to Dodge an Opponent

Setting: A group of five or six children, half with hockey sticks and balls; the others positioned as obstacles, holding hockey sticks in their hands and wearing armbands or other identifying clothing (Figure 27.3). Space will need to be defined depending on the size of the group.

Cues	
Heads Up	(Always look up to avoid collisions.)
Dodges	(Use stopping/starting, both sides of the stick, changes of speed, and turns to avoid obstacles.)
Lead Receiver	(Pass to an open space ahead of the receiver.)
Angles	(The receiver should be in an open space to the side and in front of the passer.)

Tasks/Challenges:

T This is a dodging task. We've done activities like this before but without equipment. To begin, those of you wearing blue will be the obstacles; the rest of you will be dodgers. Obstacles, find a self-space and stand there. Dodgers, try to cross the room without coming near an obstacle. The obstacles have the right to steal the ball if it comes within their area. Their area is that space they can reach while keeping one foot glued to the floor. The dodgers' goal is to get to the other end of the space without having the ball stolen. The group gets five tries and then switches places.

Figure 27.3 Arrangement for dribbling and dodging activity.

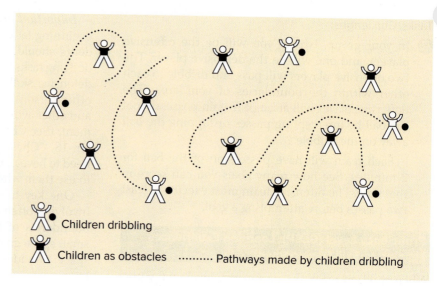

Children dribbling
Children as obstacles   ·········· Pathways made by children dribbling

C We're going to change the experience a little this time. Instead of the dodgers each having a ball, they're going to have only one ball. Their job is then to get the ball to the other end, as a team. The obstacles still have the same rule: They can take the ball only when it comes into their area. After four tries, switch places.

? *Teacher Observation.* At this point children should be demonstrating their ability to use skills and strategies to avoid other players. A teacher observation of the use of the critical elements (Heads Up, Dodges, Lead Receiver, and Angles) would be appropriate before advancing to more complex tasks.

Keep-Away

Setting: Groups of four: three players on the outside standing about 20 feet apart and one in the middle; each player with a hockey stick; one ball or puck per group

Cues

Offense
Don't Pass Until the Defense Commits (Control the ball until the defense makes you pass by coming close to you.)

Receivers to Open Space (Receivers should move to an open space at an angle from the passer.)

Stay Away from Passer (Receivers shouldn't go close to the passer.)

Defense
Play the Ball (Play defense on the person with the ball.)

Tasks/Challenges:

T This is like Keep-Away, except that it's played with hockey sticks. There will be four in a group: three on the outside standing about 20 feet apart, and one in the middle. The three on the outside pass the ball back and forth; the one in the middle tries to intercept the pass. After eight successful passes or four interceptions, trade places. You must stay in the boundaries of your space. There is no contact.

? *Video/Digital Analysis.* As children learn to play in dynamic situations, it helps them immensely to watch their own performance and analyze the use of the offensive and defensive cues.

Small-Sided Hockey Invasion Game

Setting: Groups of four or six, two or three players on each team; hockey sticks for every player; one ball or puck per group; milk crates, cones, or boxes for goals; a space at least 20 feet by 15 feet

Cues

Offense
Don't Pass Until the Defense Commits (Control the ball until the defense makes you pass by coming close to you.)

Receivers to Open Space (Receivers move to an open space at an angle from the passer.)

Stay Away from Passer (Receivers away from passer.)

Defense
Ball First; Player Second (First play defense on the person with the ball; then cover the receivers.)

Hustle Back (When you lose the ball to the offense, hurry back on defense.)

Tasks/Challenges:

C This game is called Mini Hockey. The objective is to strike the ball into the opponent's goal. Here are the rules:

1. The players on the teams decide the boundaries and width of the goal. There should be one goal on each end of the space. Use milk crates, cones, or boxes for the goals.
2. One team gets the ball first.
3. The ball can be stolen only on the pass.
4. No contact.
5. Everyone must be playing—no standing around.
6. Make up your own form of scoring (if you want to keep score).
7. Make up any more rules you need.

C We're going to change the game a little this time. Instead of one goal on each end of the field, there will be two.

Striking with Long-Handled Implements—Bats

If only everyone could enjoy a backyard game of softball! The skill theme of batting can lead to that as well as participation in games in more traditional sports like baseball, cricket, and a myriad of "made-up" games. A sidearm pattern is used when striking a ball with a bat to keep the bat at the same distance from the ground and in a horizontal plane throughout the swing. We have identified the equipment used as a bat, though you could easily substitute a tennis racket for a bat.

It is important that the teacher is familiar with the critical elements needed for quality instruction, demonstration, and observation of the skill. Throughout the chapter are sample cues (short phrases or words summarizing these critical elements). Ideally, if the cue is the last thing a teacher repeats before sending the students to practice, the learner will be cognitively focused on the critical elements.

The critical elements for striking with a long implement, sidearm pattern, are:

- Bat up and back in preparation for striking action
- Step forward on opposite foot as contact is made
- Coil and uncoil the trunk for preparation and execution of the striking action
- Swing the bat on a horizontal plane
- Wrist uncocks on follow-through for completion of the striking action

See Box 27-2 for the correct form for striking sidearm. Remember, striking a pitched ball with a bat is one of the last skills that children develop. Our progression spiral for striking with bats provides activities that will lead to skill development.

Box 27-2

Critical Elements: Side-Armed Striking Pattern (Batting)

©Derek Sine & Van Tucker

Skill Theme Development Progression

Striking with Long-Handled Implements—Bats

Proficiency Level

One-Base Baseball
Six-player striking and fielding in a game-like situation
Directing the pathway, distance, and speed of an object

Utilization Level

Batting, combining distance and placement
Hitting a pitched ball to open spaces
Striking a pitched ball varying the distance
Directing the placement of an object
Grounders and flies

Control Level

Striking a pitched ball
Striking a self-tossed ball for accuracy
Striking a self-tossed ball to different distances
Striking a self-tossed ball
Hit and Run
Striking suspended objects
Striking a stationary ball for distance
Level swings
Striking a stationary ball

Precontrol Level

Striking off a batting tee

Implements for Batting

While we refer generically to bats in this chapter, there are a variety of "bats" that may be used and that, at times, may be more appropriate as well as more challenging for youngsters. These "bats" may include traditional plastic bats, large plastic bats, flat-sided plastic bats, and cricket bats.

Striking Off a Batting Tee

Setting: Preferably outside in a large open space; for at least every two children (but preferably for every child), a box containing five plastic balls or 5- to 7-inch high-density foam balls or beach balls (indoors), a plastic bat, and a batting tee

Each individual should have a personal "striking zone" defined by markers to ensure that children do not crowd each other or are hit by someone else's bat. Be aware of right- and left-handed children who are next to each other.

Tasks/Challenges:

🅣 This time, you're going to hit a big ball off a tee with a plastic bat. Stand to the side of the tee and facing the tee so you are batting to the field. Now line up facing the same way, so you won't hit one another. Hit all the balls in your box, and then wait until I give the signal before collecting them. Remember: Hit hard. *(If a partner is used, the partner should be positioned "in the field" a good distance away from the hitters behind a safe zone marked by the teacher. After the signal, both partners can collect the balls and change places.)*

🅒 Practice hitting until you can hit the ball three times in a row.

🅣 Now see how far you can hit the ball.

Batting tees are helpful for children at the precontrol level who are unable to strike a moving ball and for children at the control level who are practicing ball placement. Figure 27.4 provide options for batting tees.

Precontrol Level (GLSP): Experiences for Exploration

Learning experiences at the precontrol level ask children to explore all varieties of striking with bats. At this level, a chopping, downward swing is typical for any striking pattern. Children struggle just to make contact between the ball and the striking instrument. Therefore, we give children tasks and challenges that let them explore striking with the added length that comes with bats—and the greater demands that length places on their hand–eye coordination. Due to the difficulty of the skill, tasks are developed using large objects to be struck.

All learning experiences at this level need to be done with balls of various sizes. For beginners, large plastic balls are easier because they're larger and move more slowly.

Control Level (GLSP): Learning Experiences Leading to Skill Development

At the control level, children begin to develop mature striking patterns used in increasingly complex contexts. They can be challenged with tasks requiring them to include one or two other variables besides striking such as striking a pitched ball for distance.

A note about cues: *Although several cues are listed for many of the learning experiences, it's important to focus on*

only one cue at a time. This way, the children can really concentrate on that cue. Once you provide feedback to the children and observe that most have learned a cue, it's time to focus on another one.

Striking a Stationary Ball

Setting: Preferably a large, open, outdoor space big enough for every child to hit against a backstop or a wall; children about 15 feet from the backstop or wall

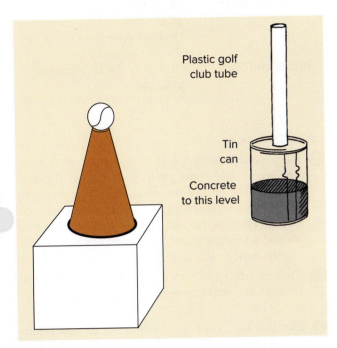

Figure 27.4 Construction of a batting tee.*
The easiest way to make a batting tee is to use a large (36-inch) traffic cone, which is high enough for young children. Increase the height by placing the traffic cone on a cardboard box. A batting tee can also be made out of a tin can and a plastic tube.

Materials
    Large tin can (available from the school cafeteria)
    Plastic golf club tube (obtained from a sporting goods store)
    Sack of ready-mixed concrete (1/10 to 1/8)

Directions
1. Place the golf club tube into the tin can.
2. Add water to the concrete mix and fill the tin can approximately half full.
3. After a few minutes, when the concrete begins to harden, make sure the golf club tube is not leaning to the side. Once the concrete dries, the batting tee is ready to use.

You can vary the heights of the batting tees by shortening the plastic golf club tubes before inserting them into the cans. We try to have batting tees of three different heights.

*Prior to constructing equipment we recommend you check with school administration to be certain that district policy permits homemade equipment.

with their individual striking zones defined by ropes or markers (or place a line on the ground about 15 feet from the batting positions for children to hit over); a box of about five balls (large, light plastic or beach balls [indoors], high-density foams balls, and whiffle balls), bats, and batting tees for each child or pair of children

Cues	
Side to the Field	(Turn your side to the target or field.)
Bat Back, Elbow Up	(Bring the bat way back over your shoulder so your back elbow is level with your shoulder.)
Watch the Ball	(Keep your eyes on the ball all the time.)
Level	(Extend your arms to swing flat as a pancake.)

Tasks/Challenges:

Ⓣ When we explored batting, you practiced hitting a ball off a tee. We're going to practice that again. Check your personal space to make sure you have plenty of room. Let's just practice the swing. If you do not have a bat, you will do an "air swing" until your turn with the bat. **Take a batting grip** (Figure 27.5) where your preferred hand is on top. (If you are having a hard time remembering which hand to put where on the bat, an easy way to remember is that the bottom hand on the bat is the same side as facing the field—so if your left side faces the field, your left hand is the bottom hand on the bat.) Let's practice five times, each time pretending you are looking at the ball being pitched to you. Let your partner try.

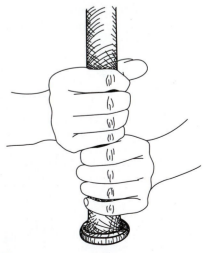

Figure 27.5 Batting grip.

T We are going to continue our practice swings, but this time, we want to hit the imaginary ball hard and far. Assume the same starting position with your bat up and back over your shoulder. This time, twist your body back a little and as you swing, untwist, and step on your front foot (the direction you are "hitting"). A *demonstration is important here.* Practice this motion keeping that level swing for five times. Let your partner try.

T Now practice striking off the tee. Use a plastic ball or a beach ball. Stand about a bat's length away and to the side of your batting tee. **If you are batting the ball correctly, your swing will follow through over your other shoulder.** *Note: It may be necessary to have the children strike all the objects they have and wait for a teacher signal to collect them.*

C Practice until you can hit the plastic ball 10 times in a row off the tee.

T When you can hit the plastic ball 10 times in a row, trade it in for a whiffle ball. Now practice with that ball.

T Hit the ball so hard that it goes in the air to the wall (over the line).

C Practice hitting with the bat until you can hit five times in a row so the ball hits the wall (lands over the line).

Increasing the size of the ball reduces the complexity of the task. Increasing the size of the bat does the same thing. Some teachers also use soap bubbles for children to practice striking. One partner blows bubbles; the other gets to swing away, trying to pop the bubbles as they fall. It works!

? What is the most important cue for making contact with the ball? What is one hint that will help you do this?

Level Swings

Setting: Ropes suspended from the ceiling or a line hung across the room to about children's shoulder height (Figure 27.6); batting tees, plastic balls, and bats for each child. Individual striking zones defined by ropes or markers.

Cues	
Side to the Field	(Turn your side to the target or field.)
Bat Back, Elbow Up	(Bring the bat way back over your shoulder so your back elbow is level with your shoulder.)
Watch the Ball	(Keep your eyes on the ball all the time.)
Level	(Extend your arms to swing flat as a pancake.)
Rotate and Shift	(Roll over the shoelaces of your back foot.)

Tasks/Challenges:

T Place your batting tee directly under your rope. The tee should come up to your knees. The area between the end of the rope and the top of your tee is your strike zone. Step up to the tee and swing. There is no ball for this task. Your swing should go through the strike zone without touching the rope or the tee.

C Practice until you can get three strikes in a row through the strike zone without touching the rope or the tee.

T (For this task, each child will need an equal number of plastic or foam balls.) Place a ball on top of the tee. Hit all the balls and wait for my signal to collect them.

? *Teacher Observation.* At this point, it is appropriate to conduct a teacher observation of the use of the critical elements for batting before proceeding to a more complex use of the skill.

Figure 27.6 Setup for level swings.

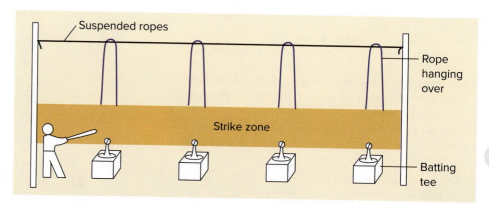

Striking a Stationary Ball for Distance

Setting: Partners, each pair with a batting tee, three whiffle balls or high-density foam balls, and a bat; batters in a circle in the middle of the playground facing out with individual striking zones defined by ropes or markers (Figure 27.7); fielders about 30 feet (or whatever is appropriate) in front of their partner; zones marked at 10-foot intervals around the center circle

Cues

Watch the Ball	(Keep your eyes on the ball all the time.)
Bat Back, Elbow Up	(Bring the bat way back over your shoulder so your back elbow is level with your shoulder.)
Side to the Field	(Turn your side to the target or field.)
Level	(Extend your arms to swing flat as a pancake.)
Rotate and Shift	(Roll over the shoelaces of your back foot.)

Tasks/Challenges:

T Stand inside the circle about a bat's length away from your tee with your side to the field. You are going to practice batting the ball in the air. There's enough room to hit as hard as you like. Your partner will collect the balls. After three hits, trade places. Remember, watch the ball.

T This time, have your partner stand where your ball landed. Try to hit the next ball farther. The partner moves to that spot. Try again to hit farther than the previous hit. After three hits, trade places with your partner.

T Bat the ball as far as possible. Remember the zone in which the ball first lands. Bat three times, each time trying to improve your distance. Trade places.

C Try to bat the ball so it lands in the same zone three times.

In conjunction with these tasks, you may want to add the following: Twisting While Striking with a Bat (Chapter 19, page 248).

Striking Suspended Objects

Setting: Whiffle balls suspended about waist height from strings (see Figure 26.2) around the practice area;

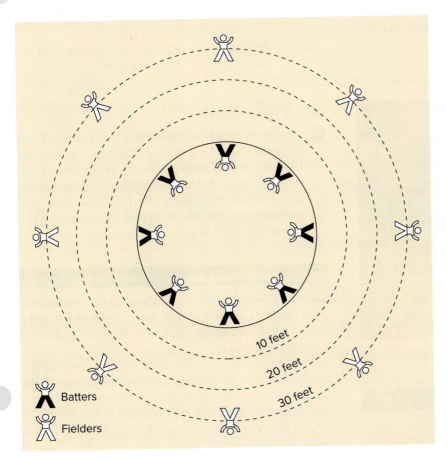

Figure 27.7 Setup for striking a stationary ball for distance.

10 feet

20 feet

30 feet

Batters

Fielders

a bat for each child and individual striking zones defined by ropes or markers

Cues	
Side to the Field	(Turn your side to the target or field.)
Bat Back, Elbow Up	(Bring the bat way back over your shoulder so it so your back elbow is level with your shoulder.)
Watch the Ball	(Keep your eyes on the ball all the time.)
Level	(Extend your arms to swing flat as a pancake.)
Rotate and Shift	(Roll over the shoelaces of your back foot.)

? How does rolling over your shoelaces help you bat?

Tasks/Challenges:

T This task is a little harder than the last one. Instead of hitting balls that don't move from batting tees, you're going to hit balls that are hanging from strings. Stand to the side of the ball about a bat's length away. Practice hitting the ball. Remember, stop the ball still before you hit it again.

T Practice batting until you can hit five balls in a row without missing.

C Now the game changes a little. See how many times you can strike the ball in a row without missing.

Balls suspended on strings give youngsters the opportunity to practice swinging level.

©Barbara Adamcik

Hit and Run

Setting: Partners with individual striking zones defined by ropes or markers; plastic or high-density

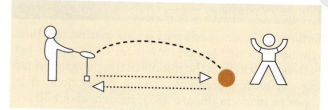

Figure 27.8 Setup for Hit and Run.
Source: Holt/Hale, S. and Hall, T. (2016) *Lesson Planning for Elementary Physical Education: Meeting the National Standards & Grade-Level Outcomes.* SHAPE America. Champaign, IL: Human Kinetics.

foam ball, bat, batting tee, and spot for each set of partners (set up as in Figure 27.8)

Cues	
Bat Back, Elbow Up	(Bring the bat way back over your shoulder so your back elbow is level with your shoulder.)
Watch the Ball	(Keep your eyes on the ball all the time.)
Side to the Field	(Turn your side to the target or field.)
Level	(Extend your arms to swing flat as a pancake.)
Rotate and Shift	(Roll over the shoelaces of your back foot.)

Tasks/Challenges:

T Partner A stands at the batting tee; partner B, on the spot about 15 feet away. Partner A strikes the ball off the tee, hitting it as far as possible. Then partner A runs to the spot and back to the batting tee. Partner B collects the ball and runs and replaces it on the tee. Switch places after each hit. Be careful: Both of you are running.

Striking a Self-Tossed Ball

Setting: Preferably a large outdoor space, where children can bat against a wall or fence; a plastic bat and a ball for each child and individual striking zones defined by ropes or markers
For this task and beginning tasks that involve hitting a pitched ball, sock balls work quite well. They won't travel too far, allowing children to focus on the swing. To make a sock ball, stuff an old sock with other socks and tie off. Cut off the tail. Alternatively, high-density foam balls work equally well.

Cues

Bat Back, Elbow Up	(Bring the bat way back over your shoulder so your back elbow is level with your shoulder.)
Watch the Ball	(Keep your eyes on the ball all the time.)
Side to the Field	(Turn your side to the target or field.)
Level	(Extend your arms to swing flat as a pancake.)
Rotate and Shift	(Roll over the shoelaces of your back foot.)

Tasks/Challenges:

T You're going to practice hitting a ball you throw into the air yourself. In your own space facing the wall (fence) and about 10 feet from it, toss a ball up into the air and then hit it with the bat. You must have both your hands on the bat when you hit the ball, so you'll have to work quickly. *(Demonstrate.)* Explore which hand is best for you to use for the toss.

C Now practice trying until you can hit the ball five times in a row

In conjunction with these tasks, you may want to add the following: Twisting While Striking a Tossed Ball (Chapter 19, page 348).

Striking a Self-Tossed Ball to Different Distances

Setting: Lines marked on a field for distance measurement; a number of whiffle or high-density foam balls and a plastic bat for each child; batting tees (optional); each child's individual striking zones defined by ropes or markers

Cues

Bat Back, Elbow Up	(Bring the bat way back over your shoulder so your back elbow is level with your shoulder.)
Watch the Ball	(Keep your eyes on the ball all the time.)
Side to the Field	(Turn your side to the target or field.)
Level	(Extend your arms to swing flat as a pancake.)
Rotate and Shift	(Roll over the shoelaces of your back foot.)

Tasks/Challenges:

T Now we're going to add something you worked on before: striking to different distances. This involves using different amounts of force to hit the ball. There are a lot of lines on the field; you can use them to judge how far you hit the ball. Each time you hit a ball, see how far you can make it go. If you hit it over one line one time, try to hit it over the next line the next time you hit. *You may choose to give students the option of using the tee if they are struggling with a self-tossed ball.*

C Pick out a line you know you can hit the ball past. Try to hit the ball past that line five times in a row. After you've practiced at one line, pick another line and try again.

Striking a Self-Tossed Ball for Accuracy

Setting: Preferably a large outdoor space, where children can bat against a wall or fence; large round targets on the wall; a plastic bat and a ball for each child and individual striking zones defined by ropes or markers

Cues

Bat Back, Elbow Up	(Bring the bat way back over your shoulder so your back elbow is level with your shoulder.)
Watch the Ball	(Keep your eyes on the ball all the time.)
Side to the Field	(Turn your side to the target or field.)
Level	(Extend your arms to swing flat as a pancake.)
Rotate and Shift	(Roll over the shoelaces of your back foot.)

Tasks/Challenges:

T To begin you are going to practice what you have done before. In your own space facing the wall (fence) and about 10 feet from it, toss a ball up into the air and then hit it with the bat. You must have both your hands on the bat when you hit the ball, so you'll have to work quickly. *(Demonstrate.)*

T Now practice trying to hit the large circle on the wall.

C Score 5 points for every ball that hits the target; 3 points for every ball that hits the wall but misses the target; and 1 point for every ball you hit that doesn't hit the wall. Try to get to 21 points.

Striking a pitched ball is much more complex than striking off a tee; regression in the execution of the strike is to be expected.

©Barbara Adamcik

Striking a Pitched Ball

Setting: A large outdoor space, marked as follows: a pitcher's square and a batting box for each group of two, each batter's box marked with "neat feet" in the correct batting position (Figure 27.9); a skilled thrower (older student, classroom teacher, parent, or grandparent) as a partner for each child; one plastic, high-density foam or sock ball and a bat for each pair

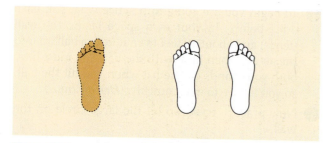

Figure 27.9 "Neat feet" for a right-handed striking action. You can easily make "neat feet" by painting them in the correct position on a rubber mat. Challenge the children to move the left foot to the position of the dotted foot as they swing.

Cues

Bat Back, Elbow Up	(Bring the bat way back over your shoulder so your back elbow is level with your shoulder.)
Watch the Ball	(Keep your eyes on the ball all the time.)
Side to the Field	(Turn your side to the target or field.)
Level	(Extend your arms to swing flat as a pancake.)
Rotate and Shift	(Roll over the shoelaces of your back foot.)

Tasks/Challenges:

T Before, you hit a ball off a batting tee or from a self-toss. This time you're going to practice batting a ball that's pitched by a "big" partner. Your big partner will be the pitcher, and you will get to bat all the time. Your big partner stands on the pitcher's square and pitches the ball to you. You stand on the batter's square and try to hit the ball. The batter's square has a secret help in it: pictures of feet that show you exactly where to stand so you have the best chance of hitting the ball. Just try to hit the ball; it doesn't have to go far. *Note: Pitches from skilled throwers enhance the learning of batting skills.*

C Try to hit five balls in a row.

©Barbara Adamcik

This youngster has clearly rotated his hips forward by "rolling over his back shoelaces."

? *Homework.* The same task of striking pitched balls could be done as a homework assignment. The assignment could be in the form of a task card that includes the cues and asks a parent, grandparent, or older brother or sister to pitch 20 balls to the child. The parent would check on every fifth throw whether the cues were used.

A New Cue

The idea of shifting weight forward on a batting swing has long been accepted. Recently an accomplished softball coach told us a new (and probably more effective) cue for this. Instead of telling children to step forward or shift their weight, tell them, "Picture a shoe with the laces tied, facing upward as usual. As the hips rotate and the weight shifts during the swing, the back foot should roll so the laces almost face the ground." This not only forces the rotation of the hips but also automatically causes the weight shift.

? *Student Report.* Partners digitally record each other while striking a ball resting on a batting tee (five times) and while striking a ball thrown by a pitcher (five times). They review the recording with their partner and self-assess according to criteria presented to them in class. Based on this information, they write a description of the following: the critical elements of batting; the consistency of their hitting; and practice suggestions for improvement in each skill.

Criteria for Assessment

a. Accurately describes the criteria for good batting.
b. Accurately assesses their own consistency of performance.
c. Selects appropriate practice options based.

Adapted from: NASPE (1995, pp. 48–49).

Utilization Level (GLSP): Learning Experiences Leading to Skill Development

At the utilization level, children are able to control a ball in the space around them and strike consistently with the appropriate striking pattern. We challenge them to use their striking skills in more dynamic and unpredictable situations.

A note about cues: *Although several cues are listed for many of the learning experiences, it's important to focus on only one cue at a time. This way, the children can really concentrate on that cue. Once you provide feedback to the children and observe that most have learned a cue, it's time to focus on another one.*

Grounders and Flies

Setting: Groups of three or four: one batter and one pitcher per group, the rest are fielders; a space large enough for all groups to bat without interfering with the others and defined by markers or ropes; five high-density foam or plastic balls and a plastic bat for each group

Cues	
Under the Ball	(Hit the ball slightly below its center for a fly ball.)
Behind the Ball	(Hit directly behind the ball for a line drive.)
Over the Ball	(Hit near the top of the ball for a grounder.)

Tasks/Challenges:

T So far you have practiced hitting from behind the ball. This usually makes the ball travel in a straight aerial pathway—a line drive. Yet, there are times when you will need to hit balls high, and other times when you will need to hit grounders. That is what we will practice first—grounders. Hit the pitches so they hit the ground about 6 to 10 yards away. After five hits, switch places.

T The next practice will be for fly balls. Practice hitting these pitches so they don't hit the ground until past the baseline. They should go higher in the air than a line drive.

T This time the pitcher will challenge the pitcher and call out line drive, pop fly, or grounder, and the batter has to hit that kind of ball. After five hits, switch places.

C This time the batter calls out the type of hit before the ball is pitched. The batter gets one point for each hit that goes the way it was called. See how many you can get out of five pitches.

Directing the Placement of an Object

Setting: Partners, each pair with a batting tee, a bat, a cone, a hoop, and a plastic or high-density foam ball; each pair with enough space to bat for distance and defined with markers or ropes. (See Figure 27.10 for setup.)

Cue	
Step Toward Target	(Remember to step toward your target as you strike.)

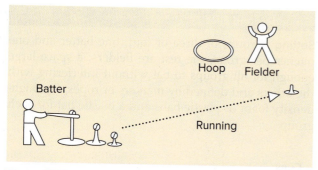

Figure 27.10 Setup for directing the placement of an object.

Tasks/Challenges:

T Before, you practiced hitting fly balls, grounders, and line drives; this time, you're going to practice hitting the ball to different places. To start, one person will be at bat, and the partner will be in left field. The batter first tries to hit five balls off the tee to left field (for right handed batters) or right field (for left handed batters), aiming for her or his partner. If everything works correctly, the partner shouldn't have to move very far to catch the balls. After the first five hits, the partner moves to center field, and the batter tries to hit the next five balls to center field. Then switch places. You'll know you're really good when your partner doesn't have to move too many steps to catch the balls.

T This time, the fielder is going to make it harder. After every hit, the fielder moves to a new position, and the batter tries to hit the ball close to the fielder. The fielder can choose any place to go. After 10 hits, trade places.

T Now that you've gotten the hang of placing the ball, you're going to try to hit where the fielder isn't. In softball, you want to be able to hit to open spaces so you can get on base. Hit three balls off the tee, trying to send them to different places in the field. The fielder will collect them. After three hits, trade places.

C As you hit the three balls this time, call out where the hit will go. You get one point for every hit that goes where you indicated. Try for a perfect three.

T Now, you get to run as well. Bat the ball. As soon as you bat the ball, run around the cone and try to get home before the fielder has the ball in the hoop. After three hits, trade places.

Note: Either through teaching by invitation or intratask variation (Chapter 7), the difficulty of this task can be increased by striking a pitched ball.

In conjunction with these tasks, you may want to add the following: Twisting for Placement When Batting (Chapter 19, page 349).

Striking a Pitched Ball Varying the Distance

Setting: A large outdoor space; groups of three or four with a bat in an individual striking zone defined by ropes or markers and five balls

Cues	
Full Swing	(Swing quickly all the way through to send the ball a long way.)
Medium Swing	(Swing at a medium speed all the way through to send the ball a shorter distance.)

Tasks/Challenges:

T This time, you're going to practice hitting a pitched ball different distances. To begin, one of you will pitch, one will hit, and others are fielders. Batter, your task is sometimes to hit the ball short so it lands near the pitcher and at other times to hit it long so it goes to the outfield. Try to decide ahead of time where you want the ball to go, and then hit it there.

T Now, to show how good you are, call out where the ball is going—a short or a long distance—before you hit it. Do this 10 times, and then switch places.

T This task is a little different from the last one. Instead of the batter calling out where the ball is to go, the pitcher calls out where the ball is to be hit. Change places after five hits.

Hitting a Pitched Ball to Open Spaces

Setting: A large outdoor area; children in groups of three or four, each group with a bat and a ball and individual striking zone defined by ropes or markers

Cue	
Step Toward Target	(Remember to step toward your target as you strike.)

Tasks/Challenges:

T You're going to practice hitting a pitched ball and try to make it go to open spaces. One of the fielders will become the pitcher. All pitches must be easy so they can be hit. The batter will try to hit the outfield and have the ball hit the ground before the fielder can touch it. After 10 hits, switch places.

C You get one point for every ball that hits the ground untouched. Try for 6 points. Every 10 hits, trade places.

Batting, Combining Distance and Placement

Setting: A large open space where children can bat balls safely in their individual striking zones defined by ropes or markers; bases marked in a diamond pattern; children in groups of four or five; appropriate bats and balls for each group

Cues

Step Toward Target	(Remember to step toward your target as you strike.)
Full Swing	(Swing quickly all the way through for hits that go a long way.)
Medium Swing	(Swing at a medium speed for shorter hits.)

Tasks/Challenges:

Ⓣ In your group, one of you will be the pitcher, one of you the batter, and the rest fielders. You're now going to combine hitting for distances and hitting to open spaces. The pitcher will pitch 10 balls to the batter, who tries to hit the balls to where no one is standing. Some hits need to be short and others long, but all hits should be to empty spaces.

Ⓒ This is a pretend baseball game. You are at bat; you get five swings. You will try to place each of the hits to advance the make-believe base runners. Your first two hits should be short, near the pitcher or third base. Your third swing is for a hit and run—try to place a ground ball between second and third so a runner could advance to second. Your fourth hit should move the runner to third—so hit a grounder between first and second. Your last swing is to score the run—hit a long fly ball to the outfield.

❓ *Homework.* Students at this point can profit from watching skilled players. An appropriate homework assignment would be to watch a baseball game (live or on television) and record all the places to which two selected players hit the ball (e.g., left field, bunt down third-base line).

Proficiency Level (GLPS): Learning Experiences Leading to Skill Development

When children reach the proficiency level, many possess mature striking patterns, and striking becomes a skill that can be used in complex, unpredictable, game-like situations. At this point, children are able to incorporate previous experiences into situations that involve strategic and split-second decisions. At this level, children are given situations that facilitate development of the ability to strike with implements while focusing on the strategy and outcome of the action and on their skill. The focus at this level is the attainment of consistency and accuracy. Cues are focused on the use of the skill rather than on the skill itself.

As with other skill themes, at the proficiency level, many appropriate learning experiences call for the use of striking skills in dynamic game-like skill development situations. It can be quite tricky to keep these tasks and challenges developmentally appropriate, especially in terms of active participation for all children. There are several solutions here. One is to set up multiple playing areas around the space. Another option is to have stations, several of which offer game-like learning experiences and several of which have practice opportunities that are more invariant requiring less space and setup. Finally, you could have peer assessment opportunities; within small groups, half will play and half observe, and then they switch. Regardless of the solution, all dynamic game-type and game-playing learning experiences should be appropriate for all children. See Chapter 31 for more information on game options in physical education.

A note about cues: *At the proficiency level, tasks are more complex, typically requiring children to coordinate several movements simultaneously in a dynamic context. A list of cues is provided to assist the children in being more successful in the learning experiences. The challenge is in determining which cue will be most beneficial for each child—and when. Thus, careful observation and critical reflection become very important as you watch the children move and then decide which cue will be the most helpful to move each learner to a higher level.*

Directing the Pathway, Distance, and Speed of an Object

Setting: Groups of five: one batter, one pitcher, and three fielders; one plastic bat and ball per group; a space large enough for groups to bat without interfering with other groups marked with ropes or markers

Cues

Quick Swing	(Quick swing = long.)
Medium Swing	(Medium swing = short.)
Below, Over, Behind the Ball	(Below = fly ball; over = ground ball; behind = line drive.)

Tasks/Challenges:

T For this task you will use a plastic bat and ball. The practice goes like this:

1. There are five people in a group: one batter, one pitcher, and three fielders.
2. Before the pitcher pitches the ball, she or he calls out the type of hit and the placement. The batter has to hit the ball the way the pitcher calls it.
3. Change batters after five hits.

C Now that you have the hang of it, each player keeps his or her own score—one point for every ball that was hit as the pitcher called it.

Six-Player Striking and Fielding in a Game-like Situation

Setting: Groups of six players, three-person teams; bases as in softball, but with the distance between each reduced to make the game challenging for the group; one bat, ball, and tee per group; sufficient space so children can bat without interfering with one another, with each field defined by markers or ropes

Cues	
Batters	
Hit to Open Spaces	(Always hit to open spaces.)
Fielders	
Throw Quickly	(Throw the ball as soon as you get it.)
Have a Plan	(Know where the runners are; plan where to throw the ball.)

Tasks/Challenges:

C This game involves the skills of striking, throwing, and catching. The objective is to place a batted ball, catch and throw, and run bases. Here are the rules:

1. There are three players on each team.
2. The batter strikes the ball from the tee and tries to run the bases.
3. The fielders try to catch or collect the ball and throw it to one another so all three players catch the ball before the batter finishes running the bases.
4. Each player on a team bats, and then the teams switch places.

During the class, we focus on each child's individual improvements rather than on class or individual competition. Many children (and faculty!) enjoy voluntary tournaments after school or at lunch.

One-Base Baseball

Setting: Groups of six or eight, three- or four-person teams; one base, one bat, and one ball per group; a field set up (see Figure 27.11) defined with ropes or markers

Cues	
Batters	
Hit to Open Spaces	(Always hit to open spaces.)
Fielders	
Throw Quickly	(Throw the ball as soon as you get it.)
Have a Plan	(Know where the runners are; plan where to throw the ball.)

Tasks/Challenges:

C You're going to play One-Base Baseball. The objective is to get to the base and back before the pitcher gets the ball. Here are the rules:

1. Each team has three or four people.
2. The batter bats and then tries to run to the base and back to home plate before the pitcher gets the ball again.
3. Each person on a team bats, and then the teams trade places.

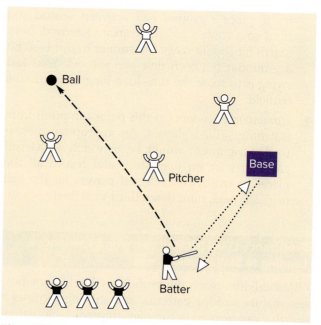

Figure 27.11 Setup for One-Base Baseball.

Striking with Long-Handled Implements—Golf Clubs

Hitting a golf ball and actually having it travel the intended direction and distance never fails to excite the player. The golf swing is unique to golf but can be used in a variety of circumstances from playing 18 holes of regulation golf, to three par courses, to the "back nine," to the driving range, or even putt-putt. Wherever and whatever, golf requires the use of swing in a vertical plane to strike a stationary ball. Our skill development progression spiral provides basic tasks and challenges for learning to use a golf swing from precontrol to utilization. Although there a few tasks that focus on a full swing, due to space, safety, and expertise issues, most of the tasks concentrate on a half swing and a putting action.

Precontrol Level (GLSP): Experiences for Exploration

Learning experiences at the precontrol level ask children to explore striking with golf clubs. At this level, a chopping, downward swing is typical for any striking

pattern. Children struggle just to make contact between the ball and the striking instrument. Therefore, we give children tasks that let them explore striking with the added length that comes with golf clubs—and the greater demands that length places on their hand–eye coordination. Ideally you want to have golf clubs available in a variety of lengths for different height children. There are a variety of "traditional" clubs available as well as plastic versions. Due to the difficulty of the skill, tasks are developed using large objects to be struck.

Putting

Setting: Inside in a gym or on a carpeted surface. Each child has a putter, a ball, and about a 12-inch-diameter ring made of rope or plastic. Use a poly spot to mark a distance about 5 feet from the ring. Set up as many stations as you can—cup, putter, ball for each child, and spot.

Tasks/Challenges:

Ⓣ Today we are going to get a chance to practice putting like in golf. Look around the gym and you will see holes set up. Each hole has a putter, a ball for

Modified equipment allows for swings with golf clubs to be practiced indoors.

©Lars A. Niki

each of you, a cup, and a starting spot (poly spot). Your goal is to experiment striking the ball toward the ring. Try to make it go to the ring. Explore how much force you need. Try and just use short strokes.

Setting: If possible, set up individual striking areas in large, open outside space for each child defined by ropes and markers. Plastic golf clubs and high-density foam balls for each child (or pair). If you are using partners, switch, when you give the signal, every five swings. Lines on the ground about 10 yards in front of where the children are hitting.

If you do not have enough clubs for each child, then define an area safely behind the children who are striking with golf clubs for their partners to stand a safe distance away. You will need to use keen observation skills to be certain they remain in their zones and do not change until you give them the signal to do so.

Tasks/Challenges

Ⓣ Do you see the line in front of you? See if you can hit the ball past the line? (The line should be about 10 yards in front of the children who are striking.)

Note: At the precontrol level, the children are just discovering the sensations associated with striking a ball with a golf club, so provide them with plenty of opportunities to swing the club before you start teaching them the cues that will lead to better golf swings.

Control Level (GLSP): Learning Experiences Leading to Skill Development

At the control level, children begin to develop mature striking patterns that are used in increasingly complex contexts. They can be challenged with tasks that require them to include one or two other variables besides striking such as striking a whiffle golf ball for distance.

A note about cues: *Although several cues are listed for many of the learning experiences, it's important to focus on only one cue at a time. This way, the children can really concentrate on that cue. Once you provide feedback to the children and observe that most have learned a cue, it's time to focus on another one.*

Striking a Ball so It Travels in the Air: Air Ball

Setting: Plastic golf clubs and high-density foam or whiffle balls; striking zones defined with ropes and/or markers; children about 10 feet from the wall; marks on the wall about 3 feet off the floor if inside. If outside, you can use ropes in cones, hurdles, or chairs to make a tar-

get to hit over about 3 feet high. If inside, you will need something to protect the floor and the club (e.g., mats, nonskid pads, old rugs, turf squares, carpet samples).

Cues	
Stance	(Feet shoulder width apart, knees bent.)
Grip	(Thumbs pointing slightly to the sides—one o'clock and eleven o'clock for right handers—not straight down the shaft; all fingers touching.) (Figure 27.12)
Circle Swing	(Turn shoulders away from the target and toward the target)

Setting: Children in their individual striking zones defined by ropes and markers. Ideally a club for each child and plenty of high-density foam or whiffle balls.

If you use partners, be sure to define a zone that the children who are not swinging a club must remain inside of so they do not accidentally run into someone swinging a club.

Tasks/Challenges:

Ⓣ Do you see the line (rope, chairs, hurdles) in front of you? It is about 3 feet high. We are going to practice hitting balls with a half swing over this line. *(This will need to be demonstrated.)* To do so, you will need to get the ball into the air. To do this, you will need to keep your knees bent throughout the swing. Go ahead and start hitting.

Ⓒ Try to send the ball in the air so it hits above the mark (over the hurdle) three times in a row. If you do, tell the teacher your favorite golfer—or if you don't know a golfer, your favorite kind of ice cream.

Ⓣ This time we are going to use a half swing back and full swing forward. To do this, you will need to keep your knees bent throughout the swing. *(A demonstration will be needed.)*

Figure 27.12 Golf club grip.

Striking to Varying Distances

Setting: Preferably a large outdoor space; a golf club and a bucket of plastic balls for each child; all children facing the same direction in their individual striking zones defined by ropes and markers, with at least 6 feet between them; large buckets or other targets at various distances from the children who are striking

Cues	
Setup	(Legs form an A, arms and shaft of the club form a Y. Knees bent.)
Circle Swing	(Shoulders turn away from the target, club sweeps low, and then shoulders turn back toward the target.)

Tasks/Challenges:

(T) Use the golf grip (Figure 27.12). You're going to be practicing a golf swing. Let's practice first without the ball. Stand to the side of the make-believe ball, side to the target (field), and take a full backswing, bend your knees, swing, and follow through. Make five practice swings and then start hitting balls. Remember, only swing in your individual striking zone.

(T) There are markers (buckets, hoops) on the field to help you judge the length of your hits. Hit the ball, and then try to hit the next ball farther. Try to find your maximum distance. If working in partners, switch after 10 to 15 swings. Be sure the partners remain in their own zone when they are not hitting.

(C) Every time you hit the ball longer then you have before, jump in the air three times and say "YES!"

Putting for Accuracy

Note: This task can be used at the utilization level also.

Setting: Inside in a gym or on a carpeted surface. Each child has a putter, a ball, and a plastic cup. Use a poly spot to mark a distance about 5 feet from the cup. Set up as many stations as you can—cup, putter, ball for each child, and spot.

Cues	
Grip	(Both thumbs straight down the shaft.)
Wrists	(Stiff, as if in a cast.)
Swing	(Like a pendulum, back and through.)

Tasks/Challenges:

(T) Today we are going to practice golf putting. Look around the gym and you will see holes set up. Each hole has a putter, a ball for each of you, a cup, and a starting spot (carpet square or poly spot). Your goal is to put the ball so it goes into the cup in as few strokes as possible. A perfect score would be a 1. Remember not to swing your putter—but just use it for the putting stroke, which is much shorter than the full swing.

(T) Begin by putting into your own cup. Demonstrate and remind them of the cues as they practice—one cue at a time.

(C) Now we are going to play a game. You are going to play three times (holes) into your own cup. See how few putts you can take for the three holes. What would a perfect score be? Right: a 3.

(T) Now look around the gym and you will see that the holes are numbered (on the cups and by the poly spots). This time you are going to start at your hole and then proceed to the next number hole. So, if the number on your cup is 5, you will start there; once the ball is in the cup, you will go to the next highest number. When you finish putting at hole number 30 (the highest hole), you will go to hole 1.

(C) On the scorecard I have provided, use the pencil to write down your score for each hole. How many putts did it take you to go through the entire course? A good score would be two putts a hole. So if there are 15 holes, a score of 30 would be a good score. (*Note: This score will depend on the GLSP of the children and also the distance from cup to cup. Higher-skilled children will be challenged by setting a lower target score and/or moving the cups a further distance from the starting point.*)

Striking for Accuracy

Setting: If possible, set up individual striking areas in large open outside space for each child defined by ropes and markers. Plastic golf clubs and high-density foam balls for each child (or pair). If you are using partners, switch, when you give the signal, every five swings. Hoops on the ground about 10 yards in front of where the children are hitting.

Cues	
Stance	(Feet shoulder width apart, knees bent.)
Grip	(Thumbs pointing slightly to the sides—one o'clock and eleven o'clock for right handers—not straight down the shaft; all fingers touching.)
Circle Swing	(Turn shoulders away from the target, club sweeps low, and then toward the target.)

Tasks/Challenges

C Do you see the hoops in front of you? See if you can hit the ball into or past the hoop? *(After all the children have had 20 to 30 swings, move the hoops to different distances—some closer, some farther away.)* Now aim for different hoops—but remember to try to hit the ball so it goes past the hoop.

Utilization Level (GLSP): Learning Experiences Leading to Skill Development

At the utilization level, children are able to control a ball in the space around them and strike consistently with the appropriate striking pattern. We challenge them to use their striking skills in more dynamic and unpredictable situations.

A note about cues: *Although several cues are listed for many of the learning experiences, it's important to focus on only one cue at a time. This way, the children can really concentrate on that cue. Once you provide feedback to the children and observe that most have learned a cue, it's time to focus on another one.*

Playing Hoop Golf

Setting: A plastic golf club and ball for each child. Children can share clubs if there are not enough. You will need to designate a hitting zone and a standing zone for the partners—one hits, the other one stands on a poly spot a safe distance from the tee (cone). Only introduce this task if the students in the class have learned to work safely and follow directions (Chapter 7).

Cues	
Grip	(Thumbs pointing slightly to the sides—one o'clock and eleven o'clock for right handers—not straight down the shaft; all fingers touching.) (Figure 27.12)
Stance	(Legs form an A, arms and shaft of the club form a Y. Knees bent.)
Circle Swing	(Shoulders turn away from the target, club sweeps low making a circle, and then shoulders turn back toward the target.)

Tasks/Challenges:

T The starting point for each hole is a tee. The "hole" is a hoop. The object is to strike the ball into the hoop in as few strokes as possible. If you are hitting your ball too far, don't turn your shoulders as much. If you want to hit it farther, turn your shoulders more.

C Play the hole three times. Each time you hit the ball counts as 1 point until the ball stops inside the

hoop. What is your score for three holes? What would a perfect score be? Right: a 3. Now I want you to switch to a different hole and tee (and hoop). Play the hole three times. Is your score better or worse than the score on the last hole you played?

T Now find a partner. Play the same hole. What is your total score between the two of you? Remember to count each hit (stroke). Now can you and partner make an even better score? If your total score is 2, then you need to move the hoop farther away.

T Now you and your partner can join up with two other partners. You can play for a total score (all four of you) and see if you can improve. Or you may want to play a game where you and your partner try to make a lower score then your opponents. Remember, you have to count each swing—even if you miss the ball.

Whiffle Ball Golf

Setting: A Whiffle Ball Golf course (Figure 27.13); a golf club and whiffle ball for each child. Cones or large balls mark the tees.
This task can be adapted for use with control- or utilization-level students.

Cues	
Grip	(Thumbs pointing slightly to the sides—one o'clock and eleven o'clock for right handers—not straight down the shaft; all fingers touching.) (Figure 27.12)
Stance	(Legs form an A, arms and shaft of the club form a Y. Knees bent.)
Circle Swing	(Shoulders turn away from the target, club sweeps low, and then shoulders turn back toward the target.)

Tasks/Challenges:

T The game you're going to play is Whiffle Ball Golf. It's played just as regular golf is played. The objective of the game is to get the ball to land in the hoop with as few strokes as possible. Each of you will start at the hole I assign you and then go to the next higher numbered hole. Each hole has a tee area from which to start: This area is marked with big rubber balls to guarantee that everyone starts from the same place. When you get to hole 9 (or however many holes you set up), go to hole 1. Keep score by counting the shots it takes you to go around the entire course.

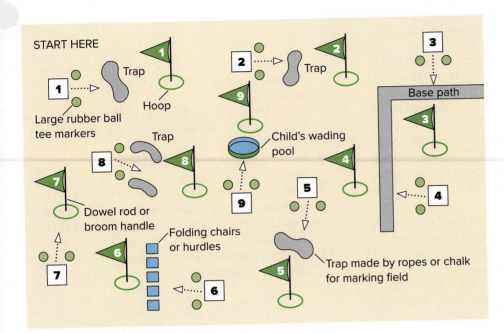

Figure 27.13 Whiffle Ball Golf course.

C You may want to have the children play alone or with (or against) a partner. You may also want to have two partners play the course challenging another pair for the lowest score.

Box Golf

Setting: Boxes of various heights set up throughout the entire space. A tee that marks the starting point; a golf club and a ball for each child. As always you will have to be clear about where the children stand to swing the club and where children who are not hitting need to stand (inside a hoop, for example, several feet from the tee where the child is swinging the club). *Note: This is an appropriate task-teaching station instructional approach as well as an example of a child-designed instructional approach. (See Chapter 9 for more information on these teaching approaches.)*

Cues	
Knees Remain Bent	(Remember, keep your knees slightly bent as you swing.)
Hinge and Hold	(Make an L with your arms as you swing back, swing low, and try to hold the L in your arms on the follow-through.) *(You want the children to avoid scooping the ball when their hands get ahead of the ball and "top" the ball.)*
Follow Through	(Swing all the way through and over your shoulder.)

Tasks/Challenges:

T Try to hit the ball so that it lands in the box. When the ball lands in the box three times in a row, move your tee one giant step away from the box and try again.

C Design your own box golf game. You may have up to three players in a group. When you are finished, write down the rules for the game. *(See Chapter 31 for details about how to help children design their own games.)* Do you want to give different points for hitting the box and for making the ball stop inside the box? How many swings will each of you get?

? *Event Task.* The written self-designed game is an appropriate assessment task to be included in a child's portfolio.

Proficiency Level (GLSP): Learning Experiences Leading to Skill Development

When children reach the proficiency level, many possess mature striking patterns, and striking becomes a skill that can be used in complex, unpredictable, game-playing situations. Because of time limitations, equipment and facility requirements, safety aspects, and the normal student–teacher ratio, we do not teach golf skills at this level. However, if you have students who have progressed to this level, encourage them to pursue out-of-school golf activities in the local community. These activities allow children to increase their skill level beyond what we can do in a class setting.

Reading Comprehension Questions

1. What are the two swing planes one will use for striking with long-handled implements? Which swing planes are used with which implements?
2. Which implement is used for an underhand swing pattern?
3. What is the purpose of introducing children to striking with long-handled implements?
4. What can be the long-term result when children try to swing implements that are too heavy or too long?
5. Describe the correct form for striking a ball with a bat. See if you can find a group of children playing baseball (or softball). Do their forms match those in the photo sequence (Box 27-2)?
6. How does the idea of "roll over shoelaces" to enhance the cue of "rotate and shift" promote a mature striking pattern with a bat?
7. Why do we recommend that children initially practice striking with hockey using yarn or plastic balls?
8. Describe two examples, one for bats and one for hockey sticks, of contexts that are unpredictable or changing.
9. In using a hockey stick to handle a ball, what do the terms *give* and *control* mean?
10. Find a picture that illustrates what the cue of "Legs form an A, arms and shaft of the club form a Y" looks like in the set up for a golf swing. Label the A and the Y.
11. List three safety cues for striking with long-handled implements.

References/Suggested Readings

Holt/Hale, S., and T. Hall. 2016. *Lesson planning for elementary physical education: Meeting the national standards & grade-level outcomes*. Champaign, IL: Human Kinetics.

[NASPE] National Association for Sport and Physical Education. 1995. *Moving into the future: National standards for physical education*. St. Louis, MO: Mosby.

[SHAPE America] Society of Health and Physical Educators. 2014. *National standards & grade-level outcomes for K-12 physical education*. Champaign, IL: Human Kinetics.

Skill Theme Application

Now that we have introduced you to the movement concepts and skill themes in the previous two sections, we want to focus on their application in different contexts in physical education. Chapter 28 defines fitness for children, revisits the differences between physical activity and physical education, and discusses the interrelatedness of physical education, physical activity, and wellness for children. The chapter describes how health-related fitness concepts are interwoven throughout our lessons and provides numerous examples of ways children can increase their physical activity and improve fitness both within and beyond the school day.

Chapters 29, 30, and 31 discuss how dance, gymnastics, and games, respectively, are developed in the skill theme approach. You will not, however, find a series of rules for games, steps for dance, or specific gymnastics stunts in these chapters. To do so would violate the very premise on which *Children Moving* is based—children have different needs and interests! Thus, these three chapters are designed so that the skill themes and movement concepts most associated with educational gymnastics, dance, and games are combined and developed in that context. For example, Chapter 30, "Teaching Educational Gymnastics," links the skill themes of jumping and landing; balancing; transferring weight and rolling; and the actions of bending, stretching, twisting, and curling in gymnastics settings. The concept of skill theme development and application in these context areas is explained in depth in Chapter 2. The three chapters on dance, games, and gymnastics focus on predesigned and child-designed curriculum experiences, with child-designed experiences being the underlying focus of all our work in *Children Moving*.

The final chapter in this part—Chapter 32, "Integrating the Skill Theme Approach Across the Curriculum"—offers valuable insights into classroom teachers and physical education teachers working together to develop integrated, or interdisciplinary, learning experiences for children.

Teaching Physical Fitness, Physical Activity, and Wellness

Intelligence and skill can only function at the peak of their capacity when the body is healthy and strong.

—JOHN F. KENNEDY

©Nathan Patton

Physical fitness, like educational gymnastics, games, and dance, should be child-centered. Physical fitness is not about test scores and records posted on gymnasium walls; it is about helping all children become healthy, physically active individuals. That is the approach to fitness within this chapter: the importance of becoming and remaining physically fit, the knowledge and skills for achieving fitness, and the role of physical activity within fitness.

Just as it takes a village to raise a child, it takes an entire school community to provide the daily recommended physical activity for children. The Comprehensive School Physical Activity Program (CSPAP) presented in this chapter outlines the various school, home, and community resources for physical activity for children and their interrelatedness in meeting this critical need for children's health.

Fitness for children is more than just physical fitness; it is the total well-being of each child. It is wellness. This chapter concludes with a discussion of wellness as the child-centered approach to a lifetime of good health and well-being.

Parents, school administrators, and even some physical education teachers often confuse physical education, physical fitness, and physical activity, assuming that there is no distinction between the three. We, as teachers of elementary physical education, must be diligent in making this distinction (see Box 28-1). While the goals of each are intertwined, they should never be used interchangeably (i.e., physical activity and physical education are not the same). Teachers of elementary physical education design each and every lesson of educational gymnastics, dance, and games learning experiences with the relatedness of the physical education curriculum, physical fitness, and maximum physical activity in mind.

Box 28-1

Physical Education, Physical Fitness, and Physical Activity: How Are They Different?

- **Physical education** has a definite purpose and long-term goals and is developmentally and instructionally appropriate. It is an instructional program taught by teachers with professional credentials in physical education and includes instruction and time to practice and apply skills and knowledge within a school setting (SHAPE America 2009).
- **Physical fitness** is the capacity of the heart, blood vessels, lungs, and muscles to function at optimum efficiency in work and leisure activities, to be healthy, to resist hypokinetic diseases, and to meet emergency situations (Corbin et al. 2015). Physical fitness is divided into health-related and skill-related fitness. Although skill-related fitness is a by-product of teaching for skill acquisition, health-related fitness is the focus of quality physical education programs:
  - Health-related fitness: cardiorespiratory fitness, muscular strength, muscular endurance, flexibility, and body composition.
  - Skill-related fitness: agility, balance, coordination, speed, power, and reaction time.
- **Physical activity** is any bodily movement produced by skeletal muscles that requires energy expenditure (WHO 2017). Participating in physical activity provides an important component of physical education, as well as a means of achieving a healthy fitness level (SHAPE America 2009).

Fitness: Past and Present

The first alarm on children's physical fitness was sounded in the mid-1950s in response to a comparison of fitness levels of American and European children. The Kraus-Weber test battery had a significant impact on physical education programs in schools, resulting in increased emphasis on exercises to improve physical fitness in children and youth, and fitness as the major curricular focus for physical education.

The second alarm on children's fitness was sounded with the linkage of physical fitness in childhood to the prevention of cardiorespiratory and coronary disease in adults, as well as of the degenerative diseases of hypertension and diabetes. The result was a curricular shift to health-related fitness and a renewed emphasis on activities to boost fitness components.

The alarm sounding today focuses on children's lack of physical activity and the increase in overweight and obese children. Childhood obesity has reached epidemic proportions. According to the Department of Defense, approximately one in three of all 17- to 24-year-olds in the United States are disqualified from entering military service due to being overweight (Murrie 2018). Physical fitness has been, and continues to be, a critical component of good health.

Health-Related Fitness for Children

Quality physical education contributes to increased physical activity, improved self-concept, increased self-efficacy, improved motor skills, increased enjoyment, increased motivation, and a reduction in sedentary behavior (LeMasurier and Corbin 2006). Competence in motor skills and early motor skills proficiency are related to the health-related aspects of fitness and to fitness in adolescence and beyond (Cattuzzo et al. 2016). Physical activity is a preventive for degenerative diseases and obesity. With the importance of physical education and physical activity well documented in the research (see Chapter 1), what then is the role of health-related physical fitness for children? What is the role of health-related fitness in our physical education programs?

In some elementary physical education programs, fitness is *the* focus of physical education, with the curriculum devoted almost entirely to activities that promote specific areas of physical fitness. In other programs, a segment of every class is devoted to fitness, with a specific number of minutes targeting a fitness component, or every physical education class begins with exercises. We, the authors of *Children*

Box 28-2

Health-Related Fitness, Physical Activity, and Wellness in the *National Standards & Grade-Level Outcomes for K–12 Physical Education*

Fitness, physical activity, and wellness are referenced in the *National Standards & Grade-Level Outcomes for K–12 Physical Education* (SHAPE America 2014) under Standards 3 and 5, with an emphasis on knowledge and skills relating to physical activity, fitness, assessment, program planning, nutrition, and the benefits of physical activity:

- Standard 3: The physically literate individual demonstrates the knowledge and skills to achieve and maintain a health-enhancing level of physical activity and fitness.
- Standard 5: The physically literate individual recognizes the value of physical activity for health, enjoyment, challenge, self-expression, and/or social interaction.

Moving, do not support either of these stances; we believe that fitness is interwoven into our educational gymnastics, dance, and games lessons with planned learning experiences to teach fitness knowledge, skills, and values. See Box 28-2 for physical activity and fitness components in the *National Standards & Grade-Level Outcomes for K–12 Physical Education* (SHAPE America 2014).

The *National Standards* include grade-level outcomes within the following categories:

- Physical activity knowledge (K–5)
- Engagement in physical activity (K–5)
- Fitness knowledge (K–5)
- Fitness assessment (4–5; introduction 3)
- Nutrition (K–5)
- Health (K–5)
- Challenge (K–5)
- Social interaction (3–5)

Health-Related Fitness Components Fitness concepts for each of the components of health-related fitness center on children's understanding of that component, its linkage to good health, and activities that promote that area of health-related fitness. Here we highlight concepts associated with muscular strength, endurance, flexibility, aerobic fitness, and body composition as they relate to elementary school children (SHAPE America 2011).

Muscular Strength and Endurance Muscular strength is the ability of a muscle or muscle group to exert a maximal force against a resistance one time through the full range of motion; muscular endurance is the ability of a muscle or muscle group to exert a sub-maximal force repeatedly over a period of time. To children, this may mean they can pick something up that they perceive as heavy without assistance. The following are important concepts for teachers to remember:

- Activities that require children to move and lift their body weight, as opposed to forced exercise and conditioning, are desirable at the elementary school level.
- While adolescents may benefit from appropriately designed programs, strength training is not appropriate for elementary students.
- Lack of upper-body muscular strength can be very discouraging for children; therefore, focus on praise for progress.

Flexibility Flexibility is the ability to move a joint through its full range of motion. To children, this means they can bend, stretch, curl, and twist. Children should understand these critical concepts about flexibility:

- You must continue to exercise to maintain flexibility.
- Stretching should be done slowly, without bouncing.
- Flexibility is important for all activities, but especially so for gymnastics and dance.

Aerobic Fitness Aerobic fitness is the ability to perform large-muscle, dynamic, moderate- to high-intensity exercise for prolonged periods. To children, this may mean playing longer before becoming tired. Children should understand these important concepts about aerobic fitness:

- The heart is a muscle that benefits from exercise, as do other muscles.
- Endurance running is not sprinting; pacing is important for endurance activities.
- Being on an athletic team doesn't automatically increase your aerobic fitness; active participation is necessary.

In addition, teachers should remember that participation in continuous aerobic activities of long duration is not desirable for elementary-school-age children.

Body Composition Body composition is the amount of lean body mass (all tissues other than fat, such as bone, muscle, organs, and body fluids) compared with the amount of body fat, usually expressed in terms of percent body fat. Children will likely only associate this with how big they perceive themselves and others

to be. The important concepts to remember about body composition are:

- A certain amount of body fat is needed for good health.
- Body weight and body composition are not the same.
- A good balance of body fat and lean tissue is attained by good nutrition and physical activity.
- Body composition is influenced by physical activity and the other fitness components.
- Body composition is affected by heredity, nutrition, and lifestyle.

FITT for Children

The principles of fitness training (frequency, intensity, time, and type) must be used with caution when working with children. Children accept what adults say, especially teachers and coaches they respect, quite literally. If we say eight push-ups are good for arm strength, but 50 will be even better, their goal is 50 push-ups each and every day. Pain is not the name of the game in fitness for children. Figure 28.1 presents the FITT guidelines as they apply to aerobic fitness for youngsters, ages 5–12.

The principles of fitness training when applied to children were best stated years ago by Corbin (1986) and are still very applicable today; the principles of fitness training for children are fun, intrinsic motivation, and the 2 Cs: competence and confidence. If fitness activities are fun and if children experience success, they will be intrinsically motivated to be physically active. They will be motivated to improve themselves. Children who participate in developmentally appropriate physical education will develop confidence in themselves as they develop competence in physical education skills. This combination of competence and confidence motivates children to adopt lifestyles that include moderate to vigorous activity on a regular basis. Our task as physical education teachers is to provide programs that give children skills, confidence, and enjoyment; by doing so, we instill in our students a desire to continue physical activity, accompanied with the skills and knowledge for fitness.

Fitness in the Physical Education Curriculum

Physical fitness is interwoven in the educational gymnastics, dance, and games learning experiences of physical education at the elementary school level. Physical fitness concepts center around children's

Figure 28.1 FITT Guidelines Applied to Aerobic Fitness

	Children (5–12 years)
Frequency	• Developmentally appropriate physical activity on all or most days of the week. • Several bouts of physical activity lasting 15 min or more daily.
Intensity	• Mixture of moderate and vigorous intermittent activity. • Moderate includes low-intensity games (hopscotch, Four Square), low-activity positions (goalie, outfielders), some chores, and yard work. • Vigorous includes games involving running or chasing and playing sports.
Time	• Accumulate at least 60 min, and up to several hours, of activity per day. • Up to 50% of minutes should be accumulated in bouts of 15 min or more.
Type	• Do a variety of activities: play games, ride a bike, jump rope, hike, different sports. • Continuous activity should not be expected for most children.

Source: Adapted from Society of Health and Physical Educators (SHAPE America), *Physical Education for Lifelong Fitness*, 3rd ed., ed. S. F. Ayers and M. J. Sariscsany (Champaign, IL: Human Kinetics, 2011); Society of Health and Physical Educators (SHAPE America), *Physical Activity for Children Ages 5-12: A Statement of Guidelines*, https://www.shapeamerica.org/standards/guidelines/pa-children-5-12.

understanding of fitness, an awareness of the linkage of fitness to good health, and a working knowledge of the activities that contribute to fitness. The following fitness concepts are appropriate for elementary-age children:

Physical Fitness Concepts

- It's okay for your heart to beat rapidly when you run and play.
- Sweat is a good thing.
- The heart is a muscle; it gets stronger with physical activity and exercise.
- Body size does not determine fitness; being thin does not mean you are fit.
- Good exercise and physical activity habits begin in childhood.
- Exercise and physical activity should be a daily habit, like brushing your teeth.
- Fitness doesn't just happen; you prepare and practice.
- Skill-related fitness is different from health-related fitness.

- Fitness has several components, and a truly physically fit person is healthy in each area.

In addition, the following are important concepts for teachers to remember:

- An emphasis on conditioning for sports is not appropriate at the elementary-school-age level.
- Given the opportunity to be active, most children will do so.
- Physical activity participation declines as boys and girls reach adolescence; teaching the concepts and behaviors of fitness and physical activity in the elementary school years can play an important role in reversing this trend.

Fitness is a personal matter; its goal is self-improvement toward healthy living. Within our elementary physical education curriculums, we can teach basic concepts of fitness, design our lessons to promote physical activity, and help children build a repertoire of skills for their personal use.

The skill themes, Chapters 17–27, are rich with tasks and challenges that develop the components of fitness, such as "Traveling with a Partner: Changing Speed and Direction" (Chapter 17), "Locomotors and Rhythm: The Follow-Me Dance" (Chapter 17), "Chasing and Dodging Simultaneously" (Chapter 18), Stretching, Curling, and Twisting into Weight Transfers" (Chapter 19), "Stretching to Catch Against an Opponent" (Chapter 19), "Jumping Rhythmically" (Chapter 20), "Transferring Weight to Hands" (Chapter 22), and "Transferring Weight Onto and Off Equipment" (Chapter 22). Cardiorespiratory fitness, balance, and flexibility are easily targeted within our skill theme and movement concept lessons.

An example of this integration of skill themes and fitness was observed in a fourth-grade physical education class. The theme was dribbling; the movement concept was pathways. The lesson began with a brief discussion of heart rate and the children counting their pulse before activity began. On the music signal, the children began dribbling in different pathways (straight, curved, zigzag). When the music stopped the children went to a nearby station where an upside-down cup had a fitness activity taped inside, such as "Do high-five push-ups with your partner in the position of your choice." When the music began, cups were returned to their original position and the dribbling in pathways resumed. Each time the music stopped, the children found another cup for the fitness activity. The children counted their pulse several times during the class. The class culminated with a discussion of the various activities and changes in heart rate.

> *The use of calisthenics is unacceptable in children's physical education. Formal exercises are unrelated to child life situations and have very little, if any, carry-over value.*
>
> —NEILSON AND VAN HAGEN (1935)

Focus Lessons

The components of health-related fitness are introduced to children through focus lessons, distributed throughout the year. The first of these lessons will center on the concept of fitness; other lessons will focus on one of the components of health-related fitness: aerobic capacity/cardiorespiratory fitness, muscular strength and endurance, or flexibility and body awareness. It is important that the fitness terminology be developmentally appropriate for the children's understanding and that the tasks and challenges support the fitness component that is the focus of the lesson. The following example illustrates a focus lesson:

The concept of physical fitness is chosen as the theme for the lesson. The concept is introduced with a brief discussion of children's perceptions of a physically fit person: What does a physically fit person look like? Do you know one? How do you know he or she is physically fit? Various activity areas/stations are set up around the teaching space, providing active participation, targeting each of the health-related fitness components. Children working with partners discuss and answer questions regarding the activity and its contribution to fitness. Following participation at each of the stations, younger children draw a picture to illustrate a physically fit person; older youngsters write two or three sentences in their journals describing what it means to be physically fit. The lesson concludes with children's responses to a definition of physical fitness. *Plan the focus lesson with the amount of time needed for children's understanding of the fitness component, i.e., meeting the objective of the lesson. Lessons will vary in length depending on the component of fitness that is the focus and depending on the grade level.* Review of the fitness concept or health-related fitness component will be woven into the skill theme and movement concept lessons throughout the year.

Additional strategies for teaching fitness to elementary-age children include the following:

Bulletin Boards and Posters Bulletin boards highlight the targeted fitness concept, linkage cues are given during instructional physical education, and the concept is revisited and/or expanded throughout the year. Colorful displays outlining health-related fitness concepts and definitions can provide a helpful visual for students. These visuals also provide diagrams (i.e., heart) or types of activities that correspond with health-related fitness components.

Checking for Understanding Checking for the understanding of fitness concepts can take place at any time during a lesson (e.g., set induction, transitions between tasks, closure). This occurs through brief question-and-answer sessions that align with the newly introduced concept(s). Examples of questions the teacher could ask to increase fitness concept comprehension include: What sort of activities increase flexibility? Why does your heart beat faster when you perform vigorous activities? What types of tasks or movements should you do to make your muscles stronger?

Worksheets/Assessments Fitness concepts can be built upon across lessons using worksheets and various assessments (see Chapter 12 for assessment examples). These learning and assessment tasks allow students to apply their knowledge gained in lessons throughout the year and provide a record of their comprehension with which to design future lessons. Additional lessons that focus on the teaching of fitness can be found *in Lesson Planning for Elementary Physical Education* (Holt/Hale and Hall 2016) and in *Physical Best Activity Guide* (SHAPE America 2011).

Use of Technology To aid in the teaching of fitness concepts, teachers are increasingly turning to technology. Children today are digital natives and have grown up with technology—they don't know a time when technology wasn't part of their daily lives. Pedometers, heart rate monitors, fit trackers, apps, Web sites, video resources, and exergames are just some of the technology resources available to assist teachers. With any technology, use due diligence to determine if the information is developmentally appropriate and aids in the teaching of concepts.

Assessing Health-Related Fitness

Health-related physical fitness assessment has become commonplace as an important part of physical education, almost too important in many instances. Physical fitness is now a requirement in approximately one-fourth of the states in the United States (Corbin et al. 2014; SHAPE America 2017; SHAPE America and Voices for Health Kids 2016). For many school administrators, fitness is equated with physical education for two reasons: (1) that is what the program administrators

Activity Trackers and Pedometers

Activity trackers (e.g., Fitbit, Garman) and pedometers can be excellent instruments for increasing children's awareness of their physical activity level. Wearing them during physical education, recess, and after school or at home will assist children in assessing their individual levels of activity and the amount of cumulative activity they attain in a given time period and in different environments (e.g., on the playground, in organized sports, in free play).

Activity trackers, also known as fitness trackers, are often worn like a watch for monitoring and tracking a variety of fitness-related metrics. These metrics vary by model but often include distance walked or run, calories burned, heart rate, and even sleep. These devices, while intended for 24/7 use, may be used in physical education class to help students track their activity and to understand how different types and intensities of movement influence their results.

Additionally, children enjoy charting their steps (tracked via pedometers) for "A Walk Across America," calculating the miles (and steps) to various destinations within the state, or climbing Mt. Everest. Classroom teachers appreciate the reinforcements of mathematics and geography lessons. It is important to remember that 10,000 steps as a daily goal is a target number of steps set for adults. It is a goal that is too high for sedentary individuals or those with chronic diseases. It is a number that is low for many children during an average day; their goal is 12,000. If pedometers are used to motivate children for increased physical activity, it is important to set personal goals after establishing baseline steps for the child, specific health goals, and sustainability of the goal for that child in a routine day (Tudor-Locke 2002).

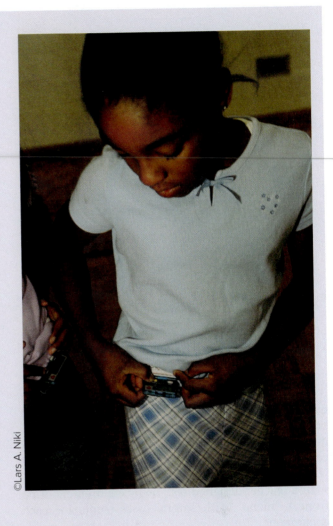

©Lars A. Niki

had when they were in school and (2) fitness assessments provide concrete results that can be easily reported to parents and local school boards to show student growth. The authors of *Children Moving* do not view fitness and physical education as synonymous, neither do we think fitness assessment scores should be the measure of a program nor of a teacher's effectiveness. However, fitness assessment can provide measures of student growth if child-centered in the assessment approach. This section is devoted to child-centered assessment of fitness in elementary school; remember that the assessment is for upper-elementary children only, grade 4 and above.

Proponents of fitness education have provided a useful eight-step process (Figure 28.2) that demonstrates the practices needed to ensure meaningful fitness instruction (Corbin et al. 2012). This process was designed to support students in learning the concepts and skills needed to attain and maintain a health-enhancing level of physical activity and fitness. Practices for meaningful fitness instruction include the following eight steps:

1. Students first learn fundamental fitness concepts.
2. Once aware of the purpose of testing, students prepare for the tests, including practicing the correct form for each test item.
3. Once steps 1 and 2 are successfully completed, students engage in fitness testing.
4. Students use results to determine what areas their scores are in healthy zones, set goals, and create personalized programs for improvement.
5. Students track their progress using self-monitoring.
6. Students retake fitness testing periodically.
7. After retaking the tests, students refine personal goals and fitness programs as appropriate.

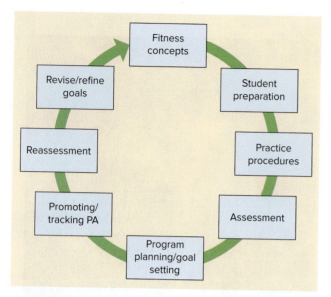

Figure 28.2 Eight-step fitness education process.

Source: C. B. Corbin, G. J. Welk, W. R. Corbin, and K. Welk, *Concepts of Physical Fitness: Active Lifestyles for Wellness*, 17th ed. (Columbus, OH: McGraw-Hill Education, 2012.

©Lars A. Niki

Simple playground activities lead to fitness.

The components of fitness (muscular strength and endurance, flexibility, cardiorespiratory fitness, and body composition) are assessed with a battery of tests designed to measure a child's performance on each component. Fitness assessment may be conducted with a commercial packaged assessment program, with a teacher-designed test, or by children choosing from a "menu" with several assessments for each component.

Physical fitness assessments can be used to culminate a unit, to motivate students, as diagnostic screening instruments, and/or as an ongoing process throughout the year. Physical fitness assessment is part of the overall fitness education for upper-elementary children, providing information on their levels of health-related fitness and the linkage between physical activity and improvements in fitness. If the fitness

The most widely adopted commercial assessment for physical fitness is FitnessGram, a non competitive health-related assessment based on scientifically established Healthy Fitness Zone criterion-referenced standards. FitnessGram, developed by the Cooper Institute, measures the five elements of health-related fitness: aerobic capacity, muscular strength, muscular endurance, flexibility, and body composition.

Source: http://www.cooperinstitute.org/fitnessgram

assessment is to be child-centered, we must then provide assistance for those students whose scores fall below the desired range for good health (FitnessGram). The following strategies will assist in providing remediation for student growth:

1. If the physical fitness assessment is to be used as a diagnostic tool, administer the test in early fall. You can then use the test results to help develop yearly plans, assist children in establishing personal fitness goals, and plan remedial programs for individual students. We recommend that children who have extremely low scores be given remedial fitness programs—individualized physical education programs (IPEPs)—for their area(s) of weakness. The physical education teacher can counsel these students individually on ways to improve fitness through physical activity. In doing so, teachers not only teach their students how to assess their own fitness, students also learn how to set goals based on their assessment and create action plans to

achieve their fitness goals. Programs of activity and exercise can be designed for use at home, and parents can become active participants with their child.

2. Children with extremely low scores reflecting an area of fitness that is of concern can benefit from experiences in a school fitness lab. Schools with available space and staffing can create a fitness/wellness lab to which children can come for physical activity and exercise designed for their areas of weakness. Working on their personal fitness plans, under the supervision of a trained volunteer and/or the physical education teacher, children follow their prescribed programs of activity, record the activity in their fitness logs, and describe feelings via journal entries.

3. We have found activities to do at home that focus on a particular fitness component and family activities to promote fitness and physical activity for everyone to be extremely beneficial. At-home "prescriptions" can be written, for which children complete the activities along with their parents. A monthly calendar can be provided for the child to code (with color, star, or sticker) at the completion of the activity each day. We have found the at-home prescriptions to be an excellent introduction to family fitness as parents and children take part in the activities together. Examples of prescription activities and exercises for flexibility, muscular strength, and cardiorespiratory fitness as well as family fitness activities can be found in Appendices 28A and 28B at the end of this chapter.

Physical fitness assessment can be very time consuming, resulting in frustration for both students and the teacher: students lose valuable physical activity time and the teacher loses valuable instructional time. Careful planning and organization for the assessment, the use of stations for assessment and/or skill-related practice, and acceptance of responsibility by students will greatly facilitate efficient assessments of the fitness components. Even with the best organization, fitness assessment is time consuming; parent volunteers, who are properly trained, can greatly reduce the time factor. And finally, just as there should be no waiting in line during physical education classes, there should be no waiting your turn for assessment.

Whether the physical fitness assessment is used as a screening tool in the fall, as a culminating experience for children, or as an ongoing process, it should be an educational endeavor. Each test item should be carefully explained, emphasizing the particular component being tested. All too often, children do poorly on an assessment because they do not understand the directions. Sufficient time should be allowed for practice so children understand the proper techniques and stretch their muscles. The purpose of the test is to motivate the children to do their personal best, not to trick them.

After the Assessment

The purpose of all assessment is to provide feedback to both the student and the teacher; the test itself is of little, if any, value if not used for teacher reflection on his or her teaching and to guide students in their learning. What is important in fitness assessment for children is not the test itself, but what is done after the test is completed. Fitness assessment should be an educational experience for the child, the parents, and the teacher. Simply sending home scores on a report card or at the end of the semester is of very little benefit to anyone. The recording of scores should be done in a manner that provides ownership to children, is personal and private for each individual, and assists children in setting fitness goals. Children can be active participants in recording their fitness scores following test completion. Scores may be recorded with computer programs or with teacher- and child-designed activity sheets, both providing interactive participation for the children. With commercial programs, students enter their test scores in the computer program and receive the printout of physical fitness assessment; some commercial programs also provide suggestions for improvement in low score areas.

We have found children enjoy recording their fitness scores with bar graphs and bright colors. A simple graph can be designed listing test items (Figure 28.3). After the fitness screening in the fall, each child is provided his or her scores from the assessment. Using a highlighter, the child colors in the portion of the bar corresponding to the score for each test item—upper bar for fall scores. Completion of the graph provides a visual representation for the child of the areas of fitness in the health fitness range, those above, and those needing remediation. When the children have recorded their scores and reflected on the assessment results, they can write in their journals their feelings about their test results and record their personal fitness goals for the year. When the fitness assessment is repeated in the spring, each child again colors the portion of the bar corresponding to spring scores (lower bar for spring scores), using a different color highlighter. A comparison of fall and spring scores shows changes in fitness and progress toward personal goals established in the fall. *Note: A simple turning of the paper reveals for each child a bar graph of the year's fitness assessments and opportunity for an integrated mathematics lesson.*

Figure 28.3 Personal fitness profile.

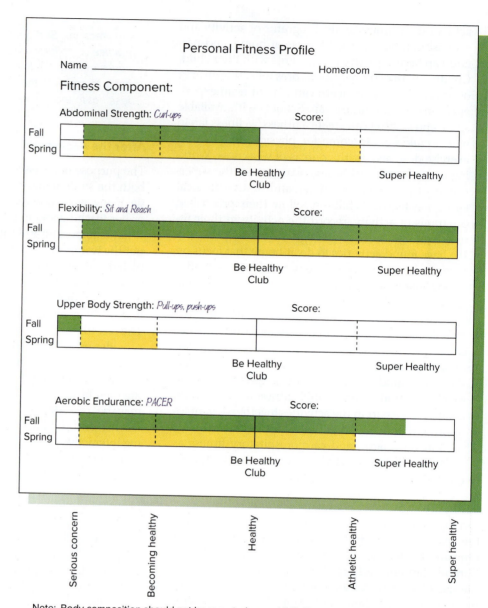

Note: Body composition should not be reported on a child's Personal Fitness Profile.

The focus of elementary physical education is the child; the focus of physical fitness should also be the child. Physical fitness, as is true for all areas of elementary physical education, is child-centered, with learning experiences and assessment focused on the child and his or her needs. No child should be asked to give more than his or her personal best. Scores from the assessment test are personal; they are not to be compared with other children's scores. We recommend the following guidelines for the assessment of children's physical fitness:

- Keep test results confidential. They should never be announced to the class or posted publicly.

- Assist the children in setting their personal fitness goals. Following the fall screening and graphing of scores, have the children record in their journals their personal goals for the year. Young children often need teacher assistance in setting realistic goals. All too often, the school athlete is the measure of success for children. Instead, goals should be based on a reflection of assessments and increments of success.
- Praise children's accomplishments at the lower end of the spectrum, as well as those at the high-performance level. Never post achievement charts on the wall for fastest runner, highest number of pull-ups, etc. Recognize all children and their personal growth.

Box 28-3

Appropriate and Inappropriate Physical Education Practices

Component: Developing Health-Related Fitness

Appropriate Practice

- The health-related component of fitness is the focus on fitness activities. Skill-related components of fitness are emphasized in their relation to skill development.
- The teacher helps students interpret and use assessment data for setting goals and helping to develop a lifelong fitness plan.

Inappropriate Practice

- Fitness activities are random and unrelated to lifelong learning benefits. Physical fitness activity consists of mass exercises following a designated leader or standard routine.
- The teacher conducts the fitness assessment but never uses results to set goals or to design a personal fitness plan.

Component: Fitness Testing

Appropriate Practice

- Physical educators use fitness assessment as part of the ongoing process of helping students understand, enjoy, improve, and/or maintain their physical fitness and well-being (e.g., students set goals for improvement and they are revisited during the school year).
- As part of an ongoing program of physical education, students are physically prepared in each fitness component so they can safely complete the assessments.

Inappropriate Practice

- Teachers use fitness test results to assign a grade.
- Students are required to run a mile without appropriate conditioning or acclimatization.

Source: SHAPE America. 2009. *Appropriate instructional practice guidelines, K-12: A side-by-side comparison* (Reston, VA: Author).

Appropriate and inappropriate practices with regard to physical fitness and fitness testing are summarized in Box 28-3.

Final Thoughts on Fitness

The goal of physical fitness for children is to enable them to develop health and physical activity habits that will become lifestyles. The two most important factors in attaining this goal at the elementary school level are (1) enjoyment of physical activity and (2) mastery of the basic skills of physical education that will enable them to participate successfully in physical activities that promote fitness. Only if physical activity and fitness are fun will children pursue them outside the time they are with us in physical education. Therefore, we focus on the teaching and learning of skills, knowledge, and behaviors that will enable children to value physical activity and be physically active today, tomorrow, and throughout their adult lives.

If we at the elementary level can provide enjoyment in activity, a solid cognitive base of the importance of fitness for good health, and the skills with which to be active, we will have made tremendous strides in children having the competence, confidence, and acceptance of the personal responsibility for their fitness as adolescents and young adults.

Importance of Physical Activity

> *Physical activity is the closest thing we have to a wonder drug.*
>
> —DR. TOM FRIEDEN, DIRECTOR OF CENTERS FOR DISEASE CONTROL AND PREVENTION

Physical activity is the medium for the development of fitness in children; however, physical activity is more than just the path to fitness. Physical activity is now recognized as a preventive for disease and a formula for good health (Shephard 2005; Strong et al. 2005; Watts 2005; Welk and Blair 2000). Childhood obesity and preventable degenerative diseases have reached epidemic proportions in the United States. The health risks of obesity can be largely managed through physical activity and good nutrition. The health risks of degenerative diseases, appearing in children as early as age eight, can be prevented through daily physical activity.

The following are statements regarding the obesity and degenerative diseases epidemic:

- Young children are predicted to not outlive their parents (CDC 2017).
- Childhood obesity has more than tripled in the past two decades (USDHHS 2010).
- There is $117 billion in annual health care costs associated with inadequate physical activity (CDC 2017).
- One in three children born in 2000 and beyond are predicted to develop type 2 diabetes (McConnaughey 2003).

Obesity is a health issue, an emotional issue, and a social issue. Here are some of the facts relating to obesity:

- Ninety percent of our children are born healthy and are genetically predisposed to lead normal lifestyles (Seffrin 2010).
- Birth weight has not changed significantly in more than 300 years (Seffrin 2010).
- The prevalence of obesity has remained fairly stable at about 17% and affects about 12.7 million children and adolescents (CDC 2017).
- The prevalence of obesity is higher among Hispanics and non-Hispanic blacks than among non-Hispanic whites (CDC 2017).
- Culture plays a significant role in attitudes toward exercise, food and nutrition, and body image (Peralta 2003).
- Inactivity is both a contributing cause of excess weight and a consequence of being overweight (Welk and Joens-Matre 2007).
- Obese children feel alienated and isolated. The emotional, social, and health issues of being overweight begin in elementary school; they are no longer confined to adolescence and adulthood.

For elementary-age children, the focus should be on good health, not on size or weight. A positive focus contributes to emotional wellness and self-esteem as well as increased physical activity for students who are overweight. Excellent resources are *Real Kids Come in All Sizes* (Kater 2004), *Supersized P.E.* (Trout and Kahan 2008), and *Teaching Overweight Students in Physical Education: Comprehensive Strategies for Inclusion* (Li 2017).

Physical Inactivity

Physical inactivity is a health issue, an environmental issue, and an emotional issue. As a health issue, we now know inactivity is a contributing factor in children being overweight and obese. Increases in physical inactivity have been linked to increased screen time (i.e., television time, video games, and computers)—that is, increases in sedentary time. Less outdoor play, due to a variety of reasons including unsafe neighborhoods, has also contributed to the increase in physical inactivity. A drive through any neighborhood provides a very vivid visual of the decrease in children's physical activity.

Hypokinetic diseases are those diseases or conditions associated with lack of physical activity or too little regular exercise.

—Corbin et al. 2008

Physical inactivity increases with age; girls are less active than boys. Minority children are less likely to be active, with the highest rate of physical inactivity among minority females. The percentage of physically inactive minority females who become less active as they grow into adolescence is of clinical and public health significance (Crespo 2005). Self-confidence and self-esteem are consistently mentioned as important predictors of physical activity, or lack of activity, in both boys and girls, increasing in importance as children reach upper-elementary school. Self-confidence is linked as a protective factor against obesity and depression (Dunton et al. 2006). Confidence in self breeds increased activity; a lack of confidence breeds a lack of activity, leading to less activity and increased weight gain. The negative cycle is as follows: Inactivity leads to more inactivity, to obesity and degenerative disease, to low self-esteem and fear of failure, and thus to increased inactivity. The positive cycle is very different: Physical activity leads to more activity, serves as a preventive for obesity and degenerative disease, and increases self-esteem and emotional, as well as physical, health.

Enjoyment and skill development are the two key factors children and adolescents give as reasons to engage in and maintain programs of physical activity (Bengoechea et al. 2010; Gao, Lodewyk, and Zhang 2009; Lohman, Going, and Metcalfe 2004). Perceived competence of that skill development greatly affects participation in physical activity (Davison, Downs, and Birch et al. 2006; Fairclough and Stratton 2006). It is important for us as teachers to remember the word is *perceived*. Children may be very capable of successful participation in a variety of activities but do not view themselves as having the skills for success. Very young children think they are very skilled, capable of conquering the highest climbing wall, shooting at the tallest basket, and performing at the highest level on all measures of physical ability. As children progress through elementary school, this perception begins to match against the reality of the performance and the comparison to others, which all too often results in a decrease in perceived competence and confidence that leads to a decrease in willingness to participate and a decrease in the joy in doing so. Our task as teachers is to provide developmentally appropriate activities, in a "differentiated, inclusive learning environment" (Dunton et al. 2006) to assure children's enjoyment, confidence, and competence in physical activity.

Guidelines for Physical Activity

One of the most reliable predictors for lifelong physical activity is the power of early physical activity experiences (Ennis 2010). Youth who are regularly active tend to be active as adults, and thus have a better chance of a healthy adulthood. That activity should be developmentally appropriate, enjoyable, and contribute to the child's skillfulness in physical activities. The recommendations for children's physical activity are included in the newly released *Physical Activity Guidelines for Americans (2nd edition)* (USDHHS 2018) and include 60 minutes of moderate- or vigorous-intensity aerobic physical activity daily, muscle-strengthening activities at least three days a week, and bone strengthening activities at least three days a week.

The *Physical Activity Guidelines* are based on children's needs and developmental characteristics; the guidelines focus on developmentally appropriate physical activity, skill development, and fitness through activity. Physical education provides the tools; physical activity provides the arena for good health and fitness development.

Key concepts from the *Physical Activity Guidelines* include:

- Children and adolescents should have 60 minutes or more of physical activity daily.
- Aerobic activities increase cardiorespiratory fitness.
- Vigorous activity comes in short bursts for children, accumulated throughout the day.
- Vigorous-intensity activities are important as they result in more improvement in cardiorespiratory fitness.
- Bone strengthening is especially important for children; the majority of peak bone mass is obtained by the end of adolescence.
- Children do not need formal muscle-strengthening programs, e.g., lifting weights.
- Children doing moderate-intensity activities will notice their hearts are beating faster than normal and they are breathing harder.
- Children doing vigorous-intensity activities will feel their hearts beating much faster than normal, and they will breathe much harder than normal.
- A variety of activities is important to reduce the risk of overtraining or injury.
- Physical activity is important for children with disabilities; when possible the same *guidelines* should be met.

Figure 28.4 provides examples of moderate- and vigorous-intensity activities as well as muscle- and bone-strengthening activities for children.

The Physical Activity Guidelines for Americans *provide toolkits for schools, families, and communities to support physical activity for children and adolescents, ages 6 through 17.*

SOURCE: HTTPS://HEALTH.GOV/PAGUIDELINES/

Figure 28.4 Sample Activities for Children (pre adolescents)

Type of Physical Activity	Children
Moderate–intensity aerobic	• Active recreation, such as hiking, skateboarding, rollerblading • Bicycle riding • Brisk walking
Vigorous–intensity aerobic	• Active games involving running and chasing, such as tag • Bicycle riding • Jumping rope • Martial arts, such as karate • Running • Sports such as soccer, ice or field hockey, basketball, swimming, tennis • Cross-country skiing
Muscle-strengthening	• Games such as tug-of-war • Modified push-ups (with knees on the floor) • Resistance exercises using body weight or resistance bands • Rope or tree climbing • Sit-ups (curl-ups or crunches) • Swinging on playground equipment/bars
Bone-strengthening	• Games such as hopscotch • Hopping, skipping, jumping • Jumping rope • Running • Sports such as gymnastics, basketball, volleyball, tennis

Source: U.S. Department of Health and Human Services, *Physical activity guidelines for Americans* (U.S. Department of Health and Human Services: 2008).

Comprehensive School Physical Activity Program (CSPAP)

With the importance of physical activity and health consequences of physical inactivity well established, professionals are actively seeking ways to increase physical activity in children's lives to the recommended level of 60 minutes per day. Realistically children cannot meet this expectation during physical education alone. Therefore, it is essential to develop a systematic approach by which schools use all opportunities for school-based physical activity (SHAPE America 2015). Programs before and after school, in school, and at home are essential to successful promotion of daily physical activity. Lee and Solomon (2007) term this the "whole-school approach," involving all school clients—students, physical education specialists, classroom teachers, and parents—in the promotion of physical activity for children. In response to calls for a whole-school approach, SHAPE America and the Centers for Disease Control and Prevention (CDC) (2013) have provided guidelines for the creation of the whole-school programs, using the term Comprehensive School Physical Activity Programs (CSPAPs).

With quality physical education and daily programs of physical activity both inside and outside the school, children can meet the recommendation of 60 minutes or more of daily physical activity. A commitment from everyone—students, parents, classroom teachers, and the physical education specialist—is critical to attaining the goal. We as teachers must believe we can make a difference in the lives of children and that we can have a positive effect on children's present and future ability to attain and maintain physical activity and good health.

Goals of CSPAP

In their position statement on CSPAP, SHAPE America (2015, p. 3) identifies that the goals of a comprehensive program are to:

- Provide a variety of physical activity opportunities throughout the school day, with a high-quality physical education program as the foundation.
- Provide physical activity opportunities both before and after school, so that all students can participate in at least 60 minutes of physical activity daily.
- Incorporate physical activity opportunities for faculty and staff members, as well as for families.
- Encourage and reinforce physical activity opportunities in the community.
- Coordinate among the CSPAP components to maximize understanding, application, and practice of the knowledge and skills learned in physical education, so that all students are physically educated and motivated to pursue a lifetime of physical activity.

CSPAP in Elementary Schools

What does CSPAP look like in an elementary school? Identifying the components of such programs, Rink, Hall, and Williams (2010; p. 78) described the following elements:

- Quality physical education programs
- Physical activity opportunities before, during, and after school
- Daily recess
- Activity breaks in the classroom and opportunities to learn academic content through movement
- Collaboration with community programs and events
- Parental participation

Quality physical education programs. Physical education is the cornerstone of any CSPAP effort. Ideally, physical education would be required of students every day and, therefore, could provide a significant amount of children's daily recommended physical activity. This however, is not the reality in most schools, and therefore, physical education efforts must be supplemented with additional physical activity opportunities within and outside of schools. A detailed account of the characteristics of quality elementary physical education programs is provided in Chapter 1. To summarize, quality programs provide 150 minutes of instructional physical education per week and provide learning opportunities, appropriate instruction, meaningful and challenging content, and student and program assessment (SHAPE America 2010). Ultimately, the goal of elementary physical education is to teach students the foundational movement skills, knowledge, and dispositions to be physically active.

Physical activities before, during, and after school. Before and after school programs are effective ways to provide additional physical activity opportunities. These formal or informal programs are most often conducted by both physical educators and other school faculty and staff. Additionally, they may include community members as well as parent volunteers. Activity clubs, intramurals, active commuting, and youth sports and other physical activities are all examples of before, during, and after school ideas used by many schools:

Activity Clubs

- Jump rope clubs organized at different skill and interest levels. These clubs are organized for full participation by all students, in comparison to a jump rope team with selected students.
- Jogging/walking clubs with an emphasis on jogging or walking for distance, as opposed to running for speed. These clubs can focus on total miles completed for each student, matching the miles of a friend/parent/community volunteer on a hiking trail, or walking/jogging across the state.

Intramurals

- Intramural programs provide opportunities for students to practice fundamental movement skills learned in physical education. Intramural planning should be informed by student interest. Consider surveying your students to find out what activities they would like to participate in and be sure to include ideas that are not just sport focused, including options for free play and instructional activities. Physical activity choices may include sports (e.g., soccer, volleyball), lifetime activities (e.g., walking), and classes or lessons (e.g., dance or gymnastics).

Active Commuting

- The decrease in physical activity noted in this chapter is, in part, an environmental issue. We are seeing a lack of play spaces, safety concerns for children at play, fewer children riding bikes or walking to school, and fewer neighborhood schools within walking distance for children. Encouraging active commuting by walking and/or biking to school is another strategy to encourage students' physical activity.

Youth Sports and Other Physical Activities

- These community-based programs are provided at the schools and include organized physical activity experiences in both competitive and noncompetitive environments. A variety of developmentally appropriate sports, gymnastics, cheerleading, and dance may be offered before or after school. Community organizations such as YMCA, parks and recreation departments, and boys' and girls' clubs are typically the facilitators of these school-based opportunities.

Daily recess. Recess offers an excellent opportunity to help children discover enjoyable physical activities to increase their motivation to engage in more movement. As such, schools have the obligation to devote daily time to recess as well as adequate resources in terms of permanent and manipulative equipment and adequate, safe play spaces. It is important to note that recess must not be substituted for physical education. Instead, recess should be child-directed and provide children an unstructured break. Recommendations for recess include using strategies to encourage active play, thoughtfully scheduling recess, teaching children playground games, and designating equipment and play areas for use during recess (Rink et al. 2010). Additionally, promoting children's physical activity–related autonomy (i.e., give choices about the nature and type of activities), competence (i.e., present tasks that vary in difficulty so children can be successful), and relatedness (i.e., provide social opportunities in a physical and emotionally safe environment) have been identified as critical element in getting children active during recess (Stellino and Sinclair 2008).

Breaks in the Classroom and Movement Opportunities to Teach Academic Content

The physical activity recommendation of 60 minutes per day is cumulative and may not be completed in extended physical activity sessions. Instead, the recommendation is for short bouts of multiple activity breaks. Classroom activity breaks are just that, short activity breaks that take the form of transitions between content areas, recess, and the use of physical activity to teach academic content (Rink et al. 2010). With respect to the impact of activity breaks, research indicates that benefits include fitness gains, improved attention spans, and increased physical activity levels (Erwin et al. 2009; Erwin et al. 2011). Examples of activity breaks include walking breaks, games, and simple dances (Rink et al. 2010). Furthermore, integrating movement into the occasional lesson can be an effective tool to enhance classroom learning as well as an opportunity for physical activity. For specific examples of movement opportunities to teach academic content, see Chapter 32.

Community Programs and Events

A key component of CSPAP is establishing relationships with the community to work cooperatively to address the physical inactivity of both children and adults. The reality, however, is that most schools operate independently from what is happening around them. Therefore, schools should become aware of community programs and events and become part of these initiatives whenever feasible, involving children and their families. Examples include Saturday activities such as "Bark in the Park," which invites children to bring along their dogs for the activities. Other possibilities include active field trips to parks, bowling centers, and hiking trails. Community recreational opportunities encourage children and adults to play

---

Physical Activity Beyond Physical Education

- A before-school activity program*
- Family Fun and Wellness Education nights*
- A before-school coed dance program*
- A town-wide exercise program for students, families, dignitaries, and friends*
- Fitness homework calendars*
- A Run/Walk Club at recess*
- Nonelimination games, physical activity choices for recess
- Integrated movement/academics activities for classroom
- Classroom activity breaks

*Susan Donovan, Director of Physical Activity and Physical Education Specialist, Guiteras Elementary School

together in an environment that is emotionally safe and fosters confidence and competence.

Working with Parents

Several of the physical activity opportunities mentioned previously (i.e., fitness clubs, physical activity clubs, and playgrounds) provide additional physical activity for children and involve their families in the physical activity. Awards systems often give double points for parental participation. Family physical activity nights, fitness fairs, and fitness/health checks bring families together to participate in physical activity, as well as to learn the current information on physical activity, fitness, nutrition, and good health. Parents can also be involved by using physical activity calendars (https://www.shapeamerica.org/publications/resources/teachingtools/teachertoolbox/activity-calendars.aspx) as well as assigning active homework

Physical activity leads to fitness and wellness.

©Lars A. Niki

that requires physical activity outside of class. Parental involvement, activity choice, and encouragement of extracurricular participation are characteristics of active homework (see Figure 12.8, page 199, for an example). Parents are the number one influence in the lives of elementary-age children. Parent involvement may well be the best way to establish the habits and instill the importance of physical activity for good health.

CSPAP: Who Is Responsible?

Schools are ideally positioned to influence children's health through physical activity participation because school is where most children spend the majority of their time outside the home (SHAPE America 2015). It is therefore the responsibility of the entire school to work with young children who are forming habits that will remain with them for a lifetime. While everyone in the school needs to be united in the goal of daily physical activity for all children, it is the physical education teacher who will take the lead in designing and/or coordinating the CSPAP effort. The physical education teacher is the expert at the school and thus becomes the school's "Physical Activity Director" as well as the teacher of physical education, designing comprehensive programs of physical activity both within and beyond the school day. The physical education teacher, with support of the administration, will engage others in the CSPAP. In fact, school wellness councils were mandated by the federal government to play a significant role in the CSPAP, and the physical activity director plays the major coordinating role (Rink et al. 2010). The role of the school wellness council and wellness for children will be addressed in the wellness section later in this chapter. Classroom teachers are also directly involved through their work with students in the classroom and recess. Lastly, parents and community volunteers play a supervisory role when called upon.

Getting Started with CSPAP

Getting CSPAP started at your school is a task that will require much planning. There are several publications and training resources that can provide additional information on CSPAP:

- Comprehensive School Physical Activity Programs: http://www.shapeamerica.org/CSPAP/
- Centers for Disease Control and Prevention Web page on CSPAP: https://www.cdc.gov/healthyschools/physicalactivity/cspap.htm

The development of skill promotes increased physical activity; increased physical activity promotes increased fitness.

©Lars A. Niki

- CSPAP Professional Development: https://www.shapeamerica.org/cspap/prodev.aspx
- Rink, J. E., T. J. Hall, and L. H. Williams. 2010. *Schoolwide physical activity.* Champaign, IL: Human Kinetics.

> *Thomas Jefferson introduced pedometers to America. They came into the commercial market in Japan in 1965 under the name of manpo-meter (manpo in Japanese means 10,000 steps).*
>
> —HATANO AND TUDOR-LOCKE (2001)

Active Schools

- With the physical education specialist as director of physical activity and a school committed to meeting the recommended requirement of physical activity for good health, schools can become "active schools" designed to maximize school-based opportunities for reinforcing the relevance and value of physical activity for all children (Fox, Cooper, and McKenna 2005). We as physical education teachers, in collaboration with classroom teachers, parents, and community leaders, can design and promote our schools as active schools with the following strategies:
- Develop "safe routes" for walking and riding bikes to school.
- Develop and maintain safe, developmentally appropriate playgrounds at school and in the community.
- Permit access to the gymnasiums and school playground after school hours and on weekends.
- Work with classroom teachers to incorporate physical activity breaks during the day and "active" lessons.
- Mark outdoor paved surfaces for game play.
- Adopt a policy of daily recess for all children (CDC and SHAPE America 2017).
- Promote the value of physical education and the importance of physical activity in each school newsletter.
- Ensure safe play during recess, both physically and emotionally.
- Market the school as being healthy, active, and safe.

Technology in Fitness/Wellness Education

The world of technology relative to fitness/wellness education has exploded in recent years. Fitness technology now includes electronic portfolios, activity trackers, and heart rate monitors for upper-elementary students, equipment for fitness/wellness labs, interactive video games, the storage and analysis of fitness data for both students and teachers, and a wealth of information via the Internet. Jogging/walking club members can now connect with other students around the world charting mileage and comparing adventures. The list of Internet resources is almost limitless in fitness, nutrition, and other areas of wellness. We encourage you as physical education teachers to explore the use of technology in your teaching of physical education; however, we caution you to use technology to enhance your program of physical education, not as a substitute for quality teaching.

Wellness for Children

Physical activity, physical education, and fitness come together in the concept of wellness—the child's total well-being. The dimensions of wellness for children translate into mental/emotional health; personal and social responsibility; personal safety (bicycle, auto, water, and fire); risks of drugs, alcohol, and tobacco abuse; and nutrition, as well as physical activity and fitness.

All the dimensions of wellness are critical to a child's well-being. Crisis in any dimension leads to a breakdown in that child's optimum health. The total package comes to school; the total package comes to physical education each time a child enters our class. Our task is teaching the skills of physical education while not neglecting any dimensions of the total child. This focus on the total child often adds to the curriculum for teachers of elementary physical education as they are asked to address health, safety, and nutrition as well as physical education, physical activity, and fitness. Collaboration with classroom teachers and integration of concepts/benchmarks within the curriculum will preserve quality time for teaching the skills of physical education.

School Wellness Programs

Coordinated School Health was established by the CDC in 1998 to promote student health and wellness by "putting it all together to help students grow strong and healthy." Two of the eight components of Coordinated School Health are nutrition and physical education. The Child Nutrition and WIC (Women, Infants, and Children) Reauthorization Act of 2004 mandated that all school districts receiving federal monies for food services establish wellness policies regarding nutrition and physical activity, and set goals for nutrition education, food provision, and physical activity for students and employees. Both Coordinated School Health and the Child Nutrition Act emphasize school-based wellness councils composed of teachers, parents, and community leaders and collaboration to promote wellness for children. Physical education teachers can and should be vital members of each.

Noted as an essential part of CSPAP (see above), the school wellness plan should be developed by the school wellness committee and the resulting plan should be a part of the school improvement plan. The overall success of the school wellness program is dependent on gaining stakeholder support and involving administration, teachers, parents, and community leaders. This plan, which reflects a school culture of physically active and healthy behaviors and attitudes, must also include ideas to overcome barriers to success (i.e., lack of time, support from administration, funding, student involvement and interest, and accountability) (Rink et al. 2010).

Mental and Emotional Health

Emotional security ranks second only to food and shelter as the individual's most basic needs. The need to be loved and accepted moves quickly to the top for children as the basic needs of food and shelter are met. What happens in the life of children at home, on the way to school, at breakfast, and in the classroom affects their emotional health when they are with us for physical education. Emotional health affects their learning. What happens in our gymnasiums and on our playgrounds affects the child's emotional health in the classroom, for the day, and beyond the school day.

The foundation of young children's emotional health is self-esteem—how worthy and valuable they consider themselves (Anspaugh and Ezell 2012). We as teachers play a critical role in how children view themselves. Our reactions to their skill or lack of skill and our reaction to their mistakes and sometimes loss of control greatly affect their view of themselves. Children's opinions of themselves are established early and are very fragile. A quick, negative response can have a lasting effect on a child. Children with a strong sense of worth and importance are free to develop their potential, better able to resolve personal and interpersonal conflicts, and free to establish their independence and self-expression.

As teachers we need to remember:

- Acceptance of children, even on their worst days, is critical.
- What happens in elementary school affects children throughout life.
- The most important influences in young children's lives are their parents; the most powerful influences at age 11 and older are their peers.
- Perception of self may or may not match reality; perception of self greatly affects self-esteem.

Page and Page (2014) offer the following suggestions to foster a positive climate for emotional wellness:

- Quickly learn the names of students, call them by name; show respect for each child.
- Be sensitive to diverse cultures, ethnicities, and races; strive to view children from their perspectives rather than your own.
- Expect students to be competent, capable, and eager to learn … and they will.
- Create an atmosphere in which children feel at ease.
- Arrange for a high ratio of successes to failures.

We are teachers of children; our interactions with them, our actions, and our language affect not just the moment, not just their time in physical education, but their lives.

Personal and Social Responsibility

The gymnasiums and playgrounds of our schools provide a rich environment for the development of personal and social responsibility. The physical activity setting provides a mini-world of emotional, interactive situations. Within this world of competition and cooperation, success and failure, and fast-moving action, children make a multitude of decisions on a daily basis. The development of personal and social responsibility—and its importance to the future of our society—is a reminder that we are teachers of children, not just teachers of skills, gymnastics sequences, games, and dances.

Personal and social responsibility stem from acceptance of two basic concepts:

- I will respect myself and others.
- I am responsible for myself, my actions, and my behavior.

Responsible adults develop from responsible children who have had opportunities to make decisions, to experience success and failure, to be accepted, and to accept others. Acceptance of self and others leads to respect for self and others and to personal and social responsibility. These attributes do not just happen, but rather require a school focus that includes clear personal and social responsibility expectations and reinforcement.

Safety (Bicycle, Auto, Fire, Water) The concepts of safety relative to helmets and safe riding of bicycles, rollerblades, and skateboards; the buckling of seat belts at all times when riding in automobiles; how to respond when in a fire emergency; and water safety for swimming and recreational outings/sports are all matters of personal responsibility. Each of these areas of personal responsibility and safety presents excellent opportunities for collaborative endeavors with community agencies as schools and agencies come together to present programs, sponsor community events, and provide hands-on demonstrations of safety for children. Again, we cannot assume that young children know the safety concepts for each of these areas; they must be taught. We do know that when learned at an early age, the lessons of "helmets, seat belts, and life jackets" become habits for a lifetime.

Drug, Alcohol, and Tobacco Abuse With children experimenting with drugs, alcohol, and tobacco at increasingly younger ages, it is never too early to educate them on the risks of use and dangers of substance abuse. We can no longer pretend that drug and alcohol use and abuse are limited to older adolescents and young adults. Nor can we pretend that abuse and overdose happen only somewhere else. Elementary-school-age children are experimenting with drugs and alcohol. No socioeconomic level is immune to substance abuse. A significant resource for teaching students decision-making skills to help lead safe and healthy lives is the widely adopted program called D.A.R.E. (Drug Abuse Resistance Education): https://dare.org. The success of this program has led to it being implemented into 75% of U.S. school districts.

Physical educators serve a key role for children in the area of substance abuse. With daily reports of professional athletes and media celebrities involved in substance abuse, children receive a confusing message regarding the dangers of drugs and the consequences of use. We can provide positive role models and clear, consistent messages regarding abstinence. Responsible decisions and personal responsibility begin with a solid knowledge base provided by adults who are respected and viewed as important in a child's life. We as teachers are second only to parents in the potential influence we have on young children.

Much research and thought have been given to the reasons individuals use drugs. Two of those reasons are boredom and low self-esteem. A youngster actively involved in physical activity and sports is an active youngster. A youngster involved in a quality physical education program develops the skills for successful participation in a variety of sports and physical activities. A solid movement-skills base provides a positive self-image in this important area for children. Thus, physical education has the potential to contribute directly to a healthy, drug-free world for children.

Fire Safety Should Be a Part of All Elementary School Curriculums

The concept of fire safety can be addressed via a school assembly and hands-on activities conducted by the local fire department personnel. We have found fire fighters eager to come to the schools; they bring trucks and ladders for demonstrations, provide active participation in "stop, drop, and roll" and "stay low," and teach the basic critical emergency response, "911."

Nutrition

The importance of nutrition as a contributor to a child's well-being cannot be overestimated. Nutrition contributes to cognitive learning in the classroom and in the gymnasium. Nutrition contributes to a child's physical development and to his or her physical activity. Lack of good nutrition contributes to obesity and numerous health problems.

A number of factors have contributed to the existing state of poor nutrition among school-age children in the United States. A large number of children are responsible for their own meals, especially breakfast and after-school snacks. Children do not choose fruits and vegetables as a favorite snack; young children do not have the knowledge or skills to prepare healthy meals or snacks. For many children, the foods needed for good nutrition are not available in their homes. Thus, by choice and by circumstance, many children are the victims of poor nutrition.

Busier schedules and more fast-food meals have also contributed to a decrease in good nutrition for America's families. A positive increase in physical activity—that is, organized sports, dance, and gymnastics clubs for children—has been coupled with a decrease in family meals at home. All too often the quickest meal is one from a drive-through, one that is high in fat and low in the balance of nutrients needed for good health.

Although elementary-age children may not be interested in nutrition for good health (after all, they are immortal), we have found they are very interested in nutrition as it relates to running, jumping, throwing, and being better athletes. Thus the appeal of athletics opens the door to educating children about the importance of eating fruits and vegetables, decreasing fats, attaining healthy body weight, and maintaining a balance of physical activity and nutrition as a daily pattern, a childhood pattern that becomes a lifestyle for wellness.

MyPlate

Children at the elementary level need an understanding of nutrition, the contribution of the major essential nutrients to building and maintaining healthy bodies, and the role of nutrition in overall good health.

My Plate (Figure 28.5) has been designed for easy understanding of food portions and the relationship of the food groups. Children easily visualize the plate and are quick to educate their parents on the recommended portions. MyPlate (www.choosemyplate.gov) includes suggestions for increasing physical activity and interactive games and projects for teachers, children, and families. The role of nutrition in achieving and maintaining good health was recognized in 2011 by the President's Council on Physical Fitness and Sports (PCPFS), which was renamed the President's Council on Sports, Fitness, and Nutrition. The emphasis for children is the nutritional balance for good health. This is increasingly important for upper elementary

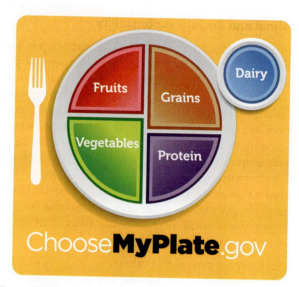

Figure 28.5 MyPlate.
Source: www.choosemyplate.gov

students as puberty approaches. At this stage in their development, maintaining a healthy body weight takes on an all new emphasis as students may become increasingly concerned with social acceptance.

The Good Health Balance

Physical activity and good nutrition are the essential ingredients for the body's good health balance. Envision a young child first learning to walk a balance beam; the arms are extended outward on either side of the body for good balance. If neither arm is extended or if the extension is only on one side, the child's balance is in jeopardy. In adults, we speak of the match between caloric intake and daily energy expenditure—that is, energy balance. In children, we call it the *good health balance* (Graham, Holt/Hale, and Parker 2006).

Adults in the United States have a tremendous mismatch between caloric intake and energy expenditure, the results of which are the obesity epidemic and the health risks associated with obesity. A combination of larger food portions, more readily available food, a lack of knowledge regarding portion sizes and number of servings within containers, and the abundance of high-fat, high-calorie food mean energy expenditure—that is, physical activity—must increase. However, advances in technology and automation have created just the opposite—an environment that supports less physical activity. The same mismatch exists for children. We as teachers must take the lead in creating the good health balance for children—a balance of daily physical activity and good nutrition that leads to

The good health balance.

©Derek Sine & Van Tucker

children becoming, and remaining, physically active for a lifetime.

A Final Note on Wellness

Many elementary and middle schools are "community centers for learning." Hours are extended to include adult education, physical activity in gymnasiums, nutrition classes for parents, and in many schools, a health service center. District educational administrators and community leaders, recognizing the importance of wellness, are working together to provide optimal learning communities for children and their families. Physical education professionals are regarded as leaders in these endeavors. Our task is to embrace the challenge and assist all children in reaching their potential in all areas of learning and development—wellness for all children.

Summary

Physical activity is a preventive for disease and a formula for good health. Physical activity and fitness are products of competence and confidence in the skills of physical education. The *Physical Activity Guidelines for Americans* provide the framework for the daily amounts and types of activity children need.

Physical fitness is the capacity of the heart, blood vessels, lungs, and muscles to function at optimum efficiency in work, in leisure activities, and in emergency situations. In previous years, fitness was defined as the capacity to carry out the day's activities without undue fatigue; we are now recognizing that this condition may not be sufficient for healthy hearts and lungs. Optimum efficiency is the key. That efficiency also includes resistance to hypokinetic diseases.

Fitness is a process and the product of a physically active lifestyle; a physically active lifestyle is the product of movement competency and knowledge gained through quality physical education and positive participation in physical activity.

Physical fitness for children includes a health-related screening each fall, setting individual goals, a cognitive understanding of the components of fitness, and moderate to vigorous activity on a regular basis. It involves the physical education specialist, the classroom teacher, the child, and the parent(s). Physical fitness can be incorporated into the theme of study, added to the lesson as a group activity, and increased through before- and after-school programs. The focus of physical fitness for the elementary school child is the development of a positive attitude toward an active lifestyle, a knowledge of the concepts of fitness, and an understanding of how to attain and maintain personal fitness.

Because children cannot realistically meet daily physical activity expectation during physical education alone, CSPAP has been developed as a systematic approach by which schools use all opportunities for school-based physical activity (SHAPE America 2015).

Physical activity, nutrition, and physical education culminate in well-being for children, i.e., wellness.

Wellness is optimal health and well-being (physical, emotional, mental, spiritual, interpersonal/social, and environmental well-being). Physical education must be child-centered, educating the whole child in his or her quest for wellness and a lifetime of physical activity.

Reading Comprehension Questions

1. Define physical education, physical fitness, physical activity, and wellness? How are they different and what is their relationship?
2. Why is physical inactivity called an environmental, an emotional, and a health issue?
3. Why is physical activity considered a preventive for disease and a formula for good health?
4. Design a program of physical activity beyond physical education classes for elementary-age children.
5. Define physical fitness. Why can we no longer define the level of fitness as the capacity to carry out the day's activities without undue fatigue?
6. What is the difference between health-related and skill-related fitness?
7. Why do we emphasize health-related fitness in our programs?
8. What is the focus of fitness at the elementary-school level?
9. Discuss the linkage of physical activity to physical fitness and wellness. Why is this relationship so important to children in our elementary schools?
10. Describe the options for physical fitness assessment for children.
11. Why do the authors of *Children Moving* not recommend testing of children for fitness below the fourth grade?
12. What are the key elements of CSPAP? What is the role of physical education?
13. What is meant by the term *good health balance*? Why is it important for children?
14. How do the FITT guidelines affect the fitness for children?
15. Give two examples of tasks/challenges from the skill themes to illustrate each FITT guideline.
16. What is meant by the term *active schools*? Design a collaborative project for working with community leaders, the parent–teacher organization, or local agencies to increase physical activity for children.
17. Define wellness. What are the components of wellness for children at the elementary-school level?
18. Choose one wellness component. Design a strategy for working with the classroom teacher to teach that component. Include in your action plan the integrating of the component into physical education.

References/Suggested Readings

Anspaugh, D. J., and G. Ezell. 2012. *Teaching today's health*. 10th ed. New York: Pearson.

Bengoechea, E. G., C. M. Sabiston, R. Ahmed, and M. Farnoush. 2010. Exploring links to unorganized and organized physical activity during adolescence: The role of gender, socioeconomic status, weight status, and enjoyment of physical education. *Research Quarterly for Exercise and Sport* 81(1): 7–16.

Cattuzzo, M. T., R. S. Henrique, A. H. Ré, I. S. de Oliveira, B. M. Melo, M. de Sousa Moura, R. C. de Araújo, and D. F. Stodden. 2016. Motor competence and health related physical fitness in youth: A systematic review. *Journal of Science and Medicine in Sport* 19(2): 123–9.

[CDC] Centers for Disease Control and Prevention. 2013. *Comprehensive school physical activity programs: A guide for schools*. Atlanta, GA: U.S. Department of Health and Human Services.

[CDC] Centers for Disease Control and Prevention. 2017. Prevalence of childhood obesity in the United States, 2011-2014. https://www.cdc.gov/obesity/data/childhood.html.

[CDC] Centers for Disease Control and Prevention and [SHAPE America] Society of Health and Physical Educators. 2017. *Strategies for recess in schools*. Atlanta, GA: Centers for Disease Control and Prevention, US Department of Health and Human Services.

Cooper Institute. 2017. *FitnessGram administration manual*. 5th ed. Champaign, IL: Human Kinetics.

Corbin, D. B. 1986. Fitness is for children: Developing lifetime fitness. *Journal of Physical Education, Recreation and Dance* 57(5): 82–84.

Corbin, C. B., W. R. Corbin, G. J. Welk, and K. A. Welk. 2008. *Concepts of fitness and wellness: A comprehensive lifestyle approach*. 7th ed. New York: McGraw-Hill.

Corbin, C. B., G. J. Welk, W. R. Corbin, and K. A. Welk. 2015. *Concepts of fitness and wellness: A comprehensive lifestyle approach*. 11th ed. New York: McGraw-Hill.

Crespo, C. J. 2005. Physical activity in minority populations: Overcoming a public health challenge. *PCPFS Research Digest* 6(2).

Davison, K. K., D. S. Downs, and L. L. Birch. 2006. Pathways linking perceived athletic competence and parental support at age 9 years to girls' physical activity at age 11 years. *Research Quarterly for Exercise and Sport* 77(1): 23–31.

Dunton, G. F., M. Schneider, D. J. Graham, and D. M. Cooper. 2006. Physical activity, fitness, and physical self-concept in adolescent females. *Pediatric Exercise Science* 18(2): 240–51.

Ennis, C. D. 2010. On their own: Preparing students for a lifetime. *Journal of Physical Education, Recreation and Dance* 81(5): 17–22.

Erwin, H. E., M. G. Abel, A. Beighle, and M. W. Beets. 2009. Promoting children's health through physically active math classes: A pilot study. *Health Promotion Practice* 12: 557–66.

Erwin, H. E., A. Beighle, C. F. Morgan, and M. P. Noland. 2011. Effect of low-cost, teacher directed classroom intervention on elementary students' physical activity. *The Journal of School Health* 81: 455–61.

Fairclough, S., and G. Stratton. 2006. Physical activity, fitness, and affective responses of normal-weight and over-weight adolescents during physical education. *Pediatric Exercise Science* 18(1): 53–63.

Fox, K. R., A. Cooper, and J. McKenna. 2005. The school and promotion of children's health-enhancing physical activity: Perspectives from the United Kingdom. *Journal of Teaching in Physical Education* 23(4): 338–58.

Gao, A., K. R. Lodewyk, and T. Zhang. 2009. The role of ability beliefs and incentives in middle school students' intention, cardiovascular fitness, and effort. *Journal of Teaching in Physical Education* (28): 3–20.

Graham, G., S. Holt/Hale, and M. Parker. 2006. *Children moving: A reflective approach to teaching physical education.* 8th ed. New York: McGraw-Hill.

Hatano, Y., and C. Tudor-Locke. 2001. *Pedometer-assessed physical activity: Measurement and motivations.* Paper presented at the American College of Sports Medicine Meeting, Baltimore, MD.

Holt/Hale, S., and T. Hall. 2016. *Lesson planning for elementary physical education: Meeting the national standards & grade-level outcomes.* Champaign, IL: Human Kinetics.

Kater, K. J. 2004. *Real kids come in all sizes: Ten essential lessons to build your child's body esteem.* New York: Broadway Books.

Kennedy, J. F. 1960. The soft American. *Sports Illustrated* 13: 15.

Lee, A., and M. Solomon. 2007. School programs to increase physical activity. *Journal of Physical Education, Recreation and Dance* 78(5): 22–24.

LeMasurier, G., and C. B. Corbin. 2006. Top 10 reasons for quality physical education. *Journal of Physical Education, Recreation and Dance* 77 (6): 44–53.

Li, W. 2017. *Teaching overweight students in physical education: Comprehensive strategies for inclusion.* New York: Routledge.

Lohman, T. G., S. B. Going, and L. Metcalfe. 2004. Seeing ourselves through the obesity epidemic. *PCPFS Research Digest* 5(3): 1–6.

McConnaughey, J. 2003. CDC diabetes warning for children. *Associated Press,* June 16.

Murrie, E. 2018. Law requiring PE will help US military. *Knoxville News Sentinel,* May 18.

Neilson, N. P., and W. Van Hagen. 1935. *Physical education for elementary schools.* New York: A.S. Barnes.

Page, R. M., and T. S. Page. 2014. *Promoting health and emotional well-being in the classroom.* 6th ed. Boston: Jones & Bartlett.

Peralta, R. L. 2003. Thinking sociologically about sources of obesity in the United States. *Gender Issues* 21(3): 5–16.

Rink, J. E., T. J. Hall, and L. H. Williams 2010. *Schoolwide physical activity.* Champaign, IL: Human Kinetics.

Seffrin, J. R. 2010. *Address to the American Alliance for Health, Physical Education, Recreation and Dance.* Indianapolis, IN, March.

Shephard, R. J. 2005. The obesity epidemic: A challenge to pediatric work physiologists? *Pediatric Exercise Science* 17(1): 3–17.

[SHAPE America] Society of Health and Physical Educators. 2009. *Appropriate instructional practice guidelines, K-12: A side-by-side comparison.* Reston, VA: SHAPE America.

[SHAPE America] Society of Health and Physical Educators. 2010. *Opportunity to learn: Guidelines for elementary, middle & high school physical education—A side-by-side comparison.* Reston, VA: SHAPE America.

[SHAPE America] Society of Health and Physical Educators. 2011. *Physical Best activity guide: Elementary level.* 3rd ed. Champaign, IL: Human Kinetics.

[SHAPE America] Society of Health and Physical Educators. 2014. *National standards and grade-level outcomes for K-12 physical education.* Champaign, IL: Human Kinetics.

[SHAPE America] Society of Health and Physical Educators. 2015. *Comprehensive school physical activity programs: Helping all students log 60 minutes of physical activity each day [position statement].* Reston, VA: SHAPE America.

[SHAPE America] Society of Health and Physical Educators. 2017. *Appropriate and inappropriate practices related to fitness testing.* Reston, VA: SHAPE America.

[SHAPE America] Society of Health and Physical Educators. 2018. *PE metrics: Assessing student performance using the National Standards & Grade-Level Outcomes for K-12 Physical Education.* 3rd ed. Champaign, IL: Human Kinetics.

[SHAPE America] Society of Health and Physical Educators and Voices for Healthy Kids. 2016. *Shape of the nation: Status of physical education in the USA.* Reston, VA: SHAPE America.

Stellino, M. B., and C. D. Sinclair. 2008. Intrinsically motivated, free-time physical activity. *Journal of Physical Education, Recreation and Dance* 79(4): 37–40.

Strong, W. B., R. M. Malina, C. J. Blimkie, et al. 2005. Evidence based physical activity for school-age youth. *Journal of Pediatrics* 146: 732–37.

Trout, J., and D. Kahan 2008. *Supersized P.E.: A comprehensive guidebook for teaching overweight students.* Reston, VA: National Association for Sport and Physical Education.

Tudor-Locke, C. 2002. Taking steps toward increased physical activity: Using pedometers to measure and motivate. *PCPFS Research Digest* 3(17): 1–6.

[USDHHS] U.S. Department of Health and Human Services. 2018. *Physical activity guidelines for Americans, 2nd edition.* Washington, DC: U.S.

[USDHHS] U.S. Department of Health and Human Services. 2010. *Healthy people 2020: Improving the health of Americans.* www.healthypeople.gov

Watts, K., et al. 2005. Exercise training in obese children and adolescents. *Sports Medicine* 35(5): 375–92.

Welk, G. J., and S. N. Blair. 2000. Physical activity protects against the health risks of obesity. *Research Digest* 3(12): 1–8.

Welk, G. J., and R. Joens-Matre. 2007. The effect of weight on self-concept, and psychosocial correlates of physical activity in youth. *Journal of Physical Education, Recreation and Dance* 78(8): 43–47.

[WHO] World Health Organization. 2017. *Global strategy on diet, physical activity and health.* https://www.who.int/dietphysicalactivity/pa/en/

Appendix 28A: Family Fitness Activities

Strength and Endurance Activities

Wake-up Time

- Before getting out of bed, tighten all the muscles in your body, rest your muscles, then tighten them again—hard! Can you tighten one part of your body at a time?

Getting Ready

- While you're wringing out the washcloth, squeeze and twist it as hard as you can. What does this movement strengthen?
- After putting on your shoes, lift both your feet and legs up and down from a sitting position. How many times can you do this without stopping? Can you hold both legs in the air for 30 seconds?

Going to School

- Hold a heavy book in one hand and see how many times you can lift it up and down by bending your elbow. Try lifting the book while keeping your arm straight.

- On the bus, put your feet underneath the seat in front of you and tighten your leg muscles to make them straight and stiff.

Studying

- Hold the sides of your chair and pull as hard as you can, but don't bend your back.
- How hard can you push down on the desk with your hand and arm? Push and hold for 30 seconds.

Screen Time

- Lie on your side, and lift one leg up and down in the air. Can you do each leg for a whole commercial?
- Lie on your back with knees bent, feet flat on the floor, and arms at your sides. Tighten your abdominal muscles and raise your arms, shoulders, and head slightly off the floor. Hold that position for a couple of seconds.
- Lie on your back. Place a pillow between your knees and try to curl up in a ball so your nose touches the knees. How many times can you do this during one commercial?

Flexibility Activities

Wake-up Time

- Stretch all your body in all different directions; then wiggle like Jell-O on a plate.
- Lie on your stomach, and then reach back and grab your feet with your hands. Try to make a bowl shape with your body by raising up your chest and legs and rocking on your stomach.

Going to School

- Keep one arm straight, and swing it in a big circle from the front of your body to the back. Hold on tight to your books.
- Shake your leg each time you take a step. If you're wearing long socks, try to shake them down to your ankles. The vibration of the skin and muscles will help loosen you up.

Studying

- Hold your hands together behind your chair, keeping your arms straight. Can you feel which muscles are being stretched?
- Let your head fall to one shoulder, and then roll it around to the other shoulder. Be limp, but don't fall asleep.

In the Kitchen or Den

- Stand about 3 feet from the kitchen counter or a table. Lean toward it, holding on to the edge of the counter or table. Can you keep your legs straight and your feet flat on the floor?

Screen Time

- Sit on the floor and pull your feet up to your body with the bottoms of your feet together. Hold on to your feet; then use your elbows to push your knees to the floor. Next, try to touch your chest to your feet. What do you feel stretching this time?

Family Time

- Sit facing a partner with your legs spread apart and your feet touching your partner's feet. (If you're doing this exercise with your father or mother, your feet may touch only their ankles because their legs are much longer.) Hold hands; one partner leans back and slowly pulls the other partner so he or she is stretching. Take turns stretching your partner.

Cardiorespiratory Activities

Wake-up Time

- Before getting out of bed, lie on your back and kick your legs up in the air. Keep kicking them as fast and as long as possible, or move them in a circular motion, as if you were riding a bicycle.

Getting Ready

- Stand in front of the mirror and pretend you're boxing with yourself. How quickly can you swing and punch? How long?

Going to School

- Walk, skip, ride a bicycle, or even jog to school or the bus stop.
- If you ride in a car pool, run to the car before mom or dad gets there, and then count the number of times you can jump up and down before she or he arrives.

Family Time

- Put on some upbeat music and dance. See who can move around the most, longest, and best.

Appendix 28B: Prescriptions for Fitness

Activities/Exercises for Abdominal Strength and Endurance

Wall Push Stand with your back against a wall, your feet only a few inches from the wall. Your knees should be slightly bent, with your arms at the sides of your body. Pull in your abdomen and press your shoulders, small of back, and buttocks against the wall. Hold the position for 5 seconds.

Untimed Sit-ups Lie flat on your back with your knees bent and your arms crossed on your chest. Gradually perform sit-ups.
 Sit-up variations:

- Extend your arms forward. Shake your hands and arms as you curl up.
- Extend your arms forward. Clap your hands on the floor as you curl back to the mat.

Finger Walk Lie flat on your back with your knees bent in the sit-up position. Extend your arms at your sides. Walk your fingers forward on the mat in the direction of your feet as you tighten your stomach muscles and raise your shoulders slightly off the mat. Gently lower your shoulders to the mat and repeat.

Activities/Exercises for Upper-Body Strength and Endurance

Flexed-Arm Hang In a pull-up position, palms facing forward, chin above the bar (Figure 28.6), hold the position for 5 to 8 seconds without letting your chin touch the bar or drop below the bar. When holding for 8 seconds feels comfortable, increase the duration to 15 seconds.

Figure 28.6 Correct position for flexed-arm hang.

 The flexed-arm hang should not be held for extended periods because of the possibility of elbow injury and/or extreme muscular fatigue.

Reverse Pull-ups Hold the bar as in the flexed-arm position, chin above the bar, palms either forward or reversed. Slowly lower your weight to a hanging position by straightening your arms.

Walking Hands Assume a push-up position with your body fully extended and your hands on the floor behind a line or tape mark (Figure 28.7). Walk your hands forward and backward over the line as you count 1-2-3-4; aim for 60 counts. Variation: Time for 60 seconds.

Figure 28.7 Weight on hands improves upper-body strength.

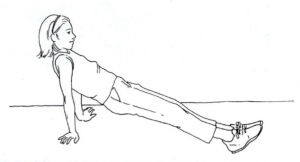

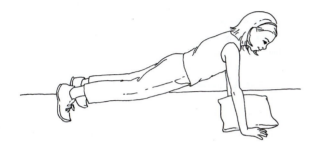

Figure 28.8 Correct position for pillow push-ups.

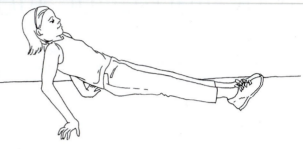

Figure 28.9 Correct position for belly-ups.

Pillow Push-ups In a push-up position (Figure 28.8), hands shoulder-width apart, fingers forward, slowly lower your body toward the floor until your chest gently touches the pillow. Straighten your arms to raise your body back to starting position. We have found that children have a fear of crashing to the floor when attempting a push-up. Placing the pillow under the chest eliminates this fear. You may begin with a modified push-up—knees bent—if you wish; when you are confident and ready, switch to the regular position—legs straight.

Belly-ups Sit on the floor with legs extended forward, arms at the side, hands flat on the floor, with your fingers pointing away from your body (Figure 28.9). Raise your hips, extending your body—straight like a board. Bend your elbows to slowly lower your body toward the floor; do not allow your buttocks to touch the floor. Return to the extended starting position by pushing your body upward. Bending the elbows to lower the body is the key to building the arm muscles.

Activities/Exercises for Shoulders, Lower Back, and Hamstring Flexibility

Trunk and Shoulder Extensions Slowly extend both your arms overhead as high as possible and hold them for 10 seconds. Gently lower arms; repeat extension.

Trunk and Shoulder Rotation With your right arm at shoulder level, look and slowly turn to your left; hold 10 seconds. Repeat the movement in the opposite direction.

Inner-Thigh Stretch Sit on the floor with your legs spread apart and extended. Slowly lean forward with one arm on each side of one leg and hold the position (Figure 28.10). Repeat the exercise on the other leg.

Lying Knee Pull Lie flat on your back with your legs extended and arms straight at your sides. Bring your left knee to your chest, grabbing under the knee with both your hands (Figure 28.11). Pull and hold your knee for 5 seconds. Repeat the exercise with your right leg. Remember, keep your extended leg straight and on the floor.

Figure 28.10 Student performing the inner-thigh stretch on the right leg.

Figure 28.11 The lying knee-pull exercise.

Teaching Educational Dance

One of the great values in the education of children comes from the experience of making their own forms to express, to communicate, to enjoy. Each child is unique in his individualism and in his environment. He needs a chance to say what he is, how he feels, what his world means to him.

—RUTH L. MURRAY

Drawn by children at Monfort, Chappelow or Shawsheen Elementary Schools, Greeley, CO.
Courtesy of Lizzy Ginger; Tia Ziegler.

Key Concepts

- Dance experiences should give children freedom in movement, confidence in their movement, and most important, an enjoyment of dance.

- Dance in elementary physical education includes both predesigned and child-designed learning experiences.

- Predesigned dance for children includes rhythmic experiences and cultural dance.

- Child-designed dance for children includes creative rhythmic experiences and creative dance.

- Rhythmic experiences for children are designed to assist them in becoming competent and confident in recognizing and moving to internal and external rhythms.

- Cultural dances can be studied in their authentic form as the cultural dances of a society, or they can be studied for their composition/component parts, leading to children's creation of new dances, thus moving from predesigned to child-designed dance.

- The focus of creative dance is performing movements to communicate an idea or message and to express feelings and emotions through movement.

D ance is as natural to young children as the air they breathe. They jump and hop; they swing and sway. They move to their internal rhythm; no music is necessary. Dance can provide enjoyment, health benefits, and opportunities for social interaction to all ages. Yet many teachers are hesitant to include dance in physical education. Somehow in the process of becoming adults, the natural love of free movement can be lost (Box 29-1). Dance allows us to reconnect to the "child within us."

None of the authors of this text were professional dancers; neither were we professional athletes nor Olympic gymnasts, and yet we have each found the skills of educational gymnastics, dance, and games/sports to all be integral components of our physical education programs. *Children Moving* is designed to provide a rich program of skills, including dance, for all children.

As discussed in Chapter 2, skill themes and movement concepts form the curricular base for elementary physical education, with educational gymnastics, dance, and games as the contexts, or settings, in which these skills and concepts are applied. The area of application, i.e., educational gymnastics, dance, or games, is

Box 29-1

The Movement Movement

When we are children, most of us can run and tumble and roll in the grass. We can yell and laugh and cry. We can sing our inner songs and dance our personal dances. Our feelings are visible in our actions. When we're unhappy, we stomp and mope. When we're happy, we turn cartwheels and splash in puddles. Our imaginations have a direct line to our arms and legs. We can take giant steps and be giants. We can flap our arms and they will fly us away over houses and mountains. We can do all of this and more, for a while.

And then, somewhere between 5 and 20, we stop.

We stop running just for the fun of it. We stop letting out the shouts and belly laughs. We stop looking at the tree-tops and start walking the city sidewalks staring at the pavement. We begin, somewhere along the line, to "keep a stiff upper lip," to put "starch" in our spines, to speak softly and when spoken to. Our behavior becomes "acceptable" and, in the process, we are cut off bit by bit from ourselves and therefore from each other. If my impulses can't get through to me, how can I possibly share them with you? As we lose touch with our bodies, our heads take over and begin to monitor our actions, to restrict our responses until the simple interaction of children becomes an elaborate and inaccurate communication system between brain A and brain B.

Jules Feiffer pictures one of these disconnected, clever heads floating around complaining about its headless, funny-looking, malfunctioning body. "It's lucky," Feiffer's head says, "that I need my body to carry my head around . . . otherwise . . . out it would go."

Too drastic.

We can fit our heads back onto our bodies. We can rediscover the links between the headbone and the toebones. We can regain the freedom to spread our arms out wide; to run and shout without feeling awkward or embarrassed. We can learn to fall down, jump up, and bend over without breaking. We can unlock the sounds of our sadness and our joy. We can tune in to the beat of our pulse and stamp our feet to our inborn sense of rhythm. We can explore the sounds and the gestures of our feelings and our dreams. We can reclaim our bodies and our voices; free them to rediscover our inherent sense of balance and design, and use them to show each other who we are and what we hope to be.

Source: Ken Jenkins, The movement movement, *California Living: The Magazine of the San Francisco Sunday Examiner and Chronicle*, January 25, 1976, 19. Used with permission.

selected by the teacher after the skills are initially taught in isolation and then combined with other skills and movement concepts (see Figure 2.3, page 27).

This chapter is designed to provide the guidelines for application of these skill themes and movement concepts into educational dance. See Box 29-2 for information on dance in the *National Standards & Grade-Level Outcomes for K–12 Physical Education* (SHAPE America 2014) in the elementary school.

The Purpose of Dance in Elementary School

One key to providing children with successful dance experiences is to develop an understanding of dance and its purpose in an educational program. Dance experiences in physical education classes are designed to provide children with:

- An introduction to using their bodies and imaginations to express feelings
- The ability to interpret and move to different rhythms
- Enjoyment and appreciation of dance
- Another avenue to develop fundamental movement skills and apply movement concepts
- An opportunity to use higher order, critical thinking skills

We have all seen the video clips where a toddler hears music and starts moving. A few years later when the child enters school, he or she will most likely still be in tune with his or her body as an instrument of expression. Young children appear to love moving to music. Weikert (2006) states that rhythmical qualities are not innate; yet, they can be nurtured and developed through a variety of dance experiences. Sue Stinson (1988) referred to it as rediscovering the magic deep inside and using the magic to transform movement into dance. The reverse can happen without dance opportunities. By including dance in our curriculums, we are able to help children develop or maintain an awareness of their bodies as instruments for the expression of feelings and ideas. Dance for many children is their sport; they excel in its creation and performance, "for enjoyment, self-expression, and/or social interaction" (SHAPE America 2014).

The Content of Dance

The movement framework, depicting the interaction of skill themes and movement concepts (Chapter 3), is used as the foundation for dance experiences for children. The locomotor skills within the skill theme of traveling (walking, sliding, hopping, skipping, leaping, and galloping); the nonmanipulative skills of balancing, transferring weight, jumping, and landing; and the actions of stretching, curling, bending, twisting, and turning are all used in dance (Chapters 17 and 19–22). All of the movement concepts (Chapters 14–16) are used to enhance the child's ability to move in a variety of dance experiences. Dance experiences for children can be classified into two types: predesigned and child-designed.

Box 29-2

Dance in the *National Standards and Grade-level Outcomes for K–12 Physical Education*

Dance is referenced in the *National Standards & Grade-Level Outcomes for K–12 Physical Education* (SHAPE America 2014) with grade-level outcomes for Standards 1, 2, and 5. Sample grade-level outcomes* include:

- Performs locomotor skills in response to teacher-led creative dance (K)
- Combines locomotor and nonlocomotor skills in a teacher-designed dance (1)
- Performs a teacher- and/or student-designed rhythmic activity with correct response to simple rhythms (2)

- Performs teacher-selected and developmentally appropriate dance steps and movement patterns (3)
- Combines locomotor movement patterns and dance steps to create and perform an original dance (4)
- Combines locomotor skills in cultural as well as creative dances with correct rhythm and pattern (5)
- Analyzes movement situations and applies concepts (e.g., force, direction, speed, pathways, extensions) in dance (5)
- Expresses via creative dance the enjoyment and/or challenge of participating in a favorite physical activity (5)

*Suggested grade-level outcomes for student learning.

Predesigned Dance Experiences

Predesigned dance experiences include rhythmic experiences and cultural dances (e.g., folk, ethnic, square, line, hip-hop) in which the composition of the dance is set or the teacher modifies the rhythmic experience or dance. Rhythmical experiences provide opportunities for students to move to different rhythms and develop beat competence. Collaboration with the music teacher will greatly enhance the development of beat competence in children. In cultural dances, children are taught dances that are part of a society's heritage. Many of these dances have been taught for years and passed on from generation to generation. Others are currently being developed. The teaching of cultural dances may be coordinated with social studies units in the classroom—for example, the culture of Greece or the pioneer period of American history (Chapter 32).

Rhythmic Experiences Rhythmic experiences for children are designed to assist them in becoming competent and confident in recognizing and moving to rhythm. Rhythm is defined as a strong, regular repeated pattern of movement or sound that includes beat and tempo. Rhythm is part of everyday movement. Young children walk, skip, and gallop to their internal rhythm; they later respond to the beat and the tempo of an external rhythm. Early rhythmic experiences in physical education are chosen to build upon the natural rhythms of children and to reinforce the movement concepts and themes the children are already studying. For example, after experiencing the locomotor movements freely at their own tempo, children may be asked to walk three beats in one direction and change directions on the fourth beat. In this combination of skill (walking) and movement concept (direction), children are now matching the tempo of their movements to that imposed by the external beat.

Children may echo the beat by moving body parts or swinging the total body at fast or slow tempo to match a teacher's count. Moving body parts in self-space in accompaniment to a beat enhances children's rhythm awareness and beat competence. Once children are able to move to an external beat imposed by the teacher's voice or a simple instrument (e.g., a drum, shaker, clacker; Figure 29.1), music may be introduced. The music should have a steady beat; although it provides the beat for the movements, it should accompany, not dominate, the children's movements. The learning experience Traveling with Music (Chapter 17, page 309) is a good example of how children can explore even and uneven rhythms using locomotor skills.

As children grasp the basic concepts of rhythm and are able to respond correctly to different beats, they enjoy the addition of a manipulative to the rhythmic experiences. Streamers, scarves, cardboard pizza circles, rhythm sticks, and playground balls are examples

The teacher challenges a class to rhythmic movement at a high level.

©Barbara Adamcik

DRUMS

Tin can drum

Remove the top and bottom on any size tin can. Cut two circles, about an inch larger in diameter than the tin can, from an inner tube. Punch about six small holes around the edge of each rubber circle. Place one circle over each end of the can. Tighten by lacing strong string or nylon cord through the holes. Bells or bottle caps may be added for additional sound.

Bleach (or milk) jug drum

Screw top of jug and secure with tape or glue. Hit with dowel rod. The children can decorate the jug with paint or colored tape.

SHAKERS

Tube shaker

Cover one end of an empty paper towel tube with heavy paper or aluminum foil. Fill with small round stones or dried beans. Then cover the other end. The children can decorate the shaker.

Pie pan shaker

Place small round stones or dried beans in an aluminum pie pan. Staple another pie pan of the same diameter onto the top of the first pan.

Balloon shaker

Pour sand, rice, beans, or a combination of these ingredients into a balloon. Partially inflate the balloon and tie the end.

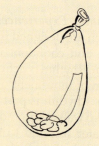

CLACKER

Cut two pieces of board to the same size. Drill holes in one end of each board and join the boards with nylon cord or wire. The children can decorate the boards.

Cup shaker

Partially fill a paper or plastic cup with small stones, beans, or bottle caps. Tape another cup on top of the filled cup.

---

of equipment that we have discovered enhances rhythmic experiences for children. Initial activities focus on individual exploration and responses to rhythm. Following this exploration phase, teacher-designed routines are used to elicit a group response to a given rhythm. These experiences are designed to involve the children in working together with partners or in a small group, responding correctly to the rhythm (suggested 4/4 beat), and memorizing a sequence of movements and/or actions to be performed.

Examples of teacher-designed rhythmic routines (rhythm/Lummi sticks, Chinese ribbons/streamers, and jump ropes) can be found in Appendix 29A at the end of this chapter; a group routine for ball gymnastics can be found in *Lesson Planning for Elementary Physical Education* (Holt/Hale and Hall 2016). Rhythmic group routines are excellent for promoting physical education at assemblies, parent–teacher association/organization (PTA/PTO) programs, and community functions (see Chapter 33).

Cultural Dance Experiences Cultural dances (e.g., ethnic, folk, square, line, and hip-hop) are just that— the cultural dances of a society, the heritage of a people, the representation of the diversity in a school community. Cultural dances range from simple to very complex; some are designed for partner and group formation, while others have a focus on individual creativity. These dances involve a series of actions with one or more of the following: a stated progression, verses and a chorus, locomotor and nonmanipulative actions, formations, changes in directions, right and left discrimination, and a range of rhythmic and musical selection.

Cultural dance in its authentic form is introduced only when children are competent and comfortable with the locomotor skills, movement patterns, and movement concepts (pathways, directions, time, etc.) of the dance. When upper-elementary children have acquired competence in rhythm and the specific dance movements, they are ready to learn formations for dances, moving to musical phrases, and repetition of movement patterns. They're able to analyze cultural dances according to spatial awareness, effort qualities, and relationships.

When children participate in cultural dance as an integrated study of a culture, the dances are performed in their traditional form with attention to maintaining the authenticity of the dance. This is also true when cultural dances are performed for a PTA/PTO program or school assembly for parents and community. The dance is representative of the culture and, as such, is often demonstrated with children in the costumes of that culture. The focus is a demonstration of the enjoyment of dance from different cultures and dance as part of the heritage of the people.

When we have children participate in cultural dances as a study in dance form, we approach them differently. As teachers, we may change the formation of the dance from circle to line or scattered. We may change the way partners are selected or do the dance without partners. We may change the travel patterns or actions of the dance. We may combine components of different dances or combine types of dances. These dances, although altered by the teacher, still have set travel patterns and actions, repetition of sequences, and correct responses to rhythm. The teacher adaptations allow for success and developmentally appropriate experiences. The focus is the study of dance, the enjoyment of participation in dance, the feeling of success, and the freedom of movement and confidence in that movement. Box 29-3 includes a variety of appropriate cultural dances for children that can be altered or taught in their existing form.

With the richness of diversity increasing in our schools (Chapter 10), it is important that we as teachers recognize the diversity within our classes, the wealth of dances the children bring to us, and the appreciation for dance and cultures that can be gained by learning from each other. Dance provides the

Box 29-3

Traditional Cultural Dances

Here are some examples of beginning and intermediate cultural dances appropriate for elementary school-age children with no previous dance experience:

Beginning Dances

Seven Jumps (Denmark)
Chimes of Dunkirk (Belgian)
Jump Jim Joe (United States)
Kinderpolka (Germany)
Cshebogar (Hungary)
Shoemaker's Dance (Denmark)
Patti Cake Polka (United States)

Intermediate Dances

Greensleeves (England)
Teton Mountain Stomp (United States)
Virginia Reel (United States)
Gustav's Skol (Sweden)
Kavelis (Lithuania)
LaRaspa (Mexico)
Troika (Russia)
Mayim! Mayim! (Israel)
Funga African Dance (West Africa)
Irish Stew (Ireland)
D'Hammerschmieds G'Sellin (Germany)
Jamaican Holiday (Jamaica)
Scattered Square Dance (United States)

platform to learn about one's own culture, maintain a cultural connection, or learn about different cultures (Ward 2007).

Child-Designed Dance Experiences

Child-designed dance experiences are invented or created by the children. We divide them into creative rhythmic experiences and creative dance. In creative rhythmic experiences, children develop an awareness of rhythm and the ability to move in a variety of ways in relation to various beats. Predesigned rhythmic experiences call for a specific response; in child-designed experiences, there are multiple responses. In creative dance, children express feelings and ideas through movement. Whereas predesigned dances call

These youngsters enjoy matching rhythms.

©Lars A. Niki

one's own rhythm with creative expression. For early creative rhythmic experiences, we are not concerned with the rhythmical accuracy of the movement. There is no incorrect response; each child moves to his or her internal rhythm. When first introduced to rhythmic and dance experiences, many children are concerned that their response will be incorrect, that their movement does not match the beat imposed by the rhythm instrument or the music; thus, they are hesitant to participate in the dance experience. Our goal is for each youngster to be comfortable when exploring rhythms in physical education.

When children are comfortable exploring rhythm, they are then introduced to the timing of the movement, the beat of the instrument or music. Following the exploration of rhythm and teacher-designed rhythmic experiences, we progress to the child-designed rhythmic experiences involving children alone, with a partner, or in a group, designing routines with rhythmical accompaniment; this accompaniment may be in the form of the human voice/rapping, hand jive (a pattern of hand moves and claps at various parts of the body), rhythm instruments, or music. The rhythmical routine may be without accompaniment, such as a ball dribbling or jump rope routines (see Appendix 29A for rhythmical learning experiences).

Children in the upper-elementary grades focus on creating new rhythm routines (e.g., rhythm sticks, clap, or stomp), designing individual and partner jump rope or jump band routines (see Chapter 17, page 319), and using ball-handling skills in routines to music, like the learning experience Child-Designed Dribbling/Passing Routines (Chapter 25, page 533). Children transition

for a correct response, there are multiple answers in creative dance. Children are asked to provide interpretations or responses to a particular problem or situation (see guided discovery in Chapter 9). Individual responses are encouraged; diversity is valued.

Creative Rhythmic Experiences   The content of creative rhythmic experiences centers around moving to

For these partners, jumping rope becomes a creative rhythmic experience.

©Barbara Adamcik

Table 29.1 Overview of the Content and Rationale of Teaching Creative Dance to Children

We Want Children to Acquire:	By Learning a Movement Vocabulary of:	That Can Be Used to Express Emotions and Thoughts Such As:	Stimulated by Catalysts Such As:
An ability to use their bodies as a means of expression	Movement concepts	Friendship	Sounds
The sense of self-satisfaction that can be derived through expressive movement	Space awareness	Warmth	Music
	Effort	Anger	Poetry
	Relationships	Unhappiness	Art
An enjoyment and appreciation of dance	Skill themes	Peace	History
	Locomotor	Hostility	Movies
An ability to interpret and move to different rhythms	Nonmanipulative	Joy	Personal experiences
		Satisfaction	
		Harmony	

Source: Adapted from K. R. Barrett, Educational dance, *Physical education for children: A focus on the teaching process,* ed. B. Logsdon, K. Barrett, M. Ammons, M. Broer, L. Halverson, R. McGee, and M. Roberton (Philadelphia: Lea & Febiger, 1984).

from predesigned to child-designed rhythm experiences as they create new routines. They combine various movement qualities and patterns with their manipulative skills—for example, floor patterns, directions, levels, phrases, and variations in rhythm, such as double time, half time, and so on.

Rapping

One of the earliest forms of rhythmic accompaniment for young children is their own voices. Observe preschoolers at play, and you will hear them talking and singing as they move. The popular pastime of rapping is a rhythmic expression of voice and actions. Its popularity is confirmed with a quick browse of YouTube. Children should be encouraged to use the human voice to accompany their rhythmic and expressive dance experiences as appropriate.

Creative Dance Experiences The focus in creative dance is not on executing a particular movement; it is communicating through movement. The beauty of a child creating a dance is that although the child is not concerned with a particular movement, he or she is also not concerned with controlling an object or working with another person. The focus is on self and the movement. The resulting body awareness and control of movement transfer to gymnastics, games, sports, and everyday play.

As in predesigned dance experiences, locomotor and nonmanipulative movements are the foundational skills of creative dance. A functional understanding of the movement concepts is essential for creative dance experiences. The movement concept of effort (Chapter 15) has numerous creative movement experiences designed to teach students the concepts of time, force, and flow (see Box 15-4 and Following Flow

Sentences in Chapter 15, page 270). Virtually all of the movement concepts can be used to heighten and expand the child's ability to express feeling and emotion through movement (see Table 29.1).

Teachers must guide students into the quality movements that will be used in more complex creative dance experiences. For example, children are initially exposed to turning actions combined with the concept of time: slow, hesitant turns or fast, sudden turns are two possibilities. Eventually these qualities of turning can be used to express inner feelings. Slow, hesitant turns might be used to depict sadness or uncertainty; sudden, quick turns could be used to express anger, frustration, or perhaps joy. Turning, by itself, communicates little. It's the quality of the turn that communicates a message, just as it's the quality of any movement that gives it expression.

Creative dance at the precontrol level includes learning experiences encouraging the child to explore and experiment with both imagination and movements. At the control level, the movements appear to be understood and intentional in design. At this level, dance movements become more abstract as children respond to images, to poetry, and to stories. The Neighborhood Friendship Dance (Appendix 29C) is an example of a control-level creative dance guided by the teacher. In the dance, the teacher uses life experiences familiar to the children and guides them to create and cultivate combinations of locomotor and nonmanipulative skills and movement concepts as a story is told. Later, students are guided to the culminating dance.

Creative dance for the utilization and proficiency levels increases in complexity as children design and choreograph the dance from beginning to ending pose. At these levels, children are ready to combine locomotor skills with movement concepts in complex patterns and actions to express ideas, portray emotions, contrast ideas, and interpret their own writings and poems. When children fully transition into creative dance, they will be able to design, (choreograph) a dance. Creative dance for proficiency level may also include studying a dance in its original form and then using the components of the predesigned dance to create or design a new dance.

The Teaching of Predesigned and Child-Designed Dance

Teaching Predesigned Rhythms

Rhythmical experiences for children include sequences of movement in which children move to their internal rhythm and routines in which children move to an external rhythm. When children first experience rhythm in physical education, the teacher provides the feedback for each child to establish comfort in moving, without being overly concerned about the beat of the movement. As children progress into experiences with external rhythms, the teacher's role becomes that of helping each child respond correctly to a given beat. We have found that a steady beat with a 4/4 rhythm is the easiest for children to grasp; this now becomes the external rhythm established by the teacher. As children respond with hand or thigh claps, snaps, stomps, and so forth, they begin to attain competence in the beat and are ready to add locomotor and manipulative movements to match the beat.

Predesigned routines with Lummi sticks, Chinese ribbons/streamers, jump ropes and parachutes are provided in Appendix 29A. Performing Rhythmical Patterns: Jump Bands/Aerobic Tinikling can be found in Chapter 17, page 319.

In predesigned rhythmical experiences, all of these decisions are made by the teacher as he or she composes the routine. The routine is practiced in parts and then as a total when children have mastered all of the components. The rhythmical accompaniment is selected by the teacher, e.g., music, percussion, human body. Instruction may be first to the class as a whole, followed by practice of components individually and/or at stations, and then large group practice for the total routine. Even though the routine is teacher designed, intratask variation will provide competence for each child at his or her skill level. Teacher observation and individual feedback with encouragement are critical to predesigned group experiences in rhythms.

Teaching Predesigned Cultural Dance

Before learning structured (predesigned) dance forms, children need experiences in locomotor movements and responses to rhythm. They need a functional understanding of the movement concepts as well as the actions of bending, stretching, curling, and twisting. Children are first guided to explore specific predesigned dance movements in self space before they are asked to move within the set formations of circles, squares, or lines.

The following guidelines may be beneficial when introducing students to predesigned dances.

- Choose developmentally appropriate dances or modify the dance. Choose dances:
  - that do not specify the use of the right or left foot.
  - that can be easily modified for beginners (e.g., fewer steps to remember).
  - that do not require younger children to do complex footwork, rhythms, or changes in direction.
  - with a repetition of sequences; sequences should be short and uncomplicated.
  - that initially require neither partners nor holding hands.
- Show a video of the dance (many can be found on YouTube) or demonstrate the dance in its entirety (see Box 29-3 for appropriate examples).
- Allow the students to hear the music and establish the rhythm (clap hands, clap thighs, stomp, snap, etc.).
  - Select music with a strong underlying beat; the musical phrases should be distinct and in groupings of 8 or 16 beats, with no resting beats.
  - Younger children need a slower tempo (less than 120 beats per minute).
  - Make sure you use the music during practice (e.g., practice part of the dance without music; practice it with music, and then practice the next part without music; then, with music; continue).
- Teach the steps in personal space or general space first. Add partners or formations when students demonstrate competency.
  - Single circles are less complex than double circles.

Technology and Dance

There are a multitude of electronic gaming devices (e.g., XBox, PlayStation, Wii, Nintendo, SEGA, Dance Dance Revolution) with "dance" applications. These programs provide an exciting venue for children to refine and apply the skill themes associated with dance (and fitness) in after- or before-school programs, during in-school activity breaks, or at home.

Dance experiences provide movement and joy for children.

©Lars A. Niki

- Use "windows." With line formation make sure each row can see the teacher rather than be positioned directly behind other students.
- Use clear cues and demonstrations to help students learn the steps.
  - Use both mirroring and matching techniques.
  - Call the cues in advance. (e.g., on count 7 of the eight-count grapevine step, announce the next step of "heel-toe").
- Teach the dance in the tempo in which it will be performed.
- If the dance is in parts, teach in a progression: Part A, B, A + B, C, A + B + C.
- Spend extra time on combination and transitional moves; they are typically the most complex.
- Repetition is critical for memorization.

Teaching Child-Designed Rhythms

In the early stage of children experiencing rhythms, predesigned and child-designed rhythmical movements merge. As mentioned earlier, once children are confident in moving to their internal rhythms, the teacher introduces external rhythm. The response of the child is to the beat imposed by the teacher verbally, with instruments or with music. As was true for predesigned rhythms, a steady beat with a 4/4 rhythm is the easiest for children to grasp with confidence and competence.

The following examples may assist you in teaching child-designed rhythmical experiences. A simple teacher prompt (fill in the blank) allows for creative movement at the precontrol level to the teacher-imposed beat:

_____ to the beat.

- Move your hand only (elbow, foot, head, etc.)
- Stretch (twist, bend, curl)
- March in place (hop, jump)
- Walk and move arms in general space (gallop, skip, slide)

A good way for children to explore rhythm while adding creativity at the control level is through the use of rhythmical movement sequences. The following example involves the teacher using a drum or other musical accompaniment to do continual 4/4 counts. Each movement in the sequence is done for four counts. *Walk, Turn, Stretch Wide, Freeze, Collapse to the Floor, Rise.* Repeat all of the above in the same order until memorized.

The creative rhythmical challenge continues as the teacher asks the students to repeat the above sequence with any or all of the following movement concepts:

- Slow motion
- Fast motion
- Large movements
- Small movements
- Light force
- Strong force
- Bound, jerky
- Free and flowing, graceful

Students can move to their internal rhythm, or the teacher may play music.

Children at the utilization and proficiency levels are asked to choreograph their own rhythmical movement sequence after reviewing a sequence similar to the above. The students are instructed to include one shape, one locomotor skill, one nonmanipulative movement, some type of turn, and one change of levels. We have found the teacher establishing the beat and the number of sequences/phrases to be included in the routine provides the framework within which children best design their rhythmical routines. After creating and writing their routines, each student is paired with another student. They then teach each other their sequences. Finally, they combine the two for an ABAB choreography to perform for another group.

As is true with gymnastics sequences and original games, children will need guidance in the transition from predesigned/teacher-directed to child-designed dance experiences. As in the movement sequence specified earlier, we provide a template for the learning experience. This is also true for child-designed rhythmical routines with hands (hand jive) or manipulatives (e.g., balls, Lummi sticks, jump ropes, jump bands). The teacher may include the following components, with variations from predesigned routines:

- Beat—4/4 rhythm, eight-count sequences
- Group composition—alone, partner, group of no more than six
- Formation—side by side, mirroring, etc. (Chapter 15)
- Skills—locomotor, manipulative

While the components of the routine are the same as those of predesigned rhythms, responsibility shifts from the teacher to the child, as the student makes decisions regarding group, formation, and skills. The posting of teacher and student requirements on a whiteboard or chart frees the teacher for feedback, refinement, and student questions.

One of the most difficult parts of child-designed rhythmic experiences is the time factor—that is, the matching of the length of the routine to the length of the music. Children often need guidance in choosing whether to add skills, repeat phrases, or repeat the entire routine.

Teaching Creative Dance

Teaching creative dance is different from teaching predesigned structured dance. Predesigned dance movements are performed correctly or incorrectly, and the teacher's task is to guide the child toward an appropriate execution. Dance movements performed to express an idea or emotion are more difficult to define clearly, and so the teacher's task is different. Guided discovery or teaching through questioning is the most effective instructional approach for creative dance (Chapter 9).

Because the child is trying to express a feeling or an idea, observation and feedback are also more complex. In games and gymnastics, the purpose of a movement is obvious; this isn't true in creative dance. However, the purpose or goal of each creative dance experience must by identified by the teacher and communicated to the students. During the lesson, the teacher encourages, expands, and embellishes the responses rather than correcting or refining. The intent typically begins with exploration and then must advance to an understanding of the expression and control of the movement. Finally, the students must be guided to put the movement in a completed form.

Early experiences in creative dance may be as simple as shapes and actions guided by the teacher into sequences to express the child's interpretation of the dance stem. These early experiences may center around single words that elicit the movement creativity or a story read or spoken by the teacher to which the children respond. Numerous action words that illicit a variety of creative movements can be found in Chapter 15 (Box 15-4). In the Dance of Colors (Holt/Hale and Hall 2016), young children will respond to the color red with the shapes and actions of playground balls that bounce, fire engines that move very quickly, etc. Young children are still very much in the concrete stage of child development; their dances reflect that developmental stage. The teaching of creative dance at the precontrol level will focus heavily on open-ended questions and "Show me" statements that provide and promote each child's interpretation. Machines, flowers, and snowflakes come to life as young children

©Barbara Adamcik

Youngsters explore the expressive possibilities of partner formation.

Box 29-4

Expressive and Communicative Activities

Time

- Travel or gesture in slow motion.
- Travel to an externally imposed beat or rhythmic pattern, such as a handclap or drumbeat.
- Rise and sink suddenly or slowly.

Flow

- Combine two travel skills, such as running and leaping, always moving smoothly.
- Display hesitant, jerky, mechanical flow to create the illusion of being a robot.
- Feel and observe the differences in combining a step with a turn, first with smooth, continuous flow, then with pauses (stillnesses) interspersed between each step and turn.

Force

- Travel or perform nonlocomotor actions to a strong beat.
- Travel or perform nonlocomotor actions to light, gentle, delicate music.
- Freeze in a strong, dramatic pose.

Relationships

- Experience the sensation of matching, mirroring, or shadowing the movements of a partner.
- Explore the expressive possibilities of group formations—for example, sculpture for the city park, or a mountain range.
- Experience the feeling of contrasting the movements of a partner—for example, as one partner rises the other sinks, or one partner travels in a geometric path (square) while the other travels in a random path.

respond to the teacher's lead. Numerous creative dance ideas can be found in Chapter 17 ("Traveling").

At the control level, we begin to clarify for children the expressive and communicative aspects of movement. As children enter the abstract stage of child development, this focus of their creative dance now centers more on the effort and relationship concepts (Chapters 15 and 16). Box 29-4 provides examples for how the effort and relationship concepts are used for creative dance. Through these concepts, movement is explored as a tool for expressing an idea, attitude, or feeling. Movement is no longer studied primarily as an entity in and of itself; it's viewed as a medium of expression. In the earlier example of the Dance of Colors, the children's interpretation now becomes abstract; red may be interpreted as a range of emotions from compassion to anger.

Children at the utilization level have learned to efficiently perform the movements studied at the control level and to modify the movements to meet the intent of the dance. The teacher focus for feedback is on refinement of the movement concepts to enhance the aesthetic quality of the dance. At this level, we guide children as they begin to structure their communicative movements into choreographed dances (see Traveling to Tell a Story: The Fountain of Youth Dance in Chapter 17, page 317).

Dance making is the focus at the proficiency level. When children reach this level of creative dance, they have progressed from teacher designed dance, to the sharing of decisions with the teacher's guidance, to complete ownership of the choreography of the dance. Choreographed dances include all of the following components from theme selection to concluding statement:

1. Selection of the purpose, idea, or theme of a dance
2. Identification of appropriate movements and movement concepts to express the intended idea, feeling, or theme
3. Design of a powerful opening statement for the dance
4. Design of a series of actions rising to a climax
5. Design of the portion of the dance that is to be the climax or peak of the action
6. Design of the concluding statement of the dance

Traveling with Shapes and Actions: A Story Without Words (Chapter 17, page 318), Body Shapes and Group Travel: A Study in Form (Chapter 17, page 318), and Freedom (Appendix 29B) are examples of child-designed dances in which students are responsible for the design and the choreography of the dance in its entirety.

- *A Story Without Words* tells the story of primitive tribes. Children are introduced to primitive living through pictures. They are prompted to create through movement the life of two different tribes. The story is developed from the life of the tribes to the conflict between the tribes.

- *A Study in Form* is an example of a creative dance designed to portray emotions. It is an abstract dance contrasting tradition with the forces of change. One group arranges itself as a solid square facing in one direction. Symmetrical movements prevail; actions are firm and sustained. The other group is scattered widely, facing in random directions. Nonsymmetrical movements, free use of space, and variety are used.
- *Freedom* is an expressive dance based on the theme of freedom and the journey of a people to freedom. The story of Rosa Parks and her refusal to ride in the "back of the bus" led children to create a dance portraying the struggles of African Americans during slavery, their freedom from slavery, the struggles after emancipation, and their strengths as individuals and as a people united.

The transition from teacher-designed to child-designed creative dance does not happen automatically. This dance-making process occurs somewhere on a continuum between teacher input and student creativity with the idea to progress toward increasing student independence. The Spaghetti Dance (Appendix 29C) is a fun and simple learning experience with decisions shared by the teacher and students; it can be used to illustrate this transition. The teacher's decisions include the movement concepts of shapes, levels, and pathways combined with travel. The children are responsible for adding variety to their unique movement; thus, the teacher and the children work together to create the Spaghetti Dance.

The Homework Machine (Appendix 29C) illustrates decisions placed on the students as well as a collaborative group expectation.

The teaching of dance can be a very fulfilling experience for both teacher and students; it can also be overwhelming for teachers without a strong background in dance. We have found the following suggestions to be helpful when teaching dance to children.

Use Books or Stories

Children's literature can be an excellent stimulus for creative dance. Young children enjoy the interpretation of a story that you as the teacher create or read to them. The movements are in response to pictures and stories generated by words, e.g., snowflakes, flowers, animals in motion. Quality creative dance experiences go beyond simply reading the story and having children imitate the movements. For example, if the story is about a lion, the students will begin moving on

---

Box 29-5

Suggested Literature for Creative Dance

The following are excellent examples of the many books available for young children's experiences in creative dance:

Appelt, K. *Bats Around the Clock*. 2000. New York: Scholastic.

Appelt, K. *Elephants Aloft*. 1997. New York: Houghton Mifflin.

Bond, F. *Tumble Bumble*. 1997. Cambridge, MA: Barefoot Books.

Carle, E. *From Head to Toe*. 1997. New York: HarperCollins.

Carle, E. *The Tiny Seed*. 1987. Natick, MA: Picture Book Studio.

Fleming, D. *In the Small, Small Pond*. 1993. New York: Henry Holt.

Fleming, D. *Where Once There was a Wood*. 2000 New York: Square Fish.

Fox, M. *Straight Line Wonder*. 1996. New York: Mondo.

Lionni, L. *Swimmy*. 1963. New York: Pantheon.

Marzollo, J. *Pretend You're a Cat*. 1990. New York: Scholastic.

Pandell, K. *Animal Action*. 1996. New York: Scholastic.

Ryder, J. *Night Gliders*. 1996. Mahwah, NJ: Bridgewater Books/Troll Communications.

Steinberg, D. *The Turkey Ball*. 2005. New York: Penguin Young Readers Group.

Tankard, J. *Grumpy Bird*. 2007. New York: Scholastic.

Walsh, E. S. *Hop Jump*. 1993. San Diego: Harcourt Brace.

---

hands and feet. They may begin to roar. Despite the simplicity of this concept, there are many possibilities the students can explore. Questioning should elicit different shapes, levels, and directions (e.g., Can you make the lion stretch, twist, and pounce? How would that lion look at a high level? Can the lion move backward?) as well as actions such as on the prowl, attacking prey, and sleeping. Help the students go deeper into the movement until the movement becomes their own interpretation (Joyce 1994). The dance becomes the feeling of the animal rather than an imitation. See Box 29-5 for examples of books that serve as excellent creative dance stimulus for young children.

Use Imagery

Imagery is the use of a creative stimulus as a catalyst for movement. Many people believe, inaccurately, that imagery provides the content of dance. The content of creative dance is movement; imagery is a helper. Asking children to use imagery as the content of creative dance is similar to asking children to write a story when they have a vocabulary of only 50 words. One or two extraordinarily intelligent pupils might do well. Most, however, would fail miserably because they hadn't yet acquired the tools needed for successful story writing.

The same principle can be applied to creative dance. Children must be provided with the tools of dance—the ability to use a variety of movements effectively. Only when children have developed these skills can they successfully combine the movements into dances that express what they want to communicate. Movement vocabularies, however, aren't acquired through imagery, as the following example illustrates.

A teacher focusing on the concept of slow, heavy movement may ask children to travel as if the floor were coated with six inches of peanut butter. Using the peanut butter image without first teaching the concept of slow and heavy travel is of little value. Children who are adept at such movements at the beginning of the class will remain adept. Those individuals who were unable to travel slowly and heavily might move in the desired manner when stimulated by the image of a peanut butter floor, but they will not have acquired a functional understanding of slow, heavy movement as a concept that can be transferred to other movement situations. (See Chapter 15, page 268, for an array of imagery examples in the learning experience called Showing Contrasts of Force.) In short, imagery can be useful to reinforce certain movements, but imagery by itself doesn't enhance the quality of children's expressive movement.

Begin Gradually

The class's first experiences with creative dance need not last for an entire class session. A few minutes at the beginning or end of a class are often sufficient to introduce creative movement concepts—and simultaneously build your confidence as a teacher of creative dance. A short creative dance activity at the beginning of class can serve as a review of a concept related to the skill theme for the day—for example, twisting and turning actions as if doing a Karate Dance before their use in the skill theme of balance. A short creative dance activity at the conclusion of an active lesson can also be effective. While the children lie on the floor, eyes closed, ask them to move only their fingers (toes, arms, legs, elbows) to the music. Short segments of lively music are most effective. The children, whose eyes are closed, are less inhibited; the teacher, whose eyes are open, sees the creative dance potential of the young child.

Start with a Cooperative Class

If you are unsure of yourself when first teaching dance, select a class that is generally cooperative as the first one to which you'll teach creative dance. While we want all children to experience dance, it is always a good idea to try something that is new to you with just one class. Select a cooperative class and try a fun-filled dance such as the Spaghetti Dance (Appendix 29C). This first experience in teaching creative dance may well give you the confidence you need, especially when you observe the movements uninhibited young children can do and the joy in their expressions.

Start with Exciting Movement Experiences

Fast, vigorous, large movements are attractive and appealing to young children. A lesson that focuses on running, leaping into the air, landing, and rolling evokes the exuberance associated with speed and flight. Gradually the teacher can begin to focus on the quality of the leaps, the effectiveness of the landings, and the use of gestures while in flight.

Dance to the Music

One of the most devastating experiences for poorly skilled or less confident children occurs when a teacher plays some music and simply says, "Today is a dance lesson. Go ahead and dance anyway you would like to the music." This can be a terrifying task for youngsters with no background or confidence in creative movement and no vocabulary of functional movements. The challenge "Move to the music" is only appropriate when children have created movements and are ready to apply them to music.

Hesitant Learners

When it comes to dance, some older students may be reluctant to participate. The following may be helpful for encouraging these students:

- Be enthusiastic. A student's attitude can be influenced by your attitude.
- Provide a positive "try again" atmosphere in predesigned dance while acknowledging their effort.
- In child-designed dance, remember that creativity is encouraged; preconceived notions of a teacher may limit the creative aspect.
- Ask students to journal about their dance experiences. The *telling* may be different when not in the presence of a peer.
- Start with dances you are confident the children will enjoy and can learn easily. When their confidence increases, so too can the complexity of the dance experiences.

Final Thoughts

Dance and Fitness

Once children have learned a predesigned dance, they can perform the dance for the full length of the music. Most predesigned dances last two to four minutes and are highly aerobic. These dances can then be used for warm-ups, as instant activity, or shared with the classroom teacher to use for activity breaks during the day. Dance goes beyond cardiorespiratory endurance; the movements of dance contribute to the development of balance, strength, and flexibility.

Dance and the Affective Domain

Dance and rhythmic activities provide a rich environment for fostering positive social interaction and respect for differences among people. As youngsters actively participate in dances from different cultures, they expand their understanding of others and broaden their cultural world. As they cooperate in creating dance sequences and rhythmic routines, they develop cooperative skills and respect for others. Responsible social behavior, understanding and respect for others, and positive social interaction are important for all children (SHAPE America 2014).

Creative dance can be an avenue for a child to gain self-understanding and personal values. Through exploring ideas, feelings, and emotions and then sharing them with others, creative dance learning experiences help develop imaginations, creative thinking, and self-esteem. In a world where many children are experiencing troublesome lives, creative dance may well be an opportunity to help them release emotions and cope in their world. Our goal in dance and rhythms is the same as it is in all areas of physical education: to assist each and every child in developing the skills, the confidence, and the enjoyment for a lifetime of participation in this rich movement environment.

Summary

Dance for children in our programs of physical education includes both predesigned and child-designed experiences. Predesigned dance centers on rhythmic experiences and cultural dance. In predesigned rhythmic experiences, children learn the rhythm and the timing of movements to match rhythms; these range from movement responses with hands and feet, to responses with manipulatives (e.g., rhythms sticks and jump ropes), to routines designed for display of children's learning of rhythm and movement. Cultural dances (folk, ethnic, square, line, or hip-hop) are part of a society's heritage. Many of these dances have been taught for years and passed on from generation to generation. A new one is most likely being created today.

Child-designed dance centers on creative rhythmic experiences and creative dance. The focus is on children creating the rhythmic routine—the dance—within the perimeters set by the teacher. Children are free to use their bodies to express emotions and feelings and to communicate an idea or message, integrating the skill themes and movement concepts with their design of the dance. Creative dance transitions from teacher designed, to sharing of decisions with the teacher, to total choreography by the children.

Dance within our programs of elementary physical education provides children one avenue to enhance the joy of movement. In dance, children can, "explore the sounds and gestures of their feelings and their dreams. They are free to discover their inherent sense of balance and design, and use them to show who they are and what they hope to be" (Jenkins 1976, 19).

Reading Comprehension Questions

1. What should dance in the elementary school provide for children?
2. What are the two types of dance experiences for children? Where does each form fit into the curriculum, and why?
3. What skill themes and movement concepts generally appear in creative dance content?
4. Name three settings for cultural dance in elementary school. Choose a cultural dance and describe its development in each of the three settings.
5. What is the focus of creative dance?
6. What is the role of imagery in dance? What must children possess before they can effectively use imagery?

7. What is the primary focus of creative dance? How does the purpose of creative dance differ at each skill progression level?
8. What is choreography? What steps must be included in choreography?
9. Choose a theme for a creative dance for children. Outline the dance to show beginning and ending shapes, locomotor movements, travel pathways, and concepts that express the theme.
10. What hints do the authors give for starting to teach creative dance?

References/Suggested Readings

Barrett, K. R. 1984. Educational dance. In *Physical education for children: A focus on the teaching process*, ed. B. Logsdon, K. Barrett, M. Ammons, M. Broer, L. Halverson, R. McGee, and M. Roberton. Philadelphia: Lea & Febiger.

Bennett, J. P., and P. C. Riemer. 2006. *Rhythmic activities and dance*. 2nd ed. Champaign, IL: Human Kinetics.

Boorman, J. 1969. *Creative dance in the first three grades*. New York: McKay.*

Carroll, J., and P. Lofthouse. 1969. *Creative dance for boys*. London: MacDonald & Evans.*

Cone, T., and S. Cone. 2012. *Teaching children dance*. 3rd ed. Champaign, IL: Human Kinetics.

Fleming, G. A. 1976. *Creative rhythmic movement*. Englewood Cliffs, NJ: Prentice Hall.*

Fleming, G. A., ed. 1981. *Children's dance*. Reston, VA: American Alliance for Health, Physical Education, Recreation and Dance.

Gilbert, A. G. 2015. *Creative dance for all ages*. 2nd ed. Champaign, IL: Human Kinetics.

Holt/Hale, S., and T. Hall. 2016. *Lesson planning for elementary physical education*. Champaign, IL: Human Kinetics.

Jenkins, K. January 25, 1976. *The movement movement, California Living: The Magazine of the San Francisco Sunday Examiner and Chronicle*, p. 19.

Joyce, M. 1993. *First steps in teaching creative dance*. 3rd ed. New York: McGraw-Hill.

Little, S., and T. Hall. 2017. Selecting, teaching and assessing physical education dance experiences. *Journal of Physical Education, Recreation and Dance* 88(3): 36–42.

McGreevy-Nichols, S., H. Scheff, and M. Sprague. 2005. *Building dances: A guide to putting movements together*. 2nd ed. Champaign, IL: Human Kinetics.

Russell, J. 1975. *Creative movement and dance for children*. Boston: Plays.*

[SHAPE America] Society of Health and Physical Educators. 2014. *National standards and grade-level outcomes for K-12 physical education*. Champaign, IL: Human Kinetics.

Slater, W. 1974. *Teaching modern educational dance*. London: MacDonald & Evans.*

Stinson, S. 1988. *Dance for young children: Finding the magic in movement*. Reston, VA: American Alliance for Health, Physical Education, Recreation and Dance.

Ward, S. A. 2007. Why we all should learn to dance: Reflecting on the African cultural heritage. *Journal of Physical Education, Recreation and Dance* 78(5): 3–5, 47.

Weikart, P. S. 2006. *Teaching movement and dance*. 6th ed. Ypsilanti, MI: High Scope Press.

*The skills/movement concepts foundation for creative dance for children.

Appendix 29A: Rhythmic Routines

Lummi Sticks

Lummi sticks for elementary-age children are usually 12 inches long and 1 inch in diameter. They may be made from rolled newspaper sealed with tape or cut from wooden broom and mop handles or dowel rods. We have found it best to have children practice with the paper sticks until they master the basic patterns. Each child needs two sticks. The routine that follows is designed in two parts. First, children learn the basic patterns without tossing the sticks; then they work with a partner to add tossing and catching the sticks in the rhythm of the pattern.

Basic Patterns

Pattern 1: Hold sticks together vertically, one in each hand. Tap sticks down, tap sticks together, extend right hand forward. Tap down, tap sticks together, extend left hand forward. Repeat entire pattern two times.

Pattern 2: Hold sticks vertically, one in each hand. Tap both sticks down, tap them together, extend right hand, extend left hand. Repeat pattern four times.

Pattern 3: Hold sticks horizontally, with front tips extending toward the floor. Touch the edge of the sticks to the floor, and then half-flip the sticks, catching the sticks in your hands. Hold sticks vertically for one count. Repeat pattern 2. Touch edge of sticks to floor; half-flip the sticks, hold sticks one count. Then repeat pattern 2: Tap down, tap sticks together, extend right hand, extend left hand. Repeat entire pattern four times.

Pattern 4: Hold sticks horizontally on each side of your body. Touch the edge of each stick on the floor, and then half-flip the sticks. Bring sticks in front of you and perform pattern 3: Side touch, flip; front touch, flip; tap down, tap together, extend right hand, extend left hand. Repeat entire pattern four times.

Pattern 5: Hold sticks horizontally on each side of your body. Touch side front, side back, side front. Bring the sticks in front of your body; touch front, cross your arms over, touch on opposite side, uncross arms and touch. Repeat pattern 2: Side, touch front, back, front; front, side, cross, side. Tap down, tap together, extend right hand, extend left hand. Repeat entire pattern four times.

Tossing to a Partner   Children sit facing a partner, approximately 3 feet from the partner. Patterns are the same basic patterns, except that instead of an

Student-designed Lummi stick routine, to be performed with a partner.

extension of the arm, the stick is tossed to the partner, who catches it.

Chinese Ribbons/Streamers

Chinese ribbons or streamers for elementary school students are 8 to 12 feet long and made of plastic. Crepe paper can be used, but it doesn't withstand children's practice or rough handling. Streamers can be made by attaching the plastic to a 12-inch dowel rod with either an eyelet and screw or a swivel hook and nylon fishing line.

In time with the music, the streamers are twirled in front of the body, to the side, or over the head. The following patterns represent a combination of skills suited for control level. Routines become more advanced as locomotor skills are added.

Pattern 1: Side circles—right side, left side

Pattern 2: Front circles

Pattern 3: Figure 8s—in front of the body

Pattern 4: Helicopter—circles overhead

Pattern 5: Lasso—front circles near the floor

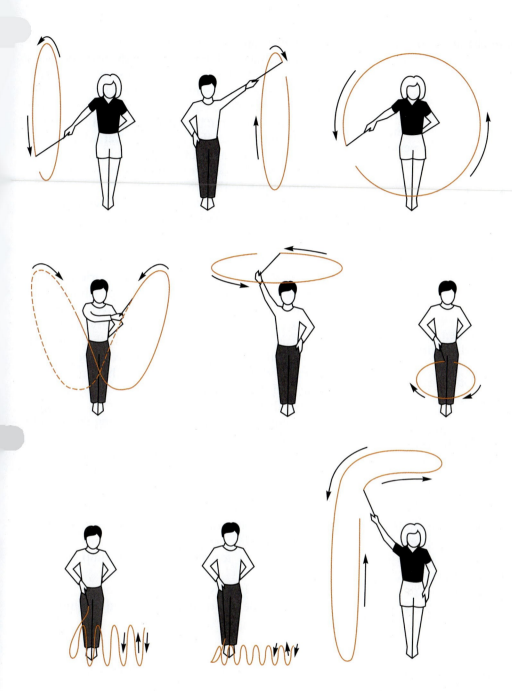

Chinese ribbon patterns.

Pattern 6: Walk the Dog—waist-high vertical movements in front, to the sides

Pattern 7: Snake—forward, backward movements near the floor, in front, to the sides

Pattern 8: Mountain Peaks—slow vertical movements, high to low levels

The ribbon routines of rhythmic gymnastics in the Olympics are examples of this skill at the proficiency level. Visuals and educational materials relating to rhythmic gymnastics are available from the U.S. Olympic Committee (www.olympic.org).

Musical Parachute

Parachute routines are combinations of locomotor and nonlocomotor actions. Sample skills include:

Waves: Shaking the parachute up and down

Umbrella: Raising the parachute high overhead

Mountain: Bringing the umbrella down to touch the edges on the floor

Merry-go-round: Locomotor actions moving the parachute clockwise and counterclockwise

Floating cloud: Umbrella with release of the parachute

Mushroom: Inflating the umbrella and moving forward to a mushroom shape

Music that is flowing, smooth, and expressive with a strong underlying beat is good for parachute routines. The best music is a song with meaningful lyrics and expressive movements in the format of the music. Routines should be easy to understand and perform, with creative movements and shapes that flow and change with the music. We have found it best to begin with instrumental music; words can be a distraction to the routine directions. After the students have mastered the routine, the music can be either instrumental or vocal.

The following routine is designed for students whose skills are at the control level and is done to the music "Pop Goes the Weasel":

- Children sit around the parachute and face clockwise. They hold the parachute in their right hands. The children are numbered 1 and 2, with 2 being behind 1, who is the partner.
- Start the introductory music ("Pop Goes the Weasel"). The children stand up on the first "pop," still holding the parachute with their right hands only.
- The children march clockwise in time with the music until they hear "Pop Goes the Weasel," at which point the 1s let go of the parachute and walk under the chute and behind their partners. Now the 2s are in front.
- Students march clockwise. On the next "pop," the 2s let go of the chute and go under the chute and behind their partners. Now the 1s are in front again.
- Children now skip clockwise. On the "pop," the 1s go under the chute and behind their partners.
- The children continue skipping. On the "pop," the 2s go under the chute and behind their partners.

- Students now face the center of the circle, holding the parachute with both their hands. Slide sideways clockwise. On the "pop," children stop, then repeat the slide sideways counterclockwise. They stop again, raise the parachute high in the air, and bring it back to the tuck position; they don't let go of the chute.
- Students wait for the next "pop," at which point they raise the parachute high in the air, walk forward three steps, and then pull the parachute down behind them so they're "in the cave."
- Students wait quietly in the cave. When they hear the final "pop," they come out of the cave.

Jump Rope

Jump rope routines are rhythmical experiences that students enjoy creating in small groups (three to six students). The routines should be relatively short and include only the basic jumps that everyone in the group can do. As a child-designed rhythmic experience, a group jump rope routine involves executing the jump rope skills correctly, staying in rhythm with the music, and staying in time with others in the group.

Music that has a strong beat and generates energy is best for jump rope routines. Encouraging students to include a basic single-bounce jump between skills aids them in staying on beat. The following is an example of a group jump rope routine for children at the control level; it is designed for 4/4 rhythm:

- Basic single-bounce jump for eight counts
- Skier (two-foot side to side) jump for eight counts
- Basic single-bounce jump for eight counts
- Bell (two-foot forward/backward) jump for eight counts
- Basic single-bounce jump for eight counts
- Side-straddle (apart/together) for eight counts

Children Designing Their Own Dance: A Description of a Process

One goal in teaching dance is to work with children so they learn to design dances to express feelings or thoughts that are important to them. This description of the process of creating a dance tells how one teacher worked with a group of upper elementary children, assisting them to create their own dance. The description is intended to reveal the process of creating dances; it isn't presented as a predesigned dance to be taught to other children.

Background

The population of the community in which the children in this class lived was predominantly African American. The eight children in this group wished to create a dance that expressed pride and respect for their African American heritage.

We began by using several methods to develop an outline for the dance:

- One student wrote a short paper describing what he considered the most important events in African American slavery.
- The school media specialist provided several sources of information. Individual students read and outlined these sources for the remainder of the group.
- Several students interviewed teachers and classmates about their family backgrounds. They also asked people to describe what emotions they had about their heritage.

The pride and courage of many of their descendants were the qualities the children wanted most to exhibit in their dance.

An Outline of the Dance

After gathering and reviewing this information, the students discussed a sequential outline for the dance. It was agreed that:

1. They would begin by depicting, in some way, the period of slavery.
2. The arrival of freedom would be expressed next. Interestingly, the children didn't want this portion of the dance to be happy or exhilarating, for several reasons. They felt that blacks were always free, despite slavery, that many freedoms were long in coming, and that the struggle for equality continues today.
3. Upon arrival of freedom, it was important to display the pride and courage of African Americans in overcoming many injustices, both as individuals and as a people.

4. The conclusion of the dance would be spiritual, exhibiting respect and thankfulness to God for blessing a cherished people.

Creation of the Dance

Children focused on each section of the dance before putting it all together. For each portion, the youngsters needed to decide upon and write down the following:

1. Beginning location of each dancer
2. Sequential travel pathway of each dancer or of the entire group

Travel Pattern for "Freedom"

Travel pathways
    Random: Dancers weaving in, out, and around one another
Qualities
    Smooth, wavy, uncertain, looking to others for help
Actions
    Wavy gesturing of arms, held upward for protection or reaching out
    Slow stepping, with changes in direction and levels

3. Expressive qualities they intended to exhibit in their movements
4. Sequence of specific gestures and travel skills incorporated to express desired qualities

Once the group could perform one section to the teacher's and their own satisfaction, work began on the next phase of the dance.

Slavery

After discussing the accumulated information, the children agreed to begin the dance by exhibiting the qualities and actions of field slaves laboring under a hot sun.

Freedom

This phase of the dance was the most difficult for the children. After experimenting with several ideas, the youngsters asked if they could select music to serve as background for the dance. They thought that if they had appropriate music as a stimulus, they would be able to solve their dilemmas. After listening to several cuts from the *Roots* soundtrack, the children unanimously agreed that the words and slow pulse of the song "Many Rains Ago (Oluwa)" was perfect for their purposes.

(continued)

They decided to express freedom by simply putting down their tools and slowly and smoothly beginning to interweave with one another, making eye contact with others for the first time. This was intended to express changed circumstances in which they were free and proud but still struggling. During this phase, the youngsters' facial features exhibited fear and uncertainty about the future. The travel pattern was random.

Gathering Together: Strength as a People

To express their solidarity and pride as a people, the children's random travel began to be directed toward the center of the room where they gathered one by one, grasped one another's hands tightly, and formed a strong, unified statue.

From this point the youngsters were able to complete their dance with little teacher suggestion or intervention.

Dispersing: Strength as Individuals

Youngsters dispersed from the center of the room with new vigor and traveled along definite travel patterns.

Gathering Again: Strength, Pride, Confidence

Children leaped to the center of the room, where suddenly and simultaneously they clasped hands with one another overhead and formed a statue.

Respect and Thankfulness to God

From the statue position, youngsters slowly bowed and traveled to semicircle formation. Slowly they dropped to their knees, and then slowly they raised their hands and heads upward.

Conclusion: We Are Strong and Proud

Youngsters slowly bent to curled position. . . . Suddenly and simultaneously, they rose on knees to grasp one another's hands to form a statue as a final statement of strength and pride.

Travel Pattern for "Gathering Again: Strength, Pride, Confidence"

Travel pathways
  All dancers suddenly and simultaneously gather in the middle with a run, leap, and turn
Qualities
  Strong, confident, proud, smooth, and fluent
Actions
  Smooth, fluent leap and landing when dancers grasp each other's hands overhead and freeze into a stillness

Neighborhood Friendship Streamer Dance

Skills and concepts: Skip, gallop, slide sideways, hop, turns, levels, pathways

Equipment: Streamers of four different colors (e.g., ribbons, survey tape, crepe paper). Distribute the streamers to the children so there is approximately the same number of each color.

Introduction: Inform the students that today they will be doing a dance about friendships in their neighborhood.

Exploration: (Guide the students with the following tasks.)

In your personal space, explore making curved pathways in the air with your streamer.

- Move the streamer around your body and in front of and behind your body as you explore curved pathways.
- Make both large and small movements.
- Make both slow and fast curved pathways.
- Now travel in general space, skipping as you make your curved pathways. Try a gallop; now slide sideways.

Development of Dance Parts: (These are the specific movements that will be a part of the dance. Guide the students through the following practice tasks.)

- In your own personal space, spin in a circle with your streamer.
- Now try a jump turn. You can do a full jump turn or just part of the way. Remember to bend your knees and land safely on your feet.
- For the third turn, keep one foot still and make a wide shape. Keeping that one foot still and the wide shape, turn in a circle. Remember to use your streamer.
- The final turn is going to be really slow, and you will change levels as you turn. Your streamer will also change levels.
- Take a couple of minutes and practice all four turns.
- Now that you know all four turns, we are going to add different locomotor skills. Skip in general space four times and then stop and perform one of your turns. Try four gallops and another turn. Slide sideways four times and use a third turn. Hop on one foot four times and try the last turn. *(You can direct the turns or allow the children to select one each time.)*
- Our last task is to throw the streamer into the air and let it fall to the floor. Make your body in the same shape next to the streamer. Try this a couple more times. Your streamer may be twisted, curled, or straight. Your body will be the same shape as you lie on the floor next to the streamer.

The Dance: (Guide the students through the dance. They typically enjoy doing it a couple of times.)

- Starting formation: Children divided in four groups by color in the four corners of the room. Those with red streamers live on Red Street, yellow on Yellow Street (in the corner to the right of Red Street), blue on Blue Street (diagonally across from Red Street), and green on Green Street (diagonally across from Yellow Street).
- Tell the story of the Neighborhood Friendship Dance and provide the directions for each part. The dance begins with each group galloping to the middle of the room and showing off their turns. *(Call one group at a time to gallop to the center of the room and do a turn before returning to their corner.)*
  - Red group gallops and performs a spin turn with the streamer before galloping home.
  - Yellow group repeats with the jump turn.
  - Blue group is next with the wide shape turn.
  - Finally, the green group gallops to the center and performs the slow change of levels turn before galloping home.
- Suddenly the red group decides it wants to know how the blue group lives (group diagonally across the room). Strangely, at the same time, the blue group is wondering what it is like on Red Street. Both groups slide sideways and change places. They wave their streamers to each other as they pass.
- Then, the green and yellow groups wanted to explore each other's streets. They each slide sideways across to the opposite neighborhood and wave as they pass.
- Next, the red and blue groups decide to return home and slide sideways back to their street, waving again as they pass. Yellow and green groups do the same after red and blue return home.
- Red Street then decides it would be fun to have a big neighborhood party. Two people from the red group lead the red group one behind the other skipping to Yellow Street and wave their streamers saying, "Join us for a party." The two combined groups skip to Blue Street and invite them to the party. They continue to Green Street and invite them. A big circle is formed with all of the students.

(continued)

- With the two leaders from Red Street, the circle moves around the room until the leaders slow down to a stop; facing each other, they hold the ends of the streamers, making a doorway into the party. Each person goes through the doorway and spreads out to spin and turn with their streamers. They can dance alone or with someone with a different color streamer.
- On a signal (drum, tambourine, clap, etc.), everyone throws their steamer into the air and then sinks to the floor, making the same shape as their streamer.

With or without music, ask the children to repeat the dance. Provide guidance as needed; some children may have difficulty remembering all the parts of the dance. The idea is for them to tell the story with their dance without you telling the story.

Closure: What did you think about the Friendship Dance and what was your favorite part? When you get home, teach the dance to your family.

(Adapted from Cone, T. P., and S. L. Cone. 2012. *Teaching children dance*. 3rd ed. Champaign, IL: Human Kinetics.)

The Spaghetti Dance

Skills and concepts: Jump, shapes, levels, pathways, directions, actions of bending, curling, stretching

Equipment: Drum or wooden block, music with a steady beat ("Hot, Hot, Hot" by The Merrymen is one recommendation), a circle marked in the middle of room

Introduction: Today, we will be doing a dance about narrow and curled body shapes. We are going to create shapes and movements that tell a story about making spaghetti.

Exploration: *(Guide the students with the following tasks.)*

In your personal space, explore making narrow and curved shapes with your body.

- Make a narrow shape with your body. Make a narrow shape with your body at a high level; now a low level.
- Make a curled shape with your body. Make a curled shape at a medium level; now a low level.
- Start in a narrow shape. I am going to beat the drum four times (four counts), and you will slowly move into a curled shape. I will strike the drum four more times for you to return to the narrow shape. This time, I will beat the drum eight times and you will move from narrow to curled and back to narrow without a pause.
- Now we will explore moving our shapes. Walk in a straight pathway with your body in a narrow shape. Repeat the pathway as you travel backward; now sideways. Explore different ways you can use your arms while maintaining a narrow shape. On the signal (one drum beat), jump barely off the ground while maintaining your narrow shape and then continue your straight pathway travel. Every time you hear the single drum beat, show me that narrow jump.
- Next, we will explore ways we can use our curled shapes and travel in curved pathways. You may travel forward, backward, or sideways. You can change the levels as you

travel. Remember to keep the body moving as you explore the different curled shapes you can make. You may want to run and jump, making a curled shape in the air. Remember, uncurl and bend your knees to land safely.

Development of Dance Parts: *(These are the specific movements that will be a part of the dance. Guide the students through the following practice tasks.)*

We are now ready to create the movements to our spaghetti story.

- Spread out standing along one of the walls (or outer perimeter of the room). Pretend you are a piece of spaghetti in a box. Good, I see everyone in narrow shapes. Keep that shape as you jump out of the box and travel in a straight pathway to the center circle.
- On my signal (one beat), keep the narrow shape and jump into the circle.
- As the spaghetti cooks, I will strike the drum, creating a rumbling sound. Travel within the circle, in and around each other, and slowly change into a curled shape. Your travel is now in a curved pathway as you move about in the pot. Start your curled shape by bending at your legs, curling your back, bending your arms, and finally curling you neck and tucking your chin. Change levels as your travel.
- On my signal, eight beats that get louder and louder, pretend a big bubble is forming in the middle of the pot and is getting bigger and bigger, pushing the spaghetti out of the pot. When you hear the last really loud beat, jump out of the pot. Travel in curved pathways keeping the curled shapes and return to the wall, but this time, pretend to stick to it.
- On the next beat, the spaghetti maintains the curled shape returning to the middle of the room and slowly collapsing on the plate.

(continued)

Appendix 29C *(continued)*

The Dance: *(Guide the students through the dance.)*

- Starting formation: Children divided in four groups, one group in each corner representing boxes of spaghetti. The children are lined up one behind the other.
- On the drum beat, the first person begins traveling to the center pot for cooking. Remember to keep the narrow shape and walk a straight pathway. As soon as one person begins walking, the next person in line can begin, ending with all spaghetti standing around the pot.
- On the drum beat, everyone takes a small jump into the pot and very slowly transforms from the narrow uncooked spaghetti to the curled cooking spaghetti. Remember to change slowly, use different curled shapes, and travel in curved pathways and at different levels.
- I will now get in the middle of the pot in a curled shape at a low level. Watch as I slowly rise and make my shape bigger and bigger becoming a big wide bubble. I will now pretend to push you out of the pot. Move to the edge of the pot as I push and push with the big bubble. When I wave my arms at you, jump out. First, I will wave at one side and then another until all of the spaghetti is out. You may travel anyway you wish but remember to use curled shapes as you find a place on the wall to stick.

- Now I will make a curled shape in the center of the circle, like a giant meatball on the plate. Return to the plate in your curled shape and slowly collapse to the floor. The dance ends when all of the spaghetti is on the plate.

Repeat the dance, but ask for one volunteer from each corner to be the bubble and the meatballs this time. Give them a couple of minutes to decide how they will communicate and work together to be the big exploding bubble that sends the spaghetti out of the pot. Then, once all of the spaghetti is stuck to the wall, the same four volunteers will become the four delicious meatballs that signal the others to come to the dinner plate. These four will lead the dance as you, the teacher, step back and watch the performance.

Repeat the dance with music.

Closure: What did you think about the Spaghetti Dance, and what was your favorite part? Maybe you can go home and create a dance about your favorite meal. Your family will delight in this "after-dinner" entertainment.

(Adapted from Cone, T. P., and S. L. Cone. 2012. Teaching children dance. 3rd ed. Champaign, IL: Human Kinetics.)

The Homework Machine

Skills and concepts: Cooperation, collaboration, creation of repetitive movements

Equipment: Drum or wood block, music with a steady beat or a metronome (purchased or downloaded version), whiteboard or chart paper, two sets of premade signs attached to cones naming the parts of the machine (in slot, smoother, computer, checker, out slot, finished homework)

Introduction: Today and in the next class period, you will work together in small groups to create repetitive movements, movements that are done the same way over and over. You will use these movements to create a dance about a machine that does your homework. I'm guessing you like that idea.

Day 1

Exploration: *(Guide the students with the following tasks.)*

In your personal space, make up a movement with your arms and do it over and over the same way. Try to make your movement different from the movements of other people around you.

- Try the arm movement to the beat of my drum. *(You may choose to use a metronome or music that changes tempo.)*

- Now take a step forward on each beat of the drum. As I change the tempo of the beat, step to that beat. Change directions, sometimes moving forward, backward, or sideways, but continue to stay with my tempo.
- Create a repetitive movement with your head and follow the beat; try your shoulders, one arm, alternating arms, and the legs. Make the movement match my tempo of fast or slow.
- Choose two of the movements and combine them. For example, eight beats with the head and then eight beats with one arm.

Development of Dance Parts: *(These are the specific movements that will be a part of the dance. Guide the students through the following practice tasks.)*

Students select a partner (teacher may assign partners). For each movement, the partners will communicate and collaborate as they create a repetitive movement sequence that later will combine with other sequences for the homework machine dance. Each sequence below is titled as one of five parts of the machine and should be written on the white board or on chart paper.

(continued)

Each sequence must include three different eight-count movements. The partners will create the movements and practice performing in unison to the tempo of the metronome or the music. After several minutes of creating and practice, one set of partners will perform their sequence for another set of partners. Observation is to ensure that the sequence is in unison and that there are three different movements of eight counts each. After one group receives feedback, the other group takes their turn. This observe and perform pattern continues through the following movement sequences. *Hints are provided for each sequence; they may be written on task cards or used for guided discovery.*

- Part 1: The *In Slot* pulls the homework into the machine.
  - (Hints: Reaching, pulling, small to large movements, forward and backward steps)
- Part 2: The *Smoother* smooths out the homework after it comes out crumpled from your backpack.
  - (Hints: Change levels, use different body parts)
- Part 3: The *Computer* does the homework for you.
  - (Hints: Big movements, use the whole body, exaggerate the movements, do not think just fingers working a computer)
- Part 4: The *Checker* makes sure the homework is correct.
  - (Hints: What movements can you make to show success?)
- Part 5: The *Out Slot* pushes the homework out of the machine.
  - (Hints: Push the homework out, use different body parts, vary the force)

Children will need practice each of these movement challenges; provide sufficient practice time for each.

Day 2

The Dance: *(Guide the students through the dance.)*

- Starting formation: Children are divided into two large groups (approximately 10–14 students per group). One group is called the Monday homework machine, and the other is called the Tuesday homework machine. They are given one part of the teaching space with the cones (names of the machine parts are written and attached to cones) arranged in a semi-circle in order. Each group is given the following child-designed tasks:
  - The group decides who will perform each of the machine parts (list all parts here).
  - Practice the working of the machine by pretending that one person (representing the homework) is passing through the machine. The *In Slot* begins, and then shortly after, the *Smoother* begins, and each part after joins one after the other.

- When ready, the Tuesday group will visit the Monday homework machine and pretend to be the homework that travels one behind the other through the Monday homework machine. The homework begins in a crumpled curled shape. As you reach the *Smoother*, show how your shape may stretch and change. As you continue through the machine, you can be creative in your movements using different locomotor movements, changing levels, turning, spinning, etc. When you exit the homework machine, skip or run and pretend to play outdoors because your homework is finished.
- When the last person passes each part, the machine slowly shuts down part by part starting with the *In Slot.*
- The Monday group now visits the Tuesday homework machine, and they are reminded of the movements listed above for the role of the homework. However, first they must listen to the following story before going through the machine.
  - The homework begins and is moving slowly and effectively until the last homework has passed through.
  - This time, the homework circles back around to go through as if a second round of homework. With the overload of homework, the machine starts working faster and faster (the tempo of the metronome or music will increase). Suddenly, the machine explodes and breaks apart. The machine parts scatter all over the area but are continuing to make their same movement. The movement slows and slows until the machine parts all collapse to the ground.
  - The homework desperately waves to the machine parts to come back. The parts slowly return, reassemble, and finish the homework.
  - The dance ends as the finished homework finds a space in the room and sinks to the floor. The machine slowly stops part by part as the last homework passes through and each machine part freezes in a shape created by their last move.

Ask the children to repeat the dance all the way through. Provide guidance as needed. The idea is for them to tell the story with their dance not with you telling it.

Closure: What did you think about the Homework Machine, and what was your favorite part? Sadly, you must do your homework and can only imagine the homework machine doing it. Go home and create a dance about a machine someone else in your family would want.

(Adapted from Cone, T. P., and S. L. Cone. 2012. *Teaching children dance.* 3rd ed. Champaign, IL: Human Kinetics.)

Teaching Educational Gymnastics

If gymnastics is to be for everyone then all children cannot be asked to do the same gymnastic movement at the same time, in exactly the same way, for clearly some children are going to be underchallenged and some are going to be overchallenged.

—Andrea Boucher (1978)

Drawn by children at Monfort, Chappelow or Shawsheen Elementary Schools, Greeley, CO. Courtesy of Lizzy Ginger; Tia Ziegler.

As discussed in Chapter 2, skill themes and movement concepts form the curricular base for elementary physical education, with educational gymnastics, dance, and games as the contexts, or settings, in which these skills and concepts are applied. The area of application, i.e., educational gymnastics, dance, or games, is selected by the teacher after the skills are initially taught in isolation and then combined with other skills and movement concepts (see Figure 2.3, page 27). Educational gymnastics integrates the skill themes of traveling, jumping and landing, balancing, transferring weight, and rolling; the body actions of bending, stretching, curling, and twisting; and the movement concepts of space awareness, effort, and relationships. This chapter is designed to provide the guidelines for application of these skill themes and movement concepts into educational gymnastics.

The Nature of Gymnastics

The self-testing nature of gymnastics is challenging to children. They constantly ask themselves, "Can I balance in this position without falling? Can I walk this curb? Can I cross the monkey bars? Can I climb this tree and hang upside down on the limb? Can I turn a somersault underwater?" These self-testing challenges are a part of their daily lives and clearly connect to gymnastics experiences.

First, children receive immediate feedback regarding the skill: "Yes, I can do a headstand," or "No, I am still losing my balance when I try a headstand." Second, the feedback is personal and not dependent on others; children do not have to rely on others to determine whether they are successful at the task. Third, the self-challenging tasks of gymnastics are a natural part of children's world, coupled with their curiosity and love of movement. This creates multiple opportunities for climbing, hanging, supporting weight on different body parts, balancing, rolling, and so on. Finally, the self-testing nature of gymnastics permits younger children who are still in the egocentric stage of development to participate fully and successfully in a personal challenge without the necessity of team play or cooperative work with other children.

Gymnastics in Elementary School

The purpose of educational gymnastics as taught in elementary physical education is to provide our students with a foundation of gymnastics experiences that

©Barbara Adamcik

Young children enjoy the challenge of balancing on different body parts.

©Barbara Adamcik

Moving in relation to apparatus is part of educational gymnastics.

increases their skills and introduces them to the types of experiences characteristic of gymnastics. The *National Standards & Grade-Level Outcomes for K–12 Physical Education* (SHAPE America 2014) support the inclusion of educational gymnastics in elementary physical education. You will find these grade-level outcomes relating to gymnastics in the skill themes of Bending, Stretching, Curling, and Twisting (Chapter 19), Jumping and Landing (Chapter 20), Balancing (Chapter 21), and Transferring Weight and Rolling (Chapter 22). The *National Standards* also include grade-level outcomes with combinations of skill themes for educational gymnastics (Box 30-1).

Educational gymnastics is both child-centered and child-designed with tasks and challenges appropriate for each child at his or her skill level as well as sequences and routines created by the children. *Children Moving* includes many balance and transferring weight learning experiences matched to individual skill levels and in appropriate floor and modified apparatus environments. In contrast, Olympic-style/club gymnastics centers on defined skills with specific performance expectations and complex routines.

Children may be exposed to advanced, competitive gymnastics through media coverage of the Olympics, as well as by watching peers involved in local club gymnastics show their skills on playgrounds and in their neighborhoods. Children without a background of gymnastics experiences often enter our gymnasiums saying, "I can't do those things," or asking, "Will we do back handsprings today?" Our task is to present gymnastics for children in a way that is both challenging and appropriate for all students in our classes.

Educational gymnastics programs are designed to assist all children, regardless of ability, to improve their gymnastics skills. Educational gymnastics follows appropriate practices for school physical education programs (see Box 30-2). The skills for competitive gymnastics are reserved for club gymnastics and after-school programs with trained gymnastics specialists and coaches. These programs provide the training needed for advanced stunts and required routines on both the floor and apparatus.

Do we exclude Olympic stunts from our curriculum? Not at all. Children at the utilization and proficiency levels, who have a background in gymnastics experiences and the proper body control, often use Olympic stunts as a response to a gymnastics task. When children use a handstand, walkover, or cartwheel, for example, the maneuver should be identified as such. With children who have a background in gymnastics, we discuss the actions they have chosen in response to the task given. As teachers, we decide whether the response is appropriate for physical education class or best reserved for club gymnastics. For example, does the stunt require a spotter and will the other children be tempted to imitate a stunt beyond their capabilities that could result in injury?

An illustration will clarify this point. If we ask the children in a class to "transfer from feet to hands to feet in a different location," there are a variety of ways to do this. Some children might do a cartwheel, a round-off, or even a handspring. Others may simply place their hands on the grass or floor and lift their feet only a few inches from the ground and, with a slight twist, land only about a foot from where they started. All are "correct" responses! If you ask the entire class to do a cartwheel, those children who are unable to do so may feel as if they have failed. In contrast, the "gymnasts" in the class would be bored if they were asked to only lift their feet a few inches from the ground.

Creating a Safe Learning Environment

Some teachers avoid gymnastics because they are concerned about the children's safety and are afraid that children might be injured; some administrators are hesitant to include gymnastics in the curriculum for the same reasons. Injury is always a possibility in physical education classes. When the focus is on educational gymnastics (as opposed to Olympic-style/club gymnastics actions) and with the establishment of procedures for safe practice, gymnastics is no more dangerous than other physical education learning experiences. To children, the self-testing, risk-taking nature of gymnastics brings excitement; to the teacher, it brings the challenge of creating a safe environment. We as teachers must always be sure the expectations for safety are enforced and consistently reinforced. Additionally, the arrangement of equipment and selection of tasks maximize safety for our students. The

following ideas relating to the learning environment and the teaching of educational gymnastics help create successful and safe experiences for children. Taken together, these suggestions, along with the safety emphasis icon (⚠️) used in the skill theme chapters, will help establish a safe learning environment for teaching educational gymnastics.

Expectations of Safe Practice

From the initial lessons, children learn spatial awareness of their movements and the movements of others. Children are taught not to interfere with others attempting their gymnastics work, either by touching or talking to them. Concentration on the task is essential in gymnastics.

An appropriate learning environment in gymnastics emphasizes safety throughout. Encourage the children to be responsible for their own safety. Stress that if they don't think they can do something, they should either not do it or ask you for help. Games of I Dare You and Follow the Leader are inappropriate in gymnastics lessons. Remember, following the progression outlined in the spirals for gymnastics skills and mastering a skill before attempting the next are critical for safety. Gymnastics lessons are not the place for off-task behavior; being off task in games or dance may result in inappropriate behavior, but off-task behavior in gymnastics can lead to injury. When we encourage children to be responsible for themselves, they tend to rely less on us and more on themselves to determine what is appropriate. Acceptance of responsibility and self-reliance are affective goals of physical education; they are major goals in teaching gymnastics.

Safety Check

Teach children very early in gymnastics to do a "Safety Check" before they begin work at any station: mats correctly placed under equipment, adequate space surrounding the equipment. In the beginning, stop the class frequently and ask the children to do a "Safety Check," visually scanning the working area for space and equipment safety.

Gymnastics Equipment

The type and organization of gymnastics equipment are important considerations when planning gymnastic lessons. Use of mats under or around equipment and the spacing of equipment are important teacher decisions. Movement of equipment is another variable. Gymnastics apparatus can be heavy, cumbersome, and difficult for one person to move. In some situations, gymnastics would never be taught if the teacher had to move the gymnastics equipment alone. Children can practice moving gymnastics equipment correctly during the first few lessons in which the apparatus is used. Once they learn to maneuver the apparatus safely and efficiently, the children can set up or take down a gymnastics environment in a short time. The following guidelines should be used when children move gymnastics apparatus:

- An adequate number of children (as determined by the teacher) must be present before equipment can be moved.
- Children are to lift the equipment together and lower it together, being careful of toes and fingers.
- Each piece of apparatus has its own storage space to which it is to be returned.

Moving gymnastics apparatus correctly is as important a part of the children's learning in educational gymnastics as working safely on the apparatus. Taking the time during the initial lessons to teach them the proper procedures will help create a safe environment for gymnastics and increase valuable instructional time in subsequent lessons.

Check with your school for district policy regarding children moving equipment.

Selection of Tasks

The teacher's knowledge of individual students and selection of developmentally appropriate tasks and challenges are critical for positive learning experiences and safety. There has to be a match between student and task to allow for individual differences. The skills are designed to progress from simple to complex, and the students must experience success before moving to the more complex tasks. The mastery of gymnastics skills is a slow process and must not be rushed by us as teachers or by our students.

Safety Rules

Rules for working safely on mats and apparatus should be explained, demonstrated, and enforced very carefully. We suggest posting the rules where the children can see them as they work. (See Chapter 7, "Establishing an Environment for Learning," for additional suggestions.)

In educational gymnastics, we never ask all students to perform a task the same way. For example, some students do not have the upper body strength to take weight on hands. Others may have the strength but are experiencing anxiety about the task. Still others

Children are encouraged to be responsible for themselves and their own safety.

©Barbara Adamcik

have the strength, balance, and confidence. A task of placing both hands on the mat and trying to kick up one leg followed by the other may result in one child barely leaving the floor and another kicking into a full handstand. This child-centered approach provides for tasks that are challenging to the less skilled, yet not boring to the highly skilled. The selection of tasks may mean that sometimes a single task is presented with the expectation of different responses from students; other times, children are given different tasks.

Safety Rules

Teaching gymnastics is different from teaching either dance or games because of the self-testing nature of gymnastics and because apparatus is often used. Using an educational gymnastics approach, successful teachers are able to provide a safe learning environment and match interesting and challenging tasks to the children's ability levels.

The Content of Educational Gymnastics

The content of educational gymnastics is based on the skill themes of balancing (Chapter 21) and transferring weight and rolling (Chapter 22) in combination with jumping and landing (Chapter 20) and traveling (Chapter 17). Tasks and challenges within each skill theme are the foundation of quality educational gymnastics learning experiences. This example using the skill theme of balancing illustrates this idea. An understanding of the concept of balance is a prerequisite to applying the skill in educational gymnastics—maintaining stillness in a position and holding that position for three to five seconds. Many children can take weight on their hands momentarily or balance in a headstand for one to two seconds but cannot hold the position stationary for five seconds. Children also need experiences in aligning body parts for balance and in tightening the muscles to maintain balance as prerequisites to skill themes in educational gymnastics. Children often fall out of inverted balances because the body parts are not properly aligned over the base of support and muscular tension is not sufficient to hold the proper alignment. These foundational lessons are essential to a higher level of gymnastics learning experiences.

Educational gymnastics content also includes movement concepts such as directions, levels, pathways, time, shapes (Chapters 14, 15, and 16), and the actions of bending, stretching, curling, and twisting (Chapter 19). These movement concepts and actions are incorporated into the gymnastics themes only after children have experienced them in isolation or combined with another skill theme. For example, children do not study twisting into and out of balances before they have an understanding of the action of twisting.

Educational gymnastics can be divided into floor experiences and apparatus experiences. *Floor* experiences are movements executed on grass, floor, or mats that don't require equipment to enhance the challenge. Apparatus experiences involve moving in relation to one or several pieces of equipment (tables, benches, beams, bars, vaulting boxes, and playground apparatus). *Although apparatus adds excitement to gymnastics, children can experience challenging, rewarding work in educational gymnastics with floor experiences only.*

Floor Experiences

Children at the precontrol level in educational gymnastics explore balancing on different body parts as bases of support, balancing on wide bases, and balancing in different shapes. They learn to curl their bodies into rounded shapes and to maintain the rounded shape for rocking and rolling.

Control-level experiences include rolling from different positions and in different directions. Inverted balances are introduced, with a strong emphasis on alignment of body parts and muscular tension to maintain balance. The concept of stillness is studied in combination with weight-transfer actions and as a contrast to rolling. Beginning at the control level, children are challenged with combinations of skills and the combination of skills and concepts—for example, moving from a two-part balance into a three-part balance on new bases of support or balancing in a wide body shape at different levels. These combinations lead to application of the skills in gymnastics sequences.

Utilization-level floor experiences include transferring weight on hands and twisting, maintaining weight on hands, and exploring the state of being "almost off balance." Students at this level enjoy focusing on the quality of movement execution in gymnastics, as well as increasing the complexity of balances and transfers. *Transferring weight and rolling experiences at the proficiency level are reserved for club gymnastics.*

Floor experiences in educational gymnastics progress from exploration of balancing and transferring weight, to children controlling their bodies in these self-imposed challenges, to combinations of skills and concepts. These skills and concepts are then applied in gymnastics sequences and to apparatus experiences.

Exploring basic shapes on apparatus follows balances on the floor/mats.

©Barbara Adamcik

Apparatus Experiences

Once children demonstrate control of their bodies in educational gymnastics floor experiences, have an understanding of safety in gymnastics, and understand the concept of sequences, we introduce them to experiences on apparatus. Balance beams, parallel bars, side horses, vaulting boxes, and still rings are Olympic or club gymnastics equipment. Some elementary schools have this official gymnastics apparatus, but many elementary school programs use benches, tables, wooden boxes, the edge of a stage, climbing ropes, climbing walls, and climbing frames to provide gymnastics experiences on apparatus. Unofficial equipment is often more compatible with the children's abilities, and children have fewer preconceived notions about what is expected when they practice movements on an unfamiliar or nontraditional piece of equipment. *Any equipment used as gymnastics apparatus should be checked for stability and safety.*

Even in a program rich in gymnastics apparatus, children need to spend a large amount of time on floor experiences before they begin work on apparatus. Success should occur with balancing, transferring weight, and rolling actions on the floor before they are attempted on low or high gymnastics apparatus. Many of the movements performed on the floor will be replicated on apparatus, but the height and narrowness of the surfaces will increase the difficulty of the task. Students begin apparatus work on low, larger surfaces—that is, boxes, low beams, and benches—before they work on higher, narrower pieces of apparatus.

You can introduce the children to a piece of apparatus by encouraging them to explore the equipment and to discover safe ways for getting on and off. Children at the precontrol level can start by walking along a low beam or bench, jumping from a wooden box or low table, hanging from a climbing rope at a low height, or traveling on a climbing frame or climbing wall. Obstacle courses designed from available equipment—tables, benches, hoops, ropes—are also challenging to children at this level as they learn the concepts of under, over, on/along, and through in a new setting. Some children will immediately begin to explore the apparatus; other children will be more cautious. Never force any child onto a piece of apparatus.

Children at the control level, while continuing to explore apparatus, can begin to focus on different ways to move in relation to the equipment. They can try different ways of traveling on or along a beam, hanging from a bar or rope, jumping from a table or bench, or traveling from side to side on a climbing frame or climbing wall. They can balance on different bases of support and combine traveling with stationary balances on apparatus.

Weight on hands is a challenge on apparatus.

©Barbara Adamcik

Children at the utilization level can try different ways to get onto equipment, vault over equipment, and form shapes in flight while moving from apparatus to the floor. Apparatus experiences that involve supporting weight on different body parts, transferring weight on equipment, nonsymmetrical balances, and inverted balances are also appropriate for children at this level.

When children reach the proficiency level, they should continue to focus on increasingly demanding balances, shapes, ways of traveling, and ways of supporting body weight, with complex transferring weight and rolling actions reserved for club gymnastics.

Creating Sequences

Creating and performing individual gymnastics sequences are often the highlight for children in educational gymnastics. The educational gymnastic sequence is the child's expression of self—a portrayal of self in gymnastics showing skills and concepts that flow together smoothly and fluently.

Teaching sequences may begin with a simple combination of two skills in which the focus is on making smooth transitions connecting the skills. The students will need guidance and experience in determining how to go from one skill to another. The actions of stretching, curling, and twisting will aid in linking many combinations. Following are examples of combinations:

- Balance at a low level in a narrow body shape; slowly curl into a different balance.
- Roll sideways in a narrow body shape; stretch and balance on just your stomach.
- Jump and land off the wooden box; roll in a forward direction.
- Choose an inverted balance of your choice; curl and roll out of it.

The creation of sequences in educational gymnastics, like dance, has a clear beginning, middle, and end. The beginning is the starting point that announces, "I am ready to begin my performance." This may be a particular body shape or simply standing erect. The purpose of the ending shape is to state "I am finished." Children often end their sequences in a different shape or pose than the starting position or with the "Ta Da" pose used in Olympic gymnastics routines. In the middle of the sequence, children are given options that can include combinations (e.g., travel, balance, weight transfer, and rolls). Beginning-level sequences may be as simple as the following:

- Beginning shape
- Three balances on different bases of support
- Ending shape

As children become more competent in gymnastics and more confident in the process, sequences become increasingly complex, with combinations of transfer actions and stillness, movement concepts (e.g., changes in levels, variations in speed), and transitions as illustrated with the following sequence:

- Beginning shape
- Three balances
- Two rolls or weight transfers
- Ending shape

The teacher may add that each balance has to be on a different base of support using at least two levels (low,

middle, high) and the sequence should have smooth transitions. Children should be encouraged to use only movements that exhibit safe and controlled movements (e.g., if the child is unable to hold a headstand still for three to five seconds, he or she should consider another balance until the child has the opportunity to master that skill). From the beginning, children should be encouraged to focus on the quality of their movements and to be creative and versatile in their sequence composition. Multiple examples of sequences can be found in Chapters 21 and 22.

Children also enjoy the challenge of creating partner sequences. Partner sequences can be enhanced with the relationship movement concepts of meeting, parting, mirroring, and matching (Chapter 16). These sequences require students to respect differences in others as they compose safe and creative movements.

Both individual and partner sequences can be created on the floor and on apparatus. Sequence work on apparatus might include transferring weight onto the apparatus, balancing and traveling on the apparatus, and traveling off the apparatus. Skills that were mastered during the floor experiences present a new challenge to children as they combine them for sequences on various pieces of gymnastics apparatus.

A sequence in gymnastics can be compared to a recital piece in music. Once the children have designed the sequence, they are to memorize and repeat it in exactly the same order with exactly the same balances and actions. This is one of the most difficult parts of sequencing for children. They enjoy creating but not memorizing for repetition. Recording the sequences with paper and pencil helps children retain them. The children may record their gymnastics sequences with drawings and stick figures. We call them stick figures; the art teacher calls them pictographs. There are many approaches to recording gymnastic sequences: You as a teacher may develop a method of recording sequences that will be used in all your gymnastics classes. The children may create their individual notation systems, or each class may devise a system of notation for balances and actions. Chapter 21 (Figure 21.14) illustrates one child's sequence notation.

Individual, partner, or apparatus sequences are challenge tasks that can be used for both informal and formal assessment. Examples of sequence assessments appear in Chapters 21 and 22. Additional guidance in assessment can be found in Chapter 12.

Outdoor Play Equipment as Gymnastics Apparatus

Outdoor playground equipment can serve as gymnastics apparatus in schools that have no indoor equipment or indoor physical education facility and as an additional avenue of exploration for children who have experienced indoor gymnastics. Children at the pre-control and control levels can focus on body control on various pieces of equipment. Children at the utilization level will be challenged by the complexity of structure, the number of bars, the distance between bars, and the variety of levels on playground equipment. Horizontal ladders, parallel bars, jungle gyms, monkey bars, balance beams, landscape logs, and railroad ties can be used for rolling, balancing, and transferring weight on apparatus. (See Chapters 21 and 22 for these learning experiences.) Very often the key to successfully teaching gymnastics on the playground is the positioning of the playground equipment, with grouped equipment being more conducive to teaching than isolated pieces of equipment. If the playground equipment is grouped, several pieces can easily accommodate a class of 25 to 30 children. But if the playground arrangement is such that instruction of the group as well as individuals on various apparatus isn't possible, cable spools and milk crates can be added to supplement large apparatus.

Children's work on playground apparatus should begin with a study of the proper use of the equipment—the acceptable and unacceptable tasks on the apparatus—and correct ways of getting on and off the apparatus. Early in the school year, let the children explore the various pieces of apparatus; this will lead to questions from the children and class discussions about what is permitted during both physical education class and recess. Any safety rules needed should be developed cooperatively by teacher and students; the rules may vary for younger and older children.

The use of playground equipment in physical education class will lead to increased use of that equipment during recess, which may make classroom teachers uncomfortable with children on the equipment. However, the rules established for physical education class and for recess will help the classroom teacher be more at ease. The use of apparatus during physical education can be very different from the use of apparatus during recess; it's our responsibility to be sure children understand the difference.

The Teaching of Educational Gymnastics

Initial gymnastics lessons for children focus on floor experiences with large-group instruction. During this time, the children learn how to control their bodies when balancing, transferring weight, and rolling; they also learn about safety in gymnastics and working independently. While the instruction is large-group in nature, the responses are child-centered. Each child is

Rolling on a bench is a challenge for this utilization student.

©Barbara Adamcik

encouraged to respond as appropriate with his or her skill level. The teacher's observation of those responses leads to individual inquiry for refinement and challenge.

When all the children in a class are expected to perform the same skill the same way, two things are likely to happen. Many of the children in the class will be bored because they can already perform the task successfully. Some of the children will be frightened because the task is too difficult for them, and they

These youngsters enjoy creating matching balances.

©Lars A. Niki

know it. When you offer children choices about how they'll perform a task, each child can select a developmentally appropriate response. This is child-centered gymnastics, i.e., educational gymnastics. For example, it's unlikely that all the children in a particular class will be able to do a handstand. Some children may not be strong enough to support all their body weight on their hands; some won't be able to land safely if they lose their balance. Instead of telling the entire class to do a handstand, you could tell the children to find a way to place some or all of their weight on their hands. An instruction that allows for individual differences in ability affords all children an opportunity for success.

Does presenting choices in a task performance mean that you do not expect quality in their movement? Absolutely not. Perhaps a comparison of the above educational gymnastics task to teaching a child to throw will help. Teaching a precontrol level child to throw begins with exploratory learning experiences (Chapter 24). The tasks presented to a child at control level begin to focus on teaching the mature pattern of the throw. The teacher holds the student accountable for stepping with opposition, emphasizing this cue over and over. Quality of movement is the teacher's focus in each task presented. In educational gymnastics, although the tasks presented are not asking for a specific skill, the quality of the movement is still expected. Using the earlier handstand example, a teacher would instruct the students to "Find a way to place some or all of your weight on your hands." After some exploratory time, the teacher would add, "Kick up and stretch your legs toward the ceiling. Tighten

your stomach muscles to help maintain your balance a little longer each time." The starting position for one child may have been squatting with hands on the mat, whereas another child may have started in a standing position before transferring weight to hands, yet the expectation to focus on those tight muscles is there for both children.

Demonstrating

Some teachers feel that because they aren't skilled gymnasts themselves, they won't be able to teach gymnastics effectively. Certainly a thorough background in a teaching area is an asset in teaching, but even teachers who aren't skilled gymnasts can provide children with appropriate educational gymnastics experiences. In educational gymnastics, the instructor doesn't need to be able to demonstrate a skill correctly because the children are never expected to perform the same skill the same way. However, to emphasize a particular movement quality such as "use of free body parts and extensions," to demonstrate a safety quality such as "chin on chest and stay round," or to show several examples that are "sample correct responses" to a task, you can invite, or pinpoint, a few children to demonstrate for the rest of the class. Asking several children to demonstrate eliminates the desire to copy one child's response and reinforces that everyone can do gymnastics, not just the highly skilled.

Stations

Following the initial gymnastics lessons with a focus on floor experiences, children are ready for work on gymnastics equipment/apparatus. After children demonstrate the ability to work safely and independently, allowing the class to work at stations (learning centers) can be a most efficient method of providing maximum participation on gymnastics apparatus. The stations are set up in different parts of the teaching area (see Chapter 9), with groups working on the same or different skills on the various pieces of equipment. Sample tasks include jumping from a low table onto a mat, landing, and rolling; traveling different ways along a bench or beam; climbing a rope; practicing taking weight on hands; and traveling onto and off a table or bench.

This method of organization allows the use of various pieces of equipment and eliminates waiting in line. Tasks for the stations can be posted on the wall near each station. This increases practice time because the children can read the directions and begin work immediately. Teachers can vary the tasks posted within a station to meet the individual skill levels. The number of stations and complexity of the setup are guided by answers to the following considerations:

- How many stations will the total available space accommodate?
- Are there enough mats to place under and around each piece of equipment?
- Is the space surrounding the station adequate for the children to practice getting off the equipment— for example, jumping, landing, and rolling—safely?
- Is the space between the stations sufficient to allow the children to work without interfering with those at the adjoining station?
- Does the setup provide the teacher the freedom to move throughout the learning environment, giving individual assistance as needed?
- Does the setup provide the teacher a view of all children and stations all of the time?

Transferring weight from feet to hands is a control-level skill that can later be used in gymnastics routines.

©Lars A. Niki

Club Gymnastics

Some of the children in your classes may be studying gymnastics independently, perhaps in a club or recreation program. Most of the club gymnasts are more skilled than the other children—many are at the proficiency level in many skills. Their skills in gymnastics may exceed your teaching knowledge and ability in this area. Because you're responsible for the safety of all the children, the activities of these club gymnasts may cause you some uneasiness.

If you explain your concern to these children, you'll find they appreciate your candor. Tell these young gymnasts you're working to learn about the movements they're practicing. Assure them that once you're skilled enough to help them practice appropriately and safely, you'll be delighted to have them resume practice in class.

This approach makes it clear you aren't criticizing but instead are respecting their proficiency. Students will, in turn, respect you for acknowledging your limitations and seeking their cooperation, and teacher–student rapport will be enhanced.

Spotting

Spotting—the practice of physically assisting children as they perform a movement—isn't commonly used in educational gymnastics classes. Children who depend on such help are likely to be unsure and even afraid unless a teacher is nearby. And, conversely, spotting encourages children to attempt movements they may not be ready for. We've observed a number of programs, including our own, in which children have progressed to a relatively high level of skill proficiency without any spotting. Even though we do not "spot" children when they are performing skills in educational gymnastics, we strongly believe in safety for all children in the gymnastics setting. Throughout the skill themes for gymnastics (Chapters 17, 19–22), you will have noted the safety icon (⚠) emphasizing safety tips for the teacher.

The other children will look to the club gymnasts as models and sources for new ideas. The presence of club gymnasts in physical education results in an interesting blend of child-created gymnastics skills and

The Little Gymnast

Come with us, now, to a very nice place where little children swing on rings.

Where laughter is king—and happiness queen—and everyone likes who they are.

On a little green island called Mercer, in a big blue Washington lake surrounded by trees, is a wonderful building assembled by people who think it's important for children to play. And learn. And find out what they can do.

The building is called the Jewish Community Center, and children come from miles around to follow a Pied Piper of a man named Robin West.

Robin grew up in South Africa and then went to college at the University of Saskatchewan in Canada. Now he teaches movement, tumbling, and gymnastics to hundreds of boys and girls in the United States. One of his favorite classes is "kiddie gymnastics," for little gymnasts, four to six.

Most four-year-olds already know how to run, jump, and play when they come to their very first day of kiddie gymnastics. But in no time at all, Robin can open their eyes to hundreds of new ways to move, swing, roll, bend, and balance their bodies with success.

"Success for everyone" is the motto in kiddie gymnastics. It's such a simple motto—so easy to follow—that sometimes even Robin and the children's parents must stop to remind themselves of its magic.

A child is a butterfly in the wind. Some can fly higher than others; but each one flies the best way it can. Why compare one against the other? Each one is different. Each one is special. Each one is beautiful.

In kiddie gymnastics, everyone flies and nobody fails. There's plenty of praise for the attempt well-tried. To balance on a beam for the very first time is discovery. To be praised and applauded for the very same motion is joy.

In just a few short weeks the children in Robin's class have learned to move with a confidence, poise, and imagination that surprises and pleases both themselves and their parents.

But they've also learned something else along the way. You can see it in their eyes when they tug so gently on Robin's bushy black beard. You can see it in the way they lie on their backsides and stare at the ceiling and giggle. It's as if they've learned something deep and exciting about themselves.

"I'm me . . . I'm special . . . I can try."

"If I make a mistake, it's all right. I'll start over . . . I'll learn . . . I'll get better."

"Look at my friend. I'm helping him stand on his head. He's special, too."

"We're good. We're children. We're okay."

—Dan Zadra

Source: Dan Zadra, The little gymnast, *Young Athlete Magazine* (June 1976), 8. Reprinted with permission.

Olympic/club gymnastics skills, providing an interesting dimension to gymnastics lessons.

A Final Thought

Teaching educational gymnastics is, in the beginning, perhaps more difficult than teaching Olympic-style/club gymnastics. In Olympic/club gymnastics, the desired outcomes are clear—the teacher wants the children to execute predetermined skills in specific ways. He or she then teaches, observes, and assesses the children's responses based on that predetermined outcome. In educational gymnastics, the desired student responses aren't predetermined, nor are they to be performed in one correct way. Instead, the teacher helps the children improve their balance and weight transfer abilities, gain self-confidence and self-reliance in interpreting tasks, and determine the best ways to execute skills. Often, it's more difficult for a teacher to state a task and determine if the variety of student responses are quality decisions than it is for a teacher to state a task and expect all to perform it the same. You'll find, however, that the process of sharing decisions in educational gymnastics can be exciting for you, the teacher, and rewarding for the children, regardless of their gymnastics abilities.

Summary

Because of the self-testing nature of gymnastics, children are fascinated by the challenges of balance and weight transfers. It's important in our physical education programs to distinguish educational gymnastics from Olympic/club gymnastics. Educational gymnastics is child-centered, focusing on tasks and challenges appropriate for each child at his or her skill level. Olympic/club gymnastics emphasizes defined stunts performed the same way by all children. *Children Moving* focuses entirely on educational gymnastics.

Many gymnastics movements are learned on the floor (mats) first and then practiced on apparatus. Gymnastics apparatus can be purchased, or equipment available in schools—such as tables, wooden boxes, and benches—can be adapted to serve the same purposes.

It's important to establish a safe learning environment for all gymnastics work. Games like Follow the Leader or I Dare You have no place in the gymnastics environment. The teacher's knowledge of individual students and the selection of developmentally appropriate tasks are critical for this safety.

Reading Comprehension Questions

1. Why do children find balancing, transferring weight, and supporting weight on different body parts fascinating skills?
2. What do we mean by "Gymnastics is self-testing in nature"?
3. Why is safety emphasized so heavily in the teaching of gymnastics?
4. What are the purposes of Olympic/club gymnastics and educational gymnastics?
5. Why do we choose educational gymnastics for children in our physical education programs?
6. How are children introduced to equipment?
7. Can children experience a gymnastics curriculum without equipment?
8. Why are equipment arrangement, class organization, and selection of tasks extremely important in the teaching of educational gymnastics? Explain the significance of each in establishing the learning environment.
9. Why is teaching Olympic/club gymnastics somewhat easier than teaching educational gymnastics?

References/Suggested Readings

Boucher, A. 1978. Educational gymnastics is for everyone. *Journal of Physical Education and Recreation* 49(7): 48–50.

Cameron, W. McD. and P. Pleasance. 1971. *Education in movement–gymnastics*. Oxford, England: Basil Blackwell.*

Carroll, M. E., and D. R. Garner. 1984. *Gymnastics 7–11: A lesson-by-lesson approach*. London: Falmer Press.*

Holbrook, J. 1974. *Movement activity in gymnastics*. Boston: Plays.*

Holt/Hale, S. and T. Hall. 2016. *Lesson planning for elementary physical education*. Champaign, IL: Human Kinetics.

Mauldon, E. and J. Layson. 1965, 1979. *Teaching gymnastics*. London: MacDonald & Evans.*

Morison, R. 1969. *A movement approach to educational gymnastics*. London: Dent.*

Nilges, L. M. 1997. Stages of content development in educational gymnastics. *Journal of Physical Education, Recreation and Dance* 68(3): 50–55.

Nilges, L. M. 1999. Refining skill in educational gymnastics: Seeing quality through variety. *Journal of Physical Education, Recreation and Dance* 70(3): 43–48.

[SHAPE America] Society of Health and Physical Educators. 2009. *Appropriate instructional practice guidelines for elementary physical education*. Reston, VA: Author.

[SHAPE America] Society of Health and Physical Educators. 2014. *National standards & grade-level outcomes for K-12 physical education*. Champaign, IL: Human Kinetics.

Trevor, M. D. 1985. *The development of gymnastics skills*. Oxford, England: Basil Blackwell.

Werner, P. H., L. H. Williams, and T. Hall. 2012. *Teaching children gymnastics*. 3rd ed. Champaign, IL: Human Kinetics.

Williams, J. 1974. *Themes for educational gymnastics*. London: Lepus Books.*

Zadra, D. 1976. The little gymnast. *Young Athlete Magazine* (June): 8.

*The foundation of educational gymnastics for children.

Teaching Educational Games

The game is not sacred; children are.

—JIM STIEHL

Megan C.

Key Concepts

- The purpose of educational games in the elementary curriculum is for youngsters to become versatile, adaptable, and skillful games players in meaningful game situations.

- The content of games is largely based on the manipulative skills themes.

- You will not find "traditional games" in this chapter or in the skill theme chapters, but you will find experiences that allow children to apply their skills in a variety of developmentally appropriate games-playing situations.

- Skill themes are applied to the context of games in three different types of experiences: invariant game skill experiences, dynamic game-like experiences, and games-playing experiences.

- In the invariant game skill experiences, the focus is practicing isolated skills in an unchanging situation and the "game" takes the form of self-testing challenge activities.

- The dynamic game-like experiences include using skills in a changing (open) environment, combining skills, and developing tactics.

- The games-playing experience can be predesigned or child-designed and involves playing games that conform to all that is known about appropriate practices in physical education.

- Predesigned games-playing experiences include ready-made games, modified ready-made games, and teacher-designed games. Child-designed games-playing experiences include teacher/child-designed games and games designed by children.

- The process of teaching games experiences includes both planning and teaching considerations to ensure that the game is a learning experience.

Fifth-Grade Definitions of a Game

- A game is something which you can play for fun or for something serious. It is to learn sometimes, too. —*Jennifer*
- A game is a thing where you have fun. It involves two or more people. You play with a set of rules till the time runs out or some amount of points are scored. —*Alfie*
- A game is an activity that involves one or more people to play. There are many different kinds of games. A lot of games involve running, catching, throwing, and dodging, but not all of them. Some need teams and some don't. —*Danny*
- A game is an action of play that almost all the time has rules. —*Merrell*
- A game is something you play. It's when you learn to play something with other people. You run in some; in some you throw and catch; in others you hide. You have partners. You can do lots of things when you play a game — you walk, you kick, you dodge. —*Leisel*
- A game is something that you do. You sometimes have bases or balls or different equipment. —*Nancy*

What is a game? The concept of a game holds a very different connotation for children than it does for adults. Children tend to view games as play-like, challenging, vigorous, skillful, and having rules. These activities may or may not look like adult versions of sports. Although youth versions of sports exist, sports are generally designed for adults and require a level of technical expertise to which many children will never aspire. When created by or designed for children, games may use the same basic skills as many sports but lack the institutionalized rules and procedures. Quite often, children call their games by names similar to those of standardized sports, and their games may use equipment similar to that of standardized sports; however, the "game" is quite different.

Games are appropriate elementary school content; sports in their common form are not.

Initially in the skill theme approach, we focus on children acquiring the building blocks, the fundamentals of movement that provide the foundation for a lifetime of enjoyable physical activity—in this case, games. These movement fundamentals are studied and practiced in different games contexts and settings and, over time, develop from isolated skill tasks with a "games" focus to games tasks that use selected skills. For example, traveling in straight, curved, and zigzag pathways while dribbling a ball becomes the means to scoring a goal in either soccer or basketball. As such, it is not the game that is important, but the application of skill themes in game settings. The "game" allows children to apply the skills they have learned in a dynamic environment. Our goal, then, is to provide games experiences for children in a way that is both challenging and appropriate for all students in our classes. Thus you will not find "games" in this chapter or in the skill theme chapters, but you will find learning experiences that allow children to apply their skills in a variety of developmentally appropriate games-playing situations.

The Nature of Games

Games always seem to take us back. They take us back to our own childhood, when we played for hours on the school playground, in the streets, and in our

neighborhood backyards. We played our made-up games; we played games with names like Red Rover and dodgeball that we had learned somewhere, and we played games that were called by "real" names such as baseball and football. Our games playing is steeped in tradition. And tradition can be good or bad. It is good when it enables us to pass on the best of what games have to offer—friendship, skill practice, teamwork, camaraderie, and the sheer excitement of playing.

Yet all too often, games playing seems to be the content area that traps us in the negative aspects of our tradition. We are trapped by the same tradition that brought us joy, trapped into thinking that what gave us excitement and satisfaction will also bring excitement and satisfaction to all of today's children. That entrapment lets us forget how we were often the highly skilled players and how even we changed those games. We become so ingrained in the tradition that we forget how we made constant adjustments to all our games to make them "our own" and to meet our needs and the needs of others.

We made the games fit us, rather than fitting ourselves to the games. Rarely, if ever, did we play on regulation fields with regulation equipment with the "right" number of players or by any rules other than our own. We had bricks for bases, four players on a baseball team, imaginary runners, and no gloves, and we played with whatever bat and ball we could find. We didn't have people sit out—they were all our friends. Yet somehow when we teach games to children, we tend to get caught in the rules we learned later in life, rules we played by as teenagers and adults. Our challenge is to help all children enjoy playing games that are theirs, not ours, and to help prepare them to want to play games forever—whatever those games may be. Our challenge is to make the games-playing experience fit the child.

The Purpose of Games in the Elementary School

Our view of games is what can be called educational games (Rink 2008). While the primary focus of educational games is skill acquisition, when children progress to the utilization and proficiency levels, they also learn to become versatile and adaptable games players. Educational games can be grouped in a variety of ways; most often by either the skill used or the tactics involved. If grouped by tactics, games are classified such as invasion, net/wall, target, striking/fielding, and individual games (Almond 1986; Mauldon and Redfern 1969; Mitchell, Oslin, and Griffin 2013). However, we develop games around the skill theme used

(e.g., throwing, catching, striking, dribbling) that provides the foundation to be later transferred and applied for use in invasion, net, target, or striking games. Games experiences should help children apply the cognitive, affective, and psychomotor skills they have acquired in an effort to become competent and knowledgeable games players. Our responsibility is to provide experiences that allow this to happen and are appropriate for all children. As a result of participating in physical education games experiences, children should be excited about participating in games on their own. In short, games should be a good learning experience, characterized by the following: (1) the potential to improve motor skills; (2) maximum participation for all children; (3) the appropriate experiential level of all children; and (4) the possibility of integrating cognitive, psychomotor, and affective learning (Rink 2014).

What Is a Good Game?

- Contributes to skill development
- Is safe
- Includes and does not eliminate
- Has high participation rates
- All children are successful and being challenged

Source: P. Hastie, *Student-designed games* (Champaign, IL: Human Kinetics, 2010).

The *National Standards & Grade-Level Outcomes for K–12 Physical Education* (SHAPE America 2014) support the inclusion of games experiences in elementary physical education. Box 31-1 lists the sample grade-level outcomes specific to games in the elementary school curriculum.

In addition, *Appropriate Instructional Practice Guidelines for Elementary School Physical Education* (SHAPE America 2009) provides a useful analysis of the appropriateness of games in different situations. It is our responsibility as physical educators to teach developmentally appropriate games (Box 31-2).

Content of Games

The manipulative skill themes and movement concepts combined with the locomotor skill themes of traveling, chasing, fleeing, and dodging are largely applied in the context of games. For example, a player is asked to travel while dribbling a ball, using changes in speed and direction to dodge an opponent, all the while being aware of where a teammate is. Dance combines skill themes and movement concepts into both

Box 31-1

Games in the *National Standards & Grade-Level Outcomes for K–12 Physical Education*

Games are referenced in the *National Standards & Grade-Level Outcomes for K–12 Physical Education* (SHAPE America 2014) under Standards 1, 2, and 5. The intent of these standards includes the following: (1) competency in a variety of motor skills and movement patterns (Standard 1); (2) application of concepts, principles, strategies, and tactics related to movement and performance (Standard 2); and (3) recognition of physical activity for health, enjoyment, challenge, self-expression, and/or social interaction (Standard 5).

Sample grade-level outcomes from the *National Standards** include:

Standard 1

- Combines locomotor and manipulative skills in a variety of small-sided practice tasks/games environments (5)
- Combines jumping and landing patterns with locomotor and manipulative skills in dance, gymnastics, and small-sided practice tasks in games environments (5)

- Performs curling, twisting, and stretching actions with correct application in dance, gymnastics, small-sided practice tasks, and games environments (5)

Standard 2

- Combines spatial concepts with locomotor and nonlocomotor movements for small groups in gymnastics, dance, and games environments (5)
- Recognizes the types of kicks needed for different games and sports situations (4)
- Recognizes the type of throw, volley, or striking action needed for different games and sports situations (5)

Standard 5

- Identifies physical activities that provide self-expression (e.g., dance, gymnastics routines, practice tasks in games environments) (2)

*Suggested grade-level outcomes for student learning.

Box 31-2

Appropriate and Inappropriate Physical Education Practices

Component: Productive Learning Experiences

Appropriate Practice

- Teachers select, design, sequence, and modify games to maximize the attainment of specific learning, fitness/skill enhancement, and enjoyment.
- Teachers modify the rules, regulations, equipment, and playing space to facilitate learning by children of varying abilities or to focus learning on particular games or skills components.

Inappropriate Practice

- Teachers use games with no obvious learning purpose or goal other than to keep children "busy, happy, and good."

Component: Maximizing Participation

Appropriate Practice

- Physical educators use small-sided games (1 v. 1; 2 v. 2; etc.) or mini-activities that allow students ample opportunity to participate.

Inappropriate Practice

- The teacher consistently uses only one ball for most activities that involve playing with a ball (e.g., soccer, softball). In game situations, most players rarely touch the ball.

Component: Competition and Cooperation

Appropriate Practice

- Physical educators develop learning experiences that assist students to understand the nature and the different kinds of competition. For example, the students may elect to keep score or play for skill practice in selected situations.
- Physical educators create a mastery learning environment that encourages students to compete against previous personal performances or against a criterion score. Children are given the opportunity to choose their competitive environment.

Inappropriate Practice

- Students are required to always keep score and participate in activities that publicly identify students as winners or losers (e.g., relay races, elimination tag).
- Teachers focus on the production of full-scale competition and limited skill instruction (e.g., teachers play 11 v. 11 soccer instead of modifying the game to 2 v. 2).

SHAPE America, *Appropriate instructional practice guidelines, K-12: A side-by-side comparison.* Reston, VA: SHAPE America, 2009. Copyright ©2009 by SHAPE America. Reprinted with permission from SHAPE America - Society of Physical Educators, 1900 Association Drive, Reston, VA 20191, www.shapeamerica.org.

predesigned and child-designed experiences that encourage children to use their bodies and imaginations to express feelings as well as gain the ability to interpret and move to different rhythms, and gymnastics uses skill themes and movement concepts for children to maneuver their bodies against gravity both on the floor and on apparatus. Game situations, however, require players both to combine skills themes and apply them to outsmart and outplay an opponent. It is precisely the use of skills at the appropriate time and in the appropriate way that makes games difficult to teach well. Thus, although many of us are most comfortable and familiar with the games context, and although a game tends to be self-propelling once students grasp the basic concepts, the game context is complex and takes the same care in planning as gymnastics and dance.

Games experiences for children can be classified into three types: (1) invariant skill development experiences, (2) dynamic game-like skill development experiences, and (3) games-playing experiences. Games playing can be either predesigned or child-designed. Historically, our teaching starts with invariant skill development experiences (unchanging) and then immediately moves to the games-playing experiences. The middle type of experiences, dynamic game-like skill development, which focuses on the combination of skills and the progressive use of those combinations in changing conditions, is often omitted. As teachers, we have done little to help children learn how to combine skills and use the combinations effectively. The bottom line is this: Just because a skill is linked to a context area (games, dance, or gymnastics), this doesn't mean that by acquiring the skill one can use it appropriately in games, dance, or gymnastics settings. Teaching throwing and catching is one thing; learning how to throw and catch in a game situation is another. Some skill development results from playing games, but game playing isn't the most efficient way for all children to improve the motor skills used in games.

One implication teachers often draw from these three types of games experiences is that children must do boring "practice" tasks before "playing the game" or that until children become exceedingly proficient during dynamic game-like skill development experiences and approach the proficiency level of skill development, they shouldn't play games. That is exactly what skill themes are not about. Although invariant and dynamic skill development experiences are largely hierarchical, games-playing experiences are not. Children should have games-playing experiences on a continuous basis; however, what that games-playing experience looks like changes as children's skills develop. Isolating skill development and keeping children in invariant games-playing experiences over a long period of time is just as inappropriate as teaching games playing before children possess the prerequisite skills. There is no clear line of demarcation for moving from one type of experience to another—it depends on students' development level. Thus, the games-playing experience offered is constantly changing, depending on what is to be taught and students' level.

A broad rule might be that for children at the precontrol and early control levels of development, invariant skill development experiences are appropriate (remember, youngsters will most often think of the challenges used in this phase as games) because they are trying to master a skill. Players at control and utilization levels benefit from dynamic game-like experiences. Utilization- and proficiency-level players will find games-playing experiences exciting and engaging. This does not mean you never return to invariant game experiences (think of how many Olympic-caliber athletes practice basic skills for hours daily); it means you can gradually make the invariant skills more complex so they approach an increasingly changing situation. As with dynamic game-like experiences, as students become more proficient players, you gradually extend the challenges used in games playing to make it more complex while ensuring it remains developmentally appropriate. It also means that at the control level games-playing experiences are simple and static to match the skill of the child.

The instructor who teaches children to play games successfully and effectively creates a variety of learning opportunities and situations in which children combine skills into game-like situations, as well as situations in which children play games and in which they practice skills. The children in such programs acquire a foundation of movement skills that enables them to participate successfully in a broad variety of games and sports. Once children have acquired the prerequisite game skills, sport becomes an attractive leisure-time alternative for them throughout their lives.

Invariant Game Skill Development Experiences

Invariant skill development involves practice of the isolated skills used in games in relatively closed or unchanging situations. These experiences really don't look like games at all to adults—they look like skill development, which is what they are. The "games" focus is the potential use of the skill in games playing that will emerge later. The "game" experience here is that of a self-testing or challenge activity.

Trying to roll a ball through a target is an example of invariant game experience.

©Lars A. Niki

Learning experiences during invariant skill development experiences allow the students to gain control of an object using a specific motor pattern (Rink 2014). The experience is structured so the task is as identical as possible each time—the experience is invariant in that the child isn't required to predict the flight of a ball or the movement of an opponent, for example. At this point, refinement is the major emphasis. For example, the task progression of "Continuous Dribbling" (Chapter 25, page 522) is an example of an invariant skill development experience. The challenge tasks of "Practice until you can dribble the ball five times without losing control of it" and "Say one letter of the alphabet for each time you dribble. Can you get to Z?" are perceived as "games" for the children performing them. Remember, a challenge task that allows a child to "self-test" is easily viewed by the child as a "game" as the focus is shifted from practicing the skill to using the skill. See Chapters 6 and 7 for more on the development of challenge tasks.

Such experiences are appropriate for a child who is at the precontrol or control level of skill proficiency and who would have difficulty executing a skill in a dynamic or moving situation. As a child's proficiency in a skill increases, you can increase the difficulty of the tasks while retaining the relative predictability of the skill. For example, when a child is learning to throw a ball to hit a stationary target, you can increase the distance to the target. If the child is learning to run and leap over a low obstacle, increase the height of the obstacle.

When a child who isn't able to perform a basic skill consistently (precontrol level) is placed in a situation (often a game) that requires the skill and the ability to perform it in a changing environment, the results are often counterproductive. A child in that situation often fails and becomes frustrated because of continuing inability to execute the prerequisite movements of the game. The child may then become a self-proclaimed, permanently terminated games player or a teenager or adult who vows to never again play in a game situation. And the other children are frustrated as the lesser skilled player interrupts the flow and their enjoyment of the game.

Dynamic Game-like Experiences

A second example of applying skill themes in the context of games provides children with dynamic game-like experiences. These experiences may look and feel like games to children, but they are designed to teach three things: (1) the use of basic skills in a changing environment, (2) combinations of skills, and (3) simple offensive and defensive tactics. During these experiences, "games" are small-sided with restricted rules (two passes before a shot; no more than three dribbles before a pass) and limited space. They have clear learning goals and are permeated by stops and starts to refine skill and provide cues. In the beginning, they are often cooperative; they develop into competitive games when children no longer find cooperative experiences challenging. Dynamic game-like experiences are appropriate for children at the upper control, utilization, and proficiency levels.

For example, the task of "Maintaining Possession While Dribbling and Passing" (Chapter 25, page 533) would be a dynamic game-like skill development experience. The task states that: "Working in your group of three, two of you will dribble and pass while the third player tries to steal the ball. We'll rotate the interceptor [defender] every 2 minutes. Remember, you must either be dribbling or passing the ball. You may not hold it; no touching." The children completing this task would view it as a game, while the purpose would be the development of passing and dribbling skills

Dribbling a ball past a defender into a goal is a dynamic game-like skill experience.

©Barbara Adamcik

competent games players. Yet it is precisely these experiences that are usually omitted.

Skills in a Changing Environment

Research suggests that a child has little chance of actually being able to use basic skills in a game environment unless he or she has first practiced them in an open, changing, and dynamic situation (Schmidt 1977). The skill acquired by a child who throws and catches a yarn ball may transfer minimally to the skill of throwing and catching used in, for example, baseball or basketball. For this reason, as soon as a child displays a minimum level of mastery in an invariant situation, it is necessary to create situations that are progressively and increasingly complex and in which skills are used in combination as they occur in games-playing situations. For example, dribbling the ball on the ground (Chapter 23, page 454) is a skill different from playing two-on-one soccer (Chapter 23, page 454) while being guarded by an opponent.

against a defender. The implication is that as the child slowly becomes more adept at using a motor skill or combination of motor skills, the child is simultaneously learning games-playing tactics to accompany the skill.

These three different and equally important aspects—the use of skills in a changing environment, the use of combinations of skills, and the development of game tactics—like games experiences themselves, are developmental but not hierarchical. In actual practice, they intermingle greatly. Teaching skills in an open environment and teaching combinations of skills, as well as tactics, are critical to children learning to be

Combinations of Skills

When children are involved in dynamic game-like experiences, they need to be exposed to experiences that relate to a variety of types of games. The infinite combinations of and linkages between skills have to be taught. Skill combinations might include dribbling and passing, shooting off a pass, receiving a pass and dribbling, receiving a pass and passing, and the like. Practicing skills in combinations is a critical and often neglected aspect of

Young children's games rarely have game-playing qualities

©Barbara Adamcik

learning how to play games. It is critical because it is the transition between the two skills that makes the combination skillful and effective. To make the transition well, preparation for performing the second skill must occur while the first skill is being performed. For example, when young players are learning receiving and passing with the feet, they commonly receive the ball, stop, move into position to pass, and then pass. The skilled player moves the ball into position to pass as he or she is receiving it and passes without stopping. The difference is the transition. For players to be successful in games situations, they have to learn the transitions after they learn the skills. The focus at this point is on the transition, not on the two isolated skills. Tasks and cues can be developed that focus on the transition. For example, in the dribbling and passing with a partner task on page 531 in Chapter 25, the focus is on the cues that allow the motion to be continuous: the receiver being ahead of the passer, the pass leading the receiver, both players constantly moving, and smooth transitions between the dribble and the pass.

Tactic or Strategy—What Is the Difference?

Tactics can be defined as an understanding of what to do during game-play situations or the problems players need to solve to be successful in game play (Mitchell, Oslin, and Griffin 2003). Tactics generally involve how to score and how to prevent scoring from occurring. Strategy, on the other hand, is an overall game plan and would include the use of a variety of tactics.

Tactics

The third critical and often neglected aspect that occurs in dynamic games skill experiences is learning simple offensive and defensive tactics that allow players to use the skills they have learned to outwit others. At this point, children shouldn't have to devote their attention to controlling objects. They should already know to how to do a skill; their focus is now on when to use that skill. The attention to tactics is not to suggest that skills are neglected or that overdue attention is placed on tactics; just that if you have the contact time to get to utilization-level tasks with your students, learning and employing simple tactics allow for increased enjoyment of using skills in game-like experiences. Thus, it is wise to teach tactics when children's skills are at the utilization level. Tactics, like basic skills, can be taught and have critical elements. One example might be learning to create space in an invasion-type activity using dribbling with the feet. For example, in the "Playing Mini Soccer" task (Chapter 23, page 456), students can play a game-like activity that asks them to provide a 45-degree passing

angle for their partner. The focus is on the angle for passing and when to pass rather than the pass itself. As with skills, it is best to learn these activities in less complex situations first, then gradually increase the complexity. For example, the idea of passing angles can first be learned with no defense, then with a passive defense or in a two-on-one situation, and then with an aggressive defense such as in the "Playing Two-on-One Soccer" task from Chapter 23 (page 454). Complexity can be increased by adding players, boundaries, or scoring. The key aspect here is to add complexity very gradually. The utilization- and proficiency-level learning experiences described in the manipulative skill theme chapters contain cues for simple offensive and defensive tactics.

During these experiences, many teachers use inquiry teaching to teach tactics (Mitchell, Oslin, and Griffin 2003, 2013). For example, in a one-on-one situation of striking over a net, you are trying to teach the idea of hitting to open spaces and covering space. Children already can keep the ball going back and forth to each other. A teacher may stop the lesson and ask, "Where do you have to hit to make your opponent miss?" Answer: "Open space" (most often phrased as "where they are not"). "Where do you have to be to prevent your partner from having a lot of open space to which to hit?" Answer: "Home" (middle of court just behind center). Then the teacher sends the students back to practice doing those things, even giving them points for doing those things. Tactics can also be taught through direct instruction, but it lends itself well to the inquiry approach as it is a cognitive concept as well as a physical ability.

Games-Playing Experiences

Unlike the two previous games experiences that are characterized by starts and stops, games-playing experiences are somewhat different as they allow children to focus on gaining knowledge and enthusiasm for playing a developmentally appropriate game while using the skills and tactics previously learned. The enjoyment and satisfaction derived from playing games frequently are products of playing a game with fewer interruptions. This does not mean the teacher does nothing during games-playing experiences or never stops the game. It is a great opportunity to observe the types of skill work that children need as they're playing games and to focus on those needs at convenient breaks. Games-playing experiences may occur at all levels of skill proficiency, yet it is the skills within the game that are different. At the precontrol/control levels, the game contains invariant skills, whereas at the upper control, utilization, and proficiency levels, the skills are in a dynamic and changing environment. Remember, games-playing experiences don't occur in every lesson; they are only a part of the total physical education program.

We have divided games-playing experiences into pre-designed experiences and child-designed experiences. Each has its own inherent strengths and weaknesses.

Predesigned Games-Playing Experiences

There are three types of predesigned games-playing experiences: ready-made, modified ready-made, and teacher-designed.

Ready-Made Games   Ready-made games are often taught to children without modification. Some games resources imply that such games will be appropriate, as well as interesting, for children. Brownies and Fairies; Duck, Duck, Goose; Red Rover; Four Square; and Steal the Bacon are well-known ready-made games.

Ready-made games are easy to teach because they require little preparation or teaching skill. The teacher selects a game and explains it to the children. When the children understand the game, they start to play, and the game continues until the lesson ends or the teacher changes the activity.

It has been our experience that few ready-made games are appropriate for all the children in a class. A few skilled children often dominate such games, whereas others are minimally involved, both physically and emotionally. Some (Belka 2004b) say these games

---

So What's Wrong with Playing "the" Game?

This question invariably arises. And yes, there are multiple answers. Here are just a few:

- The actual time a child is involved in activity is minimal.
- The game is not appropriate for all children in the class—in terms of physical, psychological, or skill readiness.
- The equipment is not appropriate for all children.
- Children are eliminated from play (and these are the children who need to play the most).
- Children are spotlighted for their lack of skill (or their skillfulness).
- Winners and losers rate one child or group of children better than the others.
- When teams are chosen some children are publicly humiliated.
- The game is often just played to play a game; it is not linked to skill development.

The list can go on. For a more extensive discussion of the inappropriateness of playing "*the*" game see Neil Williams's "Hall of Shame" articles in *Journal of Physical Education, Recreation and Dance* (1992; 1994; 1996).

---

should be discarded. However, you may occasionally encounter a situation in which a particular ready-made game is appropriate for a class or group of children. Usually, though, you'll find that although many of the ideas in a ready-made game are worthwhile, you have to extensively modify the structure of the game to the abilities and interests of different children.

When observing a game of kickball played by a group of third and fourth graders under the supervision of the classroom teacher, it was detected that:

- Less than half of the game was actually spent using the criterion skills.
- The average number of catches attempted in the kickball games was slightly more than two—35 percent of the children never caught the ball. Of the children who didn't catch the ball, 83 percent were girls.
- The average number of throws made in the kickball games, excluding those made by the pitcher and catcher, was slightly more than one—52 percent of the children never threw the ball at all during the entire game, and 67 percent of those who never threw the ball were girls.

Wilson, N. 1976. The frequency and patterns of selected motor skills by third and forth grade girls and boys in the game of kickball. Unpublished master's project, University of Georgia, Athens.

Modified Ready-Made Games   Modifying ready-made games requires greater planning and organizing ability. Yet by modifying a ready-made game, you can do much to make the game address a specific lesson objective and thus be more appropriate for a particular class.

Both Rink (2014) and Stiehl, Morris, and Sinclair (2008) provide useful ideas for modifying ready-made games. The teacher can change the rules (e.g., allow two tries instead of only one); the equipment used (e.g., larger and lighter); the number of players involved (generally, it's best to decrease the number); the playing area (e.g., larger or smaller); or the skills involved (e.g., throwing instead of striking). Many teachers modify one aspect of the game at a time until it provides an experience appropriate for the children's skill level (see Table 31.1). The task of "Volleying Game: Modified Teacher-Designed Game" in Chapter 25 (page 519) is an example of a modified ready-made game. A good rule to follow is to change or eliminate anything that impedes or slows the flow of a game.

Teacher-Designed Games   Sometimes a teacher can't find a ready-made game appropriate for a particular class, and modifications of ready-made games don't seem effective. In such a situation, the teacher may design a game that satisfies a specific goal. Designing a game places a greater demand on a teacher's creative

Table 31.1 **Game Aspects That Can Be Modified**

Aspect	Possible Changes				
Players	Reduce the number of players	Increase the number of players	Mix skill levels	Combine like skill levels	
Purpose	To practice skill	To practice combined skills	To practice strategy	To play games	
Player Movement	Restrict the movement of some players	Allow some players to move			
Equipment	Use smaller equipment	Use larger equipment	Use lighter equipment	Use heavier equipment	Use more (or less) equipment
Organization	Define the organization—circle, etc.	Let the organization be random			
Space	Increase the space	Decrease the space	Make the space long and narrow	Make the space short and wide	
Rules	Omit rules that restrict the flow	Add rules to enhance opportunities			
Skills	Reduce the number of skills involved				

abilities than do either of the game lesson structures already discussed.

The teacher needs to understand the children's skill abilities and interests and be able to use this knowledge to design a game form that the children will find interesting and enjoyable. For example, a teacher could design a game to focus on striking a ball with a bat. The object would be to strike a pitched ball and then run around a cone and back before the other players catch or collect the ball and touch the home base with the ball. If the children used rather narrow boundaries and played in small groups, they would get more striking, throwing, and catching opportunities than the standardized nine-per-side version of softball provides. The teacher could design the game to be played by two teams or design it so each child goes back "to the field" once she or he hits the ball and runs around the cone. "Punting for Distance and Accuracy: Punt Over" (see Chapter 23, page 466) is an example of a teacher-designed game.

Child-Designed Games

Each of the three game lesson structures in predesigned games places the responsibility for selecting or designing a game on the teacher. One advantage of these games structures is that the children spend most of the time–once the game has been explained and organized–playing the game. But the children don't contribute to the design of the game, nor do they have anything to say about whether they would like to continue playing the game as is or change the game to make it better. The previous three game designs are direct instructional approaches; the following two child-designed game structures, by contrast, involve the children in the design of the game. They would be classified as inquiry or child-designed approaches and require more advanced teaching skills. (See Chapter 9 for a discussion of instructional approaches and the skills necessary to use each.)

Child-designed games include those designed by the teacher and children working together and those designed by the children with teacher support and structure.

Teacher/Child-Designed Games When the children and the teacher design a game together, the teacher presents the purpose of the game and the restrictions. The children and the teacher then work cooperatively to decide the rules, scoring, and equipment to be used. The whole class plays in small groups.

You'll find it's wise to stipulate that once the game has begun, only the team with the ball (or the advantage) can stop play to suggest a change. (Unless the children are restrained by this rule, they're likely to stop the game and suggest a change every time the other team gains an advantage.) After a brief discussion of the proposed change, the class or group votes, with the majority decision prevailing. If a rule needs to be made to ensure safety, offer solutions to be voted on or ask the children to propose a solution.

One example of a teacher/child-designed game is Magladry Ball, which the children named after their school. The teacher was concerned about the children's inability to travel and pass a ball or other object to a teammate who was also traveling, particularly when an opponent attempted to intercept or prevent the pass from being made. After describing the purpose of the game, the teacher imposed two restrictions: Children couldn't touch each other; and once the ball (object) touched the ground, it was automatically in the possession of the team that didn't touch it immediately before the object hit the ground. The object of the game was to throw the ball (beanbag, flying disc) through a hoop suspended from a goal post by a rope at either end of a field. Once the game began, children made decisions about how long one child could remain in possession of the ball (object); what type of ball (object) to play the game with; boundaries, violations, and penalties; and scoring.

Teacher/child-designed games evolve slowly, and you may spend several lessons creating games children are excited about and enjoy playing. Once the time and effort to create a game have been spent, the children will want to have opportunities to play it.

Games Designed by Children   The underlying assumption of ready-made games, modified ready-made games, teacher-designed games, and teacher/child-designed games is that the entire class is playing the same game, in small groups. In child-designed games, however, we assume that many games are being played simultaneously and that few, if any, are identical. Such an environment is a far more complex one in which to teach (Hastie 2010). The teacher is assisting groups of children to develop different games and is also responsible for observing a number of different games and assisting or staying away when appropriate.

Games designed by children have some definite advantages. Children in groups of similar skill ability (given a choice, children typically choose to be with others of similar ability) are allowed to design games that are interesting and exciting to them. These may be cooperative or competitive, active or passive, depending on the children's intent.

Initially, children need help in creating their own games. Teachers who've met with success in using child-designed games have found that in the beginning it's helpful to suggest a structure for the game—that is, the purposes, boundaries, and rules. For example, the teacher may say, "Make up your own striking game. There may be up to four people in the group. All of you must play at once; there's to be no waiting in line. And the space can be no larger than 15 feet by 15 feet." The teacher can also help the children organize the game by asking them to identify their rules, either verbally or in writing (Figure 31.1). Three child-designed games for volleying and dribbling are illustrated in Figure 25.6 (page 514).

As children learn to make decisions about their games, the amount of imposed structure can be decreased. If children are to make significant and worthwhile decisions about their game, you must stay out of as many decisions as possible; this is just as

Figure 31.1 Example of a child-designed game—sixth grade.

important as providing proper initial guidance. Even if you're certain some idea won't work, it's no longer your role to tell them so (except in the case of safety). They'll find out soon enough.

You may consider it a disadvantage that some children take a great deal of time to create games. Children who've had little experience in creating their own games may spend as much as half of a lesson seriously working out the way they want a game to be played, perhaps without ever actually playing the game. But you'll find that as students gradually become more adept at creating games, playing time increases substantially.

Most children enjoy participating in the creation of their own games. But the children must be ready—they must be able to function successfully in a small group (two or three is an appropriate number) when playing a game they know before they can begin to design games (see Chapter 9 for more detail on the skills a teacher and the children need in order to implement child-designed activities). Some teachers, even of younger children, can use child-designed games from the time they begin teaching and have exciting, successful lessons. But when a teacher—even one who believes in the philosophy represented by child-designed games—tries to have children design their own games before the children (and the teacher) are ready, the outcome can be a disaster.

I would like to contrast the richness of children's natural play with the stultifying rigidity of play that is organized by adults. No better example can be found than that of the Little League, for what boys, left to their own devices, would ever invent such a thing? How could they make such a boneheaded error as to equate competition with play? Think of the ordinary games of boys—in sandlots, fields, parks, even stickball in the street. They are expansive and diverse, alternately intense and gay, and are filled with events of all kinds. Between innings the boys throw themselves on the grass. They'll wrestle, do handstands, turn somersaults. They hurl twigs and stones at nearby trees, and yell at the birds that sail by. A confident player will make up dance steps as he stops a slow grounder. If an outfielder is bored, he does not stand there pulling up his pants and thumping his glove, but plays with the bugs in the grass, looks at the clouds. . . . There is almost always a dog on the field, and no part of the competition is gayer or more intense than that between the boys and the dog, who when he succeeds in snapping up their ball, leads them off in a serpentine line that is all laughter and shouts, the dog looking back over his shoulder and trotting with stiff legs, until finally he is captured and flattens his ears as they take back their ball. No one has forgotten the score or who was at bat. The game goes on. The game goes on until darkness ends it, and the winners can hardly be distinguished from the losers, for by then everyone is fumbling the ball and giggling and flopping on the grass.

—**George Dennison,** *The Lives of Children* (1969)

The ecology of the particular teaching situation determines which game design is best. When selecting a design for a class to address the learning objective of the lesson, consider the purpose for playing the game, the skills required, the children's interests and abilities, the playing area and equipment available, and your skills as a teacher. We try very carefully to match the skills required in the games-playing phase to the children's skills. Nothing is as counterproductive as having children participate in games for which they don't possess the prerequisite skills. The teacher who has closely assessed the children's skill level can discover and/or design well-matched games-playing situations to ensure the children's success and pleasure.

The Teaching of Invariant Games Skill Development, Dynamic Game-like Skill Development, and Games-Playing Experiences

Teaching Invariant and Dynamic Game-like Skill Development Experiences

The type of experience selected for a class—invariant games skill development, dynamic game-like skill development, or games playing—is the first critical aspect in the process of teaching games. The teaching of the invariant and dynamic game-like skill development experiences requires the use of the all the planning and teaching skills discussed in Chapters 6 to 11 because, at this point, the lessons contain isolated or combinations of skills with a "games" focus. Tasks within these experiences are generally appropriate for children at the precontrol and control levels of

Children enjoy playing a self-created game

©Lars A. Niki

proficiency. As such, you must decide the learning objectives for the experience, determine the instructional approach or approaches to be used, develop the content through an appropriate sequence of tasks, communicate effectively, provide specific congruent feedback, and accommodate individual differences. Remember that at these stages challenge tasks are often considered "games" by children; all you have to do is call them that.

Teaching Games-Playing Experiences

When the focus of a lesson turns to games-playing experiences, however, some additional teaching considerations are required. Although we have not addressed each category of games-playing experiences separately, the fundamental instructional pieces discussed in the following paragraphs are paramount to making the type of game selected "work" for a group. If your choice of game is perfect for a class but the instructional aspects contradict your game choice, the class climate negates the content.

It is hard to modify the content without modifying the instruction, yet we have seen it done. It is our thought that for the games playing to be effective, instruction has to be modified as well. Teaching games-playing experiences that meet children's developmental needs is not as simple as it initially appears. For many of us, game playing is so intertwined with deeply embedded sport experiences that it is difficult to "see differently." To see differently, we must focus on the type of games-playing experience best suited to meet the lesson objective, our role as a teacher, and whether the experience is truly a learning experience. It is only then that we truly start to look at the child first and the game second.

In the following section, we provide some concrete strategies for teaching games playing. Both planning considerations as well as considerations while actually teaching are presented. When carefully considered, these strategies provide for more meaningful games experience for you and your students.

Considerations for Planning

Effective teachers do a myriad of things to enhance learning experiences well before their interactions with students. Planning that provides structure for essential learning is perhaps the most essential. While planning and developing the content is addressed in a previous chapter (see Chapter 6), we highlight several key aspects for games here. Key games elements to consider before instruction include alignment with learning objectives, whether or not a game is a true learning experience, the equipment used, what we call the game, the number of players involved, and whether or not the game is competitive.

Alignment of the Game with the Learning Objectives The first planning decision that must be made with a games-playing experience is that it must match the learning objectives that children have been working on in class. We have often seen games in elementary physical education "thrown in" as the last task of a lesson, and they may (or may not) relate to the content being taught. For example, if students have been practicing "Dribbling Against an Opponent: One-on-One (Chapter 25; page 531), then a game of Dribble Tag (Chapter 25; pages 532–533) would be appropriate; however, a game of Dribble/Pass Keep-Away (Chapter 25; page 534) would not be appropriate because the children have not been practicing the combination or dribbling and passing.

A Learning Experience or Not? Games for children in physical education should be learning experiences. We come back here to Rink's (2014) criteria for a learning experience presented on page 665. When planning, be sure to determine if the game: (1) has the potential to improve motor skills; (2) provides for maximum participation for all children; (3) is at the appropriate experiential level of all children; and (4) contains the possibility of integrating cognitive, psychomotor, and affective learning.

Games Equipment The equipment used to play games most certainly affects the quality and difficulty of the game. Large, regulation-size sports equipment slows the play and promotes the use of incorrect skills. Equipment manufacturers design equipment for children: foam paddles, balls, and hockey sticks are three examples. Smaller, lighter, more colorful balls that don't hurt reduce the fear of catching. Basketball goals that can be adjusted to multiple heights (not just one or two) allow all children to be able to shoot at an appropriate basket. The bottom line is this: Adult equipment is almost always inappropriate for elementary school children. Make sure the equipment matches the child.

> *A true game is one that frees the spirit—the true game is the one that arises from the players themselves.*
>
> **—PETER OPIE AND IONA OPIE,** *Children's Games in Street and Playground* (1969)

The Name of the Game   By calling a game by the name of the sport with which its skills are usually associated, we effectively limit children's options. The skilled children think they have to play by the rules of the sport, and the unskilled unconsciously evaluate themselves against some external standard, whether or not they really know much about the sport. As a result, some children are disenfranchised and others are frustrated. We have found children are much more creative and open in their games playing if we refer to the experience by a new name or by the name of the skill. This is why in the index you will find games linked to the skill theme they are used to develop but not listed separately by their name.

Group Size   To many, there is a "right" number of players for a game. Because of our conscious or unconscious sport orientation, the "right" number of players is often the number of players associated with the sport in which the skill is most commonly used. And because predesigned games are usually designed for entire classes, they often call for 15, 20, or more players. Rarely does either of the preceding scenarios contain the "right" number of players for games appropriate to the elementary school setting. Games experiences should never involve more players than can be active at any one time, or so many that the flow of the game is slowed. We have found this usually means four to six (and maybe eight) players as a maximum in any games experience (e.g., three versus three or four versus four). The small group size we recommend implies that more than one game will be played simultaneously. Having several games going on at one time, however, can be uncomfortable for many of us. If this is true for you, we suggest you begin slowly. Start with a class you are confident with, and have only two games play concurrently. As you feel more confident, gradually add more games. Amazingly, more games actually decrease many potential management problems. Because more children are actively and appropriately involved in playing and are spending less time waiting or otherwise unengaged, the amount of off-task behavior is substantially reduced.

Cooperative or Competitive? Score or No Score?   Much has been written about cooperative games versus competitive games. Competition is not inherently bad for children; inappropriate competition is. Children should never be forced to compete against another child until they are ready, and all children are not ready at the same time. Therefore, to have an entire class playing by the same rules of competition disenfranchises many children. We have found two guidelines that work for us. First, let children choose whether or not they want to be in a competitive situation. If there are multiple small-sided games occurring simultaneously, then some could be competitive and some cooperative. Second, cooperative experiences always precede competitive experiences. It is only when cooperative experiences are no longer challenging that competitive experiences are appropriate (Rink 2014). Children, when left to their own devices, almost always follow this maxim.

Cooperation and competition also impact several other aspects of physical education classes. Research clearly indicates that children learn best in a mastery climate focusing on cooperation, hard work, learning, and task mastery (Biddle 1999; Standage, Duda, and Ntoumanis 2003). On the other hand, learning is diminished in classes where children are compared to each other, where there is a focus on competition between children, and where mistakes are punished. In addition, there is recent evidence that during cooperative, nonelimination games, children accrue more moderate and vigorous physical activity than in elimination games (Bruggeman et al. 2008).

Competition/Cooperation

Some children love to compete; others prefer (and seem to learn better in) games that encourage cooperation. We attempt to respect each child's preference by giving choices and trying never to place an entire class in a competitive situation. Instead, we let children choose between two or more games or ask them to make up their own games. The teachers heighten or lessen the degree of competition. Teachers who constantly shout out the score, post team win-and-loss records, and reward the winners (thereby punishing the losers) place an emphasis on competition for which some children aren't ready. If you don't believe us, talk to the thousands of adults who were unskilled as children and yet were placed in highly competitive situations. They can describe, in vivid detail, the feelings of being picked last, shouted at for dropping a ball, and ridiculed for "letting the team down." Such distasteful experiences usually have lasting and negative influences on the individual's willingness to participate in sports.

Considerations While Teaching

Once teachers make important decisions about planning, there are a number of additional considerations while teaching games playing. As authors and teacher educators, we frequently observe the common misconceptions among teacher candidates that once a game begins, the teacher's only role is to observe and maintain safety. What follows are several consider-ations and suggestions for active teaching while games are in progress?

Provide Feedback or Not? Take your cue from the children in determining when to provide feedback. A lull in the game, a water break, the end of class, or other natural interruption provides an opportunity to check with the children and offer guidance if needed. Try not to stop or interfere in the children's games to teach skills, unless the game has become unsatisfying and boring because of lack of ability. Adults prefer not to be interrupted during a game, even by someone who wants to provide feedback. Children share this feeling, and teachers must respect it if they want to create posi-tive attitudes toward games.

"It's like baseball but better! We took out all the boring stuff and we only need six friends to play!"

Freeze Frame Though it is true that game interrup-tions should be kept to a minimum, there are instances where it is beneficial to stop a game and confirm posi-tive attributes and/or identify areas of improvement. These stoppages, or freeze frames, must be strategically used to improve game play. For example, maintaining appropriate spacing is a frequent break down during many games. When this happens, teachers may choose to "freeze" the game and have a brief discussion about how to refine the students' performance, exploring options for getting open and using the entire activity space to create passing opportunities. It may also be

helpful for the teacher to have children physically point to open space. This exercise helps children look for open areas as well as plan their next move once the "go" signal is given.

Questioning An additional strategy for games teach-ing is the use of questioning to help guide students in identifying solutions to the tactical problems presented in games (Mitchell et al. 2013). Questioning may occur during "freeze frames," as previously described, or it may happen at the conclusion of the game. Addition-ally, the use of questions (e.g., What made you success-ful in that game? When you made a successful pass or scored, what did your team do well?) may happen with the members of one small-sided game, or they may be posed to the entire class during a stoppage of play. The number and types of questions are identified by the teacher based on the success of the game and the les-son's learning objectives.

Role of the Teacher As authors of this text, we advo-cate that teachers take an active role to ensure a quality learning environment. Active teaching is particularly important in games teaching. To ensure maximum activity and practice attempts, multiple small-sized games are necessary. These games require thoughtful planning as well as teacher awareness. Active teaching requires observing multiple games at once and provid-ing feedback and or game modifications as needed. However, there are some aspects of active teaching that vary between predesigned games and child-designed games.

Predesigned Games-Playing Experiences. During these experiences, you explain the game and intervene only when it is necessary to keep the game going. Eval-uating the game is more complex. You also have to decide, after observing the children, whether the game should be modified further or is satisfactory as cur-rently structured. As a teacher, you may be tempted to become a game participant; we do not recommend this strategy. While this may be motivating to some chil-dren, when you are playing, you are no longer actively teaching. Also to be considered is whether to serve as an official (or not). We address this here as we have so often seen the teacher as the referee in children's games. Quite simply, we do not believe in officiating children's games. Officiating does several things that detract from the ultimate value of the games-playing experience. First, officiating places the responsibility for coming to decisions about the process of the game on the teacher, taking away all responsibility and deci-sion making from the children. The end result is that they can "blame the teacher" for what happened and avoid learning to cooperate and decide for themselves. Second, officiating takes the teacher out of the teaching role and limits the teacher's ability to provide feedback and instruction—our primary goal. Third, a teacher can only be in one place. If we officiate, only one game can be occurring; this means that all the children aren't active and that more than likely we have created an inappropriate games environment. We have been very successful in letting children "call" their own games. They not only adapt the rules to fit their situation but also develop decision-making and cooperation skills. The flow of the game is also generally more continuous; they stop only when they need to.

Child-Designed Games-Playing Experiences. The role of the teacher changes in child-designed experiences. Helping children design their own games is skill in and of itself. We have learned from experience (the hard way) that just telling children to make up their own game without any structure or guidance leads to chaos and an unproductive experience. Start with the design you think is most appropriate to a class and situation and proceed from there. See Box 31-3 for suggestions on helping children create their own games.

The instructor in child-designed approaches to games serves as a facilitator, enhancing and expanding ideas rather than imposing personal ideas on the children. The teacher helps the children modify the games, offers suggestions, and manages a group of charged-up children who are eager to get the game going again. This isn't an easy task, and it often takes some time to master this approach. See Chapter 9, "Instructional Approaches," for more information about teaching in child-designed environments.

After-School Sport Programs

Many children in your classes may be participating in various sport programs. Often these children are very skilled—many are at the proficiency level of the skills involved in their sport—and so provide an interesting dimension to games lessons. We have found that by using small groups for games-playing experiences, intratask variation, and teaching by invitation, these students can be challenged in our classes just as any other student can be. For example, if students are allowed to design their own game, they can (and will) make it more or less competitive to meet their needs.

Child Development and Games

The research on child development (Piaget 1962) and the development of reasoning (Kohlberg and Mayer 1972) further supports placing children in game situations designed to accommodate their skills, interests, and abilities. For moral and social development and growth to occur, a motivation to change must exist. This motivation requires both developmental readiness and opportunity (Brustad and Parker 2005). Game situations provide an attractive opportunity for children to develop their social skills and reasoning when the situations are developmentally appropriate. Before the age of eight, children are in the egocentric stage. They have a personal conception of reality; the world centers around self. There's no sense of obligation to rules, no desire to check for accuracy. "I" am right at all times. Whatever meets the needs at the present time is what is true. Following rules is fine if it serves the purpose at the time. The concept of cheating doesn't exist because rules constantly change to fit the child's needs. At this stage, the child feels that everyone completely understands him or her and is in agreement with what the child wants. Imagine placing 25 youngsters in a traditional group game when each child thinks he or she is completely understood and in agreement with all!

Piaget (1962) described the game play of the young child (from the child's viewpoint) as a situation in which everyone plays the game as each understands it, with no concern for "checking" on others. Nobody

---

Box 31-3

Helping Children Create Their Own Games

1. Limit group size to six or less.
2. Provide structure:

   - Identify and limit the equipment that can be used.
   - Identify and limit the skills and movements to be included.
   - Identify and limit the space each group may use and have them mark the space.

3. Allow adequate time:

   - Provide time for thinking and creativity, but then indicate a time needed to start play.
   - Provide time for "sorting out" the game as they play.
   - Provide time for playing.

4. Create accountability:

   - Have children name their game.
   - Have children identify the rules.
   - Have children teach others.
   - See if children are able to and want to play the game another day.
   - Have children write their game down.

loses and everybody wins at the same time because the purpose is to have fun (Piaget and Inhelder 1969).

Children between 8 and 11 have a strong social need. To be a part of the group, to belong, is extremely important to children in the upper elementary years. In the early phases of this stage, however, children still have strong egocentric tendencies. Group interaction is desired, but they also desire to cling to the comfortable self-centered view. The earlier "absolute" view is now confronted with the viewpoints of others, viewpoints perhaps not in agreement with one's own. How many children do we see get upset and leave the game when things don't go their way or when they're asked to sacrifice themselves for the good of the team? Cooperative game situations with small groups of children can facilitate establishing the child as a member of the group and foster acceptance of differing points of view.

Students entering the higher level of cognitive development, ages 11 and above, begin to create strategies and mentally test their abilities. They enjoy group activity and respect the physical and mental skills of others in the game situation. The game no longer rules the group; the game is made for the use of the group—to be adapted as needed.

A Final Thought

In this chapter, we have made a case for the inappropriateness of adult versions of sports for children. The child who seeks sport experiences can find them outside the school, and most communities in the United States offer adequate sports at the middle and high school levels, in after-school programs, and in programs sponsored by youth agencies.

Tyson-Martin (1999) has challenged us to refocus, recycle, reorganize, and restructure games for children. It seems an appropriate challenge to take. Physical educators have a responsibility to provide instruction for all children and to help them become skillful games players who enjoy participating in games and are eager to play games on their own time. We must do more than produce a few good athletes. In a successful physical education program, all the children improve their games-playing skills and are eager and excited about playing games. The purpose of this chapter has been to provide an overview of the teaching of games in the elementary school. See Box 31-4 for more resources on children's games.

Box 31-4

Resources for the Teaching of Children's Games

Almond, L. 1983. Games making. *Bulletin of Physical Education* 19(1): 32–35. (This is a classic, but if you can find a copy it is worth the effort.)

Belka, D. 2000. Developing competent games players. *Teaching Elementary Physical Education* 11(3): 6–7.

Belka, D. 2004a. Combining and sequencing games skills. *Journal of Physical Education, Recreation and Dance* 75(4): 23–27.

Belka, D. 2004b. Substituting developmental for traditional games in elementary physical education. *Teaching Elementary Physical Education* 15(4): 21–24.

Casey, A., and P. A. Hastie. 2011. Students and teacher responses to a unit of student-designed games. *Physical Education and Sport Pedagogy* 16(3): 295–312.

Casey, A., P. Hastie, and I. Rovegno. 2011. Student learning during a unit of student-designed games. *Physical Education and Sport Pedagogy* 16(4): 331–50.

Doolittle, S., and K. Girard. 1991. A dynamic approach to teaching games in elementary physical education. *Journal of Physical Education, Recreation and Dance* 62(4): 57–62.

Hastie, P., and M. H. Andre. 2012. Game appreciation through student designed games and game equipment. *International Journal of Play* 1(2): 165–83.

Hastie, P. 2010. *Student-designed games.* Champaign, IL: Human Kinetics.

Mauldon, E., and H. Redfern. 1969. *Games teaching.* London: MacDonald and Evans. (Another classic that is worth the search.)

Mitchell, S., J. Oslin, and L. Griffin. 2003. *Sport foundations for elementary physical education: A tactical games approach.* Champaign, IL: Human Kinetics.

Mitchell, S., J. Oslin, and L. Griffin. 2013. *Teaching sport concepts and skills: A tactical games approach for ages 7 to 18.* 3rd ed. Champaign, IL: Human Kinetics.

Stiehl, J., G. S. Morris, and C. Sinclair. 2008. *Teaching physical activity: Change, challenge, choice.* Champaign, IL: Human Kinetics.

Todorovich, J. R., J. P. Fox, S. Ryan, and S. W. Todorovich. 2008. A dynamic-rules game for teaching striking-and-fielding game tactics. *Journal of Physical Education, Recreation, and Dance* 79(5): 26–33.

Summary

Because games playing is the context with which we are most comfortable, some teachers find games easier to teach than dance or gymnastics. This deceptive ease, however, is an educationally unacceptable rationale for curricular decision making. Games in the elementary school allow children to become versatile, adaptable, and skillful games players in meaningful game situations. Thus teachers need to provide children with developmentally appropriate experiences that lead to the acquisition of games-playing skills. In the context of games, skill themes are developed in three types of experiences: (1) invariant skill development, (2) dynamic game-like skill development, and (3) games playing. Invariant games experiences focus on skill acquisition in a predictable, unchanging environment in which the movement is essentially the same each time. Dynamic game-like skill development experiences require children to use skills in a changing environment and to use combinations of skills in situations that resemble those found in games-playing experiences. Games-playing experiences are designed to expose children to the joy and satisfaction that can be found in games. In these experiences, children use skill and sometimes tactics in an attempt to outwit an opponent. These experiences are divided into predesigned games and child-designed games. The predesigned games include ready-made games, modified ready-made games, and teacher-designed games, whereas child-designed games incorporate both teacher/child-designed games and games designed by children.

Several variables affect the process of teaching games to children. The type of game selected can influence the success of the experience. Other factors to be considered when teaching games to children are the alignment of the games with a lesson's learning objectives, equipment used, the number of children in the game, the role of the teacher, whether the game is cooperative or competitive, when to provide feedback, the name of the game, and whether the game provides the opportunity to learn.

The role of games in elementary physical education is to provide all children the chance to be successful in playing in dynamic, unpredictable situations that challenge them to outwit their opponents. It is the teacher's responsibility to design game experiences that meet the needs of all students.

Reading Comprehension Questions

1. What is meant by the statement, "It is not the game that is important but the use of skills in game settings"?
2. What is the purpose of educational games in elementary school? How does that differ from more traditional approaches to games?
3. What are the characteristics of developmentally appropriate and inappropriate games for children? Identify one activity that you know is appropriate and one that is inappropriate.
4. Skill themes in games are developed through three types of experiences. How does each experience differ? Provide an example from one of the skill theme chapters.
5. What happens when we place children in dynamic situations before they're ready?
6. When is it appropriate to move children from the invariant skill development experiences to dynamic game-like skill development experiences? Why is such movement necessary?
7. What is the difference between predesigned games and child-designed games? From your own experience, identify a game that fits each category.
8. Using the ready-made predesigned game you identified in the previous question, modify it into a game that is more appropriate for a class of 25 control-level children.
9. How would you go about helping children design a striking with paddles game?
10. What factors should be taken into account in the process of teaching in the games-playing phase?
11. How is the role of the teacher different between the predesigned and child-designed games-playing experiences?
12. Why do we recommend small group sizes and multiple games in physical education class?
13. What do you think are the three most important points for the teaching of games? Why did you choose those three?

References/Suggested Readings

Almond, L. 1986. Reflecting on themes: A games classification. In *Rethinking games teaching*, ed. R. Thorpe, D. Bunker, and L. Almond, 71–72. Loughborough, England: University of Technology.

Belka, D. 2000. Developing competent games players. *Teaching Elementary Physical Education* 11(3): 6–7.

Belka, D. 2004a. Combining and sequencing games skills. *Journal of Physical Education, Recreation and Dance* 75(4): 23–27.

Belka, D. 2004b. Substituting developmental for traditional games in elementary physical education. *Teaching Elementary Physical Education* 15(4): 21–24.

Biddle, S. 1999. The motivation of pupils in physical education. In *Learning and teaching in physical education*, ed. C. Hardy and M. Mawer, 105–25. Philadelphia: Falmer Press.

Bruggeman, K., D. Dzewaltowski, T. Behrens, and A. Jager. 2008. The effects of elimination and non-elimination games on physical activity and psychosocial responses in children. Paper presented at the Annual Meeting of the American College of Sports Medicine, Indianapolis, IN.

Brustad, R., and M. Parker. 2005. Enhancing positive youth development through sport and physical activity. *Psychologia* 39: 75–93.

Casey, A., and P. Hastie. 2011. Students and teacher responses to a unit of student-designed games. *Physical Education and Sport Pedagogy* 16(3): 295–312.

Casey, A., P. Hastie, and I. Rovegno. 2011. Student learning during a unit of student-designed games. *Physical Education and Sport Pedagogy* 16(4): 331–50.

Dennison, G. 1969. *The lives of children*. New York: Random House.

Doolittle, S., and K. Girard. 1991. A dynamic approach to teaching games in elementary physical education. *Journal of Physical Education, Recreation and Dance* 62(4): 57–62.

Hastie, P. 2010. *Student-designed games*. Champaign, IL: Human Kinetics.

Hastie, P., and M. H. Andre. 2012. Game appreciation through student designed games and game equipment. *International Journal of Play* 1(2): 165–83.

Kolhberg, L., and R. Mayer. 1972. Development as the aim of education. *Harvard Educational Review* 42(4): 449–96.

Mauldon, E., and H. Redfern. 1969. *Games teaching*. London: MacDonald and Evans.

Mitchell, S., J. Oslin, and L. Griffin. 2003. *Sport foundations for elementary physical education: A tactical games approach*. Champaign, IL: Human Kinetics.

Mitchell, S., J. Oslin, and L. Griffin. 2013. *Teaching sport concepts and skills: A tactical games approach for ages 7 to 18*. 3rd ed. Champaign, IL: Human Kinetics.

Opie, P., and I. Opie. 1969. *Children's games in street and playground*. New York: Oxford University Press.

Piaget, J. 1962. *Play, dreams, and imitation in childhood*. New York: Norton.

Piaget, J., and B. Inhelder. 1969. *The psychology of the child*. New York: Basic Books.

Rink, J. 2008. *Designing the physical education curriculum*. New York: McGraw-Hill.

Rink J. 2014. *Teaching physical education for learning*. 7th ed. New York: McGraw-Hill.

Schmidt, R. 1977. Schema theory: Implications for movement education. *Motor Skills: Theory into Practice* 2: 36–48.

[SHAPE America] Society of Health and Physical Educators. 2009. *Appropriate instructional practice guidelines for elementary physical education*. 3rd ed. Champaign, IL: Human Kinetics.

[SHAPE America] Society of Health and Physical Educators. 2014. *National standards & grade-level outcomes for K-12 physical education*. Champaign, IL: Human Kinetics

Standage, M., J. Duda, and N. Ntoumanis. 2003. A model of contextual motivation in physical education: Using constructs from self-determination and achievement goal theories to predict physical activity intentions. *Journal of Educational Psychology* 95(1): 97–110.

Stiehl, J., G. S. Morris, and C. Sinclair. 2008. *Teaching physical activity: Change, challenge, choice*. Champaign, IL: Human Kinetics.

Tyson-Martin, L. 1999. The four "Rs" of enhancing elementary games instruction. *Journal of Physical Education, Recreation and Dance* 70(7): 36–40.

Wilson, N. 1976. *The frequency and patterns of selected motor skills by third and forth grade girls and boys in the game of kickball*. Unpublished master's project, University of Georgia, Athens.

Integrating the Skill Theme Approach Across the Curriculum

When asked what I teach, I like to respond "children."

—JOHN HICHWA (1998)

Key Concepts

- Interdisciplinary learning connects content from at least two subject areas in an attempt to promote learning in both subjects.
- Making connections between the cognitive and psychomotor domains and between content areas, such as mathematics and reading, is motivating to children and helps them see connections in what they are learning.
- When integrating lessons, we cannot lose sight of the educational goals we want to accomplish in our physical education programs, but we can effectively reinforce important concepts taught in other subject areas across the curriculum.
- Three approaches—content linkage, shared integration, and the thematic unit—all connect curricular content from at least two subject areas.
- For successful integration, we need knowledge of and an appreciation for other subject area content and an understanding of the scope and sequence of the subjects being integrated.
- Recent research suggests there is a connection between physical activity and academic performance.

This chapter will help you better understand how the classroom teacher and physical educator can integrate physical education concepts and skills with those from other subject areas throughout the elementary curriculum. Three approaches to integrating skills and concepts are discussed—the content linkage approach, the shared integration approach, and the thematic unit approach. Examples from different content areas are used to illustrate how these approaches work.

The chapter ends with a review of recent literature that makes the connection between physical activity and successful performance in the classroom, including research suggesting an important link between movement and brain function. Both the connection between physical education and other areas of school curriculum and the connection between physical activity and academic performance reinforce the importance of an effective physical education program in all elementary schools.

Connecting Physical Education and the Classroom Curriculum Through Interdisciplinary Learning

Any time we can make learning more relevant and personally meaningful to the child's life, it has a more profound effect and will be remembered longer (Roberts and Kellough 2006). For many learners, the connections are best made through movement.

Defining Interdisciplinary Learning

A major thrust in curriculum development in schools today is the integration of subject content across the curriculum (Wood 2009). "Interdisciplinary learning is an educational process in which two or more subject areas are integrated with the goal of fostering enhanced learning in each subject area" (Cone, Werner, and Cone 2009). Integration helps kids make sense of what they know as it pertains to them and their world. The terms *interdisciplinary* and *integration* are usually considered synonymous and will be used interchangeably in this chapter.

Benefits of Interdisciplinary Education

Integration enhances and enriches students' learning by:

- Encouraging critical thinking skills.
- Reinforcing curriculum content in a variety of educational settings.
- Supporting children to transfer what is learned in one setting or situation to new settings and situations, adding meaning to what is being learned.
- Providing children with multiple opportunities to practice particular skills and concepts.
- Encouraging children to better understand and to see the connectedness of what they are learning and how it relates to their own world.

As a result of the connections between academic areas, children often see the knowledge gained as having more importance in the real-life context. For example, students who are normally unenthusiastic about physical education may be motivated by the integrative activities that allow them success in both the cognitive and psychomotor domains, such as learning to swim while studying water in science. By the same token, students who excel in physical activities but are less interested in other academic areas may find an

It has been said that learners retain:

- 10 percent of what they read
- 20 percent of what they hear
- 30 percent of what they see
- 50 percent of what they hear and see at the same moment
- 70 percent of what they hear, see, and say
- 90 percent of what they hear, see, say, and DO

Source: B. Fauth, Linking the visual arts with drama, movement, and dance for the young child. In *Moving and learning for the young child*, ed. W. J. Stinson (Reston, VA: American Alliance for Health, Physical Education, Recreation and Dance, 1990), pp. 159–87.

Integrating Physical Education and Other Curricula Content

Physical education as part of an integrated curriculum can work in two ways—integrating core subject-matter content into the physical education lesson, or integrating physical education skills and concepts into other curriculum areas in the classroom. (See Table 32.1.)

Physical education as well as various forms of physical activity can be integrated with any other content area in the curriculum, including math, reading/language arts, social studies, science, health, technology, music, and art. Integration examples are provided throughout this chapter as a guide in helping teachers develop integrated lesson ideas for connecting physical education/activity to any other subject-specific standard.

Benefits of Integration

It is important to understand why integrating subject areas is worthwhile and to reflect on the benefits of integration for both physical education and other subject content areas. Following are some of the most notable benefits—from both the physical education class and the classroom perspectives.

interesting connection that motivates them to learn other subject-specific content. One example might be the student who is struggling with reading but is excited to complete a reading assignment about a famous hockey player while learning the skill of striking with a hockey stick in physical education class. In either case, the integrated approach increases the potential for motivating children to learn.

As part of health class, students are learning about nutrition and physical activity.

©Lars A. Niki

Table 32.1 Example of Two-Directional Integration Between Physical Education and Science

Physical Education	integrated → into	Science	Plan a hike through a nearby part to identify trees, flowers, and other plants
Science	integrated → into	Physical Education	Children use different locomotor movements to travel through a large replica of the heart on the gym floor to show the pathway of blood flow

Benefits of Integrating Other Subject Skills/Concepts into the Physical Education Class

- Children learn best by seeing connections in what they are learning. For most children, physical education is fun! A quality physical education program helps them to become proficient in many skills, and most elementary children are innately inclined to be physically active at every given opportunity. Kinesthetic learning of other subject content often helps children grasp concepts in language arts, science, and math that they might otherwise struggle with in a more inert classroom environment.

Benefits of Integrating Physical Activity in the Regular Classroom

- It is recommended that children be physically active at least 60 minutes a day (IOM 2005; SHAPE America 2015). Schools should strive to meet as much of this time recommendation as possible during the school day. As outlined in Chapter 28, a comprehensive school physical activity program encourages physical activity opportunities throughout the school day.
- Physical activity breaks in the classroom not only contribute to increased daily physical activity time but also have been shown to improve classroom attentiveness and behavior (Mahar et al. 2006).
- Several studies have described benefits associated with including short physical activity breaks throughout the school day, including fitness gains, improved attention spans, and increased physical activity levels (Erwin et al. 2009, 2011).
- By integrating physical activity with other subject areas, children are able to simultaneously practice motor, language arts, and math skills, for example, while also gaining the benefits of being physically active. In addition, short activity breaks every 20 to 30 minutes help children concentrate and make them more ready to learn.
- Children love to move! For children, movement is a critical means of communication, expression, and learning. The active rather than passive involvement in learning that movement allows often makes children more excited and motivated to learn.

Important Considerations

Before deciding to use an interdisciplinary approach in your program, there are some important considerations to ponder. For successful integration, you should have knowledge of and an appreciation for other subject area content, be prepared to put forth more effort, and always keep your goals in mind.

Standards-Based Instruction Integrating physical education and other subject content is not always easy. Physical educators will have to become familiar with the state or district standards in other subject areas in order to promote real learning. Classroom teachers will have to do the same when integrating physical education concepts and skills. Before planning interdisciplinary learning activities for your children, you (and any other collaborating teacher) should identify standards for each discipline, determine the assessment to be used to show what students know or can do at the end of the lesson(s), and then plan the appropriate activities and tasks. As with all standards-based curricula, the learning goals, tasks, and assessments should align with each other.

Knowledge of Students Knowing where students are developmentally in academics can be a challenge, especially for beginning physical education teachers. Classroom teachers likely will struggle with the reality of where students are motorically and even emotionally in regard to physical activity opportunities. The reciprocal relationship works best when the teachers from the two areas can inform each other. For example, providing the teacher with the *Appropriate Instructional Practice Guidelines for Elementary School Physical Education* (SHAPE America 2009) may be a first step.

Extra Effort Developing effective interdisciplinary learning experiences, as with any curricular innovation, requires effort and time. You may have to rearrange the order of your teaching to coincide with the lesson concept or theme the classroom teacher is teaching, and vice versa. Some learning experiences will be successful; others may not be. Be prepared to reflect on the learning experience, make changes, and try again.

Your Goals One challenge of interdisciplinary teaching is not to lose sight of the educational goals and objectives you want to accomplish as you plan integration activities with other subject areas. Always assess the potential benefits of the proposed integrative learning experience or unit, and if educational goals and objectives are not met, then it should not be considered a worthwhile endeavor. Remember, it is through the physical education program that children learn to perform locomotor, nonmanipulative, and manipulative movements proficiently, which will enhance their interdisciplinary learning.

The Process of Teaching Using an Interdisciplinary Learning Approach

A variety of interdisciplinary models have been introduced over the years. As we gain experience in integrating lessons, we typically develop and name our own models that guide us. We have chosen three approaches to discuss in this book that we hope will give you a general understanding of subject integration from simple to more complex. Other models and a more detailed breakdown of the approaches we are discussing here can be found in the related literature recommendations.

The three approaches—**content linkage, shared integration,** and **thematic unit**—all combine the teaching of skills and concepts from at least two subject areas. The content linkage approach can be used by one teacher independently, while the shared integration approach and the thematic unit approach both require a collaborative effort between at least two teachers from different subject areas in the school curriculum.

Content Linkage Approach

The *content linkage approach* is used by one teacher to connect content from at least two subject areas. One content area may be the primary focus of the lesson, but skills/concepts from another subject area enhance the learning experience and provide practice opportunities for learning the skills/concepts in the other subject area. Physical education teachers can find ways to reinforce classroom content without jeopardizing their primary focus of teaching skill themes, movement concepts, and fitness concepts using the content linkage approach. For example, the physical education teacher teaching a kindergarten class might reinforce the math concept of counting from 1 to 30 while focusing on traveling to pick up beanbags to transport across the gym.

Other examples are depicted in Figure 32.1, which shows how content-specific skills for fourth graders might be integrated in the physical education curriculum while focusing on practicing the skill theme of dribbling with hands.

Likewise, classroom teachers can use movement to teach specific concepts in subject areas throughout the curriculum. For example, a classroom teacher who is teaching a language arts spelling lesson might have her fourth graders throwing and catching a ball with a partner while spelling a specific word or group of words.

Shared Integration Approach

Another strategy for connecting more than one subject-specific content area is the shared integration model. In this approach, two teachers work together to provide a lesson or multiple lessons that focus on shared concepts from the two distinct disciplines. (For a comparison between this approach and the content linkage approach, see Table 32.2.) This type of lesson integration can be used readily in both the classroom and the physical education setting to reinforce skills and concepts. When teachers work together to teach and reinforce related skills from two or more subject areas, it helps integrate the cognitive, affective, and psychomotor domains of learning.

An example of shared integration is a lesson in Box 32-1 called "Stepping Across the U.S.," for fourth or fifth grades. This learning experience reinforces three physical education goals—teaching children about (1) the importance of physical activity, (2) what activities promote more movement and therefore more pedometer steps, and (3) the amount of physical activity needed to reach a set goal during each day. In addition, this learning experience reinforces the social studies concepts of geography—location, distance, and facts about the states across the country. It could also be used to practice the math skills of estimation and comparison. This lesson would require both the physical education teacher and the classroom teacher to work together to equally reinforce these concepts.

Developing an Integrated Learning Experience

Once you have chosen a class or grade level with which you wish to teach an integrated lesson(s) using the

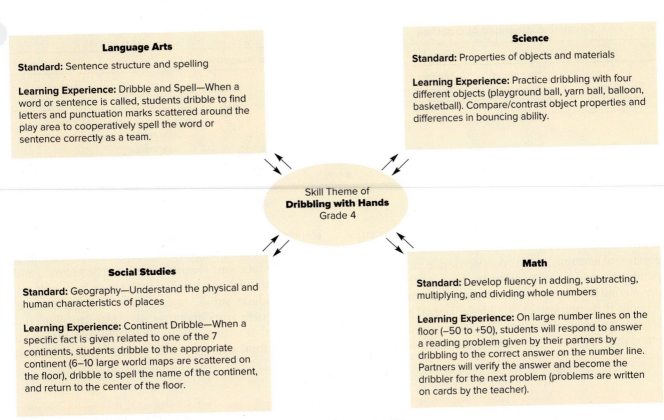

Language Arts

Standard: Sentence structure and spelling

Learning Experience: Dribble and Spell—When a word or sentence is called, students dribble to find letters and punctuation marks scattered around the play area to cooperatively spell the word or sentence correctly as a team.

Science

Standard: Properties of objects and materials

Learning Experience: Practice dribbling with four different objects (playground ball, yarn ball, balloon, basketball). Compare/contrast object properties and differences in bouncing ability.

Skill Theme of
Dribbling with Hands
Grade 4

Social Studies

Standard: Geography—Understand the physical and human characteristics of places

Learning Experience: Continent Dribble—When a specific fact is given related to one of the 7 continents, students dribble to the appropriate continent (6–10 large world maps are scattered on the floor), dribble to spell the name of the continent, and return to the center of the floor.

Math

Standard: Develop fluency in adding, subtracting, multiplying, and dividing whole numbers

Learning Experience: On large number lines on the floor (−50 to +50), students will respond to answer a reading problem given by their partners by dribbling to the correct answer on the number line. Partners will verify the answer and become the dribbler for the next problem (problems are written on cards by the teacher).

Figure 32.1 Examples of other subject content integrated with the skill theme of dribbling.

content linkage approach, you will first need to review the grade-specific content scope and yearly pacing guide for the integrated subject and compare those with your own. Then choose the concepts/skills for each subject you wish to integrate, and you are ready to design an appropriate learning experience that focuses on the chosen concepts. (Use the format applied to the "Stepping Across the U.S." lesson as a guide.) Before implementing your lesson, share it with a teacher(s) of the other content area for awareness and feedback. After teaching the lesson, assess the success of the learning experience.

For the shared integration approach, both teachers should share the program scope and pacing guide and identify targeted standards, discuss possible integration experiences and assessment strategies, and decide which skills/concepts will be targeted. Together, write an appropriate lesson experience(s) that equally focuses on at least one skill/concept from each of the subject areas being integrated. Decide on the implementation date so lessons can be adjusted, if necessary.

Criteria for Integrated Lesson Development When preparing and implementing learning experiences using either the content linkage approach or the shared

integration approach, ask yourself the following questions. Does the integrated lesson:

- Provide developmentally and instructionally appropriate tasks (for grade, for individual children)?
- Focus on a skill theme, movement concept, and/or fitness concept that is consistent with the program scope and pacing guide?
- Reinforce specific content standard(s) in all subject area(s) being integrated, and is it consistent with the specific program scope and pacing guide for that grade?
- Include assessment strategies for assessing student learning in both subject areas?

Thematic Unit Approach

In the third approach to content integration, the thematic unit approach, teachers overlap the content across the curriculum over a set period while focusing on one theme. Many educators believe that integrating subjects such as physical education, art, and music with the core subject areas of math, science, social studies, and language arts using a thematic approach should be considered in school curricula (Roberts and Kellough 2006; Wood 2009).

Table 32.2 Comparing Integrated Approaches

| | Comparison of Content Linkage and Shared Integration | | | |
Approach	Number of Subject Areas	Number of Teachers Needed	Time	Focus
Content linkage	2 or more	1	Usually during 1 lesson	Primary focus on 1 content area, with another subject area used to enhance
Shared integration	2 or more	2 or more	Could be for 1 lesson, but often extends over a longer period	Equal focus on shared concepts from two distinct disciplines

One thematic approach in physical education currently gaining momentum proposes that social and emotional learning such as cooperation, courage, independence, and responsibility be used as themes for organizing the physical education curriculum. In many schools, this approach or one similar is used as a whole school management system. The interdisciplinary thematic unit approach is also being incorporated in many elementary school curricula to help connect student learning across a number of subject areas, including physical education. Thematic units can be planned and implemented by one teacher with his or her students, but to include subject areas across the curriculum, most teachers work together as a team to plan and implement learning experiences centered around a theme or topic over a specific period. A thematic unit

---

Box 32-1

Example of a Shared Integration Learning Experience

Stepping Across the U.S.

Grade level: 4–5

PE skill/concept focus: Fitness and wellness concepts

PE content standard: Exhibits a physically active lifestyle

Social studies skill/concept focus: Geography—U.S. states

Social studies content standard: Understands the physical and human characteristics of places

Math skill/concept focus: Convert steps to miles, estimate, compare stats, add class miles/steps

Math content standard: Computes fluently and makes reasonable estimates

Materials needed: Pedometers for each child, paper logs or daily access to **PE Central Log It** (www.peclogit.org), maps for classroom and gym to track class progress, state facts, flags, etc.

Description of activity: Children are given a pedometer by the physical education teacher to be worn on weekdays for 3 consecutive weeks. The classroom teacher has the students log their steps each day on paper logs, or at **PE Central Log It** (www.peclogit.org). Students convert steps to miles using the conversion of 2,000 steps = 1 mile. Total class miles are calculated each day, and the class moves across the U.S. map according to the miles accumulated. When a new state capital is reached, both the classroom teacher and the physical education teacher will reinforce state facts such as the state seal; flag; bird; flower; animal; and the location, area, and population of the state, etc. Daily or weekly goals can be set, and estimation and comparisons can be taught. The physical education teacher should instruct students to set daily goals, to identify activities that promote the most physical movement by monitoring steps after specific activities, and to participate in physical activity outside of school.

Note: Using **PE Central Log It** to record pedometer steps allows students to record their steps daily, compare their stats with others, and take a "virtual hike" around the United States. When a new state is reached, students are able to see state information online, as well as see how many miles their class must log to travel to the next state. Individual goal setting is built into the Web site, and students earn certificates for reaching daily goals. Teachers must register their classes online.

Assessments:

- Check written logs for math accuracy in converting steps to miles, calculating total steps/mile, totaling and averaging group steps/mile, setting reasonable daily goals, and meeting them.
- Student worksheets should identify states traveled and list their state capitals.

of instruction might be a one-week study, or it might focus on a theme on an ongoing basis over many weeks. An example of a theme that might be used to connect different subject content in a kindergarten class is "The Jungle." Young children are interested in and intrigued by animals. This theme could easily incorporate lessons related to jungle animals, including characteristics of different types of animals, the jungle habitat, math concepts such as measuring and comparing (i.e., elephant foot to human foot), and many of the movement concepts (space awareness, relationships, and effort).

Included in this chapter are two examples of how thematic units can be developed to include a variety of subject areas, including physical education, connected through a theme. The thematic unit "Recreation in (Your State)" in Table 32.3 was designed for grades 5 and 6 and focuses on the study of recreational areas in a state and incorporates six subject areas that revolve around the theme. The "Wild Wild West" thematic unit in Table 32.4 is based on the westward expansion of America and incorporates four content areas. These examples illustrate only an overview of the partial unit but will help you see how learning across subject areas can be interconnected and how children might better "connect" their learning in ways that are more meaningful to their everyday experiences.

Tips for Developing an Interdisciplinary Thematic Unit

1. Choose a theme, together with your students, that is motivating to them and that can incorporate skills/concepts from a variety of subject areas. If you are working with another teacher, include him or her in the theme selection process.
2. Inform school administrators and other teachers of your intent and ask for their support and assistance. (Team teaching may require special planning time; outside speakers may be asked to come into the classroom; field trips may be planned, etc.)
3. Form a teaching team of interested teachers from other content areas. The team will:
   - Share content materials and brainstorm ideas for the unit.

Table 32.3 Thematic Unit: Recreation in (Your State) (Grades 5–6)

Overview: This thematic unit focuses on the study of recreational areas in your state. Learning activities include students working in groups to study and report on a specific recreational area, preparing a budget associated with participating in the recreational opportunity, and practicing motor and fitness skills necessary for successful participation in the physical activities of that area.

Social Studies	Math	Science	Language Arts	Physical Education	Health
Locate recreation opportunities throughout the state on the map; research each park or recreational area; determine distance from home area to each recreational area; study economy of the area; in a group, prepare a PSA or commercial to promote the area and its recreational opportunities.	Choose a recreational area that the class will visit; prepare a budget for a trip to the area, including cost of the trip (transportation, lodging, meals, fees), equipment, clothing, and any other costs associated with participating in the physical activity.	Decide what muscles need to be developed to prepare to participate in the physical activity.	Prepare a group report and poster about one recreational area in the state; use the Internet to read specific information about the recreational area you will visit.	Choose one recreational sport (e.g., snow skiing) and discuss and practice the motor skills and fitness levels necessary to enjoy participating in the sport.	Determine benefits of the physical activity; determine preferences; set personal goals—proper diet and activity; learn and practice basic first aid.

Culminating event: Plan a field trip to one of the recreational areas in the state and participate in recreational opportunities in that area; utilize prepared budget, and apply the knowledge of the area and the physical activity.

Parental and community involvement: Parents join in on the trip, help organize and make arrangements for the trip; community resources that will be utilized are local recreation agencies, which will provide informational pamphlets, and clothing/equipment catalogs or retailers.

Source: B. McCracken, *It's not just gym anymore* (Champaign, IL: Human Kinetics, 2001).

Table 32.4 Thematic Unit: The Wild Wild West (Grade 4)

Overview: This thematic unit focuses on the westward expansion of America during the 19th century. The unit connects content in social studies, language arts, fine arts, and physical education.

Social Studies	Language Arts	Physical Education	Fine Arts
Map making of the U.S., locating landmarks and cities that travelers would see traveling west	"Wild West" theme folders to include a vocabulary list, daily journal entries as a frontiersperson, and other related activities	Introduction to orienteering—map reading, compass reading	Art: Begin to create a quilt and discuss the history of quilt making
Identify famous people involved in the settlement of the Old West; hardships of the early settlers	*How the Settlers Lived* by George and Ellen Laycock	Complete an orienteering activity, using landmarks that represent the Old West	Art: Incorporate *The Quilt Story* by Tony Johnston
The Oregon Trail computer software (The Learning Co. Inc.) takes you on an educational adventure	Prepare and rehearse oral presentations on various aspects of the Wild West	Participate in simple folk and square dances representative of that period	Music: Video musical *Oklahoma*—socializing aspects and time period comparisons

Culminating event: The Wild Wild West Celebration will conclude the thematic unit, with demonstrations of quilting, square dancing, storytelling, and oral presentations by the students. Displays of student work will be shown. Parents will be invited and all will be invited to wear period clothes and bring period items to share, such as old hats, pictures, lanterns, and other unique items.

Parental and community involvement: Parents are invited to be guest storytellers, observers, and participants in the final celebration. They are asked to help with their child's period costume. Local media are invited to attend the culminating event.

Source: Developed by Brenda Cannon, Kevin Hutchinson, Rick Spreeder, and Shannon Owen, Concord University, Athens, WV.

- Develop an overview of the unit, goals, instructional objectives, and final assessment.
- Develop the theme-based learning experiences that meet subject area content standards and those of the thematic unit, including a culminating event, assessment strategies, and timelines.

4. Inform parents and seek parental involvement. For example, parents may be asked to assist their children with special projects, bring expertise on a particular topic to the class, join the students for a special presentation, and so forth.

5. Locate instructional resources for the unit, including community resources. For example, if you are planning a unit around the theme of "Heart Health," you might have a pediatric cardiologist speak to the class, take children to a local park to explore physical activity possibilities, organize a field trip to the grocery store to analyze food selections, and have local athletes come to talk with the children about tobacco avoidance.

6. Implement the interdisciplinary thematic unit and assess the success of the unit (student learning).

©Lars A. Niki

Pedometers can be used to teach important concepts in mathematics.

Box 32-2

Examples of Integrating Reading/Literacy and Physical Education

Making connections between books and movement can help enhance reading comprehension and promote physical activity. Here are some examples:

Grade: *K*

Book: *The Silly Tail Book* (Marc Brown)
Lesson Idea: Read the story and discuss the different kinds of tails that jungle animals have. As the teacher pulls different tails from the bag, the children identify the animal to which it belongs, and then move through the jungle (classroom or cones on the gym floor) as that animal would move (e.g., elephant, giraffe, snake, panther, monkey, etc.).
Source: Debra Williamson, Concord University, Athens, WV.

Grade: *1*

Book: *Stellaluna* (Janell Cannon)
Lesson Idea: Have children recollect the beginning of the story when the baby bat, Stellaluna, is knocked from her mother's safe grasp by an angry owl one night while looking for food. In Stellaluna Steal Tag, four taggers (owls) try to tag mother bats carrying their young (a beanbag). If tagged, owls take the baby bats to the "baby bat bin," and they are rescued by their mother as she travels in various pathways to the bin. *Source:* www.activeacademics.org—Dorothy Reynolds, creator.

Grade: *1–2*

Book: *Going on a Bear Hunt* (Rosen and Oxenbury)

Lesson Idea: After reading the book to the students, read again, this time allowing children to "act out" the story as the children and their father go through the tall grass, over the river, through the mud, etc. *Source:* www.activeacademics.org.

Grade: *2–3*

Book: *Brand New Kid* (Katie Couric)
Lesson Idea: After reading the book about a boy who comes to a new school and is not readily accepted by his classmates, the children can discuss how his soccer skills impressed one of his classmates and helped her encourage others to accept him. Children can practice soccer dribbling skills like Lazlo and discuss ways to make others feel less lonely and less scared in any kind of "scary" situation. *Source:* www.activeacademics.org.

Grade: *4–5*

Book: *Backyard Birding for Kids* (Fran Lee)
Lesson Idea: This book will help teach children to appreciate birds and will help them to identify birds through sight and song. It identifies birds common to the city, the woodlands, the country, the wetlands, the seashore, and the desert. Helping children learn to appreciate birds can lead to an outdoor hobby of birdwatching. If appropriate at your school, take your class on a "mini field trip" around campus to look for birds, and to begin a birdwatching journal. Assign children birdwatching walks outside of school (with a family member) to add more birds to their journals. *Source:* www.activeacademics.org.

Understanding the Scope and Sequence of Subject Area Content

For teachers to effectively integrate subject area content, they must be knowledgeable in the scope and pacing guide of the subjects being integrated. In their text *Interdisciplinary Elementary Physical Education*, Cone et al. (2009) have reviewed textbooks and projects in the content areas of math, language arts, social studies, science, and the arts and have compiled a scope and sequence for each area in grades K–6. Table 32.5 is provided to help you better understand the skills/concepts taught at each grade level in math. *Interdisciplinary Elementary Physical Education* also offers many suggestions in each subject area for active learning experiences that would be helpful to any

physical education teacher planning interdisciplinary learning experiences.

Integrating physical education concepts with learning in other subjects in the school curriculum can be considered a viable approach to help physical education teachers enhance what is being learned in other subject areas and to help classroom teachers promote healthy lifestyles and physical activity. But clearly, it is the teachers who make integration work. If teachers recognize the contributions each field of study can make to the others and strive to make connections between the subject areas, then student learning can be enhanced in new ways. Children benefit from seeing teachers working together to focus different subject areas on a common theme and reinforce what they are learning across the curriculum.

Table 32.5 Example of Scope and Sequence of Mathematical Concepts Taught in Elementary Schools

Concept	K	1	2	3	4	5	6
							Grade
Numbers	X	X	X	X	X	X	X
Meaning of numbers 1–12	X						
Meaning of numbers through 99		X					
Meaning of numbers through 999			X				
Meaning of addition and subtraction		X					
Addition and subtraction computation			X				
Meaning of numbers through 100,000				X			
Meaning of multiplication and division				X			
Meaning of numbers through 1,000,000					X		
Multiplication and division computation					X		
Meaning of decimals through hundredths					X		
Meaning of decimals through thousandths					X		
Meaning of addition and subtraction of fractions and decimals						X	
Number theory						X	
Meaning of multiplication and division of fractions and decimals						X	
Integers and ratios							X
Percents							X
Measuring and graphing	X	X	X	X	X	X	X
Geometry	X	X	X	X	X	X	X
Patterns and functions	X	X	X	X	X	X	X
Probability and statistics	X	X	X	X	X	X	X
Logic		X	X	X	X	X	X
Algebra		X	X	X	X	X	X

Source: T. Cone, P. Werner, and S. L. Cone, *Interdisciplinary elementary physical education: Connecting, sharing, partnering.* 2nd ed. (Champaign, IL: Human Kinetics, 2009.)

The Connection Between Physical Activity and Academic Performance

Educational reform movements, including the Every Student Succeeds Act (ESSA 2015), have placed increased emphasis on math and reading for all grades, and schools and teachers are being held more accountable for adequate student progress toward achievement of state standards. With high-stakes testing programs taking precedence across the nation, some administrators are tempted to reduce, or even eliminate, physical education as a solution to improve test scores. Recent evidence suggests this is ill advised. In fact, students who have regular physical education, are more physically fit, and have more opportunities to be physically active may do better in school than those who are deprived of these valuable experiences.

What the Research Suggests: Physical Activity, Fitness, and Physical Education

Introduced in Chapter 1, physical activity can have both immediate and long-term benefits on academic performance (Active Living Research [ALR] 2014). Almost immediately after engaging in physical activity, children are better able to concentrate on classroom tasks, which can enhance learning. Regular physical activity participation and higher levels of physical fitness have been linked to improved academic performance and brain functions (i.e., attention and memory). Long-term studies have also reported that increases in physical activity, resulting from greater time spent in physical education, were related to improved academic performance. Even single bouts of physical activity have been associated with better scores on academic tests, improved concentration, and more efficient transfers of information from short- to long-term memory (ALR 2014).

Two recent reviews of literature (ALR 2014; Donnelly et al. 2016) also indicated positive associations among physical activity, fitness, cognition, and academic achievement. The authors of these papers reported, however, that when comparing the results of the reviewed studies, the findings were inconsistent, and the effects of several elements (i.e., type, amount, frequency, and timing) of physical activity on cognition remain largely unexplored. Regardless, there is no indication that increases in physical activity negatively affect cognition or academic achievement. The authors concluded that physical activity has a positive influence on cognition as well as brain structure and function; however, more research is necessary to determine mechanisms and long-term effect as well as strategies to translate laboratory findings to K–12 school settings.

Other researchers have also found compelling evidence that supports the relationship between physical activity and enhanced learning in the classroom, including the following:

- Integrating physical activity within the elementary curricula had a positive influence on fluid intelligence and academic achievement of third-grade students (Reed et al. 2010).
- After walking on a treadmill for 20 minutes at a moderate pace, children responded to test questions (in the content areas of reading, spelling, and arithmetic) with greater accuracy and had a more intense response within the brain than children who had been sitting (Hillman et al. 2009).
- Among 5,316 students in grades K through 5, the frequency and duration of physical education class were positively associated with standardized test performance among girls but not boys. This relationship may have been attributed to a lower beginning level of fitness for female students, which shows that the girls may have had more to gain from physical education participation (Carlson et al. 2008).
- In a group of diverse, urban school children, the odds of passing academic achievement tests in both math and English increased as the number of fitness tests passed increased (Chomitz et al. 2009).
- Children in the third and fifth grades who scored better on the aerobic fitness and the BMI (body mass index) components of a fitness test tended to have higher standardized test scores in reading and math (Castelli et al. 2007).
- Children who participated in four times as much physical activity per day as previously reported, through exposure to a designated 14-week physical education program, showed improvements in fitness, classroom behavior, and academic performance (IOM 2005).
- Allocating less time for physical education, art, and music did not relate to higher standardized test scores (Graham et al. 2002).
- Allocating twice as many minutes per week to physical education for a control group did not show it interfered with standardized reading or math scores (Sallis et al. 1999).

- Increased physical activity time during the school day led to higher test scores in math (Shephard 1997).
- An intense school physical activity program had a positive effect on math, reading, and writing test scores (Symons et al. 1997).
- Canadian children who spent an extra hour a day in physical education class performed higher on exams than their less active counterparts (Hannaford 1995).

The obesity epidemic currently plaguing our nation focuses increased interest on the physical activity levels of children. As school administrators begin to be held accountable for the amount of physical activity time provided for children during the school day, this body of research will become increasingly important to support daily physical education.

What the Research Suggests: Brain-Based Learning

Brain researchers believe that exercise contributes to optimal brain functioning and optimal learning, and the evidence is mounting to make their case. In *Learning with the Body in Mind* (2000), author Eric Jensen reported that:

- Vigorous daily physical exercise can promote new brain cell growth.
- Exercise and aerobic conditioning may help improve memory and strengthen other areas of the brain.
- Downtime, such as recess, is necessary for children to learn. It allows for the "strengthening of synaptic connections in the brain that solidify prior learning" (p. 66).
- Exercise of longer durations creates more cognitive boosts.

Dr. John Ratey, author of the seminal book *Spark: The Revolutionary New Science of Exercise and the Brain* (2008), draws together emerging findings from science and educational research that correlate physical activity and brain functioning. Dr. Ratey connects physical activity to improving attention (including attention deficit hyperactivity disorder [ADHD]), reducing anxiety and depression, and in general, optimizing the brain for learning.

Hannaford, Jensen, and Ratey all support the need for quality physical education programs in all schools and additional physical activity time throughout the day for all children to promote learning and, therefore, increase student achievement. Integrating physical activities with the core subjects helps students engage both their bodies and their brains in learning, as suggested in the brain research. The skill theme approach

Box 32-3

Examples of Brain-Enhancing Activities

Tracking activities help prepare the eye muscles for reading. An example is following the flow of a scarf, a bubble, or a feather as it falls to the ground, or tracking a balloon as it is struck with a racket from one side of the body to the other.

Cross-lateral movements enable the brain to cross the midsection from the right side across the center to the left side, which is important for allowing the brain to be ready to read and write. Examples of cross-lateral activities include basic scarf juggling, elephant walks, windmills, and rhythm ribbons.

Rhythmic movements such as tapping rhythms, moving body parts to the beat, moving equipment to the beat, and marching are all ways to stimulate the frontal lobes and can potentially enrich language development.

- *Using music.* Research on music and learning has shown that music improves learning and memory and increases optimum functioning.
- *Teaching personal goal setting.* Goal-setting skills help students to "think smart."
- *Reinforcing good eating habits.* To "eat smart," students should always eat breakfast, consume sugar and carbohydrates in moderation, and increase fruit and vegetable intake.
- *Reinforcing water consumption.* Children should drink plenty of water throughout the day to avoid dehydration and less than optimal learning.
- *Remembering the importance of first and last.* We remember most what is presented first and last. Have powerful beginnings, present new information early, and always review important information during lesson closure.
- *Having fun.* Laughter lowers stress and contributes to a relaxed learning environment.

A Final Thought

In concluding this chapter, we would like to reemphasize that in physical education, the teacher places the goals of physical education, as expressed in national and state standards, as the top priority just as the classroom teacher must make the standards-based goals in her classroom the priority. When the two can successful integrate learning, it becomes a "win-win" for the students. In addition, the integration of physical activity in the classroom helps to get classroom teachers involved in the comprehensive school physical activity program (Chapter 28). This increased activity time can potentially lead to better health, better academic performance, and better motor skill levels.

readily lends itself to "brain activities" and to promoting both cognitive and psychomotor learning.

The skill theme approach emphasizes many of the concepts that brain researchers say are so important to brain development and learning. Skills such as balancing, tracking, moving cross-laterally, and moving rhythmically are all included within the movement concepts and skill themes. (Some examples of brain-enhancing activities are included in Box 32-3.) In addition, Prigge (2002) suggests other ways we can increase "brain power" through physical education programs. These ideas include:

Summary

Interdisciplinary teaching and *integrated teaching* are terms used to describe teaching subject matter from two different disciplines within the same lesson, thereby promoting learning in both subjects simultaneously and, when physical education is involved, making connections between the psychomotor and cognitive domains. Three approaches to interdisciplinary learning are described in the chapter—content linkage, shared integration, and thematic units. It is important that the teacher have a mastery of the subjects to be taught if the lessons (units) are going to be effective and maximize learning. The chapter also includes overviews of research related to the relationships between academic performance, optimal brain functioning, and human movement and physical fitness.

Reading Comprehension Questions

1. Define *interdisciplinary learning.* What are some advantages of using this approach to teaching/learning?

2. How does integration enhance learning?
3. How does the skill theme approach support interdisciplinary learning?

4. Describe and discuss three unique benefits for both classroom teachers and physical educators for integrating physical education with other subject areas.
5. Identify three approaches to integration discussed in this chapter. What are the characteristics of each? How are they alike/different?
6. What are some examples of two-directional integration between physical education and math? Language arts? Social studies? Science?
7. Briefly describe an integrated learning experience using both the content linkage approach and the shared integration approach.
8. Briefly describe a thematic unit overview that includes at least three subject areas for a primary or intermediate grade.
9. Briefly summarize key points made in the recent literature about the connection between physical education and academic performance.

References/Suggested Readings

Active Living Research. 2014. *Active education: Growing evidence on physical activity, and academic performance.* Research brief. Robert Wood Johnson Foundation.

Carlson, S., J. Fulton, S. Lee, L. Maynard, D. Brown, H. Kohl, and W. Dietz. 2008. Physical education and academic achievement in elementary school: Data from the Early Childhood Longitudinal Study. *American Journal of Public Health* 98(4): 721–27.

Castelli, D., C. Hillman, S. Buck, and H. Erwin. 2007. Physical fitness and academic achievement in third- and fifth-grade students. *Journal of Sport and Exercise Psychology* 29: 287–88.

Chomitz, V. R., M. M. Slining, R. J. McGowan, S. E. Mitchell, G. F. Dawson, and K. A. Hacker. 2009. Is there a relationship between physical fitness and academic achievement? Positive results from public school children in the northeastern United States. *Journal of School Health* 79: 30–37.

Cone, T., P. Werner, and S. L. Cone. 2009. *Interdisciplinary elementary physical education: Connecting, sharing, partnering.* 2nd ed. Champaign, IL: Human Kinetics.

Donnely, J. E., C. Hillman, D. Castelli, J. L. Etnier, S. Lee, P. Tomporowski, K. Lambourne, and A. N. Szabo-Reed. 2016. Physical activity, fitness, cognitive function, and academic achievement in children: A systematic review. *Medicine and Science in Sports and Exercise* 48(6): 1197–222.

Erwin, H. E., M. G. Abel, A. Beighle, and M. W. Beets. 2009. Promoting children's health through physically active math classes: A pilot study. *Health Promotion Practice* 12: 557–66.

Erwin, H. E., A. Beighle, C. F. Morgan, and M. P. Noland. 2011. Effect of low-cost, teacher directed classroom intervention on elementary students' physical activity. *The Journal of School Health* 81: 455–61.

Every Student Succeeds Act. 2015. S. 1177-114th Congress: Every Student Succeeds Act. www.govtrack.us/essa.

Fauth, B. 1990. Linking the visual arts with drama, movement, and dance for the young child. In *Moving and learning for the young child*, ed. W. J. Stinson, pp. 159–87.

Reston, VA: American Alliance for Health, Physical Education, Recreation and Dance.

Graham, G., J. M. Wilkins, S. Westfall, S. Parker, R. Fraser, and M. Tembo. 2002. The effects of high-stakes testing on elementary school art, music and physical education. *Journal of Health, Physical Education, Recreation and Dance* 73(8): 51–54.

Hannaford, C. 1995. *Smart moves: Why learning is not all in your head.* Arlington, VA: Great Ocean Publishers.

Hichwa, J. 1998. *Right fielders are people too.* Champaign, IL: Human Kinetics.

Hillman, C., M. Pontifex, L. Raine, D. Castelli, E. Hall, and A. Kramer. 2009. The effect of acute treadmill walking on cognitive control and academic achievement in preadolescent children. *Neuroscience* 159: 1044–54.

[IOM] Institute of Medicine. 2005. *Preventing childhood obesity: Health in the balance.* Washington, DC: National Academies Press.

Jensen, E. 2000. *Learning with the body in mind.* San Diego, CA: The Brain Store.

Mahar, M., S. Murphy, D. Rowe, J. Golder, A. Shields, and T. Raedeke. 2006. Effects of a classroom-based program on physical activity and on-task behavior. *Medicine and Science in Sport and Exercise* 38(12): 286–94.

McCracken, B. 2001. *It's not just gym anymore.* Champaign, IL: Human Kinetics.

Prigge, D. 2002. 20 ways to promote brain-based teaching and learning. *Intervention in School and Clinic* 37(4): 237–41.

Ratey, J., with E. Hagerman. 2008. *Spark: The revolutionary new science of exercise and the brain.* New York: Little, Brown.

Reed, J., G. Einstein, E. Hahn, S. Hooker, V. Gross, and J. Kravitz. 2010. Examining the impact of integrating physical activity on fluid intelligence and academic performance in an elementary school setting: A preliminary investigation. *Journal of Physical Activity and Health* 9: 343–51.

Roberts, P., and R. Kellough. 2006. *A guide for developing interdisciplinary thematic units.* Upper Saddle River, NJ: Prentice Hall.

Sallis, J., T. McKenzie, B. Kolody, M. Lewis, S. Marshall, and P. Rosengard. 1999. Effects of health-related physical education on academic achievement: Project SPARK. *Research Quarterly for Exercise and Sport* 70(2): 127–34.

[SHAPE America] Society of Health and Physical Educators. 2009. *Appropriate instructional practice guidelines for elementary school physical education.* Champaign, IL: Human Kinetics.

[SHAPE America] Society of Health and Physical Educators. 2015. *Comprehensive school physical activity programs: Helping all students log 60 minutes of physical activity each day* [position statement]. Reston, VA: Author.

Shephard, R. 1997. Curricular physical activity and academic performance. *Pediatric Exercise Science* 9: 113–26.

Symons, C., B. Cinelli, T. James, and P. Groff. 1997. Bridging student health risks and academic achievement through comprehensive school health programs. *Journal of School Health* 67(6): 220–27.

Wood, K. E. 2009. *Interdisciplinary instruction for all learners K–8: A practical guide.* 4th ed. Upper Saddle River, NJ: Merrill Prentice Hall.

The Future

Courtesy Children at Monfort, Chappelow or Shawsheen Elementary Schools, Greeley, CO

Basket ball

Our last two chapters emphasize future directions in physical education. Chapter 33, "Building Support for Your Program," describes how teachers can work with seven different populations to gain support for their physical education programs. We offer practical ideas for working with other teachers in the school, the principal, parents, the school board, legislators, the children themselves, and the community at large.

Chapter 34, "Physical Education for Tomorrow's Children," is in many ways our favorite chapter. We end the book by focusing on the future, presenting some of our thoughts. We hope our ideas will encourage you to dream too.

Building Support for Your Program

Many parents, students, teachers, and administrators do not know how physical education contributes to an individual's growth. The lack of a public relations plan can result in an absence of communication between the physical educator and the public, thereby hampering the growth of the physical education program.

—MICHAEL TENOSCHOK AND STEVE SANDERS (1984)

Physical education has undergone major changes in the past decade. So have its consumers. In order for physical education to be viewed as an integral part of the educational process, more attention must be paid to the marketing of tangible and intangible benefits.

—ALLISON MCFARLAND (2001)

Drawn by children at Monfort, Chappelow or Shawsheen Elementary Schools, Greeley, CO.
Courtesy of Lizzy Ginger; Tia Ziegler

Key Concepts

- Successful teachers, in addition to everything else they are asked to do, must also successfully market or build support for their programs.
- Physical education programs need to be marketed to several populations—school and district administrators, other teachers in a school, parents, the school board, the community at large, and legislators.
- Teachers who create positive, enjoyable, and productive programs are building support with their most important population—the children they teach.

When the first edition of *Children Moving* was published in 1980, there was a need to convince parents that regular physical activity was important for their children. Since the publication of the Surgeon General's report in 1996 (USDHHS 1996) documenting the scientific evidence of the value of physical activity, we have a strong research base that physically active children, as well as adults, derive significant benefits from being physically active (Reiner et al. 2013). Thus, the role of the physical educator today is to convince the seven populations described (i.e., children, school and district administrators, other teachers in a school, parents, the school board, the community at large, and legislators) that quality physical education programs can lead to a lifetime of enjoyable participation in physical activity (Stodden et al. 2008).

Most teachers need support from a variety of sources to develop the type of programs they want for their children. This is especially true in physical education, for two reasons. First, even with the scientific evidence about the value of physical activity for children and adults (CDC 2018), many continue to regard physical education as less important than other subjects, such as reading and math. Second, physical education is a relatively expensive program to conduct because of the necessary equipment involved. (It's important, however, that we continually remind others that physical education is for every child in the school—for the entire five or six years they are in attendance.)

While we wish it wasn't necessary to convince these various populations of the value of a quality physical education program, this becomes an important and necessary part of the job today. Notice that we continue to use the term "quality physical education." Unfortunately, many of the populations with whom you are working may have experienced a different type of program than the one we have been describing in this text and described by SHAPE America (2015). Thus, it's necessary to cultivate support from the various segments of a school community who have the potential to be allies in our quest for improved programs. The seven related populations we have identified who need to be aware of and supportive of our program are the school administration, especially the principal; other teachers in the school; parents; the school board; the community at large; legislators, in some instances; and the children.

This chapter discusses ideas for building support within each of these seven populations. However, note that it's important that a teacher first build a quality physical education program. Even with limited resources, it's possible to begin a good program, and this is a necessary first step because much of the work that will go toward building more support involves opening the program to administrators, parents, and the community in general. Obviously, if the program doesn't get off to a good start, you won't want visitors.

Once the program is off to a reasonable start, however, the teacher can invite observers to visit the classes. It may take months before the program is ready; the learning environment has to be established first, with the children and teacher working together comfortably, before visitors are welcome. Once the teacher is ready, the principal and other teachers in the school will probably be the first visitors. You might want to consider your answers to the questions in Box 33-1 as you begin to build support for your program.

The Principal

Principals are critical in building support for your program (Giles-Brown 1993; Rink, Hall, and Williams 2010). Many principals, through no fault of their own,

The principal is an important component of a quality physical education program.

©McGraw-Hill Education

Building Support Through Social Media

Facebook, Twitter, Instagram, and other social media have the potential for informing parents, colleagues, and the administration about many of the good things you are doing in your program. We have several suggestions for using social media in a school setting.

- Before using any social media, be sure to discuss it with your principal.
- It would be wise to set up separate accounts for use at your school. For example, use a different Facebook account than the one you use with your friends. While the parents and children you teach might be interested in seeing pictures of what you and your friends did on Saturday night, it is probably not a good idea.
- Some of the parents and children at your school may want to "friend" you on Facebook. The decision to become their "friends" should be made cautiously and should probably be discussed with your principal. Remember, you are a teacher and a professional, not their buddy.
- Twitter is a great tool to let others know what you are doing in your program, to inform them of student accomplishments, and to remind them of upcoming events. When appropriate, include a link to a news release containing information that people will find interesting.

however, know very little about quality physical education programs—especially the approach we're advocating in *Children Moving*. Thus, it's important not to take for granted that the principal knows and understands the program you're trying to develop. We suggest the following ideas for working with your principal. The ideas aren't arranged in order of implementation, and we don't suggest they all need to be done. We've simply listed practical suggestions you may find helpful for your school.

- Invite your principal to observe the skill theme approach at a nearby school with you. Sit with your principal, and be certain that he focuses on the aspects of the program that are critical to the growth of your own program, e.g., equipment, class size, development of the content, instructional strategies. Be certain to schedule a visit with the principal at the school you're observing so the two administrators can discuss their programs and your principal can ask questions.

- If you are new to a school, or you are changing your program, invite your principal to a class or two that is beginning to work the way you intend. Be certain to follow up regarding this visit so you can answer any questions that may have arisen. Some administrators, for example, are unaccustomed to seeing every child with a ball and may be concerned about the "chaotic" appearance of a class that differs from their experiences in which there was only one ball for an entire class—and most children were waiting in lines.

- If you're able to obtain digital recordings of other skill theme teachers, invite your principal to view one of the recordings with you. Be sure to comment on the critical aspects of the program and relate them to your needs. Remember, the principal is busy, so you may want her to watch only certain key features, not the entire recording. There are also videos of parts of lessons on PE Central (https://www.pecentral.org/mediacenter/videos.html) and supportREALteachers.org (www.supportrealteachers.org) that will provide insight into quality teaching and the equipment needed.

- Occasionally give your principal a copy of an article or book you think is particularly well done and relevant to your program. Be certain to discuss the document after your principal has had a chance to read it. This is especially important if, for example, you're teaching 12 classes a day and you're able to locate a publication that recommends 9 classes a day as a complete load for a physical education specialist. We recommend the publication by the Society of Health and Physical Educators (SHAPE), *Appropriate Instructional Practice Guidelines for Elementary School Physical Education* (SHAPE America 2009). It provides important guidelines written in an easy-to-understand format. It can be obtained from the Web site for SHAPE (http://www.shapeamerica.org). Also be sure to share overviews of the 1996 Surgeon General's report (USDHHS 1996), the *National Standards & Grade-Level Outcomes for K–12 Physical Education* (SHAPE America 2014), and your state standards with your principal. Another good source of information for you, and your principal, is supportREALteachers.org (http://www.supportreal-teachers.org/).

- Be on the lookout for research you can use to support the importance of physical education, especially if your principal is feeling pressure to increase test scores in reading, math, and science. For example, SHAPE America has many advocacy resources (www.shapeamerica.org/advocacy) available including infographics summarizing the research recognizing the benefits of health and physical education to students

Figure 33.1 SHAPE America infographic for physical education.

SHAPE America—Society of Health and Physical Educators, *PE + Health = Student Success infographic.* (Reston, VA: Author, 2018). Copyright ©2018 by SHAPE America. Reprinted with permission from SHAPE America - Society of Physical Educators, 1900 Association Drive, Reston, VA 20191, www.shapeamerica.org.

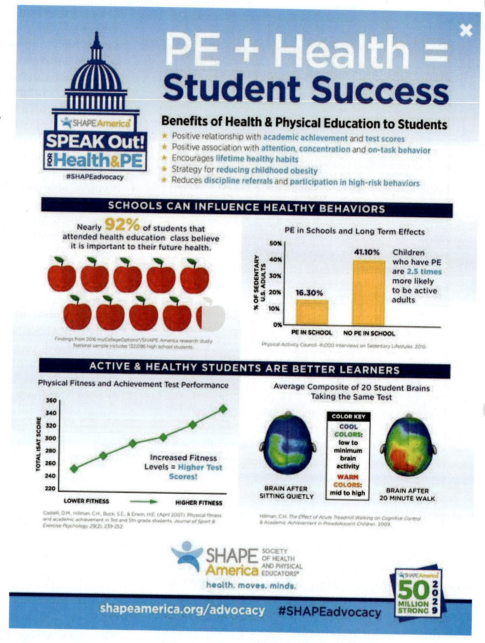

(see Figure 33.1). You may also want to share a copy of the book *Spark* by a Harvard professor about the important relationship between exercise, the brain, and academic achievement (Ratey 2008).

- Seek quality Web sites with advocacy resources and toolkits. For example, SHAPE America (www .shapeamerica.org/advocacy) and supportREAL-teachers.org (http://www.supportrealteachers.org/ how-to-advocate-for-your-program.html) have a variety of free resources available to build support for your program.

Try to avoid falling into the trap of thinking your principal really doesn't like your program, or physical education in general, if she isn't initially enthusiastic. It takes some principals several years to become active supporters of a program. In fact, we've worked with principals who took several months to find time to come view our programs. Eventually, however, they did support our program and came to view it as an asset to the school.

Teachers in the School

As you build your program, it's important that other teachers in the school understand and support your efforts. You'll certainly want to invite these teachers to observe your classes. Some of the ideas you use with your principal can also be used with your colleagues. Physical education specialists also find the following ideas helpful:

- Develop a thematic approach to an integrated curriculum in which the entire school or a certain grade level focuses on an idea or theme as suggested in the last chapter. With this approach, content in all disciplines is centered around the same selected theme. This is quite a natural fit for music, art, and physical education, but it can also be used in a total-school or grade-level approach. (See Cone, Werner, and Cone [2009] for more information on integrating curriculum.) Remember, when developing an integrated curriculum, content should be integrated in a manner that does not compromise physical education content, force integration, or sacrifice the existing curriculum.
- On a smaller scale, work in conjunction with a classroom teacher on certain projects (Chapter 32). Child-designed games, for example, provide marvelous opportunities for writing, math, and art projects. Expressive dance is an excellent catalyst for creative writing.
- If you require your students to keep student logs or do written assignments (Chapter 12), some classroom teachers will provide class time for students to do the writing immediately after physical education class. This really serves to educate teachers about physical education due to their "sneak peaks" at student journals!
- Arrange for several of the primary grades to view the last 10 minutes of an intermediate grade's lesson to show the younger children the progress the older children have made. This motivates the younger children, encourages the older children, and provides some extra physical education for the younger children who attend this viewing.
- When a class has done a particularly good job on a physical education project, it's a treat for the classroom teacher to share in the children's efforts. Invite her to observe the last 10 minutes of a class while the children demonstrate their progress—for example, child-designed games or gymnastics sequences. This also has the added incentive of encouraging the classroom teacher to observe your physical education program.
- When feasible, try to eat with other teachers in the lunchroom. This not only helps to fight isolation but also develops rapport and helps them see you as a caring person and a professional.
- Hold a physical activity session for teachers before or after school. Doing so helps to build rapport and break any barriers, which may lead to more support and engagement in physical education.

The classroom teacher's support of the physical education specialist is important. Classroom teachers who understand that physical education is educational, not simply recess, will be less likely to keep children "in" to complete math or reading assignments. They also respect the fact that the physical education program has certain time limits, so make sure their children arrive on time and are ready to return to the classroom on schedule. This may seem to be a minor point, but it can be a source of considerable friction when all the teachers in a school aren't working together to provide the best possible program for children. When teachers understand the value and quality of a physical education program, their support is easier to obtain.

Parents

The physical education teacher must be sure to establish administrator and colleague support before beginning a major program to cultivate enthusiasm among parents. Parental support is important, but it's not enough without the assistance of the principal and the other teachers. If "internal" support doesn't exist, a principal might feel you're going "over her head" by appealing to parents, which can be disastrous for a new program. Once the administration understands your program and its needs, in many instances, the principal will encourage you to generate parent support. And parent support can be especially helpful in obtaining funds that aren't available in the school's budget. There are many ideas for generating support among parents. Try a few of the following one year, a few the next year. Be sure to adapt the suggestions to match the needs and interests of parents in your community.

- Attend parent–teacher association/organization (PTA/PTO) meetings regularly, even if you aren't required to. Try not to sit in the back corner with the other teachers; take the time to meet some of the parents—introduce yourself, tell them what you teach, and invite them to observe your classes. This isn't necessarily the most enjoyable part of building a program, but it certainly can be a major factor in creating support.
- If you're invited to do a presentation for the parents' group, try to involve as many children as possible to ensure a large turnout for your program. Be certain to include children at all skill levels, not only the utilization- and proficiency-level youngsters—and if possible, relate your program to the 1996 Surgeon General's report (USDHHS 1996) and your state standards.

- Send a letter home at the beginning of the year. Tell parents about your program and the general rules the children will be expected to follow (for example, shoes for physical education class). Invite parents to visit. Share an e-mail address with parents and invite them to contact you if they have questions about the program or your policies.
- Most elementary schools today have a Web site for the school. If your school has one, be sure to take advantage of the opportunity and keep it up to date (Figure 33.2). Include items such as community programs of interest, books and articles to read, special accomplishments of the children, upcoming television programs of interest, and future programs you've scheduled. Also include a brief sketch of what you've been working on in physical education and suggest activities for the parents and the children to do together—for example, include the directions from this text for making a nylon-hose racket or short-handled paddle, and suggest several activities for the parents to do with their children. Be careful to proofread what you have written before you submit it so there aren't any spelling or grammatical errors.
- Bulletin boards are a great way to let parents know about your program. If you don't have the skills to make attractive bulletin boards, try trading with

Figure 33.2 Example of a physical education newsletter.
Source: S. Diller, Newsletters make parents and professionals take note, *Strategies* 8(1): 18–20.

The Physical Education Quarterly Report

While some schools view physical education merely as a good break time for teachers or a time for students to blow off a little steam, this is not true for us at Davis. Physical Education is a necessary and integral part of the total curriculum and is viewed with the same seriousness as any other subject matter. One of my primary goals is to provide each student with specific instruction to enable them to become more skillful movers. As students become more proficient in the various motor skills taught in class, I hope that they will enjoy using these skills on a regular basis. Medical and exercise science research indicates that regular physical activity contributes to a healthier and more enjoyable lifestyle while decreasing the incidence and seriousness of various illnesses and diseases. This report will help you know more about the activities in which your child has been instructed this last quarter of the school year.

Space

The second grade students began the school year by reviewing the spatial awareness concepts related to safe, efficient movement. Some of these concepts included moving in personal and general space where students attempt to move either alone or among others without interfering with the others' movements. Additional space concepts included movement at different levels (low, medium, and high), in different directions (forward, backward, sideways, up, and down), and in pathways (straight, curved, and zigzag). A proper understanding and use of these movement concepts permit children to move more safely and effectively in all settings. Games like "Bridges & Boulders," "High-Five Freeze Tag," and "Octopus" made this learning a lot of fun for everyone. Ask your second grader how to play these games and which one they enjoyed the most.

Throwing and Catching

The students also worked on tossing, the underhand throw, the overhand throw, and catching. To help students learn these skills, we use learning cues, key words that help students remember how to perform a skill. Learning cues can also be used to prompt students when they are practicing these skills. The learning cues for the underhand throw are:

- arm back
- step (on opposite foot)
- swing, and
- throw (the ball toward target)

The cues for the overhand throw are:

- cock (arm back in ready position, elbow out)
- step (on opposite foot)
- twist (upper body in direction of throw), and
- throw (the ball toward target)

To put these steps together into a smooth progressive action was not easy, but a lot of practice helped!

The learning cues for catching are:

- watch (the ball)
- reach (for the ball)
- grab, and
- give (with the ball to absorb the ball's force and slow it down)

Students participated in various activities to further develop throwing and catching for accuracy, distance, and with partners. "Throw and Go" and "Bombs Away" were two of the most popular games. Play these games with your students; you will have fun.

Jump Rope & Kicking

We are currently refining and extending jump rope skills during the warm-up portion of class. We work on kicking skills for the remainder of the lesson. The kicking skills students are learning are most related to soccer, such as dribbling (with the feet) trapping, juggling (thigh and foot), and kicking with various amounts of force using the instep.

The Best

As teachers and parents, we want the very best for our students. One thing we desire most is for our students to be healthy, to enjoy the benefits of good health throughout their entire lives. You can help them establish healthy levels of physical activity and support the physical education program by encouraging your children to view physical education as a place to learn, to have a serious learning aptitude, to always try their best, and to practice at home to facilitate the learning process and insure success.

Our own example is one of the most important influencing factors in the lifestyle habits passed on to our children. We must take care of ourselves. Take time to go outside and play with your children—play ball or tag, jump rope, go roller skating. These are all fun ways to stay fit and show your children that good health is in many ways a matter of what you do, as well as what you do not do.

Feel free to contact me if you would like to know more about our program. Thanks for your support!

Scott Diller, Physical Educator
Davis Elementary School

another teacher—for example, one week of bus duty for one bulletin board. In many communities, there are retail stores for teachers that have very attractive bulletin board letters, pictures, backgrounds, and so on, that even the least skilled person can use to make an appealing bulletin board. Written student assessments, illustrated with their drawings, make appealing bulletin boards. PE Central also has great examples of bulletin boards physical educators have created (www.pecentral.org).

- Send a "good news" note home with the children that informs the parents of their children's accomplishments in physical education class. Design and print a supply of notes at the beginning of the year so it won't take long to send several every week (Figure 33.3). These notes are particularly effective for the children who work hard but rarely get noticed. E-mail also works well for "good news" notes.

- Some teachers use positive texts or phone calls or email to communicate with parents about the program. A positive phone call is just a brief phone call to tell a parent how pleased the teacher is about the child's progress (attitude, effort) in physical education. It doesn't take long, but the fact that the teacher takes the time to make the call means much to the parent. In many instances, it's also unexpected because most contacts from the school tend to be negative. Challenge yourself to make two positive contacts to parents per week.

Pete Tamm, a physical education teacher at Michael McCoy Elementary School in Orlando, Florida, wrote letters to his students (Tamm 1993). During a three-year period, he averaged more than 1,000 letters a year to his children. Figure 33.4 contains several examples of his letters.

- Several nights a year, hold an open house for parents and the children. The children must have adults with them to gain admittance. At the open house, equipment is available, and the children show the adults what they've been practicing in physical education. Other ideas include mother–daughter, father–son, mother–son, and so forth, open houses. Some teachers hold these open houses on Saturday mornings because many of the parents work nights. If you schedule the open houses informally, parents are free to stay a few minutes or an hour, depending upon their schedule. The PE Central Challenge (http://www.pecchallenge.org/) is another popular event for a parents' night. Be sure to provide concrete information to parents about what their child has learned (i.e., standard or learning indicator based).

- Once a year, schedule a parent work evening in which parents can help build, repair, and paint equipment for the physical education program. The advantage of such an evening is that it gives parents an understanding of the need for physical education equipment. Make sure the evening is well organized; two hours is adequate.

Figure 33.3 Examples of "good news" notes.

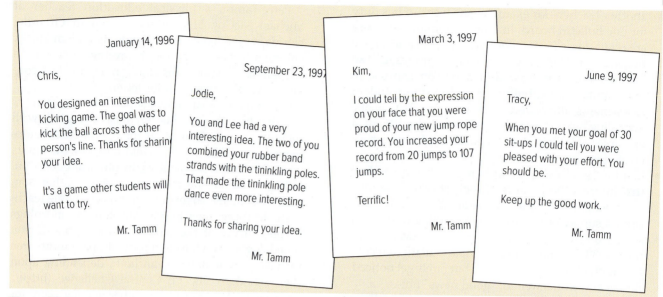

Figure 33.4 Letters to students.
Source: P. Tamm, Dear physical educator: Writing letters makes a difference, *Strategies* 6, no. 8 (1993).

- Walking is so popular today that parents may enjoy a family walk once the children have built up their ability to walk (or run) a limited distance. It's important to explain that it isn't a race but just a chance to get together and walk or run. A local celebrity walker makes an appropriate guest for such an event.
- Schedule a speaker for parents only. For example, you might invite a child psychologist, a medical doctor, or a former athlete. Be certain that you've heard the speaker personally—don't trust someone else's opinion. The speaker has to be worthwhile if the parents are going to enjoy and benefit from the talk. The entire program should run a maximum of 60 minutes. Make sure the speaker understands the difference between physical education and physical activity.
- Invite parents with special skills—for example, a mountain climber, dancer, self-defense expert, or triathlete—to visit your physical education classes and discuss their sport.
- Report cards can also be used as a way to advocate for your program. Obviously you will need to design the report card with this in mind so it communicates the progress a child is making but also educates the parents about your program (Sims and Dowd 2010). SHAPE America also has a helpful document, *Standards-Based Physical Education Student Progress Report: Introduction & Guidance on Usage* (2016), available on its Web site (https://www.shapeamerica.org/uploads/teachersToolbox/Standards-Based-Student-Progress-Report-FULL-web-version-locked.doc).

The School Board

Another obviously important factor in building support for your program is the school board. Although the board members may seem far removed, they're the ones who ultimately determine whether a school district will employ physical education specialists for their elementary schools. The time to gain the board's support is not when it's considering eliminating the physical education program at the elementary schools—that's often too late. Get to know the members, and let them get to know you and your program long before then.

- Attend one or two school board meetings each year, or more if possible. You will learn much about how decisions are made in school districts. If there's an opportunity, try to speak to one or more of the board members so you get to know them. Don't ask for anything; just introduce yourself and talk about the current business before the board. If you ever have an occasion to speak to the board, the fact that you understand how the meetings are conducted and know a few members of the board will make things substantially easier for you.
- Whenever you're offering a special program at your school, send the board a written invitation. Be sure you've attended enough board meetings so you can recognize the members and call them by name if they come to your program. If you know in advance that the members will attend, try to have someone, such as the principal or another teacher, available to serve as a host.

Why Should My Child Take Physical Education?

As you consider ways to build support for your program, it helps to formulate answers to the questions that a parent (administrator, board member) might ask:

- Why should my children take physical education?
- What benefits is he or she gaining from participating in your program?

Today we are able to suggest that quality physical education has the potential to lead youngsters to a lifetime of physical activity. Every parent wants these benefits, outlined by the Centers for Disease Control and Prevention (CDC 2018), for their children. There is scientific evidence suggesting that if you regularly participate in physical activity, you can:

- Control your weight
- Reduce your risk of cardiovascular disease
- Reduce your risk for type 2 diabetes and metabolic syndrome
- Reduce your risk of some cancers
- Strengthen your bones and muscles
- Improve your mental health and mood
- Improve your ability to do daily activities and prevent falls, if you're an older adult
- Increase your chances of living longer

Another good resource is the SHAPE America Web site (www.shapeamerica.org). The CDC Web site (www.cdc.gov) is especially helpful if you are searching for PowerPoint slides about the obesity epidemic to share with parents.

- If you come across an article you think the school board members should read, send them a copy with a brief note. The article should be short, well written, and important to the board members.
- SHAPE America's Web site (www.shapeamerica.org) contains "advocacy resources" if you need up-to-date facts and figures for a presentation to the school board or a legislative group.

Your relationship with the school board will be somewhat distant. It's important, however, to cultivate a relationship if your program of physical education is going to thrive within a school district.

The Community at Large

Realistically, the community at large is less important than the populations discussed so far. You can potentially enhance your program, however, by conducting a program with community appeal. Typically, these are major undertakings that require substantial time and effort. The workload can be lightened by conducting programs with other schools in your district.

- If your community has a shopping mall, check with the managers; the managers of malls are often looking for demonstrations. Such a presentation will give your program a great deal of public visibility. It's a good idea to have handouts available so that people who stop by for a few minutes to watch the program know exactly what they're watching. The children who aren't currently in action can distribute these leaflets.
- The halftime of basketball games is a good opportunity for displaying some of the highlights of your program. For the program to be effective, the announcer's script needs to be well done and rehearsed. Many children from different grades will make the program more appealing for the spectators. Contemporary loud music is also stimulating. Be sure to include the younger children because they have enormous crowd appeal to help get your message across. Also, the children really enjoy performing, and their parents, grandparents, friends, and neighbors enjoy watching them.

Legislators

One of the eternal truths about teaching physical education is the seemingly endless need to convince others that physical education is important in the lives of children. There are times when, in addition to parents, administrators, and school boards, it is important to contact a legislator about an impending bill that will have an impact on physical education programming. To do so requires that teachers are "policy active." That is, they must be proactive in creative policy, not simply reacting to it. To support advocacy for quality physical education, SHAPE America facilitates a SPEAK Out! Day each year. This member advocacy event in Washington, D.C., recently brought more than 150 health and physical education advocates from 42 states to meet with members of Congress to advocate for quality school health and physical education (https://www.shapeamerica.org/events/speakoutday/default.aspx).

The need for such advocacy is apparent, as some states have recently considered legislation to substitute activities such as marching band, athletics, and/or Reserve Officers' Training Corps (ROTC) for secondary physical education. If this happens in your state, contact your legislator(s) to explain why you do not support a particular piece of legislation. In response to increased prevalence of substitutions, waivers, and exemptions, SHAPE America recently created a position statement entitled *Physical Education Is Essential for All Students: No Substitutions, Waivers or Exemptions for Physical Education* (2018), providing a strong rationale for why school policies should not allow substitutions, waivers, or exemptions for physical education courses, class time, or credit requirements. If you are faced with the prospect of waivers, there are a number of Web sites that list the contact information for both state and national legislators. When you do contact legislators, there are several guidelines to follow.

- Mention the legislation specifically by its title—for example, House Bill 402.
- Be certain the letter or e-mail is well written. Be especially careful that all words are correctly spelled and that the grammar and format follow recommended guidelines.
- Be concise and straightforward. Legislators may receive hundreds of letters about a piece of legislation, and long rambling letters are not as effective as ones that stick to the facts.
- Often a form letter is circulated by a professional association to be sent to legislators. Although it is acceptable to use the form letter, it is probably less effective than modifying the letter to make it more personal and unique.
- A handwritten letter may attract more attention than a typed letter. It will stand out from computer-generated letters.

- Finally, if it can be arranged, a personal visit is the most effective way to advocate for legislation. Again, it is best to be concise and straightforward as the visit will be limited in length and you will need to know your facts.

Children as Advocates

We've saved the most important component until the end: the children. Obviously, if you hope to build support from the six populations just described, the children will have to benefit from and enjoy the program. If the children aren't avid supporters of your program, you'll have difficulty gaining support from others in the immediate community.

Children become advocates and talk positively about teachers who help them learn and improve in

Advocacy Resources

The following are a few of the many excellent resources available for physical education advocacy:

- SHAPE America Web site:
  - Legislative Action Center: https://www.shapeamerica.org/advocacy/
  - Guidance Documents and Position Statements: https://www.shapeamerica.org/advocacy/positionstatements/
  - SPEAK Out! Day for Health and Physical Education: https://www.shapeamerica.org/events/speakoutday/default.aspx
- supportREALteachers.org Web site:
  - The Importance of Physical Education: https://www.supportrealteachers.org/the-importance-of-quality-physical-education.html
  - Advocacy Resources and Toolkits: https://www.supportrealteachers.org/how-to-advocate-for-your-program.html
- Supporting and Defending Your Physical Education Program: https://www.pecentral.org/professional/defending/defendingpemenu.html
- Articles/Books:
  - Le Masurier, G., and C. B. Corbin. 2006. Top 10 reasons for quality physical education. *Journal of Physical Education, Recreation and Dance* 77(6): 44–53.
  - Kretchmar, R. S. 2006. Ten more reasons for quality physical education. *Journal of Physical Education, Recreation and Dance* 77(9): 6–9.
  - Ratey, J. J., and E. Hagerman. 2008. *Spark: The revolutionary new science of exercise and the brain.* New York: Little, Brown and Company.

Legislative Advocacy

Legislative endeavors take time. We will not accomplish change within a single contact to a legislator. Be patient, be well informed, and be passionate. Network with outside agencies who support physical education for children; build strong, positive relationship with all the support groups mentioned earlier.

In 2018, the state of Tennessee passed a legislative bill requiring all children in elementary schools be provided 2 days per week of instructional physical education with a certificated physical education professional, with a minimum of 60 minutes of physical education per week (Tom Cronan Physical Education Act, SB 558, TN).

any subject, not only physical education. In any school, the best teachers are both known and respected by the children, other teachers, and the principal. The word gets out when a teacher and a program are good.

Unfortunately, building a quality program of physical education requires more than being a successful teacher. To cultivate all the other populations that contribute to the success of a program, a teacher also needs to be part politician, part public relations director, and part fundraiser. Some teachers find that part of the job distasteful, but it is necessary, especially when one is beginning a program of physical education.

Summary

One important activity teachers of successful physical education programs perform is generating support for their programs. Seven different populations need to be aware and supportive of physical education if the programs are to be successful: school administration, other teachers in the school, parents, the school board, the community at large, legislators, and the children. Children are the most important advocates of a program, so a program must be of high quality if support from the other six groups is to be developed. Remember, the perception of physical education held by administrators, school board members, legislatures, and even parents is most often formed by their experiences in elementary school physical education. We are not only educating children in our programs, we are also educating adults. Use every opportunity to education and advocate for quality physical education.

Reading Comprehension Questions

1. Why are seven different populations identified for building support for a program? Which of the seven do you think is least important? Why?
2. What's the first step a teacher must take to develop a program with widespread support?
3. What does the phrase *principal education* mean? Why do you think many principals are not well informed about quality physical education programs?
4. Locate two elementary school Web sites from your state that have a physical education section. Write a brief review of the physical education section. Was it helpful? Comprehensive? Did it answer questions parents might ask?
5. Why is the school board so important to the success of a physical education program?
6. Why are the children the most important factor in developing support for a program?

References/Suggested Readings

[CDC] Centers for Disease Control and Prevention. 2018. *Physical activity and health: The benefits of physical activity.* https://www.cdc.gov/physicalactivity/basics/pa-health/index.htm.

Cone, T., P. Werner, and S. L. Cone. 2009. *Interdisciplinary elementary physical education: Connecting, sharing, partnering.* 2nd ed. Champaign, IL: Human Kinetics.

Diller, S. 1994. Newsletters make parents and professionals take note. *Strategies* 8(1): 18–20.

Giles-Brown, E. 1993. Teach administrators why physical education is important. *Strategies* 6(8): 23–25.

McFarland, A. 2001, December. Developing a marketing plan for physical education. *The Physical Educator.*

Ratey, J., with E. Hagerman. 2008. *Spark: The revolutionary new science of exercise and the brain.* New York: Little, Brown.

Reiner, M., C. Niermann, D. Jekauc, and A. Woll. 2013. Long-term health benefits of physical activity: A systematic review of longitudinal studies. *BMC Public Health* 13: 1–9.

Rink, J. E., T. J. Hall, and L. H. Williams. 2010. *Schoolwide physical activity.* Champaign, IL: Human Kinetics.

Sims, S., and K. Dowd. 2010, July/August. Using a report card as an advocacy tool. *Strategies* 36–37.

[SHAPE America] Society of Health and Physical Educators. 2009. *Appropriate instructional practice guidelines for elementary school physical education.* Champaign, IL: Human Kinetics.

[SHAPE America] Society of Health and Physical Educators. 2014. *National standards & grade-level outcomes for K-12 physical education.* Champaign, IL: Human Kinetics.

[SHAPE America] Society of Health and Physical Educators. 2015. *The essential components of physical education.* Reston, VA: Author.

[SHAPE America] Society of Health and Physical Educators. 2016. *Standards-based physical education student progress report: Introduction & guidance on usage.* Champaign, IL: Human Kinetics.

[SHAPE America] Society of Health and Physical Educators. 2018. *Physical education is essential for all students: No substitutions, waivers or exemptions for physical education.* Champaign, IL: Human Kinetics.

Stodden, D. F., J. D. Goodway, S .J. Langendorfer, M. Roberton, M. E. Rudisill, C. Garcia, and L. G. Garcia.

2008. A developmental perspective on the role of motor skill competence in physical activity. *Quest* 60(2): 290–306.

Tamm, P. 1993. Dear physical educator: Writing letters makes a difference. *Strategies* 6(8): 13–15.

Tenoschok, M., and S. Sanders. 1984. Planning an effective public relations program. *Journal of Physical Education, Recreation and Dance* 55: 48–49.

[USDHHS] U.S. Department of Health and Human Services. 1996. *Physical activity and health: A report of the Surgeon General.* Atlanta: Centers for Disease Control and Prevention, National Center for Chronic Disease Prevention and Health Promotion.

Physical Education for Tomorrow's Children

Some see things as they are and say why. I dream things that never were and say why not.

—ROBERT F. KENNEDY

Courtesy Children at Monfort Elementary School, Greeley, CO; Lizzy Ginger

Key Concepts

- Successful children's teachers are by nature optimists and innovative thinkers who dream about the future.

- This chapter provides a series of dreams with the hope that it will stimulate readers to develop their own dreams about the future of physical education for children.

- Since the first edition of Children Moving was published in 1980, some of these dreams have become realities for some teachers and children.

This final chapter in *Children Moving* is different from what you will find in most books. We are dreamers. We want the best for children and their teachers, so we continue to dream about how things might be. Since 1980, when the first edition of *Children Moving* was published, the profession of physical education has made great progress. Today, as never before, the important benefits of becoming and remaining physically active for a lifetime are widely understood. There is also an increasing recognition that the skill theme approach, as described in *Children Moving*, has the potential to provide the movement foundation critical for enjoyable and ongoing participation in physical activity and sport as adolescents and adults. We are delighted with the progress that has been made. Yet, we are not satisfied. We will continue to dream about ideal physical education programs and want to share those dreams with you as the last chapter in the book. Some will call our dreams unrealistic, perhaps even unnecessary. We hope you will understand, however, the feeling that exists so strongly in us to never be satisfied with anything but the best.

Perhaps our hopes for the future will stimulate you to think and dream about the way things could be. The following dreams describe the world of children's physical education as we would like it to be—for every child and every teacher.

- Quality daily physical education, designed for learning of the knowledge, skills, and dispositions that provide the foundation for a lifetime of enjoyable physical activity, would exist for all children.
- Stakeholders, parents, and administrators would understand that quality programs of physical education consist of far more than physical activity and require specialized teachers to implement these programs.
- Children's physical education would be guided by clear learning outcomes, and progress toward those outcomes would be shared with parents—and the children.
- Every physical education program would be designed for all children, not only the athletes and physically fit youngsters.
- The public would continue to understand and value the important role regular physical activity can play in the prevention of cardiovascular disease, diabetes, certain types of cancer, alcohol and drug addiction, and obesity.
- K–12 physical education would be designed to assist children to discover their personal tendencies, interests, and joys related to physical activity and then guide them to develop the competence that leads to confidence and regular participation in a sport or physical activity.
- Parents would limit "screen time" (television viewing and computer usage) and encourage their youngsters to use the extra time to increase their physical activity at home.
- Children would play more often outdoors in our neighborhoods and playgrounds, as opposed to spending so much time indoors.
- Negative physical education programs that discourage and humiliate youngsters would be banned from schools, along with their teachers.
- All physical education programs, recreation programs, and youth-serving agencies would collaborate to provide interesting, enjoyable, and easily accessible opportunities for children to be physically active outside of the school day.
- All parents would become involved in their children's physical education. The concepts and skills introduced at school would be valued, enhanced, and embellished at home, through parent–child activity nights, after-school programs for parents, and parent volunteer programs.
- Children would control technology, as opposed to being controlled by technology.
- Children would be grouped—by interest in a specific activity, by ability, by experience—to accomplish the specific goals of a series of lessons, then regrouped when the teacher decides to move to a new skill theme. For example, some upper-grade children might be interested in putting on a dance performance for lower-grade children. Those upper-grade children could be grouped to meet together for two weeks to prepare their dance and perform it. When they accomplish that goal, they could be regrouped as appropriate for another activity.
- There would be time during the day for teachers to cooperatively plan a personalized curriculum with each child. This would help children learn to make

significant decisions about what they want to learn and how they want to learn it.

- All children, regardless of culture, fitness level, socioeconomic status, religion, gender, or disability, would be included in physical education and would benefit from programs and activities designed specifically for them to help them lead physically active lives.

- Discrimination of any type would no longer exist in physical education.

- There would be times during each school day, beyond scheduled physical education classes, when children could choose to come to the gymnasium to practice skills or activities in which they were interested.

- Classes would be scheduled to facilitate cross-age teaching— for example, fifth graders working with first graders, or children at the proficiency level working with those at the precontrol level.

- Classes would be scheduled so that beginnings and endings were determined by the children's interest and involvement in a lesson rather than by an impersonal and insensitive time schedule.

- Teachers would have adequate time between classes to jot down a few notes about the progress the last class made, rearrange equipment, review lesson plans, and shift their thoughts to the next class.

- Administrators and others who schedule classes would understand that physical education is an educational experience, not a loosely organized recess. This understanding would be reflected by scheduling only one class rather than two or three classes with 60 or even 90 children at a time. The time limit would be developmentally appropriate (e.g., pre-K–2 for 30 minutes; grades 3–5 for 30–45 minutes).

- Teachers would have access to ongoing and sustained quality professional development and opportunities that would include frequent visits to other schools and teachers to gain new ideas for their programs.

- Teachers would be able to make arrangements to switch teaching assignments with other teachers for a day or a week. This would provide more experiences working in different environments and with children from various cultural and socioeconomic backgrounds.

- Teachers would collaborate and organize their curriculum into organic, natural contexts (consistent with the way children view the world), rather than artificially separating learning into compartmentalized subjects such as reading, mathematics, art, and physical education. For example, building a house involves reading, mathematics, climbing, balancing, and cooperating with others.

- All classroom teachers would understand that a quality program of physical education can significantly contribute to children's total development, including cognitive and social learning. Children would not be denied physical education class because they hadn't finished their work or because they misbehaved.

- Whole school physical activity programs (e.g., Comprehensive School Physical Activity Program) would be fully implemented as designed with physical education recognized as a necessary educational component.

- All colleagues, parents, and administrators would be vitally interested in our teaching and physical education programs. They would demonstrate this interest by visiting our classes regularly, not only at the first parent–teacher meeting of the year or during school lunch week.

- It would be common practice for individuals from the community to share their expertise and experiences with children. Children might learn about rock climbing walls, hang gliding, hiking, outdoor adventure, and skateboarding, for example.

- Schools would become community centers that involve parents and children in educational projects of mutual interest and benefit. These would include child/parent-designed and -constructed playscapes, child/parent-designed and -implemented field days for preschool children or underserved children, and child–parent programs designed for senior citizens.

- There would be no more grades in elementary physical education. Children's progress would be reported to parents communicating what was to be learned and what children had learned, i.e., through practical assessments.

- Physical education, in both elementary and secondary schools, would receive as much emphasis as high school athletics. Communities would understand that an appropriate program of physical education for every child is as important, if not more so, as athletic programs for the gifted.

- All schools would have appropriate equipment, facilities, and budgets for physical education programs.

- Every school would have a gymnasium designed specifically for children's physical education that would not have to be vacated for lunch, school assemblies, or plays.

- All school districts would understand the differences between teaching children and teaching adolescents and would refuse to hire individuals whose primary interest and expertise is in coaching or teaching at a high school. Instead, school districts would hire, as elementary instructors, only reflective teachers who are professionally qualified and dedicated to a career of teaching physical education to children.

- Preservice teachers would work in elementary schools for several years before going to college so they learn the right questions to ask about children and teaching when they enter college.
- Teacher-education institutions would offer professional preparation programs for elementary school physical education specialists; these programs would be different from those for secondary school physical education teachers.
- College teachers would regularly trade teaching assignments with elementary school teachers, allowing the teachers to study current theories and practices at a college and share their wisdom with preservice teachers while giving the professors realistic opportunities to translate their theories into practice and gain experience about teaching today's children.
- Teachers and professors would collaborate and be supported to collaborate in the development of professional learning groups aimed at discovering better ways to enhance the learning experiences of children, preservice teachers, and in-service teachers.
- Teachers would be involved in conceptualizing and conducting action research. The resulting studies would have the potential for finding answers to the questions that teachers want answered.
- Research results would be disseminated in forms that teachers of children would find useful, practical, and interesting, for example, in weekly pamphlets, newsletters, or podcasts that would use layperson's language, not professional jargon or advanced concepts related to experimental design or statistics.
- Every school would have the quantity and variety of equipment that would allow every child maximum practice at his or her level of physical development.
- Schools would continue to use digital technologies with the children, and physical educators would continue to discover ways to use these technologies to enhance learning and motivate and encourage children to become and remain physically active.
- Portable environments would be made available to schools throughout the year. Children would have

opportunities to use portable swimming pools for swimming lessons, portable ski slopes for skiing lessons, and portable antigravity chambers to experience moving in a weightless atmosphere.

- A national association designed specifically for teachers of children's physical education would be started. The conferences, newsletter, research, and other functions would be designed to specifically address and answer the questions teachers in the schools are asking.
- Mentors would be available to teachers who want to improve their teaching effectiveness and be supported in their early years of teaching.
- Adequate funds would be made available for resource centers operated by teachers for teachers. Such centers would offer assistance in making materials or equipment, opportunities to hear visiting lecturers, professional development activities, and up-to-date professional libraries.
- Technologies would be readily available in gyms for children to keep track of their own progress and for teachers to design better programs and report the children's progress to the parents.
- All gyms would be equipped with the latest technology, including audio systems, digital video and still cameras, permanently mounted television monitors, pedometers, heart rate monitors, and classroom response systems (at a minimum), to facilitate teaching and learning.
- Physical educators would continue to find ways to use social media to enhance their programs and meet and keep in touch with other educators.
- The childhood obesity epidemic would no longer exist.
- All children would be skillful movers.
- Physical education teachers would gain the respect and admiration of the children they teach, their parents, their colleagues, and the community. They deserve it!

One other dream emerged as we were writing this book. Wouldn't it be great if the ideas from our book help you become a more effective teacher of children? We've done our part—now it's up to you. Make a positive difference in the lives of the children you teach! We wish you all the best!

Note: Page numbers followed by italicized letters refer to boxes (*b*), figures (*f*), or tables (*t*)